CHINA

CHINA'S ECONOMIC SYSTEM

HISTORY, PHILOSOPHY, ECONOMICS

CHINA: HISTORY, PHILOSOPHY, ECONOMICS

I	The Chinese Economy	*Adler*
II	A Documentary History of Chinese Communism	*Brandt et al*
III	China's Economic System	*Donnithorne*
IV	A History of China	*Eberhard*
V	The Spirit of Chinese Philosophy	*Fung*
VI	Chuang Tzŭ	*Giles*
VII	People's War	*Girling*
VIII	China's Regional Development	*Goodman*
IX	Health Care and Traditional Medicine in China	*Hillier & Jewell*
X	The Political Philosophy of Confucianism	*Hsü*
XI	Religion in China	*Hughes & Hughes*
XII	Ta T'ung Shu	*K'ang*
XIII	China's Foreign Relations since 1949	*Lawrance*
XIV	Confucian China and its Modern Fate V1	*Levenson*
XV	Confucian China and its Modern Fate V2	*Levenson*
XVI	Confucian China and its Modern Fate V3	*Levenson*
XVII	Crisis and Conflict in Han China	*Loewe*
XVIII	The Performing Arts in Contemporary China	*Mackerras*
XIX	The Rulers of China	*Moule*
XX	The Fading of the Maoist Vision	*Murphey*
XXI	The Grand Titration	*Needham*
XXII	Within the Four Seas	*Needham*
XXIII	Education in Modern China	*Price*
XXIV	Sino-Russian Relations	*Quested*
XXV	Contest for the South China Sea	*Samuels*
XXVI	The Classical Theatre of China	*Scott*
XXVII	Macartney at Kashgar	*Skrine & Nightingale*
XXVIII	The Analects of Confucius	*Waley*
XXIX	Ballads and Stories from Tun-Huang	*Waley*
XXX	The Book of Songs	*Waley*
XXXI	Chinese Poems	*Waley*
XXXII	The Life and Times of Po Chü-i	*Waley*
XXXIII	The Opium War Through Chinese Eyes	*Waley*
XXXIV	The Real Tripitaka	*Waley*
XXXV	The Secret History of the Mongols	*Waley*
XXXVI	Three Ways of Thought in Ancient China	*Waley*
XXXVII	The Way and its Power	*Waley*
XXXVIII	Yuan Mei	*Waley*
XXXIX	Confucius and Confucianism	*Wilhelm*
XL	Sociology and Socialism in Contemporary China	*Wong*

CHINA'S ECONOMIC SYSTEM

AUDREY DONNITHORNE

LONDON AND NEW YORK

First published in 1967

Reprinted in 2005 by
Routledge
2 Park Square, Milton Park, Abingdon, Oxfordshire, OX14 4RN

Routledge is an imprint of the Taylor & Francis Group

First issued in paperback 2016

© 1967 George Allen & Unwin Ltd

All rights reserved. No part of this book may be reprinted or reproduced or utilized in any form or by any electronic, mechanical, or other means, now known or hereafter invented, including photocopying and recording, or in any information storage or retrieval system, without permission in writing from the publishers.

The publishers have made every effort to contact authors/copyright holders of the works reprinted in *China: History, Philosophy, Economics*. This has not been possible in every case, however, and we would welcome correspondence from those individuals/companies we have been unable to trace.

These reprints are taken from original copies of each book. In many cases the condition of these originals is not perfect. The publisher has gone to great lengths to ensure the quality of these reprints, but wishes to point out that certain characteristics of the original copies will, of necessity, be apparent in reprints thereof.

British Library Cataloguing in Publication Data
A CIP catalogue record for this book
is available from the British Library

China's Economic System
ISBN 0-415-36147-8

China: History, Philosophy, Economics

ISBN13: 978-0-415-36147-7 (hbk)
ISBN13: 978-1-138-99127-9 (pbk)

中國經濟制度

董有德

CHINA'S ECONOMIC SYSTEM

by
AUDREY DONNITHORNE
Reader in Chinese Economic Studies
University of London

London
GEORGE ALLEN AND UNWIN LTD
RUSKIN HOUSE · MUSEUM STREET

FIRST PUBLISHED IN 1967

This book is copyright under the Berne Convention. Apart from any fair dealing for the purposes of private study, research, criticism or review, as permitted under the Copyright Act, 1956, no portion may be reproduced by any process without written permission. Inquiries should be addressed to the publisher.

© *George Allen & Unwin Ltd, 1967*

Preface

An explanation, if not an apology, may be demanded for attempting so ambitious a task as delineating, sector by sector, the economic organization of China. This is an age of specialized monographs, and it might be thought advisable to await the appearance of separate studies of the various sectors of China's economy before embarking on a more general work. However, the significance of trends in the different sectors cannot be understood unless they can be fitted into an overall picture. Patterns emerge which are not apparent when parts of the economic system are studied in isolation.

This work deals mainly with the institutional side of the Chinese economy rather than with the quantitative. Sometimes, however, reference must be made to quantitative data in order to assess and understand the institutional framework. The study of economic institutions is at present unfashionable. Some would indeed say that it is not 'proper economics', a branch of knowledge which is deemed to be restricted to what is quantifiable. Preoccupation is all with growth, and with the rates of change. The institutional economist can point out, with the reassuring support of Adam Smith, the father of economics, that growth may be dependent on organizational factors. 'China', Smith wrote, 'seems to have been long stationary, and had probably long ago acquired that full complement of riches which is consistent with the nature of its laws and institutions. But this complement may be much inferior to what, with other laws and institutions, the nature of its soil, climate and situation, might admit of.'[1] An economist must be rash, we may suggest, who excludes 'the laws and institutions' of China from the ambit of our discipline and, more particularly, from that part of it concerned with economic development.

The disreputable status so often accorded to the study of economic institutions is particularly strange in view of the importance now attached to interdisciplinary studies, and the increase, at least in Britain, of joint degree courses involving several branches of knowledge. For the study of economic institutions can serve as a bridge between economics and other social sciences, notably anthropology, sociology, social geography and politics, thus avoiding the danger that threatens, of economists becoming increasingly incapable of communicating with students of these adjacent disciplines.

Nowhere is an interdisciplinary approach more needful than in studying the contemporary Chinese scene. In a country in which, at least fitfully, 'politics is in command', the economic and the political can scarcely be disjoined. When a government's economic policy has among its objects the remoulding of social life and customs, anthropology and sociology are at once involved.

Another reason for studying the institutional features of the Chinese economy lies in the lack of statistics to enable other types of economic studies to be done. The peculiar difficulties in working on matters concerning modern China must be mentioned. The use of Chinese newspapers and periodicals as

[1] A. Smith: *The Wealth of Nations* (ed. E. Cannan, 6th Edition, London, 1950) p. 96.

source material will be treated in the introductory chapter. Here it must be noted that, beginning from around 1959–60 all local newspapers, from the provincial press downwards, have been banned for export, at least, to the West.[1] The same has also applied to many journals, particularly those dealing with finance, statistics and economic planning. This blackout has been mitigated, but not dispelled, by the ingenuity of smugglers.

The refusal to give visas for visits to China to many students of the contemporary Chinese scene, including the present author, puts further obstacles and frustrations in the way of the study of Chinese affairs. Even those who are permitted to visit China as tourists are severely circumscribed in the areas to which they may travel and in facilities for contact with fellow scholars and with the populace at large. A change in this restrictive policy would lead to greater goodwill among a group of scholars who, whatever Peking may think of them, are in a position to exert some influence on China's image in the world. Most of this band have deep respect and affection for China, for its people and its civilization, while for some of us it is the land of our birth.

This volume attempts, despite increasing difficulties, to depict China's economic organization down to the close of 1966. While something is said of the earlier years of the Communist government, the focus of attention is on the period from 1957–8 onwards. No attempt is made to treat of the Taiwan province of China where, for reasons of politics, the economic system is very different.

For the titles of Chinese papers, journals and books, the new system of romanization has been used, because many publications carry on their covers the title so romanized. For personal names, and the names of places, the older system most widely used in English-speaking lands has been employed, or the conventional spelling, if this differs from both. Thus, the capital is given as Peking, not Beijing or Peiching. This, too, follows the present practice of the Chinese authorities in their English language publications. Where only the translation of a Chinese or Russian source has been available, an indication is given by quoting in the reference the abbreviated name of the translation series—e.g. SCMP, JPRS, etc. In other cases, the original has been consulted.

The reader will soon be made aware of the exploratory nature of this work. However, before he ever plunges into it, this fact must be brought to his attention. In existing circumstances, a study of this nature can only be tentative. Fuller knowledge is bound to indicate errors of fact and of omission. Nevertheless, this would not seem sufficient reason to abandon the attempt to gain some understanding of the economic system, or absence of system, in which a quarter of our fellow men are living.

There remains the pleasant duty of thanking all those whose co-operation made this study possible. Professor G. C. Allen has read the whole manuscript, at one stage or other of its composition, and I am deeply grateful for his criticisms and suggestions, as well as for his encouragement in the writing of this book, and on many other occasions since I joined the staff of his department as a new graduate in 1948. This work appears at the time of his retirement and I should like to pay tribute to the distinction and the kindliness

---

[1] Recently my attention has been drawn to the collection of Chinese local newspapers of 1960–5 in the library of the Institute of the Peoples of Asia, Moscow.

which have marked his tenure of the headship of the Department of Political Economy at University College. To the study of the economies of both Britain and the Far East he has brought a compassionate realism, leavened with humour; an appropriate outlook for surveying the human scene, and one which deserves to be continued.

Without the constant devoted assistance of Mrs Tsu-t'ung Emslie, this book would never have been completed. To her knowledge, skill, patience and hard work my debt is incalculable and I thank her very warmly. I wish also to thank all those friends who have read various chapters and given me the benefit of their criticism. They include Professor Ronald Hsia of the University of Hong Kong, Miss Anne Martin of Lady Margaret Hall, Oxford, Mr Michel Oksenberg of Stanford University, Dr Leslie Pressnell of the London School of Economics, Mr Herbert Tout of University College, London, Mrs Sybille van der Sprenkel of the University of Leeds, Miss Barbara E. Ward of the School of Oriental and African Studies, London, Professor Peter Wiles of the London School of Economics and members of the China Department of the Institute of the Peoples of Asia, Moscow. Mr Hugh Collar of the China Association has often come to my help with his knowledge and experience. I am also indebted to many others, especially to members of various groups which have met at Chatham House, and to those attending the Seminar on Modern China at University College. To each and all I am deeply grateful. Gratitude is also due to the many librarians in Britain, Hong Kong, Japan, the United States, the Soviet Union, Poland and elsewhere who, on so many occasions, have given their help. I wish also to thank very warmly all those who have typed successive drafts of atrocious manuscript; notably Mrs Barbara Abel, Miss Molly Harris and Mrs L. Hazel. To their patience and care I owe much.

The Houblon-Norman Fund made a generous grant which enabled me to spend a year in Hong Kong and Japan in 1959–60, while to the Leverhulme Foundation I am indebted for a grant which enabled me to attend the Golden Jubilee Congress of the University of Hong Kong in 1961 and to prolong my stay to further my research.

One other debt I wish to acknowledge. It is to the scholars in Mainland China on whose works I have drawn in writing this book. Despite the barriers between us, I salute them as colleagues and hope one day to know them as friends.

It is usual at this point for an author to assume complete responsibility for any errors or omissions in the book being prefaced. I shall break this convention. I willingly and fully exempt from responsibility those whose names I have mentioned. However, I cannot exempt from blame for the defects of this book, those who, by preventing export of publications and entry of qualified observers, try to separate the Chinese people from the rest of their fellow men.

AUDREY DONNITHORNE

University College, London
December 1966

Preface

Preface to the Second Impression

Two main reasons, apart from continued requests for copies of a book out of print for some years, prompted this new impression.

First, this book depicts China's economy in the period of Liu Shao-chi's dominance in the mid 1960s. The manuscript was completed at the outbreak of the Cultural Revolution when that movement was still sufficiently new for its name to be in quotation marks. Recently, under the guidance of Liu's henchman, Teng Hsiao-ping, the economy has been passing through a neo-Liuist era in which many mid-1960s features have been revived and developed. This gives the present volume current relevance.

Secondly, I intend to write a sequel to update the picture. In the sequel I do not want to repeat at length information given in the present work, although frequent reference will have to be made to it, which makes its availability the more desirable.

Changes in China have happily made parts of the old preface out of date. No longer am I barred from visiting China to collect information on the spot. A three-week trip in 1973, followed by a far more satisfactory visit of seven weeks in 1980, have brought the pleasure of meeting many people connected with economic life—economists in academic and government positions, other officials and many more people besides. The second visit, as a guest of the Chinese Academy of Social Sciences, enabled me to collect material which will be used in the sequel to this volume.

Australian National University AUDREY DONNITHORNE
Canberra
January 1981

Contents

PREFACE	page 7
TABLE OF MEASURES	13
ABBREVIATIONS	13
GLOSSARY	14
1. Introduction	15
2. Collective Agriculture I	31
3. Collective Agriculture II	65
4. State Farms, Agricultural Machinery Stations and Forestry	92
5. Water Conservancy and Electric Power	124
6. The Organization of Industry	140
7. Industrial Labour and Management	176
8. Handicrafts, Small-Scale Industry and Urban Communes	219
9. Mining	237
10. Transport	251
11. Internal Trade	273
12. Foreign Trade	318
13. State Procurement of Agricultural Produce	337
14. The Fiscal System	365
15. Banking, Currency and Credit	402
16. Price Policy	434
17. Economic Planning	457
18. Conclusions	496

APPENDICES
1. Remittances from Overseas Chinese	513
2. Insurance	515
3. State Council Offices, Ministries and Bureaux	517
BIBLIOGRAPHY	530
INDEX	572
MAP	end paper

Table of Measures

1 *mow*	$\frac{1}{15}$ hectare, $\frac{1}{6}$ acre
1 *chin*	$\frac{1}{2}$ kilogram
1 *liang*	50 grams
1 *tan*	50 kilograms
1 *ch'ih*	$\frac{1}{3}$ metre
1 *li*	$\frac{1}{2}$ kilometre

N.B. These are the official equivalences. In practice the Chinese measures are sometimes subject to local variation.

Abbreviations

BBC	British Broadcasting Corporation
CB	Current Background
CCP	Chinese Communist Party
CPPCC	Chinese People's Political Consultative Conference
ECMM	Extracts from China Mainland Magazines
ECMP	Extracts from China Mainland Publications
JPRS	Joint Publications Research Service
NCNA	New China News Agency
NPC	National People's Congress
PLA	People's Liberation Army
SCMM	Selections from China Mainland Magazines
SCMP	Survey of China Mainland Press
URI	Union Research Institute

Glossary

Chen	Market town
Chü	Bureau of central, provincial or *hsien* level government
Ch'u	Sub-division in local government departments
Ch'ü	District between *hsien* and *hsiang* levels or a sub-division of municipality
Chuan ch'ü	Special district (administrative unit under province)
Hot'ung	Contract
Hsiang	Rural district under *hsien* administration
Hsien	County (administrative unit under province and special district)
Kuanlichü	Administrative bureau which administers enterprises of a special branch of industry, e.g. coal, railways, etc.
Kungsze	Corporation
Paokan chihtu	Responsibility system
Paokung	A type of contractual arrangement
T'ing	Bureau or department of provincial level government
Tsungchü	General bureau

Chapter 1

INTRODUCTION

> ... I see a myriad hills all tinged with red,
> Tier upon tier of crimsoned woods
> On the broad stream, intensely blue,
> A hundred jostling barges float; ...
> I ask the great earth and the boundless blue
> Who are the masters of all nature?
>
> MAO TSE-TUNG

An economy close to the border of subsistence narrowly limits the play of economic policy. Where agriculture bulks large, much is unpredictable, for mastery of natural vagaries is more difficult than of industrial techniques. Economic planning in these conditions cannot be certain or precise, nor can rash adventures be afforded.

The Chinese country folk, by ingenuity and diligence, coax the soil to yield the rice, wheat, maize, millet and sweet potatoes which, with beans, peanuts and green vegetables, provide the normal diet. Cotton gives clothing; stalks and grass, with charcoal, the fuel; while from the beneficent bamboo derive building materials, furniture, utensils, chopsticks, as well as pen and paper—and inspiration to poet and artist to use both. On days of festival, pork, rice-wine and fireworks give that change from routine, that sense of occasion which prevents human nature from sinking into torpor. Simple needs, yet often unsatisfied: drought, flood and harsh rule can negate the results of much diligence. The Chinese cultivator is as skilful as any in the arts of pre-scientific agriculture but even so, his toil produces little surplus over and above the needs of his own family.

A surplus from agriculture is needed to free and feed the labour for industrialization. Industrialization is the goal towards which national pride has been urging China for decades in order to get equal with the upstart West and its Japanese pupil. Nor is it only sentiment that impels the need for industry. The knowledge of the higher standard of living enjoyed elsewhere arouses discontent with traditional ways of life. Even were this not so, old methods of production would no longer be sufficient to maintain even the former levels.

Modern health measures and, after 1949, the restoration of peace, raised the rate of natural increase of population. The growth of one factor—in this case population—eventually necessitates a change in the whole structure of the economy, and makes it impossible to continue in the old grooves even if nothing else caused a desire for change.

In Europe, the Industrial Revolution followed after the great improvements in agriculture. In China, as in most of Asia, impatience for industry means that its advance is planned simultaneously with agricultural advance. As the speedy promotion of industry is easier than that of farming, what in fact is liable to happen is that industry outstrips agriculture until it becomes hamstrung by its own disproportionate growth. At this stage no further workers can be spared from the still labour-intensive methods of cultivation, nor are crops of industrial raw materials sufficient to provide a basis for the continued expansion of light industry.

Before the war, modern industry in China had been confined very largely to the great sea ports, Shanghai notably, and Tientsin, and also to Japanese-held Manchuria. Much of this peripheral industry was, too, in foreign hands. Thus the programme of industrialization appealed to patriotism as well as arousing that ferment of excitement which comes from the first substitution of machinery for muscle. It is difficult for those from long industrialized countries to appreciate this excitement. The prospect and process of enrichment both exhilarate although affluence, when attained, may be found to pall. Citizens of rich lands extol the beauties of unspoilt nature compared to which the trappings of industry seem dreary and sordid. Not so those villagers whose backs have ached under heavy loads, who have felt the weight of bucketfuls of water pulled from deep wells and know how little can be made in a long day's work by unaided human hands. The sense of power bestowed by elementary mechanical skills makes everything seem possible and instils optimism, even arrogance, in the face of difficulties. Especially is this true for youths of initiative to whom the old country life offered little scope or prospect of honour and advancement except that brought at long last by old age. To this inherent excitement of the industrial revolution is added the bustling vitality which strikes all strangers on their first impact with Chinese life—with Chinese life as lived under Communist, Kuomintang, or colonial rule alike: intense individual purposefulness combined with at least outwardly harmonious co-operative relations within small groups, and all shot through with evident energy and zest.

There is, of course, another side. Despite high expectations, country workers find adapting to urban ways an uncomfortable process. Old habits are out of place, personal relationships are replaced by impersonal ties; rigid daily time-keeping instead of the routine of the seasons. This first generation of industrial labour is inefficient, lacking the necessary disciplines, hence the constant complaints of poor care of machinery, and low quality of products. At a higher level, analogous deficiencies are found among administrative staff. Few are competent in the accountancy demanded for a large concern, or in methods of stock-taking or of control of labour. Material conditions in the sprawling towns of early industrialization are often dreary and whole communities lack roots.

Most of these factors, good and bad, are common to the process of industrialization, whether in Victorian England, Soviet Russia, Congress India or Maoist China. Distinguishing features are added by the political complexion of the government concerned, but even more by national temperament and tradition.

The immensity of China must never be forgotten, nor the multi-dimensional nature of this immensity, embracing both space and time. Duration, extent and population are all vast and together convey an overpowering sense of self-sufficiency. Once away from the coast and the cities, even a foreigner can find it difficult to envisage that outside China the world exists at all. This sense of China being a world in itself, or even the world in itself, assumes as axiomatic the unity of China. The converse is the extreme diversity contained in this vastness. The sea freezes along the northern coast, while pineapples and rubber trees thrive in the tropical south. Great deserts stretch over the northwest in contrast to the lush well-watered valley of the Yangtze. Apart from natural conditions, inadequate transport leads to local disparity so that plentiful supply in one place cannot always relieve shortage in another, even when separated by no great distance. Human differences, in character and tradition, also distinguish provinces and regions. All this makes generalization about China more than ordinarily dangerous.

In October 1949, when the Communist leaders established the People's Republic of China, already they had behind them long years' experience of rule. The early 'liberated areas', however, were all in the interior, bereft of industry and other modern devices. Many of the problems the new rulers faced in 1949 were, therefore, strange to them. However, in the period of rehabilitation, from 1949–52, they acted with decision and success. By the close of 1952, China had regained the pre-war (i.e. c. 1937) economic level despite strain caused by the Korean war. Inflation had been curbed, transport restored, dykes repaired, and industry refurbished. A revolutionary land reform had also been carried out, while in industry and commerce the state had extended its control. The First Five Year Plan period (1953–7) was a time of centralization. Heavy industry received the bulk of investment funds (including Soviet aid) and made notable advances, while agriculture and consumer goods were relatively neglected. In these years, agriculture was collectivized. After land reform, the peasants were encouraged to form mutual aid teams and co-operatives, first small and then larger. Before the end of 1956 almost all the peasants of China had been organized into agricultural producers' co-operatives.

At the end of the First Five Year Plan period, measures were promulgated to decentralize economic authority, primarily from the central government to the provinces. However, owing to an apparent change in the balance of power within the Chinese Communist Party, 1958 (the first year of the Second Five Year Plan) became a year of unparalleled centralization of policy. A decision had evidently been taken to attempt a short cut to economic development by diverging from the Soviet model to an indigenous alternative in which labour-intensive small-scale industry was stressed (the policy of 'walking on two legs'—i.e. using both modern and old style methods) and in which political pressure was to take the place of material incentives. In many spheres direct action by party organs ousted the machinery of government and the administration of economic enterprises. In the countryside, agricultural producer co-operatives were amalgamated to form new multi-purpose units, the people's communes. It was a year of frenzied activity, both political and economic, the year of the 'Great Leap Forward', encouraged by a bountiful harvest and by industrial output augmented with production from many newly completed plants. Reports and statistics, however, far exceeded reality and had to be revised in the following year.

By 1959, too, the unwisdom of some of the policies of the Great Leap had begun to be realized—such as the over-centralized campaigns on agricultural techniques and also, the proliferation of small iron and steel furnaces. These mistakes aggravated the difficulties caused by bad weather and poor harvests in 1959–61. During this period of crisis, a fundamental switch was made in economic policy. Agriculture replaced industry as the first priority. Investment was cut and industrial production fell steeply from the record levels reached during the Great Leap. Consumer goods industries lacked agricultural raw materials, while producer goods were no longer in demand. Industrial workers were laid off and, with other urban residents, ordered to the countryside to boost the labour force on the land.[1] Political pressure was somewhat eased, material incentives became respectable once more and skill and experience again brought reward. 'Consolidation' and 'adjustment' were the slogans of these years, meaning caution and retrenchment.

The structure of the communes underwent great changes, the village and smaller groupings coming back into their own, together with those other local units, the county (*hsien*) and the market town (*chen*). In other ways, too, traditional patterns and methods re-asserted themselves.

From 1962 the situation eased. Better harvests put spirit into workers in fields and factories, while more relaxed policies began to bear fruit. Some new industrial investment was taken in hand, particularly in lines such as fertilisers and farm machinery which served agriculture. Output of consumer goods rose, with more reliance on plastics and other non-agricultural raw materials. Investment policy in agriculture from 1964 was to concentrate funds on areas with high and stable yields.

After the débâcle of the Great Leap, little was heard of the Second Five Year Plan or indeed of any plan. Improvisation was the keynote. The Third Five Year Plan was postponed and did not begin until January 1966. It has been learned by hard experience that the road to industrialization will be slow and arduous, only achieved in the course of generations. Perhaps this helps to explain why the period of political pressure, marked by the 'Great Proletarian Cultural Revolution' has not, to the time of writing, being accompanied by a parallel economic campaign.

A brief summary of the political organization of the country is essential to an understanding of China's economic system.

Power at all levels of government has lain with the Communist Party, which has branches in every type of organization and enterprise—economic, administrative and social, the key official being the secretary of the committee of the branch. In addition, special political departments were established in 1963–4 in a number of economic ministries. A close connection exists between the Party and the Army; in the intra-Party dissensions that came out into the open in 1966, one facet of the struggle was that between the military elements in the Party and some of the Party's civilian groupings. In

---

[1] For an interpretation of the years 1958–60 in terms of boom and depression, see *China Quarterly* No. 17, Jan-March 1964, pp. 49–52, W. W. Hollister: 'Capital Formation in Communist China.' For a comparison of the period 1961–3 with the Soviet New Economic Policy, see Ibid., pp. 65–91, F. Schurmann: 'China's "New Economic Policy"—Transition or Beginning?'

1964 (the last date for which we have this figure) the Chinese Communist Party claimed a membership of 18 million. It includes an overwhelming proportion of those in the leading positions in the country.

The Party Congress elects the Central Committee of the Party which, in turn, elects the Politburo. By the Party's Constitution, the National Party Congress should be convened once a year by the Central Committee, although 'under extraordinary conditions', the Central Committee may postpone it. Plenary sessions of the Central Committee are supposed to be convened at least twice a year.[1] Both these provisions have been honoured in the breach and long periods have elapsed without any recorded meeting of Congress or Committee. The Standing Committee of the Politburo is the highest policy-making body in China. Mao Tse-tung is Chairman of the Central Committee. A large proportion of the Party's leaders come from the provinces of the interior and especially from Mao's own province, Hunan. The Secretariat of the Party has under it departments dealing respectively with organization, propaganda, united front work (i.e. with the small 'democratic' parties), rural work, industrial work, communications work and finance and trade. The geographical organization of the Party rests in the first place on six regional bureaux, the existence of which was first reported in 1961. Below these come the Party committees of the provinces, autonomous regions and centrally controlled cities, and of the lower local authorities. These committees have their own specialized departments under them for such matters as agriculture, industry and transport.

From the end of 1963 onwards, there were established within the Central Committee of the Party, Political Departments for Finance and Trade, Industry and Transport, and Agriculture and Forestry respectively. It is not known whether these replaced the previous departments of the Central Committee or were additional to them. At the same time, as already mentioned, new political organs were set up in economic organs alonside the old Party committees. This development will be discussed in Chapter 7; it is connected with the intra-Party dissensions of the period.

The two hierarchies, that of the Party and that of the government administration, run alongside each other throughout both the political and economic systems, right down to the lowest units of local authority and to individual enterprises and institutions. The Party is organized both territorially and by production branches; after the administrative decentralization of 1957-8, the territorial organs of the Party became of paramount importance. Of the two hierarchies, that of the Party has ranked the higher. The system of dual hierarchies is, of course, copied from the Soviet Union where the Party committee at each level has usually been more influential than the corresponding government organ. The tendency towards direct Party control in economic matters has been stronger in China because that country has had proportionately fewer educated people than the Soviet Union, even than the Soviet Union in its early days; hence the maintenance in China of fully-staffed dual hierarchies is difficult, if not impossible. Another reason for the tendency is no doubt the more recent date of the Chinese Revolution and the necessity of continuing to employ as managers and professional personnel many members

[1] *The Constitution of the Communist Party of China*, Peking, 1965. Articles 31 and 36.

of the old bourgeoisie who cannot be considered politically reliable. The Party therefore, keeps a tight rein on their activities.

Anent the machinery of government, as distinct from that of the Party, the Constitution of 1954 lays down that the National People's Congress is the highest state organ. The Congress elects the Chairman of the Republic (who, after Mao retired from the Chairmanship in 1959, was Liu Shao-ch'i) and has legislative authority. It is supposed to meet annually, although it did not do so in 1961. When the National People's Congress is not in session its authority is exercised by its Standing Committee. The State Council is both the executive organ of the National People's Congress and also the highest administrative organ of the state. It is composed of the Premier (Chou En-lai), the Vice-Premiers, ministers, heads of commissions and the Secretary-General. The State Council, operating through its six offices, exercises immediate control over ministries and also over various commissions, bureaux and other bodies.[1] The six Offices of the State Council are those of Internal Affairs, Agriculture and Forestry, Industry and Communications, Finance and Trade, Culture and Education, and of Foreign Affairs; they are in the position of overlords, each (with the exception of the Office of Foreign Affairs) controlling a group of subordinate ministries. Each ministry has one minister and usually half a dozen or so vice-ministers. The more than thirty other organs that come directly under the State Council include such bodies as the State Planning Commission, the State Economic Commission and the People's Bank of China, of which we shall treat in subsequent chapters.

Nowhere have we found set out the functions of the Offices of the State Council. Together with the more important commissions, they are probably the chief policy making organs, with ministries playing a distinctly secondary role. The most important measures are usually announced as coming jointly from the Central Committee of the Party and the State Council (in that order), those of the next importance from the State Council; in neither case is there mention of the particular State Council Office concerned with the topic. The detailed regulations ensuing may then be issued by the relevant ministry. The State Council offices have a co-ordinating role in respect of the ministries under them. For example, a State Council office sometimes convenes a conference on a topic of common interest to a number of its subordinate ministries to which each sends representatives.

From 1949 until their abolition in 1954, China was divided into six great administrative regions (*ta hsingcheng ch'ü*).[2] In 1958, press references began to appear to the country's seven economic co-ordinating regions (*chingchi hsiehtso ch'ü*). We have not been able to trace any mention of their establishment. After 1958 references became fewer, but no announcement of their demise has come to our notice. The mysterious rise and disappearance of governmental organs without public notification is a feature of the Chinese scene which we shall be meeting on more than one occasion.

Apart from these entities, the highest authorities under the central government have been the provinces, autonomous regions and the municipalities

---

[1] See Appendix I.
[2] Their original responsibilities had been reduced in 1952. Chou Fang: *Our Country's State Organs* (in Chinese), Peking, 1957, p. 107.

INTRODUCTION 21

under direct central control. All of these will be known collectively in this work as the provincial level (or major) local authorities. In the early years of the regime, these were subject to various divisions and amalgamations.[1] After the abolition of the great administrative regions in 1954, the number of provincial level authorities was reduced; but it was stabilised after 1955, except for the demotion of Tientsin and the revival of Ninghsia, both in 1958. Since the latter date, these authorities have comprised 21 provinces (22 with Taiwan), five autonomous regions, and the two great cities of Peking and Shanghai. Autonomous regions (Sinkiang, Inner Mongolia, Ninghsia, Kwangsi and Tibet[2]) are established where minority nationalities form a significant part of the population;[3] special small units of local government (autonomous *chou* and autonomous *hsien*) being set up in some places for the same reason. Many of the provinces and autonomous regions, it must be borne in mind, are in size or population, or both, counterparts of any of the countries of West Europe.

Provincial level authorities have their own specialized departments (*t'ing*), bureaux (*chü*), divisions (*ch'u*) and commissions, roughly corresponding to the ministries and commissions of the central government, although sometimes a joint provincial department, e.g. for agriculture and forestry, may be set up, with scope corresponding to more than one ministry.[4] A central government ministry, together with the enterprises immediately under it, its corresponding local departments and their subordinate enterprises, are known collectively as the ministry's 'system' (*hsit'ung*). This term is sometimes used to denote vertical (production branch) control from the ministry downwards, in contrast to horizontal (territorial) control by local authorities.[5] On occasion references are found to the 'finance and trade system,' thus aligning the 'system' to the sphere of a State Council office and not to an individual ministry; at other times, however, the Ministry of Commerce's 'system' is mentioned on its own.

It should be noted that the boundaries of Peking and Shanghai municipalities were expanded in 1958 to embrace large rural areas, thus including several *hsien* within their borders.[6] This was done to increase local self-sufficiency, a trend which we shall see was pronounced at that time.

[1] For details see Chou Fang: op. cit., pp. 107–108 and T. Shabad: *China's Changing Map*, London, 1956, pp. 25 and 28.

[2] Tibet did not become a fully fledged autonomous region until 1965.

[3] These minorities constitute some 6 per cent of the total population of China, the remaining 94 per cent being Han Chinese.

[4] *Collected Laws and Regulations of the People's Republic of China* (in Chinese), Vol. I, pp. 154–6. Sometimes provincial departments (*t'ing*) are paralleled by bureaux (*chü*) in the directly controlled municipalities. See Ibid., Vol. 5, p. 146. This may be a continuance of similar differences in nomenclature before 1949. However, both *chü* and *t'ing* are to be found in provinces (as distinct from municipalities). See, e.g. *Coal Industry* (*Meitan Gongye*) No. 12, June 25, 1959, p. 29.

[5] e.g. *Collected Laws and Regulations*...Vol. 8, p. 124. A ministry's *hsit'ung* may include the Party and trade union organs operating in it, although we have not seen this specifically stated.

[6] Compare the area of Peking Municipality given in *People's Handbook* (*Renmin Shouce*) *1958*, p. 650. (4,700 sq. km.) and that given in ibid., 1959, p. 209 (17,100 sq. km.). The 7,400,000 population of Peking Municipality in 1963 included 300,000 families engaged in agriculture. A. L. Strong: *Letter from China*, No. 11, October 25, 1963, p. 2. See also A. L. Strong: *The Rise of the Chinese People's Communes—and Six Years After*, Peking, 1964, p. 111.

The Constitution promulgated in 1954 stipulated four levels of administration over most of the country: central, provincial, county (*hsien*) and on the same level municipalities (*shih*), and then on the fourth level, rural districts (*hsiang*) and market towns (*chen*).[1] In autonomous regions, an additional level was laid down—the autonomous *chou*, which came below the autonomous region and above the autonomous *hsien* but which is not invariably to be found.[2] In fact, however, there are two additional levels in the provinces, making a total of six. Immediately beneath the province comes the special district (*chuan ch'ü*—sometimes known in English as the administrative district) while the district (*ch'ü*) is found between the *hsien* and the *hsiang* levels. (The term *ch'ü*, it must be noted, also means a sub-division of a municipality.) In 1964 there were a total of 152 special districts; these were found in every province except Tsinghai and also (alongside autonomous *chou*) in every autonomous region apart from Inner Mongolia. Throughout the country there were, in 1964, altogether 2,052 *hsien* and 166 municipalities under provincial level authorities.[3]

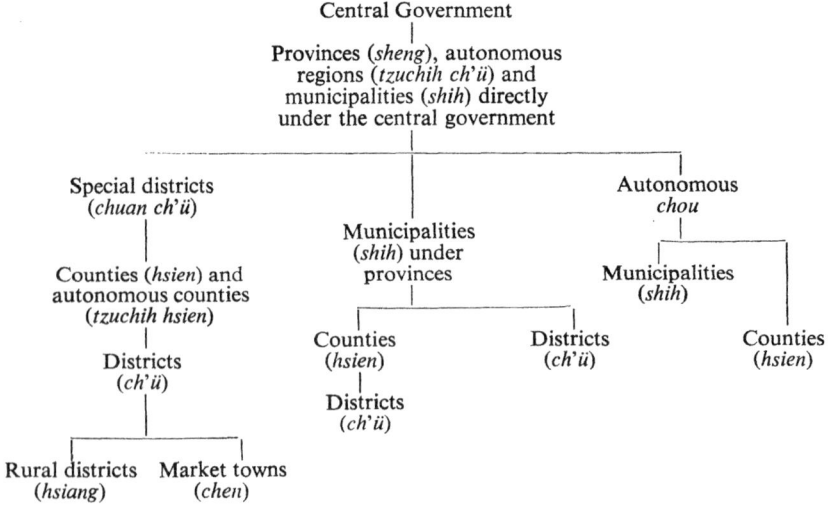

In certain parts of China (e.g. in Inner Mongolia), local authorities carrying special designations are to be found. Other variations also exit and this chart must be taken as a diagrammatic simplification.

For the ups and downs of local authority units below the *hsien*, the reader is referred to a study by R. Hofheinz.[4] Here it is sufficient to mention that on the establishment of the people's communes in 1958, the *hsiang* level ad-

---

[1] *Constitution of the People's Republic of China*, Peking, 1954. Article 53. The term 'administrative village' is sometimes used as the equivalent of *hsiang* (*The Agrarian Reform Law of the People's Republic of China* [in Chinese], Peking, 1950, p. 5). This usage pertains especially to N. China (I am indebted to John Chiu-hon Wong for this information).

[2] Chou Fang, op. cit., p. 106.

[3] *People's Handbook* (*Renmin Shouce*) *1964*, pp. 263–9.

[4] *China Quarterly*, No. 11, July–September 1962, pp. 140–59. R. Hofheinz: 'Rural Administration in Communist China.'

ministration was merged with that of the commune, while the next higher unit, the *ch'ü*, disappeared. In cases where communes were based on *ch'ü*, both the *hsiang* administration (if any) and that of the *ch'ü* was absorbed into the commune,[1] and the market towns (*chen*) also lost their standing. However, during the crisis years some of the old administrative structure re-appeared. By 1960–2 the market town was regaining its importance, and in places the *ch'ü* and *hsiang* were mentioned once more.

Sometimes, even in official regulations, local authorities are referred to by the vague term *ti-fang* (literally 'place'), without specifying the particular level which should undertake the task mentioned. This habit springs from the fact that in Chinese practice each level of administration has an overall responsibility for its subordinate levels, while having direct dealings only with those levels immediately below and above it. Following from this, the central government deals only with the provincial level,[2] and it seldom distinguishes between the rights and duties of, for example, the province and the *hsien*.

We have already touched on the intended role of the Communist Party and of the Army as centralizing forces; nor must the public security system be forgotten in this connection. Economic institutions, such as the banks and modern transport systems, which work in the same direction, will be the subject of subsequent chapters. Indeed the pull between centripetal and centrifugal forces is one of the main themes of this study. Here must be noted certain administrative methods and techniques for maintaining contact between different levels and areas of the Party and of the administration. These include conferences (both actual gatherings and also telephone conferences), exhibitions visited by relevant persons from all over the country or from particular districts, and the Press and other mass media. Policies are also propagated by means of special campaigns, during which the machinery of Party and government devotes a large part of its energies, with intense fervour, to urging a certain line of action or certain attitudes on the populace at large or on certain groups.

A lack of precision evidenced in regulations and directives, stems partly from the need to allow local authorities to adapt them to local situations, but also from the attitude to law rooted in Chinese society, an attitude which attaches much less importance to enacted law (*fa*) than to customary norms of behaviour (*li*); or rather, makes no clear distinction between the two.[3] This, in turn, is connected with a blurring (from the Western point of view) of the distinction between the state and society. Thus the responsibility of those in authority at every level has been to ensure the appropriate and correct

---

[1] See p. 48 below.

[2] However, the appointment of *hsien* magistrates was put under the control of the Personnel Bureau of the State Council (see p. 177 below). This continued the old imperial Chinese tradition by which these appointments were centrally controlled in order to ensure that *hsien* magistrates were not employed in their home districts. It is not known if this or a similar ban is now enforced; nor is it clear if appointments at the *hsien* level are effectively, as distinct from nominally, under central control.

[3] Under the Ch'ing Dynasty, the General Code of Laws made it a criminal offence to 'do what you ought not to do'. G. Jamieson: *Chinese Family and Commercial Law*, Shanghai, 1921, p. i.

behaviour of their charges. Although contrary currents of thought have occurred at times in China, this has been the dominant outlook. Under the Communist government, it has been carried to the extent of having laws on only a few topics, such as those on marriage, on counter-revolutionaries and on labour; apart from which there is no published civil or criminal code, nor a system of case law.[1] In practice, Party policy is considered of greater significance than law.[2] Law, in any case, is regarded as primarily a weapon in class struggle.

The ambiguities surrounding the idea of law are shown by the uncertainty about who is empowered to make laws, whether only the central government (the People's Congress, or the State Council, ministries and other central organs) or local authorities too.[3] A number of volumes have appeared of collected laws and regulations, which we shall often have occasion to quote. These, however, are mainly administrative measures. The terms by which they are described share in the general aura of uncertainty. We have not been able to attach precise shades of meaning to the various words used for official orders, which will here be englished, therefore, somewhat indiscriminately as regulations, decrees, directives and so on. Perhaps a detailed and comprehensive study, which we have not had time to make, could indicate significance in the exact term used in any particular case.

Because of the vagueness surrounding the notion of law, in China even more than elsewhere it is likely that there will be a divergence between what is laid down and what actually occurs. In our study we have tried, as far as possible with the material at our disposal, both to give the regulations in force and also to draw attention to indications of what was happening in actual fact; frequently both are but dimly discernible. Once again the size and variety of China must be kept in mind. Regulations often do not come into force simultaneously all over the country, nor are they necessarily enforced with equal rigour in all places.

An issue that constantly arises is that of assessing the degree of compulsion exercised at any time in any particular sector or instance. We have seen that China has never been run by clear-cut rules and enactments, but by infinitely subtle ways of conveying commands, threats and approbation. Communism has not changed this but has added yet other complicating elements. Thus a considerable degree of confusion and bewilderment is the lot of anyone trying to understand the Chinese economy, and while apologies are due for any confusion that may have been introduced unnecessarily, it must be insisted that

---

[1] Court decisions are not normally published. In 1957 Chou En-lai announced that a draft criminal code was ready and a civil code was being drafted but these have not, to our knowledge, been published. *People's Handbook* (*Renmin Shouce*), *1958*, p. 210.

[2] *People's Daily* (*Renmin Ribao*), July 24, 1962. p. 5. 'A Discussion of the Nature and Function of Socialist Law in Our Country by the Law Faculty of Peking University' and E. Szczepanik (ed.): *Symposium on Economic and Social Problems of the Far East*, p. 335–6. Luke R. C. Lee: 'Towards an Understanding of Law in Communist China' and *Journal of the International Commission of Jurists*, Vol. 4, No. 1, Summer 1962, p. 47. C. S. Leng: 'The Lawyer in Communist China' and *Harvard Law Review*, Vol. 79, No. 3, January 1966, pp. 469–533. J. A. Cohen: 'The Criminal Process in the People's Republic of China: An Introduction'.

[3] *Kuang Ming Daily* (*Guangming Ribao*), September 17, 1962, p. 2.

if this study is to be a serious work and not just a 'child's guide', a certain amount of confusion is inevitable.

The Constitution touches on matters of civil law. It declares that four 'basic forms of ownership of means of production' existed at the time of its promulgation in 1954: state ownership, co-operative ownership (defined as 'collective ownership by the working masses'), ownership by individual workers, and capitalist ownership. State ownership, described as 'ownership by the whole people', covers *inter alia*, all mineral resources and waters as well as forests and undeveloped land.[1] Central government control is not necessarily implied by state ownership: control may be by any level of the administration down to the *hsien*. Enterprises controlled below this level are not considered state enterprises, but units of the collective economy; their profits, therefore, are not remitted to the state but form part of the income of the collective unit controlling them.

Within the economic sphere, state ownership is exercised through enterprises (*ch'iyeh*), which are juridical persons, 'the basic units of the national economy in material production';[2] enterprises, however, are also found in commerce and transport and similar service industries, not falling within the communist definition of 'material production'. Sometimes a number of enterprises are grouped under the control of a corporation (*kungsze*). This term, *kungsze*, is also, on occasion, appended to the name of, and denotes, a single enterprise. A leading Chinese economist, Hsü Ti-hsin, director of the Central Administration of Industry and Commerce, borrows direct from the Soviet *Textbook of Political Economy* his description of the essential features of state enterprises: all their means of production are owned by the whole people, they are directly subject to state planning, are managed by state appointees, and their output is state property, available for distribution by the state at official prices.[3] Enterprises' profits are therefore state property, to be handed over to the state treasury, except for sums specifically assigned for retention by the enterprise earning them. Workers in state enterprises are remunerated by wages.

While the assets of an enterprise are state property, the enterprise has nevertheless a certain independence in their use and they are to that extent its 'own' assets. These assets fall into two categories: fixed assets (*kuting tzuch'an*), the equivalent of the Soviet *osnovniye fondi*, and working capital (*liutung tzuch'an*). Fixed assets cover property worth over ¥500 (before 1957 over ¥200) with a working life of over a year, and the term includes factory

[1] *Constitution of the People's Republic of China*. Articles 5 and 6.

[2] *Economic Research* (*Jingji Yanjiu*) No. 3, March 1964, p. 4. Li Ch'eng-jui: 'An Exploratory Discussion of the General Equilibrium of the Budget, Credit and Material Supplies.' Schools, hospitals, etc., and other 'state budgetary organs', i.e. concerns depending on budgetary grants for their expenses, are also juridical persons; collectively these are often known as *shihyeh* which may be translated as 'institutions', or 'undertakings'. See Education Research Department of the Central School for Political and Legal Cadres (ed.): *Basic Questions in the Civil Law of the People's Republic of China* (in Chinese), Peking, 1958, p. 68 and *Finance* (*Caizheng*) No. 13, November 24, 1958, p. 1. Kwangtung Provincial Department of Finance: 'Promote the Development of Undertakings through Budgetary Responsibility and Financial Decentralization.'

[3] Hsü Ti-hsin: *An Analysis of China's Economy in the Transitional Period* (in Chinese). Revised Edition, Peking, 1959, pp. 44–5.

buildings, residential accommodation, roads, vehicles and machinery.[1] Enterprises pay no interest on that part of their capital represented by fixed assets. Working capital, both the 'self-owned' category, which forms part of an enterprise's assets, and that part deriving from the bank, will be discussed in Chapter 15./ Enterprises are subject to the 'economic accounting system' (*chingchi hosuan chihtu*). This system, copied from the Soviet *khozrashchët*, requires that 'an enterprise bears complete responsibility for the management of its activities and that the results of its own operations be shown independently;'[2] the purpose of this system is to facilitate the fixing of responsibility on an enterprise for the use made by it of the state capital with which it is entrusted for the fulfilment of its allotted duties. An economic accounting unit has its own capital, both fixed and working, its own production and financial plans handed down from higher levels, its own account with the People's Bank (in some cases with other state banks), and the right to negotiate short-term bank loans and to sign contracts for the supply of raw materials and for the disposal of finished products.[3] While most enterprises are under an obligation to fulfil plans for profits (as well as production plans), under certain conditions planned losses are allowed. All enterprises have, of of course, the obligation to preserve their capital.[4]

Something on the lines of the economic accounting system had been encouraged during the war in the areas held by the Chinese Communists, but the chief channel through which it came to be introduced into China was Manchuria, notably through the joint Sino-Soviet administration of the Changchun Railway in the early days of the regime.[5] In this, as in other ways, the North East acted as a testing ground for new practices in those early years, more specially for methods introduced from the Soviet Union. The economic accounting system underwent a process of adaptation, requiring 'a long period of repeated practice to harmonize foreign experience with our country's conditions'.[6]

The collective or co-operative sector of the economy covers units of collective agriculture (agricultural producer co-operatives,[7] people's communes, production brigades and production teams, although as we shall see,

[1] *Basic Questions in the Civil Law of the People's Republic of China*, p. 243. See also Choh-ming Li: *Economic Development of Communist China*, Berkeley, 1959, p. 113, fn 6, where certain reservations are stated to the pre-1957 definition.

[2] *Economic Research* (*Jingji Yanjui*), No. 4, April 1962, p. 4. Ho Chien-chang, Kuei Shih-yung and Chao Hsiao-min: 'The Content of Economic Accounting of Socialist Enterprises.'

[3] *Ta Kung Daily* (*Dagong Bao*), Peking. June 4, 1962, p. 3. Tso Ch'un-t'ai: 'The Institution and Development of the Economic Accounting System in Our Country', Part 2.

[4] *Kuang Ming Daily* (*Guangming Ribao*), February 25, 1963, p. 4. Hsiang Ching-ch'üan: 'A Draft Discussion on the Function of Price in Promoting Agricultural and Industrial Production at the Present Time', and *Ta Kung Daily* (*Dagong Bao*), Peking, July 6, 1962, p. 3. Ch'en Tsu-wen: 'The Conservation of State Capital.'

[5] *New China Monthly* (*Xinhua Yuebao*) No. 38, December 1952, pp. 138–42. (Reprint of *People's Daily* [*Remnin Ribao*] November 5, 1952, Editorial) and *Stand in the Forefront of the North East's Economic Construction:* Report by Comrade Kao Kang to the CCP North East Region's First Congress 1950, Canton, pp. 20–22.

[6] *Ta Kung Daily* (*Dagong Bao*) Peking, June 1, 1962, p. 3. Tso Ch'un-t'ai: 'The Institution and Development of the Economic Accounting System in Our Country', Part I.

[7] The earlier 'lower' agricultural co-operatives in which ownership of land remained in private hands, although it was worked collectively, cannot strictly be called collective units.

communes were at first held to partake somewhat of the nature of 'ownership by all the people') handicraft co-operatives, supply and marketing co-operatives and credit co-operatives. Many of these are closely integrated with the state-owned sector of the economy. Workers in collective undertakings normally receive a share of a residual income (total income less expenses and other deductions). In those undertakings closely assimilated with the state sector, however, wages may be paid instead.

'Individual ownership by the working people' comprises dwelling houses, peasants' private plots, domestic handicrafts and small workshops. As far as is known, there is no explicit ban on the private hiring of labour (except by members of the Communist Party)[1] for the purposes of non-agricultural production;[2] in this, China differs from the Soviet Union. Any private producer who employs more than three persons is, however, categorised as a capitalist, so presumably his undertaking would be liable to 'socialist transformation' into a joint state-private enterprise. In 1966 it was reported that some Red Guards demanded the deletion from the Constitution of the clauses protecting private property. Our discussion of the role of law in contemporary China will have indicated that the constitutional position may not be a matter of great practical significance, more important in this respect being the political atmosphere at any given time.

Capitalist ownership, mentioned in the Constitution of 1954, was in the following years transformed into joint state-private ownership, with the state as the dominant partner.

Certain other fundamental concepts in the Chinese economy must be defined. Capital investment (*chipen chienshe*—literally basic construction; the equivalent of the Russian *kapitalnoye stroielstvo*) is defined as the act of increasing, repairing and purchasing fixed assets. Specifically it covers building, the acquisition and installation of machinery and other equipment; such designing, scientific research and geological surveying as directly serve investment purposes; compensation to previous inhabitants dislodged from the site of projects and the training of cadres to staff enterprises after completion.[3] In agriculture, capital investment also includes the construction and repair of water conservancy projects, the opening and settlement of new land, the purchase of draught cattle and livestock for breeding purposes and of saplings, as well as of machinery and tools.[4]

Another concept, not dissimilar from economic accountability, is what we may call the 'responsibility (or guarantee) system' (*paokan chihtu*).[5] This,

[1] For reference to this ban, see Chao Shu-li's novel *Sanliwan Village* (English edition), Peking, 1953, pp. 79–80.

[2] In agriculture, the practice of richer peasants employing others on their private plots is sometimes denounced.

[3] The training of the initial complement of staff only would appear covered, and not that of those subsequently appointed; however, this is not altogether clear.

[4] *Basic Questions in the Civil Law of the People's Republic of China*, p. 243 and *Simple Explanation of Terms Used in the First Five-Year Plan for the Development of the National Economy of the People's Republic of China* (in Chinese), Peking, 1955, p. 42, and *Collected Laws and Regulations* ... Vol. 2, p. 545.

[5] This term was also used to denote the 'supply system' in operation until 1955, by which cadres received their keep, or allowances in lieu, instead of wages. *Collected Financial Laws and Regulations of the Central Government* (in Chinese) 1955, p. 459, and p. 210 below.

however, is of native provenance, although the same notion appears all over the world as circumstances require. As employed by the Chinese Communists, the concept has been embellished by borrowing from Soviet practice, particularly in the application of 'responsibility systems' to individual workers, whereas in China the idea had more collective connotation.[1] Under the responsibility system, in the old Chinese sense, a unit guarantees performance in a certain sphere to the authorities of the level immediately above it, in return for which it is allowed a very wide latitude in the conduct of its internal affairs, including its relations with its lower units, without interference from superior authority. According to this traditional system, so long as a province, lineage, village or other group fulfilled its obligations to the outside world, it would be left alone in peace to deal with its members or subordinates as it thought best. This satisfied the Chinese attachment to the notion of harmonious self-sufficient groups. At the same time, it was an eminently practical arrangement in a society where direct administration down to the grass roots was impossible. This 'responsibility system' is so taken for granted in China that it is seldom explicitly spelled out, but it is something we shall often have occasion to recall.

In conflict with this complex of ideas are the demands of the Party, which set out to be a movement corrosive of the ties of small traditional groups. It demands the direct allegiance of the individual, an allegiance prior to that given to family, lineage or locality. Much of the impact of Communism on the Chinese scene, and its interaction with Chinese society, can be seen in the antithesis of these two notions of the responsibility system and of the claims of Party allegiance.

Another term to which we must allude is that of 'contract' (*hot'ung*). Lengthy studies have been made of the nature and significance of contracts in China.[2] Here we will but note that contracts are used to fill in the particulars which state economic plans are too generalized to detail and that contracts are made between and within units at all levels. Contracts are thus 'the method of harmonizing state economic planning and enterprises' economic accountability.'[3] While the need for voluntariness in contracts is sometimes affirmed, it must not be assumed to exist, especially when the parties are under obligation to conclude contracts in fulfilment of their economic plans.

Contracts are made in the course of production, sale, and transport of goods. While private enterprises still existed, the state used contracts placed with them as a means of control and direction. Contracts are also used, as a flexible means of planning, in the state and collective sectors. The use of contracts as instruments of planning is found in the Soviet Union and the Chinese

---

[1] For Soviet influence on the Chinese Communist concept of the 'responsibility system', see F. Schurmann: op. cit., pp. 242–53.

[2] *China Quarterly*, No. 14, April–June 1963, pp. 153–77 and ibid, No. 15, July–September 1963, pp. 115–39. R. M. Pfeffer: 'The Institution of Contracts in the Chinese People's Republic', Parts I and II, and *California Law Review*, Vol. 53, No. 4, October 1965, pp. 1029–60. Gene T. Hsiao: 'The Role of Economic Contracts in Communist China', Berkeley. See also *Political and Legal Research* (*Zhengfa Yanjiu*), No. 2, April 1959, pp. 41–3. Hsieh Ming: 'On the Contract System.'

[3] *Economic Research* (*Jingji Yanjiu*), No. 10, October 1962, p. 20. Kao Hsiang: 'The Functions of the State Bank in Socialist Construction.'

Communists undoubtedly transplanted it. What is difficult to ascertain is how much the system owes to traditional Chinese concepts of contract.

Something must be said about the material used for writing this book. The chief source has been Mainland Chinese newspapers, journals and other publications. It may be wondered how useful such sources can be. Their limitations must be acknowledged. They contain a large ideological element and often exaggerate achievements, while there is usually no method of getting an independent check on the facts they state. At the same time, it must be realized that newspapers and journals form a vital link between the central government and its widespread cadres.[1] ('Cadre' in current Chinese usage denotes anyone in a responsible position, in any organization of party, government, collective agriculture, industry, cultural life, etc.)[2] Local and specialized journals fulfil this same function within their own spheres. This means that the problems discussed in the Press must be real problems on which the centre wishes to give guidance; this prevents too extreme a separation of the Press from actual life.

The four main national daily newspapers published in Peking in recent years are the *People's Daily* (organ of the Central Committee of the Chinese Communist Party), the *Ta Kung Daily*, which dealt mainly with economic affairs, the *Daily Worker*[3] (published by the All-China Federation of Trade Unions) and the *Kuang Ming Daily*, which specializes in cultural matters and is directed at intellectuals. The *Ta Kung Daily* ceased publication in the autumn of 1966. The Party Central Committee also publishes the journal, *Red Flag*.

In keeping with the empirical and concrete character of Chinese thought, approval and disapproval of policies are normally expressed in the Press not only in the abstract but accompanied by examples to be followed or scorned.[4] As all publications in fact if not in theory are official, such approval or disapproval must be taken (to a greater or lesser extent, according to context) as an expression of policy. Sometimes, particularly in specialized journals, an author may be permitted to float a suggestion—e.g. for a new pricing policy for coal—before the authorities have reached any final decision on the matter. Also, in the brief 'Hundred Flowers' period in 1957, frank opinions were published on many matters. Normally, however, anything in the Press may be considered either as official policy or as an idea that might be officially adopted. Editorials and articles in, for example, the *People's Daily* and *Red Flag*, have had, in effect, the force of official directives. The same is true of articles in 'house journals' published by various commissions and ministries,

[1] e.g. some tax collectors in Kwangsi, who spent one day in ten on studying 'directives from higher levels, official documents and relevant editorials from newspapers and journals'. *Ta Kung Daily* (*Dagong Bao*), Peking, July 16, 1962, p. 2. Liang Hung-mou and Lung Cheng-yuan: 'The Completion of Tax Collection Tasks in Successive Years by Muko Tax Office.'

[2] J. W. Lewis: *Leadership in Communist China*, Ithaca, New York, 1963, pp. 186-9. See also F. Schurmann: op. cit., pp. 162-72.

[3] From January 1, 1967, the *Daily Worker* changed its title to *Chinese Workers' Paper*.

[4] We can only speculate about the art of 'getting a favourable mention' in the Press in China, but suspect it may be highly developed. How are examples to be followed, or scorned, chosen? Are there the equivalent of public relations officers, who try to get a good image projected of particular factories, particular Party committees, etc?

e.g. *Planned Economy* (published by the State Planning Commission) and *Finance* (by the Ministry of Finance).[1]

Frequently in this book an individual example will be instanced to illustrate some point. Sometimes this may be because insufficient information is available to warrant generalization so that the best that can be done is to let the reader see the clues obtained. When the meaning of a statement is ambiguous, as often happens, we have usually felt it preferable to give it in quotation, passing on the ambiguity to the reader, rather than to endow it with a meaning which may be incorrect.

Notwithstanding the defects of the Chinese press as source material, it is in general more useful than the accounts of foreign visitors to China, although these can sometimes supplement it. The Press, as we have said, normally deals with real problems, while visitors' contacts are commonly superficial and marginal to a society which they are often not equipped to interpret.

Useful statistical information about the Chinese economy is even more difficult to obtain than other types of material. Since 1960 very few nationwide statistics have been published. In any case interpretation of statistics presents many problems which have been thoroughly expounded in Chohming Li's book, *The Statistical System of Communist China*. These difficulties arise not only from political bias but more fundamentally from the inherent perils of statistical data collected in a large and under-developed country, where subsistence agriculture forms a major part of economic activity. A preindustrial society seldom thinks in precise quantitative terms. Units of measurement often give rise to difficulties. Officially the metric system was adopted in 1959, but the old Chinese measures are still widely used, and local usage may vary from place to place or according to circumstances. The Chinese authorities are well aware of the problem these attitudes present, but changing them can only be a slow process.

Finally a word must be said about the arrangement of the chapters in this book. It might be thought that the most obvious order would be to begin with an account of economic planning and of other of the more centralized activities, and then work outwards, so to speak, to agriculture and industry. However, this would give the impression of an economy whose dominant note was one of centralization. Although in the years since 1949 China has been much more centralized than ever before, yet the country remains primarily one of small scattered rural communities, a far cry from the picture of a monolithic planned economy.

Thus it will be easier to get the picture in focus if we begin with agriculture. Water conservancy follows on naturally, and with it is combined electric power, the two being closely connected through multipurpose river conservancy schemes, and jointly supervised by a single ministry. Then we shall consider industry and mining, before turning to communications and trade. Procurement of agricultural produce overlaps both with trade and with taxation, but it is of such importance as to warrant a separate chapter. Financial and planning activities are then discussed, before we finally draw together our conclusions.

[1] On the role of the Press in China, see F. Schurmann: op. cit., pp. 62–8.

Chapter 2

COLLECTIVE AGRICULTURE I

1. THE RURAL BACKGROUND

The great majority—some 85 per cent—of China's population is engaged in agriculture and of these farmers, again the great majority work the arable 11 per cent or so of the country's area. The rest of China, through lack of water or difficulty of terrain or of access, supports no agriculture save the scattered herding of livestock.

The concentration of a farming population of over 500 million on a cultivated area of 1,600 million *mow* (*c.* 107 million ha.) necessitates intensive husbandry; indeed, through multiple cropping, the cropped acreage is raised over 40 per cent above this figure. Before the successive reorganizations of agriculture brought about by the Communists, the average size of farms was very small. A sample survey in twenty-two provinces made by J. L. Buck in 1929-33[1] gave the mean size of farms as 25·4 *mow* (approximately 1·7 ha.), the median as 20·1 *mow* (1·3 ha.) and the mode as 24·3 *mow* (1·6 ha.). In the wheat region of north China, the mean, median, and modal sizes of farms were 34·2 *mow*, 21·6 *mow* and 33·4 *mow* respectively, notably higher than in the rice-growing south, for which the corresponding figures were 19·1 *mow*, 13·8 *mow* and 18·2 *mow*.[2]

According to Buck's survey, 54 per cent of the farmers owned all the land they worked, 29 per cent owned part and rented part, while 17 per cent were wholly tenants. Another survey in the same period gave the owners as 46 per cent, part-owners 25 per cent, and tenants as 29 per cent. In north China the proportion of owners was double that in the south. Little difference in size of farms was found between owners and part-owners, but tenants had on average about 17 per cent less land than the other two categories. Over China as a whole, in Buck's sample, a little under 75 per cent of the farm land was owned by those who worked it.[3] Land holdings were fragmented and scattered; this caused waste of land in boundaries and of time in going from one small plot to another. In some parts of China, in Kwangtung for example, much land was owned by corporate groups, such as localized lineages.

---

[1] J. L. Buck: *Land Utilization in China*, Nanking, 1937 (reprinted New York, 1964), pp. 268–9. Although this study was made 16–20 years before the Communist victory, no great changes occurred in the organization of Chinese agriculture, or in its methods, until those introduced by the Communists. The mode was estimated from a sample taken from twenty provinces; the mean and median from a sample from twenty-two provinces. It should be noted that some Chinese social scientists consider that Buck's sample had an inbuilt bias towards the better-off peasants, owing to the greater feasibility of surveying the more peaceful areas and the more prosperous households.

[2] Ibid. [3] Ibid., pp. 194–7.

Rent took several different forms. In 51 per cent of Buck's cases, the tenant paid a fixed quantity of produce or its cash value; fixed cash rents applied to 25 per cent of the tenancies. Share rent, by which the landlord claimed a fixed proportion of the main crop (thus sharing the harvest risk) was found in 22 per cent of the sample, being commoner in the north where agricultural risks rank high.[1] The usual practice in share cropping was for the landlord to take 40 per cent of the main crop, but in some places this went up to 90 per cent.[2]

The burden of rent was often made weightier by the system of rent deposits on entry to tenancies and by levies of government and military (although land tax was officially borne by the landlords). Payment of these exactions frequently led peasants into debt, thus adding to their troubles.

In the mid-1930s, the chief sources of rural credit were merchants, landlords, rich peasants and shopkeepers, in that order; in 1934 these together were reckoned to have provided 80 per cent of the total. In the next ten years their relative share lessened and that coming from banks increased.[3] Most loans were incurred not for productive purposes, which would have raised borrowers' capacity to repay, but for imposts such as those described, for the celebration of weddings, birthdays and funerals, and to buy food in the lean pre-harvest period. Buck found that the rate of interest charged per month averaged 2·7 per cent (3·2 per cent in the wheat region and 2·3 per cent in the rice region).[4]

Apart from providing credit on such terms, and as we have seen, in some cases sharing harvest risks, landlords seldom had any positive economic function. While large landholdings were by no means unknown, they were seldom worked as one estate but were normally rented out to a number of tenants. This suggests that economies of scale in Chinese agriculture may not be great, at least after a relatively small size has been reached.

The average size of farm families, in Buck's sample, was just over five persons. Total population growth in China between 1865–1953 was relatively low, at an estimated average annual rate of 0·4–0·5 per cent.[5] Some 45 per cent of the rural males and 9 per cent of the rural females over seven years of age were found by Buck to engage exclusively in agricultural occupations of all kinds, while another 27 per cent of the men and 20 per cent of the women supplemented agriculture with other work. Non-agricultural tasks (including household duties) were the sole occupation of 20 per cent of males and 59 per cent of females, while only 7 per cent and 11 per cent of each sex respectively were idle throughout the year. Men were responsible for 80 per cent of all

[1] Buck: pp. 197–8. The remaining 2 per cent of tenants were croppers, who provided only the labour and received only a very small proportion of the crop.

[2] T. H. Shen: *Agricultural Resources of China*, Ithaca, New York, 1951, p. 98.

[3] Yen Chung-p'ing and others (ed.): *Selected Statistical Material on the Modern Economic History of China* (in Chinese), Peking, 1955, pp. 345–6. Buck's figures for sources of credit in 1929–33 are analysed differently but are generally consonant with those given by Yen. See Buck: op. cit., p. 465.

[4] Buck: op. cit., p. 462. The higher interest rates in the wheat region were due to the lower level of economic development and the higher risks of farming in north China, ibid, p. 463.

[5] Buck: op. cit., p. 368, and Ping-ti Ho: *Studies on the Population of China 1368–1953*. Cambridge, Massachusetts, 1959, p. 277.

farm labour, women for 13 per cent, and children for 7 per cent. Two man-equivalent labour units were employed on average per farm, of which family labour accounted for 1·7 units and hired labour for only 0·3 per cent of a unit.[1] It is to be expected (although no study on this point is to hand) that women's contribution to agriculture has increased, in numbers working and even more in effectiveness, since the decline of the custom of footbinding, a decline which was rapid after the 1911 Revolution.

In the winter season, from November to February, agricultural work is slack; time spent at this period accounted, according to Buck, for 80 per cent of the 1·7 months of idleness averaged by able-bodied men of working age.[2] The greatest annual festival, the lunar New Year, occurs in January or February.

Shortage of labour at the peak seasons of agricultural activity (harvesting, transplanting of rice and irrigation) was found by Buck to be widespread.[3]

In harvested tonnage, rice is the chief staple crop of China, followed by coarse grains (maize, millet, and kaoliang) tubers and wheat. By area of cultivation, however, coarse grains come first, and then rice, wheat and tubers. The chief rice areas are in the Yangtze and Pearl River basins, where in some places up to three crops a year may be grown. In recent years, the northern limits of rice cultivation have been extended and also the areas of multiple cropping. The north China plain is the main area for wheat, although this crop is found in every province.

Maize, millet and kaoliang are more resistant to drought and water-logging than rice and wheat; consequently they are grown on land unsuited to either of those preferred crops. Coarse grains, with potatoes, are considered inferior foodstuffs, and have traditionally been the fare of the poor. Sweet potatoes are the most widely grown tubers. Their acreage is reported to have been considerably extended in the 1950s.

Rice is a highly labour-intensive crop. The seeds are sown in dry seedbeds, and later the seedlings are planted out one by one into flooded fields. Rice fields must be encompassed with small dykes, in order to retain the water in which the rice plants grow. These dykes have constantly to be watched for damage, and quickly repaired, as a single breach might cause the loss of all the water. Because of the water, rice fields must be flat; in hilly areas this means that small terraces have to be carved out and maintained; in 1929–33 about 25 per cent of all the land was estimated to be terraced.[4] Without perpetual watchfulness, disaster can quickly occur.

'The core of Chinese agriculture has been its cropping system.'[5] Past improvements in farming have largely taken the form of developing new systems of crop rotation and new strains of rice, wheat, and other crops, which enable these to be grown more quickly and in wider areas. New crops have been introduced over the centuries and the area of multiple cropping extended. The government at times took the lead in promoting these innovations.[6]

Chinese agriculture is chiefly arable, due to the necessity of producing the maximum amount of food from every piece of land. Livestock rearing pre-

[1] Buck: op. cit., pp. 292 and 372.
[2] Ibid., pp. 294–5.
[3] Ibid., p. 299.
[4] Buck: op. cit., p. 192.
[5] Ping-ti Ho: op. cit., p. 169.
[6] Ibid., Chapter 8, passim.

dominates only in those peripheral areas of the country which are unsuited for crops; herding of sheep, goats, cattle, horses or yaks is there the main occupation. Over the rest of China, the most common farm livestock are poultry, pigs, and draught animals. In Buck's sample, 75 per cent of the farms in the rice region kept chickens, 13 per cent ducks, 58 per cent pigs, 33 per cent oxen and 30 per cent water buffaloes. Among farms in the wheat region, 60 per cent had chickens, 26 per cent pigs, 39 per cent donkeys, 36 per cent oxen and 12 per cent mules. On an average, a draught animal in China is reckoned to be able to work 30 *mow* (2 ha.) of land; therefore owing to the small size of the farms and the poverty of the peasants, such animals were often owned in partnership by two or more farmers.[1] The significance of livestock in the arable areas of China lies perhaps as much in the manure as in the labour or food they provide.

The importance of irrigation in the rice region can scarcely be overstated. On the basis of Buck's studies, estimates of irrigated land were then between 38–47 per cent of the total cultivated area; almost all the rice land was irrigated. Water for irrigation is derived from streams, ponds, wells, and ditches, streams being most important in the rice region and wells in the wheat region. Great ingenuity has been shown in the control and pumping of water supplies. Many irrigation tasks have always been undertaken by community action, and the same holds true of flood control schemes.[2]

The Chinese peasant has always exercised great economy in returning all waste matter to the soil. The main fertilizers are animal and human excreta, green manure, mud from ponds and rivers, and soya bean cake. Chemical fertilizers are still in very short supply and are allocated by the government mainly for cotton and other special crops, and for special areas. Chinese soils are generally deficient in nitrogen, less so in phosphate, and least in potash.[3]

Less skill has been shown in improving farm tools than in working out cropping and irrigation systems or in utilizing organic waste. 'The native farm implements', according to a leading Chinese expert, 'have a low working capacity and consequently reduce the working efficiency of human and animal labour; they handicap the quantity and quality of the work done, affect the growth of crops, and cause damage and loss.'[4] Practically no farm machines had been introduced into Chinese agriculture before the Communist era, except on some of the large former Japanese farms in Manchuria. The mechanization of rice culture in any case poses special problems. Rural transport has always been very crude. Where no waterways exist, a large proportion of goods is carried either by wheelbarrow or by human carriers using shoulder poles or baskets on the back.

The shortage of capital exemplified in the small number of draught animals and poor implements and means of transport, has been a characteristic of Chinese farming. A peasant too poor to own a draught beast might exchange

[1] Buck: op. cit., pp. 245–6 and *Collected Laws and Regulations of the People's Republic of China* (in Chinese), Vol. 7, p. 301.
[2] Buck: op. cit., pp. 186–7.
[3] See H. L. Richardson: *The Use of Fertilizers in the Far East*. Paper read before the Fertilizer Society in London, 1956, pp. 27–30 for a discussion of the usage of fertilizers in China.
[4] T. H. Shen: op. cit., pp. 117-118.

his labour for the loan of one from a richer neighbour. Another indication of the peasant's lack of capital is that farm implements, stores of grain, and also livestock were wont to be kept in the farmstead, frequently in bedrooms, living rooms or kitchens.

Studies by Buck in certain districts of north and east-central China and east China in the 1920s found the average farm family gained 25–67 per cent of its income, depending on locality, from sales of output, the rest of its income being taken in the form of self-consumed home produce. In the northern localities surveyed, the proportion of sales was positively correlated with income, while the reverse held in the one district south of the Yangtze included in the sample. In some areas, peasants purchased a high proportion of the foodstuffs they consumed.[1] Almost two-thirds of the farm output sold went through middlemen, while the rest was purchased directly by consumers.[2] Over 44 per cent of peasants' sales of farm produce were made at market towns (*chen*), 29 per cent in *hsien* cities, while 19 per cent was sold in or near the producer's own village and 8 per cent at distant places.[3] Near cities, the commercialization of agriculture would naturally be greater than average. Here peasants have always concentrated on intensive growing of vegetables, made possible by the availability of large supplies of nightsoil. Thus cities are surrounded by circles of green, gradually shading off into ordinary farmland.

The significance of the market towns has been not only as the chief sales places for surplus farm output, but also as social centres for the area each serves. The role of these 'standard market towns', (defined as those which cater for the normal needs of peasant households) and of their dependent 'standard marketing systems', estimated to total some 58,000 in the whole of China in 1949, has been explored by G. W. Skinner,[4] and we will have occasion to discuss this topic further. Here we need but note that in addition to standard markets, are those of a higher level in which wholesaling is an important, though not the sole, activity. These Skinner calls intermediate markets, those above them he designates as central markets.

The rural population of China before the Communist changes has been commonly analysed (especially in Communist writings) into five main categories, according to their relation to land. Landlords gained their livelihood by renting out land and by employing labourers to work the land they retained. Rich peasants themselves worked their own land, but supplemented family labour with permanent hired hands. Middle peasants neither employed others to work their land nor themselves took employment on the land of others.[5] Poor peasants were those who could not make a living from working their

[1] *Soviet Studies*, Vol. XVI, No. 2, October 1964, pp. 223–5. J. Gray: 'Political Aspects of the Land Reform Campaign in China, 1947–52.' (Calculations based on J. L. Buck: *China's Farm Economy*, Nanking, 1930, p. 66.)

[2] J. L. Buck: *Land Utilization in China*, p. 350.

[3] Ibid., p. 349.

[4] *Journal of Asian Studies*, Vol. XXIV, No. 1, November 1964, No. 2, February 1965, and No. 3, May 1965. G. W. Skinner: 'Marketing and Social Structure in Rural China', Parts I, II, and III. The 58,000 standard systems of 1949 (Ibid., No. 2, February 1965, p. 228) included those depending on larger towns which, while perhaps being intermediate markets, also served as 'standard marketing towns' to their immediate environs.

[5] Middle peasants are often, in Chinese Communist parlance, sub-divided into 'upper middle' and 'lower middle' peasants.

own scanty holdings, but had to spend part of their time working for others. At the bottom of the social scale, landless labourers depended for their whole livelihood on hiring out their labour. These categories were not in real life as distinct as in exposition.

Studies made in various places between 1925 and 1937 indicate that landlords formed from 0·5 per cent to 7 per cent of all rural households, rich peasants between 1–11 per cent, middle peasants from 6–43 per cent, poor peasants 43–80 per cent and others (e.g. landless labourers, or non-agricultural) between 3–21 per cent of all rural households.[1] The richer classes, especially the landlords, constituted a higher percentage of the rural population than of rural households because their prosperity meant that they were more likely to support the extended family of Chinese tradition or at least a stem family, while the nuclear family was in fact usual among the peasants.

The class structure in the Chinese countryside was by no means clear cut or rigid. Division of property among all the sons of a family meant that large estates did not often last long and that there was always a good deal of social mobility. Ties of kinship might exist between members of all classes: landlords, peasants of all grades and landless labourers could be found within a single lineage. Thus there was not the social polarization of the pre-revolutionary Russian villages.[2] However, during the twentieth century, economic polarization had been increasing in rural China.

Social groupings, often with economic functions, included not only kinship groups and villages, but also various types of village association, whose functions might include crop protection and irrigation. Nor must the secret societies be forgotten.

The condition of the peasants had deteriorated in the first half of the twentieth century. Decades of warlord rule and civil and international warfare had disrupted transport and irrigation and led to the press-ganging of many rural youths and to large and arbitrary tax demands. Peasant indebtedness grew heavier. In some districts, taxes were levied for forty years in advance. Tenancy increased and in many places rents rose: these circumstances were particularly in evidence in the vicinity of the large port cities.

Sun Yat-sen, the leader of the 1911 Revolution, called for land 'to the tiller'. The Kuomintang included rent reduction in its programme but did not implement it.

In their rule of the 'early liberated areas' before 1949, the Communists had experimented with various types of land policy. During the Sino-Japanese War, confiscation and redistribution of land gave way to the more moderate policies of reduction of rent and of interest, but the former drastic measures were resumed after the Japanese defeat. By July 1950, when an agrarian reform law was promulgated, much of the country had already experienced land reform.[3] In the course of the next two-and-a-half years, land reform was

---

[1] Yen Chung-p'ing and others (ed.), op. cit., p. 261.

[2] *The Political Quarterly*, Vol. 35, No. 3, July–September 1964, p. 277. J. Gray: 'The Communist Party and the System of Government.'

[3] In this and succeeding paragraphs, I am much indebted to an unpublished University of London Ph.D. Thesis (1966) by John Chiu-hon Wong, entitled *A Study of Communist Land Reform in Post-War China with Special Reference to Policy and Its Implementation*.

carried out in the rest of China. It was a piecemeal operation, the administrative level being the *hsien* (county) with the *hsiang* (rural district) being normally taken as the operational unit. The way land reform was implemented might vary very considerably from place to place. The deliberate emphasis on class struggle was, however, common to all areas and many landlords were killed after summary 'popular' trials.

Land distribution, done as it was in a rough and ready fashion, consisted of confiscating the above-average quantity of land, draught animals, implements and houses of the landlords, and also some of the land owned by rich peasants but not worked by themselves. The confiscated assets were then distributed among poor peasants and landless labourers. In the process, 40–50 per cent of the arable land of the country was said to have been redistributed with some 60–70 per cent of the rural population as beneficiaries.[1] The result, however, was not egalitarianism; the rich and middle peasants still had greater than average holdings, as well as more and better equipment and animals. They, too, were more likely to be literate than their poorer fellows; this advantage was even more probably possessed by landlord families. The more prosperous members of the rural community also would have had more experience in dealing with affairs and with outsiders and, since some class mobility had existed, they may well, on an average, have been of higher than normal drive and ability.

One of the immediate results of land reform was a rise in the numbers and in the relative importance—social and economic—of the middle peasants.[2] Another result, stemming from the downfall of the landlords and merchants, who had been important sources of loans to the peasants, was the occurrence of an acute credit crisis. Many of the holdings resulting from land reform were too small to be viable, especially as the redistribution of draught animals and of farming implements was not as far-reaching as the redistribution of land. Therefore the poor peasants and former landless labourers remained short of animals and equipment. At the same time, their opportunities for employment by others had diminished, as more prosperous peasants became chary of hiring labour for fear of political ostracism and possible higher reclassification in the social scale.[3]

In order to fill the credit gap, the government encouraged the formation of various types of credit co-operatives, including some based on traditional practices and others which were departments of supply and marketing co-operatives. For a solution to the problem of the disparate needs of poor peasants on the one hand and of rich and middle peasants on the other, the traditional practice of bringing together several families to form mutual aid was refurbished, and mutual aid teams were established, at first temporarily, during the busiest farming seasons, but before long on a permanent basis. These teams might undertake subsidiary occupations (e.g. handicrafts) as well as farming. They were formed by the participating households pooling labour, draught animals and equipment, so that one might supply what the

---

[1] Tung Ta-lin: *Agricultural Co-operation in China*, Peking, 1959, p. 7.
[2] *Soviet Studies*, Vol. XVI, No. 2, October 1964. J. Gray, loc. cit., p. 228, and John C. H. Wong: op. cit.
[3] John C. H. Wong: op. cit.

others lacked, while yet retaining private ownership both of the assets pooled and of the land worked. Such teams, as well as being traditional in some parts of the country, had also been established by the Communists in the 'early liberated areas'. Before long some mutual aid teams began to acquire new property which was owned in common—a buffalo perhaps, or some implements; the teams also tended to grow larger, from about four households in the early days up to about ten.[1]

While mutual aid teams were yet being formed, experiments were under way with a larger and closer unit of organization, the agricultural producer co-operative. Some of these too had been established earlier in areas of China long under Communist rule. Even when leaving these parts out of the question, there was an overlap in time between the first three major organizational changes that the Communists introduced in Chinese agriculture—land reform, mutual aid teams and producer co-operatives. Whilst, for example, land reform was still being implemented in one place, others might have advanced to mutual aid teams or even to co-operatives.[2]

The agricultural producer co-operative involved the pooling of land as well as of labour, draught animals and implements. In the 'lower' agricultural producer co-operatives, as the first 'semi-socialist' type to be formed were called, a share of the crop, usually 30–60 per cent, was paid out as dividends on the land so pooled, while the rest (after payments for animals and implements) was distributed according to the labour performed. The trend in these lower co-operatives was towards reducing the proportion awarded to land, especially when production increased. In the 'higher' agricultural producer co-operatives (sometimes known as 'collectives' to distinguish them from the earlier type of co-operative) this trend was taken to the point where no payments were made for land which thenceforward was collectively owned and not just co-operatively worked; the whole income of the co-operative, net of taxes and other expenses, and of payments into certain collective funds, was distributed as remuneration of labour, calculated either on a simple time basis or on the basis of individual norms, piece-work or contract work.

We have seen that the various stages of Communist agrarian policy overlapped in time. Another feature was that the changes did not proceed smoothly over time but with pauses for checking. 'Whenever a batch of co-operatives have been established in a province or county, there must be a time when progress is held up for a check-over before a new batch of co-operatives is formed.'[3] Thus before the autumn of 1954, three batches of agricultural producer co-operatives had been formed—numbering 300, 13,700 and 86,000 respectively. A fourth group, of 550,000, was set up in 1954–5.[4]

In July 1955 Chairman Mao stated that by the spring of 1958 some 55 million peasant households (i.e. half the total rural population, according to

[1] J. Gray: 'Collectivization in China: the Experimental Year, 1952.' (Unpublished paper given to a working group at the Royal Institution of International Affairs, London); and John C. H. Wong: op. cit.

[2] *Mao Tse-tung: On the Question of Agricultural Co-operation.* (A Report delivered at a Meeting of Secretaries of Provincial, Municipal, and Autonomous Region Committees of the Communist Party of China on July 31, 1955). English Edition, Peking, 1962, pp. 3–5.

[3] Mao Tse-tung: op. cit., p. 25.

[4] Ibid., p. 7. Exact dates are not given.

Mao) would have been organized into lower agricultural producer co-operatives.[1] In the event, as can be seen from the following table, already by 1956 over 96 per cent of the peasant households were in co-operatives, and higher co-operatives accounted for the great majority. Not all areas passed through every stage; in some cases a transition straight from mutual aid teams to higher co-operatives might be made; also it must be borne in mind that the transitions from one stage to another were not necessarily abrupt. As the mutual aid team accumulated common property, it became increasingly similar to a lower co-operative. The lower co-operative, in turn, as the proportion of its income distributed as dividends to capital declined, could move smoothly towards the next stage, that of the higher co-operative. Nevertheless, even making allowance for this, the speed of change was very rapid between 1953, when only 40 per cent of households were in mutual aid teams and 1956, when 88 per cent were members of higher agricultural co-operatives.

Percentage of Peasant Households in Mutual Aid Teams and Agricultural Producer Co-operatives, 1950–6

	Mutual Aid Teams	Lower Agricultural Producer Co-operatives	Higher Agricultural Producer Co-operatives	Total per cent in Mutual Aid Teams and Agricultural Co-operatives
1950	10·7	—	—	10·7
1951	19·2	—	—	19·2
1952	39·9	0·1	—	40·0
1953	39·3	0·2	—	39·5
1954	58·3	2·0	—	60·3
1955	50·7	14·2	—	64·9
1956	—	8·5	87·8	96·3

Source: *Ten Great Years*, Peking, 1960, p. 35.

Throughout all the stages of the formation of mutual aid teams and agricultural producer co-operatives, the official statements emphasized that participation must be voluntary and to the mutual benefit of all who joined, i.e. not only to the benefit of the poor peasants. However, as we mentioned earlier, in present circumstances in China, voluntariness is an elusive concept, and it is clear that great pressure was exercised in pushing through each successive stage of the government's programme. In any case, once a large part of any village had been formed into a co-operative, it must often have been very difficult for a few peasants to keep out, owing to mutual dependence in irrigation and other matters. Inducements, in the form of easier access to state credit or to marketing facilities, probably played only a minor role in prompting peasants along the route charted for them. The impetus for all the changes, from land reform to the communes, came from above. A pre-determined pattern of change was, at each stage, imposed from the centre although scope was left for local variations on the pattern. The speed and scope of the successive changes, however, give rise to doubts of how thorough-reaching they were in all cases.

Peasants were supposed to be free to withdraw from mutual aid teams and

---

[1] Mao Tse-tung: op. cit., p. 28.

co-operatives and indeed some such instances occurred. However, demands for withdrawal were liable to be denounced as 'agitation' and those making such demands were categorized as 'landlords, rich peasants, counter-revolutionaries and bad elements'. Cadres known to be lukewarm towards co-operativization were also likely to be condemned as rightist opportunists, as for example P'an Fu-sheng, First Party Secretary of Honan Province.[1]

The overall motive of the Communists for moving towards agricultural collectivization was, of course, ideological. Their step-by-step progress towards their goal can be attributed to tactical reasons. The land hunger of the peasants was one of the forces which propelled the Communists to power and hence land reform was the policy publicized during the struggle with the Kuomintang, and in the early years of Communist government; only when and where their rule had been consolidated could the next stages be pushed. By that time too, it had become evident to the peasants that land reform was no panacea. The authorities no doubt hoped that the inner logic of the situation would lead the peasants willingly to accept the transition to mutual aid teams and then to co-operatives. In this hope they were not wholly justified, but it is true to say that up to the formation of the communes, of which we shall speak in the next section, the drive towards collectivization did not disorganize agriculture to the extent that had occurred in the Soviet Union.

It is a disputable question how far the Chinese Communists were influenced in their agrarian policy by Soviet experience. Certainly they were in the habit of alluding to it, both as holding out an example to be followed or by illustrating dangers to be avoided.[2] These allusions, however, seem to be more for the sake of making points in arguments with opponents than for actually giving guidance in making decisions.

On the practical level, two considerations may have influenced the Communist leadership in its successive decisions to speed up the pace of agrarian reorganization after land reform. The first of these was the need to extract a sufficient surplus of farm output from the peasants and the second, the fear of the revival of a 'rich peasant economy' in the countryside.

Land reform diverted a considerable part of the farm surplus, which had formerly been paid to landlords as rent, to the poor peasants, who may be assumed to have had a high income elasticity of demand for food. The lack of suitable industrial goods for sale in rural areas in those years must have intensified the poor peasants' preference for consuming the extra food themselves, rather than marketing it. This was a major contributory cause of the grain crisis of 1953 which led to the introduction of compulsory sales of grain to the state. The government hoped that the co-operatives would be instruments of control over the peasants, enabling more of the surplus to be siphoned off the farms.

The authorities also hoped that co-operatives would be more efficient at producing food. The effect of land reform and the formation of co-operatives on agricultural output is difficult to disentangle from the operation of other

---

[1] *Honan Daily* (*Honan Ribao*), July 4, 1958 (CB No. 515). P'an was condemned as a rightist in 1958, but later rehabilitated; by 1966 he was First Party Secretary of Heilungkiang province.

[2] e.g. Mao Tse-tung: op. cit., pp. 18–23.

factors, including the natural fluctuations of the harvest. The period during which land reform was put into effect undoubtedly saw a substantial rise in farm production. But this period was also the time of the restoration of law and order, the repair of dykes and irrigation works, and the rehabilitation of transport. During the First Five Year Plan period (which covered the latter part of the movement to form mutual aid teams, as well as the establishment of the agricultural producer co-operatives) grain output, on official estimates, rose by 20 per cent.[1] It is, nevertheless, difficult to see any correlation between the rather jerky upward trend of grain output and the no less jerky organizational changes or even to decide whether without these changes, the rise would have been greater or less.

The number of draught cattle declined seriously after collectivization, owing both to slaughter by the peasants and to failure to rear young beasts. Their rate of increase fell from 1953, and in 1956 an absolute decline in numbers set in which continued in 1957. The resulting shortage was particularly acute on the north China plain; here it meant that human labour had to be substituted for animals in pulling ploughs.[2] It also led to a decline in manure supplies.

We have seen that land reform did not usher in an era of equality in rural China. In the succeeding years, indeed, inequalities began to grow greater. The maintenance of peace and order must have made it more worth while for industrious and intelligent peasants to work hard, and thus to widen the difference between their wealth and that of their less enterprising fellows. 'Every one has noticed in recent years', reported Mao in 1955, 'that new rich peasants have sprung up everywhere, and that many well-to-do middle peasants are striving to become rich peasants. On the other hand, many poor peasants, lacking sufficient means of production, are still living in poverty; some are in debt, others are selling or renting their land. If this tendency goes unchecked', Mao continued, 'the bipolar differentiation in the countryside will get worse day by day.'[3] The fear that this situation would get out of hand prompted the authorities to take drastic action, by speeding up their timetable for collectivizing the peasants. When we take up the story of agrarian collectivization in greater detail in the next section, we will see that the formation of the communes represented an attempt at even greater acceleration of change.

Before concluding this section, something must be said about the Party and government organs concerned with agriculture at central and other levels.

The Central Committee's Rural Work Department and Agriculture and Forestry Political Department, are the highest Party organs charged with supervision of all facets of life in the countryside. Their counterpart in the government is the State Council's Office of Agriculture and Forestry (the former Seventh General Office) which controls the Ministries of Agriculture, Forestry, State Farms and Land Reclamation, and Aquatic Products, as well as the Central Bureau of Meteorology. The exceptionally close interlocking of

[1] *Ten Great Years*, p. 120.
[2] *Collected Laws and Regulations* . . ., Vol. 7, p. 301.
[3] Mao Tse-tung: op. cit., p. 27.

Party and governmental hierarchies in agriculture was demonstrated by the fact that for some years before 1962 the directorships of the Rural Work Department and of the State Council Office of Agriculture and Forestry were held concurrently by Teng Tzu-hui. No other example is known of dual tenure of two such posts. The Department and the Office also had two deputy directors in common, one of these two being Liao Lu-yen, Minister of Agriculture. In 1962 T'an Chen-lin succeeded Teng Tzu-hui as Director of the State Council Office. Whether Teng still remains Director of the Rural Work Department is not known. No announcement was made that he had been succeeded by T'an in this second appointment, so it may be supposed that the two positions were from 1962 held by different men, a development which may betoken the less political approach adopted towards agriculture at that time.

Functional bureaux within the Ministry of Agriculture exist for such matters as soil utilization, seed control, plant protection and industrial crops. The territorial network supervised by the Ministry includes bureaux and offices at the level of provinces, districts and *hsien*. In 1963 it was announced that special organs concerned with rural subsidiary production (i.e. everything excluding arable farming) had been set up in many areas at the provincial, administrative district and *hsien* levels;[1] it was not stated whether these were to come under the Ministry of Agriculture.

The Ministry of Agriculture controls the Chinese Academy of Agricultural Sciences, which was established in 1957. This academy operates specialized research institutes, and also co-ordinates the research programmes of agricultural colleges and other bodies in this field. Each of the provincial level authorities has its own agricultural research institute. In addition, the State Council's Commission for Science and Technology interests itself in agriculture as well as in other spheres.

The reported activities of the Ministry of Agriculture are mostly of a routine nature. The Ministry holds conferences, for example, to formulate details of national plans and issues instructions to local authorities on such topics as measures against pests and plant diseases.

The Central Bureau of Meteorology, founded in 1954, comes directly under the aegis of the State Council. Soviet methods have been adopted and at one time a Soviet adviser was attached to the Central Bureau.[2] A nationwide system of weather observation reaches down to *hsien* observatories and to outposts in communes.

Agriculture in China today falls into three divisions—state farms, collective agriculture, and private plots. State farms are owned and operated on behalf of the government. Collective agriculture accounts for the greatest part of the country's agricultural activity. This category, comprising the people's communes, the production brigades and the production teams, implies collective ownership and operation by members of these bodies. Private plots, together with privately raised livestock, handicrafts and other sideline occupations, are those means of livelihood currently carried on by individual rural households, almost all of which are members of agricultural collectives

[1] *Ta Kung Daily* (*Dagong Bao*), Peking, October 10, 1963, p. 1. Editorial.
[2] *Science News* (*Kexue Tongbao*), No. 10, 1954, p. 56 and No. 12, 1955, p. 54.

under people's communes. It is to collective agriculture, together with the private plots of its participants, that we shall now direct our attention.

2. THE EVOLUTION OF THE COMMUNE

By March 1957 some 97 per cent of China's rural population were organized in 752,000 agricultural producer co-operatives, of which 668,000 were of the higher (and larger) type and 84,000 of the lower category.[1] The higher co-operatives at that time averaged something over 170 households each, against 54 for the lower co-operatives. A reaction set in before long in favour of a smaller size for the higher co-operatives. In a directive of September 1957 it was suggested that the higher co-operative should normally be co-terminous with a village of a hundred or more households, with the proviso that large villages might be kept as one co-operative or might be split into several, and small villages might be combined into one co-operative. Beneath the large co-operative it was laid down there should be production brigades (*sheng-ch'antui*) consisting of about 20 households each; no additional levels of management should be allowed apart from those of the co-operative and the brigade, and third and fourth levels, where they existed, should be abolished. Once this system of management had been settled, it was to be announced that no further change would take place for the space of ten years.[2]

Whether this directive had any effect in reducing the size of the co-operative is doubtful. The 740,000 agricultural co-operatives, all apparently of the higher type, which existed in January 1958 still averaged about 170 households each.[3] In 1956 complaints were made of encroachment by agricultural co-operatives on the sphere of the *hsiang*, the lowest unit of rural administration. In some places, indeed, *hsiang* and agricultural co-operatives had actually amalgamated; hence some agricultural co-operatives comprised several thousand inhabitants. By the summer of 1958 credit co-operatives had, in certain areas, been incorporated into the agricultural co-operatives, and with official approval.[4] Despite earlier misgivings, it had come to be realized by 1958 that competent cadres were so scarce in the countryside that it was impossible to staff several sets of organizations—the *hsiang* and the various types of co-operative. This was especially the case in financial matters. One of the narrowest bottlenecks in all sectors of the Chinese economy in recent years has been, as we shall often have cause to note, the supply of accountants,

[1] H. Yin and Yi-chang Yin; *Economic Statistics of Mainland China*, Cambridge, Mass., 1960, p. 38.

[2] *New China Fortnightly* (*Xinhua Banyuekan*), No. 117, October 10, 1957, p. 137. Directive of the Central Committee of the Chinese Communist Party, September 14, 1957.

[3] *Red Flag* (*Hongqi*), No. 1, January 1, 1959, p. 14. Liao Lu-yen, Minister of Agriculture: 'The 1959 Task on the Agricultural Front.'

[4] *Study* (*Xuexi*), August 1956, p. 27. Hsüeh Ch'iu-lun: Reply to a Question Whether the *Hsiang* Organization Remains Necessary Where Co-operatives Have Been Formed; and *People's Daily* (*Renmin Ribao*), December 24, 1958, p. 7. Chao Han: 'Government and Commune May be One, but Party and Commune May Not be One'; and *Ta Kung Daily* (*Dagong Bao*), Peking, August 8, 1958, p. 2. Mei Chi-lun: 'Some Questions on the Work of Credit Departments.' In some parts of Shantung no distinction was made in 1957 between the Party, the government, and the agricultural co-operatives. R. MacFarquhar; *The Hundred Flowers*, London, 1960, p. 211.

for whom numeracy as well as literacy is required. This shortage had delayed the setting up of financial organs in the *hsiang*, as well as being a cause for the absorption of some credit co-operatives into agricultural co-operatives.¹

The *hsiang*, like the agricultural co-operative, had experienced several vicissitudes within a few years. At the time of land reform, the size of the *hsiang* was ordered to be reduced (and thus their number increased). By the end of 1955 there were altogether around 210,000 *hsiang*. Policy was then reversed in favour of larger *hsiang*, and it was laid down that the population of *hsiang* in plain, hilly and mountainous areas should be respectively of the order of 10,000–20,000, 5,000–8,000 and 2,000–3,000 or less.² By August 1958 and perhaps before, amalgamations had reduced the number of *hsiang* to something over 80,000.³ The intention may well have been to enable each new and larger higher agricultural co-operative to be comprised within a single *hsiang*, as well as to bring about a coincidence of the administrative system with the marketing systems.⁴ The responsibilities of the *hsiang* at this period apparently included the development of agriculture, of rural industry and of education.⁵

In the summer of 1958 a great movement was launched to amalgamate agricultural co-operatives and *hsiang* into larger bodies, called 'people's communes'. These communes were to combine political and economic functions and be 'both basic economic units and basic units of state power'.⁶ The communes were to be multi-purpose units for management of agricultural, industrial, commercial, cultural and military affairs. They were to achieve this multi-purpose nature by absorbing or amalgamating with the various basic level organizations operating in the countryside—which included the officially sponsored co-operatives for supply and marketing, credit and handicrafts, and the local branches of the People's Bank.⁷ Sometimes, if not always, market towns were incorporated into communes and at least temporarily lost their administrative identity and much of their economic stand-

¹ See p. 400, below.

² *Handbook of Current Affairs* (*Shishi Shouce*), No. 14, July 25, 1956, translated in Chao Kuo-chun: *Agrarian Policies of Mainland China: A Documentary Study* (1949–56), Cambridge, Mass., 1957, p. 259 and *China Quarterly*, No. 11, July–September 1962, pp. 143 and 146. R. Hofheinz: 'Rural Administration in Communist China.'

³ *Economic Research* (*Jingji Yanjiu*), No. 8, August 1958, p. 40. Wang Shao-fei: 'Collectivization as Seen from the Viewpoint of a *Hsiang* Federation of Co-operatives.'

⁴ *Journal of Asian Studies*, Vol. XXIV, No. 3, May 1965, pp. 367–8. G. W. Skinner, loc. cit.

⁵ *People's Daily* (*Renmin Ribao*), June 23, 1958, in *People's Handbook* (*Renmin Shouce*) *1959*, p. 362. Speech by Ma Ming-fang, Minister of Commerce; and *Finance* (*Caizheng*), No. 9, September 5, 1958, p. 18. Tuan Li-chün: 'Waste Land and Pasture Are Transformed into Riches, Ponds and Rivers Are the Source of Funds'; and *Economic Research* (*Jingji Yanjiu*), No. 8, August 1958, pp. 38–43, Wang Shao-fei: loc cit.

⁶ NCNA, Oct. 27, 1958.

⁷ *People's Handbook* (*Renmin Shouce*) *1959*, pp. 32–4. Resolution on the Establishment of the People's Communes in Rural Areas, passed by the enlarged Conference of the Political Bureau of the Central Committee of the Chinese Communist Party at Peitaiho, Hopei, on August 29, 1958. It should be noted that the commune movement was signalled by a resolution of the Central Committee of the Party and not by a decree of the Government which in 1958 came to be overshadowed by the Party; and *Red Flag* (*Hongqi*), No. 2, January 16, 1959, pp. 1–2. Li Hsien-nien, Minister of Finance: 'How to Recognize Improvements in the Management of Rural Finance and Trade.'

ing.[1] The communes were to be the basic units of taxation.[2] Nor was this all, for they were also to have the declared intention of promoting collective living. An upsurge of the apocalyptic element in Chinese thought is visible in the declaration that communes represented a new phase in human progress as 'sprouts of communism'.[3] This traditional apocalyptic element springs from the concept of *tat'ung*: 'a legendary golden age of social equality and harmony ... in which everyone is unselfish and all men work for the common good rather than for their own interests or that of their families. It is one in which there is care for the old, the young and the sick, and employment and an equal share of property for all men and women.'[4] This 'seems to have been part of a complex of cosmological and religious ideas which were incorporated into Confucian philosophy during the third and second centuries BC' despite their divergence from Confucian ideas on the family.[5] Thus, much of the euphoric utterances on the communes in 1958 was a deliberate appeal to native Chinese sentiments and an assertion of their superiority over the Soviet model of socialism. This must be linked up with the early smoulderings of conflict between the two powers which we now know had already been ignited by 1958.

The claim that communes were 'sprouts of communism' rested chiefly on two grounds: first that they included an element of 'all-people ownership' instead of the collective ownership which had prevailed under the co-operatives, and second because a part of the income of the commune members was to take the form of free meals and sometimes of other goods and services to be distributed on the basis of need rather than of work. The establishment of the communes was made the occasion of a drastic reduction of private property among the peasants. Private plots were abolished or curtailed, while livestock, many agricultural implements, and even cooking utensils were made over to the commune. In any case campaigns for greater production and frequent political meetings left the peasants very little time for working on their own account.

The formation of the communes must be seen in the context of both the decentralization of 1957–8 and of the Great Leap of 1958. Decentralization demanded strong basic authorities to shoulder the responsibilities devolved on to them. Neither the *hsiang* nor the agricultural co-operatives fitted this role. The Great Leap put the development of small labour-intensive industry, especially rural industry, as a major part of its programme, and this was made one of the chief tasks of the new communes. The manner in which

[1] Cases are known of communes in 1958 which included six *hsiang* but only one market town, or eight *hsiang* and two market towns, which makes it clear that many market towns must have been excluded. *Economic Research (Jingji Yanjiu)*, No. 1, January 1960, p. 23. Ho Chi: 'The Superiority of the People's Communes as Seen from Hohsiang Commune', and *Finance (Caizheng)*, No. 15, December 24, 1958, p. 10. CCP Committee of Paikao Commune, Macheng *hsien*, Hupeh: 'The Circumstances in which Paikao Commune Implemented the "Two Transfers, Three Unifications and one Guarantee".'

[2] NCNA Chengchow, August 21, 1958. 'Structure of the People's Communes Outlined.'

[3] *China Youth (Zhongguo Qingnian)*, No. 22, November 16, 1958, p. 8. Fang Ch'ün: 'Be a Zealous Upholder of all Sprouts of Communism.'

[4] From a paper by Martin Bernal to be published in J. Gray (ed.): *China's Search for a Political Form*.

[5] Ibid.

the communes were launched and the exaggerated reports made of their ideological and economic achievements also bore all the symptoms of the Great Leap.

The commune movement was claimed to be a spontaneous upsurge of the peasantry, who had found the co-operatives too small for their purposes, especially in the sphere of water conservancy. Certainly the blurring of the distinction between the *hsiang* and the agricultural co-operative, which at first met with disapproval, had every appearance of being a spontaneous tendency, necessitated by shortage of staff, with the central authorities giving *post-facto* approval to what they could not prevent. No doubt also the feeling of disappointment at the slow rate of agricultural progress was shared by the cadres in the field as well as in Peking. However, other aspects of the commune movement bore signs of central direction. Not only was a strong multipurpose basic unit demanded by the administrative decentralization of the time, but also the Party authorities seem to have controlled the movement all along.[1] As in the case of land reform and the agricultural co-operatives, public announcement of the policy did not come until it was already being implemented.

Once official promulgation came in the form of the Central Committee resolution of August 29, 1958, the speed of the movement (or the rate at which achievement was reported) rose strikingly. In the course of September the proportion of rural households claimed to be in communes increased from 30 to 98 per cent.[2] Fourteen provinces and one autonomous region (Kwangsi) reported 100 per cent membership, while the lowest returns were 31 per cent from Yunnan and 59·3 per cent and 67·3 per cent from Sinkiang and Ninghsia respectively. From all other provinces and autonomous regions the figure was over 90 per cent.[3] Thus the 2 per cent of rural households remaining outside communes were mainly in the national minority areas on the periphery of China. In 1966, agricultural co-operatives were still reported to exist in some of these areas. (Tibet, even in 1966, had not yet reached the stage of communes but statistically this is scarcely significant in relation to China as a whole.)

The original Central Committee resolution in August 1958, on the formation of communes, gave a figure of around two thousand households as being a suitable size for a commune. In the same sentence it also laid down that usually one *hsiang* and one commune should be equated. In 1958, as we have seen, there were approximately 80,000 *hsiang* in China, while the rural population comprised some 120 million households. Therefore, on the basis of 'one *hsiang*, one commune', some 80,000 communes averaging around 1,500 households each might have been expected. Instead, by the end of September 1958 the previous 740,000 agricultural co-operatives had been merged into some 26,400 people's communes.[4] Thus on an average around

[1] For a fuller discussion of these points, see *Pacific Affairs*, Vol. XXXII, No. 4, December 1959, pp. 339–53. A. Donnithorne: 'Background to the People's Communes: Changes in China's Economic Organization in 1958.'
[2] A. L. Strong: *The Rise of the Chinese People's Communes—and Six Years Later*, Peking, 1964, p. 28, and *Statistical Work (Tongji Gongzuo)*, No. 20, October 29, 1958, p. 23.
[3] *Statistical Work (Tongji Gongzuo)*, No. 20, October 29, 1958, p. 23, loc. cit.
[4] Ibid.

three *hsiang* appear to have been incorporated into each commune. The average, however, concealed wide differences. The average number of households per commune for the whole of China at the end of September 1958 was estimated to be 4,600, varying from 1,400 in Kweichow to 9,800 in Kwangtung, while in the country districts within the municipalities of Peking and Shanghai, the number of households per commune exceeded 11,000.[1] Before long the average size of communes grew still larger, for in 1959 their number fell to something over 24,000.[2]

A certain pattern emerges from the figures which we have for September 1958 for the average size of communes (in numbers of households) for each provincial level authority. The largest average size of communes measured by number of households was found in the environs of Peking and Shanghai and after that in Kwangtung. Communes of much above average size were also found in the provinces on the great plain of north China, in the two provinces adjacent to Shanghai and in the two provinces contiguous to the great central China industrial city of Wuhan. The common factor of all these areas is that they are the most modernized parts of China and enjoy the best transport facilities. Conversely, the seven provincial level authorities with the smallest average number of households per commune were all relatively undeveloped and sparsely populated.[3]

From knowledge available (full data being limited to the province of Hunan) the same pattern seems to be reproduced within each province, with the average population per commune being the highest in the more modernized areas nearer urban centres, and lowest in the least developed parts.[4] The conclusion drawn by G. W. Skinner in the first of a distinguished series of articles on marketing systems in China is that, disregarding the earlier declared intention of equating *hsiang* and commune, the cadres 'were under pressure to make communes as large as prevailing conditions allowed'.[5] This may be ascribed to the ascendant 'leftist' drive of 1958 which thought that by shaking free of local particularisms, both political and economic advance might be achieved. The leaders of this movement were themselves working in north China, a region where the larger size of commune was less impracticable than in more backward parts, and this predisposed them to depict the ideal commune as being large. However, even in 1958 reality placed certain constraints on action and in less modernized and less populated areas communes with such large populations were clearly impossible to administer and their size had to be adapted accordingly. The influence of natural conditions, however, cannot alone account for all the differences in size of communes. Some must be ascribed to differences of policy between the controlling cadres in one province and another. In Szechuan, for example, there is evidence to suggest that in 1958 there was a close correspondence between standard marketing area, *hsiang* and commune.[6] In this connection it should be noted

[1] *Statistical Work* (*Tongji Gongzuo*), No. 20, October 29, 1958, p. 23, loc. cit.
[2] *Economic Research* (*Jingji Yanjiu*), No. 11, November 1959, p. 34. Chai Mao: 'The Superiority of the People's Communes from the Viewpoint of Finance and Trade.'
[3] *Statistical Work* (*Tongji Gongzuo*), No. 20, October 29, 1958, p. 23, loc. cit.
[4] *Journal of Asian Studies*, Vol. XXIV, No. 3, May 1965, p. 391. G. W. Skinner, loc. cit.
[5] Ibid.   [6] Ibid., passim.

that the original Resolution on the Establishment of People's Communes of August 1958 specifically stated that the size of communes was a matter to be decided at the provincial level.

While in some places the commune in 1958–9 may have been equated with the *hsiang*, in Fukien and possibly elsewhere the new unit corresponded to the former *ch'ü*, a local authority intermediate between the *hsiang* and the *hsien*, while the production brigades were based on the *hsiang*.[1] It should be noted that in Fukien the 1958 communes were a little below the all-China average in number of households. The relative significance and role of *ch'ü* and *hsiang* had varied in different parts of the country (in some the existence of the *ch'ü* seems to have been shadowy) and this no doubt influenced the local cadres in fixing the old unit, if any, to which the communes should correspond.

The urge towards large communes, already mentioned as according with the spirit of 1958–9, was carried in places to the extreme of equating the commune with the *hsien*. The 'one *hsien* one commune' system was reported more especially from Honan, a province which set the pace for the commune movement, where by the end of 1958 this system was reported in force in 6 *hsien*, while in addition, 95 *hsien* federations of communes had been established.[2] 'One *hsien* one commune' was held preferable on ideological grounds as involving a higher degree of ownership by the whole people and it was predicted that in future all communes would develop in this direction. However, in 1958–9 this system was said to be no more than a 'creative experiment', less practical for the immediate future than the system of a federation of the communes of a whole *hsien*.[3] Soon 'federations of communes of a whole *hsien*' ceased to be mentioned, but the *hsien* itself regained some of its old prominence: which came to the same thing, as the 'federations' envisaged would be nothing but the *hsien* under a new guise.

In the subsequent years official thought on communes began to move in the opposite direction, towards smaller rather than larger communes. Secret instructions from the Central Committee to rural cadres issued in May 1961 recommended that, in general, communes should be made equal to the former (or the original—the Chinese here is ambiguous) higher agricultural cooperatives, which had numbered 740,000, or to the *hsiang* in either their original or their subsequent larger form (i.e. 210,000 or 80,000 units in total); different versions of these secret instructions differ in regard to the unit to which the commune was to be equated.[4] In the next sentence these instruc-

---

[1] *Mainland Today* (*Jinri Dalu*), No. 176, January 25, 1963, p. 8. Ch'iu Fang-chen: 'A Report on Conditions in Red Star People's Commune, Kwangtse *hsien*, Fukien.'

[2] *Honan Daily* (*Honan Ribao*), January 14, 1959 (SCMP 1965). 'CCP Honan Provincial Committee's Plan on Overhaul, Consolidation and Elevation of People's Communes this Winter and next Spring, December 23, 1958.' It should be noted that in the course of 1958 the size of the *hsien* had been increased, and the numbers of *hsien* reduced, in many parts of the country.

[3] *Red Flag* (*Hongqi*), No. 10, October 16, 1958, p. 4. Li Hsien-nien, Minister of Finance. 'A Look at the People's Communes', and *Financial and Economic Research* (*Caijing Yanjiu*), No. 9, December 1958, p. 11. Chao Fu-chi: 'The One *Hsien* One Commune System as Demonstrated by Chaoyuan *Hsien* Commune.'

[4] Chinese Communist Party Central Committee: *Draft Articles on Rural Communes* (in Chinese), Peking, 1961. Article 5. An edition from Union Research Institute, Hong Kong,

tions go on to say that, notwithstanding what had just been said, communes, brigades and teams might all be of various sizes—large, medium or small: a degree of vagueness that no doubt accorded well with the situation (and with the variations in different versions of the document itself) and which was probably as much a description of fact as a statement of policy.

The difficulties encountered by the communes in 1958–61 were, as suggested by G. W. Skinner, aggravated by their large size and 'the failure to align the new unit with the natural socio-economic systems shaped by rural trade',[1] i.e. in general with the standard marketing area. By 1961, hard-learned experience had brought these natural social systems back into favour, resulting in the decision to reduce the size of communes.

No mention of the total number of communes had been made for some years until 1963 when 74,000 were stated to be in existence.[2] In 1966 the number was put at 70,000–80,000 ranging in size 'from a few hundred hectares of farmland with several thousand members to almost 10,000 hectares (150,000 *mow*) with a population of as much as 100,000'.[3] This shows that the reduction in size of communes had proceeded very unevenly and that in some parts no reduction may have taken place; which accords with the latitude deliberately allowed by the 1961 instructions. G. W. Skinner, after presenting various hypotheses on alignment between communes and natural marketing systems, thinks that of the 58,000 communes he estimates to have existed in 1964 in 'agricultural China' (i.e. excluding the peripheral pastoral regions) some 42,000 were aligned with basic level commercial systems (37,000 with standard marketing systems and 5,000 with intermediate ones). The 16,000 communes not so aligned are, according to Skinner's exposition, accounted for mainly by two classes of exception—one being areas 'where population is dense and agrarian modernization advanced' and where communes exist which are larger even than intermediate trading systems; the other exception being in 'sparsely settled, inaccessible and relatively unmodernized areas' when more than one commune may be found in a single standard marketing area.[4] Skinner estimates that by 1964, 16,000 communes had been established in 'non-agricultural China' and that 'communes now very nearly exhaust the

---

gives the higher agricultural producers' co-operative, while an edition from Taiwan mentions the *hsiang*, as the unit with which the commune should be equated. The ambiguity about whether the *former* (i.e. the immediately pre-commune) or the *original* higher co-operatives were meant, may not have been serious because, as we have seen, the directive of September 1957 suggesting a reduction in size in co-operatives does not appear to have had much practical effect—see p. 43 above.

[1] *Journal of Asian Studies*, Vol. XXIV, No. 3, May 1965, p. 394. G. W. Skinner, loc. cit.
[2] *Peking Review*, November 1, 1963, p. 9. Liao Lu-yen, Minister of Agriculture: 'Collectivization of Agriculture in China.' On p. 7, of the article, Liao said that 'over 70,000 people's communes were formed ... in the second half of 1958'. However, on January 1, 1959, the same author had stated that there were something over 26,500 communes. *Red Flag* (*Hongqi*), No. 1, January 1, 1959, p. 14. Liao Lu-yen, loc. cit. In 1962 a Japanese source had given the number of communes as nearly 100,000. See *The New China Yearbook: 1962*, Tokyo, pp. 19–20, quoted in J. L. Buck, O. L. Dawson and Y. L. Wu: *Food and Agriculture in Communist China*, New York, 1966, p. 95.
[3] NCNA, Peking, March 22, 1966.
[4] *Journal of Asian Studies*, Vol. XXV, No. 2, February 1966, pp. 320–1. Communications: Note by G. W. Skinner in reply to note by A. Donnithorne.

landscape of China, with the obvious exceptions of Taiwan and Tibet/ Chamdo', and that in particular the 'non-Han areas of non-agricultural Szechuan were almost completely formed into communes by 1963'.[1] However, in 1963 and later the minority peoples of Szechuan were reported to be still organized in agricultural co-operatives, not communes.[2] In Yunnan both agricultural co-operatives and communes are reported from minority areas in recent years. It is interesting to note that communes have been formed among the Yi nationality in Yunnan,[3] but not apparently among the same people in the neighbouring province of Szechuan. It may be wondered what actual difference there was between a commune in 1965 and an agricultural co-operative. While confessing this a difficult question, the fact is that for some reason (perhaps because of the unpopularity that had become attached to the name of commune) the authorities saw fit to continue the old name in certain tribal areas.

The continued use of the term 'agricultural co-operative' is also relevant when we examine the development of communes in Szechuan. It has already been noted that in 1958 there may have been an equivalence between *hsiang*, standard marketing area and commune in this province. By September 1958 a total of 4,800 communes were reported to have been formed in Szechuan, comprising over 99 per cent of the peasant households.[4] By 1963 'more than 7,000' communes were reported in Szechuan,[5] an increase of 60–70 per cent over 1958. Great commercialization and population increase in the intervening five years (which included the post-Leap period of hardship) cannot have been sufficient to have caused a 60–70 per cent increase in the number of standard market areas: on Skinner's calculations their increase between those years was 500 for Szechuan, excluding the minority areas.[6] Thus, whatever occurred to the Szechuan communes between 1958–63, there must have been a considerable change in the degree of their alignment to standard marketing areas. This suggests that for China as a whole the number of communes not aligned with basic level commercial systems is more than Skinner's estimate of 16,000.

A note of cynicism may be sounded about the figures (74,000 in 1964 or the 70,000–80,000 of 1966) reported for the total number of communes in China. It is not so much that the figures may be false as that they may be meaningless. We shall see that the concepts and functions of communes have become so variable that it is difficult to define the unit at all. An aggregate of such dissimilar units with disparate functions might not appear to be of great significance. The vagueness that exists may be reflected in the report that 'nearly

[1] *Journal of Asian Studies*, Vol. XXV, No. 2, February 1966, pp. 321 and 323.
[2] NCNA Chengtu, December 17, 1963, and *Peking Review*, No. 1, January 3, 1964, p. 43, and NCNA Chengtu, March 3, 1965, and NCNA Chengtu, July 18, 1965, and NCNA Chengtu, July 19, 1965, and NCNA Chengtu, August 21, 1965, and NCNA August 28, 1965, and NCNA September 22, 1965.
[3] NCNA Kunming, July 26, 1965.
[4] *Statistical Work* (*Tongji Gongzuo*), No. 20, October 29, 1958, p. 23, loc. cit.
[5] *People's Daily* (*Renmin Ribao*), October 5, 1963, p. 2.
[6] *Journal of Asian Studies*, Vol. XXV, No. 2, February 1966, p. 323, loc. cit. Skinner considered that the additional new communes in Szechuan were those established in minority areas. However, we have seen that co-operatives still continued in these areas.

10,000' communes existed in Kwangsi in 1964,[1] 'ten thousand' having in Chinese the connotation of a large number.

No less scepticism must remain when now we turn to considering changes in the status of the constituent units of communes.

Beneath the commune there were to be two lower tiers of management. The unit directly beneath the commune (i.e. the intermediate unit) was at first called the production brigade (*shengch'antui*);[2] this was already in December 1958 in the Central Committee's Resolution on Certain Problems in the Communes, designated as the economic accounting unit, while in August 1959 it was also declared to be the basic level of ownership.[3] The status of economic accounting unit is important in that this is the unit by and within which distribution of collective income is effected. A literal translation of the original name of the lowest unit of a commune was 'production small brigade' (*shench'an hsiaotui*) although in English it was frequently known as the 'production team'. Changes occurred in the Chinese nomenclature and as these are relevant to the changes in the status of the constituent units of the communes, they must be mentioned here. The first change was made in April 1961, when an editorial in the *People's Daily* referred to 'the production great brigade (formerly called the production brigade)' and 'the production brigade (formerly called the production small brigade)'. At the beginning of 1962 the new-style 'production brigade', i.e. the lowest level, was mentioned as being the basic economic accounting unit.[4] Probably the motive of this change in appellation was to enable the lowest unit to be recognized as the basic accounting unit without formally having to go back on an earlier declaration that the intermediate unit held this position. By this means the name of the basic unit (production brigade—*shengch'antui*) remained the same while the transfer from the second to the third tiers was effected. In this study, for clarity, the intermediate level will be known throughout as the production brigade, or for short, the brigade, while the third will be called the production team; the term 'agriculture collective' will be used to cover communes, brigades and teams indiscriminately, corresponding to the sometimes vague allusions in the Chinese sources. It is envisaged by the Communist authorities that in some distant future first the production brigade, and then later the commune, will be made the basic accounting unit.[5] If all this, and the changes

---

[1] *Peking Review*, June 12, 1964, p. 20. A. L. Strong: 'Some Comments on the Chinese People's Communes.'

[2] In the early days of the communes a number of different names for the sub-divisions of communes were in vogue in different places. See T. A. Hsia: *The Commune in Retreat as Evidenced in Terminology and Semantics*, Berkeley, 1964, p. 36. The expression *shengch'antui* occasionally occurs in pre-commune days e.g. *New China Fortnightly* (*Xinhua Banyuekan*), No. 93, October 6, 1956, p. 55.

[3] *People's Handbook* (*Renmin Shouce*) *1959*, p. 43. Resolution of the Central Committee of the Chinese Communist Party of December 10, 1958 on Certain Problems of the People's Communes and *New China Fortnightly* (*Xinhua Banyuekan*), No. 163, September 12, 1959, p. 3. Resolution of the Eighth Plenary Session of the Chinese Communist Party on Developing the Movement for Economy, August 16, 1959.

[4] *People's Daily* (*Renmin Ribao*), April 2, 1961, p. 1, Editorial, and ibid., January 1, 1962, p. 1, Editorial.

[5] *Peking Review*, April 10, 1964, p. 20, T'ao Chu, First Secretary of the Kwangtung Provincial Party Committee: 'The People's Communes Forge Ahead'—Part II.

in rural organization detailed below, appear to be somewhat confusing, the reader is begged to remember that the reality of the situation is probably even more confused.

Communes, even at the same period of time, have differed widely in the number of production brigades and teams beneath them. Some have had only a handful of these lower units while, in contrast, cases are on record of communes with 365 teams, and with 47 brigades and 440 teams.[1]

If any type of commune has been regarded as 'standard' at any time, it has been a commune equated with a *hsiang*, its production brigades equated with higher agriculture co-operatives and its production teams with lower agricultural co-operatives. None of these particulars, however, has been invariable, whether in precept or in fact. Sometimes the production brigade is equated with a natural village, while in other cases several villages are comprised within one brigade.[2] In the latter case the production team might be equated with the village. If there is, as already suggested, some doubt about the number and identity of communes, much greater uncertainty must exist about lower units. In 1963 a Taiwan journal reported the existence of 700,000 production brigades and more than five million production teams in Mainland China,[3] but it is difficult to know how much significance to attach to this report. As mentioned below, by 1963 in some places production brigades had lost many of their functions and were thus liable to be somewhat nebulous bodies, although in other places they remained important. The growing importance of job groups under production teams meant that in places these (and neither brigades nor teams) had become *de facto* 'economic accounting units'. Indeed it must be difficult at any moment of time to know which 'job groups' have reached this stage.

The three-tier system of commune, brigade and team has itself been by no means universal. In 1958 opinion differed on the advantage of 'two level', 'three level' and 'four level' systems of management; the last, however, being considered suitable only for communes equivalent to a whole *hsien*.[4] In 1963, when the Minister of Agriculture spoke of the increased number of communes, he added that the bigger ones had beneath them the two levels of brigade and team, while the smaller ones had only teams. Usually, according

[1] *China Reconstructs*, June 1964, p. 24. 'Report from Huatung Commune—II: How Farmers Distributed Their Income', and *Southern Daily* (*Nanfang Ribao*), August 21, 1962 (SCMP 2814) K'uang Ch'ang-ch'eng, First Secretary, CCP Toushan Commune Committee, Toishan *hsien*, Kwangtung: 'Production Teams that Have Increased Output Should Not Distribute and Consume All Their Output.'

[2] For example of four, six and eight natural villages respectively in single production brigades, see the following three sources: J. Myrdal: *Report from a Chinese Village*, London, 1965, p. 196, and *China Youth* (*Zhongguo Qingnian*), No. 13, July 1, 1965, p. 28. Chao Ch'uang-shih, Secretary of the League branch of Miaoti Production Brigade, Ch'engkuan Commune, Juich'eng *hsien*, Shansi: 'Our Young People Here Are Very Lively', and *Red Flag* (*Hongqi*), No. 1, January 1, 1966, p. 30. Wang Yung-hsing, Secretary of the General Party Branch, Hsiatingchia Production Brigade, Talüchia Commune, Huanghsien, Shantung: 'We Cannot Sit and Wait for Socialist Undertakings to Develop.'

[3] *Communist Affairs Research* (*Feiqing Yanjiu*) VI, No. 20, December 31, 1963, quoted in *Journal of Asian Studies*, Vol. XXIV, No. 3, May 1965, p. 398, fn. 277 and p. 399, fn. 279. W. G. Skinner: loc. cit.

[4] *People's Daily* (*Renmin Ribao*), December 2, 1958, p. 3. Rural Work Dept. CCP Liaoning Provincial Committee: 'The System and Organization of the Communes.'

to the Minister, the team owned and managed all the means of production and was the basic unit for the distribution of income. In a few cases, however, these functions of ownership, management and distribution were in the hands of brigades and in still fewer cases, in those of the commune as a whole.[1] This statement represents the position reached after several years of retreat from the 1958 emphasis on the importance of communal ownership; in 1960 ownership by the brigade was officially the correct element to stress while from 1962, at least in some areas, the brigade's position waned[2] and the team was accorded the predominant role in ownership of assets and in distribution of income. The retreat from the centralized commune came about because the methods of production in Chinese agriculture necessitate management by small units. At the same time, peasants' private plots were once more restored to favour. This important development will be treated more fully in the next chapter.

All along, the production teams have normally been the units in charge of day-to-day collective farming operations, except in so far as the teams have handed these over to smaller informal job groups: as already noted, the distinction between these two may sometimes be blurred. In places, a team comprises a single localized lineage, a phenomenon particularly common in Kwangtung province. In accordance with the responsibility system, the team —and sometimes the job group—is given an agricultural tax obligation (in kind) and a procurement quota to fulfil. For this task, and also to provide for its own needs of food and cash, it employs its 'four fixed' (i.e. assigned on a long-term basis) factors of production (labour, land, animals and tools). The quota obligations are frequently given the form of contracts between the higher unit allotting the task and the lower unit to which it is allotted. The job group can, when appropriate, assign responsibility to households and individuals. Giving responsibility to job groups simplifies administration. Incentives work more powerfully in a small group, whose remuneration depends on results and within which it is easier to exert pressure on the slothful, so that there is 'no longer anybody sneaking off to rest in the shelter of the trees'.[3]

[1] *Peking Review*, No. 44, November 1, 1963, p. 9. Liao Lu-yen: loc. cit.

[2] Brigades, according to complaints by some brigade cadres, had become mere 'transportation stations' for the further transit of compulsory deliveries of crops. *Southern Daily* (*Nanfang Ribao*), April 8, 1962 (SCMP 2733). 'How Production Brigade Cadres Should Approach Their Duties.'

[3] *Yunnan Daily* (*Yunnan Ribao*), July 30, 1959. (SCMP 2091) Ch'engchiang *hsien* Work Team, Rural Work Dept., CCP Yunnan Provincial Committee: 'Ch'engchiang *hsien's* Preliminary Experience of Improvement of Labour Organization.' On operational groups, see also *Peking Daily* (*Beijing Ribao*), July 3, 1961. (SCMP 2545) 'Four Production Teams of Chaochiawu Production Brigade Effect Division of Authority between Production Teams and Job Groups', and *Daily Worker* (*Gongren Ribao*), December 15, 1961, p. 3. Ts'ai Shih: 'The Benefits to be Gained by Production Teams from Contracting Work for a Short Period, a Season or a Whole Year', and *People's Daily* (*Renmin Ribao*), July 22, 1960, p. 2. Chang Hua, Yang Kun-ch'uan and Li Kuang: 'An Introduction to the Leadership Methods of Three Production Teams', and *People's Daily* (*Renmin Ribao*), June 4, 1961, p. 1. 'Assign Summer Transplanting to Job Groups', and *People's Daily* (*Renmin Ribao*), June 30, 1961, p. 4. 'The Contract Responsibilities of Small Groups are Clearly Delineated', and *Current Events* (*Shishi Shouce*), No. 18, September 21, 1961 (SCMM 288). Chen Chih: 'How to Strengthen and Perfect the Responsibility System in Production Teams.'

In some places, even as early as 1959, tasks had been devolved right down to the household, although this was at that time considered ideologically distasteful. The practice was sufficiently widespread to be attacked in the *People's Daily* and the *Red Flag* in 1959–60, and instances are quoted of backward peasants demanding such a devolution.[1] In 1961, however, contracting jobs down to the household appeared to be an accepted practice in Paoan *hsien*, Kwangtung,[2] although in the following year disapproval of it was expressed in Fukien.[3] However, three years later, in the spring of 1963, it was quite respectable to talk of assigning jobs to individuals under the responsibility system,[4] while in 1966 even obligations for tax grain had apparently been devolved down to individual peasants (or presumably households).[5]

In the early days of the commune movement, the need for centralization within the commune was emphasized.[6] Formal constitutions were proposed, such as that drafted for the Weihsing (Sputnik) Commune in Honan, which was regarded as a model. This constitution provided for all important affairs to be discussed by a congress of commune members which was to comprise representatives of all production teams and of all social groups including women, youth, old people, cultural, educational, and so forth. This congress was to elect an administrative committee, which should include the director and deputy directors of the commune. Under this committee several departments or committees were to be established to take charge of various aspects of the commune's affairs, such as agriculture, water conservancy, forestry, livestock, industry and communications, finance and grain, credit, commerce, education and culture, labour, defence, planning and scientific research. This formidable apparatus was to be kept up to the mark by an elected supervisory committee.[7] It is improbable that any sustained attempt was made to operate such a constitution at all widely and its main interest lies in exemplifying the ambitions of that high summer of 1958.

In actual fact, the type of administrative machinery possessed by any individual commune must depend on what functions that particular com-

---

[1] *People's Daily* (*Renmin Ribao*), December 31, 1959, p. 7. Chou Lin: 'The Struggle between the Two Forces of Old and New in the Great Leap Forward,' and *Red Flag* (*Hongqi*), No. 1, January 1, 1960, p. 17. Wu Chih-pu: 'The Strengthening and Development of the People's Communes', and *Yunnan Daily* (*Yunnan Ribao*), July 30, 1959. (SCMP 2091). 'Rapidly Establish Reasonable Labour Organization', and *Shensi Daily* (*Shanxi Ribao*), November 4, 1959. (SCMP 2210) 'Actively Develop the Socialist and Communist Education Campaign in Rural Areas.'

[2] *Paoan Bulletin* (*Baoan Tongxun*), No. 64, October 6, 1961, p. 4, and ibid., No. 73, November 18, 1961, p. 1.

[3] Intelligence Bureau, Ministry of Defence, Taiwan (ed.): *The Collected Documents obtained by the Anti-Communist Guerrillas in the Raid on Lienchiang, Fukien* (in Chinese), Taipei, 1964 (*the Lienchiang Papers*), pp. 36–7.

[4] *Southern Daily* (*Nanfang Ribao*), February 1, 1963 (SCMP 2964), loc. cit., on the responsibility system, see pp. 27–8 above.

[5] *People's Daily* (*Renmin Ribao*), April 14, 1966, p. 6. Wang Lien, Secretary of Party Branch of Tungshihtzukou Brigade, Shihtzukuo Commune, Chungli *hsien*, Hopei: 'A Party Branch Must Conscientiously Control and Educate Party Members.'

[6] Ibid., February 25, 1959, p. 7. T'ao Chu, First Secretary of CCP Kwangtung Provincial Committee: 'Report on a Survey of Humen Commune.'

[7] *Red Flag* (*Hongqi*), No. 7, September 1, 1958, p. 18. 'Provisional Regulations (Draft) of the Ch'ayashan Weihsing People's Commune,' Article 12.

mune performs, and similarly with the production brigades and teams. These functions differ from instance to instance, as we shall see below. Presumably all units have leaders (who should, at least in theory, be elected by all members) and also some form, however crude, of financial management. Both these topics will be studied in the following chapter.

The series of amalgamations that occurred in the countryside in 1958, between the new communes and the former *hsiang*,[1] and between the communes and the co-operatives for credit, supply and marketing and handicrafts led some to suppose that amalgamation ought also to occur between the organs of Party and commune. In some places the Party organs were actually merged with those of communes. This met with official disapproval. The secret Party directive of 1961 on rural communes (the 'Sixty Articles') explicitly stated that the Party organization was not to undertake the work of the commune administration at its various levels.[2] But although Party and administration were kept formally distinct, the Party in 1958 took the initiative in carrying out many governmental functions, eclipsing the administrative organs. This was especially the case in the countryside, where this tendency continued in the following years. Here once again, the shortage of competent people may have been a major reason, making it even more difficult in the countryside than in the towns to staff a dual hierarchy of Party and state. Thus cadres had often to hold posts in Party branches and in commune administrations concurrently.[3]

The lowest level at which effective Party organs are found in rural areas varies, like everything else, from place to place. Often it would seem to be at the level of the commune or production brigade, but where communes are small and Party membership weak, it is possible that few active branches exist below the level of the *hsien*. In other areas effective branches, or at least cells, may operate in production teams.

Party secretaries and committees take executive action on many practical matters in agriculture. To quote a few examples among many, the decision to release water from a reservoir in Kwangtung to fight drought was reported to be made by the Party committee of a commune,[4] while a brigade CCP Secre-

---

[1] As we have seen, in most cases the original communes must have corresponded to several *hsiang*. This does not mean they did not absorb the *hsiang* administrative organs, such as they were.

[2] *People's Daily* (*Renmin Ribao*), December 24, 1958, p. 7. Chao Han, loc. cit., and *People's Handbook* (*Renmin Shouce*) 1959, p. 44. 'Resolution on Certain Problems of the People's Communes,' loc. cit., and *Draft Articles on Rural Communes*, op. cit. (Taiwan ed.), Article No. 56, and *Red Flag* (*Hongqi*), No. 19, October 1, 1961, p. 28. Huang Chih-kang: 'Strengthen Leadership of Study by basic Level Rural Cadres.'

[3] See *People's Daily* (*Renmin Ribao*), July 28, 1959, p. 6, for an account of steps taken by a particularly efficient Party committee of a *ch'ü* in the suburbs of Peking to end the concurrent holding of such posts. 'Previously some of the Party branches in the *ch'ü* were short of hard core cadres and in many places the heads of production brigades were concurrently Party branch secretaries and in some places there was a joint Party branch for two to four brigades.' Therefore the *ch'ü* Party committee trained 170 hard core cadres to be Party branch secretaries, thus making it possible for a separate branch to be established in each brigade with full-time branch secretaries. Not all areas had such effective Party organizations.

[4] *Red Flag* (*Hongqi*), No. 4, February 26, 1964, p. 16. Chang Han-ch'ing: 'Huahsien has Truly Changed into a Flowery *Hsien*.'

tary in Chekiang was responsible for classifying the land of the brigade production teams into categories for assignment of quotas for compulsory sales.[1] Many other examples of this type of direct action by the Party could be given. In addition, Party committees play a supervisory role. For example, the check-up of the communes, ordered by the CCP Central Committee in December 1958, was entrusted to local Party committees and secretaries.

In the mid-1960s, a major responsibility of the Party has been to allay discontent among young people 'sent down' to the countryside for agricultural work instead of obtaining coveted urban employment. Many cultural clubs are reported to have been opened by the Communist Youth League to cater for them. Another task given to the Party has been the drive against old customs surrounding weddings and funerals and other occasions, which are reprobated on grounds of economy and ideology.

The bare outline of the development of the communes presented above must now be discussed in terms of the functions of the various units of collective farming. The recent history of rural China can then be seen as a moulding of the administrative framework by the realities of agriculture, thus forcing an alignment of the superstructure into a form consistent with the existing state of productive forces.

Routine agricultural operations in Chinese conditions demand a small unit of control. This is more particularly the case in the rice region where, as we have seen, technical reasons often dictate that fields remain small. This sets severe limits to the extent of change in field layout which can be brought about by collectivization. Pictures and reports of large fields made by amalgamating small plots come mostly from the wheat region.

Intensive farming, of the types common in China, also requires small units for management of labour. Supervision of the care and use of draught animals is best done by a small unit, as is, too, the collection and distribution of manure, both animal and human. The production team is the largest unit that can exercise any direct oversight over the employment of these four factors of production—land, labour, draught animals, and manure—and even it, as we have seen, has often to devolve many functions to smaller units—operational groups and even households. The role of the team in water conservancy and in land reclamation may be great or small according to local circumstances. Among the chief responsibilities carried directly by the team are decisions on cropping and on the distribution of the net income of the team. In addition, teams may control various forms of subsidiary production.

The team's authority to decide crops to be grown is limited by obligations imposed by the state (transmitted through the communes) to deliver certain quantities of grain (or other staple) in payment of agricultural tax, and other quantities of specified crops in fulfilment of compulsory sales quotas. From what we know, it may be surmised that the annual compilation of agricultural plans by the commune authorities now consists mainly of allocating these tax and sales quotas between the constituent units of the commune. Agricultural planning in general remains rudimentary.[2] Similarly in the distribution of the harvest, these obligations have to be met as well as any

---

[1] *People's Daily* (*Renmin Ribao*), September 19, 1961, p. 2. Shao Ch'ang: 'The Masses are Sages.'   [2] See pp. 486–90, below.

contributions payable to the brigade or commune. The residual is then at the team's disposal to allocate between reserves, investment and division among members of the team. These transactions will be treated in the next chapter.

The selection of seed, from the best strains of the past harvest or from special seed cultivation plots, is usually undertaken at the team level,[1] although this function is shared with state seed farms.

Production teams and peasant households are the main owners of grain stocks, apart from the stocks of 'public grain' collected by the state through agricultural tax and compulsory sales.[2] Before 1962, stocks had been held by all levels of local government but in that year, after the team had been recognized as the basic accounting unit, the holding of grain reserves was forbidden to special districts, *hsien*, communes, and brigades (with the exception of those brigades which were still basic accounting units).[3] Previously, when these other authorities had also held grain stocks, the standard of storage may have been low.[4] The production team, being closer to the ultimate consumers, might be expected to have a more immediate incentive to exercise good care of stocks. However, by 1962 most collective mess halls had been shut, and grain for peasant consumption was distributed by the team to each household. It seems that teams retained little, if any, reserves themselves, but households accumulated sufficient to cause 'the rise of a spontaneous tendency towards capitalism'.[5] As a cure, the authorities pressed teams to set up their own reserves. However, by 1964, two years after the directive appointing them the sole holders of collective grain, production teams with grain reserves were still sufficiently rare to merit special commendation.[6] The reserves which the team were urged to accumulate in 1964 might either be kept by the teams themselves or, if they had inadequate storage space, reserves might be handed over to state food departments for storage.[7]

Considerable confusion still reigned in 1965 over the question of responsibility for collective grain reserves. Evidently the ban on certain administrative units holding grain reserves had been lifted by that time, as praise was given to *hsien* and communes which had accumulated such reserves.[8]

The relationship between the team and its individual members and households (the last two are not always readily distinguishable in this context) is sometimes crystallized in typical fashion in the form of 'four fixed', echoing

[1] *People's Daily* (*Renmin Ribao*), June 8, 1962, p. 1. Editorial; and ibid., September 8, 1962, p. 1. Editorial; and ibid., August 26, 1963, p. 2.

[2] Insufficient state granary capacity was probably a major reason for the shortfall in state procurement of grain in 1958. See p. 89, below.

[3] *People's Daily* (*Renmin Ribao*), November 27, 1962, p. 2. Editorial.

[4] *Ta Kung Daily* (*Dagong Bao*), Peking, March 20, 1962, p. 2, suggests that this may have been the case.

[5] *Ta Kung Daily* (*Dagong Bao*), Peking, October 26, 1964, p. 1. Editorial. In one team, the accumulation of collective grain reserves was said to have brought to an end 'activities in which grain is used for speculation or for lending out at high interest rates'. *People's Daily* (*Renmin Ribao*), November 22, 1964, p. 2.

[6] *Ta Kung Daily* (*Dagong Bao*), Peking, October, 26 1964, p. 1. Editorial.

[7] Ibid., p. 1. Editorial, and ibid., December 11, 1964, p. 1. Letter from a Correspondent.

[8] NCNA, June 14, 1965, and *BBC Summary of World Broadcasts*, Second Series. FE/W337/A/4 (Nanchang, October 11, 1965), and *Ta Kung Daily* (*Dagong Bao*), Peking, July 23, 1965, p. 2. Editorial.

at this lowest level the 'four fixed' which regulate relations between teams and commune. These other 'four fixed' are the fixed number of work days required, the fixed quantity of manure to be accumulated for the team, the fixed quantities of subsidiary products to be sold by the household to the state and the fixed rations to be provided by the team.[1] These are the chief points of contact between the peasant household and the national economy.

Participation in collective work is obligatory for women as well as for men, although women are normally required to put in fewer days. This has extended the practice of women working in the fields from south China, where it had been customary, to the north. The resumption by the individual family after the Great Leap of its old tasks of preparing meals and undertaking various forms of sideline production has presumably lessened the amount of time which housewives spend in the fields.

The peasant is paid for the factors of production (labour and manure)[2] he is required to contribute towards collective farming. A conflict of interest arises because these factors of production yield a higher return to the peasant when applied to his private plot. Therefore supervision is constantly required to ensure labour attendance and the delivery (and non-dilution) of manure.[3] According to one survey, peasants' household manure (probably including both human and animal) accounts for a third to a half of all manure available and 60–70 per cent of this household manure had to be sold to the team. This survey was made in Kwangtung, but a production team in Honan required its members to deliver about the same proportion, 60 per cent, of their manure.[4] The remaining 30–40 per cent would ensure that the peasants' private plots were much more heavily manured than the collective fields. This is a major reason why vegetable growing is concentrated on private plots except near cities where collective vegetable growing, using urban nightsoil and the manure of a dense pig population (fed on urban swill), is undertaken on a large scale. Both nightsoil and swill are probably delivered by municipal agencies to the units of collective agriculture (sewage is pumped out of some large cities) thus making possible collective production of vegetables and pigs on a larger scale than where manure and swill derive in greater measure from peasant households. The collective pigs, in turn, increase still further the amount of manure available for collective crops.

The sources of manure under the immediate control of production teams include collectively reared draught cattle and pigs, public latrines, and pond and river mud dredged, and green manure grown, by collective labour. Experience with collective rearing of livestock has not, on the whole, been happy and there have been many reports of heavy mortality among cattle and pigs.

---

[1] *Southern Daily* (*Nanfang Ribao*), June 21, 1962. (SCMP 2789). Editorial.

[2] Payment for labour is by work points and will be further considered below. Payment for manure may be either by work points or by cash. *People's Daily* (*Renmin Ribao*), August 26, 1962, p. 1, and *Southern Daily* (*Nanfang Ribao*), June 21, 1962 (SCMP 2789). Editorial, and *Southern Daily* (*Nanfang Ribao*), August 7, 1962 (SCMP 2834).

[3] *Southern Daily* (*Nanfang Ribao*), July 20, 1962. (SCMP 2804) K'ung Fan-chi: 'Rates of Work Attendance and Manure Delivery Must be Fixed Seriously to Improve the Relationship between Public and Private Interests.'

[4] *Southern Daily* (*Nanfang Ribao*), August 7, 1962 (SCMP 2834), and *People's Daily* (*Renmin Ribao*), August 26, 1962, p. 1.

The unremitting attention needed is more likely to be given when the animals are owned by the peasants themselves or, if publicly owned, are cared for by peasant families under contract. With draught cattle, ownership seems to be normally by the team, at least in Kwangtung, with the care being frequently entrusted to individual households who are paid by work points according to the animals' condition.[1] In north China ownership and care of draught cattle by the brigade may be more common.[2]

During the Great Leap, collective rearing of pigs was promoted and private rearing discouraged. Since then the pendulum has swung in the opposite direction and private ownership and rearing of pigs would seem the norm; sometimes, however, ownership and rearing are separated, with peasant households being entrusted with the care of pigs owned by the team. Sows may often be found under collective management of the team, while teams, brigades, and communes sometimes keep boars for stud purposes. Large pig farms do not seem to be common, except in the vicinity of cities, where they are run by brigades or communes,[3] and probably utilize urban garbage for feed.

Water conservancy projects and rural industrialization figure prominently among the original purposes of the commune movement. It was hoped that by mechanizing agriculture, large numbers of workers could be released for other tasks. Indeed, even without waiting for mechanization, many communes in the autumn of 1958 switched 30–50 per cent of their labour force to mining and the making of coke, charcoal, and the smelting of iron and steel in small primitive furnaces. 'If the commune movement had not occurred', wrote the Minister of Agriculture, 'it would have been impossible to withdraw such a large amount of manpower from the agricultural front to the industrial front during the tense, brisk autumn season.'[4] The failure to gather in much of the 1958 harvest which resulted from this over-assurance, led to a reversal in policy. By 1960, at least in Kwangtung province, it was considered advisable that around 90 per cent of the total manpower should be at the disposal of the production teams for agricultural work.[5]

Since then work on water conservancy projects and similar labour-intensive schemes has normally been restricted to the slack winter months. The importance of the commune as a unit in initiating and executing these works has depended on irrigation and water control problems in the locality concerned. A commune that is the right size for one type of responsibility may not be the right size for another. Thus, a commune which is convenient as an

---

[1] *Southern Daily* (*Nanfang Ribao*), July 6, 1962 (SCMP 2793) 'Why Are Cattle Markets Not Regularly Open?' And ibid., August 5, 1962 (SCMP 2806), Huang Chung-hsiang: 'Persistently Hold Examination and Rating, Firmly Carry Out the Party's Policy.'

[2] *People's Daily* (*Renmin Ribao*), February 21, 1963, p. 2. Hsiao Mei and Yü Ch'ing: 'Economic Aid to Production Teams Must Fit the Actual Circumstances.'

[3] *Southern Daily* (*Nanfang Ribao*), September 15, 1963 (SCMP 3085), and *Ta Kung Daily* (*Dagong Bao*), Peking, July 17, 1964, p. 3. Chang Ying: 'A Discussion of Some Problems in Rearing Pigs', and ibid., August 14, 1964, p. 3. Ching Tung: 'Why Should Private Ownership Still Predominate in Pig Rearing?' And ibid., August 21, 1964, p. 3. Ching Tung: 'Some Problems in Developing Collective Pig Rearing.'

[4] *Red Flag* (*Hongqi*), No. 1, January 1, 1959, pp. 14–15. Liao Lu-yen, loc. cit.

[5] *Southern Daily* (*Nanfang Ribao*), October 28, 1960 (SCMP 2401) Chang Ken-sheng: A Report Delivered at the Conference of Directors of Rural Work Departments of the CCP District and *Hsien* Committees in Kwangtung Province.

administrative unit (as might be claimed for those co-terminous with *hsiang* and standard marketing areas) may be too small for necessary water conservancy schemes. In places, some particular project is of such over-riding importance that the commune was tailored to fit: for example, it was reported that sixty agricultural co-operatives north of Canton were united in one commune in order to build a stretch of an irrigation canal.[1] More often a number of communes, their sizes determined by other considerations, have co-operated in some project.

By the autumn of 1959, a degree of disillusionment had set in on the efficiency of communal enterprise in water conservancy. Instead, a greater role began to be played by water conservancy departments of provinces and by specialized units, some with long histories, known as 'irrigation districts'.[2] However, communes are still frequently reported as significant units in improving local irrigation facilities, sometimes through co-ordinating the activities of their constituent brigades and teams.

Mechanized cultivation has as yet made little headway in collective agriculture in China, except in a few favoured areas. In these it had, from 1958, been the policy to hand tractor stations over to the communes. From about 1961, policy seems to have changed in favour of state ownership of tractor stations. This may have been for one of the same reasons as caused the similar policy change in water conservancy—because of poor management by the communes. Another factor probably was the inability of many communes to buy the machines and also, perhaps, their unwillingness to do so as fees charged by the state tractor stations were often below cost. Still a third reason may have been the incompatibility in scale between a commune and the usually much larger area (150,000–300,000 *mow*) which was considered the optimum to be served by a tractor station.[3] The trend towards smaller communes from around 1961 probably caused the change in policy on the management of tractor stations. However, even after that date some communes with 150,000 *mow* of land were to be found,[4] and these probably accounted for the commune-operated tractor stations which continued to exist. By 1966, policy in some parts of the country at least, came to favour the smaller scale management of tractors, leading to stations and sub-stations, or even individual machines, being operated by communes and brigades.[5]

In the early 1960s, it came to be realized that over much of China agricultural mechanization was a distant prospect and that less capital-intensive forms of technical improvement must be promoted to raise farm output. Some of the more advanced communes have their own agricultural extension centres and experimental farms but in general this is a sphere more appropriate

[1] This much visited commune has been described in *China Reconstructs*, June 1964, pp. 18–25. Chang Yen: 'The Commune Gave Us Wings: Report from Huatung Commune,' I. and *Far Eastern Economic Review*, December 17, 1964, pp. 564–7. D. Davies: 'A Kwangtung Commune', and A. L. Strong, op. cit., pp. 175–81. It should be noted that the overall direction of the canal project was in the hands of the *hsien* which co-ordinated the work of the communes through which it was to extend.

[2] See p. 129 below.

[3] See p. 116 below. *Chinese Agricultural Journal* (*Zhongguo Nongbao*), No. 11, November 1963, p. 7. Chang Ch'ing-t'ai: 'The Problems of Consolidating the Operational Management of Tractor Stations.' Extracts from a Speech to the Liaoning Provincial Conference on Tractor Station Work.   [4] See p. 49 above.   [5] p. 118 below.

to the resources of the provincial or *hsien* departments of agriculture.

Fishing is managed by different levels of rural administration as conditions warrant. Sometimes a commune, brigade or team devotes almost all its energies to fishing; in other cases fishing is combined with agriculture, either seasonally or intermittently through the year.[1]

The dream of rural industrialization as envisaged during the Great Leap soon faded. By the spring of 1959, most of the small primitive iron and steel furnaces had ceased to operate. Some of the small factories and workshops of 1958 persisted and others were established later. The unit, (*hsien*, commune, brigade or team) best fitted to manage these enterprises depends, of course, first on the size and administrative competence of these respective units in any particular locality, and second on the capital requirements, scale, type and local circumstances of the enterprise concerned. With the revival in the position of the *hsien* in the period after the Great Leap, this has been a significant level for the management of many types of rural industry.

Other concerns, of smaller size, are best operated at communal level: these include small power plants, plants for making chemical fertilizers, or for polishing rice, sawmills, small opencast mines and foundries and workshops for making farm implements. Enterprises requiring somewhat smaller investments may be under the management of a brigade or jointly operated by a group of teams. These undertakings may include brick and tile works, sugar and oil seed presses, pottery and lime kilns, and the working of salt fields. Still smaller and simpler forms of enterprise, especially those which do not employ a permanent labour force, may be operated by production teams or by peasant households. These include repairs and crafts of various kinds (including those traditionally carried out by itinerant artisans) straw plaiting, the making of chopsticks, brushes, and a host of minor products.

Some of the commune enterprises had previously been managed by the *hsien* and had been handed down to the communes in 1958 as a consequence of the decentralization measures. As far as new enterprises were concerned, the original capital was normally found by the commune, brigade, team or household managing them to which also the profits accrue; expansion being financed by ploughed back profits. In some cases, commune-level industries have received state grants, and in the early days of the commune movement, communes raised levies for such purposes from their brigades.

Ownership and management at the level of the commune have been of greater importance in rural industry than in agriculture. As we have seen, from 1959 onwards the communes as such did not have direct control over most agricultural operations. A survey published in October 1959 found that some 58 per cent of the total value of industry in the communes studied came from enterprises operated directly by a commune, or jointly by several communes.[2] In 1960, it was estimated that industry comprised some 80 per cent

[1] In addition, state fishing enterprises, under the Ministry of Aquatic Products, engage in fishing in the sea and on the bigger lakes. Such trawlers as exist are owned by state enterprises, while collective fishing uses mainly old-style junks and other sailing vessels, although some motorized junks are employed.

[2] *People's Daily* (*Renmin Ribao*), October 26, 1959, p. 7. Sun Chih-yuan, Vice-chairman, National Economic Commission: 'The Great Historical Significance of Industry of the People's Communes.'

(presumably by value of output) of the economic activities controlled at the commune level in Honan.[1]

Local branches of both supply and marketing co-operatives and of credit co-operatives were to be transformed, according to the directives of 1958, into departments of the new communes. In the event, commune managements were as little able to cope with these as with some of the other responsibilities with which they had been saddled at their birth. By 1961, both types of co-operative had been reconstituted and were functioning again as entities separate from the communes.[2] Concerning the area covered by the revived credit co-operatives, little information is to hand except that there were wide variations, and that supervision has tended to be by the *hsien*.[3] The post-1961 supply and marketing co-operatives were reported to have been organized to correspond with a commune or with a *ch'ü* or to be based on a market town. The last two types enjoyed economies of scale, but since they covered several communes their existence led to a weakening of the authority of the party committees of individual communes.[4]

The communes were originally intended to be instruments of collective living. Linked with this, in the early enthusiasm of the commune movement, was the talk of free provision for many needs. Few communes can ever have set out to provide all the services mentioned—free meals, clothing, children's nurseries, old people's homes, baths and hairdressing, and fewer still maintained them for any time. Meals in collective mess halls were the most widespread form of 'free supply'. Collective feeding arrangements, in the first period of the commune movement, operated on a year round basis in many places, and elsewhere just during the busy farming seasons. Although more elaborate buildings existed in certain model communes, the mess halls often seem to have been crude sheds, consisting of a rough thatch roof supported by poles. The advantages of collective feeding were that it freed women for collective work (although the mess halls themselves absorbed quite an amount of labour), that it made it easier to enforce rationing and harder for the peasants to hoard grain, since any grain found in their homes might be claimed to be stolen from the collectives, that fuel was saved and that the mess halls provided good opportunities for political instruction and control. The importance attached to the political and social role of mess halls is seen in the frequent references to the high ideological level required in their workers and also by the fact that cadres sent to the countryside in 1960–1 were often appointed managers of mess halls.

Collective feeding proved unpopular with the peasants, except possibly at the peak agricultural periods. The rural cadres also disliked the mess halls, as they were under constant pressure from higher authority to eat at them and even to take turns at cooking, a circumstance which is unlikely to have raised culinary standards.[5] When rations were cut in the difficult years after the

[1] Ibid., March 14, 1960, p. 7. Shih Hsiang-sheng, Secretary of the Secretariat, CCP Honan Provincial Committee: 'Some Problems Concerning the Consolidation and Development of People's Communes.'
[2] See p. 302 and p. 410 below.   [3] See p. 410 below.   [4] Pp. 303–4 below.
[5] *Southern Daily* (*Nanfang Ribao*), April 3, 1960 (SCMP 2262), Chao Tzu-yang: 'We Must Surely Make a Success of the Mess Halls.'

Great Leap, corruption among mess hall workers is reported to have increased. Then, when peasants were allowed once more to raise their own pigs and poultry, they needed their own domestic scraps. The large stoves of the mess halls required coal, while often the peasants in their homes used stalks and grass as fuel. The consequent need to supply coal to scattered points in the countryside aggravated transport problems. In the north China winters, in any case, peasants had to have fires in their homes. In the peasant houses there the flue from the stove passed under the brick bed, heating it and the rest of the house. Thus fuel was not saved when the stove ceased to be used for cooking. Often, too, the cooking might be done by an old woman who would not be much use in the fields and whose work points would not compensate the family for the extra expense of mess hall meals.[1]

In the course of 1961 mess halls closed down— certainly in Kwangtung and probably also in other provinces. (Later reports tell of mess halls being opened to feed the young people 'sent down' to the countryside from the towns and who, therefore, had no families with which to eat).[2] Grain, and sometimes other farm products, were distributed to peasants as part of the remuneration for their labour, but meals were cooked and eaten in their own homes. The peasant household re-established itself as the basic unit of consumption.

Other forms of collective life established in the communes included nurseries for children and homes for old people without families; like the mess halls, these often were rudimentary.

When the communes were first founded, press publicity—both in China and abroad—was given to a higher degree of collective life in the communes, a re-organization of living accommodation so that even husbands and wives were separated, and the family unit abolished. While the authorities may well have wished, for reasons of political control, to have carried out such a policy on a wide scale, in fact it must have been limited to a very few cases, if any. The speed and extent of the commune movement would show the improbability of any total remoulding of social life. When in a province of the size and population of a western European state, it is announced that the entire rural social structure has been fundamentally changed in a period of three weeks, scepticism must be profound.

The communes and their constituent units share with the *hsien* responsibility for rural schools and health services. In 1964 communes and production brigades were reported to run 22 per cent of the primary schools in rural areas,[3] and some communes also finance a middle school. Primary education is not yet universal, except in certain areas; efforts to supply gaps include the opening of many part-time schools.[4] The secret directive of 1961 on rural communes laid down that all middle schools run by communes should become spare-time only, with all students participating in labour; also that school

[1] I. and D. Crook: *The First Years of Yangyi Commune*, London, 1966, pp. 157–8.
[2] *Ta Kung Daily* (*Dagong Bao*), Peking, April 29, 1966, p. 3.
[3] NCNA Peking, May 26, 1964.
[4] e.g. it was claimed that in Kiangsi (whether excluding or including the towns is not clear) children of school age attending school rose from 59 per cent in 1963 to 75 per cent in 1964 after the opening of part-time schools. *BBC Summary of World Broadcasts*, Second Series, FE/1894/B/1 (Nanchang, June 9, 1965).

fees should normally be payable by the pupil's families.[1] Adult classes to impart literacy and knowledge of improved farming methods are also held by communes. Rural hospitals are usually run by *hsien*, although some large and prosperous communes have their own; communes and brigades sometimes possess simple clinics and health centres.

Communes, brigades, and teams are responsible for the construction and repair of minor roads, and for the provision of local transport, as conditions require.

The commune unit now finds its main function as a level of local administration and of Party organization. This should not be set in contrast to economic functions, because all local authorities in China today have important economic functions, including the control of industrial and other enterprises. However, the commune's originally envisaged role as a basic unit for the direct control of all types of rural economic, political, and social operations was impracticable because the optimum size for different types of activities within these spheres is dissimilar. Thus communes are usually too large to direct routine agricultural operations, and only on occasion the right size for particular water conservancy projects or for managing a tractor station. Some of these activities, and also rural commerce and credit, can usually be better run by specialist organs. The early visions of collective life soon vanished. Only as an initiator of rural industry has its original economic role still remained in varying degrees, according to local circumstance.

On the other hand the commune has continued to carry out its tasks as a local authority, both in those parts where it is equated with the *hsiang* and elsewhere.[2] Indeed, with allowance for its status as the lowest local authority, it appears to function on lines similar to its superiors. Like them, it bears responsibility for the tax payments of its constituent units, and has a share in running certain social services. Like them, too, it controls and receives the profits from those industrial and other enterprises appropriate to management at its level. As economic units the communes fall within the collective sector, not that of the state, and their budgets are not incorporated in the state budget as are those of local authorities from the *hsien* upwards. However, despite this, the formation of the communes represented in fact the first substantial extension of the state apparatus to levels below the *hsien*, for this had not been effected by the *hsiang* of pre-commune days. Beyond this, little can be said unequivocally about the commune: over a country of China's range there is much necessary variation in the lowest local authority.

[1] *Draft Articles on Rural Communes*, op. cit. (Taiwan edition), articles 30 and 33.
[2] In some places (e.g. where communes are very small) the *hsiang* may have revived, comprising several communes.

Chapter 3

COLLECTIVE AGRICULTURE II

1. RURAL CADRES

The term 'cadre', it will be remembered, is applied in China to anyone in a position of responsibility in any type of organization.¹ The cadres of communes, production brigades and teams are the instruments through which higher authorities exert such control as they can over the countryside.

Rural cadres comprise those of the Party, of the Young Communist League, of the government administration (including specialists such as accountants, storekeepers and health workers) and of the militia;² those of the Party and the administration (taken to include communes and their component units) being the most significant. Posts in the Party and administration are often held concurrently (e.g. the same man might be both Party secretary and the chairman of a commune)³ and executive decisions on practical matters are frequently reported as being taken by Party officials. The Party and government organs are not clearly differentiated at the lower levels of rural life. The secretary of the Party committee usually wields the chief authority in any commune,⁴ and the senior cadres of the commune and brigade, and often of the team as well, are likely to be Party members.

The administrative cadres of communes, brigades and teams are supposed to be elected annually by representative meetings of members of the collective unit concerned: it may be expected that such elections are usually held under firm Party control.

The number of cadres of production brigades and teams in the whole of China in 1963 was reported to exceed twenty million.⁵ No estimates are available of the number of commune level cadres. The number of cadres in any commune, brigade or team depends on the size of the unit and on the number and complexity of the operations it directs; in all these there are wide variations.

A continual struggle is waged against the proliferation of cadres. In 1960 the Kwangtung CCP Provincial Committee, quoted approvingly by the *People's Daily*, directed that full-time cadres of the commune and brigade

---

¹ p. 29 above.
² *Mainland Today* (*Jinri Dalu*), No. 180. March 25, 1963, p. 8. Ting Yueh: 'The Disintegration of Commune Cadres under Restrictions.'
³ e.g. *Red Flag* (*Hongqi*), No. 24, December 16, 1961, p. 32. Chou Li-po: 'On a Sunday', and see p. 19 above and p. 198 below.
⁴ *Southern Daily* (*Nanfang Ribao*), March 21, 1962 (SCMP 2722), Che'en Yi-yen: 'Whose Words Are Final?'
⁵ *People's Daily* (*Renmin Ribao*), July 4, 1963, p. 1. Editorial.

level should normally not exceed 0·6 per cent, or in special cases 1 per cent, of the population of the units concerned.[1]

The chief Party and governmental cadres at the commune level are 'state cadres', that is officials with salaries applicable to their grades.[2] A Western visitor noted a great change in commune-level cadres between 1960 and 1964; in the earlier years they had been informal peasants, but in 1964 they had changed into uniformed government officials.[3]

The most important cadres of brigades also rank as state cadres, but not the lower ones, nor cadres of production teams.[4] At these lower levels the cadres are local peasants who are awarded compensatory 'work days' or 'work points' for time spent on official duties, while engaging in agriculture for the rest of the time. The value of a work day or a work point depends on the total distributed income of the collective unit concerned and on the total number of work points by which it is divided. This means that the income of the lower rural cadres is directly linked with the incomes of the peasants: both parties benefit from a higher value of work days and work points, but the ordinary peasants will suffer if the value of these units of payment is devalued through large numbers being awarded to cadres for non-productive tasks. This latter circumstance produces a conflict of interest between cadres and peasants but against this must be set the fact that these lower cadres are local people, chosen from among the villagers in the place where they were already living. Their ties with the peasants, to many of whom they may be related, are closer than their obligations to the impersonal authority of Party and state. In any conflict between the peasants and the authorities, the sympathies of the lower cadres are likely to be with their families and friends, even though they may circumspectly pay verbal tribute to the other loyalties. However, at the same time, if a conflict arises between the cadres' own interests and those of the other members of the collective, the cadres' position gives them much opportunity for making their own interests prevail.

In some production teams, a single family has acquired a dominant position, supplying a large proportion of the team's cadres.[5] In addition there are teams composed each of a single localized lineage (as found especially in Kwangtung province) where all the team cadres are necessarily related.

It can be seen that a significant dividing line runs between those who are 'state cadres' and who look to higher rungs of Party and state hierarchies for the approbation which can further their careers and the lower cadres who are first and foremost local peasants, subject to pressures from their fellows.

[1] *People's Daily* (*Renmin Ribao*), July 11, 1960, p. 2.
[2] See p. 21 fn. 4 above, and *Mainland Today* (*Jinri Dalu*), No. 180, March 25, 1963, p. 8. Ting Yueh: loc. cit., and A. L. Strong: *The Rise of the Chinese People's Communes—And Six Years After*, Peking, 1964, pp. 172 and 195. According to this source, some of the salaries are paid by the *hsien* and others by the commune. On occasion, a report of a model commune will mention that none of the cadres receive state salaries, but that their work is rated for wage points which are paid out of profits of communal enterprises. *Red Flag* (*Hongqi*), Nos. 13–14, July 10, 1963, p. 47. Wang Luan-sheng, Tu Chia-hsing and Hsiang Shao-t'ang: 'Give a Lead to Production by Participation.'
[3] Private communication to the author.
[4] *Mainland Today* (*Jinri Dalu*), No. 180, March 25, 1963, p. 8. Ting Yueh: loc. cit.
[5] J. W. Lewis: *Leadership in Communist China*, Ithaca, New York, 1963, p. 238.

The decentralization of authority from the commune to the production team between 1958 and 1962 effected a transfer of power to those cadres most nearly identified with the local people. The team cadres, for example, are likely to be more responsive to price incentives when taking decisions on production matters than would be the case with state cadres.[1] Presumably this is one reason which has led to greater reliance on price incentives and less on direct orders for the extraction of an agricultural surplus.

The higher authorities have wanted the lower cadres to be dependable instruments for implementing policies which are often unpopular among the peasants. Yet they have been reluctant to allow them sufficient material incentive to endure this invidious position, because a large gulf between their standard of living and that of the rest of the peasants would have aggravated rural discontent. Hence the demand that cadres should live like peasants, eating at the public mess halls while these still existed, and participating as much as possible in farm work. The cadres responded in two ways: first by apathy, by carrying out orders only superficially while colluding with peasant evasion; second, by corruptly securing personal advantage.

Officially, cadres' remuneration is austerely restricted. The draft regulations of the model Weihsing Commune in 1958 ruled that payment of administrative personnel should not exceed 1 per cent of total payments made to commune members; while the secret directive on rural communes issued by the CCP Central Committee in 1961 laid down that compensatory work points of brigade and team cadres together should not normally be more than 2 per cent of the total work points given in the brigade concerned.[2] In practice, these limits must often be exceeded, partly because of the amount of time spent on official duties and partly because cadres are apt to be over-generous in awarding themselves compensatory (and other) work points. One team leader said he had been getting between two and three times as much cash (reckoned in labour days) and over 70 per cent more grain than the average peasant, as well as other privileges; yet his cash income was less than half that of the salaried brigade chief. In addition, cadres obtained supplies of various commodities unavailable to the ordinary peasants.[3]

The senior rural cadres are often veteran Party members, steeled in long years of revolutionary struggle. Now they are ageing, so the recruitment of their successors is an urgent matter. Official preference is for cadres of poor and lower middle peasant origin, and cautionary tales are told of collectives controlled by rich middle peasants, or even by rich peasants and ex-landlords. (It might be thought that class classification would have ceased after collectivization. However, as we shall further note below, considerable differences in income still exist, often reflecting former class background; due, for example, to superior equipment and skill. However, apart from this, former

[1] D. H. Perkins: 'Price Formation in Communist China' (unpublished Ph.D. Thesis, Harvard University 1963), pp. 171–2.
[2] *People's Communes in China*, Peking, 1958, p. 72, *and* Chinese Communist Party Central Committee: *Draft Articles on Rural Communes*, Peking, 1961 (Taiwan ed.), article No. 43.
[3] *Mainland Today* (*Jinri Dalu*), No. 180, March 25, 1963, p. 8. Ting Yueh, loc. cit. However, it must be noted that this journal is published in Taiwan, and may, therefore, exaggerate the favourable position of cadres relative to peasants.

classifications tend to be retained for political reasons: thus, the status of 'ex-landlord' or 'rich peasant' can seldom be shaken off and even clings to the new generation. Criteria currently taken for rural class determination are confused; both living standards and political activities are sometimes used. A CCP Central Committee directive of 1963 gave the correct criteria as being the amount owned of means of production and the degree of exploitation, e.g. employing others, or lending money, undertaken. Children of landlords and rich peasants are not supposed to be basic level cadres in their own districts, nor to be accountants or work point recorders or store keepers;[1] however, exceptions are allowed for those thought to be adequately reformed. It has not always been possible to insist on evidence of such reform before employing persons of families considered untrustworthy.)

Cadres of the desired poor and lower middle peasant background are often completely uneducated, so there has been pressing need to train them. Special arrangements for this purpose have been made at *hsien* and other levels. Short training courses and spare-time classes are the usual methods although for a selected few—mainly local Party secretaries and directors of key communes—the Peking Agricultural University began in 1960 a one-year course in commune management.[2] Special urgency has been attached to the training of accountants to improve the very poor state of financial management in collective agriculture. Local training schemes are organized and, in addition, the Peking Correspondence College gives postal instruction in agricultural accounting and statistics as well as in commune management.[3]

In the 1960s a new source of cadres, with both education and correct class background, appeared in the form of young people directed to take up agricultural work after leaving school. Some became Party secretaries, leaders of production teams, accountants and storekeepers,[4] while many have been trained as technicians. However, the authorities have shown anxiety about the political attitudes of this new generation.

Demobilized soldiers have provided another and politically more reliable supply of rural cadres. In 1963 they were estimated to account for about 30 per cent of the cadres in the communes of Shantung province.[5]

Many and varied duties are expected of the cadres in rural collectives. They have to see that peasants turn up for work and assess their work points, give orders for and supervise the operations of the agricultural year (to the extent that these are not delegated to groups and individuals under the responsibility system), ensure payment of taxes and the making of compulsory deliveries, operate the various collective enterprises of commune, brigade or team as well

[1] Chinese Communist Party Central Committee: *Policy Directive on the Socialist Education Campaign in Rural Communes* (Draft), (in Chinese), 1963. (Published by National Security Bureau, Taipei, Taiwan.)

[2] *Red Flag (Hongqi)*, No. 24, December 16, 1959, pp. 7–8. An Tze-wen: 'Further Strengthen the Role of the Party Organization in the People's Communes', and NCNA Peking, April 15, 1960.

[3] *Ta Kung Daily (Dagong Bao)*, Peking, February 18, 1963, p. 2, and *People's Daily (Renmin Ribao)*, March 26, 1963, p. 2.

[4] *People's Daily (Renmin Ribao)*, May 16, 1962, p. 1, editorial, and ibid., November 27, 1963, p. 5. Chin Chao, Sung Kuai-chih and Hao Hsien-pin: 'Growing Up Steeled in Struggle.'

[5] Ibid., January 17, 1963, p. 1.

as collective welfare arrangements, keep the accounts, press on with the political education of themselves and their flocks, keep abreast of the latest directives, and prepare the many reports demanded by higher levels—all this while they themselves are often barely literate. In addition, the cadres have had to attend innumerable conferences. An analysis of the working time of nine brigade cadres in May 1961 showed that each had spent an average of eleven days of that month at commune and brigade conferences.[1] These meetings appeared to serve no purpose, and to ramble on too long.[2] Chairmanship must have been notably deficient.

Fully occupied by attending such meetings and by paper work, cadres have tended to lose touch with actual farming, while peasants grow discontented at the devaluation of their own work points by the large numbers awarded to cadres. The higher authorities' anxiety over this situation led them in the early 1960s to renew pressure on cadres to take part in agricultural work, a practice which had been encouraged at least since the Central Committee directive on the subject in 1957,[3] but which appears to have been frequently neglected, owing both to the distaste of cadres for such pursuits and to their chronic overwork on official business.

The Central Committee secret directive of 1961 on rural communes laid down that cadres of commune level should devote at least 60 days a year to manual labour; brigade and team cadres should work as ordinary peasants, receiving a limited number of compensatory work points for time spent on official duties.[4] Productive labour for a minimum of 120 days a year was the standard mentioned in 1965 for brigade cadres.[5] From the flood of exhortations and reports of cadre participation in labour, it is difficult to conclude how much this has in fact been put into practice at the different levels. In 1963, after the movement had been in full spate for some years, cadres were still treating it with scepticism as a temporary craze of their superiors to which over much attention need not be given.[6] Two years later, in 1965, rural cadres were still reported to be avoiding manual labour.[7]

The attempt to insist on participation in farm labour was one of the factors which led to a serious decline in the morale of rural cadres; a decline demonstrated by numerous lower level cadres being among the Kwangtung country folk thronging into Hong Kong in May 1962.

The higher authorities tried to shift on to the lower cadres much of the blame for the agricultural disasters of the post-1958 period. Consequently the cadres felt themselves ground between unreasonable superiors and a discontented peasantry and their resentment bred listlessness. The cadres of pro-

---

[1] *People's Daily* (*Renmin Ribao*), June 28, 1961, p. 3.
[2] *People's Daily* (*Renmin Ribao*), February 27, 1962, p. 2.
[3] *New China Fortnightly* (*Xinhua Banyuekan*), No. 109, June 10, 1957, pp. 11–12.
[4] *Draft Article on Rural Communes* (Taiwan ed.), Articles Nos. 43 and 44.
[5] *People's Daily* (*Renmin Ribao*), May 21, 1965, p. 2.
[6] *Southern Daily* (*Nanfang Ribao*), July 13, 1963 (SCMP 3039) Fang Nan: 'For Those Who Are Drifting with the Main Current: On Cadres' Participation in Collective Labour.'
[7] *People's Daily* (*Renmin Ribao*), August 19, 1965, p. 2, and *Southern Daily* (*Nanfang Ribao*), November 26, 1963 (SCMP 3130), '*Hsien*-Level Cadres in Enping *Hsien* Take Part in Labour.' A Party secretary in this *hsien* 'thought that this instruction was like those given previously, only verbally emphasizing the importance of labour'.

duction brigades, in particular, felt that their position had been undermined by the devolution of power to the teams. 'Now that production brigades have been deprived even of the authority over production and distribution, ... what should we do if a production team does not listen to us?' ... 'When there is no rice in your hands, not even the chickens will come to you.'[1]

During the Great Leap, cadres had been guilty of an overbearing attitude towards the peasants and of giving irrational orders. In subsequent years they were accused of relaxing control and of a lack of courage to take the lead.[2] Insinuations were also made of corruption in various forms: speculation, awarding themselves too many work points, favouritism to their relatives, false reports to superiors, extravagance in putting up unnecessary buildings or indulging in feasts and giving favours in return for hospitality and gifts.[3]

The higher authorities also discovered wide-ranging collusion between rural cadres and peasants in circumventing state regulations on such matters as compulsory sales of crops. In order to put an end to this state of affairs, a campaign called 'the four cleansings' was put in operation from the autumn of 1964. In certain provinces large numbers of students and others were dispatched to the countryside, not primarily to work in agriculture but just to keep a watch on the peasants' activities and report on them.[4] This whole movement was intended to be hidden from foreigners and it is impossible to estimate the campaign's degree of success. In any case, no answer satisfactory both to government and peasants yet appears to have been found to the problem posed by the ambiguous position of the rural cadres.

The radio and the telephone have enabled orders to be transmitted easily to rural cadres. By 1960 every commune and most production brigades were said to have telephones.[5] But supervising the implementation of orders remains difficult. This is partly because both administrative techniques and rural transport have not improved in step with tele-communications, and in part because of the inherent difficulties of supervising widely dispersed activities. The campaigns to make higher officials undertake manual labour in the villages were aimed among other reasons, at supplying this deficiency. However, if much of their time is spent this way, administration suffers. Hence the attempt to use students as supervisors: their efficiency in this role has yet to be proven, as has also the permanence of results of short-term campaigns such as that of 1964.

[1] *Southern Daily* (*Nanfang Ribao*), April 8, 1962 (SCMP 2733).
[2] Ibid., April 6, 1962 (SCMP 2733).
[3] e.g. *Southern Daily* (*Nanfang Ribao*), March 20, 1963 (SCMP 2960), and ibid., July 13, 1963 (SCMP 3039), Fang Nan: loc. cit., and *People's Daily* (*Renmin Ribao*), October 20, 1964, p. 2, and ibid., December 14, 1964, p. 1. 'Is This a "Token of Affection" or Poison?'—letter from a reader, and *Draft Articles on Rural Communes*, Articles Nos. 25 and 52, and Intelligence Bureau, Ministry of Defence, Taiwan (ed.) *The Collected Documents Obtained by the Anti-Communist Guerrillas in the Raid on Lienchiang, Fukien* (in Chinese), Taipei, 1964 (*The Lienchiang Papers*), pp. 52–3, and Chinese Communist Party Central Committee: *Policy Directive on the Socialist Education Campaign in the Rural Communes* (Draft) 1963, loc. cit.
[4] *New York Times*, November 15, 1964, and *Far Eastern Economic Review*, June 9, 1966, pp. 479–84, H. Munthe-Kaas: 'China's "Four Clean-Ups".'
[5] *Peking Review*, October 11, 1960, p. 5.

The economic role of the rural cadres has largely been to act as expensive substitutes for the working of market pressures. In the past no one had to tell the peasants to go out in the field to labour, nor was it necessary to assess anyone for work points; accounts were kept in people's heads and paper work was almost non-existent. When, as during the Great Leap, the cadres were compelling peasants to adopt agricultural practices which, in many localities, were actually harmful (e.g. close planting and deep ploughing), the economic damage done was far greater than the actual burden of the cadres' keep. At such a time the cadres may well have been an even heavier incubus on the rural economy than were the landlords they displaced. In so far as the cadres, in the years after the Leap, have acted more reasonably—and particularly perhaps where they have sided with the peasants in mutual defence against economically harmful directives from higher authorities—they may have made a positive contribution to rural advancement.

2. FINANCE AND REMUNERATION OF LABOUR IN COLLECTIVE AGRICULTURE

The establishment and maintenance of an ordered financial system in communes, brigades and teams has been beset with the same difficulty as, before 1958, had hampered a similar development in the *hsiang*, that is by the lack of people in the countryside with even the most elementary ability to keep accounts.[1] Hence what is considered desirable in the way of financial control and methods of payment for labour has had continuously to give way to what is feasible.

Policy promulgated in 1958 on communal finance and trade was summed up in the slogan 'two decentralizations, three centralizations and one guarantee'. This referred to the decentralization of the personnel and assets of the state's rural financial and trade organs (such *hsiang* and *ch'ü* financial organs as existed, together with credit co-operatives and supply and marketing co-operatives) to the communes, the 'three centralizations' of economic policy, of planning and of management of working capital, with which communes had to comply, and the guarantee by the communes to pay the required taxes.[2]

The basic level financial and trade organs, now intended to be converted into departments of the communes, were still to be subject to direction by the higher levels of the relevant state organs. The communes' financial departments were to handle receipts and expenditures while the credit departments, which acted as branches of the People's Bank of China, dealt with deposits and loans.[3] All the spare cash, except for day to day requirements,

---

[1] e.g. in a production brigade in Kwangtung in 1962, seventeen out of the nineteen production teams were not able to produce accounts. *People's Daily (Renmin Ribao)*, June 21, 1962, p. 2. In another case not one out of ten teams had proper accounts in 1963. *Southern Daily (Nanfang Ribao)*, June 22, 1963 (SCMP 3022), Lin Ch'eng-ts'ai: 'Strengthen Guidance over Financial Work in Production Teams.'

[2] *Red Flag (Hongqi)*, No. 2, January 16, 1959, p. 1. Li Hsien-nien, Minister of Finance: 'How to Recognize Improvements in the Management of Rural Finance and Trade.' The slogan had been in use at least since October 1958.

[3] In 1958-9 the practice of communes issuing their own currency was sufficiently widespread to merit condemnation by the Minister of Finance. See *Red Flag (Hongqi)*, No. 2,

belonging to the commune and its constituent units, had to be deposited with the credit departments. These credit departments, and also the trade departments of communes, soon regained their previous organization as co-operatives; we shall trace this development in the chapters on Banking and on Internal Trade respectively.

The fiscal guarantee demanded from communes—a guarantee to pay the required taxation—might, as originally laid down in 1958, take the form of an absolute sum or, alternatively, of a fixed proportion of a commune's income. The guarantee covered agricultural tax, with local surtax, industrial and commercial tax and other payments hitherto collected by the state in rural areas and the profits of enterprises transferred from higher levels to communes under the decentralization measures of 1957–8.[1] We have seen that on the formation of the communes the emphasis was on the obligation of the commune, as a unit, for tax payments, but that as first the brigade and then the team became the basic economic accounting unit, the primary responsibility for tax payments and for compulsory sales of produce rested with these in turn. The commune kept an overall responsibility for seeing that these lower units fulfilled their obligations in the same way that higher local authorities, such as provinces and *hsien*, are responsible for the obligations of the units below them. It is to be presumed that when the supply and marketing co-operatives were re-established, the responsibility for payment of industrial and commercial tax reverted to these bodies.

The commune originally exercised a redistributive function in relation to its brigades through the levying and expenditure of funds for investment, welfare and reserve purposes: the richer brigades contributing disproportionately and the poorer benefiting the more. In this way it was intended to reduce differences in living standards within each commune. However, the disincentive effects of such a tendency on the more prosperous brigades provoked a reaction and warnings were issued against egalitarianism. Peasants were reminded that they had 'not yet attained a socialist economy owned by the whole people but were at the lowest stage of common ownership, still retaining distinctions between poor and rich communes and between poor and rich brigades'.[2]

The commune, as we have already seen, came to draw much of its income from the profits of its own industrial and other enterprises, rather than from levies from its brigades and teams, although some part of the reserve funds of the lower units were still supposed to be paid into the general reserve fund of

---

January 16, 1959, p. 5. Li Hsien-nien: loc. cit., and *Ta Kung Daily* (*Dagong Bao*), Peking, February 7, 1959 (SCMP 1989). From 1955 onwards, some agricultural producers' co-operatives are said to have issued currency. F. J. Durand: *Le Financement du Budget en Chine Populaire*, Hong Kong, 1965, p. 61.

[1] *New China Fortnightly* (*Xinhua Banyuekan*), No. 147, January 10, 1959, p. 63. These various taxes and payments, together with compulsory sales to the state, will be discussed in Chapters 13 and 14 below.

[2] *Daily Worker* (*Gongren Ribao*), July 19, 1961, p. 3. Lo Keng-mo: 'The Nature of Rural People's Communes at the Present Stage.' Examples of poorer brigades being helped by their communes, however, were still reported—e.g. NCNA Wuhan, September 16, 1964. 'Poorer Areas Helped Forward by Central China Commune.'

the commune. Apart from this, all transactions between a commune and its constituent units, and between these constituent units, should be on a business footing, on a basis of 'parity of exchange of material supplies and labour'.[1]

The production team, as the basic economic accounting unit, is responsible for the distribution of its income—both of that portion of income which is distributed in kind and of the team's cash receipts. These cash receipts derive from sales to the state (compulsory and voluntary) and on the free market; also some teams receive cash for the labour of their members contracted out to state agricultural machinery stations, state forest farms, nearby factories and other undertakings, as well as certain payments by members who ply their trades outside the team.[2] For the distribution of a production team's income, the method usually reported is for certain deductions to be made from the team's total income and then for the residual to be divided among team members according to work performance. Allowance, however, has to be made for the crudity of teams' accounts and the system must often be far less smooth than as here described.

The proportion of gross income accounted for by deductions before payments to members has been subject to great variations. In 1961 the Minister of Agriculture considered that this proportion should be around 35 per cent[3] but this figure, as we shall see, has often been exceeded. The deductions are for taxes, expenses of production and administration (including the servicing and repayment of loans), and for the collective accumulation and welfare funds. Agricultural tax and local surtax are discussed in Chapter 13 below; during the First Five Year Plan period these totalled some 11–13 per cent of the output of the main crop. Production expenses cover requirements for working capital; they may, according to reported cases, comprise anything from 13–57 per cent of gross income. Expenses for any year are supposed to be provided from the previous year's income, rather than from loans which, in any case, are severely rationed.[4] Figures quoted for administrative expenses range from less than $0 \cdot 2$ to 5–6 per cent of gross income; $0 \cdot 2$ per cent was mentioned in 1962 as the normal limit[5] although it is difficult to envisage how the figure could be kept so low, and it must be noted that the chief item in administrative expenses, the compensatory wage points for cadres, would usually alone exceed this percentage of total income.

The public accumulation fund (sometimes translated as the 'reserve fund') is the chief source of investment funds for the team, while the welfare fund is

---

[1] *Ta Kung Daily* (*Dagong Bao*), Peking, June 15, 1962, p. 3. Chiang Hsüeh-mo: 'A Discussion on the Use of the Law of Value in the Economy of the Rural People's Commune.'

[2] See pp. 81–2 below.

[3] *Red Flag* (*Hongqi*), No. 3–4, February 1, 1961, p. 28. Liao Lu-yen, Minister of Agriculture: 'Summon up Vigour, Energetically Win a Bountiful Harvest.'

[4] *Ta Kung Daily* (*Dagong Bao*), Peking, November 25, 1962, p. 2. Feng Ch'un-lin: 'Retain Enough Funds for Expenses of Agricultural Production.' On rural credit see pp. 408–11 and 425–33.

[5] *People's Daily* (*Renmin Ribao*), July 1, 1960, p. 4. Wang Te-ho: 'Some Understanding Gained by Being Secretary of a Party Branch', and *Southern Daily* (*Nanfang Ribao*), October 28, 1960 (SCMP 2401), Chang Ken-sheng: A Report Delivered at the Conference of Directors of Rural Work Departments of the CCP District and *Hsien* Committees in Kwangtung Province, and *People's Daily* (*Renmin Ribao*), June 16, 1962, p. 2. Lin Hsi: 'What I Have Seen, Heard and Thought about in Places Where I Once Worked.'

used for providing medical facilities, help for old people without support, and similar purposes. The accumulation and welfare funds are now retained for the most part by the production teams, although in some cases a portion may still be handed over to the brigade or commune. The proportion of gross income going to these funds has fluctuated widely with the prosperity of year and place. In 1957, agricultural co-operatives in the country as a whole were said, on an average, to have set aside some 10 per cent of their total income for welfare funds, while in the same year a survey of twenty co-operatives in Hupeh indicated that about 25 per cent of their incomes went to the accumulation fund.[1] During the Great Leap, targets for saving, like all the other targets, were raised to exaggerated levels. For example, in Hupeh it was recommended that accumulation should account for between 40–70 per cent of total income; this corresponded to marginal rates of saving of between 40–90 per cent of the expected rise in income in 1958 over the previous year.[2] Such rates were unreasonable and the agricultural crisis of the following few years quickly forced a reappraisal. As a result, in 1960 it was recommended that accumulation and welfare funds together should take some 5 per cent of total income.[3] This would accord with reports of teams putting 3 and 4 per cent into accumulation funds in 1961 and 1962 respectively.[4] In 1964 it was recommended (in Heilungkiang province) that the proportion of gross income allotted to the accumulation fund should range from zero (in a bad year) to a maximum of 20 per cent.[5] However, rates above 20 per cent have on occasion been reported even after the Great Leap.

Accumulation funds must not be equated with net saving by agricultural collectives, even after making allowance for contributions to state investment from taxes remitted by them to the state. On the one hand, few agricultural collectives make provision for depreciation, even when they possess large items of equipment.[6] On the other hand, in addition to monetary investment,

[1] *Collected Laws and Regulations of the People's Republic of China* (in Chinese), Vol. 7, p. 254, and *New China Fortnightly* (*Xinhua Banyuekan*), No. 144, November 25, 1958, p. 92. CCP Hupeh Provincial Committee, Rural Work Department: 'Report of a Survey on the Relation between Accumulation and Expenditure in Agricultural Co-operatives.'

[2] *New China Fortnightly* (*Xinhua Banyuekan*), No. 144, November 25, 1958, p. 91. CCP Hupeh Provincial Committee Rural Work Department, loc. cit.

[3] *Red Flag* (*Hongqi*), No. 22, November 16, 1960, p. 38. Chin Ming: 'The Way in Which Financial Work in People's Communes Serves Distribution.'

[4] *Southern Daily* (*Nanfang Ribao*), August 21, 1962 (SCMP 2814). K'uang Ch'ang-ch'eng, First Secretary CCP Toishan Commune Committee, Toishan *hsien*, Kwangtung: 'Production Teams that Have Increased Output Should not Distribute and Consume All Their Output.'

[5] *People's Commune Construction* (*Renmin Gongshe Jianshe*), No. 21, November 5, 1964 (SCMM 452). Work Team, Agricultural Work Department CCP Heilungkiang Provincial Committee: 'A Survey of the Method of Setting Aside Reserve Funds in Communes.' (One passage in this article suggests that 20 per cent to the accumulation fund applies only to increments of income. Another passage, however, would seem to lay down a maximum of 20 per cent of total income), see also *People's Daily* (*Renmin Ribao*), February 5, 1963, p. 2. Hsing Huan and P'ei Ch'uan: 'When the Root is Firm, the Branches Will Flourish.' In the brigade (formerly a higher co-operative) instanced here, 'accumulation' amounted to 8, 19, 22·5, 12 and 17 per cent total income in 1957, 1958, 1959, 1960 and 1961 respectively.

[6] *Economic Research* (*Jingji Yanjiu*), March 1965, p. 54. Shih Che: 'Preliminary Examination of Certain Questions Concerning Accumulation and Expenditure in Rural People's

there have been contributions made to investment projects (especially water conservancy) by the labour of peasants, for which they are usually remunerated with work points (i.e. this portion of investment is paid for by inflating the number of work points, thus reducing the value of each point: this amounting in effect to a proportionate income tax).[1]

Loans from credit co-operatives and from banks (the Agricultural Bank, in periods when such has been in existence, and from the People's Bank at other times) have been available both for agricultural working capital and for investment in water conservancy projects, afforestation, for purchases of livestock and machinery, and for rural industrialization. During 1958, such loans were given recklessly,[2] but from 1959 credit was tightened again and greater selectivity shown in loan extension. In addition, the state has at times made non-repayable grants to agriculture, including ¥2,500 million to communes in 1959–60. However, all these sources of finance together are small in relation to requirements. The major part of both short and long term capital for collective agriculture has to be self-supplied and the necessity for accumulating this capital is constantly being urged on the communes and on their lower units. Economy in current expenses, the development of subsidiary production, self-sufficiency in tools and livestock rearing, in fertilizers and seed, and the encouragement of personal savings are the chief methods envisaged for achieving this end.

A question which we may here raise is the extent to which higher authorities can influence the quantity and direction of investment by communes, brigades and teams. Methods by which they might do so include direct pressure on cadres, pricing policy (prices of various types of farm produce and of means of production), the extension of credit and its conditions and terms and, of course, the availability of investment goods. Nor should the provision of consumer goods suited to rural needs be overlooked, for their incentive effect in increasing production and hence indirectly investment, can be most important. The 'state cadres' who head communes and brigades, are presumably more amenable to pressure from above than the lower ranks of peasant cadres. Pricing policy, we shall see, is used to promote the output of desired products and thus indirectly those forms of investment (water conservancy projects, soil improvement measures, machinery) which assist their production, while in the aid agriculture campaign of the early 1960s, prices of farm machinery were lowered to encourage purchase, and industrial policy was directed to making such equipment, together with chemical fertilizers and

---

Communes.' In 1965 the People's Bank and the Agricultural Bank were experimentally encouraging a system of depreciation for draught animals and major farm tools. *Ta Kung Daily (Dagong Bao)*, Peking, May 21, 1965, p. 2.

[1] Sometimes alternative methods are practised, such as setting an obligatory number of work days on investment projects without any remuneration, or making payment from the collective reserve funds, but these are said to be less satisfactory than payment with work points. *Economic Research (Jinghi Yanjiu)*, No. 9, September 1965, p. 9. Agricultural Economics Unit of Shantung Provincial Economic Research Institute: 'Rely on Accumulation by Labour for Agricultural Irrigation and Other Forms of Capital Investment.'

[2] It is not known what proportion went to communes of the People's Bank loans of ¥2,000 million to aid the 1958 iron and steel campaign. See p. 429 below.

insecticides, more widely available. Allocation policy, notably of fertilizers, has favoured particular crops and, from 1963 onwards, high yielding areas. Credit policy will be discussed in Chapter 15. Here it may be noted that in the mid-1960s loans for draught animals accounted for some 60 per cent of the bank loans extended every year to production teams for capital equipment, while loans for working capital were spent largely on fertilizer.[1] The desirability of acquiring more and better draught animals would not need to be driven home to the peasants, but is something on which both the government authorities and the production team members would agree. Machinery and chemical fertilizers may need more selling, but at present both are in short supply. In the 1960s the incentive role of consumer goods came to be more fully appreciated, and steps were taken to improve supplies in the countryside.

To compute remuneration of labour, that part of the team's income to be distributed among members (i.e. gross income net of the deductions listed above) is divided by the total number of work points or work days credited to members; this determines the value of a work point or work day in that team for the year concerned. (Ten work points are reckoned for a standard work day in the system commonly reported, although variations exist.) Then each member receives the payment to which he is entitled by the number of work points he has to his credit. Earnings are computed for each individual worker. These are supposed to be paid to the individual and not to the head of the household; however, this is not necessarily done in practice.[2] Payment is made usually after the second harvest, in cash[3] and in kind—normally in the local staple grain which, for account purposes, is probably reckoned at or near the state's compulsory purchase price (perhaps net of cost of transport to the state purchasing point);[4] sometimes other farm products, such as vegetable oil, are also distributed. The distribution in kind is effected mainly 'according to need' by the number and ages of persons in each family, i.e. it is a form of rationing of grain and other staples and peasants may not take more than a fixed amount of their remuneration in kind, although additional bonus grain is sometimes given as a reward. The greater part of the variation in payments for labour is expressed in the cash component of distribution. In the case of large families with few able-bodied workers, or more generally in bad years, the payments in kind may exhaust all the remuneration due and little or no cash may be payable at all. Many refugees reaching Hong Kong from Kwangtung in 1960–1 said they had received no cash.

On the first formation of the communes, it was intended that a large part,

---

[1] *Ta Kung Daily* (*Dagong Bao*), Peking, September 25, 1964, p. 3. Chang Shu-jen: 'A Short Cut Solution to the Problem of Funds for Draught Cattle', and ibid., May 8, 1964, p. 1.

[2] J. Myrdal: *Report from a Chinese Village*, London, 1965, p. 29.

[3] In some exceptionally well-organized collective units, monthly cash payments have been made. *People's Daily* (*Renmin Ribao*), August 8, 1960, p. 3. Wang Shih-hsin: 'Open the Source and Economize the Flow: Pay Wages Monthly in Advance.'

[4] *Ta Kung Daily* (*Dagong Bao*), Peking, December 18, 1961, p. 3. Li Hai: 'The Organization of Rural Handicrafts.' The statement that 'the peasants' grain is calculated according to the state's official purchasing price' would seem in the context to apply for computation purposes to grain retained in the collective for self-consumption as well as to that actually sold to the state.

sometimes put at half, of distributable income should be given out in the form of 'free supply': free meals at the mess halls, in some cases also free clothing and other benefits allotted according to need and not according to work. This diminished incentive to work and encouraged wasteful consumption. So no sooner had it been announced that 'free supply' was in force in all rural areas (whether or not this had actually been achieved) than counteracting tendencies came into play. The CCP Central Committee's Resolution of December 1958 laid down that for some time to come in the communes distribution of income must be primarily according to labour and the cash component of personal income must increase faster than the amount given in free supply.[1] At this period the generally recommended proportion between 'free supply' and cash remuneration was 3:7. The secret directive of 1961 reiterated that a minimum of 70 per cent of the total should be in the form of wages. The giving of grain ration 'according to need' was modified in the course of the years of agricultural disaster. The 1961 directive permitted the provision of free or subsidized rations to those incapable of work, but all others were to receive supplies only 'according to labour'.[2]

The average value of a work day has varied greatly from place to place and year to year. For the period 1962–4 the lowest figure reported for a work day that has come to our knowledge is ¥0·65 in a team in Kwangtung and the highest ¥3 in a commune in Heilungkiang. However, many cases may have occurred of average values outside these limits.[3] The average annual income (per worker, from the context, rather than per commune member) in the Heilungkiang commune cited was ¥200 while, in an exceptionally successful Kwangtung team with a work-day worth ¥2 in 1962, the annual *per capita* income reached ¥221 (¥792 a household):[4] in the northern province of Heilungkiang, farm work was, of course, possible on fewer days than in the south.[5] The average annual *per capita* income of a cotton-growing brigade in Honan was reported in May 1963 to have risen in the previous six years from

---

[1] *People's Handbook* (*Renmin Shouce*) *1959*, p. 41.

[2] *Draft Articles on Rural Communes* (Taiwan ed.), Article No. 33. See also *Paoan Bulletin* (*Baoan Tongxun*), No. 71, November 14, 1961, p. 3, and ibid., No. 78, December 14, 1961, p. 1.

[3] *Southern Daily* (*Nanfang Ribao*), August 21, 1962 (SCMP 2814), K'uang Ch'ang-ch'eng: loc. cit., and *People's Daily* (*Renmin Ribao*), April 6, 1964, p. 1.

[4] *People's Daily* (*Renmin Ribao*), April 6, 1964, p. 1, and *Southern Daily* (*Nanfang Ribao*), December 21, 1962 (SCMP 2899), Ho Chen-lu and Li Hui-chao: 'The Origin of the Evaluation of a Work-Day at ¥2.'

[5] Some uncertainty surrounds the question of the number of days worked in total, and on collective tasks, by peasants. For 1929–33, J. L. Buck estimates 1·7 months idleness and 0·2 months sickness per able-bodied man a year, i.e. over ten months full-time work. (J. L. Buck: *Land Utilization in China*, Nanking, 1937, reprinted New York, 1964, p. 294). However, in 1957 a writer in a Chinese statistical journal stated that peasants worked an average number of 'labour days' equivalent to less than 150 days a year. (*Statistical Work*, *Tongji Gongzuo*, No. 16, August 29, 1957, p. 33. Hsü Kang: 'Some Views on How to Compare Standards of Living of Workers and Peasants.') Possibly the last source was considering collective work only but even so, it must leave unexplained a wide divergence between the 1957 estimate and that of Buck. Perhaps the explanation is that many farm workers (women, the young and the old) are not reckoned to do a labour day equivalent in one day's work. In the early days of the communes, the time worked by peasants is likely to have increased above the 1957 level, although later it may well have declined.

¥86 to ¥141.¹ A visitor in 1965 met variations in payments between ¥600 a year in a commune near Peking to ¥50 a year near Kunming.² The above figures are for total income, cash and kind. Cash payments, as indicated, would normally be much less: a large family in Anhwei province with few active members, which had previously received no cash, in 1962 earned ¥22 after cost of meals had been deducted.³ Cash receipts per worker varied between ¥10 and ¥200 in communes (presumably of above-average prosperity) visited by a Western traveller in the autumn of 1964.⁴

That these payments are below what peasants can earn from working on private plots and other subsidiary occupations must be presumed from the evident unwillingness of peasants to turn up for collective work. Low attendance rates have been disapprovingly but widely reported—as low as eight days a month in 1962 for a team in Fukien, for example.⁵ As well as relative material receipts from working for the collective or on their own plots, the intangible preference for being one's own master must also be borne in mind.

No study of inter-regional differences in peasant income since the Great Leap, comparable to that made by P. Schran⁶ for 1955–7, has come to our knowledge. Schran found significant regional differences in both monetary and real earnings of the peasantry; differentiated expenditure had, however, been restricted to less essential goods and (through variations in agricultural tax rates and in compulsory deliveries) differentiated consumption of own produce even more severely limited.⁷ Schran was concerned with comparisons between four large geographic regions (the north west, the north east, the central plains, and the south).⁸ Not all his conclusions would necessarily hold off inter-local comparisons on a smaller scale, e.g. within his geographic regions. Since land reform, local differences in rural gross incomes have been greater than before, as there are no longer differential rent payments to compensate for varying qualities of soil and situation.⁹ A substantial part of the higher national ground rent enjoyed by the more favoured units of collective agriculture goes (as Schran found) to the state as agricultural tax and compulsory deliveries at prices lower than would educe voluntary sales. However, it would seem probable that considerable differences in standards of living (both in peasant expenditure and even in consumption of own produce) between certain types of district must exist and have increased since the Great

---

¹ *People's Daily* (*Renmin Ribao*), May 29, 1963, p. 2.

² *New Statesman*, September 3, 1965, p. 321. K. S. Karol: 'Maoism: China's Secular Religion. A Twentieth-Century Experiment in Puritan Ethics.'

³ *China Youth Newspaper* (*Zhongguo Qingnian Bao*), May 15, 1962. (SCMP 2753). Shang Hsiu-lien: 'Farmers with Culture Needed for Agricultural Work.'

⁴ Private communication to the author.

⁵ *Lienchiang Papers*, p. 37.

⁶ Peter Schran: *The Structure of Income in Communist China*. (Unpublished Ph.D Thesis, University of California, 1961.) I am grateful to Victor Funnell for bringing this thesis to my attention.

⁷ Ibid., pp. 244–5.

⁸ Ibid., p. 144.

⁹ The more remote parts of the country, however, benefited (at least during the First Five Year Plan period) from a deliberate narrowing of the 'scissors' differential in those areas relative to that in other areas. Improved transport contributed to this end. See p. 456 below.

Leap. We have seen that the attempt to even out such differences within communes was halted. The especially favoured districts would be those near cities and in areas designated as being of 'high and stable yield'. These areas have profited from priority for state and municipal investment funds and for agricultural machinery and fertilizers, as well as being the first to benefit from rural electrification. Better transport and proximity to urban markets means that peasants get better prices for free market sales, and also obtain many consumption goods at lower prices and in greater variety. Education and health facilities must also be of a higher standard than in more remote areas. In order to get the greatest return from its investment in priority rural areas in the 1960s, the state in all probability has given incentives, by permitting retention of part of extra output as well as by the more plentiful provision of consumer goods.

If such local differences in rural standards of living do not occur, it is unlikely that so much theoretical attention would have been given to the topic of rural rent differentials and their compatibility with Marxist theory.[1] The non-payment of rent runs parallel to the absence of interest charges for industrial fixed capital in China. However, in the case of industry the bulk of the residual profits go to the state, while in collective agriculture they go to the peasants. In both cases, the economy suffers by the absence of the allocatory functions played by rent and interest respectively, in ensuring that capital (land or investment funds) is directed towards the most productive uses: it must, of course, be remembered that before 1949 the market for land was far from perfect.

Most of the methods for allotting work points in the communes had also been used in the agricultural producer co-operatives.[2] The difficulty has lain in finding a system which combined ease of assessment with the provision of the maximum incentive for skill and hard work. The levelling tendencies of 1958 came out not only in the provision of 'free supply' according to need but also in the preference for time wages rather than piece rates, a preference which was evidenced too in industrial wages in that year. Under the time wages system, which had the advantage of relative simplicity, each worker was assessed for skill, strength, and attitude to labour, and then assigned to a particular grade. If he performed the required number of days' work a month, the fixed amount of work points for his grade would be recorded in his labour handbook and eventually he would be paid according to that year's value of a work point in his team, with bonuses awarded by the cadres for good work. Six to eight grades were the number officially recommended with the wages of the highest grade set at four or more times that of the lowest.[3]

The deleterious effect of 'free supply' on incentives was aggravated by the

---

[1] *Kuang Ming Daily* (*Guangming Ribao*), September 18, 1961, p. 4. Wang Chieh: 'Views on Differential Ground Rent', and ibid., September 18, 1961, p. 4. Yen Yung-ch'ien: 'A Tentative Discussion on Differential Net Land Rent and Its Distribution', and ibid., January 4, 1962, p. 3, and ibid., August 6, 1962, p. 4. Hou Chih-yüan: 'The Reason for Differential Rent in Rural People's Communes at the Present Stage', and *Red Flag* (*Hongqi*), No. 23, December 1, 1961, pp. 39–41 Ku Ming (ed.): 'A Discussion of the Question of Differential Rent in Rural People's Communes.'

[2] Tung Ta-lin: *Agricultural Co-operation in China*, Peking, 1959, pp. 124–30.

[3] *People's Handbook* (*Renmin Shouce*) *1959*, p. 42. Resolution of the Central Committee of the Chinese Communist Party, December 10, 1958.

similar tendency of time wages. By 1961, not only had 'free supply' come to an end with the closure of the mess halls, but in agriculture, as in industry, piece work had been restored to favour. Piece work has taken several forms, but they all involve assessing the appropriate number of work points for a given task, and then making sure that the task has been accomplished up to standard. Because of the number and complexity of farm jobs, and the constant changes of weather and other factors, setting of norms is notoriously difficult in agriculture. Irrational norms distort distribution of labour by making people unwilling to work on tasks thought to have been underrated. Supervision, too, has peculiar problems: the dispersed nature of much farm work makes on the spot supervision difficult and subsequent inspection slow; also farming operations cannot be judged for results on a day-to-day basis. Sometimes special 'quality control workers' are employed, a job which one holder admitted to be 'most embarrassing' and fruitful of quarrels.[1]

It should be noted that even in collective work the better-off peasants have an advantage. Small farm implements usually have to be provided by the workers using them, and the more prosperous families have more and better implements and are thus able to earn more work points than their poorer fellows.[2] The recording of work points, due to the low level of literacy, has often been chaotic and sometimes not even attempted. When it is possible to find a competent recorder, his illiterate fellows will not be able to check him and this may engender suspicion, even if no cause for it exists.[3] This task, although it requires great tact and ability to deal with people, often has to be performed by teenagers because they are more frequently literate. At other times, the only competent people for the job may be members of former landlord and rich peasant families, who are liable to be mistrusted by Party cadres.

All these difficulties have strengthened the tendency for tasks to be set for long periods, sometimes—as we have seen—by giving contracts for a season or more to operational groups or even to individuals. (Presumably payment for contracts is made by the award of so many work days but no reference to this has been found.) This cuts the amount of clerical work, as points do not have to be recorded for each short job, and lessens the frequency of inspection needed. However, not all farm tasks are suited to long-term contracts. For those not so suited either the assessment of norms job by job or some system of time wage has still to be practised.[4]

Artisans and handicraftsmen present special problems, for not all can

[1] *BBC Summary of World Broadcasts*, Second Series, FE/2147/B/8. (Canton, April 14, 1966.)

[2] *Rural Finance* (*Nongcun Jinrong*), No. 10, May 21, 1965 (SCMM 477). Correspondence Team of Huailai Branch, Agricultural Bank of China: 'Help Poor and Lower Middle Peasants Obtain All the Small Tools They Need.' A survey in a *hsien* in Chekiang showed that the disparity in equipment was increasing as upper middle peasants bought the tools of poorer and lower middle peasants. *Economic Research* (*Jingji Yanjiu*), June 1965, p. 50. Yueh Wei: 'A Discussion of Socio-Economic Research Surveys.'

[3] *Southern Daily* (*Nanfang Ribao*), October 6, 8 and 15, 1961 (SCMP 2816). 'Questions and Answers Concerning Commune Management', and *China Youth* (*Zhongguo Qingnian*), No. 1, January 1, 1965, p. 12. Hsüeh An-fu: 'Wholeheartedly for the Thirteen Households of Poor Peasants.' Before this author went to a certain village as a teacher, nobody there was capable of recording and settling work points.

[4] *Southern Daily* (*Nanfang Ribao*), October 6, 8 and 15, 1961 (SCMP 2816), loc. cit., and

conveniently be employed on work for the collectives. To exclude those not so employed from membership of production teams would introduce a diversive element into what is supposed to be a comprehensive unit and might be held to encourage capitalist tendencies in the countryside. These artisans ply their trade or sell their wares for cash and are required to surrender a fixed sum of cash to the production team for each working day. In return the team credits them with the equivalent number of work days (presumably according to the grade to which they are assigned). As we have seen, the value of the team's work day is paid net of deductions (tax, administrative expenses, public accumulation and welfare funds), and bears a further incidence of tax through being largely based on state compulsory purchasing prices, while artisans' earnings represent free market prices. In addition, the value of a work day is lowered through the granting of work days for work on investment projects or, as we shall see, for reasons other than remuneration (e.g. to retired servicemen, etc.). Therefore it is considered appropriate that the team should claim from the artisan cash of 50–100 per cent greater value than that of the work day with which he is credited in exchange.[1] This practice amounts to commutation of collective labour obligations for cash, a line of conduct which has been sternly forbidden to peasants wishing to engage in commerce.[2] It gives scope to the handicraftsmen's 'spontaneous inclination to capitalism' which aroused official anxiety in 1964–5, when special attempts were made to integrate them more closely into the communal organization.[3]

Rural artisans may regard the practice of commutation of labour obligations as a valued concession, allowing them to retain anything above the sum agreed.[4] Alternatively, they may contrast their lot, shouldering a daily tax, with the improved prospects of urban handicraftsmen in the early 1960s.[5] This may have prompted them to leave the countryside for market towns or cities. While, in general, peasants have been discouraged, forbidden, or prevented from flocking to the cities since the Great Leap, it is not known how

---

Kuang Ming Daily (*Guangming Ribao*), May 20, 1963, p. 4. Ts'ai Yüan-yüan and Teng Tse-hui: 'An Exploratory Discussion on Methods of Calculating Labour Remuneration in People's Communes—The System of Recording Work by Piece-Rate.'

[1] *Ta Kung Daily* (*Dagong Bao*), Peking, December 18, 1961, p. 3. Li Hai: loc. cit. See also ibid., April 17, 1961 (SCMP 2499) The Central Correspondence Unit of the CCP Wuhsiang *Hsien* Committee, the Work Unit of the Department of Commerce of Shansi Province and the Correspondence Unit of the Bureau of Commerce of Wuhsiang *hsien*: 'Implement the Policies, Strengthen the Leadership, Make Trade through Rural Markets Brisk without Becoming Chaotic', and see *Southern Daily* (*Nanfang Ribao*), July 5, 1962 (SCMP 2799) 'Fengyunghsin Production Team Develops Diversified Economy According to Local Conditions to Increase Income and Build the Production Team into a Consolidated Unit of Production': here it is stated that work points for artisans working outside the team are 'calculated according to the amount of money earned'. This might mean that they get the equivalent of the whole of what they earn, or get a fixed proportion of it.

[2] *Southern Daily* (*Nanfang Ribao*), June 20, 1962 (SCMP 2781). 'The Success of a Production Team in Developing Collective Economy.'

[3] *Ta Kung Daily* (*Dagong Bao*), Peking, February 15, 1965. Editorial, p. 1.

[4] Certainly it is an improvement for them on the severe reduction of income they experienced on the formation of the communes in 1958. On this, see P. Schran: op. cit., p. 336.

[5] See pp. 232–4 below.

far this policy has been applied to artisans moving, for example, to a market town. If the net result of the assessment of cash payments from rural craftsmen is that they pay heavier taxes than their urban fellows, this is likely, in the absence of strong institutional barriers, to bring about a changed distribution of workers of this type.

Demands for excessive payments in exchange for 'work days' can lead to a fall in supply of the skills concerned. Thus a report from Kwangtung tells of traditional veterinarians who were assessed at sums greater than their earnings for each day spent outside the team on their speciality. As a result the veterinarians were unwilling to offer their services or to take on apprentices.[1] In other instances, when demand for the service is inelastic, this policy may cause a sharp rise in prices charged for it. For example, a certain ferryman had to pay his production team ¥100 a month 'greatly in excess of the cost of maintaining a ferry boat', with the result that ferry fares rose steeply.[2]

Work points are awarded not only for labour but also in payment for household manure; this sometimes accounts for a high proportion of total work points given in the collective unit concerned.[3]

As well as the work points awarded to factors of production (labour and manure) others are sometimes given without any compensatory productive return. These include work points credited to crippled ex-servicemen and to service dependants. Work points are also given for labour on road repairs and water conservancy projects, which may increase the team's income in the long run but not necessarily in the year in which the work points are earned. By adding these types of work points to those earned in the ordinary way, the value of each point participating in the general share out is diminished; these charges are in this way met by what in effect is a proportionate income tax on income from collective sources, but not on income from private sidelines.[4] This provides yet a further reason for the peasants' preference for private occupations over collective work. It is to these private sidelines that we must now direct our attention.

3. PRIVATE PLOTS AND SUBSIDIARY OCCUPATIONS OF RURAL FAMILIES

As well as remuneration in cash and kind from collective agriculture, peasants have other sources of income in their private plots, livestock and domestic handicrafts.

Private plots are the pieces of land assigned to members of production

---

[1] *Southern Daily (Nanfang Ribao)*, May 18, 1962 (SCMP 2766).

[2] *People's Daily (Renmin Ribao)*, December 14, 1962, p. 2.

[3] Ibid., August 26, 1962, p. 1. In the brigade instanced here, work points given for manure accounted for 54 per cent of all work points awarded in 1961.

[4] *Agricultural and Forestry Work Bulletin (Nonglin Gongzuo Tongxun)*, No. 6, June 1964 (SCMM 430). Rural Work Department, CCP Yunghsiu *Hsien* Committee: 'Spread the Work of Distribution of Income over the Whole Year.' In this team the work points representing welfare expenditure, such as payments to school teachers, did not participate in the general share out, but 'were dealt with in accordance with the principle of letting those pay who receive the benefit'—presumably by making the families of the pupils pay, in cash or kind, the value of these work points.

teams, normally on a household basis, for their own use. Frequently they consist of scattered fragments of land, sometimes including newly opened waste land and often of poorer quality than the collective fields. Ownership of the land remains collective. The individual or family concerned has a right to the produce of the plot, but may not rent out the land, sell it, mortgage it, or give it to others.[1] No mention has been found of a right of inheritance, but if the plot is implicitly or explicitly given to the family as such, and not to an individual, this might normally be presumed.

For an extensive study of the role of private plots in Chinese agriculture and of some of the changes in official policy towards them, the reader may consult the book by K. R. Walker.[2] Here only a brief sketch of their significance and history can be given. For most of the period since 1956, under both the co-operatives and the communes, the official criterion for the size of private plots was that they should not exceed 5 per cent of the arable area in any locality. We shall note below that for a short period in 1957–8 this figure was raised to 10 per cent, while at times the plots were (at least widely) abolished. Apart from occasional aberrations by local cadres, no cases are known where plots have reached the maximum size officially permitted, the normal range being between 2·5–3 per cent of the arable area (in absolute size, plots reported in north China in 1956–7 averaged some 483 square metres a household against 87 square metres in the south).[3] Walker estimates that from this 2·5–3 per cent of the arable acreage derived an average of 14 per cent of the calories in the peasants' diet in 1956 and between 9 per cent and 60 per cent of total peasant income in 1956–7.[4] This indicates the degree to which peasants lavish labour, manure and entrepreneurial ability on their plots.[5] The general pattern is that peasants get most of their staple foodstuffs from collective distribution, while obtaining marketable produce and subsidiary foods from private sidelines, including handicrafts. 'We depend on the collective for grain, but on ourselves for cash.'[6]

Despite official provision for private plots in model regulations promulgated in 1956 for higher agricultural co-operatives, policy as implemented in that year was unfavourable to the private sector in agriculture. Plots were restricted and, in some cases, abolished, while privately-owned pigs, poultry and equipment were confiscated. Fear of further confiscation and lack of the fodder previously obtained from their plots, together with diminished sales

---

[1] *New Construction (Xin Jianshe)*, No. 1, January 1964, p. 9. Liu Shih-pai: 'A Tentative Discussion on Remnants of Private Ownership under the Socialist System', and *Daily Worker (Gongren Ribao)*, August 2, 1961, p. 3. Kung Wen: 'Sideline Occupations of Rural Households: Part I', and NCNA, February 19, 1966.

[2] *Planning in Chinese Agriculture: Socialization and the Private Sector.* London, 1965.

[3] K. R. Walker: op. cit., p. 25.

[4] Ibid., pp. 32 and 33. The present author disagrees with some of the assumptions on which these calculations are based, but considers that the orders of magnitude are reasonable.

[5] In the Soviet Union in 1956, private holdings of collective peasants comprised less than 4 per cent of the sum of collective land plus these holdings, and contributed about 30 per cent of all Soviet agricultural production in that year. A. Nove: *The Soviet Economy* (Revised ed.), London, 1965, p. 29. In 1962 collectivized peasants in North Vietnam are estimated to have obtained over 55 per cent of their real incomes from private plots and other non-collective sources. *China News Analysis*, No. 460, p. 6.

[6] *People's Daily (Renmin Ribao)*, November 20, 1964, p. 2.

outlets owing to restrictions on rural markets, led peasants to slaughter large numbers of their remaining livestock. The difficulties that followed led to privately-owned plots and livestock being regarded with more favour in the latter part of 1956 and in 1957, to an increase in the official purchasing price for pigs, and to the raising of the upper limit on plots' size to 10 per cent of the agricultural land in any area. At the same time, some restrictions on rural markets were lifted. Towards the end of 1957 an official pronouncement deplored excessive severity towards private plots and urged that they be expanded.[1] These instructions scarcely had time to yield results when they were overtaken by the commune movement in the summer of 1958.

The establishment of the commune was made the occasion for widespread confiscation of private plots and other assets of peasant families. The original Central Committee Resolution on Communes, of August 1958, said in guarded language that, in general, private plots might be taken into collective management, while scattered fruit trees should temporarily remain in private ownership, as should also private financial holdings. In any case, nothing should be done in a hurry.[2] The draft regulations for model Weihsing Commune, issued in September 1958, laid down that peasants joining the commune should turn over private plots, houses, trees and most livestock to collective ownership (this property, however, to be considered an investment made by its former owners on which, it might be implied although not explicitly stated, they would receive interest). Peasants were to be allowed to retain a small number of domestic animals and poultry as private property.[3]

In the months that followed, many local cadres exceeded instructions and confiscated not only peasants' private plots but also their personal chattels. Domestic sideline occupations, too, were widely suppressed. In addition, such were the demands made on the peasants in the early days of the communes, that they can have had little time for anything other than collective work. The closure of rural markets also had its influence.

Although these extreme measures may not have been universally implemented, the ban on subsidiary agricultural activities was sufficiently effective to cause extensive economic dislocation. In many places no arrangements had been made for the collective pursuit of these activities nor of domestic handicrafts which fell under similar official displeasure in 1958. Hence severe shortages developed of pigs, poultry, vegetables and fruit, as well as of such items as straw sandals, coir brooms and raincoats, bamboo hats and baskets.[4]

These developments impelled the Central Committee, in its Resolution of

---

[1] K. R. Walker: op. cit., pp. 62–3 and 67–70, and *Collected Laws and Regulations* . . . Vol. 7, pp. 293–4.

[2] *People's Handbook* (*Renmin Shouce*) *1959*, p. 33. Resolution on the Establishment of the People's Communes in Rural Areas, passed by the enlarged Conference of the Political Bureau of the Central Committee of the Chinese Communist Party at Peitaiho, Hopei, on August 29, 1958.

[3] *Red Flag* (*Hongqi*), No. 7, September 1, 1958, p. 18. 'Provisional Regulations (Draft) of the Ch'ayashan Weihsing People's Commune.'

[4] *Ta Kung Daily* (*Dagong Bao*), Peking, February 20, 1959 (SCMP 1980). Li Ch'eng-jui and Yang Ch'un-hsü: 'Apply the Contract System Extensively.'

December 1958, to condemn the wholesale confiscation of personal property that had occurred. This resolution laid down that in the communes all privately owned means of livelihood (a term defined to include houses, clothes and furniture) together with bank and credit co-operative deposits, should remain in private ownership in perpetuity. With owners' consent, houses surplus to private needs might be used by communes, but the ownership was to remain unimpaired. The peasants might continue to own odd trees around their houses, tools and small farm implements, small domestic livestock and poultry. So long as it did not interfere with collective work, they were also permitted to continue their small-scale domestic side occupations.[1] Following this resolution, in January 1959 an article in *Red Flag* recommended that, among other things, peasants should be allowed to grow some vegetables around their houses.[2] Private pig raising, too, began to be encouraged, partly to supply the lack of manure caused by the decline in pig population.[3]

These small concessions whetted the appetite for more. Towards the end of 1959, reports came in of peasants demanding additional private land.[4] In some cases, local cadres weakened, as in one production team where over a quarter of the cultivated land was given back to individuals to the neglect of collective production.[5] Perhaps it was fear of such relaxation that lay behind a movement in 1960 to take private plots away from the peasants once more and give them to the public mess halls to use for growing vegetables and other auxiliary foodstuffs for their own use.[6] Many mess halls were at that date developing into significant corporate units, apart from their obvious canteen functions. They had been ordered to produce non-staple foodstuffs for consumption in the halls, but some had gone further and—against official policy—had engaged in production for sale, this money being then divided among their members.[7]

The dissolution of the halls in 1960–1 put an end to these developments. It is not a coincidence that these years also saw the revival of private plots and private livestock-rearing, as well as of the rural markets where peasants could sell their produce. The CCP Central Committee's secret directive on rural

---

[1] *People's Handbook* (*Renmin Shouce*) *1959*, p. 42. Resolution of the Central Committee of the Chinese Communist Party of December 10, 1958, on Certain Problems of the People's Communes.

[2] *Red Flag* (*Hongqi*), No. 2, January 16, 1959, p. 10. Chen Cheng-jen: 'Start Up a Large-Scale Mass Campaign to Get the People's Communes in Order.'

[3] K. R. Walker: op. cit., p. 81.

[4] *Inner Mongolia Daily* (*Neimenggu Ribao*), November 15, 1959 (SCMP 2159). Wang To, Secretary of the Party Committee of Inner Mongolia: 'Deepen the Socialist Education Movement Centred on Waging a Struggle between Two Roads and on the Implementation of the General Line', and *Kiangsi Daily* (*Jiangxi Ribao*), December 3, 1959 (SCMP 2166): 'The Idea of Extending the Responsibility System for Work and Production to the Households is a Reactionary Idea Aimed at Restoring the System of Exploitation.'

[5] Ibid.

[6] *Southern Daily* (*Nanfang Ribao*), April 3, 1960 (SCMP 2262). Chao Tzu-yang: 'We Must Surely Make a Success of the Mess Halls', and *Liaoning Daily* (*Liaoning Ribao*), May 24, 1960. (SCMP 2289). Work Groups, CCP Liaoning Provincial Committee: 'Report on Conditions in Rural Community Mess Halls.' (Excerpts.)

[7] *Liaoning Daily* (*Liaoning Ribao*), May 24, 1960 (SCMP 2289). Work Groups, CCP Liaoning Provincial Committee: loc. cit.

communes of 1961 stipulated that private plots normally equivalent to 5 per cent of total cultivated land should be allowed to peasant families on a long-term basis.[1] This was reiterated in the Central Committee's directive of 1963 with an added gloss that if plots slightly exceeded the maximum laid down, the excess should not be confiscated if it did not harm the collective economy.[2] In the course of 1961 a number of articles appeared in the national press justifying and commending private plots and domestic handicrafts, which were held to be 'an essential supplementary part of the socialist collective economy . . . completely socialist in nature' and in no way a remnant of the old order.[3] Policy on pig-rearing was reversed, the private sector now being recognized as the main supplier of pigs.[4] One corollary of the change in official attitudes to private plots at this time was their exemption from agricultural tax and (in theory) from compulsory sales, to which they had previously been liable. The exemption for compulsory sales appears commonly to have been honoured in the breach,[5] despite instructions in the secret directive of 1961 that grain (and, therefore, presumably the less important crops also) grown on private plots should be excluded from both collective distribution and compulsory purchase.[6]

The relaxation in favour of private enterprise in 1961 was followed by a notable improvement in the rural economy, and there was truth in the saying by which private plots, private reclamation of land, family subsidiary occupations, and rural markets were dubbed the 'four great magic wands'.[7] The advantages of such a revival to the government are obvious. So long as appropriate consumer goods are put on sale in the countryside (and this was increasingly achieved by the growth of the plastics and metalware industries in the early 1960s) the peasants willingly sell vegetables, fruit, and livestock products to the urban market. Many of the products grown mainly on private plots, it should be noted, are important export commodities.

The authorities also sense dangers in these developments. For ideological reasons they regard it as imperative that the greater part of agriculture, including most of the grain and cotton cultivation, should remain collectivized. This is in direct competition with the private plots for labour and manure, both of which yield higher returns to the peasants when applied to their own plots rather than to collective fields. Combined with the poor morale of rural cadres since the Great Leap, this has often resulted in low rates of attendance for collective work and of delivery of household manure. Consequently a marked contrast has occurred in rates of growth of productivity in collective agriculture and in the private sector, a contrast which was reflected in the continued rationing of grain and cotton, while subsidiary farm produce came

---

[1] *Draft Articles on Rural Communes* (Taiwan ed.). Article No. 37.

[2] *CCP Central Committee: Policy Directive on the Socialist Education Campaign in the Rural Communes* (Draft) 1963, p. 12.

[3] *Ta Kung Daily (Dagong Bao)*, Peking, June 12, 1961, p. 3. Yao Fang-yü: 'My Views on the Nature of Private Plots.'

[4] K. R. Walker: op. cit., pp. 90–1.

[5] See pp. 352–3 below.

[6] *Draft Articles on Rural Communes* (Taiwan ed.), Article No. 38.

[7] *Southern Daily (Nanfang Ribao)*, November 10, 1962 (SCMP 2881), Ch'en Yi-yen: 'On the So-Called Four Magic Wands and the Like.'

into plentiful supply in the towns. The desire of the peasants to use collectively owned draught animals and implements on their private land has provided other occasions of dispute.¹

The conflict of economic interests between collective and private cultivation is not the only reason which has caused the authorities anxiety over private plots. Opportunity for peasants to earn incomes from private sources increases class polarization in the countryside. The former rich and upper middle peasants still retain more and better livestock, fruit trees, implements for farming and handicrafts and above all, superior agricultural knowledge and efficiency. Their material superiority, compared with poor peasants, is enhanced by the lack of any institutionalized source of long-term credit to individual peasants. The credit co-operatives which handle such loans are restricted to one year's term.² There remains only private money lending at high rates of interest; as such loans are presumably made by richer peasants to their poorer fellows, this only serves to raise the relative position of the former. Rich peasants employ others to help with their sidelines and tend to have more land due to private reclamation.³ The greater the peasants' private output, the greater importance they attach to rural markets and other opportunities of trade, which are now once again the recognized road to wealth.⁴ The government has tried to counter these developments by spasmodic encouragement of collective rather than private sidelines (in the face of economic advantage which, in most cases, lies decisively with the latter), by helping poor peasants to take up subsidiary occupations (e.g. by selling them piglets on credit) and by political campaigning (demonstrated in frequent newspaper articles from 1963 onwards) on the need for continued class conflict in the countryside, including the formation in many places of special associations of poor peasants. In 1966, reports from Kwangtung and other parts spoke of private plots being restricted or even abolished. At the time of writing, it is too early to say how far the authorities will be willing to sacrifice the advantages to the economy of private plots in order to curb the political tendencies to which they give rise.

The government's dilemma is that, while the rural upsurge from 1962 has greatly improved livelihood in both town and country, it has done so by giving scope to private initiative and ambitions which, if allowed to continue unchecked, may undermine the political foundations of the regime. The situation has been made more dangerous by the government's own policies. The severe restrictions on trade in staple crops, for which only a marginal free market exists and of which the great bulk has to be sold to the state at lower than free market prices, the fact that agricultural tax falls only on collective

---

¹ *Southern Daily* (*Nanfang Ribao*), January 25, 1963 (SCMP 2959). The Correspondence Section of the CCP Suihsi *Hsien* Committee: 'Poor and Lower Middle Peasants Must Be the Masters of the House', and *Current Scene*, Vol. II. No. 32, May 1, 1964, quoting *Asahi*, December 6, 1963.

² See p. 411 below. Even credit co-operatives sometimes prefer to lend to richer rather than poorer peasants. *Ta Kung Daily* (*Dagong Bao*), Peking, March 10, 1965, p. 2.

³ *People's Daily* (*Renmin Ribao*), November 14, 1963, p. 1, and *New Construction* (*Xin Jianshe*), No. 1, January 1964, p. 13. Liu Shih-pai: loc. cit.

⁴ *Southern Daily* (*Nanfang Ribao*), February 20, 1963 (SCMP 2945) Fang Nan: 'Common Prosperity and Individual Riches.'

production and that this also bears a disproportionately large share of compulsory sales—all these diminish still further the relative returns to the peasant of working on and applying manure to collective land and strengthen his inclination to devote all the resources he can muster to producing goods for his family consumption and for sale. The very successes of the government have worked against their policy, for the bright new consumer goods, specially planned to stimulate peasant incentives, have sharpened the desire for cash, a desire which is fulfilled more certainly and swiftly by the cultivation of individual plots than by labouring for the collective.

4. THE COMMUNES: 1958 AND 1966

How far, looking back on the first eight years of the communes' history, can it be said that they fulfilled the hopes placed on them by Party and government in 1958?

In 1958 the communes were heralded as strong multi-purpose basic units of rural life, political, economic and social. They have succeeded in many areas in extending the state apparatus to levels below the *hsien*, where previously it had scarcely penetrated.[1] In other words, the communes have been less shadowy entities, on the whole, than had been the *hsiang* and *ch'ü* in former days.

The organization of agriculture, is, in the main, back to where it was under the lower agricultural co-operatives: that is, the small natural village (or a section of larger ones) is the normal, but not invariable, unit of farm management, except in so far as it has contracted its responsibilities down to even smaller groups or to households and except also that a considerable share of farm output comes from private plots. Another exception must be made for 'suburban' areas around cities, where easier transport, larger markets and more commercialized agriculture, together with greater supplies of manure and pigswill under collective control, facilitate larger units of farm management and the collective operation of certain lines, such as pig rearing and vegetable-growing, for which deeper in the countryside, the advantage lies with the private producer. The fact that these suburban communes differ radically from other communes is seen in their tendency, in some instances, to be absorbed into state-owned commodity bases.[2]

The communes have not been as multi-purpose as intended. They have not proved effective units for the management of trade or credit, nor usually of tractor stations. Even for water conservancy, they have frequently had to give way to units of more appropriate size. This is partly, as already noted, because the indivisibilities of scale of all the functions originally intended for the communes have proved mutually incompatible, and partly because the weakness of commune management, especially in financial matters, has inhibited them from undertaking many of these responsibilities. Rural industrialization has not made the headway expected in 1958, but many communes have successfully promoted this development and much of the cost of

[1] The role of communication techniques, particularly the telephone, in making this possible, must be stressed.
[2] See p. 102 below.

commune level administration is met from the profits of such enterprises. One limiting influence on the communes' participation in commerce and small-scale industry has been the revival of the market towns as units in their own right and as centres for such activities; although some market towns were still, in 1965, integrated with communes which have their headquarters in them.[1] The development of the market towns will be charted further in Chapter 11.

The authorities hoped, in 1958, that the communes would prove useful and compliant instruments in mobilizing and extracting rural savings which could then be channelled into industry and, in real terms, that they would provide the agricultural surplus necessary to feed the growing urban sector. The responsibilities for guaranteeing tax and procurement quotas, and assigning them to brigades and teams, still rests with the communes and is probably the most important duty generally remaining to them. In the event, the communes in their early days developed a high degree of self-sufficiency and in 1958 the government was not able to procure as much grain as had been hoped. In the 1958 harvest, for perhaps the first time in Chinese history, a considerable gap emerged between biological and barn yield, owing to diversion of labour to the iron and steel campaign, and to other distractions.[2] Even as a proportion of barn yield, the government probably collected less than it might have done, simply because of the shortage of storage space under its control. In the old days, large quantities of grain (in aggregate) were stored in private premises of peasants, landlords and merchants. After the trade in grain and other staples became a state monopoly from 1953 onwards, a grave shortage of granary space under state control became apparent.[3] As long as the grain had to be kept in scattered storerooms and granaries owned by villages or private individuals, state control could not be complete. Something was done to alleviate this shortage before 1958, but the exceptional harvest of that year precipitated a crisis. In August 1958 an announcement was made that farm products purchased by the state might be left with the co-operatives (news of the communes had not yet been released) until warehouse space and transport facilities enabled it to be moved.[4] From reports of extravagant food consumption in 1958, it may be presumed that peasants took advantage of this situation (in any case the fantastic efforts demanded of them in 1958 must have raised their calory requirements) and that some of the stocks nominally collected by the state never actually left the villages (this raises the question whether the 53 million tons of grain reported[5] to have been procured by the state in tax and compulsory sales is the nominal or the actual quantity procured: probably the former). In addition, great losses occurred in storage.

[1] *Literary Gazette* (*Wenyi Bao*), No. 10, October 1965, p. 2. 'Acclaim the New Achievements of Small Modern Revolutionary Operas.'

[2] Choh-ming Li: *The Statistical System of Communist China*, Berkeley, 1962, pp. 95–6.

[3] *People's Daily* (*Renmin Ribao*), February 10, 1954, Editorial (reprinted in *New China Monthly* [*Xinhua Yuebao*], No. 53, March 1954, p. 158), and *People's Handbook* (*Renmin Shouce*) *1957*, p. 496. Chang Nai-ch'i, Minister of Food: 'Grain Work in the Past Year.' Report to the 3rd Session of the 1st National People's Congress, and Sun Ping-yen: *The Communist System of Food Grain Control* (in Chinese), Taipei, 1958, pp. 132–3.

[4] *Ta Kung Daily* (*Dagong Bao*), Peking, August 10, 1958, p. 1.

[5] *Ten Great Years*, Peking, 1960, p. 169.

Sweet potatoes comprised an unusually high proportion of 'grain' output in 1958 and they keep badly; carelessness at harvest time in that year meant that crops were stored in a damp condition, nor was inspection adequate.[1] In 1959 a crash campaign was put in hand to build granaries and storage bins.[2] In 1962, as we have seen, the basic accounting units (i.e. normally the production teams) were designated the sole licit owners of rural grain reserves, apart from peasant households.[3]

The suppression of private plots and domestic sidelines in 1958, together with the closure of rural markets and the dislocation of traditional trading patterns, reduced the agricultural surplus and aggravated the trend to self-sufficiency.[4] When, from 1961, both private plots and rural markets were restored, the flow of subsidiary farm produce to the towns grew larger. But the output of the staple commodities which the government was most anxious to obtain—grain, vegetable oil and cotton—proved most difficult to raise. The direct result of the policies adopted to procure them (virtual state monopoly of purchase at prices below free market levels) meant that their cultivation was less attractive to the peasants than that of commodities which could be sold on the free market. This in turn led to the marginal productivity (to the peasants) of factors of production applied to collective activities—among which the growing of these staples predominated—being depressed relative to their use on private plots and other household subsidiary occupations. As a result, vegetables, fruit, pork, and eggs came into plentiful supply in the cities, while grain, vegetable oil and cotton goods remained rationed. The rise in official procurement prices for grain in the 1960s,[5] however, must have done something to counteract this.

The demoralization of the lower rural cadres after the Great Leap and the subsequent collusion between cadres and peasants to disregard regulations, made it more difficult for the government to extract a surplus from agriculture on terms unacceptable to the peasants. At the same time, this disregard of unwise orders has assuredly been a major factor in the subsequent revival of the rural economy, by enabling economic incentives to operate in spheres where their action was supposed to be non-existent or minimal. In short, it is now seen to be impossible to operate an all-embracing command economy in the countryside. This has wide-reaching consequences on the government's ability to control investment in the agricultural sector and, through it, the rate and direction of increase in rural output and incomes.

It was originally hoped that differences in standards of living within each commune would be levelled out. This aim, we have seen, was abandoned because it conflicted with the need to provide each unit with sufficient incentive to raise its output. On a wider scale, local inequalities of income must have increased in rural China, not only because of the absence of differential rent but also due to the special advantages, above those of natural endowment, accruing to areas of high and stable yield and to rural areas near cities.

Finally the communes were meant to promote collective living—not in the crude way sometimes stated of breaking up families into separate dormitories,

---

[1] *Ta Kung Daily* (*Dagong Bao*), Peking, March 2, 1959 (SCMP 2020). Editorial.
[2] NCNA, May 13, 1959. [3] See p. 57 above.
[4] See pp. 291–301 below on the rural markets. [5] See p. 360 below.

but in providing at least a number of goods and services 'according to need'. Something of this remains in the distribution of part of the remuneration of labour in kind and with some relation to size of household, and therefore to need. The collective mess halls have been swept away, except in places where they are revived in the busiest farming seasons or for special categories of persons. Communes and their constituent units make provision for unsupported old people and share with higher local authorities the task of providing such education and health facilities as exist, although the beneficiaries are often charged. In the old days some of these functions were undertaken by lineage associations and other bodies, whose property has now been collectivized.

In the years since the Great Leap, 'sprouts of communism' in the communes have been less in evidence than 'sprouts of capitalism', real or suspected, in the economic activities of the peasant household: the private plots, private livestock, domestic handicrafts and commerce at rural markets. These activities have been largely responsible for the rural revival after 1962. The resurgence of the rural family as the basic unit of consumption and of a considerable part of production, has been the most striking feature in China's countryside. Its efficiency as an economic unit is due to the immediacy of the incentives to hard work and thrift and to the convenient way in which its multifarious aspects dovetail into each other. Domestic swill feeds livestock, manure nourishes land; farm and handicraft products can be taken together to market; the surveillance of children, of livestock and of cooking, can be carried on simultaneously with the production of handicrafts or care of vegetables and fruit trees near the house. Thus, odds and ends of materials and of the time of young and old are used to better advantage than when these varied activities are carried on in specialized fashion by different people. Greater differentiation of roles must await changes in productive methods.

'Historical materialism informs us that new relations of production can be built only when productive forces make new demands.' From this was argued the objective necessity, the inevitability, of the communes. 'Their establishment was like the falling of a melon when it has ripened and like the filling of a ditch when water comes.'[1] But over most of the Chinese countryside the productive forces of peasant agriculture have not changed. The scientific revolutions that altered Western farming have made as yet small impact on the paddy fields and vegetable plots, on the pig pens and scrawny fowl of rural China. Thus, even in the theoretical framework of the country's rulers, their original intentions for the communes were bound to frustration: the melon had not ripened nor had the water come to fill the ditch.

[1] *Daily Worker* (*Gongren Ribao*), November 7, 1961, p. 3. Hsüeh Nung: 'The Objective Necessity of Rural People's Communes.'

Chapter 4

STATE FARMS, AGRICULTURAL MACHINERY STATIONS AND FORESTRY

1. STATE FARMS

State farms are defined as 'socialist agricultural enterprises under ownership by all the people'.[1] This ownership status is the feature which distinguishes them from collective agriculture. The management of state farms may be subject to an organ of either the central government or of a local authority down to the level of *hsien*.[2] State farms are the equivalent of the Soviet *sovkhozy* and, in their early days, owed much in concept, and sometimes also in organization, to these prototypes.[3] Another debt, this time unacknowledged, was to the large mechanized farms established by the Japanese in Heilungkiang as well as to the great sheep farms opened in 'Manchukuo' by the puppet government of that territory and by the Japanese-owned South Manchurian Railway.[4]

By virtue of their 'ownership by the whole people' state farms enjoy an ideological superiority: they realize here and now the position which collective agriculture is held destined to attain some time in a future ever more remote. Another distant objective of the regime is to bridge the gap between the rural population and urban workers: here state farms are to

[1] *Economic Research* (*Jingji Yanjiu*), No. 12, December 1963, p. 15. Ting Lü-ch'u: 'An Exploratory Discussion of the Rational Management of State Farms.'

[2] Below this level, any agricultural concern is usually connected with a unit of collective agriculture and, therefore, is not under 'ownership by all the people'.

[3] A model *sovkhoz* was provided by the Sino-Soviet Friendship Farm, established near the Sino-Soviet frontier in Heilungkiang in 1954 with the help of a team of Soviet experts and with a considerable array of Soviet tractors, combine harvesters, and other farm machinery. This farm in 1961 covered 40,000 ha. with a population of 60,000, and produced wheat, soya beans and livestock. It must have exercised a considerable influence through the flow of trainees and visitors (some 5,000 in the first five years of its existence), who came from as far as Hainan Island in the south and Sinkiang in the north west. In addition, members of the farm's own staff were dispatched to state farms elsewhere to pass on what they had learned. A similar function on a lesser scale was performed by the Sino-Czech Friendship Farm established in 1956 on the north China coast. *People's Daily* (*Renmin Ribao*), November 12, 1959, p. 4. Chang Lin-ch'ih, Vice-Minister of State Farms and Land Reclamation and First Secretary of the CCP Hokiang District Committee, Heilungkiang, and Wang Cheng-lin, Director of the Yu-yi State Farm: 'The Yu-yi State Farm—A Model and a Training Centre for Mechanized Farms', and NCNA, Harbin, July 18, 1961, and *Kuang Ming Daily* (*Guangming Ribao*), September 27, 1961, p. 2, and NCNA Tientsin, September 20, 1961. In June 1960, when all Soviet experts were recalled from China, three were working in the Ministry of State Farms and Land Reclamation. *Far Eastern Economic Review*, May 28, 1964, p. 422. Daniel Wolfstone: 'Economics of the Split.'

[4] On the Japanese farms in 'Manchukuo', see E. B. Schumpeter (ed.): *The Industrialization of Japan and Manchukuo 1930–40*, New York, 1940, pp. 309–10.

help by habituating farm workers to machinery, and by the creation in agriculture of a class of wage earning employees. Originally workers on state farms, like workers in state factories, were remunerated by wages, not by a residual (as are peasants on collectives) while the net profits and losses accrued to the state (either central or local authorities as the case may be). We shall see that in course of time there has been a movement to assimilate methods of labour remuneration on state farms to those obtaining in collective agriculture, but in general the assimilation has probably been incomplete and some difference remains. Paid employees, rural as well as urban, are considered intrinsically more reliable in their political outlook than peasants, even collectivized peasants, who are believed more likely to retain the individualistic leanings of their origin.

These ideological advantages have been reinforced by practical considerations. State farms, coming under the immediate control of public authorities, might be assumed more amenable to planning directives; thus it should be easier to make them switch to whatever crop is at any time most urgently needed. They have enjoyed priority in obtaining tractors, other farm machinery and chemical fertilizers, and have been the recipients of considerable investment from central and local government resources. This fact, together with their larger scale and what was hoped would be more efficient methods, was intended to make state farms yield a relatively larger surplus of output over subsistence needs than could be expected from the great bulk of peasant farming. Their higher technical level was meant to provide a model for the collectives and be a practical proof of the superiority of ownership by the whole people. State farms have been an important instrument for the large-scale reclamation of waste land, especially in the peripheral regions of China. Linked to this is their function of settling 'Han' Chinese (i.e. of the majority race), both ex-servicemen and civilians, in these parts, and thus promoting migration from densely peopled provinces to the sparsely populated borderlands, where the earlier inhabitants are mainly of minority races; a migration of political and strategic, as well as of economic, import.[1]

The earliest Chinese Communist state farms were set up during the Sino-Japanese war by the army to provide for its own support.[2] From 1949–56 state farms came under the Ministry of Agriculture. In 1956 the Ministry of State Farms and Land Reclamation was established to take charge of state farms as well as of the settlement of waste lands.[3] Since its establishment, the Ministry has been held by Wang Chen who, as a former Party First Secretary of Sinkiang, has had first-hand experience of one of the main areas of his Ministry's operations.

[1] On the superiority and role of state farms, see the speech of Wang Chen, Minister of State Farms and Land Reclamation, to the First National Congress of the Chinese Agricultural and Water Conservancy Workers' Trade Union on January 30, 1958. *Daily Worker* (*Gongren Ribao*), February 1, 1958. (Quoted from *New China Fortnightly* [*Xinhua Banyuekan*], No. 127, March 10, 1958, p. 135.)

[2] *Peking Review*, September 25, 1964, p. 26.

[3] *Collected Laws and Regulations of the People's Republic of China* (in Chinese), Vol. 3, p. 81. The literal translation of the Chinese title of this Ministry is 'Ministry of Agricultural Reclamation'. However, official Chinese publications in English translate it as 'Ministry of State Farms and Land Reclamation' and this title will be used here.

In addition to the state farms coming under the Ministry of State Farms, there are various other state-owned agricultural enterprises (including those under departments of local authorities) detailed below, which are controlled by one or other of the Ministries of Agriculture, Public Security or Internal Affairs or by the Overseas Chinese Affairs Commission. State forestry farms, together with game farms and reserves, come under the Ministry of Forestry and will be separately discussed. In official Chinese pronouncements, the term 'state farm' normally, but not invariably, refers to those under the Ministry of State Farms and Land Reclamation; the term includes both arable farms and livestock ranches. Definitional discrepancies complicate the facing table:

Sources:

1949–58: *Ten Great Years*, Peking, 1960, p. 134, which gives figures for 'state farms and livestock farms under the Ministry of State Farms and Land Reclamation'. According to *Red Flag* (*Hongqi*), No. 7, April 1, 1961, p. 1. (Wang Chen, Minister of State Farms and Land Reclamation: 'Strengthen the Building Up of State Farms') the figures for the state farms in 1957 given in *Ten Great Years*, p. 134 (and by implication all the other figures for the years 1949–58 printed opposite) are for large farms, excluding state farms coming under special districts and *hsien*. For the 1952 figure for the grain output of state farms, I am indebted to V. Kurbatov of the Institute of the Peoples of Asia, Moscow.

1960: *Red Flag* (*Hongqi*), No. 7, April 1, 1961, p. 1 and p. 5. Wang Chen: loc. cit. This passage suggests that the figures also apply only to 'large state farms', as for 1957.

1961: *Peking Review*, July 28, 1961, p. 4. These are specified as 'big state farms'; of the total, 260 were under the Ministry's direct administration.

1962: *People's Daily* (*Renmin Ribao*), March 14, 1964, p. 1. Output of grain and soya bean in 1963 given as 26 per cent more than in 1962. The 1962 grain figure is calculated from that of 1963 on the assumption that grain and soya bean separately rose in roughly the same proportion.

1963: *People's Daily* (*Renmin Ribao*), March 14, 1964, p. 1. Cultivated Area stated to be more than twice that of 1957 and grain output over three times as much.

1964: Number and Cultivated Acreage of State Farms: *BBC Summary of World Broadcasts*, Second Series, FE/W282/A/8 (Peking, September 15, 1964), gives the number as upwards of 6,400 'with more than 62 million *mow* of crop fields and more than 8,200,000 *mow* of cultivated forest land'. *People's Daily* (*Renmin Ribao*), September 19, 1964, p. 1, states the number as nine times that of 1957 with over four times the cultivated acreage. *Peking Review*, September 25, 1964, p. 26, says that the number of state farms has doubled since 1957, and that their cultivated area has increased 2·3-fold. Presumably these divergencies are due to differences in definition, although these are not stated. It may be inferred that forest farms, coming under the Ministry of Forestry, are included in the 6,400. Early in 1964, the existence of 2,000 'large mechanized state farms' in China, cultivating 60 million *mow*, is reported. *Far Eastern Economic Review*, October 28, 1964, p. 351. P. H. M. Jones: 'Creeping Modernization.' This figure is difficult to reconcile with the figures for 1964 in the Table.

Peking Review, January 29, 1965, p. 29. The 1964 figure for output of 'grain and soya' is given as 14 per cent above 1963. The 1964 figure for grain output is based on the assumption that the output of grain and soya bean separately rose in roughly the same proportion.

1965: NCNA, September 29, 1965: 'China today has more than 2,000 big state farms.'

State Farms 1949–65

(For definitions, see under Sources)

	Unit	1949	1952	1957	1958	1959	1960	1961	1962	1963	1964	1965
Farms	Number	18	404	710	1,442		'over 2,490'	2,500			'over 6,400' (2,000)	(2,000+)
Cultivated Area	Thousand *mow*	460	3,820	15,380	34,080		'over 78,000'			'over 30,760'	'over 62,000'	
Reclaimed Area	Thousand *mow*		2,240	4,060	12,430							
Employees	Thousands	4	390	500	990		2,800					
Grain Output	Thousand metric tons		193	595			'over 2,500'		1,417	'over 1,785'	2,035	

Problems of definition mar the attempt to reckon the average size of state farms for some individual years and even more the observation of changes in the average between different years. If, however, the 710 'large state farms' of 1957 are comparable with the 2,000 'large mechanized state farms' of 1964, the average size of this category of state farm increased from roughly 22,000 *mow* to 30,000 *mow*. However, the 2,240 'big state farms' of 1961 are said to have ranged in size from 30,000 *mow* to more than 1,500,000 *mow* each, which implies an average size greater than in 1964.[1] We are even less in a position to estimate the modal or median sizes of state farms at different times.

Paucity of statistics also makes it difficult to calculate the state farm's share of Chinese agriculture. The most that can be hazarded is that in 1964 the farms under the Ministry of State Farms and Land Reclamation cultivated not more than 4 per cent of China's total cultivated area, and less of the total sown area owing to a lower multiple cropping ratio on state farms (many of them being in the north of the country). In 1964 state farms produced little more than 1 per cent of China's total grain output.[2] It must be remembered that much of the land worked by state farms was previously uncultivated because of difficulties of situation, soil, or lack of water, which helps to account for their relatively low unit area yields. In 1964 state farms were reported to dispose of 32 per cent of the total tractor power of Chinese agriculture, 50 per cent of the mechanical farm tools, 82·5 per cent of the combine harvesters, and 68 per cent of the heavy duty motor vehicles used in agriculture.[3] In that year, state farms on the plains of north China were said to be 'basically mechanized' for the main agricultural operations with over 80 per cent of the ploughing, harrowing, and sowing of cotton on state farms being done by machinery. State farms in south China, growing rice and tropical produce, were not so highly mechanized but their degree of mechanization was increasing.[4] Greater mechanization of state farms compared with collective agriculture has led to a much higher output per worker. In 1958 the output of grain per man-day on state farms was reported to be 43·5 kg. against only 14 kg. in collective agriculture, the relative advantage of the state farms over collectives being much greater for wheat than for rice.[5] On certain state farms in Inner Mongolia in 1964 the average annual output per

[1] *Peking Review*, July 28, 1961, p. 4.

[2] See p. 95 above and p. 357 below. In the First Five Year Plan Period (1953–7) the state-owned sector of agriculture was reported to account for a little over 1 per cent of the total value of agricultural output. *People's Handbook* (*Renmin Shouce*) 1958, p. 23. Li Fu-ch'un: 'Report on Achievements of Our First Five Year Plan and Future Tasks and Aims of Socialist Construction.'

[3] *Technology of Agricultural Machinery* (*Nongye Jixie Jishu*), No. 11, November 13, 1964 (SCMM 451). Shang Chih-lung and Ma Ching-p'o: 'Fifteen Years of Agricultural Mechanization on State Farms.'

[4] *People's Daily* (*Renmin Ribao*), September 19, 1964, p. 1, and NCNA Urumchi, October 22, 1964.

[5] *People's Daily* (*Renmin Ribao*), March 12, 1959, p. 7. Hsieh Yin-chi: 'Ways to Increase Productivity in Agriculture in Our Country.' For wheat the output per man-hour was ten times and for rice four times that in collective agriculture. The relative advantage of state farms in production of other grains or potatoes (which in Chinese statistics are included in grain, converted on a basis of 4 kg. of potatoes equalling 1 kg. of grain) must have been much less to pull down the average for all 'grain' to about three times the commune level.

worker exceeded 30 metric tons.[1] The higher output per man on state farms means that their 'commodity rate' (the percentage of crops going in tax and in off-farm sales) is higher than in collective agriculture. In 1959 the commodity-rate for grain on mechanized state farms was reported to be 74 per cent, and on semi-mechanized state farms 60 per cent, against a nation-wide average within the range of 22–29 per cent for that year.[2]

The last available analysis of state farms by province, region or municipality, is for 1957 and applies only to the 710 farms under the jurisdiction of the Ministry of State Farms and Land Reclamation in that year, as follows:

Province, Region or Municipality	Number of State Farms Total	Arable	Livestock
Sinkiang	102	44	58
Kwangtung	87	81	6
Heilungkiang	57	42	15
Inner Mongolia	46	5	41
Liaoning	37	19	18
Kirin	37	10	27
Kwangsi	36	27	9
Yunnan	30	28	2
Kansu	30	12	18
Kiangsi	27	10	17
Kiangsu	25	12	13
Hopei	22	9	13
Szechuan	20	4	16
Hupeh	19	7	12
Tsinghai	19	—	19
Shantung	18	10	8
Anhwei	16	8	8
Honan	16	7	9
Shansi	13	4	9
Fukien	11	5	6
Chekiang	9	5	4
Shanghai	9	—	9
Kweichow	8	2	6
Shensi	7	2	5
Peking	3	3	—
Tientsin	3	3	—
Hunan	3	2	1
Tibet	—	—	—

Source: *People's Daily* (*Renmin Ribao*), March 18, 1958, p. 2.

While the number of farms is no necessary guide to their size or importance, the table indicates the large number situated in the north western and northern extra-mural regions and in the far south. In the north west and north east are found the reclamation areas under the direct control of the Ministry of State Farms and Land Reclamation. In 1961 these comprised the areas cultivated by the People's Liberation Army (PLA) Production and Con-

---

[1] *People's Daily* (*Renmin Ribao*), September 19, 1964, p. 1.
[2] Ibid., August 26, 1960, p. 7. Niu Chung-huang: 'The Technical Transformation of the Agriculture of Our Country.' See pp. 355–6 below for a discussion of this reference. See p. 357 below for national average percentage of state procurement of grain.

struction Corps in Sinkiang,[1] the Moutankiang and the Hokiang Reclamation Areas both in Heilungkiang province and the Hulunbuir Reclamation Area in a frontier district of Inner Mongolia; altogether these four areas included 260 farms.[2] By the end of 1963 the North East General Bureau of Land Reclamation had been established and apparently controlled, *inter alia*, the Moutankiang and Hokiang Reclamation Areas.[3] Probably both strategic and economic motives account for the continued retention directly under the Ministry of the organs controlling state farms in these areas. Originally settled by ex-servicemen in military units, they are situated in important frontier regions and have been the recipients of heavy state investment.

State farms outside these four reclamation areas are managed by different levels of local government, from the province down to the *hsien*. Sometimes control has been devolved from higher levels (similarly to what occurred with other types of state enterprises)[4] as when in 1958 the management of reclamation farms in Kiangsi was transferred from the province and special districts to the *hsien*.[5] In other instances, the farms were originally established by the local authority which still controls them.

State farms have been used as instruments in promoting internal movements of population. Overland migration, undertaken throughout the centuries under pressure of necessity, has seldom exerted a positive attraction on the Chinese people. Young men in Kwangtung and Fukien might dream of fortunes to be made in the 'southern seas' but no such prospects beckoned the peasants of Shantung and Honan to make the trek to the north east in the earlier years of this century. Only because conditions in their own provinces were so harsh did even the inhospitable spaces of Manchuria seem preferable. Since 1949 the government has sought, for economic and strategic reasons, to do something to correct the demographic disequilibrium of China by encouraging migration into the sparsely populated peripheral regions which comprise some 60 per cent of China's area. This vast territory, collectively known as the 'frontier regions', includes Heilungkiang, Inner Mongolia, Ninghsia, Kansu, Sinkiang, Tsinghai, Tibet and Yunnan, together with the island of Hainan. It was claimed that by the close of 1958 over 1,400,000 settlers, both civilians and servicemen, had gone to these regions,[6] and in

[1] The districts in Sinkiang in which Corps farms are known to be situated are Ili, the Mannass River Basin in Dzungaria, and the edges of the Taklamaklan Desert (Tarim Basin). In addition to the Corps farms, there are other state farms in Sinkiang controlled by local authorities.

[2] NCNA Peking, July 10, 1961, and *Peking Review*, July 28, 1961, p. 4.

[3] *Daily Worker* (*Gongren Ribao*), December 5, 1963, p. 2. At this date the North East General Bureau of Land Reclamation was reported to control 853 farms.

[4] See p. 151 below. Some of the discussion in Chapter VI on the control and management of state enterprises applies to state farms.

[5] *Kiangsi Daily* (*Jiangxi Ribao*), February 28, 1959 (SCMP 2027). Lin Chün-hsiu, Secretary, CCP Kiangsi Provincial Committee: Report delivered to the Kiangsi Provincial Representatives' Conference of State Owned Comprehensive Reclamation Farms and the Communist Labour University on February 13, 1959.

[6] *China Youth* (*Zhongguo Qingnian*), No. 1, January 1, 1959, p. 24. Hsü Li-chih, Deputy Director, Resettlement Bureau, Ministry of State Farms and Land Reclamation: 'Reply to Young Friends Clamouring to Go to the Frontiers.'

At times the migration to the north west exceeded the government's wishes, especially when it was directed mainly to the industrial centres there. See the State Council's Directive

subsequent years the flow continued. Honan, Hupeh, Hunan, Kiangsu and Anhwei seem to have provided the greatest number of migrants. Control of both recruitment and resettlement appears to have been largely in the hands of Party organs.[1]

In the 'Great Northern Waste' of Heilungkiang, demobilized troops of the Army's Railway Corps have been responsible for reclamation as well as for building railways and roads; their first farm was opened in 1954. Wheat and soya bean have been the major crops grown.

The troops in Sinkiang, many of whom were former members of the Kuomintang armies, had begun land reclamation in 1950. In 1952 they were reorganized into a number of agricultural and engineering reconstruction divisions, except for some units for which garrison duties remained paramount. Two years later, a further reorganization resulted in the formation of the Sinkiang Production and Construction Corps of the People's Liberation Army, which in 1961 was stated to cultivate over a third of the arable acreage of Sinkiang.[2] A report in 1966 said that the Corps had established more than 100 state farms, covering 660,000 ha. of land.[3] It is interesting to note that a Deputy Commissar of Corps, Chang Chung-han, has been concurrently a Vice Minister of State Farms and Land Reclamation. In addition to agriculture (in which wheat, cotton and livestock have predominated), the Corps has been responsible for considerable industrial development, said to have been made by ploughing back its own profits. Some enterprises were handed over to the local authorities but at the end of 1961 the Corps still owned several hundred industrial and mining concerns. The Corps entered the field of urban development, being acclaimed as the 'creator of the new Urumchi', while it has also been responsible for building and administering the new city of Shihhotzu between Urumchi and Wusu.[4] Altogether, there-

---

on Preventing the Blind Migration of Rural Population of December 1956 in *Collected Laws and Regulations* . . . Vol. 4, p. 225.

[1] *Nationalities Unity* (*Minzu Tuanjie*), No. 1, January 6, 1960. (ECMM 201). Yang Hu-ch'en, Director, Resettlement Bureau, Ministry of State Farms and Land Reclamation: 'The Great Victory in Mobilizing Youth to Participate in Borderland Nationalities Areas.'

[2] NCNA Urumchi, September 10, 1959. Wu Ying-t'ang: 'The Production and Construction Corps of the PLA in Sinkiang', and *People's Daily* (*Renmin Ribao*), July 31, 1960, p. 7. Chang Chung-han, Deputy Commissar of the Sinkiang Production and Construction Army Corps and Vice Minister of State Farms and Land Reclamation: 'The Production and Construction Corps in Sinkiang', and *Nationalities Unity* (*Minzu Tuanjie*), No. 12, December 6, 1961. (SCMM 301). Wang Chi-lung, Director of Political Department, Sinkiang Production and Construction Army Corps: 'Strive to Strengthen Further the Solidarity of All Nationalities in Building a New Sinkiang Together.' However, in 1963, the PLA farms in Sinkiang produced only 20 per cent of the region's grain output, which suggests either that they are situated on the more marginal land or are cultivated less intensively or produce proportionately more cotton or other non-grain crops. NCNA Urumchi, April 28, 1964.

[3] NCNA, March 17, 1966.

[4] *Nationalities Unity* (*Minzu Tuanjie*), No. 12, December 6, 1961. (SCMM 301) Wang Chi-lung: loc. cit., and *China News Service*, Peking, April 7, 1959 (SCMP 2018). Li T'i: 'Shihhotzu: A New City to the North of the Tienshan', and *Daily Worker* (*Gongren Ribao*), April 13, 1961, p. 2. Shih Man: 'The Bright Youthfulness of an Ancient City—Urumchi.' The Corps runs its own Agricultural College in Sinkiang, which is reported to have trained over 5,000 agronomists between 1952–62. NCNA Urumchi, August 1, 1962.

fore, the Corps has grown into a powerful verticalized organization, controlling a substantial part of Sinkiang's economy.

As the years go by, the labour force on the military farms in Heilungkiang and Sinkiang is constantly being replenished by young civilian Han Chinese immigrants. Numerous civilian migrants to Sinkiang, however, have been settled on state farms by the local authorities, and on collective agricultural undertakings. The task has been rendered more difficult by the resentment of the local people who 'with special malice attack the Production Corps' and 'slanderously say "the Han nationality has brought calamity to Sinkiang".'[1]

It was hoped that the state farms in the outlying pastoral areas of China would spontaneously multiply, 'expanding in neighbouring districts by using the method known as "hens lay eggs" . . . old farms build up new farms, and big farms assist small farms'.[2] State farms in these regions formed centres around which permanent villages grew up of herdsmen who had abandoned their nomadic life for settled agriculture.[3] The settlement and control of nomads was also furthered by the foundation of joint state-private livestock farms in Tsinghai and Inner Mongolia. In all these frontier regions, the state farms have tended from necessity to be self-sufficient by undertaking other functions in addition to agriculture. In Tsinghai, for example, state farms have been encouraged to open transport services.[4]

On China's south-western frontier, in Yunnan, there were at the beginning of 1960 reported to be over 110 state farms 'of a larger scale', opened in the border regions and other parts of the province. The workers on the farms, who include ex-servicemen, numbered 200,000, estimated at about 3 per cent of the agricultural labour force of Yunnan. Some farms were mixed, others devoted exclusively to economic crops, such as sugar cane, or to livestock, while those near towns supplied the needs of urban residents.[5]

In addition to the settlement of immigrants on the special farms for Overseas Chinese in Kwangtung, about which more will be said below, migrants were also sent to state farms and communes in the less developed parts of that province, particularly to Hainan Island. The state farms in Hainan at first specialized in tropical crops such as rubber, which called for technical skill and long-term investment (and which substituted for imports), while the com-

---

[1] *People's Daily* (*Renmin Ribao*), February 14, 1958, p. 10. Pathan Sugurpaev: 'To Build Socialism Well in Sinkiang, We Must Depend on Support from the State and from the Han Nationality.' (Speech to 5th Session of the First National People's Congress), and *Sinkiang Daily* (*Xinjiang Ribao*), March 11, 1959 (SCMP 1998). Sung Chun, Deputy Director, United Front Work Department, CCP Committee of Sinkiang Uighur Autonomous Region: 'Resolutely Change our Political Stand and Take the Road of Socialism under Party Leadership.' (Report to Joint Enlarged Conference of the Chinese People's Political Consultative Congress, Sinkiang Committee and Sinkiang Islamic Federation.)

[2] *People's Daily* (*Renmin Ribao*), July 11, 1960, p. 7. Kao Feng, First Secretary, CCP Tsinghai Provincial Committee: 'Energetically Open Waste Land, Quickly Develop Agriculture and Ensure the Continuous Leap Forward of the National Economy.'

[3] *People's Daily* (*Renmin Ribao*), September 26, 1960, p. 7. Kao-wan-pao-cha-pu, First Secretary, CCP Committee for Silongol League: 'A Great Victory Achieved for Agriculture on the Grasslands.'

[4] *Tsinghai Daily* (*Qinghai Ribao*), June 2, 1959. (SCMP 2081.)

[5] *Yunnan Daily* (*Yunnan Ribao*), February 2, 1960. (SCMP 2241.)

munes devoted their attention to grain and the simpler perennials.[1] Later with the crisis in food production, these state farms were urged to diversify and to become at least self-sufficient in grain.

The role of state farms in Kiangsi has been distinctive—or at least they have enjoyed more publicity than in other provinces. In the winter of 1957-8 the Kiangsi provincial authorities sent 50,000 cadres to mountainous districts to reclaim land. By January 1962, 286 state farms had been opened in the province, with 3,200,000 *mow* of arable land and 25,000,000 *mow* of forest, and with a total population (local people and new settlers) of nearly 1,500,000.[2]

While most of the farms are in mountainous districts, some are situated in low-lying land near the Poyang Lake. The devolution of control over the farms from the province and special districts to the *hsien* which occurred in 1958, did not prove altogether satisfactory in Kiangsi because it led in some places to cadres, equipment and funds being diverted from the farms to other purposes. To rectify this, certain important aspects of planning and management were restored to the Provincial Department of Agriculture, Forestry, and Land Reclamation.[3]

The chief functions of the Kiangsi state farms have been to reclaim and settle the mountainous and other sparsely populated districts of the province. In addition they are credited with fulfilling a large part of the province's compulsory deliveries of pigs and poultry.[4] No doubt it was found easier to obtain these commodities from enterprises under closer official control than from units of collective agriculture or from individual peasants.

One type of state farm is that set up near large cities to supply their markets with vegetables and other non-staple foodstuffs. These were mostly established from 1958 onwards as one aspect of the growth of local self-sufficiency which

[1] *Southern Daily* (*Nanfang Ribao*), February 13, 1960 (SCMP 2220), and *China Youth Newspaper* (*Zhongguo Qingnian Bao*), January 11, 1959 (SCMP 1956).

[2] *Chinese Agricultural Journal* (*Zhongguo Nongbao*), No. 1, January 1962, pp. 2-3. P'eng Men-yü, Vice Governor of Kiangsi Province: 'Struggle to Consolidate and Improve State Farms.' Kiangsi province also operates fifty-three fish farms; the people on these are included in the population figures above. These figures must not be compared with the figures for state farms in the Table on p. 95 as the Table (see sources) refers, for the most part, to large farms, excluding those run by local authorities below the provincial level. An organization known as the Communist Labour University was established in 1958 to provide political and technical instruction on the Kiangsi state farms; by December 1959 it was reported to have eighty-eight branches, as well as sixteen labour technical schools, with a total staff and enrolment of 55,000, although in subsequent years the numbers declined. It is responsible for running a number of farms. *Kiangsi Daily* (*Jiangxi Ribao*), December 15, 1959 (SCMP 2217). Wang Tung-hsing: 'The Struggle for the Construction of Strong and Modernized Socialist State-Owned Bases for the Production of Commodities', and *China's Agricultural and Land Reclamation* (*Zhongguo Nongken*), No. 1, January 5, 1965 (SCMM 466). Chang Yü-ching: 'The Great Victory of the Half-Work (Farming) and the Half-Study Educational System—Introducing Kiangsi Communist Labour University', and *People's Daily* (*Renmin Ribao*), April 17, 1965, p. 6. Liu Chün-hsiu, Secretary, CCP Kiangsi Provincial Committee and Principal of the Communist Labour University: 'How We Founded the Communist Labour University', and NCNA Nanchang, March 25, 1965.

[3] *Kiangsi Daily* (*Jiangxi Ribao*), February 28, 1959 (SCMP 2027). Liu Chün-hsiu: loc. cit.

[4] *People's Daily* (*Renmin Ribao*), December 25, 1960, p. 7. Shao Shih-ping, Secretary, CCP Kiangsi Provincial Committee: 'Push on the Construction of Great Undertakings in Mountainous Districts.'

made municipalities want to have sources of food supply under their immediate jurisdiction. Sometimes these farms (also known as 'commodity bases') absorbed communes, 'in this way raising the proportion of ownership by the whole people'.[1] These farms are usually controlled by the municipalities they serve; it is not clear how many of them are enumerated among the state farms under the Ministry of State Farms and Land Reclamation. Other farms are controlled by food-processing factories in order to have at least part of their raw material supplies in their own hands.[2] Such farms would come under the ultimate control of the Ministry of Light Industry.

The drive for self-sufficiency also led to the opening of farms by public offices, schools, factories and mining enterprises, to provide for their own needs. In so far as all these are state undertakings, the farms might be described as 'owned by all the people' but they would not normally be known as state farms.

The larger state farms have been directed primarily to increasing agricultural production and reclaiming and settling new land; any help given to collective farming has been secondary to these aims.[3] In addition, however, a whole range of experimental, demonstration, and seed farms have been developed for the purpose of improving peasant agriculture by scientific bodies and by various levels of the state administration, more especially by *hsien* authorities;[4] those under communes, production brigades or teams are, of course, an integral part of collective agriculture. These undertakings, both state and collective, grew in number and importance in the 1960s, with the greater attention being given to scientific agriculture. It seems probable that most of these come under the supervision of the local departments of agriculture. While the majority of these concerns were specially opened for their present functions, some existing state farms were apparently turned over to these purposes.[5] By the end of 1964, some 1,700 state seed farms were in operation, but all told they produced only between 1–2 per cent of the country's seed requirements.[6] In 1963 it was decided to set up ten 'big multi-purpose agricultural experimental centres' and by October 1964 farms answering to this description had been established near Peking, and in the north east, the north west, the Szechuan basin, the Taihu Lake area in Kiangsu, the Pearl River Delta in Kwangtung, and in Hainan Island.[7] Four

[1] *People's Daily* (*Renmin Ribao*), February 12, 1960, p. 7. Yang Yi-ch'en, Secretary, CCP Heilungkiang Provincial Committee: 'On Establishing a Network of Commodity Production Bases', and NCNA Peking, August 24, 1962, and *Peking Review*, January 15, 1965, p. 23. Chen Hsüeh-nung: 'Full Market Counters in Peking.'

[2] *Ta Kung Daily* (*Dagong Bao*), Peking, December 6, 1961, p. 3. Chin Chüeh: 'The Question of Raw Material Bases for Light Industry.'

[3] The First Five Year Plan, however, included agricultural extension work for local peasants among the tasks of local state farms which at that time, before the decentralization measures, would generally comprise only the smaller farms. *First Five Year Plan for Development of the National Economy of the People's Republic of China in 1953–57*, Peking, 1956, p. 127.

[4] In 1963, central policy favoured the merging of the various units of this type controlled at the *hsien* level. *Ta Kung Daily* (*Dagong Bao*), Peking, October 31, 1963, p. 1. Editorial.

[5] *Red Flag* (*Hongqi*), No. 20, October 16, 1962, p. 6. Editorial.

[6] *People's Daily* (*Renmin Ribao*), October 8, 1963, p. 2, and NCNA Peking, November 13, 1964.

[7] *People's Daily* (*Renmin Ribao*), October 25, 1964, p. 1. Editorial.

of these farms were in areas designated as being of 'high and stable yield',[1] thus conforming to the programme of concentrating state agricultural investment in such areas.

From 1958 onwards 'large numbers' of tea and mulberry plantations are reported to have been established by the state as well as by units of collective agriculture. State silk farms also participated, along with peasants, in the cultivation of tussah silk in north China.[2] The state tea and mulberry plantations probably come under the local departments of the Ministry of Agriculture, as this is the Ministry charged with supervising the production of raw silk and of tea.

The Overseas Chinese Affairs Commission of the State Council administers a special category of state farms in Kwangtung, Fukien, Kwangsi, Yunnan and Kweichow. In addition to their functions as agricultural enterprises, these farms are 'bases for the reception, resettlement, organization for work and for the education' of returned Overseas Chinese.[3]

The first Overseas Chinese farms were established in 1951 to receive deportees from Malaya and by May 1959 nine had been opened. Their great development occurred in 1960 and 1961 with the inflow of Chinese from Indonesia. Another much smaller stream of settlers came in 1963 with the repatriation of Chinese from India as a result of Sino-Indian hostilities. By the beginning of 1965, thirty-eight Overseas Chinese farms were operating, of which more than ten were in Fukien and at least six in Kwangsi; the latest figure from Kwangtung was in 1962, when there had been ten in that province. More than 60,000 returned Overseas Chinese were settled on the farms by 1965, bringing their population, including local peasants who had been absorbed, to over 110,000.[4] The area brought under cultivation was reported to have exceeded 400,000 *mow* by the end of 1961 out of the 2,280,000 *mow* (of which 1,400,000 were estimated to be cultivatable) of land held by the farms.[5]

The Overseas Chinese farms are headed by managers, 'under the collective

[1] *Peking Review*, December 11, 1964, p. 27. Hu Chi: 'How Industry Helps Agriculture.'

[2] *People's Daily (Renmin Ribao)*, March 26, 1963, p. 2, and *Ta Kung Daily (Dagong Bao)*, Peking, December 17, 1963, p. 2. Ho Cheng: 'Energetically Develop the Production of Tussah Silk', and ibid., January 25, 1964, p. 2. Editorial.

[3] *Overseas Chinese Affairs Journal (Qiaowu Bao)*, No. 6, December 6, 1961, p. 4. Editorial. As well as state-owned Overseas Chinese farms, there are also farms opened under the Regulations governing the Application by Overseas Chinese for the Use of Wasteland of the State, promulgated in 1955, and farms opened by Overseas Chinese investment companies. These farms, which may be operated as co-operatives or as joint state-private enterprises, were reported variously to number twenty-six or twenty-eight in 1959. Privately-owned farms, permitted under the 1955 regulations, had apparently been transformed by 1959 into joint state-private enterprises. *Collected Laws and Regulations* . . . Vol. 2, pp. 845-7, and *People's Daily (Renmin Ribao)*, May 3, 1959, p. 11. Wang Yuan-hsing and Yu Yang-tsu: 'Overseas Chinese Farms in the Great Leap Forward'—a joint statement at the National People's Congress, and *Overseas Chinese Affairs Journal (Qiaowu Bao)*, No. 9, September 1959, p. 35. Editorial Department: 'Replies to Questions about Overseas Chinese Farms', and Appendix on Remittances from Overseas Chinese, pp. 513-4 below.

[4] *People's Daily (Renmin Ribao)*, May 3, 1959, p. 11. Wang Yuan-hsing and Yu Yang-tsu: loc. cit., and NCNA Peking, September 14, 1964, and *China News Service*, Canton, December 30, 1962, and *China Youth Newspaper (Zhongguo Qingnian Bao)*, July 28, 1962 (SCMP 2803), and *Overseas Chinese Affairs Journal (Qiaowu Bao)*, No. 1, February 1965, p. 12.

[5] *Overseas Chinese Affairs Journal (Qiaowu Bao)*, No. 6, December 1961, p. 3. Editorial.

leadership of the CCP Committees' and are intended to be self-contained communities with their own schools, shops and other facilities. Their production and development plans were said in 1961 to need the approval of the central and provincial organs dealing with Overseas Chinese affairs, after which they were not supposed to be altered by any other department (e.g. by provincial agricultural bureaux) without permission.[1]

As the easily cultivatable land in Kwangtung and Fukien, where most of the farms lie, is densely inhabited, the new arrivals were settled on difficult terrain, often barren mountain sides, lacking water and other facilities. State investment in construction (residential, agricultural and other) in 1960-2 is said to have amounted to ¥37 million, or some ¥340 a head of population on the farms. Little mechanical equipment has, however, been available to clear the waste land or work the farms.[2] They enjoy low priority for agricultural machinery and chemical fertilizer. In 1963, when supplies of both were increasing, it was expected that Overseas Chinese farms would be allocated less machinery than in 1962 and only 'a little more' fertilizer: in contrast the state farms in north east China received twice as much chemical fertilizer in 1963 as in 1962 and a large quantity of machinery.[3] This low priority is not surprising because marginal productivity of investment in Overseas Chinese farms must be lower than elsewhere. Not only are they situated on poor land, but most of the settlers had no previous experience in agriculture, nor was much attempt made to instruct them in its arts;[4] nor to give them positions of responsibility. Even on one of the best established farms, after ten years it was considered noteworthy that the proportion of Overseas Chinese among the responsible cadres had nearly reached a third.[5]

The original intention had apparently been that Overseas Chinese farms, like many of the ordinary state farms in south China, should concentrate on tropical and other cash crops, such as coffee, cocoa, tea, tobacco, sugar, peanuts and fruit. Food shortage in 1961-2, however, caused them to divert attention and resources to growing grain for their own consumption.[6] They were urged to become self-sufficient in grain and by the spring of 1962 these farms were reported to be 40-50 per cent of the way to this goal.[7] By the autumn of 1964 most Overseas Chinese farms were stated to have attained self-sufficiency in grain, or even to have a surplus.[8]

State subsidies towards current expenses, in addition to capital grants,

---

[1] *Overseas Chinese Affairs Journal* (*Qiaowu Bao*), No. 6, December 1961, p. 5.

[2] *China Youth Newspaper* (*Zhongguo Qingnian Bao*), July 28, 1962. (SCMP 2803), and *Overseas Chinese Affairs Journal* (*Qiaowu Bao*), No. 2, April 1962, p. 6. Liu Ch'ing: 'Always Remember to Rely upon the Masses.'

[3] *Overseas Chinese Affairs Journal* (*Qiaowu Bao*), No. 6, December 1962, pp. 16-17. Editorial, and NCNA Shenyang, February 17, 1964.

[4] *Overseas Chinese Affairs Journal* (*Qiaowu Bao*), No. 2, April 1962, p. 6. Liu Ch'ing: loc. cit., and NCNA Peking, September 14, 1964. A few Overseas Chinese settlers had valuable experience to offer. One from Sarawak, for example, was an expert in pepper-growing. Ibid.

[5] *Southern Daily* (*Nanfang Ribao*), November 13, 1962 (SCMP 2877). Chang Ch'iu: 'Ten Years of Hard Work and Happiness.'

[6] *Overseas Chinese Affairs Journal* (*Qiaowu Bao*), No. 6, December 1962, p. 16. Editorial.

[7] China News Service, Peking, March 4, 1962.

[8] NCNA Peking, September 14, 1964.

STATE FARMS, AGRICULTURAL MACHINERY, FORESTRY   105

have been given to Overseas Chinese farms, at least for a farm's first years.[1] The standard of living on Overseas Chinese farms has been deliberately kept above the prevailing level in the neighbouring rural districts. In September 1959 the average monthly income per person on Overseas Chinese farms was given as ¥40.[2]

In a special category of state farms are the so-called labour reform farms, under the Ministry of Public Security and its local departments. These farms, together with associated industrial and other concerns, make use of the forced labour of political, religious, and other prisoners. There are two degrees of forced labour—the more punitive is unpaid while the other is paid but at lower than normal rates. Labour reform farms are frequently established 'beside rivers or lakes, in saline areas and in arid districts with very inconvenient communications' to which it would, therefore, be difficult to attract migrants with any pretence of voluntariness.[3] Labour reform prisoners in sparsely populated places where settlers are required, may have to stay there on expiry of their sentences.[4] Convict labour is probably as economically wasteful in China as under similar conditions it proved to be in the Soviet Union. Yet the authorities may consider the expenditure worth while if lesser degrees of pressure would be ineffective to recruit workers for these places or tasks, or if economic incentives to work there would have to be even more extravagant. According to another account, relegation to labour camps before 1962 was for an indefinite period, but after that date may have been limited to three years.[5]

In addition to prisoners on special labour reform farms, some recalcitrants are sent to ordinary state farms or to units of collective agriculture, to undergo labour reform.[6]

The Ministry of Internal Affairs, together with local bureaux of civil affairs, also run certain categories of state farms. Some of these are penal,[7] while

[1] NCNA Peking, October 9, 1962.

[2] *Overseas Chinese Affairs Journal* (*Qiaowu Bao*), No. 9, September 1959, p. 35., loc. cit. and ibid., No. 6, December 1961, p. 4. Editorial.

[3] *Political and Legal Research* (*Zhengfa Yanjiu*), No. 5, October 1958, p. 68. Meng Chao-liang: 'Basic Conditions of Labour Reform Work in the Last Nine Years', and ibid., No. 3, June 1959, pp. 47-9. Meng Chao-liang: 'Preliminary Achievements of Labour Education', and *Kiangsi Daily* (*Jiangxi Ribao*), December 17, 1959 (SCMP 2230). Chou K'e-yung, Deputy Commissioner, Department of Public Security, Kiangsi: 'The Great Achievement Made in the Work of Reforming Criminals through Labour', and *People's Handbook* (*Renmin Shouce*), *1955*, pp. 359-66.

[4] E. Snow: *The Other Side of the River*, London, 1963, p. 360, and *People's Handbook* (*Renmin Shouce*), *1955*, p. 365.

[5] *Harvard Law Review*, Vol. 79, No. 3, January 1966, pp. 491-2. J. A. Cohen: 'The Criminal Process in the People's Republic of China: An Introduction.'

[6] *People's Daily* (*Renmin Ribao*), December 24, 1958, p. 7. Chao Han: 'Government and Commune May Be One, but Party and Commune May Not Be One', and *Red Flag* (*Hongqi*), No. 4, February 26, 1964, p. 12. T'ao Chu, First Secretary, CCP Kwangtung Provincial Committee: 'The People's Communes are Progressing', and *Southern Daily* (*Nanfang Ribao*), September 2, 1964 (SCMP 3312). Work Team of the Agricultural Committee of the Central-South Bureau of the CCP Central Committee, and a Work Team of the CCP Kwangtung Provincial Committee: 'The Pearl River State Farm—a Red Flag.'

[7] *China Weekly* (*Zuguo*), No. 505, September 17, 1962, pp. 13-16. Lien Lan: 'Inside the "Labour Education" Camps of Canton Municipality', and *People's Daily* (*Renmin Ribao*), March 14, 1964, p. 1, and *Southern Daily* (*Nanfang Ribao*), November 17, 1964 (SCMP 3373).

others may include farms established for dependants of servicemen and for ex-servicemen, for both of which categories this Ministry has a special responsibility.

Apart from the PLA Production and Construction Corps in Sinkiang, the Army itself directly operates farms to supply its needs, relying largely on the labour of soldiers. This activity grew very rapidly in importance during the austere years of shortage after the Great Leap. In January 1961, the Army controlled more than 700 farms covering an area of over 1,100,000 *mow* which, by August 1961, had increased to 1,660,000 *mow*. Most of the increase was due to reclamation of wasteland.[1]

The internal organization of state farms must differ very considerably with the great differences in size, type, and circumstance of the farms concerned. Under the managers, cadres are responsible for the running of a farm. Ex-servicemen appear to form a considerable proportion of state farm cadres and not only on those farms founded by army units in Sinkiang and Heilungkiang. In Kiangsi, superfluous civilian officials 'sent down' to the countryside have been prominent. Despite the educational use made of the Sino-Soviet Friendship Farm, which drew on Soviet experience, only a small proportion of state farm cadres would seem to have had previous professional training or expertise in agricultural management and techniques. Managerial weaknesses (including financial management) have been a constant problem besetting the state farms. As in collective agriculture, cadres have tended to proliferate, despite restraining efforts from higher levels. In 1957 administrative staff accounted for over 10 per cent of total employees on state farms, the figure rising on some farms to 24 per cent.[2] This would give a total of some 50,000 state farm cadres in that year.[3]

Management of state farms, as of the archetypal commune, has commonly been organized on three levels—headquarters, branch stations, and production teams (sometimes known as 'basic-level stations'); attempts have sometimes been made to reduce these to only two levels.[4]

Managerial difficulties led to a decentralization of authority in state farms, similar to that which occurred in communes. In 1957 the solution, at least in Heilungkiang, was thought to lie in reducing the size of farms.[5] The increase in the number of farms under the North East General Bureau of Land Reclamation in 1963 compared with those under the Moutankiang and Hokiang Reclamation Areas two years previously,[6] might suggest that the advice had been followed: contrariwise, the increase may be due to boundary changes

[1] *Work Bulletin (Gongzuo Tongxun)*, No. 1, January 1, 1961, p. 23. Supplement to Report of the Party Committee of the Rear Services Department on the Energetic Continuation of the Economy Movement, and ibid., No. 30, August 26, 1961, p. 2. Supplement to the Report on the Conference on the Work of the Army's Rear Services Department.
In November 1961, 100 big Army farms existed in the north east and 120 medium and small ones near the Fukien coast. NCNA, November 14, 1961. Some also are in Tibet.
[2] *People's Daily (Renmin Ribao)*, March 11, 1957, p. 1. Editorial.
[3] See table on p. 95 above.
[4] *Tsinghai Daily (Qinghai Ribao)*, October 12, 1959 (SCMP 2149), and NCNA Harbin, November 5, 1957. (Quoted in R. Carin: *State Farms in Communist China*), Hong Kong, 1962, pp. 213–14, and *Mainland Today (Jinri Dalu)*, July 25, 1963, p. 22. Wang Hsing-k'ung: 'Communist China's State Farms.'
[5] NCNA Harbin, November 5, 1957, loc. cit. [6] See p. 98 (text and fn. 3).

of the Areas concerned, leading to additional farms being included in the 1963 figures. We have seen above that the average size of state farms—at least those of the larger category—appears to have risen between 1957 and 1964. Thus, it seems probable that diseconomies of scale were attacked by decentralization within farms rather than by reducing the size of farms.

A study published in *Economic Research* in 1963 concluded that for a production team in a mechanized state farm, the optimum size (for yield per *mow* and per worker and for percentage of 'commodity' grain, i.e. surplus above the farm's own needs) was around 15,000 *mow* and that this was in fact the approximate size of successful production teams on state farms under the Heilungkiang Provincial Land Reclamation Bureau.[1] This is, of course, very much larger than the average area farmed by production teams in collective agriculture, but then the type of extensive mechanized farming practised by the state farms in Heilungkiang is very different from that obtaining in most parts of China.

By 1962, decentralization in both the ordinary and the Overseas Chinese state farms had led, as in communes, to the production team being the basic unit for production, charged with guaranteeing fulfilment of financial and production targets under the 'responsibility system'.[2] In the general run of farms under the Ministry of State Farms the production team, while described as the 'foundation of the state farm', does not seem to have been specifically designated an economic accounting unit, as it had in many Overseas Chinese farms. Thus, as far as the Ministry's farms were concerned, the farm continued to be the unit for reckoning profit and loss.[3]

Remuneration on state farms was, at least for some years, considerably higher than that of the peasantry at large, perhaps because of the analogy drawn between state farm employees and urban workers. In January 1958 the Minister of State Farms and Land Reclamation said that on an average each worker on state farms earned ¥479 a year (presumably including bonuses, although this is not specifically stated) which was 52 per cent above the estimated average income at that time for a *household* in agricultural co-operatives, while if staff wages were taken into account, the average wage for state farms would be ¥537 a year.[4] However, it must be remembered that workers on

[1] *Economic Research* (*Jingji Yanjiu*), No. 12, December 1963, p. 17. Ting Lü-ch'u: loc. cit. The farms under the Heilungkiang Provincial Land Reclamation Bureau may comprise those farms in Heilungkiang which do not come under the North East General Bureau of Land Reclamation; alternatively the Provincial Bureau itself may come under the General Bureau.

[2] *Ta Kung Daily* (*Dagong Bao*), Peking, November 4, 1962, p. 2. Chu Nai-k'ang: 'Strengthen Financial Work in Production Teams of State Farms', and *Overseas Chinese Affairs Journal* (*Qiaowu Bao*), No. 3, June 1962, p. 4. Wan Hsing: 'The Problem of Wages on Overseas Chinese State Farms.' A conference in February 1962 had decided to institute a responsibility system in Overseas Chinese farms, giving more power to production teams.

[3] *Economic Research* (*Jingji Yanjiu*), No. 12, December 1963, p. 16. Ting Lü-ch'u: loc. cit., and *Overseas Chinese Affairs Journal* (*Qiaowu Bao*), No. 6, December 1962, p. 16.

[4] *Daily Worker* (*Gongren Ribao*), February 1, 1958. Wang Chen, Minister of State Farms and Land Reclamation. 'Exert Revolutionary Zeal, Make State Farms Take a Great Leap Forward.' Quoted from *New China Fortnightly* (*Xinhua Banyuekan*), No. 127, March 10, 1958, p. 137. In speech to First National Congress of the Chinese Agricultura land Water Conservancy Workers' Trade Unions.

state farms include many mechanics and tractor drivers, and the average level of skill must be above that of workers in collective agriculture. The Minister, nevertheless, considered that wages were too high and that bonuses, amounting to 12·5 per cent of basic wages, had been paid 'indiscriminately according to the methods used in industrial enterprises'. He declared that in the next few years the wages of existing workers should 'basically not increase' while new workers should be paid on the State Council scales for young apprentices and unskilled labourers. Bonuses would in future not exceed 6–8 per cent of basic wages.[1] According to another source, a few months earlier, the average wage for new workers on state farms was to be less than ¥20 a month.[2]

Complaints were also voiced at the end of 1957 that the method of remuneration on state farms, by fixed wages, was unsuited to the vagaries of agriculture and that a system of contracting for specific pieces of work would be desirable.[3] More than a year later, 'a relatively fixed wage system' was still in force in Kiangsi province, where the wage level was said to be approximately the same in all state-owned agricultural concerns.[4] Within the next few years, especially from 1962 onwards, the more flexible system of norms and work points became the general rule on state farms, including the Overseas Chinese farms.[5]

In 1966 the change over appears still to have been in process, because an editorial in the *People's Daily* exhorts state farms 'to implement gradually the fixed norm method of recording work points and to carry out a policy of remuneration according to work points within a rationally determined sum for wages'. By that date, the income of state farm workers was said to be generally the same as that of collective peasants.[6] However, while payments for similar work may have been brought into equivalence, the greater number of skilled workers on state farms presumably still ensures a higher average income for their employees.

No information has come to our knowledge of the effect of this wage reduction on the financial position of the farms. Before, high wages not fully compensated by the higher productivity per worker, and lax management[7]

---

[1] *Daily Worker* (*Gongren Ribao*), February 1, 1958, Wang Chen: loc. cit. Quoted from *New China Fortnightly* (*Xinhua Banyuekan*) No. 127, March 10, 1958, pp. 136–7.

[2] *People's Daily* (*Renmin Ribao*), November 14, 1957, p. 3. Teng Tzu-hui, Director of the Rural Work Department of the CCP Central Committee: Speech at 3rd Plenum of CCP Central Committee.   [3] Ibid.

[4] *Kiangsi Daily* (*Jiangxi Ribao*), February 28, 1959 (SCMP 2027). Liu Chün-hsiu: loc. cit.

[5] *Southern Daily* (*Nanfang Ribao*), September 2, 1964. (SCMP 3312). A Work Team of the Agricultural Committee of the Central-South Bureau of the CCP Central Committee, and a Work Team of the CCP Kwangtung Provincial Committee: loc. cit., and *Ta Kung Daily* (*Dagong Bao*), Peking, November 4, 1962, p. 2. Chu Nai-k'ang: loc. cit., and *Overseas Chinese Affairs Journal* (*Qiaowu Bao*), No. 3, June 1962, p. 4. Wan Hsing: loc. cit., and *Chinese Agriculture and Land Reclamation* (*Zhongguo Nongken*), No. 2, February 1965 (SCMM 478). Bureau of People's Communes, Ministry of State Farms and Land Reclamation: 'The Policy of Self-Reliance and Running Enterprises with Frugality and Industry Works Well on the Nantakang Farm.'

[6] *People's Daily* (*Renmin Ribao*), April 1, 1966, p. 1. Editorial.

[7] *Tsinghai Daily* (*Qinghai Ribao*), September 12, 1956 (SCMP 1433). Ma Shang-wu, Councillor, Tsinghai Provincial People's Council: 'Views on Resettlement and State-Operated Farms in Tsinghai,' see also *Overseas Chinese Affairs Journal* (*Qiaowu Bao*), No. 3, June 1962, p. 3. Liu Ch'ing: 'Train Accountants and Take Inventories of Warehouses.'

were responsible for the persistent losses made by many farms. Poor maintenance of machinery and defective agricultural methods have also contributed. After two or three years of cropping, the fertility of newly reclaimed land drops steeply. Some farms had set out to be virtual grain factories, neglecting other branches of agriculture such as livestock; in a country short of chemical fertilizers, this monoculture defeated its own end and had to be modified. In Heilungkiang, for example, a decision was taken in 1957 that all state farms were to go over to mixed farming, although continuing to make grain production their main task.[1] High initial costs, attributed in part to inessential building and extravagant construction standards, were another element in the farms' financial difficulties. Although no interest charge was made for the original capital investment,[2] the farms were nevertheless saddled with heavy depreciation payments for buildings and machinery; this was reflected in production costs which often have been above those of collective agriculture.[3] In 1957 an investigation of 220 state farms showed that a third were operating at a loss, and in January 1965 'a minority' was reported as still doing so.[4] If full costs (including capital charges) had been charged, the proportion making a loss would probably have been much higher, although it must be remembered that the profit and loss accounts of the farms include payment of agricultural tax and reflect compulsory sales to the state at below free market prices.

State farms, like collective agriculture, are subject to agricultural tax in the form of a percentage of their notional fixed yield, not of the actual yield. Since 1958, local authorities have been empowered to fix different rates of tax for different kinds of agricultural undertakings on the basis of the average and maximum rates set by the central government. Also like collective agriculture, state farms have obligations for compulsory sales of output to the state at official prices. After these obligations have been fulfilled, the surplus produce of state farms has been permitted (at least in Kwangtung province) to be sold to supply and marketing co-operatives at a mutually agreed price, or to be sold through state stores, but was forbidden to be sold directly on the market.[5]

In addition to grants to state farms to cover losses and for capital purposes (figures for these are not given separately in the budget), the state has allocated considerable funds to be used for loans to them for working capital.

---

[1] *People's Daily* (*Renmin Ribáo*), August 9, 1961, p. 1, and NCNA Harbin, November 5, 1957, loc. cit.

[2] The average cost of land reclamation stood in 1957 at around ¥100 a *mow*. *People's Daily* (*Renmin Ribao*), July 24, 1957, p. 2.

[3] *Chinese Agricultural Journal* (*Zhongguo Nongbao*), June 25, 1953. (Quoted in Carin: op. cit., p. 51), and *Report of the Indian Delegation to China on Agricultural Planning and Techniques*, Delhi, 1956, p. 165.

[4] *People's Daily* (*Renmin Ribao*), March 11, 1957, p. 1. Editorial, and ibid., January 9, 1965, p. 2.

In 1957 Liu P'ei-chih, Assistant to the Minister of State Farms and Land Reclamation and Secretary of the Party Committee of the Ministry, was denounced for declaring that state farms made losses every year and that they were 'a bottomless pit'. See *Kuang Ming Daily* (*Guangming Ribao*), August 25, 1957, p. 4.

[5] *Nanfang Daily* (*Nanfang Ribao*), May 15, 1963 (SCMP 3003).

The terms and channels of these loans will be discussed in the context of the banking system as a whole.[1] Up to the end of 1957, the state had granted loans totalling ¥200 million to state farms. In 1958, budgetary provision was made for an increase of ¥100 million in such loans.[2] Additions to working capital for state farms made available from the budget in 1959 amounted to ¥300 million (probably the realized figure) and in 1960 to ¥540 million (budgeted estimate).[3] These figures probably refer only to those loans made to state farms under the Ministry of State Farms and Land Reclamation.

Before 1958, the sums allocated by the state for loans to state farms comprised only 5 per cent of the total of such allocations to agriculture; in 1958 this figure rose to 25 per cent.[4] Changes in budgetary presentation prevents similar comparison being made for 1959 and 1960 and after 1960 no figures for such budgetary items have been disclosed.

The great increase in the total of loanable funds available to state farms in the period 1958 to 1960 must be related to the development of state farms in those years. It will be remembered that figures reported for 1958 indicate that both the number of farms and their cultivated area more than doubled in that year compared with 1957.[5]

There has been a tendency for state farms to grow more similar to collective agriculture. In Kiangsi, and on the Overseas Chinese farms, this tendency appears to have been carried further than elsewhere. In some districts, shifting has occurred between one category of organization and the other. On the formation of the communes, some state farms were amalgamated with the new units and lost their identity as state farms.[6] In Kiangsi at the same period, certain former agricultural co-operatives were incorporated into state farms while remaining separate economic accounting units and not immediately acquiring the status of 'ownership by all the people'.[7] By 1959, the distinction between state farms and collective units in Kiangsi had become blurred. 'All the (state) reclamation farms in the province', it was reported, 'are practising the combination of farms, *hsiang* and communes . . . the farms may act in any of the three names—*hsiang* people's council, reclamation farm and people's commune.'[8]

In the state farms, as in the communes, much authority has been delegated, under the responsibility system, to production teams and the same methods of wage calculation are widely used in both state and collective farming. Efforts have, however, been made to prevent such a luxuriant development of private activities by state farm employees as has come about among collectivized peasants. While workers on state farms have private plots, they are,

---

[1] See p. 418 passim.
[2] *Collected Laws and Regulations* . . . Vol. 7, p. 137.
[3] Ibid., Vol. 11, p. 43.
[4] Ibid., Vol. 7, p. 137.
[5] See p. 95 above.
[6] NCNA Chengchow, September 1, 1958, and NCNA Peking, September 3, 1958. (Both references quoted from R. Carin, op. cit., p. 236.)
[7] *Kiangsi Daily (Jiangxi Ribao)*, February 28, 1959 (SCMP 2027). Lin Chün-hsiu: loc. cit. and ibid., December 15, 1959 (SCMP 2217). Wang Tung-hsing: loc. cit.
[8] *Kiangsi Daily (Jiangxi Ribao)*, February 28, 1959 (SCMP 2027). Lin Chün-hsiu: loc. cit.

at least on some farms, strongly discouraged from selling their own produce except to state agencies.[1] On Overseas Chinese farms, policy on this, as in other respects, is more liberal.[2]

It has been a hard, and often losing, struggle to maintain state farms as instruments of introducing urban proletarian attitudes into the ideologically backward sphere of agriculture. The contrary trend of the assimilation of state farms to collective agriculture has been at least as strong. Therefore no radical change need be seen in the announcement of the Kwangtung Provincial CCP Committee in August 1966 that 'state farms, forestry and reclamation farms must also, at the same time, be people's communes'.[3] This represents no more than the continuation of earlier trends to their logical conclusion.

If the Chinese government has had scant ideological return for its investment in state farms, financially, as we have seen, it has not done much better. From the broader economic viewpoint, the gains are no doubt more substantial. Investment in opening new land and in internal migration cannot be expected to show short-term profit, yet its long-term economic benefits may be great. In addition, the higher 'commodity ratio' of the state farms and their greater amenability to planning directives—as illustrated, for example, by their swift expansion of cotton growing in 1964[4]—may outweigh some degree of financial unprofitability.

Strategic interests probably counted as heavily as economic in the opening of state farms near China's north west and northern frontiers. Even although, when the farms were first established, relations with the Soviet Union were cordial, yet any government of China must inherit an underlying historic sense of insecurity about those regions which have seen so many barbarian forays. Settlement of frontier areas by soldiers and civilians (including convicts) is a long-standing Chinese tradition.

Finally, state farms have been used as a solution of certain specific and pressing problems. Provision has to be made for the livelihood of ex-servicemen and for repatriated Overseas Chinese, while criminals and recalcitrants need (from the viewpoint of the Chinese authorities) to be reformed through labour. Experimental, demonstration and seed farms are required in the interests of national agriculture as a whole, while suburban state farms reflect the policy of encouraging local self-sufficiency. The advantage of state farms to the government in these and other matters lies in their greater responsiveness to orders compared with collective agriculture. The government has had to pay heavily for these advantages, but the basis on which official decisions rest in China, as in other countries, is seldom strictly economic.

[1] Workers on the Pearl River State Farm in Kwangtung, for example, were informed that while it was legal for them to sell their own produce at the rural markets, 'advanced workers should consciously refrain from doing so'. Thereafter, we are told 'no one on Pearl River Farm has ever sold anything at rural markets'. The cadres on this farm are reported not to have private plots nor to visit the rural markets.
Southern Daily (Nanfang Ribao), September 2, 1964 (SCMP 3312). A Work Team of the Agricultural Committee of the Central-South Bureau of the CCP Central Committee and a Work Team of the CCP Kwangtung Provincial Committee: loc. cit.
[2] *Overseas Chinese Affairs Journal (Qiaowu Bao)*, No. 6, December 1962, p. 16. Editorial.
[3] *Summary of World Broadcasts*, Second Series, FE/2247/B/5. (Canton, August 13, 1966.)
[4] *People's Daily (Renmin Ribao)*, January 9, 1965, p. 2.

2. AGRICULTURAL MACHINERY STATIONS

In 1964 some 32 per cent of China's total tractor park was employed by state farms.[1] The remaining 68 per cent served collective agriculture and was mainly operated by agricultural machinery stations, previously known as tractor stations;[2] the new name betokens a widening of functions. The majority of agricultural machinery stations are under state ownership, the rest being owned by large and prosperous communes or jointly by state and commune.[3]

State agricultural machinery stations probably fall within the sphere of the Eighth Ministry of Machine Building which was established by January 1965 and is surmised to be the successor of the former Ministry of Agricultural Machinery. The Ministry of Agricultural Machinery had been established in 1959 to supervise the process of agricultural mechanization and the actual use of machinery in agriculture. It was also responsible for the manufacture of agricultural machinery and for the training of tractor drivers and other personnel to operate such machinery.[4] These functions had previously been undertaken by a bureau of the Ministry of Agriculture.[5] The setting up of a separate ministry in 1959 was linked with the switch to reliance primarily on home production for supplies of agricultural machinery.[6] It is not certain if the Eighth Ministry of Machine Building has succeeded to all the responsibilities of the Ministry of Agricultural Machinery, or whether there has been a re-allocation of duties.

The total number of tractors reported employed in Chinese agriculture both on state farms and collective agriculture is given in the table on p. 113.

It is not possible to ascertain with any accuracy the number of physical units (actual tractors) represented in any year by a given number of 'standard units' of 15 h.p. In 1965 the six types of tractors being manufactured in quantity were of 100 h.p., 75 h.p., 54 h.p., 35 h.p., 28 h.p., and 7 h.p. respectively;[7] the 'mix' turned out in any period is not known. However, some foreign observers have estimated that 100,000 standard units may be equivalent to 50,000 physical units and there is evidence that for rough calculations the Chinese sometimes reckon two standard units for every physical unit.[8]

[1] *Technology of Agricultural Machinery* (*Nongye Jixie Jishu*), No. 11, November 13, 1964 (SCMM 451). Shang Chih-lung and Ma Ching-p'o: loc. cit.

[2] *Kuang Ming Daily* (*Guangming Ribao*), November 30, 1964, p. 6. Wang Yi-ming and Liu Hua-chen: 'The Nature and Tasks of Our Country's State Agricultural Machinery Stations.'

[3] Ibid., and *People's Daily* (*Renmin Ribao*), December 22, 1962, p. 5. Hsiang Nan: 'Certain Problems in the Mechanization of Agriculture.'

[4] *New China Fortnightly* (*Xinhua Banyuekan*), No. 163, September 12, 1959, p. 24, and *China Youth Newspaper* (*Zhongguo Qingnian Bao*), July 18, 1960 (SCMP 2324), and *Daily Worker* (*Gongren Ribao*), January 5, 1963, p. 1. Chang Feng-shih, Vice Minister of Agricultural Machinery: 'The Technical Transformation of Agriculture Must Be Better Served by the Agricultural Machinery Industry.'

[5] *Report of the Indian Delegation to China on Agricultural Planning and Techniques*, op. cit., p. 167.

[6] *Daily Worker* (*Gongren Ribao*), January 5, 1963, p. 1. Chang Feng-shih: loc. cit.

[7] NCNA Peking, May 19, 1965.

[8] e.g. *Chinese Agricultural Journal* (*Zhongguo Nongbao*), No. 11, November 1963, p. 7. Chang Ch'ing-t'ai: 'The Problems of Consolidating the Operational Management of Tractor Stations.' Extract from a speech to the Liaoning Provincial Conference on Tractor Station Work.

STATE FARMS, AGRICULTURAL MACHINERY, FORESTRY

'Standard Units' of 15 h.p each
(figures rounded off to the nearest hundred)

Year	Units	Year	Units
1949	400	1957	24,600
1950	1,300	1958	45,300
1951	1,400	1959	59,000
1952	2,000	1960	73,800
1953	2,700	1961	98,100
1954	5,100	1962	100,000
1955	8,100	1963	103,300
1956	19,400	1964	123–150,000
		1965	135,700

It should be remembered that some tractors used, e.g. for large land reclamation and water conservancy schemes, would not be reckoned to be employed in state or collective agriculture and are presumably excluded from these figures.

Sources: 1949–58: *Ten Great Years*, p. 135.

1959: *Red Flag (Hongqi)*, No. 4, February 16, 1960, p. 6. Ch'en Cheng-jen, Minister of Agricultural Machinery: 'Speed Up the Technical Transformation of Agriculture.'

1960: *People's Daily (Renmin Ribao)*, February 3, 1962, p. 5. Hua Kuo-chu: 'Raise the Utilization Rate of Tractors,' states that in 1960 there were three times as many tractors as in 1957.

1961: *Daily Worker (Gongren Ribao)*, January 18, 1962, p. 1. Chang Feng-shih, Vice Minister of Agricultural Machinery Industry: 'Produce Suitable Agricultural Machinery to Support Agriculture.' 40,000 new units supplied since 1959. Allowance made for scrapping of tractors ten years old (i.e. those added in 1950).

1962: *Ta Kung Daily (Dagong Bao)*, Peking, June 9, 1963, p. 3. Shih Yen-nung: 'Some Problems in Raising the Utilization Rate of Tractors.'

1963: *Peking Review*, May 10, 1963, p. 13. Chung Huang: 'Basing Industry on Agriculture.' '4·2-fold as many tractors working as in 1957.'

1964: *People's Daily (Renmin Ribao)*, October 20, 1964, p. 1. 'More than six times the 1957 number.' However, the Prime Minister, Chou En-lai, two months later, reported that the number of tractors employed in agriculture in 1964 was five times the 1957 figure. *People's Daily (Renmin Ribao)*, December 31, 1964, p. 1.

1965: *People's Daily (Renmin Ribao)*, April 13, 1966, p. 2. 'The number of tractor standard units owned by tractor stations and state farms in 1965 was 6·96 times that of 1956.'

The number of tractors in operation at any one time has been considerably below the number in existence. Owing to the low level of care and maintenance, unavoidable in the early stages of industrialization, tractors are often out of order. At some tractor stations the proportion incapacitated sometimes exceeds half.[1] We shall later refer to the shortage of mechanics which contributed to this state of affairs. Another cause has been the lack of spare parts. However, urgent attention devoted to the provision of spare parts in the early 1960s has probably improved the situation. In the same period, priority for investment funds was given to plants making farm machinery accessories.[2] Thus, although the total number of tractors increased but slightly in 1962 and 1963, their effectiveness may have risen considerably.

[1] *Chinese Youth (Zhongguo Qingnian)*, No. 15, August 1, 1960, p. 15. Li Wei-fu, Deputy Secretary of CCP Committee of Changshih Commune, Shaokuan, Kwangtung: 'Agriculture Needs More Educated Young People', and *Daily Worker (Gongren Ribao)*, May 17, 1962, p. 1. Kuo Kuo-sheng: 'Development of Tractor Ploughing Potential from the Viewpoint of Two Tractor Stations.'

[2] At the end of 1963, however, a severe shortage of tractor accessories was reported from Honan. *People's Daily (Renmin Ribao)*, December 16, 1963, p. 2. Li Ch'ao-jui: 'Fully Develop the Use of Tractors for Ploughing.'

Despite the large increase in the number of tractors since 1949, less than 10 per cent of the total cultivated area of China was worked mechanically in 1962.[1] Tractors have been concentrated predominantly in the north east (where in 1962 Heilungkiang province alone had nearly 20,000 standard units of tractors (20 per cent of the national total),[2] in the north west (with 10,000 standard units in Sinkiang in 1965)[3] and on the north China Plain (over 8,000 standard units in Shantung in 1963).[4] These regions enjoyed priority for tractor allocations in 1964, together with Hupeh, the Chengtu Plain in Szechuan and the deltas of the Yangtze and Pearl Rivers in Kiangsu and Kwangtung respectively;[5] the last four, as well as parts of the north China Plain, being among the key areas of 'high and stable yields' designated for priority investment and allocations under the policy enunciated in 1964.[6] These areas are important producers either of grain surpluses or of cotton and other 'economic crops'. The outskirts of large cities also receive priority for tractors.[7] As a general rule tractors have been considered more appropriate to the labour-extensive agriculture of thinly populated regions, while in the densely inhabited wet rice areas, irrigation and drainage are held to be the first operations to mechanize.[8] This distinction is not absolute; three of the districts listed above as having priority for tractors are major paddy areas where, despite large populations, seasonal pressures can cause labour shortages which make the use of tractors beneficial. A considerable number of tractors are employed in these localities, but technical problems in the use of tractors in irrigated, and often small, fields have not been satisfactorily solved.[9] In addition to the saving of labour, increased yields of the order of 10 per cent are claimed as a consequence of mechanized ploughing. On demonstration farms, rises in output of 20–40 per cent are said to have resulted from mechanization.[10] The labour saved by mechanization is reported to be used for intensifying agriculture by such measures as raising the multiple cropping index and increasing the time given to subsidiary farm products and occupations.[11]

The agricultural machinery stations, which as we have seen, serve collec-

[1] *People's Daily (Renmin Ribao)*, November 9, 1962, p. 1. Editorial.
[2] NCNA Peking, January 2, 1963.
[3] NCNA Peking, September 29, 1965.
[4] NCNA Tsinan, October 22, 1963.
[5] *People's Daily (Renmin Ribao)*, October 20, 1964, p. 1.
[6] *Peking Review*, December 11, 1964, p. 27. Hu Chi: loc. cit.
[7] *Red Flag (Hongqi)*, No. 7–8, April 20, 1964, p. 60. T'ao Ting-lai: 'The Direction and Order of Our Country's Agricultural Mechanization Development.'
[8] *Economic Research (Jongji Yanjiu)*, No. 12, December 1963, p. 77. Chung Chieh: 'A Discussion of the Modernization of Agriculture in Our Country.'
[9] *People's Daily (Renmin Ribao)*, July 2, 1963, p. 5. Sha Yao-chien: 'The Problem of Tractors in the Paddy Fields of Our Country', and *People's Daily (Renmin Ribao)*, November 4, 1964, p. 5. Teng Cho-jung and Feng Wu-ch'u: 'Investigation on Tractors for Wet Rice Areas in Our Country.'
[10] *Economic Research (Jingji Yanjiu)*, No. 2, February 1964, p. 15. Meng Ch'ing-p'eng: 'Some Problems of Agricultural Mechanization', and NCNA Changchun, February 18, 1965.
[11] *Economic Research (Jingji Yanjiu)*, No. 2, February 1966, p. 18. The Agricultural Economics Group of the Shantung Provincial Institute of Economic Research and the Politics and Economics Teaching Research Office of Shantung University: 'A Survey of the Formation of a New Socialist Countryside by the Tungkuo Production Brigade.'

tive agriculture, date from 1950 when one was set up in Liaoning.[1] Their numbers are reported as follows:

	Number of Agricultural Machinery Stations	Per cent of total tractors employed in Agriculture which are controlled by Agricultural Machinery Stations
1953	11	
1955	138	
1957	383	49
1964	over 1,500	68
1965	2,263 or 1,488	
1966	over 2,200 in addition to communes' own tractor stations.	

Sources:
1953: *New China Monthly* (*Xinhua Yuebao*), No. 62, December 1954, p. 152.
1955: *Chinese Agricultural Journal* (*Zhongguo Nongbao*), No. 8, 1956, p. 10. Quoted from *China Weekly* (*Zuguo*), No. 583, March 9, 1964, p. 7. Ma Ch'ang-tsung: loc. cit.
1957: *People's Daily* (*Renmin Ribao*), January 18, 1958, p. 2.
1964: *People's Daily* (*Renmin Ribao*), October 20, 1964, p. 1, and *Technology of Agricultural Machinery* (*Nongye Jixie Jishu*), No. 11, November 13, 1964 (SCMM 451). Shang Chi-lung and Ma Ching-p'o: loc. cit.
1965: *People's Daily* (*Renmin Ribao*), April 13, 1966, p. 2, states that 'by 1965 a total of 2,263 agricultural machine stations have been set up in more than 1,300 *hsien* (and municipalities)' in addition to tractors on state farms. However, ibid., August 31, 1965, p. 2, gives the number of agricultural machinery stations serving communes as 1,488.
1966: NCNA, May 12, 1966.

It will be noticed that the proportion of tractors in collective agriculture rose steeply between 1957 and 1964. This probably reflects the fact that state farms in the priority areas were already relatively well mechanized in the earlier year. Since 1957, an increased share of new tractors has been going to collective agriculture. The sharp rise (according to one source) in the number of agricultural machinery stations in 1965 may reflect definitional changes, perhaps combined with changes in policy. Thus the sub-stations set up at that time in some areas to serve individual communes may each have been counted, and the same might even apply to the instances when machines were allocated to production brigades on a 'fixed' basis.[2] Such figures as we have of the distribution of agricultural machinery stations between provinces, indicates that the general pattern resembles, perhaps in an accentuated form, that for total tractor power. Thus in 1962 nearly 500 such stations were situated in Heilungkiang and 400 in Liaoning; two thirds of the total were probably in the three north eastern provinces.[3] By 1964 more than 70 per cent of the *hsien* in China were reported to have at least one agricultural machinery station each.[4] In the provinces of Heilungkiang and Shantung and in the rural areas of Peking Municipality, they are stated to be found in every *hsien*, and in almost every *hsien* in Hopei, Kirin and Ninghsia.[5]

[1] *China Weekly* (*Zuguo*), No. 583, March 9, 1964, p. 7. Ma Ch'ang-tsung: 'Communist China's Agricultural Machinery Stations.'
[2] *People's Daily* (*Renmin Ribao*), April 13, 1966, p. 2.
[3] Kirin reported agricultural machinery stations in most *hsien* and in many communes in 1965. NCNA Changchun, February 18, 1965, and NCNA Shenyang, August 26, 1962, and NCNA Harbin, September 17, 1962.
[4] *People's Daily* (*Renmin Ribao*), October 20, 1964, p. 1. This statement appears to be incompatible with the figures given in the previous sentence and in the table above.
[5] NCNA Harbin, September 20, 1963, and NCNA Tsinan, October 22, 1963, and NCNA Peking, September 25, 1962, and NCNA Tientsin, September 7, 1964, and NCNA Changchun, February 18, 1965, and NCNA Yinchuan, December 8, 1964.

State agricultural machinery stations are defined as 'socialist agricultural enterprises equipped with modern agricultural implements'. They have no land or products of their own, but for standardized charges (to be discussed below) sell services to units of collective agriculture.[1] Before 1957, these stations confined themselves mainly to ploughing, raking and sowing, but later, as they acquired more machinery, they began to undertake more varied types of work, including levelling of fields and the processing of non-staple agricultural produce.[2]

In 1963 a sample survey of seven agricultural machinery stations in north and north east China gave an average for each station of some 100,000 *mow* ploughed by 40 standard units of tractors.[3] A normative statement, made in Liaoning province in the same year, mentioned 150,000–300,000 *mow* (10,000–20,000 ha.) of land within a radius of up to 10 km. as the area that ought to be worked by one tractor station, which should possess 60–100 standard units of tractors.[4] A model station, with 45·8 standard units, is cited as ploughing 270,000 standard *mow*,[5] but here the achievement was obviously exceptional.[6] As a rule, 3,000 *mow* per standard unit of tractor when only ploughing was done, or 1,500 *mow* with multiple operations, has been an accepted norm.[7]

Competent tractor drivers and mechanics have been in even shorter supply than tractors. In some areas, especially on the ex-servicemen's farms in Heilungkiang and Sinkiang, former military truck and tank drivers were available,[8] but elsewhere peasants lacked mechanical skills. Three years was the time thought necessary in 1961 to learn to operate an agricultural machine efficiently;[9] later this period may have been shortened when youths with primary or middle school education, denied urban employment, were available in larger numbers. Most training has been given on the job, supplemented by classes run by communes or *hsien* and, for an elite, short courses at provincial colleges.

---

[1] *People's Daily* (*Renmin Ribao*), June 30, 1964, p. 5. Li She-nan: 'Some Problems in Lowering Operational Costs of Agricultural Mechanization.'

[2] Ibid., October 20, 1964, p. 1.

[3] *Economic Research* (*Jingji Yanjiu*), No. 6, June 1963, p. 11. Yang P'ei-hsin: 'The Problem of Financing the Process of Agricultural Mechanization in Our Country.' It is not stated if the sample was random or how it was obtained.

[4] *Chinese Agricultural Journal* (*Zhongguo Nongbao*), No. 11, November 1963, p. 7. Chang Ch'ing-t'ai: loc. cit.

[5] 'A standard *mow* is a uniform unit used to measure the amount of work done by a tractor engaged in different operations. It assumes a tractor in normal use and proper technical state, pulling a complex plough to cultivate land (the soil having a specific resistance of 0·45 to 0·5 kg. per square cm.) to a depth of 20–22 cm; over an area of one *mow*.' *People's Daily* (*Renmin Ribao*), June 30, 1964, p. 5. Li She-nan: loc. cit.

[6] *Chinese Agricultural Journal* (*Zhongguo Nongbao*), No. 2, February 1964, p. 47. Wuan *hsien* Tractor Station, Hopei: 'The Experience of the Wuan Tractor Station in Practising Cost Accounting at Three Levels.' Figures of up to 7,000 standard *mow* a standard unit have been reported—ibid., No. 8, August 1964, p. 24. Investigating Group of Peking Municipal Agricultural Mechanization Research Institute: 'Some Problems of Raising the Utilization Rate of Tractors.'

[7] *Economic Research* (*Jingji Yanjiu*), No. 6, June 1963, p. 11. Yang P'ei-hsin: loc. cit.

[8] NCNA Peking, January 2, 1963.

[9] *People's Daily* (*Renmin Ribao*), February 28, 1961, p. 1. Editorial.

Because of the seasonal nature of the work, policy is to retain only a nucleus of permanent skilled men at each station, to be supplemented by temporary workers hired on contract with local communes or production teams.[1]

Policy on the ownership of agricultural machinery stations has undergone a number of changes. In 1958, just before the formation of the communes, a decision was reported to transfer ownership of these stations from the *hsien* (which appear to have owned most of them at that time) to the agricultural co-operatives. This step was taken because of the poor standard of management and the financial losses of the stations under the existing system and their failure to meet the needs of the co-operatives.[2]

At the beginning of 1959, it was stated that 30 per cent of the tractors concerned had not been transferred to the communes, while some tractor stations were reported to be under nobody's care, as the *hsien* authorities had relaxed control without alternative arrangements being made.[3] One of the reasons for the continued existence of some state tractor stations was probably that many agricultural collectives could not afford to buy the machines from the stations, even after the establishment of the communes might have made this more feasible. Also, there was little financial incentive for collective purchase: fees charged by state tractor stations were usually below costs, even when costs excluded depreciation.[4] Another factor was incompatibilities of scale. Until mechanical skills are more widespread in the Chinese countryside, there are great advantages in concentrating machinery at stations, with their own tractor crews, mechanics, and repair shops. For economic operation, such machinery stations need to work areas larger than the total land farmed by individual communes in most parts of China, especially after communes were reduced in size.[5] Consequently, in 1961 a reversion of policy occurred and *hsien* tractor stations were re-established to assume control over machinery formerly dispersed among separate communes.[6] Thereafter, state ownership became the general rule, with control vested in the *hsien*. Sometimes stations were operated jointly by the state and a commune or, more rarely, by a commune on its own.[7] The latter was more common in those areas, such as north

[1] *Ta Kung Daily* (*Dagong Bao*), Peking, November 6, 1964, p. 3. In 1961 the stipulated ratio of men to machines was six drivers and operators and one mechanic to each tractor (presumably physical unit). *People's Daily* (*Renmin Ribao*), February 28, 1961, p. 1. It is not known what proportion of these would be temporary workers.

[2] *Chinese Agricultural Journal* (*Zhongguo Nongbao*), No. 5, 1958, p. 8, and *Study* (*Xuexi*), Nos. 10–11, May 31, 1958, p. 29. Li Chien-pai, First Secretary, CCP Heilungkiang Provincial Committee: 'Some Problems of Agricultural Mechanization.'

[3] *Agricultural Mechanization* (*Nongye Jixie*) No. 1, January 15, 1959 (ECMM 161). Li Ching-yu: 'A Summary of the Conference on Agricultural Mechanization and Electrification.'

[4] *Economic Research* (*Jingji Yanjiu*), No. 2, April 1957, p. 24, fn. Nan Ping and So Chen: 'Some Problems in the Pricing of Producer Goods.'

[5] *Economic Research* (*Jingji Yanjiu*), June 1963, p. 11. Yang P'ei-hsin, loc. cit.

[6] *People's Daily* (*Renmin Ribao*), November 23, 1961, p. 1. This refers to Anhwei. That it was not an isolated occurrence can be seen from references to Hopei where, in March 1961, we read of tractor stations set up in the past few years 'mostly by the communes, and some by the state', while in December 1961, most of the tractors in Hopei were reported to be operated by state tractor stations. NCNA Peking, March 19, 1961, and NCNA Tientsin, December 12, 1961.

[7] *People's Daily* (*Renmin Ribao*), December 22, 1962, p. 5. Hsiang Nan: loc. cit.

China, where communes large both in area and population were to be found even in the mid-1960s, and in regions such as north east China and Sinkiang where the ratio of land to labour is high. In 1965–6 there may have been another swing in policy on the management of agricultural machinery stations, with the state giving greater help and encouragement to communes to set up their own tractor stations.[1] A similar result was obtained by state agricultural machinery stations opening sub-stations with one commune as a unit or even by allocating certain machines to production brigades on a 'fixed' basis,[2] (an echo of the 'four fixed' factors of production controlled by production teams). In some parts of the country, the relatively large units of management for tractors previously considered desirable (with, as we have seen, concentrations of some 60–100 standard units of tractors) were apparently no longer thought necessary and brigades were encouraged to buy, for example, just one ordinary tractor and a couple of hand-pushed ones.[3] Perhaps this is a sign that mechanical skills had become more common among the peasants than had been the case a few years previously.

No doubt the method of control of agricultural machinery stations varies in different parts of the country (as well as over time) with the province probably being the significant level for decisions on such matters. In Liaoning (which has more tractors than any other province) the rule in 1963 apparently was to have a three-tier organization, with a headquarters tractor station in every *hsien*, ordinary tractor stations beneath it, and mechanized farming teams below them; *hsien* with fewer tractors operated a two-tier system.[4] The most effective technique of management in this, as in other spheres, is believed to be the responsibility system, whereby the province charges the *hsien* with certain specific responsibilities in respect of its tractor station, the *hsien* in turn the sub-station, and the sub-station the mechanical farming team. Special personnel assume full care for each machine and the personnel of each tractor works a certain area permanently and takes full responsibility for the tasks, cost and quality of the work.[5]

Agricultural machinery stations conclude contracts with the agricultural collectives whose land they are to work. Standard fees are set, apparently by the provincial authorities,[6] for each operation in each area. Sometimes instead of contracting to perform services, the stations rent out their machinery,[7] but the other would seem the usual practice.

From 1962 onwards, experiments were made in associating communes and

[1] NCNA, May 12, 1966.

[2] *People's Daily* (*Renmin Ribao*), April 13, 1966, p. 2.

[3] *Yangch'eng Evening Paper* (*Yangcheng Wanbao*), April 4, 1966 (SCMP 3679). 'Postulation by the CCP Hupeh Committee Concerning the Gradual Realization of Agricultural Mechanization.'

[4] *Chinese Agricultural Journal* (*Zhongguo Nongbao*), No. 11, November 1963, p. 7. Chang Ch'ing-tai: loc. cit.

[5] *People's Daily* (*Renmin Ribao*), December 22, 1962, p. 5. Hsiang Nan, loc. cit., and ibid., November 26, 1963, p. 1, and *Chinese Agricultural Machinery* (*Zhongguo Nongye Jixie*), No. 6, June 1963 (SCMM 374). 'News About Agricultural Machines.'

[6] *People's Daily* (*Renmin Ribao*), June 30, 1964, p. 5. Li She-nan: loc. cit. Here reference is made to 'the average standard fee for a standard *mow* fixed by Shensi province' for a particular area.

[7] *People's Taxation* (*Renmin Shuiwu*), No. 18, September 19, 1958, p. 10.

production brigades more closely with the management of state-owned tractors. This was done by allocating a number of tractors to work in a particular brigade for a comparatively long period (i.e. on a 'fixed' basis as noted above) and by giving bonuses both to the team of tractor drivers and to the production brigade when operational costs of the tractors fell below the set standard.[1]

Managerial and financial acumen in agricultural machinery stations has been at least as scarce as technical skills. Frequent complaints occur of organizational weaknesses and the managers, appointed perhaps because of political experience, have often found themselves out of their depth. 'When the peasants will not work we lecture them on Marx-Leninism, when the draught animals will not work we give them a beating', remarked some rural cadres, 'but when the machines do not work, there is nothing we can do about it.'[2] Mechanization necessitates new techniques of management.

Fees charged by agricultural machinery stations for their services are deliberately set at a low level: peasants are not always convinced of the desirability of employing the tractor stations' services, nor could they always afford to do so unless fees were low. Depreciation of tractors has been excluded from costs, but even on this definition, costs are often not covered and some stations even exclude wages and administration expenses from costs.[3] Articles in 1964 and 1965 complained that some people considered that it was of the nature of agricultural machinery stations to make losses and be recouped with state subsidies.[4]

The importance of the province in matters of agricultural mechanization has been noted in respect of the pricing of services of agricultural machinery stations, as well as in the establishment of provincial training schools for their staff. The methods of organizing and managing tractor stations also seem to be a matter of provincial policy. Provincial economic commissions decide which agricultural operations most need mechanizing in their areas, while types of tractors for local production are approved by provincial authorities.[5] Each province and autonomous region has its own farm machinery research institute.[6] The medium and small sized agricultural machinery plants have been under provincial control since 1957-8, and the province is better placed

---

[1] *People's Daily* (*Renmin Ribao*), July 28, 1965, p. 2. Chang K'uang-yu and T'an P'ei-ch'uan: 'A Revolutionary Agricultural Machinery Station', and NCNA Peking, April 12, 1966.

[2] *People's Daily* (*Renmin Ribao*), October 25, 1957, p. 4. Huang Ching, Chairman of the State Technological Commission: 'Problems of Agricultural Mechanization in our Country.'

[3] *Ta Kung Daily* (*Dagong Bao*), Peking, November 6, 1964, p. 3. Yü T'ung-li: 'A Short Cut to the Reduction of the Operating Costs of Tractor Stations,' and *Economic Research* (*Jingji Yanjiu*), No. 2, April 1957, p. 24, fn. Nan Ping and So Chen: loc. cit.

[4] *Kuang Ming Daily* (*Guangming Ribao*), November 30, 1964, p. 6. Wang Yi-ming and Liu Hua-chen: loc. cit., and *Economic Research* (*Jingji Yanjiu*), No. 7, July 1965, p. 60. Li She-nan: 'Some Problems in the Economic Accounting of Agricultural Machinery Stations.'

[5] *China Reconstructs*. December 1964, p. 35. Chang Chi, Vice-Chairman of Hupeh Provincial Economic Commission: 'Hupeh Begins to Mechanize its Farming', and NCNA Nanking, February 27, 1965, and *Yangch'eng Evening Paper* (*Yangcheng Wanbao*), April 4, 1966 (SCMP 3679), loc. cit.

[6] NCNA, February 7, 1966.

than the central authorities for supervising the process of agricultural mechanization.

In the Soviet Union, collectivization and mechanization of agriculture were introduced simultaneously. In China, as we have seen, this has not been the case. A decade after collectivization was virtually completed, mechanization was still of only marginal importance over most of China's agriculture. Ideologically, however, hope was still pinned on it to transform the nature of the peasants. 'Only mechanization and electrification can finally consolidate the collective economy, abolish the material basis on which individual peasant economy exists and block access by the peasants to the road of working as individuals.'[1] A long pull remains before this goal is attained.

3. FORESTRY

Shortage of timber is chronic over much of China. Some 1,400 million *mow* (about 9 per cent of the country's surface) is covered by forests and timber reserves are estimated at around 5,000–6,000 million cubic metres,[2] but these resources are low relative to population. Most of the forests are found on the periphery of the country, thus aggravating transport problems. Heilungkiang, Kirin, and Inner Mongolia together provide half of China's timber output,[3] while forests are also found in the mountainous regions of West Szechuan and Yunnan, on the south China ranges, and on the Tienshan Mountains in Sinkiang.

A wide variety of trees are comprised in China's forests, corresponding to the divergent climatic belts across which they stretch. Conifers are found in both north and south China and hardwoods are also widespread. The bamboo (not strictly a tree) is found throughout south and central China.

Output of timber was reported to have risen from 5·7 million cubic metres in 1949 to 35 million cubic metres in 1958.[4] The main uses for timber are for pit props (the coal industry being responsible for 17·6 per cent of total consumption of timber in 1957),[5] railway sleepers, building, paper manufacture,[6] farm tools, artificial fibres, firewood and charcoal. Efforts are made to restrict the use of wood as fuel in forest areas; elsewhere unavailability and price severely limit such use.

In addition to timber, China's trees yield many secondary products, including tung oil, camphor, tallow, nuts and fruit. Forests also serve to shelter farmland from wind and sand, and to prevent soil erosion. Large-scale protective belts have been planted since 1949, especially on the edges of the deserts of north China, in the upper reaches of the Yellow River and along certain

---

[1] *Economic Research* (*Jingji Yanjiu*), No. 12, December 1963, p. 74. Chung Chieh: loc. cit.

[2] *China's Coal Industry, Part III*, p. 26 (published by Joseph Crosfield & Son, Ltd. Warrington, 1961.)

[3] *People's Daily* (*Renmin Ribao*), April 10, 1963, p. 1. Editorial.

[4] *Ten Great Years*, p. 96.

[5] *China's Coal Industry, Part III*, op. cit., p. 26.

[6] Wood comprised about 27 per cent and bamboo 3 per cent of the raw materials for the paper industry in the 'past few years' before 1962. *Ta Kung Daily* (*Dagong Bao*), Peking, August 22, 1962, p. 1.

STATE FARMS, AGRICULTURAL MACHINERY, FORESTRY   121

stretches of coast. Impressive achievements in this direction do not seem to have been altogether matched by care of existing forests, where the rate of felling has tended to exceed regeneration and serious loss has occurred through fire, clearance of trees for agriculture and low utilization rate of timber.[1]

The Ministry of Forestry is charged with the general supervision of forestry, both that undertaken by state enterprises and that controlled by agricultural collectives. From 1956–8 a separate Ministry of Forestry Industry was established to take over from the Ministry of Forestry the responsibility for lumbering, processing, transporting and marketing timber, and for chemical industries subsidiary to forestry (e.g. resin). The division of duties evidently proved unsatisfactory and the two ministries were re-united in 1958, since when the Ministry of Forestry has controlled both the care of the forests and their utilization.[2] Through its Hunting Control Bureau, the Ministry is responsible for the protection of wild animals and their hunting, whether for fur or for other purposes.[3]

Provincial departments of forestry, and similar organs at lower levels of local government, have been established where circumstances warrant. In 1957–8 all except a few enterprises under the Ministry of Forests were decentralized, being put under the control of local authorities.

The territorial network under the Ministry and local authorities consisted until 1964 of forestry bureaux, each administering operations within a given forest area, and having under them forestry farms, lumber yards and woodworking and other plants. Often bureaux had to construct considerable lengths of roads and narrow gauge railways before lumbering became possible. Special administrative provision was made for exceptionally large forests. In China's largest single forest in the Great Hsingan Mountains, for example, a number of forestry bureaux were grouped under the Greater Hsingan Forestry Bureau, with its headquarters at Yakoshih. This town, the largest of a dozen that had sprung up in these mountains by 1959, boasts a complex of factories producing wood alcohol, tannin and other chemicals, machinery for lumbering and for railways, as well as a paper mill, tool repair shops and a thermal power station. The Greater Hsingan Forestry Bureau (which controls all these and also local transport) had—like the PLA Corps in Sinkiang—become a major verticalized authority, controlling almost the whole economic life of its area.[4]

In 1964 certain changes evidently occurred in the system of forest administration as 'the newly established forestry bureaux' were contrasted with the

[1] *China's Forestry* (*Zhongguo Linye*), No. 5, May 1963 (SCMM 367). Ministry of Forestry: 'Summing Up Afforestation Work in the Past Thirteen Years', and NCNA Peking, June 19, 1956. Liang Hsi, Minister of Forestry: 'The Forestry Situation in China.' Report to 3rd Session of 1st National People's Congress.'
[2] *Collected Laws and Regulations* . . . Vol. 3, pp. 80–1 and ibid., Vol. 7, p. 62.
[3] NCNA Peking, November 13, 1963, and *Nationalities Unity* (*Minzu Tuanjie*), Nos. 2–3, February/March 1964, p. 8. Hunting Control Office, Ministry of Forestry: 'A Discussion on the Development of Hunting in National Minority Areas.' In 1963 there were reported to be fifty-eight game preserves and national game parks and 130 deer-raising farms. NCNA Peking, November 13, 1963.
[4] NCNA Huhehot, September 20, 1959, and *People's Daily* (*Renmin Ribao*), December 4, 1960, p. 7. Chao Hsiang and Ai Ting: 'Technical Innovations Introduced by Workers in the Greater Hsingan Forestry Area', and NCNA Huhehot, November 8, 1961.

'old bureaux now present'.[1] No explicit account of the change has come to our knowledge, but in 1965 the Greater Hsingan forests were apparently directly controlled by the Forestry Bureau of Inner Mongolia.[2] Possibly the old *ad hoc* forestry bureaux had grown too independent and the new arrangement was for the purpose of assimilating them more closely with provincial administrations.

State forest farms, the basic units of management of state-owned forests, increased in number from about 30 in 1949 to over 500 in 1957. By 1965 they totalled over 3,500 and managed several hundred million *mow* of forests.[3] State forestry technical aid stations provide extension services to help local peasants engaged in forestry. In 1957 some 5,000 of these stations are said to have existed, but in subsequent years their activities diminished, although by 1965 a subsequent revival may have been under way.[4]

In 1959 state-owned enterprises were reported to account for some two-thirds of China's timber production.[5] Felling and regeneration in the great forests, as well as the more ambitious schemes of afforestation, are usually undertaken by state enterprises. Units of collective agriculture (communes, brigades and teams) also engage in forestry work and in 1964 were reported to operate 30,000 forest farms,[6] most of which were probably very simple undertakings.

State forestry enterprises are generally more highly mechanized than those of collectives and have higher per unit area costs:[7] it was hoped that these would be justified by lower operating costs. Uncertainties about ownership have at times led to neglect of forests. As a remedy for this situation, the policy of 'assigning ownership to those who cultivate the forests' was adopted for existing forests, while for new plantings ownership was to go to the planters—state organs or enterprises, agricultural collectives, or (for trees around their houses) private individuals. In the case of agricultural collectives, decentralization of the care of forest land to production teams was urged.[8]

[1] *China's Forestry* (*Zhongguo Linye*), No. 3, March 1964 (SCMM 414): 'Exploit the Victories and Advance, Strive for Greater Victories in Capital Construction'—a summing up of the National Conference on Capital Construction in Forestry (excerpts).

[2] *People's Daily* (*Renmin Ribao*), April 1, 1965, p. 2. 'We Staunchly Protected the State's Interests.'—a letter.

[3] *China's Forestry* (*Zhongguo Linye*), No. 5, May 1963 (SCMM 367). Ministry of Forestry: loc. cit., and *Ta Kung Daily* (*Dagong Bao*), Peking, January 27, 1964, p. 3. Te San: 'On Afforestation in Our Country', and *Economic Research* (*Jinghi Yanjiu*), No. 4, April 1965, p. 28. Jen Yuan-shou: 'Arouse the Masses, Plant Trees and Create Forests.'

[4] *China's Forestry* (*Zhongguo Linye*), No. 5, May 1963 (SCMM 367). Ministry of Forestry: loc. cit., and NCNA Peking, March 11, 1965.

[5] *People's Daily* (*Renmin Ribao*), June 27, 1959, p. 1. Editorial.

[6] NCNA Peking, September 26, 1964.

[7] *Ta Kung Daily* (*Dagong Bao*), Peking, August 22, 1962, p. 2, and NCNA, Harbin, October 17, 1963, and NCNA, Huhehot, April 1, 1964. For 1950–62 the cost of regeneration in state forests averaged ¥30 a *mow*, while in 1962 afforestation by state forest farms was estimated to average around ¥20–25 a *mow*. *China's Forestry* (*Zhongguo Linye*), No. 5, May 1963 (SCMM 367). Ministry of Forestry, loc. cit., and *Ta Kung Daily* (*Dagong Bao*), Peking, August 22, 1962, p. 2.

[8] *China's Forestry* (*Zhongguo Linye*), No. 5, May 6, 1963 (SCMM 367). Ministry of Forestry: loc. cit., and *People's Daily* (*Renmin Ribao*), February 11, 1962, p. 2, and NCNA Peking, June 22, 1963. Felling of its own trees by an agricultural collective for self-consumption is officially subject to approval by the *hsiang* or *hsien*, according to the quantity to be felled. NCNA Peking, June 22, 1963.

Sometimes state lumbering enterprises contract to fell collectively-owned trees.[1] Conversely, a state enterprise may make contracts with agricultural collectives by which the latter will provide the bulk of the labour for forestry operations, the state enterprise itself employing only a small nucleus of skilled personnel. Under these contracts, the collective unit concerned will assume responsibility for specified areas of forest farms.[2]

Even when a state forestry enterprise employs direct labour, activities are apt to be verticalized on an area basis, with each work team, of perhaps fifty men, being responsible for all operations, from cutting to transport; this method or organization is said to prove more efficient than horizontal specialization of function.[3] Thus, in the case of state forestry enterprises, as also with state farms, there has been a tendency to convergence with collective agriculture in the form of organization adopted. This, of course, springs from the fact that both state and collective concerns are faced with the same fundamental problems of production under rather primitive conditions. In the more mechanized state lumbering enterprises, we may expect to find a different tendency, with greater horizontal specialization of function due to the need to confine scarce-skills to the type of operation for which they are essential.

The operations of production teams, whether in state or collective enterprises, in the simpler forms of forestry, exhibit verticalization on a small scale corresponding to the larger scale verticalization of forestry bureaux. Yet another form of verticalization is demonstrated by the encouragement given to major timber users—railways, mines, enterprises manufacturers of paper and of synthetic fibres—to plant their own special purpose forests; the railways have also planted millions of trees along railway lines to provide their requirements of timber for sleepers.[4] This trend to verticalization and that to operation by small groups, are manifestations in the sphere of forestry of characteristic features of Chinese economic organization.

[1] NCNA Peking, June 22, 1963.

[2] *People's Daily* (*Renmin Ribao*), October 12, 1964, p. 1, and ibid., January 23, 1965, p. 5. Joint Survey Team of Ch'eng-te Special District Office, Hopei, and Forestry Bureau of Hopei Province: 'A Survey Report on the "Afforestation as Well as Agriculture" Contract Labour System Used by the Huangtuliang State Forest Farm.'

[3] Ibid., December 18, 1964, p. 2. Chi Hsi-ch'en and Li Chi-ch'eng: 'Innovations in Forestry.'

[4] Ibid., February 11, 1962, p. 2, and *Ta Kung Daily* (*Dagong Bao*), Peking, August 22, 1962, p. 2, and *China's Forestry* (*Zhongguo Linye*), No. 5, May 1963 (SCMM 367). Ministry of Forestry: loc. cit., and A. I. Il'yin and M. P. Voronichev: *Railroad Transport of the Chinese People's Republic*, Moscow, 1959 (translated from the Russian in JPRS 3484), p. 53.

Chapter 5

WATER CONSERVANCY AND ELECTRIC POWER

Water conservancy has ever been a touchstone for judging the competence of China's rulers. It vitally affects the life and livelihood of the people at several points—flood prevention, irrigation, navigation, while to these three has now been added a fourth, hydro-electricity. Large-scale water conservancy projects have been undertaken almost exclusively by the state at all periods of Chinese history.[1]

The importance of hydro-electricity has led to both large water conservancy projects and the supply and distribution of electricity being brought under a single ministry. This administrative arrangement explains why these two topics are treated together in this chapter. It must, however, be borne in mind that the discussions of the nature and responsibilities of state enterprises, which follows in Chapter 6, and of labour matters in Chapter 7, apply to the enterprises with which we are now concerned, especially electric power plants which organizationally have a close resemblance to manufacturing industry.

Years of wartime neglect left dykes, canals and irrigation ditches in disrepair by 1949. Plans for harnessing rivers and watering plains existed in abundance—drawn up by the Nationalist government and its American advisers, either in the hopeful years of the early 1930s or during the war—but the plans remained on paper awaiting the coming of peace. After 1949, the Communist government acted in this sphere with all the vigour traditionally expected of a new dynasty. Soon the work of restoration, both of water conservancy facilities and of power plants, was completed and, in the First Five Year Plan period, the way lay open to expand power generating capacity and to embark on new and ambitious projects of water conservancy; some of these latter were drawn, without acknowledgment, from the old blue prints while others were undertaken on the advice of Soviet experts. In the impatience of the Great Leap in 1958, this advice was disregarded and projects were undertaken hastily and without proper investigation, thus aggravating the difficulties of the ensuing period. In the early 1960s more cautious policies prevailed. Maintenance and improvement of existing water conservancy facilities were emphasized, rather than the undertaking of large new projects.[2] In keeping with the priority newly given to agriculture, the chief developments in the power industry lay in the field of rural electrification, particularly in the spread of powered irrigation and drainage pumps. This was aided by the decline in urban demand for electricity with the industrial setback

---

[1] Chi Ch'ao-ting: *Key Economic Areas in Chinese History*, 2nd edition. New York, 1963 p. 70.

[2] e.g. *People's Daily (Renmin Ribao)*, November 30, 1963, p. 1. Editorial.

of the early 1960s. Despite the increasing role of mechanized pumping, the continued importance of the water wheel (both old type and improved) in Chinese irrigation must not be overlooked.

The total irrigated area in China was said to be nearly 500 million *mow* in 1964.[1] This is below the 520 million reported in 1957 and less than half the 1,000 million *mow* claimed in 1958, and the 1,070 million *mow* reported in 1960.[2] The disparity probably indicates the degree to which statistical reporting had sobered by 1964, rather than any actual decline.[3] More difficult to explain is the fact that by the 1964 figure, irrigated land is only some 31 per cent of total cultivated acreage (1,600 million *mow*) as against the 38–47 per cent estimated by Buck.[4] Here again, the figures may well be explained by problems of estimation or definition rather than by a real decline.

Some 75 per cent of the 1964 irrigated acreage was watered by natural flow from rivers, streams, ponds and reservoirs, 7 per cent from wells and other underground sources, and 18 per cent by motor-driven pumps.[5] By the end of 1964 the total capacity of mechanized rural pumps (electric, diesel, turbine, etc.) was reported to exceed 7 million h.p., thirteen times as much as in 1957. Mechanized pumps irrigated an area of around 100 million *mow* which, however, represents only around 6 per cent of China's total cultivated acreage. Some 90 per cent of the *hsien* in China were said to have such equipment.[6] The efficacy of these water pumps has been diminished by the shortage of spare parts causing many to be unserviceable.[7] Electric pumping stations are especially numerous in certain key grain and cotton areas, most of which also enjoy priority for tractors and fertilizers; they include the deltas of the Yangtze and Pearl Rivers, the area around the Tungting Lake in Hunan, and the Chengtu Plain in Szechuan.[8]

By 1964 the standard of flood control said to be generally attained was the provision of defences against flood levels occurring once every twenty years.[9]

For a full discussion of capacity and output in the electrical power industry in China from 1936 to 1960, reference should be made to Yuan-li Wu's *Economic Development and the Use of Energy Resources in Communist China*.[10]

[1] *China Reconstructs*, November 1964, p. 15. Su Tsung-sung: 'Irrigation Renews the Land.'

[2] *Ten Great Years*, Peking, 1960, p. 130, and NCNA Peking, April 9, 1960.

[3] 'Only about one-third of the present total cultivated acreage of the country is *effectively* irrigated.' *People's Daily (Renmin Ribao)*, November 30, 1963, p. 1. Editorial (our italics), i.e. the 480 million *mow* added in 1958 were, for one reason or another, ineffectively irrigated, see *Asian Survey*, Vol. IV, No. 5, May 1964, p. 854. Kang Chao: 'Economic Aftermath of the Great Leap in Communist China.'

[4] See p. 34 above.

[5] *China Reconstructs*, November 1964, p. 16. Su Tsung-sung: loc. cit.

[6] NCNA Peking, September 20, 1964, and NCNA Peking, December 27, 1964, and NCNA Peking, July 16, 1965.

[7] *People's Daily (Renmin Ribao)*, April 12, 1966, p. 2.

[8] NCNA Peking, December 27, 1964.

[9] *New Construction (Xin Jianshe)*, No. 10–11, October/November 1964, p. 153. Chan Han-ying: 'Agricultural Water Conservation and Fields of High and Stable Yields.' Frequency of occurrence is a common measure of flood severity. Thus, defence against floods occurring once every twenty years betokens a higher standard than defence against floods occurring once every ten years.

[10] Published New York, 1963.

Total electric power capacity and output is estimated as follows:

	Capacity[1] Million kW	Gross Output Thousand million kWh	
1953	2·4	9·3[2]	
1957	4·7	19·7[2]	
1958	6·6	28[2]	
1959	9·8	42·2[2]	
1960	14·3	56–9[2]	
1962		45[3]	30[4]
1963			31[4]
1964			32[4] / 55[5]

Sources:

[1] Wu: op. cit., p. 14. Table I, Column III. Figure for 1960 is based on *planned* capacity.
[2] Ibid., p. 19. Table III, Column V.
[3] *Communist Affairs Research* (*Feiqing Yanjiu*), Vol. V, No. 12, December 25, 1962, p. 96. (I am indebted to Yuan-li Wu of Stanford University for this reference.)
[4] *Current Scene*, Vol. III, No. 17, April 15, 1965, p. 10.
[5] *1965 Yearbook of the Great Soviet Encyclopaedia* (in Russian), Moscow, 1965, p. 283.

The Soviet figure may be preferred to Western estimates because of the superior background information gained as a result of Soviet experts having worked in China up to 1960. The supposition that the gap between the two estimates is accounted for by the power used for China's nuclear programme depends on China's arrangements for processing uranium which, at the time of writing, are the subject of speculation.

Overall administrative responsibility in the spheres treated in this chapter is divided between the Ministry of Water Conservancy and Electric Power and the Ministry of Agriculture. The Ministry of Water Conservancy and Electric Power was formed in 1958 by the merger of the Ministry of Water Conservancy and the Ministry of Electric Power; this step was probably due to the added importance being given to hydro-electric power in the Second Five Year Plan. The Ministry of Electric Power had dated from 1955, when the Ministry of Fuel Industries was abolished and in its place were set up three separate Ministries of Coal, Petroleum, and Electric Power. The Ministry of Water Conservancy had been among the original ministries established in 1949. This Ministry, and the joint Ministry which succeeded it, have all along been held by one man, Fu Tso-yi. Fu was the Kuomintang general who, in 1949, surrendered Peking to the Communists without a fight; it may perhaps be speculated that his former troops provided the nucleus of the labour force for some of the earlier water conservancy tasks. In 1958, when the Ministry of Water Conservancy and Electric Power were established, the Agricultural Land Water Conservancy Bureau and the Irrigation Control Bureau of the former Ministry of Water Conservancy was transferred to the Ministry of Agriculture, which was henceforth to be responsible for agricultural irrigation and also for the construction of small scale rural hydro-electric projects, while larger ones came under the new ministry. The Ministry of Water Conservancy and Electric Power was charged with plans for the basins of larger rivers (in consultation with the Ministry of Agriculture where planning touched on agricultural irrigation); with the design of large-scale engineering works in this sphere and with giving technical guidance to the local authorities who bore the immediate responsibility for plans for smaller rivers and for the designing of less important projects. Disputes between provincial level authorities over water for urban, industrial, and mining uses were to be settled by the Ministry of Water Conservancy and Electric Power and over water for agricultural purposes by the Ministry of Agriculture.[1]

The Ministry of Geology is responsible for preparatory surveying before the construction of reservoirs, hydro-electric plants and similar projects, and for prospecting for underground water.[2] The Ministry of Communications is concerned with navigational aspects of canal building. The First and the Eighth Ministries of Machine Building are thought to be concerned with equipment of power plants and with agricultural pumping equipment respectively. Two other relevant bodies giving guidance at the national level are the National Water and Soil Conservation Commission, established in 1957 directly under the State Council, and the Central Flood Prevention Headquarters: routine activities in these two fields are the responsibility of the Ministries of Agriculture and of Water Conservancy respectively, except that water and soil conservation in the middle reaches of the Yellow River Basin was to come under the Yellow River Water Conservancy Commission. Where apposite, provinces and lower local authorities were ordered to set up soil and water conservation commissions or bureaux.[3] Scientific advice on water conservancy is given by the Chinese Academy of Science and the Chinese Academy of Agricultural Science.

The Ministry of Water Conservancy and Electric Power operates both through its specialized bureaux in Peking and through local organs, of which the most important are the provincial departments of water conservancy and electric power, and the commissions for individual river valleys. These commissions, successors of similar bodies under the Kuomintang government, are responsible for formulating and executing the plans for their respective rivers. Chief among them are the Yellow River Water Conservancy Commission, the Huai River Water Conservancy Commission and the Yangtze River Planning Office. In the case of the Heilungkiang (Amur River), the surveying and planning for its development was undertaken by a joint Sino-Soviet scientific expedition in keeping with the two countries' interests in the valley. The river valley schemes with which these commissions are charged are of such importance that separate mention must be made of some of the largest before discussing the functions of the water conservancy and electric power departments of the provinces and other local organs.[4]

---

[1] *State Council Bulletin* (*Guowuyuan Gongbao*), No. 140, April 11, 1958, p. 322, and ibid., No. 149, July 7, 1958, pp. 497–8.

[2] NCNA Peking, April 28, 1959. Li Szu-kuang, Minister of Geology: 'Current Geological Work in China', and *Red Flag* (*Hongqi*), Nos. 9–10, May 5, 1961, p. 43. Ho Ch'ang-kung: 'Survey Underground Water Resources and Help Agricultural Production.'

[3] *People's Daily* (*Renmin Ribao*), July 8, 1957, p. 6. 'Soil and Conservation Work in the Middle Reaches of the Yellow River Must Be Carried Out Firmly.'—Speech by Li Fu-tu, Vice-Chairman of the Yellow River Water Conservancy Commission, and *State Council Bulletin* (*Guowuyuan Gongbao*), No. 149, July 7, 1958, p. 498, and *Collected Laws and Regulations of the People's Republic of China* (in Chinese), Vol. 6, pp. 433–4.

[4] For a fuller discussion of river valley schemes and other water conservancy and hydro-electric projects, see R. Carin: *River Control in Communist China*, Hong Kong, 1962, and E. S. Kirby (ed.): *Contemporary China II*, Hong Kong, 1958, pp. 36–53. T. J. Lindsay: 'Water Conservancy and Hydro-Electric Schemes in China', Part I, and ibid., III, Hong Kong, 1960. pp. 163–80, T. J. Lindsay: ibid., Part II.

The plan for harnessing the Yellow River, although not the biggest is, in many ways, the most spectacular of these schemes. This river, long known as 'China's Sorrow' from its history of flood and drought, presents peculiar difficulties. The rainfall in its basin is highly seasonal and the river carries an exceptional load of silt eroded from the loess lands of the north-west and later deposited as the river crosses the north China Plain. Here the river bed has built itself high above the surrounding countryside, which is swiftly submerged if the retaining dykes are breached. A special body, the Yellow River Administration, had been established in the seventeenth century under the Ch'ing dynasty.[1] During the disturbed years before 1949, the river defences and irrigation systems had been neglected. With the help of Soviet experts, the new government drew up a plan, which was adopted by the State Council in 1955, for controlling and exploiting the Yellow River. Erosion was to be prevented by afforestation and other measures, check dams built to eliminate silt, major dams on the upper and middle reaches would provide power for the industrial centres planned in those regions, as well as water for irrigation, while navigation was to be improved to enable 500-ton vessels to reach Lanchow at all seasons.[2] The Yellow River Conservancy Commission was charged with the overall responsibility for this programme, but without being given effective power.[3] The key to the first phase of the Yellow River plan was the Sanmen Gorge project; its completion was delayed by trouble over silting, by the sudden withdrawal of Soviet experts in 1960 and by the Soviet refusal for some years to supply promised equipment. In the early 1960s little was heard of the progress on implementing the Yellow River plan. The existence of nuclear programme installations at Lanchow indicates that hydro-electric projects in that area have been completed. The contrast between the lack of authority ascribed to the Yellow River Water Conservancy Commission and the apparent efficiency with which the project or projects powering Lanchow were constructed, suggests that these latter may have been undertaken by a special *ad hoc* body—perhaps that (the Second Ministry of Machine Building) in charge of the nuclear weapons programme as a whole. If this surmise is true, the fact that control of operations on these upper reaches of the river is taken out of its hands, would inevitably weaken the Commission.

The Yangtze is China's longest river and some 300 million people inhabit its basin. The Yangtze River Plan, also compiled with Soviet help (but doubtless drawing, too, on an earlier plan made by the Kuomintang government and its American advisers) includes dams on both the main river and its tributaries. Not much has so far been reported about the activities of the Yangtze River Planning Office, which is responsible for work on these schemes. A proposal for linking the Yangtze River system with that of the Yellow River, for the purpose of channelling the abundant water of Central China to

---

[1] *Far Eastern Quarterly*, Vol. XIV, No. 4, August 1955, pp. 505–8. Ch'ang-tu Hu: 'The Yellow River Administration in the Ch'ing Dynasty.'

[2] Teng Tzu-hui: *Report on the Multiple Purpose Plan for Permanently Controlling the Yellow River and Exploiting Its Water Resources*, Peking, 1955, passim.

[3] *People's Daily (Renmin Ribao)*, July 8, 1957, p. 6. Li Pin-tu: 'The Necessity of Pushing on Unremittingly in Water and Soil Conservation in the Middle Reaches of the Yellow River.' Speech at the 4th Session of the 1st National People's Congress.

the arid regions of the north was mooted in the heady days of the Great Leap,[1] but later little was heard of the scheme.

As early as 1950 a decision was taken to make a comprehensive plan to harness the Huai River which, with its tributaries, drains much of Honan, Anhwei and Kiangsu, and is very liable to flood and water-logging. Under the Huai River Conservancy Commission, reservoirs and flood prevention basins have been built, the water thus stored being used for irrigation and the generation of power.

The river commissions are organs of the central government's Ministry of Water Conservancy and Electric Power, while the provincial water conservancy departments are guardians of local interests. Thus, the water conservancy departments of Honan, Anhwei and Kiangsu all complained that the claims of their respective provinces had been given insufficient weight in the Huai River Plan.[2]

In addition to the river commissions and to the water conservancy departments of local authorities, from the province downwards, all of which are, of course, under the supervision of the Ministry of Water Conservancy and Electric Power, there exist administrative units called irrigation districts (*kuanch'ü*), each responsible for supervising irrigation within its boundaries; these units come under the Ministry of Agriculture.[3] While normally the phrase 'irrigation district' appears to mean a definite operational unit, sometimes it is used in a loose sense to imply merely a district which is irrigated. Irrigation districts (in the stricter sense) are delineated according to natural conditions and technical requirements, and thus are normally not co-terminous with particular local authorities. Some irrigation areas are the continuation of old-established units, while others are newly created. A revealing comparison was made in 1962 between two irrigation districts, one 300 years old and the other existing for only seven years. The old district had a smooth-running organization in which all knew their roles and a responsibility system was operated. Representative meetings examined and adopted major operational and financial measures and elected a canal control committee. The 450 and more irrigation teams in the district were responsible for routine maintenance of canals, while every 200 *mow* of the whole irrigation district was under the care of a designated person. In contrast, the new irrigation district suffered from bad management. It lacked co-ordination, canals were in disrepair and water wasted.[4] These irrigation districts usually seem to be of a size between a *hsien* and a commune. Sometimes the term is applied to a larger area as, for

---

[1] *People's Handbook* (*Renmin Shouce*), *1959*, p. 459, and *Red Flag* (*Hongqi*), No. 17, September 1, 1959, p. 36. Wang Hua-yün: 'The Glorious Ideal of Diverting Southern Waters Northwards.'

[2] *Chinese Water Conservancy* (*Zhongguo Shuili*), No. 3, March 14, 1958, pp. 4–5. Sung Hsien-min, Deputy Director, Honan Department of Water Conservancy: 'Some Views on Controlling the Upper Reaches of the Huai River', and ibid., pp. 10–14. Anhwei Department of Water Conservancy: 'The Circumstances of Controlling the Hua River in Anhwei in the Past Seven Years and Some Views on this Work from 1958 to 1962', and ibid., pp. 5–9. 'The Views of Kiangsu Province on the Project for Controlling the Huai River.' A Report edited by Ch'eng Chih-ting and Hsu Yin-t'ung.

[3] e.g. *People's Daily* (*Renmin Ribao*), February 21, 1961, p. 1. Editorial, and ibid., January 24, 1962, p. 1.

[4] Ibid., January 24, 1962, p. 1.

example, in the case of the Urumchi River, Sinkiang, where the irrigation works are comprised in one irrigation district, with subordinate irrigation stations and teams, under the Urumchi River Administrative Bureau.[1]

During 1958 in water conservancy, as in many other fields, 'mass campaigns' were set in motion, with the purpose of substituting the intensive use of unskilled labour for capital equipment and technical expertise. Both large schemes under the central or provincial authorities and small works under special districts, *hsien* and communes, were covered by the campaign, although the emphasis was on the small type. In remote districts, soldiers and prisoners formed a major element in the labour force; in densely settled areas, the workers were mostly local peasants, together with surplus urban residents, students and officials 'sent down' for work in the countryside. The new communes became an instrument for switching peasant labour to water conservancy works.

A feature of the Great Leap was that Party organs came to overshadow the parallel government bodies, and also to take over the management of enterprises and other concerns. This happened in water conservancy, leading to neglect of technical standards and the hasty adoption of schemes without proper investigation. Party Committees overrode the professional skill and experience which the river commissions had carefully built up.[2] The results were reflected in the agricultural disasters of 1959–61. Badly co-ordinated water conservancy projects undertaken by inexperienced people caused a rise of the water table which led to alkalization and salinization of the soil over much of the north China Plain. In some places water-retaining strata were breached and much water was lost. Meanwhile elementary precautions for conserving the soil were neglected, notably by cultivating steep slopes.[3] A reasoned attack on the deficiencies of water conservancy policies during the Great Leap was made in 1959 by the leader of the Soviet advisers on water conservancy. Poor management was singled out for special criticism, the validity of which was recognized by the Chinese authorities in 1962.[4] The lack of competent planning of the large multi-purpose water conservancy schemes, notably the Yangtze Plan, had earlier been attacked by the veteran economist Ma Yin-ch'u.[5]

Managerial weakness was very evident in the water conservancy works undertaken by communes, whether singly or by several together. Small schemes at this level had, as we have seen, been favoured in 1958. By the next

[1] *People's Daily* (*Renmin Ribao*), March 29, 1962, p. 1.

[2] *Red Flag* (*Hongqi*), No. 2, June 16, 1958, pp. 6–7. Tseng Hsi-sheng: 'The Two Roads in Water Control Problems', and *People's Daily* (*Renmin Ribao*), February 11, 1960, p. 3.

[3] *Kuang Ming Daily* (*Guangming Ribao*), April 10, 1962, p. 1, and *People's Daily* (*Renmin Ribao*), May 25, 1962, p. 2. Su Tsung-sung, Irrigation Research Institute of the Chinese Academy of Agricultural Science: 'Adapt to Local Conditions the Measures to Curb Salinization and Alkalization in Irrigated Areas', and *Red Flag* (*Hongqi*), No. 9–10, May 5, 1961, pp. 44–5. Ho Ch'ang-kang: loc. cit., and *People's Daily* (*Renmin Ribao*), March 23, 1962, p. 2, and ibid., May 18, 1962, p. 2, and ibid., July 14, 1962, p. 2.

[4] *Water Conservancy and Electric Power* (*Shuili yü Dianli*), No. 4, February 20, 1959, pp. 19–24. Korniev: 'Some Problems in the Further Development of Water Conservancy in China', and *People's Daily* (*Renmin Ribao*), April 10, 1962, p. 1. Editorial.

[5] Ma Yin-ch'u: *My Economic Theory, Philosophical Ideas and Political Standpoint* (in Chinese), Peking, 1958, p. 18.

year official opinion had swung towards control being vested in the hands of larger units such as special districts and *hsien* which might be hoped to muster more skill and executive ability than was available to communes. Three provinces—Shantung, Hupeh and Honan—were commended for restoring the previous administrations of the irrigation districts placed under commune control in 1958.[1] Higher authorities were asked to supervise and inspect the irrigation activities of agricultural collectives.[2] Continued deficiencies in management are evidenced by complaints made in 1965 that many small water conservancy projects had no one in charge, with consequent damage and loss.[3] (In some instances, of course, communes have proved themselves satisfactory units for undertaking various schemes for water control and distribution.) These defects contributed to the surprising fact that at least until the end of 1961, almost a direct correlation has been found between the increase in area irrigated and in the area affected by drought.[4]

Investment in water conservancy is financed, according to size of the project concerned, by the state (i.e. by authorities from the central government down to the *hsien*), by the state and communes jointly, by several communes, or by a single commune, brigade or team. Sometimes the main body of a project may be constructed by the state, while subsidiary parts are built by communes and their constituent units.[5] Usually, these provisions result in the collectives shouldering the bulk of the cost, apart from certain exceptional projects. Thus, in one locality in Kwangtung Province where the irrigated area was reported to have been doubled, some 30 per cent of the cost came from the state and the remaining 70 per cent from agricultural collectives.[6] In the case of a district in Liaoning, where extensive irrigational work had taken place, state appropriations accounted for roughly 20 per cent.[7] Investment by collectives often takes the form not of cash but of peasant labour, compensated by work points. Thus, for projects of similar total cost, state grants and loans are more likely to be necessary in the case of electrical irrigation and drainage stations, where purchase of equipment represents 70–90 per cent of the investment, than for construction of canals and reservoirs where labour accounts for 70 per cent of the total.[8]

The general principle enunciated has been that whoever builds a project,

---

[1] *Chinese Agricultural Journal* (*Zhongguo Nongbao*), No. 17, September 8, 1959, p. 19. Ho Chi-feng, Vice-Minister of Agriculture: 'Energetically Continue to Build Water Conservancy Projects.'

[2] *People's Daily* (*Renmin Ribao*), February 21, 1961, p. 1. Editorial.

[3] *Ta Kung Daily* (*Dagong Bao*), Peking, January 8, 1965, p. 3. Yi Hsin: 'Give Serious Consideration to the Management of Water Conservancy Work.'

[4] *China Quarterly*, No. 23, July–September 1965, pp. 45–51. Wen-shun Chi: 'Water Conservancy in Communist China.'

[5] *Finance* (*Caizheng*), No. 3, February 7, 1963 (SCMM 360). Tseng Chih, Vice Minister of Finance: 'Exercise Strict, Practical and Proper Control over Appropriations for Capital Construction, Increase the Return on Investments.' Speech to Branch Managers of the Construction Bank, and NCNA Peking, December 27, 1964.

[6] *Red Flag* (*Hongqi*), No. 4, February 26, 1964, p. 8. T'ao Chu, First Secretary CCP Kwangtung Provincial Committee: 'The People's Communes are Progressing.'

[7] *People's Daily* (*Renmin Ribao*), March 13, 1964, p. 2.

[8] *Finance* (*Caizheng*), No. 3, February 7, 1963 (SCMM 360). Tseng Chih: loc. cit.

should reap the benefit from it and be responsible for its maintenance.[1] Consequently, when a project is built by an authority higher than the basic economic accounting unit (which in collective agriculture is normally the production team) the production teams which benefit are charged either on the basis of the area of each team irrigated by the project or on the actual volume of water used. All water charges are, by a State Council decree, to be used exclusively for the maintenance and improvement of water conservancy projects and these funds are not to be raided for fiscal purposes.[2]

Irrigation districts are supposed to be self-supporting, depending on water charges for the cost of maintenance. However, many receive some state subsidy, the achievement of financial independence being sufficiently exceptional to be commended.[3]

'Communism means sovietization plus national electrification.' The Chinese Government, heeding Lenin's dictum, has attached great importance to the development of electric power. Most of the pre-1949 generating capacity had been foreign owned, mainly by Japanese, and was situated in the north eastern and coastal areas. After the war, the Japanese plants were confiscated and in 1950 roughly three-quarters of the total power capacity was state owned or under joint state-private ownership. By 1956 all privately owned plants had been transformed into joint state-private concerns.

The bulk of electricity generation and supply is ultimately controlled by the Ministry of Water Conservancy and Electric Power and more directly by the corresponding local departments under provinces, *hsien* and other local authorities; the river valley commissions are responsible for the hydro-electric projects which form part of their schemes. In addition, however, are the power plants built and operated by industrial, mining and other enterprises for their own needs; some of these plants must be of considerable importance. Ultimate control of these would be by the ministry controlling the parent enterprise.[4]

China has no national grid. In 1958 there existed thirty-six separate power supply zones,[5] which very likely represented the separate local grids. The oldest of these local grids was originally developed by the Japanese in Manchuria, and then under the Communists passed to the control of the North East Electricity Administration.[6] Other large local grids existing already in

---

[1] *Water Conservancy and Electric Power (Shuili yü Dianli)*, No. 13, July 5, 1963 (SCMM 380). Chao Ming-fu, Vice-Chairman, Yellow River Conservancy Commission: 'Water and Soil Conservation in Regions along the Middle Reaches of the Yellow River.'

[2] *People's Daily (Renmin Ribao)*, March 10, 1963, p. 2. Wang Ch'ing and Kung Ch'eng-hua: 'Economic Rationality Is the Best Policy', and ibid., April 25, 1964, p. 4.

[3] Ibid., December 13, 1963, p. 2. Huimin North Canal United Water Conservancy Administrative Committee: 'When the Masses Manage an Irrigation District Themselves, the Development of Production Is on a Firm Basis.'

[4] See e.g. reference to power stations under the Ministry of Coal: *Coal Industry (Meitan Gongye)*, No. 13, July 10, 1959, p. 6, and to 'the Karamai Power Plant of the Sinkiang Petroleum Administrative Bureau'. *BBC Summary of World Broadcasts*, Second Series, FE/W354/A/27 (Urumchi, November 5, 1965).

[5] *People's Power Industry (Renmin Dianye)*, No. 19, October 1958, p. 4. Editorial.

[6] The existence of the Anshan Electricity Administration was reported in 1966. (NCNA, June 23, 1966.) Presumably it is subordinate to the North East Electricity Administration, unless the latter has been split up.

1957 included that linking Peking, Tientsin and Tangshan, the Shanghai-Nanking grid and the one covering part of Anhwei province.[1] The main integrated power systems planned for development under the Second Five Year Plan were those for Shensi-Shansi-Honan, centring on the Sanmen Gorge project (still incompleted in 1966), for Kansu-Tsinghai (the Liuchia project, presumably completed and supplying Lanchow), Kiangsu-Chekiang (in operation, powered from Sinankiang), for Yunnan (Liho project), and for Sinkiang (Urumchi). It was envisaged that a national grid might be inaugurated after the completion of the main Yangtze hydro-electric schemes which, however, is not likely to occur in the near future.[2] Most of the power systems mentioned above, together with those of the river conservancy commissions, cut across the normal framework of provincial administrations.[3] This may be one reason for defects in the planning of power supplies. As late as 1959, a Soviet adviser was urging that every province and special district should draw up a preliminary plan for a power system based on the planned distribution of industry, in order to facilitate co-ordination between local authorities and major power stations under the central government, and to prevent the building of small power plants in places which could be supplied by the transmission lines planned for the future.[4] Such plans might not be easy to co-ordinate with plans for supplying power to more than one province from a large hydro-electric plant. A few months later, in April 1959, a Chinese engineer took up the same theme of the inadequacy of plans for this industry. Basic information had not yet been collected for estimating future electricity loads: 'in the middle of the Great Leap it was not possible to have a firm grasp of research material'. He demanded that the Ministry of Water Conservancy and Electric Power should be consulted when factories were being built.[5]

The development of medium and small hydro-electric plants had a major role in the Great Leap drive towards rural industrialization. Medium-sized plants, with capacities ranging up to 10,000 kW. were put in hand by *hsien* and other local authorities.[6] The new communes were active in constructing smaller 'native' plants, usually of less than 50 kW. capacity, often much smaller. Many were crude, made for example by linking up an old water wheel with a dynamo. While many of the medium-sized hydro-electric plants proved useful, the small commune projects for generating power were in general disappointing.[7]

A more systematic movement for rural electrification began in the early 1960s, with the development of power networks stretching out from cities to

[1] *Collected Laws and Regulations . . . Vol.* 7, p. 224.

[2] S. H. Gould (ed.): *Sciences in Communist China*, Washington D.C., 1961, p. 756. T. C. Tsao: 'Electrical Engineering.'

[3] These large systems were among the undertakings excluded from decentralization in November 1957. See p. 152 below.

[4] *Water Conservancy and Electric Power* (*Shuili yu Dianli*), No. 4, February 20, 1959, p. 15. Pieh-szu-to-fu-szu-chi (name transliterated), Chief of the Team of Soviet Electric Power Experts: 'Some Important Problems in Development and Investment in China's Power Industry at the Present Time.'

[5] *People's Daily* (*Renmin Ribao*), April 28, 1959, p. 12.

[6] NCNA Peking, September 25, 1958.

[7] *China Quarterly*, No. 17, January–March 1964, pp. 141–2. T. C. Kuo: 'Agricultural Mechanization in Communist China.'

the neighbouring countryside. This was a by-product of the industrial recession of that time. Power shortages in the towns had been serious throughout the First Five Year Plan period and were aggravated by the industrial upsurge of the Great Leap. Much new urban capacity was installed (in addition to the rural plants just mentioned) but in 1960 power supply was still considered a weak link in the economy and the budget of that year made increased provision for investment in it.[1] The steep fall in industrial and mining activity from 1961 led to under-utilization of the expanded generating capacity in the cities. As part of the new policy of priority for agriculture, a programme was put in hand for the installation of high tension transmission lines from industrial and mining centres with surplus generating capacity to the surrounding rural areas.[2] This added yet another factor to the preferential position enjoyed by agriculture near cities. These power networks include those stretching from Shanghai to the Yangtze delta, from Canton to the Pearl River delta, from Wuhan, Paotow, Kunming, Taiyuan, and many other centres. In areas remote from cities, and especially in those important as producers of grain, cotton and other industrial crops, policy has been to build power stations of at least 500 kW. capacity, with the intention of linking them to a larger power system when feasible.[3] The very small plants of 1958 are no longer favoured. The main long distance high power transmission lines are built by the state (i.e. normally by provinces and *hsien*) with units of collective agriculture being responsible for the smaller lines.[4]

The technical ignorance of the peasants poses serious problems for rural electrification. While some training schemes have been operated, reports speak of places with thousands of electric motors but no technicians.[5]

The benefits of powered irrigation are not only that it frees a large amount of labour from very tiring tasks and makes it available for alternative occupations but that also it often performs these tasks more effectively. The full benefits of chemical fertilizers and other measures to raise agricultural yields in many cases accrue only when used in conjunction with mechanized irrigation.[6]

[1] *People's Handbook* (*Renmin Shouce*) *1960*, p. 185. Li Hsien-nien, Minister of Finance: Report on Final Accounts for 1959 and Draft Budget for 1960.

[2] *Economic Research* (*Jingji Yanjiu*), No. 3, March 1963, pp. 10 and 12. Tso Hu: 'Several Problems of Agricultural Electrification.' Over 70,000 km. of high tension transmission lines in rural areas were installed in the period from the summer of 1958 to the summer of 1963, mainly in the latter part of the period. In 1957, only 18,500 km. existed. Yuan-li Wu, op. cit., p. 29, and *Daily Worker* (*Gongren Ribao*), September 24, 1963, p. 2. Wang Wen: 'A Continuous Supply of Electricity for the Villages.' Another source (NCNA Peking, March 13, 1963), states that '70,000 km. of high-tension transmission lines radiating from the big centres of power to the villages' had by 1963 been installed *since the liberation* (our italics). Perhaps scarcely any going to the villages had been installed before 1958.

[3] NCNA Peking, March 13, 1963, and *People's Daily* (*Renmin Ribao*), September 12, 1963, p. 5. Huang Ching-ya: 'Certain Problems in the Development of Agricultural Electrification.'

[4] *New Construction* (*Xin Jianshe*), No. 11-12, December 1965, p. 68. Sung T'ao: 'The Problem of Accumulation and Investment by Production Teams.'

[5] *Peking Review*, February 22, 1963, p. 4, and *Water Conservancy and Electric Power* (*Shuili yu Dianli*), No. 7, April 5, 1963 (SCMM 372). Chu Huai-chen: 'Some Problems on Rural Electrification: Views for Deliberation.'

[6] *Economic Research* (*Jingji Yanjiu*), No. 3, March 1963, p. 11. Tso Hu: loc. cit.

Distribution of Electric Power by Sectors as Percentages of Net Domestic Supply.[1]
(Figures for later years subject to revision, in view of subsequent information about China's nuclear weapon programme—see pp. 136–7.)

	1953	1957	1960	1962	1964
Industry	83·0	88·2	92·6	88·8	
Agriculture	0·5	1·3	1·7	3·8	17·1
Transport	1·4	0·8	0·6	0·7	
Household	14·6	10·6	5·4	6·7	
	99·5	100·9	100·3	100·0	
Net Exports	0·5	−0·9	−0·3		
Net Domestic Supply	100	100	100		

[1] i.e. excluding consumption by power plants themselves and loss in transmission. For 1962 and 1964, percentages are of net domestic *output* as figures for net exports are not available for those years.

Sources:

1953, 1957 and 1960: Yuan-li Wu, op. cit: p. 85.

1962: Yuan-li Wu, F. P. Hoeber and M. M. Rockwell: *The Economic Potential of Communist China*, Vol. III, Menlo Park, California, 1963, p. 108.

1964: 4·75 million kWh (derived from *Peking Review*, January 1, 1965, p. 8) as percentage of net domestic supply (i.e. 32 million kWh.—see p. 126 above—less difference between net and gross supply: for this the 1958 ratio is used. See Yuan-li Wu: op. cit., pp. 68–70.)

Irrigation has had priority for the use of electric power in the countryside. However, its needs are seasonal and, at least in the slack season, in many places power is also supplied to agricultural processing industries.[1] When agricultural processing, such as grinding flour and milling rice, is mechanized, the time saved enables women to take a greater share in farm work.[2]

While the large regional grids cut across provincial boundaries, the greater part of the rural electrification movement reinforces the tendencies to provincial self-sufficiency. The networks often radiate from provincial capitals, and in any case seldom seem to stretch into other provinces.[3] Irrigation equipment, electrical and other, is commonly produced and used within the same province, production being arranged by provincial planning bureaux and allocation being by provincial organs.[4]

Consumption of electric power by different sectors of the economy changed considerably in the early 1960s with the decline in industrial intake and the growth of rural electrification. In 1965, twenty-five times as much power was reported to have been supplied to rural areas as in 1957;[5] this would give the

[1] *Economic Research (Jingji Yanjiu)*, No. 3, March 1963, p. 11. Tso Hu: loc. cit.

[2] *People's Daily (Renmin Ribao)*, April 9, 1966, p. 2.

[3] An exception is the Yangtze delta which is divided between three provincial level authorities (Shanghai, Kiangsu and Chekiang) and is served by a network of transmission lines radiating from the large Sinankiang Hydro-electric Station and from thermal stations. NCNA Shanghai, December 27, 1965.

[4] *Collected Laws and Regulations* . . . Vol. 9, p. 168, and *Machine Building Industry (Jixie Gongye)*, No. 3, February 1963 (SCMM 362). Shih P'ing: 'Some Suggestions Concerning the Use and Study of Electrical Appliances for Farming Purposes.'

[5] *People's Daily (Renmin Ribao)*, September 7, 1965, p. 1. Editorial. This increase showed very great local variations. In Shansi, for example, agricultural electricity consumption was reported early in 1960 to be 487 times as high as in 1957, and ibid., February 6, 1966, p. 3.

1964 supply to agriculture as around 5·4 million kWh. on the assumption that power supplies to agriculture increased in the same proportion as total supplies to rural areas.[1] Unfortunately, we do not have figures of supplies to other sectors in 1964 for comparison.

More than 10,000 power-driven pumping stations were said to have been set up by the state by 1963.[2] Government policy, however, has favoured ownership by communes or production teams as the normal rule for pumping stations, with state ownership limited to a few key instances.[3] It is not known if the state had greater success in selling collectives its pumping stations than it had with a similar policy for the sale of tractor stations.[4] Quite possibly it did, because with pumping stations the indivisibilities of scale are less serious in that one pumping station usually does not serve anything like as large an area as a tractor station. Electric pumping stations can be made of a size appropriate to irrigating the land owned by one production team.[5] Another factor which makes electric irrigation equipment more suitable than tractors for ownership by communes and production teams is that electric pumps are relatively easier to maintain and service and do not require fuel oil (also the manufacture of electric motors is better developed in China than that of tractors).[6] However, once again, difficulties are inherent in management at this level, often leading to inefficient use of equipment.[7]

Although China has vast hydro-electric resources, estimated in 1963 at 580 million kW.,[8] the greater part of power generation is, and always has been, by thermal plants because of their lower capital costs. No great change has occurred in the reported proportionate output of thermal and hydro-electric plants since 1952, as can be seen from the table on p. 137.

In 1959, hydro-electric capacity accounted for 18 per cent of total capacity, the same proportion as for output.[9]

The considerations which led to only 20 per cent of total investment in the power industry during the First Five Year Plan period going on hydro-electricity are treated in Y. L. Wu's study, already mentioned.[10] It was intended to increase the relative proportion of hydro-electric capacity during the Second Five Year Plan Period,[11] but according to the figures below this was not achieved. The decline in industrial activity after the Great Leap did away with the need for most of the planned increase in generating capacity. Alternatively, it is possible that the power output from the Luchia Gorge project is, for

---

[1] Yuan-li Wu: op. cit., p. 80. However, this figure must be treated with caution as the 1957 figure on which it is based is an interpellation. Ibid., p. 78.

[2] NCNA Peking, September 30, 1963.

[3] *Ta Kung Daily* (*Dagong Bao*), Peking, October 23, 1964, p. 3. Ho Hui: 'Rely on the Masses, Emphasize Self-Dependence and Small-Scale Production.'

[4] See p. 117 above.

[5] *Economic Research* (*Jingji Yanjiu*), No. 3, March 1963, p. 14. Tso Hu: loc. cit.

[6] Ibid., p. 10 and p. 13.

[7] *Water Conservancy and Electric Power* (*Shuili yu Dianli*), No. 7, April 5, 1963 (SCMM 372). Chu Huai-chen: loc. cit.

[8] *Popular Science* (*Kexue Dazhong*), No. 5, May 1963, p. 9. Hsü Shou-po: 'Rural Electrification.'

[9] Yuan-li Wu: op. cit., p. 170.

[10] Ibid, pp. 160–4.

[11] Ibid., p. 164.

security reasons (or just because it may come under the Second Ministry of Machine Building instead of under the Ministry of Water Conservancy and Electric Power) omitted even from the figures circulated within China, on which the 1963 percentages, given below, are based. If this is so, it means that all figures previously accepted for power output and capacity in the early 1960s, and especially those for hydro-electricity, will need to be raised.

Plants of 500 kW. and above

	Thermal per cent of total output	Hydro-electric per cent of total output
1952	82·7	17·3
1957	78·4	21·6
1958	79·4	20·6
1959	82	18·0
1963	82	18·0

Sources:
1952–9: Wu, op. cit., p. 167.
1963: *People's Daily (Renmin Ribao)*, November 27, 1963, p. 5.
Figures subject to revision in view of China's nuclear weapon programme—see discussion above.

Other sources of power—tidal, wind, and nuclear—have not yet been developed on a significant scale in China.

A number of the projected large hydro-electric projects, by their size and siting, are likely to supply parts or the whole of more than one province. Their influence would thus counter any tendency to provincial self-sufficiency. The failure to expand the relative proportion of hydro-electric power may therefore act to maintain this tendency.

The average capital cost per kilowatt capacity in hydro-electric plants built in 1953–7 was ¥17 more than that for thermal plants built in the same period, while annual average operating costs of hydro-electric plants were from ¥0·0211 to ¥0·0278 a kWh. below the cost of thermal stations.[1] Although capital costs are not taken into account in China in reckoning profit and loss,[2] notice is in fact taken of them in making investment decisions. Thus, the decision to increase the proportion of hydro-electric capacity in the Second Five Year Plan was greatly influenced by lower estimates made, perhaps fallaciously, of future capital costs of this type of power plant.[3]

The general trend of both operating costs and prices of electricity was downwards during the First Five Year Plan period. No constant relationship between cost and price was evidenced, the annual average rate of profit on cost varying between 52 and 99 per cent.[4] This is not surprising, as the annual averages concealed wide local divergences in both costs and prices.[5] It may

---

[1] Yuan-li Wu: op. cit., pp. 162 and 133. For operating costs of different types of power plant in 1963, see *People's Daily (Renmin Ribao)*, September 12, 1963, p. 5. Huang Ching-ya: loc. cit. Costs include industrial and commercial tax which in 1958 was fixed at 5 per cent of cost (inclusive of the tax itself) for electric power. *Collected Laws and Regulations* . . . Vol. 8, p. 136.

[2] See pp. 161–2 below.

[3] Yuan-li Wu: op. cit., pp. 168–72.

[4] Ibid., p. 130.　　　　　[5] Ibid., p. 258.

be surmised that the units for pricing policy are the separate power supply zones, which, as we have seen, are probably based on the local grids. Sometimes this may result in a common provincial price or sometimes in uniform charges within smaller or larger geographical units.

Discriminating pricing according to user is practised.[1] No case has come to our notice of charges being varied according to peak periods (daily or seasonal) but a suggestion was made in 1963 for preferential off-peak prices for agriculture.[2] Load-spreading, however, occurs and is presumably achieved by direct means—by command, negotiation or a mixture of the two.

While irrigation, especially powered irrigation, presents enormous possibilities of improving China's agriculture, it must once again be stressed how relatively little has apparently been done in recent years. The achievements of 1949–52 in rehabilitation should not be overlooked. Since then, however, the picture has been patchy. Against important advances in some directions must be set the nil or negative entry of much of the Great Leap efforts in irrigation and rural electrification. Despite the more sensible measures in these spheres in the early 1960s, grain production apparently rose little between 1957 and 1964, although labour input in agriculture has presumably increased with rising population and checks on migration to the cities.[3]

If agricultural output is to keep up with population increase, greater production of chemical fertilizer is needed. This industry is highly power-intensive. In addition, as we have seen, the use of electricity in agriculture is being promoted. If all these power requirements are to be met, together with the demands made by industry and the nuclear weapons programme, it would seem that China's hydro-electric resources must speedily be developed.

The scope of large hydro-electric projects, as noted above, frequently cuts across provincial boundaries. Thus, their execution would mean giving real authority—not just nominal responsibility—to supra-provincial bodies such as the river valley commissions. At all levels, effective control of water conservancy undertakings often demands *ad hoc* bodies, with boundaries drawn according to particular natural circumstances. These frequently do not correspond with the boundaries of local authorities or communes which have usually been determined primarily by other considerations. Some exceptions are found with certain new administrative units in areas where water conservancy is an exceptionally pressing matter; one example quoted is of an certain special district in Kwangtung which was created in 1963 for the express purpose of flood control,[4] and instances have already been given of communes of which this is true. Research might, of course, show that some older units, such as *hsien*, originally had their boundaries fixed with a view to their suitability as units for control of water. At the present day, however, the

[1] Yuan-li Wu, op. cit., p. 89, fn.
[2] *Economic Research* (*Jingji Yanjiu*), No. 3, March 1963, p. 15. Tso Hu: loc. cit.
[3] See pp. 183–6 below. An increase in population does not, of course, necessarily or usually mean an *immediate* increase in the labour force. Much of the rise must have resulted from a decline in infant mortality after the restoration of peace in 1949. These larger age groups would not be old enough to make a significant contribution to agriculture until the mid-1960s.
[4] A. L. Strong: *The Rise of the Chinese People's Communes—and Six Years After*. Peking, 1964, p. 163.

tendency of local authorities towards economic self-sufficiency for purposes of administrative convenience would seem to conflict with the requirements for the effective utilization of China's water resources for irrigation and hydroelectricity.

Chapter 6

THE ORGANIZATION OF INDUSTRY

1. INTRODUCTION

Industry, in contemporary Chinese parlance, includes not only manufacturing, but also handicraft production, mining, the generation and supply of electric power and other public utilities (water and gas, but not transport). Handicrafts, mining and electric power are considered separately in this study on account of their special features. However, what is said in this chapter on the general organization of industry and of industrial enterprises applies also to mining and power; handicrafts are in a different category because of the small size of production units and their status as, for the most part, collective, not state-owned, undertakings.

The system of industrial organization, on the level of the country as a whole, on that of major local authorities, and on that of the individual enterprise, must claim our main attention to this chapter. These subjects cannot, however, be properly discussed without some brief allusion to other matters: general policy towards industry, the changes in absolute and relative importance in the national economy of industry in general and of its separate branches, and shifts in industrial location.

First we must examine the meaning of certain Chinese terms used in discussing industry.

The distinction between heavy and light industry is by no means clear cut. In popular publications, heavy and light industry are in general identified with producer and consumer goods industries respectively.[1] For a more sophisticated readership it was argued in 1957 that such a clear identification was false; heavy industry was defined to include the production of capital equipment, motive power and fuel, mineral raw materials, cement and other intermediate goods and defence industries, but to exclude certain producer goods reckoned as falling under light industry (e.g. some types of chemicals and glass, printing, as well as producer goods made by the handicraft industries).[2] However, this definition, while winning praise abroad,[3] did not

---

[1] e.g. *Explanation of Certain Terms Used in the First Five Year Plan* (in Chinese), Peking, 1955, p. 10, and *Simple Explanation of Terms Used in the First Five Year Plan for the Development of the National Economy of the People's Republic of China* (in Chinese), Peking, 1955, p. 1.

[2] *Statistical Work* (*Tongji Gongzuo*), No. 18, September 14, 1957, pp. 13-14. Li Hui-hung, Sung Chi-jen and Wang Hua-hsin: 'Some Opinions on the Division Between Light and Heavy Industry.' In 1961, producer goods used in heavy industry were estimated to represent 20 per cent of the output by value of 'light industry', thus implicitly accepting the definition of light industry given in the reference above. *Daily Worker* (*Gongren Ribao*), September 7, 1961, p. 1. Editorial.

[3] P. J. D. Wiles: *The Political Economy of Communism*, Oxford, 1962, p. 281.

carry the day in China. Six years later, in 1963, a Chinese economist complained, with examples, of 'lack of rigid, scientific criteria of classification' between the terms heavy and light industry.[1]

Basic industries are defined as that part of heavy industry which produces 'the material basis for the development of industry, especially of heavy industry'. Basic industries include mining and timber, metallurgical, chemical and building material industries and machine building for the equipment of heavy industry.[2]

For planning and statistical purposes, the distinction between large- and small-scale industrial enterprises depends, for those using mechanical power, on whether the number of employees is 16 or more; 31 or more in the case of those enterprises without mechanical power. Independent power plants (i.e. those not forming part of any other economic accounting unit) are reckoned as large-scale enterprises if their generating capacity is 15 kW. or more, regardless of number of employees. The dividing line between small-scale industrial enterprises and individual handicrafts is drawn so that an undertaking counts as a unit of individual handicrafts if it depends mainly on the labour of one individual and his family and does not employ more than three hired workers and apprentices.[3]

Yet another classification (used in the following table) is between modern industry and handicrafts; this normally hinges on whether mechanical power is employed in the main operations.

The fluctuations in industry's proportionate contribution to net national product between 1952 and 1962 are estimated as follows:[4]

Per cent of Total Net National Product

	1952	1957	1960	1962
Modern Industry (Manufacturing, Mining and Public Utilities)*	11	20	35	15
Handicrafts	7	6	4	6
Agriculture	49	39	24	47
Other Sectors	33	35	37	32
	100	100	100	100

* Electricity, gas and water.

Between 1960 and 1962 net national product is reckoned to have fallen by a third.[5]

Within the industrial sector, estimates of the contribution of different types of industry are shown as follows:[6]

---

[1] *Economic Research (Jingji Yanjiu)*, No. 4, April 1963, p. 16. Wang Hu-sheng: 'Problems in the Classification of Heavy and Light Industry.'

[2] *Kuang Ming Daily (Guangming Ribao)*, February 22, 1965, p. 4. Hu Feng-chi: 'Why Should the Development of Basic Industries be Further Speeded Up?'

[3] *Simple Explanation of Terms* . . . p. 2.

[4] Derived from Y. L. Wu, F. P. Hoeber, and M. M. Rockwell: *The Economic Potential of Communist China*, Vol. I. Menlo Park, California, 1963, p. 241.

[5] Ibid.   [6] Ibid., p. 233 (derived).

Per cent of total Net Value added in Industrial Sector

	1952	1957	1960	1962
Modern Manufacturing Industry	49	63	67	55
Public Utilities	3	4	6	3
Mining	11	11	15	12
Handicrafts	37	22	12	30
	100	100	100	100

Estimates for output of certain major products are as shown on p. 143 (as few official statistics have been published since the Great Leap, estimates of foreign observers have had to be used for more recent years).

During the First Five Year Plan period, industrialization was the paramount economic aim, with priority given to the development of heavy industry. This accorded with the early Soviet pattern which regarded industrial growth as a prerequisite of agricultural improvement. At this time, large capital intensive factories and mines were preferred over small labour intensive enterprises. Considerable Soviet aid in the form of plants and equipment financed by loan, and of technical advice, helped to make this programme possible. By 1958 impatience set in with the slow rate at which industrialization would be realized by these means, and it was decided to embark on a drive for small-scale rural industry, notably small iron and steel furnaces, while continuing to build modern industrial plants: the policy of 'walking on two legs'. At the same time, greater effort was to be put into agriculture in an attempt to raise output by cheap methods, among which ideological enthusiasm ranked high, without waiting on the growth of heavy industry. Agricultural problems had come sufficiently to the fore by the autumn of 1959 for 'the speedy development of agriculture' to be put on an equal footing with 'priority for heavy industry' as national aims. In 1960 agriculture was accorded the first priority while industry's foremost task was to come to its aid by providing machinery, tools, fertilizers and consumer goods as well as training in mechanical skills. Even more emphasis was given to this policy in the succeeding two years, while, in view of the cut in capital investment, light industry—especially that based on non-farm raw materials—was to have priority over heavy industry. The relative facility with which plants for the manufacture of chemical fertilizer and of agricultural machinery can be adapted to the production of military supplies and equipment, may have been a factor in winning acceptance for the switch in favour of industries auxiliary to agriculture.

The reason behind the change in the relative priorities of industry and agriculture was partly the grave difficulties caused by the bad harvests of 1959–61 (which had necessitated heavy imports of grain) and partly the fact that industrial growth required a parallel increase of farm output to provide raw materials for many branches of light industry as well as for exports to make possible the import of capital equipment. The check to industrial development caused by the withdrawal of Soviet assistance in 1960 must have been a contributory factor in this reversal of policy. When, towards the end of 1963, the worst of the agricultural crisis had passed, a slight modification of priorities was signalled by the slogan 'agriculture as the foundation and

	Unit	1953	1957	1958	1959	1960	1961	1962	1963	1964	1965
Steel	million metric tons	1·77[1]	5·35[1]	11·08[1] (8·00 modern)	13·35[2]	18·45[2]	11–12[3]	7–8[3]	8–9[3]	10[3] 9·5[4]	12[3]
Chemical Fertilizers (Nitrogen content)	million metric tons	0·25[5]	0·87[5]	1·46[5]	1·78[5]	2·00[5]	1·45[5]	2·17[5]	2·92[5]	3·40–3·60[9]	4·5[6]
Cement	million metric tons	3·88[7]	6·86[7]	9·3[7]	12·27[8]	13·5[9]		6·0[9]	7·0[9]	8·0[9] 11·5[4]	
Lorries	thousand units		7·5[9]	16·0[9]		29·0[9]		3–5[9]	10–15[9]	20–25[9]	

[1] *Ten Great Years*, Peking, 1960, p. 95.
[2] *Peking Review*, March 24, 1961, p. 16. Chu Chi-lin: 'The Great Victory in Steel.'
[3] *Far Eastern Economic Review*, March 31, 1966, p. 623. H. Munthe-Kaas: 'China's Steel.'
[4] *1965 Yearbook of The Great Soviet Encyclopaedia* (in Russian), Moscow, 1965, p. 283.
[5] *China Quarterly*, No. 24, October–December 1965, p. 32. Jung-chao Liu: 'Fertilizer Application in Communist China.'
[6] *Far Eastern Economic Review*, February 3, 1966, p. 154. However, a Chinese source has stated that output of chemical fertilizer in 1965 was 3 million tons more than in 1964. NCNA Peking, June 6, 1966.
[7] *Ten Great Years*, p. 96.
[8] *Peking Review*, April 5, 1960, p. 6. Li Fu-ch'un, Chairman of the State Planning Commission: 'Report on the Draft 1960 National Economic Plan.'
[9] *Current Scene*, Vol. III, No. 17, April 15, 1965, p. 10. (The 1960 figures have appended to them the note that they represent a 'Great Leap' claim and should be heavily discounted.

industry the leading factor'. Those sectors of heavy industry which directly served agriculture, notably chemical fertilizers and agricultural machinery, were expanded. These policies were confirmed in 1964–5. While the order of priority was still 'agriculture, light industry, and heavy industry', heavy industry was to provide increasing quantities of means of production to agriculture and to light industry. Therefore it was considered essential to speed up the development of heavy industry and, first and foremost, of the basic industries.[1]

2. LOCATION OF INDUSTRY

The concentration of modern industry in Shanghai, Tientsin and the former Manchuria, where it developed under foreign protection, had long rankled with patriotic Chinese, The Communists determined from the first, from motives of economics, sentiment, and strategy, to effect a more widespread industrial distribution. The majority of large new industrial projects of the First Five Year Plan were located in the interior where Wuhan, Paotow, Chungking, Lanchow, Taiyuan[2] and Loyang grew into sizeable centres of heavy industry. Encouragement was also given to light industry to develop inland, near sources of raw materials and markets for finished goods. Some manufacturing enterprises from Shanghai, with their equipment and skilled workers, were even moved to remote provinces such as Kwangsi and Ninghsia. As a result of all these efforts, the provinces of the interior (that is excluding the seven coastal provinces) were reported to produce over a third of the country's gross industrial output by value in 1958 compared with less than a quarter in 1949.[3]

The balance of industrialization, however, still lay heavily in favour of the coastal areas. By 1956–7 it had come to be realized that quicker returns could be gained by making full use of their long-established manufacturing facilities which had been somewhat neglected during the First Five Year Plan period. The development of the interior, still regarded as highly desirable, was acknowledged to be essentially a long-term proposition.[4] While the simpler forms of manufacture could be developed in every part of China, the importance of Shanghai and the eastern cities in the more highly skilled branches of industry was no longer overlooked. In the mid 1960s, policy appears to have been to give these 'old industrial bases' priority for industrial investment.[5] Shanghai added important steel, machine-building and chemical

[1] *Peking Review*, January 1, 1965, p. 10. Chou En-lai: Report on the Work of the Government at the 1st Session of the 3rd National People's Congress.

[2] This development in Taiyuan had begun under the war lord Yen Hsi-shan in the 1930s. See *Journal of Asian Studies*, Vol. XXIV, No. 2, February 1965, pp. 245–59. D. G. Gillan: 'China's First Five Year Plan: Industrialization Under the Warlords as Reflected in the Policies of Yen Hsi-shan in Shansi Province 1930–7.'

[3] *Ten Great Years*, p. 49.

[4] *The Eighth National Congress of the Communist Party of China*, Vol. II, Speeches. Peking, 1956, pp. 296–7, and *Planned Economy* (*Jihua Jingji*), No. 8, August 1957, pp. 13–14. Yang Ch'ing-wen: 'Two Problems of Industrial Location', and *New China Fortnightly* (*Xinhua Banyuekan*), No. 99, January 10, 1957, pp. 70–1.

[5] *People's Daily* (*Renmin Ribao*), July 20, 1964, p. 5. Ch'en Pao-sen: 'A Preliminary Discussion of the Renewal and Technical Transformation of the Equipment of Industrial Enterprises.'

industries to its former textile and consumer goods manufactures. By 1962 heavy industry accounted for around half of Shanghai's total industrial output.[1]

General policy on industrial location is, of course, the responsibility of the Central Government which, owing to its control over 'above-norm' capital projects,[2] has direct charge of the construction of major industrial bases. The First Five Year Plan provided for some 530 of the planned 825 'above-norm' projects to be located in the interior.[3] The organ of the Central Government which is charged with questions of industrial location, is probably that which controls investment plans, i.e. the State Construction Commission. This is borne out by the fact that in March 1959, Ch'en Yün, then head of the State Construction Commission, wrote in *Red Flag* on the distribution of industry.[4] For smaller projects, the central government appears to determine only general policy, leaving details to local authorities. Thus, when factories from Shanghai moved to Kwangsi, it was the Kwangsi Department of Light Industry which decided their locations within that region.[5]

3. INDUSTRIAL OWNERSHIP AND CONTROL

By the end of 1956 virtually no industrial enterprises larger than workshops licitly remained under private control.[6] Around two-thirds of China's industry, by value of total output, belonged wholly to the state, while almost all the rest was under joint state-private ownership, except for the 2 per cent owned by co-operatives.[7] Foreign factories and plants had suffered severely in the war and never regained their former position. Within a few years after the Communists came to power all were squeezed out by various forms of pressure: one last woollen mill remained under British management until 1959.

Industry under state ownership inherited by the Communists in 1949 from their Nationalist predecessors, accounted for more than a third of industrial output by value in that year; much of this consisted of confiscated ex-enemy assets, mainly Japanese plants in Manchuria (although these had been despoiled of much of their equipment by Soviet forces immediately after the war), north China and Shanghai. These assets included all the non-ferrous metal and petroleum undertakings, almost all the iron and steel concerns and two-thirds of the electric power capacity; a substantial share of the country's coal mining, shipping, cement and textiles were also comprised in this legacy. (State-owned industry, in the days of the Kuomintang—as of the Communists

[1] *Peking Review*, October 9, 1964, p. 20. Ts'ao Ti-ch'iu: 'Shanghai—Growth of a Socialist Industrial Centre.'
[2] See p. 473 below.
[3] *Planned Economy (Jihua Jingji)*, No. 8, August 1957, p. 13. Yang Ch'ing-wen: loc. cit.
[4] *Red Flag (Hongqi)*, No. 5, March 1, 1959, pp. 2–8. Ch'en Yün: 'Some Important Problems in Capital Investment at the Present Time.'
[5] NCNA Nanning, January 29, 1962.
[6] *Ten Great Years*, p. 38. In Sinkiang, 'socialist transformation' of private enterprise was not completed until 1958. (NCNA Urumchi, September 21, 1965.) This may have been true of other remote areas as well. However, no sizeable private industrial enterprises are likely to have existed in such parts of the country.
[7] *People's Handbook (Renmin Shouce) 1958*, p. 23. Li Fu-ch'un: 'Report on Achievements of Our First Five Year Plan and Future Tasks and Aims of Socialist Constructions.'

—included enterprises under provincial and other local authority ownership, as well as under the central government.) In addition to these enterprises wholly under state ownership, in 1949 official control extended over a further 10 per cent of industry (by value of output), either through state participation in capital, or by virtue of private firms depending on state contracts.

Private industry existing in 1949 was augmented by a flood of enterprise unleashed by the ending of the civil war in that year. Large numbers of privately owned undertakings—including iron foundries, machine-building plants and coal mines—were established in the period 1949–53, while existing private concerns expanded.[1] Private industry in China was usually under some form of personal ownership.

Forms of pressure used by the Communists in the early days of the regime to expand the category of joint state-private ownership included the 'five antis' campaign,[2] while the giving of orders to private industry by state commerce and state contracts for processing state-supplied raw materials were other means used to integrate private concerns closely with the state sector.[3]

At first the transformation to joint state-private ownership[4] was made enterprise by enterprise, but in 1956 whole trades and branches of industry, locality by locality, were changed in batches from private to joint ownership. Specialized local state-owned corporations were established to promote 'socialist transformation' in different branches of industry, as well as in commerce, transport, communications, and service trades.[5] By the end of 1956, when, as we have seen, the process was effectively completed (except for illegal concerns), enterprises with private capital totalling more than ¥2,000 million had been turned into joint state-private concerns.[6] Another change dating from 1956 was the substitution of fixed interest, generally 5 per cent per annum, on shares representing the private assets, in place of the dividends previously paid to the former owners.[7] These interest payments were supposed to terminate in 1962 but were renewed for a further three years, after which

[1] Hsü Ti-hsin: *An Analysis of China's Economy in the Transitional Period* (in Chinese). Revised Edition. Peking, 1959, p. 270, and P. Schran: *The Structure of Income in Communist China* (unpublished Ph.D Thesis. University of California, 1961.) pp. 78–80.

[2] A campaign launched early in 1952 against bribery of officials, tax evasion, theft of state assets, fraud in fulfilling state contracts, and theft of official secrets. The charges were so framed that few firms escaped. Offenders were heavily fined; this depleted their resources, and forced them to accept capital from the state. This campaign, aimed at private enterprise, followed the 'three antis' campaign, which was directed against state concerns and officials. See Y. L. Wu: *An Economic Survey of Communist China*, New York, 1956, pp. 228–9.

[3] Kuan Ta-t'ung: *The Socialist Transformation of Capitalist Industry and Commerce in China*, Peking, 1960, pp. 59–60.

[4] Provisional regulations on organization, management, and operations of joint state-private industrial enterprises, promulgated in 1954, are given in *New China Monthly* (*Xinhua Yuebao*), No. 60, October 1954, pp. 233–4.

[5] *New Construction* (*Xin Jianshe*), No. 2, February 1957, p. 12. Wang Hung-ting: 'The Nature and Functions of Specialized Industrial Companies', and Kuan Ta-t'ung: op. cit., p. 87.

[6] *Finance* (*Caizheng*), No. 18, September 24, 1959, p. 20. Jung Tze-ho, Vice-Minister of Finance: 'China's Finance in the Past Ten Years.'

[7] Kuan Ta-t'ung: op. cit., pp. 86–7. On the pre-1956 system of dividends to former owners, see ibid., p. 70.

their continuance was to be further considered.[1] The rate of interest, while nominally constant at 5 per cent per annum, appears in effect to have been lowered to 3¼ per cent in 1957; possibly this was done by reassessing the capital stock values, thus nominally retaining the 5 per cent rate unchanged.[2] After the fixed interest system was introduced, the joint state-private undertakings were made subject to the financial discipline applicable to state-owned enterprises, the remaining profits, apart from certain deductions, being remitted to the state.[3] In the mid-1960s, there were reported to be around a quarter of a million ex-capitalist recipients of dividends in China.[4] One reason for continuing to pay interest to former capitalists may be that it provides evidence which can easily be pointed out to show that classes, and therefore class struggle, still exist.[5]

In many cases the former owners were retained as managers of joint state-private enterprises in order to benefit from their experience and technical knowledge; their position, however, was very weak. Individual businesses were frequently amalgamated or brought together under some degree of common control, sometimes being grouped under the specialized corporations, already mentioned, 'equivalent to trusts, but of a socialist nature'.[6] The management of joint state-private concerns became progressively assimilated to that of state-owned enterprises, and in 1960 an authoritative work from Peking stated that 'these joint enterprises have become state enterprises owned by the whole people, except for the fixed interest paid by the state to the holders of private shares'.[7] In this context, state-private ownership is put forward as a device for transforming existing private enterprise. Reports, however, tell of new undertakings, notably restaurants, founded (in the early 1960s) as joint undertakings from their first establishment and here the private element appears to be more prominent. However, no example has come to our knowledge of any industrial concern recently founded on a joint state-private basis.

Two organizations are specifically engaged in the control of joint state-private undertakings. The first is the Central Administration for Industry and Commerce, an official organ of government directly under the State Council, and which also has other duties; the second is the All-China Federation of Industry and Commerce, the membership of which comprises the former private owners of the joint enterprises. In addition, to facilitate the manage-

---

[1] *Peking Review*, April 20, 1962, p. 6. 'Press Communique on the National People's Congress.' Nothing more has been heard about this matter at time of writing, although in 1966, in the 'great socialist cultural revolution', the discontinuance of these interest payments was demanded.

[2] P. Schran: op. cit., p. 97.

[3] *Finance (Caizheng)*, No. 19, October 9, 1959, p. 18. Chen Chi, An Pai-k'ang and Liu Hsing-san: 'A Review of Honan's Finance in the Past Ten Years.'

[4] Private communication to the author.

[5] For an example of this use, see Intelligence Bureau, Ministry of Defence, Taiwan (ed.): *The Collected Documents Obtained by the Anti-Communist Guerrillas in the Raid on Lienchiang, Fukien* (in Chinese), Taipei, 1964. (*The Lienchiang Papers*), p. 29.

[6] *Study (Xuexi)*, No. 1, January 1956, p. 7. Hsü Ti-hsin: 'Advance the Transformation of Capitalist Industry and Commerce to a New Stage.'

[7] Hsüeh Mu-ch'iao, Su Hsing and Lin Tse-li: *The Socialist Transformation of the National Economy in China*, Peking, 1960, p. 226.

ment of large numbers of formerly private concerns, certain changes in central government ministries were made in 1956, in which the Ministry of Local Industry and the Third Ministry of Machine Building were abolished and their work parcelled out among more specialized industrial ministries, both new and old.[1] It should be noted that joint state-private enterprises are more important in some parts of the country (for example, Shanghai) where private industry was formerly prominent than in other parts (the north east for example) where this was not the case.

The smaller private, as well as co-operative industrial ventures, of which great numbers still exist in China, will be discussed in Chapter 8.

Overall direction of industry is in the hands of the State Council's Office of Industry and Communications, under Po I-po. This office was formed in 1959 by a merger of the former Third, Fourth and Sixth General Offices, which had dealt respectively with heavy industry, light industry and transport and communications. In the Party headquarters, however, industrial work and communications work still form separate departments. The Director of the Party Industrial Work Department is Li Hsueh-feng, who also holds the position of First Secretary of the North China Party Regional Bureau and First Secretary of the Peking Municipal Party Committee. Alongside the Central Committee's two separate Work Departments for Industry and for Communications, there now also exists under the Central Committee, a combined Industry and Communications Political Department, of which Ku Mu is Director.

Control of industrial enterprises in China is divided between the industrial ministries of the central government and the corresponding organs of local authorities. Before 1957–8, the industrial ministries of the central government (such as the Ministry of Light Industry, the Ministry of Textiles, and others which will be mentioned below) exercised from Peking direct control over great numbers of individual factories and mines all over China. Permission from the ministries, to quote one instance, was required before these enterprises acquired fixed property of more than ¥200 in value.[2] This centralization may have been necessary in the early years of the regime, among other reasons because of administrative weakness at the provincial level. Nor did it pose such problems as later because, in 1949, there were only 3,145 state and joint state-private industrial enterprises; by the beginning of 1958 the total number of sufficient importance to be entered in state plans was 60,000.[3] Not all of these were directly controlled by the central ministries, many being even then under local authorities. However, the increased numbers of enterprises under central control overstrained the administrative apparatus and had an inhibiting effect on development. The Soviet Union had shortly before put into effect far-reaching changes in economic administration. This may have influenced Chinese developments, although the obvious requirements of the situation in China were almost certainly of greater moment and the topic

---

[1] *Collected Laws and Regulations of the People's Republic of China* (in Chinese), Vol. 3, pp. 80–1.

[2] *People's Daily* (*Renmin Ribao*), November 18, 1957, p. 1. Editorial.

[3] *Economic Research* (*Jingji Yanjiu*), No. 3, March 1958, p. 33. Ch'en Ta-lun: 'The Change in Our Country's Industrial Administrative System.'

had been mooted in public since 1956. In any case, the form which the Chinese reorganization took was different from that in the Soviet Union. In the Soviet Union the territorial principle was substituted for the production branch principle, the industrial ministries were abolished and control of most enterprises was handed over to new regional economic councils, the *sovnarkhozy*; while in China the central government's industrial ministries were retained, although direct control over many enterprises was handed over to the corresponding provincial departments.

These industrial ministries must now be detailed. Particulars of the many changes in number and name which they have undergone may be seen in Appendix 3. In February 1958, consequent on the decentralization decrees and the reduction in the number of enterprises under central control, the number of industrial ministries, through amalgamations, was reduced by seven.[1]

In broad terms three ministries—Textiles and the two Ministries of Light Industry—now supervise the production of most consumer goods, while heavy industry falls under twelve ministries; the eight ministries of Machine Building, and the Ministries of Metallurgy, Chemical Industry, Construction Engineering and Building Materials.

The Ministry of Textiles is responsible for manufacture of all types of textiles: cotton, wool, silk, coarse fibres and synthetic; in 1956 it took over those textile enterprises formerly under the Ministry of Local Industry. The Ministry of Textiles also engages in the production of textile machinery.

Virtually all manufactured consumer goods, other than textiles, are the responsibility of the Ministries of Light Industry. In 1956 the Ministry of Light Industry (there only being one at the time) assumed responsibility for all undertakings, other than textile mills and food processing plants, that had previously been controlled by the Ministry of Local Industry; in 1958 it also absorbed the Ministry of Food Industry.[2] In 1965, the Central General Bureau of Handicraft Industry, which had at one time been controlled by the Ministry of Light Industry, was abolished and simultaneously (presumably to replace it) a second Ministry of Light Industry was established.[3] The original Ministry—now named the First Ministry of Light Industry—has a wide range of interests which include paper, soap, matches, rubber shoes, bicycles, sewing machines, crockery and porcelain, pots and pans, socks, leather goods, watches and clocks, salt, certain other chemicals such as alcohol, glycerol and some fertilizers and insecticides (based on waste products of food factories), processed foodstuffs including sugar, oils and fats and a host of other

---

[1] Those suppressed as separate ministries were the Ministries of Building Materials and Urban Construction (merged with the Ministry of Construction Engineering); the then Second Ministry of Machine Building and the Ministry of Electrical Equipment (absorbed by the First Ministry of Machine Building); the Ministry of Food Industry (amalgamated with the Ministry of Light Industry); the Ministry of Electric Power (amalgamated with the Ministry of Water Conservancy to form the Ministry of Water Conservancy and Electric Power) and the Ministry of Forestry Industry (amalgamated with the Ministry of Forestry). *Collected Laws and Regulations*... Vol. 7, p. 61.

[2] *People's Handbook* (*Renmin Shouce*) *1959*, p. 257, and *Collected Laws and Regulations*... Vol. 3, p. 81.

[3] *Ta Kung Daily* (*Dagong Bao*), Peking, February 21, 1965, p. 1.

miscellaneous articles, some of which—such as certain types of paper and chemicals—come into the category of producer goods.[1]

By 1956 the former Ministry of Heavy Industry had grown unwieldy and was abolished, its duties being divided among the newly-established Ministries of Metallurgy, Chemical Industry and of Building Materials.[2] The Ministry of Metallurgy is responsible for the processing of iron and steel, aluminium, tin and other metals up to the intermediate stage; its sphere also covers most mining operations except for coal and petroleum.[3]

The scope of the Ministry of Chemical Industry includes chemical fertilizers, industrial chemicals, plastics, synthetic rubber, the more general aspects of natural rubber manufacture (as distinct from the production of specific articles which come under the First Ministry of Light Industry) and pharmaceuticals. Before May 1956 the Ministry of Light Industry had controlled both the rubber and the pharmaceutical industries.[4]

In February 1958 the Ministry of Construction Engineering, established in 1952, absorbed the Ministries of Building Materials and of Urban Construction (which included town planning), both dating from 1956.[5] In 1965 the Ministry of Building Materials was revived, a step presumably influenced by the resumption of capital investment at that time.

Responsibility for the production of machinery rests in the main with the eight Ministries of Machine Building. Other ministries, including Communications, Railways, Coal, Petroleum, Textiles and Construction Engineering, engage in certain activities in this line ancillary to their principal functions.

The Ministries of Machine Building have a tangled history, of which the outlines may be traced in Appendix 3. The official announcements of the establishment, amalgamations and revivals of these several ministries never state their respective functions which have, therefore, been the subject of considerable detective work by foreign observers. The responsibilities of the eight Ministries of Machine Building may be surmised to have been as follows in the autumn of 1966:

First Ministry of Machine Building: Civilian machinery of most types, including motor vehicles, electrical and transport equipment, mining and other heavy machinery, machine tools (excluding agricultural machinery).
Second Ministry of Machine Building: Nuclear weapons.
Third Ministry of Machine Building: Conventional armaments, not otherwise covered.
Fourth Ministry of Machine Building: Communications equipment (military and civilian).
Fifth Ministry of Machine Building: Artillery equipment.
Sixth Ministry of Machine Building: Naval shipbuilding.
Seventh Ministry of Machine Building: Military aircraft.
Eighth Ministry of Machine Building: Agricultural machinery.

[1] *Red Flag* (*Hongqi*), No. 6, March 16, 1961, pp. 9–17. K'ung Hsiang-chen, Vice-Minister of Light Industry: 'A Short Cut Solution of the Raw Material Supply Problem of Light Industry.'
[2] *Collected Laws and Regulations* ... Vol. 3, pp. 80–1.
[3] See p. 247 below.
[4] *Collected Laws and Regulations* ... Vol. 3, p. 81.
[5] Ibid., Vol. 7, p. 61.

Ministers, vice-ministers, and their immediate subordinates in the industrial ministries usually appear to be non-technical men, but the levels next below these are frequently staffed by technologists, often trained in the Soviet Union or elsewhere abroad.

In addition to the industrial enterprises controlled by the industrial ministries and their local counterparts are those under the aegis of non-industrial ministries and organs. These include the processing and other plants run by the Ministries of Commerce, Food, Foreign Trade, Aquatic Products and Forestry,[1] the machine-building enterprises already mentioned of various transport, mining, construction and other ministries, the factories under the Overseas Chinese investment corporations,[2] and those operated by institutions of higher learning.[3] Industrial undertakings under the People's Liberation Army include iron and steel, cement, tools and spare parts:[4] these are apparently distinct from and additional to factories controlled by those Ministries of Machine Building engaged on military work. The Ministry of State Farms and Land Reclamation may perhaps be the controlling ministry for the factories and plants operated by the PLA Construction Corps in Sinkiang,[5] although this is uncertain.

The existence of this, in aggregate, considerable amount of industrial activity outside the industrial ministries is one aspect of the tendency to verticalization—to building up self-contained enterprises and empires—which we shall consider below. The result is that many products may be made in enterprises controlled by one of several different ministries. While duplication may lead to waste, it can introduce an element of competition into the economy.[6] In passing, it can be hazarded that statistics for the output of commodities ancillary to the main function of the ministry or other organ controlling their production, may be less complete and less accurate than those for production of the same type of goods by the ministry primarily responsible for them.

The reform of the industrial management system, decreed in November 1957, had two declared objectives: to increase the power of major local authorities in the management of industry by handing over to their control many enterprises previously managed by the industrial ministries of the central government and by giving these authorities a bigger role in the allocation of materials;[7] and secondly to give more autonomy to enterprises by reducing

---

[1] *Collected Laws and Regulations* . . . Vol. 7, p. 322, and *People's Handbook (Renmin Shouce) 1959*, p. 361, and p. 121 above.

[2] See Appendix I.

[3] *People's Daily (Renmin Ribao)*, February 1, 1965, p. 4, carries an advertisement for the products of the chemical factory of Nankai University, Tientsin.

[4] *Work Bulletin (Gongzuo Tongxun)*, January 1, 1961, p. 26.

[5] See p. 99 above. These were developed from scratch with local resources, e.g. 'The officers and men decided to get no new military hats for a year. Using the hat money they had saved they built the first group of small and simple factories.' *People's Daily (Renmin Ribao)*, October 14, 1963, p. 2.

[6] . . . 'the machines made by the Ministry of Railways and the Ministry of Fuel Industries were cheaper than those made by the First Ministry of Machine Building'. *Economic Research (Jingji Yanjiu)*, No. 3, June 1957, pp. 54–5. Fan Jo-yi: 'A Further Discussion of Price Policy for Products of Heavy Industry.'

[7] A tentative beginning of this policy had been made before 1957. *People's Handbook*

the number of their mandatory targets. As far as manufacturing industry was concerned, the decentralization was principally to affect factories making consumer goods. The major local authorities were to take over most of the undertakings formerly controlled by the Ministry of Light Industry. The regulations stated that for the time being only a small number of textile enterprises were to be decentralized; however, by June 1958 all factories in the textile industry were said to have been handed down.[1]

Most plants of importance in the producer goods industries were by the decree of November 1957 to be retained under direct control of the central ministries. These included large-scale metallurgical and chemical enterprises, oil refineries, large and important mining concerns, large power stations and electricity networks, factories making large and precision machines, electric motors and instruments, military equipment and other technically complex branches of industry. Apart from these, the decree laid down 'all other factories suitable for decentralization are gradually to be decentralized according to actual conditions'.[2] In the event, in heavy industry, too, the decentralization was reported in fact to have covered a wider range of plant than indicated by the original decree; excluded were only a few of large size, or of an experimental or other special character.[3]

Even enterprises still retained under the control of central ministries were to be subject to greater local influence. For these enterprises, 'the central-local dual leadership system' was to be followed, 'with the central authority as the main', while 'the leadership and supervision exercised by local authorities over these enterprises' was to be strengthened.[4] In other words, the production branch vertical (*t'iao t'iao*) links were to be paramount for these centrally controlled enterprises, but the local horizontal (*k'uai k'uai*) ties were to be stronger than before. Horizontal control came in the next few years to be identified with control by local Party committees and the strength of these ties seems to have increased over that period beyond what was originally envisaged in the decentralization decrees. This theme will be taken up again in our concluding chapter.

According to the Chinese press, decentralization proceeded with considerable rapidity for so large a change. Before the end of June 1958, some 80 per cent of the enterprises and institutions controlled in 1957 by the industrial ministries of the central government had been handed over to provinces,

---

(*Renmin Shouce*) *1958*, p. 220. Li Hsien-nien, Minister of Finance: Report on Final Accounts for 1956 and Draft Budget for 1957, and *Finance* (*Caizheng*), No. 18, September 24, 1959, p. 21. Jung Tze-ho, Vice-Minister of Finance: loc. cit.

[1] *People's Daily* (*Renmin Ribao*) June 25, 1958, p. 1. Also by this date, all factories under the Ministry of Light Industry had been transferred except for five in, or connected with, paper manufacturing. A decree of April 1958 had laid down that decentralization was to be effected first in light industry and only later in heavy industry. *Collected Laws and Regulations* . . . Vol 7, p. 331.

[2] *Collected Laws and Regulations* . . . Vol. 6, p. 392. 'Those parts of construction enterprises which were engaged in civil engineering' were, according to the decree of November 1957, to be handed down to local authorities in many (unspecified) places. Ibid., Vol. 6, p. 392.

[3] *People's Daily* (*Renmin Ribao*), June 25, 1958, p. 1.

[4] *Collected Laws and Regulations* . . . Vol. 6, p. 392.

autonomous regions and directly-administered cities.[1] The proportion of industry decentralized by value of output, would have been much less than by number of enterprises, as the most important enterprises in capital goods industries, as well as some of the largest in other branches, were reserved to the central government.

Local authorities received all the profits of the enterprises that were formerly already under their control. The decree of November 1957 stipulated that profits of enterprises decentralized to them should be divided, 20 per cent going to the local authority concerned and 80 per cent to the central government. This provision was expanded to state that all enterprises formerly under central government ministries might divide profits with local authorities in the same proportion, except for those enterprises under the Second Ministry of Machine Building, the Ministry of Posts and Telecommunications, the Ministry of Railways, departments of civil aviation, inter-provincial coastal and Yangtze shipping concerns, oil mining and refining, large mines, metallurgical and chemical plants, extensive power networks, big motor electrical machinery factories and the Ministry of Foreign Trade's overseas sales organs—all these were to pay their whole profits to the central government and not to divide them with local authorities. In those enterprises in which local authorities were entitled to share profits, the 20:80 ratio for their division was to remain unchanged for three years. No information is available about the ratio obtaining from 1961 onwards.[2]

In the following month, December 1957, another decree elaborated the regulations on the division of enterprises' revenue for the year 1958. This 20:80 division, it was now stated, was to apply not only to profits but also to basic depreciation funds and to the income arising from price changes of fixed assets (e.g. on the sale of capital assets at above book value).[3] This time the list was given of ministries whose enterprises were to divide profits. This was followed by a long list of categories and individual enterprises which were to be exceptions to this rule and were to continue to remit all revenues to the central government.[4] However, should any enterprise on the excepted list

---

[1] *People's Daily* (*Renmin Ribao*), June 25, 1958, p. 1.
[2] *Collected Laws and Regulations* ... Vol 6, p. 394.
[3] Ibid., Vol. 7, p. 224, and Ko Chih-ta: *China's Budgets during the Transition Period* (in Chinese), Peking, 1957, pp. 82–3.
[4] The list of ministries whose enterprises (both state-owned and joint state-private) were to divide revenues, reads as follows: Ministry of Metallurgy, First Ministry of Machine Building, Ministries of Electric Power, of Chemical Industry, of Building Materials, of Electrical Equipment, of Petroleum, of Coal, of Forestry Industry, of Textiles, of Light Industry, of State Farms and Land Reclamation, of Food Industry, of Commerce, of Urban Services, and of Aquatic Products. Also to divide profits were the food processing enterprises under the Ministry of Food, the home sales side of the Ministry of Foreign Trade, and the Medicinal Materials Corporation of the Ministry of Health. The list of those not to divide revenues with local authorities covered the construction units controlled by the construction contracting enterprises internal to each ministry, the surveying units of the Ministry of Geology; the Ministry of Metallurgy's large iron and steel enterprises at Anshan, Penhsi, Taiyuan and Shihchingshan; the First Ministry of Machine Building's Changchun Motor Plant and five named engine works under the same ministry, four specified power grids under the Ministry of Electric Power, the Ministry of Chemical Industry's large chemical works, the extracting and refining enterprises of the Ministry of Petroleum, three named large engine works coming under the Ministry of Electrical Equipment,

later be handed down to the control of a local authority, division of profits would then apply to it.[1] Provincial level authorities might share their proportion of the profits with lower local authorities.[2]

The municipalities of Peking, Tientsin and Shanghai, and the province of Liaoning were deemed to have sufficient revenues already, so that the stipulated division of revenues was not to apply in their case.[3]

The upshot of all these regulations of November and December 1957 would seem to be that division of profits between central and local authorities was to apply to a wider range of enterprises than was originally intended to be affected by decentralization. Perhaps this was one factor which led to the scope of decentralization within the next few months apparently being, as we have noted, wider than at first laid down. More recently, however, the trend may have gone the other way. At the beginning of 1965, the First Ministry of Light Industry (which in 1958 had transferred almost all its enterprises to local authorities) was reported to have under its direct control sixteen concerns in North East China alone.[4]

The relative positions of central ministries and provincial authorities after the regulations of November 1957 is difficult to gauge with any precision. Some of the wording, notably on local influence over central enterprises, is vague; purposefully no doubt, in order to permit wide latitude of interpretation to fit differing situations. The extent of provincial autonomy in respect of enterprises handed down to them, and the degree of provincial authority over those still under central ministries, must depend on the ministries and provinces concerned, on intra-party tensions, on the enterprises, the matters at issue and the personalities involved. The fact that two provinces and one autonomous region (Yunnan, Kweichow and Ninghsia—all among the more backward parts of China) were temporarily excepted from taking over certain coal mines from central ministries on the grounds that their administration was not yet competent to do so,[5] suggests that among the other provinces and equivalent authorities, there may be a wide variation in efficiency, as might be expected in so vast a country.

Leading on from these considerations is the question of what role remains to the industrial ministries, especially those such as the Ministries of Textiles and of Light Industry, which have (or at one time had) lost direct control of almost all their productive enterprises. A pronouncement of April 1958 said that in future some 30–40 per cent of the duties of central industrial ministries would be concerned with national plans, the direct control of large enter-

---

thirty-four listed mines of the Ministry of Coal, together with five engine and machine works of the same Ministry, the commercial enterprises under the Ministry of Food, the foreign sales side of the Ministry of Foreign Trade and any enterprise operating on a planned loss, regardless of which ministry it came under. Surplus working capital remitted back by any enterprise was also not subject to division. *Collected Laws and Regulations* . . . Vol. 7.

[1] Ibid.
[2] Ibid., p. 227.
[3] Ibid., p. 225.
[4] *Economic Research (Jingji Yanjiu)*, No. 2, Feb. 1966, p. 42. T'ung Wan: 'The Problem of Fixed Point Supply of Third Category Raw Materials for Enterprises in Light Industry.'
[5] *People's Daily (Renmin Ribao)*, June 25, 1958, p. 1.

prises and the promotion of scientific research, while the remaining 60–70 per cent would consist of helping local authorities to manage their enterprises efficiently, especially in such ways as supplying technical materials, giving guidance in technical specifications and in the training of technical personnel, and spreading the knowledge of advanced experience.[1] A few months later, in June 1958, an editorial in the *People's Daily* argued that while the direct burden on central ministries had been lightened, their responsibilities for socialist construction in general had become heavier. Ministries had now to 'concentrate their energy on overall planning, organize nation-wide co-ordination and balancing ... manage "experimental plots", keep a firm grip on key enterprises, draw conclusions from and publicize advanced experience, organize research in and application of new techniques and effectively guide and raise technical levels'.[2] They are also supposed to exercise a general supervisory role over their respective industries and to conduct investigations.[3] As we shall see later, the industrial ministries have the function of distributing bonuses and a share of profits among enterprises, of allocating machinery and equipment specific to the industries with which they are concerned, while in 1961 they were made the channel through which 80 per cent of fixed quota working capital has passed from the Ministry of Finance to enterprises.[4] In addition the ministries were to be the organs to which provinces and equivalent local authorities applied for allocations of raw materials for enterprises within their areas. Their part in economic planning will be examined later.

As the June 1958 editorial, quoted above, suggests, the central ministries have considerable responsibilities in the field of research and of higher technical developments. The research institutes of ministries undertake the more practical lines of research, leaving theoretical branches to institutes of research under the Academy of Sciences. Institutes of engineering design usually fall directly under the appropriate ministry. The shortage of competent scientists and designers was a major factor in causing these functions to be in large measure centralized at national level, at least in the early years; a wider dispersal was possible at a later date.[5] Even so, there were many types of designing which could not be done in China and for which Soviet and other East European aid was essential. During the First Five Year Plan period, foreign designs had to be used for projects representing half the investment made by eight industrial ministries.[6] Later the proportion of designing work accomplished in China rose considerably.

Among other responsibilities in the technical field assigned to ministries is that of nation-wide technical standards for their own branches of the economy.

[1] *Collected Laws and Regulations* ... Vol. 7, p. 332.
[2] *People's Daily* (*Renmin Ribao*), June 25, 1958, p. 1. Editorial.
[3] *Economic Research* (*Jingji Yanjiu*), No. 11, November 1958, p. 48. Lin Yün: 'The 1958 Reform of our Country's Financial Management System', Part 2.
[4] p. 423 below.
[5] *New China Monthly* (*Xinhua Yuebao*), No. 39, January 1953, p. 120, and *Planned Economy* (*Jihua Jingji*), No. 7, July 1958, pp. 8–9. Hsiao Lu: 'The Problem of Building Industrial Bases and the Balanced Development of Local Economies.' On this topic, see also *The China Mainland Review*, Vol I, No. 2, September 1965, pp. 1–9. Y. L. Wu: 'Expansion of the Chinese Research and Development Industry.'
[6] *New China Fortnightly* (*Xinhua Banyuekan*), No. 89, August 6, 1956, p. 148.

In the case of the most important technical standards of significance to the whole economy (the 'state standards'), after being drafted by the appropriate ministries, these had, by regulations of 1962, to be submitted, according to their type, either to the State Council or (for industrial and agricultural products) to the Commission for Science and Technology or (for civil engineering and construction) to the State Planning Commission (in 1962 there was no State Construction Commission) while the State Economic Commission and the Offices of the State Council for Finance and Trade, and for Agriculture and Forestry, are also concerned. For technical standards of somewhat lesser importance and limited to one industry or occupation ('ministry standards') the ministries had merely to report them to the Commission for Science and Technology or to the State Planning Commission. For all products and projects not covered by state and ministry standards, 'enterprise standards' are to be adopted. Rules governing these have to be enacted by the various ministries in conjunction with local authorities and then to be reported to the appropriate commission as for 'ministry' standards.[1]

The Commission for Science and Technology was formed in November 1958 by a merger between the State Technological Commission and the Commission for Scientific Planning. A few months previously the State Bureau of Weights and Measures had been put under the State Technological Commission, which had also been charged since its creation in 1956 with the application and popularization of technical knowledge, the provision of technical evidence, the formulation of five year and perspective plans for technical development, the unification of technical standards and the approval of industrial rules for new factories, the organization of experimental manufacture of new products, the fostering of international exchange and co-operation on technical matters, and in general with taking measures to raise China's technical level. Actual negotiations with foreign countries on technical exchanges and co-operation were, however, to be undertaken by the Ministry of Foreign Trade.[2]

An assessment of whether the measures of decentralization improved efficiency in either central ministries or in enterprises is difficult to make, partly because of the general lack of reliable information from China and also because over the next few years normal economic activity was superseded by the frenzy of the Great Leap and by the years of shortage and retrenchment that followed. Those branches of light industry not dependent on agricultural raw materials achieved notable increases in output in the years after decentralization and this may have been due in some measure to the fact that they were no longer closely controlled from Peking.[3]

Provinces and other local authorities down to the *hsien* have their own departments and bureaux of industry (*t'ing* and *chü*—or occasionally *ch'u*)[4] or, according to local circumstance, more specialized organs—of light industry, chemical industry, building engineering and so forth. Sometimes a provincial

---

[1] *People's Daily* (*Renmin Ribao*), December 16, 1962, p. 2.
[2] *Collected Laws and Regulations* . . . Vol. 3, p. 82. Ibid., Vol. 7, p. 64 and ibid., Vol. 8, p. 95.
[3] Choh-ming Li: *The Statistical System of Communist China*, Berkeley, 1962, p. 70.
[4] See p. 21 above.

department of industry will have under it administrative bureaux (*kuanli chü*) for special branches of industry and mining, such as coal, oil, or electric power. A local bureau of industry often has under it corporations (*kungsze*) each of which controls a group of factories. In this case each corporation plays a large part in the management of its factories, shifting labour between them as need arises and dividing among them the bonus fund which would accrue in the first instance in the form of an overall sum to the corporation. However, the scene in China by the mid-1960s is subject to sharp local variations. While in some provinces and municipalities the organization is three-tiered as just described, with bureaux of industry, corporations and factories, other places have abolished one of these tiers. In some cases it is the bureaux that have been done away with, in others the corporations.[1]

In 1959 a visitor to China reported that policy making and planning in provincial departments of industry was in the hands of executive committees, the majority of members being political people with the addition of certain specialists (e.g. designers, production men, construction men, perhaps economists, etc.). The day to day technical work would be undertaken by the expert members of this body.[2] These provincial departments have directly under them the larger productive enterprises in their areas, other than those controlled by the central ministries. Smaller concerns fall under the industrial bureaux of lower local authorities, notably of *hsien* and of communes.

The regional, provincial, and other local Party committees also have bureaux of industry concerned with enterprises in their respective areas. One sequel of the transfer of control of an enterprise from a ministry of the central government to a local authority was to transfer immediate control of the enterprise's Party committee from the Party committee of the ministry to that of the local authority.[3] Thus, the decentralization of 1957-8 had the effect of greatly increasing the economic importance of provincial and other local Party committees and of their secretaries.

4. THE OPERATION OF ENTERPRISES

The nature of state-owned enterprises has already been reviewed.[4] It will be remembered that each enterprise, being an economic accounting unit, has its own fixed and working capital and that on capital invested in fixed assets (as defined on pp. 25-6 above), no interest is payable. Fixed capital, and part of working capital, derive from the state budget and the remainder of working capital from bank loans or ploughed back profits.[5] Sometimes several enterprises may be controlled by one corporation coming between the individual enterprise and its controlling ministry or local authority depart-

---

[1] I am indebted to Barry M. Richman, Chairman, Management and Industrial Relations Division, Graduate School of Business Administration, University of California, Los Angeles, for the information in the last five sentences.

[2] Private communication to the author.

[3] *People's Daily* (*Renmin Ribao*), April 7, 1960, p. 10. 'Long Live the Urban People's Communes.'

[4] See pp. 25-6 above.

[5] Allocation and control of capital investment will be treated in Chapter 17 and control of working capital in Chapter 15.

ment. Enterprises are under obligation to fulfil certain production and financial plans; while enterprises' annual plans constitute their formal plans as laid down by the state and usually attract most publicity, it is probably the quarterly—or sometimes monthly—plans that are operational.[1] The plans specify certain targets, or success indicators for the enterprises to attain. However, in China, even more perhaps than in the Soviet Union and East Europe, it is very difficult first to find targets which will produce desired results and then to enforce the fulfilment of plans. One problem has been that of getting accurate statistical returns from enterprises. Ch'en Yün, soon to be appointed Minister of Commerce, addressing the Eighth Congress of the CCP in 1956, realized these limitations. He stated that for most consumer goods, no detailed production plans were made; the plan only specified the value of their annual output, and for the ministries responsible, targets are set for cost reduction, for labour productivity, and for the amount of profits to be remitted to the treasury. Ch'en admitted that these plans were based on shaky statistical data and, when handed down to individual enterprises, led to concentration on the quantity and profit targets, to the neglect of consumer satisfaction. Therefore, he declared that in future 'these targets in the state plan should be taken merely as figures for reference. Factories manufacturing articles of daily use should be allowed to make their own production plans in the light of market conditions, without being tied down to the reference figures in the state plan. As for the profits to be handed over to the state treasury, the amount should be determined by the factories' actual receipts at the end of the year'.[2] This acceptance of practices which were not adopted in the Soviet Union until the following decade, and which are usually associated with Liberman's pioneering campaign, may be taken as one example of the short-lived Chinese 'revisionism' of 1956, soon to be swept away. On the other hand, Ch'en's statement might, with perhaps more truth, be considered a realistic acceptance of what the state was powerless to prevent. The Great Leap, with the chaos ensuing on the attempt to set targets for activities of all kinds, may be held to have proved Ch'en's views correct in this particular as in others.[3]

These reflections must be borne in mind when now we go on to consider formal regulations about enterprises' targets. In general it will be found that

---

[1] According to a decree of November 1957, ministries were to decide which enterprises' quarterly and monthly plans were to be determined by the ministries concerned or their subordinate bureaus, and which enterprises might be left to draw up these for themselves. These short-term plans were not included in the formal state plans. *Collected Laws and Regulations* . . . Vol. 6, p. 396. In 1964 we read that 'the plans for industrial enterprises distinguished according to duration are the long period plan, the annual plan, and the operational plan'. *Economic Research (Jingji Yanjiu)*, No. 7, July 1964, p. 14. Ma Wen-kuei: 'The Characteristics, Responsibilities and Methods of Planning for Socialist Industrial Enterprises.' For difficulties in the way of making annual plans operational, see J. Kornai: *Over-Centralization in Economic Administration*, London, 1959, pp. 2–17. The author writes of Hungary, but most of the difficulties he cites would be at least as great in China.

[2] *The Eighth National Congress of the Communist Party of China*, Vol. II. Speeches, pp. 173–4.

[3] Ch'en Yün was one of the relatively moderate men who came under a cloud during the Great Leap.

current economic circumstances and political atmosphere have a greater role in determining the significance of any type of target than has the existence of these formal regulations. When Ch'en spoke, enterprises were (despite his statement) officially subject to twelve mandatory targets which were not supposed to be changed without the consent of the State Council. The directive of November 1957 reduced these to four: the total quantitative output of major products, total number of employees, total wage bill, and profit.[1] (Some enterprises in China, as in the Soviet Union, operate on the basis of a 'planned loss'[2]. In such cases, fulfilment of the profits plan would consist in keeping losses down to the planned figure. In 1961, all industrial economic accounting units making losses were ordered to shut down;[3] later, however, they may have been permitted to operate again.) The other eight previously mandatory but henceforward (after 1957) non-mandatory targets were the total value of output, new varieties to be trial-manufactured, important technical and economic norms, rate of reduction of cost, amount of reduction of cost, number of manual workers at the end of the year, average wage and labour productivity. These non-mandatory targets were still to be entered into the plans, but the 1957 regulations permitted enterprises to amend them in the course of plan implementation. Industrial ministries and provincial level authorities might set additional mandatory targets.[4] Many instances have in fact occurred of such targets being used as determinants of enterprises' bonuses.

Quantitative targets have tended to engross attention in China, as at one time in the Soviet Union, to the detriment of other targets. While this was particularly the case during the Great Leap, the tendency continued despite official disapproval. Editorials in the *People's Daily* denouncing it in 1959 and 1960 insisted that plan fulfilment should cover all production targets, including those of quality, variety, and cost;[5] it will be noted that this list of targets does not coincide with the mandatory list of 1957, although no change in official regulations in the meantime has come to our notice. In the following years, when lack of raw materials often prevented fulfilment of output plans, it was increasingly realized that cost and profit targets provide subtler success indicators than quantity.[6] More will be said about this important train of thought. First, however, it must be noted that the modish success indicators in 1963 were 'fixed norms': labour norms, norms for use of raw material, fuel and equipment, quality norms, cost norms, norms for working capital and profits.[7] Some of these appear to be technical co-efficients. In

[1] *Collected Laws and Regulations* ... Vol. 6, p. 395.
[2] *Economic Research* (*Jingji Yanjiu*), No. 11, November 1962, p. 68. Chin Li: 'A Recent Discussion among Economists on Problems of Socialist Economic Accounting.'
[3] *Seventy Important Points of Communist Industrial Policy*, 1961. (From Taiwan source). No. 9.
[4] *Collected Laws and Regulations* ... Vol. 6, p. 395.
[5] *People's Daily* (*Renmin Ribao*), November 26, 1959, p. 1. Editorial, and ibid., July 21, 1960. In 1965, some still considered 'output to be a "rigid" target and quality a "soft" target.' *People's Daily* (*Renmin Ribao*), June 2, 1965, p. 1. Editorial.
[6] *People's Daily* (*Renmin Ribao*), July 19, 1962, p. 5. Yang Jun-jui and Li Hsün: 'A Tentative Discussion of Economic Accounting in Industrial Enterprises.'
[7] *Kuang Ming Daily* (*Guangming Ribao*), March 4, 1963, p. 4. Chang T'ing-tung: 'Fixed Norm Management in Industrial Production,' and *Ta Kung Daily* (*Dagong Bao*), Peking,

large enterprises, such as modern steel mills, such norms may be a feasible way of assessing a plant's performance, although not, apart from the profits norm, of deciding whether it is producing what is needed. But for great numbers of smaller concerns, using equipment of varying age and efficiency and a wide range of types and qualities of raw materials, it would be extremely complex and laborious to fix technical norms.

An economist, writing in 1964, stated that the composition of production, technical and financial plans varied with different industrial enterprises, but that these plans usually included the following nine items: production and supplementary production plans (presumably meaning quantitative output of major and minor products), equipment maintenance and repair plan, labour and wages plan, plan for supply of raw materials, transport plan, cost plan, financial plan (probably profits) and 'technical organization measures' plan (see p. 165 fn. 1 below for the meaning of this term). To these were added, where relevant, a new products trial manufacture plan and a capital investment plan.[1] No suggestion was made that some of these targets were 'flexible' and once again the divergence from the list of 1957 will be noted. Industrial ministries and local authorities had presumably used freely their right to add to the number of non-flexible targets.

In the mid-1960s, the quantity of output sold appears, at least on occasion, to be used as a success indicator. Three enterprises producing aerated water in Kwangtung 'competed fiercely with each other for the market under the cloak of overfulfilling the state plan'. Since price competition was presumably ruled out, this competition took the form of lengthening the period of quality guarantee and of giving presents to retailers of their goods. This was considered most reprehensible.[2]

The use of other types of targets also produced undesired side effects. Thus profits as a success indicator, in the absence of free market prices, led to an enterprise refusing to make goods having a low profit margin 'although they were urgently needed by the masses'. A textile enterprise, for which quality, defined as the absence of imperfections, was evidently an important target, achieved this very efficiently by cutting out all imperfections so that every length of cloth was dotted with holes.[3]

The difficulties experienced by the Chinese in devising the type of targets that should be embodied in enterprises' plans will not surprise those familiar with Soviet and East European attempts to solve this problem. The reader is referred to the literature on this topic.[4]

As P. J. D. Wiles notes, 'the essence of the indicator problem is, what is its influence on the sortament and other decentralized decisions?'[5] A quantity

---

October 4, 1963, p. 3. Wang Tsu-k'ang: 'Certain Problems of Fixed Norm Management in Industrial Enterprises.'

[1] *Economic Research* (*Jingji Yanjiu*), No. 7, July 1964, p. 14. Ma Wen-kuei: loc. cit.

[2] *Southern Daily* (*Nanfang Ribao*), January 14, 1966, p. 1.

[3] Ibid.

[4] For the Soviet Union—A. Nove: *The Soviet Economy* (revised ed.), London, 1965, pp. 161–73. For Hungary: J. Kornai: op. cit. A more theoretical exposition is given in P. J. D. Wiles: op. cit., Chapter 4.

[5] P. J. D. Wiles: op. cit., p. 82.

target may be achieved at the expense of quality[1] or by providing a product mix that does not satisfy consumer demand, as when enterprises concentrate on products for which labour productivity is higher, but demand weak.[2] More crudely, it may lead to false claims to overfulfilment.[3] Almost any success indicator (except for profits, if success is rewarded by a constant percentage of profits earned) makes it advantageous for an enterprise to have its targets set low and Party branches are supposed to counteract the tendency to try to get an 'easy plan'.[4]

After the Great Leap, as we have seen, financial targets, notably cost reduction and profit, were put forward as better tests of enterprises' performance. We must first define these terms as used in China before their significance as targets can be discussed. Costs, following Marxist usage, are taken to be 'the comprehensive indicator of the expenditure of labour time' and are listed under four main heads: wages and supplementary benefits; raw and processed materials and fuel; depreciation (including the major repairs fund), and fourthly, management expenses.[5] Depreciation is (or was according to a work of 1952) reckoned on a straight line basis, as in Soviet practice; that is, original capital cost plus cost of disposal when scrapped, minus estimated scrap value is divided by estimated years of utilization, giving equal annual charges (two variants on this method are permitted). In addition to this 'basic' depreciation fund, enterprises also have what is called a 'major repairs fund', sometimes known as 'major repairs depreciation fund'. Depreciation rates vary from one section of the economy to another, but around 1956–7 commonly came to 4–5 per cent of total capital value of the asset concerned for both the basic depreciation and the major repair funds together.[6] In 1962 it was mentioned that in most industries depreciation accounted for less than 10 per cent of total costs; however, it was higher in power generation and in extractive mining.[7]

It will be noted that, apart from depreciation, no capital elements are included in costs; this has sometimes led to extravagant standards of construction, and enterprises have needed to be enjoined to discover and catalogue what they possess in the way of fixed assets.[8] Profit is reckoned for

---

[1] *Ta Kung Daily* (*Dagong Bao*), Peking, July 16, 1962, p. 3. Yang Fang-hsün: 'Determine Price According to Quality—Higher Price for Higher Quality.'

[2] Niu Chung-huang: *Accumulation and Consumption in the National Income of Our Country* (in Chinese), Peking, 1957, p. 103, and *People's Daily* (*Renmin Ribao*), September 4, 1965, p. 1.

[3] *Tsitsihar Daily* (*Qiqihaer Ribao*), January 19, 1957 (SCMP 1481). The most widespread example of such an abuse occurred in agricultural statistics in 1958, see Choh-ming Li: op. cit., p. 85.

[4] *Ta Kung Daily* (*Dagong Bao*), Peking, April 16, 1962, p. 1.

[5] Ibid., Peking, December 10, 1962, p. 3. Li Ch'eng-jui: 'Socialist Economic Accounting', and *Collected Laws and Regulations* . . . Vol. 10, pp. 258–61.

[6] P'an Hsü-lun and Yu Wen-ch'ing: *Principles of Accounting for State Enterprises* (in Chinese), Shanghai, 1952, p. 39, and *Collected Laws and Regulations* . . . Vol. 10, p. 259, and Ko Chih-ta: op. cit. pp. 81-2.

[7] *Economic Research* (*Jingji Yanjiu*), No. 4, April 1962, p. 6. Ho Chien-chang, Kuei Shih-yung and Chao Hsiao-min: 'The Content of Economic Accounting in Socialist Enterprises.'

[8] *People's Daily* (*Renmin Ribao*), December 9, 1964, p. 2. Ch'en Yang-p'ing and Liao Yen-chih: 'On What Principles Should Office Blocks be Built?' and *Red Flag* (*Hongqi*),

F

accounting purposes as a percentage of costs (as in the Soviet Union) and not as a percentage of capital (as in the West). Profit is calculated on sales, not output, in the current period; therefore, it does not take into account the running down or building up of stocks.[1] This again reflects the Soviet example and means that the fulfilment of the profits plan is not directly linked with the fulfilment of the output plan.[2]

At least in the case of some manufacturing enterprises, profit targets are said to be increased proportionately with production increases, thus keeping constant the remitted profit per unit of output.[3] This by itself would be liable to cause production to cease before the point where total profit is maximized (i.e. where marginal cost equals price or marginal revenue): however, this tendency would be counteracted if the achievement of maximum output ranked as a more important target, carrying greater material or political incentives.

Profit targets, like other targets, are capable of abuse. An enterprise with a lax bank manager may remit profits to the state according to plan with the aid of a bank loan when it has not fulfilled output and sales plans.[4] Profits to be remitted might be decreased by the wrongful inclusion in costs of items which should not have been entered or by using prices lower than those actually obtained by sales in calculating profit to be remitted.[5] References occur to enterprises being willing to produce only those goods yielding high profit to the neglect of others perhaps more urgently required with lower profit margins.[6] This illustrates the limitations of profit as a target when the absence of a free market prevents demand being reflected in higher prices and greater profit margins. Sometimes producing enterprises have had considerable latitude in setting their own prices, but usually their initiative in this is severely restricted.[7]

However, despite limitations caused by shackling the price mechanism, considerable advantages may be claimed for profit targets over targets of other types. In China, as in the Soviet Union, this train of thought has given rise to a lively controversy from 1962 onwards. The innovators (led in the Soviet by Liberman and in China by Sun Yeh-fang and Yang Chien-pai) have demanded the use of profit on capital as the chief success indicator for enterprises; some protagonists of the new ideas even favoured making profit on capital the criterion for investment.[8] In China, contrary to the outcome in the

---

No. 19, October 1, 1961, p. 21. Li Ch'eng-jui and Tso Ch'un-t'ai: 'Some Problems Concerning Economic Accounting in Socialist Enterprises.'

[1] *Economic Research* (*Jingji Yanjiu*), No. 11, November 1962, p. 68. Chin Li: loc. cit.
[2] A. Nove: op. cit., p. 136.
[3] *China Reconstructs*, August 1965, p. 32. Chang Chuan-wen: 'How Higher Production Targets are Fulfilled.'
[4] *People's Daily* (*Renmin Ribao*), July 5, 1964, p. 5. Teng Chia-jung: 'The Relationship Between the Work of Economic Ministries and the Issue of People's Currency.'
[5] D. H. Perkins: *Market Control and Planning in Communist China*, Cambridge, Mass., 1966, pp. 127–8.
[6] *Economic Research* (*Jingji Yanjiu*), No. 3, June 1957, p. 65. Fan Jo-yi: loc. cit.
[7] See p. 446 below.
[8] *Economic Research* (*Jingji Yanjiu*), No. 12, December 1963, pp. 40–56. Yang Chien-pai: 'The Problem of National Economic Equilibrium and "Production Price".' and ibid., No. 5, May 1964, pp. 12–20. Ho Chien-chang and Chang Ling: 'A Tentative Discussion on "Production Price" in the Socialist Economy.' ('Production price' is a term

Soviet Union, official backing has gone to the opponents of this proposal, the outcry against it, and the school of thought it represented, reaching a ferocious pitch in 1966-7 during the 'Cultural Revolution'; this must not, however, be taken to mean that thenceforward the concept of the rate of profit on capital was ignored in practical decisions. The chief argument used against these ideas is ideological—that they would involve the collapse of socialism; for the use of profit on capital as the major success indicator is considered intrinsically capitalist.[1]

During the turmoil of the 'great socialist cultural revolution' of 1966-7, attacks were made on those who 'advocated profit and money being in command' and opposed 'the thoughts of Mao Tse-tung and politics being in command'.[2] Visitors to China in the summer of 1966 corroborated reports in the Chinese press at that time that factories considered political activities more important than plan fulfilment or the achievement of other economic targets.[3] How deep or how long lasting the effects of this movement have been in this respect cannot, at the time of writing, be confidently judged.

We must now turn from theoretical discussion on profits to more practical matters concerning them.

Profits of state enterprises, together with depreciation charges, income arising from changes in price of fixed assets, and surplus working capital,[4]

---

meaning price formed with a profit mark up which is reckoned as a percentage of capital and not of costs. Ibid., No. 12, December 1963, p. 42. Yang Chien-pai: loc. cit.) Sun Yeh-fang, until 1966 Director of the Economics Institute of the Chinese Academy of Sciences, was vitriolically attacked during the 'Cultural Revolution' of 1966-7 for advocating a 'revisionist' economic policy, see, e.g., *Peking Review*, October 21, 1966, pp. 21-5, Meng Kuei and Hsiao Lin: 'On Sun Yeh-fang's Reactionary Political Stand and Economic Programme.'

[1] On this controversy, see *Economic Research* (*Jingji Yanjiu*), No. 4, April 1962, pp. 1-10. Ho Chien-chang, Kuei Shih-yung and Chao Hsiao-min: loc. cit., and *People's Daily* (*Renmin Ribao*), July 19, 1962, p. 5, Yang Jun-jui and Li Hsün: loc. cit., and *Economic Research* (*Jingji Yanjiu*), No. 1, January 1963, p. 61. Chin Li: 'A Discussion in Recent Years of Our Country's Economists on the Question of Socialist Economic Results', and ibid., No. 4, April 1964, pp. 1-14. Ho Kuei-lin, Hsüeh Chung-chang and P'eng Chen-yüan: ' "Production Price" Cannot Form the Basis of Socialist Price Formation', and ibid., No. 5, May 1964, pp. 1-11. Yü Lin: 'The Correct Manner of Determining Prices of Different Kinds of Products', and ibid., No. 6, June 1964, pp. 6-15. Pai Hung: 'Further Comments on the Basis of Price Formation under the Socialist System', and ibid., No. 9, September 1964, pp. 1-11. Tai Yüan-ch'en: 'A Criticism of "Production Price" and the Theory of Equalizing Profit on Capital', and *Kuang Ming Daily* (*Guangming Ribao*), October 12, 1964, p. 4. Lin Chai-mu and Wu Shu-ch'ing: 'Do Not Let the Equalizing of Profit and "Production Price" Choke up the Socialist Economy', and *Economic Research* (*Jingji Yanjiu*), No. 1, January 1965, pp. 10-19. Ts'ai Chien-hua: 'Controverting the "Production Price" Theory of Comrade Yang Chien-pai and Others', and ibid., pp. 20-5. Ho Kuei-lin: 'The True Quality of the "Theory of Socialist Production Price",' and ibid., No. 2, February 1965, pp. 50-3. 'The Economic Research Institute, Nankai University, Criticises the "Theory of Production Price".' See *Kuang Ming Daily* (*Guangming Ribao*), November 30, 1964, p. 6. For a discussion on the desirability of a fixed charge (a tax in the form of a capital levy) on enterprises' capital.

[2] *Red Flag* (*Hongqi*), No. 8, August 1966, p. 7. Editorial.

[3] I am indebted to Barry M. Richman of the University of California, Los Angeles, for this information.

[4] *Collected Laws and Regulations* . . . Vol. 5, p. 124. On income arising from changes in price of fixed assets, see p. 153 above.

have to be remitted to the treasuries of the central government or of local authorities as the case may be. These items are frequently lumped together as 'revenue from state enterprises'. Regulations on the remittance of profits often cover, explicitly or implicitly, the lesser items as well. Together they form the largest single contribution to the revenue of the Chinese government comprising 46, 53 and 62 per cent of the total in 1957, 1958 and 1959 respectively and a budgeted 65 per cent for 1960. More on this topic will be said in Chapter 14.[1] Here we will confine ourselves to regulations on profits, as they have affected individual enterprises.

First, however, a significant divergence from Soviet practice should be noted. While the major repairs fund is retained by the enterprise concerned in a special bank account in its own name, the 'basic depreciation' charges are remitted to the treasury and form part of the national revenue; the individual enterprise loses any particular claim on them.[2] This circumstance makes Chinese enterprises more dependent than their Soviet counterparts on budgetary grants for expansion. However, it is probable that other sources of funds (e.g. retained profits, licit or illicit) under enterprises' control are relatively larger in China; certainly, as we shall see, many factories have expanded enormously by ploughing back profits. In addition, the industrial and commercial tax paid by Chinese enterprises is relatively lighter than the turnover tax levied from Soviet enterprises (i.e. taxes form a smaller proportion of enterprises' total payment to the state, and profit remittances a larger proportion in China than in the Soviet Union). This results in less pressure on Chinese enterprises to lower costs because higher costs disadvantage primarily the state treasury not the enterprise[3] (especially at periods when profits have not been a major success indicator).

Before 1958, enterprises had to remit to the state all their profits except that in the case of overfulfilment of the profit plan, certain payments were made to the enterprises' bonus funds and that 40 per cent of the above-plan profits (reckoned after deduction of these bonus payments) accrued to the central ministry or local authority controlling the enterprise.[4] In 1957 such bonuses paid to central and local enterprises together were estimated to account for 2·8 per cent of their total profits and the central ministries' share of above-plan profits to 4·5 per cent of total profits of central enterprises.[5] On the supposition that local departments' share of above-plan profits of local enterprises came to a similar percentage of the total profits of their enterprises as that which accrued to the central ministries from central enterprises, it can be seen that 92·7 per cent of total profits would have been remitted to the state treasury. After remitting profits, an enterprise (or ministry) could claim

---

[1] Realized revenue and expenditure for 1960 have not been published so the budgeted percentage is given instead. No figures for any subsequent year are available. The Chinese budget includes revenues and expenditures of local authorities as well as of the central government.
[2] See p. 369 below.   [3] D. H. Perkins: op. cit., pp. 113–14.
[4] *Collected Laws and Regulations* . . . Vol. 5, p. 121, and *New Construction* (*Xin Jianshe*), No. 8, August 1959, p. 17. Lo Keng-mo: 'The Problem of the Transition from Socialism to Communism.' The ratio 40:60 for the division of above-plan profits was already in force in 1954. *Collected Laws and Regulations* . . . Vol. 2, p. 523.
[5] *New Construction* (*Xin Jianshe*), No. 8, August 1959, p. 17. Lo Keng-mo: loc. cit.

a refund of sums spent on four special items: 'technical organization measures',[1] trial manufacture of new products, labour protection measures and certain miscellaneous purchases.[2]

The directive of November 1957 on the reform of the industrial management system, and the more detailed regulations laid down six months later, were intended *inter alia* to increase the powers of enterprises' managements. In future a percentage of the profits of an enterprise was to be left at its disposal to be used by it for certain specified purposes. This percentage was to be determined thus: for all the enterprises under any one industrial ministry, the totals which had accrued during the First Five Year Plan period of enterprises' bonuses, enterprises' 40 per cent share of above-plan profits, and the four items of refundable expenses were to be added together; then the percentage was to be calculated which this sum represented of the total profits made by that ministry during the same period.[3] Thereafter for a period originally fixed at three years, but by February 1958 changed to five years, the ministry concerned was to be allowed to retain that fixed percentage of all the profits made by its enterprises. Enterprises would no longer be able to claim refunds for the four special items nor for enterprise bonus funds.[4]

Each industrial ministry, provided it kept within its total permitted retainable sum calculated as stated, was to fix different percentages of retainable profits for the enterprises under it according to individual circumstances. (For enterprises controlled by local authorities, this function was to be performed by the appropriate local department.) As far as joint state-private enterprises were concerned, 'special investigations should be conducted and suitable methods stipulated in determining the percentage of profits receivable by them'. Because these enterprises had been 'transformed' to their joint state-private status at different times, the percentage of retainable profits should be based on the figures for 1957 and not, as in the case of other enterprises, for the First Five Year Plan period as a whole.[5]

If an enterprise failed to attain targets set by the state (not only the profit target), its retainable percentage of profits was to be reduced as circumstances

---

[1] A term which covers a multitude of measures to improve efficiency, e.g. by raising labour productivity, lowering costs and wastage, etc. Twelve items are included under this term in *Simple Explanation of Terms Used in the First Five Year Plan for the Development of the National Economy of the People's Republic of China*, p. 47. (Compare the Russian *Organizatsionno-teknichiskie meropriyatii*.)

[2] *Collected Laws and Regulations* . . . Vol. 6, p. 396.

[3] The directive of November 1957 had stated 'the total profit *transmitted to the state* by that ministry' (our italics) while the regulations of May 1958 merely said the 'total realized profit', the difference being the enterprises' bonuses and share of over-plan profits which were not remitted to the state. *Collected Laws and Regulations* . . . Vol. 6, p. 396, and ibid., Vol. 7, p. 240.

[4] Ibid., Vol. 6, p. 396, and Vol. 7, p. 240. Different provisions were to apply to enterprises under the Ministry of Construction Engineering and the Second Ministry of Machine Building. In the case of the latter (believed to be concerned with nuclear weapons), it was said that 'expenditure on the trial manufacture of new products is relatively large and profit relatively small'. *Collected Laws and Regulations* . . . Vol. 7, p. 242.

[5] *Collected Laws and Regulations* . . . Vol. 6, p. 397, and ibid., Vol. 7, pp. 239–42, and ibid., pp. 136–7. Li Hsien-nien: 'Report on Final Accounts for 1957 and Draft Budget for 1958', and *Ta Kung Daily* (*Dagong Bao*), Peking, May 12, 1961, p. 3. Sung Hsin-chung: 'The System of Enterprises' Retainable Percentage of Profits.'

warranted. In the event of an enterprise's profits being notably affected, favourably or unfavourably, by changes in price policy or taxation, or by natural disaster and similar external occurrences, the retained percentage of profits might be appropriately revised. For a ministry as a whole such adjustments should not exceed 5 per cent of the original planned profits, subject to a state guarantee that in these circumstances the sum retainable by the ministry should not be below the figure for the previous year.[1]

In the case of enterprises which divided profits between the central government and local authorities, the enterprises' retainable share of profits was to be deducted from the 80 per cent going to the centre.[2]

It should be noted that under the new system, retained profits were calculated as a fixed proportion of *total* profits. Before 1958 they had been a fixed proportion of *above-plan* profits, and hence dependent on the profit plan set each year; large above-plan profits in one year might lead to a raising of the profit plan for the next year. Now for a period fixed in February 1958, as we have seen, for five years, the retainable proportion of total profits was not to be altered. (However, in 1961 the proportion was in fact reduced.) The change from using above-plan profits to total profits as the basis for calculating retainable profits, must have increased the incentive to maximize profit.[3]

The changes in the financial administration of enterprises in 1958 were intended to give greater incentive to make profits and in addition to cut out the work and delays involved in applications for repayments of the four items of expenditure which were now to be met from enterprises' own revenues. The diminution of red tape may have been a real enough benefit, but the actual increase in the proportion of profits at the disposal of the industrial ministries and enterprises was not over substantial. It has been seen that in 1957 enterprises' bonuses and ministries' and local departments' share of above-plan profits may have amounted to 7·3 per cent of total industrial profits. In his budget report in February 1958, Li Hsien-nien, the Minister of Finance, estimated that in 1958 enterprises' share of profits would amount to 10 per cent of the total, this of course to include provision for the four items previously refundable.[4]

Although no great increase occurred in the retainable proportion of profits in 1958, the Great Leap and the consequent rise in profits of enterprises meant that in absolute terms the sums rose very considerably and were alleged to 'exceed actual requirements'. This provided an excuse for a reduction being made in 1961 in the percentage of retainable profits, the reduction being larger for those ministries with high profits than for those whose profits were lower.[5] By 1961 profits must have fallen very steeply owing to the decline in economic activity, with a serious result on government revenues which it was evidently hoped to make good in some part by reducing the percentage of profits retainable by enterprises. The government's ability to enforce any

[1] *Collected Laws and Regulations* ... Vol. 7, p. 241.
[2] Ibid., Vol. 7, p. 226.
[3] *The China Mainland Review*, Vol. I, No. 4, March 1966, pp. 9–10. E. R. Lim: 'The Role of Profit in China's Industrial Planning.'
[4] *Collected Laws and Regulations* . . . Vol. 7, p. 136. Li Hsien-nien: loc. cit.
[5] *Ta Kung Daily* (*Dagong Bao*), Peking, May 12, 1961, p. 3. Sung Hsin-chung: loc. cit.

discipline on enterprises in respect of the division of profits appears to have been weak,[1] but at least it may have hoped to add somewhat from this source to its depleted revenues. When political pressure mounted in the mid-1960s, the retainable percentage of profits was in some places reduced.[2]

The regulations of 1958 laid down that the greater part of retained profits was to be used for productive purposes, notably for the four special items enumerated above, for making good inadequacies of both working capital and planned capital investment and, with permission, for other capital outlays. Expenditure from retained profits up to a maximum of 5 per cent of an enterprise's total wage bill might be made for 'socialist emulation prizes' and other bonuses (individual or collective) and for employees' welfare.[3]

In addition to the retainable proportion of profits, enterprises can receive rewards for fulfilling targets of various types (output, variety, quality, economy in raw materials, etc.), such rewards being reckoned as a percentage of the enterprise's wage bill. By 1962 sometimes the only target taken into account was the rate of profit (both the rate reckoned on capital and that reckoned on cost). In this case both types of enterprise reward schemes would be dependent on the profits achieved. Some of the schemes for rewarding enterprises operated in the mid-1960s were of considerable complexity and sophistication.[4]

Whatever reward system has operated in any instance, there is no disputing the importance attached for at least a period from 1961 to the profits target as a success indicator for enterprises. 'Enterprises which are not making profits have no vitality',[5] declared an article in that year in the Central Committee's journal *Red Flag*; and in their devotion to the profit motive as a spur to enterprises' efficiency, the Chinese at that time were not behind the Soviet Union and East Europe.[6] Later, the 'proletarian cultural revolution' of 1966–7 may have abated the zeal for profit maximization.

These rewards of which we have been speaking are made (in the first place at least) to the enterprise as a collective unit. Quite separate is the fund for those individual bonuses, fixed as a specified percentage of an enterprise's total wage bill, which an enterprise distributes among meritorious employees, regardless

[1] See p. 389 below. See also *Ta Kung Daily* (*Dagong Bao*), Peking, April 26, 1961, p. 3. Wang Cho: 'A Discussion of Some Problems of Financial Management', where an allusion is made to excessive profit retention by enterprises.

[2] I am grateful to Barry M. Richman of the University of California, Los Angeles, for this information.

[3] *Collected Laws and Regulations*... Vol. 7, pp. 240–1.

[4] *Ta Kung Daily* (*Dagong Bao*), Peking, August 22, 1962, p. 3. Ch'en P'ei-yi: 'A Tentative Discussion of Certain Practical Problems in the Bonus System', and *Labour* (*Laodong*), No. 8, August 1964, pp. 27–9. Chang Feng-lin: 'Distribute Enterprises' Bonus Funds Reasonably', and *Economic Research* (*Jingji Yanjiu*), No. 10, October 1965, p. 39. Ch'ai Yen-hsieh: 'Some Problems in Correctly Regulating the Financial Relations between the State and State Enterprises.' On the bonus system up to 1956, see *Finance* (*Caizheng*), No. 3, December 5, 1956, pp. 9–12. T'ao Sheng-yü: 'A Study of Enterprise Bonus Funds for State Enterprises.'

[5] *Red Flag* (*Hongqi*), No. 19, October 1, 1961, p. 21. Li Ch'eng-jui and Tso Ch'un-t'ai: loc. cit.

[6] 'All the signs are that the major success indicator of the enterprise in China today is enterprise profit.' *Annals of the American Academy of Political and Social Science.* Vol. 349. September 1963, p. 63. F. Schurmann: 'Economic Policy and Political Power in Communist China.'

of the achievement of the enterprise as a whole.¹ These individual bonuses will be discussed in the following chapter.

Retained profits were an important means of industrial expansion, especially in the years 1958–60 before their reduction by recession and official cuts. Numerous examples are known of self-financed growth of enterprises. A photochemical plant in Swatow, for example, grew in eight or nine years from a small laboratory to a modern plant with an annual output valued at ¥70 million in 1960; in the five years before 1960 the state had invested only ¥1,300,000 in this concern.² Typical was the instrument and tool factory at Chengtu, which used retained profits to verticalize production by establishing numerous ancillary plants making pig iron, steel, carbon rods and so forth.³

In 1964, when economic recovery was well under way, funds for 'technical organization measures' (perhaps more widely defined than above) were augmented by the inauguration of special loans for these purposes to small and medium sized local industrial enterprises, in Shanghai and possibly elsewhere as well.⁴

5. VERTICALIZATION

Self-finance through the ploughing back of licit or illicit retained profits was responsible for much of the industrial verticalization which has been a notable feature of the Chinese economic scene. However, from the First Five Year Plan period onwards,⁵ at least to the mid-1960s, many new factories were built as self-sufficient units from the outset. In any under-developed country, a large plant may have to undertake ancillary operations which would be contracted out to others in a more advanced economy, so there was nothing unusual about this situation. The defects of the allocation system, which have encouraged vertical integration in the Soviet Union, must have worked even more strongly to the same end in China; this was most evident during the Great Leap. When outside supplies cannot be relied on for raw materials and components, it becomes essential for an enterprise to produce them for itself. Before 1958, the tendencies towards verticalization were not considered inherently beneficial and indeed sometimes met with criticism, as when one argument advanced against high transfer prices for capital goods was that this encouraged self-sufficiency, entailing higher costs and unnecessary duplication.⁶ Any inhibitions against verticalization were, however, discarded in

[1] *Ta Kung Daily* (*Dagong Bao*), Peking, August 22, 1962, p. 3. Ch'en P'ei-yi: loc. cit.

[2] *Red Flag* (*Hongqi*), No. 12, June 16, 1960. p. 8. T'ao Chu, First Secretary, CCP Kwangtung Provincial Committee: 'Some Problems of Leadership over Factory and Mining Enterprises.'

[3] *People's Daily* (*Renmin Ribao*), June 24, 1960, p. 1. CCP Committee for the Measuring Instruments and Cutting Tools Factory, Chengtu: 'A New Example of the Socialist Enterprise Management System.' For further information on profit levels in industry, see p. 371 and p. 450 below.

[4] *People's Daily* (*Renmin Ribao*), March 19, 1965, p. 2.

[5] *Ta Kung Daily* (*Dagong Bao*), Peking, July 10, 1964, p. 3. Lo Ching-fen: 'Actively Develop Specialized Production in the Machine Building Industry.'

[6] *Economic Research* (*Jingji Yanjiu*), No. 3, June 1957, p. 60. Fan Jo-yi: loc. cit., and ibid., No. 2, February 1959, p. 35. 'Comrades from Economic Ministries Discuss Distribution and Pricing of Industrial Goods.'

1958 when each enterprise attempted to push up its output regardless of assured supplies. Some remarks of Chairman Mao commending the verticalized Wuhan iron and steel complex,[1] were seized on to give moral support for what was happening.

Certain other trends, however, might be set against the encouragement of verticalization during the Great Leap. The great growth of 'street industry' treated in Chapter 8, increased the use made by factories of outworkers. These small urban workshops were used by larger concerns to make components and for undertaking processing and repairs. This was encouraged by the provisions of the new consolidated industrial and commercial tax, promulgated in September 1958. It might also be thought that the reported method of computing an enterprise's output (gross of purchases from other enterprises, but net of internal transfers of intermediate products) would encourage the tendency towards vertical disintegration,[2] especially at a time, such as 1958, when output targets were all-important. However, no mention has been found of this acting as a brake on the predominant trend. Although there was a growth in the use by large factories of small workshops, these workshops stood to them in a largely dependent status. If these goods or services had previously been provided by independent outside enterprises, this development would indeed have increased verticalization. In any case it is compatible with the decline of independent specialized manufacturing concerns.

By 1959, economists were warning against indiscriminate verticalization.[3] The general tenor of official opinion throughout 1959 and 1960 continued, however, to encourage vertical integration.[4] In sophisticated Shanghai the pendulum had already in 1960 begun to swing in the opposite direction towards specialized enterprises.[5] In Peking, Tientsin and Shenyang a reorganization in this direction began in the spring of 1964. Then, at the end of 1964 and in 1965 when the movement was well under way in these big cities, a vigorous press campaign spelled out the advantages of specialized production, which

---

[1] *People's Daily* (*Renmin Ribao*), September 29, 1958, p. 1.

[2] Ta-chung Liu and Kung-chia Yeh: *The Economy of the Chinese Mainland: National Income and Economic Development 1933–59*, Vol. I, p. 81. Rand Corporation, Santa Monica, 1963.

[3] *Red Flag* (*Hongqi*), No. 9, May 1, 1959, pp. 18–21. Niu Chung-huang: 'The Composite Economic Management of Large-scale Factories and Mines', and *Economic Research*, No. 6, June 1959, p. 11. Wang Cho: 'My Views on the Planned and Proportionate Development of the National Economy.'

[4] e.g. in May 1960, the Changchun Automobile Plant inaugurated a drive for self-sufficiency. *Red Flag* (*Hongqi*), No. 19, October 1, 1960, p. 36. The CCP Committee of the First Automobile Plant, Changchun: 'Promote Multiple Utilization of Factors of Production and Develop Many Kinds of Operation.' The first half of 1960 saw a continued increase in verticalization in Heilungkiang. *People's Daily* (*Renmin Ribao*), October 8, 1960, p. 7. Li Hsi-mu: 'Many-sided Operation is the Road to the Development of Greater, Quicker, Better and More Economical Production by Industrial Enterprises', and ibid., June 15, 1960, p. 1. Editorial.

[5] *People's Daily* (*Renmin Ribao*), April 12, 1965, p. 5. Lü Liang-p'ing: 'With Revolutionary Energy Organize Specialization and Co-operation in Processing Industries.' For an account of the different types of specialized factories in Shanghai, see ibid., June 10, 1965, p. 5. Fan Jung-k'ang and Ch'en Ch'ih: 'Bring About Co-operation Between Large, Medium and Small Concerns, Take the Road of Specialized Production and Co-ordination.'

included rises in productivity, reduction in both investment and operating costs, avoidance of duplication of investment, improvement in quality and variety. Specialization was put forward as applicable primarily to large cities and not suitable for rural areas. After the reorganization had been tried out in Peking, Shanghai, Tientsin, and Shenyang, the State Economic Commission summoned a national conference at Tientsin to discuss the matter. Meanwhile a number of other industrial centres had begun to encourage specialization.[1]

If the campaign against verticalization succeeds, it will suggest that, at least in the larger cities, the difficulties which had led to its rise have been overcome. Articles advocating specialization have stressed the demand it makes for better co-ordination between enterprises; also that changes in taxation and price policy will be needed.[2] As Chinese industry develops, specialization may be expected to increase, but the process is likely to be slow. A Japanese visitor in 1964 considered that China was one or two generations behind Japan and the West in the division of production between manufacturing concerns.[3]

6. CAPITAL INVESTMENT PROJECTS

Special note must be made of the organization of capital investment projects and more particularly those that involve construction and the installation of equipment.[4] Construction and installation may either be 'self-managed'—that is, undertaken directly by the enterprise, the 'construction unit'[5] concerned, or may be done under contract by an enterprise specializing in these tasks. The latter method accounted for over 70 per cent of such work according to a book published in 1958. The specialist enterprise may either be part of the 'system' of the same ministry as the construction unit (an 'internal contract') or come under the Ministry of Construction Engineering (an 'external contract').[6] Sometimes a contract may also be made

---

[1] *People's Daily (Renmin Ribao)*, May 12, 1965, p. 5.

[2] Ibid., February 20, 1965, p. 5. Chi Ch'ung-wei, Li Lan-ch'ing and Lo Ching-fen: 'Specialization and Co-operation are an Important Short Cut to Greater, Faster, Better, and More Economical Development of Industrial Productive Capacity', and *Ta Kung Daily (Dagong Bao)*, Peking, March 5, 1965, p. 3. Ku Lien-ch'i and Chu Tso-ch'un: 'Why Must Industrial Production Take the Road of Specialization and Co-ordination?'

[3] *Current Scene*, Vol. II, No. 32, May 1, 1964, p. 4.

[4] For the Chinese definition of capital investment, see p. 27 above. Around 1958, construction and installation accounted for 50 to 60 per cent of the total value of capital investment. *Basic Questions in the Civil Law of the People's Republic of China* (in Chinese), Peking, 1958, pp. 243–4. On the planning and control of investment projects see pp. 472–82 below.

[5] The term 'construction unit' (*chienshe tanwei*) can mean either the enterprise for which the project is being made or the actual project itself. *Simple Explanation of Terms Used in the First Five Year Plan for the Development of the National Economy of the People's Republic of China*, p. 42, and *Basic Questions in the Civil Law of the People's Republic of China*, p. 244.

[6] *Basic Questions in the Civil Law of the People's Republic of China*, p. 244. The existence of building co-operatives and 'small building production groups' is known from a single reference stating that, at the end of August 1958, these two categories together counted some 670,000 workers. *Statistical Research (Tongji Yanjiu)*, No. 9, September 1958, p. 10. Editorial Information Room: 'The Great Leap Forward in Basic Construction.'

with a designing unit for its services. The Construction Bank, established in 1954, exercises general supervision over both construction units and the specialist contracting enterprises.[1] Thus the execution of a capital project may involve close co-ordination between four parties—the construction unit, a specialist construction enterprise, a designing unit, and the Construction Bank.[2] In the case of self-managed projects, the construction unit might contract work down to lower levels inside its own organization. The Shihchingshan Iron and Steel Plant, for example, had a four-tier arrangement of contracts, from the plant itself to its engineering office, from that to the work sections, and thence to the small teams.[3]

A change in the system of contracts for investment projects was propounded in an editorial in the *People's Daily* in November 1965. 'The development of our construction strength', it stated, 'must gradually become fixed according to localities. The contract system by which A and B make contracts with each other must be completely reformed.' A start had already been made, for from the beginning of 1965 'some units have done away with this system, and in accordance with differing conditions, adopted either the construction unit complete responsibility system or the contracting unit complete responsibility system, or the responsibility system of the department involved on the construction site. Basically this has unified leadership on construction sites.'[4] This appears to represent an extension of horizontal local authority at the expense of functional specialization.

Budgetary funds for capital investment are channelled through the Construction Bank. Before 1958 the general rule was that expenditure under different headings in any one capital project should be controlled from above. In July 1958 a new method, the 'responsibility system for capital investment',[5] previously tried out on an experimental scale, was made nation-wide in scope.[6] Under this system, the construction unit and its ministry were to be allowed freedom to use as they wished the sum provided by the budget for any given investment project, so long as they guaranteed to complete the project by the prescribed date with no reduction in its planned productive capacity and without increasing the proportion of construction for non-productive purposes or overstepping the total expenditure laid down. Thus, subject to these conditions, they were permitted to switch expenditure from one item to another and to retain for their own use (which had, however, to be mainly for productive construction) any sums saved on the project as a whole. Balances remaining at the end of a year no longer had to be returned to the treasury

---

[1] On the Construction Bank, see p. 411 below.
[2] *Economic Research (Jingji Yanjiu)*, No. 3, March 1960, p. 14. Ku To-ching: ' "Responsibility for Investment" is a Very Important System for Regulating Production Relationships and for Developing Productive Capacity in Capital Construction.'
[3] *People's Daily (Renmin Ribao)*, July 15, 1958, p. 1.
[4] Ibid., November 30, 1965, p. 1. Editorial.
[5] This is sometimes translated as 'the contract system of capital investment' which, however, blurs the distinction between '*paokan*' ('responsibility') and '*paokung*' ('contract'). The latter is a legalistic phrase, while the former has wider connotations—see pp. 27–8 above.
[6] *Economic Research (Jingji Yanjiu)*, No. 2, February 1961, p. 11. Chi Ts'ai-ch'eng: 'The Form of Comprehensive Financial Plans and the Inter-Relations Between Items in Them.'

but might be carried down for future use: this was to put an end to lavish expenditure before the end of the year, of funds which would otherwise have to be returned to the state.[1] Grants for capital purposes were in future to be channelled horizontally from the financial department of the appropriate local authority (presumably via the local branch of the Construction Bank) to the construction unit and not vertically through the unit's ministry.[2]

These provisions for capital investment were in line with the decentralization measures promulgated in 1957–8 in respect of other economic activities. They gave greater authority to the management of enterprises and to local authorities, and permitted greater flexibility in the employment of investment funds. The 150 per cent rise in investment grants in the twelve months ending October 1958[3] must in any case have made detailed supervision of this expenditure even harder than before. As with other of the decentralization measures, national promulgation of this decree had been preceded by some months of experimentation. In this case the Ministry of Metallurgical Industry, and in particular the extension of the Shihchingshan Iron and Steel Plant, had been chosen to pioneer the new system. It was claimed that the desired economies of expenditure had been achieved.[4]

The new regulations were implemented only gradually, despite the original intention that they should go into force immediately.[5] By December 1959, nearly eighteen months after their promulgation, the new system had been universally adopted only in Kwangtung. In Liaoning, Kansu and Sinkiang it had become effective for 50–60 per cent of total investment by value, and in Hopei, Shensi, Ninghsia, Heilungkiang, Kirin and Shangtung for 35–45 per cent. Analysed according to sectors, implementation was 85 per cent complete for hydro-electricity and oil, 75 per cent for metallurgy, coal and chemicals, and 30 per cent for railways.[6] A hint that snags had occurred is indicated by supplementary regulations of May 1959 designed to prevent enterprises using their new powers over investment funds in such a way as to negate economic planning.[7] Control over unplanned investment by enterprises has all along proved very difficult to exert, as will be seen in subsequent chapters. In 1961 all capital work in progress and all plans for investment projects were, apart from special cases, ordered to be discontinued.[8] It is not known how long the ban remained in force or how universal was its implementation. Probably its removal occurred in piecemeal fashion.

---

[1] *Collected Laws and Regulations* . . . Vol. 8, pp. 123, and *People's Daily* (*Renmin Ribao*), December 15, 1957, p. 1.

[2] *Collected Laws and Regulations* . . . Vol. 8, p. 124.

[3] *Finance* (*Caizheng*), No. 12, December 1958, p. 11. Investment Finance Office of the Ministry of Finance: 'Actively Organize the Supply of Capital: Sustain Investment with All One's Strength.'

[4] *People's Daily* (*Renmin Ribao*), July 15, 1958, p. 1.

[5] *Collected Laws and Regulations,* . . . Vol. 8, p. 124.

[6] *Economic Research* (*Jingji Yanjiu*), No. 3, March 1960, p. 11. Ku To-ching: loc. cit.

[7] *Collected Laws and Regulations,* . . . Vol. 9, pp. 135–6.

[8] *Seventy Important Points of Communist Industrial Policy*, 1961. (From Taiwan Source), Nos. 3 and 4.

7. ALLOCATION OF RAW MATERIALS AND OTHER PRODUCER GOODS TO ENTERPRISES

The nationwide allocation of raw materials and producer goods, the development of control over the distribution of major commodities, and the responsibilities of different organs of commerce, will be treated in subsequent chapters. Here we are concerned with the distribution of raw materials and producer goods at a lower level, more especially as it faces the individual enterprise.

In the course of the First Five Year Plan period there had developed a distinction between certain major commodities, the allocation of which was supposed to be controlled by some organ of the central government[1] (State Planning Commission, State Economic Commission, or one of the ministries, according to commodity) and other goods of lesser importance which were not so subject.[2] However, those quantities of these major commodities destined for small enterprises were not formally allocated—the planning system being quite inadequate to deal direct with small concerns—but were put at the disposal of the Ministry of Commerce to allocate or sell through its organs in the ordinary line of business.[3] Policy on the degree of control over commodities of lesser importance varied over time. In 1956, in a period of relatively liberal economic policy, Ch'en Yün (soon to become Minister of Commerce) declared that 'with the exception of the raw materials in short supply, which are distributed by the estate alone, all other raw materials should be purchased by the factories on the free market'.[4]

Before 1959 enterprises under the direct control of central ministries had to apply for their requirements of materials through their own ministries. Local concerns applied to their local authorities.[5] For supplies of commodities controlled by the State Planning Commission or by central ministries, local authorities were supposed to apply to these bodies on behalf of those local enterprises designated as 'planned units' (i.e. those which figured in the national plan); in the case of the other local enterprises, the 'unplanned units', the Ministry of Commerce was the channel for obtaining supplies.[6] The regulations of November 1957 left these arrangements unchanged except for the proviso that when local conditions and urgent needs demanded, provincial level authorities might adjust the quantities, varieties and time of use of

---

[1] For difficulties and abuses of the allocation system in the First Five Year Plan, see *Planned Economy* (*Jihua Jingji*), No. 2, February 1957, pp. 8–11. Men Tso-min: 'Learn from the Experience of Supplying Raw Materials in 1956.'

[2] See p. 284 below.

[3] See *Statistical Work* (*Tongji Gongzuo*), No. 13, July 14, 1957, p. 30, for figures of quantities of steel, non-ferrous metals, machine tools, forging and rolling equipment, timber and cement distributed by allocation and through the market respectively in 1953–6.

[4] *The Eighth National Congress of the Communist Party of China*, Vol. II. Speeches, p. 164.

[5] *Planned Economy* (*Jihua Jingji*), No. 9, September 1958, p. 13. Wang Kuei-wu: 'An Important Change in the Method of Drawing Up Annual Plans.' Only from 1955 did allocation extend to enterprises controlled at levels below the province. *Statistical Work* (*Tongji Gongzuo*), No. 13, July 14, 1957, p. 31.

[6] *Planned Economy* (*Jihua Jingji*), No. 10, October 1958, p. 34. She Yi-san: 'A Discussion of the Change in the Allocation System for Raw Materials.'

materials applied for and received by all enterprises in their areas, including those controlled by central ministries.[1]

A year later this extension of local power over material allocation was carried further. From 1959 even central government enterprises were to apply to the planning organs of provincial and equivalent local authorities for supplies. Exceptions to this were made in the case of 'commodities required for a few special ministries and for special purposes', such as raw materials for the needs of the armed forces, armament industries and the railways, fuel for civil aviation and materials for export, foreign aid and stockpiling purposes, for which requisition should continue to be made to the ministries concerned. So far as local authority enterprises were concerned, the distinction between planned and unplanned units was abolished. At the same time, the number of commodities under central control was reduced, thus further increasing provincial responsibilities.[2]

When the main allocation decisions have been taken by the national or local organs concerned, their implementation is arranged by contracts at lower levels. 'General contracts', concluded between central organs of the supplying or producing ministry and the ministry requiring some commodity, are followed by detailed 'particular contracts' between the actual enterprises producing and consuming it. In some cases 'direct contracts' may be made between the two enterprises without any 'general contract' between their superiors.[3] Inter-enterprise contracts are, in many instances, made on a long-term basis. For example, enterprises consuming large quantities of any product often sign contracts for long-term direct supply with factories or mines producing it.[4] By 1965 at any rate, enterprises sometimes had considerable latitude in choosing the producers with which to place contracts. In that year, for example, dissatisfaction with the quality of alloy steel tubes from Anshan led to custom being switched to a plant in Shanghai.[5]

In many instances, especially when enterprises buy in small quantities, supplies of raw materials and semi-finished goods do not pass directly, as in the cases above, between producer and user. Instead, they may be sent by the producer to a godown, from which they are eventually dispatched to the consuming enterprise. These godowns may be controlled by the consuming enterprise's ministry or local department, in which case they hold a wide range of supplies needed for enterprises of the ministry or department in the area. Alternatively, for certain commodities, special godowns or other storage facilities exist, confined to the one type of product, from which are supplied enterprises controlled by many different ministries; petroleum products are a

---

[1] *Collected Laws and Regulations*, . . . Vol. 6, p. 393.

[2] Ibid., Vol. 8, p. 101, and *Planned Economy (Jihua Jingji)*, No. 10, October 1958, p. 34. She Yi-san: loc. cit., and ibid., No. 9, September 1958, p. 13. Wang Kuei-wu: loc. cit.

[3] *Economic Research (Jingji Yanjiu)*, No. 2, February 1965, p. 34. Sung Chi-shan: 'A Brief Discussion of the Nature and Function of Industrial Contracts in our Country.'

[4] Ibid., No. 4, April 1965, pp. 1–5. Weng Chan: 'The Problem of Developing Fixed Co-operation and Fixed Point Supply in Local Industry.'

[5] *People's Daily (Renmin Ribao)*, December 8, 1965, p. 2. Hsü An-ch'eng, Assistant Manager, Seamless Steel Tube Plant, Anshan Iron and Steel Works: 'When Our Consumers Are Satisfied, We Shall Be Satisfied.'

notable example in this category.¹ More will be said about this subject in Chapter 11.

Sometimes raw materials are supplied by an undertaking to an enterprise making goods for it. In 1964 it was stated that when they have fulfilled their production plans, enterprises may undertake other tasks for units which can supply them with the necessary raw materials but that such raw materials must not include any subject to allocation by state plans.²

Apart from those raw materials and other supplies obtained by enterprises through the allocation system, and those imported (for which special provisions exist),³ some commodities are supplied, as already mentioned, through regular commercial channels or by enterprises when placing an order for goods to be made while, in addition, another and separately listed category is given as those for whose supply 'light industry enterprises must find their own solution',⁴ a phrase which covers a multitude of free-ranging activities, which would include illicit commercial dealings⁵ and, as already noted, verticalized production within the enterprise,⁶ barter deals⁷ and various unofficial methods. A tea house in Shanghai grew into a centre for transactions in certain types of equipment.⁸ Procurement or purchasing agents, the equivalent of Soviet *tolkachi*, are known to be active. In some cases these informal arrangements are officially permitted, while in others they are reprobated. The flexibility provided by such improvisation must be an invaluable element in the economy.

Provinces vary greatly in efficiency. The large authority for material allocation delegated to them from 1959 onwards is likely to be reflected in greatly differing stringency of control in this sphere. It may be surmised that a tighter hold can be and is maintained over inter-provincial movement of raw materials and producer goods than over intra-provincial deals.

¹ *Economic Research* (*Jingji Yanjiu*), No. 3, March 1960, p. 44. Chi Kuang: 'Problems of Distributing Productive Materials.'

² *People's Daily* (*Renmin Ribao*), March 3, 1964, p. 5. Ma Wen-kuei: 'The Nature and Tasks of State Industrial Enterprises in our Country.'

³ See p. 324 below.

⁴ *Red Flag* (*Hongqi*), No. 6, March 16, 1961, p. 11. K'ung Hsiang-chen: loc. cit.

⁵ We have seen that commercial organs receive allocations of centrally controlled raw materials as being the most convenient channels for supplying these to small consumers. Large enterprises are not supposed to buy such materials on the market, but this is difficult to prevent. *Collected Laws and Regulations*, . . . Vol. 5, p. 180.

⁶ e.g. a machine building plant which in one quarter was allocated enough materials for two months' requirements only; whereupon 'they immediately used their own initiative to get raw materials, energetically put up satellite factories . . . already in a few months they have produced twelve kinds of materials including steel and silicon iron'. *People's Daily* (*Renmin Ribao*), June 15, 1960, p. 1. Editorial.

⁷ e.g. A Peking radio factory is mentioned as having negotiated supplies of chemicals with the Municipal Party Committee when the usual suppliers, in Tientsin, wanted a barter deal. See p. 290 below.

⁸ See p. 290 below.

Chapter 7

INDUSTRIAL LABOUR AND MANAGEMENT

In this chapter we shall consider the official machinery, both governmental and trade union, for dealing with labour questions; the distribution, recruitment, training, organization and payment of non-agricultural labour; the position of managers, administrative staff and technical personnel in industry, and the role of Party branches in enterprises. Space forbids the consideration of several related topics of great import, such as population changes, general (as distinct from technical) education, and welfare services.

1. GOVERNMENTAL APPARATUS

The Ministry of Labour comes under the State Council's Office for Industry and Communications. The Ministry is charged with all matters concerning labour, including recruitment, systems of remuneration, technical training and safety measures.[1] Since 1954 the Ministry has been held by the same man, Ma Wen-jui.

The Chinese Constitution lays down that appointments at ministerial level should be made by the Chairman of the Republic in accordance with decisions of the National People's Congress or of its Standing Committee.[2] Below this level, the State Council has the formal power of appointment and dismissal of officials in central government ministries down to the level of directors and deputy directors of bureaux, and also of provincial level bureaux, and of certain other officials including the principals and vice-principals of institutions of higher learning.[3] The State Personnel Organization Commission, directly subordinate to the State Council, presumably is responsible for the exercise of some of these powers.[4]

Below the officials under the jurisdiction of the State Council are others who come under the jurisdiction of individual ministries, each of which has its own personnel bureau. In this sphere of personnel, as we shall later note, the role of the Party is particularly dominant, with the state organs merely giving formal effect to Party decisions. However, first we must briefly note certain salient organizational changes in respect of control of higher grades of personnel in administrative and economic life.

[1] *Collected Laws and Regulations of the People's Republic of China* (in Chinese), Vol. 4, pp. 194–6.
[2] *Constitution of the People's Republic of China*, Peking 1954. Article 40.
[3] *Collected Laws and Regulations* ... Vol. 1, p. 122.
[4] Ibid., Vol. 13, pp. 57–8, and F. Schurmann: *Ideology and Organization in Communist China*, Berkeley, 1966, pp. 184 and 196, fn. 7.

From 1955 to 1959 the Personnel Bureau of the State Council had responsibilities in connection with the appointment and dismissal both of officials coming under the State Council and also of those of the rank of *hsien* magistrate and higher (probably this would include the top staff of some state enterprises). In addition, the Personnel Bureau was put in charge of salary and welfare matters of state officials as well as of compiling statistics of cadres in state organs, enterprises and institutions. It also had the task of placement of cadres leaving the armed forces. In 1959 the Personnel Bureau was abolished and its duties taken over by the Ministry of Internal Affairs.[1] Probably, on the establishment of the State Personnel Organization Commission in 1963, the new body took over these responsibilities, although the Ministry of Internal Affairs may still have some duties concerning ex-servicemen.

In addition to these special central organs for personnel, local authorities of different levels also have personnel bureaux of their own.

Technical and scientific manpower comes under the Scientific and Technological Personnel Administrative Bureau, which was established in 1964 to take over tasks in these matters which had, since 1959, been done by the Commission for Science and Technology. Between 1956–9 these tasks had been the concern of the Bureau of Experts (the pre-1956 Bureau of Experts being re-named the Bureau of Foreign Experts) which was responsible for supervising and co-ordinating the execution of policy on experts and higher intellectuals[2] (probably meaning graduates of institutions of higher education). The Bureau of Foreign Experts remains under the direct control of the State Council.[3] After the Soviet and East European experts left in 1960, there were still a number of other foreign experts in China, including those working in the Foreign Languages Press and Institute.

The industrial decentralization directive of November 1957 increased the authority of provinces and other local authorities in personnel matters. In enterprises now handed down to them, they were to have the same authority over personnel as they already had in existing local enterprises. Even in the case of enterprises that remained in the control of central ministries, local authorities were permitted 'to adjust the cadres appropriately' so long as they did not weaken the staff of major factories and mines. When transferring cadres of grades controlled by the State Council, local authorities were supposed to get approval from the State Council; consultation with the central ministries was required when local authorities transferred cadres of those categories falling under the jurisdiction of these ministries.[4] The directive also laid down that the enterprises themselves should have greater powers over their own staffing. The enterprise was now to have control (presumably implying power to appoint and dismiss) over all personnel except for the

---

[1] *Collected Laws and Regulations* . . . Vol. 2, p. 103, and ibid., Vol. 9, p. 109.

[2] Ibid., Vol. 4, p. 202, and ibid., Vol. 9, p. 109, and *People's Handbook* (*Renmin Shouce*) *1957*, p. 322. See also *People's Daily* (*Renmin Ribao*), July 14, 1957, p. 2, for an account by the anthropologist Fei Hsiao-t'ung (at that time a vice-Director of the Bureau of Experts; later denounced as a rightist) of how he was sent by the Bureau of Experts to investigate the way in which policy on intellectuals was carried out in Szechuan and Yunnan.

[3] *Collected Laws and Regulations* . . . Vol. 9, p. 110, and NCNA, April 29, 1966.

[4] Ibid., Vol. 6, p. 394.

manager, assistant manager, accountant, assistant accountant and the chief technical staff.[1]

2. THE DISTRIBUTION AND MOVEMENT OF LABOUR

After the decentralization measures of 1957–8, the chief items of planning that were to remain under central control included the allocation of scientific and technical manpower and the overall arrangements for the enrolment plan for institutions of higher education and for the plan for dispatch of students abroad.[2]

In 1956 the State Economic Commission was entrusted with planning the employment distribution of new graduates, the actual task of assignment being in the hands of the Ministry of Higher Education.[3] Certain ministries and local departments have run specialized middle schools and other training establishments to cater for their own needs. The graduates of these institutions, according to information of 1957, are subject to assignment by the ministry or department concerned.[4]

It is difficult to assess how effectively the assignment of graduates and other cadres to specific posts is enforced. Probably enforcement is more rigid in the case of new graduates' first jobs than in their subsequent employment. Annually, towards the close of the academic year, meetings lasting several days are held in institutions of higher education for graduates and on occasion for their parents also, at which intensive 'ideological education' is given on the need to comply with state assignment to jobs, to whatever part of the country or type of work they are sent; simultaneously, press campaigns are run with the same theme. (It has been noted that members of the Party and of the Young Communist League tend to be assigned to cities and large towns, while non-Party graduates are more often given the less popular postings to smaller places.)[5] Despite the injunction that for students with higher education 'obedience to the state's unified assignment to posts is the minimum demand of state and the people',[6] a small minority are said to refuse assignments, sometimes remaining unemployed for a long period.[7] An

[1] *Collected Laws and Regulations* ... Vol. 6, p. 397.

[2] See pp. 461–2 below. Probably an exception continued to be made for graduates of teacher training colleges, who were reported (in 1956) to be subject to assignment by local authorities, with adjustments being made by the central authorities. Chang Chien: *The Question of Cadres in the Socialist Construction of our Country* (in Chinese), Peking, 1956, p. 47.

[3] *Collected Laws and Regulations* ... Vol. 4, pp. 419–21. In 1956 the supervision and re-posting of dissatisfied graduates after assignment was transferred from the Ministry of Higher Education to the State Council's Personnel Bureau. Ibid., Vol. 4, p. 434.

[4] *Planned Economy (Jihua Jingji)*, No. 4, April 1957, p. 9.

[5] R. MacFarquhar (ed.): *The Hundred Flowers*, London, 1960, p. 101. See also: S. Lindqvist: *China in Crisis*, London, 1965, pp. 54–5. 'Allocating people to jobs rationally, without considering their own preferences at all, has some advantages, but a number of irrational factors come into play. ... A Chinese student, about to sit for an examination, hears a host of conflicting rumours, suggesting that anyone who does well in this or that subject will be sent here or there. Everyone has his own theory about it, and the student takes care not to risk showing too much ability in certain papers. This does not make it any easier for the planners, whose job is in any case almost impossibly difficult.'

[6] *Kuang Ming Daily (Guangming Ribao)*, July 3, 1963, p. 1. Editorial.

[7] *China Youth Newspaper (Zhongguo Qingnian Bao)*, May 30, 1963 (SCMP 3000). Teng Ying-ch'ao: 'Greetings to University Students Who Are to Graduate This Year.'

announcement in 1956 merely stated that it would be in the interests of socialist construction if arrangements could be made for those now wanting work who had previously not complied with their assignment, left their posts of their own accord or overstayed their leave and failed to return.[1] The impression given is that these cases are not abnormal. With respect to those at a later stage in their career, reports coming out of China suggest that it is difficult for anyone on the staff of an organization of any sort to get released to take alternative work or for other reasons, without getting a chit from his present employers. Probably the truth is that smart people know how to pull the right strings in the right organizations to obtain the sort of postings they want—an art of universal utility but brought to a fine pitch of perfection in a system like that of China. Without the backing of an organization, the individual would appear helpless and at the mercy of the bureaucratic machine, but the very proliferation of this bureaucracy creates opportunities of playing one part of it off against the other.

Stringent controls on emigration enable China, unlike many other countries, to prevent a drain of graduates abroad, although a good number, of course, fled or remained abroad when the Communists first came to power.

Another category for whom special arrangements are made for assignment to jobs are ex-servicemen. In their case, much more freedom of choice is allowed and it is difficult to judge how far official preoccupation with their employment is of the nature of the normal advisory facilities provided for discharged servicemen in many countries, or the extent to which deliberate direction is employed. It is probably hard, in the circumstances, to distinguish between the two. In 1957 it was laid down that 'servicemen changing their occupations are to be assigned work by the ministries connected with their new occupations. Discharged ex-servicemen still unplaced in 1956 are to be dealt with by provincial and municipal authorities.'[2] We have already noted that at that date the State Personnel Organization Commission also had responsibilities in this respect.

The importance of ex-servicemen as Party officials, commune cadres, and in other managerial positions, and also as settlers in Sinkiang, Heilungkiang and elsewhere, has been or will be mentioned in this study. Here it should be remarked that the armed forces must be a major—probably the major—ladder of upward mobility in China today. There is, therefore, no reason to discount reports of youthful eagerness to enlist.

Behind the state apparatus for the assignment of officials lies that of the Party which is particularly active in all matters affecting personnel. In the Soviet Union the Party controls the distribution of cadres through the *nomenklatura* system. *Nomenklatura* means a list of appointments in the state administration, in enterprises, trade unions and other bodies, which specified Party committees are responsible for making; the word is also used to signify the list of persons qualified to hold these posts.[3] Little information is available

---

[1] *Collected Laws and Regulations* . . . Vol. 4, pp. 433–4.
[2] *Planned Economy (Jihua Jingji)*, No. 4, April 1957, p. 9.
[3] A. Nove: *The Soviet Economy* (revised ed.), London, 1965, p. 101. See also *Problems of Communism*, Vol. 8, No. 5, September–October 1959, pp. 56–9. J. F. Hough: 'Technical Elite Versus the Party—A First-Hand Report.'

on this topic in respect of China, but it is almost certain that a similar system is in operation. A provincial report in 1958 mentions 'that the appointment or dismissal of cadres must first of all be decided by the Party committees'[1] and this must imply an apportioning out of the responsibility among Party committees at different levels according to the importance and type of the appointments to be made.

Now we must turn from graduate and other cadres to consider the degree of control that is exercised over ordinary employees. It was officially laid down in regulations promulgated in 1954 that workers should comply with a definite transfer procedure and get permission from their employing enterprise or organization before leaving their employment. Employees vital to the enterprise who leave without permission forfeit their right to severance pay, but otherwise their conduct apparently entails no official penalty.[2] However, they may find themselves in difficulty over their residence cards, without which they cannot get ration cards and may be forced to leave the cities.[3] This deterrent may have been weakened by the mid-1960s, owing to more plentiful supplies of unrationed foodstuffs. In any case, it is improbable that much trouble would be taken to retain unskilled or semi-skilled workers who wished to leave as the supply of those who would like to work in modern industry, with its higher wages and other attractions, greatly exceeds the jobs normally available; also the administrative task of detailed control of labour, as existed for example in war-time Britain, would scarcely be feasible in China. The most that the authorities can aspire to accomplish, with regard to unskilled labour, is to control the flow to and from the cities and this, as we shall see, only with very moderate success.

The distribution of China's non-agricultural labour force must now be briefly surveyed. For fuller information the reader is referred to the study by J. P. Emerson.[4] The tables on the opposite page summarize Emerson's findings.

The figures given for each branch of the economy are those reported or estimated for workers and employees plus those engaged in traditional non-agricultural work who were not classified as workers and employees.[5] The phrase 'workers and employees' (*chihkung*) implies working under contract for wages; thus it excludes members of collective bodies and those working on their own account.[6] In this sense 'workers and employees' includes the staff of enterprises as well as manual workers and clerks. In other contexts,

[1] *Kansu Daily* (*Gansu Ribao*), August 16, 1958 (CB 528). Report by Chang Chung-liang, First Secretary of the CCP Kansu Provincial Committee. It should be noted that the term *pienchih*, translated as 'Personnel Organization' in the title of the State Personnel Organization Commission, is the Chinese term used to translate '*nomenklatura*'. F. Schurmann: op. cit., p. 186, fn. 7.

[2] *New China Monthly* (*Xinhua Yuebao*), No. 58, August 1954, p. 187, and *Collected Laws and Regulations* ... Vol. 7, p. 410.

[3] *China News Analysis*, No. 454, February 1, 1963, p. 6.

[4] J. P. Emerson: *Non-Agricultural Employment in Mainland China 1949–58*, US Bureau of Census, Washington, DC, 1965.

[5] J. P. Emerson: op. cit., p. 145. (Agricultural workers include those in forestry as well as those in collective agriculture and state farms.) See also *Statistical Work* (*Tongji Gongzuo*), No. 1, January 1957, pp. 19–20. Ch'en Chih-ho: 'The Scope of Employment Statistics in Our Country at the Present Time.'

[6] J. P. Emerson: op. cit., pp. 41–2.

Distribution of Civilian Non-Agricultural Employment by Branch of the Economy
Absolute Figures (in thousands)

Branch of the Economy	1952	1957	1958	1959	1960	1961
Handicrafts (and carrier services)[1]	7,364	6,560	1,465			
Salt extraction	500	500	700			
Fishing	1,336	1,500	2,000			
Industry (including mining)	5,263	7,907	23,734			
Water conservancy	134	340	1,360			
Capital construction	1,048	1,910	5,336			
Transport, posts and telecommunications	4,655	4,417	5,823			
Trade and the food and drink (i.e. catering, etc.) industry	9,900	7,819	7,500			
Finance, banking and insurance	351	621	400			
Sundry services[2]	443	489	489			
Traditional medicine	746	1,363	1,607			
State education, medicine, public health and cultural affairs	2,392	3,211	3,811			
Government administration	1,523	1,698	1,183			
Mass organizations	1,053	1,184	1,281			
Urban public utilities	41	133	150			
Meteorology	3	15	28			
Total	36,752	39,667	56,867	55,000	52,500	45,500

[1] Carrier services are included in the 1952 figure only. See J. P. Emerson: op. cit., p. 159 note 3.
[2] Workers in hotels, bathhouses, barber shops, etc.

Percentage Distribution of Non-agricultural Employment by Branch of the Economy

Branch of the Economy	1952	1957	1958
Handicrafts and carrier services	20·0	16·5	2·6
Salt extraction	1·4	1·3	1·2
Fishing	3·6	3·8	3·5
Industry (including mining)	14·3	19·9	41·7
Water conservancy	0·4	0·9	2·4
Capital construction	2·9	4·8	9·4
Transport, posts and telecommunications	12·7	11·1	10·2
Trade and the food and drink (i.e. catering, etc.) industry	26·9	19·7	13·2
Finance, banking and insurance	1·0	1·6	0·7
Sundry services[1]	1·2	1·2	0·9
Traditional Medicine	2·0	3·4	2·8
State education, medicine, public health and cultural affairs	6·5	8·1	6·7
Government administration	4·1	4·3	2·1
Mass organizations	2·9	3·0	2·3
Urban public utilities	0·1	0·3	0·3
Meteorology	([2])	([2])	([2])
Total	100·0	100·0	100·0

[1] Workers in hotels, bathhouses, barber shops, etc.
[2] Less than one-half of 0·1 per cent.

Sources: J. P. Emerson: op. cit., p. 128, except for figures for 1959–61 which are from *Current Scene*, Vol. 1, No. 30, April 20, 1962, p. 5. J. P. Emerson: 'Chinese Communist Party Views on Labour Utilization before and after 1958.'

however, 'workers and employees' may be set in antithesis to staff members (*kanpu*—also translatable as cadres).[1]

Women were reported to comprise 11·7 per cent of the non-agricultural labour force in 1957, rising to 13·5 per cent in 1957 and to 15·5 per cent in 1958;[2] the rise between 1957 and 1958 was presumably due in some measure to participation in 'street factories'.[3] The female percentage may have fallen in subsequent years when this form of industrial activity declined but the secular trend is likely to be upward.

The number engaged in non-agricultural work may be estimated, very roughly, to form around 15–20 per cent of China's total labour force which has been reckoned in the mid-1960s at about 300 million.[4] Those in urban employment are in a way a privileged elite, into which many a peasant's child would wish to climb. They work and live in more secure and comfortable conditions than the agricultural population and in general receive much higher cash remuneration, as well as labour insurance and medical benefits; this applies more particularly to the regular workers in modern enterprises who are an elite within an elite. The converse of this is, of course, that the factory hand works much more intensely for many more days a year and in a much more disciplined manner than his cousins on the land: this may not be fully appreciated by these cousins who aspire to join him. Their ambitions have meant that industrial enterprises could be very selective in recruiting new workers who thus have tended to be above average in education, health and intelligence.

The competition to obtain jobs in towns brought, however, its problems. Throughout the First Five Year Plan period, the authorities struggled to enforce an orderly system of recruitment to urban employment. Enterprises sometimes recruited new workers from those peasants who had made their own way to the cities and sometimes drew labour direct from the countryside. In the winter and spring of 1956–7 (when agricultural collectivization had recently been completed), the number of country people, including cadres and discharged soldiers, flocking townwards rose markedly. The migrants came preponderantly from the great plain of north and east China (from the provinces of Hopei, Honan, Shantung, Anhwei and Kiangsu) and made more especially for the rising industrial centres of the north west in Shensi, Kansu and Sinkiang.[5] (This rather unusual preference for those regions may be because they were favoured in the 1956 wage increase, but on this see p. 208 below.) Employment opportunities in these and other cities did not increase correspondingly, while agricultural production suffered, causing difficulties which led two Vice-chairmen of the State Planning Commission to urge the halting of this migration.[6]

---

[1] e.g., see *People's Handbook* (*Renmin Shouce*) *1959*, p. 363. 'It must be established that workers and employees (*chihkung*) participate in the management of enterprises and that staff (*kanpu*) participate in labour.'

[2] *Ten Great Years*, Peking, 1960, pp. 180 and 182.

[3] See pp. 228–9 below. [4] J. P. Emerson: op. cit., p. 1.

[5] *Collected Laws and Regulations* . . . Vol. 4, p. 225, and ibid., Vol. 6, pp. 229–30.

[6] *Planned Economy* (*Jihua Jingji*), No. 8, August 1957, p. 7. Wang Kuang-wei: 'Opinions on the Arrangement of Agricultural Labour', and *Labour* (*Laodong*), No. 21, October 4, 1957, pp. 3–4. Sung P'ing: 'The Problems of Employment.'

In December 1956 the State Council, and in December 1957 the Central Committee and the State Council together, issued directives to regulate the 'blind flow' of peasants to the towns. Enterprises were ordered to channel recruitment through the local departments of labour and, in the case of hiring workers from the countryside, the support of the agricultural co-operatives concerned had to be obtained. *Hsiang* authorities and agricultural co-operatives were forbidden to hand out identity papers on demand to would-be migrants. Public security and other departments were to establish posts at railway and bus stations and at ports to intercept the travellers and send them back again. In cities, the public security organs were directed to ferret out those who had come without authorization and dispatch them to their homes in the country, meting out punishment to the recalcitrant. Snap checks were made on houses at night to discover unauthorized persons staying in them. The rationing system was also used to round up illegal migrants, as most ration cards in China are valid only for one particular place. Urban workers were enjoined to refrain from bragging tales of city life which might unsettle their rural relatives.[1] Lack of liaison between the dispatching authorities and the rural reception areas was found to hamper the implementation of this directive and some cadres in the country made difficulties for homecomers.[2]

Despite these measures, 1958 saw a record increase, estimated at 15·6 million, in the urban population, of which over 10 million is estimated to have resulted from migration from the countryside. The rise in industrial employment (including mining) was officially reported to exceed 234 per cent in the one year, the total of industrial workers jumping from 9 million in 1957 to 25·6 million in 1958; a Western estimate gives the growth as from 7·9 million in 1957 to 23·7 million in 1958.[3] Of course, a good part of this increase in 1958 was due to the development of rural industry, one of the advantages of which was that it provided an alternative to migration to the towns for underemployed labour in the countryside. In 1958 the Director of the State Statistical Bureau reckoned the growth in China's total labour force at about 10 million a year.[4] Therefore, with a rise in the industrial labour force of between 15–17 million, labour to sectors other than industry dropped absolutely as well as relatively in 1958. Rural industry had drawn not only on the pool of underemployed rural labour (which, in any case, was mainly seasonal) but also on that which was normally employed in farm work. The failure to gather in all the 1958 harvest resulted largely from this.

Whatever the correct figures may be, the fantastic movement to the towns at the time of the Great Leap was beyond the powers of the administrative machinery to control; especially inasmuch as it was not evenly spread over the country but affected certain areas in disproportionate degree. In some towns the labour force was reported to have been trebled or quadrupled in the course of a year or less.[5]

[1] *Collected Laws and Regulations* . . . Vol. 4, pp. 225–6 and Vol. 6, pp. 229–32.
[2] Ibid., Vol. 7, pp. 194–5.
[3] *Ten Great Years*, p. 183, and J. P. Emerson: op. cit., p. 128, and *Current Scene*, Vol. 1, No. 30, April 20, 1962, p. 6. J. P. Emerson: loc. cit.
[4] *Study (Xuexi)*, No. 3, February 3, 1958, p. 14. Hsüeh Mu-ch'iao: 'National Construction and the General Arrangement of the People's Livelihood.'
[5] *Anhwei Daily (Anhui Ribao)*, March 15, 1959 (SCMP 1993). Ch'eng Hsi-hai, Secretary,

By no means all the entrants to large-scale industry during the Great Leap were drawn straight from the fields. Many came from the ranks of handicraftsmen—nearly five million in 1958 alone, according to one Western calculation.¹ The First Secretary of the CCP Kiangsi Provincial Committee said that of the new workers in factories, mines, and other enterprises in that province in 1958 and the first half of 1959, 70 per cent had come from agriculture and handicrafts and over 20 per cent from schools, offices and the armed forces. Repair and service trades also lost workers to industry.²

The pressure for higher output no doubt caused enterprises to engage great numbers of new workers. Meanwhile the formation of communes and other rural campaigns in 1958, following on after the drastic curb on free marketing of many agricultural products (instituted in August 1957)³ and the accelerated collectivization of 1956, must have impelled many of the more enterprising peasants to make their way townwards. Relatively to life in the country, the glamour of even the not very bright lights of the cities exercised a more powerful attraction than ever. A considerable wage differential existed between town and countryside, a phenomenon about which the authorities expressed regret and issued directives but which they did not seem able to abolish, although there was a reduction in the wages of the lowest grade industrial workers in 1958.⁴ Many of the migrants to the towns had relatives and friends there already, the substantial urban migration of the First Five Year Plan period producing in this way a snowball effect. However, there was no assurance of employment when the newcomers arrived in the towns.

For most of their years in power, urban unemployment has been a problem to the Chinese Communists,⁵ but estimates of its dimensions have been vague. A survey in 1956 found that the majority of urban unemployed were unskilled and relatively old, but that they included some youngsters educated to higher primary standard or above.⁶ The political and social dangers presented by urban unemployment have occasioned greater anxiety than has unemployment or under-employment in rural areas. It is not, however, true to say that

---

CCP Huainan Municipal Committee: 'How Was Labour Organization Overhauled in Huainan Municipality?' And *Daily Worker* (*Gongren Ribao*), August 9, 1959 (SCMP 2097). Li Ming-hsin, Chairman of the Changchiak'ou Municipal Federation of Trade Unions: 'Pay Attention to All Aspects of the Training of New Workers.'

¹ *Current Scene*, Vol. 1, No. 30, April 20, 1962, p. 6. J. R. Emerson: loc. cit., and *People's Daily* (*Renmin Ribao*), April 26, 1959, p. 9. Sung Yi-p'ing: 'Street Industry—A New Force Not to Be Neglected.' In Wuhan 70,000 workers were said to have moved from 'street industry' to modern industry in 1958.

² *Daily Worker* (*Gongren Ribao*), July 14, 1959. (SCMP 2069). Yang Shang-k'uei, First Secretary, CCP Kiangsi Provincial Committee: 'Care for and Educate New Workers, Strengthen and Raise the Ranks of Workers', and *Chinese Worker* (*Zhongguo Gongren*), No. 13, July 12, 1959, p. 18. Mao Ch'i-hua, Vice-Minister of Labour: 'The Way to Treat the Problem of Adjusting Organization of Labour.'

³ See p. 292 below.

⁴ *China Quarterly*, No. 7, July–September 1961, p. 78. J. P. Emerson: 'Manpower Absorption in the Non-Agricultural Branches of the Economy of Communist China 1953–8', and *New China Fortnightly* (*Xinhua Banyuekan*), No. 122, December 25, 1957, p. 92.

⁵ D. H. Perkins: *Price Formation in Communist China*, p. 184. (Unpublished Ph.D Thesis, Harvard University, 1963.)

⁶ *Collected Papers of the Third Session of the First National People's Congress* (in Chinese), Peking, 1956, p. 742. Speech by Ma Wen-jui, Minister of Labour.

the Chinese Communists have ignored the latter[1] although realization that the rural unemployed will be supported by their families, that such unemployment is mainly seasonal, and that the marginal productivity of labour in agriculture is seldom zero[2]—all these factors make the Chinese government less troubled about unemployment in the country than in the towns.

Overstaffing of factories and other enterprises has been chronic, judging from the Chinese press. This, however, is certainly not a deliberate policy to deal with urban unemployment. On the contrary, such practices have frequently been condemned and enterprises enjoined not to hoard labour. In the early 1960s some enterprises were reported not to know how many employees they had, nor the total of their wage bill, although these figures comprised two of the four targets that remained mandatory for all enterprises after 1957.[3]

The approved policy for dealing with the urban unemployed, at least from 1957 onwards, was to reverse the migration to the towns by the 'sending down' (*hsiafang*) movement. The movement called by this name consisted in fact of several different strands with disparate motives. First there was the permanent 'sending down' to the countryside of urban unemployed or potential unemployed (e.g. primary and secondary school leavers);[4] second, the periodic 'sending down' of cadres of various types for shorter or longer spells of agricultural labour, after which they return to their former posts (in addition, many Party and government cadres were 'sent down' permanently along with other townsfolk); third, the 'sending down' of students for temporary work in the countryside, either during vacations or for longer periods. The last two types of 'sending down' are primarily political in aim and only secondarily economic.

To return to the economically-motivated 'sending down' of urban unemployed, this was given an added impetus during the aftermath of the Great Leap when factories had to cut production through lack of agricultural raw materials and when the excesses of 1958–9 had shown how easily the rural labour surplus could be turned into a labour deficit. Between 1959 (when the movement first reached large proportions) and late 1963, the urban population was reported to have been reduced by the 'sending down' movement from 130 to 110 million.[5] However, the government had great difficulty in enforcing

---

[1] References to the problem occur in Chinese official documents, e.g. the Directive on Employment approved by the Government Administrative Council (the predecessor of the State Council) in 1952. See *Labour Laws and Regulations of the People's Republic of China*, Peking, 1956, p. 76.

[2] T. Schultz: *Transforming Traditional Agriculture*, New Haven, 1964, p. 58.

[3] *Labour* (*Laodong*), No. 14, August 18, 1962, pp. 22–3. Hsiang Kan-ch'eng: 'Control the Wage Fund Severely and Use It Rationally' and *Collected Laws and Regulations . . .* Vol. 6, p. 395. Among the other targets for enterprises which had previously been mandatory but were henceforth to be non-mandatory (although they might be made mandatory by individual ministries or local authorities), were the number of manual workers at the end of the year, the average wage, and the productivity of labour.

[4] Senior middle schools and higher educational institutions had, by 1957, become over full and in that year reduced their intake at a time when the number of teenagers was increasing. *People's Handbook* (*Renmin Shouce*) *1958*, pp. 205–6. Chou En-lai: 'Report to the 1957 Session of the National People's Congress on the Work of the Government.'

[5] A. L. Strong: *Letter from China*, No. 13, December 30, 1963, p. 2. Four million were stated to have been dispatched back to the country by July 1959. *People's Handbook* (*Renmin Shouce*) *1960*, p. 154.

this policy and in 1961 country people were still said to be swarming into Shanghai.[1] In 1961 recruitment of rural labour for industry was banned for three years;[2] it is not known how effectively this was enforced.

The reasoning behind the policy of 'sending down' was that the rate of increase of the urban population should not exceed the rate of increase of the procurement of major farm crops, especially grain.[3] Once the unemployed were back in their villages, the responsibility for feeding them rested primarily with themselves, their families and production teams, all of which thus had a direct incentive in increasing production for their support. So long as these people lived in towns and cities, the government, at either central or local level, had to provide them with rations which (granted the government was unwilling to use the price mechanism to increase voluntary sales of crops by the peasants) meant additional compulsory procurements of output from the producers which, in turn, diminished their incentive to produce.

The criteria for selection for sending down was in general that the most recent arrivals in the towns should be sent back first and that those most fitted for factory work, notably the literate, should be retained. As for the others, in addition to severance pay based on length of employment, they were also to be given travelling allowances and in at least one locality it was laid down that 'farewell meetings and forums are to be held in their honour'.[4] This was obviously to mitigate the loss of face they would experience in returning to their villages empty handed, after having left for the towns with high hopes. The unpopularity of the movement is widely attested. The ranks of the 'sent down' provided many of the refugees who thronged the Hong Kong border in May 1962. Urban school-leavers 'sent down' between 1962–5 are said to have numbered one million, in addition to their many more numerous fellows of peasant parentage who had to return to their villages after finishing their studies. In 1964 some 30 million young people who had completed higher primary schooling were reported to be working in the countryside, about half of whom had either returned to their homes there or been 'sent down' from 1961 onwards.[5] These youngsters were by no means always easy to fit into rural life. Local branches of the Young Communist League were especially charged with their care. Travelling theatrical troupes, 'rural clubs', 'study rooms' and a variety of part-time educational facilities (including part-time agricultural technical schools and colleges) were provided, in order to sweeten the pill of enforced rustication.

Where industry's demands for labour cannot otherwise conveniently be met, special contract schemes for recruitment from agriculture are operated. Several variants of these contract labour schemes have been employed, from

---

[1] *Current Scene*, Vol. 1, No. 6, July 10, 1961, p. 3.
[2] *Seventy Important Points of Communist Industrial Policy* 1961. (From Taiwan source.) No. 32.
[3] *Kuang Ming Daily* (*Guangming Ribao*), October 7, 1963, p. 4. Hsüeh Cheng-hsiu: 'Tentative Discussion of the Relationship Between the Increase in Population in Socialist Cities and the Development of Industrial and Agricultural Production.'
[4] *Anhwei Daily* (*Anhui Ribao*), March 15, 1959 (SCMP 1993). Ch'eng Hsi-hai: loc. cit.
[5] *China Youth* (*Zhongguo Qingnian*), No. 4, February 16, 1964, p. 17. Huang T'ien-hsiang: 'Energetically Develop Spare Time Education for Rural Young People', and NCNA Peking, September 25, 1965.

the Great Leap in 1958 onwards. Usually contracts are concluded between an industrial enterprise and a unit of collective agriculture, binding the latter to supply a stipulated number of long-term, short-term, or seasonal workers. Sometimes it is specified that they may be sent home whenever the factories no longer require them or that they should be given leave during the busy agricultural seasons.[1] In some places secondment from agriculture is for a period of years, as in the case of girls employed in certain cotton mills and silk filatures,[2] an arrangement similar to that long practised in Japan. The financial provisions of the schemes also vary, but commonly they provide that the workers receive board and lodging and that at least part of their money wages is remitted back to the agricultural collective to which they continue to belong.[3] Meanwhile the workers' dependants remain in their villages, thus reducing the urban influx.

The purpose of all these contract labour schemes has been to provide a body of workers to act as reserves for both industry and agriculture, transferable between the two as pressure of work demands, and at the same time not to increase the permanent urban population. Certain similarities are apparent between these contract (*hot'ung*) labour schemes and those contract labour systems (*paokung*) operated in China, more especially in foreign concerns, in days past, under which the enterprise did not deal directly with the workers, but instead only with the contractor who remained responsible for them. Without further knowledge of the way in which the present-day contract labour schemes function, it is not possible to know how far the parallel can be drawn.[4]

3. INDUSTRIAL TRAINING

The general and political education and technical training of the industrial labour force were, in 1950, entrusted primarily to the trade unions. The trade union organizations in enterprises were to be 'responsible for the carrying out of spare-time education for workers and staff there under the direction of the local spare-time education committees'.[5] Before long, enterprises' managements came to control workers' general and technical studies; political education, however, remained in the hands of the trade unions. During the Great Leap, trade unions are reported to have regained responsibility for the whole field of workers' education.[6] But whichever agency has at any time

---

[1] *People's Daily* (*Renmin Ribao*), June 7, 1958, p. 3, and *Daily Worker* (*Gongren Ribao*), June 10, 1958 (SCMP 1797), and *People's Daily* (*Renmin Ribao*), July 17, 1964, p. 1, and ibid., August 28, 1964, p. 5. Chao Jung-an and Wang Chao-lin: 'A Labour System Mutually Beneficial to Industry and Agriculture', and ibid., October 22, 1964, p. 2, and *New Construction* (*Xin Jianshe*), No. 1–2, February 1966, pp. 57–67. Chang Ho-wei: 'An Outline Discussion of the Worker-Peasant System in Finance and Trade.'

[2] *Chinese Textiles* (*Zhongguo Fangzhi*), No. 1, January 10, 1965 (SCMM 465).

[3] J. P. Emerson: op. cit., p. 48.

[4] See p. 209 below on the use of the contract system (*paokung*) in the remuneration of labour.

[5] *Labour Laws and Regulations of the People's Republic of China*, p. 86.

[6] *Current Scene*, Vol. III, No. 15, March 15, 1965, pp. 2–3. P. Harper: 'Closing the Education Gap.'

been in the ascendant, the bulk of industrial training has been given inside industry. Apprenticeship schemes exist[1] but more important have been spare-time and half-time classes and schools operated within enterprises for their employees. Technical schools and colleges, whole or part-time, are also run by local authorities.

The great influx of raw workers in 1958 created massive problems for factory educational and training schemes, while the difficulties of the succeeding years hit the movement severely. However, between 1949–60, 5·6 million skilled workers were reported to have been trained in industry, mining and communications.[2] The definition of 'skill' is not given and is unlikely to equal that of skilled men in long industrialized countries; nevertheless, a large body of workers has been made familiar with industrial techniques. Since many workers were initially illiterate, their enterprises (or the unions in the enterprises) had to teach them the rudiments of learning as well as of technical proficiency. Illiterate and semi-illiterate employees are claimed to have dropped from 70–80 per cent in the early years of the regime to only 20 per cent by 1964.[3] Part of this rise in educational standards is likely to have resulted from discrimination in favour of the better-educated when the labour force was cut after the Great Leap.

It is inevitable that such a large and rapid programme of training should be of uneven quality. However, to set against such weaknesses, it must be repeated that the ordinary industrial labour force in a Chinese factory includes individuals of high intelligence, who would be less likely to become manual workers in countries with more adequate educational facilities. Lack of early opportunities for study, and of other ways of occupying leisure hours, as well as the incentive of need and the high traditional esteem of learning in China, are apt to give rise to far more zeal by workers for evening classes than could be found in their Western counterparts. The young average age of Chinese industrial workers must also help.

All these factors have facilitated internal promotion from the ranks, a policy fostered by necessity as well as by choice. Another source of technicians and higher staff has been large well-established plants, especially in Shanghai and the north east. Sometimes workers from elsewhere are sent to these places to gain experience before returning. In many instances, a group of skilled men trained and experienced in such undertakings as the Anshan Steel Works, the Kirin Chemical Corporation, or the Changchun Motor Corporation, is sent to a new plant to form a nucleus which in turn will train local workers.

Skilled factory workers are given the formal title of technician. This also is the grade which new graduates from engineering colleges enter. After a few years these graduates are likely to be promoted to be engineers, a rank which

---

[1] Apprenticeship systems in the past were connected with the guilds. No trace of the guilds in contemporary China has come to our knowledge; earlier they had been dealt a severe blow by measures taken by the Kuomintang. Chang Kia-ngau: *The Inflation Spiral*, London, 1958, p. 343.

[2] *China Reconstructs*, August 1960, p. 24. Wen Yu: 'The New Generation of Skilled Workers.'

[3] *Daily Worker* (*Gongren Ribao*), January 26, 1964, p. 1. Editorial.

carries great prestige and which is also open to technicians promoted from the ranks.

Apart from training provided within industrial enterprises, technical and other vocational education is given by ministries and local departments to fulfil their own requirements for skilled men. However, these sectoral training facilities often are unable to supply the great variety of specialists that are needed by a single ministry. For example, the Ministry of Coal requires the services of 60 to 70 different types of middle-ranking technical personnel, but in 1957 the Ministry's own training establishments were turning out only 10 to 20 different types.[1] The decentralization of 1957-8 may have aggravated this problem. The general rule, as we have seen, has been that whatever organ runs a training institution controls assignment of its graduates.[2] Thus a province which is not self-sufficient in all the specialists it needs (and few, if any, provinces can be) must depend on a supply of graduates from institutions outside its control. Local quotas appear to exist for enrolment in certain national institutions of higher education and each province may well have a claim on all or some of its own quota of students. Also inter-provincial agreements may perhaps exist for provinces to allot places to outsiders for training unavailable in their provinces of origin. Very little information has come to our knowledge on this topic.

4. TRADE UNIONS

The All-China Federation of Trade Unions was established by the decision of a congress held in Harbin in 1948, as a revival of an organization of the same name which existed in the 1920s,[3] but which later had to go underground. For a period until 1954 the Minister of Labour was concurrently Chairman of the Federation.

Trade unions are organized on both an industrial and regional basis. In 1965 the Federation was listed as having sixteen constituent industrial unions, including unions of workers in education and finance and trade, as well as in sectors concerned with material production. These industrial unions operate at national and provincial levels. In addition, trade union councils, embracing activities of all unions within a given area, exist at provincial, municipal and county levels.[4] The primary or basic level organizations at places of work numbered 160,000 in 1965.[5]

[1] *Planned Economy* (*Jihua Jingji*), No. 4, April 1957, p. 19. Huang Tsu-yu: 'The Problem of the Training and Distribution of Middle-Ranking Specialist Cadres.'

[2] Ibid., p. 9. 'An Explanation of the Basic Circumstances of the Implementation of the 1956 National Plan and of the Draft Plan for 1957.' It may be surmised that the blows struck at the universities in 1966 during the 'cultural revolution', led to a growth in the relative importance of the politically less exposed ministry schools, perhaps accompanied by a movement to them of university students and staff.

[3] *People's Handbook* (*Renmin Shouce*) *1950*, pp. '*chi*' 9-10, and *Peking Review*, April 30, 1965, p. 22.

[4] *Peking Review*, April 30, 1965, pp. 23-4. Sometimes trade union councils also exist at the levels of special district and market town. The phrase 'trade union council', used of local bodies, can be translated as 'federation of trade unions' or 'general trade union'. Here we follow the usage of English language publications from Peking.

[5] Ibid., p. 24.

Total membership has grown as follows:[1]

	Million members	
1948	2·83	
1953	10·2	
1957	16·3	(of which 3·89 million were 'activists')
1963	20·8	
1965	20·8	

By the Trade Union Law of 1950 all employed persons, whose wages constitute their sole or main means of livelihood, are eligible to join; those engaged in, for example, collective agriculture or handicraft co-operatives, are ineligible; but workers in supply and marketing co-operatives, these being closely assimilated to state commerce (e.g. remitting profits to the state) are eligible for membership.[2] The total number of employees, therefore, sets an upper limit to potential union membership. However, even after deducting those ineligible for union membership from the employment figures on p. 181 above, the number eligible would appear consistently to exceed by a wide margin the reported membership. The discrepancy is perplexing, as normally it seems that membership is compulsory, comprising in the basic trade union organization all the regular workers in the work place concerned. Part of the gap must be accounted for by casual, contract and other short-term workers who either are ineligible or are not pressed to join.[3] The stability of the membership total between 1963 and 1965 may reflect success for the policy of stabilizing total urban employment; alternatively, it may just come from a failure to revise statistics of membership.

Figures for total numbers of trade union cadres have not been found. Ratios between the number of employees at any place of work and the number of full-time trade union officials were laid down in the 1950 Trade Union Law and repeated in the Secret Instructions of December 1961 known as the Seventy Points on Industrial Policy, but it is uncertain how far these have been observed.[4] The chairmen of basic level trade unions can be either full time or part time.[5] Full-time trade union officials, like other cadres, are expected to undertake manual work from time to time.[6]

Chinese trade unions derive their funds from membership dues, officially fixed at 1 per cent of a member's wage, but sometimes reported to exceed that

---

[1] *Sources: 1948, 1953* and *1965*, ibid., p. 22. *1957*, ibid., p. 23, and *Constitution of Chinese Trade Unions* (in Chinese), Peking, 1957, p. 62. *1963 China Reconstructs*, May 1963, p. 27.

[2] *Labour Laws and Regulations of the People's Republic of China*, p. 5. 'The Trade Union Law . . . 1950.' On p. 7 of this source, mention is made of 'trade unions in enterprises operated by the state or by co-operatives'—presumably this refers to such co-operatives (e.g. supply and marketing) which are almost identical with state enterprises. In practice, at least, workers in other types of collective seem to be excluded. See J. P. Emerson: op. cit., p. 47, and *China News Analysis*, No. 482, August 23, 1963, p. 2.

[3] *China News Analysis*, No. 482, August 23, 1963, p. 2; see *Current Scene*, Vol. I, No. 22, January 5, 1962, p. 5, for an example of an unskilled labourer who said he had no difficulty in finding a job without joining a union.

[4] *Labour Laws and Regulations of the People's Republic of China*, pp. 10–11, and *Seventy Important Points of Communist Industrial Policy*, No. 65.

[5] *Daily Worker (Gongren Ribao)*, July 24, 1963, p. 1. Editorial.

[6] Ibid., August 17, 1963, p. 1. Editorial.

rate; from registration fees on entry, officially fixed at 1 per cent of the entrant's previous month's wages, from payments equivalent to 2 per cent of their total wage bills from enterprises and other employers; from state subsidies; from profits derived from catering, sporting and cultural activities; and from profits of political, technical, and other publications, including the *Daily Worker* (*Gongren Ribao*).[1]

Trade unions are organized on the principles of 'democratic centralism'; that is, they are run at every level by committees elected under Party guidance and which remain under the control of the corresponding Party committee. It seems usual for the chairman of the trade union branch to be a member of the Party committee in the enterprise.

The task of a trade union is 'to play the part of a strong assistant of the Party',[2] and more especially to promote 'production, welfare and education, with production paramount'.[3] Wage negotiations are no part of a trade union's functions in China, and workers are discouraged from discussing wages among themselves.[4] Together with the Young Communist League, the trade unions are intended to be 'transmission belts between the Party and the masses', to launch labour emulation campaigns and to mobilize workers to fulfil plans and to observe labour discipline.[5] The responsibilities of unions for social welfare are intimately connected with the aim of increasing output: there is no need to think that the importance attached to this side of their activities is purely for propaganda. In the early stages of industrialization in any country, with raw workers crowding into factories and mines, the general social inadequacy of the labour force is a most serious factor inhibiting rises in output. In the decade before the Communist victory, a Chinese factory manager had remarked that 'if the present experiment of national enterprise fails, the failure will not come from our technical incompetence but from our unpreparedness to deal with human factors'.[6] The same could be said with truth of the drive to industrialize under the Communist regime.

The social matters with which trade unions, together with Party committees and others, have to deal include industrial safety, mess halls, clinics, hostels (many factories and mines house their own workers, as occurred also in pre-Communist China), creches, clubs, sanatoria and rest homes, sparetime education, physical culture, libraries, loans for children's school fees, marriage guidance, and the settling of domestic disputes, advice and assistance to the dependants of workers, and the payment of pensions to the retired. The

---

[1] *Constitution of Chinese Trade Unions*, p. 38, and *Labour Laws and Regulations of the People's Republic of China*, pp. 14–15, and E. Snow: *The Other Side of the River*, London, 1963, p. 239, where it is reported that a small percentage of enterprises' profits (amounting to 0·015–0·03 per cent of the total wage bill in 1960) was returned by the state to enterprises' trade unions. This may be the form which the state subsidies (stipulated in the Trade Union Law of 1950) have taken, or it may be some additional payment.

[2] *Chinese Worker* (*Zhongguo Gongren*), No. 19, October 12, 1959, p. 7. Ku Ta-ch'un: 'Trade Unions Must Energetically Take the Initiative to Be Good Assistants of the Party.'

[3] *Daily Worker* (*Gongren Ribao*), June 23, 1961, p. 1.

[4] *New Statesman*, September 3, 1965, p. 320. K. S. Karol: 'Maoism: China's Secular Religion.'

[5] *Labour Laws and Regulations of the People's Republic of China*, p. 8, and *Daily Worker* (*Gongren Ribao*), June 27, 1958 (SCMP 1809). Editorial.

[6] Shih Kuo-heng: *China Enters the Machine Age*, Cambridge, Mass., 1944, pp. 168–9.

unions administer workers' insurance and other welfare funds on behalf of the state. Members of trade unions are entitled to free medical care and insurance against sickness, accident and old age. Reports indicate that in some places this is still only an ideal (see p. 213 below for divergence between total trade union membership and total numbers covered by labour insurance and full medical care). No doubt in this, as in other respects, conditions are patchy, varying widely with the locality, the industry and the enterprise.

In addition to these domestic functions, trade unions play a significant representational role in foreign affairs, by frequent sending and receiving of delegations.

It is not easy to draw clear dividing lines between the duties of trade unions, managers of enterprises, and Party committees. The lack of independence of the trade unions is obvious. Lai Jo-yu, the then Chairman of the All-China Federation of Trade Unions, in his speech to the Eighth National Congress of the CCP, in 1956, argued the case for trade unions continuing to have a function to fulfil. Although under socialism, 'the fundamental task of management coincides with that of the trade unions, that is fulfilment of the state plan, yet due to the difference in the nature of their work, and the difference in their approach towards problems, the trade unions and management differ in their views on a number of matters'. However, the tendency for unions to participate in governmental functions, 'such as fixing wage scales and the work norms, taking charge of labour insurance, supervising safety and sanitation measures in production' was increasing and this must be regarded as normal.[1] Lai deprecated the growth of bureaucracy and 'commandism' in the unions.

Complaints against union bureaucracy and 'commandism' were voiced with considerably more vigour in 1957, during the short spell of free speech known as the 'Hundred Flowers' period. In a graphic expression, unions and managements were said to 'breathe through one nostril'.[2] However, at times some trade union officials have spoken up for the workers and for more freedom for the unions, being denounced in 1958 for so doing.[3] In February 1964 the Finnish Communist leader, Kuusinen, referred to the abortive attempts of Chinese trade unions to voice workers' demands.[4]

5. MANAGEMENT AND STAFF

The shortage of educated people is one of the gravest obstacles to development in all parts of the world. China lacks engineers, agriculturalists, doctors, teachers—persons of all kinds competent in the techniques of modern life. In no sphere is this deficiency felt more than in the management of large-scale enterprises; a capacity which cannot be acquired so rapidly as technical qualifications.

Personal ties have always counted for much in Chinese economic life and

---

[1] *The Eighth National Congress of the Communist Party of China*, Peking, 1956. Vol. II, Speeches, pp. 241 and 245.
[2] *People's Daily* (*Renmin Ribao*), May 20, 1957, p. 1.
[3] *Daily Worker* (*Gongren Ribao*), June 27, 1958 (SCMP 1809). Editorial.
[4] *Soviet News*, March 27, 1964, p. 124.

weakness in the management of large impersonal organizations bedevilled attempts to modernize the country from the nineteenth century onwards.[1] Before the war with Japan broke out in 1937, a measure of success had been achieved by Chinese undertakings of some size in various sectors of economic life, but managerial skills, especially on the financial side, together with a sense of responsibility for impersonal organization, were still critically inadequate.

After 1949 the small pool of professional, technical and managerial manpower was depleted by flight to Taiwan and Hong Kong and by continued residence abroad of many Chinese who were at that time studying in America and Europe. The great majority of well-qualified people, however, stayed in China from choice as well as from necessity, despite the fact that their family backgrounds (achieving higher education normally implied prosperous parentage) frequently subjected them to suspicion by the new rulers. The educated classes themselves by no means wholly reciprocated these suspicions, especially in the case of those whose assets consisted chiefly of their qualifications and ability. These people had become thoroughly disillusioned with the Kuomintang; they, more than others, realized the need to modernize the country, they had suffered severely in the war and post-war inflation, and their inclination was to give the new regime the benefit of any doubts they may have nursed.

The shortage of higher managerial and technical staff was aggravated by the withdrawal of the Japanese who, before 1945, had operated many of the modern plants and other enterprises in Manchuria and north and east China. In addition, the measures taken by the Communist government necessitated more managers and organizers capable of running large undertakings. Collectivization was usually accompanied by an increase in the size of individual units in industry. Family handicraft concerns were combined into co-operatives, private firms on being transformed into joint state-private undertakings were often amalgamated with others. In each case the new set-up made extra demands on administrative ability. The old type of working proprietor, who may have kept the accounts in his head, was not equal to the changed situation. New and more complex forms or organization demanded new and more specialized skills. Yet the men with these skills did not exist. This no doubt was one argument that weighed in favour of the encouragement given to small-scale industry during the Great Leap and to the development of small handicraft undertakings at a later date—that, whatever their other defects, they made use of a type of entrepreneurial ability which is in plentiful supply in China.

The new government put in hand a programme of rapid development of higher education, so that the total number of graduates (new and old) of institutions of higher education increased from around 150,000 in 1949 to an estimated 625,000 by 1960.[2] Engineers constituted over a quarter of the 1960

[1] See A. Feuerwerker: *China's Early Industrialization*, Cambridge, Mass., 1958.

[2] L. A. Orleans: *Professional Manpower and Education in Communist China*, Washington, DC, 1961, pp. 126–7. Between 1949 and 1963, 1·1 million students (370,000 being engineers) are reported to have graduated from institutions of higher studies. *Far Eastern Economic Review*, February 6, 1964, p. 310. Colina MacDougall: 'The Reds and the Experts.'

G

total, compared with about one-sixth in 1949; the proportion in medicine and education also rose. Graduates in finance and economics slightly increased their proportional share of the total, while those in other social sciences, in law and liberal arts declined proportionately.[1] While the standards of the best institutions remained high, the large increase in numbers of those receiving higher education was accompanied by a widespread fall in quality. It is not possible in this study to consider in greater detail the growth of higher education in China since 1949 or the contribution made by those educated abroad: for this the reader is referred to two studies on this subject.[2] In addition to educational developments in China, between 1950–8 some 38,000 Chinese technicians were trained in the Soviet Union, as well as 6,500 students who were sent there for higher studies.[3]

China's nuclear programme is considered by one observer to have required only 3·4 per cent of the available scientists and engineers in the relevant fields. 'But this figure substantially underrates the manpower costs, since the Chinese have had to use many of their best scientists and engineers—particularly from the fields of chemical and electric engineering, which have been lagging in China.'[4]

During the years 1949–59 over 10,800 Soviet experts, as well as more than 1,500 others from East Europe, worked in China for longer or shorter spells.[5] This went some way towards mitigating the urgent need for trained manpower in economic life and in higher education. These specialists won a reputation for competence, although their advice was not always thought relevant to the Chinese situation. In this latter respect, the older men who had known the earlier and rougher days of the Soviet economy, were found to be more adaptable than their younger colleagues.

Directors and deputy directors of factories are drawn from several different sources. Many, especially in joint state-private enterprises, are former owners or salaried managers who continued to be employed after their businesses had undergone 'socialist transformation'. Others are demobilized army officers and veteran Communist cadres (who also figure prominently among Party secretaries in enterprises) while in course of time a number of ordinary factory workers have been promoted to be directors or heads of workshops or to other responsible posts.

In 1955, 56 per cent of chief engineers in factories were graduates of institutions of higher learning.[6] Probably such graduates, both technical and others, will come to fill an increasing proportion of senior positions in industry.

The staff of factories and similar enterprises in China fall into three main

[1] L. A. Orleans: op. cit., pp. 127–30.
[2] Ibid., and Cho-yuan Cheng: *Scientific and Engineering Manpower in Communist China 1949–63*, Washington, DC, 1965.
[3] *New Hunan Daily* (*Xin Hunan Bao*), February 13, 1960 (SCMP 2232).
[4] M. H. Halperin: *China and the Bomb*, London, 1965, p. 74.
[5] I. A. Lysenko: *Economic Co-operation between China and the Countries of the Socialist Camp* (in Russian), Moscow, 1960, p. 60.
[6] *New China Fortnightly* (*Xinhua Banyuekan*), No. 100, January 25, 1957, p. 89. Statistical Work Bulletin Information Room: 'The National Figures, Composition and Distribution of the Employed Labour Force in 1955.'

categories: administrative, technical and political.[1] The enterprise is headed, at least nominally, by a manager. His two chief executives are the chief engineer, in charge of the technical side, and (at least since new regulations promulgated in 1961) the chief accountant, controlling the financial administration and having certain powers independent of the manager. This triangle of top management resembles that in the Soviet Union and East Europe.

Two-, three- or four-tier administration exists or has existed in different factories at different times since 1949. Policy on this has shifted; probably practice has at most times varied considerably between factories. However, before 1958, three-level administration—factory, workshop and work sector—was considered standard at least in heavy industry.[2] From 1958 'small production groups' (sometimes called 'shift groups') smaller than work sectors (which commonly counted more than fifty, and sometimes several hundred workers) were encouraged as 'basic levels' of factory organization in which all could participate.[3] As a result, some factories developed four levels of management, leading to a proliferation of administrative work and bureaucratic rules. In 1965 a movement was reported for streamlining factory organization by reducing the number of administrative tiers; this was connected with the encouragement of vertical disintegration, resulting in smaller and more specialized plants. In consequence, the intermediate level or levels between the factory and the small group were in some cases abolished.[4]

A visitor to China in 1965 remarked on the relative autonomy of the workshops, with collective determination of wages and distribution of tasks and collective bonuses.[5] This is in accordance with the Chinese tradition of decentralized small groups using the methods they prefer so long as they fulfil allotted responsibilities. However, vertical 'responsibility systems' cutting across horizontal lines were also acknowledged and even the need to define the specific responsibility of each worker.[6]

Parallel to an enterprise's administration is the Party committee of the enterprise, headed by the Party secretary. According to the constitution of the Chinese Communist Party, the tasks of 'primary Party organizations' in

[1] *People's Daily (Renmin Ribao)*, May 12, 1964, p. 5. Wu Hsing-feng, Director, Political Department, Ministry of Petroleum: 'Deal Satisfactorily with the Problem of the Orientation of Socialist Enterprises.'

[2] *New China Monthly (Xinhua Yuebao)*, No. 51, January 1954, p. 147.

[3] *Economic Research (Jingji Yanjiu)*, No. 6, June 1960, p. 36. Production Study Group at the Chengtu Measuring Instruments and Cutting Tools Factory of the Szechuan Finance and Economics Institute, Industrial Economics Department, Class 56: 'Small Group Administration in Industrial Enterprises Is a Necessary Product of the Political and Economic Development of Our Country.'

[4] *People's Daily (Renmin Ribao)*, September 24, 1965, p. 1. Editorial. And ibid., March 13, 1965, p. 5. Yang Ch'eng-min, Vice-Mayor of Tientsin: 'Organize the Machine-Building Industry on the Basis of "Small but Specialized" and "Medium-Sized but Specialized" Units', and *Ta Kung Daily (Dagong Bao)*, Peking, April 18, 1965, p. 2. K'ung Hsiang-chen: 'Organize a High Tide in Production and Construction in Light Industry in Harmony with the General Line', and *BBC Summary of World Broadcasts*, Second Series, FE/W325/A/21 (Changsha, July 12, 1965), and ibid., FE/W333/A/18 (Peking, July 7, 1965).

[5] *New Statesman*, September 3, 1965, p. 320. K. S. Karol: loc. cit.

[6] *Chemical Industry (Huaxue Gongye)*, No. 1, January 6, 1964 (SCMM 406). Editorial. And *Economic Research (Jingji Yanjiu)*, No. 4, April 1965, p. 13. Tung Yang: 'Establish a Job Responsibility System and Strengthen the Management of Industrial Enterprises.'

factories, mines and other basic units of economic and social life include the strengthening of labour discipline and ensuring fulfilment of plans, as well as the more purely political functions of ideological guidance and control. Party committees have also been charged with running mess halls and welfare work.[1] In their responsibilities the Party committees are assisted by branches of the Young Communist League and, as we shall further note below, by trade unions.

In 1956 the number of Party members in industry and mining in China was reported to be 1,121,000, representing according to the report some 15 per cent of the total employees working in these sectors.[2] Another source for the same year states that 10–20 per cent of the workers in enterprises of all kinds (i.e. including all state and joint state-private enterprises but excluding workers in units under collective ownership) were Party members as were the majority of cadres (i.e. staff) in such enterprises.[3] By 1964 total Party membership of the Chinese Communist Party had risen to 18 million,[4] but no analysis of this total according to occupation or sector of the economy has come to our knowledge.

We do not know the number of full-time political cadres in enterprises of all kinds or of particular types, but the total must be very considerable. In 1957 the Changchun Motor Plant was reported to have more than a hundred full-time Young Communist League Cadres;[5] the number of Party cadres was probably even greater.

Policy on the relationship within enterprises between management and Party committee has swung more than once from one direction to another under the influence of nation-wide political and economic trends. The Director of the Party Central Committee's Department of Industrial and Communication Work, Li Hsueh-feng, speaking in 1956, gave an account of the shifts in policy up to that date. During the rehabilitation period, from 1949–52, the Party committees took the lead, the system being described as 'collective leadership of the Party combined with individual responsibility'. 'But in carrying out this system there was a tendency on the part of the Party committee to take over all the work of the management, and this caused some confusion.' Beginning in 1953, a new system, 'unified leadership under a single head', was introduced, to give more authority to the managers of enterprises. This policy was held in 1956 to have been effective 'up to a point' in redressing the lack of clear cut responsibility, but it 'wrongly emphasized that the man responsible for the management of the enterprise had full authority, that the duties of the Party organization were only to guarantee production

[1] *The Eighth National Congress of the Communist Party of China*, Vol. I, p. 165, and *Seventy Important Points of Communist Industrial Policy*, 1961. (From Taiwan source), No. 60.
[2] E. S. Kirby (ed.): *Contemporary China*, Vol. II, Hongkong, 1958, p. 141, taken from *Current Events (Shihshih Shouce)*, No. 18, September 25, 1956.
[3] *Documents of the Eighth National Congress of the Chinese Communist Party* (in Chinese), Peking, 1956, p. 463. Speech by Li Hsueh-feng, Director of the Central Committee's Department for Industry and Communications.
[4] *Pravda*, April 28, 1964, p. 5. This figure is given as 'over 17 million' in *People's Daily (Renmin Ribao)*, July 1, 1961, p. 2. Speech by Liu Shao-chi.
[5] *Shenyang Daily (Shenyang Ribao)*, June 11, 1957, quoted in R. MacFarquhar (ed.) *The Hundred Flowers*, p. 109.

and give general supervision, and that the director or manager need not carry out the resolutions of the Party organization if he disagreed with them'.[1] In these circumstances, it is not surprising that 'unprincipled disputes' were apt to occur between Party committee secretaries and managers of enterprises.[2] The system recommended by Li Hsueh-feng and ordered to be put into effect by the Central Committee was that of combining the 'collective leadership of the Party with individual responsibility'. All major questions in an enterprise were to be decided by the Party committee after which 'the comrades in charge of management should ... be entrusted with the task of making arrangements to carry out the decisions'. The managers were to be solely responsible for routine administrative and technical tasks.[3]

It proved impossible to draw a clear line in this way between the responsibilities of managers and of Party committees. Managers often found themselves torn between the demands of higher authorities of their enterprises' controlling ministries to fulfil plan targets and the conflicting demands of enterprises' Party committees which might be more interested in, for example, some current campaign. Not knowing which master to serve, managers sometimes considered the safest line of conduct to be 'blind production', that is to concentrate on maximizing output, regardless of other considerations. Therefore to correct this tendency, emphasis was laid on certain 'key tasks'. The Party committees, being better placed to determine these than the managers, gradually took over more administrative authority; so that even before the Great Leap the Party committees had come to make the important decisions in enterprises.[4] Thus when the Directive of November 1957 on the Reform of the Industrial Management System gave more latitude and initiative to the individual enterprise,[5] these enhanced powers accrued to the Party committees and Party secretaries of enterprises, rather than to the nominal managers. The policy of 'combining the collective leadership of the Party with individual responsibility' was re-interpreted as 'the responsibility of the factory manager under the leadership of the Party committee'.[6] Presently we shall have more to say on the fall in status of both managerial and technical staff in 1958-9. Here we will but note that the supercession of administrators by Party officials characterized all spheres of Chinese life at this period.

A few examples will suffice to show how far in 1958-9, Party committees in enterprises concerned themselves with details of production and welfare. A worker in Kweichow received from the Party committee of his plant an assignment to invent a special alloy rod; a safety campaign in a Shanghai engineering works was initiated, and action laid down, by its Party committee; when a

---

[1] *The Eighth National Congress of the Communist Party of China*, Vol. II. Speeches, p. 305.

[2] *People's Daily* (*Renmin Ribao*), March 27, 1955, p. 1. Editorial.

[3] *The Eighth National Congress of the Communist Party of China*, Vol. II, Speeches, pp. 304-6.

[4] *Annals of the American Academy of Political and Social Science*, Vol. 349, September 1963, p. 53. F. Schurmann: 'Economic Policy and Political Power in Communist China.'

[5] See pp. 151-2 and 165 above.

[6] *Red Flag* (*Hongqi*), No. 15, August 1, 1960, p. 11. Wang Ho-feng, Secretary, CCP Heilungkiang Provincial Committee: 'Strengthen and Develop the "Two Participations, One Reform and Three Co-ordinations"': Improve all Aspects of Enterprise Management.'

Shansi paper mill ran short of raw materials, its Party committee organized a search for supplies.[1]

On occasion the tendency of the Party committee to usurp managerial functions has been carried to the length of having one person concurrently holding the posts of Party secretary and administrative head of the unit concerned. The examples of this phenomenon that have come to our attention are mainly from agriculture, education and political administration, but one striking case of its occurrence in industry was at the Wuhan Iron and Steel Corporation where, at one time, the First Secretary of the Party General Branch was concurrently general manager of the Corporation.[2] We have been informed by Soviet economists that such a combination of posts would be unthinkable in the Soviet Union.

In 1961, under the pressure of economic crisis, the authority of managers of enterprises was once again affirmed. A 'strict responsibility system' was demanded, by which the duties of manager, technologist and Party committee would be clearly defined.[3]

The policy propounded in 1961 would have the Party committee of an enterprise act in relation to the manager as an ever present board of directors. It was exhorted to reserve its energy for the more serious decisions and not get involved in routine matters, lest it be 'demoted to the status of an ordinary operational department and its leadership role weakened'.[4] The manager was charged with the disposition of labour, materials, and financial resources in accordance with state plans, with directives of higher Party and of government organs and with resolutions of the Party committee of his own enterprise.[5] It was not said how he should act if these were mutually inconsistent. Great importance was attached to clear cut allocation of duties through 'a whole set of responsibility systems', from the 'responsibility system of the factory manager' downwards, 'clearly specifying the responsibility of the cadres at every level and the responsibility of every organization so that every man may have a special job to do and everything may have a special man to take care of it'.[6] In all spheres of life, after the Great Leap, this desire to nail down specific responsibilities was a reaction to the confusion of 1958–9 when, as we shall further note, workers of all grades were encouraged to participate in management, so that everyone's responsibility become no one's.

The policy of 'the manager's full responsibility under the collective leader-

---

[1] NCNA Peking, November 5, 1959, and *Daily Worker* (*Gongren Ribao*), June 14, 1959 (SCMP 2047), and ibid., September 13, 1959 (CB 601) Tu Yen-ch'ing, Chairman of the National Committee of the China Light Industry Trade Union: 'Struggle to Produce More and Better Light Industry Products.'

[2] Union Research Institute, Hong Kong: *Who's Who in Communist China*, Hong Kong, 1966, p. 347. See under Li I-ch'ing. A more recent example of the concurrent holding of two such posts is the reference to a certain Chen Hsin-yu, 'Party Branch Secretary and Manager of the Tehsin Metallurgical Works in Shanghai, a fine Party branch secretary and an outstanding representative of the national industry and communications front.' NCNA, February 22, 1966.

[3] *People's Daily* (*Renmin Ribao*), February 22, 1961, pp. 1 and 4. Editorial.

[4] *Liberation* (*Jiefang*), No. 7, June 5, 1961 (SCMM 312). 'Perfecting the Responsibility Systems.'

[5] *People's Daily* (*Renmin Ribao*), August 4, 1961, p. 7.

[6] *Liberation* (*Jiefang*), No. 7, June 5, 1961 (SCMM 312), loc. cit.

ship of the Party committee' has not, at the time of writing, been officially rescinded although in 1963 and 1964 some increase in Party control may have occurred. In the 'great proletarian cultural revolution' in 1966, political pressures and incentives appear to have become paramount.[1] The attempt to prevent Party committees of enterprises from being absorbed into the ordinary administration was apparently not successful[2]—in any case from 1964 it was thought necessary to provide additional political leadership in economic life through establishing special 'political work organs', first at national level, but before long at provincial and *hsien* levels as well, inside the ordinary administrative departments, of finance, commerce, industry and communications. New political work organs were also formed inside some corporations (*kungsze*) presumably alongside their Party committees, while in some places special 'guides' or 'instructors' were assigned to individual enterprises by political departments of *hsien* or higher level.[3] Clearly it was felt that the strictly political tasks had been neglected and that a stiffening of the political element was needed throughout the economy. These political work organs come under the political departments mentioned in Chapter 1 which were set up within the central committee from the end of 1963.

Doubt may be permitted on whether these political work organs in their turn, may not go the same way as the Party committees. As long as the main task of Party organs in economic sectors is to produce certain economic results, so long must the leading elements in these Party organs concentrate their energies on economic matters. Even if their tasks are expressed in political terms, success in these may be measured by the degree of subsequent economic success—i.e. the attainment of targets is the most easily ascertainable proof of ideological zeal.[4] This inevitably involves taking sides on economic issues, for example which method of production to prefer in a given instance. Before long these problems engross the group which has to decide them and mould it rather than the group moulding the economic matters with which it deals. That the group in question continues to repeat the approved political slogans may disguise rather than demonstrate its chief preoccupations. This trend may be hastened, if, as often seemed to occur, new industrial recruits

[1] For an account for foreign consumption of policy on factory management early in 1965, see *Peking Review*, February 26, 1965, pp. 20–4. Ma Wen-kuei: 'Industrial Management in China.' For the various swings in policy on the role of factory managers, see F. Schurmann: *Ideology and Organization in Communist China*. Chapter 4, and D. H. Perkins: *Market Control and Planning in Communist China*, Cambridge, Mass., 1966. Chapter 6.

[2] In 1966 articles were still appearing to warn Party Secretaries not to take over too much administrative responsibility in their enterprises to the neglect of political duties, e.g. *People's Daily* (*Renmin Ribao*), April 6, 1966, p. 5. Meng Shao-wen: 'Do Not Forget Party Work.'

[3] *Ta Kung Daily* (*Dagong Bao*), Peking, June 16, 1965, p. 1. Editorial and news item. See also *China News Analysis*, No. 581, September 17, 1965. From 1954 to 1957 similar special political organs, alongside Party committees, existed within the Ministry of Communications' 'system'. *People's Water Transport Paper* (*Renmin Hangyün Bao*), October 19, 1957. (I am indebted to Victor Funnell of the Flinders University of South Australia for this reference.)

[4] 'Whether or not an enterprise is able to fulfil the whole of the plan laid down by the state is the chief way of determining if theoretical political work in the enterprise has been done well or badly.' *Labour* (*Laodong*), No. 8, August 1964, p. 27. Chang Feng-lin: 'Distribute Enterprises' Bonus Funds Reasonably.'

to the Party have been chosen in great measure for their competence in their jobs, and whose interests may therefore be more professional than political.

In any case, the new political work organs can only be as effective as the quality of their staff permits. Figures available for one province, Heilungkiang, show that the majority (54 per cent) of the new political instructors assigned to the particularly sensitive sector of finance and trade, were secretaries of Party branches—i.e. from the category whose defects presumably made the new departments necessary, 10 per cent were chosen from administrative staff, and 32 per cent were ex-servicemen.[1] It is on the last category that the most sanguine hopes have been placed; a corollary of the national campaign to emulate the political zeal said to characterize the armed forces. Yet the ignorance of economic affairs of the ex-service cadres is likely to weaken their ability to enforce political control over economic life.

These considerations suggest that whatever may officially be at any given time the respective roles of Party secretary, 'political guide' or enterprise manager, in actual fact the situation in any particular enterprise must depend largely on the personalities, competence and individual Party standing of those concerned, and on the plant's position in respect to local and national political currents. Such factors are important in the Soviet Union;[2] in China, where everything is less settled, they must carry even greater weight.

The conflict between the need for, and the suspicion of, expertise in the administrative and technical control of enterprises, shows itself not only in relations between management and Party, but also in the linked, but not identical, question of relations between management and workers. In the early years of the Communist regime, all state-owned enterprises set up workers' representative conferences with consultative functions. This consultation with the workers ceased, in reality if not in theory, during the First Five Year Plan as the authority first of the managers, then of the Party committees, grew greater. In 1958 the situation changed. There was in the air at that time a boundless trust in the ability of Party and people to work economic wonders, untrammelled by the traditions which restricted experienced managers and experts, a Rousseau-like belief in the virtue of unsophistication. General meetings of workers were summoned and a system was proclaimed of 'two participations, one reform and three co-ordinations'—that is, the participation of staff in manual tasks and of workers in management, the reform of established procedures and the joint discussion of problems by administrative staff, technical experts and workers.[3]

Managerial and technical staff were relegated to an inferior position during the Great Leap. On the other hand, no responsibility was considered too great, no process too complicated for the ordinary unlettered workers to undertake. The fact that most Chinese manual workers had never had access to an educational ladder meant that unskilled workers might be of higher average intellectual ability and drive than is usual in societies with more wide-

[1] *Ta Kung Daily* (*Dagong Bao*), Peking, June 16, 1965, p. 1.
[2] A. Nove: op. cit., p. 100.
[3] *People's Daily* (*Renmin Ribao*), November 27, 1958 (SCMP 1914), and *Red Flag* (*Hongqi*), No. 15, August 1, 1960, pp. 6–15. Wang Ho-feng: loc. cit.

spread opportunities for education. This circumstance gave some justification to the attitudes of the Great Leap.

Higher authority sometimes had to issue rebukes at the length to which egalitarian tendencies were carried in 1958. In a certain rubber factory the title 'management personnel' was changed to 'service personnel', the secretary of the Party committee at the factory being 'Service Personnel No. 1', and the factory manager, 'Service Personnel No. 2'. 'According to some comrades the main job of these service personnel should be labour, and their subsidiary job, performance of their official or professional duties, and a principal part of "labour" should consist of making beds for the workers and bringing them tea and hot water.' The result was that not only management but even Party leadership in that factory disappeared, together with all rules, regulations, and systems of management.[1] In another factory, the secretary of a Party branch wrote that 'the administrative set-up in an industrial enterprise is in essence a legacy of the system of bourgeois authority' and should be abolished. The *People's Daily* condemned this attitude,[2] but the force of feeling behind it cannot be understood without a knowledge of how deep the gulf between staff and workers had always been in China. A study of a state-owned factory in Kunming during the Sino-Japanese War revealed this as a major cause of resentment.[3] Also there is no doubt that before 1958 factories had been top heavy with managerial staff, so the anti-managerial movement was directed, amongst other things, to pruning the bureaucracy. Thus, in the Shanghai Diesel Oil Engine Plant, administrative personnel had made up over a quarter of the total payroll and had included 147 test and inspection staff, 'as if only these personnel would attach importance to quality. They often came into conflict with . . . the workers'. In 1958, this factory went to the other extreme, 'the masses' claiming competence to take over technical control, against the opposition of the technical staff.[4] As a result of such tendencies, technical standards fell sharply in many plants; for example, in the Shenyang Transformer Factory where workers suggested that silicon steel sheets need be dipped in varnish only once and 'although it was evident that it would affect the quality of the products, nobody ventured to say it would not do'.[5] Objection, in the atmosphere of 1958, would have been held tantamount to 'conservatism'.

The re-thinking of economic policy brought about by the disasters of 1960–1 led to a change in these attitudes. The importance of systematic technical control of industrial operations again became accepted. The restoration of technical men to favour was made even more necessary by the sudden withdrawal of Soviet experts in 1960. Their talents and skills had to be put to proper use: '. . . technical staff currently on non-technical work must, as far as possible, be allowed to return to technical work . . . the top jobs on the technical side should generally be held by technical men and technical problems

[1] *People's Daily* (*Renmin Ribao*), October 27, 1958 (SCMP 1907).
[2] Ibid.
[3] Shih Kuo-heng: op. cit., pp. 116–23.
[4] *People's Daily* (*Renmin Ribao*), November 27, 1958 (SCMP 1914).
[5] *Electric Motor Industry* (*Dianji Gongye*), No. 10, May 25, 1959, p. 2. Eighth Bureau of First Ministry of Machine Building: Directive on the Swift Adoption of Measures to Maintain the Quality of Electrical Goods.

must be solved primarily by them'.¹ The public image of the technologist was felt to be in need of refurbishing. 'The odds are one to a million against technical personnel being portrayed as good men in novels, films, plays or operas. In almost every instance they are cast in the role of a villain . . . over the past three or four years (this appeared in August 1962) this tendency has been more or less universal.' The 'worker-peasant masses' are depicted as courageously pioneering innovations, while authors 'always create a conservative, backward, passive and selfish image for technical personnel'.² To counteract these views, a press campaign was conducted in 1962, urging due recognition and respect for technologists.³

Special attention was given at this time to securing the position of the chief engineer of a plant, particularly in relation to the manager or deputy manager in charge of production. This relationship was clearly fraught with difficulty especially when, as often happened, the manager was a Party member and the engineer was not. Suggestions were made that the posts of chief engineer and deputy manager in charge of production should be combined, a practice already followed in a number of enterprises.⁴

Accountants were another group of specialists whose functions were emphasized in the years after the Leap. Their position in enterprises was strengthened at the end of 1962 by the promulgation of 'Provisional Regulations Governing the Authority of Accounting Personnel'.⁵ It has been seen how severe a problem was set in collective agriculture by lack of even the simplest skills in accountancy. The same difficulties were met in other sectors of the economy. So acute was the shortage of accountants that we read of even agricultural technicians—a category of specialists in urgent demand in their own spheres—being transferred to work in accountancy.⁶ This illustrates the extreme lack of trained people, that staffing in one priority field could be improved only by drawing personnel from another equally vital sector; it also

¹ *Red Flag (Hongqi)*, No. 8–9, April 25, 1962, p. 44. Shih K'e-chien: 'Fully Tap the Strength of Technical Staff.'
² *Daily Worker (Gongren Ribao)*, August 5, 1962, p. 2. (Trans. partly from SCMP 2805.) Lin Chiang, member of the technical staff of the Red Flag Chemical Fertilizer Factory, Yangchow: 'Technologists and "Conservatives".'
³ Ibid., June 19, 1962, p. 2. Wang K'ai, Chief Engineer, Kuanghua Timber Plant: 'Some Preliminary Considerations', and ibid., Wang Ch'ung-lun, Deputy Chief and Engineer, Tool Shop, North Machine Repair Plant, Anshan Iron and Steel Corporation: 'Be Friendly Towards Engineers and Technologists', and ibid., June 21, 1962, p. 2. Chou Yung-liang, Assistant Secretary, CCP Committee, Ming-sheng Pharmaceutical Manufacturing Factory, Hangchow: 'They Are Working Class Intellectuals', and ibid., June 26, 1962, p. 2. Chang Hung-hsing: 'We Must Humbly Listen to the Opinions of Technologists.'
⁴ Ibid., July 3, 1962, p. 2. Kao Jun-chih, Deputy Chief Engineer, Shihchingshan Iron and Steel Corporation, Peking, and Deputy Manager, Steel Refinery: 'How to Train and Employ Technical Personnel', and ibid., July 19, 1962, p. 2. Ch'en Mao-li, Engineer and Deputy Manager, Steel Refinery, Wuhan Iron and Steel Works: 'Competent, Responsible and with Authority', and ibid., August 14, 1962, p. 2. Feng Ta-chih: 'The Need to Make a Good Job of a Four-sided Relationship.' For an account of a play on the theme of tension between manager and chief engineer, see *Report of the Indian Delegation to China on Agriculture Planning and Techniques*, Delhi, 1956, pp. 17–18. This shows that the problem was already attracting attention in the First Five Year Plan Period.
⁵ *People's Daily (Renmin Ribao)*, December 14, 1962, p. 1.
⁶ Ibid., February 3, 1963, p. 2.

exemplifies the traditional Chinese attitude that educated persons should be able to turn their hand to any intellectual task regardless of specialization.

While attitudes towards management and staff underwent great modification after 1958, the policy of 'cadres' participation in labour and workers' participation in management' was still officially maintained. The approved methods for bringing this about have been the regular or sporadic 'sending down' of enterprise staff to do manual jobs and the calling of conferences or 'representative meetings' of workers to discuss matters concerning the enterprise. Both of these methods pre-date the Great Leap.

The 'sending-down' movement was set in operation by a Central Committee directive of May 1957. This was followed in September 1958 by a joint decree of the Central Committee and the State Council in which it was laid down that all staff of ministries, enterprises, and other undertakings should, unless exempt by age or health, spend one month a year doing manual work.[1] Since then, these orders have been constantly repeated with the assertion that 'the participation of cadres in labour is one of our basic national practices'.[2] In some cases, office workers leave in rotation for one year or so to work on the land or in factories; in others, all spend one month a year in such work; instances are often reported of managers and engineers doing one day a week at a workbench in their own factories. These practices are known to be unpopular among cadres, and it appears that frequently they are disregarded or complied with in letter but not in spirit.[3]

For managerial, technical, and professional people (as well as students) to spend considerable time in manual labour may seem a glaring extravagance in a country where the scarcity of such people seriously hampers the rate of development, However, in view of the contempt in which educated people in China previously held these jobs and the difficulty they had in applying theoretical knowledge to practical problems, some sympathy must be felt for the present government's attempts to bridge this social gap.

The 'participation of labour in management' through workers' representative conferences had been important in state enterprises in the early days of the regime, when these conferences may have had genuine consultative functions. In the course of the First Five Year Plan period, more authority passed to enterprises' management. By 1956 these meetings had become 'a platform for the cadres only'.[4] During the Great Leap, much use was made of workers' conferences to publicize campaigns; like much else at that time, this appears to have been overdone and led to indifference or antipathy towards meetings of all sorts. The number of meetings was diminished after the Leap, but complaints were being made in 1964 of numerous and unnecessary conferences in factories.[5] Trade union branches in enterprises have the

[1] *New China Fortnightly* (*Xinhua Banyuekan*), No. 109, June 10, 1957, pp. 11–12, and *Collected Laws and Regulations* . . . Vol. 8, pp. 17–18.

[2] *People's Daily* (*Renmin Ribao*), February 25, 1965, p. 1.

[3] *Southern Daily* (*Nanfang Ribao*), November 2, 1964 (SCMP 3358), and *Far Eastern Economic Review*, March 12, 1965, p. 440. J. Ashdown: 'China's Proletarian Problems.'

[4] *The Eighth National Congress of the Communist Party of China*, Vol. II. Speeches, p. 243. Speech by Lai Jo-yu.

[5] *People's Daily* (*Renmin Ribao*), June 21, 1964, p. 6. Chin Chang-chün, Tientsin 4th Metal Wire Factory: 'Numerous Conferences Are Bad for Production.'

responsibility for organizing workers' conferences. These conferences are nominally empowered to demand the dismissal of the factory manager and other members of the staff.[1]

6. WAGES, BONUSES AND OTHER INCENTIVES

Chinese wage policy has had as its main objective the keeping of wages down to a level which enabled a high rate of investment to be maintained without inflation while, at the same time, attempting to provide sufficient incentives for work. In addition, such subsidiary aims as the maintenance, increase or reduction of differentials between regions, economic sectors and industries have had to be borne in mind. The shifting of declared wage policies between these objectives in response to ideological campaigns or economic needs has been marked; the actual changes in practice, however, have been less notable.

Among the chief targets to remain under central government control after 1958 was that of the total expenditure on wages, and that of the total number of employees.[2] Like other targets, these were to be settled after consultation with the provinces and equivalent local authorities who were responsible, within their own areas, for keeping to the figures each had agreed with the central government. Before 1959, two labour plans had co-existed—one vertical, drawn up by industrial ministries and applicable to the enterprises under their direct control and the other horizontal, covering enterprises of all types controlled by a single local authority. As a result, great differences in wages for similar jobs might exist between factories in the same industry and town if some of the enterprises concerned were controlled by a central ministry and others by a local authority. The two labour plans were merged in 1959, both forming part of the local authorities' plans;[3] a step which was intended to facilitate the introduction of uniform local wage levels.

The central government lays down general policies on wages and related topics, which the provinces are then supposed to work out and apply according to local conditions. When, for example, in 1958 the State Council decreed that the real wages of unskilled urban workers should not be much higher than the income of local peasants, it specifically declared that the actual wage scales should be formulated by the people's councils of the provinces and equivalent authorities.[4] Other matters dealt with similarly include regulations for apprentices, for leave arrangements of workers separated from their families, and for retirement pensions.

Systems of wage payments in force when the Communists took over were a hotchpot of devices made necessary by rampant inflation. As this inflation was brought under control, a series of wage reforms were undertaken.[5]

---

[1] *Seventy Important Points of Communist Industrial Policy*, 1961. (From Taiwan source), No. 58.

[2] *Collected Laws and Regulations* . . . Vol. 8, p. 97, and p. 462 below.

[3] *Planned Economy (Jihua Jingji)*, No. 9, September 1958, p. 13. Wang Kuei-wu: 'An Important Change in the Method of Drawing Up Annual Plans.'

[4] *New China Fortnightly (Xinhua Banyuekan)*, No. 122, December 25, 1957, p. 92.

[5] *People's Handbook (Renmin Shouce) 1958*, p. 209. Chou En-lai: 'Report to the 1957 Session of the National People's Congress on the Work of the Government', mentions reforms of the wage system occurring in 1950 and 1952. For references to regional wage

Subsequently a wage system using wage points was in wide use. Workers were graded (commonly into eight grades) according to skill, with each grade being awarded a fixed number of wage points a month. The value of a wage point varied according to the local cost of five staple commodities.[1] This system, however, was considered only transitional because it commonly included elements of non-labour income, such as traditional gratuities (especially New Year bonuses) and cost-of-living allowances, because it did not provide incentives for high output and innovation, and because some of the differentials it embodied (e.g. favouring light industry and the coastal areas) ran counter to government policy.[2] However, the prevalence of this type of wage payment in the early 1950s, must not be exaggerated because even as early as 1952 some 35 per cent of 'production workers' in state enterprises were said to have been on piece rates.[3]

The State Council directive of June 1956 on the reform of the wage system in state organs, undertakings, and enterprises (including joint state-private enterprises and enterprises under supply and marketing co-operatives) was a landmark in Communist Chinese wage policy. Perhaps, however, it was more in the nature of a standardization and culmination of tendencies already operating than the initiation of a new trend. Its main provisions were that increases in remuneration should be related to, but less than, increases in productivity; that the former wage point system with cost-of-living differentials should be abolished (although a cost-of-living subsidy separate from the wage scale would be paid in certain places); that the system of grading workers should be reformed, with a reduction in the number of grades but an increase in differentials according to skill, type, and conditions of work; that the piece rate system should be extended and that, in the course of 1957, it should come to cover all or most types of work to which it was applicable, and that scales should be so changed that piece workers should earn more than equivalent workers on time rates; and that each ministry should overhaul and rationalize bonus systems in its subordinate enterprises.[4] The pronouncements on wage policy in 1956 were accompanied by a move to standardize hours of work in state enterprises, as will be mentioned below.

For the previous two years, 1954 and 1955, wages had risen little, despite

---

reforms in 1950-3, see P. Schran: *The Structure of Income in Communist China* (unpublished Ph.D Thesis, University of California, 1961), p. 257. D. H. Perkins argues (*Journal of Political Economy*, Vol. LXXII, No. 4, August 1964, p. 364) that wage policy played no part in bringing the initial inflation under control, because wages were tied to the cost of living, while inflation was controlled by tackling the root cause, the insufficiency of government revenues. However, if wage policy prevented real wages rising in step with increases in productivity (at least for workers not on piece rates), this would have been one factor helping to bring government revenue and expenditure into balance, especially as productivity must have risen fast during the rehabilitation period.

[1] *Industrial Relations*, Vol. 3, No. 2, February 1964, p. 84. C. Hoffman: 'Work Incentives in Communist China.'

[2] P. Schran: op. cit., pp. 249–50.

[3] *Economic Research (Jingji Yanjiu)*, No. 4, April 1959, p. 19. Sun Shang-ch'ing: 'Current Problems Concerning the Nature and Destiny of Piece-Work Wages in Our Country.'

[4] *Collected Laws and Regulations* ... Vol. 4, pp. 408–10.

large increases in productivity. The wage reform directive of 1956 was made more palatable and the attempt to rationalize differentials made easier by incorporating in the directive a proposal for a wage increase, which averaged 13 per cent for all staff and workers, or 14·5 per cent if new workers, recruited in 1956, were excluded from the reckoning. Wage rises were to be relatively large for heavy industry, for key investment areas, for higher technical and scientific staff, for primary teachers, for workers in supply and marketing co-operatives, and for rural cadres. Lower than average rises were the rule in the coastal cities which had previously enjoyed above-average wage levels.[1] Also, some of the highest salaries—those of managers of enterprises and senior government officials—were 'controlled or lowered'.[2] One difficulty smoothed over by the wage rises of 1956 was that the former private undertakings, which by the close of 1956 had almost all been transformed into joint state-private enterprises, had often been paying wages above the level prevailing in the state sector; this was because private concerns had had less power to resist demands for wage increases.[3]

By the 1956 wage reform the extra month's pay traditionally given at the New Year was to be abolished;[4] presumably the 13 per cent (or 14·5 per cent) average wage rise was reckoned after taking this loss into account. The exceptionally large number of promotions on the grade scale which occurred in 1956 must have boosted the rise in average wages; therefore the actual increase in the rate for each grade must have been lower than indicated by the percentages specified. The span between the wages of the highest grade of operatives (the eighth in most industries) and the lowest was increased by the measures of 1956;[5] it was widened still further by the cut in the wages of the lowest-paid groups which probably occurred in the latter part of 1957 or soon afterwards.[6] A publication in 1959 stated that grades were commonly so ordered that the workers in the top grade received about three times the pay of those in the lowest.[7] This grading system, like the other provisions of the 1956 directive, applied to office employees as well as to manual workers.

That this directive was more of a codification than a signal to change is

---

[1] *Collected Laws and Regulations* ... Vol. 4, pp. 407–8. In 1955 measures had been taken to reduce inter-regional price differentials (see below p. 454), and *Collected Papers of the Third Session of the First National People's Congress*, pp. 733–43. Speech by Ma Wen-jui: loc. cit.

[2] *People's Handbook* (*Renmin Shouce*) *1958*, p. 208, Chou En-lai: loc. cit. However, a large part of the emoluments of these groups took the form of non-monetary privileges of various kinds. See R. McFarquhar (ed.) op. cit., pp. 75, 211 and 222.

[3] P. Schran, op. cit., pp. 275 and 279.

[4] *Collected Papers of the Third Session of the First National People's Congress*, p. 733. Ma Wen-jui: loc. cit. In 1966 mention was made of barbers and others in Shanghai receiving an annual 'assistance' at Chinese New Year. This amounted to less than one month's pay. *Far Eastern Economic Review*, March 3, 1966, p. 415.

[5] *Collected Papers of the Third Session of the First National People's Congress*, p. 737. Ma Wen-jui: loc. cit.

[6] *New China Fortnightly* (*Xinhua Banyuekan*), No. 122, December 25, 1957, p. 92. The difference in standards of living between unskilled urban labour and peasants has been a chronic complaint of the latter. See ibid., and *Work Bulletin* (*Gongzuo Tongxun*), No. 1, January 1, 1961, p. 14.

[7] Hsü Ti-hsin: *An Analysis of China's Economy in the Transitional Period* (in Chinese). Revised edition. Peking, 1959, p. 167.

seen from the fact that when the percentage of piece workers reached a peak in the same year, 1956, this was 42 per cent of the total work force, compared with 35 per cent of state 'production workers' in 1952. From 1957, the percentage began to fall.[1] After piece rates had been adopted, norms were frequently revised upwards to the detriment of workers who, out of chagrin, went slow in order not to provoke further revisions, or who kept output low when making new products in anticipation of being put on piece rates.[2] The system was also said to lead to concentration on quantity at the expense of economy in raw materials and tools. Piece rates were acknowledged to have increased the productivity of labour, encouraged the adoption of new techniques, and reduced absenteeism.[3] These very successes, however, had led to invidious divergences within individual enterprises between the wages of those on piece rates and of those who had, by the nature of their work, to remain on time rates.[4]

Piece work was also open to political objection, in that it inclined workers to mercenary and unsocialist attitudes of mind. This argument carried particular weight in 1958, since one of the chief features of the Great Leap Forward was to put 'politics in command': a corollary of this was to rely on non-material incentives such as mass campaigns, emulation drives, and the more lavish awarding of titles, such as 'model worker' and 'labour hero'. In addition, the spurt in production raised piece work wages still further above the level of time workers and of what the government thought desirable in view of the inflationary pressures of the time. Hence the policy of payment by results was reversed and the use of piece rates declined in favour of time rates. In the summer and autumn of 1958 reports came from factory after factory that workers were 'spontaneously' and 'unanimously' demanding an end to piece rates.

As so often found in China, the changes made in practice were not so sweeping as those that had been proclaimed. Although there was a switch from piece work to hourly wages in many factories in 1958, this change was by no means universal nor persisting. The well-known economist and official, Hsü Ti-hsin, in a work published in 1959, reported that both piece rates and time rates, the latter often in conjunction with bonus schemes, were currently operating.[5] This shows that material incentives had already been restored to favour, a fact confirmed in subsequent years. In contrast to the violent policy swings between various wage systems which had characterized the period 1956–8, discussion in the early 1960s had become much more tentative and empirical, in line with similar tendencies in regard to other economic matters. It was recognized that different forms of wage payments might be appropriate in different circumstances. Incentive bonuses were favoured for their flexibility. The importance of careful setting of labour norms had come to be

---

[1] *Economic Research* (*Jingji Yanjiu*), No. 4, April 1959, p. 19. Sun Shang-ch'ing: loc. cit.

[2] P. Schran: op. cit., p. 305, and *Daily Worker* (*Gongren Ribao*), August 29, 1958 (SCMP 1862). Chao Te-huan, Jen Chung-te and Ma Yu-t'ien: 'How Do We Rouse the Masses to Cancel the Piece Wage System?'

[3] *Economic Research* (*Jingji Yanjiu*), No. 4, April 1959, p. 20. Sun Shang-ch'ing: loc. cit.

[4] P. Schran: op. cit., p. 306.

[5] Hsü Ti-hsin: op. cit., pp. 165–67.

appreciated, with the difficulties that this involves. Piece rates were seen to be applicable only where a sufficient standard of management had been attained, with sound statistics of output and with quality inspection.¹

In the mid-1960s and especially with the stormy political campaigns of 1966, the pendulum swung in the opposite direction. Material incentives were out of favour. Wage differentials came to be reduced by lowering the salaries of staff, while staff bonuses were abolished, at least in some factories.²

Regional wage differentials, as mentioned above, were reduced in 1956 when the areas which previously had relatively high wages, received less than average increases. A report in 1960 said that (in addition to special allowances for regions such as Tibet, Sinkiang and the Tsaidam Basin in Tsinghai) the country was divided into eleven wage regions, the highest being 30 per cent above the level of the lowest; a span probably no greater than justified by cost-of-living differentials.³

In 1963 the first widespread rise in wages since 1956 was reported, affecting 40 per cent of the labour force⁴ and presumably reflecting the rise in productivity during recovery from the post-Leap depression.

In absolute terms, the average wage over the whole non-agricultural labour force was increased, by the 1956 wage rise, from about ¥45–¥50 a month to around ¥50–¥55.⁵ (Wages are paid monthly.) Reports in 1964 indicate an average wage for factory workers (usually earning above the level of the non-agricultural labour force as a whole) of around ¥60–¥70 a month, which suggests that factory workers were not among those benefited much by the 1963 rise. Factory managers and senior technical staff in 1964 were getting salaries within the range of ¥200–¥250 a month. Early in 1965 higher salaries are reported to have been cut.⁶ This no doubt accounts for the fact that in factories visited by a Western observer in 1966 managers' salaries seldom exceeded two to two and a half times the pay of an ordinary worker.⁷

In considering wage rates, it must be borne in mind that on the one hand they are frequently subject to compulsory savings, and on the other that rent usually accounts for only a very small percentage (usually not more than 5 per cent) of income. Type of accommodation, coupons permitting the purchase of goods in short supply and other facilities are allotted according to the job.

Bonuses did not come into prominence until 1956. The trend towards their

---

¹ *People's Daily* (*Renmin Ribao*), October 28, 1961, p. 7. Lin Fang: 'A Tentative Dissertation on Forms of Wages', and ibid., March 6, 1962. p. 5. Shih Hsiu-lin: 'A Tentative Dissertation on Industrial Enterprises' Bonus Systems', and *Ta Kung Daily* (*Dagong Bao*), Peking, May 14, 1962, p. 3. Shih Hsiu-lin: 'Some Problems of Enterprises' Bonus Systems', and ibid., May 30, 1962, p. 1. Editorial, and ibid., November 2, 1962, p. 3. Chou Yen-pin: 'The Conditions for Implementing the Piece Wage System.'

² Information kindly supplied by B. M. Richman, Graduate School of Business Administration, University of California, Los Angeles.

³ P. Schran: op. cit., pp. 271–2. The division into eleven wage regions may have dated from 1956, see *Finance* (*Caizheng*), No. 6, June 1957. p. 14. Yang Pang-ch'un: 'Enterprises' Bonus Fund Should Be Based on the Numbers of Productive Workers.'

⁴ *Peking Review*, December 6, 1963, p. 7.

⁵ *Collected Papers of the Third Session of the First National People's Congress*, p. 734. Ma Wen-jui: loc. cit.

⁶ Information privately supplied to author.

⁷ I am indebted to Barry M. Richman for this information.

greater use predated by a few months the wage reform directive of that year.¹ This directive specified that bonus schemes should be instituted to encourage trial manufacture of new products, economy in raw materials, fuel and power, the raising of quality, and the exceeding of output quotas.² Which of these indicators is used in any enterprise as a basis for awards depends on what targets the management wishes to emphasize: this is a matter in which enterprises have considerable latitude.³ By the Directive on the Reform of the Industrial Management System of November 1957, all bonuses were thenceforward to come from retained profits. In Chapter 6 we saw that from 1958 an enterprise was permitted to use from this source a sum equivalent to not more than 5 per cent of its total wage bill on 'socialist emulation prizes', other bonuses and on employees' welfare.⁴ Bonuses may be given to enterprises collectively, to groups of workers (shifts or working groups) or to individuals.⁵ Awards to enterprises have been discussed in Chapter 6. Bonuses to groups of workers may be based on indicators mentioned above. Alternatively, the equivalent of a bonus scheme may be achieved through giving a group of workers a task to complete on contract (*paokung*) for a fixed remuneration.⁶

The maximum sum an enterprise may expend on bonuses for its workers was, we have just noted, laid down as a fixed percentage of its total wage fund,⁷ although some would have preferred it to be based on the total number of its workers.⁸ In one province for which we have information, the number of workers in an enterprise receiving bonuses might, in 1959, be up to 70 per cent of the total.⁹ The distribution of bonuses among individual workers is often left to the small production groups within which personal relationships would be important. This might be one reason for the tendency, officially condemned, for bonuses to be given automatically and to be regarded as an integral part of a wage.¹⁰

In the years after the Great Leap, conditions governing the award of bonuses became more complex and subtle, in line with the general development of economic policy. The 'comprehensive bonus system' favoured at that

---

¹ P. Schran: op. cit., pp. 302–3, and *Labour (Laodong)*, No. 5, March 3, 1957, p. 14. Weifang Diesel Engine Factory: 'The Circumstances and Problems of Instituting a Staff Bonus System in Our Factory.'

² *Collected Laws and Regulations* ... Vol. 4, p. 410.

³ Wu Tan-ko: *Labour and Wages under the Socialist System* (in Chinese), Shanghai, 1956, p. 50.

⁴ p. 167 above.

⁵ Wu Tan-ko: op. cit., p. 51.

⁶ Ibid., and see p. 187 above on the contract labour system.

⁷ The wage fund is defined as including all wages, bonuses akin to wages, and those subsidies laid down by government regulations. It excludes the following items: once for all bonuses made from an enterprise's bonus fund, expenditure on labour insurance, trade union management expenses, medical facilities, welfare grants, industrial safety measures, travelling expenses, and certain other minor payments. *Simple Explanation of Terms Used in the First Five Year Plan for the Development of the National Economy of the People's Republic of China* (in Chinese), Peking, 1955.

⁸ *Finance (Caizheng)*, No. 6, June 1957, pp. 13–14. Yang Pang-ch'un: loc. cit.

⁹ *Labour (Laodong)*, No. 9, May 3, 1959, pp. 29–30. Hsiang Kan-ch'eng, Deputy Director, Kirin Provincial Department of Labour: 'The Great Superiority of Comprehensive Bonuses.'

¹⁰ *Ta Kung Pao (Dagong Bao)*, Peking, August 22, 1962, p. 3. Ch'en P'ei-yi: 'A Tentative Discussion of Certain Practical Problems in the Bonus System.'

time could be adapted to take into account, besides the fulfilment of quantitative targets, any other indicators appropriate to particular activities as well as general compliance with current official policy.¹

In the course of the 1963 wage rise, bonuses were also raised² and in 1964 a visitor reported that workers at Anshan received bonuses of up to 14 per cent of their basic wages. Workers' bonuses are normally reckoned and paid on a monthly basis, while bonuses for staff are sometimes calculated on a longer period.

We must now consider the system of remunerating the staff of enterprises. The principle was laid down in 1956 that in order to encourage cadres to take up such appointments, the administrative staff of state economic enterprises should be paid more than their opposite numbers in government offices.³ (These latter had, in 1955, been transferred from the 'supply system' by which they were provided with their keep, or allowances in lieu, to fixed cash wages plus local cost-of-living allowances.⁴ In 1956, when they benefited from the general wage rise—*hsiang* cadres' pay being increased by 69 per cent—cost-of-living allowances were dropped.) Above-average rises were granted in 1956 to higher scientific research workers, to technologists, and to 'higher intellectuals'. Within enterprises, technical staff were to receive more than the corresponding administrative personnel. The pay of enterprises' staff, both administrative and technical, was to be aligned more closely with their actual position and responsibilities, and not just with their nominal grading.⁵

Differences of opinion have existed on whether enterprises' cadres—political, administrative, and technical—should be eligible for bonuses. In 1956 it was announced that the rules on bonuses had been omitted from the draft constitution of the Chinese Communist Party, and that Party members did not work for such considerations.⁶ Nevertheless, in 1957, Party cadres in enterprises are mentioned as receiving bonuses. The fact that these bonuses were assessed within the enterprise by enterprise staff must have been an important factor in causing these political cadres to identify themselves with the enterprise management, thus tending to lose their separate identity.⁷

---

¹ *Labour (Laodong)*, No. 4, February 18, 1962, pp. 24–5. Wages Office, Technical Organization Bureau, Ministry of Commerce: 'Certain Problems in Improving the Comprehensive Bonus System in State Commerce', and ibid., No. 17, November 18, 1962, pp. 20–1. Shen Chen-hsin: 'Improve the Bonus System for Administrative Personnel According to the Special Features of the Job.'

² *Peking Review*, December 6, 1963, p. 7.

³ *Collected Papers of the Third Session of the First National People's Congress*, p. 735. Ma Wen-jui: loc. cit.

⁴ The regulations of 1955 divided government employees (other than those in economic enterprises) into thirty grades from the President of the Republic at ¥560 a month to menials at ¥18. *Collected Financial Laws and Regulations of the Central Government* (in Chinese), 1955, p. 466.

⁵ *Collected Papers of the Third Session of the First National People's Congress*, p. 735–8. Ma Wen-jui: loc. cit., and *Chinese Industry (Zhongguo Gongye)*, No. 2, 1956, pp. 1–8. Ho Po: 'A Tentative Discussion of the System of Determining the Wages of Senior Administrators, Engineers, and Staff of Industrial Enterprises according to Positions Held.'

⁶ *Documents of the Eighth National Congress of the Communist Party of China* (in Chinese), Peking, 1956, pp. 104–5.

⁷ *Labour (Laodong)*, No. 11, June 3, 1957, p. 17. Yü Shu-fang: 'Enterprises' Political and Mass Organization Cadres Who Are Not Engaged in Production Should Not Receive

Bonuses given to the administrative, technical and political staff of enterprises in 1956–7 appear to have been on a notably more generous scale than those of ordinary workers. At one mine, for example, it was reported that senior staff received bonuses equal to 8–15 per cent of their basic wages if the plan was fulfilled, and 25–40 per cent for overfulfilment, but that ordinary production workers were given bonuses equivalent to only 2·5–3·5 per cent of their wages.[1] The bonus schemes were worked out inside the enterprises by the staff members themselves, subject only to the approval of the ministries or local departments to which they were subordinate and which did not appear, in this and other matters, always to be able to exercise sufficient control. It may be surmised that some extra-budgetary funds[2] (whose growth in 1957–8 was another indication that enterprises had got out of control) also went to swell the bonuses of workers and more especially of enterprises' staff.

These abuses, together with reports that because staff bonuses were dependent on plan fulfilment, managers tried to wangle a low target figure,[3] provided occasion in 1957 for debate on whether administrative, technical and political cadres should be eligible for bonuses.[4] During 1958 material incentives were under a cloud and at least in places bonuses were abolished. However, within a short period, sometimes no more than three months, they were reinstituted for both staff and workers; political incentives alone had proved insufficient.[5] Again, as political tension mounted in the mid-1960s, staff bonuses were for a second time, at least widely, discarded;[6] whether this time they will be as speedily revived, still remains to be seen.

Here we must remark that little is known about the motivation of managers in China. Managerial bonuses have not normally been as large nor evidently as significant as in the Soviet Union and East Europe. The marginal utility of money must be low due to the lack of outlets for expenditure together with discouragement of conspicuous consumption and the absence of channels of private investment. This is not to say that staff bonuses have been of negligible importance, or managers would not have been accused of malpractices caused by a desire for bonuses. The status of a manager of a factory directly under

---

Bonuses.' The author argues the case against these cadres receiving bonuses, but assumes it is still an open question, although mentioning the 1956 disapproval of the bonus system for Party members. He writes: 'At present bonuses for Party and mass organization cadres not engaged in production are decided by the manager of the enterprise, or even by the wages department, or some are not even assessed by anyone. Thus, the work of such cadres is not judged by higher levels of the Party, Youth League, or trade union.'

[1] *Labour* (*Laodong*), No. 11, June 3, 1957, p. 16. Hsieh Kuang-ch'eng: 'After Implementing the System of Production Bonuses for Senior Personnel.'
[2] See pp. 389–93 below.
[3] *Labour* (*Laodong*), No. 11, June 3, 1957, p. 16. Hsieh Kuang-ch'eng: loc. cit.
[4] Ibid., p. 17. Yü Shu-fang: loc. cit., and ibid., p. 18. Tsao Hai-chung: 'Bonuses to Technical Administrative Staff for Fulfilling Tasks Should be Abolished', and ibid., p. 19. Lei Chih-p'ing: 'Technical and Administrative Staff and Political and Mass Organization Cadres Ought to Get Bonuses.'
[5] *Labour* (*Laodong*), No. 13, July 3, 1959, p. 14. Working Group of Kirin Provincial Labour Department and Kirin Municipal Federation of Trade Unions and Bureau of Labour: 'After Kirin Municipal Wooden Implement Factory Had Experimented with Comprehensive Bonuses.'
[6] Information from B. M. Richman gratefully acknowledged.

the central government ranks higher than that of a manager of a local authority's plant, and ambition for promotion on this ladder is another managerial incentive.[1]

An important type of incentive payment is the awards given for inventions and technical improvements. Provisional regulations governing this subject were issued in 1954 and definitive regulations promulgated by the State Council in 1963. Inventions and improvements are by these regulations divided into several categories, carrying both graded monetary and non-monetary rewards.[2] From time to time special campaigns to encourage innovations have been launched. The existence of these rewards helps to explain the very large number of technical innovations reported—more than 90,000 for example, in Shanghai alone in the first five months of 1965.[3] Technical innovations seen by East European technicians when working in China were of uneven merit. Some they considered 'pretty old hat by European standards' while others 'were worthy of introduction even in industrial Czechoslovakia'.[4] In China no patent rights are given to any enterprise or industrial inventor.[5]

The field of non-material incentives has been assiduously developed in China. These include emulation drives, in which factories and groups of workers compete in raising output or in achieving other goals; mass participation in special campaigns; and the award of titles, such as 'model worker' or 'five good worker' (good at political thought, completion of tasks, observance of regulations, at regular study, and at mutual help). Special conferences are held at national, provincial, and other levels, of award-winning workers where they receive great publicity and are sometimes received by national leaders. Nor are the benefits attached to such awards entirely non-material, for award holders have privileges in labour insurance and medical treatment.[6] Outstanding workers may also be seconded by their enterprises or units for higher education. Also they are likely to be encouraged to join the Communist Party, thus smoothing their entry into the managerial elite, and leading to promotion, either in industrial administration or as cadres in the Party or trade unions.

Neither must the force of non-material *dis*incentives be overlooked. Public criticism at meetings or on wall-newspapers can be a severe penalty for slackness, carelessness, and other misdemeanours, especially in a society so traditionally devoted to the maintenance of external appearances as China. However, even in China it may be surmised, non-material incentives and disincentives have been pushed to a point where they produce diminishing

[1] *Southern Daily (Nanfang Ribao)*, January 14, 1966, p. 1.

[2] *Labour Laws and Regulations of the People's Republic of China*, pp. 54–64. 'Provisional Regulations on Awards for Inventions, Technical Improvements and Rationalization Proposals Concerning Production', issued by the Government Administration Council, 1954, and *People's Daily (Renmin Ribao)*, December 2, 1963, p. 2. 'Regulations on Awards for Inventions', and ibid., 'Regulations on Awards for Technical Improvements.'

[3] *Daily Worker (Gongren Ribao)*, July 14, 1965, p. 1. Ma T'ien-shui, Secretary of the Secretariat, CCP Shanghai Municipal Committee: 'Strengthen Mass Work and Fundamental Work: Promote Technical Innovation and Technical Revolution.'

[4] *Far Eastern Economic Review*, January 19, 1961, p. 80.

[5] *BBC Summary of World Broadcasts*, Second Series, FE/W365/A/22. (NCNA, April 30, 1966.)

[6] *Labour Laws and Regulations of the People's Republic of China*, pp. 46–7.

returns. Boredom, indifference, and even counter-suggestion may frustrate these methods of raising productive efficiency.

The figures for workers covered by labour insurance and by free medical care are officially reported to be as follows: (figures for trade union membership and for total non-agricultural employment are given alongside for comparison).

Year	Total Civilian Non-Agricultural Employment	Total Trade Union Membership	Number of Workers and Other Employees Covered by Labour Insurance	Number of Workers and Other Employees Covered by Free Medical Care
		(millions)		
1952	36·8		3·3	4·0
1953		10·2	4·8	5·5
1957	39·7	16·3	11·5	6·6
1958	56·9		13·8	6·9

Sources:
Civilian Non-Agricultural Employment, p. 181 above.
Trade Union Membership, p. 190 above.
Number of Workers covered by Labour Insurance: *Ten Great Years*, p. 218.
Number of Workers covered by Free Medical Care, 1952, 1957 and 1958. Ibid., p. 219.
Number of Workers covered by Free Medical Care. 1953. *Statistical Work (Tongji Gongzuo)*. No. 14, July 29, 1957, p. 13.

The reasons for the gap between total non-agricultural labour force and trade union membership has already been discussed. It will be more surprising that, while the administration of labour insurance schemes (accident, sickness, maternity, old age and death) forms a large part of the duties of trade unions, in 1957 scarcely more than 70 per cent of their members can have been covered by these schemes, while only 40 per cent enjoyed free medical care.[1] Labour insurance, at least in 1953, was limited to factories and mines with over 100 workers, to modern transport and communications workers, and to large construction enterprises.[2] Despite any subsequent extensions which may have come about, comprehensive coverage of the labour force was not approached in any year for which figures are available. Numbers benefiting from free medical care were even more restricted and increased much more slowly than in the case of labour insurance. Shortage of qualified medical personnel and of other facilities accounted for this.[3]

Labour insurance and workers' medical benefits and other welfare provisions are financed from payments into the funds concerned, by the enterprise, of sums equal to fixed percentages of total wage payments. Altogether, during the First Five Year Plan period, the total of these stipulated payments (including the equivalent of 2 per cent of total wages paid as dues to the trade unions) amounted to the equivalent of 15·5–17·5 per cent of the total wage bill, with actual payments reaching 20 per cent.[4] Presumably this 20 per cent

[1] These percentages assume that a negligible number of non-members of unions will have been covered by either of these schemes.

[2] *Important Labour Laws and Regulations of the People's Republic of China*, Peking, 1961, p. 11. 'Labour Insurance Regulations of the People's Republic of China' promulgated as amended January 1953.

[3] P. Schran: op. cit., p. 312.

[4] *Important Labour Laws and Regulations of the People's Republic of China*, p. 13. 'Labour

covered payments for certain items which, from 1958, were to be met from a sum, out of retained profits, not exceeding 5 per cent of the total wage bill of the enterprise concerned.[1]

Retirement is officially at the age of 50 for women manual workers, 55 for women staff members, and 60 for men. Pensions, for those covered by labour insurance, range from 50–70 per cent of previous wage.[2] Severance pay is given on retirement to those ineligible for pensions and to others who leave their jobs with official permission; according to regulations of 1958 it can total up to 30 months' pay.[3] For medical benefits, unlike labour insurance, dues are deducted every month from workers' wages. The extent and quality of medical and welfare provision varies widely from enterprise to enterprise.[4]

Labour conditions also tend to be patchy, ranging from good to poor. A Japanese reporter, seeing what were presumably above-average factories in China, described them as 'dimly lit, lacking colour, squalid, overstaffed, and with no basic safety precautions'.[5] Other visitors have been better impressed. In 1956 a labour protection inspectorate apparently had not yet been established.[6] We have not heard when or if this was subsequently done.

Workers in the state sector of the economy have, since 1956, been supposed normally to work eight hours a day six days a week; shift working is common. Longer hours are in fact often worked, especially towards the end of any 'plan period'. In 1958–60 very long hours, such as 16–18 a day, were reported in some factories.[7] At many periods, workers have in addition been obliged to participate in political activities. In the more moderate atmosphere of the early 1960s, efforts were made to cut down on these demands.[8]

Insurance Regulations' . . . loc. cit., and *Planned Economy (Jihua Jingji)*, No. 5, May 1958, p. 12. Wei Li: 'The Supplementary Wage System Must Be Radically Reformed.' We have not been able to discover if the changes called for by this author (greater centralization of provision for labour insurance and health, together with greater economy all round) were ever implemented. See also *People's Daily (Renmin Ribao)*, November 21, 1957, p. 1. Editorial, in which 'supplementary wages and welfare benefits' during the First Five Year Plan period are stated to have been equivalent to 19·2 per cent of the wage bill.

[1] See p. 167 above.
[2] *Important Labour Laws and Regulations of the People's Republic of China*, pp. 72–4. 'Provisional Regulations of the State Council Concerning the Retirement of Workers and Staff Members', as amended February 1958. Lower ages of retirement apply to certain occupations. In addition, different figures for retirement ages and for pensions are sometimes quoted.
[3] *Collected Laws and Regulations* . . . Vol. 2, pp. 711–12, and ibid., Vol. 4, p. 437, and ibid., Vol. 7, pp. 406–12.
[4] *Current Scene*, Vol. III, No. 6, November 1, 1964, p. 9. M. Sieh: 'Medicine in China: Wealth for the State', Part II.
[5] *Current Scene*, Vol. II, No. 32, May 1, 1964, p. 4: 'A Japanese View of China.'
[6] *Collected Papers of the Third Session of the First National People's Congress*, p. 740. Ma Wen-jui: loc. cit., where he states that: 'A labour safety inspectorate must quickly be established.'
[7] Ibid., p. 739, and *Labour Laws and Regulations of the People's Republic of China*, p. 71, and Ta-chung Liu and Kung-chia Yeh: *The Economy of the Chinese Mainland: National Income and Economic Development 1933–59*, Rand Corporation, Santa Monica, 1963, p. 192, fn. 102, and *China News Analysis*, No. 434, August 24, 1962, p. 4.
[8] *People's Daily (Renmin Ribao)*, August 10, 1965, p. 1. In a Shanghai textile mill, 'previously, after working hours there were classes on Mondays, Party and Young Communist League activities on Tuesdays, mass activities (sc. political) on Wednesdays and Thursdays,

In 1957 the non-agricultural labour force was estimated to work 306 days a year, with holidays on Sundays and on seven national festivals. Those working at a distance from their immediate families are entitled to annual home leave, but pressure is sometimes exercised to persuade them not to take it; while this was especially the case during the Great Leap, it was still occurring in 1965.[1] Absenteeism has been sufficient a problem for some enterprises to institute bonuses for regular attendance. Cotton mills in Shanghai, and presumably elsewhere, experience higher absenteeism in the summer, a common phenomenon in all newly industrializing lands where factory workers still have close ties with the agricultural economy.[2]

A few general observations on the wage policy of the Chinese Government must conclude this chapter. It is generally agreed that throughout most of the time since 1949, the rise in wages has been kept below the average increase in labour productivity, although not always to the extent needed to avoid inflationary pressures. While the high rate of investment during the First Five Year Plan period required a large margin to be maintained between rises in productivity and in wages,[3] in practice this was hard to reconcile with the need to provide incentives and to keep the labour force reasonably contented. For the years 1953–6, gross earnings (including bonuses, labour insurance benefits, and enterprises' expenditure on welfare) were officially estimated to have risen by an average of 7·1 per cent a year, or by nearly 95 per cent of the 7·5 per cent average annual increase in productivity per worker in

---

classes on Fridays and production activities on Saturdays. Meetings were crammed in. . . . Now we have laid down that meetings must be combined where possible, and attended only by those people concerned. There are to be no meetings for mid-day and night shifts.'

[1] *Statistical Work* (*Tongji Gongzuo*), No. 16, August 29, 1957, p. 33. Hsü Kang: 'Some Views on How to Compare Standards of Living of Workers and Peasants', and *Yangch'eng Evening Newspaper* (*Yangcheng Wanbao*), January 19, 1965 (SCMP 3391).

[2] *Labour* (*Laodong*), No. 8, August 1964, p. 30. Cheng Ch'i-chang: 'Regular Attendance Bonuses Are Very Harmful and Have Few Advantages', and *Chinese Textiles* (*Zhongguo Fangzhi*), No. 1, January 10, 1965 (SCMM 458).

[3] It is sometimes inferred (e.g. *New Construction* [*Xin Jianshe*], No. 12, December 1956, p. 21. Yuan Fang: 'The Relationship between Increases in Labour Productivity and in Wages in Our Country') that the First Five Year Plan laid down that wages should rise at only about half the rate of labour productivity. This is mistaken. The Plan assumed a 64 per cent increase in labour productivity in *state-owned industries* and a rise of about 33 per cent 'in the average wage of *workers and staff members* in state, co-operative and joint state-private enterprises, *state organs, people's organizations, and cultural, educational and public health departments*'. (Our italics.) (*First Five-Year Plan for Development of the National Economy of the People's Republic of China in 1953–7*, Peking, 1956, pp. 171 and 193.) The method usually employed in China to calculate labour productivity in industry is to divide the value of the total product by the number of productive workers (i.e. excluding those not directly engaged in production). See Niu Chung-huang: *Accumulation and Consumption in the National Income of Our Country* (in Chinese), Peking, 1959, p. 100. The rise in productivity of industrial workers directly engaged in production is likely to have been faster than that of non-productive industrial workers or of workers in other sectors of the economy. Therefore on the basis of the figures given in the First Five Year Plan, the rise in labour productivity in state industry was expected to be more than double the rise in *industrial* wages (27·1 per cent. See *First Five Year Plan*, p. 194). The general rise in productivity of the whole labour force, however, would, on the figures given, be likely to be a good deal less than twice as fast as wages.

non-agricultural employment in the state and collective sectors.[1] Most of the rise in earnings was concentrated in 1956; thus for the years 1953–5 productivity kept well ahead of wages, while in 1956–7 wage policy added to the inflationary tendencies that built up towards the end of the First Five Year Plan period.

During the Great Leap, average productivity of non-agricultural labour must have fallen, owing to the influx of raw hands[2] and to lower productivity in small-scale industry which expanded particularly fast at that time. The reduction of the non-agricultural labour force from 1959 onwards by the dismissal of the less competent workers and the closing of many of the small industrial concerns established in 1958, will have tended to reverse this trend; although the effect was at least partially offset by irregularity in raw material supplies in the years of agricultural disaster. From 1962 onwards, when raw materials became easier, the rise in the productivity of labour must have been considerable. The growth of incentive methods of payment limited, but did not abolish, the use which could be made of wage policy as an anti-inflationary weapon. By 1962 the need was recognized of keeping wage increases related not just to increases in non-agricultural productivity, but even more to increases in the productivity of agricultural labour and in the commodity rate (i.e. rate of off-farm procurement and sales) of agricultural output.[3]

At least until the mid-1960s, the successes of the Chinese wage policy have come from the willingness to use draconian measures—(a virtual wage stop during some years of rapidly rising productivity, and then later a drastic cut in urban employment), while its failures have lain in its weakness in employing more subtle means of control. Whether or not in China, as in the Soviet Union, 'the upper limit on the wage bill' may well be 'perhaps the most frequently violated of all indicators',[4] the Chinese authorities have in any case been unable to prevent widespread overspending of the wage fund. The overspending sometimes comes about by paying excessive bonuses out of retained profits, by hiring labour without permission for unauthorized investment projects, or by taking on more workers than permitted (especially auxiliary workers not directly engaged in production, who were not counted when reckoning an enterprise's fulfilment of its target for rise in labour pro-

---

[1] Niu Chung-huang: *Accumulation and Consumption in the National Income of Our Country*, p. 106. The productivity indices calculated by W. Galenson and J. R. Eriksson in 'Industrial Labour Productivity in Non-Western Countries Since 1945' (paper presented to the International Economic Association's International Congress on Economic Development, Vienna, 1962). Appendix, p. 10, are for industrial labour only and therefore, as might be expected, show a higher rate of increase. Their estimates are as follows:

1953	100
1957	170·9
1958	131·9
1959	163·6

[2] W. Galenson and J. R. Eriksson's calculations for the average productivity of industrial labour in China show a fall of 23 per cent for 1957 to 1958, with a partial recovery in 1959, loc. cit.

[3] *People's Daily* (Renmin Ribao), April 6, 1962, p. 5. Wang Cho: 'Financial and Currency Work in Relation to the Policy of Taking Agriculture as the Foundation.'

[4] P. J. D. Wiles: *Political Economy of Communism*, Oxford, 1962, p. 85.

ductivity).¹ Although these abuses were particularly flagrant around 1957–8, they were still to be found in later years.² One fundamental difficulty has been that sometimes enterprises' record keeping and accounting was so bad that they did not know the number of their workers or the total of their wage bill.³

The incentive role of wages was undoubtedly sharpened by the introduction of piece rates, which culminated in the 1956 wage reform. During the Great Leap of 1958 and its aftermath, this role ceased to be so important. This was probably due first and foremost to a shortage of consumer goods, leading to a fall in the marginal utility of money, and only secondarily to the suppression of piece rates (which, as we have seen, was not universal) or to a substitution of political incentives (which are likely to have had steeply diminishing returns). When consumer goods became more plentiful from 1962 onwards, the renewed encouragement of incentive wage systems was able to produce results and no doubt contributed to economic revival.

The question arises whether wages have played a significant part in the allocation of labour between regions, between the industrial and agricultural sectors of the economy, or between different types of urban employment. We have already suggested that the flow of migrants from rural areas in east China to the cities of the north-west in 1956–7 may have been influenced by the relatively large wage increases brought about in that region by the 1956 wage reform. However, this is only an hypothesis and it may well be that migration turned in that direction because control on entrants into the cities there was, or was believed to be, less stringent than in the cities of east China. The greater part of inter-regional migration since 1949 would appear to have been brought about by non-material pressures of various types. In so far as material incentives operated to encourage such movement, they are more likely to have done so in the shape of a general prospect of a more prosperous future, or of the possibility of exchanging collectivized agricultural work for secure wage-remunerated urban (or even non-urban) employment, than specifically by higher ruling wage rates in the region to which the migrants went. For professional and other skilled workers, official direction to posts in other parts of the country may be surmised to have been more important than wage differentials in bringing about the inter-regional mobility which has characterized this category of labour in recent years. It is, of course, possible that promotion prospects are better in remote areas, and the influence of patriotism and other high motives should not be discounted. However, in contemporary China, the advice 'go West, young man' has probably, more often than not, been backed by explicit orders.

Wage policy was never used as a deliberate instrument to attract labour from agriculture into industry, because for most of the period since 1949 the authorities have been embarrassed by an excessive number of would-be recruits for industry. The fact that, for other reasons, despite intentions to narrow it, the

[1] Niu Chung-huang, op. cit,, p. 106,

[2] *Finance* (*Caizheng*), No. 7, July 1957, p. 31. Chang Pen-lien: 'Some Questions Influencing the Raising of the Profit Level in the State Coal Mining Industry', and *Southern Daily* (*Nanfang Ribao*), May 15, 1962 (SCMP 2757). Editorial.

[3] See p. 185 above, and *Red Flag* (*Hongqi*), No. 19, October 1, 1961, p. 22. Li Ch'eng-jui and Tso Ch'un-t'ai: 'Some Problems concerning Economic Accounting in Socialist Enterprises.'

differential between agricultural and industrial incomes may have been widened by the wage reform of 1956 and the concomitant wage rises, was perhaps one cause of the great migration to the towns of 1956–8; but agricultural collectivization probably had more influence in this respect. Even without such a differential, the attractions and opportunities of urban life would probably weigh overwhelmingly with many rural youths. The government has attempted to keep down the wages of unskilled urban workers because of anxiety over the gap between their standard of living and that of local peasants. This anxiety to prevent excessive differentials between peasants and workers in any one area may have lessened the government's freedom of action in regard to differentials between different parts of the country for urban employment.[1]

There remains to be considered the degree to which wages have acted to allocate urban labour between different occupations and industries. The government set differential rates for different industries, favouring heavy industry for example, so presumably these differentials were intended to enable the favoured industries to have the pick of the labour force, especially of skilled men; similarly with the differential benefiting cadres in state economic enterprises. Even in a command economy where direction of labour is possible, it is less clumsy to use wage policy to bring about the desired allocation of workers, at least on the margin. Except on the margin, however, wage policy has not been important in labour allocation.[2]

[1] P. Schran: op. cit., p. 270.
[2] On this topic see D. H. Perkins: op. cit., Chapter 7.

Chapter 8

HANDICRAFTS, SMALL-SCALE INDUSTRY AND URBAN COMMUNES

1. INTRODUCTION

Modern industrial development attracts publicity both within and outside the country in which it takes place. Less attention is commonly given to that other sector of industry, comprising handicrafts and small workshops, which in many parts of the world touches the ordinary life of the people more closely than the activities of large factories.

The definition of handicrafts in contemporary China is beset with ambiguities and complexities.[1] The distinction between individual handicrafts and small-scale industry has already been mentioned.[2] In this instance, with the definition hinging on the major part of the work being done by the handicraftsman and his family, the emphasis is on property relationship—on the individual nature of the undertaking in contrast to capitalist, co-operative or state production. The phrase 'handicraft workshop' (*kungch'ang shoukungyeh*), however, denotes a technical level—labour by hand and not by machine. This implication is not inherent in other uses of the term 'handicraft'. A handicraft co-operative may still be denoted as such, although it is mechanized.[3] We have already seen that the technical criterion is used in distinguishing handicrafts from 'modern industry'.[4]

Handicraft production, carried on by rural families for their own use or by way of preliminary processing of farm produce, is reckoned as an agricultural subsidiary occupation, and the output is included for statistical purposes with agricultural output. This is also the case where farm families process materials provided by a customer-consumer. However, rural handicraft production for the market is excluded from agricultural output and is counted as handicrafts.[5] These various definitions are not consistently followed in statistics or in general usage in China.[6] Added to this, in writings on handicrafts the definition being used is often not given, and rests on some commonsense basis which may well differ from occasion to occasion. All this must be borne in mind in perusing the rest of this chapter.

We have seen in Chapter 6 that handicrafts are reckoned to have accounted for 37 per cent of total net value added in the industrial sector in 1952, falling to 12 per cent in 1960 but then rising again to 30 per cent in the

---

[1] See C. T. Lu: *An Interim Understanding of the Concept of Handicraft as the Term Is Used in Communist China.* (Mimeographed paper prepared for the First Research Conference of the Social Science Research Council Committee on the Economy of China, Berkeley, California. January–February 1963.)
[2] p. 141 above.
[3] C. T. Lu: op. cit., passim.
[4] See p. 141 above.
[5] C. T. Lu: op. cit., pp. 10–11.
[6] Ibid., passim.

industrial recession.[1] However, handicrafts have formed a much higher percentage of everyday consumer goods. In 1962 they were said to account for 67 per cent of the 'goods for production and livelihood' sold by supply and marketing co-operatives, the main organs of rural commerce. In the case of certain important commodities, the proportion of handicrafts was even greater. In 1962 over 80 per cent of small farm tools was reported to be made by handicraftsmen.[2]

In some branches of Chinese industry, handicrafts have largely yielded to machine manufactures: the spinning and weaving of cotton are notable examples of this tendency. In many cases, however, scarcity of capital combined with high density of population is likely to ensure the continued importance of labour intensive handicrafts for many years to come. The range of handicrafts includes consumer goods and services of many types: textiles and clothing, plastic ware, agricultural tools, the processing of various agricultural products, the making of sundry intermediate goods and spare parts for large-scale industry, and repairs of all kinds. Traditional arts and crafts, for both home and export markets, figure in the list.[3] Juxtaposition of small old-style industry with highly-capitalized modern factory production is found in almost all countries in the process of rapid industrialization. It characterizes the economy of even so technically advanced a land as Japan.[4]

2. THE COLLECTIVIZATION OF HANDICRAFT PRODUCTION

From time immemorial handicrafts had been undertaken on a family basis, either by peasant households who took their wares to market along with their surplus farm products, or by town-dwellers who sold their finished goods from a shop at the front of their house. Often members of the family would supply all the labour, with son being apprenticed to father, or sometimes a few outside workers would also be employed. Such businesses made the minimal demands on administrative ability and accountancy. Very likely the working proprietor kept the accounts in his head. Incentive to satisfy consumer need was strong and immediate, transmission of skills presented no problem or expense, and the maximum use was made of the spare moments of housewives by the ease with which production could be dovetailed with domestic tasks.

These simple virtues were easy to overlook, especially for the new regime in its first fervent decade, when the ideological vices and political dangers of independent artisans appeared very obvious. After the peasants, these were the most numerous representatives of individual enterprise and of private ownership of the means of production, while their output did not conform to any officially conceived plan. Consequently handicraftsmen and small manufacturers of all kinds had logically to be collectivized. In addition, the

---

[1] p. 142 above.
[2] *Economic Research* (*Jingji Yanjiu*), No. 7, July 1962, p. 5. Hu Jui-liang and Yuan Tai-hsu: 'A Discussion of Handicraft Industry and Its Economic Forms', and *People's Daily* (*Renmin Ribao*), October 27, 1963, p. 1. Editorial.
[3] On the official dividing line between handicrafts and the arts, see C. T. Lu, op. cit., pp. 22–4.
[4] G. C. Allen: *Japan's Economic Recovery*, London, 1958, pp. 74–6.

government thought that only collectivization would enable it to acquire for its own purposes any considerable share of the profits of these small enterprises, which are notoriously hard to tax effectively.

Producer co-operatives were not an entirely new phenomenon in China. During the war with Japan, the China Industrial Co-operatives, with considerable support from individual foreigners, had encouraged the formation of co-operatives to operate workshops and small industrial establishments. However, political difficulties with the Nationalist Government, as well as the lack of competent managers and honest accountants, had inhibited their progress.

These war-time efforts had been well-meaning but weak attempts to kindle interest in co-operative enterprises at the grass roots level. After 1949 the tables were turned and the movement was developed from above. Producers' co-operatives, under political control, were considered the ideologically preferable form of organization for handicrafts and small workers. Consequently the co-operative movement was launched on a national scale. The setting up of co-operative arrangements for supply of raw materials and for sale of finished products was usually the first step, to be followed closely by the establishment of fully fledged producers' co-operatives.[1] Eventually, in 1955–6, the movement was given such an impetus that by the close of 1956 over 90 per cent of handicraft workers were enrolled as members of co-operatives. The progress of the movement of collectivization is shown in the following table:

Date	Number of handicraft producer co-operatives	Number of handicraft workers in co-operatives	Handicraft workers in co-operatives as per cent of total handicraft workers
1949	300[1]	88,000[1]	
1952	3,000[1]	c. 250,000[1]	3·1[2]
1953			3·9[2]
1954			13·6[2]
1955			26·9[2]
1956	c. 100,000[2]	Over 5,000,000[2]	91·7[2]

[1] NCNA Peking, December 16, 1957.
[2] *Economic Research* (*Jingji Yanjiu*), No. 7, July 1962, p. 6. Hu Jui-liang and Yuan Tai-hsu: loc. cit.

Statistics relating to handicrafts are frequently unreliable owing to difficulties of definition and collection. Thus, while the 'over 5 million' collectivized handicraftsmen of 1956 were said to constitute 91·7 per cent of the total engaged in this sector of the economy, in the following year the total of full-time handicraftsmen was given as eight million, with another twelve million engaged part-time in these occupations.[2] There is, however, reason to believe that the number engaged in handicrafts rose in the latter half of 1956 and the first part of 1957, when they were able to sell their products on the reopened rural markets.[3] It will be remembered that in Chapter 7 the

---

[1] Hsüeh Mu-ch'iao, Su Hsing and Lin Tse-li: *The Socialist Transformation of the National Economy in China*. Peking, 1960, pp. 147–50.
[2] *People's Handbook* (*Renmin Shouce*) *1958*, p. 487.
[3] *Planned Economy* (*Jihua Jingji*), No. 12, December 1956, p. 6. Sung Yi-min: 'Strengthen Leadership Over the Free Market.'

number of handicraft workers was given as 6,560,000 in 1957 falling to 1,465,000 in 1958. A good part of this sudden decline must be ascribed to definitional changes when, as we shall see, handicraft co-operatives were merged to form local state enterprises. An estimate of nearly six million full-time handicraftsmen in the whole country was made in 1962, the total being brought up to some twenty million if those combining agriculture with handicrafts were included; this figure of twenty million whole and part-time handicraftsmen was repeated in 1964.[1] A survey made in 1961 and described as incomplete recorded over 60 per cent of the full-time handicraft workers as being in urban areas.[2]

The handicraft co-operatives are organized into federations, first at the level of the municipality or *hsien*, and then into provincial federations; these, in turn, come under the All China Federation of Handicraft Co-operatives. This body held its first National Congress in December 1957. A Preparatory Committee for the Federation had been elected three years earlier at the fourth meeting of the All China Handicrafts Co-operatives; among its declared functions were to assist the formation of and give a lead to handicraft co-operatives at all levels, and to improve the management and technical standards of the handicraft industry. The Preparatory Committee, together with the Central Handicrafts Administrative Bureau (see below), took a prominent part in the collectivization movement. Between 1955 and 1957 the Committee had disposed of a total income of nearly ¥49 million drawn from government subsidies, profits (source unspecified) and sums derived from co-operatives themselves and from the subordinate federations. These funds provided for the operational expenses of the central and provincial federations as well as for 'advance payments for the purchase of iron and steel for local production and for expenses for various undertakings'.[3] More recent reports of the activities of the All China Federation are of its exhortatory functions—issuing appeals for priority to be given to production for agriculture or calling for improved management of co-operatives and putting forward criteria of efficiency.[4] In October 1963 the All China Federation held its Second National Congress.

The All China Federation of Handicraft Co-operatives is, at least nominally, the representative body of the handicraft co-operatives. The Central Handicrafts Administrative Bureau was constituted after the promulgation of the constitution in 1954 as the government organ for the supervision of the handicraft industry. Originally this bureau was immediately subordinate to the State Council. In March 1958 it was put under the Ministry of Light Industry. No further information was available about its demise or revival until the announcement in October 1961 that a Central General Bureau of Handicraft Industry was to be established directly under the State Council 'in order to

[1] *People's Daily* (*Renmin Ribao*), June 30, 1964, p. 5. Ho Ju: 'The Positive Role of Handicrafts in Our National Economy.'

[2] *People's Daily* (*Renmin Ribao*), April 19, 1963, p. 5. Shao Yen: 'Wholeheartedly Encourage the Role of Handicraft Industry in Aiding Agriculture.'

[3] NCNA Peking, December 20, 1957, and *People's Handbook* (*Renmin Shouce*) *1957*, p. 278, and *Collected Laws and Regulations of the People's Republic of China* (in Chinese), Vol. 2, pp. 617–20, and ibid., Vol. 3, pp. 271–2.

[4] *Ta Kung Daily* (*Dagong Bao*), Peking, November 11, 1962, p. 1.

strengthen guidance of the handicraft industry'.[1] For some undisclosed reason a year elapsed before the State Council appointed the Director and Deputy Director of the restored Bureau and then the choice fell on Teng Chieh and T'ien P'ing respectively.[2] Teng was concurrently Chairman of the All China Federation of Handicraft Co-operatives and also a Vice Minister of Light Industry while T'ien was a Vice Chairman of the All China Federation. This illustrates the very close links that existed between the Bureau and the Federation, both being in effect official bodies charged with the execution of government policy towards the handicraft industry. It also showed that the ties between the Bureau and the Ministry were still close despite the fact that the former was no longer under the latter. In 1965 the Bureau was abolished and at the same time a Second Ministry of Light Industry established; presumably the control of handicrafts was among its duties. This change may have been a recognition that as operations in many handicraft co-operatives became mechanized, the dividing line between handicrafts and industry was no longer realistic.

In the provinces and lower units, local handicraft administrative organs, corresponding to the Central Bureau, appear to have existed widely, at least after 1954. Continuity may in some cases have been broken, perhaps during the 'Great Leap': in 1959 we read that in Kwangtung 'handicraft administrative organs were re-established'.[3]

In 1959 three main types of handicraft co-operatives were distinguished: the small group, the supply and marketing producers' co-operative and the producers' co-operative pure and simple. The small group, based on independent craftsmen or family enterprises, was linked with state enterprises, supply and marketing co-operatives or producer co-operatives for the purpose of obtaining raw materials or goods to be processed and of selling output. Only the master craftsman or the head of a family actually became a co-operative member. One step nearer socialism stood the handicraft supply and marketing producers' co-operative under which individual artisans or small groups were more closely connected with the co-operative; in some cases this involved centralized production in one place as well as common purchasing and sales arrangements. In this form of organization, all the participants—family members, apprentices and assistants—became members of the co-operative. Co-operatives of this type could gradually transform themselves into proper socialist enterprises through using collective funds to buy collectively-owned tools, thus becoming full producer co-operatives. In 1956 this highest type, the producers' co-operatives, were said to have accounted for 76·6 per cent of the total labour force and 89·5 per cent of the value of output of all handicraft co-operatives.[4]

In the collectivization of handicraft enterprises no attempt appears to have been made to adopt the size of unit best fitted to the needs of production. A

[1] *Collected Laws and Regulations* . . . Vol. 1, p. 151, and ibid., Vol. 7, p. 64, and NCNA Peking, October 5, 1961, and *People's Handbook (Renmin Shouce) 1962*, p. 50.

[2] NCNA Peking, November 8, 1962.

[3] NCNA Canton, July 21, 1959, and *Collected Laws and Regulations* . . . Vol. 1, p. 154.

[4] Hsü Ti-hsin: *An Analysis of China's Economy in the Transitional Period* (in Chinese), Revised Edition, Peking, 1959, pp. 104–5, and *Economic Research (Jingji Yanjiu)*, No. 7, July 1962, p. 6. Hu Jui-liang and Yuan Tai-hsu: loc. cit.

policy of amalgamation and centralized management was followed, with the different concerns thus drawn together pooling their profits and losses and losing their status as independent accounting units. The damage done by such measures was realized in the highest quarters even at a time when the collectivization campaign was barely over. This is seen in the speech of Ch'en Yün to the Eighth National Congress of the Chinese Communist Party in September 1956. He stated that the amalgamation of handicraft enterprises had been over-emphasized and had brought 'many inconveniences' to both workers and customers; it was the reason why 'some handicraft products have deteriorated in quality or become less varied since the handicraftsmen ceased working on their own'. Domestic industries in rural districts had also declined as a result of official neglect in the course of the collectivization of agriculture.[1]

Despite this strong criticism of the policy of amalgamating small handicraft concerns, there seems to have been no reversal of it during the next few years. The economic realists in high places, of whom Ch'en Yün was one, were overshadowed as a result of the shift of power in the inner councils of the Party. In the Great Leap of 1958, led by the extremists, there was little place for old-fashioned handicraft production carried on in a decentralized fashion. The policy of 'walking on two legs' certainly laid stress on small-scale industry, but organized in quite a different way: centralized under the commune and its constituent units in the countryside and under the street association, and later under the urban commune, in the towns. By May 1959 only 13·3 per cent of the over five million handicraft co-operative members of 1956 were reported to be still in co-operatives of the old types. Slightly more (13·6 per cent) were in units amalgamated to form co-operative factories, 37·8 per cent worked in what had now been designated locally-controlled industry while 35·3 per cent were employed in commune factories.[2]

In the course of the Great Leap the type of products demanded from small workshops also changed: consumer goods were neglected in favour of producer goods. The most notable instance of this was the campaign for 'backyard' iron and steel in the summer and autumn of 1958. Some of the poor quality metal thus turned out was used for farm tools and other rural purposes, but no systematic attempt had been made to relate supply to potential demand in either type or quality. Not only was raw material wasted, but also labour power. In addition to workers drawn from agriculture, at the cost of leaving ungathered some of the record harvest of that year, artisans were taken from their former trades to turn their hands to making iron and steel. At the same time craftsmen provided an obvious source of recruits for engineering and similar branches of industry.[3]

The shortage of handicraftsmen was aggravated by the decline in the number of apprentices after collectivization. The spirit of the age militated against the system of apprenticeship. Reports came of apprentices asking

[1] *The Eighth National Congress of the Communist Party of China*, Vol. II. Speeches. Peking, 1956, p. 163.

[2] *People's Daily* (*Renmin Ribao*), September 17, 1959, p. 4. Teng Chieh: 'The Great Victory of the Socialist Transformation of China's Handicraft Industry.'

[3] *Ta Kung Daily* (*Dagong Bao*), Peking, August 28, 1961, p. 3. Feng P'ing-fei: 'Handicraft Industry is an Important Component of the National Economy.'

excessive wages, 'demanding absolute equality, quarrelling with their masters and being disrespectful to them and even regarding their masters as exploiters'. The formation of co-operatives had not improved this situation and skilled men became unwilling to take on apprentices.[1] Sometimes they were not permitted to do so; in other cases they could not select their own apprentices but had them assigned by the labour department which might reassign them elsewhere after a year or two.[2]

As a result of the diversion of handicraftsmen and their potential apprentices to other occupations, many products became unobtainable and certain services were in short supply. Distribution of skilled artisans became very uneven. Excessive numbers in certain trades might be found in places which were grievously short of others. 'In Hsilo commune (Hunan) there are more than enough carpenters, shoemakers, painters and dyers . . . but there is an acute lack of blacksmiths, rope makers and coopers.' To get a hoe repaired might involve going ten miles to find a blacksmith and spending one or two days on the round trip. 'The masses find this inconvenient.'[3] Shortage of blacksmiths was also a serious problem in parts of Shansi in 1962. A visit to four communes with nineteen production brigades revealed not one furnace. Peasants had to go to the towns to have their tools made.[4] This was only four years after the nation-wide campaign for iron and steel smelting during which almost 30,000 furnaces (nearly one to every five hundred inhabitants) were reported to be in operation in this very province of Shansi.[5]

A Chinese returning from abroad noted the disappearance of a multitude of small trades and services. 'Now the children were deprived of toys and firecrackers, the girls of ribbons and trinkets, the weddings of the spangled bridal sedan-chair, the streets of the bright signs and advertisements, the New Year of its snack booths and theatrical performances, the roads of their tea-houses and wine-shops, the villages of their local festivals, the birthdays of their celebrations and story-tellers.'[6] These small items could not be incorporated into economic planning, at least with the planning techniques available in China. Consequently their production lacked the public acclaim and glamour that surrounded those branches of industry with widely proclaimed targets. As a result there came about a diversion of labour and raw materials from the old handicrafts into the more fashionable types of production.[7]

---

[1] *People's Handbook* (*Renmin Shouce*) *1958*, p. 497. Report by Chia T'o-fu, Director of the Fourth Office of the State Council, on Handicraft Co-operatives.

[2] *People's Daily* (*Renmin Ribao*), March 21, 1962, p. 2. An Hsing-ts'un: 'Make Full Use of Old Craftsmen in Arts and Crafts.'

[3] *Ta Kung Daily* (*Dagong Bao*), Peking, May 29, 1961, p. 3. Shang Chien-ming: 'Some Problems in Organizing and Developing Rural Handicraft Production.'

[4] *People's Daily* (*Renmin Ribao*), May 10, 1962, p. 2. Letters from readers.

[5] NCNA Taiyuan, November 26, 1958. It is realized that the two types of furnace, for making farm tools and for producing iron and steel, are not identical. However, the skills required are similar and one purpose of the 1958 rural iron and steel campaign was to encourage local manufacture of farm tools.

[6] Mu Fu-sheng: *The Wilting of the Hundred Flowers—Free Thought in China Today*, London, 1962, p. 196.

[7] Cf. P. J. D. Wiles: *The Political Economy of Communism*, Oxford, 1962, p. 250: ' . . . while an advanced manufacturing sector produces greater variety than artisans, an immature one produces less'.

The rapid growth of modern factory industry during the First Five Year Plan period, and more especially in 1958–9, led to a greatly increased demand for accessories and components, while the ever-increasing amount of mechanical equipment in use necessitated more spare parts and an expansion of repair facilities. Previously it may have happened that a factory in one place depended for these requirements on suppliers elsewhere. The greater powers granted to local authorities in 1957–8 meant that they were henceforth in a stronger position to accord priority to local needs when allocating the output of enterprises in their area, while giving only later consideration to customers in other places. At a time of chronic shortages, this meant that outside customers were often neglected. Therefore it frequently became necessary to improvize local sources for products previously bought from elsewhere. This tendency was aggravated by the transport bottlenecks which grew worse in 1958–9. All these factors—the decentralization measures, the nature of the planning system and the deficiencies in transport—made for a growth in local self-sufficiency. The next development in small-scale manufacture which must now be considered traces its origin to this situation, as well as to that created by the decline in handicrafts which has already been recounted.

3. URBAN COMMUNES

In 1958–60 a large number of small industrial undertakings in towns—mainly workshops—were established or expanded under the aegis of street associations and urban communes. The street associations (also known as residents' associations) are organs of social and political control, embracing all the inhabitants of one street, group of small streets or section of a large one. They owe something to the concept of the old *paochia* system, by which the population was divided into units of ten and a hundred families, for registration, policing, and other purposes.[1] Street associations also undertake social welfare, rationing, and security functions. The increased importance of street associations at this time arose from the new responsibilities they acquired under the decentralization measures of 1957–8 when certain state and joint state-private economic enterprises, and also schools and medical agencies were transferred to their management.[2] The renaming of street associations as urban communes (for this in fact is what the urban commune movement often amounted to) may have been a recognition of the more varied nature of the duties then assumed. Alongside the greater importance of the basic local unit in towns, went an increase in the power of the Party committee at the corresponding local level. As long as local factories were controlled by different central ministries and provincial bureaux, the Party committees of these factories were independent of local Party committees. When however, the factories were taken over by street associations or urban communes, the factory Party committees became subordinate to local Party committees.[3]

[1] This system varied greatly in both theory and fact at different periods in Chinese history and learned opinion about its origin and operation is also divergent.

[2] *Teaching and Research* (*Jiaoxue Yu Yanjiu*), No. 11, November 1958 (ECMM 163). Wang Hai-p'o: 'Questions Concerning the Establishment of People's Communes in Urban Streets.'

[3] *People's Daily* (*Renmin Ribao*), April 7, 1960, p. 10.

It is not clear what proportion of 'street industry' represented new concerns, initiated in accordance with the policy of 'walking on two legs' and how much was already in existence but previously under the control of ministries and bureaux. Probably the new ventures received more than their share of publicity.

In 1958, when the rural communes were being formed, reports came of communes being established in a few cities as well. The director of a particularly famous urban commune in Chengchow told a foreign visitor at that time that the change made no difference, 'just another damn committee with me as chairman and the secretary of the trade union as deputy'. The visitor however remarked that with the formation of the commune, private ownership of houses and shops came to an end.[1] Whatever either the intention or the actuality of the early urban communes had been, it was soon decided, for reasons which are still the subject of speculation, that the time was inopportune for their wider establishment. The Central Committee of the CCP, in its resolution on the communes adopted at the Wuhan Conference in December 1958 stated that 'we ... should not be in a hurry to set up people's communes on a large scale in the cities. Particularly in the big cities, this work should be postponed except for the necessary preparatory measures.' From the close of 1958 until the spring of 1960 there was virtually no news of urban communes. However, in the intervening period much was heard of 'street factories' opened by street associations in Chungking, Wuhan, Changchun and elsewhere. These reports continued into 1960 even when the revivified movement for the formation of urban communes was in full spate.

This movement was heralded by a speech to the National People's Congress in March 1960 by Li Fu-ch'un, the Chairman of the State Planning Commission, and by an editorial in the *People's Daily* on the next day. The speech stated that 'all the cities' were currently setting up people's communes while the editorial mentioned that for nearly two years urban communes had been progressing steadily.[2] Since the difference between street associations and urban communes appears to be largely one of definition and nomenclature, the date at which any urban commune can said to have been founded is a concept of some elasticity. One feature of the movement which must be noted is the wide divergence in time of the reported establishment of communes in different cities; a contrast to rural communes which were said to have become almost universal within a few weeks. Local delays were sometimes explained in terms of the misgivings of bourgeois elements in towns. This would suggest that the change from organization by street associations to the setting up of urban communes was, in fact, or was at least anticipated to be, more than a change in name. We shall not know the truth about the circumstances surrounding these events until an account is obtained of the cross currents in the Party at the time. To hazard a guess, the formation of the urban (as of the rural) communes may have become a symbol of victory for the extremists, both nationally and on the local level, and as such was opposed by those who did not share their aims. On this interpretation, the extremists won a token victory, but the moderates—or rather the pressure of reality—were able, as

[1] *Encounter*, March 1959, p. 19. R. H. S. Crossman: 'Chinese Notebook.'
[2] *Peking Review*, April 5, 1960, p. 7, and *People's Daily* (*Renmin Ribao*), March 31, 1960, pp. 1–4.

we shall see, to ensure that this was short-lived. It is noteworthy that in the city of Shanghai, as distinct from its suburbs, urban communes were not reported to have been set up, apart from one experimental commune, although there were often rumours of their imminent formation. Street organizations were said to have been active in Shanghai, but in that politically sensitive city the authorities at that time shrank from the appellation of commune.

North and north-east China, especially the provinces of Honan, Hopei and Heilungkiang, were the scene of the first urban communes. Later they were established more widely. By May 1960, over 1,000 urban communes with over 42 million inhabitants were reported to have been established throughout China; this amounted to about 60 per cent of the city population.[1] In October of that year, reference was made to 'the more than 1,000 urban communes'[2] in existence, which suggests that not many had been formed after May. While most reports of urban communes came from sizable cities, they were not unknown in *hsien* towns as well.[3]

Urban communes were not invariably as all-inclusive as their rural counterparts. While in some cities, such as Shenyang, 100 per cent membership was claimed,[4] in others this was not the case. This difference arose from the variety of types of urban commune, the main kinds being those consisting of the employees of one large factory, colliery or government organization and their families, those comprising the residents of one sector of a city and those communes on the outskirts of towns which included some agricultural land although being mainly urban. Urban communes varied greatly in size and organization. A commune in Kaifeng, Honan, had 16,000 inhabitants in December 1959, while the pioneer Red Flag commune of Chengchow, in the same province, was reported to have expanded until by October 1960 its members numbered 150,000.[5] Chungking, with 2,200,000 inhabitants in 1958, was by 1961 divided into thirty-nine urban communes while in the same year Harbin, with a population of 1,800,000 in 1961, had only seven.[6] In Harbin the communes were based on the former *ch'ü* (wards),[7] a practice which was followed in a number of other cities.

During the years 1959–61, the phenomenon known as 'organizing the economic life of the urban people' was taken in hand in cities throughout China whether they were controlled by urban communes, street associations or other forms of organization (in some places local commercial departments were particularly prominent). This involved (as in the rural communes) the enlistment of the housewives for productive work in small factories and workshops and in the various social agencies which were established to enable

[1] *People's Daily (Renmin Ribao),* June 5, 1960, p. 2. Speech by Li Hsien-nien.
[2] *Peking Review,* October 25, 1960, p. 5.
[3] I. and D. Crook: *The First Years of Yangyi Commune,* London, 1966, p. 230.
[4] *Liaoning Daily (Liaoning Ribao),* April 28, 1960 (SCMP 2283).
[5] *Honan Daily (Honan Ribao),* December 16, 1959 (SCMP 2220), and *Peking Review,* October 25, 1960, p. 5.
[6] NCNA Chungking, April 30, 1961, and ibid., Harbin, April 28, 1961, and M. B. Ullman: *Cities of Mainland China 1953 and 1958,* US Department of Commerce, Washington, DC, 1961, pp. 35–6.
[7] *Daily Worker (Gongren Ribao),* September 6, 1961, p. 3. Tso Chi: 'Strengthen Planning, Promote Initiative.'

women to leave their homes. Such social agencies included mess halls, nurseries, homes for the aged and livelihood service stations—these last undertaking a variety of services such as laundry, shopping and repairs. The mess halls, as in the country, were a means of stricter enforcement of food rationing as well as of political control. The new services had almost invariably to be paid for by the individual consumer and must often have absorbed almost the whole of the housewife's wage packet. Unlike the practice in the first days of the rural communes, 'free supply'—the provision of food and other goods and services without payment—appears to have been unusual in urban communes. At the same time great efforts were made to see that any surplus cash possessed by city dwellers was absorbed by savings campaigns.

The street factories and workshops to which the housewives and others were recruited, usually had little machinery, at least in the early stages. Most of these factories fell into one or other of two broad categories: those acting as outworkers of large state-owned factories in the same town, making spare parts or ancillary products on contract, often using waste products of the larger factories as raw material and perhaps receiving technical help from them; and those manufacturing for local use small consumer goods which had been in short supply as these did not warrant inclusion in economic plans. Some of the new undertakings were occupied with repair work of one type or another, a sector of economic life which had been seriously neglected during the years of the Great Leap. A survey made in the spring of 1961 in eight widely-scattered cities showed that roughly 50 per cent of the workers in commune industry were making consumer goods, about 40 per cent producing for industrial requirements, while the remaining 10 per cent were engaged on making goods required for agricultural production or for export.[1]

The general purpose of street and communal factories was in fact to impart a degree of flexibility into the local economy. These small and informal concerns could switch more easily than large enterprises to the production of whatever commodity happened to be in short supply in any town or meet more quickly some urgent demand for spare parts or repairs for a nearby factory. Thus they exemplified both the growth in local self-sufficiency which re-asserted itself in the Chinese economy from 1958 and also the tendency towards vertical integration by the development of clusters of ancillary undertakings around and connected with large enterprises. In January 1961 it was reported that as a result of urban commune industries some places had become entirely self-sufficient in small consumer goods and that the past situation of 'large goods from Tientsin and Shanghai, small commodities from Soochow and Hangchow' had been transformed.[2]

The high proportion of non-employed dependents in the urban population, a corollary of the fact that in 1957 women formed only 13·5 per cent of the non-agricultural labour force, provided another motive for the opening of the commune or street factories.[3]

---

[1] *Daily Worker* (*Gongren Ribao*), September 5, 1961, p. 3. Tso Chi: 'Production of Small Commodities Should Be the Main Task of Urban Commune Industry.'
[2] *Ta Kung Daily* (*Dagong Bao*), Peking, January 25, 1961, p. 1. Editorial.
[3] p. 182 above, and P. Schran: *The Structure of Income in Communist China*. (Unpublished Ph.D Thesis, University of California, 1961), p. 358.

Reports of the opening of commune factories lay stress on the informal and spontaneous nature of the action. For example, nine women in a Peking commune are said to have borrowed two pairs of bellows and two broken cooking-pots, gathered some broken bricks and built two stoves. They used ¥2·40 of their own money to buy gloves and mouth covers, got some waste sulphuric acid from a nearby nail plant and scrap iron from a machine tool plant, and thus they set up a small enterprise to make insecticides. From the same commune came the news of 200 housewives who worked hard for three days carrying earth and bricks and re-built a derelict house. They earned some money by processing discarded sulphuric acid and scrap iron into iron sulphate and with the proceeds bought equipment and raw materials to set up a book-binding and toy-making enterprise.[1]

If these and similar stories of the origin of commune factories are typical, the original capital for many of them was of the scantiest, scraped together by the participants. The same enthusiasm is reported to have led to a willingness to work for very small or even no wages in the initial stages until an enterprise was on its feet; even then wages in urban commune industry did not usually exceed ¥20–30 a month, a level below that prevailing in state industrial undertakings. The more successful of these small enterprises are reported to have grown by the ploughing back of profits until they became sizeable factories.

The decline of the urban communes was, to the outside observer, a process wrapped in even greater mystery than their original development. In the course of 1961 less was heard of them, and after the end of that year they were scarcely mentioned. The social and political functions of the urban communes duplicated those of the organs of municipal government and were thus superfluous. The shortage of raw materials, due to agricultural disasters and transport deficiencies, hit urban commune industry with especial severity. In the category of light industry, priority for the allocation of raw materials was given to 'advanced enterprises'—that is to large-scale concerns—on account of their more efficient use of materials and their lower costs. Urban commune industries were told to use initiative in discovering new sources of supplies, but these could be of no more than marginal importance. The decline in industrial activity in many branches of heavy as well as light industry reduced the demand for ancillary goods while large factories which could not provide sufficient employment for their regular labour force would be less likely to put jobs out on contract to outworkers. A report from Shanghai of street industry in this predicament tells of cadres encouraging housewives to stay at home because of the heavy nature of their household duties.[2] In Shanghai and no doubt in other places, the earlier exhortation to eat at mess halls was muted before long, with the result that fewer people used them, thus making it more difficult for housewives to go out to work. The changes in the mess hall situation must not, however, be exaggerated. In most towns there were never

[1] NCNA Peking, April 18, 1960, and *People's Daily* (*Renmin Ribao*), May 1, 1960, p. 7.
[2] *Current Scene*, Vol. I, No. 6, July 10, 1961, p. 3, and *Daily Worker* (*Gongren Ribao*), September 8, 1961, p. 3. Tso Chi: 'How Should the Problem of Raw Materials be Solved?', and *Ta Kung Pao* (*Dagong Bao*), Peking, August 26, 1962, p. 1. Editorial. Another reason for discouraging housewives from continued employment may have been that their additional nutritional requirements when employed were greater than foreseen. E. Snow: *The Other Side of the River*, London, 1963, p. 627.

enough canteens to feed the whole population. After a time some were closed, but the more successful often continued in existence.

Shortage of raw materials and of orders from large factories, combined with waning enthusiasm and lessened ideological pressure, were major factors in bringing about a decline in urban communes and their industrial enterprises. In addition, the movement suffered from that defiant amateurism which had marked the period of the Great Leap. Housewives completely new to industry set about finding ways of manufacturing quite complex products and in next to no time were managing medium-sized factories. Probably much talent was thrown up which had previously been hidden through lack of education and customary barriers to women's employment and promotion; but the opportunity provided little time for ability to mature with experience or for the sifting out of those with sound judgment and managerial potential from those who had been thrust forward for political reasons. The more successful of the new enterprises continued in existence and sometimes expanded into sizable factories controlled by the appropriate bureau of the municipal government.

In Tientsin, the decline of the urban communes was followed, in 1962, by the establishment of neighbourhood women's committees. These committees, which numbered nearly 1,500, comprised a total of some 28,000 housewives. Each committee maintained contact with 300–400 households, for which it provided certain welfare and advisory services. Public health, the upbringing of children and help with housework fell within the activities mentioned, but these were not reported to include industrial production.[1] A similar development occurred in Peking. Street associations and similar bodies continued their activities in cities throughout the country.

As the economic situation improved again after the post-Leap recession, street industries revived. Greater supplies of raw materials and renewed activity in large factories were probably the chief forces behind this renewal, which occurred from 1963 onwards.[2] Politics also played a part, but perhaps more in the greater publicity given to street industry in 1966 than in the increase in its actual operations. This small, simple, yet collective type of workshop production was more consonant with the political atmosphere of 1966, as of 1958, than was the larger, modern, foreign-style industry.

4. THE REVIVAL OF THE HANDICRAFTSMAN

The decline of the urban commune industries was accompanied by a revival, in both town and country, of interest in the older forms of handicrafts and of small-scale manufacturing and service enterprises. We have seen that a diversion of skilled artisans to other forms of employment had taken place during the period of the First Five Year Plan and had reached a climax in 1958. A reaction began in 1959 and in the next few years strong official encouragement was given to the return of handicraftsmen to their old occupations and to the taking on of apprentices. No figures are available to show the success of these

[1] NCNA Tientsin, April 2, 1963.
[2] *Far Eastern Economic Review*, July 28, 1966, pp. 134–5. H. Granquist: 'Urban Leap', and NCNA Peking, March 31, 1966, and NCNA Canton, April 1, 1966, and NCNA Nanning, May 17, 1966, and NCNA Lanchow, June 9, 1966.

appeals. Reduced employment in many branches of modern industry must have compelled workers to go back to handicrafts, although some were loth to do so after having become familiar with the use of machinery.[1] At the same time, efforts were made to ease the raw material position for handicrafts. In 1961, in spite of shortages, handicrafts were allocated more centrally-controlled materials such as steel, pig iron and timber, than in any previous year.[2] The revival of rural fairs also helped the handicraft industry by providing ready outlets for its products. Before long, some handicrafts were in much more plentiful supply and by 1963 customers could afford to be choosey and refuse low-quality goods.[3]

The type of small-scale industry associated with the Great Leap declined. The small iron and steel furnaces, for example, ceased to exist. Those that had proved themselves were developed into medium-sized enterprises, while the rest were closed. In a number of other branches of industry, too, the economies of large-scale modern operations were recognized. Restrictions on raw material supplies were used to limit handspinning and weaving, which are extravagant of raw cotton compared with machine production. The revival of handicrafts was not motivated by sentimentality.

The position of handicraftsmen in rural areas has already been considered.[4] In cities and market towns the handicraft producers' co-operatives (each being an independent accounting unit)[5] were still the main type of organization envisaged in this branch of production. Indeed, secret instructions issued to cadres in December 1961 ordered that, except in special cases, the local state industrial workshops, formed in 1958 by the amalgamation of co-operatives, should gradually be divided up again and resume their identity as separate co-operatives.[6] Eventual transition to all-people ownership was declared inevitable, but such a transition on a large scale was ruled out for a long time ahead and permission was explicitly given for the continuation of individual handicraft enterprises. The emphasis now was on the diversity of the industry and the need to respect this by allowing a multiplicity of organizational forms. Empiricism must be the test of policy: what needed centralization must be centralized, what needed dispersal must be dispersed.[7]

Lavish praise was given to the traditional domestic organization of handi-

---

[1] *Ta Kung Daily* (*Dagong Bao*), Peking, July 15, 1959, p. 1. Editorial, and *Daily Worker* (*Gongren Ribao*), September 20, 1961, p. 1. Teng Chieh, Chairman of the All China Federation of Handicraft Co-operatives: 'Be Content and Skilful in the Production of Small Things.'

[2] *Ta Kung Daily* (*Dagong Bao*), Peking, August 28, 1961, p. 3. Feng P'ing-fei: loc. cit. It will be remembered from p. 173 above that normally small enterprises are supplied with these commodities through the Ministry of Commerce. Presumably the allocation mentioned here refers to certain quantities of these materials being given to the Ministry of Commerce to distribute specifically to handicraft producers.

[3] Ibid., August 31, 1963, p. 2. 'Handicraft Production After the Late Autumn Harvest.'

[4] See pp. 81–2 above.

[5] *Ta Kung Daily* (*Dagong Bao*), Peking, September 17, 1963, p. 3. Shao Yen: 'A Preliminary Discussion of Some Problems Concerning Handicraft Co-operatives.'

[6] *Seventy Important Points of Communist Industrial Policy 1961*. (From Taiwan Source), No. 12.

[7] *People's Daily* (*Renmin Ribao*), March 2, 1962, p. 1. Editorial, and ibid., October 27, 1963, p. 1. Editorial, and p. 2. Report by Ch'en Yi-fan.

crafts. 'Our country's handicraft industry has many traditional ways of doing business. In the hardware, small farm tool, clothing, shoe and hat trades, there used to be shops in the front of the houses while production was carried on at the back, and in this fashion orders were taken, sales and manufacture carried on, guarantees given for goods and repairs. . . . Tinkers, crockery-menders, knife and scissor grinders and others engaged in repairs used to go around the streets and the countryside, to the customers' doors. Some opened stalls at fairs . . . all these traditional business methods . . . are a precious national heritage. In order to develop production, it is important to encourage their continuance.'[1] These features were never properly appreciated until the great loss occasioned by their absence. One aspect of the 'traditional ways of doing business' specially singled out for praise was that of having very few administrative personnel, in sharp contrast, it was noted, to the situation prevailing in the handicraft co-operatives.[2] No report has been heard of any revival of the old artisans' guilds of former days. Absence of information must not, however, be taken to signify that they have vanished without trace; they may well have re-established themselves under some other guise.

The encouragement given to domestic handicraft enterprises would make it seem probable that in many cases the functions of the co-operatives are now limited to providing capital and to being the channel for the distribution of materials. A co-operative in Fukien which in 1961 received favourable mention in the *People's Daily*, responded to the desires of its members and customers by setting up eleven production groups on a family basis (nine being 'husband and wife teams'). Each group was to be responsible for its own profits and losses; some profits, however, had to be handed over to the co-operative. Capital and rationed raw materials were obtained from the co-operative which also maintained reserve and collective welfare funds drawn from its members. Each of these groups sold its products to the public from a sales counter at the front of the house. In this way the activities of different members of the family could conveniently be co-ordinated. Wang, a copper-smith, 'energetically carries out production while his wife and children help in cleaning the shop and putting everything in order . . . he is welcomed by the masses'. Another family group engaged in soldering, 'while the wife carries out production at home and looks after the shop, the husband goes out in all directions to get raw materials. He contacts public offices and units in order to procure empty milk tins and broken jars, from which he makes kerosene lamps for the countryside.'[3] Such instances may seem trivial but repeated throughout the country they represent a vast liberation of initiative and of entrepreneurial ability to respond to the needs of consumers.

Frequently it must occur that the co-operative is left an empty shell with no real functions to fulfil. Workshops such as those mentioned need little capital and if they expand it is likely to be through the ploughing back of their own profits. Many make no use of rationed materials. This would leave a number of co-operatives with little justification for existence save that of giving

[1] *Daily Worker* (*Gongren Ribao*), November 21, 1961, p. 2. Ho Yi-fu: 'Encourage Traditional Business Methods.'
[2] *People's Daily* (*Renmin Ribao*), September 13, 1961, p. 3.
[3] Ibid., September 1, 1961, p. 3.

a veneer of collective respectability to a multitude of private enterprises.

Those handicraft co-operatives which still play an active role find this role largely in acting as a link between the individual handicraftsmen or small group and the local department of commerce. Materials under state allocation are supplied through commercial departments which also take quantities of the finished products. By their orders for goods the commercial departments can thus strongly influence the direction of handicraft production.[1] Some of the more important types of handicrafts (approximately 25 per cent by value of total handicraft production in 1962) were reported to be under central control, but commercial plans were the chief instrument for connecting the bulk of the handicraft industry to the national planning system,[2] to the extent to which it was so connected at all. Official tribute is still paid to the ideal of ownership by the whole people, towards which the handicraft co-operatives are claimed to be evolving. Such an evolution may be occurring in the case of those already mentioned as being under direct central control, especially if the adoption of modern production techniques increases economies of scale. In the case of other handicraft co-operatives the trend appears to be in the opposite direction, although this may be cloaked by verbal disguise. Some forms of mechanized production, such as the use of simple electrically-powered tools, may be compatible with very small-scale operation. The development of these small concerns must have been forwarded by the easing up of the previous power shortage, with its consequent restrictions on the use of electricity by non-priority consumers, when larger industrial enterprises cut their activities after the Great Leap.

Many of the old familiar problems still remained. Dishonest co-operative officials and misuse of funds give cause for anxiety. An illiterate or semiliterate membership cannot check figures. Experiments have been made in drawing up accounts in the clearest and simplest ways. This is a matter in which local federations of co-operatives can provide a useful service.[3]

The revival of old handicrafts and the recall of the artisans represented one part of the movement for the reinstatement of the professional after his denigration during the Great Leap. We have seen that such a tendency occurred with regard to engineers, technicians and accountants. The return to his bench of the hereditary craftsman may have been no less significant for the economy of China.

5. PRIVATE ENTERPRISES

In noting the revival of family handicraft production, it must not be overlooked that all the time, even in the days of tightest collective control, numerous private undertakings continued to survive. It is difficult to chronicle their story, for many were illegal and most were probably very small workshops.

[1] *Ta Kung Daily* (*Dagong Bao*), Peking, October 27, 1963, p. 1. Editorial, and ibid., September 17, 1963, p. 3. Shao Yen: loc. cit.

[2] Ibid., March 23, 1962, p. 3. Ch'en Hung-yung: 'Handicraft Production: at the Same Time Both Planned and Adaptable.'

[3] Ibid., January 20, 1964, p. 2. Accounting Department of the Hunan Provincial Federation of Handicraft Co-operatives: 'In What Ways Should a Handicraft Co-operative Publish Its Accounts?'

The re-opening of the free market in July 1956 gave an impetus to these individual enterprises by making it easier to get raw materials and sell their finished goods. In October 1957, 'incomplete statistics' from eleven provinces and municipalities (including Shanghai, Peking, Tientsin, Canton, Sian, Kiangsu and Liaoning) found some 150,000 independent handicraftsmen and 'spontaneous industrial' artisans in 80,000 workshops. Among these, the new 'spontaneous industrial workshops' denoting, it seems, illegal enterprises, outnumbered the 'handicraft workshops' that had legally escaped collectivization. The 'spontaneous industrial workshops' were mostly run by handicraftsmen, 'relatively few being capitalist enterprises'; and they used mainly waste articles and scrap material. The proprietors had acumen as well as courage for 'their products were cleverly made and in great variety and met the demand of the market at the right time'.[1]

Some of these entrepreneurs were drawn from clerks or workmen previously employed by the private side of the management of joint state-private enterprises, or were 'small owners [sic] of handicraft co-operatives' and co-operative members. Some were accused of acting in collusion with employees of joint state-private enterprises and handicraft co-operatives to engage in speculation, illicitly obtaining raw materials, corrupting cadres and using underhand means to get the services of workers from state and co-operative concerns.[2]

In 1957–8 an attempt was made to put these 'spontaneous workshops' under control; after re-organization some were licensed to continue production, presumably subject to the discriminatory taxation on independent handicraftsmen and capitalists, imposed in June 1958.[3] In May 1958 a total of 57,000 'spontaneous' industrial concerns were estimated to be still in existence in sixteen of the largest cities in the country.[4] Private industrial and commercial undertakings all over China were believed to total 'several millions' in 1959.[5] In 1960 it was reported that in the city of Wuhan, in addition to some legitimate independent artisans, petty merchants and hawkers, there were still 'a very small handful of illegal underground factories and feudal bosses exercising control over hand-cart pullers'.[6] According to one report some of these small private businesses were regularized by transformation into street factories. However, the problem still remained serious and in September 1962 the Plenary Session of the Party Central Committee thought it necessary to refer in its communique to the 'spontaneous tendency towards capitalism among part of the smaller producers'.[7]

We have seen that the 1956 re-opening of the free market was followed by

---

[1] *New Construction (Xin Jianshe)*, No. 3, March 1958, p. 19. P'an Ching-yuan: 'The Struggle Between the "Two Roads" on the Free Market.'

[2] Ibid.

[3] Ibid., and *New China Fortnightly (Xinhua Banyuekan)*, No. 134, June 25, 1958, p. 89.

[4] *Finance (Caizheng)*, No. 5, May 1958, p. 18. Wen Ping-yuan: 'A Discussion on the Trial Reform of the Industrial and Commercial Tax System.'

[5] Ibid., No. 18, September 24, 1959, p. 30. Shen P'ing: 'Our Country's Industrial and Commercial Tax in the Past Ten Years.'

[6] *Yangtze Daily (Changjiang Ribao)*, May 6, 1960 (SCMP 2276). Wen Li: 'The Superiority of Large-Sized Urban People's Communes.'

[7] NCNA Peking, September 28, 1962.

an increase in private manufacturing activity. Similar consequences are likely to have followed the 1959 free market revival. It may be that with the more moderate and relaxed economic policy of the subsequent period, the distinction between licit and illicit private production was blurred. With official approval given to household groups operating almost independently under the general umbrella of a handicraft co-operative, and presumably exempt from the heavy taxation aimed against independent handicraftsmen, there remained less reason for a would-be entrepreneur to evade the process of collectivization. The term 'household member' is capable of elastic interpretation, especially as artisans were now encouraged to take apprentices. Very likely some 'spontaneous workshops' that had led an underground existence were able to regularize their status without changing their essential nature.

Chapter 9

MINING

The organization of mining and of enterprises engaged in it follow the general lines of industrial organization which we have already surveyed. The special features of the mining industry, however, necessitate separate discussion.

Since 1949 output of most minerals has increased very considerably. Production of some major products dropped significantly in the 1960s from their Great Leap peak; petroleum output, in contrast, registered a notable increase. Official figures published during 1958–60 must be regarded with great wariness: since that time no absolute production figures have been published by the Chinese authorities and consequently estimates by foreign observers have had to be used in the table on page 238.

The Ministry of Geology has had the main responsibility for the ambitious programme of geological surveying and prospecting, which has led to the upward revision of estimated reserves of many minerals. Hydro-geological investigations for water conservancy purposes are included among the Ministry's activities. Like other ministries, the Ministry of Geology supervises a countrywide network of departments at provincial and lower levels. In addition to the Ministry of Geology, other bodies concerned with geological surveying include the Chinese Academy of Sciences and the Ministries of Metallurgy, Coal and Petroleum.

In 1965, the Ministry of Geology established five research institutes covering different branches of geological studies. The Chinese Academy of Sciences also has its own Geological Institute. A desire to emulate the Soviet example promoted this proliferation of research bodies. However, during the period of free speech in the spring of 1957, a research geologist in one of these institutes said that this mushroom growth had been premature. The numerous bodies in this field in the Soviet Union, he pointed out, were not created all at once, but grew out of one original Institute of Geology as circumstances warranted. Visiting Soviet geologists had reminded them of this. 'In the development of scientific work', the Chinese critic continued, 'our failure to consider this point has given rise to some difficulties.' He instanced the case of four of the research institutes, which all operated in the same building, but each of which had its own administrations with consequent waste of personnel, equipment and room space.[1] The speaker went on to discuss the training of geologists in several of the geological academies, which he considered had been too

---

[1] *People's Daily* (*Renmin Ribao*), March 12, 1957 (CB 443). Hsieh Chia-jung: 'Close Co-ordination of Geological Work with State Demand.' (Speech to the 3rd Session of the 2nd CPPCC National Committee on March 11, 1957), and *Mining Engineering*, March 1960, p. 249. Eugene A. Alexandrov: 'Red China Steps Up Its Geological Service.' (Based on Soviet Sources.)

Production of Minerals in Mainland China
(Thousand Metric Tons)

	Coal	Petroleum (Crude)	Iron Ore	Manganese Ore	Tin	Antimony
Pre-1949 Peak	62,000[1]	320[6]	11,000[6]	80[6]	15[6]	40[6]
1949	32,000[2]	121[2]	590[6]	1[6]	4[6]	4[6]
1952	66,000[2]	436[2]	4,290[6]	191[6]	10[6]	8[6]
1957	130,000[2]	1,458[2]	15,000[6]	700[6]	24[6]	15[6]
1958	270,000[2]	2,264[2]	30,000[6]	850[6]	25[6]	15[6]
1959	347,800[3]	3,700[3]	45,000[6]	1,000[6]	26[6] or 21[7]	15[6]
1960	425,000[4]	4,500[4]	55,000[8]	1,200[8]	24[7]	15[8]
1961			35,000[8]	800[8]	24[7]	15[8]
1962	190,000–200,000[4]	5,300[4]	30,000[8]	800[8]	24[7]	15[8]
1963	210,000[4]	5,900[4]	35,000[8]	1,000[8]	24[7]	15[8]
1964	220,000[4]	6,000–7,000[4]				
	209,000[5]	8,400[5]	37,000[8]	1,000[8]		15[8]

(Thousand Metric Tons)

	Copper (Refined)	Lead (Refined)	Zinc (Refined)	Aluminium	Tungsten (Concentrate)
Pre-1949 Peak	3[6]	12[6]	7[6]	9[6]	15[6]
1949	2[6]	2[6]	None[6]	None[6]	5[6]
1952	10[6]	7[6]	9[6]	None[6]	20[6]
1957	50[6]	45[6]	37[6]	20[6]	15[6]
1958	70[6]	60[6]	41[6]	27[6]	15[6]
1959	80[6]	75[6]	60[6]	60[6]	15[6]
1960	100[8]	70[8]	70[8]	80[8]	20[8]
1961	100[8]	85[8]	90[8]	100[8]	20[8]
1962	100[8]	85[8]	90[8]	100[8]	20[8]
1963	100[8]	90[8]	90[8]	100[8]	20[8]
1964	100[8]	100[8]	90[8]	100[8]	18[8]

Sources:

[1] *Statistical Research* (*Tongji Yanjiu*), No. 4, April 1958, p. 19. Editorial Information Department: 'The Basic Circumstances of Our Country's Coal Industry.' The figure is for 1942.

[2] *Ten Great Years*, Peking, 1960, p. 95.

[3] NCNA Peking, January 21, 1960.

[4] *Current Scene*, Vol. III, No. 17, April 15, 1965, p. 10. This source says that the 1960 figures should be heavily discounted.

[5] *1965 Yearbook of the Great Soviet Encyclopaedia* (in Russian), Moscow, 1965, p. 283.

[6] US Bureau of Mines: *Mineral Trade Notes Special Supplement*, No. 59. March 1960, p. 10.

[7] International Tin Council: *Statistical Bulletin*, December 1963, p. 7. Estimated Figures.

[8] US Bureau of Mines: *1964 Year Book* (preprint). K. P. Wang: 'The Mineral Industry of Mainland China', p. 4.

specialized, thereby rendering them incapable of research. Thus it had become necessary for the geological departments of certain universities to attempt to fill the gap by providing wider courses.[1] The other ministries concerned with mining also have their institutions for research and training in addition to the research on these matters which is carried out by organs of the Academy of Sciences.

[1] *People's Daily* (*Renmin Ribao*), March 12, 1957 (CB 443). Hsieh Chia-jung: loc. cit.

Whatever geological personnel may lack in quality, their numbers have certainly been impressive. Writing in October 1959, a Vice-Minister of Geology, Ho Ch'ang-kung, claimed that over 400,000 were employed in geological surveying, including nearly 50,000 with technical qualifications.[1]

The amount of prospecting to be accomplished forms part of the general economic plan, and is apportioned between the provinces and by them, in turn, between the lower local authorities. In 1958 a mass movement for prospecting was launched, and all local authorities down to communes were mobilized. This represented the application of the 'walking on two legs' principle in the sphere of geological work. 'Under the direct leadership of the local Communist Party committees, thousands of people have combed the mountains for minerals needed for industrial development.'[2] This movement must have been educational in making the country people conscious of the mineral potentialities of their districts. However, in economic terms, the amount of time needed to be spent by trained personnel in investigating the finds of the amateurs may have outweighed the value of any discoveries made. Professional geologists are reported to have been unenthusiastic about the campaign, although in the previous year there had been support among them for the opinion, voiced by the visiting Soviet Minister of Geology, Antropov, that cheaper and quicker methods than those hitherto used in the Soviet Union might be effective.[3]

The comprehensive method of survey and prospecting which the Ministry of Geology prescribed in 1959, aimed at speeding the work by a system of combining geological, geophysical and geochemical prospecting with prospecting engineering.[4] In a developed country this might be considered wasteful of personnel, but in China it may have been a reasonable way of using the services of a large number of narrowly specialized geologists.

Considerable achievements have resulted from all this activity. A national geological map on the scale of 1:3,000,000 has been plotted, beside larger scale maps of particular localities.[5] New deposits of many types of minerals have been discovered and China's mineral reserves are now considered much more promising than hitherto. Abundant reserves have been proved of antimony and tungsten (thought to be the largest in the world) and also of iron ore, coal (including coking coal), tin, bismuth, molybdenum, mercury, graphite, fluorite, salt, magnesite, limestone, and talc, with a sufficiency also of manganese, aluminium, phosphates, magnesium, alum, borax, asbestos, gypsum, quartz and mica. Reserves of both petroleum and copper are larger than was previously believed, while reports tell of uranium deposits in south China. Other minerals found in moderate quantity include gold and silver, lead, zinc, sulphur, potassium ores, silica and diamonds.[6]

[1] *People's Daily* (*Renmin Ribao*), October 11, 1959, p. 6. Ho Ch'ang-kung, Vice Minister of Geology: 'The Glorious Road of Our National Geological Work.'

[2] NCNA Peking, December 27, 1958.

[3] *Mining Engineering*, March 1960, E. A. Alexandrov: loc. cit., and *People's Daily* (*Renmin Ribao*), March 20, 1957 (CB 443). Hsieh Chia-jung: loc. cit.

[4] *Kuang Ming Daily* (*Guangming Ribao*), July 23, 1961, p. 1.

[5] *People's Daily* (*Renmin Ribao*), October 11, 1959, Ho Ch'ang-kung: loc. cit. (quoted from *People's Handbook* [*Renmin Shouce*] 1960, p. 55).

[6] US Bureau of Mines: *Mineral Trade Notes Special Supplement*, No. 59, March 1960,

Soviet help was substantial and Soviet methods were adopted in the general organization of surveying. Large numbers of Soviet geologists worked in China during the 1950s—over 200 in the province of Hunan alone.[1] A noteworthy example of Sino-Soviet co-operation was the Joint Sino-Soviet Scientific Expedition which, from 1956-9, surveyed the basin of the Heilungkiang (Amur River) and among other objectives, explored the mineral resources of that area.[2]

Most mining enterprises come under the Ministries of Coal, Metallurgy or Petroleum. Some non-metallic mines are operated by various other industrial ministries, including the Ministries of Chemical Industry (e.g. potash and pyrites) and of Building Materials.[3] The People's Bank is closely concerned with gold production.[4] The Ministry of Light Industry deals with salt mining. Uranium mines are the responsibility of the Second Ministry of Machine Building, which administers the nuclear weapon programme.[5] Crystal mines, as far as is known, fall under the First Ministry of Machine Building.[6] The Ministry of State Farms and Land Reclamation may possibly be the central organ ultimately responsible for those mines operated by the PLA Production and Construction Corps in Sinkiang.

From 1950-4 two joint Sino-Soviet companies engaged in mining petroleum, and non-ferrous and rare minerals respectively in Sinkiang. From 1955 the Chinese Government took over the Soviet share, which it paid for by instalments over the next few years. Since then all mining enterprises in China have been exclusively Chinese-owned. Assistance, in the form of equipment and advice, was given in mining matters by the Soviet Union and East European lands.

In administrative status and in their relationship to their respective central ministries and to local authorities, mining undertakings closely resemble factory enterprises. Indeed in many cases the same set of regulations covers

---

p. 12. Figures for reserves are even more uncertain than output figures. Coal reserves were in 1957 reckoned to be 1·5 million million metric tons; at later dates, 9-10 million million metric tons were mentioned, of which 100,000 million tons were reported to have been verified as recoverable. Y. L. Wu, F. B. Hoeber, and M. M. Rockwell: *The Economic Potential of Communist China*, Vol. I, Menlo Park, California, 1963, pp. 112-13, and *Far Eastern Economic Review*, November 18, 1965, p. 341. In 1959 oil reserves were thought to amount to some 5,900 million metric tons. Y. L. Wu et. al., p. 114. Tin reserves have been estimated at between 650,000 and 1,900,000 metric tons. J. J. Schanz: *The United States and a Postwar Tin Control Agreement*, p. 30. (Unpublished Ph.D Thesis, Pennsylvania State University, 1954.)

[1] *New Hunan Paper* (*Xin Hunan Bao*), February 13, 1960 (SCMP 2232).
[2] NCNA Peking, December 15, 1959.
[3] *Kuang Ming Daily* (*Guangming Ribao*), September 2, 1963, p. 4.
[4] *New China Fortnightly* (*Xinhua Banyuekan*), No. 117, October 10, 1957, p. 141, and *BBC Summary of World Broadcasts*, Second Series, FE/W344/A/27. (Sian, November 25, 1965).
[5] *Far Eastern Economic Review*, December 9, 1965, pp. 476-81. H. Munthe-Kaas: 'Easy Atoms.'
[6] *Collected Laws and Regulations of the People's Republic of China* (in Chinese), Vol. 4, p. 343. In 1956 crystal mines came under the Second Ministry of Machine Building, which was later absorbed by the First Ministry. Diamonds come (or did in 1956) under the Ministry of Metallurgy.

both. The 'socialist transformation' of 1955–6[1] and the decentralization movement of 1957–8, for example, affected mines and factories very similarly. Hence, it is not necessary here to repeat the provisions laid down for the administrative changes that occurred, except to mention that according to the regulations of November 1957 control over large and important coalfields, and over enterprises engaged in the extraction and refining of petroleum, was not to be decentralized but to remain with the ministries of the central government. Fresh regulations promulgated in April 1958 would appear to have lessened the number of enterprises, including mines, to remain under centralized control.[2] In Ninghsia, Yunnan and Kweichow certain newly opened coal mines were to remain directly under the Ministry of Coal because the local administrations were not competent to assume responsibility for them.[3] A list was given of enterprises that were in 1958 to remit all their profits to the central treasury and not to divide them with provincial local authorities, it included four verticalized mining and manufacturing complexes under the Ministry of Metallurgy (Anshan, Penhsi, Taiyuan and Shihchingshan), thirty-four named coal mines, and the Ministry of Petroleum's extracting and refining concerns.[4] The list is probably shorter than the list of enterprises remaining under central control; while all decentralized enterprises were to divide profits, this may have also been the case with some that were not decentralized.

In mining, as in industry, numerous small 'native' enterprises were developed in 1958 under the lower local authorities, especially the communes. This movement had been heralded by a State Council directive of April 1957 on the development of small coal pits; after that the output from mines operated by agricultural co-operatives and handicraft co-operatives had risen steeply.[5] Thus the campaign for small-scale mines in 1958 was an acceleration of a development already under way. In the course of 1958 some 100,000 small coal pits were said to have been opened[6] in addition to great numbers of small iron, copper and non-ferrous mines; the working of many small-scale oil deposits and oil seepages was also put in hand. Coal mines operated by communes in seventeen provinces and municipalities were reported to have supplied over 25 million tons of 'crude coal' in 1958.[7] One reason for the importance attached to small local coal mines in 1958 was that rural demand for coal rose in that year. This was partly because collective cooking on big stoves in the mess halls necessitated the use of coal whereas formerly the peasants had

[1] In 1953, 857 privately-owned coal mines were reported to exist, of which 374 had been opened after 1949. Hsü Ti-hsin: *An Analysis of China's Economy in the Transitional Period* (in Chinese). Revised Edition, Peking, 1959, p. 270.

[2] *Collected Laws and Regulations* ... Vol. 6, p. 392, and ibid., Vol. 7, p. 331, and *People's Daily (Renmin Ribao)*, June 25, 1958, p. 1.

[3] *People's Daily (Renmin Ribao)*, June 25, 1958, p. 1.

[4] *Collected Laws and Regulations* ... Vol. 7, p. 224.

[5] *Planned Economy (Jihua Jingji)*, No. 2, February 9, 1958, p. 14. Ho Pai-sha, Director, Coal Industry Planning Bureau, State Economic Commission: 'Increase Local Initiative, Energetically Develop Coal Mines.'

[6] NCNA Peking, February 10, 1959.

[7] *People's Daily (Renmin Ribao)*, October 26, 1959, p. 7. Sun Chih-yuan, Vice Chairman, National Economic Commission: 'The Great Historical Significance of Industry of the People's Communes.'

used small firewood and straw and partly because the substitution of sweet potatoes for crops with stalks had in any case reduced the supply of stalks for fuel.[1] This increased demand for rural consumption came on top of rising demands from industry. Financial and transport difficulties also, as we shall see, encouraged the development of small mines in 1958.

The local Party committees, which came so notably to the fore at this time, took the lead in the opening of small mines. For example, the Party committee of Tangshan, Hopei, where the great Kailan Mines are situated, established a headquarters to direct the operation of small pits. 'This has helped to link the work of the small pits with that of the big collieries.'[2] Here we see an example of a Party committee acting as a bridge between a large enterprise intended, according to the original decentralization measures of 1957, to be retained under predominantly central control and small concerns under local authorities. Special requests were made in 1958 to central government organs and enterprises to help small mines, especially in such matters as staff training and technical designing.[3] This occurred not only in the coal industry, but also in other forms of mining. Thus, for example, the long-established Yenchang oilfield in Shensi sent prospectors to help to look for oil in 1958 and even handed over more than forty oil wells to agricultural collectives.[4]

The development of small primitive mines was an answer to the financial difficulties experienced by the coal industry in 1956–7. The emphasis during the First Five Year Plan period had been on opening large mines, many of which were coming into operation around 1956–7. Their production costs per ton were commonly two or three times, and sometimes even up to six times, the costs of the old mines. This was partly due to extravagance, but partly because some capital expenditure was wrongfully included in production costs which, in China as in the Soviet Union, are supposed to represent working costs only.[5] The high costs of the new large-scale mines was no doubt one cause influencing the shift to small-scale 'native' mining in 1958.

The financial difficulties of the coal industry must also be attributed in part to a cause outside its own control, that is to the low prices, relative to other sources of energy or to other commodities (compared with pre-war relative prices), set for coal, especially before 1958;[6] profits in coal mining have, as a result, been considerably lower than in other branches of industry. This question will be treated further in Chapter 16. The confluence of all these factors resulted in half China's coal mines working at a loss (on the Chinese method of calculation) in 1957.[7]

---

[1] *People's Daily* (*Renmin Ribao*), October 25, 1961, p. 2. Li Ho-t'ing, Yin Chün-k'ai, Hsieh Hung-te, Tseng Li-t'ing and Mao Shih-sheng: 'A Report of a Survey of Flexibility in Planting Crops in Aikuo Commune', and ibid., March 28, 1962, p. 2, and I. & D. Crook: *The First Years of Yangyi Commune*, London, 1966, p. 157.

[2] NCNA Peking, December 20, 1958.

[3] *Planned Economy* (*Jihua Jingji*), No. 2, February 1958, p. 13. Ho Pai-sha: loc. cit.

[4] NCNA, Sian, August 15, 1958.

[5] *Finance* (*Caizheng*), No. 7, July 1957, p. 30. Chang Pen-lien: 'Some Questions Influencing the Raising of the Profit Level in the State Coal Mining Industry.'

[6] Ibid., No. 3, March 1958, pp. 14–15, Chang Meng-tseng: 'Price Problems of the Products of the State Coal Mining Industry.'

[7] Ibid., see pp. 161–2 above on method of calculating profits and losses.

The campaign for developing small mines continued through 1959 and into 1960, but emphasis came to be placed on rationalization, modernization and improving the quality of products. The most inefficient small mines were closed, and attempts made to mechanize at least some of the better ones. The metallurgical industry had grown beyond the capacity of the mining industry to supply, particularly as regards iron ore and coking coal. Also damage had been done during the Great Leap by concentration on immediate increases in mineral output at the expense of long-term considerations. Hence, after the Leap, at a time when the further development of heavy industry was being soft-pedalled, priority was given to mining. An editorial in the *People's Daily* in July 1960 summoned the railways, power stations and the machine industry to regard assistance to mining as an urgent task. Industry was exhorted to release labour for mining but was not, however, to draw workers from agriculture, a sphere of even higher priority. In some places, for example in Nanking, factories were linked directly with mines for the better supply of mutual needs, a development connected with the growth at that time of local self-sufficiency.[1]

By the summer of 1960 the output of small coal mines (both 'modern' and 'native') was estimated to account for about a third of the country's total production, while for iron ore, the proportion from small mines was put at over half.[2] The quality of the small mines' output left much to be desired, judging by the constant Press insistence that it ought to be improved; special importance was attached to setting up dressing plants to remove impurities from coal and ore. In subsequent years the proportion of output from small mines probably declined.

The broad categories into which the coal industry is divided are sometimes given as large mines on the one hand, and medium and small on the other, or modern and 'native', or central and local; the several terms being used with little consistency.[3] According to the decree of November 1957, as we have seen, large coalfields were to be retained under central control; however, by June 1958, decentralization appears to have been going further than envisaged under this decree. The organs through which the central Ministry of Coal administered the industry had been the administrative bureaux (*kuanli chü*) each of which was responsible for the industry within a large area. The administrative bureaux usually bore the names of large towns, some of which were provincial capitals but others not. Towards the end of 1958 and in 1959 a change was made which, as far as can be traced, occurred piecemeal. Instead of administrative bureaux carrying the names of towns, these organs came to be known under provincial designations. In some provincial level units the title thence forward used was 'coal industry bureau', in others 'coal industry administrative bureau' or 'coal mine administrative bureau'. Each province or autonomous region appears to have used one such title consistently. Probably the status of these organs was in every case roughly the same, coming under the provincial level department of industry; exceptions to this were those provinces, including Fukien, Heilungkiang and Tsinghai, where the

[1] *People's Daily* (*Renmin Ribao*), July 11, 1960, p. 1. Editorial.
[2] Ibid.
[3] *The China Quarterly*, No. 19, July–September 1964, p. 179. Review by F. Delbridge.

bureaux of coal mining came under a special bureau or department of fuel industry.[1]

The naming of these coal-mining organs according to provinces instead of towns probably denoted a transfer of authority over the industry to the provincial level. In the spring of 1958 provinces were encouraged to set up administrative organs for 'local coal mines'[2] that is for those coal mines which at that time were under their control. In the course of 1958 great stress was laid, as we have seen, on co-operation between large and small mines, and this may have led to the extension of provincial authority over the larger units in the industry. Some such extension seems to have occurred (presumably in 1958–9 when appellations of the local administrative organs were changed) for we read of provincial bureaux supervising and controlling the mining bureaux and mines directly under the Ministry of Coal.[3] These bureaux and mines may have been subject to the system of dual subordination to both the Ministry and to provincial administration bureaux, with the latter playing a more prominent part than originally envisaged; this is suggested by the nature of some references which imply jurisdiction by the provincial organs over even important mining bureaux. However, an uncertainty here remains unresolved.

Beneath the provincial level bureaux come units known as 'mining areas' (*k'uangwu ch'ü*) each administered by a mining bureau (*k'uangwu chü*).[4] In October 1959 the Minister of Coal referred to fifty-five mining areas with an annual output of at least a million tons of coal each; the number, if any, of smaller mining areas was not specified.[5] The figure of fifty-five corresponds to the number of named mining bureaux we have been able to trace in the Ministry of Coal's journal *Coal Industry* (*Meitan Gongye*) in late 1958 and in 1959. In 1965 there were said to be 'over forty large mining bureaux'.[6] These forty-plus large mining bureaux may be roughly the equivalent in average output of the fifty-five mining areas producing a million tons or more coal in 1959; the reduction in the number of mining areas in this category being linked with the decline of total coal output between those dates.

Beneath each mining bureau come three or four lower levels of organization: the mine (*k'uang*); the pit (*k'eng* or *ching*)—this level is not always found nor is it clear how it differs from the mine, possibly the organizational mine may

---

[1] *The Coal Industry* (*Meitan Gongye*), 1957–9, passim.

[2] Ibid., No. 7, April 4, 1958, p. 5. Local Industry Bureau of the Ministry of Coal: 'Energetically Develop the Local Coal Industry.'

[3] e.g. *People's Daily* (*Renmin Ribao*), May 19, 1961, p. 2. Wang Yu-chang, Tieh Yün, Hsieh Feng, Lo Hsuan and Yeh Chien-yün: 'Make Careful Arrangements for the Livelihood of Employees', and *Ta Kung Daily* (*Dagong Bao*), Peking, December 23, 1965, p. 1.

[4] In the case of the Kailan Mines, Hopei, special provision appears to have been made, for in 1958–9 references occur to Kailan Coal Mining General Administrative Office (e.g. *Coal Industry* (*Meitan Gongye*), No. 24–5, November 2, 1959, p. 23.)

[5] *People's Daily* (*Renmin Ribao*), October 7, 1959, p. 7, Chang Lin-chih, Minister of Coal: 'Struggle for the Swift Development of the Coal Industry.' In 1958 provinces were told they might establish mining bureaux for areas with an annual coal output of 3–5 million tons, *Coal Industry* (*Meitan Gongye*), No. 7, April 4, 1958, p. 5. Ministry of Coal, Bureau of Local Industry: loc. cit. This suggests that there were unlikely to be mining bureaux with less than 1 million tons output a year.

[6] *People's Daily* (*Renmin Ribao*), August 23, 1965, p. 2.

comprise several pits; the area or sector (*ch'ü* or *tuan*) and the team (*pantsu*).[1] Some coal mines seem to be independent of mining bureaux. Presumably these are isolated mines in areas where total output is not sufficient to warrant the existence of a bureau.

Smaller coal mines are administered by lower local authorities: down to the *hsien* level in the case of underground mines, according to official advice in April 1958, while opencast mines might be operated by *hsiang* or by agricultural producer co-operatives,[2] and later by communes and their constituent units.

While subsequently, as we have seen, the distinction between central and local coal mines may have become blurred, originally in 1958 a clear division of function had been envisaged for the two categories. The Director of the Coal Planning Bureau of the State Economic Commission laid down that the central government mines should be built 'in coal bases with plentiful reserves and in large coalfields that produce coking coal' and should supply big enterprises and major cities. Small coalfields ought to be worked by local mines and 'the coal used by local industry and handicrafts. Small towns and villages should be supplied chiefly by local mines and supplemented by central mines'.[3] Coal from central government mines, and from more accessible local mines, was subject to allocation.[4] The extension of provincial control over more of the industry may have been connected with a growing importance of effecting 'provincial balances' for coal when provincial self-sufficiency became an important objective; more will be said about this below. Coal from the less accessible local mines was distributed through the market, the chief agent for this being the Coal Construction Company.

In 1960 some 80 per cent–94 per cent of China's energy production was probably based on coal.[5] Distribution of coal in 1960 is estimated to have been as follows:—51 per cent to industry, 24 per cent to households, 7 per cent to transport, and 18 per cent to stocks.[6]

The decentralization of 1957–8 augmented the powers and duties of the local administrative bureaux of the coal industry. Before this, the Ministry of Coal had contained three 'general bureaux' (*tsung chü*) of geological prospecting, design and capital construction. In January 1958 it was announced that

[1] *Coal Industry* (*Meitan Gongye*), No. 22, November 19, 1957, p. 30.

[2] *Coal Industry* (*Meitan Gongye*), No. 7, April 4, 1958, p. 5. Chang Ch'ing-jen: 'The Creative Conditions for a Great Development of Local Coal Mining.' Speech to a conference of Responsible Officials of the departments of Industry of several provinces, called by the Ministry of Coal.

[3] *Planned Economy* (*Jihua Jingji*), No. 2, February 1958, p. 12. Ho Pai-sha: loc. cit.

[4] *Economic Research* (*Jinji Yanjiu*), No. 2, February 1959, p. 35. 'A Discussion among Staff of Economic Departments on Problems of Distribution and Pricing of Industrial Commodities.' It should be noted that Julia Berezina in *Power Resources of the Chinese People's Republic* (in Russian), Moscow, 1959, p. 21, gives the production from centrally controlled coal mines in 1957 as 71·6 per cent of the total output; this, of course, was before the decentralization measures.

[5] Y. L. Wu: *Economic Development and the Use of Energy Resources in Communist China*, New York, 1963, p. 216, gives coal as the source of 94 per cent of total energy production in 1960. However, Wu's work was published before the latest Soviet estimate of China's electric power output was available (see pp. 126 and 136–7 above). In the light of this, his previous estimate of hydro-electric output may need to be raised.

[6] Ibid., p. 119.

the enterprises and other units directly under the general bureaux of geological prospecting and basic construction, together with some of the colleges of design administered by the general bureau of designing, would now be placed under the authority of the local administrative bureaux and of the mining bureaux. More responsibility for planning finance, supplies, personnel, and other matters would, at the same time, be devolved from the Ministry to administrative bureaux and also to individual enterprises and units in the industry. The three general bureaux that had previously existed within the Ministry, and which had now lost much of their purpose would, it was announced, be amalgamated. The result of this change was that in future the administrative bureaux controlled both production and capital construction.[1]

The provincial administrative bureaux, therefore, came to have under them not only mining bureaux but also engineering departments, machinery repair plants, shaft-building companies, designing institutes, finance and costing units and so forth. Mining bureaux in their turn control various concerns of these types as well as coal dressing plants. It is not known what, if any, machinery factories are still directly subordinate to the Ministry of Coal. In December 1957 five such plants were listed among enterprises which were to continue to remit all their profits to the central government.[2]

The administrative bureaux appear to have a degree of autonomy in such matters as wage determination, safety regulations, and welfare benefits, although for some things (e.g. the maximum coal and silicon dust per cubic metre of air) national regulations are laid down; implementation may not, however, be uniform. The freedom of action of local organs, in mining as in other spheres, has also been limited by the campaigns and movements emanating from Peking; this was especially the case during the Great Leap.

Hostel accommodation is provided for such workers as do not have homes in the vicinity. Reports indicate that the Party and trade union branches in the enterprises undertake much of the responsibility for the administration of these hostels.

In 1960 the average rate of attendance for all the mining bureaux directly controlled by the Ministry of Coal was said to be about 85 per cent–86 per cent. Absenteeism rates seem to vary considerably from mining area to mining area and from mine to mine, depending largely on the local Party and trade union activity. In one mine, these organizations had been so successful that during the Spring Festival, the great traditional holiday of the Chinese year (which occurs in January or February), attendance reached, or was reported to have reached, 98 per cent.[3] Fuller treatment has been given in Chapter 7 to questions relating to labour.

Originally, the mining bureaux were designated as the economic accounting units in mining. This gave scant incentive to individual mines or auxiliary plants to improve their record, because the overall level of the whole bureau

---

[1] *Coal Industry (Meitan Gongye)*, No. 2, January 19, 1958, p. 2. The Decree of the Ministry of Coal Concerning the Regulations for Reforming the Administrative System of Its Enterprises and Units, and ibid., p. 3. Editorial, and ibid., No. 22, October 13, 1959, p. 5. Chung Tze-yün, Vice Minister of Coal: 'Current Problems of Capital Construction in Coal Mining.'

[2] *Collected Laws and Regulations* . . . Vol. 7, p. 224.

[3] *People's Daily (Renmin Ribao)*, May 19, 1961, p. 2. Wang Yu-chang, et al.: loc. cit.

might be dragged down by more inefficient units. Therefore, from July 1956, the Ministry of Coal selected fourteen mining bureaux to operate experimentally the system of taking single mines or plants as separate economic accounting units.[1] By the end of 1957, the new system had been adopted throughout the coal industry and in some cases had been carried further by taking as the economic accounting unit an even lower unit of operation, such as the pit or team.[2] One of the desired objects was to align the economic accounting unit with the unit taken for labour emulation campaigns, prizes being awarded for both activities.[3]

The encouragement of local self-sufficiency was especially marked in the case of coal, for reasons of transport. Coal transport poses heavy problems in China, owing to the concentration of coal mining in the north and north-east. From 1954 onwards, schemes were put in hand to lessen local disequilibria between supply and demand for coal.[4] In 1958, the hope was expressed that by 1962 all but eight provinces would be self-sufficient in coal.[5] Special efforts were made to develop coal mining in south China, where the lack of coal necessitated long hauls from the north. By 1964, Kwangtung province was said to be producing enough coal for industrial use throughout the province, and for household use in the towns;[6] rural households, in any case, are more likely to use other forms of fuel, such as stalks and firewood. Szechuan province was in 1958 divided into nine zones for coal distribution, according to sources of supply and transport routes,[7] and this may have been done in other provinces as well.

The Ministry of Metallurgy has the dual role of operating mines (except those, as mentioned, for coal, petroleum, and certain other minerals) and of processing ores into iron and steel, aluminium and other intermediate products.[8] This vertical nature of the Ministry is reflected in the fact that many of the largest units under it are, for technical and administrative convenience, similarly organized. The great Anshan Iron and Steel Works, for example, has its own mines which supply part of its ore needs. The major enterprises in this branch of the industry may be presumed to be still primarily in direct subordination to the Ministry of Metallurgy.

Very little information is available about the organization of tin mining

---

[1] *Finance* (*Caizheng*), No. 7, July 1957, pp. 30–1. Chang Pen-lien: loc. cit.

[2] *Coal Industry* (*Meitan Gongye*), No. 22, November 19, 1957, pp. 29–30. Sun Ting: 'The Need to Strengthen and Promote Economic Accounting by Teams', and ibid., p. 30. Chang Chung-lien: 'A Consideration of Basic Level Accounting in the Coal Industry.'

[3] Ibid., No. 22, November 19, 1957, p. 29. Sun Ting: loc. cit.

[4] *Planned Economy* (*Jihua Jingji*), No. 10, October 1957, p. 24. Chang Shih: 'A Major Problem in Promoting a Rational System of Coal Transport.'

[5] Ibid., No. 2, February 1958, p. 13. Ho Pai-sha: loc. cit. In addition Shanghai would still need to draw its coal from elsewhere.

[6] *Southern Daily* (*Nanfang Ribao*), July 21, 1964 (SCMP 3281). No mention was made of Kwangtung's requirements of coal for railways and for ship bunkering, unless these were included in industrial uses.

[7] *Coal Industry* (*Meitan Gongye*), No. 7, April 4, 1958, p. 6. Li Tse-wen, Szechuan Provincial Department of Industry: 'Certain Measures Taken by Szechuan Province to Develop the Local Coal Industry.'

[8] *Red Flag* (*Hongqi*), Nos. 15–16, August 10, 1961, p. 46. Kao Yang-wen: 'Put Mining in the Forefront of the Metallurgical Industry.'

since 1949. Before the war, some 80 per cent of China's tin output came from Yunnan province, notably from the two large mines near Kochiu. The Yunnan provincial government before 1949 had a 40 per cent interest in these mines, the remaining 60 per cent being divided equally between the Bank of China and the Nationalist Government's National Resources Commission.[1] This demonstrates that the idea of 'dual subordination' of enterprises to a local authority and to an organ of the central government, predates the Communist era.

The Ministry of Metallurgy played a parallel role in the encouragement of small 'native' metallic mining (especially iron and copper) during the Great Leap, to that of the Ministry of Coal in respect of small coal mines. In 1961, when the less efficient small mines had been closed, the Ministry laid down the order of priority for the mechanization of those small mines that were to be retained.[2]

The People's Bank, as well as the Ministry of Metallurgy, is closely involved with gold production. This activity (not one of any great scale in China) is divided between mines under the control of provinces and of lower authorities, and gold-washing by peasants in collective agriculture.[3] Information on silver mining is even scantier than that on the mining of gold.

In 1957 some 85 per cent of China's salt derived from sea water, the rest coming from ponds, wells and mines. Much was produced on a small scale by units of collective agriculture or by specialized salt co-operatives. The larger units of salt production of all types are managed by local authorities. From 1954 the production and trade in salt (which in 1950–4 had been under separate auspices) were both made the responsibility of the producing ministry, the Ministry of Food Industry, which later was amalgamated with the Ministry of Light Industry. From 1958, most of the Ministry's operational responsibilities in respect of salt were handed down to the provinces.[4]

The Ministry of Petroleum is responsible for both the mining and refining of petroleum, for the production of shale oil (in co-operation with the Ministry of Coal) and for mining natural gas. On account of the military importance of petroleum supplies, the Ministry has close links with the People's Liberation Army: the (1966) Political Commissar of the Army's Rear Services Department was formerly Minister of Petroleum, a position subsequently filled by his predecessor as Political Commissar.[5] The Ministry of Petroleum is also involved in the production of chemicals.[6]

There are five major oilfields in China: Yümen in Kansu, Tach'ing in Heilungkiang (the newest), the Tsaidam basin in Tsinghai, Karamai in Sinkiang and Nanch'ung in Central Szechuan. All these oilfields have their

[1] J. J. Shanz: op. cit., pp. 18 and 286.
[2] *Red Flag (Hongqi)*, No. 15–16, August 10, 1961, p. 50. Kao Yang-wen: loc. cit.
[3] *Collected Laws and Regulations* . . . Vol. 6, pp. 403–9, and *BBC Summary of World Broadcasts*, Second Series. FE/W344/A/27. (Sian, November 25, 1965.)
[4] *Collected Laws and Regulations* . . . Vol. 6, p. 401, and ibid., Vol. 7, p. 287, and J. P. Emerson: *Non-Agricultural Employment in Mainland China 1949–58*, US Bureau of Census, Washington DC, 1965, p. 84.
[5] Unpublished paper by John Gittings.
[6] e.g. at Lanchow Oil Refinery—*BBC Summary of World Broadcasts*, Second Series, FE/W347/A/48–9. (Sian, December 16, 1965.)

own refineries. However, much of the oil from Yümen, and some from Tsaidam and Karamai, is sent to the great refinery built with Soviet help at Lanchow, the nodal point of the railway system of north-west China. Some oil from Tach'ing, the new field responsible for the great rise in petroleum output in the 1960s, is sent to the refinery at Shanghai. Another big refinery is situated at Nanking. The main shale oil centres are at Fushun in Liaoning and at Maoming in Kwangtung. The chief natural gas field is found in Central Szechuan.

Oil production, like coal mining, is controlled at the provincial level by administrative bureaux, presumably also coming under provincial departments of industry except where separate departments of fuel have been set up. However, it may be assumed that the central government exerts very considerable control over major oilfields. As oil production is less widely dispersed throughout China than coal-mining, oil administrative bureaux—as far as can be gleaned from Press references—exist only in a few provinces and regions, including Sinkiang, Szechuan, Tsinghai and Kweichow. The East China Oil Administrative Bureau apparently covers all the oil-deficient eastern part of the country where provincial bureaux would be superfluous. The administrative bureau controlling the Yümen oilfield bears the name of that centre and not of the province of Kansu. This may be because its activities are reported to extend into Sinkiang,[1] although this reference may be an example of the important training functions performed by Yümen, China's oldest established oil centre, on behalf of newer oilfields and prospecting areas as well as for the small local mines in 1958.[2]

Mining bureaux have commonly been established beneath administrative bureaux in oil as in the coal industry. Oil prospecting bureaux also exist; presumably they too come below the administrative bureaux, as do also the undertakings charged with capital construction, which are variously denoted as corporations, brigades, or by other titles. Responsibility systems for the various levels and organs in oil administration have been widely operated.[3]

The three older oilfields—Yümen, Karamai and Tsaidam—are situated far from the major centres of oil consumption in the industrialized coastal cities.

---

[1] In 1959 the Yümen Oil Administrative Bureau was said to be planning to drill wells in the Turfan Basin, Sinkiang, hundreds of miles north-west of Yümen (NCNA Urumchi, February 20, 1959). If oil operations in this area come under Yümen, this would leave the Sinkiang Oil Administrative Bureau to concentrate mainly on the Karamai oilfield. This spread of Yümen's sphere may have occurred in April 1959, when the Yümen Mining Bureau ceased to be mentioned, being replaced by the Yümen Oil Administrative Bureau. *Oil Prospecting* (*Shiyou Kantan*), No. 6, March 17, 1959, p. 39, and ibid., No. 8, April 17, 1959, p. 26.

[2] e.g. see *People's Daily* (*Renmin Ribao*), November 6, 1960, p. 7. Liu Chang-liang, First Secretary of CCP Yümen Municipal Committee, Secretary of CCP Committee of Yümen Petroleum Administrative Bureau: 'Extend the Functions of the Petroleum Base', and NCNA Lanchow, March 9, 1964.

[3] *Oil Refining* (*Shiyou Lianzhi*), No. 10, October 9, 1958, p. 13. The Fifth Oil Factory: 'A Summary of the Progress in Basic Construction in the Fifth Oil Factory in 1958', and ibid., p. 14. The Sixth Oil Factory: 'An Introduction to Experience in Decentralizing and Enforcing the Responsibility System from Level to Level', and *Daily Worker* (*Gongren Ribao*), July 17, 1962 (SCMP 2794), and *Red Flag* (*Hongqi*), No. 20, October 28, 1964, p. 32. Li Chih-sheng: 'Co-ordinate Revolutionary Responsibility and the Responsibility System.'

This has put added pressure on the overloaded railways. The Szechuan oilfield, developed in the 1950s, is better situated but even it is not well placed to serve the east and south. Part of the significance of the Tach'ing oilfield, held up as the country's pride in the mid-1960s, has been its convenient situation to supply some of the most industrialized areas of China and thus to lessen the strain on the transport system. It is to transport that we will now turn our attention.

Chapter 10

TRANSPORT

Attention to transport, as well as to water conservancy, has characterized strong Chinese governments through the centuries, at once both a cause and an effect of their strength. Without good means of communication the distant provinces would soon break loose from central control. Modern technical improvements in transport and telecommunications have enabled this control to be more effective than in olden days. The Communist regime has been the first government of China in a position to benefit by these developments over any considerable period of time, and in so doing it obtained a tighter and more penetrating hold over the country's life than was wielded by any of its predecessors.

In addition to the importance of transport for political and economic reasons, the expansion of rail and shipping services under Chinese ownership and control has been of symbolic significance. In the century of weakness following the Treaty of Nanking in 1842, foreign powers obtained rights of navigation on Chinese rivers and also, through concessions and loans, came to control the construction and operation of many of the principal railway lines. As a result, steamships and trains were introduced into China at an earlier date than if matters had been left to indigenous initiative, but at the cost of deep emotional resentment. On a practical level, this course of events had the disadvantage that development occurred piecemeal and the country's transport needs were not studied as a whole. No national railway system came into being, only a collection of lines 'each as distinct as if existing on separate islands'.[1] An attempt by the Chinese authorities to weld the railways into one system was nullified in the 1920s by civil war. In the next decade, the Kuomintang's rehabilitation of the railways was interrupted by the Japanese invasion. After the war there was a general determination to exert Chinese authority over all forms of internal transport. Foreign shipping was banned from inland navigation by the Kuomintang Government, and the Communists continued the ban; after the transfer to China of the Soviet share in the Changchun Railway and in the Sinkiang airline in 1952 and 1954 respectively, no foreign control remained of any transport undertaking internal to China.

The Communist Government, on winning power, found that the country's transport facilities—which at best were scanty—had been rendered chaotic. Railways were fragmented by years of guerilla warfare, many ships and civil aircraft had been taken to Taiwan by the retreating Nationalists. The rehabili-

---

[1] *Annals of the American Academy of Political and Social Science*, Vol. 152, November 1930, p. 168. J. E. Baker: 'Transportation in China', see also G. C. Allen and A. G. Donnithorne: *Western Enterprise in Far Eastern Economic Development: China and Japan*, London, 1954, pp. 140–1.

tation of transport was a major preoccupation of the early days of the regime. The process of 'socialist transformation' was less significant in this sector than in others, for even in 1949 nearly 89 per cent of modern transport capacity (measured by freight turnover) was state-owned. By 1957 this figure was reported to have risen to 99·7 per cent, the minute remainder being under joint state-private ownership.[1]

In China the railways carry by far the greater portion of long-distance traffic, both freight and passenger. In 1957 they were responsible for 135,000 million ton-km. of freight, out of a total of 173,000 million ton-km. by all forms of modern surface transport; ships and barges accounted for 34,000 million ton-km. and motor vehicles for the remaining 4,000 million ton-km. In the same year the railways' share of passenger traffic was 36,000 million passenger-km. out of a total (here including civil aviation as well as motor and water transport) of 49,000 million.[2] This great preponderance of the railways may seem strange in an under-developed country crossed by numerous rivers. It reflects the lack of north-south river communication and also the fact that one of the great east-west waterways, the Yellow River, has as yet been of little value for navigation, although the plan for its development, published in 1955, envisages a change in this state of affairs. Another reason, discussed below, is that during the 1950s freight rates by water were above those by rail.

The State Council's Office of Industry and Communications, under Po I-po, has general control over the ministries concerned with transport and communications, in addition to its industrial responsibilities. Before 1959 one of its predecessors, the Sixth General Office of the State Council, was concerned exclusively with transport and communications. The Director of the CCP Central Committee's Communications Work Department is Tseng Shan, who concurrently holds a post in the government as Minister of Internal Affairs, while the Central Committee's Industry and Communications Political Department is headed by Ku Mu. Under the State Council Office, the Ministry of Communications deals with road and water transport. Two bureaux within the Ministry, the General Bureau of Highways and the General Bureau of Sea and River Navigation, are concerned with these two divisions. The present (1966) Minister, Wang Shou-tao, was formerly director of the State Council's Sixth General Office: his predecessor at the Ministry, Chang Po-chun, was dismissed as a rightist in 1957. During the 'Hundred Flowers Movement' in the spring of 1957—when, for a brief period, criticism of the government was permitted—both Chang and members of his staff spoke very freely, throwing light on the inner workings of the Ministry and on its relations with superior organs. Chang complained that his Ministry was treated as a forwarding office, without scope for initiative, and subject to telephone instructions from the Sixth General Office of the State Council. Chang mentioned three major projects—the Szechuan–Tibet Highway, the Tangku New Harbour, and the Tsamkong Harbour—for which his Ministry had solely the function of contractor.[3] One of Chang's subordinates complained of bureaucratic inefficiency and over-staffing in the Ministry, instancing the

[1] *Ten Great Years*, Peking, 1960, p. 41.
[2] *Ibid.*, pp. 148 and 150.
[3] *People's Daily* (*Renmin Ribao*), May 20, 1957, p. 1.

General Bureau of Highways with its director and six vice-directors and over thirty departmental chiefs.[1]

The other two ministries concerned with this sector of the economy are the Ministry of Railways and the Ministry of Posts and Telecommunications. Civil aviation is controlled by the Civil Aviation General Administration of China. In April 1962, this body was placed directly under the State Council. Previously it has been under the Ministry of Communications for a period although, when it was first established in 1954 (as the China Civil Aviation Bureau), it was immediately subordinate to the State Council.[2] Between 1954-9 there existed a Central Bureau of Confidential Communications directly under the State Council and not subordinate to any of the ministries concerned with transport and communications.[3] It is uncertain what functions it performed: it may have been the handling of secret cables. In 1964 the State Maritime Bureau was established, also directly under the State Council; no indication of its duties is available to us.[4]

Close co-operation between the ministries concerned with transport and between them and other ministries is clearly desirable. Various efforts have been made to these ends, especially during the transport crisis in 1959 which resulted in large measure from the excessive burden thrown on the railways and on rural transport by the Great Leap. At that time a body called the Central Transport Headquarters, and its subsidiary, the Joint Office for Short Distance Transport, were active. These both were closely linked, and probably were subordinate to, the Ministry of Communications, but also enjoyed the collaboration of other ministries.[5] Local transport headquarters were similarly established by provinces and lower local authorities at this time, for the purpose of settling freight priorities, unifying transport rates, and co-ordinating facilities.[6] More recently nothing has, to our knowledge, been heard of these *ad hoc* organs at either national or local levels. Joint conferences, such as that held in 1959 on the 'one dragon' system of through shipments of freight by different forms of transport (e.g. water transport connecting with rail), are another device for bringing about co-ordination between ministries.[7]

Provincial level authorities have their own departments of communications, as have also the local authorities under them, down to *hsien* and even to people's communes. Provincial departments of railways were in 1959 mentioned in Liaoning and Kirin and in 1966 in Shensi; it cannot be said with

[1] *People's Daily* (*Renmin Ribao*), May 24, 1957, p. 3.
[2] NCNA Peking, April 16, 1962, and E. S. Kirby (ed.): *Contemporary China*, Vol. I, Hong Kong, 1956, p. 223
[3] *Collected Laws and Regulations of the People's Republic of China* (in Chinese), Vol. 1, p. 151 and Vol. 9, p. 109.
[4] *People's Daily* (*Renmin Ribao*), June 6, 1964, p. 1.
[5] *Highways* (*Gonglu*), No. 11, November 1959, p. 3, and NCNA Peking, October 27, 1959.
[6] *Ta Kung Daily* (*Dagong Bao*), Peking, July 26, 1959, p. 1, and *People's Daily* (*Renmin Ribao*), September 23, 1959, p. 9. Wang Shou-tao, Minister of Communications: 'Raise High the Banner of the General Line: Speed Up the Development of Transport Undertakings', and *Highways* (*Gonglu*), No. 12, December 1958, for mention of articles by the Hopei and Anhwei provincial transport headquarters.
[7] *People's Daily* (*Renmin Ribao*), December 2, 1959, p. 1. Editorial.

certainty whether they are additional to the railway bureaux (of which more below) or whether they are the bureaux under another name.

The Ministry of Railways, although affected, as we shall see, by the decentralization movement, still remains more centralized than most industrial ministries. This springs from the inter-connecting nature of the national railway network, which necessitates a higher degree of supra-provincial control than is the case, for example, with most forms of manufacturing industry. It should also be noted that the Ministry of Railways has been closely linked with the Army.[1]

Under the Ministry of Railways, the national network is divided organizationally into separate 'railways', each comprising one 'railway administration' under a 'railway bureau'. Before the Communists came to power, each railway line was indeed separate, with its own administration; at that time there was no uniformity between them. In 1950 an overall operational unity was instituted and through freight wagons could be dispatched from Canton in the south to Manchouli on the Soviet border. In the same year, railway administrative bureaux (*t'iehlu kuanli chü*) were set up.[2] In 1953, the Chinese railways were described as falling into three main divisions—the north-east (the former Manchuria), the north and the south. Control of the railways of the north-east was divided among four railway administrations, of which one— that of Harbin—was the organizational successor to the Changchun Railway; five railway administrations existed in north China and three in the south. These twelve administrative bureaux came directly under the Ministry of Railways and had forty-six sub-bureaux beneath them. In addition, two outlying railway bureaux (*t'iehlu chü*) at Chungking and Kunming, controlled isolated lines not yet linked to the national system; these two bureaux likewise were under direct control by the Ministry. The administration of two lines in northwest China in course of construction in 1953 was in the hands of the North-West Trunk Lines Engineering Bureau.[3] Fifteen railway administrative bureaux, with forty-four sub-bureaux, were in existence at the end of 1957, when it was decided to abolish the sub-bureaux in order to streamline railway management, improve local co-ordination and reduce the total number of staff. Some of these former subordinate organs were, however, to be elevated to the rank of bureau.[4]

Railways were not listed among the economic activities to be decentralized in 1957–8. The volume and turnover of railway freight figured with the economic planning targets which continued to be set by the central authorities.[5] It will, however, be remembered that even those undertakings retained under the control of central ministries were to have a twofold subordination, to their ministry first and foremost, but simultaneously also to their appropriate provincial level authority.[6] This was the case with the railways, and was described by two Soviet writers as a 'characteristic peculiarity' of Chinese

---

[1] F. Schurmann: *Ideology and Organization in Communist China*, Berkeley, 1966, p. 345.
[2] *People's Handbook* (*Renmin Shouce*) *1958*, p. 565.
[3] Chi Yu: *New China's Railway Construction* (in Chinese), Peking, 1953, pp. 4–7.
[4] *People's Handbook* (*Renmin Shouce*) *1958*, pp. 564–5.
[5] See p. 462 below, and *Collected Laws and Regulations* . . . Vol. 8, p. 97.
[6] See p. 152 above, and *Collected Laws and Regulations* . . . Vol. 6, p. 392.

railway organization.[1] Dual subordination applied to the individual railway administrations which, in 1959, numbered twenty-eight, to railway construction bureaux, to plants making and repairing locomotives and rolling stock and to the higher educational institutions of the Ministry of Railways. Some unspecified individual railway undertakings were, however, to be subordinate only to the Ministry.[2]

All profits earned by the Ministry of Railways were, by the 1957 regulations, to continue to accrue to the central treasury and were not to be divided with local authorities.[3]

The Ministry of Railways' duties (to take only those reported as being exercised after 1958) include the laying down of operational regulations for the whole national railway system and the compilation of timetables, at least for the main express trains, together with the carrying out of the standardization programme for locomotives, wagons, signalling apparatus and other equipment, a programme necessary for welding the former separate lines into a national system. In 1958 the Ministry was responsible for the allocation of locomotives, rolling stock and steel rails, although since that date local railway administrative bureaux have been given room for initiative in this respect,[4] and some have their own plants to manufacture these items. However, the Ministry of Railways' allocatory and other powers should be sufficient to enable it to maintain a firm control of its subordinate railway administrations. The Ministry of Railways also controls locomotive, carriage and wagon construction and repair plants. (Wheels and some other components are made for the railways by the First Ministry of Machine Building.)[5]

Each railway bureau has under it locomotives, rolling stock and large stretches of track. The administrative bureaux are responsible for inspection, maintenance and repair of the track, for business and technical management, and sometimes, as we have noted, also for the manufacture of rolling stock and in some cases even of steel for their own use. They control engineering works, cement plants, and other industrial establishments.[6] In the course of the decentralization movement, the Ministry delegated more authority to the bureaux. They were now permitted, for example, to readjust their targets within limits as by altering the planned turn-round time of wagons in stations.[7]

---

[1] A. I. Ilyin and M. P. Voronichev: *Railroad Transport of the Chinese People's Republic*, Moscow, 1959. (Translated from the Russian in JPRS 3484), p. 39.

[2] Ibid., pp. 39–40.

[3] *Collected Laws and Regulations* . . . Vol. 6, p. 394.

[4] *Collected Laws and Regulations* . . . Vol. 8, pp. 100–1, and NCNA Tsinan, April 3, 1959, and ibid., Peking, July 6, 1959, and ibid., Peking, May 31, 1961, and *Daily Worker* (*Gongren Ribao*), February 23, 1962, p. 1, and *Peking Review*, No. 6, February 8, 1963, p. 20, and *News from Chinese Regional Radio Stations*, No. 141, January 20, 1966, p. 55. (Chengtu, January 11, 1966.)

[5] *Daily Worker* (*Gongren Ribao*), April 6, 1965, p. 1.

[6] *People's Daily* (*Renmin Ribao*), February 1, 1961, p. 2, and *Railway Weekly* (*Tiedao Zhoukan*), No. 32, August 19, 1959 (ECMM 188). Editorial, and *Red Flag* (*Hongqi*), No. 22, November 16, 1960, pp. 41–5. CCP Committee of the Chinchow Railway Administrative Bureau: 'Continuously Raise the Quality of Equipment: Realize the Potential of Rail Transport', and NCNA Peking, November 21, 1960, and *People's Daily* (*Renmin Ribao*), April 21, 1964, p. 2.

[7] *Railway Weekly* (*Tiedao Zhoukan*), No. 32, August 19, 1959, loc. cit.

A change in nomenclature also dates from the time when decentralization measures were becoming operative. In 1957-8, ministerial directives were usually addressed to 'railway administrative bureaux'. From 1959 the mode of address changed to 'railway bureaux', except for certain individual bureaux (e.g. Canton and Shanghai) which continued to be known by the old style. (Shanghai was sometimes called a 'general bureau').[1] It may be that the change denotes that these organs are subordinated in some respects to provincial departments of industry. Apart from this, it is not certain what, if any, conclusions about organizational changes can be drawn from the change in usage; nor is the relationship between railway bureaux and provincial level authorities at all clear. In 1958-9 there was, outside the north-east, one railway administration to each provincial level authority, except that Peking and Hopei appear for this purpose to have been regarded as one unit.[2] The north-east, with three provinces has six railway administrations,[3] but then that region is in railway matters exceptional in China; the provinces of Heilungkiang and Liaoning which in 1959 were reported to possess three and two railway administrations respectively, having greater lengths of line than any other provinces.

It is not always possible for railway administrations to correspond exactly with provinces because a single (organizational) railway may extend through more than one province. Therefore we hear of railway bureaux in one province having branches or sub-bureaux (these having apparently been revived) in other provinces.[4]

In 1958, when greater local freedom was given in the matter of specifications of investment projects, it was laid down that those for railway lines running through more than one province or autonomous region, should require central government approval.[5] This would cover most railway lines of importance, but would exclude some, such as the Chengtu-Chungking Railway, which lie within the confines of a single province. This suggests, what is highly probable, that the degree of autonomy of any single railway depends considerably on its inter-provincial or intra-provincial nature.

The partial re-organization of the railways under provincial control had as one of its objects their alignment with local Party organization—as was occurring in 1957-9 in almost all spheres of economic and political life. Without such alignment, Party control over any sector of the economy is difficult to implement.[6] However, the degree of fragmentation brought about

[1] See issues of *Journal of Railway Commerce* (*Tielu Shangwu Zhuankan*).
[2] A. I. Il'yin and M. P. Voronichev: op. cit. (JPRS 3484), p. 40. There is no railway administration corresponding to Ninghsia in the list of railway administrations given in this source, but the Ninghsia Autonomous Region was not established until October 1958. If a railway administration was subsequently established to correspond to Ninghsia, it might have been too late to figure in Il'yin and Voronichev's list.
[3] Ibid.
[4] e.g. The Taiyuan (Shansi) sub-bureau of the Peking Railway Bureau (*BBC Summary of World Broadcasts*, Second Series, FE/W351/A/25); Hsuchow (Kiangsu) branch of the Tsinan Railway Bureau (in Shantung). (Ibid. FE/340/A/39) and the Henyang (Hunan) sub-bureau of the Canton Railway Bureau (in Kwangtung). (NCNA Canton, February 5, 1964.)
[5] *Collected Laws and Regulations* ... Vol. 8, p. 103.
[6] *People's Handbook* (*Renmin Shouce*) *1958*, p. 565.

in the administration of the railways, limited although it was, may have provided a contributory cause of the breakdown in rail transport which occurred when, during the Great Leap, the volume of freight shipments rose steeply.[1]

The earliest use of the economic accounting system in China was on the Changchun Railway under its joint Sino-Soviet administration in 1950–2.[2] Its adoption throughout the Chinese railway system was, however, slow, as in 1959 it was mentioned in a Soviet work as 'now being introduced' in the various units that constitute the railway system. It is not clear if each railway administration comprises a separate economic accounting unit; more probably it seems that these units are smaller, such as individual repair shops and stations.[3] It is possible that administrations and lower units are both economic accounting units; a similar arrangement occurs in commerce where both the national corporations and their subordinate local corporations are economic accounting units.[4]

The Railway Engineering Corps of the People's Liberation Army has engaged in rail and road construction, especially in remote regions. Labour reform units have also been employed on this task. In Sinkiang the PLA Production and Construction Corps has been responsible for building some stretches of the railway. In more densely populated areas much of the building and maintenance of railways and roads is done by local peasants under the traditional system of compulsory labour. The total length of China's railway tracks, excluding small local lines, was reported in 1965 to exceed 36,000 km.[5] It is not proposed here to list the railways built since 1949,[6] but some indication must be given of the main accomplishments. A new rail connection with the Soviet Union was opened in 1959 with a line via Ulan Bator, capital of the Mongolian People's Republic. Another rail link with the Soviet was planned through Sinkiang and by 1961 it was reported to have reached Urumchi. The Sino-Soviet conflict has evidently caused a suspension of the original plans for extending it to the frontier. Szechuan province has been linked by rail with Shensi in the north (and thence with the whole of the north and north-west), while southward lines are under construction from Szechuan to Yunnan and Kweichow: indeed, in 1966 it was surmised that the latter had been opened. The long-awaited Chengtu-Chungking railway, connecting the two chief cities of Szechuan, was completed in 1952; the original proposals for this line had been an indirect cause of the outbreak of the 1912 revolution. A railway east to west across south China will, when completed, link Kunming with Shanghai. The line built from Nanking to Amoy via Yingtan (whence it connects with Shanghai) is of obvious military, as well as economic, significance because of the exposed situation of the coast facing Taiwan. Kwangsi obtained its first railway to the sea and also a line to North Vietnam. A line from Wuhan to north-west Hupeh was completed in 1960. A railway has been

[1] F. Schurmann: op. cit., p. 209.
[2] See p. 26 above.
[3] A. I. Il'yin and M. P. Voronichev: op. cit. (JPRS 3484), p. 88.
[4] p. 276 below.
[5] *BBC Summary of World Broadcasts*, Second Series, FE/W342/A/32 (Peking, October 31, 1965).
[6] See *Ten Great Years*, p. 70, for a list of the principal new railways built 1950–8.

built from Paoki in Shensi and Lanchow in Kansu to Sining, capital of Tsinghai, whence it was to be extended to the Tsaidam oilfield; and at one time a southward extension to Lhasa was rumoured.

It appeared to have been overlooked that the building of new railways would place an intolerable pressure on the existing lines connecting with them which were already working at maximum capacity. Now these had to bear the extra load of traffic originating from or proceeding to the new lines. This was particularly true of the Lunghai Railway, the east-west line crossing north China, which is now linked with both Sinkiang and Szechuan. A new line from Paotow to Lanchow relieved it of some of the traffic but the situation still remained serious. By 1959 the double tracking of key railways had become an urgent need and the Lunghai, the Peking-Canton, and the Tientsin-Shanghai lines were taken in hand for this purpose.

The transport crisis in the last quarter of 1958 was caused not only by the sheer bulk of what had to be carried, but also by inefficiency leading to counterflow of goods and unnecessarily long hauls. 'The chief reason for the backflow, counterflows, overlapping and excessively long hauls of transport', stated an article in 1959, 'still rests with weaknesses in planning and organization of production, supply and transport, together with continuing deficiencies in the allocation of raw materials, imperfections and instability in the distributive system, and dislocations between production, supply, transport, and sales'. Since 1954, this article continued, attempts had been made to minimize transport difficulties by effecting local balances of major commodities (i.e. by encouraging local self-sufficiency) and this policy should continue to be implemented.[1] Another answer to this difficulty was looked for in the application of linear programming to transport problems.[2] A more immediate solution to the crisis was sought from the beginning of 1959 in raising the norms for loading freight wagons.[3]

Apart from the national railway network, small local railways have been constructed by local authorities. The first went into use in July 1958 in Shansi, and by the end of 1959 more than 400 such railways had been built or were under construction by local authorities, with a total length exceeding 2,400 km. open to traffic and a further 3,600 km. in process of completion.[4] Their rails were made of locally produced steel or pig iron, or even of timber, while locomotives had gas, diesel, motor or small steam engines.[5] These lines could be constructed in a few months and cost little either to build or to run. A Vice-Minister of Railways, speaking in April 1960, recommended the construction of light railways of this type on rural transport routes carrying between

---

[1] *Economic Research* (*Jingji Yanjiu*), No. 7, July 17, 1959, pp. 3–4. Kao Yü-Huang: 'The Need for Vigorous Organization of Rational Transport in the Economic Activities of the Nation.' See also *Planned Economy* (*Jihua Jingji*), No. 10, October 1957, p. 24. Chang Shih: 'A Major Problem in Promoting a Rational System of Coal Transport.'

[2] *Red Flag* (*Hongqi*), No. 20–1, November 1, 1960, p. 45. Liu Chi-p'ing, Secretary of the Secretariat of the CCP Shantung Provincial Committee: 'Extensive Use of Operations and Programming in the Service of Socialist Construction.'

[3] A. 1. Il'yin and M. P. Voronichev: op. cit. (JPRS 3484), p. 81.

[4] *People's Daily* (*Renmin Ribao*), April 9, 1960, p. 10. Lü Cheng-ts'ao, Vice-Minister of Railways: Speech to Second Session of Second NPC.

[5] Ibid., December 16, 1959, p. 1. Editorial, and NCNA Peking, November 20, 1958.

100,000 tons and a million tons of goods a year.[1] The railway administrative bureaux of the modern national railway system were urged to give technical guidance and other assistance.

The first local railways were built to connect mines and factories with the ordinary railways or with navigable waterways; some were also constructed within mining areas, state farms and forests and large industrial plants by these concerns to serve their own internal needs. It would seem that these lines come under the enterprises concerned and not under the Ministry of Railways. Some local lines are built by the Railway Corps of the Army[2] which also, as we have seen, is responsible for constructing some railway lines of the national system. It was hoped that the local lines would later be developed into networks linking one *hsien* city with another, and with major communes. Some, it was envisaged, would eventually be replaced by ordinary railways.[3] When considering the results of this and other aspects of the mass campaign for rural transport in 1958 to 1960, it must be borne in mind that, according to the admission of the Minister of Communications himself, much of what was done was of low quality.[4] Nevertheless, this does not mean that the results were necessarily negligible; no doubt wide local variations occurred.

Coal forms by far the largest item of railway freight in China, accounting (around 1959 and 1960) for some 40 per cent of the total volume (whether of turnover or of ton-kilometres is not said). The uneven distribution of coal resources necessitates long hauls, especially from north to south. Pig iron comes second, followed by building materials of mineral origin. In 1959 it was stated that no other commodity accounted for as much as 10 per cent of the rail freight deliveries (presumably of freight turnover).[5] The four commodities of steel, coal, grain and cotton were estimated in 1959 to form some 60 per cent of the 'total highway transport work' and in water transport, about 40 per cent.[6]

The Ministry of Communications, through its General Bureau of Highways, concerns itself with the overall direction of policy on road transport. Road transport, by its nature, lends itself to decentralized control more readily than do the main line railways and this is strengthened by the fact that in China road transport deals chiefly with short distance movements. Thus most road transport undertakings, apart from those ancillary to other enterprises, are managed by organs of local authorities from the provincial level downwards; every local authority, down to people's communes, is supposed to have a special department for transport. Road freight charges, too, are normally subject to local, not central control.

In 1949 less than 81,000 km. of highways were said to exist. By September

[1] *People's Daily* (Renmin Ribao), April 9, 1960, p. 10. Lü Cheng-ts'ao: loc. cit.
[2] *Peking Review*, January 17, 1964, p. 31.
[3] *People's Daily* (Renmin Ribao), March 15, 1960, p. 1. Editorial, and ibid., April 9, 1960, p. 10. Lü Cheng-ts'ao: loc. cit.
[4] Ibid., September 23, 1959, p. 9. Wang Shou-tao: loc. cit.
[5] NCNA Peking, March 31, 1959. Po I-po, Director of State Council Office of Industry and Communications: Speech to National Radio Conferences on the Emulation Drive among Railway Workers, and NCNA Peking, August 19, 1960, and NCNA Peking, April 25, 1959. Lü Cheng-ts'ao, Vice-Minister of Railways: Speech to First Session of Second NPC.   [6] NCNA, February 4, 1959.

1959 the total length was reported as over 400,000 km. Both figures are beset by problems of definition. Many of these roads are of a rudimentary character: in 1961 the Minister of Communications admitted that on rainy days about half the country's highways were impassable.[1] Foreign visitors have reported that asphalted roads are rare and that only a modest volume of road traffic is to be seen.

According to regulations of 1960, highways are divided into three categories for administrative purposes. The first category, trunk roads, are those which—for political, economic, strategic or cultural reasons—are judged to be of national or provincial significance. The second category, local roads, are those of lesser importance and may come under either *hsien* or communes. The third category, specialized roads, are those specifically serving mining, agricultural, forestry and other undertakings. Provincial level units are enjoined to set up special organs with technical staff to maintain trunk roads. *Hsien* authorities are charged with organizing communes and production brigades to form regular maintenance squads to look after roads coming under *hsien*. Both provinces and *hsien* may also call on mass labour by the local population as well and this is the mainstay of the commune roads. Sometimes production teams are entrusted by *hsien* with road upkeep on a contract basis at a fixed sum per kilometre. The maintenance of the specialized roads is the responsibility of the undertakings (e.g. mines, factories, state farms, or forestry concerns) they serve, although these may pay to have them looked after by local authorities.[2]

Similarly, responsibility for building roads has been divided between different administrative levels. Certain major highways, notably those of strategic importance in the remote parts of the country, are built and maintained by the central government. In Tibet, the PLA Railway Engineering Corps and in Sinkiang the PLA Production and Construction Corps have participated in the building of roads. These strategic new roads include the three highways to Tibet from Tsinghai, Szechuan, and Sinkiang (via Ladakh) respectively. The PLA Railway Corps has also built roads in the forest areas of north-east China. Highways of lesser importance, or in more densely populated areas, are built by provincial, *hsien*, or other local authorities, while the construction of smaller rural roads is left to communes and their constituent units.

Regulations on road tax levied on vehicles, issued in 1960 jointly by the Ministries of Finance and Communications, stipulated that provincial departments of finance and transport should draw up road tax budgets separate from their ordinary budgets (i.e. the road tax should be extra-budgetary). All the proceeds from road tax should be expended on roads and should not be diverted to other purposes.[3]

[1] *Ten Great Years*, p. 144, and NCNA Peking, September 26, 1959, and *People's Daily* (*Renmin Ribao*), May 26, 1961, p. 7. Wang Shou-tao, Minister of Communications: 'Continuously Develop Communications and Transport Undertakings: Improve Service to Production and Livelihood.'
[2] *Collected Laws and Regulations* . . . Vol. 11, p. 166, and *Ta Kung Daily* (*Dagong Bao*), Peking, October 12, 1964, p. 1.
[3] *Collected Laws and Regulations* . . . Vol. 11, pp. 161–4. See pp. 289–93 below for a discussion of extra-budgetary funds.

Some 250,000 to 300,000 lorries were estimated by foreign observers to be in service in China in 1966, as well as around 10,000 buses and 40,000 to 50,000 passenger cars.[1] In 1958 motor vehicles were reported to be responsible for 28 per cent of the freight handled by all forms of modern transport, but in terms of ton-kilometres for only around 3 per cent of the total.[2] More plentiful and cheaper supplies of petroleum may have increased the share of freight carried by motor vehicles, but they are still mainly restricted to short-distance transport, except in the remote areas of the west and north-west of China. In 1949 75 per cent of the lorries in China were privately owned. By 1955–6 most had been placed under joint state-private ownership and before long under state-owned enterprises.[3] Lorries are now owned either by companies established under departments of communications of local authorities of different levels, or by other government organs and enterprises for their own use. Many of China's motor vehicles are old and have been subject to intensive use on poor roads; hence they require constant maintenance. Provision of spare parts presents another problem. Chinese mechanical ingenuity is, however, capable of remarkable feats, even if one suspects the record of the lorry which earned for its driver the title of 'labour hero' by covering 400,000 km. in difficult country without accident or major overhaul.[4]

Most motor bus services are operated by local authorities from the province downwards. In 1963, ninety inter-provincial bus services were being run. These appear to be a direct concern of the Ministry of Communications, for the Ministry is reported to have made a special allocation of vehicles for them.[5]

The manufacture of motor vehicles comes under the First Ministry of Machine Building. The Ministry of Communications controls certain factories (sometimes in conjunction with other ministries), making, for example, motor parts and accessories. For these particular items a centralized production and allocation system has been jointly operated by the Ministry of Communications and the First and Eighth Ministries of Machine Building.[6]

The lowest level of transport, such as the carriage of agricultural produce from the point of production to the points where supplies are concentrated for movement to other localities, is handled mainly by communes and their constituent units, using largely the part-time labour of peasants. For the next stage in the process of transport—from the concentration points to cities, railway stations and ports—specialized transport teams (such as communes were encouraged to form in 1959) as well as part-time transport groups, are employed.[7] In some places the specialized transport teams are organized as

[1] *Far Eastern Economic Review*, February 17, 1966, p. 326. H. Munthe-Kaas: 'Roads and Rails in China.'
[2] *Ten Great Years*, pp. 146 and 148.
[3] *People's Daily* (*Renmin Ribao*), September 23, 1959, p. 9. Wang Shou-tao: loc. cit.
[4] NCNA Urumchi, September 26, 1958.
[5] NCNA Peking, February 3, 1963.
[6] *Ta Kung Daily* (*Dagong Bao*), Peking, May 3, 1962, p. 1. At that time, the subsequent Eighth Ministry of Machine Building was entitled the Ministry of Agricultural Machinery.
[7] *People's Daily* (*Renmin Ribao*), February 20, 1963, p. 1. Editorial, and *Red Flag* (*Hongqi*), No. 17, September 1, 1959, p. 31. Chang Pang-ying: 'Transport Undertaken by People's Communes.'

transport co-operatives, which are sometimes grouped into local federations of transport co-operatives.¹

In the absence of roads in many country areas, much of the Chinese peasant's working life has always been taken up with carrying heavy loads on the back or by shoulder pole. Surveys in different places have shown that a third, or even a half or more, of the man-days of labour available (varying according to terrain and type of agricultural activities) may be spent in this way.² Thus even minor improvements in traditional means of transport may effect great savings in time and energy and bring about increases in efficiency out of all proportion to the costs involved. The introduction of rubber tyres for carts, the fitting of wheelbarrows with ball bearings and the use in hilly areas of chutes and overhead cables, together with similar devices, came within the scope of the movement for technical innovations.

Shipping, like road transport, falls under the aegis of the Ministry of Communications which attends to this branch of its responsibilities through its General Bureau of Sea and River Navigation. At the end of 1965, according to one report, China's merchant fleet comprised over 220 ships totalling around 600,000 tons.³ However, another foreign observer thought that the total tonnage in 1966 might be approaching one million, while the ocean-going merchant fleet might number 150–200 vessels.⁴ Possibly some difference in definition may be involved.

According to official Chinese statistics, in 1957 ships and barges were responsible for 20 per cent of freight ton-kilometres carried by modern means of transport in China. In that year, navigable inland waterways were reported to extend 144,000 km. (almost double the 1949 figure); however, only 40,000 km. were accessible to steamships;⁵ this is in addition to the 14,000 km. coastline. The increase in navigable inland waterways was said to have resulted from improvements made on both large and small waterways. Half the Sungari River was reported navigable in 1962, compared with less than a quarter a decade earlier; a large part of the middle reaches of the Yellow River was opened for passenger traffic; navigable waterways in Szechuan were announced to have increased by a third between 1957 and 1961 and similar reports are made from other provinces.⁶ As well as opening new stretches of river, improvements have been effected in those already in use. One result is that the Upper Yangtze between Ichang and Chungking, through the steep gorges, is now navigable at night, thus halving the time necessary for the journey.

The three most important navigation regions for coastal and inland services

---

¹ *Ta Kung Daily (Dagong Bao)*, Peking, July 13, 1963, p. 2. Editorial.

² *People's Daily (Renmin Ribao)*, December 8, 1960, p. 4. Ch'iu Hsien-chung, Deputy Director, Communications Department, Szechuan Province: 'Improve Field Transport and Save Labour', and ibid., June 6, 1964, p. 5. Chang Wu-tung and Yang Kuan-hsiung: 'Function of Transport in the Development of Agricultural Production.'

³ *China Association Annual Report 1964–5*, p. 8, and ibid., *1965–6*, p. 6.

⁴ *Far Eastern Economic Review*, March 3, 1966, p. 399. H. Munthe-Kaas: 'Chinese Afloat.'

⁵ *Ten Great Years*, pp. 144 and 148.

⁶ NCNA Shenyang, April 24, 1962, and NCNA Peking, May 29, 1962, and NCNA Peking, September 4, 1961.

are the north and south China coasts and the Yangtze River. The Shanghai and the Canton Sea Transport Administrative Bureaux and the Yangtze Navigation Administrative Bureau control shipping in these three areas respectively and come directly under the Ministry of Communications.[1] There is, however, some indication that central control of south China shipping services has been less far-reaching than those of the north.[2] Other local navigation organs directly under the Ministry of Communications have included the Heilungkiang and the Pearl River Navigation Administrative Bureaux.[3]

The jurisdiction of the Shanghai and the Canton Sea Transport Administrative Bureaux do not connect, because the blockade operated in the Taiwan Straits by the Nationalists has prevented ships under the Chinese Communist flag sailing through those waters. Hence, as far as such vessels are concerned, coastal shipping routes are divided into two separate zones: the northern zone, centred on Shanghai, and the southern zone, centred on Canton with services extending to Hong Kong and North Vietnam as well as along the south China coast.[4] Even foreign-flag tonnage under Chinese charter avoids the Taiwan Straits where possible; however, voyages by such ships from Shanghai to Hong Kong would normally be run through the Straits.

The Yangtze Navigation Administrative Bureau, the central government's organ for the operation and control of shipping on the Yangtze, has its headquarters at Wuhan, with branch offices at Shanghai and Chungking. In addition to the Bureau's own vessels, joint state-private shipping companies and companies owned by local authorities also run ships on the river. In 1956 three large state-private shipping companies operating on the Yangtze were brought under unified management by the Yangtze Navigation Administrative Bureau.[5]

Some local navigation bureaux come under the provincial departments of communications. Shipping concerns may also be controlled by lower local authorities, such as *hsien*. At one time shipping co-operatives were reported to exist. In 1959 we read that Honan province set up six shipping communes,[6] i.e. people's communes with shipping instead of agriculture as their economic basis.

In 1958 a Grand Canal Committee was established to implement plans for the improvement of the facilities for navigation as well as for water conservancy on the Grand Canal, the traditional route between the capital and the Yangtze

[1] *Ta Kung Daily* (*Dagong Bao*), Peking, July 9, 1963, p. 2.
[2] According to regulations of 1959, the Ministry of Communications was to make plans for the transport of salt by north China and Yangtze services, while provincial level departments of communication were to plan for its carriage in south China coastal and inland waters. *Collected Laws and Regulations* ... Vol. 9, p. 213.
[3] *Water Transport* (*Shuiyun*), March 1958, pp. 6–7.
[4] *Geographical Knowledge* (*Dili Zhishi*), No. 3, March 1958, p. 101. Chang Yuan-kuang: 'New China's Sea Transport.'
[5] *People's Daily* (*Renmin Ribao*), September 23, 1959, p. 9. Wang Shou-tao: loc. cit., and ibid., October 25, 1961, p. 3, and *China Reconstructs*, March 1960, pp. 22–4. Tung Shaosheng, Vice Director of the Yangtze Navigation Administrative Bureau: 'The Yangtze Belongs to the People', and *Daily Worker* (*Gongren Ribao*), August 10, 1961, p. 2, and *People's Daily* (*Renmin Ribao*), September 2, 1956, p. 1.
[6] *Water Transport* (*Shuiyun*), January 1959, p. 10.

Valley. This committee was chaired by the Minister of Communications and its members included a Vice Minister of Water Conservancy and Electric Power and Vice Governors of Kiangsu, Chekiang, Shantung and Hopei. Also set up at the same time were the Grand Canal Engineering Headquarters and equivalent provincial bodies in the provinces concerned.[1] By 1963 a 400 km. section of the Grand Canal in north Kiangsu had been reconstructed so as to be able to take larger ships, as well as to provide for flood protection and irrigation.[2] The importance of improving navigation on the Grand Canal lies in the fact that one of the severest transport bottlenecks has been the carriage of freight, particularly coal, from north to central and south China. This problem, as it concerns south China, has, of course, been aggravated by the division of coastal shipping into two zones by the blockade.

For trans-ocean shipping China has depended mainly on chartered vessels and on foreign shipping services. The China Ocean Shipping Co., which operates the Chinese-owned ships in this service is, however, increasing its tonnage both with ships built in China and with new and secondhand vessels purchased from abroad. In 1961 the Chinese and Albanian governments signed an agreement to form a Sino-Albanian joint stock shipping company, but this may be thought of greater political than economic significance. A similar agreement between China and Tanzania was concluded in 1966.

Most of China's trans-ocean cargoes are handled by the Sinofracht Chartering and Shipbroking Corporation (also known as the China National Chartering and Shipbroking Corporation) and the China National Foreign Trade Transportation Corporation. Sinofracht charters vessels and books space for cargoes and for these purposes has agencies in many parts of the world, while the CNFTTC with branches in the chief ports of China, is responsible for operations subsequent to the chartering of shipping space, such as insurance, loading and customs clearance.[3] China became very active in chartering foreign tonnage in 1958, when the severance of commercial relations with Japan led to increased trade with remoter lands, and in 1960 the repatriation of Overseas Chinese from Indonesia led to another burst of chartering. Heavy imports of grain in subsequent years, together with a switch in Chinese trade from the Soviet Union (with which much trade had gone by land) to more distant trade partners, led to further chartering. For some consignments, use is made of foreign shipping, including conference lines. The Chinese Government's monopoly of the country's foreign trade puts it in a strong position for hard bargaining over rates.

In 1958 the State Council established a Maritime Arbitration Commission within the China Council for the Promotion of International Trade.[4]

The responsibilities of the Ministry of Communications include ports, each of which is administered by a port bureau (*kangwu chü*). Some of these port

[1] *People's Daily* (*Renmin Ribao*), May 17, 1958, p. 1.

[2] *China Reconstructs*, July 1963, pp. 5–7. Chi Yu-ching: 'Rebuilding the Grand Canal.'

[3] *Far Eastern Economic Review*, October 1, 1959, p. 533. Kayser Sung: 'Shipping—Charter, Purchase, Construction, Salvage.'

[4] *People's Daily* (*Renmin Ribao*), January 24, 1959, p. 6. In November 1958 the State Council authorized the Commission's establishment and in January 1959, its rules were adopted.

bureaux were decentralized to local authorities in 1957-8, but others evidently remained under the Ministry's direct control.[1]

All sea ports are officially open to foreign shipping. Those at which foreign ocean-going vessels are accustomed to call are Shanghai, Hsinkang (for Tientsin), Dairen, Chinwangtao, Whampoa and Canton, and Tsamkong; some smaller sea ports are occasionally visited by foreign coastal vessels. Foreign ships are not permitted to call at inland ports. The China Ocean Steamship Agency handles the clearing of foreign ships and agency work at all ports. No foreign line has independent agents, with the possible continued exception of a Polish agency at Shanghai. The port bureaux enforce regulations stringently and, on the whole, have earned a reputation for efficiency. At certain major ports it is claimed that the greater part of loading and unloading merchandise has been mechanized.

Control of dockyards has been divided between the Ministry of Communications, with dockyards engaged mainly in repairs, and the First Ministry of Machine Building which is concerned, among other activities, with shipbuilding. In 1957, during the 'Hundred Flowers' period, this division of responsibility was criticized as leading to duplication and under-utilization of facilities,[2] but it is not known that any change has been made in these arrangements. The Shipbuilding Industry Research Centre was established by the two ministries jointly.[3] Cement boats for agricultural use are made, at least in some areas, by local departments of building construction, and not by departments of communications.[4] Until the end of 1954 the Dairen dockyards were owned by a Sino-Soviet joint-stock company, the Soviet share consisting of Japanese assets expropriated by the Soviet military authorities. As in the case of the Changchun Railway, the Chinese Government bought out the Soviet interest on an instalment basis.[5] The largest ships built in Chinese dockyards have been around 10,000 tons deadweight.

Quantitatively, civil aviation plays a small role in China compared with other means of transport. In 1958 it accounted for a turnover of 13 million ton-km. of freight and 109 million passenger-km.: less than one-hundredth of 1 per cent and less than three-tenths of 1 per cent of the respective railway figures for that year.[6] However, from the point of view of providing political and administrative links, especially with remote parts of the country, the significance of air travel is very considerable. By the end of 1964 the length of China's internal civil aviation routes was reported to total 39,000 km.[7] The development of civil aviation in China was for long restricted by the shortage

[1] *Collected Laws and Regulations* ... Vol. 6, p. 392.
[2] *People's Daily* (*Renmin Ribao*), March 24, 1957, p. 11. Wang Chi-yi: Speech to the 3rd Session of CPPCC 2nd National Committee of March 18, 1957, 'Give Overall Consideration When Planning Dockyards.'
[3] Ibid., May 5, 1959, p. 9. Yang Chün-sheng and Sa Pen-hsin: Speech to 1st Session of 2nd National People's Congress, 'New Achievements of China's Shipbuilding Industry.'
[4] *Economic Research* (*Jingji Yanjiu*), No. 8, August 1965, p. 39. T'ao Yu-liang: 'A Good Way for Departments of Building Construction to Help Agricultural Production.'
[5] A. Eckstein: 'Moscow-Peking Axis: The Economic Pattern' in H. L. Boorman, A. Eckstein, P. E. Mosely and B. Schwartz: *Moscow-Peking Axis*, New York, 1957, p. 91.
[6] *Ten Great Years*, pp. 148, 150 and 152.
[7] *Far Eastern Economic Review 1966 Yearbook*, p. 137.

of petroleum. The rise in China's petroleum output in the 1960s has made possible an increased activity in this sphere.

The most important pre-1949 civil aviation concern, the China National Aviation Corporation, was a joint venture in which the Chinese Government had a controlling interest and Pan American Airways a minority holding. After 1949 its aircraft passed into the hands of the Nationalist Government in Taiwan. The Communists established the China Civil Aviation Bureau to operate civil aviation. In 1954 this Bureau was placed directly under the State Council. It was subordinated to the Ministry of Communications in 1958[1] and re-named the Civil Aviation Administration of China. Then in April 1962 it was again made directly subject to the State Council and re-named the Civil Aviation General Administration of China.[2] Local bureaux of civil aviation are established at the provincial level.

Between 1950 and 1954 a joint Sino-Soviet airline operated services within Sinkiang and between north China, Sinkiang, the Mongolian People's Republic and the Soviet Union. In December 1954 the Soviet shares were transferred to the Chinese Government.[3]

In 1964 the national network of air services linked Peking with some seventy cities in China, as well as with the Soviet Union, Mongolia, North Korea, North Vietnam, and Burma. In addition, in 1966, Soviet, Pakistani, French, Korean and Cambodian air lines had regular services into China. From 1958 onwards, provincial air services are reported to have been extensively developed under the local bureaux of civil aviation.

Civil aircraft undertake a considerable volume of work on behalf of agriculture and forestry. Bureaux of civil aviation in many parts of the country have set up special offices for this purpose. Aircraft are used to spray insecticides, sow seed, apply fertilizers, and report forest fires. Other functions performed include the making of surveys to aid mineral prospecting and the selection of routes for roads and railways and of sites for water conservancy and industrial projects.

In 1956, Wang Shou-tao, at that time Director of the Sixth Office of the State Council, announced that the Ministries of Railways and Communications were to draft a measure for a division of labour between rail, water and road transport, with a special view to the greater use of waterways.[4] A step towards this had been taken by an adjustment of freight rates in 1955–6 to correct previous regional discriminations which for the railways had favoured the north-east (the former Manchuria) and for water transport the north China services as a whole. The new rates, which were on average lower than those they replaced, applied to the whole national railway system and to all steamers on the coastal and Yangtze services, whether the vessels were owned by the state, local authorities, joint state-private companies, or by co-operatives. At that time the ton-km. operating costs (excluding harbour charges) of steamers

[1] *Collected Laws and Regulations*... Vol. 7, p. 64.
[2] NCNA Peking, April 16, 1962.
[3] *New China Monthly (Xinhua Yuebao)*, No. 61, November 1954, pp. 33 and 175, and A. Eckstein: loc. cit.
[4] *New China Fortnightly (Xinhua Banyuekan)*, No. 88, July 21, 1956, p. 133. Wang Shou-tao, Director of the Sixth Office of State Council: 'Develop Transport, Postal and Telecommunication Undertakings.' Speech to 3rd Session of 1st NPC.

were 81 per cent of rail costs for coastal services, but 142 per cent of rail costs on the Yangtze. This discrepancy between coastal and Yangtze costs was due to the great expense of navigation on the upper Yangtze; on the lower Yangtze alone, costs were below those of railways. Rates were adjusted to reflect this, so that by the end of 1956 those on the upper reaches of the river were between 144 per cent–258 per cent of those on the lower river.[1]

Local shipping enterprises on the Yangtze were hard hit in 1955–6 by the application of the new rates to them. Due to the age of their vessels and defects of management, their costs were in some cases 20 per cent–100 per cent above those of the central government concerns and in 1956 most local enterprises were making losses on short distance Yangtze services. The new rates did not apply to steamers on the Yangtze tributaries nor in any case to junks. So the departments of communication of the Yangtze riparian provinces diverted junks from the tributaries to the main river from which their steamers in turn were switched to the tributaries where they charged rates 70 per cent–180 per cent above those on the Yangtze, making profits in some instances exceeding 30 per cent of costs. Meanwhile, on the Yangtze itself short-distance services were seriously depleted, until in 1959 short-distance freight rates were raised.[2]

This adjustment of Yangtze freight rates, accompanied by a halving of insurance rates was made, presumably by design, at about the time (July 1956) of the completion of the Paoki-Chengtu railway,[3] which linked Szechuan with north and north-west China, and indirectly with much of the rest of China as well. This introduced competition with the Yangtze shipping services to and from Szechuan and in 1957 it was found cheaper to send fertilizer from Nanking (on the lower Yangtze) to Chungking (on the upper Yangtze) by a circuitous railway route, rather than ship it by river.[4]

This development intensified the already severe pressure on the Lunghai Railway which carried these new freight loads to Paoki. The transport plan for 1958 provided for about 65 per cent of the freight tonnage to and from Szechuan to go by the Yangtze and for some 30 per cent or more to go by the railway. In that year freight rates between Paoki and Chungking were 15 per cent–30 per cent above the normal rates on the national railways.[5] It cannot be said how far this was to compensate for higher costs on this line (which included the first electrified stretch of railway in China, and which was reported to have suffered various mishaps in its early days) and how far to lessen its attractiveness relatively to that of the Yangtze route: both considerations may have weighed. That the latter was not absent may be judged from the simultaneous reduction of freight rates up river between Ichang in

[1] *Planned Economy (Jihua Jingji)*, No. 12, December 1956, p. 13. Chu Yen: 'A Preliminary Consideration of Certain Problems in Planning Transport Rates', and *People's Handbook (Renmin Shouce) 1956*, p. 510.
[2] *Planned Economy (Jihua Jingji)*, No. 12, December 1956, pp. 12–14. Chu Yen: loc. cit., and *People's Daily (Renmin Ribao)*, June 1, 1959, p. 2.
[3] *People's Handbook (Renmin Shouce) 1957*, p. 529. Regular services, however, were not announced until January 1958. (ibid., *1958*, p. 563) and were rumoured to have been intermittently suspended at later dates.
[4] *People's Daily (Renmin Ribao)*, August 18, 1957, p. 5.
[5] *Planned Economy (Jihua Jingji)*, No. 3, March 1958, p. 23. Hsü Fen and Li Yuan: 'Why Is the Cost of Yangtze River Transport Higher than that of Railway Transport?'

Hupeh and Luhsien in Szechuan to the level of the down-river rates for this particularly difficult reach: a reduction which would benefit the river services that competed directly with the new railway. Specially low Yangtze freight rates (some 20 per cent below rates by rail) were introduced for thirty unspecified commodities.[1]

This process was carried further in 1959 when, despite the greatly disparate costs on different stretches of the Yangtze, a uniform tariff was introduced for the whole river, replacing the separate rates for the upper, middle and lower reaches respectively. At the same time an average reduction of 15 per cent was made in the Yangtze rates as a whole. This brought about a fall of nearly 37 per cent in rates for shipments on certain runs on the upper Yangtze.[2] It seems possible that this may have involved certain upper Yangtze services running at a loss. Whether or not such pricing is rational depends on the rationality of the various prices that enter into the costs of these services. Before passing judgment, it would also be necessary to know whether the rates charged by the railways reflect the social costs of marginal additional quantities of freight on a line (the Lunghai) which at times has been on the verge of breaking down through pressure of traffic.

In discussing the relative costs of rail and water transport, it must be remembered that China copies the Soviet Union in excluding from costs any interest payment by an enterprise on its capital, which is provided free (although subject to amortization charges) by the state or a local authority. The effects of this on railways is greater than on river transport as, on the Western definition of costs, capital charges form a higher proportion of rail costs than of the costs of river transport (especially by junk).[3] This factor has not escaped attention in China where in 1956 it was being argued that despite the relatively high cost of freight carriage on the Yangtze, nevertheless greater use should be made of that river as the investment required by water transport was small and state funds could thus be saved by its development. 'In order to maintain a rational relationship between rates of rail and water transport, the profit level on river transport should be lowered, while that on rail transport must be maintained relatively high.'[4] In 1956 the rate of profit reckoned on cost made by Yangtze shipping services was only about one-third of that earned by the railways (the whole national railway system seems to be implied). Thus higher profit margins are used as a way of imposing heavier capital charges on the more capital intensive means of transport. However, even profit reckoned on capital was in 1956 lower for Yangtze shipping services compared with profit on capital for railways (9·6 per cent compared with 11·2 per cent).[5]

[1] *Planned Economy* (*Jihua Jingji*), No. 3, March 1958, p. 23. Hsü Fen and Li Yuan: loc. cit. These specially low rates may have been withdrawn in the following year, in the course of the adjustments in rates which then occurred. *People's Daily* (*Renmin Ribao*), June 1, 1959, p. 2.
[2] *People's Daily* (*Renmin Ribao*), June 1, 1959, p. 2.
[3] The accounting cost of river transport has been inflated as ships are amortized over a forty-year period while their actual serviceable life in China is greater. *Planned Economy* (*Jihua Jingji*), No. 3, May 1958, p. 22. Hsü Fen and Li Yuan: loc. cit.
[4] *Planned Economy* (*Jihua Jingji*), No. 12, December 1956, p. 13. Chu Yen: loc. cit.
[5] Ibid., No. 3, 1958, p. 20. Hsü Fen and Li Yuan: loc. cit.

In the case of freight rates by rail, a discount (i.e. a tapering of rates) is given up to a certain maximum length of journey. Very long hauls are penalized in order to encourage the development of local sources of supply. Penal rates have also been imposed on 'irrational transport' such as the shipment of goods to places where such goods are produced. However, it is difficult to determine administratively what constitutes a reasonable transport distance, or direction of flow.[1] The same question arose in connection with freight policies in the Soviet Union —as P. Wiles commented about Moscow region coals 'the "zone of their rational use" is only to be discovered if a single c.i.f. price reigns in Moscow for coal from all coal fields, and if transport rates subsidize no particular locality. . . . The "limiting distance over which transportation is rational" will certainly not be discovered by raising instead of tapering haulage rates in direct contradiction of cost behaviour'.[2]

The desire to eliminate long hauls led to attempts already mentioned,[3] to achieve local self-sufficiency in major commodities, such as coal and grain. As more authority was devolved to local authorities, local self-sufficiency came to mean. self-sufficiency within administrative units, from the province down. This, in its turn, led to new irrationalities of commodity flows, as when goods were supplied from distant parts of the same province instead of from across the nearby border of another province. This phenomenon became especially common m the period 1958 to 1960. From 1962, again in the interests of 'rational transport', an effort had to be made to counteract this tendency.[4]

Some rate discrimination has been practised between different types of freight: A writer in 1956 stated the general principle that rates must vary according to the Importance of a commodity to the national economy. The lowest rates should apply to raw materials, such as minerals, coal and coke, iron and steel and building materials, which are vital to national economic construction; the next most favoured should be goods needed for agricultural purposes, such as farming implements and fertilizers. Goods for which conditions of transport are similar—e.g. machinery of different types should generally enjoy similar rates. However, consideration must also be given to charging what the traffic will bear, e.g. rates for scrap rubber must be below those for raw rubber, for inferior coal lower than for ordinary coal, for miscellaneous grains lower than for wheat, and for cotton yarn and steel higher than for raw cotton and cast iron respectively.[5] These principles appeared in the form of recommendations and it is uncertain how far they were ever embodied in actual freight rates; however, we know that freight rates have at times been lower for raw materials of mineral origin, and for certain products of heavy

[1] People's Railway (Renmin Tiedao), No. 9, 1952. 'Policy and Function of Railway Freight Rate Determination.' (JPRS/NY Report No. 478), and *Planned Economy (Jihua Jingji)*, No. 12, December 1956, p. 14. Cbu Yen: loc. cit., and A. I. Il'yin and M.P. Voronichev : op. cit. (JPRS 3484), p. 83.

[2] P. J. D. Wiles : *The Political Economy of Communism*, Oxford, 1962, p. 125.

[3] p.258 above. See also Wang Shou-tao, Director of the Sixth Office of the State Council: Speech in *Documents of the Eighth National Congress of the Communist Party of China* (in Chinese), Peking, 1956, pp. 532-3.

[4] See p. 308 below.

[5] Planned Economy (Jihua Jingji), No. 12, December 1956, p. 14. Chu Yen: loc. cit.

industry and of agriculture.[1] In September 1966, at a meeting called by the State Economic Commission, it was decided to carry free of charge, by all means of transport and by post, the works of Chairman Mao, his printed portraits and paper machine impresses of his works; priority was also to be accorded to these goods.[2]

The central government's responsibility for providing investment funds for transport probably extends to major projects on the national railway system (excluding local railways), and also to certain major highways, notably those of political and strategic importance,[3] to the centrally controlled civil aviation services and presumably, as well, to those ocean, coastal and river shipping services under its direct control.

	State Investment in Transport, Posts and Telecommunications (million yuan)		*State Investment in Transport Posts and Telecommunications as percentage of total state Investment	*State Investment in Railways only as percentage of total state Investment	State Revenue (i.e. profits) from Transport, Postal and Telecommunication enterprises under its ownership (million yuan)
	Total	Railways only			
1953	1,070[1]	650[1]	13	8	
1954	1,500[1]	950[1]	17	10	
1955	1,760[1]	1,220[1]	19	13	
1956	2,610[1]	1,760[1]	18	12	2,132[4]
1957	2,070[1]	1,340[1]	15	10	2,265[5] (budget)
1958	3,400[1]	2,030[1]	13	8	2,388[6] (budget)
1959	4,950[2]		19		
1960 (budget)	6,810[3]	5,000[3]	21	15	

* The 1960 figures specifically exclude 'self-provided' investment funds raised by local authorities and enterprises (*Peking Review*, April 5, 1960, p. 11), i.e. they exclude extra-budgetary funds. *People's Handbook* (*Renmin Shouce*) *1960*, p. 185. This exclusion is not specifically stated for the earlier figures, but probably holds for them too.

Sources:
[1] *Ten Great Years*, pp. 58–9.
[2] *Peking Review*, April 5, 1960, p. 16. Li Fu-ch'un, Director, State Council Office of Industry and Communications: Report on Draft 1960 National Economic Plan.
[3] Li Hsien-nien, Minister of Finance: Report on Finance to NPC. *People's Handbook* (*Renmin Shouce*) *1960*, p. 185.
[4] Ibid., *1958*, p. 214 (figure given is for final accounts).
[5] Ibid., p. 218 (budgeted figure only).
[6] Ibid., *1959*, p. 229 (budgeted figure only).

The 1960 investment figures are for (*ex ante*) budgeted investment as figures for realized investment were not published. For other years figures are for realized investment. For an explanation of the financial terms and concepts used in this Table see Chapter XIV. State revenue figures include depreciation charges and certain other funds as well as profit remittances; tax receipts are excluded.

[1] A. I. Il'yin and M. P. Voronichev: op. cit. (JPRS 3484), p. 83.
[2] NCNA, September 8, 1966.
[3] In 1957 one of the charges against the General Bureau of Highways of the Ministry of Communications was that for the construction and repair of roads of equivalent categories its costs were above those of local authorities. *People's Daily* (*Renmin Ribao*), November 16, 1957, p. 4.

These figures show a steady increase in absolute terms in the investment in transport and communications between 1953 and 1960 except for 1957, a year of inflationary pressure and shortages of raw materials. The percentage formed by investment in this sector to total investment from the central government's budgetary funds fell in general between 1955 and 1958, but rose to a record level in the 1960 budget. The predominant position of railways as a recipient of investment funds in the transport sector is clearly evident; throughout the First Five Year Plan period they took between 60 per cent–70 per cent of the sector's investment allocation, the figure falling slightly below these limits in 1958 but rising to 73 per cent in the 1960 budget, in which railways (together with power and non-ferrous metals) were mentioned as weak links to be strengthened.[1] During the Great Leap, in the years 1958 and 1959, when investment in railways rose sharply, the average cost of railway construction fell from ¥544,000 a km. to ¥380,000, a decline of over 30 per cent.[2] The total length of new track laid in 1958 (information for 1959 is not available) increased considerably, but it is difficult to relate construction total, total expenditure and average kilometre cost in the different years as the proportion of new, restored and double-tracked length in the total changed from year to year.[3]

A notable feature of the increase in central government investment in transport and communications in 1958 is that it rose very much more steeply than budgeted profits received from the same sources (by 64 per cent compared with 5 per cent); inevitably in a year of heavy investment, which would not have time to produce an operating profit before the end of the year. As a result, in 1958 this sector was (on the basis of budgeted revenue) a net recipient of resources on a large scale, whereas before, its net absorption of funds was much smaller, and in the exceptional year of 1957, its profits more than covered its investment programme so far as central government funds were concerned. Despite annual fluctuations, a large part of the capital requirements of transport development have been self-generated.

Investment in transport has produced high returns in economic benefits although this, of course, is also true of investment in many other sectors in China as in most other countries at a similar stage of economic development. For example, it was estimated that the whole cost of the Yangtze bridge at Chungking would be recovered within one year by the saving on unloading and re-loading the freight which used to be ferried across the river.[4] Instances of even higher rates of return in industry have, however, been reported on occasion.

The remoulding of China's transport administrative system in the 1950s was done very largely on Soviet lines. Similarly many of the technical changes were based on Soviet experience. The Changchun Railway, under joint Sino-Soviet administration from 1950 to 1952, adopted many Soviet practices, including the economic accounting system, which were later extended

---

[1] *People's Handbook (Renmin Shouce) 1960*, p. 185. Li Hsien-nien: loc. cit.
[2] Ibid., p. 183. Li Hsien-nien: loc. cit.
[3] *Ten Great Years*, p. 69.
[4] *China Reconstructs*, February 1960, p. 10.

throughout the economy.[1] While the 'Hundred Flowers' bloomed in the spring of 1957, complaints were made that the Ministry of Communications had too slavishly modelled itself on Soviet patterns, which were not practical in actual circumstances.[2] This theme, unlike other criticisms made in the same period, was heard again in 1958, when the opinion was aired that overmuch had been copied from the Changchun Railway.[3]

As far as road transport is concerned, in May 1959 the Director of the General Bureau of Highways in the Ministry of Communications paid a tribute to the Soviet experts under whose direction 'we settled our plans of work, decided the form of organization of the highway departments, and fixed the system of management and the technical norms'.[4] Soviet experts supplied the answer to many technical problems occurring in various branches of transport, such as railway construction in desert areas, methods of tunnelling, the designing of the great Yangtze bridges at Wuhan and Chungking, methods of road surfacing and the system of lighting on the upper Yangtze. 'Volga-type' passenger ships for the Yangtze run were built in China, while Soviet blueprints were also employed for building ocean freighters, as well as electric locomotives.

Both strategic and economic motives have dictated the general pattern of the development of the transport system. Previously modern communications had been concentrated in the east, especially in the north-east region. Since 1949, most of the effort has been directed to building railway lines and roads in the interior, where much of the new industrial development has taken place. Reports tell of greatly increased economic activity in areas newly opened by railway and roads. This must have contributed towards the improvement in the standard of living which occurred during the First Five Year Plan period.

The Communist regime has been the first government of China in modern times both to plan a comprehensive nationwide transport system and to have the opportunity to put it into effect. Its achievement in carrying this out was rewarded by a firmer control of the country than that enjoyed by any of its predecessors. Great shortcomings have been apparent in the organization of transport, but these do not obliterate the economic advantages derived from the general improvement in communications.

[1] See p. 26 above, and *People's Railways* (*Renmin Tiedao*), No. 3, March 1952, pp. 38–9. 'The Economic Calculation System of the Chinese Changchun Railway.' (JPRS/NY Report No. 478), and *People's Daily* (*Renmin Ribao*), November 5, 1952 (reprinted in *New China Monthly* (*Xinhua Yuebao*), No. 38, December 1952, pp. 138–42).

[2] *People's Daily* (*Renmin Ribao*), May 24, 1957, p. 3.

[3] *Philosophical Research* (*Zhexue Yanjiu*), No. 4, August 10, 1958, p. 22. Wu Wen-pin: 'Irrational Regulations and Systems Must Be Reformed.'

[4] *Geographical Knowledge* (*Dili Zhishi*), No. 9, September 1959, p. 398. Lien Po-sheng: 'The Past Ten Years' Achievements in Building Highways.'

Chapter 11

INTERNAL TRADE[1]

A description of the Chinese commercial system is beset by a problem of definition, because in contemporary China it is hard to draw the dividing line between trade and taxation. While a part of the harvest is taken by the state without payment as agricultural tax in kind, and therefore clearly falls into the category of taxation, a further share is compulsorily bought by the state at prices below free market levels, thus partaking of the nature of both trade and taxation. The close connection between trade and taxation is seen in the fact that ever since 1954 both have come under the same office of the State Council and under the same department of the Central Committee of the Party. Agricultural taxation and the compulsory procurement of farm produce will be dealt with in Chapter 13, although these topics must necessarily be mentioned when describing the organization of trade.

Another definitional problem arises from the circumstance that in China a large proportion of goods are distributed by direct allocation. In this case, the formal transaction is between the producing ministry and the consuming ministry (or between their local counterparts) while details may be written into contracts between the two enterprises concerned and the goods probably pass direct from one to the other of these (this latter, of course, may also happen with goods not subject to allocation). The allocatory system is discussed on the micro-scale, as affecting the individual enterprise, in Chapter 6, and on the macro-scale, in the context of Economic Planning, in Chapter 17. References to it will, however, occur in this chapter. Matters of pricing are inevitably mentioned, too, but will be treated more fully in Chapter 16.

The growth of a strong merchant class in China had been stunted by the official bureaucracy, who were unwilling to leave in private hands undertakings of any size or significance. In any case, long before the Communist victory in 1949, the pre-war pattern and organization of China's internal trade had been shattered by international and civil war. The country's economy had become even more locally fragmented than was traditional, the role of the foreign merchants had declined and that of the state commercial bodies had grown. Outside the Treaty Ports and their environs, most parts of China always had a high degree of self-sufficiency. Factory-made textiles and certain other consumer goods, such as kerosene and cigarettes had, however, penetrated even the remoter districts, but the turmoil of the war years arrested these developments. Local produce replaced goods from the ports or from abroad. Linked with this was the decline in the part taken by the foreigners in internal

[1] Portions of an early draft of this chapter appeared in E. Szczepanik (ed.): *Symposium on Economic and Social Problems of the Far East*, Hong Kong, 1962, and in *China Quarterly*, No. 8, October–December 1961.

trade, a function which had been an offshoot of their activities in the import and export trades or of foreign manufacturing operations in the Treaty Ports. When Free China was largely cut off from the outside world and the coastal districts, private Western participation in China's internal trade almost ceased. The extensive networks that had been established throughout the country to sell oil, cigarettes and dyes now atrophied; and an end came, also, to the complicated system of relationships that had grown up between foreign buyers of Chinese produce and the native dealers. To meet the difficulties of economic isolation and to combat inflation, the government, then at Chungking, established companies to procure and sell certain essential commodities —mainly food, cotton and fuel, and to assume monopoly powers in the case of some goods. However, the scope of these companies was limited to a few large towns.

In Japanese-occupied China, Western merchants had their activities curtailed even before the outbreak of the Pacific War brought them to an end, at least as far as allied nationals were concerned. Japanese commercial operations naturally increased in importance but were suddenly and completely obliterated in 1945.

In the years of civil war between 1945 and 1949, little could be done to pick up the threads of pre-war economic life. After the Communist victory, two of the war-time tendencies already noted in China's internal trade were accentuated: the decline of the foreign merchant and the increased participation of the government. The third tendency mentioned—that of local fragmentation —was reversed in the early years of the new regime with improved internal security and the rehabilitation of the transport system.

1. CENTRAL COMMERCIAL ORGANS

In the first years of Communist rule, the Ministry of Trade controlled both internal and external trade. Under its direction, specialized corporations were established in 1950 to deal in the main categories of goods, separate corporations being formed for domestic and foreign trade. In 1952 the Ministry of Trade was divided into the Ministry of Commerce, the Ministry of Food and the Ministry of Foreign Trade; the specialized corporations were put under the appropriate ministries. In July 1955 a Ministry for the Purchase of Agricultural Produce was established. Later, in May 1956, a Ministry of Urban Services was set up to control trade in subsidiary foodstuffs (i.e. excluding the most important items, especially grain) and service trades; however, no Minister was appointed until November 1956. In that month the Ministry for the Purchase of Agricultural Produce was abolished and its Minister transferred to head the Ministry of Urban Services. In February 1958, the Ministry of Urban Services was absorbed into the All-China Federation of Supply and Marketing Co-operatives (which was established in 1954 and is charged with the supervision of collective, as distinct from state, commerce), the combined body coming under the newly-established Second Ministry of Commerce; the original ministry thereupon became known as the First Ministry of Commerce. A few months later, in September 1958, the two ministries were united in a single Ministry of Commerce. One of the questions at issue in these changes was whether rural and urban trade should come under the same ministry. From 1956 to 1958 Ch'en Yün was Minister of Commerce (First Minister of Commerce from February to September 1958) and his term of office covered a period when the free market was temporarily revived. On the merging of the two Ministries of Commerce in September 1958, Ch'eng Tzu-hua was appointed Minister and Ch'en Yün became head of the State Construction Commission which was established the following month. In February 1960, Yao Yi-lin succeeded Ch'eng Tzu-hua as Minister of Commerce, a post which from January 1966 he held concurrently with the Directorship of the Political Department for Finance and Trade of the CCP Central Committee. As we shall see below, several other ministries have also engaged in commercial activities.

Another body, the Central Administration for Industry and Commerce, is charged *inter alia* with the supervision of joint state-private enterprises in commerce as in industry. In addition, a Ministry for the Allocation of Materials was established in 1964, succeeding a bureau of a similar name.[1]

The Ministries of Commerce, of Food and of Foreign Trade, together with the Ministry of Finance, the People's Bank of China, and the Agricultural Bank of China, come under the immediate control of the State Council's Office of Finance and Trade. The Director of this Office, as of its predecessor the Fifth General Office of the State Council, is Li Hsien-nien, who also holds the post of Minister of Finance. The parallel Party organs are the Central Committee's Finance and Trade Work Department and its Finance and Trade Political Department headed by Ma Ming-fang and by Yao Yi-lin (the Minister of Commerce) respectively.

The duties of the Ministry of Trade (as it was then called) were laid down in 1950 and are given here as in essence they are now the same although, as we shall see, other ministries have subsequently shared responsibility for trade with the Ministry of Commerce. The 1950 list of duties was as follows:—

i. To draft and carry out the general plans for state and co-operative trade with the approval of the Government Administrative Council (the predecessor of the State Council) and in accordance with its economic and financial plans.
ii. To approve the business and financial plans of the specialized trading corporations and to supervise their execution.
iii. To manage and regulate state commercial capital and stocks throughout the country.
iv. To fix wholesale prices of state trading corporations at the major markets of the country.
v. To guide private trade throughout the country and to give guidance on market control to local authority departments of trade at all levels.
vi. To promulgate regulations for commercial accounting throughout the country.[2]

The national corporations set up for internal trade initially numbered six, dealing respectively in grain, cotton (raw, yarn and cloth), general goods, salt, coal and building materials, and native products.[3] Each of these nationwide

[1] See p. 477 below.
[2] *New China Monthly (Xinhua Yuebao)*, No. 6, April 1950, p. 1408.
[3] Ibid.

corporations was, in turn, to establish regional corporations in each large administrative region.[1] The regional corporations were to be under the joint leadership of their respective national corporations and of the regional departments of commerce. For grain, general goods and native products, separate corporations were to be formed in each province under the joint supervision of the regional corporations concerned and of the provincial departments of commerce. In the case of commodities for which no provincial corporations were established, the regional corporations were to set up branches in large towns in their region, or appoint the provincial corporations of other national companies as agents.[2] Later, more national corporations were established, covering many other branches of trade.[3]

The economic accounting system, as operated in other branches of economic life,[4] was introduced into commerce in 1953. The specialized corporations were established as independent accounting units, as were also their subordinate components. For example, not only was the China General Goods Company an independent accounting unit, but so were the regional and provincial corporations under it, its central and regional wholesale depots and its retail stores at provincial and equivalent level.[5]

Subject to the approval of the Ministry of Trade and later its successor ministries, each of the specialized national corporations had to draft and execute its own plans, arrange its own organization and personnel, manage and regulate its own capital and working funds and enforce a unified system of accounts and reports.[6] Regulations were laid down for the control of the capital of the specialized corporations at different levels. All cash from sales and other sources had to be deposited with the People's Bank of China. The regional and provincial departments of trade had to supervise and co-ordinate the operations of the specialized corporations in their respective areas, fix prices for the corporations at the medium and smaller centres and control private trade within their regions or provinces.[7]

At first the direct operations of state commerce were mainly confined to the large towns. In March 1956 a beginning was made with establishing state commercial organs at the *hsien* level and in the more important market towns beneath the *hsien*.[8] As far as rural trade was concerned, the state's chief instruments of control were, as we shall see, to be the supply and marketing co-operatives.

The central government ministries concerned with trade ('the commercial ministries')[9] together with their provincial and other local departments and

[1] In 1950 China was divided into six large administrative regions. These were abolished in 1954. See p. 20 above.
[2] *New China Monthly* (*Xinhua Yuebao*), No. 6, April 1950, p. 1408.
[3] See *People's Handbook* (*Renmin Shouce*) *1951*, Vol. 2, p. '*shen*' 24, ibid., *1952*, p. 277, and ibid., *1956*, p. 524.
[4] See p. 26 above.
[5] *New China Monthly* (*Xinhua Yuebao*), No. 38, December 1952, p. 153.
[6] Ibid., No. 6, April 1950, p. 1408.
[7] Ibid.
[8] *New China Fortnightly* (*Xinhua Banyuekan*), No. 83, May 6, 1956, p. 84.
[9] In addition to the ministries for which trade is the main activity (the Ministries of Commerce, of Food and of Foreign Trade) several other ministries have responsibilities for certain branches of trade (see p. 286 below). These include the Ministries of Light

the specialized state corporations, are collectively referred to as the state commercial organs.

2. THE DIVISION BETWEEN STATE, CO-OPERATIVE, AND PRIVATE TRADE

The state corporations quickly gained a large share of the market. By 1954, 83·8 per cent of China's wholesale trade was reported to be conducted by state concerns compared with 10·2 per cent by private enterprise, 5·5 per cent by trading co-operatives and the remaining 0·5 per cent by 'state-capitalist and co-operativized commerce'; this last phrase apparently covers former private commercial enterprises which had undergone 'socialist transformation', the larger ones then becoming 'state-capitalist' (i.e. joint state-private) enterprises and the smaller ones being changed into co-operatives. In the same year, in retail trade the corresponding figures were: state concerns 22·2 per cent, private enterprise 26·4 per cent, co-operatives 45·8 per cent and 'state-capitalist and co-operativized commerce' 5·6 per cent.[1] The reported share of private commerce in retail sales (reckoned on another basis)[2] was 25·6 per cent in 1954 and declined to 17·8 per cent in 1955, 4·2 per cent in 1956 and 2·7 per cent in 1957. The figures for sales by state concerns in retail trade indicated a slight decline in their relative position between 1954 and 1957; while the share of 'state-capitalist and co-operativized commerce' rose considerably in retailing as seen on page 278.

By 1954, therefore, state commerce was overwhelmingly important in wholesale trade. The organization of wholesaling in the state commercial system was based on a hierarchy of wholesale depots, aligned with the political administrative system. In the course of time, provincial corporations in each line of trade came to have under them Grade 2 wholesale depots in each special district and Grade 3 depots at the *hsien* levels.[3] This was at variance with the traditional marketing system in which G. W. Skinner's researches have suggested that 'only a minority of intermediate market towns serve as capitals of *hsien* or higher level administrative units.'[4] In the mid-1960s, as we shall see, the realignment of the commercial wholesaling system in accordance with natural economic areas, rather than with administrative units, came to be encouraged, but how far such a realignment has actually been effected is uncertain.

Co-operative commerce refers to that conducted by the supply and market-

---

Industry, of Health, of Aquatic Products and of Forestry. The term 'commercial ministries' appears to refer to all these ministries in their commercial aspects.

[1] *New China Fortnightly* (*Xinhua Banyuekan*), No. 91, September 6, 1956, p. 46.

[2] *Ten Great Years*, Peking, 1960, p. 40. No explanation is given of the difference in basis between these two sets of figures.

[3] *Southern Daily* (*Nanfang Ribao*), September 29, 1962 (SCMP 2864). Lu Ch'i-mo and Li Ch'ung-ch'ing: 'Why the Delay in Sending Industrial Products to Rural Areas?', and *Ta Kung Daily* (*Dagong Bao*), Peking, October 27, 1964, p. 2. Ch'i Yen-yung: 'What Is the Rational Disposition of Grade 2 Wholesale Depots?', and ibid., April 8, 1965, p. 2.

[4] *Journal of Asian Studies*, Vol. XXIV, No. 1, November 1964, p. 9. G. W. Skinner: 'Marketing and Social Structure in Rural China', Part 1. On the various levels of marketing systems, see p. 35 above.

1. Percentage Distribution of Wholesale Sales

Year	State Commerce	Co-operative Commerce	State-Capitalist and Co-operativized Commerce	Private Commerce
1950	23·2	0·6	0·1	76·1
1952	60·5	2·7	0·5	36·3
1953	66·3	2·9	0·5	30·3
1954	83·8	5·5	0·5	10·2
1955	82·2	12·6	0·8	4·4

Source: New China Fortnightly (Xinhua Banyuekan), No. 91, September 6, 1956, p. 46. For wholesale sales, unlike retail sales, figures are not given in *Ten Great Years*. The possibility that private wholesaling may have revived between July 1956 and September 1957 is raised by Choh-ming Li: *Economic Development of Communist China*, Berkeley, 1959, p. 26.

2. Percentage Distribution of Retail Sales

A.

Year	State Commerce	Co-operative Commerce	State-Capitalist and Co-operativized Commerce	Private Commerce
1950	9·7	6·7	0·1	83·5
1952	18·2	23·8	0·2	57·8
1953	19·5	29·9	0·3	50·3
1954	22·2	45·8	5·6	26·4
1955	31·6	35·7	15·2	17·5

Source: New China Fortnightly (Xinhua Banyuekan), No. 91, September 6, 1956, p. 46.

A later and somewhat divergent set of figures for the percentage distribution of retail sales is given in *Ten Great Years*, p. 40, as follows:

B.

Year	Socialist Commerce	State-Capitalist and Co-operative Commerce	Private Commerce
1950	14·9	0·1	85·0
1951	24·4	0·1	75·5
1952	42·6	0·2	57·2
1953	49·7	0·4	49·9
1954	69·0	5·4	25·6
1955	67·6	14·6	17·8
1956	68·3	27·5	4·2
1957	65·7	31·6	2·7

3. Retail Sales handled by Socialist Commerce, 1950=100

Year	Index
1950	100
1951	233·2
1952	505·6
1953	774·7
1954	1,220·0
1955	1,230·0
1956	1,480·0
1957	1,470·0
1958	2,020·0

Source: *Ten Great Years*, p. 39.

ing co-operatives which were established all over the country soon after the Communists came into power. Although nominally collective bodies, the co-operatives come under close state control and are in fact little different from state organs. (Sometimes, nevertheless, relations between co-operative and state commercial organs are strained.)

Even before 1949 supply and marketing co-operatives had existed in the old Communist areas. Total membership grew from something over 10 million at the end of 1949 to over 25 million in 1950, over 79 million in 1951; over 138 million in 1952, to over 149 million in 1954, and 156 million in 1955, which probably meant that by that time one representative of almost every peasant household was, at least nominally, a member.[1] By the autumn of 1954, when the period of rapid growth in numbers of basic-level supply and marketing co-operatives was over, there were some 29,600 throughout the country with 2,005 federations at the level of the *hsien* and twenty-six at provincial and equivalent level. In July 1954 a national body, the All-China Federation of Supply and Marketing Co-operatives, was established to promote and supervise the development of co-operative commerce. The movement is predominantly rural, more than 90 per cent of the 1954 membership being peasants.[2]

During the development period of the supply and marketing co-operatives, their growth was encouraged by preferential treatment in respect of taxation, loans and transport as well as by enabling the co-operatives to buy goods from state commerce at between 2 per cent and 6 per cent below normal wholesale prices. This situation was ended in 1955 and supply and marketing co-operatives were ordered to bring their retail prices in line with those of state commerce.[3]

The co-operatives engage in both buying and selling. By 1955 they had opened more than 200,000 retail outlets and purchasing points. On the sales side, they deal in consumer goods and also in supplies and equipment for agriculture. In purchasing, the co-operatives buy from the peasants on behalf of the state. Already by 1953 the co-operatives were responsible for 75 per cent of total state purchases, including almost all those of the main agricultural commodities. Much of the processing of agricultural produce was by then also in their hands.[4]

The 2·7 per cent of retail sales reported to be conducted by private enterprise in 1957 presumably excluded the unlicensed hawkers and similar operators. These had increased in numbers after agricultural collectivization and the re-opening of the free market in 1956 (see below) which made it easier for them to obtain goods. It was estimated that in eleven large cities in 1957 some 130,000 unlicensed traders were active; 20,000 were to be found in Peking alone. In one part of Hopei it was reported in that year that un-

---

[1] *People's Handbook (Renmin Shouce) 1955*, p. 461. Ch'eng Tze-hua, Chairman, All-China Federation of Supply and Marketing Co-operatives: 'The Development of Supply and Marketing Co-operatives in the Past Five Years.' Speech to the National People's Congress, September 1954, and ibid., *1956*, p. 525. Ch'eng Tze-hua: 'Struggle to Fulfil the Task Assigned to Supply and Marketing Co-operatives by the National First Five Year Plan.'

[2] Ibid., *1955*, p. 461. Ch'eng Tze-hua: loc. cit., and *New China Monthly (Xinhua Yuebao)*, No. 61, November 1954, p. 163.

[3] *New China Monthly (Xinhua Yuebao)*, No. 65, March 1955, p. 148.

[4] *People's Handbook (Renmin Shouce) 1955*, p. 461. Ch'eng Tze-hua: loc. cit., and ibid., *1956*, p. 525. Ch'eng Tze-hua: loc. cit.

licensed traders were twice as numerous as private traders had been before 'socialist transformation'.[1] Pedlars made their profits from the large local price differentials which existed for many products, thanks to the high overheads and other deficiencies of state and co-operative commerce.[2] The most startling case reported is that of a woman merchant, Yang Hsiu-ying, who began as a trader in Chungking with ¥300 and had accumulated a large amount of capital. She operated on a wide front, covering all the north-west, as well as the cities of Chungking, Chengtu, Wuhan, Canton and Tientsin. With her title of 'guerilla commander' no wonder she is described as a 'terrifying' phenomenon: clear evidence that 'spontaneous capitalism' still survived.[3] And her case was said to be far from unique. The existence of such activities must be kept constantly in mind while reading about the progress of 'socialist transformation' and the growth of state monopolies.

3. COMMERCIAL LABOUR FORCE

Figures for commercial employment are given by J. P. Emerson[4] as follows:

	1952	1955	1956	1957	1958
Trade	8,450	6,473	7,002	6,719	6,400
Food & Drink Industry (i.e. catering)	1,450	1,350	1,083	1,100	1,100
Total	9,900	7,823	8,085	7,819	7,500

In addition to employed workers in these activities are the self-employed, notably pedlars, both licensed and unlicensed, which one estimate gives as between 5 and 6 million for the years 1955 to 1957.[5]

Problems of estimating the numbers engaged in commerce are complicated by the employment of peasants on a part-time basis. This suits well the sporadic nature of rural trade, with its market days and seasonal pressures. From 1965 onwards particular encouragement was given to the development of part-time rural commercial employment.[6]

4. RELATIONS BETWEEN COMMERCE AND INDUSTRY

The relation between state commerce and industry between 1953 and 1956 was moulded by the desire to curb the initiative of private enterprise in both

---

[1] *Collected Laws and Regulations of the People's Republic of China* (in Chinese), Vol. 6, p. 376, and *New Construction* (*Xin Jianshe*), No. 3, March 1958, pp. 18–19. P'an Ching-yüan: 'The Struggle Between "Two Roads" on the Free Market.'

[2] *Planned Economy* (*Jihua Jingji*), No. 12, December 1956, p. 6. Sung Yi-min: 'Strengthen Leadership Over the Free Market.'

[3] *New Construction* (*Xin Jianshe*), No. 3, March 1958, p. 19. P'an Ching-yüan: loc. cit.

[4] *Non-Agricultural Employment in Mainland China 1949–58*, US Bureau of Census, Washington DC, 1965, p. 128.

[5] Ta-chung Liu and Kung-Chia Yeh: *The Economy of the Chinese Mainland: National Income and Economic Development 1933–59*, Vol. 1. Rand Corporation, Santa Monica, 1963, p. 97.

[6] *Ta Kung Daily* (*Dagong Bao*), Peking, October 8, 1965, p. 1. Editorial, and *New Construction* (*Xin Jianshe*), Nos. 1–2, February 1966, pp. 57–67. Chang Ho-wei: 'An Outline Discussion of the Worker-Peasant System in Finance and Trade.'

commerce and industry. A purely passive role was forced on those factories still in private ownership which were supplied by state commerce with raw materials for processing to its specifications at a fixed charge, the finished goods being marketed exclusively, or at least underwritten, by state commercial organs, thus edging out private wholesalers. Higher level state wholesaling concerns allocated goods to those under them until, in turn, state retail stores had to accept whatever they were sent.

By 1956, with the 'socialist transformation' of large-scale commerce and industry virtually completed, the situation was recognized to have changed. A new policy on the relations between industry and commerce was outlined in speeches by Ch'en Yün and Tseng Shan (whom Ch'en was about to succeed as Minister of Commerce) to the Eighth National Congress of the Chinese Communist Party. For major and relatively simple consumer goods, such as sugar, cotton yarn and cloth, paper, coal, cigarettes and matches (which altogether accounted for some 70 per cent–80 per cent of the value of goods handled by state commerce) the old system was to be retained by which state commerce was the exclusive purchaser or underwriter, although certain modifications in the relations between commerce and industry were to occur even with respect to these items. For 'commodities supplied in fragmentary quantities and of varied and complicated patterns', a change was gradually to be introduced. Factories in future were to manufacture these goods for their own account. State commerce was to have priority for their purchase which would be on a selective basis. What was not bought by state commerce might be marketed by the factories themselves or consigned by the factories to state commerce to be sold on a commission basis on behalf of the factories. At the same time, except for materials in short supply which were to remain under state allocation, factories were to fill all their other raw material requirements by purchases on the free market.[1] The higher state wholesaling organs were no longer to allocate goods to their subordinates for sale but retail stores were to be permitted to buy as they thought fit from any wholesaling organ in the country, or to purchase direct from factories. It was hoped that the new system would lead factories to pay closer attention to consumer demand.[2]

In June 1958 selective buying by retail stores was reported to be in force.[3] However, in the subsequent years of shortages it appears to have lapsed. Not until goods became more plentiful again in 1962 were shops in Peking, usually one of the best supplied places in the country, allowed to buy selectively and then only in the case of certain commodities of relatively small importance.[4] Rural areas were not so fortunate. The cumbersome state commercial machinery, with wholesale depots at three levels, often failed to transmit consumers' desires back to the producers and failed to operate the system of

---

[1] *Eighth National Congress of the Communist Party of China*, Vol. II. Speeches, Peking, 1956, pp. 164–5. Speech by Ch'en Yün, and *Documents of the Eighth National Congress of the Communist Party of China* (in Chinese), Peking, 1956, pp. 640–3. Speech by Tseng Shan, Minister of Commerce.

[2] *Eighth National Congress of the Communist Party of China*, Vol. II. Speeches, pp. 164–5. Speech by Ch'en Yün.

[3] *Financial and Economic Research* (*Caijing Yanjiu*), No. 3, June 1958, p. 64. Hsiao Lin: 'Commercial Work in the Great Leap Forward.'

[4] *Ta Kung Daily* (*Dagong Bao*), Peking, January 11, 1963, p. 1.

selective purchase. By the autumn of 1962 the situation had improved, at least in Kwangtung where 'the practice of rigidly accompanying one kind of commodity with another no longer exists as it used to'. The improvement may have been due to the revival, decreed in May 1962, of the specialized corporations which in 1957-8 were amalgamated with commercial departments: these developments will be further treated below. However, much room still remained for improvement because 'when commodities are purchased, what is usually done is to allow people merely to choose among major categories and to leave them no choice with regard to types or designs'. As a result some *hsien* wholesale departments had to scrap their original plans and buy goods which were not of the kind required by local consumers.[1] Despite the larger amounts of industrial consumer goods becoming available from the early 1960s onwards, supplies to rural areas continued to be inadequate[2] and at times unsuitable, although—as we shall later see—some attempts at market research into peasant requirements have been made.

Turning to relations between state and commerce and factories, it is difficult to assess how far the policy statements made by Ch'en Yün and Tseng Shan in 1956 were in fact implemented. Nine months later, in June 1957, when tighter economic policies were coming into vogue, a writer in *Economic Research* mentioned one school of thought that held that factories and mines should be restrained or prohibited from direct dealings with outsiders.[3] This suggests that such dealings were in fact occurring.

In any case, earlier policies were soon overtaken by the attitudes of the Great Leap, when higher production was encouraged regardless of the suitability of what was being produced—the corollary of this, presumably, being that commercial departments must not dampen factories' enthusiasm by declining to take their output. In the post-Leap period, the shortage of consumer goods might have made it possible for industry to have adopted a 'take it or leave it' attitude, disregarding requests from commercial departments on types of goods. This is borne out by the secret instruction of December 1961, known as the Seventy Points on Industrial Policy, which stipulated that market satisfaction should be industry's primary object.[4] The commercial departments, nevertheless, drew strength from their control of the supply of many scarce raw materials (apart from those subject to direct allocation). By 1964, at any rate, some factories were once again manufacturing to the specification of commercial bodies,[5] with their production supervised by commercial representatives on the factory floor.[6] We hear of a dyestuffs fac-

[1] *Southern Daily* (*Nanfang Ribao*), September 29, 1962 (SCMP 2864). Lu Ch'i-mo and Li Ch'ung-ch'ing: loc. cit. See also *Ta Kung Daily* (*Dagong Bao*), Peking, February 24, 1963, p. 1. Editorial, and ibid., March 22, 1963, p. 1.

[2] *Ta Kung Daily* (*Dagong Bao*), Peking, November 28, 1964, p. 1. Editorial, and ibid., June 23, 1965, p. 1. Editorial, and *Far Eastern Economic Review*, February 18, 1965, p. 290. A. Close: 'Correcting the Cadres.'

[3] *Economic Research* (*Jingji Yanjiu*), No. 3, June 1957, p. 55. Fan Jo-yi: 'A Further Discussion of Price Policy for Products of Heavy Industry.'

[4] *Seventy Important Points of Communist Industrial Policy*, 1961. (From Taiwan source.) No. 2.

[5] *Ta Kung Daily* (*Dagong Bao*), Peking, January 2, 1964, p. 2. Editorial.

[6] *New Statesman*, September 3, 1965, p. 321. K. S. Karol: 'Maoism: China's Secular Religion—A Twentieth-Century Experiment in Puritan Ethics.'

tory which had itself to find buyers if it decided to raise output,[1] and of a steel tube plant losing customers to a rival whose goods were of a better quality.[2] Other factories were denounced for giving presents to retailers to win their goodwill.[3]

Bound up with the relations between industry and commerce is the question of overlap between the two. At least, in the early 1950s, before Ch'en Yün's policy statement in September 1956, the official attitude as far as consumer goods were concerned was that industry should not market products and that commerce should not undertake industrial tasks. This attitude tended to lengthen the series of commercial links between producer and ultimate consumer,[4] a condition which was endemic in Chinese commerce long before the arrival of the Communists and has by them been transmogrified but not checked.

Despite earlier policy, commercial organs certainly did control industrial concerns during the First Five Year Plan period, because the decentralization measures of 1957–8 made express provision for them. Many of these industrial undertakings were plants processing agricultural produce, but others evidently did not come within this category.[5] In the Great Leap, when units of all types were urged to take up industrial production, it is not surprising that commercial departments were actively encouraged to do so, especially in the countryside. Enterprises they controlled included plants processing agricultural produce and pioneering concerns established to provide models in rural areas (e.g. fertilizer plants).[6]

In 1958, some agricultural processing plants were handed over from commercial organs to communes. Very likely some of these later reverted to commercial control. However, others continued to be operated by units of collective agriculture, and this was further encouraged in 1966 by the 'worker-peasant' movement to combine agricultural labour with industrial labour.[7]

5. DIVISION OF COMMODITIES INTO CATEGORIES AND BETWEEN MINISTRIES

At first, except for certain metals and ores,[8] the state commercial organs operated alongside private merchants. From 1951 they became the sole buyers of cotton yarn,[9] and from 1953 they had a monopoly of dealings in many

[1] *China Reconstructs*, August 1965, p. 32. Chang Chuan-wen: 'How Higher Production Targets Are Fulfilled.'
[2] *People's Daily (Renmin Ribao)*, December 8, 1965, p. 2. Hsü An-ch'eng, Assistant Manager, Seamless Steel Tube Plant, Anshan Iron and Steel Works: 'When Our Customers Are Satisfied, We Shall Be Satisfied.'
[3] *Southern Daily (Nanfang Ribao)*, January 14, 1966, p. 1.
[4] *Economic Research (Jingji Yanjiu)*, No. 3, June 1957, p. 60. Fan Jo-yi: loc. cit.
[5] *Collected Laws and Regulations of the People's Republic of China* (in Chinese), Vol. 6, p. 356, and ibid., Vol. 7, p. 322.
[6] *People's Handbook (Renmin Shouce) 1959*, p. 361. Speech by Ma Ming-fang, Director of the CCP Central Committee's Finance and Trade Work Department.
[7] *New Construction (Xin Jianshe)*, Nos. 1–2, February 1966, p. 58. Chang Ho-wei: loc. cit.
[8] Choh-ming Li: op. cit., p. 20, fn. 50. In 1950 state companies were given a monopoly of the purchase, supply and export of wolfram, aluminium and tin ore and ingots.
[9] *People's Handbook (Renmin Shouce) 1955*, p. 457.

other important commodities with the introduction of two practices known respectively as 'planned purchase and planned supply' and 'unified purchase'.[1] Under both practices the commercial departments of the state, together with the supply and marketing co-operatives, were the sole authorized buyers of the specified commodities. In the case of 'planned purchase and planned supply', in addition, supply was rationed to the consumer: the goods falling under this system were those considered most essential to control—food grains, edible oils, raw cotton, cotton yarn and cotton cloth. The distribution of commodities under 'planned purchase and planned supply' was controlled by the State Council, acting originally through the State Economic Commission, the task being transferred to the State Planning Commission in the course of 1958.[2]

Agricultural produce subject to 'unified purchase' covered items next most significant to the national economy for consumption or export including, by 1957, cured tobacco, kenafe, ramie, hemp, sugar-cane, domestic silk cocoons (together with native-type silk), tea, live pigs, wool, cowhide and other important kinds of skins, native-type paper and sugar, tung oil, certain kinds of bamboo products, lacquer, walnuts, almonds, melon seeds, chestnuts, major timber products from regions of concentrated production, certain important Chinese medicinal materials, and apples and oranges for export. Aquatic products for export or for supplying large cities (from certain fishing regions), scrap copper, scrap aluminium, scrap lead and scrap steel also fell into this category. The distribution of commodities subject to 'unified purchase' was controlled by various central government ministries (see below); these goods were, therefore, sometimes called 'ministry-controlled materials'.[3] Provincial authorities were empowered to make additions to the list. Goods subject to distribution according to 'planned purchase and planned supply' and 'unified purchase' have been known respectively as first and second category commodities, with less important agricultural produce coming under a third category, not subject to central distribution. Local authorities have had responsibility for any control thought necessary for third category commodities.

Industrial goods were divided into two categories: first, those distributed by the Ministry of Commerce and the specialized national corporations which local authorities were forbidden to buy direct from centres of production and, second, those not subject to this restriction.[4]

These classifications were not always observed or perhaps even understood by those engaged in commerce. In 1956, for example, some industrial and mining areas were being forced to buy all their vegetables through the state

---

[1] The use of these terms varied at different dates, e.g. in *New China Monthly (Xinhua Yuebao)*, No. 71, September 1955, p. 160, the term 'unified purchase and unified supply' is used in the case of grain.

[2] *Collected Laws and Regulations* . . . Vol. 6, pp. 366–9, and *Planned Economy (Jihua Jingji)*, No. 10, October 1958, p. 34. She Yi-san: 'A Discussion of the Change in the Allocation System for Raw Materials'.

[3] *Collected Laws and Regulations* . . . Vol. 6, p. 368, and *Planned Economy (Jihua Jingji)*, No. 1, January 1958, p. 38. Sun Hui-ch'ing: 'Lecture No. 13: Charts of Supply Plans of Raw Materials and Technical Equipment'.

[4] *Collected Laws and Regulations*, . . . Vol. 6, pp. 369–70.

vegetable company, instead of being allowed to buy direct from the peasants as should have been permitted in the case of third category farm products.[1]

In February 1959 the division of commercial commodities into three categories was promulgated afresh in greater detail, presumably on the basis of the experience of the past two years and in the light of changing priorities. It should be noted that the same categories now covered many industrial as well as agricultural goods. The first category comprised thirty-eight products 'of the greatest importance to national planning and the people's livelihood'. The targets for their purchase, sale, transfer, import, export and stockpiling were to be controlled by the State Council. Included in the first category were those goods under 'planned purchase and planned supply' and a number of others, such as petroleum and petroleum products, sugar, tobacco, edible salt and various commodities of special significance as exports (e.g. hides and skins, pig bristles, carpets, silk, and some minerals).[2] (It will be noted that some very important raw materials, including steel, iron, coal, machinery and cotton yarn, are not included in this list. These are allocated by organs of the central government direct to the major consumers and provincial level authorities, thus bypassing commercial channels. Hence they are not considered 'commodities', except for the minor quantities which are distributed through the market, on which see below.)

The second category covered goods of a lesser but still considerable importance, to the total of 293 commodities. Among them were items which figured prominently among exports or which gave rise to particular problems of distribution because their production was concentrated and their consumption widespread or vice versa. The State Council was to lay down policy in respect of these products and effect 'balance transfer' (i.e. control the quantities subject to inter-provincial allocation, plus exports).[3] Some of these second category commodities might need a further degree of control which would be undertaken by the relevant ministry (see below). Second category commodities included various fibres, tea, live pigs, beef, mutton, poultry, eggs, woollen cloth, machine-made paper, rubber shoes, bicycles, chemical fertilizers and agricultural chemicals. All commodities that were not in the first and second categories, nor separately notified, were to come within the third category, and were subject to a number of different types of control as befitted their varied nature.[4]

The division of commodities among the categories was not immutable. In 1958 the first two categories together comprised 417 items. By February 1959 this number had been reduced to 331.[5] At the end of 1960 an article in a

---

[1] *Documents of the Eighth National Congress of the Communist Party of China* (in Chinese). Speech by Yao Yi-lin, Vice Minister of Commerce, p. 791.
[2] *Collected Laws and Regulations* . . . Vol. 9, pp. 159–63.
[3] In the case of some goods, the State Council would control only 'balance transfer' between major centres of production and consumption. On the somewhat blurred division of responsibility between different organs of the State Council for carrying out such allocatory duties see pp. 477–8 below.
[4] *Collected Laws and Regulations* . . . Vol. 9, pp. 159–63.
[5] *Planned Economy (Jihua Jingji)*, No. 10, October 1958, p. 34. She Yi-san: loc. cit. This source had envisaged a reduction in the number of commodities in these two categories in 1959 to only 132, and *Collected Laws and Regulations* . . . Vol. 9, p. 159.

Kwangtung paper states that some goods formerly belonging to the second category might be transferred to the third.[1] No list of commodities according to category of a date later than 1959 has come to our notice and it is possible that the division between second and third category goods now rests with the provincial level authorities.

Commodities were divided not only according to these three categories, but also according to which ministry was to control them. The Ministries of Commerce, Food, Foreign Trade, Forestry, Health, Aquatic Products and Light Industry all have their own commercial networks. By far the greatest volume of trade comes under the Ministries of Commerce and of Food. The Ministry of Commerce controls a large assortment of products including cotton (raw, yarn and cloth), and other fibres, tobacco, sugar, petroleum, meat, eggs: it appears to have all those items which are not, for one reason or another, connected with some other ministry.[2] Among the goods distributed by the Ministry of Commerce are the quantities set aside for the market of certain important raw materials such as coal, tin and steel, of which, as we have seen, the major quantities are subject to direct allocation. Smaller consumers cannot conveniently be supplied by allocation and so a proportion of such materials is put aside for the general market, to be distributed through the commercial system.[3] Each of the 'commercial ministries' has responsibilities shared with local authorities for effecting local balances and arranging transfers between localities of the commodities with which it is concerned.[4]

The Ministry of Food has under it the all-important trade in food grains, as well as vegetable oils, edible and non-edible. The Ministry of Light Industry controls the trade in edible salt (which it had taken over on absorbing the former Ministry of Food Industry) but apparently no other commodity. A wide selection of goods that figure prominently among Chinese exports come under the Ministry of Foreign Trade in respect of internal as well as of external trade. The Ministry of Health is charged with the trade in many medicines and medicinal raw materials, while commerce in fish is controlled by the Ministry of Aquatic Products.[5] In 1960 the Ministry of Forestry took over from the Ministry of Commerce the distribution of timber.[6] The Ministry of Culture controls the Hsin Hua (New China) Book Store, with branches all over the country, which is responsible for the sale of books, newspapers and periodicals. In China these are not reckoned as commercial commodities and therefore the Ministry of Culture does not figure among the commercial ministries.

The system of dividing commercial responsibilities among a number of ministries (some of which were primarily engaged in other tasks) was not a new departure in 1959, but merely confirmed an existing practice which probably dated from 1956. Indeed there is evidence that with the devolution of commercial activities to local authorities in 1957–8, which we shall soon

[1] *Southern Daily* (*Nanfang Ribao*), December 28, 1960 (SCMP 2429). Ch'en Yi-yen: 'Small Freedoms and Spontaneous Influences'.
[2] *Collected Laws and Regulations* . . . Vol. 9, pp. 159–63, and ibid., Vol. 11, p. 127.
[3] *Statistical Work* (*Tongji Gongzuo*), No. 13, July 14, 1957, p. 30.
[4] *Collected Laws and Regulations* . . . Vol. 8, p. 99.
[5] Ibid., Vol. 9, pp. 160–3.
[6] Ibid., Vol. 11, p. 127.

discuss, the trade networks of some ministries may have been reduced in scope.¹

6. THE DECENTRALIZATION OF COMMERCE

The Decree on the Reform of the Commercial Management System, promulgated in 1957, was in line with the general decentralization of economic administration that was put in hand at this period. At a meeting of the heads of provincial level departments of commerce, held in August 1957, a decision was reported to go ahead with decentralization on the basis of experience gained in pilot experiments.² The actual measures to be taken were published three months later, in November 1957.

The chief effect of these measures was to devolve authority from Peking to the provinces and the lower local authorities. Previously, Grade 1 wholesale depots, large refrigerating plants and granaries had been under the sole control of the central authorities; now these were placed under dual central and provincial level control, although the central government was to remain the senior partner. (In a similar fashion, provinces were to share with lower authorities control over Grade 2 wholesale depots.) Processing plants belonging to commercial ministries of the central government were, with certain exceptions, to be transferred to the control of the commercial departments of local authorities. However, the central government ministries were to retain far-reaching powers over the operations of concerns thus transferred. The number and complexity of the annual targets fixed by the State Council for commercial work were to be reduced, parallel to the similar reduction in targets for industrial establishments which occurred at this time. In each case the targets were now to number only four, and for commerce these were to be the purchasing plan, the selling plan (we are not told in what form the purchasing and sales targets were to be couched), the total number of employees and the amount of profits. The local authorities were given a latitude of 5 per cent in either direction in fulfilling the plans for buying and selling. However, as far as goods controlled by the central government's commercial ministries were concerned, permission had to be gained before making any alteration affecting them; while in the case of food grain, oils and cotton, the approval of the State Council was ordinarily necessary before any changes were made, although in special circumstances a province might act without this and subsequently report its action to the State Council. The targets for profits would be given by the central government to the provincial level authorities, but these authorities were not to transmit profits targets

---

¹ *Collected Laws and Regulations*...Vol. 8, pp. 172–3 on the partial dismantling of the local levels of the Ministry of Foreign Trade's 'system'. In 1956 the Ministry of Commerce was reported to have been 'divided into six ministries'. (Ibid., Vol. 6, p. 360.) This presumably referred to the division of commercial responsibilities among several ministries. In 1959 a reference occurs to 'six ministries' engaged in commerce, meaning the ministries of Commerce, Food, Foreign Trade, Health, Aquatic Products, and Light Industry (ibid., Vol. 9, pp. 165 and 158). The six of 1956 were probably not identical with this list, e.g. because of the existence, at that time, of the Ministry of Urban Services.

² *People's Handbook* (*Renmin Shouce*) *1958*, p. 550. The local experiments, confined to some *hsien*, were announced in the spring of 1957. NCNA Peking, March 7, 1957.

downwards to commercial enterprises. Nevertheless, commercial enterprises were not, on their own initiative, to cause their profits to be lowered. The new departure, by which target figures for commercial profits were not notified to the basic level enterprises, was made to avert undesirable practices to which these had resorted in efforts to reach the targets. The change was regarded as an important one which should be put into practice on an experimental scale before being extended to the whole country.[1]

Profits of enterprises under commercial ministries of the central government were by the decree of 1957 to be divided between the central treasury and the provinces and equivalent authorities in the ratio of 80:20 as in the case of industrial undertakings. An exception was made for the grain trade, all of whose profits were to go to the central government, as was that portion of the profits on foreign trade which derived from sales abroad.[2] The 1957 decree also provided for the partial decentralization of price control. This will be treated in Chapter 16.

The local specialized corporations were to be merged with the local commercial departments; some large cities and certain other unspecified places were exempt from this provision if investigation showed it to be impracticable.[3] It appears that a parallel merger took place at the national level between the national specialized companies and the ministries engaged in commercial activities.[4] These changes resulted in a great loss of authority for the Ministry of Commerce. It had controlled many of the national corporations which, in turn, controlled the local corporations. Now the local corporations were absorbed by local departments, over which the Ministry of Commerce could exercise small influence.[5] One result was that after the decentralization measures came into force, very considerable divergences developed between the commercial systems of different localities.[6] In Chapter 6 we have seen that in industry, likewise, local differences have occurred in the respective roles of local corporations and local departments.

It must not be imagined that these administrative decrees went into practice immediately and with equal thoroughness all over the country. Both on grounds of general reasoning and from internal evidence it seems that at first the implementation was local and tentative; and, in some cases, the intention that this should be so was explicitly stated.

7. URBAN COMMERCE

While rural markets and supply and marketing co-operatives are, as we shall see, the most important channels of trade in the countryside, state commercial bodies predominate in urban trade.

The responsibilities of municipal departments of commerce have often

---

[1] *Collected Laws and Regulations* . . . Vol. 6, pp. 355–7. See also p. 315 below.
[2] Ibid., pp. 356–7.
[3] Ibid., p. 355.
[4] We learn this from announcements in 1959 and 1962 of the re-establishment of national trading corporations, see *Collected Laws and Regulations* . . . Vol. 11, p. 128, and ibid., Vol. 13, p. 138.
[5] F. Schurmann: *Ideology and Organization in Communist China*, Berkeley, 1966, p. 208.
[6] *Collected Laws and Regulations* . . . Vol. 8, p. 172.

extended far beyond the normal scope of trade. They were reported, for example, to have played a great role in the life of the urban communes as in the street associations which preceded them. From 1958 onwards, local commercial departments were prominent in 'organizing the economic life of city dwellers'.[1] Their sphere included the provision of many of the collective services which made possible the mobilization of the housewives for work outside their homes. The Minister of Commerce, Yao Yi-lin, speaking in April 1960, gave the special tasks of commercial organs in urban communes as helping to establish mess halls, nurseries, service and welfare facilities, and the distribution of commodities, including the operation of a rationing system for non-staple consumer goods.[2] Commercial bodies were also expected to play an active part in developing production. The exact role of the commercial departments has varied greatly from city to city—in some cases they have been reported responsible for much of economic life, while in others they have had scant mention. In Chungking, where the commercial organizations have been particularly prominent, the comprehensive stores, one of which was opened in each street committee's area, became keypoints in economic life; the Party organizations of the comprehensive stores and of the streets keeping in close contact through inter-locking secretariats.[3] The area stores in Chungking stood at the head of a network of 'service stations' and personnel, including women selling goods for the stores at a commission of 2 per cent.[4]

One reason for the prominence of commercial departments in urban communes was that many of the street factories which the communes controlled, were established to fill gaps in the supply of small consumer goods—to make things that proved unobtainable from other sources, or which had been omitted from the production plan. The commercial departments would naturally be in the best position to determine these gaps while also, of course, they distributed the finished products. Other street factories functioned as outworkers to large state manufacturing enterprises, supplying their needs of components and semi-manufactured goods. In both cases these small factories imparted a degree of flexibility into the distributive system which had been hampered by the rigidity of planning. Once an item had been entered into, or left out of the plans, it was difficult for any changes to be made quickly in response to market needs. In any case, the fact that the supply of goods might be planned did not necessarily mean that they became available when they should, especially if they had to come from another part of the country. Thus, the street factories, providing consumer goods for local needs on the one hand, and semi-manufactures for large factories on the other hand, solved many problems for the city commercial departments and for the supply departments of the factories.

However, not all problems of supply could be solved by this means. Some raw materials and other commodities could not be produced locally and great

[1] *People's Daily* (*Renmin Ribao*), May 19, 1960, p. 6. Editorial.
[2] Ibid., April 9, 1960, p. 2.
[3] *Red Flag* (*Hongqi*), No. 5, March 1, 1960, p. 41. Jen Po-ke: 'Organizing Urban Residents' Economic Life Is an Important Aspect of Building New Socialist Cities.'
[4] *People's Daily* (*Renmin Ribao*), March 11, 1960, p. 7. Survey Team, Finance and Trade Department, CCP Chungking Municipal Committee: 'Everyone Attends to Everyone's Business, the Masses Control the Life of the Masses.'

difficulties arose because of the increased demands made by the Great Leap and the clogging up of the transport system in 1958. These difficulties were accentuated by the general shortages of agricultural raw materials after the poor harvests of 1959–61. Factory staff had to spend much time and effort on trying to procure raw materials and, in doing so, had to go outside the official channels of commerce or of the planning system. We have an account given, quite incidentally, of how, in August 1958, a radio factory in Peking sent members of its staff to the Municipal Party Committee to negotiate a supply of industrial chemicals. The factory's usual suppliers in Tientsin had offered to provide their needs in exchange for two lorries; this was condemned as 'departmentalism'. 'These materials have previously been supplied from other places. Now in the Great Leap Forward everyone wants to supply his own local demand first. So there is a problem of supplying other places. At the same time the Peking Municipal Party Committee wants all factories to get their materials locally and to attain self-sufficiency.'[1]

In these circumstances, enterprises have sometimes to dispatch staff or agents to scour the country to get some wanted item. In May 1958 a report told of a Shanghai teahouse which, in the old days, had been a centre for rice dealers and certain other traders, but now was an acknowledged mart for metals and machinery, with patrons coming from all parts of China. For example, a man from Inner Mongolia, charged with buying a generator, had failed to get a suitable one in Peking, Tientsin, Wuhan or through usual channels in Shanghai, but succeeded when visiting this tea-house. Tea-house transactions on the whole were said to have declined in importance 'following the steady broadening of the scope of the planned market'. Shanghai, however, remained a nation-wide market where goods unprocurable elsewhere could be obtained, partly because of the large and varied stocks that were carried there, and partly because of the activities of 'a group of people acting as intermediaries for disposing or getting hold of many of the privately-held items not obtainable on the market'. Also a number of enterprises in Shanghai still distributed their own products themselves. In an attempt to maintain some control of prices, the Industry and Commerce Bureau of Shanghai Municipality set up three exchanges in tea-houses.[2] Another reason for the flourishing market in Shanghai must have been the hundreds of 'clandestine industrial establishments' existing there in 1957.[3] No doubt, in addition to that part of the market which the municipal authorities attempted to control through the tea-house exchanges, there has been a luxuriant undergrowth engendered by the 'spontaneous capitalist' forces which were denounced in vain.

The purchasing agents employed by enterprises, departments of local authorities and other bodies, perform a necessary function in the economy, as do their counterparts, the *tolkachi*, in the Soviet Union. Their job is to cut through the dilatory mechanism of the planning, allocating and commercial

[1] *China Youth (Zhongguo Quingnian)*, No. 19, October 1, 1958, pp. 39–40. Lu Mu-lan: 'An Unexpected Meeting with Premier Chou.'
[2] *Liberation Daily (Jiefang Ribao)*, May 7, 1958 (SCMP 1794). Li Yin: 'Ch'inglienko Tea-House in Shanghai Enters a New Era'.
[3] *People's Daily (Renmin Ribao)*, October 13, 1957 p. 4.

systems in order to obtain urgently needed supplies and equipment without which enterprises would be crippled or hardships caused to large numbers of consumers. Although they have no place in the official scheme of commerce, their existence is accorded a grudging recognition. In 1957 it was laid down that certain provinces and cities might be allowed to establish purchasing offices at industrial centres. It was hoped that these offices would keep purchasing agents from their respective localities under control. Purchasing agents of state and joint state-private enterprises, supply and marketing co-operatives and handicraft co-operatives had to register with the appropriate local departments where they intended to operate. They were not to buy goods subject to planned or unified purchase or commodities being processed under contract with state commercial bodies. Agents were first to approach the wholesale departments of the local state companies and if these could not supply their needs they might, with the approval of the local authorities, deal direct with enterprises producing the goods required or with the higher level of exchange markets (probably the commodity interchange meetings to be discussed below), or the wholesale market, but they were not permitted to buy from retail outlets. Apparently agents from outside had been going round buying large quantities of scarce goods by offering high prices.[1]

In addition to these agents there have also been independent brokers, working on commission. Official disapproval of them is strong, although they do not appear to have been completely forbidden. It was stipulated in 1957 that they should be controlled, 'educated' and 'transformed' and that their scope and commission might be fixed; in the markets for some commodities they might be banned, and in any case they were prohibited to deal in goods subject to planned or unified purchase. Experienced men from among them could, it was suggested, be given commercial employment.[2]

In May 1962 a State Council decree ordered that specialized corporations, which in 1957–8 had been amalgamated with the central and local commercial ministries and departments, should be revived or established anew. Three types of corporations were envisaged by this decree, differing according to the extent of vertical (from higher level corporations over local corporations) or horizontal (by local authority) control.[3]

8. RURAL TRADE

The periodic rural markets, which had formerly been of great economic and social significance in the Chinese countryside, almost ceased to exist after the introduction, in 1953, of 'planned purchase and planned supply' and 'unified purchase'. In the summer of 1956, to counter the inflationary pressures of that time, the reopening of the rural markets was encouraged. At first there was uncertainty about which commodities might be sold there; then in October 1956 a decree laid down that first and second category goods,

---

[1] *Collected Laws and Regulations* ... Vol. 6, pp. 375–6.
[2] Ibid., p. 377.
[3] Ibid., Vol. 13, pp. 138–40. The Timber Corporation had already been re-established by a decision of December 1959. Ibid., Vol. 11, p. 128.

together with some others for which 'supply does not meet demand', were to be excluded from the markets. However, this ban appears to have been modified before long and second category items permitted after compulsory sales had been fulfilled.¹

Nine provinces were reported to have re-opened rural markets in August 1956, either throughout the whole province or, more frequently, at certain places only. Between August and November the movement apparently did not spread to any other provinces,² although in subsequent months markets may have been revived more widely. As well as the basic level 'standard markets', serving the ordinary needs of the peasants, some higher level markets were also reopened.³

At the same time another traditional commercial institution was also revived, the trade warehouse (*maoyi huochan*). This wholesaling unit belies the passive sound of its literal English translation. In the old days, traders not only stored goods at these warehouses, but also did business and were boarded there; the managers too would provide them with commercial contacts. With the withering of the free market system, these warehouses had evidently ceased to operate. Early in 1957 more than 1,200 warehouses were reported to have been re-activated or newly opened in two provinces alone. Some warehouses were state-owned, others under joint state-private ownership. Some were specialized to one trade, and others catered for a wide variety. This movement had by February 1957 affected ten provinces; of the five named, four also figured among the nine provinces where free markets had been reopened by November 1956.⁴

By the summer of 1957 the government was reconsidering the policy of permitting free markets. In practice it had been found impossible to keep the relaxation within the limits laid down, and many agricultural and other products subject to unified purchase entered the market before compulsory deliveries had been completed. Even commodities subject to planned purchase were sold at the markets while, as we have seen, in many places peasants were deserting agriculture for trade.⁵ Therefore, in August 1957, the State Council issued a decree banning from the markets all agricultural produce subject to planned purchase and to unified purchase. According to this decree, if—after fulfilling their compulsory sales quotas—the peasants wished to sell any more of such commodities, they were to do so only to the state purchasing stores or other agents of the state, including supply and marketing co-operatives.⁶

¹ *Collected Laws and Regulations* . . . Vol. 4, pp. 330–1, and Vol. 6, p. 367.
² *People's Handbook* (*Renmin Shouce*) *1957*, p. 519, and *Collected Laws and Regulations* . . . Vol. 4, p. 330.
³ e.g. that at Chengtu, which attracted buyers of medicinal materials from as far as Shanghai. *People's Handbook* (*Renmin Shouce*) *1957*, p. 519. On 'standard' and higher level markets see p. 35 above.
⁴ *People's Handbook* (*Renmin Shouce*) *1957*, p. 519, and *Collected Laws and Regulations* . . . Vol. 6, pp. 379–80.
⁵ *Collected Laws and Regulations* . . . Vol. 6, p. 367, and *Planned Economy* (*Jinhua Jingji*), No. 12, December 1956, p. 7. Sung Yi-min: loc. cit.
⁶ *Collected Laws and Regulations* . . . Vol. 6, pp. 366–9. From August–October 1957 markets for grain were permitted to be opened in certain provinces where the local grain supply position was good. In the latter month this permission was revoked (ibid., pp. 368 and 353).

Below we shall be following the history of the rural markets after the formation of the communes.

The growth of local self-sufficiency, inherent in the decentralization measures of 1957–8, was carried further by the outstanding administration innovation of this period—the formation of people's communes throughout rural China in the summer and autumn of 1958. In that year, when a bounteous harvest led to the belief that problems of agricultural production were almost solved, great stress was laid on the development of rural industry of which the communes were to be the instruments. This would mean that they could supply much of their own requirements in the way of light industrial goods.

The collectivization of social life in 1958, partial and temporary as it was, lessened the scope of retail trade because it meant that many foodstuffs, and sometimes other consumer goods, went only to mess halls and other public institutions. This development, together with the increased employment of women outside the home, led to a change in the type of goods demanded: for example, large cooking utensils were required for the public mess halls, the fact that fires for cooking were no longer lit in homes led to a demand for thermos flasks in which hot water could be brought back from the mess halls; women no longer had time for making clothes, and so garments and cloth shoes had to be bought ready made. The upsurge in production in 1958, and the ambitious plans that were laid at that time, caused substantial orders to be placed for capital equipment for agriculture, water conservancy, transport and rural industry.

While the establishment of the people's communes temporarily changed the nature of the rural market, it also affected the machinery both of collection of agricultural produce and of distribution of consumer and other goods. The commune was to be an all-inclusive, basic unit of rural life, thus embracing commerce along with other activities—economic, social, and political. The exact relationship of the commercial element in the communes to the commune organization on the one hand, and to the state commercial system on the other, was not clear and doubtless varied from district to district, from province to province and from one short period to another. A good deal was written about this subject in the Chinese press, but here—as elsewhere—it is sometimes hard to decide if what was said was an account of actual circumstances or of what might ideally be desired. In many instances the common practice of the Chinese press was followed, according to which a detailed account was given of the situation in one particular area or commune (perhaps idealized in the telling), with the implication that this model was worthy to be copied. In yet other articles, couched in general terms, a number of possible solutions to the problem of commercial organization were set out. From all these sources a picture can be drawn, not in clear outline, but probably no more confused than the real situation.

The supply and marketing co-operatives, together with the lowest levels of state commerce, were to be changed into supply and marketing departments of the communes.[1] However, while they were placed under the local commune,

---

[1] In some places supply and marketing departments had been established in agricultural producers' co-operatives some months before the communes were formed. See *Ta Kung Daily* (*Dagong Bao*), Peking, April 28, 1958, p. 2. Wang K'e: 'A Tentative Discussion of

their operation was to be closely controlled from above. This was the policy of 'two decentralizations, three centralizations and one guarantee' which Li Hsien-nien, Minister of Finance, propounded in the autumn of 1958,[1]—the 'decentralizations' of personnel and assets of the state's rural financial and trade organs to the communes, the 'centralizations' of economic policy, planning and of working capital, and the 'one guarantee' being the guarantee of tax payment. According to Li Hsien-nien, 'the supply and marketing department of the commune is the organ of the commune in distributing commodities and is also the basic level organ of state commerce'.[2] The state financial and trading departments were still to maintain relations of 'professional leadership with the financial and trading organs of the communes'.[3] Contracts, according to Li, would be the main commercial link co-ordinating state and commune plans.

Sometimes the operations of state and commune commercial organs were parallel rather than combined. We read of a commune in Honan where, in September 1958, the basic level commercial machinery was split between the two systems, 'one is the commodities purchasing and supply station of the commercial departments with fourteen retail stores. The other is the system of supply and marketing departments in seventeen natural villages under the leadership of the commune'.[4] When and where the state commercial machinery should be withdrawn in order to leave the field to commune-controlled commerce was something which, it was recognized, must be decided according to circumstances.[5]

Another matter on which it was impossible to lay down a fixed rule was whether all commercial work (including distribution of commodities which in pre-commune days would have been commercial) should be channelled through the commune's commercial department. It was thought unnecessary that the commercial department should handle means of production (e.g. small farm tools) produced for use inside the same commune. It was a more complex question whether subordinate parts of a commune—production teams, for example, or the commune's industrial department—might contact the state commercial organization only through the intermediary of the commune's department of commerce. However, from the early days of the communes this was felt too cumbersome. For example, production teams had direct dealings with state commercial organs for the purpose of taking delivery of supplies, although the original indents were supposed to go through the commercial department of the commune. Similarly, deliveries of agricultural

---

Supply and Marketing Departments of Agricultural Producer Co-operatives', and ibid., May 26, 1958 (SCMP 1797). Li Jen, Kan Fu and Tsung Shun: 'Several Views on the Problem of Establishing a Supply and Marketing Department for the Agricultural Producers' Co-operatives.'

[1] *Red Flag* (*Hongqi*), No. 10, October 16, 1958, p. 7. Li Hsien-nien: 'A Look at the People's Communes.'
[2] Ibid., p. 8. See also p. 71 above.
[3] Ibid.
[4] *Commercial Work* (*Shangye Gongzuo*) September 3, 1958 (SCMP 1910).
[5] *Ta Kung Daily* (*Dagong Bao*), Peking, September 28, 1958, p. 3. Chung Fu: 'A Discussion of Some Commercial Problems in People's Communes.'

produce to the state might be made directly by production teams or by the specialized departments of the commune. It was considered superfluous for the state commercial organization to maintain its own machinery inside the communes for collection of agricultural produce, although it might need to station a few of its own workers there for liaison purposes.[1]

A matter which at first gave rise to some uncertainty was whether the commune's commercial department should buy only from the state commercial organization, or whether it might also go to other sources for its requirements. It was soon apparent that to insist that all commercial dealings by communes with the world outside should be channelled through the state commercial organization would be hopelessly restrictive. In some cases there was obvious need for direct contact with sources of supply, even when it meant bypassing the state system. There was no great enthusiasm in the early days of the communes for commercial contacts of this nature, perhaps because horizontal trade links—between communes, for instance—are more difficult to fit into a plan than vertical ones between a commune and the state commercial organization. Nevertheless, some such trade was seen to be necessary.

In these circumstances, contracts were intended as one of the principal instruments for implementing state commercial plans. The use of contracts for this purpose preceded the establishment of the communes,[2] but now more importance was attached to it than previously. The sixth plenary session of the Eighth CCP Central Committee, held in December 1958, resolved that 'to see the exchange plan is realized, the contract system should be extensively introduced between the state and communes and between different communes'. The contract system was 'an important means of implementing the state's planned leadership over the people's communes'.[3]

The nature and significance of contracts in contemporary China have already been considered[4] and we have seen that this term 'contract' does not imply a voluntary agreement as in Western usage. In rural commerce, contracts have been used to particularize the demands of the state for compulsory deliveries of agricultural products. Their importance has been especially great in the case of third category commodities, the contract system being the intended method for bringing these into the orbit of state planning. Contracts with state commercial organs are made at all levels in the rural economy, down to the production team and individual peasants. Details, such as delivery dates, can be put into contracts; so also can quality specifications, especially useful with those minor commodities which cannot be classified into broad grades as easily as, for example, grain and cotton. In some cases, peasants are given individual 'contract handbooks' in which are entered the quotas of various products they have to supply.

In 1959 the need to promote production of third category commodities was urgent. The formation of the communes had in many places put an end to the domestic manufacture of a host of small consumer goods—straw sandals and

---

[1] *Ta Kung Daily* (*Dagong Bao*), Peking, September 28, 1958, p. 3. Chung Fu: loc. cit.
[2] See e.g. *New China Monthly* (*Xinhua Yuebao*), No. 61, November 1954, pp. 163–8.
[3] *Ta Kung Daily* (*Dagong Bao*), Peking, February 20, 1959 (SCMP 1980). Li Ch'eng-jui and Yang Ch'un-hsü: 'Apply the Contract System Extensively.'
[4] See pp. 28–9 above.

other items of clothing, household implements and so forth. Some local authorities failed to make any provision for the continued production of such goods. The same held true, in places, of certain fruits and vegetables, the collection of plants, fishing and even of raising pigs and poultry.[1] Thus in the first months after the communes were established, severe shortages developed of many products of this type. By bringing third category commodities into the planning system through contracts, it was hoped to resolve these difficulties. At the same time this would help diversify the communes' economy, an aim on which great stress was laid in the early days of the commune movement.

Formalized contracts, however, were no substitute for regular rural markets in encouraging the output of all this miscellaneous produce. The restrictions re-imposed in 1957 on the types of commodities permitted to be sold at these markets had caused them to decline. In the following year, even before the formation of the communes, many had ceased to be held.[2] Then in the early days of the communes, the peasants had neither time nor produce of their own, and consequently—at least over wide areas—the traditional peasant markets disappeared. Rural life must have been much duller in their absence. In addition, the economic consequences were serious especially, as we have seen, in respect of minor farm products, the third category commodities.

Not only had the basic level markets lapsed, but wholesaling arrangements for the less important commodities had also atrophied. Trade warehouses had apparently gone out of business and the periodic markets at major centres ('intermediate' and 'central markets'[3]) had evidently also stopped business. From the summer of 1959 attempts were made to fill the wholesaling gap by organizing special 'meetings for the circulation of third category goods' at different levels. The first such meeting at the national level was convened by the Ministries of Commerce and Light Industry for two weeks in May 1959, at Shanghai, and was attended by thirty delegations from provincial level authorities. They concluded contracts for the sale and purchase of many types of goods and also made agreements for technical co-operation.[4] In February 1960 it was announced that national meetings for the circulation of third category goods would be held regularly twice a year.[5]

Similar meetings were enjoined to be held at lower administrative levels, from the province downwards, where arrangements could be made by sub-contracting down to communes, brigades, and factories, for the production and purchase of the goods promised by contract at the national meetings.[6] This type of contract was very difficult to enforce, as had already been found

[1] *Ta Kung Daily* (*Dagong Bao*), Peking, February 20, 1959 (SCMP 1980). Li Ch'eng-jui and Yang Ch'un-hsü: loc. cit.

[2] Ibid., July 10, 1958, p. 1. Editorial.

[3] *Journal of Asian Studies*, Vol. XXIV, No. 1, November 1964, p. 9. G. W. Skinner: loc. cit., Part 1.

[4] *New China Fortnightly* (*Xinhua Banyuekan*), No. 157, June 10, 1959, p. 127.

[5] *People's Handbook* (*Renmin Shouce*) *1960*, p. 387. The sponsors of these meetings had, by December 1962, come to include the State Economic Commission, the All-China Federation of Supply and Marketing Co-operatives and the All-China Federation of Handicraft Co-operatives in addition to the original sponsors, the Ministries of Commerce and Light Industry. *People's Daily* (*Renmin Ribao*), December 21, 1962, p. 2.

[6] *New China Fortnightly* (*Xinhua Banyuekan*), No. 157, June 10, 1959, p. 127.

earlier.[1] So recourse was also had to less rigid methods of obtaining the desired produce by permitting the revival of the old rural markets where goods would be offered for sale spontaneously.

In June-July 1959, a few weeks after the first national third category commodity exchange meeting, a conference convened by the Ministry of Commerce laid down that 'the rural market trade should be extended step by step'.[2] An article published at the close of the conference spoke of 'the need to restore the basic level markets in rural areas to widen the exchange of commodities and stimulate the growth of production'. First category commodities were not to enter these markets and those of the second category only to a limited degree and not until compulsory procurement totals had been fulfilled.[3] Third category commodities were to be the main objects of trade at the markets.

The revival of many rural markets occurred swiftly.[4] Certainly they were already widespread once more by September 1959, when formal Regulations on the Organization of Rural Markets were promulgated by the Central Committee of the Party and the State Council. These regulations appeared to make an important departure by permitting even first category commodities to be sold at rural markets once procurement quotas had been fulfilled. However, the importance of this permission is lessened by the ruling that all first and second category commodities must be sold at the state purchasing prices, which could destroy the incentive for selling them on the market rather than to state agencies.

Sideline and handicraft goods produced by individual commune members, whether coming under the first, second, or third category, might be offered for sale in rural markets, with the qualification that in the case of certain commodities in the first and second categories, such as pigs, commune members might be required to sell definite quantities to the state.[5]

The Regulations went on to promulgate rules on price control at the markets, on who should participate and on the control that should be exercised. The principal participants in rural markets were to be communes, production brigades, individual commune members and local state commercial departments.

Conditions laid down on the participation of outsiders in the rural markets are of particular interest because they indicate the extent to which enterprises and bodies of all kinds had been by-passing the official channels of commerce in order to buy straight from the producers. Before being allowed to take part, procurement personnel of factories, mines, enterprises, public offices, people's organizations, departments, and army units from outside had to produce letters of introduction furnished by industrial or commercial departments at, or above, the level of the *hsien* in the areas from which they came, and also seek the approval of local market control organs. Pedlars and other small

---

[1] *Ta Kung Daily* (*Dagong Bao*), Peking, February 20, 1959 (SCMP 1980). Li Ch'eng-jui and Yang Ch'un-hsü: loc. cit.

[2] NCNA, July 17, 1959.

[3] *Ta Kung Daily* (*Dagong Bao*), Peking, July 18, 1959, p. 1. Sung Chih-ho: 'On Development of a Many-Sided Economy.'

[4] However, the re-opening of some markets was delayed until the end of 1960. See *Journal of Asian Studies*, Vol. XXIV, No. 3, May 1965, p. 375. G. W. Skinner: loc. cit. Part 3.

[5] *People's Handbook* (*Renmin Shouce*) *1960*, pp. 380–1.

tradesmen might take part if they had been licensed for that particular area. They were permitted to go around buying and selling in the countryside and 'deriving a reasonable income from the difference in price between different places. But they are not permitted to do this if the two places concerned are far apart.' They were forbidden to make a profit by buying commodities and selling them at the same market. However, they were allowed more scope than communes, brigades and commune members who were not allowed to buy goods at one place and sell them at a profit elsewhere. Such activities were to be restricted (outside the state commercial organs) to specially licensed persons.[1]

Finally, the Regulations of September 1959 laid down the necessity of market management committees being set up under the authority of the local Party committees. These market management committees were to contain representatives of the relevant departments and organs including those of commerce, food, banking, revenue, industry and agriculture.[2]

The 1959 directive applied not only to the standard and higher level markets held every few days, but also to the fairs held at temples and elsewhere on festivals, and other occasions.[3]

Before long official policy appears to have diverged from that laid down in September 1959. Those regulations, as we have seen, made no distinction between first and second category commodities at rural markets. Both might be sold there after compulsory deliveries had been fulfilled, but only at state purchasing prices. Subsequent pronouncements and reports on rural markets repeatedly stressed that first category commodities must be totally excluded, and sold direct to state agencies only. However, the ban was later either rescinded or ineffectively maintained, because in 1964 references occur to grain being bought and sold on the free market, apparently with official connivance.[4] Evidently it had been found impossible to enforce a ban on the sale at free market prices of surplus grain, and other first category commodities. Even when the sale of these commodities in their original form was effectively prevented, ways could be found of getting round the ban by subjecting them to some form of processing—as for example by using grain to make rice-wine, rice-sweets, cakes (there is mention of these being sold at a market in Hupeh)[5] or the large flat biscuits which are widely eaten.

With respect to second category commodities, once the markets were revived it soon became accepted that they might be sold at above official prices, although market control committees were exhorted to see that prices

---

[1] *People's Handbook* (*Renmin Shouce*) *1960*, pp. 380–1.   [2] Ibid.   [3] Ibid., p. 381.

[4] A. L. Strong: *The Rise of the Chinese People's Communes—and Six Years After*, Peking, 1964, p. 203, where a reference is made to an apparently licit free market price of grain more than 80 per cent above that of the state price, and *Ta Kung Daily* (*Dagong Bao*), Peking, January 20, 1964, p. 3. Kao Ti-ch'en: 'Emphasize the Supply and Marketing Co-operatives' Role in Guiding Rural Market Trade', where these co-operatives are urged to engage in buying and selling grain in order to keep prices stable. In 1961, pedlars in Honan offered prices above the official level for a production brigade's surplus cotton. Some peasants held that such sales would not be contrary to official policy. However, 'the brigade Party branch strongly criticized this wrongful way of thinking, and explained over and over again the harm done by selling surplus cotton to speculative pedlars'. The Party won. *People's Daily* (*Renmin Ribao*), May 29, 1963, p. 2.

[5] *People's Daily* (*Renmin Ribao*), March 14, 1961, p. 7. Lin-Yao: 'Rely on the Masses, Uphold Policy, Activate Rural Market Trade.'

were 'reasonable'. Peasants often had to have certificates that they had fulfilled their compulsory deliveries before being allowed to take second category produce to market.

However, it must be emphasized that the bulk of the goods traded at rural markets—some 80 per cent of all the farm and rural sideline products sold at them, according to an estimate in 1962[1]—consisted of third category commodities. Essentially the markets are occasions for peasants to sell vegetables and fruit grown on their private plots, their poultry and eggs, and the products of cottage industries.[2] It is no coincidence that the revival of rural markets and of the peasants' private plots and handicrafts occurred at the same time. Without opportunities for individual and family production, there would have been little to be brought to market. Without the markets, incentive to increase output beyond a limited amount would have been lacking. Numerous reports in the Press and from visitors to China told of the rapid increase in the production of pigs, poultry and vegetables attributable to the re-opening of the markets.

In September 1961 it was estimated that some 25 per cent of rural 'commodity circulation' was transacted at the 40,000 rural markets then existing all over the Chinese countryside;[3] 'commodity circulation' probably excludes tax grain and compulsory deliveries of crops. Purchases of subsidiary farm products, by state commercial organs and by supply and marketing cooperatives together were said to account for about 10 per cent by value of sales at rural markets in 1961, while between 60 per cent–70 per cent of the value of transactions consisted of business done between individual peasants.[4] At some markets, however, organs of state commerce had a bigger share in business than these overall figures would suggest. For example, state commerce was said to have been responsible for nearly 70 per cent of the purchases of agricultural produce on the first seven occasions on which a certain market in Hupeh was held.[5]

One purpose intended to be served by the re-opening of the rural markets in 1959 was to make it easier for the state commercial organs to obtain the produce necessary to fulfil their contracts. In this, success was reported. According to an account from Hopei shortly after they had been resumed, the markets made the contract system work more smoothly, because of the greater stability of price they brought about. 'The contract system which our *hsien* commerce department previously adopted could not be successfully enforced due to unstable prices. Since the development of commune trade markets, prices have become uniform.'[6] This suggests that frequent and

---

[1] *Economic Research* (*Jingji Yanjiu*), No. 4, April 1962, p. 12. Ho Cheng and Wei Wan: 'A Discussion of Rural Market Trade'.

[2] Pigs, another important sideline product sold at rural markets, come into the second category of commodities.

[3] *Red Flag* (*Hongqi*), No. 18, September 16, 1961, p. 16. Kuan Ta-t'ung: 'Rural Market Trade.'

[4] *Economic Research* (*Jingji Yanjiu*), No. 4, April 1962, p. 12. Ho Cheng and Wei Wan: loc. cit.

[5] *People's Daily* (*Renmin Ribao*), March 14, 1961, p. 7. Lin Yao: loc. cit.

[6] *Hopei Daily* (*Hopei Ribao*), August 3, 1959 (SCMP 2134). Li Ju-mei, member of the Secretariat of the Hochien Hsien CCP Committee: 'Functions of Commune Trade Markets.'

regular sales at free market prices led to less price instability than did bilateral bargaining at infrequent intervals, a view which implies that the sellers were in a position to bargain with the organs of state commerce.

Another motive which may have been contributed to the re-opening of the rural markets was their usefulness for revenue purposes. The decline in rural trade in 1957–8, especially after the formation of the communes, had reduced state revenue from industrial and commercial taxes. Much of this must have been made good after the markets were resumed, although the assessment and collection of tax on dealings at them was no easy matter. Taxation of rural market trade will be treated in Chapter 14.[1]

The figure of 40,000 rural markets given above for 1961 deserves notice. G. W. Skinner estimates (on one set of assumptions) that around 42,900 rural 'standard rural markets' ('that type of rural market which meets all the normal trade needs of the peasant household') were in existence in China in 1948.[2] Subsequently, more standard markets may be presumed to have been formed through the intensification process described by Skinner. Others, especially in the neighbourhood of large cities, would have died out through economic modernization.[3] Much of the third category farm output produced near cities is diverted from sale at rural markets through being delivered under contract to municipal departments of commerce,[4] a development facilitated by the relative importance of suburban units of collective agriculture in the growing of vegetables.[5] This will hasten the atrophy of standard markets in these areas.

Definite attempts are being made in some places to supplant rural markets by getting state commercial bodies, or supply and marketing co-operatives, to visit villages for the purpose of buying from the peasants and selling to them.[6] In 1966, during the 'great socialist cultural revolution', rumours reported curtailment of rural markets. The motives behind such moves are mainly political, because markets are thought to foster the capitalist tendencies ever latent among the peasants. Economic conditions also play a part because time spent on trips to market could be devoted to agricultural work; however, except near the towns where alternative diversions are available, it is unlikely that this would outweigh in the minds of the peasants, the psychological and social benefits derived from the jostle and brisk dealings of market day.

The limitations on the types of participants to be allowed to do business at rural markets have been repeated many times in the Chinese press. 'Speculative activities', i.e. buying with the intention of re-sale, have been denounced with a vigour which suggests that these are difficult to suppress. Differential

[1] See pp. 376–7 below.

[2] *Journal of Asian Studies*, Vol. XXIV, No. 2, February 1965, p. 228. G. W. Skinner: loc. cit. Part 2.

[3] *Far Eastern Economic Review*, August 6, 1964, p. 231, for evidence that markets have died out in the environs of Shanghai.

[4] *China Reconstructs*, August 1963, pp. 2–5. Lung Yeh: 'Vegetables in Abundance for Peking.'

[5] p. 88 above.

[6] *People's Daily* (*Renmin Ribao*), June 4, 1965, p. 2. The Political Department for Finance and Trade, CCP Hsinhsiang Committee: 'Report on the Rural Market.' This is similar to a policy put forward but not implemented in 1956. See *Journal of Asian Studies*, Vol. XXIV, No. 3, May 1965, p. 365. G. W. Skinner: loc. cit., Part III.

taxation has been used as a weapon to curb undesired types of trade.[1] Policy towards traders and pedlars favours their eventual transformation into members of co-operatives.[2]

State commercial bodies have been encouraged to take an active part in the markets. Sometimes, as already mentioned, they buy large quantities of farm produce at these gatherings; in addition, they may sell manufactured goods, such as towels, socks, thermos flasks and footwear. State and co-operative commercial organs were urged to open trade warehouses at markets to handle purchasing and marketing orders on behalf of peasants.[3] In contrast to what was said in 1959 on the beneficial effects of rural markets on state commerce, state commercial organs in 1961, concerned only with fulfilling their purchase quotas for second category commodities, were fearing that this task would be made more difficult by the markets. As a result they failed to take a full part in the markets so that 'state commerce has not kept pace in its economic activities with rural markets and has failed to play its due role of leadership'.[4] The appearance at markets of small traders peddling goods unobtainable at state stores reflected on the efficiency of state commerce which 'should be in a position to supply in time all commodities, be they needles or thread, indispensable to the everyday life of the masses'.[5] Thus, it was hoped, the private traders would be edged out.

The state commercial agencies are supposed to work closely with the market management committees of individual markets. The chief purpose of these management committees is 'to implement Party policies thoroughly, to protect lawful trade, firmly to repress speculation and to promote the healthy development of the markets'.[6]

The traditional markets for draught cattle (and for horses in areas where these are important) were among the old channels of trade which had been blocked during the Great Leap, perhaps as a result of the 'socialist transformation' of cattle merchants.[7] In the early 1960s demands were made to revive the regular flow of cattle from the breeding areas to places where they were needed for work. Supply and marketing co-operatives were urged to help get this trade moving again. In some cases cattle and horse markets were successfully re-opened.[8] In 1966, for example, at the traditional annual fair of the

---

[1] *Ta Kung Daily* (*Dagong Bao*), Peking, September 2, 1962, p. 2. Chu Fu-lin, P'an Tsu-yi and Liu Wen-pin: 'Correctly Implement Tax Policy, Continuously Reform Methods of Working', and see p. 377 below.

[2] *New Industry and Commerce* (*Xin Gongshang*), No. 2, February 1964 (SCMM 421). Liang Yao: 'The Current Task of Supply and Marketing Co-operatives.'

[3] *Ta Kung Daily* (*Dagong Bao*), Peking, October 18, 1961, p. 1. Editorial.

[4] Ibid. March 6, 1961 (SCMP 2504). Ch'en Hsing: 'Strengthen the Economic Work of State Commerce in Trade at Rural Fairs.'

[5] Ibid.

[6] *Economic Research* (*Jingji Yanjiu*), April 1962, p. 15. Ho Cheng and Wei Wen: loc. cit.

[7] *Collected Laws and Regulations* . . . Vol. 7, pp. 304–5.

[8] *Southern Daily* (*Nanfang Ribao*), July 6, 1962 (SCMP 2793). 'Why Are Cattle Markets Not Regularly Open?', and *Daily Worker* (*Gongren Ribao*), February 12, 1963, p. 1. Liang Yao, Vice-Chairman, All-China Federation of Supply and Marketing Co-operatives: 'Improve the Supply of Means of Production for Agriculture, Help Agricultural Production and Strengthen the Collective Economy of the People's Communes', and *Red Flag* (*Hongqi*), No. 6, April 1, 1963, p. 35. Kuan Ta-t'ung: 'Our Country's Unified, Socialist Internal

Pai nationality in Yunnan, sales of over 7,600 horses and oxen were reported. Many other sorts of goods were also sold at this fair, which was said to have attracted more than half a million visitors, including twenty-four trade delegations from other provinces.[1]

The attempt to transform the old supply and marketing co-operatives into supply and marketing departments of communes ran into continuous difficulties. Probably the close ties with the commune administrations led to an inflexibility which inhibited trade and thus contributed to the exceptional degree of self-sufficiency which characterized the early communes. It must not be thought that the position of the supply and marketing departments of the communes was in fact ever clear cut. A directive of February 1960 laid down that the supply and marketing departments of communes should be under the dual leadership of the commune administrative committees and of the *hsien* commercial bureaux; responsibility for their political side should rest with the communes (i.e. they should come under the commune Party committees), but responsibility for commercial operations with the higher levels of the Party and of the state commercial system. The departments were to practise independent accounting, but at the same time their profits and losses were assessed together with those of the local *hsien* commercial bureau (the force of this sentence in the regulations is somewhat obscure). The communes to which the supply and marketing departments belonged were to be entitled to a maximum of 10 per cent of their profits. Attempts to devolve organs of commune supply and marketing departments down to production brigades and production teams were ordered by the same directive to be halted and in part reversed.[2] Evidently brigades and teams were too small to support independent commercial organs other than retail stores.

The complex arrangements envisaged by the February 1960 directive clearly proved unworkable and in any case the decline of the commune as a unit occasioned a re-appraisal of the position. No official announcement was made of the revival of supply and marketing co-operatives, if indeed they had ever been completely absorbed into the communes, but a revival was implicitly recognized in an article by Kuan Ta-tung, Vice-Director of the Central Administrative Bureau for Industry and Commerce, published in July 1961. At present, Kuan wrote, there are three important channels of trade in China: state commerce, the rural supply and marketing co-operatives, and the rural markets. These correspond to the existing three-fold system of ownership: by the state, by collectives and by individuals. State commerce, Kuan continued, is insufficient by itself and needed assistance from supply and marketing co-operatives.[3]

Market', and *Chinese Agricultural Journal* (*Zhongguo Nongbao*), No. 8, August 1963, p. 25. Chang Hou-hsing: 'Some Remarks on Problems in the Cattle Market.'

[1] NCNA Kunming, April 27, 1960.

[2] *Collected Laws and Regulations* . . . Vol. 11, pp. 130–2.

[3] *People's Daily* (*Renmin Ribao*), July 15, 1961, p. 7. Kuan Ta-t'ung: 'Strengthen Link Between Town and Country, Promote the Flow of Commodities.' On this theme, see also ibid., October 23, 1962, p. 5. Kuan Ta-t'ung: 'Commerce Should Improve Its Service to Production and Consumption', and *Red Flag* (*Hongqi*), No. 6, April 1, 1963, pp. 30–1. Kuan Ta-t'ung: loc. cit., and *Economic Research* (*Jingji Yanjiu*), No. 5, May 1963, p. 17. Chiang Huai: 'A Discussion of the Socialist Channels of Commodity Flow.'

Several reasons probably lay behind the decision to revive the supply and marketing co-operatives. First, as already mentioned, the previous attempt to put the commercial departments of communes under the joint control of the commune administration and of the *hsien* bureau of commerce, was unworkable. It is known that the authorities were worried at tendencies of self-sufficiency which had developed in the communes[1] and which had contributed to the failure of the state to get deliveries of agricultural produce from the communes in as large quantities as hoped. This suggests that the commercial supply and marketing departments of 1958-61 were too much under the power of the commune administrations for the liking of higher authorities. Also, from a purely professional point of view, the basic organs of trade may have suffered from being largely controlled by a non-commercial organ, the commune administration.

Here again the perennial note of caution is needed. While we can trace the fluctuations in official policy from 1958-61 towards basic level rural commerce, we cannot say with any assurance to what extent all these changes were in fact implemented. In August 1961, the month after Kuan's article, a certain rural supply and marketing co-operative is said to have been signing contracts 'in the past few years' which indicates that it was regarded as enjoying a continuous existence throughout that time.[2]

In the second half of 1961, after official acknowledgment of their revival, the activities of rural supply and marketing co-operatives were widely reported. There were said to be more than 30,000 basic level supply and marketing co-operatives in existence by the close of 1961, the same number as in 1955.[3] By August 1963 the figure reported was 'more than 20,000,[4] indicating a considerable decline in units, although not necessarily, of course, in business. We have other hints that between 1961 and 1963 the revived supply and marketing co-operatives may have been deliberately increased in size. An article in 1962 complained that in some places they were too small, short of capital and unable to do much trade. 'But, "although a sparrow is small, it has five viscera" and in the same manner, a small sales force requires proportionately more administrators.'[5] It is reasonable to suppose that the numerical decrease of co-operatives may have followed from amalgamations to correct these weaknesses. Administratively, three different types of rural supply and marketing co-operatives are said to have existed since 1961: those co-extensive with a commune, or with a *ch'ü* (the local authority immediately below the *hsien*) and thirdly, those based on a market town (*chen*). The significance of these latter was that they were aligned with natural economic areas rather than with administrative areas.[6] The market towns, sites of the traditional peasant markets, had lost much of their importance with the

---

[1] *Red Flag (Hongqi)*, No. 14, December 16, 1958, p. 5. Hu Sheng: 'Commodity Production in Our Country at the Present Time.'

[2] *Ta Kung Daily (Dagong Bao)*, Peking, August 27, 1961, p. 1.

[3] *Ta Kung Daily (Dagong Bao)*, Peking, January 10, 1962, p. 1, and *People's Handbook (Renmin Shouce) 1956*, p. 525.

[4] *People's Daily (Renmin Ribao)*, August 13, 1963, p. 2. Editorial.

[5] *Ta Kung Daily (Dagong Bao)*, Peking, October 25, 1962, p. 3. Tsu Chih-ch'u: 'Base the Lowest Level Supply and Marketing Co-operatives on Market Towns.'

[6] Ibid.

formation of the communes, and many had, indeed, been absorbed into the communes. In some areas attempts had been made to establish new market towns based on commune supply and marketing co-operatives, to become the economic centres of communes. 'However, things turned out in a contrary way.' The old economic unity of the market town and its surrounding countryside reasserted itself. Their long-standing existence suggested that the market towns fulfil an economic function better than new artificial centres. In addition they have a hold on the affections of country folk. 'Peasants do not like doing business at the local supply and marketing co-operatives but persist in going to the market towns to buy and sell. Therefore . . . economic centres of people's communes have not taken shape . . . all this demonstrates that we get nowhere by opposing the law of commodity flows and customary marketing practices.'[1] In addition to their economic role, the social significance of the market towns is great in that on market days their crowded streets and teahouses provide wider contacts, fun, bustle and excitement. The revival of the rural markets held at the market towns made it more appropriate that the co-operatives should be based there too. It also provided further argument for larger and more effective co-operatives as they now had a bigger job on their hands and needed greater strength 'to fight speculative pedlars':[2] evidence of the importance and ubiquity of these entrepreneurs.

The reorganization of the co-operatives on these lines would, it was admitted, pose new problems. 'A supply and marketing co-operative, based on a market town, is responsible for the trade of several communes. The leadership of Party committees of communes over supply and marketing co-operatives may therefore be weakened, and this may affect the fulfilment of purchasing plans for subsidiary agricultural products'[3]—a tribute to the vital role played by the Party in the enforcement of compulsory deliveries. We do not know how widely supply and marketing co-operatives were reorganized so as to be based on market towns. The fact that the number of co-operatives was reduced to about half the number of rural markets, argues against widespread alignment. However, market towns regained much of their previous importance in 1961–2 with the reopening of the rural markets held in them, while communes declined, so that it seems inherently probable that many supply and marketing co-operatives fell in with this change in the rural economy. In fact complaints were voiced that the supply and marketing co-operatives concentrated too much of their attention on trading at the rural markets, and neglected other retailing activities. Apparently the target for sales turnover has constituted a major success indicator for commercial work and this is more easily achieved by brisk trading at *chen* on market days than by transporting goods deep into the countryside.[4] (Profit target is another important indicator which sometimes leads to undesired effects as when it causes the co-operatives to neglect small unprofitable lines of business, which thereupon are taken up by 'capitalist elements' whose evident greater efficiency enables them to make a profit.)[5]

[1] *Ta Kung Daily* (*Dagong Bao*), Peking, October 25, 1962, p. 3. Tsu Chih-ch'u: loc. cit.
[2] Ibid. [3] Ibid.
[4] *People's Daily* (*Renmin Ribao*), December 6, 1964, p. 2.
[5] *Ta Kung Daily* (*Dagong Bao*), Peking, December 5, 1964, p. 1. Editorial.

It is interesting to speculate on the possible interconnection between the trend towards somewhat larger supply and marketing co-operatives (with the number of units falling from 30,000 to 20,000 between 1961 and 1963, probably through amalgamation) and the simultaneous trend towards smaller communes (with numbers increasing from 24,000 in 1959 to 74,000 in 1963). One point in common between the two movements may very well have been that both sets of administrative changes were subject to great geographic differentiation. Therefore it is fruitless to try to build a nation-wide model, e.g. by surmising that one co-operative usually operates within the area of three or four communes. The same reason renders it vain to trace a general correspondence between either supply and marketing co-operatives or communes and the 40,000 rural markets reported in 1961.[1]

Further complications are added by a report in 1965 of the existence of about 200,000 'supply and marketing co-operatives and departments' distributed over China's countryside. This figure included the separate retail and purchasing departments found in every market town which would be components of a supply and marketing co-operative. Presumably it also includes the 80,000 agencies mentioned in the same report as having been set up in production brigades.[2] Thus it is not possible to deduce from the figure of 200,000 what, if any, changes had occurred between 1963 and 1965 in the number of supply and marketing co-operatives. In 1966 a large part of the countryside was still not adequately covered by the supply and marketing co-operatives' network.[3]

Every supply and marketing co-operative is supposed to hold representative meetings to elect officials, but commonly this may be a mere formality.[4] Dividends should be distributed to members although there has been a tendency to neglect or postpone this in some co-operatives.[5]

We may surmise that in 1958 the federations of supply and marketing co-operatives at *hsien*, provincial and national levels lapsed into desuetude. By 1962 we hear of them once more. For example, the All-China Federation of Supply and Marketing Co-operatives exercised its supervisory function in June 1962 by circulating its member co-operatives throughout the country 'demanding that they conscientiously tighten control over funds and other financial matters, severely prevent blind purchasing and extravagance'.[6] Evidently weakness in financial management and the lack of suitable staff were as damaging here as in other sectors of the economy. In 1963 the All-China Federation undertook commercial control of eighty-two third category agricultural products as well as of certain 'outside the plan' second category farm commodities.[7]

---

[1] See pp. 299–300 above.

[2] *Ta Kung Daily* (*Dagong Bao*), Peking, September 23, 1965, p. 2.

[3] *New Construction* (*Xin Jianshe*), No. 1–2, February 1966, p. 58. Chang Ho-wei: loc. cit.

[4] *Ta Kung Daily* (*Dagong Bao*), Peking, November 10, 1961, p. 3. Li Fu-hsiang: 'Take the Mass Line and Manage Rural Supply and Marketing Co-operatives Efficiently.'

[5] *Southern Daily* (*Nanfang Ribao*), March 6, 1963 (SCMP 2948). Liang Chen-hai and Ts'en Hung-lin: 'Dividend Distribution Must Not Be Overlooked in Supply and Marketing Co-operatives.'

[6] *Ta Kung Daily* (*Dagong Bao*), Peking, June 12, 1962, p. 1.

[7] Ibid., September 11, 1963, p. 1.

In general there is supposed to be a division of labour between, on the one hand, state commercial organs which control the higher echelons of the commercial world as well as urban trade and, on the other hand, supply and marketing co-operatives which operate mainly in the countryside. Chronic friction appears to exist between the two systems and they are constantly being exhorted to co-ordinate their activities. State wholesaling bodies are blamed for reluctance to supply industrial goods to rural areas, even hiding popular articles when staff from supply and marketing co-operatives come to select goods.[1] Both types of commerce are urged to decide together on the proper distribution of goods between cities and *hsien*, and then within *hsien* between the *hsien* towns and the country areas; and to hold conferences to co-ordinate plans. The two should decide on their respective duties: 'responsibility systems for supplying and procuring goods must be settled'.[2]

The third category commodity exchange meetings and warehouse trade were both intended to put potential buyers and sellers in touch with each other on the level of wholesale trade and of purchases by enterprises and institutions. The revival of the trade warehouses in the First Five Year Plan period has already been noted. During the Great Leap their activities were muted but from 1960 onwards revived swiftly until by the beginning of 1962 around 12,000 warehouses were in business.[3] Some, with a continuous existence of many years, had been transformed from private to joint state-private ownership, while others were newly established by state commercial organs or supply and marketing co-operatives.[4]

The flexibility of trade warehouses is shown both by their forms and by their functions. They are of all sizes, some are situated in cities, others in *hsien* towns or rural areas. Some are concerned mainly with long distance trade, others with commercial dealings between a *hsien* city and its surrounding countryside. They may specialize on one type of goods or cover a wide selection, the only common factor in this being that the goods traded are mainly third category agricultural commodities (with second category after compulsory deliveries are fulfilled) and such industrial and handicraft products as fall outside state plans.[5] Sometimes their role includes assistance with tax collection at rural markets.[6] Warehouses may trade on their own account, but their major function is supposed to be acting as agent or go-between, buying and selling on behalf of others and bringing buyers and sellers together. Warehouses also arrange for the transport of goods and sometimes

[1] *Ta Kung Daily* (*Dagong Bao*), Peking, December 28, 1964, p. 2. The Study Team, General Office, Commercial Bureau, Hsinyang Special District, Honan Province: 'Use the Thought of Mao Tse-tung to Resolve Contradictions in Sending Industrial Goods to the Countryside', and ibid., December 27, 1964, p. 2, and ibid., June 23, 1965, p. 1. Editorial.
[2] Ibid., January 15, 1964, p. 5. Editorial.
[3] *Ta Kung Daily* (*Dagong Bao*), Peking, January 24, 1962, p. 3. Yi T'ung: 'Warehouse Trade.'
[4] These are sometimes known as 'service departments' or 'trustee departments'—titles deologically preferable to the old style 'trade warehouse'.
[5] *Ta Kung Daily* (*Dagong Bao*), Peking, January 24, 1962, p. 3. Yi T'ung: loc. cit. Dealings in first category produce and second category under contract to the state, may sometimes be entrusted to warehouses, but this would be by special arrangement.
[6] Ibid., May 15, 1962, p. 2. Wang Shao-min: 'Strengthen the Control of Tax Collection at Rural Markets.' See also p. 377 below.

provide lodgings for traders. On occasion they make loans to clients. Perhaps the most significant aspect of their flexibility is that their contacts are not limited by any administrative pattern; communes and their constituent units, individual peasants, handicraft co-operatives, state commercial companies, supply and marketing co-operatives and purchasing agents, for example, can deal at or through such warehouses with customers or suppliers of all categories, levels and areas. Trading warehouses can thus respond readily to the needs of trade which, as centres of commercial intelligence, they must be well placed to sense.[1]

9. ALIGNMENT OF TRADE: ADMINISTRATIVE UNITS VERSUS 'ECONOMIC AREAS'

We do not know what proportion of commercial dealings passes through the more flexible channels of trade, such as rural markets, warehouses, pedlars, and purchasing agents. In contrast to these, the official machinery of trade—the state commercial apparatus, including the supply and marketing co-operatives—has been aligned primarily with administrative units, provinces, special districts, *hsien* and so forth, even where they do not coincide with natural economic areas. This led to a diversion of trade from routes that were old and tried—and presumably economic—to new directions based primarily on administrative convenience; a trend towards self-sufficiency within provinces and lower political units which was intensified from 1958, first by the decentralization measures which increased local autonomy, and later by weaknesses in the mechanism of planning, which made it unwise to rely on supplies from other local authorities' areas. This tendency received official approval because it simplified planning and also perhaps from the mistaken view that it would reduce unnecessary transport. In 1958, for example, it was laid down that, with the exception of supplies for Peking, Shanghai and Liaoning, each provincial level authority should be responsible for supplying within its own borders, its requirements of meat, poultry and eggs, and a similar arrangement was suggested for sweet potatoes.[2]

One of the primary purposes of street factories in urban communes was, it will be recalled, to fill local demand for small consumer goods and components for industry, thus increasing municipal self-sufficiency. Meetings summoned by provinces and municipalities to organize supplies of raw materials and spare parts had the same result. In these matters, it was held in 1960 that 'where it is possible for a city to solve its own problems, these are not to be referred to the province, and when the province is able to solve its problems by its own efforts, it is not to ask help from fraternal provinces'.[3]

[1] *Ta Kung Daily* (*Dagong Bao*), Peking, January 24, 1962, p. 3. Yi T'ung: loc. cit., and *Collected Laws and Regulations*... Vol. 6, pp. 379–80, and *Ta Kung Daily* (*Dagong Bao*), Peking, February 20, 1961 (SCMP 2460). Wu Jen-k'uei, Director, Kiangsi Provincial Department of Commerce: 'Carry Out Policy, Strengthen Leadership and Enliven Trade at Rural Markets', and ibid., January 15, 1962, p. 2. Ch'en Han-ch'üan: 'How Yüant'an Commune Controls Rural Market Trade.'

[2] *Ta Kung Daily* (*Dagong Bao*), Peking, April 27, 1958, p. 2. Chu Hang: 'Suggested Solution of the Problem of the Procurement of Sweet Potatoes', and NCNA Peking, September 3, 1958.

[3] *People's Daily* (*Renmin Ribao*), January 23, 1960 (SCMP 2201). Huang Hua-ch'ing,

The Seventy Points of Industrial Policy of December 1961 laid down that each *hsien*'s industrial concerns should rely on raw materials and should produce for the *hsien*'s own needs.¹ No account was taken of comparative costs in neighbouring administrative units, nor of the most economical transport routes, nor of traditional economic links.

The problems must have been augmented by the difference, pointed out by G. W. Skinner, between the mode of articulation in administration and in marketing. 'Whereas administrative units are discrete throughout the system, each lower-level unit belonging to only one unit at each ascending level, marketing systems are indiscrete at all levels, except that of the standard market', i.e. the higher-level marketing systems overlapped and (except in the case of standard markets) one lower-level marketing system would belong to more than one higher-level system. Therefore it was 'infeasible to contain or constrain the interlocked network of natural marketing systems within the bounds of discrete administrative units'.²

By 1962 the disadvantages of aligning the commercial system with the administrative had become too evident to overlook and a reaction was evoked. 'During the past few years', wrote a *Ta Kung Daily* correspondent in the summer of 1962, 'in some places the organization of commodity circulation according to administrative areas has been stressed to the extent of disrupting the traditional and appropriate economic links between city and countryside and between different areas.'³

The same theme was taken up in an editorial in the *People's Daily* in the spring of 1963 which criticized 'some localities' which 'insist on organizing distribution and transport according to administrative boundaries, whether or not transport routes are appropriate for this'. Some *hsien* near Peking and Tientsin, for example, which had always procured goods direct from these cities, now were forced to re-route their purchases through wholesale departments at a great distance, adding unnecessarily to costs and causing delays. 'It is essential', the editorial continued, 'to use economically appropriate methods when dealing with economic matters and not depend in the main on administrative methods.'⁴ On the same lines, Kuan Ta-t'ung, writing a week later in *Red Flag*, urged the use of 'rational methods of supply which span *hsien*, special districts and provinces' in order to speed up the flow of trade, reduce intermediate links and to lessen costs and the damage to goods.⁵

First Secretary, CCP Liaoning Provincial Committee: 'Promote the Spirit of Communist Co-operation.' See also *Economic Research* (*Jingji Yanjiu*), No. 3, March 1960, pp. 45–51. Wang Shou-li: 'Certain Problems in Demarcating Economic Regions Within Provinces.'

¹ *Seventy Important Points of Communist Industrial Policy*, 1961. (From Taiwan source.) Nos. 10 and 11.

² *Journal of Asian Studies*, Vol. XXIV, No. 3, May 1965, p. 374. G. W. Skinner: loc. cit. Part 3.

³ *Ta Kung Daily* (*Dagong Bao*), Peking, July 3, 1962, p. 2. Tu Hung: 'Energetically Restore Traditional Channels of Commodity Circulation.' The disadvantages of this alignment had been noticed as early as 1956, although the alignment was to be intensified in the next few years. *New China Fortnightly* (*Xinhua Banyuekan*), No. 83, May 6, 1956, p. 83. Tseng Ch'uan-liu, Vice Minister of Commerce: 'Supply the Countryside Efficiently.'

⁴ *People's Daily* (*Renmin Ribao*), March 23, 1963, p. 1. Editorial.

⁵ *Red Flag* (*Hongqi*), No. 6, April 1, 1963, p. 35. Kuan Ta-t'ung: loc. cit.

(It must, of course, be borne in mind that in a number of cases, administrative units were originally delineated to coincide with economic areas.)

However, the deliberate restoration by administrative means of old trading patterns, as was involved in the re-siting of state commercial organs, including wholesale depots,[1] was slow and cumbersome compared with the apparently spontaneous revival of rural markets and trade warehouses, two other witnesses to the desire to get back to traditional channels of trade. In some of the more modernized parts of China—and notably in the Tangshan special district of Hopei—the realignment of trade back to its old patterns has probably gone a long way. Over the country as a whole, however, by 1965 the change back was still very far from completed.[2]

This raises the question of how far the reaction can go without causing wide repercussions, not only in the economy but also in the political structure. Since 1957–8 almost all activities occurring within a province, partially excepting the military and the most important economic enterprises, have come under the surveillance of the provincial Party committee and more especially of its first secretary. Under the provincial level, the Party committees and secretaries of lower local authorities have enjoyed a similar sway. If commerce is no longer to be based on the administrative units of province, special district and *hsien*, transport and production are likely to follow suit. The planning and fiscal jurisdictions of the units of local government will then be difficult to maintain. The real professionals in the commercial system probably hope that by basing their activities on non-political units they may lessen the hold of the political men on them. Whether the politicians, especially the provincial first secretaries, will accept this situation remains to be seen. Awareness of the political implications involved may perhaps be shown by the leading role taken in implementing the change by the regional bureaux of the Party which each control several provinces.[3] Indeed, these may see in the movement a way of limiting the power of provincial and other local Party secretaries.

10. RETAILING AND RATIONING

The scattered references already made to retailing will have served to show the variety of forms under which it has been carried on in China over the past decade. In cities, stores are operated by state commercial organs (either specialized corporations or commercial departments of municipalities or wards), by joint state-private undertakings or by co-operative concerns. In

[1] 'At present the first thing that needs doing is to improve the siting of wholesale organs ... the siting of grade 2 wholesale depots should not be restricted by administrative divisions, but should be done according to economic areas and the natural flow of trade. Within a single province, between provinces and over the country as a whole, tens and hundreds of commodity supply zones may be formed around grade 2 wholesale depots, operating "fan-shaped distribution of goods and fixed point direct transport", thus cutting out circuitous transport.' *Ta Kung Daily (Dagong Bao)*, Peking, February 24, 1964, p. 1. Editorial.

[2] *People's Daily (Renmin Ribao)*, December 8, 1965, p. 2, and *Ta Kung Daily (Dagong Bao)*, Peking, August 9, 1965, p. 1. Editorial. I am grateful to John W. Lewis of Cornell University for information on this topic.

[3] *Ta Kung Daily (Dagong Bao)*, Peking, August 9, 1965, p. 1.

the country, state stores under *hsien* commercial bureaux are established in certain market towns, while supply and marketing co-operatives sometimes have shops; many joint state-private retailers also do business. Shops are sometimes run, in towns and cities, by units of collective agriculture and state farms, presumably as retail outlets for part of their own produce. Markets account for a substantial proportion of rural retail sales. Commission shops, which buy and sell on behalf of customers, are important in places. Nor must the activities of pedlars, licit or illicit, be overlooked. Handicraftsmen, whether as individuals or in co-operatives, often sell to consumers direct, while at least some small factories are evidently able to do the same.[1] Government organs, institutions and productive enterprises often run shops for the convenience of their members and workers.

The large number of small shops struck a Russian visitor to China very forcibly as contrasting with the Soviet Union.[2] Most of these concerns are under joint state-private ownership, carried on as family businesses by their previous owners.

Local rationing of grain and of edible oil to urban residents began in 1953; for grain it was made nation-wide by a decree of August 1955. Cotton cloth was rationed to consumers from 1954.[3] Many other foodstuffs were rationed at different times. The Ministry of Food is charged with the rationing of grain[4] and vegetable oil, while rationing of subsidiary foodstuffs, cloth and other commodities comes under the Ministry of Commerce.

For goods that are under planned purchase and planned supply—the three vital items of grain, vegetable oil and cotton—rations are determined by the central government. For other commodities—for example, pork—which are controlled on a provincial basis, the provinces and equivalent authorities, acting through their commercial departments, are the rationing authorities.

The method by which consumer rationing is administered differs radically between the countryside and towns. Peasant households are classed according to whether they are grain surplus, grain self-sufficient, or grain deficient. Grain surplus peasants are subject to compulsory deliveries of grain to the state, the grain self-sufficient neither have to sell nor are permitted to buy grain, while the grain deficient—mainly in areas growing economic crops such as cotton—are provided with fixed quantities of grain, with additional bonuses to those who sell more than their quota of their own crops.

[1] *Southern Daily* (*Nanfang Ribao*), March 2, 1963 (SCMP 2946). Yeh Ta-hsin and Liu Ch'ao-yeh: 'Do Not Believe Too Much in Figures of Goods in Stock.' The reference is to a rural farm tool factory. Another reference mentions a shop which was better stocked than others 'because of its direct connection with the manufacturer'. *Ta Kung Daily* (*Dagong Bao*), Peking, August 24, 1965, p. 2. In some cases such links may have been originally forged in the days of private ownership, and carried on under joint state-private ownership. See also *Collected Laws and Regulations* ... Vol. 8, p. 140.

[2] M. A. Klochko: *Soviet Scientists in China*, London, 1964, p. 53.

[3] *New China Monthly* (*Xinhua Yuebao*), No. 54, April 1954, pp. 158–9, and ibid., No. 71, September 1955, p. 163, and *New China Fortnightly* (*Xinhua Banyuekan*), No. 116, September 25, 1957, p. 211, and T. J. Hughes and D. E. T. Luard: *The Economic Development of Communist China 1949–60*, Second Edition, London, 1961, p. 187, and Solomon Adler: *The Chinese Economy*, London, 1957, p. 174.

[4] It must be remembered that 'grain' includes sweet potatoes. During 1958 and subsequent years, sweet potatoes and inferior grains formed a high proportion of the grain ration.

Town dwellers in possession of the necessary residence cards are given ration coupons for grain, oil, cotton cloth and any other commodities which are currently rationed. This has been a useful tool for the authorities in their attempt to check unauthorized migration to the towns, although they evidently found it difficult to stop the sale of coupons to those who had come illicitly.[1] Most food coupons are valid for only one locality, special cards being issued to those duly authorized to travel. References in the Press and reports of those coming out of China indicate that a black market flourished, both in coupons and in actual commodities, in the years of agricultural disasters when rations were at their lowest. However, it is by no means always necessary to contravene the law in order to get more supplies of rationed commodities. For some things differential pricing has been used—a low fixed price for quantities obtainable on ration, with more available at higher prices or on the free market. It has also been possible to get good meals, containing rationed foodstuffs, at special expensive restaurants.

For purposes of rationing, urban residents are divided into categories—heavy, medium and light workers, higher and other intellectuals, office employees, students, children and non-producers (including housewives). Heavy and medium workers have had the highest rations, followed by intellectuals and students. The Army's ration scale is above that of the civilian population. In the years of shortages the differentials in rations between these different categories of consumers was wide. When food became more plentiful, the differences narrowed.

In the autumn of 1964, urban civilian grain rations in north China ran at between 26–30 *chin* (one *chin*=0·5 kg.) a month according to category of consumer; vegetable oil at $2\frac{1}{2}$ *liang* (one *liang*=50 grams) a month; sugar, half a *chin* a month; and cotton cloth at around 12–16 *ch'ih* (one *ch'ih*= 0·33 metres) a year.[2] Other items, except for tea, are in general no longer rationed; sugar ceased to be rationed in 1965. With more vegetables and other foodstuffs available, grain rations are normally adequate; indeed, some urban residents do not take up their full rations. The small ration of vegetable oil can be supplemented by animal fats, which are unrationed. During 1959–61, ration levels were much lower, with grain rations around 10–20 *chin* a month;[3] while cotton cloth rations at one period amounted to no more than $4\frac{1}{2}$ *ch'ih* a year.

Schools, factories, offices, military units, and other bodies often keep their own pigs and grow vegetables for the consumption of their own members. This output is exempt from the normal obligation of compulsory deliveries of agricultural produce to the state.

Scarce industrial products, other than cotton cloth, were at one time sold according to a special priority system. For urban residents, this was changed, no doubt for administrative reasons, to rationing these goods by coupons. Coupons were distributed to individuals according to their wages; in 1962 in Peking one coupon was awarded for every ¥20 earned. The number of coupons needed to buy any article (in addition, of course, to the price in money)

---

[1] *Collected Laws and Regulations* ... Vol. 6, p. 230.
[2] Private communication to the author.
[3] *Far Eastern Economic Review*, May 12, 1960, p. 935.

could be varied to maintain demand and supply in equilibrium, without altering money prices. It also permitted local flexibility as the muncipality was the unit for varying the 'cost' of any article in coupons. Goods subject to rationing by coupon included cigarettes, cooking utensils, woollen clothing, shoes, radios, and a varied collection of other articles.[1] Subsequently, such goods became more plentiful and the coupon system was discontinued. In the countryside the supply and marketing co-operatives have had the main responsibility for distributing scarce consumer goods.[2] Durable consumer goods, especially the 'four good things' (wrist watches, radios, sewing machines and bicycles) are found to be particularly powerful incentives in China as in other parts of the world. Those who sell grain to the state in excess of the compulsory quotas[3] are sometimes rewarded by being given priority for the purchase of such items. No hire purchase facilities are known to exist.

An attempt to estimate the efficiency of the rationing system and the adequacy at various dates of the rations leads into a field of controversy. Some have claimed that during the years of scarcity, from 1959 to 1961, the available supplies were fairly spread out over the country so that none actually starved. This has, however, been disproved by the publication of issues of secret military papers of 1961, which tell of numerous deaths among soldiers' families in the disaster areas.[4] Also reports coming to Hong Kong from Kwangtung province in those years spoke of extreme malnutrition and high death rates from deficiency diseases. 'Non-producers' in cities in various parts of China are also known to have suffered severely. An interim conclusion is that the food situation during the hard years, and even in more prosperous times, has been extremely patchy, that conditions have varied greatly between one part of the country and another, and even from one district to another; that variations from year to year and from season to season have been extensive and, of course, that separate categories of consumers have fared very differently. Priority groups—workers in major industries, intellectuals, those in receipt of remittances[5] or food parcels from abroad—had, on the whole, a diet adequate to maintain health throughout the time of shortage. The great coastal cities and the industrial conurbations of Liaoning benefited from the purchases of foreign grain. Some areas of lesser political and economic importance and untraversed by outside visitors, experienced much rougher conditions in the hard years.

There is general agreement that since 1962 supplies of both food and consumer goods have become much more plentiful. In that year coupons ceased to be needed, or were reduced in number, for the purchase of certain articles and in 1963 food stalls began once again to sell rice cakes and noodles free of coupons, while prices in the special restaurants were reduced.

Apart from and in addition to the rationing system, certain priorities and special measures have been observed in distributing consumer goods, both

[1] *Guardian*, January 24, 1963, S. Lindqvist: 'Inside China—2.'
[2] *Ta Kung Daily* (*Dagong Bao*), Peking, November 10, 1961, p. 3. Li Fu-hsiang: 'Take the Mass Line and Manage Rural Supply and Marketing Co-operatives Efficiently.'
[3] See p. 360 below.
[4] *Work Bulletin* (*Gongzuo Tongxun*), No. 6, January 27, 1961, pp. 15–17.
[5] A system has been operated according to which extra rations are given on a *pro rata* basis to those receiving remittances of money from abroad.

foodstuffs and manufactures, to certain places and groups of consumers. Special provision is made for supplying foodstuffs to the key cities of Peking, Shanghai and Tientsin, and also to the province of Liaoning with its great industrial centres.[1] The armed forces, naturally, are priority consumers. Special priority for the supply of various goods is given to the home towns of Overseas Chinese and commercial organs have been established to this end.[2] This is to encourage the remittance of funds by Overseas Chinese to their dependants, to persuade wealthy Chinese abroad to return to the fatherland and to create a good impression among the Overseas Chinese communities. The Nationalities Trade Bureau, under the Ministry of Commerce, supervises commercial activities in the national minority areas and controls special corporations engaged in this trade.[3]

11. CONSUMER RESEARCH AND ADVERTISING

In the absence of a market economy and the functioning of the price mechanism, commercial departments are supposed to shoulder the responsibility of acting as substitutes by reporting back the needs of the market to producing units. This has been especially so in the periods when commercial organs have been able to order goods selectively instead of having passively to accept what is allocated. Consumer research is of recognized importance in market economies, where it makes use of highly developed methods and specialist staff. It is needed all the more in economies where the working of the market is restricted.

Many complaints have appeared in the Chinese press, that goods produced do not accord with consumers' requirements and more especially that unsuitable types of commodities are dispatched for sale in rural areas.[4] Already in 1956 commercial organs were urged to make sample surveys among peasants to discover what types of goods were really needed.[5]

[1] *New China Fortnightly* (*Xinhua Banyuekan*), No. 96, November 21, 1956, p. 95, for arrangements for fish supplies to Shanghai, Peking and Tientsin, and *Ta Kung Daily* (*Dagong Bao*), Peking, April 27, 1958, p. 2, on suggested allocations of sweet potatoes to Peking, Shanghai and Liaoning, and NCNA Peking, September 3, 1958, on supplies of meat, poultry and eggs for Peking, Shanghai, Liaoning, and for exports and for the Army, and *Collected Laws and Regulations* . . . Vol. 8, p. 175, and *Ta Kung Daily* (*Dagong Bao*), Peking, December 23, 1958, p. 2, on vegetables and pigs from Heilungkiang for Peking, Tientsin and Liaoning.

[2] *Ta Kung Daily* (*Dagong Bao*), Peking, November 24, 1962, p. 2.

[3] *Nationalities Unity* (*Minzu Tuanjie*), No. 2–3, February–March 1963, pp. 10–13. Hsieh Ho-ch'ou, Vice Chairman, Nationalities Affairs Committee: 'Further Strengthen Commercial Work among Minority Nationalities', and ibid., pp. 8–10. Yü Chieh, Vice Minister of Commerce: 'Raise the Efficiency of Commercial Work among Minority Nationalities', and *Ta Kung Daily* (*Dagong Bao*), Peking, December 14, 1963, p. 1, and ibid., January 20, 1964, p. 1. Editorial.

[4] The most glaring example was the production in 1956 of over a million double-wheeled, double-share ploughs of a Soviet model. They proved unsuitable and only some 5 per cent were used. *China Quarterly*, No. 11, July–September 1962, p. 145. R. Hofheinz: 'Rural Administration in Communist China.'

[5] *New China Fortnightly* (*Xinhua Banyuekan*), No. 83, May 6, 1956, p. 83. Tseng Ch'uan-liu: loc. cit. Here the China General Goods Company is blamed for sending high-heeled shoes to the rough, remote province of Tsinghai. See also *Planned Economy* (*Jihua Jingji*), No. 4, April 1957, p. 21. Ho T'ing-shih: 'How to Compile a Survey Study of Residents' Needs of Commodities'.

Taking into account the extreme shortage of statisticians with even the most elementary training, it is unlikely that anything of a widespread or scientific nature could be achieved in the way of sample surveys. However although statistical expertise may be lacking, commercial instincts are not, especially in that great city of traders, Shanghai. From 1961-2 onwards, when consumer goods made from non-agricultural raw materials were becoming plentiful, we hear of something more than exhortations to consider consumers' needs and tastes. In Shanghai, industrial departments appear to have taken the initiative, followed by commercial departments. Factories dispatched teams composed of 'technical men and workers, usually led by the chief cadres of the factories' to visit consumer units in Shanghai and elsewhere. Although this suggests a somewhat simple and crude approach, it may have been useful in getting across to the staff of the factories the importance of keeping consumer needs in mind, as well as giving them opportunity to see the actual performance of their products.[1] As a result, changes were made in the designs of certain articles. Other industrial centres followed Shanghai's lead.[2]

Commercial advertising in China is, of course, much less developed than in Western economies, and is informative rather than persuasive in character. The media used include the Press, telephone directories, the cinema and outdoor signboards. Advertisements in the Press (apart from notices of publications and performances) are directed towards the trade customer rather than the ultimate consumer. Among the national daily newspapers, the most advertisements have been carried by the *Ta Kung Daily* (which stopped publication in 1966; it had specialized in economic matters) and the *Daily Worker* (the organ of the Federation of Trade Unions). The *People's Daily* (the organ of the Central Committee of the CCP), however, is preferred for advertisements of journals and other publications. Most press advertisements are in the name of producing enterprises, such as factories, but warehouses, municipal supply and marketing co-operatives and other commercial undertakings also advertise. Advertisers from big cities predominate, although one will sometimes hail from a remote region.[3] Foreign firms are permitted to advertise in the daily and technical press. Specialized state-owned corporations exist to handle advertising.[4]

12. COMMERCIAL FINANCE

The various organs of state and co-operative commerce cover their costs and make their profits from the margins between buying and selling prices on the

---

[1] *People's Daily (Renmin Ribao)*, June 29, 1961, p. 3. Ch'en Shih-ho: Technical Department, Shanghai Municipal Industrial Production Commission: 'Raise Quality by Interviewing Consumers.'

[2] *Kuangming Daily (Guangming Ribao)*, September 26, 1962, p. 3, and NCNA Shanghai, November 6, 1962, and NCNA Peking, December 15, 1962, and *China Reconstructs*, November 1964, pp. 18-20. Hsia Kung: 'Producing Goods for the Peasants.'

[3] e.g. the *hsien* Bureau of Commerce of Hami, Sinkiang, was evidently bent on enlarging the market for its electrical and other technical goods. *Ta Kung Daily (Dagong Bao)*, Peking, March 23, 1962, p. 3.

[4] *Far Eastern Economic Review*, August 9, 1962, p. 243, and ibid., October 29, 1964, p. 262, and ibid., March 31, 1966. p. 636, on the Shanghai Advertising Corporation.

goods they handle. Their profits, less certain deductions, are remitted to the state. Before the absorption, early in 1958, of the Ministry of Urban Services by the All-China Federation of Supply and Marketing Co-operatives, these co-operatives did not pay their profits to the state, but were subject to income tax. From January 1958 this system was changed, and they followed the practice of state-owned enterprises in handing over their profits. For capital investment and certain training schemes they were to receive budgetary allocations and they were permitted to retain for their own use a share of their profits which, calculated on a national basis, was provisionally fixed at 8 per cent,[1] and was presumably to be used for purposes similar to those for retained profits of state enterprises in general.[2]

Little information is available about commercial profit margins. In April 1958 certain supply and marketing departments of agricultural producer co-operatives were allowed a margin of 12·3 per cent between wholesale and retail prices, in addition to 4 per cent net profit, 'which together is almost as much as that of a state-run store'.[3] The sales and supply bureaux of economic ministries at all levels charge commission on the goods that pass through their hands so that the prices to the ultimate consumer may be 30–50 per cent above the prices stipulated by the state.[4]

It will be remembered that the question of profit targets for commercial enterprises had particularly exercised the mind of the government at the time of the decentralization decrees in November 1957. It was laid down that the change then made—that profit targets should not be transmitted downwards below the provincial (or equivalent) level—should be introduced on an experimental scale before being extended to the whole country. In fact even two or three years later it would seem to have been far from universally implemented. Indeed it may possibly have been decided not to go on with it, although there is no direct information that this was the case. In July 1960, a Vice-Governor of Liaoning complained that some of the municipal departments of commerce in his province put the making of profits from vegetables before encouraging their production. At the same period, certain commercial personnel were said to be against supplying producer goods to agriculture on the grounds that this business was unprofitable. In Kwangtung complaints were made that some commercial workers did not follow the policy of low profits and large sales, but preferred to raise profit rates by restricting supply.[5] It is difficult to see how provincial departments of commerce could fulfil their profit targets without in some way apportioning among their subordinate organs the total figure to be raised.

[1] *People's Taxation* (*Renmin Shuiwu*), No. 11, June 4, 1958, p. 5. Joint Notice of the Ministry of Finance and the Second Ministry of Commerce to the Supply and Marketing Co-operatives.

[2] See p. 167 above.

[3] *Ta Kung Daily* (*Dagong Bao*), Peking, April 28, 1958, p. 2. Wang K'e: loc. cit., and ibid., May 26, 1958, p. 2. Li Jen, Kan Fu and Tsung Shun: loc. cit.

[4] *People's Daily* (*Renmin Ribao*), May 17, 1962, p. 2. Wang Hsü: 'Reduce the Number of Middlemen and Lower the Cost of Timber'—a reader's letter.

[5] *Red Flag* (*Hongqi*), No. 14, July 16, 1960, p. 25. Huang Ta, Vice-Governor of Liaoning Province: 'Even Industrial Centres Can Become Self-Sufficient in Vegetables', and ibid., p. 2, Chiang Wei-ch'ing: 'Develop Widely the Mass Movement to Aid Agriculture', and *Southern Daily* (*Nanfang Ribao*), September 27, 1960 (SCMP 2377).

Sometimes commercial enterprises have operated at a loss. This might be either in pursuance of official policy or through inadvertence and inefficiency. The first type of loss is that envisaged by the Ministry of Commerce when in 1957 it promised to reimburse losses made by a trading corporation in handling high cost coal from small mines, whose output had to be maintained in the national interest.[1] In June 1962, on the other hand, commercial enterprises were castigated for the losses incurred by incompetence.[2]

No figures are available for the contributions to the state budget from commercial profits. In addition to profits delivered to the state are the sums paid as taxation by commercial bodies. Here again, no separate figures are published but 'industrial and commercial taxes' for 1960 were budgeted at ¥19,450 million.[3] The division of profits of central enterprises between central and provincial treasuries in the proportion of 80:20, decided for 1958, was to apply in the case of enterprises under the Ministry of Commerce (including joint state-private enterprises) in the same way as to industrial enterprises.[4]

The People's Bank has wide powers of supervision, which it is encouraged to use, over commerce as over other spheres of the economy. These powers derive both from the fact that all financial transactions of any size have to pass through the Bank and also from the Bank's role as a source of working capital.[5] The Bank is expected to be constantly looking out for irregularities and inefficiency. The banking authorities are supposed to report to the local Party committees when goods supplied under contract do not conform to contractual provisions. In such cases the buying unit is entitled to refuse payment, whereupon the supplier would have to draw on its liquid resources in excess of the amount originally planned. Thus the situation would be brought to the notice of the Bank which should report it to the local Party committee.[6] The Bank has to see that commercial enterprises take stock and that idle stocks are not allowed to accumulate and also to make sure that funds advanced as working capital are not used for permanent capital investment.[7]

In conclusion, several points must be emphasized in any account of China's commercial organization. First, commerce is regarded as politically a very sensitive sector of the economy. Many of the most experienced commercial staff are former private merchants or past employees of Chinese or foreign capitalist trading concerns, but even in the younger workers commerce is liable to inculcate attitudes at variance with official ideology. Perhaps this explains why commerce, together with finance, was in 1964 chosen as the first sphere in which to establish special political departments additional to the

[1] *New China Fortnightly* (*Xinhua Banyuekan*), No. 107, May 10, 1957, p. 110.

[2] *Ta Kung Daily* (*Dagong Bao*), Peking, June 20, 1962, p. 1. Editorial.

[3] *Collected Laws and Regulations* . . . Vol. 11, p. 40. Li Hsien-nien, Minister of Finance: 'Report on the Final State Accounts for 1959 and the Draft State Budget for 1960.'

[4] Ibid., Vol. 7, p. 224. For the arrangements for the division of profits of joint state-private commercial enterprises in 1957, see ibid., Vol. 5, pp. 145–7.

[5] See pp. 421–4 below on the changes that have occurred from time to time in the role of the Bank in the control of working capital.

[6] *Red Flag* (*Hongqi*), No. 16, August 16, 1960, p. 19. Huang Ya-kuang, Deputy Director of People's Bank: 'Non-Cash Settlement of Accounts through the Bank in Our Country.'

[7] *Ta Kung Daily* (*Dagong Bao*), Peking, November 24, 1959, p. 2, and *Red Flag* (*Hongqi*), No. 1, January 1, 1960, p. 12. Li Hsien-nien, Minister of Finance: 'Some Problems in Finance and Currency Work.'

ordinary Party branches.[1] Many discharged servicemen, regarded as a political elite, are assigned to leading posts in commercial work, although usually they have no relevant experience.[2]

Many of the changes in commercial administration are interpretable in terms of a conflict between the desire for tight political control of trade and the need for efficiency. Policies furthering political control include the preference for allocation over commercial exchange, the desire to confine what trade is necessary, to state organs (or those, such as supply and marketing co-operatives, scarcely distinguishable from them) rather than permitting other channels (rural markets, pedlars, warehouses) to operate; and the organization of trade according to geographic administrative units and not according to natural economic flows. Economic efficiency, however, demands the contrary policies. The apogee of attempted political control was, of course, 1958. In the hard years that followed, necessity forced a greater regard for measures favouring economic efficiency.

The second point about China's commercial system that must constantly be borne in mind is the extent of divergence in practice from any blueprint decreed from above; this we have often had occasion to note. Indeed, it may be surmised that only through frequent evasion has the system been rendered at all viable.

Thirdly, it must not be forgotten how large a part of total output never enters the market at all, nor yet is subject to allocation. Much of China's agriculture and domestic handicrafts is of a subsistence nature, being consumed by the producer. Until the productivity of the rural labour force is increased, a severe limit is imposed on the growth of trade. As the subsistence element in the economy diminishes, the organization and control of commerce will become matters of increasing complexity.

[1] *Ta Kung Daily* (*Dagong Bao*), Peking, June 7, 1964, p. 1.
[2] Ibid., October 15, 1963, p. 1, and ibid., February 29, 1964, p. 1. Editorial, and *People's Handbook* (*Renmin Shouce*) *1964*, p. 525. Yao Yi-lin, Minister of Commerce: 'Some Hopes for Commercial Work in 1964.'

Chapter 12

FOREIGN TRADE

In quantitative terms, foreign trade has always been a marginal activity in the Chinese economy. The country's total foreign trade, imports and exports together, was estimated for 1965 at less than US $3,900 million, that is at around US $5–$6 a head of the population, considerably below the *per capita* levels of India and Pakistan. Communist China has never published any detailed statistical information about its foreign trade, nor any figures at all on it in recent years. Therefore, information has to be derived from the returns of China's trade partners, an exercise fraught with statistical hazards. In addition, figures in terms of value are distorted by the use of different pricing bases in the case of trade with Communist and non-Communist countries.[1] Hence the statistics given in this chapter should be treated with considerable caution. Unfortunately, too, the lack of information on trade between China and Mongolia, North Korea and North Vietnam means that some of the more careful calculations (such as those of the *UN Statistical Yearbook* given below) include the external trade of these four countries together:

External Trade of China Mainland, Mongolia, N. Korea and N. Vietnam (excluding mutual trade between these countries)

(from Table of World Exports by provenance and destination—f.o.b.)

US $ million

	1953	1957	1958	1959	1960	1961	1962	1963	1964
Imports	1,340	1,510	1,980	2,180	2,090	1,560	1,350	1,410	1,600
Exports	1,130	1,700	1,970	2,210	2,040	1,600	1,680	1,720	1,860
Total	2,470	3,210	3,950	4,390	4,130	3,160	3,030	3,130	3,460

Source: UN Statistical Yearbook 1965, New York, 1965, pp. 399 and 404. 'Estimates based partly on import data of trading partners. Where exports to China (Taiwan) could not be distinguished from exports to China (Mainland) they are shown as exports to China (Mainland).' Ibid., p. 406, fn. 5.

The importance of China's international trade, has been out of proportion to its size. This was already true before the Second World War, in that foreign trade formed a link with the modern world economy and served as a channel for introducing new ideas and methods into China. The change in the post-1949 composition of the country's trade, more especially of imports, increased this disproportionate significance. The chief feature of the import trade in the regime's first decade was the predominance of capital goods which, in the

[1] See *China Quarterly*, No. 19, July–September 1964, pp. 47–65. Kang Chao: 'Pitfalls in the Use of China's Foreign Trade Statistics', on this involved subject.

years 1952–8, accounted for over 90 per cent value of total imports.[1] No official figures are available for subsequent years, but the large purchases of grain in 1961 and later, lowered the proportion of capital goods, as can be seen from figures given below for Chinese imports in 1965, compiled by Western observers. These grain imports are a reversion to pre-war patterns of trade when China's coastal cities imported much of their foodstuffs from abroad.

Changes in the composition of exports have also been considerable. Between 1950 and 1957, the proportion of industrial and mining products in China's exports grew, while processed agricultural products rose relatively to unprocessed. Agricultural difficulties after the Great Leap led to a fall in farm produce available for export. In the mid-1960s, raw materials—agricultural and industrial—still predominated in China's export trade. Some of the chief agricultural exports, such as poultry and pig products, are of commodities produced largely on peasants' private plots. Estimates by outside observers of the commodity composition of China's foreign trade are given in the following table:

	US $ million
Chinese Exports in 1965	
Grains	150
Meat products	150
Other foodstuffs	230
Other agricultural products	290
Industrial materials	400
Textiles	530
Others	335
Total	2,085
Chinese imports in 1965	
Grains	400
Other foodstuffs	130
Other agricultural products	150
Fertilizers	140
Industrial materials	490
Machinery and equipment (including vehicles)	340
Others	120
Total	1,770

Source: Current Scene, Vol. IV, No. 4, February 15, 1966, p. 11.

In the years after 1949 the direction of China's foreign trade underwent several changes. The Communist victory was followed by a major switch in commerce towards other Communist lands; ideological preferences were reinforced by the Western embargo imposed at the time of the Korean war. The succeeding fluctuations in the percentage of China's foreign trade conducted with Communist countries is given in the following table, to which our previous comments on distortion caused by differences in price bases is particularly relevant. The yuan-rouble rate from 1950 to 1960 overstates the

[1] *Ten Great Years*, Peking, 1960, p. 176.

percentage of trade with Communist countries; with the devaluation of the rouble in 1961, this would seem to have ceased.[1]

Percentage of China's Trade (Exports and Imports)
Conducted with Communist Countries

1950	1953	1955	1957	1959	1960	1961	1962	1963	1964
25	69	74	62	61	61	69	43	40	36

Sources: 1950–7 China Association Annual Report 1963–4, London, p. 14.
1959–62 Ibid., *1964–5*, p. 6.
1963–4 Ibid., *1965–6*, p. 8.

From 1950 to 1956 China had an import surplus with the Soviet Union on account of Soviet deliveries under the various credit agreements. From 1957 to 1965 this changed to an export surplus as China was repaying the loans, repayment being completed early in 1965. The fall in the percentage of China's trade conducted with Communist countries from 1961 onwards reflects both the heavy grain imports, obtainable only from non-Communist lands (notably Canada, Australia, France, Mexico and the Argentine) and the desire to lessen China's dependence on the Soviet *bloc* as a result of Sino-Soviet political dissensions.

This is not the place to discuss in detail the relative importance of political or economic motives in the direction and conduct of China's foreign trade. Both factors have been present in varying measure at different times and towards different countries. On the one hand the Chinese Government has shown no reluctance to trade with countries which do not recognize it. On the other, special attention has been given to parts of the world where China has wished to exert influence and where in many cases trade has been accompanied by the giving of aid. Foreign aid commitments undertaken by China between 1953 and 1960 have been estimated at US $1,200 million, to which further grants were added in subsequent years. Over 70 per cent of this total comprised promises to China's Communist neighbours (North Korea, North Vietnam and Mongolia).[2]

Not only the direction, but also the organization, of China's foreign trading system has been altered very considerably by the Communist regime. However, in many cases this represents a development of trends that were already apparent before 1949, and even before 1937. Chinese Communist writers like to contrast the control of foreign trade by foreign merchants and their Chinese hirelings, the compradores, in the earlier era, with the operations of national trading corporations in the new China. This is an over-simplification. Up to 1937, the great bulk of China's overseas trade, it is true, was in the hands of Western and Japanese companies. Nevertheless, since the 1860s,

[1] I am indebted to P. J. D. Wiles for a discussion of this point. See also P. J. D. Wiles: *Communist International Economics*, New York, 1967, Ch. 15.

[2] US Department of Agriculture: *Trends and Developments in Communist China's World Trade in Farm Products 1955–60*, Washington DC, 1962, p. 11, and A. Eckstein: *Communist China's Economic Growth and Foreign Trade*, New York, 1966, pp. 305–7. Countries to which China promised aid at various times include North Korea, North Vietnam, Mongolia, Cambodia, Laos, Nepal, Pakistan, Burma, Indonesia, Ceylon, Yemen, Kenya, Central African Republic, Tanzania, UAR, Syria, Algeria, Guinea, Mali, Somali, Cuba, Hungary and Albania.

Chinese merchants had been competing in this trade, and after 1930 on an extensive scale. In the 1930s, the Chinese Government also began to participate in direct foreign trade operations through official concerns, such as the China Vegetable Oil Corporation and the China Silk Corporation, some of which had monopoly powers. At this time, China also conducted intergovernmental barter trade with Germany.[1]

The role of the government in foreign trade was greatly augmented during the Sino-Japanese War, when the Japanese capture of the ports disrupted China's previous pattern of trade. The small foreign commerce that remained to Free China was channelled through official corporations. Nor was the position greatly changed by the defeat of Japan in 1945. The Western merchant firms had suffered severely in the war and never regained their old position.

Thus, when the new regime made international trade a virtual government monopoly, it was not merely adopting the Soviet model but also carrying further the practices of its predecessor, the Kuomintang Government. Foreign merchant houses were before long squeezed out and foreign firms trading with China were not able to maintain branch office or resident representatives in the country. The share of private Chinese traders in exporting and importing also fell swiftly from 32 per cent in 1950 to 8 per cent in 1952.[2] The bulk of the country's international commerce was conducted by the foreign trade corporations that had been established as government organs.

The government was anxious to make use of the experience and overseas contacts of the private traders, especially in view of the admitted deficiencies of the official corporations, so that foreign trade was not formally declared a government monopoly. However, no independent scope was left to these remnants of private enterprise. By 1956 they were all transformed into joint state-private undertakings and worked under such close direction of one or other of the state corporations that they could scarcely be said to have a separate existence.[3]

A certain amount of trade on traditional lines, outside the scope of the foreign trade corporations, has continued at various times since 1949 across some of the land frontiers of China. Itinerant traders from Yunnan, for example, have been encountered in north Thailand and Laos.[4] Across the Sino-Indian frontier, old style trade also continues. Little can be said about the volume or the organization of this trade but its existence must not be forgotten.

The Ministry of Foreign Trade was established in 1952 on the division of the former Ministry of Trade. The Minister, since that date, has been Yeh

---

[1] G. C. Allen and A. Donnithorne: *Western Enterprise in Far Eastern Economic Development: China and Japan*, London, 1954, pp. 43, 50–1 and 55.

[2] Hsü Ti-hsin: *An Analysis of China's Economy in the Transitional Period* (in Chinese). Revised edition, Peking, 1959, p. 221.

[3] Hsü Ti-hsin: op. cit., pp. 221–2, and *The Eighth National Congress of the Communist Party of China*, Vol. II. Speeches, Peking, 1956, pp. 167–8. Speech by Ch'en Yün, and A. Nove and D. Donnelly: *Trade with Communist Countries*, London, 1960, p. 151.

[4] Information kindly supplied by Gordon Downer of the School of Oriental and African Studies, London.

Chi-chuang, the previous Minister of Trade. Under the State Council's Office of Finance and Trade, the Ministry of Foreign Trade is charged with the planning and conduct of China's international commerce. Its responsibilities include the formulation and implementation of the national foreign exchange plans, commercial negotiations with foreign powers, the administration of the Customs and of quality inspection stations for imports and exports.

The official foreign trade corporations specializing in different types of product operate under the aegis of the Ministry of Foreign Trade. By 1955 every province had established its own bureau of foreign trade.[1] These provincial bureaux, together with those established by local authorities below the provincial level, and those set up at ports, officially come under the joint supervision of the Ministry of Foreign Trade and of the local authorities concerned. (A similar system of joint subordination to their respective ministries and local authorities operates, as we have seen in earlier chapters, in the case of all other local bureaux and departments.) The Ministry is therefore at the head of two inter-connected systems, the one (the specialized corporations) organized according to commodity and the other on an internal territorial basis.

The headquarters organization of the Ministry of Foreign Trade was described in 1962 by a Taiwan periodical which is not contradicted, and is on several points confirmed, by the scanty information on the subject available from the mainland. According to this source, there were at that time within the Ministry four divisions concerned with commercial relations with different parts of the world. The first dealt with the Soviet Union, North Korea, North Vietnam and Mongolia; the second with the Communist countries of East Europe; the third with the West and the fourth with non-Communist Asia and with Africa. In addition, the Ministry possessed a number of functional divisions: two concerned respectively with imports and exports in general, a division concerned with the import and export of complete projects and equipment; a division controlling the quality inspection stations established at ports, a division of comprehensive planning, and others concerned with technical co-operation and transport, as well as with internal administrative requirements. An institute of market research also forms part of the Ministry.[2]

A Hong Kong source reported in 1963 that the Ministry of Foreign Trade had set up in Canton an Office of a Special Commissioner for south China, with full authority to deal on the spot with questions of foreign trade.[3]

In 1953, the Maritime Customs was made subordinate to the Ministry of Foreign Trade, having previously been directly under the State Council's predecessor, the Government Administrative Council.[4] The traditional reasons for customs duties are virtually meaningless in an economy such as

---

[1] *Collected Laws and Regulations of the People's Republic of China* (in Chinese), Vol. 2, p. 594.

[2] *Mainland Today* (*Jinri Dalu*), No. 153, February 1, 1962, p. 9. Ai T'o-ya: 'The Communist Organs of Foreign Trade.'

[3] *China Weekly* (*Zuguo*), No. 554, August 26, 1963, p. 11.

[4] *New China Monthly* (*Xinhua Yuebao*), No. 40, February 1953, p. 8.

China's. Their protective function is unnecessary where the state monopolizes foreign trade and their use as a fiscal device is superfluous as the state can achieve the same end simply by raising the domestic sales prices of imports. However, import duties are retained as formal bargaining counters in trade negotiations with non-Communist lands. In 1951, a new tariff was promulgated which, *inter alia*, provided for minimum rates of duty on goods from countries giving China reciprocal most-favoured nation treatment, and general duty rates on imports from other countries.[1] It is not known if changes have been made since 1951. In reply to a request by the author in 1963, for a schedule of China's import duties, the China Council for the Promotion of International Trade said that they did not have this on hand. We shall later see that customs duties have an internal significance as providing a source of revenue under the direct control of the central government.[2]

The Ministry of Foreign Trade controls Chinese commercial attachés and representatives abroad and is also responsible for technical exchanges and for negotiations on technical matters.[3]

According to the notions of economic planning prevalent in China, as in other Communist countries, trade is a residual item, a way of making up deficiencies or disposing of surpluses after the economic plan for a country or locality has been compiled.[4] Such an attitude makes it difficult to formulate the foreign trade plan until after the rest of the plan has been drawn up. This tardiness, in turn, makes it hard to ensure supplies of goods for export; the dependence for many export commodities on the fluctuating fortunes of agriculture aggravates this difficulty.[5] As we have seen in Chapter 11, this concept of trade also gave rise to a trend towards provincial self-sufficiency which manifested itself after the decentralization of the planning system.

The residual view of trade is in conflict with the idea of comparative costs, according to which it pays to specialize on those branches of production in which relative efficiency is greatest, even if this involves importing goods which could be made at home. Some modification of this attitude, and a consideration of comparative costs, may be indicated by the decision in the mid-1960s to increase the acreage under cotton in China at the expense of wheat cultivation which was, in fact, a decision to import more wheat and less raw cotton. However, in general, price considerations have not played a major role in the planning of foreign trade. One consequence of this has been a divorce between domestic and international prices about which we shall expatiate further below.

The concept of trade as a residual item in economic planning gives the

[1] *Tariff of Import Duties of the Chinese People's Republic* (in Chinese), published by the Chinese Maritime Customs, 1951, and *Foreign Trade of the People's Republic of China*, No. 2, June 1963, p. 2. Chen Ti-pao: 'Supervision and Control of Imports and Exports by the Chinese Customs Administration.'

[2] See pp. 397–8 below.

[3] *Collected Laws and Regulations* . . . Vol. 3, p. 82.

[4] For an example of this way of thinking, see *Documents of the Eighth National Congress of the Communist Party of China* (in Chinese), Peking, 1956, p. 607. Speech by Yeh Chi-chuang, Minister of Foreign Trade.

[5] In 1956, for example, the majority of foreign trade corporations failed to fulfil their export plans. *Planned Economy* (*Jihua Jingji*), No. 2, February 1958, p. 28. Li Po-fang: 'Energetically Organize the Supply of Exports.'

Chinese authorities a strong preference for bilateral dealings, as these can be fitted into the plan more easily than is the case with multilateral trade. In the words of the Minister of Foreign Trade in 1959, 'to follow the policy of equality and mutual benefit, each making up what the other lacks and attaining a balance by barter, is our fundamental principle in foreign trade activities . . . the development of trade which meets the requirements of both parties is helpful to the development of an independent economy and conducive to payment balances of both parties. We are also willing to trade with Western countries according to this principle, so that a fundamental balance can be obtained between imports and exports.'[1]

Planning of foreign trade—both of import requirements and of export availabilities—was radically affected by the changes which were made in the economic planning system in 1958. These had the effect of restricting central government to setting figures for certain major items and for the rest, to limit itself to the control of transfer balances between provincial level units. Among the major items for which the central government was still to set targets were total imports and exports, together with the volume of important commodities figuring among them.[2] Different commercial ministries of the central government have responsibility for organizing internal trade in different commodities, and it now fell to them to effect inter-provincial transfer balances of different commodities.[3] Among these ministries, the Ministry of Foreign Trade has performed this function for certain major export commodities including skins, wool, pig bristles, intestines, feathers, carpets, silk and silk cocoons, and other products.[4]

At the same time, in 1958, another change was made in the methods of compiling import plans. Previously units wanting imported goods submitted their applications to the Ministry of Foreign Trade, after sending them for consideration to the relevant production ministries (i.e. the ministry concerned with making the type of commodities it was proposed to import). Henceforward it was to be the production ministries themselves which actually submitted to the Ministry of Foreign Trade the plans for imports. For example, in the case of iron and steel products, the import plans were to be submitted by the Ministry of Metallurgical Industry. It was hoped this would prevent the import of goods which could be produced in China, while those which could not be produced, failed to be imported.[5] Also no doubt it was intended to prevent the practice prevalent in some quarters of attempting to cut down delays by placing similar orders simultaneously at home and abroad.[6]

A parallel change was made in the export trade. All exports were to be channelled through the Ministry of Foreign Trade (presumably through the head offices of the foreign trade corporations), so that the phenomenon

[1] China News Service, Canton, September 2, 1959. Yeh Chi-chuang, Minister of Foreign Trade: 'China's Foreign Trade during the Past Decade.'
[2] See p. 462 below, and *Collected Laws and Regulations* . . . Vol. 8, p. 96.
[3] Ibid., p. 99. See also p. 286 above.
[4] *Collected Laws and Regulations* . . . Vol. 9, pp. 160–2.
[5] *Planned Economy (Jihua Jingji)*, No. 10, October 1958, p. 36. She Yi-san: 'A Discussion of the Change in the Allocation System for Raw Materials.'
[6] Ibid., No. 3, March 1958, p. 29. Wang Ti: 'Stop up Holes through which Foreign Exchange is Leaking Out to Waste.'

would not recur of goods being exported abroad from one part of the country while goods of the same type were being imported by another area.[1] This implies that previously there had been considerable local initiative in exporting. It is also interesting as giving an example of greater centralization at a time when in other spheres more powers were being handed down to local authorities. Possibly in course of time this apparent restriction on export trade conducted by local authorities was modified, in the same way as local powers appear to have increased in other economic spheres. This may be borne out by the large number of export advertisements in the official journal, *China's Foreign Trade*, which emanate from local branches of the foreign trade corporations.

State corporations for foreign trade had already existed, as we have seen, under Kuomintang rule. In March 1950, the new Communist government established or re-established six such corporations (five for pig bristles, native products, oils and fats, mineral products and tea respectively and one for imports) simultaneously with the creation of similar organs to conduct internal trade.[2] These corporations are independent economic accounting units. In subsequent years, their number was increased until in 1956 it reached sixteen. At the end of 1960, fourteen were in existence; amalgamations in the spring of 1961 reduced this total to ten; two more were established in 1965 and another at the beginning of 1966. The thirteen foreign trade corporations operating in the autumn of 1966 were:

The China National Cereals, Oils and Foodstuffs Import and Export Corporation.
The China National Tea and Native Produce Import and Export Corporation.
The China National Animal By-Products Import and Export Corporation.
The China National Textiles Import and Export Corporation.
The China National Light Industrial Products Import and Export Corporation.
The China National Chemicals Import and Export Corporation.
The China National Machinery Import and Export Corporation.
The China National Metals and Minerals Import and Export Corporation.
The China National Technical Import Corporation.
The China National Complete Plant Export Corporation.
The China National Arts and Crafts Import and Export Corporation.
The China National Garments Import and Export Corporation.
The China National Instruments Import and Export Corporation.

The China Publications Centre (*Guozi Shudian*—literally 'International Bookshop') is responsible for the export of books and periodicals. These are not reckoned to be 'commercial commodities' but 'cultural commodities'— a classification which unfortunately sometimes acts to restrict their availability to the would-be foreign purchaser.

---

[1] *Planned Economy* (*Jihua Jingji*), No. 10, October 1958, p. 36. She Yi-san: loc. cit.
[2] *New China Monthly* (*Xinhua Yuebao*), No. 6, April 1950, p. 1408: 'Decision on Measures to Unify Nation-wide State Trade.' 'Native products' covers handicrafts and articles such as indigenous medicines and certain edible products.

In addition to the national foreign trade corporations, there are two corporations engaged in transport matters relating to foreign trade—the China National Foreign Trade Transportation Corporation and Sinofracht Chartering and Ship Broking Corporation; also one of a special local character, the China Resources Company of Hong Kong which acts as agent in that colony for most of the other specialized corporations. Except for the China Resources Company, the corporations all have their head offices in Peking. Most of them have branch offices at the main ports concerned with the particular products in which they deal, and sub-branches at smaller places. It is noticeable that recent advertisements in Chinese trade promotion literature almost all carry the name of the branch of the corporation concerned to which enquiries should be made. Usually the branch is that of a port city—e.g. the Shanghai, Tientsin, Dairen or Canton branch. Sometimes, however, advertisements name provincial or equivalent branches of corporations: for example, the Hupeh Branch of the China National Cereals, Oils and Foodstuffs Import and Export Corporation or the Kwangsi Chuang Autonomous Region Branch of the China National Metals and Minerals Import and Export Corporation. These branch corporations are presumably identical with the provincial import and export corporations (e.g. the Hupeh Provincial Animal By-Products Import and Export Corporation)[1] or with the 'port corporations' (*k'ouan kungszu*)[2] mentioned on occasion in the Chinese press.

These two types of local corporations (or branches of corporations) might be thought to be different in function, the one acting as agents at a point of export, and the other operating within one particular province, although in the case of a coastal province the two might be combined. However, some inland provinces have offices of their branches of the national corporations at port cities—e.g. the Canton office of the Yunnan branch of the China National Cereals, Oils, and Foodstuffs Import and Export Corporation.[3]

Some branches of foreign trade corporations are empowered to place orders direct with foreign suppliers, instead of going through their head office in Peking. Provincial branches in different provinces are known to export tinned goods under different brand names. This degree of autonomy must be considered in conjunction with the provision of 1957 that provinces were to receive a percentage of the foreign currency proceeds of some lines of trade, a topic to which we shall revert below.

Provincial bureaux of foreign trade exercise direct control (or did in 1957) of the branches of the national import and export corporations situated within their boundaries.[4] Thus the question of the extent of provincial autonomy in matters of foreign trade cannot be separated from that of the extent of autonomy enjoyed by the branch offices of the corporations.

The foreign trade corporations are essentially agents, to which the relevant ministries and their subordinate organs and enterprises entrust tasks of buying and selling specific quantities of goods at the best prices obtainable and in

[1] *Daily Worker* (*Gongren Ribao*), August 24, 1963, p. 1.

[2] *China's Foreign Trade* (*Duiwai Maoyi*), No. 1, January 1963, p. 5. 'The China National Chemicals Import and Export Corporation and its Port Corporations.'

[3] Advertisement in *China's Foreign Trade* (*Duiwai Maoyi*), No. 3, May 1966.

[4] *Trade with China: A Practical Guide* published by *Ta Kung Daily* (*Dagong Bao*), Hong Kong, 1957, p. 34.

accordance with the economic plans of the state. Although in theory the quantities of products to be imported and exported are laid down in annual or longer term plans, actual experience has shown that planned exports have not always been available, especially during the years of agricultural disaster from 1959 to 1961; this in turn has forced the revision of import plans.

In 1957 the corporations charged ministries ordering certain types of imported goods (e.g. complete plant, most machinery, instruments and industrial raw materials) a service fee of 2 or 3 per cent of cost, and in the case of other goods, handed over the imports to the Ministry of Commerce at prices agreed by the two ministries.[1]

As a result of the divorce of domestic and foreign prices, and the overvaluation of the *yuan*, exports have usually showed a loss when the foreign exchange earned was converted into *yuan* at the official rate, while imports have showed a profit. The profits made on imports are set against losses on exports.[2] However, not all exports are made at a book-keeping loss. In 1957, woollen goods woven from imported wool were exported at a profit equal to 60 per cent of the export price. At that date certain agricultural products were also exported at a profit—soya beans, for example, at a profit of 36 per cent, peanut oil 14·2 per cent, and frozen pork 8·6 per cent (similarly, it is implied, given as a percentage of the export price.)[3] We do not have information about how this profit was calculated. It may have been reckoned on the same basis as the *preisausgleich* of East Germany, the special profit or subsidy accruing to the foreign trade enterprises as a result of trade.[4] For exports from East Germany this was the difference between the domestic transfer price (price to the producing enterprise plus turnover tax) at which the goods for export were bought, and the foreign currency proceeds of their sales abroad, converted back at the official rate; for imports this was, of course, reversed. Because of the arbitrary nature of internal pricing, the *preisausgleich* provided no reliable criterion, from the standpoint of East Germany as a whole, of what goods should be imported or exported.[5]

The Ministry of Foreign Trade and its subordinate organs were affected by the decentralization measures of 1957–8 in a way similar to the internal trading system. However, two special provisions applied to foreign trade. It was laid down that provinces were not entitled to share profits obtained from the foreign sales portion of foreign trade but that, as in the past, they were to share profits deriving from the domestic sales arising out of foreign trade.[6] This presumably means that provinces were to share profits made by organs of the internal trade system on sales of goods for export to organs of the foreign trade system, as well as those accruing from sales of imports on the domestic market.

---

[1] *People's Handbook* (*Renmin Shouce*) *1958*, p. 559. Yeh Chi-chuang, Minister of Foreign Trade: 'A Talk on Foreign Trade', Summary of Speech to the First Session of the Fourth National People's Congress.

[2] Ibid. In Shanghai there are specially designated shops where foreign seamen and tourists can buy certain commodities at half the domestic retail price. *Far Eastern Economic Review*, August 19, 1965, p. 340.

[3] *New China Fortnightly* (*Xinhua Banyuekan*), No. 108, May 25, 1957, p. 111.

[4] F. L. Pryor: *The Communist Foreign Trade System*, London, 1963, p. 101.

[5] Ibid.

[6] *Collected Laws and Regulations* ... Vol. 6, p. 356.

On foreign exchange, the new regulations stated that local authorities were to receive a definite, but unspecified, percentage of the foreign currency proceeds obtained from the export of certain (unstated) industrial and agricultural goods.[1] It was said that further instructions on this matter would be issued; these have not come our way. Reports suggest that provinces may in addition be permitted to retain foreign currency proceeds of their above-plan exports. Before the decentralization decrees took effect, we read of the Ministry of Foreign Trade allocating foreign exchange to provinces and ports for specific purposes.[2] It is not known how far this continued after decentralization or whether provinces were supposed to cater for their own import requirements with their retained percentage of foreign currency. After the decentralization of industry and trade, the import requirements (and the export capabilities) of provincial level authorities must have increased considerably.

Responsibility for organizing the internal trade in certain major export products rests, as we have seen, with the Ministry of Foreign Trade.[3] This responsibility is discharged through the Ministry's specialized corporations, listed above, whose duties include (or, at least, formerly included) the provision of credit and technical assistance to the producers when circumstances warranted.

The effect of the changes in economic organization in 1958–9 on the activities of the foreign trade corporations is illustrated by new regulations published in October 1958 on the system of collecting silk cocoons. Before 1958 the supply and marketing co-operatives formed the immediate links between foreign trade corporations and rural producers. With the absorption in that year, at least in many places, of supply and marketing co-operatives into the communes,[4] previous arrangements had to be altered. Formerly the supply and marketing co-operatives had collected fresh cocoons which were then dried in plants operated by the co-operatives, although the capital for the plants had been supplied by the Ministry of Foreign Trade. After the decentralization measures, great variations developed in local commercial arrangements. In places, the cocoon-drying plants lost their connection with the Ministry of Foreign Trade and its organs, and came instead under a local department of commerce or of industry. Where supply and marketing co-operatives had ceased to exist, the previous arrangements for the collection and processing of fresh silk cocoons broke down. The Ministry of Foreign Trade remained the legal owner of the processing plants, but as it had no organs operating at that level, this property was of little value to it. The Ministry thereupon laid down that from 1959 it would collect only dried cocoons, that the existing plants and their equipment would be handed over free of charge to the communes, which would in future be responsible for drying the cocoons and for building new plants.[5] Unfortunately we do not have information about how these regulations worked in practice, nor whether the cocoon-drying plants were the type of enterprise which continued under commune management even after the

---

[1] *Collected Laws and Regulations* ... Vol. 6, p. 357.
[2] *People's Handbook (Renmin Shouce) 1958*, p. 558.
[3] p. 324 above.
[4] See pp. 293–4 above.
[5] *Collected Laws and Regulations* ... Vol. 8, pp. 172–3.

communes had lost many of their earlier functions. Probably, as the announcement itself suggests, the widely differing circumstances and administrative developments of different districts were reflected in very divergent relations between the Ministry's organs and local producers in the case of silk-cocoons and of other products.

From 1959, the revived rural markets provided convenient centres for the purchase of agricultural output and rural handicrafts for exports. Since then the contract system has been one of the main links between the export corporations and their suppliers of industrial and farm goods.[1] Sometimes, as mentioned, credit is extended to producers by organs of the foreign trade system. For example, in 1960 in a district of Kwangtung near the Hong Kong border, the Shekki Fruit and Vegetable Export Company was making advance payments for produce to production brigades.[2] In this connection it may be noted that in the case of goods for export produced by units of collective agriculture, handicraft concerns and workshops, an exception has been made to the general prohibition of payments in advance, provided that these advances do not exceed 25 per cent of the value of the goods and that they be repaid within ten months.[3] (Advances, however, are also given for agricultural produce destined for the home market.)

Foreign merchants dealing with the Chinese import and export corporations have frequently noted a sharp distinction between the political and technical men on their staffs. The qualifications of those heading the corporations are often mainly political. However, it is generally agreed that the technical men below them are usually competent and well-versed in their trades; they include former employees of Western firms, as well as former proprietors of trading concerns, and also younger men trained since 1949. No single staff member ever appears to be empowered to come to a decision on the spot, but has to refer matters back before giving a definite answer.

Considerable interchange takes place between posts in the Ministry of Foreign Trade, the foreign trade corporations, and the commercial sections of Chinese diplomatic missions abroad.

In the period of free speech in 1957, complaints were made of discrimination against non-members of the Party in organs of the Ministry of Foreign Trade. Party members were said to be given swift promotion over the heads of others better qualified who had, in fact, to carry the burden of the work. Party members were also more likely to be sent on delegations abroad. Staff was alleged to be grossly swollen beyond requirements.[4]

The China Council for the Promotion of International Trade was established in 1952, in accordance with a resolution passed at the International Economic Conference held at Moscow in that year.[5] The Council is not officially a government organ, although it is effectively under government control. Its chief tasks are to negotiate trade agreements with foreign governments and private commercial missions, often dealing with Western countries and organizations

---

[1] See p. 295 above.
[2] *Southern Daily* (*Nanfang Ribao*), November 30, 1960 (SCMP 2412).
[3] *Collected Laws and Regulations* . . . Vol. 9, p. 142.
[4] *People's Daily* (*Renmin Ribao*), May 17, 1957, p. 4.
[5] *People's Handbook* (*Renmin Shouce*) *1953*, p. 433.

which might not want direct contact with the Chinese Government. The Council fulfils many of the functions of a chamber of commerce. It arranges Chinese participation in economic exhibitions and fairs abroad, and assists foreign organizations in holding similar exhibitions in China. The Chairman of the Council, Nan Han-ch'en, is also the Director General of the Bank of China, a bank which specializes in foreign transactions.[1]

The Foreign Trade Arbitration Commission was established in 1956 and comes under the auspices of the China Council for the Promotion of International Trade.[2] Chinese foreign trade corporations normally insist on arbitration in Peking being stipulated in contracts but, in exceptional circumstances, they have agreed to arbitration in a neutral country or in the country of the defendant. It has rarely been found necessary for disputes with the Chinese corporations to be taken to arbitration.

In January 1960 a new body, the General Bureau for Foreign Economic Relations, was set up directly subordinate to the State Council. The announcement of its creation said that the Bureau was to give added strength in shouldering the ever-increasing responsibilities of the country's foreign economic relations, but did not give any further indication of the nature or scope of its duties.[3] The occasions on which its officials are reported to be present, suggest that it is concerned with China's foreign aid programme, although it may also have other duties. This bureau, together with a number of other Chinese organs for foreign trade and for other aspects of foreign economic relations, are modelled on Soviet organs in these fields.

In their conduct of international trade, the Chinese Government has shown a strong preference for the conclusion of bilateral trade agreements. Between 1950 and 1954, China made trade agreements with all the countries of the Soviet bloc and with the other Asian Communist lands. This was followed by a swift rise in mutual commerce. These agreements were in some cases on an annual basis and, in others, for a longer term supplemented by annual protocols. For the most part they were concluded on a government-to-government footing but in 1958 two nominally non-governmental (although in fact officially controlled) bodies, the All China Federation of Supply and Marketing Co-operatives and the Soviet Central Union of Consumer Co-operatives, made an agreement for the exchange of goods between each other.[4]

While trade agreements have been of special significance in dealing with Communist countries, they have also had a part in commercial relations with other lands. The earliest of these agreements with non-Communists were made with unofficial groups (sometimes of political sympathizers) from various Western European countries. Similarly, in 1962, the unofficial Liao-Takasaki agreement provided for an expansion of Sino-Japanese trade. (In addition from 1960 onwards, China—which in 1958 had broken off almost all trade with Japan on political grounds—had designated certain Japanese companies as 'friendly firms'; a number of such firms were in fact subsidiaries specially established for the purpose by some of the chief companies in Japan.)

[1] See p. 407 below.
[2] *People's Handbook* (*Renmin Shouce*) *1957*, p. 523.
[3] *Collected Laws and Regulations* . . . Vol. 11, pp. 92–3.
[4] NCNA, July 14, 1958.

Government-to-government trade agreements have also been concluded between China and some non-Communist states.

The normal type of annual trade agreement between China and other Communist countries has specified the commodities to be exchanged and laid down terms of delivery, the currency of payment, and the method of determining prices. As well as these general agreements, there have been others of a more specialized nature concerned with matters such as credit, and also contracts relating to a single transaction. Almost all China's trade agreements have been bilateral: one exception is the triangular agreement concluded in 1952 between China, the Soviet Union, and Finland.[1] The question of price determination in trade agreements will be treated below.

The normal trade agreements are only statements of intent. On the basis of these agreements, operational contracts are concluded by the Chinese foreign trade corporations with their foreign counterparts or with private firms, as the case might be. It has been shown that in trade between European Communist countries, these specific contracts have not always tallied with the government-to-government trade agreements.[2] In China's case, the two appear to have diverged not infrequently, due in large measure to China's inability to supply goods required by its trading partners.

The Chinese Government has not shared the growing attachment to the importance of trade and of international division of labour evidenced by the Soviet Union and other members of the Council for Mutual Economic Assistance since the late 1950s. In the letter of June 14, 1963, from the Central Committee of the Chinese Communist Party to the Central Committee of the Soviet Party, the Chinese accused the Soviet Union of practising 'great-power chauvinism' in the name of 'international division of labour' and of 'specialization'. The Chinese insisted that 'every socialist country must rely mainly on itself for its construction'.[3] The ideal of the Chinese authorities is that of 'an independent and complete industrial system' which requires 'not only that we should be able to manufacture ourselves every kind of product that we need, but also that within our own country we should be self-sufficient in raw and other materials'.[4] No doubt these sentiments result not only from their views on the nature of trade, but also arise from wounded pride at having had to accept economic assistance from the Soviet Union, from resentment that Soviet aid was not greater and that it was cut off in such an abrupt manner in 1960, and from a desire to win sympathy from the less-developed countries of East Europe, such as Rumania, by echoing their fears that 'international division of labour' might be used to prevent their industrialization.

From 1956 to 1961 China and other Asian Communist lands sent observers to meetings of the Council for Mutual Economic Assistance (Comecon) which

[1] For further information on trade agreements, see C. F. Remer: *The Trade Agreements of Communist China*, Rand Corporation, Santa Monica, 1961, and C. F. Remer: 'The External Economic Relations of Communist China' in E. F. Szezepanik (ed.): *Symposium on Economic and Social Problems of the Far East*, Hong Kong, 1962, and R. F. Dernberger: 'The International Trade of Communist China', in C. F. Remer (ed.): *Three Essays on the International Economics of Communist China*, Ann Arbor, 1959.
[2] F. L. Pryor: op. cit., pp. 192–3.
[3] *Peking Review*, June 21, 1963, p. 18.
[4] *People's Daily (Renmin Ribao)*, February 10, 1966, p. 2. Editorial.

had been established in 1949 as the Soviet *bloc's* counterpart to the Organization for European Economic Co-operation. There was a period in 1958–9 when it looked as if China was going to associate herself more closely with Comecon. The fact that China did not actually belong to this body was attributed (by an Eastern European official in an interview with the author in 1958) to the Council being essentially a European organization. This excuse was hardly tenable after 1962 when Mongolia was admitted to membership, but by that time the political rift between China and the Soviet Union had become evident and Chinese observers had ceased to attend meetings of the Council although continuing for some time to be represented at sessions of certain of the specialized commissions of Comecon.[1]

Much of China's trade with the non-Communist world has been conducted without any trade agreements. One important example is trade with Hong Kong, which occupies a very significant position in the pattern of China's external commerce. Hong Kong draws a large part of its foodstuffs as well as other supplies from the Mainland and indeed in 1964 became the largest buyer of Chinese exports. The substantial favourable balances which China earns in trade with Hong Kong have been used to finance deficits with other non-Communist trading partners. Chinese willingness to benefit from multi-lateralism in this instance has not, however, affected their theoretical concepts of foreign trade.

Special measures have been taken by the Chinese Government to foster their important market in Hong Kong. An official corporation, the China Resources Company, has been established to act as Hong Kong agents for all the Chinese foreign trade corporations except for those few with separate representation in the colony. Besides the Bank of China, which has a large Hong Kong branch, a number of other banks, trading firms and retail stores in Hong Kong are effectively controlled by Peking.

Among the advantages accruing to the Chinese Government from the existence of Hong Kong, is the ability to buy urgently needed goods at short notice. It has been pointed out that the West in general provides an escape valve for the blunders of Communist planners.[2] In the case of China, Hong Kong pre-eminently fulfils this function, both directly in that many commodities can there be bought on the spot and also, indirectly, as being a convenient place for quick commercial negotiations, even with countries which do not recognize the Chinese Communist Government. Some of China's large grain purchases from 1960 onwards were settled in Hong Kong, negotiations being on occasion initiated simply by a telephone call to the local commercial representative of the country concerned.

Since 1949 it has at times been thought that the role of Hong Kong in China's import trade would decline. The authorities in Peking were anxious to cut out the merchant intermediaries and buy goods, especially capital equipment, directly from the Western manufacturers. In many lines this has

[1] For an account of Chinese relations with the Council for Mutual Economic Assistance, see M. Kaser: *Comecon*, London, 1965, pp. 63–4 and 83–9, and *The Bankers' Magazine*, April 1959, pp. 296–7. A. Donnithorne: 'The Council for Mutual Economic Aid.'

[2] F. L. Pryor: op. cit., pp. 169 and 178.

come about, but for sudden urgent requirements and for small purchases, Hong Kong's value as a shopping centre has remained high.

The possibility of constant informal contact available in Hong Kong helps to keep the trade organizations of the Chinese Government in touch with new developments in international markets. A more formal and intermittent method is provided on Chinese soil by the twice yearly export fairs held at Canton since 1957 and attended by staff members of the Chinese foreign trade corporations and by foreign merchants. While both import and export deals are made at these gatherings, the emphasis is on Chinese exports. Major import transactions, and those involving complicated plant, take place in Peking. From 1964 a more specialized gathering, the Chinese Export Garments Trade Fair, has been held twice yearly in Shanghai.

Chinese technical delegations are frequently dispatched abroad to make themselves familiar with machinery and equipment of the latest types. These delegations may place orders on the spot or may limit themselves to collecting information for later use.

Foreign businessmen often visit Peking to negotiate deals; they also send catalogues and trade journals to the Chinese foreign trade corporations and to other bodies. In recent years a number of exhibitions, sponsored by industrial and commercial interests in different lands, have been mounted in China with the object of familiarizing the Chinese with the equipment and other goods shown and thus promoting sales. Usually there is no direct contact between a Western exporter and the Chinese consuming enterprise, such as the ultimate user of imported equipment or chemicals. On rare occasions a factory in China has written directly to the supplier abroad about some problem.

Technical specialists of various nationalities have visited China, sometimes for a considerable length of time, to help with the erection and installation of capital equipment bought from abroad. As far as Westerners are concerned, these instances became more frequent when, in the mid-1960s, West European lands began to be given contracts for complete industrial plants for China as a consequence of the Sino-Soviet split. However, these cases are still exceptional. Sometimes exhibitions and technical lectures provide opportunities for contact between foreign firms and the users of their products. Ultimate users cannot, of course, import goods directly on their own account but only through the foreign trade corporations and similarly with exports.

All foreign exchange payments (except for the relatively small proportion going through the branches of the two British and three Overseas Chinese banks in Shanghai) are handled by the Bank of China, which has branches at the main Chinese ports and at various centres abroad. In respect of trade done under bilateral agreements, commercial payments should in theory balance and obviate the need of money payments, except where loans have explicitly been granted. However, the agreements generally lay down the procedure for liquidating any balances outstanding after the period of the agreement has expired. Trade between China and the European Communist states has normally used the rouble as unit of account; in trade with Asian Communist countries this has also sometimes been the case. Trade with other countries has commonly been conducted in sterling or Swiss francs.

In the course of ordinary commercial transactions, as distinct from aid agreements, the Chinese usually demand prompt payment for their exports. Credit has, however, at times been given, as for instance in trade with South East Asia. In the early days of the regime, the Chinese paid cash for their imports but from the late 1950s onwards they have tried to obtain credit where possible—up to 180 days for ordinary transactions and up to five years for capital goods.

China's trade with non-Communist countries is usually done at world market prices. There have been exceptions, such as the barter deals with Ceylon, when rice was exchanged for rubber at rates which, at least sometimes, were more favourable to Ceylon than were the ruling market prices: this was partly due to the embargo on sales to China of rubber by some of the chief producers in the early 1950s.[1]

A partiality for barter, arising from the concept of trade as a bilateral relationship, but fostered by practical considerations, was particularly evident in the early years of the regime. Distrust of foreign currency was engendered by experience at the time of the Korean War, when some of China's holdings of foreign exchange were frozen by the United States, while the purchasing power of the remainder fell. Some barter deals were concluded with both governments and private firms at that period, but in general the emphasis changed from direct barter (where goods of the same value are exchanged simultaneously) to the encouragement of linked trade, in which one transaction takes place on the understanding that eventually it will be balanced by one of roughly similar magnitude on the other side. In practice this often came to no more than that the Chinese preferred to import from firms willing to take Chinese exports.

In 1951, provisional regulations on barter trade set out four types of barter, including linked trade, and laid down that certain categories of exports could be bartered only for high priority imports, and must not be subject to 'linked barter'.[2] In actual fact, the foreign trade corporations may have behaved rather more flexibly than stipulated in these regulations. The existence of a schedule of 'value-in-exchange' of Chinese products in terms of imported goods illustrates the tendency to think of foreign trade in terms of barter. According to this schedule, for example, 400 tons of raw silk or 3,000 tons of green tea should exchange for 1 unit of 25,000 kW. thermal generating plant.[3] In recent years, instances of linked trade have been rare. Barter trade however, continues to be done on occasion with non-Communist states, as instanced by the Sino-Pakistan barter agreement of 1966.

In trade with other Communist states, conducted under bilateral agree-

[1] In 1952, when the first of these Sino-Ceylonese agreements was made, China had no alternative source of supply and the terms from 1958 to 1962 were very favourable to Ceylon. When the agreement was reviewed, the relaxation of the embargo was reflected in a lower premium for Ceylon rubber. A third agreement from 1963 to 1967 provided for only a small premium, if any. See P. Lewin: *The Foreign Trade of Communist China*, New York, 1964, pp. 65–6.

[2] *Collected Laws and Regulations on Financial and Economic Policies of the Central Government* (in Chinese), Vol. 3, pp. 344–5.

[3] *Far Eastern Economic Review*, December 17, 1959, pp. 983–4. T. C. Lee: 'China's Food, Population, Agricultural Exports—II.'

ments, the concept of barter could never be wholly absent. 'The very nature of the bilateral bargaining process makes their offer prices for exports dependent upon the prices asked by the partner country for the goods they are seeking to import. Of importance are the barter terms of trade, and not the price tags attached to the goods being exported.'[1]

The official exchange rates of the Communist countries do not reflect the relative purchasing power of their currencies, and therefore it is unrealistic to compare the value of goods being exchanged by converting domestic prices in terms of one currency into the other currency at official rates. In their mutual trade the Communist countries get over this difficulty by using world market prices. In the words of the Chinese Minister of Foreign Trade in 1957: 'Our price policy in trade with fraternal countries is for the two contracting governments to fix prices after studying capitalist world market price levels. These prices are kept stable for a given period, thus avoiding the continual fluctuations of the capitalist world markets.'[2] The result is that prices ruling in this trade lag behind world prices because the prices taken as a basis for negotiations are usually those of the previous year; and between 1953 and 1957, world market prices of 1950 were sometimes employed.[3] Frequently, prices ruling in trade with the Soviet Union were taken as the standard in agreements between China and other Communist lands.

There is known to have been considerable dissatisfaction in some quarters in China at the prices prevailing in trade with the Soviet Union. In 1957, the Minister of Foreign Trade, after discussing the price of a number of products, had maintained that taking prices of imports and exports over a period of years, the prices under the Sino-Soviet trade agreements were, in comparison with world market prices, 'fair and reasonable'.[4] However, in the very different political atmosphere of 1964, the Chinese pointed out that the prices of many of their imports from the Soviet Union were much above world market levels.[5]

Calculations made from Soviet trade returns indicate that the unit values of China's exports to the Soviet Union have been lower than in the case of similar goods sold by China to non-Communist lands, and that unit values of China's imports from the Soviet Union have been above those of West Europe's imports of similar items from the Soviet Union. Commodity quality differences are not thought to account for the whole of these differentials. More important probably has been the effect of the inclusion of long overland transport costs in prices of Chinese imports from the Soviet Union (which, in the Soviet returns, are priced f.o.b. Chinese ports or land frontiers —usually

[1] *Law and Contemporary Problems*, Vol. 24, No. 3. Summer 1959, p. 439. R. F. Mikesell and D. A. Wells: 'State Trading in the Sino-Soviet Bloc.'

[2] *Proceedings of the Fourth Session of the First National People's Congress* (in Chinese), 1957, p. 715. Speech by Yeh Chi-chuang, Minister of Foreign Trade, on July 11, 1957.

[3] *The Review of Economics and Statistics*, Vol. XLII, No. 2, May 1960. H. Mendershausen: 'The Terms of Soviet-Satellite Trade: A Broadened Analysis', and *Collected Treaties of The People's Republic of China* (in Chinese), Vols. 1–7, passim, and F. L. Pryor: op. cit., pp. 132–3.

[4] *Proceedings of the Fourth Session of the First National People's Congress*, p. 716. Yeh Chi-chuang: loc. cit.

[5] *Peking Review*, May 8, 1964, p. 13. Letter of the Central Committee of the Communist Party of China of February 29, 1964, to the Central Committee of the Communist Party of the USSR.

the latter), while prices of Chinese exports to the Soviet would, for geographic reasons, include the cost of a much shorter journey before reaching the border. Some of the differential may also be attributable to the weakness of China's bargaining position with the Soviet Union during the period when China was subject to strategic embargo by the Western powers in respect of certain goods,[1] and when in any case China had decided, for ideological reasons, to 'lean to one side' in its trading policy. In these circumstances, Chinese demand for imports from the Soviet Union was inelastic, while Soviet demand for China's exports (which were sometimes goods of low priority for the Russians and which could be obtained from other sources) was weak. It is not, therefore, surprising that the terms of trade between China and the Soviet Union were unfavourable to China.[2]

Sometimes the impression is conveyed that in matters of foreign commerce the Chinese have now reverted to the situation that obtained before 1842 and the 'opening of China'. Certain features point to this conclusion. Foreign firms may no longer establish branches on Chinese soil. Once again Chinese and Western merchants meet at biannual gatherings at Canton where, on the Chinese side, participation is limited to official monopolists—but now government corporations instead of the 'hong' merchants of the pre-Treaty Port days.

However, the parallel is far from absolute. Before 1842 foreign trade was important to the Chinese Government as a source of revenue rather than for any wider economic benefit. Indeed, the lack of demand inside China for most foreign goods—although by this time there were many lines in which Western techniques had surpassed those of China—was a major factor in the growth of trade in opium, the one product from abroad for which internal demand was strong. The demoralizing effects of this imported drug added further disrepute to the concept of foreign trade. Now the situation in this respect is radically different. Demand for foreign goods far exceeds the country's means of payment, and foreign exchange has to be allotted only for the most essential purposes. The government, therefore, has to have a more positive approach to foreign trade than that of the officials of the Ch'ing emperors.

[1] It was not difficult to circumvent the embargo although this probably added to the cost of the goods concerned. See A. Nove and D. Donnelly: op. cit., p. 112.

[2] *The China Quarterly*, No. 17, January–March 1964, pp. 174–91. Feng-hwa Mah: 'The Terms of Sino-Soviet Trade.' For a discussion of this subject, see also: A. Eckstein in H. L. Boorman et al. (ed.): *Moscow-Peking Axis*, New York, 1957, pp. 86–8, and R. F. Dernberger in C. F. Remer (ed.): *Three Essays on the International Economics of Communist China*, p. 148, and C. F. Remer in E. F. Szezepanik (ed.): *Symposium in Economic and Social Problems of the Far East*, p. 108.

Chapter 13

STATE PROCUREMENT OF AGRICULTURAL PRODUCE[1]

The process of developing China's economy requires that agriculture should produce a surplus over and above what is needed for the consumption of the rural inhabitants and their livestock and for seed purposes. This surplus is necessary to feed the population engaged in industry and mining, administration, commerce, and other non-agricultural occupations, to supply some of the essential raw materials of industry, to provision the armed forces, to export, and to build up reserves at home. Also many country dwellers, often whole districts, concentrate on non-food crops, such as cotton, and get their grain from elsewhere. The greater the quantities of agricultural produce drawn off from the cultivators, the quicker can be the development of other sectors of the economy.

In passing, it must be noted that the present need to secure a surplus from agriculture is but an accentuation of a historic problem. State appropriation of grain threads a continuous theme through Chinese history, as through those of other agricultural civilizations. The ancient reasons for it still persist—to provender the capital and the Army and to accumulate reserves, while to these have been added the demands of industrialization.

The three main methods by which the state secures an agricultural surplus are by agricultural tax in kind, by compulsory sales by the growers at official prices, and by voluntary sales. In practice the second and third methods are difficult to distinguish because contracts by which agricultural collectives or peasant households undertake to supply stipulated quantities of produce to state purchasing agencies may be concluded under varying degrees of pressure. On the other hand, some state purchases at rural markets and on other occasions may well be without any element of compulsion.

1. AGRICULTURAL TAX

The main tax on the farming population is the agricultural tax (sometimes called the grain tax) collected in kind and assessed on a hypothetical norm of output for each tax-paying unit. In areas controlled by the Communists before their final victory, and later over the whole country for some years, two main systems of assessment obtained—the one proportionate and the other progressive. In the 'old liberated areas' the 'rich peasant economy' was deemed to have disappeared, and therefore proportionate taxation was appropriate. In the areas which had come under Communist control more recently (both before and after 1949) the continuance of inequalities of ownership prompted the imposition of a progressive agricultural tax; the exact form this took

[1] This chapter appeared as an article in *Soviet Studies*, Vol. 18, Nos. 1 and 2, July and October 1966.

differed in different regions. Before land reform was completed, rates of tax varied from complete exemption for the poorest peasant households to 80 per cent of output (including local surtax) on the richest landlords. In most cases, tax rates were between 3 per cent and 42 per cent. They were reduced by 20 per cent on income earned from tilling the fields and raised by 20 per cent on income derived from rents. Another source stated that agricultural tax rates on poor, middle and rich peasants should not exceed 10, 15 and 25 per cent respectively, on landlords not over 50 per cent, and for 'special cases' not more than 80 per cent. After land reform, a narrower range of rates was applied, from 7 to 30 per cent.[1]

During the First Five Year Plan period, the total proceeds of agricultural tax was roughly stabilized at the 1952 level. This policy was followed both because it simplified administration, and also because it gave an incentive for increased production, since a rise in output did not immediately result in higher tax demands. It was proposed to repeat this arrangement in the Second Five Year Plan period which began in 1958. After an initial revaluation, in which tax norms were raised in consideration of the growth in output since they were last fixed, the figure for agricultural tax was to remain unchanged until the end of 1962.[2]

The collectivization of agriculture, completed in 1956, had fundamentally altered the circumstances in which agricultural tax was levied. After consultations between the central government and the provinces, new regulations were finally issued in June 1958. As these regulations are the fullest source of information that we have on the subject, they deserve to be treated at length. Both the revaluation that was due and the consequences of collectivization were taken into consideration. The tax was to be reckoned as a proportion of an assessed 'normal yield'. This system was to obtain throughout the country, the use of progressive rates being discontinued now that rich peasants had been eliminated. However, allowance was to be made for local differences in taxable capacity by varying the proportionate rate from province to province, and likewise within provinces. The agricultural producers' co-operative was designated as the unit responsible for tax payments, along with the remaining independent peasants, the state farms and other enterprises and institutions with an income from agriculture. In addition, members of agricultural co-operatives were separately liable to tax assessment on their private plots.[3]

Under these regulations, crops of all types—food grains and potatoes, vegetables and 'economic crops' (e.g. cotton and other fibres, tobacco, vegetable oil, sugar, etc.) were subject to tax. The 'normal yield' was to be calculated in terms of the principal grain crop in each locality. The norm for land under potatoes was reckoned according to the normal yield of grain on comparable land. The norms for cotton, other fibres, tobacco, vegetable oil and sugar were to be estimated after 'taking into consideration' the normal yield of grain on comparable land, a departure from the existing rule which

[1] *Finance (Caizheng)*, No. 19, October 9, 1959, p. 3. Li Shu-te: 'Agricultural Taxation in the Past Ten Years', and *New China's Economic Achievements 1949–52*, Peking, 1953, p. 61, Po I-po: 'On the Question of Tax Readjustment.'

[2] *Collected Laws and Regulations of the People's Republic of China* (in Chinese), Vol. 7, pp. 257–8.

[3] Ibid., pp. 245–53.

was 'according to' the normal grain yield. This change was made to enable local authorities to raise the norm somewhat in the case of 'economic crops' because on the old system those cultivating these crops were taxed considerably more lightly than those growing grains. Other 'economic crops', together with 'horticultural crops' (e.g. vegetables) were to have their norms fixed by methods determined by provincial and equivalent local authorities.[1]

On a countrywide average, the rate of agricultural tax was set in June 1958 at 15·5 per cent of the 'normal yield'; this compared with the pre-1958 average of 16·5 per cent. Meanwhile, under the new regulations of 1958, the 'normal yield' had, for the country as a whole, been raised by about 12 per cent over the previous level. In absolute terms the total tax to be levied had, therefore, been raised by just over 5 per cent.[2]

It was claimed that the so-called normal yields were in fact set at a level considerably below the actual average annual harvest yield, especially at the end of the period for which the norms were fixed. For example, the 'normal yield' for tax purposes was said to be only 69 per cent of the actual yield in 1957, a year when the harvest was about average.[3]

The tax level for each province was fixed by the State Council, the rates varying from 13 per cent for Sinkiang and 13·5 per cent for Kansu, Ninghsia and Tsinghai to 18 per cent for Liaoning, 18·5 per cent for Kirin and 19 per cent for Heilungkiang. For purposes of agricultural tax the provinces were ranged in rough order of the relative wealth or poverty of their rural inhabitants.[4]

Within each province the 1958 regulations allowed the provincial authorities to vary rates of tax from one area to another, so long as the total laid down for the province was duly paid, and similar latitude was accorded to the lower authorities: this was in line with traditional Chinese fiscal practice. No *hsien* or higher authority might, however, according to the 1958 regulations, fix a rate of more than 25 per cent for units under it. These tax differentials compensated in some measure for the absence of rent differentials in collective agriculture. The few remaining independent peasants were to pay agricultural tax at 10–50 per cent above the ordinary rates unless they were in especial difficulties. The local supplementary tax which is collected on the same basis as agricultural tax (and is additional to the agricultural tax) ought not, it was decreed, to exceed 15 per cent of the latter for any taxpayer, except that in better off 'economic crop' and horticultural areas it might go up to 30 per cent of the agricultural tax.[5]

Exemptions or reductions of tax were allowed in respect of newly opened land, areas afflicted by natural disaster or which, for one reason or another, were backward or distressed, and also for other deserving cases. Improvements resulting from water conservancy and similar projects were not to attract an immediate increase in the assessed 'normal yield'.[6]

[1] *Collected Laws and Regulations* . . . Vol. 7, pp. 245–6 and p. 256. [2] Ibid., pp. 246, 259–60.
[3] Ibid., p. 260. [4] Ibid., pp. 261–3.
[5] Ibid., p. 247. In practice the local supplementary tax is said to exceed 15 per cent of the main agricultural tax. See Unpublished Paper of Michel Oksenberg of Stanford University, relating to the financial system in Mainland China.
[6] Ibid., pp. 246–9. In some cases, instead of tax being remitted in periods of difficulty, it has been permitted to remain in arrear—*Red Flag* (*Hongqi*), No. 11, October 1, 1965, p. 10. T'ao Lu-chia: 'Let the Tachai Spirit Blossom and Bear Fruit Everywhere.'

The collection of agricultural tax was generally to take place at two seasons, summer and autumn; where summer crops were relatively unimportant, the whole tax might be collected in the autumn. Tax was normally to be paid in grain, but in case of difficulty it might be paid in other types of agricultural produce or in cash. We shall allude to this matter again. The tax payers had the obligation to deliver the tax commodities to the designated collecting centres and to pay the cost of transport up to a distance in general equivalent to one day's round trip. Above that distance, costs were to be reimbursed them.[1]

Like most such directives in China, the Regulations on Agricultural Tax passed by the National People's Congress in June 1958 deliberately allowed, as we have earlier had occasion to mention, a wide scope for interpretation and implementation by the provinces; and an even wider scope to autonomous regions.[2] The provisions issued by two provinces, Chekiang and Kiangsi, for applying the regulations within their respective borders, are available to us. In both cases, the provincial regulations are for 1959, the year following the issue of the national measures. In each, the provincial authorities laid down the rates of tax applicable to certain special products or to special types of agricultural enterprises, and the average tax rate for the whole province. The special districts and equivalent level authorities were responsible for determining the tax to be collected from each *hsien* and municipality; it must be remembered that municipal boundaries frequently include surrounding agricultural land. The *hsien* and municipalities in turn were to parcel out the tax obligation between their communes and production brigades, the tax rates to be within the range of 11–20 per cent. The tax rate given here for Kiangsi province as a whole is 16·5 per cent, while in the previous year it had been set by the State Council, ostensibly for a five-year period, at 15·5 per cent.[3] In the neighbouring province of Chekiang, it appears that the reassessment envisaged for 1958 was not undertaken until the following year, when *hsien* and municipalities were ordered to carry it out.[4]

The agricultural tax regulations of June 1958 came just before the high tide of the commune movement. The Ministry of Finance, in its announcement of October 1958 on the drafting of the 1959 budget, recognized that the formation of the communes would eventually necessitate changes in the methods of levying this tax. Meanwhile the tax on the 1958 autumn harvest and the summer harvest of 1959 was to be collected according to the old system.[5] Whatever new regulations were later issued have not come our way, but there were references in the early days of the commune movement to the commune as the 'paying unit . . . held responsible for the fulfilment of the task of tax payments in rural areas'.[6] Hsu Ti-hsin, in the 1959 edition of his *An Analysis of China's Economy in the Transitional Period*, mentions the commune as being responsible for the combined agricultural and industrial and commercial

---

[1] *Collected Laws and Regulations* . . . Vol. 7, pp. 249–50.

[2] *Finance (Caizheng)*, No. 19, October 9, 1959, p. 3. Li Shu-te: loc. cit.

[3] *Kiangsi Daily (Jiangxi Ribao)*, September 29, 1959 (SCMP 2145), and *Collected Laws and Regulations* . . . Vol. 7, p. 263.

[4] *Chekiang Daily (Zhejiang Ribao)*, August 7, 1959 (SCMP 2088).

[5] *Collected Laws and Regulations* . . . Vol. 8, p. 146.

[6] *Economic Research (Jingji Yanjiu)*, No. 10, October 1958, p. 10. Hsieh Li: 'A Preliminary Discussion of the Financial Problem of the People's Communes.'

taxes.[1] By 1959, however, according to other sources, the immediate responsibility for payment of agricultural tax had been shifted to the production brigade, although the communes had to ensure that this duty was fulfilled.[2] When in January 1962 the production team was recognized as the basic accounting unit,[3] this unit presumably had transferred to it a direct responsibility for tax payment. However, it must be remembered that at the end of 1963 the team was not in all places the basic accounting unit.[4] By 1964 teams in some parts were apparently apportioning out tax grain delivery obligations to individuals or families,[5] presumably when the care of specific fields had been devolved down to the household level.[6] However, the downward shift of tax responsibility should not be over-emphasized. The higher units, each in its turn, retained responsibility for guaranteeing that the lower units would pay the required taxes.

We have seen that under the regulations of 1958, peasants' private plots were liable to agricultural tax. Policy on this point soon appears to have changed. The regulations for the collection of agricultural tax in 1959 for Kiangsi and Chekiang provinces (and very likely for others as well) specifically exempted private plots of commune members from agricultural tax.[7] On the national level, the first reference to this exemption that has come to our knowledge dates from 1961, when it figured in the secret instructions to rural cadres known as the 'Sixty Articles' as well as in the national Press.[8] This may be a case of provincial policy giving a lead to the central government.

When we examine such information as we have about the proportion of actual output taken in agricultural tax in any area or any unit, we are up against this difficulty of ascertaining the accuracy of the output figures on which the calculation is made. Official estimates of agricultural production have sometimes tended to be over-optimistic, more especially in 1958-9. Thus in a financial study of a commune in Hupeh, published at the end of 1958, it was said that in 1959 the rate of agricultural tax would remain the same as in 1958, at 4·23 per cent, while the output figure to which this was applied would be increased by 125 per cent, that is by half the commune's 1959 planned 250 per cent increase in output.[9] This puzzling statement can

[1] Hsü Ti-hsin: op. cit., pp. 225-6. On the industrial and commercial tax, see pp. 372-7 below.
[2] *Chekiang Daily* (*Zhejiang Ribao*), August 7, 1959 (SCMP 2088), and *Kiangsi Daily* (*Jiangxi Ribao*), September 29, 1959 (SCMP 2145).
[3] *People's Daily* (*Renmin Ribao*), January 1, 1962, p. 1. Editorial.
[4] *Red Flag* (*Hongqi*), No. 23, December 12, 1963, p. 23. Teng Tzu-hui, Director of Rural Work Department CCP Central Committee: 'The Historical Mission of Credit Co-operatives in Our Country at the Present Stage.'
[5] *People's Daily* (*Renmin Ribao*), April 14, 1966, p. 6. Wang Lien, Secretary of the Party Branch of Tungshihtzukou Production Brigade, Shihtzukou Commune, Chungli *hsien*, Hopei: 'A Party Branch Must Conscientiously Control and Educate Party Members.'
[6] See p. 54 above.
[7] *Kiangsi Daily* (*Jiangxi Ribao*), September 29, 1959 (SCMP 2145), and *Chekiang Daily* (*Zhejiang Ribao*), August 7, 1959 (SCMP 2088).
[8] Chinese Communist Party Central Committee: *Draft Articles on Rural Communes* (in Chinese), Peking 1961 (Taiwan Edition), Article No. 38, and *Daily Worker* (*Gongren Ribao*), August 3, 1961, p. 3. Kung Wen: 'Sideline Occupations of Rural Households: Part 2.'
[9] *Finance* (*Caizheng*), No. 15, December 24, 1958, p. 12. 'The Circumstances in which the "Two Decentralizations, Three Unifications and One Guarantee" Are Being Implemented in Peikao Commune, Mach'eng *hsien*', by the Party Committee of the Commune.

bear more than one interpretation—either that the norm of output for calculation of tax was revised in 1958 and again, very drastically, in 1959; or that the reassessment referred to was the one ordered in the regulations of June 1958, but that here, as in Chekiang, it was not undertaken until 1959. In any case, the scale of the re-assessment, a rise of 125 per cent for 1959 over 1958, is far in excess of anything envisaged in the regulations issued only six months earlier. This illustrates the way in which restraining regulations and promises of stable taxes were brushed aside in the frenzy of the Great Leap. It also explains the difficulties that occurred when the 1959 harvest, far from continuing or accelerating the 1958 rise, proved to be considerably below that level. In these circumstances, a rate of tax which looks light, might in fact prove burdensome.

For agricultural tax paid in 1959 by the various communes he visited, Edgar Snow was given figures varying between 5·4–14 per cent of total agricultural output. In 1961, another visitor, Gilbert Etienne, was informed of levels of between 7–19 per cent in individual communes.[1] A commune in Kwangtung was reported to have paid 4·4 per cent of its gross income in tax in 1961, while in another commune in the same *hsien* in Kwangtung the teams in one brigade paid in 1963 an average of 4·8 per cent of gross income.[2]

In addition to the agricultural tax, it must be remembered that the rural population were subject to a number of other minor taxes which will be mentioned in the following chapter. They are not of great significance, except for pastoral tax which is substituted for the agricultural tax where appropriate. It must not be thought that these direct taxes represent the total incidence of taxation on the rural population. This matter will be mentioned further in Chapter 14 below.

Considering the question on a countrywide basis, agricultural tax (including local supplementary tax) was, in 1952, said to amount to 13·2 per cent of total agricultural produce, falling to 11·3 per cent (11·5 per cent in one account) in 1957 (1·3 per cent being local tax and 10 per cent the main agricultural tax).[3] As mentioned earlier, the 'average annual crop' as defined in the regulations of June 1958 was stated to be below actual yields. This explains the fact that these percentages are considerably lower than the tax proportion of 15·5 per cent of 'average crops' fixed in the regulations for agricultural tax alone (i.e. excluding local supplementary tax). In 1966, a report on communes in south China stated that agricultural tax was roughly equal to 10 per cent of the 1961 farm output, which at the current level of output, worked out at a considerably lower percentage.[4] (This suggests that the reassessment of the tax which was due in 1962 did in fact occur, using the previous year's output as basis.)

There is, however, yet another consideration that makes calculations such as these even more hazardous than might otherwise be apparent. This is the

[1] E. Snow: *The Other Side of the River*, London, 1963, p. 487.
[2] A. L. Strong: *The Rise of the Chinese Communes—and Six Years After*, Peking, 1964, pp. 179 and 196. The 4·4 per cent in 1961 represented 14 per cent of the rice crop.
[3] *Collected Laws and Regulations* . . . Vol. 7, p. 259, and *Finance (Caizheng)*, No. 19, October 9, 1959, p. 5. Li Shu-te: loc. cit.
[4] NCNA Peking, February 19, 1966.

divergence between the year, as taken for agricultural tax, and the various years used for giving output figures for crops. In addition, there are yet other years for general fiscal purposes and for government purchase of grain. The year for agricultural tax runs from the autumn to the summer (exact months unspecified) while the normal Chinese fiscal year coincides with the calendar year; however, sometimes the figures for the proceeds of agricultural tax are given for the normal fiscal year.[1] An announcement made in October 1958 envisaged a change in the fiscal period for the levying of agricultural tax for 1959, but was phrased very ambiguously, did not state what the new fiscal period would be and said that until the new measures were published, the existing fiscal period should be used.[2] The year for calculating the government purchase of grain was, in 1957-8, from July to June; by 1963 it had changed and was from April to March;[3] such a change might shift purchases from the early harvest from one year to another. For other crops different collection years have been used.[4]

In some cases, statistics for quantities normally having different 'years'— e.g. total grain output, grain purchases and tax grain—are given in one table for 'years' of the same type for them all.[5] The implication is that the necessary adjustments have been made to figures originally collected on other bases—a process which adds still further, if that is possible, to the pitfalls of Chinese agricultural statistics. The difficulty of fixing crop years faces all large countries with a variety of crops and of harvest seasons. In China, as far as the last few years are concerned, the problem has been shelved, if not solved, by the non publication of output figures.

As already mentioned, the 1958 regulations stipulated payment in grain as a normal rule, substitution by other crops or by cash being however permissible. The practice of levying in kind the main tax on agriculture had been introduced by the Nationalist Government in 1941, during the wartime inflation; or rather it had been revived, the fifteenth century having seen the lapse of an early custom which had caused the character for 'grain' to become incorporated in the character for 'tax'.[6] The ending of inflation did away with the most pressing reason for collection in kind. The Communist authorities do not seem averse to the idea of commuting grain payments into cash, although no speedy movement in this direction has been made. In 1956 it was laid down that agricultural co-operatives which found themselves short of grain might substitute cash or 'economic crops' in payment of tax.[7] An Indian delegation which visited China in the summer of 1956 reported that some 7

[1] *People's Handbook* (*Renmin Shouce*) *1959*, p. 229.
[2] *Collected Laws and Regulations* . . . Vol. 8, p. 146.
[3] Ibid., Vol. 7, p. 282, and NCNA Peking, January 27, 1964.
[4] R. Hsia: *Government Acquisition of Agricultural Output in Mainland China 1953-6* (Rand Research Memorandum, RM. 2207), Santa Monica, 1958, p. 19.
[5] e.g. *Statistical Work* (*Tongji Gongzuo*), No. 19, October 14, 1957, p. 31.
[6] Chang Kia-ngau: *The Inflationary Spiral*, London, 1958, p. 141. However, payment of land tax in kind did not completely vanish between the fifteenth and twentieth centuries, even apart from the grain tribute. See Huang Han-liang: *The Land Tax in China* (*Columbia University Studies in History, Economics and Public Law*, Vol. LXXX, No. 3, 1918), passim.
[7] *Collected Laws and Regulations* . . . Vol. 4, p. 308.

per cent of the total agricultural tax was collected in cash.[1] It may be noted that in 1958 one of the advantages claimed for the practice of basing the payment of tax in kind on monetary values, as practised in a number of provinces (i.e. accepting a smaller quantity of high quality produce in lieu of a larger quantity of poorer quality), was that it would prepare the way for a reversion to cash payments of tax.[2]

Towards the end of 1962, an article in the *Ta Kung Daily* discussed some problems arising from the payment of agricultural tax in kind. It opposed the indiscriminate acceptance of any type of produce; rather the tax payments should be in the form of products urgently required by the state, notably grain, cotton, tobacco, peanuts and fibres. 'If other farm products are accepted, it is necessary to consider facilities for collection, storage, transport and handling.'[3] The calculation and collection of the tax was still normally based on the major local grain crop. However, money values had to be used as a yardstick for comparison when payment was made in grain of different qualities, or in crops other than grain. These conversion rates between crops or into cash might sometimes be determined by local authorities or be based on prices given for compulsory sales.[4] So long as much of the trade in the main crops takes the form of compulsory sales to the state, it is to be expected that agricultural tax will continue to be paid in kind. The task of planning is facilitated when the state gains immediate possession of the foodstuffs it requires directly from the growers. However, from the point of view of optimum allocation of resources, the collection of money taxes with subsequent purchase of crops on the market, would be preferable, since then the peasants would be able to grow the crops best suited to their soil, or for which the demand was greatest, rather than those in which tax had to be paid. The state monopoly of the major crops prevents peasants buying these for the purpose of tax payment with cash earned by growing more profitable crops themselves. The full force of this argument depends on the existence of free prices for agricultural produce. The extent and degree of government control of these prices will be discussed in a subsequent chapter. Here we will but note that prices of all, or a large part of, sales of many major farm commodities are state-controlled, while official influence on prices touches many more.

One consideration which the financial authorities presumably bear in mind is the heavy administrative cost of tax collection in kind. No figures are available of the cost of collection while the Communists have been in power but under the Nationalists, in 1941 and 1943, between 12–14 per cent of total

[1] *Report of the Indian Delegation to China on Agricultural Planning and Techniques*, Delhi, 1956, p. 138.

[2] *Peop e's Taxation* (*Renmin Shuiwu*), No. 18, September 19, 1958, p. 18. Agricultural Tax Office of the General Tax Bureau, Ministry of Finance: 'The Progress of the Collection of Agricultural Tax on the Summer Crop.'

[3] *Ta Kung Daily* (*Dagong Bao*), Peking, November 17, 1962, p. 2. K'ang Li-jen: 'Some Problems in the Present Collection of Agricultural Tax in Kind.'

[4] Ibid., and *Kiangsi Daily* (*Jiangxi Ribao*), September 29, 1959 (SCMP 2145). Ko Chih-ta: *China's Budget During the Transition Period* (in Chinese), Peking, 1957, p. 58, gives the financial equivalent of the agricultural tax for 1950–5 and the budgeted estimate for 1956. Without knowing local procurement prices in different years and the weights to be given to each it is not possible to derive from these figures anything more than the average 'cash equivalent' per ton of 'grain' for the years concerned.

government expenditure went in the cost of tax-collection in kind.[1] Under the Communists the proportionate cost of collection must be deemed lower owing to their tighter administrative control of the country.

As an administrative measure, the assessment of land tax presents formidable problems; this applies also to assessment for compulsory sales which we shall soon consider. The making of a cadastral survey is a lengthy process of great complexity. Such a survey was carried out in 1951 to determine liability to agricultural tax and another in 1954–5 to provide a basis for implementing 'planned purchase and planned supply'. It is not known if the second survey replaced the first in calculating tax obligations.[2] Nor is information available on the accuracy of either survey. A nation-wide survey of agricultural output was made in 1959 under the general supervision of the State Statistical Bureau.[3] It was probably repeated in subsequent years.

The collection of agricultural tax involves close co-operation between the Ministry of Finance, on the one hand (operating through its Agricultural Tax Bureau) and the Ministries of Food and of Commerce on the other.[4] The Ministry of Finance and its local counterparts do not themselves establish collecting points for agricultural tax in kind. This is undertaken by local food and commercial departments, depending on the products concerned.[5] These departments are also responsible for buying from the peasants the output these have compulsorily to sell to the state; this includes large quantities of the same products as are paid in tax. In the case of almost all farm products, except for grain and oil-bearing crops, the actual purchasing is done by the supply and marketing co-operatives.[6] The unit responsible for the delivery of produce for compulsory sale to the state (i.e. peasant household, co-operative, commune, brigade, or team) was presumably the same, at any one time, as the unit currently responsible for tax payment, although we learn this from inference rather than from direct statement.

As the same administrative systems with their collecting stations deal both with tax in kind and with compulsory sales, there inevitably arises a tendency for the two forms of delivery to be confused. This is discouraged: ' . . . since tax collection and unified purchasing are different in nature, the distinction between them must be clear cut. This not only helps the departments of finance, food and commerce to settle their accounts for tax receipts, but also helps investigation into policy implementation.' In order to maintain the distinction, tax collection must precede purchasing. A tax paying unit 'should

---

[1] Chang Kia-ngau: op. cit., p. 127.
[2] R. Hsia: op. cit., p. 53.
[3] Choh-ming Li: *The Statistical System of Communist China*, Berkeley, 1962, Chapter X.
[4] According to a Taiwan source, the control over stocks of public grain has, since 1952, devolved on an organ subordinate both to the Ministries of Finance and of Food. See Sun Ping-yen: *The Communist System of Grain Control* (in Chinese), Taipei, 1958, pp. 9–11 and inset charts.
[5] *Ta Kung Daily* (*Dagong Bao*), Peking, November 17, 1962, p. 2. K'ang Li-jen: loc. cit. In December 1957 the Ministry of Food's enterprises engaged in the purchase and sale of grain were listed with those concerns which were not to divide profits with provinces, but to remit them all to the central treasury. *Collected Laws and Regulations* . . . Vol. 7, pp. 224–5.
[6] *New Industry and Commerce* (*Xin Gongshang*), No. 2, February 18, 1964 (SCMM 421). Liang Yao: 'The Current Task of Supply and Marketing Co-operatives.'

first discharge its liability to agricultural tax and get a receipt for the tax paid. Then on the total, net of tax, it should work out and pay its delivery quota, and get payment for it in cash.'[1]

The division of the proceeds of the agricultural tax between the central government and the provincial authorities will be treated in Chapter 14.

2. COMPULSORY SALES OF AGRICULTURAL PRODUCE

The second method by which the state obtains agricultural produce is through compulsory sales by the peasants at prices set by the state. As in the case of payment of agricultural tax in kind, this practice had been introduced by the Nationalist Government during the War.[2]

The Government Administrative Council's decree of November 1953, which instituted the system of 'planned purchase and planned supply' of grain, laid down that the peasants were to sell grain to the state according to quantities, varieties and prices fixed by the state.[3] (Grain for this purpose included both soya bean and potatoes, Irish and sweet.) The immediate cause of this measure was the food crisis of 1953, when the grain acquired by the government did not meet the need. Early in 1955 a similar crisis arose owing to the poor harvest of the previous year. Thereupon the government introduced the policy of the 'three fixed': 'fixed production, fixed purchases and fixed sales'. 'Fixed production' signified that a standard production quota would be assigned to each piece of land used for growing grain; 'fixed purchases' referred to quotas for compulsory sales to the state, and 'fixed sales' to the rations to be supplied to grain-deficient peasants.

In April 1955, it was announced that the introduction of the 'three fixed' policy was 'basically concluded' over the whole countryside. However, it was at the same time admitted that sales to grain-deficient peasants were concurrently running considerably above the determined figure.[4] The manner of implementing the 'three fixed' policy was laid down in the Provisional Methods of Unified Purchase and Unified Sales of Grain passed by the State Council in August 1955. Individual peasants and those in mutual aid teams were to be assessed for the 'three fixed' on a household basis. Where agricultural producers' co-operatives had been formed, these might be taken as the basic unit, or alternatively assessments might still be made household by household.[5] As already mentioned, a survey made in 1954-5 provided the basis for this assessment. The administrative difficulties entailed in this policy must not be under-estimated nor the opportunities, both initially and at later dates, for false reporting and statistical error.

'Fixed production' quotas were to be assessed at around the time of the 1955 spring ploughing according to area and quality of land, natural conditions and 'normal yield' of land used for grain cultivation. The needs of each household or co-operative were to be determined, on scales set by provinces

---

[1] *Ta Kung Daily* (*Dagong Bao*), Peking, November 17, 1962, p. 2. K'ang Li-jen: loc. cit.
[2] Chang Kia-ngau: op. cit., p. 141.
[3] *New China Monthly* (*Xinhua Yuebao*), No. 54, April 1954, p. 158.
[4] *Collected Laws and Regulations* . . . Vol. 1, p. 306.
[5] Ibid., Vol. 2, p. 576.

and equivalent authorities, for seed grain, grain for fodder and for human consumption. This total, together with agricultural tax grain, was to be deducted from the figure for 'fixed production' of the household or co-operative in question. As a result of this calculation, the units would be divided into those which were grain surplus, grain deficient or self-sufficient. The *hsiang* was to have the primary responsibility for effecting this classification. The grain-surplus households and co-operatives would, in general, have to sell 80–90 per cent of their surplus, thus determined, to the state; for rich peasants this proportion might be raised. The exact rate was to be fixed by provincial and equivalent authorities. In the case of state farms, both national and local, all the grain produced, other than the quantity stipulated for their own use, was to be sold to the state.[1]

While grain, soya bean and potatoes were the products specified for compulsory sales under this directive, other regulations provided for compulsory selling of cotton and oil crops.[2]

The state's annual grain purchases were to be effected either all at once or at two separate seasons, according to whether a locality was in a single or multiple cropping area.[3]

Provincial and equivalent authorities were each year to determine what constituted grain of a medium standard, taking into consideration the year's harvest characteristics in respect of size of grain, moisture content and other qualitative factors. The prices paid by the grain receiving depots were to accord with the quality of the grain and with prices announced by the state.[4]

As far as the grain-deficient peasants were concerned, 'fixed supply' was to fill the gap between their production quota and their needs of grain for seed and consumption. Grain-deficient peasants were divided into two categories; those engaged predominantly in grain production, yet not growing enough for their own needs, and secondly, those short of grain because they devoted most of their energy to the cultivation of cotton and other 'economic crops'. For the first category, consumption standards were to be slightly below those of grain-surplus peasants in the same district. Peasants growing 'economic crops', in contrast, were to enjoy rations no lower than those of local grain-surplus households. Rural residents not employed in agriculture were, in general, to be provided with grain on a standard not above that of grain-surplus peasants. Rations provided in disaster areas were to be lower than those for grain-deficient peasants in normal years.[5]

Production quotas were to remain unchanged for three years, beginning with 1955 and concluding with 1957, the last year of the First Five Year Plan. Under normal conditions, fixed purchase quotas (i.e. compulsory deliveries to the state) were also not to be changed for the same period; the qualification, as we shall see, was important. For newly opened land, no production quotas were to be assigned for the first three years of cropping. Grain-deficient peasants engaged in grain production were to be assessed annually, adding

---

[1] *Collected Laws and Regulations* ... Vol. 2, pp. 575–9. However, see p. 109 for apparently contradicting information.
[2] *New China Monthly* (*Xinhua Yuebao*), No. 60, October 1954, pp. 241 and 247.
[3] *Collected Laws and Regulations* ... Vol. 2, p. 579.
[4] Ibid., p. 580.   [5] Ibid.

each year to their production quota the planned increase in production for the year concerned. When their production quota equalled their assessed grain needs, they would pass into the category of grain self-sufficient or surplus peasants. Grain-deficient households engaged in cultivating industrial crops were once again treated more favourably; in their case, the planned production increase for yields on any acreage they had under grain would not be taken into consideration for a three-year period.[1]

Despite the emphasis on stability, provision was made in these regulations for the considerable adjustments necessitated by harvest fluctuations. Such adjustments were to be made in the first place by the *hsiang* and reported upwards to the *hsien* and the province. In the case of shortfall, the province concerned was to do all it could to meet the deficit from within its own borders, by levying extra compulsory sales from those parts of its territory which had enjoyed more favourable conditions. If the province was still unable to meet its needs, it was to report the matter with suggestions to the State Council, which had to make the final decision on action to be taken. In extreme circumstances, the State Council would direct the better-off provinces to increase their compulsory purchases to make good the deficits elsewhere. When it was necessary to levy such increases in areas with good harvests, the excess over the fixed purchase quota should not for any household exceed 40 per cent of the additional yield accruing as a result of the bountiful year.[2]

The purpose of the 'three fixed' policy embodied in the regulations of August 1955 was to limit the state's liability to supply grain-deficient rural residents and to provide an incentive for grain-surplus peasants to increase production by placing a ceiling to their liability for compulsory sales. In 1954–5 excessive levies had unfavourably affected the peasants' willingness to work and had led to the policy embodied in the directive of 1955. As a result of this policy shift, acquisition of grain by the state fell by 4–5 per cent in 1955–6 despite a good harvest. Total state sales of grain in that year decreased much more sharply, by 13 per cent, with a corresponding decrease in *per capita* grain rations of the urban population. Clearly the peasants and the reserve stocks were benefiting at the expense of urban consumption. In the following year, 1956–7, natural disasters were blamed for a further decline in total state collection of grain.[3] On this occasion stocks were run down, while urban consumption was reportedly raised.[4]

The difficulties of 1956, coming the year after the promulgation of the policy of the 'three fixed', meant that the policy was hardly instituted when recourse was had to the escape clause permitting compulsory sales to be raised by not more than 40 per cent of any increase in output.[5] At this time priorities in grain distribution were re-stated, grain for tax payment and compulsory sales

[1] *Collected Laws and Regulations* . . . Vol. 2, pp. 576–8.
[2] Ibid., p. 582.
[3] However, it should be noted that figures put out for this harvest showed a considerable increase over the previous year. See Table on p. 357 below.
[4] *Planned Economy (Jihua Jingji)*, No. 2, February 1958, pp. 24–5. Sun Wei-tsu: 'The Principles for Compiling Grain Circulation Plans.'
[5] *Collected Laws and Regulations* . . . Vol. 4, pp. 313–14, and NCNA Peking, March 6, 1957. 'Li Hsien-nien Outlines Grain Procurement, Marketing and Distribution at National Conference.'

coming before that for seed and peasant consumption.[1] In the following year, despite on the whole better crops, a State Council decree of October 1957 permitted the 40 per cent limit to be exceeded in exceptional circumstances.[2] The greater severity with which the system of forced deliveries of grain came to be operated found a parallel in the case of other crops. For example, the amount of raw cotton which cotton-growing peasants were permitted to retain was reduced from three to two catties a head.[3]

The latitude which the government allowed itself by the decree of 1957 for an upward revision of 'fixed purchase' was, as we shall see, overtaken by the inflationary effect on output figures of the Great Leap of the following year. First, however, we must mention the formal changes made at this time. In line with the other measures for economic decentralization of 1957-8, the State Council decreed in April 1958 a parallel change in grain administration. While targets for the collection and sale of grain within each province and autonomous region were still to be under central control, these figures were to be subject to adjustment at the provincial level. The main concern of the centre was to be with the inter-provincial balances—the grain to be transferred to or from each province. These balances were to be fixed for the next five years (i.e. for the duration of the Second Five Year Plan) on the basis of the estimates for the 1957-8 grain year (adjustment being permitted if that year's figures proved exceptional). As usual with such decrees, the wording left much scope for varied interpretations. While the control figures for balances were to be 'fundamentally unchanged', provinces with good harvests might 'appropriately raise' their grain purchases and reduce their sales. Provinces with bad harvests were normally to solve their problems themselves, although in the case of major natural disasters, the central government might adjust the inter-provincial balances.[4]

Thus, while the central government still nominally controlled targets for all grain procurement and sales, its attention was focused very largely on inter-provincial transfers. This was in line with the trend at this time towards the 'responsibility system', which we have come across in other contexts, by which a unit would be left to regulate its own internal affairs so long as it guaranteed the achievement of certain targets. In grain collection and supply the responsibility system was from 1958 to be operated down to the level of the agricultural producers' co-operative (this was decreed just before the commune movement) although an official pronouncement emphasized that guidance must not on that account be relaxed over distribution of grain within co-operatives.[5]

Along with the responsibility system went its corollary, the use of contracts to set down the specific obligations of various units. We have already had occasion to discuss the notion of contracts in contemporary China and to see that it does not necessarily imply that the transaction is voluntary. When

---

[1] *Collected Laws and Regulations* ... Vol. 4, p. 315.

[2] Ibid., Vol. 6, p. 352.

[3] Ibid., p. 371. In some places the retention of two and a half catties was permitted.

[4] Ibid., Vol. 7, pp. 281-2.

[5] Ibid., p. 284.

applied to defining the obligations for compulsory sales, voluntariness is clearly absent.

A description of methods adopted for implementing the responsibility and contract systems for compulsory sales, based apparently on experience in Honan, was given in June 1958. Each agricultural co-operative had to 'declare its annual task of planned purchase or planned sale, taking into consideration the change in grain production, stocks kept for their own use, purchase and sale over the past years, and the production increase plan for the current year.' The 'declarations' of tasks were, of course, liable to the same pressures and influences as the conclusion of contracts. The tasks declared by the co-operatives had to be balanced at the *hsiang* level and approved by the *hsien*. After that, the food departments (i.e. the local organs of the Ministry of Food) signed contracts with the co-operatives to guarantee the purchase or sales for that year. This system was to be enforced provisionally for one year 'during which purchase will not be increased with increase in production' although, it will be noted, planned production increase had to be taken into account in deciding the annual task.[1] The merits claimed for the system were that it provided incentive to the peasants, enabled them to plan for a year ahead and that it facilitated control over grain distribution. Previously the peasants 'still had some misgivings in their minds. They did not know how much additional purchase will be made by the state and how much more grain they will keep for their own use after production has been massively stepped up.' This, it may be observed, was exactly the situation which the 'three fixed' policy was introduced to remedy. Harvest fluctuations, as might have been foreseen, made that policy impracticable and, as a result, the state broke its undertaking to the peasants. The new arrangements were an attempt to regain their confidence by introducing what was declared to be a new system, although the changed phraseology could not remove the root of instability which had caused the 'three fixed' policy to prove abortive. However, optimism—at least of officials, if not of peasants,—is perennial. 'Now that contracts have been signed with the agricultural producers' co-operatives,' the article continued, 'these misgivings are dispelled. Many peasants commented "We know where the government stands. Purchase will not be increased along with increase in production. . . . Who will not exert his best efforts to produce?" '[2]

Nevertheless, within eighteen months the guarantee and contract system had gone the way of the 'three fixed'. Production brigades reporting good harvests had to sell grain in excess of the figures set. 'After that, they began to say that "one loses by being progressive" and "one gains by being backward".'[3] These practices, and the resulting cynicism, were sufficiently widespread in the autumn of 1959 to evoke two condemnatory articles in the *People's Daily*.

In May 1959 a directive from the central authorities stated that, in absolute

---

[1] *Theoretical Study (Lilun Xuexi)*, No. 11, June 1, 1958 (ECMM 147). Fang Ch'i-meng: 'A Necessary Understanding of the Comprehensive Guarantee System of State Grain Purchase and Supply.'
[2] Ibid.
[3] *People's Daily (Renmin Ribao)*, October 20, 1959, p. 4.

terms, compulsory sales by the peasants of the summer crops would be increased, although, it went on to say, these sales would form a smaller proportion of total output owing to the rise in production.[1] As it happened the harvest, at least for the year as a whole and probably for the summer crops by themselves, was significantly worse than that of the previous year and thus the proportionate rise of compulsory sales is likely to have been considerable. This illustrates a point which became all-important in regard to the crop deliveries demanded from the peasants, especially in 1958 and 1959. Under the influence of the Great Leap attitude of mind, official output figures (both pre-harvest estimates and post-harvest reports) greatly exceeded the actual amounts harvested. When this happened the peasants might be faced with demands of a quite arbitrary size, in conflict with the policy of the 'three fixed' and its later variations. Local cadres often yielded to the intense pressure to report high yields. They then had to extract correspondingly high output for state purchases. In other cases, cadres sympathetic to the local inhabitants might under-report, or so the Ministry of Finance in December 1958 accused some of doing,[2] although in that year it is more likely that the unfortunates were merely failing to report the swollen figures expected by higher levels.

When the Great Leap had become a thing of the past, and more moderate policies prevailed, the pressure to over-report was probably lifted and the authorities became anxious to get accurate estimates of production. Nevertheless, other pressures remained, including those to set high figures for contracts for deliveries to the state and for overfulfilling the figures agreed. This showed itself in the 'patriotic grain' movement in 1961 when peasants were urged to increase both quantity and quality of grain sales. In 1962 we hear of a production brigade 'undergoing ideological struggle' before concluding contracts to increase sales to the state, compared with the previous year, of grain, pigs, poultry, fish and fruit, as well as selling a quantity of other products which had not been included in the 1961 deliveries.[3] In 1961, extra sales to the state were reported to be made by Paoan *hsien*, a district which adjoins Hong Kong and was known at that time to be suffering from severe food shortage.[4]

Through the contract system, not only grain and other staples but, as we have just seen, products such as pigs, poultry, eggs, and vegetables, were drawn into the system of compulsory sales. This development has already been mentioned in our chapter on Internal Trade. Here three points must be made: first, the geographic limitations to these sales; second, the confusion about the scope of these compulsory deliveries; and third, the reappearance of the individual peasant household as the unit for shouldering certain of these obligations.

Not all districts appear to be subject to compulsory sales of the less important types of agricultural produce, at least in 1959. In that year, in a reference to second category agricultural produce in Honan province, 'areas

[1] *Collected Laws and Regulations*... Vol. 9, p. 154.
[2] NCNA Peking, December 19, 1958.
[3] *People's Daily* (*Renmin Ribao*), January 5, 1962, p. 1. Ts'ao Shao-ch'iung: 'Deliveries of Farm Produce—Our Glorious Duty as Commune Members.'
[4] Ibid., December 12, 1961, p. 1.

which have been allotted obligations for sales to the state' were contrasted with areas which did not have such obligations.¹ The most reasonable criterion for areas under state collection might be presumed to be the areas from which produce could be easily transported to where it was needed, in contrast to those areas not so conveniently situated; this, however, is not specifically stated.

Procurement of staple crops, such as those subject to planned or unified purchase is, for the most part, a question of relations between the state and units of collective agriculture or state farms.² A high proportion of other commodities such as eggs, poultry, vegetables and pigs is privately produced by peasant households. Some of these products are also produced for self-consumption by schools, mess halls, government offices and other concerns. The policy on whether subsidiary agricultural production from these sources should be liable to compulsory sales has changed over time, while at any one time the official line has not always tallied with actual practice. We have seen that in respect of agricultural tax no exemption for private plots was mentioned in the regulations of 1958, but that references to such exemption occur within the next few years, first in the local Press and then in 1961 in the 'Sixty Articles' addressed to rural cadres and in the national Press. A similar change in policy on exemption from compulsory sales came about over the same period. One of the charges brought in 1958 against the 'rightist opportunist' P'an Fu-sheng, former First Secretary of the Honan Provincial Party Committee, was that he favoured exempting private plots from compulsory sales.³ By the close of 1960 such exemption was being proclaimed in the provincial Press. In addition it was declared that crops from these plots were not to be included in the rations subject to collective distribution, nor should they take the place of or be counted as grain rations: in other words, they were to be disregarded in estimating the peasants' grain retention standards before liability to compulsory sales was reckoned.⁴ Here again the exemption was confirmed on a nation-wide scale in the 'Sixty Articles' and in the national Press.⁵ This was in accordance with the general line of policy in the early 1960s of encouraging the household subsidiary occupations of the peasantry and relying more on incentives than on compulsion to raise production.

In practice, the official exemption of domestic sideline production was not maintained. Procurement obligations were still incurred in respect of them. It is interesting to see that these obligations were sometimes imposed on peasant households directly by outside state organs, and not through the

---

¹ *Ta Kung Daily* (*Dagong Bao*), Peking, July 18, 1959, p. 1. Sung Chih-ho: 'On Development of a Many-Sided Economy.' From the context it can be seen that both types of place are assumed to have marketed surpluses of second category produce.

² Some grain and oil crops from private plots were bought by the state under varying degrees of persuasion or pressure. See e.g. *Ta Kung Daily* (*Dagong Bao*), Peking, February 11, 1962, p. 2. Chang Kuei-ying: 'Why I Agreed to the Children's Father Selling Castor Beans to the State.'

³ *Honan Daily* (*Honan Ribao*), July 4, 1958 (CB 515). 'CCP Honan Provincial Committee Calls Ninth Enlarged Session.'

⁴ *Southern Daily* (*Nanfang Ribao*), December 23, 1960 (SCMP 2418). Editorial.

⁵ *Draft Articles on Rural Communes*, op. cit., and *Daily Worker* (*Gongren Ribao*), August 3, 1961, p. 3. Kung Wen: loc. cit.

intermediary of the commune, brigade or team. This runs counter to the tendency we have noticed in higher spheres in the same period, which was for the 'responsibility system' to spread, and it marks a recognition of the resurgent importance of the peasant family as an economic unit.

The delineation of peasants' obligations in respect of supplying subsidiary output to the state at this time may have been a safeguard against former arbitrary demands. A report from Shansi province in 1961 stipulated that 'only the number of eggs from each hen laid down by the procurement obligation is to be sold [i.e. to the state] and the rest are to be disposed of voluntarily'. After the fixed task has been fulfilled, the peasants were to be given a premium of 10 per cent plus extra grain, for any more eggs they sold to the state of their own accord.[1]

Another example of the greater attention paid in more recent years to protecting peasants from arbitrary demands and giving them incentive is seen in a *Ta Kung Daily* editorial of November 1963 on the procurement of pigs. 'Especially when there is a shortage of meat the peasants' incentive for rearing pigs will be reduced if over many are bought without letting them keep enough for themselves. On the other hand, however, we must energetically buy the quantity which the peasants are under an obligation to sell or which they voluntarily wish to sell.'[2] The supply of consumer goods must, the editorial insisted, go hand in hand with buying farm produce, the two activities stimulating each other. This policy of combining compulsion with incentives had apparently been successful, as pigs procured in the first nine months of 1963 were reported to have risen by 140 per cent compared with the corresponding period of the previous year.[3]

In respect of the liability of rural mess halls to the levy of compulsory deliveries on goods and livestock produced for self-consumption, there appears to have been considerable variation. In regulations promulgated in Hupeh early in 1960, rural mess halls were to sell 50 per cent of their fattened pigs to the state, up to a fixed quota above which the share to be sold would fall to 40 per cent.[4] The injunction that rural mess halls should sell pigs to the state was repeated to a nation-wide audience in the *People's Daily* in 1960; as far as other mess hall production was concerned, this article merely said that the surplus should be sold to the state.[5] In Kwangtung in the same year, the provincial authorities expressly exempted oil-bearing crops cultivated by rural mess halls from compulsory sales.[6] With the subsequent closure of most rural mess halls, policy on this matter naturally lost its importance.

The 1960 Hupeh Regulations laid down that pigs reared for self-consumption by government offices, schools, army units, factories, mines, urban mess halls, and similar enterprises should not be subject to compulsory sales. Such units, however, would in due course be expected to become self-sufficient in meat.[7]

---

[1] *Ta Kung Daily* (*Dagong Bao*), Peking, April 17, 1961, p. 3.
[2] Ibid., November 26, 1963, p. 1. Editorial.
[3] Ibid.
[4] *Hupeh Daily* (*Hubei Ribao*), March 23, 1960. (Supplement to SCMP 2271).
[5] *People's Daily* (*Renmin Ribao*), June 19, 1960, p. 3.
[6] *Southern Daily* (*Nanfang Ribao*), April 3, 1960 (SCMP 2262). Chao Tzu-yang: 'We Must Surely Make a Success of the Mess Halls'.
[7] *Hupeh Daily* (*Hubei Ribao*), March 23, 1960, loc. cit.

Advance purchases of farm output by state procurement agencies will be mentioned in a later chapter in connection with agricultural credit.

3. STATE PROCUREMENT AS PROPORTION OF TOTAL GRAIN OUTPUT

Bearing in mind the caution earlier expressed on the comparability of output, tax and purchase figures for grain, we will now examine briefly such information as is available about the proportion which agricultural tax and compulsory sales take of total output of grain.

The State Statistical Bureau's communique on the result of the First Five Year Plan said that between 1953–7 the state had acquired by tax and purchase 28 per cent of total grain output of these years. After deducting grain sold in rural areas, net retention was 16·5 per cent of total output.[1] This was the proportion available for feeding the urban population and for export, and also for provisioning the armed forces. It must be remembered that many army units engage in agriculture and achieve a high degree of self-sufficiency. Some even deliver grain and other agricultural produce to the state.

For the period from July 1953 to June 1959, total state procurement of grain was said to account for 27 per cent of total output, and state retention, net of grain re-sold in rural areas, to 15 per cent of the total.[2] For the same period the grain sold by the state was reported to have been divided as follows: 46 per cent to rural households short of grain (including relief), 49 per cent to urban residents (including sales to industry) and 5 per cent for exports.[3]

An analysis of total distribution of grain collected by the state, and not only of the marketed portion is available for the four years July 1953–June 1957, as follows: 47 per cent to the rural population, 43 per cent to urban residents and the military, 4·6 per cent to exports and 4·8 per cent reserves.[4]

For the years since the Great Leap, quantitative information on agricultural procurement is very scanty. Edgar Snow, writing after his visit to China in 1960, said that out of an average crop of 180 million tons of grain, agricultural tax would be 15 million tons and state purchase something over 40 million tons. Thus, according to these figures, total procurement would in a normal year amount to at least 30 per cent of total output. Snow thought that in 1957 procurement might not have much exceeded 30 per cent, but that it may have reached a considerably higher percentage in 1958 and 1959 owing to inflated output figures. The figure of 24 million tons from agricultural tax, which he was given for 1960, suggests that the procurement ratio rose

---

[1] *People's Handbook (Renmin Shouce) 1959*, p. 11.

[2] *People's Daily (Renmin Ribao)*, October 25, 1959, p. 6. Sha Ch'ien-li, Minister of Food: 'Brilliant Achievements on the Food Grain Front.'

[3] Ibid. p. 85.

[4] *Statistical Work (Tongji Gongzuo)*, No. 19, October 14, 1957, pp. 31–2. The last two figures are derived from other information in this article. On reserves of grain, two Chinese Economists in 1957 advocated that these be built up to 35 to 50 million metric tons 'roughly equivalent to the state's requirement for one year's commodity grain'. Tso Ch'un-t'ai and Li Hai: *The Problem of Accumulating Funds for Our Country's Socialist Industrialization* (in Chinese), Peking, 1957. p. 48. However, we may be sure that reserves have not approached this level.

STATE PROCUREMENT OF AGRICULTURAL PRODUCE 355

precipitately in that year, especially if state purchases were correspondingly increased. Outside observers estimate the grain harvest of 1960 as about 13·5 per cent below that of 1957, while according to Snow, who is sympathetic to the regime and who obtained his figures from official Chinese sources, agricultural tax had been raised by some 60 per cent between the two years.[1] Contrary to this, an article in the *Ta Kung Daily* in May 1961 stated that agricultural tax grain amounts to 'only 15 million metric tons or more a year'.[2] In the spring of 1964 a United States government publication considered that the continued imports of grain 'together with fragmentary evidence about grain collections', suggested that the Chinese authorities had decided against heavy grain procurement.[3]

It was announced that the state grain purchasing target for the year April 1963—March 1964 had been fulfilled by 101·3 per cent up to January 15, 1964, which was 'the fastest annual grain buying in recent years'.[4] This may indicate the target was the most realistic in recent years. Procurement obligations in 1965 were said to have remained at the same level as in the previous year. Peasants were, however, exhorted to sell some of their increased output to the state.[5]

Until exhaustive research has been done on references to this topic in provincial newspapers, we do not have sufficient information to enable us to divide total procurement between geographical areas nor between collective agriculture and state farms. As far as the geographical division is concerned, there is reason to believe that certain districts yield to the state disproportionately high quantities of farm output—the modern equivalent of the 'key economic areas' of China's past;[6] these are the areas on which state investment in agriculture was to be concentrated according to policy propounded in 1964. As to the division between collectives and state farms, it is known that the 'commodity rate'—the proportion marketed—is much higher in the case of state farms, especially those that are relatively highly mechanized.[7] The noted economist, Niu Chung-huang, said that in 1959 the commodity rate for grain grown on state farms 'which had been basically mechanized' was 74 per cent, on semi-mechanized state farms 60 per cent and on rural communes 40 per cent.[8] The interpretation of these figures is uncertain; the commodity rate of 40 per cent for grain from communes appears to be much exaggerated. In 1958 only 15 per cent of grain grown in communes was reported to be marketed;[9] but it was not stated if this meant 15 per cent of

---

[1] E. Snow: op. cit., pp. 486–7, and 623. It is to be noted that in 1960, Chinese exports of rice and wheat products to the USSR actually fell—see *External Trade of the USSR 1960* (in Russian), Moscow, p. 170.

[2] *Ta Kung Daily* (*Dagong Bao*), Peking, May 31, 1961, p. 3. Ling Han: 'The Interests of the State, of the Collective, and of the Individual Must All Be Considered When Dividing the Income of Rural People's Communes.'

[3] *Current Scene*, Vol. II, No. 11, April 1, 1964, p. 3.

[4] NCNA Peking, January 27, 1964.

[5] *Ta Kung Daily* (*Dagong Bao*), Peking, June 22, 1965, p. 1. Editorial.

[6] See Chi Ch'ao-ting: *Key Economic Areas in Chinese History*, New York, 1963.

[7] See pp. 96–7 above.

[8] *People's Daily* (*Renmin Ribao*), August 26, 1960, p. 7. Niu Chung-huang: 'The Technical Transformation of the Agriculture of Our Country.'

[9] *Financial and Economic Research* (*Caijing Yanjiu*), No. 1, January 15, 1959, p. 10. Chih Chung: 'The Conditions for "Ownership by the Whole People" in People's Communes.'

output net of tax, i.e. if it represented state purchases only and excluded tax grain, nor whether it was gross procurement or a figure for net procurement of grain from communes after the needs of grain-deficient peasants had been supplied.

So far the discussion of the ratio of procurement to output has been confined to grain. Space forbids us here from considering other types of farm produce, but it must be noted that in the two important cases of cotton and oil crops, the proportions procured by the state have been very much higher than in the case of grain.[1] A careful study of government agricultural procurement in China concluded that from 1953–6 net state acquisition of agricultural output as a whole came to about 25 per cent.[2]

The general picture of agricultural procurement appears to be that of a moderately heavy burden during the First Five Year Plan period. During 1958 it may have lightened proportionately to output (despite Snow's surmise mentioned above) as the communes seem to have consumed in their earlier days more produce than the state intended. However, the uncertainty of total output figures for that year, as well as the divergence between barn and biological yield[3] (owing to distractions at harvest time due to the iron and steel campaign and the establishment of the communes) make the whole question difficult to assess; but it seems that the state did not accumulate as much reserves as it might have done from the exceptional harvest of that year. (Relevant to this and to the growth of provincial self-sufficiency is the fall of 1·8 million metric tons in the volume of grain transported between provinces in 1958 compared with 1957.)[4] In the following years of poor harvests but high official targets for production, procurements appear to have been exceptionally onerous. Eventually a more realistic appraisal of the situation was forced on the government by rural discontent, and by the yet lower output resulting from the disincentive of heavy exactions. As a result, the proportion taken by the state in the last few years may have declined. One corollary of this has been an effort to reduce the urban population by sending large numbers back to their native villages: returning consumers to the country may be easier than extracting produce to feed them in the towns. Another result was the lack of raw materials for certain branches of light manufacture, and the attempt to develop industries based on synthetic materials. Yet another consequence was the heavy imports of grain, imports which displaced capital equipment in the priority list for scarce foreign exchange. The inability to draw more agricultural produce from the countryside was the major limiting factor which forced a re-appraisal of China's economic strategy after the Great Leap.

[1] See D. H. Perkins: *Price Formation in Communist China* (unpublished Ph.D Thesis, Harvard University, 1963), p. 63 for cotton. According to Perkins, the percentage of cotton procured for the years 1952–8 varied between 69 to 80 per cent of output.

[2] R. Hsia: op .cit., p. 94.

[3] See Choh-ming Li: op. cit., pp. 95–6.

[4] *Economic Research (Jingji Yanjiu)*, No. 7, July 1959, p. 5. Kao Yü-huang: 'The Need for Vigorous Organization of Rational Transport in the Economic Activities of the Nation.'

'Grain':[1] Total Output and Government Collection

(All figures are official Chinese Estimates except column headed 'US estimates')

	Total Output of 'Grain' in million metric tons		'Grain' paid in tax[2] million metric tons	State purchase of 'Grain' million metric tons	Total State collection of 'Grain' million metric tons	Total State procurement as per cent of total output of 'Grain' (including quantities subsequently distributed to grain-deficient peasants)
	Chinese figures	US estimates				
1953	157[3]		20[8]	23[12]	43[13]	27
1954	160[3]		22[8]	32[12]	54[13]	34
1955	175[3]		22[8]	29[12]	51[13]	29
1956	183[3]		[9]	[9]	49[14]	23
1957	185[3]		20[10]		nearly 50[15]	
1958	250[3]	194[7]			53[16]	22 (29 on basis of US estimate of output)
1959	270[4]	168[7]				
1960	185–250[5] 150[6]	160[7]	24[11]			
1961		167[7]				
1962		178[7]				
1963		179[7]				
1964	185–200[18]	183[17]				
1965	200[18]					

[1] 'Grain' includes potatoes (sweet and Irish) converted to grain equivalent at 4:1 ratio. Unless otherwise stated, soya bean is included up to and including 1955 and excluded in later years. 'Grain' is given with husks (e.g. paddy). Up to and including 1959, output figures are given in terms of biological yield; from 1960 a change was made to barn yield. Only in 1958 is there likely to have been much divergence between the two. (See Chohming Li: op. cit., pp. 95–6.)

[2] Tax figures for 1953–5 include local supplementary agricultural tax. Sources for subsequent years do not state whether this is or is not included. R. Hsia: op. cit., pp. 82–5, gives reasons for thinking that the actual agricultural tax figures for 1953 and 1955 were higher than those given here.

[3] *Ten Great Years*, Peking, 1960, p. 119. It should be noted that Ta-chung Liu and Kungchia Yeh consider the official Chinese crop production data for 1949–55 to be gross underestimated. (*The Economy of the Chinese Mainland*, Princeton, 1965, p. 45.) This, of course, would affect the percentages in the final column.

[4] *Peking Review*, April 5, 1960, p. 6. Li Fu-ch'un: 'Report on Draft 1960 National Economic Plan.'

[5] E. Snow: op. cit., p. 623. Chou En-lai's Statement to Snow: 'The 1960 harvest was poorer than 1958 and 1959, but higher than 1957.'

[6] *Sunday Times*, October 15, 1961. Chairman Mao to Field Marshal Montgomery.

[7] *Current Scene*, Vol. II, No. 27, January 15, 1964.

[8] *Collected Laws and Regulations* . . . Vol. 3, p. 222. Li Hsien-nien, Minister of Finance: 'Report on 1955 and Budget for 1956.' 'Fine Grain' has been calculated in terms of grain with husks by use of official conversion factor of 1·1628 (see R. Hsia op. cit., p. 21).

[9] The State Statistical Bureau's Report on the Fulfilment of the First Five Year Plan gives totals for 1953–7 of 97 million metric tons for grain taken as tax and 156 million metric tons for purchases (both figures converted into grain with husks—see Note 8). *Source: People's Handbook (Renmin Shouce) 1959*, p. 11. By deduction this gives figures for 1956 of 13 million metric tons for tax grain and 45 million for purchases. These figures seem improbable and are inconsistent with the figure of 49 million for total collection in that year.

[10] *People's Handbook (Renmin Shouce) 1959*, p. 229. Li Hsien-nien, Minister of Finance: 'Report on 1957 and Budget for 1958' (figure converted as in Note 8).

[11] E. Snow: op. cit., p. 623.

[12] Estimated by subtracting tax grain from total state grain collection.

[13] *People's Daily* (*Renmin Ribao*), May 5, 1957, p. 3. T'an Chen-lin: 'A Preliminary Study of the Income and Standard of Living of the Peasants of Our Country.' Soya bean excluded for all years; 'fine grain' converted into grain with husks as in Note 8. Figures given for calendar years.

[14] *Statistical Work* (*Tongji Gongzuo*), No. 19, October 14, 1957, p. 31. Figures for year 1956–7; converted as above into grain with husks. The difference between total collection of grain in 1955 and 1956 may, however, be greater than stated in this table as the quantity procured from July–November 1956 (the main but not the entire season for grain collection) was reported to be 15 per cent below the quantity for the corresponding period in 1955. *Planned Economy* (*Jihua Jingji*), No. 12, December 1956, p. 7. Sung Yi-min: 'Strengthen Leadership over the Free Market.'

[15] *People's Daily* (*Renmin Ribao*), July 5, 1957, p. 11. Ma Yin-ch'u: 'A New Principle of Population.'

[16] *Ten Great Years*, p. 169. See p. 89 above for a discussion of the reasons for the low proportion of output procured in 1958.

[17] *Current Scene*, Vol. III, No. 17, April 15, 1965, p. 3. The Soviet estimate for Chinese grain production in 1964 is 180 million tons. *1965 Yearbook of the Great Soviet Encyclopaedia* (in Russian), Moscow, p. 283.

[18] *China News Summary*, No. 117, April 28, 1966, pp. 1–3. Quoting *Ta Kung Daily* (*Dagong Bao*), Hong Kong, April 16, 1966, which gave a statement by Yung Lung-kwei, Vice-Chairman of the China Council for the Promotion of International Trade, made to a Filipino visitor to China and which appeared first in an article in the *Manila Times Magazine*, April 10, 1966.

4. GRAIN PRICES

The policy governing prices for farm produce subject to compulsory sale to the state has to have regard to three considerations—the desirability of purchasing prices high enough to allay peasant discontent, of sales prices low enough to satisfy consumers, and of margins between the two sufficient for the needs of the national exchequer, as well as covering costs of distribution and processing. In addition, price differentials between crops have to be sufficient to guide production in the desired direction: although compulsory procurement is in force, a lack of price incentives would make control more difficult to administer. As staple foodstuffs are subject to rationing, their prices do not have to fulfil the function of keeping demand and supply in equilibrium. The government's price policy will be reviewed more fully in Chapter 16. Here we will confine ourselves to examining certain aspects of this policy in respect of agricultural products. In passing, we must note that after the runaway inflation of the 1940s, a very high priority was attached to the maintenance of stable prices: in this China resembles all nations which have lived through the experience of hyper-inflation.

In the Soviet Union, before 1958, a large contribution to the budget was made by the turnover tax on grain (i.e. the difference between procurement price plus handling costs and the state's selling price)—almost 90 per cent of the wholesale price of wheat being accounted for by tax in 1936.[1] In China the revenue obtained by state trading in grains has been proportionately much less, although in the case of some other foodstuffs the margin has been considerable.

The Minister of Food, Sha Ch'ien-li, writing in October 1959, stated that

[1] A. Nove: *The Soviet Economy* (revised ed.), London, 1965, p. 105.

STATE PROCUREMENT OF AGRICULTURAL PRODUCE 359

purchasing and retailing prices of grains were based on the free market prices of 1953. In the subsequent six years, after state monopoly of this trade had been introduced, the state purchase prices of grain had, according to the Minister, been raised by an average of 2·1 per cent, most of which was accounted for by a rise in the prices given in places deserving of special consideration—remote frontier areas, mountainous districts, revolutionary bases, and regions which were underdeveloped or inhabited by minority nationalities. Meanwhile, the state's selling prices for grain had, he claimed, been completely stabilized, even to the eliminating of seasonal price differentials.[1] In 1955 the Minister of Finance had said that seasonal differentials in state purchasing prices for staple agricultural products had been eliminated when prices stood at or near the peak levels of the year, which was the equivalent of a general increase in average purchase prices.[2] It is difficult to reconcile this with Sha's statement that the greater part of the 2·1 per cent rise in the purchase price of grains in the period 1953–9 was due to increased purchasing prices in special areas, especially in view of the fact that almost all state purchasing of staples was now done just after harvest, at the season when prestabilized prices would have been at their lowest. The puzzle may be partly solved by a statement that reductions in seasonal price differentials had been made in 1953–4 in the case of grain, cotton, peanuts and live pigs in order to curb private speculators: and that after this the cost of storage (this, together with spoilage and the loss of weight due to reduction in moisture content— both of which may be included in storage costs—accounted for a good part of the previous seasonal price differentials), had been met by increases in the margin between purchase and sales prices and in local price differentials.[3] This implies a consequent rise in sales prices. However, another source denies that sales prices were raised significantly at that time and states that the difference was made good by a state subsidy.[4] There are obvious uncertainties in this whole subject which our present information cannot explain; among other possibilities is that changes in methods of quality grading (a matter for frequent complaints) by state procurement agencies may have influenced the trend of prices.

Sha's figure of 2·1 per cent for the average rise in state purchasing prices of grain between 1953 and 1959 also appears to be out of line with index figures for grain prices computed for other years as seen in the following table:

[1] *People's Daily* (*Renmin Ribao*), October 25, 1959, p. 6. Sha Ch'ien-li: loc. cit.
[2] *The Eighth National Congress of the Communist Party of China*, Peking, 1956, Vol. 2. Speeches, p. 209. J. L. Buck, in his study made in 1929–33 found that the average seasonal variations in the price of rice ranged from 6 per cent above the annual average to 5 per cent below it. For wheat prices in the wheat region, the comparable figures were 6 per cent above and 3 per cent below the annual average. J. L. Buck: *Land Utilization in China*, New York, 1964, pp. 336–9. However, another study, made in north China in the same period, mentions a seasonal price variation for grain of over 30 per cent. S. D. Gamble: *North China Villages*, Berkeley, 1963, p. 287.
[3] *Economic Research* (*Jingji Yanjiu*), No. 2, February 1964, p. 56. Chao Lü-k'uan and Hsiang Ching-ch'uan: 'On the Objective Foundation of Commodity Price Differentials under Socialism and the Basis for Determining these Differentials.'
[4] Ibid., No. 6, June 1965, p. 40. Hu Yü-yuan: 'On the Formation of Seasonal Price Differentials of Agricultural Commodities under the Socialist System'.

*Index figures for State purchasing Prices of Grain**

1950=100

Year	Index
1950	100
1951	
1952	120·9
1953	130·6
1954	
1955	(115·7)
1956	139·9
1957	
1958	
1959	(133·3)
1960	
1961	
1962	
1963	177·54

*It must be remembered in interpreting these figures that we do not know anything about the weighting used to obtain these averages. Changes in the index figures between years may be influenced by changed weighting (e.g. for types and qualities of grain or for localities). Despite these defects, these figures give some indication of the relative magnitudes of rises in purchasing prices of grain at different periods.

Sources: These figures are calculated on the basis of figures from the following:

1952 & 1956: *Statistical Work (Tongji Gongzuo)*, No. 17, September 14, 1957, p. 5. Statistical Research Information Department: 'Changes in the "Price Scissors" Between Industrial and Agricultural Commodities Over All the Country since Liberation.'

1953: W. Hollister: *China's Gross National Product and Social Accounts 1950–7*, Glencoe, Ill., 1958, p. 19, fn.

1955: *Report of the Indian Delegation to China on Agricultural Planning and Techniques*, p. 76.

1959: *People's Daily (Renmin Ribao)*, October 25, 1959, p. 6. Sha Ch'ien-li: loc. cit.

1963: *Peking Review*, November 20, 1964, p. 7, where it is stated that between 1951–63 state purchasing prices for grain rose 61·4. The 1951 base is calculated by interpellation.

The two figures in brackets (for 1955 and 1959) are evidently out of line, although in 1955 purchasing prices of agricultural produce did fall a little; however, this is not known to have happened between 1956–9. In the early 1960s there was apparently a notable rise in prices given the peasants for grain, in line with the policy to give priority, and material incentive, to raising farm output. (It must be borne in mind that in addition to cash payments, non-monetary inducements were sometimes offered for speedy delivery of procurement quotas and for above-quota sales of farm produce: for example, industrial goods in short supply might be available as a reward.)

According to the Minister of Food in 1959, the margin between the purchase and sales price of grains in rural areas had been stabilized at about 8 per cent (whether 8 per cent of the purchase or of the sales price is not stated); this included management expenses and a small element of tax.[1] However, the industrial and commercial tax on grain had, in 1958, been fixed at 4 per cent of the purchasing price[2] (i.e. it would account for half the margin of 8 per cent). In the spring of 1958 the margin on grain was described as having been

[1] *People's Daily (Renmin Ribao)*, October 25, 1959, p. 6. Sha Ch'ien-li: loc. cit.
[2] *Collected Laws and Regulations* ... Vol. 8, p. 130.

'excessively small' in the previous few years. Indeed it was stated that before the autumn of 1955 a loss had in fact usually been incurred.[1]

The management expenses which the Minister of Food mentioned as being met out of the 8 per cent margin on grain prices in rural areas presumably referred only to trading costs, not to the cost of processing the grain. This is the only way in which an attempt can be made to reconcile such figures as we possess on this subject with the ministerial statement, and even so there appears to be a discrepancy. A difficulty in making the comparison between purchasing and sales prices arises from the fact that while we have numerous figures of official prices for the sale of rice to consumers, and for the purchase of paddy from the peasants, there are not many cases where we have both sets of prices for one place at one time. Also we do not know exactly how much weight was lost in processing paddy into milled rice in these cases nor, to set against this, the monetary value of the husks and bran produced during processing.

However, we can examine such figures as are available. In 1956, in a village in Kiangsu, the margin between the purchasing price of paddy and the selling price of rice, after allowance for loss of weight in processing, was around 17 per cent.[2] Information available in Hong Kong in 1961 indicated price margins on rice of around 15 per cent for sales in country districts in Kwangtung. If Sha Ch'ien-li's figure of 8 per cent excluded processing costs (loss of weight already having been allowed for) our figures would give these at 7-9 per cent of the original cost of paddy, which seems excessively high. We must assume that some discrepancy exists between our estimates and those of the Minister of Food.

Despite the large measure of uncertainty about the price margin on grain, the information available demonstrates that the percentage of profit accruing to the government from grain transactions has always been very much lower than the percentage that used to obtain in the Soviet Union. One reason for this, of course, is that in China the great mass of the population is much nearer bare subsistence than in the Soviet Union and that therefore the possibility of raising large sums from the most basic foodstuffs is much less.

In May 1963 the statistician, Hsüeh Mu-ch'iao, Director of the State Statistical Bureau 1952-9 who, a few months later, was made Chairman of the National Price Commission, said that direct taxation in the form of the agricultural tax was the chief source of state revenues from agriculture, 'but, in practice, the state sometimes accumulates funds through the operation of price relationships, that is to say the state slightly lowers the procurement

---

[1] *Ta Kung Daily* (*Dagong Bao*), Peking March 23, 1958, p. 4. Chiang Yen-ling: 'On the Purchase Price for Farm Products.' See also *The Eighth National Congress of the Communist Party of China*, Vol. 2, Speeches, p. 209. Speech by Li Hsien-nien, Minister of Finance.

[2] W. R. Geddes: *Peasant Life in Communist China*, Ithaca, 1963, p. 20. In the village of Kaihsienhung in Kiangsu province in 1956, paddy was bought from the peasants at ¥4 a bushel and sold as rice in the village store at 13 cents a catty, equivalent (according to Geddes) to ¥6·50 a bushel. Geddes mentions that paddy loses c. 15 per cent of its weight in husking, but says nothing about loss of weight in milling. On the supposition that total loss of weight between purchase and sale was 28 per cent (the approximate national average for 1955—see *People's Handbook* [*Renmin Shouce*] *1957*, p. 496) the margin between purchase and sale price would have been 17 per cent.

prices of agricultural products, and the margin between these prices and the "values" of the products represents state accumulation'. Hsüeh then asks whether this indirect form of taxing agriculture should be considered a normal feature of a socialist state, and leaves the query unanswered: 'these questions are still considered from different points of view and must be the subject of further full discussion'.[1]

Hsüeh's statement that commercial profit contributed only a minor portion of the state's revenue from agriculture is borne out by the figures for 1959, the only year for which we have found sufficient data to make this estimate. In that year, the target for commercial profits from grain was around ¥400 million (in any case not more than ¥410 million)[2] and the target for profits on the processing of grain was ¥130 million.[3] Together, these two total approximately ¥530 million. This compares with a total of ¥3,300 million for revenue from the agricultural tax in the budget for 1959.[4] Thus agricultural tax was budgeted to provide over eight times as much revenue as did commercial profit on grain and over six times as much as commercial and processing profits on grain combined. (In passing, it should be noted that profits and taxes on industrial goods sold to the rural population have since 1952 provided the state with more revenue than has agricultural tax.)[5]

We know that the margin on some other agricultural products was much wider than in the case of grain. The profit rates accruing to the state on the sale and processing of sugar and cotton, to name two notable examples, have been high and these two items have made important contributions to the national budget. In 1958 the difference between the purchase and selling price of native sugar (i.e. sugar refined by old methods and not in modern factories) was said to be generally about 90 per cent and in some instances over 100 per cent.[6] On the other hand, losses have at times been incurred on state trade in some subsidiary farm products. This was the case in 1963 with certain unspecified commodities, and around 1965 with pork,[7] although in both instances this may have been a purely local occurrence.

The official prices fixed for compulsory sales of agricultural produce have been considerably below free market prices. A legitimate free market in grain has existed only sporadically since 1954.[8] In 1964 a production brigade in Kwangtung was reported to have sold above-quota grain to the state at

---

[1] *Economic Research (Jingji Yanjiu)*, No. 5, May 1963, pp. 2-3. Hsüeh Mu-ch'iao: 'Some Problems Awaiting Discussion on Commodity Prices in a Socialist Society.'

[2] Commercial profit on grain for January–May 1959 amounted to ¥205 million which was 'over 50 per cent' of the year's target. *Collected Laws and Regulations* ... Vol. 10, p. 278.

[3] *Collected Laws and Regulations* ... Vol. 10, p. 279. On p. 278, however, it is stated that the ¥38,790,000 profits of the grain industry in the first quarter of 1959 fulfilled 28·11 per cent of the year's target; this would indicate a target of about ¥138 million.

[4] Ibid., Vol. 9, p. 69.

[5] D. H. Perkins: *Market Control and Planning in Communist China*, Cambridge, Mass., 1966, pp. 42–3.

[6] *Ta Kung Daily (Dagong Bao)*, Peking, March 23, 1958, p. 4. Chiang Yen-ling: loc. cit.

[7] *Ta Kung Daily (Dagong Bao)*, Peking, September 11, 1963, p. 1, and ibid., February 18, 1965, p. 2.

[8] See pp. 297–8 above.

¥9·8 per 100 catties compared with the free market price of ¥18.[1] We are not told if the state price for above-quota sales was the same as for compulsory sales, but it would certainly not be below this latter and very likely was above it. A few years earlier, during the period of bad harvests, no licit free market in grain existed but the difference in black market prices obtained by peasants and the official state purchasing prices appears to have diverged more than the free and the official prices of 1964. This change was due both to the more plentiful supplies in 1964, which must have caused free prices to fall, and also to the rise in official procurement prices for grain which, as we have noted, occurred in the early 1960s.

The influence of low official prices for the sale by peasants of all or almost all their crops of grain and other major crops has undoubtedly weakened their enthusiasm for producing these. This is especially the case when other farm produce might be sold for free market prices. It explains why vegetables, fruit, eggs and poultry have in recent years been in plentiful supply while grain, vegetable oil, and cotton remained rationed. This anomaly—that the more important any item of produce, the weaker the incentives permitted the peasant to increase its output,—is not peculiar to China. The higher procurement prices for grain of recent years have lessened the force of this circumstance, but not yet sufficiently to enable rationing to be abolished.

Further matters concerning the price of agricultural output are held over for treatment to Chapter 16 where price policy in general will be discussed.

5. SUMMARY

Agricultural tax, collected mainly in kind, is computed as a proportion of an assessed norm of output. It was apparently intended to stabilize tax yield for the duration of a Five Year Plan period. Accordingly new regulations were issued in 1958, the first year of the Second Five Year Plan. The nationwide average rate of tax was to be 15·5 per cent of the new norm compared with approximately 16·5 per cent of the old norm in 1953–7; local supplementary agricultural tax in addition might amount to 15 per cent of the main tax. In fact the yield of both agricultural and supplementary taxes together seems to have been around 11–13 per cent of actual output during the First Five Year Plan period. For the chaotic years of the Great Leap in 1958–9, estimates of tax are not at present available. In the period of disaster that followed, the actual rate of tax probably rose, as the increased assessment for the Second Five Year Plan was levied on an output which had fallen instead of achieving the planned increase. However, in general a fair degree of stability has been maintained in the absolute quantities of grain levied as agricultural tax.

Greater fluctuations have occurred in the quantities of grain procured by the state through compulsory sales. These were also supposed to be stabilized to leave peasants the incentive to increase production. However, this intention conflicted with the state's need to secure sufficient grain for its various requirements, so the authorities were constantly resorting to escape clauses or otherwise evading the declared policy of stabilization. In most years for

[1] A. L. Strong: op. cit., p. 203.

which we have been able to make the calculations, total state procurement of grain, by tax and compulsory sales together, has been between 25–30 per cent of total output.

The central government does not control the allocation of all grain procured but only the net transfer obligations of provinces. Transfers within each province are, within broad limits, left to the provincial authorities. The 5–6 million tons of grain imported every year in the early and mid-1960s were, therefore, more significant in proportion to inter-provincial transfers of grain than to total procurement.

The Minister of Food's figure of 8 per cent for the margin between purchase and sales prices of grains in the countryside would seem to be lower than is compatible with other evidence which suggests a figure of around 15–17 per cent. Even so, it is clear that in China, unlike the Soviet Union, state profit on grain sales has not been a significant source of funds for investment. On some other agricultural raw materials, notably sugar and cotton, a high rate of tax and profit is levied at the processing stage. Compulsory sales at prices below free market levels have had a discouraging influence on the production of grain and other major crops.

Chapter 14

THE FISCAL SYSTEM[1]

The financial policy of the Chinese Government is directed towards ensuring sufficient resources to carry out planned capital investment in addition to covering normal government expenditure on current account. At the same time, enough consumption goods must be provided to supply incentives for work and to absorb available purchasing power.

The budgets of central and local authorities are the main source of long and short term capital for the economy. Bank deposits, credit co-operatives, and the extra-budgetary funds of which we shall be writing below (and which include the ploughed back profits of enterprises) are other sources of capital.

The State Council's Office for Finance and Trade is the highest governmental organ in the financial sphere. As we have already seen, it is the successor of the former Fifth General Office of the State Council which from 1954 to 1959 controlled the Ministry of Finance and the People's Bank of China, as well as the ministries concerned with commerce. The Director of the State Council Office, ever since its first establishment in 1954, has been Vice-Premier Li Hsien-nien, who since 1955 has concurrently held the position of Minister of Finance. Li is reported to spend almost all his time at the State Council Office, leaving one of the Vice-Ministers of Finance, Wu Po, in virtual charge of the Ministry.[2] Ts'ao Chü-ju, the last known Director General of the People's Bank of China, held that position from 1954 to 1965, having previously been Deputy Director of the Bank. The control of financial policy in China under the Communist Government has, therefore, been marked by a high degree of personal continuity. Parallel to the State Council's Office are the Party Central Committee's Finance and Trade Work Department and Finance and Trade Political Department. The first is headed by Ma Ming-fang and the second by Yao Yi-lin, concurrently Minister of Commerce. Finance was one of the first sectors in which, from 1964, new political departments were set up at various levels alongside the Party committees.[3]

The functions of the Ministry of Finance include the compilation of the central government's annual budgets, the collection of revenue, and the supervision of the financial work of all the other ministries and of local organs of finance and taxation which are established at the different administrative

---

[1] Part of this chapter has appeared in *The China Mainland Review*, Vol. 1, No. 4, March 1966, pp. 1–5 as an article entitled 'Extra-Budgetary Funds in the Chinese Fiscal System.'

[2] Unpublished paper of Ezra Vogel of Harvard University, relating to the financial system in Mainland China.

[3] See pp. 18–19 above.

levels. The Construction Bank and the Bank of Communications have come under the Ministry of Finance, being in effect its organs for the disbursement of budgetary grants for investment purposes;[1] they will be treated in the following chapter. The People's Bank and the post-1963 Agricultural Bank both come directly under the State Council and are not controlled by the Ministry of Finance. Insurance companies fall under the aegis of the Ministry of Finance[2] as do also the Central Finance Cadres School and the Finance Research Institute.

The Ministry of Finance's most important component is the Budget Bureau which co-ordinates the compilation of the budget, balancing the various conflicting demands. Other bureaux inside the Ministry include the Main Tax Bureau, the Agricultural Tax Bureau, the various bureaux for different branches of economic construction, and the bureaux concerned with the finance of the general administration, of defence and of education and culture.[3]

Before 1958, from the provincial level downwards, the collection of revenue was handled by taxation offices, while disbursements were made quite separately by finance offices. Subsequently, when the method of direct central control over local authorities and revenues and expenditures gave way to that of limiting central concern mainly to the balances remitted between different levels of government (see below), the local revenue and finance offices were merged at the provincial level and also in most *hsien*.[4]

1. BUDGETS, STATE REVENUE AND EXPENDITURE

Up to, and including, the year 1960, the national budget for the current year and the final accounts for the previous year were presented annually by the Minister of Finance to the National People's Congress for the approval required by the Constitution. Summaries of these budget reports, containing the chief figures, were published in these years. In 1961 no meeting of the NPC was reported to have been held and no announcement about the final accounts for 1960 nor of the budgets for 1961 and 1962 has come to our knowledge. In July 1963 the Minister of Finance, Li Hsien-nien, reported to the Standing Committee of the NPC on the final accounts for 1961 and 1962. In December 1963, the National People's Congress approved the budget for 1963 and 'the preliminary plan' of the 1964 budget. In July 1964 the State Council passed the final accounts for 1963 and the draft budget for 1964 and, similarly in July 1965, the final accounts for 1964 and the budget estimates for 1965. However, at the time of writing little news, beyond the bare announcement of these reports, has been given of the budget for any year since 1960 nor of the final accounts since 1959.

Information from a former official of the Ministry of Finance tells of a drastic fall of about 50 per cent of the budgeted total in the revenues actually collected in 1960, and he thought that in the next three or four years the figure may have remained at about the same level, that is around ¥30,000 to

---
[1] The present status, and indeed existence, of the Bank of Communications is in doubt. See p. 412 below.

[2] See pp. 515–16 below.

[3] Unpublished paper of Ezra Vogel.

[4] Unpublished papers of Michel Oksenberg of Stanford University relating to the financial system in Mainland China.

¥40,000 million.[1] Official releases disclosed that in 1963 a small surplus was achieved, that 'the results in carrying out the 1964 budget were better than originally estimated' and that in the 1965 budget, both revenue and expenditure were to be increased by over 10 per cent compared with 1964, and that the budget was to be balanced.[2] An article published in 1965 stated that 'over 30 per cent' of the national income is distributed through public finance'.[3] (National income would, of course, be reckoned in the Communist manner, as exclusive of services.)

A new set of budgetary regulations was introduced in 1963, but we have found no information about them, except that they provided for certain local supplementary taxes to be entered into the 'basic financial plan'[4] which, however, is something over and above the budget, being the financial counterpart of the whole economic plan; it will be further discussed in Chapter 17.

The latest figures available for the Chinese budget are those given overleaf. For the earlier years some figures for sub-headings, e.g. individual taxes, were published as well as the main items listed in the table on page 368.

Some preliminary observations are necessary on the scope of Chinese budgets. These will be familiar to students of the Soviet economy, for the Chinese Communists took over the main lines of their budgetary system from that of the Soviet Union.

The first point is the relatively greater importance of the budget in the national economy compared with the situation in non-Communist lands. Virtually the whole of the modern sector of the Chinese economy is owned by the state (the so-called joint state-private ownership has been treated in Chapter 6) and a very large part of the investment within this sector is undertaken with funds allocated by the budget. The budget also makes provision for considerable sums for investment in the old-style sector of the economy, notably agriculture, which is mainly under collective ownership. The existence of other sources of investment funds, to be discussed later, means that there is not a complete correspondence between the sums made available by the budget for investment and the investment projects laid down in the current economic plan (much less the investment projects that are actually undertaken). The financial counterpart of the economic plan is supposed to be not just the budget, but the whole comprehensive financial plan, of which the state budget is but one component.[5] However, the techniques and practice of

[1] Richard Diao: *Communist China's Finance in 1964* (mimeographed paper published by Union Research Institute, Hong Kong), 1965, pp. 3–4. This is not far removed from the figure of approximately ¥43,000 million for the 1963 budget estimated by F. J. Durand: *Le Financement du Budget en Chine Populaire*, Hong Kong, 1965. Durand's estimate is based on a calculation which assumes that the cash equivalence of tax grain remained unchanged through a period when the price for compulsory purchase of grain rose considerably.

[2] *Peking Review*, January 3, 1964, p. 7, and ibid., July 30, 1965, p. 3, and ibid., January 1, 1965, p. 10. Chou En-lai: 'Report on the Work of the Government.'

[3] *Kuang Ming Daily (Guangming Ribao)*, February 8, 1965, p. 4. Liu Hung-ju and Tai Ch'ien-ting: 'The Stability of the *Jenminpi* Demonstrates the Incomparable Superiority of New China's Socialist System.'

[4] *Economic Research (Jingji Yanjiu)*, No. 6, June 1965, p. 20. Shen Yün: 'A Discussion on the Nature, Special Characteristics and System of Socialist National Finance.'

[5] See pp. 471–2 below.

Revenue	Final Accounts						Budget 1960	
	1957		1958		1959			
	Yuan million	% of total	Yuan million	% of total	Yuan million	% of total	Yuan million	% of total
1. Revenue from Enterprises and Institutions	14,221	46·3	22,020	52·6	33,360	61·6	45,300	64·7
2. Taxes	15,439	50·3	18,740	44·8	20,470	37·8	24,360	34·8
3. Loans	673	2·2	790	1·9	—		—	
4. Other sources	369	1·2	310	0·7	330	0·6	360	0·5
Total	30,702	100	41,860	100	54,160	100	70,020	100

Expenditure	Final Accounts						Budget 1960	
	1957		1958		1959			
	Yuan million	% of total	Yuan million	% of total	Yuan million	% of total	Yuan million	% of total
1. 'Economic Construction'	14,861	48·6	26,270	64·1	32,170	61·0	42,910	61·3
2. Social Services, Culture and Education (in 1960 'Science' was added to this heading)	4,739	15·5	4,350	10·6	5,860	11·1	8,620	12·3
3. National Defence	5,509	18·0	5,000	12·2	5,800	11·0	5,800	8·3
4. Administration	2,322	7·6	2,270	5·5	2,900	5·5	3,170	4·5
5. Repayment of Loans, domestic and foreign	1,293	4·2	1,180	2·9	970	1·8	1,200	1·7
6. Aid to foreign countries					350	0·7	500	0·7
7. Additional allotment of Credit Funds to Banks and Repayment of Bank Overdraft	1,553	5·1	1,650	4·0	4,430	8·4	5,800	8·3
8. Additional allotment to local authorities' revolving funds	73	0·2						
9. Other Expenditure	199	0·7	240	0·6	290	0·5	320	0·5
10. General Reserve	—	—	—	—	—	—	1,700	2·4
Total	30,549	100	40,960	100	52,770	100	70,020	100

Sources: Reports by Li Hsien-nien, Minister of Finance, on Final Accounts for 1957, 1958 and 1959, and on Draft Budget for 1960.
1957: *Collected Laws and Regulations of the People's Republic of China* (in Chinese), Vol. 7, pp. 117–18.
1958: Ibid., Vol. 9, pp. 63–4.
1959: Ibid., Vol. 11, p. 34.
1960 (Draft Budget): Ibid., pp. 40–1, and *Peking Review*, April 5, 1960, pp. 21–5.

planning in China are such that a great part of this planning, both economic and financial, is not of great practical importance.

While a large part of the budgetary expenditure goes on investment in state-owned enterprises, these enterprises in turn are by far the largest source of revenue. In the budget for 1960, for example, 93·4 per cent of the total revenue was to be drawn in the form of both profits and taxes from state concerns, 5·9 per cent from rural communes, and only 0·7 per cent from other sources.[1] (It must be noted that this is not identical with the actual incidence of taxation.)

Another feature which the Chinese have borrowed from the Soviet system is that the national budget has, from 1956 onwards, included under each item not only the expenditure of its own organs, but also the budgetary expenditure of local authorities. Thus the national budget becomes a grand total of budgetary expenditure at all levels of the government;[2] similarly, the budgets of local authorities include those of the lower local authorities under them. For example, investment funds provided by a provincial budget for provincially-controlled industry appear not only in the budget of that province, but also form a component of the expenditure under 'economic construction' in the national budget. Certain items of revenue accruing to local authorities or to state enterprises are, however, excluded together with expenditures made from them. These are known as extra-budgetary funds and will be treated below.

Because the state budget includes, under each item of revenue and expenditure, those sums of each that are attributable to local authorities, it cannot at the same time show transfers between the different levels of the administration. More will be said about such transfers.

We will now discuss the separate items of revenue and expenditure in the Chinese budget.

Revenue from Enterprises and Institutions

From 1958 onwards, for as far as the published figures extend, this has been the largest single item of budgetary revenue in China. It consists of the profits, depreciation reserves, income arising from changes in price of fixed assets, and surplus working capital[3] (sometimes the term 'profits' is used loosely to cover all these items) transmitted to the state, at all levels of the state administration, by state-owned enterprises and institutions of all kinds and, since 1956, by joint state-private enterprises as well.[4] It must be remembered that these profits are a function of prices commonly set by the state. (See Chapter 16.)

In Chapter 6 we reviewed the rules laid down at various dates for determining the proportion of profits to be transmitted to the state or retained by the enterprises and industrial ministries. Most enterprises have their remittances of 'planned profits' deducted automatically from their bank balances, followed later by a final settlement according to actual profits earned. However, by regulations of January 1957, this was not to apply to the Ministries of Commerce, of Urban Services, nor of Aquatic Products, presumably

---

[1] *Peking Review*, April 5, 1960, p. 24–5. Li Hsien-nien: loc. cit.

[2] *Collected Financial Laws and Regulations of the Central Government* (in Chinese), 1956, p. 43, and *Finance* (*Caizheng*), No. 1, January 1958, p. 7. Huan Wen: 'Some Problems in Local Budgetary Management after the Implementation of the New Financial System.'

[3] See pp. 153, 161 and 163 above on the last three items.

[4] From January 1958 supply and marketing co-operatives were to be treated as state enterprises in the matter of delivering profits to the state. *People's Taxation* (*Renmin Shuiwu*), No. 11, June 4, 1958, p. 5. Joint Notice of the Ministry of Finance and the Second Ministry of Commerce to the Supply and Marketing Co-operatives.

because in commerce and fisheries the forward planning of profits is even more difficult than in other sectors of the economy. These ministries were instead to base their remittances on actual profits earned.[1]

In the final accounts for 1957, the last year for which we have such an analysis for realized revenue and expenditure, revenue (i.e. profits, depreciation, etc., but not taxes) from enterprises and institutions was divided as follows: from industry (including mining) ¥6,524 million; from transport, posts and telecommunications, ¥2,276 million; and from internal foreign trade, ¥4,337 million. The sources of the balance, ¥1,084 million out of the total ¥14,221 million (which included revenue derived from a host of institutions of many kinds as well as from enterprises) were not specified.[2] In the inflationary year of 1956, revenue (excluding taxes) from industrial enterprises (including mining) provided 62 per cent of the funds invested in industry (¥5,447 million out of ¥8,828 million) rising to 80 per cent in 1957, when efforts were made to stem the inflation, and to 82 per cent in the budget for 1958.[3] For the years since 1958 no separate figures have been published for budgetary receipts and investment expenditure in respect of industry, except that the budget of 1960 provided for capital investment to the total of ¥18,948 million in industry. The amount allotted to investment in 'the textile and other light industries and aquatic products' was to be ¥1,470 million, 90 per cent of this going to local enterprise.[4]

For accounting purposes, profit is returned as a percentage of total costs. On this basis, the profit rate has been higher in heavy industry than in light, at least during the First Five Year Plan period.[5] It will be remembered that state enterprises pay no interest on their fixed capital. This circumstance provides a relatively larger hidden subsidy for capital-intensive heavy industry than for less capital-intensive branches of industry, thus making the accounting cost of heavy industry artificially low. When calculated as a percentage of capital, profit has been higher in the case of light industry. In other words light industry has provided a share of profits as well as of taxation disproportionate to the sums invested in it from budgetary sources.[6] In the First Five Year Plan period, for example, the textile industry's profits remitted to the

[1] p. 375 fn. 2 below and *Collected Laws and Regulations* . . . Vol 5, p. 118. The construction and installation enterprises under the various ministries were also to remit according to actual, not planned, profits.

[2] Calculated from figures given in *Collected Laws and Regulations* . . . Vol. 7, pp. 124–5. On revenue from institutions, see pp. 385–6 below.

[3] *Collected Laws and Regulations* . . . Vol. 6, pp. 109–10, and ibid., Vol. 7, pp. 124–6.

[4] *Peking Review*, April 5, 1960, pp. 11 and 15. Li Fu-ch'un, Chairman of the State Planning Commission: 'Report on the Draft 1960 National Economic Plan.'

[5] *Financial and Economic Research (Caijing Yanjiu)*, No. 7, October 15, 1958, p. 34. Fang Ch'eng-p'ing: 'The Fundamental Reform of the Industrial and Financial System', and *Economic Research (Jingji Yanjiu)*, No. 5, May 1963, p. 1. Hsüeh Mu-ch'iao, Vice-Chairman, State Planning Commission and former Director of the State Statistical Bureau: 'Some Problems Awaiting Discussion on Commodity Prices in a Socialist Society.' In 1955, the rate of profit on cost in heavy industry as a whole was reported to be 40 per cent. *Finance (Caizheng)*, No. 2, November 1956, p. 20. Jen Jui-lin: 'A Study of the Present Price of Timber.'

[6] *Economic Research (Jingji Yanjiu)*, No. 5, May 1963, pp. 1–2. Hsüeh Mu-ch'iao: loc. cit., and *Statistical Work (Tongji Gongzuo)*, No. 13, July 14, 1957, p. 12. Sun Yeh-fang: 'A Talk on Gross Value of Output.'

state totalled ¥2,900 million, which was reckoned to be about 2·4 times as much as the state had invested in the industry during that period.[1] The profitability (on costs) reported to be attained or expected in cotton mills in normal operation at dates between 1957–66 has been mentioned at rates from 80–300 per cent p.a.[2]

The sugar industry has been another profitable line for the budget, providing during the First Five Year Plan period about ¥2,000 in profits, depreciation and taxes (these three sources of state revenue together are sometimes referred to as the 'accumulation' of an industry or an enterprise) during the First Five Year Plan period, some 4·3 times the amount invested by the state in the sugar industry in those years.[3] Revenue considerations may have been a factor in the extension of acreage under cotton and sugar in the 1960s, even at the expense of grain. The rate of accumulation in light industries using agricultural raw materials is in general considerably higher than in those using industrial raw materials; indirectly it constitutes a tax on agriculture.[4]

Policy has favoured profits (on cost) in industry being higher than in commerce.[5] Partly this is due to the particularly strong ideological dislike of high profits in commerce, a sector held to be non-productive. However, this also once again compensates to some extent for the lack of charge for fixed capital.

The method of reckoning depreciation has been treated in Chapter 6. Depreciation funds have to be remitted to the state and become part of the state's general revenue. Major repair funds, however, are retained in special bank accounts by individual enterprises.[6] Annual remittances of depreciation charges have been estimated as follows:[7]

    1957   ¥2,457 million
    1958   ¥2,601 million
    1959   ¥3,970 million

[1] *Chinese Textiles* (*Zhongguo Fangzhi*), No. 14, July 30, 1957, p. 1. Chiang Kuang-nai, Minister of Textiles: 'Only Socialism Can Save China.' However, these figures are incompatible with a figure of ¥1,600 million given for total state investment in the textile industry in the First Five Year Plan period. *People's Daily* (*Renmin Ribao*), September 18, 1959, p. 9. Chiang Kuang-nai: 'Ten Glorious Years of the Textile Industry.' Another source gives the textile industry's total 'accumulation' (i.e. taxes as well as profits and depreciation) for the state during the First Five Year Plan period as ¥10,000 million. *Ta Kung Daily* (*Dagong Bao*), Peking, June 23, 1961, p. 3. Yeh Fang-t'ien: 'The Development of the Role of Industrial Crops Production.' This figure seems high in relation to a figure of ¥2,900 million for profits alone.

[2] *People's Daily* (*Renmin Ribao*), August 8, 1959, p. 7. Hsiao Ch'uan: 'We Should Attach Importance to the Development of Light Industry', and *Planned Economy* (*Jihua Jingji*), No. 5, May 1958, p. 35, and *Ta Kung Daily* (*Dagong Bao*), Peking, June 23, 1961, p. 3. Yeh Fang-t'ien: loc. cit., and *BBC Summary of World Broadcasts*, Second Series, FE/W353/A/28 (Canton, February 7, 1966).

[3] *Central Co-operation Bulletin* (*Zhongyang Hozuo Tongxun*), No. 59, June 11, 1959 (ECMM 194). Long Term Planning Department, Planning Bureau of the Ministry of Commerce: 'Production and Consumption of Sugar.'

[4] *Ta Kung Daily* (*Dagong Bao*), Peking, February 22, 1963, p. 3. Jung Wen-tsuo: 'Develop Light Industry Production Based on Industrial Raw Materials.'

[5] *Economic Research* (*Jingji Yanjiu*), No. 3, March 1959, p. 28. Keng Tsun-san: 'Brief Remarks on the Current Price of Coal.'

[6] See p. 161 above, and R. Diao: op. cit., p. 9, and *Taxation in Communist China 1950–1959*, p. 38. Published by Central Intelligence Agency, Washington, DC, 1961.

[7] *Taxation in Communist China 1950–1959*, op. cit., p. 35.

Taxes

Neither the published budgets, nor final accounts, give a full analysis of the total revenue from taxes, but some details were given for the earlier years shown in the table. In 1957, figures for taxes on industry and commerce (￥11,305 million) and for agricultural tax (￥2,931 million) were reported, leaving a balance of ￥1,203 from other taxes.[1] In 1958 all the agricultural taxes (i.e. presumably including the minor agricultural taxes mentioned below) were said to have brought in ￥3,260 million[2] but no further figures of proceeds of individual taxes or groups of taxes were revealed. As far as earlier years are concerned, from 1950 to 1956 separate figures were published for each year for taxes on industry and commerce, for customs duties, salt tax and agricultural tax respectively.[3]

The largest source of tax revenue is the *consolidated industrial and commercial tax*, which was promulgated in September 1958 and is payable, with certain exceptions, by all enterprises and other units in state, private, joint-state-private or collective ownership and by individuals, engaged in industrial production, the purchase of certain kinds of agricultural output, the import of goods, retail trade, transport, communications and service trades. The tax is assessed as a percentage, varying according to type of goods or services, of the total sales proceeds (in the case of industrial enterprises and retailers) or of total payments made (in the case of importers, and of purchasers of farm output) or of 'business income'—presumably, from the context, meaning total receipts—(in the case of transport, communications and service enterprises). For industrial producers, importers of non-agricultural goods and for retailers, the tax percentage is reckoned on a total inclusive of the tax itself, in this following the example of the Soviet turnover tax, on which this tax was largely modelled. The 44 per cent tax on machine refined sugar is, therefore, the equivalent of 63·36 per cent on the ex-refinery price net of tax.[4] Imported manufactured goods are assessed on a total inclusive of c.i.f. prices, customs duty, and consolidated industrial and commercial tax: imported agricultural produce on c.i.f. prices only.[5]

Exemption from the industrial and commercial tax was given to state banks, insurance concerns, agricultural machinery stations, medical and health institutions, and to income derived from experiments by scientific research bodies. Exemption or reduction might also be granted 'when encouragement is called for' in respect of income made by public mess halls and similar concerns and in certain other instances. Provinces and equivalent authorities

---

[1] Derived from figures given in *Collected Laws and Regulations* . . . Vol. 7, p. 124. Here *kungshang shui* may be translated as 'taxes on industry and commerce' and not as 'the industrial and commercial tax' promulgated in September 1958. 'Taxes on industry and commerce' include income tax collected from these sectors, as well as the four taxes later consolidated into the industrial and commercial tax.

[2] *Collected Laws and Regulations* . . . Vol. 9, p. 66.

[3] Ko Chih-ta: *China's Budget During the Transition Period* (in Chinese), Peking, 1957, p. 58.

[4] *Collected Laws and Regulations* . . . Vol. 8, pp. 126–44. On the Soviet turnover tax, see A. Nove: *The Soviet Economy* (revised ed.), London, 1965, pp. 104–6.

[5] *Collected Laws and Regulations* . . . Vol. 8, p. 140.

were allowed to give exemptions or otherwise to effect changes in the tax within limits to be laid down by the central authorities.[1]

Rates at which the consolidated industrial and commercial tax was to be levied at the time of its introduction in 1958 varied from 1·5 per cent on unbleached cotton cloth and 2 per cent on piped water to 69 per cent on top grade cigarettes. Grain carried a tax rate of 4 per cent, wheat flour of 10 per cent, vegetable oil 12·5 per cent and processed sugar from 27–44 per cent, according to type. Cotton yarn paid 23–26 per cent depending on type and count, while the rate on factory-made cotton cloth was 1·5–5 per cent. Goods which are subsequently retailed pay tax a second time, at 3 per cent of the total retail price (inclusive of tax). For certain commodities, such as some types of farm output, this is the only occasion on which tax is payable. Postal, telecommunications, and transport undertakings pay tax at 2·5 per cent and service trades at 3–7 per cent; apparently reckoned, as mentioned above, on total receipts including tax.[2]

The rates for the new consolidated tax did not in most cases diverge much from the tax burdens previously carried by the commodities or services concerned; some rates were lowered, e.g. to help enterprises which were operating at a loss or to encourage production of certain goods, such as fertilizers. Rates of tax were raised in the case of certain commodities where profit rates were high[3] (i.e. a shift from profits remittances to tax was brought about for reasons to be discussed below). Local authorities were empowered to levy for their own use a supplementary industrial and commercial tax, equal to a certain small percentage of the main tax.[4] This tax was extra-budgetary, that is, it did not figure in the budget totals.

Little information is available about changes in rates of industrial and commercial tax since 1958. In 1962 it was stated that reduction or exemption had been given to indigenous chemical fertilizers, insecticides and farm tools made by communes and production teams. In the following year, a tax reduction for unspecified new industrial consumer goods was mentioned.[5]

The regulations of 1958 laid down that the tax was not to be payable on intermediate products made by an industrial enterprise and used for its own production purposes, except in the case of cotton yarn, leather and hides, wines and spirits. But products made by an enterprise for its own capital

[1] *Collected Laws and Regulations* . . . Vol. 8, pp. 127–8.
[2] Ibid., pp. 129–37.
[3] *People's Taxation* (*Renmin Shuiwu*), No. 18, September 19, 1958, p. 12. Wu Po: Vice-Minister of Finance: 'An Explanation of the Draft Regulations of the People's Republic of China on the Consolidated Industrial and Commercial Tax.'
[4] In January 1958 the rate for the local supplementary industrial and commercial tax was fixed at 1 per cent of the total proceeds of the commodity circulation tax, the goods tax, the business tax, and the income tax; the three first mentioned of these taxes were, in September 1958, absorbed into the new consolidated industrial and commercial tax. *Collected Laws and Regulations* . . . Vol. 6, p. 332. No subsequent information on the rate of supplementary industrial and commercial tax has come to our knowledge.
[5] *Ta Kung Daily* (*Dagong Bao*), Peking, November 27, 1962, p. 2. Pi Ming: 'The Work of Tax Collection Must Serve to Aid Agriculture and to Consolidate the Collective Economy of the People's Communes', and ibid., August 8, 1963, p. 2. Tsou Ming, Deputy Director, General Revenue Bureau, Ministry of Finance: 'Energetically Organize Financial Revenues, Improve Accumulation of Funds for the State.'

construction, or for non-productive purposes were subject to the tax.[1]

The removal of tax on intermediate products also applied in the case of goods sent out by an industrial enterprise for processing elsewhere, or of spare parts made for it by other enterprises. Formerly the consignee had to pay tax, on behalf of the consignor, on such goods. This was now, under the new regulations, to cease. Nor did the consignor have to pay tax on them, except for the tax due on their eventual sale.[2] It was hoped that this provision would encourage 'co-ordinated production', i.e. the use of outside enterprises to undertake one stage of processing or to make certain components.

The consolidated industrial and commercial tax superseded four earlier taxes: commodity circulation tax, goods tax, business tax, and stamp duty. Their consolidation into one tax was intended to reduce and simplify paper work by substituting the relatively easy calculation of actual sums received ex-factory or paid out, for the previous assessments on notional wholesale prices of goods at stages of manufacture when they were not in fact being sold. Before the change in 1958, when tax was still payable on intermediate products such as raw materials, semi-finished goods, and accessories made by an enterprise for use in its own production processes, tax might often be paid several times on one product in the course of production.[3] The old system of multiple taxes had been intended to curb private enterprise. With the achievement of 'socialist transformation', its task in this respect was finished.[4]

The 1958 change in the taxation of industry and commerce was preceded by considerable discussion and experiment. For petty traders a unified industrial and commercial tax had been adopted earlier. In the spring and summer of 1958 (as a continuation of earlier experiments) the consolidated tax was tried on a national scale for certain groups of commodities and at three places for all taxable goods. Even when it was promulgated for general application in September 1958, the regulations were described as 'draft', and the system was considered to be still on an experimental basis.[5] We have not heard of these regulations being promulgated in a permanent form.

Despite the fact that the new tax was much simpler than those it had superseded, its assessment and collection gave rise to considerable administrative difficulties. Tax evasion, too, was widespread, helped by the reduction in the staff of revenue departments which occurred in many places in the course of the Great Leap.[6]

---

[1] *Collected Laws and Regulations* . . . Vol. 8, pp. 126, 129, 130, 132 and 139.

[2] *People's Taxation (Renmin Shuiwu)*, No. 18, September 19, 1958, pp. 12–13, Wu Po: oc. cit.

[3] *Financial and Economic Research (Caijing Yanjiu)*, No. 7, October 15, 1958, p. 34. Fang Ch'eng-p'ing: loc. cit.

[4] Ibid., p. 33, and *People's Taxation (Renmin Shuiwu)*, No. 18, September 19, 1958, p. 11. Wu Po: loc. cit.

[5] *Finance (Caizheng)*, No. 5, April 4, 1958, p. 17. Wen Ping-yuan: 'A Discussion on the Trial Reform of the Industrial and Commercial Tax System', and *Financial and Economic Research (Caijing Yanjiu)*, No. 7, October 15, 1958, p. 33. Fang Ch'eng-p'ing: loc. cit., and *People's Taxation (Renmin Shuiwu)*, No. 18, September 19, 1958, p. 11. Wu Po: loc. cit., and *Collected Laws and Regulations* . . . Vol. 7, pp. 236–9 and 274–8.

[6] *Finance (Caizheng)*, No. 11, June 9, 1959, p. 17. Shanghai Municipal Department of Finance: 'Strengthen Inspection, Prevent Evasion', and ibid., No. 13, July 9, 1959, p. 18. Ho Ch'eng: 'Carry Out Well the "Three Co-ordinations" in Tax Inspection.'

One factor militating against efficient collection of the industrial and commercial tax has been that revenue cadres have thought that as profits of state enterprises (and, after 1956, those of joint state-private enterprises as well) are in any case going to the state treasury, it is of little importance to make a clear distinction between tax and profits: 'both eat out of the same pot'. This attitude is strengthened by the fact that the same revenue departments are responsible for supervising the transmission of profits, as well as for the collection of taxes.[1]

Enterprises themselves naturally prefer to pay less tax and to maximize their profits, since a proportion of profits can be retained by them for various purposes. Also the time lag before payment appears to be somewhat longer in the case of profit remittances than of tax payments, especially where above-plan profits are concerned.[2] Although the difference in time lag may not be great, it evidently adds to the attractiveness of profits to enterprises. Probably this is due to the very high marginal efficiency of capital in China and the very quick returns obtainable on it; also accountancy delays may enable above-plan profit remittances to be postponed for a considerable time. Failure to collect the tax due results in an enterprise increasing its profits, and 'if the rate of profit is excessive', a Soviet adviser had written in 1955, 'then when an enterprise has sold its products it is left with a large sum of money over and above its production expenses. These funds may make it possible for an enterprise to fulfil its financial responsibilities while failing to fulfil its plan. Thus under no circumstances will the enterprise be in financial difficulties', and will therefore be less amenable to financial discipline.[3]

[1] The responsibility of revenue departments for the supervision of profits transmission was already laid down in 1957 (*Collected Laws and Regulations* . . . Vol. 5, p. 117, and Vol. 6, pp. 313 and 320). This must have been superseded, officially or unofficially, by some alternative arrangement because later it was mentioned as being introduced as a new departure in 1962. (*Ta Kung Daily* [*Dagong Bao*], Peking, November 27, 1962, p. 2. Pi Ming: loc. cit.). Possibly earlier it may have been effective only in the cities. (*Finance* [*Caizheng*], No. 11, June 9, 1959, p. 1. Editorial). It may be surmised that during the Great Leap, control by the revenue departments was relaxed, and that less profit than stipulated was transmitted to the state. Then in 1962 an attempt was made to tighten up control; this might be connected with the fact that in 1961 the state reduced the percentage of profits retainable by enterprises (see p. 166 above) and thus enterprises had stronger motives than ever for under-reporting profits.

[2] Planned profits are deducted automatically by the bank from an enterprise's account when they fall due (different types of enterprises remit profits at intervals of different lengths: monthly, semi-monthly, or thrice monthly). Final settlement of profits to be remitted is made according to *actual* (as distinct from planned) profit, and therefore has to wait until accounts for the period concerned are available. See *Statistical Work* (*Tongji Gongzuo*), No. 13, July 14, 1957, p. 10. Sun Yeh-fang: loc. cit., and *Ta Kung Daily* (*Dagong Bao*), Peking, August 5, 1962, p. 3. Kuo Hung-te and Wang Ch'eng-yao: 'The Accumulation of State Enterprises Must Be Remitted in the Two Forms of Tax and Profit', and *Collected Laws and Regulations* . . . Vol. 5, pp. 117–24, and ibid., Vol. 6, pp. 314–21. Payment of industrial and commercial tax had, by the regulations of 1958, to be made within three to five days of the end of the period for which it was due. Such periods might be one, three, five, ten or fifteen days or one month. *Collected Laws and Regulations* . . . Vol. 8, p. 141.

[3] *Economic Research* (*Jingji Yanjiu*), No. 4, October 1955, p. 8. A. M. Pilman: 'The Role of Finance in Enforcing Economy.' See also *Ta Kung Daily* (*Dagong Bao*), Peking, August 11, 1961, p. 3. Chi Ch'eng: 'Understand the Role of State Taxation Correctly', and ibid., August 15, 1962, p. 3. Kuo Hung-te and Wang Ch'eng-yao: loc. cit.

Around 1956–7, some 65 per cent of the state's net income from its enterprises was estimated to come in the form of profit remittances and 35 per cent in the form of tax payments.[1] The ratio of tax to profits has differed widely between industries. According to an article in 1957, taxes were low and profits high in heavy industry, textiles and certain light industries, while on the other hand, tobacco and spirits paid over four times as much in taxes as they transmitted in profits.[2] The Chinese industrial and commercial tax has been relatively lighter than the Soviet turnover tax, and profit remittances in China correspondingly heavier. An important reason for this has been the exceptionally wide cost disparities between enterprises in China resulting from the existence of a multitude of small primitive concerns, alongside modern plants. A high industrial and commercial tax would have involved the small enterprises making losses, with the consequent trouble of returning tax in the form of subsidies. Low taxes, with large profit remittances from the more modern enterprises, obviated this difficulty.[3]

The levying of industrial and commercial tax in the countryside has had special features, as was the case with the taxes it had superseded.[4] In the early days of the commune movement, the commune itself was the tax-paying unit and its fiscal obligations, including payment of industrial and commercial tax, might be stated either as a single inclusive sum, or as a proportion of the commune's income.[5] An article in October 1958 suggested that tax on industry should be at the rate of 7 per cent of the total value of the industrial production (apparently regardless of types of goods produced) of the commune and commercial tax at 9 per cent of total trade turnover.[6]

One of the results of the formation of communes and of their mode of organization in the early days, was a decline in rural trade, and consequently of tax raised from commerce, because what had previously been commercial transactions between neighbouring units or individuals, now became noncommercial exchange by one communal organ to another or free supply (of foodstuffs) by the commune to its members; transactions of this kind escaped tax.[7] Before long, however, as we have seen, the commune as a unit lost many of its functions to its component units, the production brigades and the production teams; when these lower units became the basic accounting unit and the basic unit for tax payments. the circumstances of pre-commune days were once again, partly, restored. In time, old commercial links were resumed and with them the former occasions for tax levies. Thus, separate taxes were

[1] Tso Ch'un-t'ai and Li Hai: *The Problem of Accumulating Funds for Our Country's Socialist Industrialization* (in Chinese), Peking, 1957, pp. 74–5.

[2] *Ta Kung Daily* (*Dagong Bao*), Peking, August 11, 1957, p. 3. Wang Wen-ting and P'eng Wei-ts'ai: 'Reform of the Tax System Must Be Done in Two Steps.'

[3] D. H. Perkins: *Market Control and Planning in Communist China*, Cambridge, Mass. 1966, pp. 113–14.

[4] *Collected Laws and Regulations* . . . Vol. 4, pp. 279–81.

[5] *New China Fortnightly* (*Xinhua Banyuekan*), No. 147, January 10, 1959, p. 63. 'Decree of CCP Central Committee and State Council on the Reform of the Administration of Finance and Trade in Rural Areas to Fit the Situation Arising from the Establishment of People's Communes.'

[6] *Economic Research* (*Jingji Yanjiu*), No. 10, October 1958, p. 10. Hsien Li: 'A Preliminary Discussion on the Financial Problems of People's Communes.'

[7] Ibid., p. 9.

levied separately instead of being compounded together as a lump sum or a fixed proportion, as suggested in the early days of the communes.

The most important aspect of the restoration of former commercial practices was the revival of rural markets. These provide useful occasions for collecting tax on commerce. From press reports it is clear that great importance is attached to these markets as sources of revenue. It is also evident that the task is complex in view of the large number of small sellers involved. The exemption from tax of output sold at rural markets by the peasant producers themselves, which was in practice by 1962,[1] must have simplified matters. Pedlars are subjected to regular fixed taxes and to a complicated system of financial surveillance. Trade warehouses have been used to supervise tax payments at rural markets.[2]

Obviously, wide local variations have existed in methods of collecting taxes from rural industry and commerce. The officials on the spot enjoy considerable latitude in the measures they take, although official pressure and encouragement indicate which methods are currently in favour.

Tax collection at rural markets is used as a weapon to combat illicit practices. 'Speculation by traders and the desertion of farming for the taking up of trade by commune members are both illegal activities. The tax organs will impose heavy taxes on this kind of illegal activity according to the law. This will not harm the development of the market but on the contrary will benefit its correct operation.'[3] Speculators, it was advised, should be taxed on a percentage basis (of excess profit?) 'in addition to the temporary commercial tax' while serious cases of tax evasion should be dealt with by judicial action.[4] As revenue cadres probably have incentives to maximize the revenues they collect, they are unlikely to be eager to tax illicit concerns out of existence, but might rather condone or even assist their continuance.

The 1958 reform of the taxes on industry and commerce was decreed some months after the decentralization measures, which we have already had many occasions to note, and the application of which to financial matters will be discussed later in this chapter. All these steps may be regarded as part of the general re-shaping of economic administration at the end of the First and the beginning of the Second Five Year Plan periods.

The *Agricultural Tax* has been discussed at length in Chapter 13. Minor taxes sometimes comprised under the general heading of agricultural taxes include the pastoral tax, fishery tax, and tax on rural sideline production. Little is known about these sources of revenue. Pastoral tax takes the form of a capital levy. In the important pastoral region of Inner Mongolia, for example, the average annual rate of pastoral tax paid between 1953 and 1958 was reported as amounting to 0·84 per cent of the total number of livestock; it was not stated whether the tax was paid in kind or in cash equivalent.

---

[1] *Ta Kung Daily* (*Dagong Bao*), Peking, November 27, 1962, p. 2. Pi Ming: loc. cit.

[2] Ibid., December 5, 1961, p. 1, and ibid., May 15, 1962, p. 2. Wang Shao-min: 'Strengthen Control of Tax Collection at Rural Markets.' On trade warehouses, see p. 292 and p. 306 above.

[3] Ibid., July 26, 1961, p. 3. Ch'en Ching-fang: 'Strengthen the Collection of Taxes in Rural Market Trade.'

[4] Ibid., November 27, 1962, p. 2. Pi Ming: loc. cit.

Arable areas in this region were exempt from pastoral tax on livestock, and agricultural tax was not levied on fodder crops in pastoral areas.[1]

Income Tax is a relatively minor source of revenue. Under the Nationalist Government, an income tax had been levied on salaries and business profits, but administrative difficulties prevented it from yielding large sums.

In the early days of the Communist Government, three types of income tax were reported: industrial and commercial income tax, income tax on interest from bank deposits and income tax on salaries and wages.[2] Since 1959 only the first type, industrial and commercial income tax (also known as enterprise income tax), has been retained.

Industrial and commercial income tax is normally payable by non-state enterprises, both private and collective (excluding agricultural enterprises), on their net profits, but not by state-owned enterprises nor by joint state-private concerns.[3]

During the first years of the regime, income tax on industry and commerce was imposed on privately-owned enterprises for political, as well as for fiscal, reasons. By 1956, virtually all private industrial and commercial establishments of any size had been put under joint state-private ownership, and in that year the dividends paid to the former owners were changed into fixed interest payments, the remaining profits being paid to the state as in the case of state-owned enterprises. At the same time, according to an economist in a prominent official position, liability of these enterprises for income tax ceased.[4] However, in Shanghai it was not until 1959 that joint state-private businesses stopped paying this tax.[5] Probably, as in many other cases, regulations did not go into effect immediately or uniformly all over the country.

In the next few years after 1956, the scope of industrial and commercial income tax diminished still further. In 1958, supply and marketing co-operatives ceased to pay income tax and instead delivered their profits to the state.[6] Also, in 1958, when many rural handicraft co-operatives were changed into commune enterprises, these were apparently no longer liable to income tax.[7] Here the customary confusion reigns as four years later, in 1962, a series of

---

[1] *Chinese Agricultural Journal* (*Zhongguo Nongbao*), No. 20, October 23, 1959 (ECMM 192). Wang Tsai-t'ien, Vice-Chairman, Inner Mongolia Autonomous Region : 'Inner Mongolia Makes Rapid Advance in Agriculture and Animal Husbandry over the Past Ten Years.'

[2] *New China Monthly* (*Xinhua Yuebao*), No. 5, March 1950, p. 1155.

[3] Hsü Ti-hsin: op. cit., pp. 224–5, and *Explanation of Certain Terms Used in the First Five Year Plan* (in Chinese), Peking, 1955, p. 53. Strangely, until 1959, factories and welfare facilities (*fuwu she*) operated by the Army were liable to industrial and commercial income tax. *Collected Financial Laws and Regulations of the Central Government* 1959, January–June, p. 120.

[4] Hsü Ti-hsin: op. cit., p. 224.

[5] *Wen Hui Pao* (*Wenhui Bao*), June 14, 1959 (SCMP 2061). Ma I-hang, Vice-Chairman of Shanghai Economic Planning Commission and Director of the Shanghai Bureau of Finance: Report on 1958 Final Accounts and 1959 Draft Budget of Shanghai Municipality.

[6] *People's Taxation* (*Renmin Shuiwu*), No. 11, June 4, 1958, p. 5. This notice of the Ministry of Finance and the Second Ministry of Commerce states that the change was to be backdated to January 1, 1958. Here again, it was not until 1959 that it came into effect in Shanghai (see last reference).

[7] *Finance* (*Caizheng*), No. 10, October 9, 1958, p. 5. Yang Ch'ing: 'The New Circumstances and Duties of Financial Work after the Formation of the People's Communes.'

new measures (possibly restricted to Kwangtung province) exempted enterprises operated by production teams from income tax, and also those operated by production brigades if they directly served agriculture.[1]

Income tax continues to be payable on profits by the remaining privately-owned enterprises, by handicraft and transport co-operatives and by street industries. In 1963 the State Council promulgated the 'Trial Decree on the Adjustment of Income Tax Burdens in Industry and Commerce and on the Reform of Methods of Tax Collection',[2] but details of this decree have not reached us.

Industrial and commercial income tax is paid on a progressive scale, with the highest rate in 1959 reported to be 34·5 per cent.[3] However, between 1956 and 1958 supply and marketing co-operatives were said to have paid 50 per cent of their profits as income tax;[4] from 1958 (or 1959) it will be remembered their liability to pay income tax ceased and instead they delivered all their profits, less certain deductions, to the state.

Handicraft co-operatives (according to a work published in 1959) paid approximately 30 per cent of their profits in income tax; for wealthier co-operatives, the percentage might be higher.[5] In 1958, it was laid down that an extra 10–50 per cent (and even more, in exceptional cases) on income tax might be levied from better-off individual handicraftsmen and pedlars, and 10–100 per cent extra (or even a higher rate) on any remaining capitalist industrialists and merchants.[6] A rate of around 20 per cent for income tax on street industry was recommended in 1959.[7] To encourage the remaining private enterprises to make certain priority goods, reductions of up to 40 per cent in income tax were permitted, while above normal rates might be charged on those engaged in lines of production not considered beneficial.[8] The general impression given is one of considerable latitude in fixing the rates of industrial and commercial income tax payable by different categories of tax payers and even by individuals.

A reference was made in 1950 to income tax on salaries and wages.[9] No later mention of this has been found and in 1964, Premier Chou En-lai stated that the present government had never levied any personal income tax.[10] The absence of tax on personal incomes is reasonable, in view of the fact that al-

---

[1] *Southern Daily* (*Nanfang Ribao*), November 13, 1962 (SCMP 2878). Wang Ju-ming, Deputy Director of Kwangtung Provincial Department of Finance: 'Financial Departments Must Provide Energetic Aid to Agriculture.'

[2] *People's Daily* (*Renmin Ribao*), April 14, 1963, p. 1, and *Ta Kung Daily* (*Dagong Bao*), Peking, August 8, 1963, p. 2. Tsou Ming: loc. cit.

[3] *Finance* (*Caizheng*), No. 18, September 24, 1959, p. 29. Shen P'ing: 'Our Country's Industrial and Commercial Tax in the Past Ten Years.' Here the author speaks as if this tax was still payable by joint state-private businesses.

[4] Hsü Ti-hsin: op. cit., p. 225. Before 1956 they had paid about 30 per cent.

[5] Hsü Ti-hsin: op. cit., p. 223, and *Collected Laws and Regulations* . . . Vol. 7, p. 267.

[6] *Collected Laws and Regulations* . . . Vol. 7, p. 267.

[7] *People's Daily* (*Renmin Ribao*), April 26, 1959, p. 9. Sung Yi-p'ing: Speech to First Session of Second National People's Congress. 'Street Industry—A New Force Not to Be Neglected.'

[8] *Finance* (*Caizheng*), No. 18, September 24, 1959, p. 29. Shen P'ing: loc. cit.

[9] *New China Monthly* (*Xinhua Yuebao*), No. 5, March 15, 1950, p. 1155.

[10] NCNA Peking, February 5, 1964.

most all wage and salary earners are employed by state concerns, or concerns which are closely controlled by the state. Therefore, a personal income tax would only be an administrative device for doing what could be done with less trouble by adjustment of the wages and salaries originally paid. Workers in the collective sector of the economy are remunerated by a share of the taxed profits or output of the co-operative or production team concerned. Enterprises in the private sector, as we have seen, pay industrial and commercial income tax: any additional tax it is desired to levy from them could be more easily done by raising rates of this tax rather than by having a personal income tax as well.

Income tax on interest (mainly on bank deposits) was, in 1955, levied at the flat rate of 5 per cent.[1] In 1959 this tax was abolished.[2] Interest earned from government bonds had not been subject to tax.

Salt tax was one of the chief sources of revenue in China before 1949. Inelastic demand, and the comparative ease of collection, have made it a favourite tax for governments of under-developed lands in many places and periods. Under the Communist Government, the relative importance of the salt tax to China's total state revenue has diminished. In 1955, the salt tax yielded ¥481,220,000, forming some 1·6 per cent of the total budgetary revenues.[3] Salt tax has been levied in the form of a specific tax per unit weight of salt for edible purposes, the tax varying by locality. According to regulations of 1957, salt for industrial uses is tax free, for agricultural uses it is taxed at 40 per cent of the rate on edible salt, and for fisheries around 30 per cent of this rate, but with local variations.[4]

The reason why salt tax has been kept distinct from the consolidated industrial and commercial tax is probably to a large extent historical. It was seen in Chapter 11 that special arrangements have also been made for the marketing of salt. Under the regulations of December 1957, the salt tax was not included among the revenues to go in whole or in part to local authorities. By 1959, this had evidently changed, the salt tax apparently forming part of the general revenue of each province, with no special provision reported for its transmission to the central government. Salt tax was in 1955 collected by the Ministry of Light Industry, which controls both the production and trade in salt;[5] its local counterparts probably continue to collect this tax.

Customs duties have been considered in Chapter 12 where we saw that while import duties are unnecessary for either protective or fiscal reasons in China today, they are retained for bargaining purposes in foreign trade negotiations, and also as a source of revenue controlled directly by the central government. In 1955 customs duties contributed ¥466,080,000 to the budgetary revenues, some 1·5 per cent of the total.[6] The Ministry of Foreign Trade is responsible

[1] *Explanation of Certain Terms* . . . p. 53.

[2] *Collected Laws and Regulations* . . . Vol. 9, p. 121.

[3] Ko Chih-ta: op. cit., p. 58, and *Collected Laws and Regulations* . . . Vol. 3, p. 206.

[4] *Collected Laws and Regulations* . . . Vol. 7, p. 288, and *Taxation in Communist China 1950-1959*, op. cit., p. 23.

[5] *Collected Financial Laws and Regulations* . . . 1955, p. 83.

[6] Ko Chih-ta: op. cit., p. 58.

for the collection of customs duties. Export duties were abolished from 1959. Previously they had been levied on certain commodities at rates from 10–55 per cent.[1]

There remain a number of minor taxes: slaughter tax, tax on cattle transactions, urban real estate tax, entertainment tax and licence fees for vehicles and boats. The revenue from these, together with income tax on interest (which was abolished in 1959), and stamp duty, were in 1958 allocated to local authorities.

Stamp duty was said to have been absorbed into the consolidated industrial and commercial tax instituted in 1958. There are known to have been a considerable variety of stamp duties[2] and possibly not all were affected by the change in 1958 or, if affected, were restored later. Reports from China subsequent to 1958 tell of stamps, sometimes to a percentage of the value of the sale but sometimes not, being affixed to documents certifying sales of any size.

Licence fees are payable on vehicles (including bicycles) and on boats.[3] In addition, a *road tax* to be used specifically for road maintenance and improvement, is imposed on motor and animal drawn vehicles outside certain exempted categories.[4]

Slaughter tax was fixed in 1959 at the rate of 10 per cent of the purchase price of the livestock, in the case of state enterprises engaged in slaughtering, when buying livestock from other provinces. Regulations for slaughter tax on livestock bought within the same province as that in which such an enterprise operated, were to be issued by the province concerned. Slaughter tax was fixed in 1959 at 8 per cent of the sales price of the meat in the case of livestock slaughtered by communes and by other bodies (enterprises, schools, etc.) for their own consumption.[5]

Bonds have not contributed much to the Chinese budget since the advent of the Communists. An issue of Victory Bonds, denominated in commodity units, was made in 1950.[6] Economic Development Bonds at 4 per cent per annum were issued annually from 1954–8. Each of the 1954–7 issues was announced to be for ¥600 million (after making allowance for the 1955 currency change on which see p. 414 below); all those for which final figures are available were over-subscribed. The 1958 issue, announced as ¥630 million, was also over-subscribed. The 1954 issue was repayable within eight years and the subsequent issues within ten years. Redemption was to be by annual instalments, drawn by lot. In the case of the bonds issued in 1954–7, it was laid down that they must not circulate as currency, nor be used as collateral with banks. The first provision was repeated for the 1958 issue but

---

[1] *Taxation in Communist China 1950–1959*, op. cit., p. 30.
[2] *Collected Laws and Regulations*... Vol. 2, pp. 537–41.
[3] Ibid., Vol. 6, pp. 321–4.
[4] Ibid., Vol. 11, pp. 161–8. See also p. 260 above.
[5] Ibid., Vol. 10, pp. 264–5. For rates and procedure before this, see ibid., p. 264, fn., and ibid., Vol. 5, pp. 127–8.
[6] For details of these and of the Production Development Bonds for the north-east raised in 1949 and 1950, see Choh-ming Li: *Economic Development of Communist China*, Berkely, 1959, p. 152, and *New China Monthly (Xinhua Yuebao)*, No. 3, January 1950, p. 656. On the Yü-T'ao Railway Repair Bonds and on the bonds issued in areas held by the Communists before 1949, see *Collected Laws and Regulations* ... Vol. 8, pp. 120–1.

not the second; instead it was stated that the bonds must not be freely bought and sold.[1]

Subscriptions to the bonds were obtained under strong pressure, so that in effect they were a form of forced savings. Privately-owned undertakings were under special obligation to subscribe, and indeed took 70·6 per cent of the 1950 issue; this percentage declined, with the decline in the position of private enterprises, to 47·5 per cent in 1954, 38·2 per cent in 1955 and to 24·1 per cent in 1956.[2]

In June 1958, it was announced that no more national bonds would be issued. Therefore, by the end of 1968 all the central government's internal debt should be paid off. From 1959, in line with the administrative decentralization of 1957–8, provincial level authorities were empowered to issue local bonds. These local bonds were to be for a shorter term (normally not more than five years) and to bear a lower rate of interest (in general not more than 2 per cent and, if considered necessary, at no interest at all) than had been the case with national bonds. The provinces were to permit the local authorities beneath them to retain for their own use the greater part of the receipts from bonds they raised.[3]

Only a few provinces took immediate advantage of the right that had been given them to issue their own bonds from 1959.[4] Presumably, tapping other sources of revenue proved less troublesome or less unpopular than raising bonds.

Savings under varying degrees of freedom and compulsion have continued through the medium of bank deposits (in towns) and credit co-operatives (in the country).

At one time, loans from the Soviet Union figured on the receipts side of Chinese budgets. They accounted for about 2 per cent of total revenue for 1949 to 1959, and all were made in the early years of this period.[5] In 1950 to 1952, Soviet loans are thought to have amounted to 28 per cent of total investment (presumably of total budgetary expenditure on investment), which illustrates their significance during the period of rehabilitation and of the Korean War.[6]

[1] *New China Monthly* (*Xinhua Yuebao*), No. 51, January 1954, pp. 165–6 for Regulations on 1954 issue, and *Collected Laws and Regulations* . . . Vol. 1, pp. 256–62 on 1955 issue, and ibid., Vol. 2, pp. 534–5 on 1956 issue, and ibid., Vol. 4, pp. 282–8 on 1957 issue, and ibid., Vol. 6, pp. 334–8 on 1958 issue. For total sums subscribed each year, see *People's Handbook* (*Renmin Shouce*) *1956*, p. 160, and ibid., *1958*, p. 214, and ibid., *1959*, p. 226, and *Collected Laws and Regulations* . . . Vol. 9, p. 64. In the *People's Daily* (*Renmin Ribao*), March 4, 1957, p. 1. Editorial (in *New China Fortnightly* [*Xinhua Banyuekan*], No. 105, April 10, 1957, p. 86), there is a reference to prize-winning savings, without specifying if these are bonds or some other form of savings; see also fn. 4 below.

[2] Hsü Ti-hsin: op. cit., p. 226.

[3] *People's Handbook* (*Renmin Shouce*) *1959*, pp. 371–2.

[4] *Collected Laws and Regulations* . . . Vol. 9, p. 69. Li Hsien-nien's Budget Speech, 1959. In *Far Eastern Economic Review*, April 11, 1963, p. 99, there is a reference to prize-winning bonds in Shanghai, possibly a local issue.

[5] *Peking Review*, November 24, 1959, p. 8. Li Hsien-nien, Minister of Finance: 'China's Great Financial Achievements during the Past Ten Years.'

[6] United Nations: *Economic Survey of Asia and the Far East, 1961*, Bangkok, p. 97. On Soviet loans to China, see *The China Quarterly*, No. 19, July–September 1964, pp. 54–64. Kang Chao: 'Pitfalls in the Use of China's Foreign Trade Statistics.'

Surveying the revenue side of the budget as a whole for the years for which we have figures, we note the rising importance of revenue from state enterprises and institutions and the declining relative, but not absolute, contribution made by taxes. More particularly, it can be seen that those traditional pillars of China's state revenues—the direct taxes on agriculture, the salt tax and customs duties—have lost much of their relative significance.

The ultimate incidence of the revenues raised is a complex matter to determine. Here space forbids an exploration of this question. Sufficient to indicate that for example, the burden of taxation on agriculture is necessarily greater than is suggested by the small percentage which agricultural taxes forms of the total revenue. Agricultural procurement prices have in general been below free market levels. Consumer industries, based on agricultural raw materials, have remitted large sums in profits to the treasury, of which a considerable part constitutes an indirect tax on agriculture, while the incidence of some of the rest falls on the rural population as consumers. In 1962, over half the total state revenue was estimated to derive directly or indirectly from agriculture.[1]

Any economy based on subsistence agriculture faces a gruelling task in raising revenues sufficient, not only for the ordinary purposes of government, but also for industrialization. China is no exception. This inadequacy of revenue was one reason for decentralizing economic administration at the end of the First Five Year Plan period. By delegating responsibility for raising funds for any item of expenditure down to the lowest appropriate level, the greatest immediacy of incentive would be provided. In these circumstances initiative to explore new ways of getting revenues or of cutting costs is engendered. Also such a delegation of authority cuts administrative expenses and the cumbersome procedures by which funds are remitted upwards and downwards between different levels of government. This theme will be developed when we come to speak of the division between central and local finance.

Expenditure
'*Economic Construction*' accounted for over 60 per cent of total budgetary expenditure for the last several years for which figures are available. Under this heading is comprised the non-returnable interest-free budgetary grants for both investment purposes and for current expenses in the economic sphere, made to the various sectors of the economy.

From 1958 the investment needs of the so-called co-operative commercial organs at the *hsien* level and above were to be supplied through the budget.[2] Another addition under the heading of Economic Construction was made in 1959 when the budget provided for ¥1,000 million for investment in rural communes, a sum which was increased to ¥1,500 million in the budget of 1960.[3]

[1] *China Youth Newspaper* (*Zhongguo Qingnian Bao*), November 22, 1962 (SCMP 2882). Hsü Ti-hsin: 'Correct Understanding of the General Policy of Developing the National Economy.' See also *Economic Research* (*Jingji Yanjiu*), No. 9, September 1963, p. 2. Tan Ku: 'Some Problems in the Determination of the Prices of Light Industrial Commodities', and ibid., No. 5, May 1963, pp. 2–3. Hsüeh Mu-ch'iao: loc. cit.
[2] *People's Taxation* (*Renmin Shuiwu*), No. 11, June 4, 1958, p. 5.
[3] *Collected Laws and Regulations* . . . Vol. 9, p. 72. Li Hsien-nien: loc. cit., and ibid. Vol. 11, p. 43. Li Hsien-nien: loc. cit.

Grants for current expenses that fall under the heading of Economic Construction in the budget include those made for expenditure on planning, on research of many types, for measures such as prevention of crop diseases, for meteorological services, for road and river maintenance and for many other lines of expenditure of economic significance that are not included in investment.

The next item, *Social Services, Culture and Education* covers both capital and current budgetary expenditure of the sectors concerned. In the 1958 budget, this heading was further analysed under the sub-headings of culture, primary and secondary education, higher education, science, public health and pensions and relief. In the 1960 budget the word 'science' was appended to the main heading: at the same time, as shown on page 368, expenditure under this main heading increased significantly, but in that year no breakdown under sub-headings was given. This has been interpreted as indicating the acceleration of the programme for the development of nuclear weapons after the Soviet refusal to supply these to China.

Apart from expenditure listed under *National Defence*, other sums expended for purposes of military significance are probably included under the headings of economic construction and science, administration, social services (pensions, assistance to dependents), and possibly higher education. Part, too, of the credit funds allotted to banks may be used to provide working capital for industrial and other enterprises of military significance.

An analysis of expenditure in the budget for 1958 shows that some 20 per cent of the budgeted expenditure on 'economic construction' was not accounted for by the items listed under this heading. It may be surmised that it was spent on items of military significance, including work on nuclear weapons.[1]

Expenditure on *Administration* covers the expenses of governmental, public security and legal organs, of the police, of foreign relations, of the 'democratic [i.e. united front] parties' and mass organizations. It also includes subsidies to Communist Party and Young Communist League organs at all levels down to the *hsien*. The Party also draws income from members' dues

---

[1] Estimates by outside observers of the cost of China's nuclear weapons programme have varied from 'more than U.S. $200 million' to 'much more' than U.S. $1,000 million. *Far Eastern Economic Review*, October 29, 1964, p. 237. A. Close: 'Bombs or Trousers?', and *Current Scene*, Vol. III, No. 16, April 1, 1965, p. 1. Morton H. Halperin in *China and the Bomb*, London, 1965, p. 73, reckons that the nuclear programme cost China the equivalent of around 2 per cent of the country's Gross National Product (taken as U.S. $35,000–45,000 million in 1957; in the early 1960s however, it must have been lower). Halperin considers that his estimated cost of the nuclear programme could be drawn from a total defence budget of something over U.S. $2,300 million. To convert this figure into Chinese *yuan* would involve discussion of the complexities of exchange rates, and cross rates, between the yuan and other currencies. Suffice here to say that the figure is compatible with the overt annual defence budgets of 1959 and 1960. Some other estimates, based on later information, put China's nuclear programme cost lower than does Halperin—see *Far Eastern Economic Review*, December 9, 1965, pp. 476 and 481. H. Munthe-Kaas: 'Easy Atoms.' There is, therefore, no inherent necessity stemming out of the size of the nuclear programme for surmising that some items of defence expenditure are concealed. However, an analysis of budgetary figures, indicates that some items are unrevealed.

and, according to one report, from royalties on the works of Chairman Mao.[1]

Repayment of loans include repayment of debts to the Soviet Union and of internal debt. Repayment of the Soviet loans was completed in 1965; with accrued interest they were reported by the Chinese to have totalled 1,406 million new roubles.[2] All central government bonds are, as we have seen, due to be repaid by 1968.

Aid to foreign countries covers both grants and loans made by China to other lands. It has been estimated that from 1953 to 1960 China promised aid to foreign countries to the equivalent of about US $1,190 million, of which some US $880 million was actually expended in that period.[3] Since 1960, China has entered into many new aid commitments.

Allotments of Credit Funds to the Bank will be discussed in the next chapter, in the context of the whole banking system. The item *Repayment of Bank Overdraft* refers to the overdraft which was one of the devices used to cover the deficit in the realized budget of 1956.[4]

The 1955 budget set up a *revolving fund for local authorities* from which they might cover temporary requirements for cash.[5] No further addition to this fund is reported in subsequent budgets.

Undertakings eligible for appropriations from the budget are known as budgetary units (*yüsuan tanwei*). They comprise three main types: enterprises (*ch'iyeh*), institutions (*shihyeh*) and administrative units (*hsingcheng tanwei*). Enterprises, which as we have seen,[6] operate under the economic accounting system (*hosuan chihtu*) receive budgetary appropriations for fixed and working capital. As well as this, they are eligible for bank loans for additional working capital. Institutions, administrative organs and individuals are ineligible for bank loans.[7]

In the case of institutions (*shihyeh*)—a term which includes schools, hospitals, cultural organs, etc., most of which cannot be expected to cover their costs—several different methods of granting appropriations and exercising financial management are, or have been, used. The first is the expenditure budget (*chingfei yüsuan*) method, by which all expenditure is met from the budget and all receipts are paid in as budgetary revenue. This method is

---

[1] Ko Chih-ta: op. cit., p. 45, and *Collected Financial Laws and Regulations*... 1956, p. 66, and *Planned Economy* (*Jihua Jingji*), No. 5, May 1958, p. 13. Wei Li: 'The Supplementary Wage System Must Be Radically Changed', for a reference to budgetary subsidies for the Party and the Communist Youth League; and Unpublished Paper of Ezra Vogel for the point on the Party receiving royalties from Mao's works. (It would be interesting to know if the amounts received by branches of the Party depend on the number of sales in a branch's area or enterprise.) This source denies that Party finances are handled through the Ministry of Finance. However, the two previous references indicate clearly that some provision is made for the Party in the state Budget.

[2] *Peking Review*, January 1, 1966, p. 19.

[3] *Far Eastern Economic Review*, January 19, 1961, p. 84. C. Garratt: 'China as a Foreign Aid Donor.'

[4] *People's Handbook* (*Renmin Shouce*) *1958*, p. 214. Li Hsien-nien, Minister of Finance: 'Report on Final Accounts for 1956 and Draft Budget for 1957.'

[5] *People's Handbook* (*Renmin Shouce*) *1956*, p. 164. Li Hsien-nien: loc. cit.

[6] p. 26 above.

[7] *China Monthly* (*Zuguo*), No. 1, January 1966, p. 6. Li Ch'a: 'Chinese Communist Plans for Industrial Finance.'

employed for institutions (such as schools and research institutes) with only small incomes of their own. As a development of this method, in 1960 a number of provinces instituted the 'expenditure budget responsibility system' (*chingfei yüsuan paokan chihtu*) under which, with local variations, an institution was given a block grant for a year, with permission to use it as desired, switching expenditure between items, so long as it fulfilled its plan. The institution was also to be allowed to retain its year end balances, although we do not know if the size of next year's grant would be influenced by the knowledge that such balances had been retained.[1]

The second method of making budgetary grants and controlling the financial affairs of institutions is the economic accounting system, as practised by enterprises. While institutions under this system may receive subsidies (as well as budgetary appropriations for fixed and working capital), in general they have the same degree of independent operation and similar duties as enterprises. Like enterprises, they pay taxes and remit profits to the state; their profits, however, are known as surpluses, as only enterprises can—according to Chinese terminology—have profits. Institutions operating under the economic accounting system are those with considerable incomes from their own activities, such as film studios, cinemas, theatres, printing works and publishing houses.[2] The reason why such concerns are classified as 'institutions' rather than 'enterprises' stems from a sentiment that cultural organs should not be considered on the same footing as ordinary economic undertakings.

The third method of relating institutions to the budget is that of 'total sum management and fixed sum subsidy' (*ch'üan e kuanli, ting e puchu*). This method is used for institutions with a certain amount of income of their own, but insufficient to meet all their needs. Some divergence between sources exists on this method of management; it has probably changed over time. It appears to involve setting a fixed figure for the size of the deficit of the institution concerned. That is, the institution is permitted to retain its own income and receives a subsidy from the budget equal to the predetermined sum allowed for its deficit. This method has probably, at least in many cases, superseded the earlier method of 'balance sum budgets' (*ch'a e yüsuan*) by which institutions' deficits were made good by budgetary grants while surpluses were paid into the budget. This system was disfavoured by the authorities as giving insufficient incentive for institutions to reduce expenditure or to increase income. Consequently, in the case of many institutions, it was changed to some other method. Those with surpluses were, as we have seen, put on the economic accounting system. For others, the device was instituted of a fixed subsidy, to be given regardless of an institution's success (at least for the current year) in cutting costs or in expanding income, a device which should provide

[1] Ko Chih-ta: op. cit., p. 120, and *Finance* (*Caizheng*), No. 12, December 1960, p. 7. Ko Fu-chih: 'Actively Implement the Expenditure Budget Responsibility System.' Some institutions had practised a variant of the new system from 1958; see *Industrial Accountancy* (*Gongye Kuaiji*), No. 6, June 1958, p. 30.

[2] Ko Chih-ta: op. cit., p. 120, and Unpublished papers of Ezra Vogel and of Michel Oksenberg. On the whole question of appropriations to institutions, I owe much to correspondence with Michel Oksenberg.

incentive for efficiency.[1] This method, like that of the expenditure budget responsibility system (and indeed also of the economic accounting system) accords with the desire of the Chinese authorities, often mentioned in this study, to assign definite responsibilities to groups and corporate bodies and to set fixed limits to the financial obligations of the state.

In addition to appropriations to institutions, expenditure from the state budget on social services includes direct grants in cash or in kind to certain categories of people, such as disabled soldiers, servicemen's dependants, victims of disaster, unemployed workers, and returned Overseas Chinese.[2]

The Chinese fiscal year runs from January to December.[3] The budget is compiled on the basis of draft budgets submitted to the Ministry of Finance from both the central government ministries and the provincial and equivalent local authorities. These draft budgets are to be drawn up in accordance with national economic plans and policies. After co-ordination and amendment by the Ministry of Finance, the budget should be 'sent down, from one level to another, to the basic level units, with guarantees for its implementation'. The central government should approve the budgets of the provincial level authorities and then each of these, 'within its approved budget, should allocate funds and approve the budgets of *hsien* and municipalities and of provincial departments'.[4]

In the process of compiling the budget, series of conferences are held at various levels. At the national level, there are usually two conferences a year on the budget. These are attended by officials from the Ministry of Finance, from the Offices of the State Council, from the State Planning Commission and the State Economic Commission and by the chief financial officials of the provincial level authorities, as well as by representatives of the People's University and the Ministry of Finance's School, the last two groups coming to learn as well as to advise.

The first of the national conferences is held before the compilation of the budget. By regulation it should meet toward the end of the previous fiscal year, in November or December; in fact it usually meets in February or March. This conference lasts for a week or ten days. After an opening report from one of the vice-ministers of finance, the gathering divides into groups of two types, based respectively on area and on function. The six area groups coincide with the areas under each of the Party's Regional Bureaux. The functional groups correspond in general with the State Council Offices. Each provincial level authority is represented at the appropriate area group and at all the functional groups. After three or four days of meetings of the small groups, the results are sent back to the Ministry of Finance and the final budgetary figures for each province are agreed after bargaining between the head of the provincial department of finance and a senior official of the central

[1] Ko Chih-ta: op. cit., p. 120, and *Collected Financial Laws and Regulations* . . . 1955, pp. 36–7, and Unpublished papers of Ezra Vogel and Michel Oksenberg.

[2] Ko Chih-ta: op. cit., pp. 120–1.

[3] *New China Monthly* (*Xinhua Yuebao*), No. 23, September 1951, p. 1080, and *People's Handbook* (*Renmin Shouce*) *1959*, p. 229. See p. 343 above on the agricultural tax year which differs from the normal fiscal year.

[4] *Ta Kung Daily* (*Dagong Bao*), Peking, June 25, 1962, p. 3. Fan Yeh-chün, Li Te-sheng and Chang Chih-tao: 'The Centralization and Unification of Financial Work.'

government's Ministry of Finance. Bargaining is often hard, with each province trying to get as low a figure as possible accepted for its revenue and as high as possible for its expenditure. A participant at some of these negotiating sessions emphasized the importance of the relative ranks (especially Party ranks) of the negotiators concerned. In this the central representatives usually have the advantage. After the national conference, each province holds conferences in a similar way for its subordinate local authorities.[1]

The second national level conference is usually held three or four months after the budget has gone into operation. On this occasion, any revisions that appear necessary in the current budget are discussed. Also preliminary consideration is given to the budget for the following year.[2]

It should be noted that the budget is not usually compiled in time to go into operation at the beginning of the fiscal year to which it applies.

The Chinese authorities consider it desirable that the original budgets (on both the national and the local levels) should be balanced, but that a surplus should accrue in the course of their implementation: this is contrasted with the chronic deficits under the previous Nationalist Government. 'The finance of a socialist state not only demands the maintenance of a balance between revenue and expenditure, but also demands a small surplus in the course of implementing the budget.' This surplus should be of the order of 3-5 per cent of the total revenue.[3]

From 1957 onwards, as far as the published budgets go, this prescription has been followed except that the surpluses achieved have been smaller. Before 1957, the (*ex-ante*) budgets were officially balanced or in surplus, but only by the device of carrying over surpluses from previous years. As these surpluses had been used to finance credit expansion through bank loans for working capital, it was misleading to enter them on the receipt side in subsequent budgets. When this item is omitted, the *ex-ante* budgets before 1957 were in deficit; the realized budgets, however, showed a surplus from 1951 to 1955 but a deficit in 1956.[4] From 1957 onwards, overall budget surpluses ceased to be carried forward as revenue for the next year. However, according to the instructions for drafting the budget for 1959, individual ministries were still permitted to carry forward to the new year any balances of budgetary funds they retained for capital purposes; other balances had to be returned to the treasury. Local authorities were allowed to retain for their own use balances left at the end of 1958 and were to incorporate these in their budgets for 1959.[5] In 1962 it was laid down that local budgetary balances carried for-

[1] Unpublished papers of Michel Oksenberg and Ezra Vogel.
[2] Ibid.
[3] *Ta Kung Daily* (*Dagong Bao*), Peking, November 17, 1961, p. 3. Ko Chih-ta and Wang Cho: 'Some Inter-relationships between Finance and Currency Work', and *Economic Research* (*Jingji Yanjiu*), No. 10, October 1963, p. 4. Ko Chih-ta: 'The Problem of Comprehensive Equilibrium of Finance, Credit and Raw Materials.'
[4] Choh-ming Li: op. cit., pp. 143-5. See also pp. 419-20 below. The willingness to run *de facto* deficits in the *ex-ante* budgets in the early 1950s may have been influenced by the import surpluses in those years: these would have counteracted the inflationary effect of budget deficits.
[5] *Collected Laws and Regulations* . . . Vol. 8, p. 148. However, not all local authorities trusted the central government's assurances about the carrying forward of balances. See *People's Daily* (*Renmin Ribao*), December 6, 1959, p. 1. Editorial. 'Some local authorities, in

ward to subsequent years might not be used without the approval of the central government.[1] Thus their use in this respect was assimilated to normal budgetary expenditure, provincial budgets having to receive central approval before becoming effective.

Extra-budgetary funds (*yüsuan wai tzuchin*), to which reference has already been made, are those items of revenue at the disposal of local authorities of different grades, or of enterprises and of institutions of various kinds, and of their controlling ministries, which are not entered in the budget and which (orginally, at least) might be used without higher authorization. The sources of these funds are many and diverse, but they include major regular revenues and not just casual items. Profits retained by enterprises and their controlling ministries (including provincial and lower level counterparts of these ministries) have formed the largest single item. Other items include local surtaxes to industrial and commercial tax, to agricultural tax and to urban public utility charges; the road tax, local budgetary surpluses carried down from previous years, enterprises' major repairs funds, labour protection and welfare funds, irrigation charges, income from the labour of students and employees of schools and other organizations, school fees, fees for admittance to parks, museums and sports grounds, income from water supplies, rents, the sale of night-soil, the hiring of halls and of vehicles and fees for the certification of weights and measures.[2] (Some of these items such as the local surtaxes, may, at one time, have been budgetary revenues but by 1958 were listed as extra-budgetary.) As well as these officially acknowledged revenues, hints are thrown out about others that are illicit, such as excess retained profits, and profits that remained uncollected because local financial departments failed to make contact with enterprises transferred to local control.[3] Other sources of extra-budgetary revenue, while not illicit were unofficial, such as the 'voluntary'

---

view of the approaching end of the year, fear that unspent balances on capital account may then have to be remitted upwards. So some have put in hand non-urgent projects. ... Not only is this unsatisfactory but also unnecessary because the state has decreed that funds for capital purposes can be carried over for use in the following year.' The central government's assurances may have been devalued by the practise of taking these balances into account when allocating central grants in the following year. See p. 395 below.

[1] *Ta Kung Daily* (*Dagong Bao*), Peking, June 25, 1962. p. 3. Fan Yeh-chün, Li Te-sheng and Chang Chih-tao: loc. cit.

[2] *Collected Laws and Regulations* ... Vol. 8, p. 146, and ibid., Vol. 11, p. 164, and *Planning and Statistics* (*Jihua yu Tongji*), No. 2, January 23, 1959 (ECMM 176). Huo Chi-ch'ao, Finance and Fund Office, Shensi Provincial Planning Committee: 'Some of the Points We Learn in Comprehensive Fiscal Planning Work', and *Finance* (*Caizheng*), No. 20, October 24, 1959, p. 30. Budget Office of Kweichow Provincial Finance Department: 'Some Problems that Must Be Solved in the Management of Extra-Budgetary Funds', and *Economic Research* (*Jinghi Yanjiu*), No. 2, February 1961, pp. 5 and 14. Chi Ts'ai-ch'eng: 'The Form of Comprehensive Financial Plans and the Interrelations between Items in Them.' The term 'self-provided funds' (*tzuch'ou tzuchin*) is sometimes used to cover a large selection of miscellaneous extra-budgetary receipts.

[3] *Finance* (*Caizheng*), No. 10, October 9, 1958, p. 2. Yang Shao-ch'iao: 'Financial Work Must Serve the Party's General Line', and ibid., No. 10, May 24, 1959, pp. 4–5. Tseng Chih: 'The Correct Disposition of Certain Relationships in Financial Work', and *Ta Kung Daily* (*Dagong Bao*), Peking, April 26, 1961, p. 3. Wang Cho: 'A Discussion of Several Problems in Financial Management.'

contributions which some *hsien* are reported at one time to have levied from agricultural producer co-operatives or the similar contributions demanded from individual officials on occasion in some places.[1] Some extra-budgetary funds are, by their origin, tied to specific expenditures. Others, notably retained profits, are not so constrained and have at times been freely used by local economic departments to forward a wide variety of developments. Even the more restricted type of extra-budgetary funds are not necessarily used as soon as collected, and meanwhile can be made available for quickly liquidating purposes; other idle balances have on occasion been put to similar use.[2] These practices have given rise to difficulties when sums invested could not be recovered as speedily as foreseen.

Thus the expenditure of extra-budgetary funds, like their sources, is composed of varied and miscellaneous items. Investigations into these funds in certain units in the municipality of Taiyuan in 1959 discovered forty-three items of expenditure and forty-four items of revenue. These items were unspecified except that we are told that 46 per cent of total expenditure from extra-budgetary funds was devoted to capital investment[3] and that 31 per cent of extra-budgetary revenue derived from retained profits.[4] Capital investment is widely mentioned as being the largest single object of expenditure from extra-budgetary funds. This development became of major importance from 1958, many of the local capital projects put in hand at the time of the Great Leap being financed from this source.[5]

Any attempt to assess the size of extra-budgetary funds, whether nationally or locally, is hampered by the fact that, of their nature, this is difficult to ascertain. Even the local financial departments are reported often to have been in the dark about extra-budgetary funds controlled by enterprises in their districts.[6] However, since figures have on occasion been given, they will be mentioned here, although with the proviso that even greater than normal caution is needed in their respect.

According to the Minister of Finance, investment out of extra-budgetary funds amounted to ¥465 million in 1957, to about ¥5,000 million in each of the next two years, and to a predicted ¥6,000 million in 1960. (For 1960 he estimated total extra-budgetary revenues, whether used for investment or for

---

[1] *Agricultural Work Bulletin* (*Nongcun Gongzuo Tongxun*), No. 4, 1956, p. 9. I am indebted to Michel Oksenberg of Stanford University for drawing my attention to this reference, as well as for many other suggestions about this chapter.

[2] *Finance* (*Caizheng*), No. 5, May 5, 1958, p. 26. Chin Chün, Shantung Provincial Finance Department: 'Use Extra-Budgetary Funds Advantageously for Developing Production', and ibid., No. 22, November 24, 1959, p. 25, Investigation Group, Shansi Provincial Finance Department: 'Some Opinions on Strengthening the Control of Extra-Budgetary Funds', and ibid., No. 20, October 24, 1959, p. 30. Budget Office of Kweichow Provincial Finance Department: loc. cit.

[3] For definition of this term, see p. 27 above.

[4] *Finance* (*Caizheng*), No. 22, November 24, 1959, p. 25. Investigation Group, Shansi Provincial Finance Department, loc. cit.

[5] *Economic Research* (*Jingji Yanjiu*), No. 2, February 1960, pp. 16–17. Ko Chih-ta and Ling Han: 'Outline Discussion of Comprehensive Financial Plans', and ibid, No. 2, February 1961, p. 4, Chi Ts'ai-ch'eng: loc. cit.

[6] *Planning and Statistics* (*Jihua yu Tongji*), No. 2, January 23, 1959 (ECMM 176). Huo Chi-ch'ao: loc. cit.

other purposes, at ¥12,000 million,[1] equal to some 17 per cent of the ¥70,000 million total *ex ante* budgetary revenues.) On these figures, extra-budgetary capital investment came to the equivalent of nearly 4 per cent of budgetary capital investment in 1957, 23 per cent in 1958, 19 per cent in 1959, and to an expected 18 per cent in 1960.

At the beginning of 1958 it was estimated that in general, for local authorities of all levels, extra-budgetary income amounted to the equivalent of some 20–30 per cent of their budgetary revenues. For *hsien* and municipalities the estimate was 40–50 per cent, rising in a few cases to as much as 70 per cent.[2] It must be remembered that, in China, budgets at each level of the administration include the budgets of subordinate local authorities. Thus if for local authorities as a whole, extra-budgetary income amounted to the equivalent of 20–30 per cent of budgetary revenues, while for *hsien* and municipalities the figures were 40–50 per cent, this would indicate that extra-budgetary funds were equivalent on an average to less than 20–30 per cent of the revenues disposable directly by provincial level authorities.

The steepness of the rise in extra-budgetary investment during the Great Leap may have been exaggerated by changes in statistical analysis or in policy regarding publication; or it may have been under-stated through lack of knowledge or other reasons. But that a great rise in total extra-budgetary funds did occur at this time is borne out by reports from certain provinces.[3] The overall rise was all the more significant because it evidently offset the disappearance of two previous sources of extra-budgetary revenue—the local authorities' share of bonds raised in their districts (due to the cessation of national bonds and the apparent unwillingness of most provinces to raise their own) and the revenue from labour reform enterprises (which from 1959 was included in the budget). In Kweichow province, the decline in proceeds from these two items was expected to halve the extra-budgetary income in 1959.[4]

The chief cause of the rise in extra-budgetary funds during the Great Leap of 1958–9 was the growth in absolute sums of retained profits of enterprises. In the case of the economic departments of many local authorities, the rise obtained from this cause was accentuated by the greatly increased number of enterprises that had come under their control as a result of the 1957–8 decentralization measures, in the retained profits of which enterprises they had a share. The reduction in the percentage of retainable profits, decreed in 1961, presumably cut extra-budgetary funds, but even more important is likely to have been the fall in profits themselves as a result of the decline in industrial output

[1] Figures derived from *Collected Laws and Regulations* . . . Vol. 7, p. 118, and ibid., Vol. 11, pp. 35, 37, 42 and 44.

[2] *Finance (Caizheng)*, No. 1, January 1958, p. 8. Huan Wen: loc. cit.

[3] *Planning and Statistics (Jihua yu Tongji)*, No. 2, January 23, 1959 (ECMM 176). Huo Chi-ch'ao: loc. cit. In Shensi, extra-budgetary income in 1956 amounted to ¥69 million (equivalent to 24 per cent of the provincial budgetary income), to ¥74 million in 1957 (27 per cent) and to ¥130 million in 1958 (17 per cent), and *Finance (Caizheng)*, No. 22, November 1959, p. 25. Investigation Group, Shansi Provincial Finance Department: loc. cit. Here we are not informed of the rise between 1957 and 1958; however, in 1959 revenue from extra-budgetary funds was stated to have risen 63 per cent over the 1958 total and to be equivalent to 18 per cent of the budgetary revenues of Shansi province.

[4] *Finance (Caizheng)*, No. 20, October 1959, p. 30. Budget Office of Kweichow Provincial Finance Department: loc. cit.

in the years immediately after the Leap. With the subsequent improvement, it might be supposed that both profits and, with them, extra-budgetary funds rose once again. However, this is a subject on which we have little information.

But whatever the situation after 1960, extra-budgetary funds formed a considerable part of both revenue and expenditure from 1958 to 1960. This had both advantages and disadvantages. These funds impart a flexibility to the economic system—it might even be said that the rigidity of the formal system makes them necessary. Small investments, perhaps overlooked in the budget, may often yield disproportionate returns, and funds free from budgetary restraints on their use can here prove very beneficial.[1] Indeed, this may have been one factor behind the rise in industrial production in 1958. Administrative convenience, too, is served by not subjecting trifling miscellaneous sums to budgetary procedures.

However, many of the sums concerned were, as has been seen, far from trifling. It is evident that their unsupervised use makes nonsense of economic planning, especially as a large portion has (at least at times) been spent on capital purposes and thus competes for scarce materials, equipment and skills with planned projects financed from the budget.

The inflationary tendencies of this additional capital expenditure are also clear. From 1958 onwards attempts were made to bring extra-budgetary funds under some kind of control. Already in October 1958 non-budgetary funds were supposed, by order of the State Council, to be included as 'a supplementary component of the state budget' and provincial level authorities were ordered to compile and report plans for these funds.[2]

Regulations on quarterly reporting of extra-budgetary income and expenditure to the Ministry of Finance were promulgated in May 1959.[3] Nevertheless, it is apparent that considerable confusion continued to surround their management. An article in May 1959 condemned the switching of items of revenue from the budgetary to the non-budgetary category, while encouraging a contrary movement[4] (as occurred with revenue from labour reform enterprises). Towards the end of 1961 the importance of a clear distinction between budgetary and non-budgetary funds was still being urged, together with the need for local authorities and ministries to draw up balanced budgets of (paradoxically) extra-budgetary funds and to include them in their financial plans.[5] This suggests that the control of these funds was still inadequate; one reason for this was that bodies possessed of sizeable extra-budgetary funds feared that if these were entered into their financial plans, they would be made

[1] *Finance (Caizheng)*, No. 5, May 5, 1958, p. 26. Chin Chün: loc. cit.

[2] *Collected Laws and Regulations* ... Vol. 8, p. 146.

[3] *Collected Financial Laws and Regulations* . . ., January–June 1959, pp. 39–40. See also *Economic Research (Jingji Yanjiu)*, No. 2, February 1960, pp. 16–17. Ko Chih-ta and Ling Han: loc. cit., and *Finance (Caizheng)*, No. 10, October 1960, p. 12. Jung Tze-ho, Vice-Minister of Finance: Speech at the National Conference for the Exchange of Experience on Budgetary Work.

[4] Ibid., No. 9, May 9, 1959, p. 23. Yin Ch'eng-chang: 'Be Efficient in Budgetary Administration and Go All Out to Fulfil the National Budget for 1959.'

[5] *Ta Kung Daily (Dagong Bao)*, Peking, November 17, 1961, p. 3. Ko Chih-ta and Wang Cho: loc. cit. A few months earlier an article had stated that only important items of extra-budgetary funds need be entered into financial plans. *Economic Research (Jingji Yanjiu)*, No. 2, February 1961, p. 5. Chi Ts'ai-ch'eng: loc. cit.

to increase their upward remittances.[1] However, with the decline in size of extra-budgetary funds at that time, the subject had probably become of lesser importance.

In 1963, a new system of budgetary management, or a new set of regulations on the budget, provided for certain local supplementary taxes which had figured among extra-budgetary funds (supplementary industrial and commercial tax, supplementary agricultural tax and supplementary urban public utility charges), to be entered into the comprehensive national financial plan, which is supposed to be the counterpart in financial terms of the national economic plan.[2]

A point of interest about investment made with extra-budgetary funds is that in this case the rate of profit (both realized profit on previous investments from these sources and expected rate of profit on new investments) is likely to be an important determinant of the amount and direction of investment. This is contrary to the official line in China that under socialism the allocation of investment funds should not be determined by the rate of profit. Investment out of extra-budgetary funds was presumably in the early 1960s affected by the same disincentives (notably a decline in the marginal efficiency of capital caused by a shortage of raw materials), as influenced investment in general in those years. However, as we have seen, the amount of extra-budgetary funds must have drastically fallen.

It is highly probable that extra-budgetary revenues have been taken into account in negotiations between the central government and the provinces on balance transfers of budgetary revenue between the two levels (see pp. 388 and 397) and likewise in the case of provinces and lower authorities. Thus a local authority known to possess ample extra-budgetary funds might lose some of its advantage through harsher assessments or smaller subsidies. A hint of how extra-budgetary funds may influence budgetary negotiations can be gleaned from the final accounts for 1956, where it was stated that it had been agreed that half the current costs of primary schools were to be met by local authorities out of the local supplementary agricultural tax: 'but because of natural calamities and other practical difficulties, part of this was covered by grants from the state budget'.[3]

The Division between Central and Local Financial Responsibility

Local budgets are compiled at two, and possibly three levels: at the provincial (and equivalent), at the *hsien* (and municipalities under provinces), and perhaps at the *hsiang* (and *chen*) level as well. When the communes were first established in 1958, they absorbed the embryo financial organs of the *hsiang*. Communes are supposed to have annual budgets, but as they are officially reckoned to be collective rather than state bodies, these budgets cannot formally be counted as a lower level of the state budget. It is possible that *hsiang*

[1] *Economic Research* (*Jingji Yanjiu*), No. 2, February 1961, p. 5. Chi Ts'ai-ch'eng: loc. cit.
[2] Ibid., No. 6, June 1965, p. 20. Shen Yün: loc. cit. On this topic, see also *Finance* (*Caizheng*), No. 10, October 1960, p. 12. Jung Tze-ho: loc. cit., and *Economic Research* (*Jingji Yanjiu*), No. 2, February 1960, pp. 16–17. Ko Chih-ta and Ling Han: loc. cit. On the comprehensive financial plan, see pp. 471–2 below.
[3] *People's Handbook* (*Renmin Shouce*) *1958*, p. 215.

budgets may now be compiled in certain places.[1] Special districts and districts (*chuan ch'ü* and *ch'ü*) do not have their own separate budgets, their expenditure being incorporated into the budgets of their immediate superior authorities. The great administrative regions, before their abolition in 1954, also had their own budgets.

The division of revenue between the central authorities and the various levels of local government has long been a problem in China. Before 1912, under the Empire, the lack of a clear assignment of revenues to each level was responsible for many of the administrative defects of that time.[2] The Nationalist Government had effected such an assignment by reserving customs duties, together with salt and commodity taxes, for central use while allocating the land tax (the predecessor of the present agricultural tax) to the provinces. When the Japanese occupied the coastal areas, the central government lost much of its revenue and had to divert the land tax back into its own coffers. The payment of this tax in kind provided a mainstay of the national treasury during the financial chaos of the closing years of Kuomintang rule.[3]

When the Communists assumed the government, the first requirement was for centralization in finance, even more than in other spheres. In 1950 it was laid down that all important local revenues should be paid into the central treasury and that authorization from the Ministry of Finance was needed for local expenditure, the necessary amounts being paid out monthly to the provincial level local authorities. As an exception to this general rule, local authorities were permitted to retain a fixed percentage of the proceeds of the agricultural tax and of the industrial and commercial taxes, from their areas. In addition, they were allowed to levy for local use taxes supplementary to, and up to a certain percentage of, these major taxes.[4]

The gradual movement towards financial decentralization may be said to have begun as early as 1951 when sources of revenue and items of expenditure were both classified according to whether they came under the central government or local authorities, or were to be divided between the two.[5]

The large programme of capital works ushered in by the First Five Year Plan necessitated greater local financial powers. These were, however, still restrained within narrow limits and the central government controlled almost every item in local budgets. While local authorities were now allowed to build up their own reserve funds, these were not supposed to be used without central permission.[6] Enterprises, too were restricted in their initiative, being forbid-

[1] See p. 400 below.

[2] Chuan-shih Li: *Central and Local Finance in China*, New York, 1922, pp. 58 and 59.

[3] Chang Kia-ngau: *The Inflationary Spiral*, London, 1958, pp. 38 and 114.

[4] *Finance (Caizheng)*, No. 19, October 9, 1959, p. 12. Hsü Fei-ch'ing: 'Centralized Leadership and Decentralized Administration Is the Correct Policy for National Budgetary Management.' In 1957 local authorities were authorized to raise a supplementary industrial and commercial tax equivalent to 1 per cent of the normal industrial and commercial taxes in force at that date. (*People's Daily* [*Renmin Ribao*], November 18, 1957, p. 3.) For rates of the supplementary agricultural tax, see p. 339 above.

[5] *Finance (Caizheng)*, No. 19, October 9, 1959, p. 12. Hsü Fei-ch'ing: loc. cit.

[6] Ibid., No. 1, January 1958, p. 1. Jung Tze-ho: loc. cit., and *Economic Research (Jingji Yanjiu)*, No. 10, October 1958, p. 37. Lin Yün: 'The 1958 Reform of Our Country's Financial Management System.' Part I.

den to acquire fixed assets worth more than ¥200 without approval of their controlling ministries.¹

By various devices, it was complained, the central government managed to retain powers which had nominally been delegated to the provinces. For example, although from 1954 onwards provincial level authorities were permitted to keep their year-end balances of funds in hand, yet in fact this right was rendered worthless because in the following year the central government reduced their grant by an equivalent amount. This resulted in provincial authorities continuing to indulge in end of year bouts of extravagance.² Central and local items of expenditure had in 1956 still not been sufficiently distinguished, with the result that responsibility for various payments was shunted from one level to another.³

We have already seen that the approach of the Second Five Year Plan provided the occasion for reshaping the structure of economic administration. In financial, as in many other matters, decentralization was decreed. The essence of this step was that the central government should no longer control the separate items of local revenue and expenditure; instead, certain sources of revenue were to be allocated to the local authorities which would then be expected to meet all their normal expenditure without recourse to central help. This general rule was, as we shall note, modified in some important respects to take into account the wide divergence in wealth of different local authorities. It must be remembered that certain sources of revenue had from 1951 onwards been assigned to local authorities.⁴ However, these revenues were relatively small. The decree of 1957 added greatly to their volume.

The regulations issued by the central government in December 1957, to operate from 1958, were directed in the first instance to provincial level authorities. It was then left to these in their turn to allot sources of revenue to lower local authorities.⁵ The central government, as we have previously noted, seldom appears to have direct financial dealings (or contact of almost any other type) with local authorities below the provincial and equivalent level. This is in accordance with the deeply rooted Chinese tradition—or ingrained manner of action—to which we have previously alluded, by which officials and organs at each level have a comprehensive responsibility for the correct behaviour of all those beneath them, but do not directly interfere unless something goes wrong.

The 1957 regulations listed local authority revenue under three headings: fixed local revenue; the local share of profits of state and joint state-private enterprises under the central government, and the adjustable share of certain revenues. Fixed local revenues comprised revenue from the state and state-

---

¹ *People's Daily* (*Renmin Ribao*), November 18, 1957, p. 1. Editorial.
² *Economic Research* (*Jingji Yanjiu*), No. 10, October 1958, pp. 38–9. Lin Yün: loc. cit. For the tug of war between centre and provinces over the disposal of year-end balances, see *Finance* (*Caizheng*), No. 8, August 1957, p. 10. Hu Tze-ming: 'A Consideration of Certain Problems in Local Budgets.'
³ *Finance* (*Caizheng*), No. 1, October 5, 1956, p. 11. Ch'en Hsüeh: 'Further Strengthen Local Responsibility for Financial Management.'
⁴ For those so assigned in the 1956 budget see *Collected Financial Laws and Regulations* . . . 1956, pp. 45 and 49.
⁵ *Collected Laws and Regulations* . . . Vol. 7, pp. 227–8.

private enterprises and institutions already under local control before the decentralization movement, the minor taxes described above (slaughter tax, tax on cattle transactions, urban real estate tax, entertainment tax, licence fees from vehicles and ships, stamp duty and income tax on bank deposit interest) and 'other local revenue' (this last is probably an elastic category left to local initiative). The original regulations of December 1957 included pastoral tax in the category of fixed local revenue. An amendment dated January 1958 stated that this was to apply to pastoral tax in autonomous regions only; elsewhere pastoral tax was to fall into the category of revenue subject to adjustable division between the centre and the provinces.[1] In Chapter 6, we discussed the method of calculating the local share of profits of central government enterprises (embracing both those enterprises which were currently being handed over to local authorities and some of those that still remained under central control).[2] The adjustable share of certain revenues that was receivable by local authorities applied to commodity circulation tax, merchandise tax and industrial and commercial tax (these three were soon to be absorbed into the consolidated industrial and commercial tax), industrial and commercial income tax, bonds, agricultural tax and, by the amendment already noted, to pastoral tax except in autonomous regions. The proportion, if any, of these sources of revenue to accrue to any provincial level authority, was to depend on the wealth of that authority. In fact, as we shall see, this principle was also to be applied to local income falling under the other two headings.[3]

Sometimes the 'normal annual expenditure' of a province or equivalent was more than covered by fixed local revenue or by this together with the local share of the profits of central enterprises. Such local authorities were to receive no share of profits nor of adjustable revenues, or no share of the adjustable revenues only, as the case might be. If even so, such a local authority had an excess of income over normal expenditure, a fixed (but unspecified) proportion of this excess was to be paid over to the central government. Under these provisions, in 1958 no profits from central enterprises, nor any adjustable share of revenues, was to be received by the municipalities of Peking, Tientsin and Shanghai, nor by the province of Liaoning. Other provincial level authorities were to receive the agreed 20 per cent of profits of central enterprises and an adjustable share of revenues determined according to the need of each province. If income received under all these headings by some provinces or autonomous regions was insufficient to meet normal annual expenditure, subsidies would be given by the central government.[4] Some outlying autonomous regions received considerable help in this way.[5]

[1] *Collected Laws and Regulations* . . . Vol. 7, pp. 223–4, and ibid., p. 221.
[2] See pp. 153–4 above. It will be remembered that in cases where profits were divided between the central and local treasuries, the enterprises' retainable share of profits was deductable from the 80 per cent going to the centre.
[3] Ibid., Vol. 7, p. 225.
[4] Ibid.
[5] Ibid., Vol. 6, p. 332, and JPRS 1070-D, p. 2. 'Sinkiang 1957 and 1958 Final Budget and 1959 Draft Budget', and JPRS 482-D, p. 4. 'Report on 1957 Final Budget and 1958 Draft Budget of the Inner Mongolian Autonomous Region.' On fiscal regulations applying to autonomous regions towards the end of the First Five Year Plan period, see Ko Chih-ta: op. cit., p. 47.

THE FISCAL SYSTEM

The crucial factor in this system is to determine both the revenue estimates and the 'normal annual expenditure' of any province; the expenditure side is apt to be the nub of the fiercest arguments.[1] All this, as we have seen, is liable to give rise to tough negotiating, and more, between the province and the central government.

The 'normal expenditure' of a province was in 1958 stated to comprise those current expenses of institutions (*shihyeh*) which fall under the heading of 'economic construction' (see p. 383 above), e.g. expenses of institutions connected with agriculture, forestry, water conservancy, communications, posts and telecommunications; expenditure on education, culture, scientific research, training of cadres, public health, relief for the less serious natural disasters, for small-scale migration and waste-land reclamation, and for levying conscripts. The accumulation of local reserve funds is also included under 'normal expenditure'. The central government would make grants for certain special items of expenditure such as large-scale resettlement and reclamation of wasteland, and relief in serious natural calamities. Provincial capital investment was also to be covered by central grants. In addition, 70 per cent of increases in working capital of local state enterprises was to be provided by central grants or by bank loans.[2]

As well as grants for these specific purposes, however, we find the central government giving *ad hoc* financial help in special cases, for example to pay for the establishment of local grain reserves, or to compensate local authorities for loss of income due to reductions in prices of machinery.[3]

In January 1958 it was laid down that in general the system of allotment of specific revenues to the major local authorities, decreed in 1957, was not to be changed for three years, although some modifications might be made after a year's trial. The duration for which arrangements were to remain unchanged was, in April 1958, extended to five years.[4]

The decree on the reform of the planning system, promulgated in September 1958, listed the chief financial targets to be controlled from the centre as the total state revenues and expenditures, local (i.e. provincial level) revenue remittances and subsidies, credit equilibrium and the distribution of capital grants[5] (the last two items, from the text, probably referred to the inter-provincial distribution of working and investment capital respectively).

In 1959 the division of local revenue into three categories was ended. Instead, the centrally approved figure for a provincial level authority's budgetary expenditure would be compared with the figure for the total revenue the authority was responsible for raising (i.e. all the revenue from its area except for customs duties and the profits of enterprises under direct central control). Approved deficits would be made up by the central government to which a proportion of any estimated excess revenue had to be transferred.[6]

---

[1] *Economic Research (Jingji Yanjiu)*, No. 10, October 1958, p. 38. Lin Yün: 'The 1958 Reform of the Financial System of Our Country.' Part 2.

[2] *Collected Laws and Regulations* . . . Vol. 7, p. 134. Li Hsien-nien: loc. cit., and *Finance (Caizheng)*, No. 1, January 1958, pp. 1–2. Jung Tze-ho: loc. cit.

[3] Ibid., Vol. 7, pp. 282 and 314.

[4] Ibid., Vol. 6, p. 332, and ibid., Vol. 7, p. 234.

[5] Ibid., Vol. 8, p. 97.

[6] *Finance (Caizheng)*, No. 19, October 9, 1959, p. 13. Hsü Fei-ch'ing: loc. cit.

Two points were emphasized in Chinese economic journals about the delegation of financial power: the need to settle definite sources of revenue on local authorities and the corollary to this, the need to increase the scope for their initiative.[1] Thus, central ministries were no longer to transmit financial plans and quotas to provincial level departments, a provision which, if observed, must have severely curtailed the powers of the ministries.[2]

The clarity of the demarcations was diminished by the provisions for depriving wealthier authorities of revenues in excess of their 'normal expenditure'. Flexibility may have been better ensured. Provincial level authorities were empowered to re-arrange revenue and expenditure so long as the approved figures for balances were not overstepped to the central government's detriment.[3] They might levy special local taxes and, in certain conditions, increase, decrease, or give exemption from the central government taxes on industry and commerce.[4]

Local authorities at all levels were given fairly free rein to use their initiative in raising funds by what devices they chose ('self-provided funds') although their methods of fund-raising were supposed to be approved by the immediate superior level. A good measure of improvization has characterized financial affairs, especially of the lower local authorities.

The financial decentralization measures are reflected in the changes in the local authority component of the national budget between 1957 and 1958. In 1957, local authorities were responsible for collecting 56 per cent of the national budgetary revenue; in 1958 this rose to 77 per cent. Local authorities' share of total budgetary expenditure grew from 28 per cent in 1957 to 44 per cent in 1958, and to 52 per cent in 1960.[5]

The excess of the relative share of local authorities in budgetary revenue over their relative share in budgetary expenditure indicates the extent to which the central government is dependent on revenues collected at lower levels. In one respect these figures underestimate the true rise in the relative financial position of the local authorities as they omit extra-budgetary funds which, as we have seen, increased very substantially at this period, especially at the lower levels.

As already mentioned, apparently the only revenues collected by the central government itself are customs duties and the profits from those enterprises it directly controls.[6]

At the end of 1961, and in 1962, a movement back towards greater financial centralization was announced. This was prompted by a desire to rectify the

[1] *New Construction (Xin Jianshe)*, No. 8, August 1958, p. 34. Ch'eng Fang: 'Balance in the Financial and Economic System and Planning.'
[2] *Finance (Caizheng)*, No. 1, January 1958, p. 3. Jung Tze-ho: loc. cit.
[3] Ibid., No. 19, October 9, 1959, pp. 13 and 15. Hsü Fei-ch'ing: loc. cit.
[4] *Collected Laws and Regulations* . . . Vol. 7, p. 266.
[5] *Finance (Caizheng)*, No. 10, October 1958, p. 1. Yang Shao-ch'iao: loc. cit., and *Collected Laws and Regulations* . . . Vol. 11, p. 41. In the year 1959, the Municipality of Shanghai transmitted 80 per cent of its revenue to the central government. *Liberation Daily (Jiefang Ribao)*, May 18, 1960 (SCMP 2291). Ma Yi-hsing: 'Report on Shanghai's Final Accounts for 1959 and Draft Budget for 1960.' Figures for the division of budgetary expenditure between central and local budgets for 1951–6 are given in Ko Chih-ta: op. cit., p. 37.
[6] *Finance (Caizheng)*, No. 19, October 9, 1959, p. 13. Hsü Fei-ch'ing: loc. cit.

misallocation of resources that had occurred during the Great Leap and subsequent period. 'Only more centralization and unification can avoid the dispersion and waste of capital', stated an article in *Ta Kung Daily* in 1962.¹

Great emphasis was now placed on financial administrative procedures instituted for such purposes as controlling, and distinguishing between, funds of different types—between working and fixed capital or budgetary and extra-budgetary funds, for example. Cost control was another object of these new procedures. They were intended to re-introduce standards of accounting that had been swept away during the Great Leap and they accompanied the re-instatement of the professional accountant which was mentioned in an earlier chapter. Abuses needed to be eradicated. The importance of 'keeping only one set of accounts, from top to bottom' was emphasized. 'Apart from the [official] budget, there must be no other budget'.² This probably refers to a system of keeping two sets of divergent financial accounts parallel to the two sets of planning targets which we shall see had come into vogue in 1958.

In the course of this recentralization movement of 1961 and 1962, the financial power of the central government was to be augmented at the expense of both local authorities and of enterprises and organs. 'In matters of financial control, the chief power must be concentrated in the central government and the power of local authorities and of economic units must be reduced.'³ More especially it was considered desirable to reduce the financial autonomy of the lower local authorities. 'Authority in the management of national finance must be concentrated in the three levels of central government, great administrative regions, and provinces; the authority in financial management of special districts, *hsien* and below must be reduced.'⁴

Regulations on *hsien* budgets were included in the rules on *hsien* organization promulgated in 1950, and in 1954 it was proposed to institute budgets at *hsien* level.⁵ When the decentralization measures first came into force at the beginning of 1958, the problem was to find ways of developing *hsien* financial initiative, especially in the poorer *hsien* which had to be subsidized by the provincial authorities.⁶ By mid-1959, however, complaints were made that some provincial and equivalent authorities were giving too much financial responsibility to special districts and *hsien*.⁷ No doubt any ensuing difficulties

---

¹ *Ta Kung Daily* (*Dagong Bao*), Peking, June 25, 1962, p. 3. Fan Yeh-chün, Li Te-sheng and Chang Chih-tao: loc. cit.
² Ibid.
³ *Ta Kung Daily* (*Dagong Bao*), Peking, June 25, 1962, p. 3. Fan Yeh-chün, Li Te-sheng and Chang Chih-tao: loc. cit.
⁴ Ibid., November 17, 1961, p. 3. Ko Chih-ta and Wang Cho: loc. cit. On the great administrative regions, see p. 20 above. The use of this phrase in the above quotation, of 1961, is strange because the great administrative regions were abolished in 1954. A different name, 'economic co-ordinating regions', was given to the supra-provincial units which existed fitfully around 1958.
⁵ *New China Monthly* (*Xinhua Yuebao*), No. 4, February 1950, p. 868, and Ko Chih-ta: op. cit., p. 35.
⁶ *Finance* (*Caizheng*), No. 1, January 1958, pp. 5–6. Jung Tze-ho: loc. cit.
⁷ Ibid., No. 11, June 9, 1959, p. 2. Editorial.

were aggravated by the loss of *hsien* financial cadres to other occupations during the Great Leap. In 1961, as we have just seen, the policy was to reduce the financial power of the lower local authorities.[1] However, the degree to which this was done, or even recommended, varied not only from province to province, but even within each province; the need for flexibility in the implementation of this policy was underlined.[2]

Since 1958 (following decentralization of control over enterprises) *hsien* have derived a high proportion of their revenue from profits and taxes of industrial and commercial enterprises. In one *hsien* in Honan, for example, 70–80 per cent of the revenue was reported to come from such sources.[3] As a result, *hsien* financial cadres devote much of their time to supervising and promoting such enterprises, in order to increase income. This involves them in problems of finding and allocating raw materials, and in methods of cost reduction. The same is true of financial personnel of municipalities and other local authorities.[4] *Hsien*, like provinces, divide certain revenue with higher level authorities according to percentages. These percentages can be changed by the higher levels, sometimes at short notice.[5] In considering the sources of *hsien* revenue, the importance of extra-budgetary funds must be borne in mind.

A national conference on *hsiang* (rural district) and *chen* (market town) finance was held in 1953. At that time little in the way of formal administrative organs existed in *hsiang* and *chen*. When *hsien* budgets came to be drawn up, they included basic level expenditure but no separate *hsiang* or *chen* budgets were compiled.[6] Financial organization in the *hsiang* level began to be set up in 1956, but was still far from complete by 1958 when the incipient *hsiang* financial structure was absorbed into the newly established people's communes,[7] as was also ordered in the case of the financial organs of the *chen*.[8] In this policy, the lowest organs of the department of finance were treated in the same way as those of other departments, such as commerce. Later, the *hsiang* and *chen* financial structures were apparently resuscitated.[9] The financial arrangements in the communes have been discussed in Chapter 3.

---

[1] *Ta Kung Daily* (*Dagong Bao*), Peking, November 17, 1961, p. 3. Ko Chih-ta and Wang Cho: loc. cit.

[2] Ibid., December 1, 1961, p. 3. Yeh Chin-t'ang: 'Concentrate Financial Authority and Strengthen Control'.

[3] *People's Daily* (*Renmin Ribao*), April 30, 1962, p. 2.

[4] e.g. *Finance* (*Caizheng*), No. 22, November 24, 1959, p. 16, and *Ta Kung Daily* (*Dagong Bao*), Peking, October 16, 1959, p. 2.

[5] *Economic Research* (*Jingji Yanjiu*), No. 1, January 1961, p. 35. Liang Chih and Kan T'ieh-ya: 'A Study in the Development of Comprehensive Financial Planning at the *Hsien* Level.'

[6] Ko Chih-ta: op. cit., pp. 35–6.

[7] *Ta Kung Daily* (*Dagong Bao*), Peking, May 29, 1958. p. 1. Editorial. In some places *hsiang* financial organizations were developed earlier than 1956—e.g. this was reported to have occurred from 1953 onwards in the Lunghsi special district, Fukien province. *Finance* (*Caizheng*), No. 11, November 1957, pp. 24–6. Huang Ying-sung, Financial Office, Lunghsi Special District, Fukien: 'Some Points on Efficiency in *Hsiang* (*Chen*) Financial Work.'

[8] *New China Fortnightly* (*Xinhua Banyuekan*), No. 147, January 10, 1959, p. 63.

[9] R. Diao: op. cit., p. 14.

2. FINANCIAL PERSONNEL

The provision of competent financial cadres, sufficient in number and politically reliable, has been a constant problem. The more efficient ones were liable to be open to 'the corrosion and influence of bourgeois ideas'[1] and often, indeed, were of bourgeois origin, while many others were poorly educated. Special training courses, full or part-time, have been held. Under the 'worker-peasant labour system', many peasants have been recruited for part-time work as tax collectors, as well as for work in credit co-operatives and commerce. The 'worker-peasants' could normally draw their grain rations from their own production teams and it was intended that the system would reduce the state's liability to supply grain to non-agricultural rural residents while also reducing costs of finance and trade organs.[2]

The neglect of financial management during the Great Leap, the disparagement of accounting techniques and the diversion of financial workers to other employment contributed to the chaos of that period. In the succeeding years, considerable efforts were made to repair this damage. A relapse may, however, have occurred in the course of the Cultural Revolution of 1966–7.

3. CONCLUSIONS

We have seen that the Chinese budgetary system is largely devoted to the transfer of resources between state enterprises. Profits and taxes levied from these enterprises are spent mainly by other state enterprises. Thus, there need be little direct taxation of the individual since the resources required are siphoned off before they reach him. The high proportion of profits and taxes that derive from industries using agricultural raw materials, makes the revenue very dependent on harvest vagaries; this dependence has, however, recently been diminished by the growth of chemical-based industries such as plastics.

The highly centralized control of revenues and expenditures that existed in the First Five Year Plan period, was brought to an end both formally by the decentralization measures and informally by the great growth of extra-budgetary funds that escaped central control. In finance, as in other spheres, a 'responsibility system' on the traditional Chinese pattern came into being. By 1961–2 decentralization had gone too far for the liking of the central government, which tried to check and in some degree to reverse the movement. We do not know what specific objectives they had in mind in this movement, nor how successful they may have been. They are unlikely, even if they wished, to regain anything like the degree of financial centralization that was attempted in the period of the First Five Year Plan.

[1] *Ta Kung Daily (Dagong Bao)*, Peking, May 24, 1961 (SCMP 2521). Wei Wen: 'Strengthen Unceasingly the Party's Basic Level Organizational Work in the Finance and Trade Departments.'

[2] *New Construction (Xin Jianshe)*, Nos. 1–2, February 1966, pp. 57 and 59. Chang Ho-wei: 'An Outline Discussion of the Worker-Peasant System in Finance and Trade.'

Chapter 15

BANKING, CURRENCY AND CREDIT

All banks in China are under complete state control, even in those cases where in theory private participation in ownership still continues. Banks have wide powers of supervision over economic enterprises and other organs, in addition to their functions of controlling the note issue, collecting deposits and extending to enterprises both credit and budgetary grants for investments.

1. THE BANKS

Before the Sino-Japanese war, banks in China fell into three main categories: foreign banks, the modern Chinese banks (some owned by the government and some by private interests) and the old-style 'native banks'. By 1937 foreign banks had lost their earlier predominance in financing the modern sector of the economy, although in the field of foreign trade they still held the foremost place. Modern Chinese banks were increasing steadily in importance. 'Native banks' (mainly the 'Shansi banks' which, at one time, controlled much of the internal remittance business, and the 'cash shop banks' which developed from money changers), had been declining since the beginning of the century.[1]

After 1945, the importance of the foreign banks had diminished further and the main distinction was between the government-owned banks (in some of which private capital participated) and private banks which included privately owned modern Chinese banks, local and native banks, and the foreign banks.[2] In addition, in the areas held by the Communists, new banks were being established, culminating in the formation, through a merger in December 1948, of the People's Bank of China.[3] After the Communist victory in the following year, this became the central bank for the whole country and played a large part in the financial unification of China and in putting an end to inflation.

The new government discriminated between the existing private banks: the big banks owned by 'bureaucrat-capitalists' were confiscated, while the surviving medium and small banks (many closed down in 1950 as a result of anti-inflationary measures) were subject to gradual 'socialist transformation' through the medium of the Joint State-Private Bank which comes under the People's Bank.[4] By the end of 1952, the only private Chinese banks not so

---

[1] G. C. Allen and A. G. Donnithorne: *Western Enterprise in Far Eastern Economic Development: China and Japan*, London, 1954, pp. 106, 117–19.
[2] Shun-hsin Chou: *The Chinese Inflation 1937–49*, New York, 1963, p. 190.
[3] *1949 Handbook (1949 Shouce)*, Hongkong, p. '*chia*' 70.
[4] *Ten Glorious Years*, Peking, 1960, p. 173. Li Hsien-nien: 'The Great Financial Achievements of the People's Republic of China During the Past Ten Years', and Hsüeh Mu-ch'iao,

transformed were a few owned by Overseas Chinese.[1] Foreign banks were virtually eliminated from China.

The theoretical attitude of the Communists towards the existing banks was that they should be taken over rather than abolished. 'Capitalism supplies the essential prerequisites for the foundation of socialism, and big banks are one of these prerequisites.' Therefore, while the proletariat must smash the bourgeois state machine, 'the big capitalist banks . . . are not abolished or simply discarded, but are grabbed as ready-made organs to serve socialism'.[2] This policy was followed in the case of two of the four great banks of the Kuomintang era—the Bank of China and the Bank of Communications. The two others, the Central Bank and the Farmers' Bank of China, were either abolished or heard of no more on the mainland (although continuing to exist in Taiwan); the old Central Bank being superseded by the People's Bank of China.

The People's Bank is subordinate directly to the State Council. It has, apparently, always been independent of the Ministry of Finance;[3] in the early days this was contrary to the then current Soviet system as the Soviet equivalent, Gosbank, was not separated from its Ministry of Finance until 1954.[4] In their first years, the Chinese Communist government borrowed extensively from the Soviet Union in methods of financial organization; so it is worthy of note that they departed from the Soviet model in this particular. A consideration advanced for making the People's Bank independent of the Ministry of Finance was that at first, both these organs, in the absence of other qualified people, had perforce to employ many former Kuomingtang officials. By dividing these officials between two separate bodies, party control over them might be thought to be easier. In addition there may have been the fortuitous circumstances that cadres in the People's Bank had sufficient influence to ensure the independence of their own institution and the consequent enhancement of their status.[5] In any case, the Bank's independence was to have important results, especially after the Ministry of Finance was affected by the decentralization measures of 1957–8. However, despite the Bank's separation from the Ministry of Finance and despite sporadic rivalry, the two institutions necessarily work in close liaison on many matters.

The People's Bank of China has under it two banks of a specialist nature which operate as its agents: the Bank of China and the Joint State-Private

---

Su Hsing and Lin Tse-li: *The Socialist Transformation of the National Economy in China*, Peking, 1960, and *Ta Kung Daily* (*Dagong Bao*), Peking, October 12, 1959, p. 3. Ts'ao Chü-ju, Director General of the People's Bank: 'Banking in the Past Ten Years.'

[1] Kuan Ta-tung: *The Socialist Transformation of Capitalist Industry and Commerce in China*, Peking, 1960, p. 76.

[2] *Red Flag* (*Hongqi*), No. 1, January 4, 1964, p. 22. Tuan Yün: 'Several Problems in Our Country's Socialist Banking.'

[3] The arrangement of the list of state organs in *People's Handbook* (*Renmin Shouce*) *1950*, p. 'ping' 3, might appear to show the People's Bank as subsidiary to the Ministry of Finance, but we prefer to follow the listing in *New China Monthly* (*Xinhua Yuebao*), No. 1, November 1949, p. 12, which puts the two organs on an equal footing.

[4] A. Nove: *The Soviet Economy* (Revised edition), London, 1965, p. 117.

[5] Unpublished papers of Michel Oksenberg of Stanford University, relating to the financial system in Mainland China.

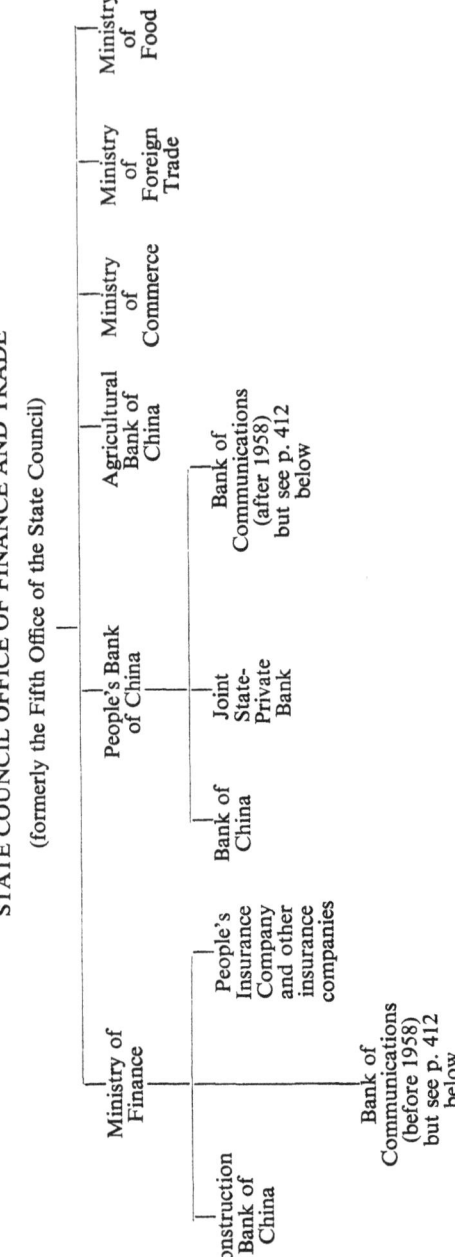

Bank. The post-1963 Agricultural Bank is, like the People's Bank, directly under the State Council, and therefore not subordinate to the People's Bank. The People's Construction Bank of China is likewise not under the People's Bank, but is an organ of the Ministry of Finance; in the same category fall the insurance companies which are classed with it as part of the Ministry's 'system'.[1] (On the status of the Bank of Communications, see p. 412 below.)

The People's Bank of China, as we have seen, was founded by the Communist authorities in 1948. It is said to be the largest and most widespread economic concern in the country with more branches and agencies than has the Post Office.[2] The People's Bank is wholly state-owned. Despite the existence of other wholly state-owned banks, it is the People's Bank which is known as 'the national bank'.[3] It is defined as being an organ of the state and not a mere economic enterprise.[4]

The People's Bank receives appropriations from the budget which (together with its own ploughed back profits and net increases in its deposits) enables it to finance credit expansion. Budgetary appropriations to the Bank are made by the central government. It is through the Bank's own mechanism that these funds are distributed over the country—first divided out among provincial level branches, by them to their subordinate branches and thus eventually to the individual enterprise which receives a loan.[5] Of course the amounts allocated to each province may well be subject to negotiations between provincial administrations and the central government rather than left to the Bank's untrammelled decision—this would seem very probable in the light of what we know of negotiations between the central and provincial level units on other matters. The important thing is that the Bank is the single channel for all these funds and that they move downwards through its hierarchical structure. (With respect to agricultural loans, made by the Agricultural Bank, an important change was made in 1965 by which local authorities began distributing the funds to be loaned. This will be discussed later.) This is very different from the budgetary system as it developed after the decentralization movement of 1957–8. As we saw in Chapter 14, as far as the state budget is concerned, the bulk of the revenues are now collected by local authorities with marginal transfers of funds being remitted upwards. The People's Bank, as far as we can tell, has been little affected by decentralization. If the Bank had been subordinate to the Ministry of Finance, it is unlikely that it would have been able to maintain its centralized structure at a time when the fiscal system was being decentralized. We shall revert to this theme in our concluding chapter.

The People's Bank is the bank of issue and its notes and coin are the sole legal tender. It keeps the government accounts and services the state bonds. Every government organ or enterprise, every military unit and every cooperative has to have an account with the People's Bank and deposit with it

[1] See Appendix 2.
[2] *Far Eastern Economic Review*, April 11, 1963, p. 99.
[3] *Economic Research (Jingji Yanjiu)*, No. 10, October 1962, p. 15. Kao Hsiang: 'The Functions of the State Bank in Socialist Construction.'
[4] *Study (Xuexi)*, No. 2, January 18, 1957, p.8. Wu Ch'ing-yu: 'Is the Socialist State Bank an Organ or an Enterprise?'
[5] Unpublished paper of Michel Oksenberg.

all cash above three days' normal expenditure or, in the case of enterprises at places with no branch of the bank, above normal expenditure for one month.[1] In a separate account, an enterprise has to deposit stipulated sums for its 'major repair fund'.[2] Individuals, too, are under strong pressure to keep money in savings deposits with the Bank. It is almost the only source of credit for the non-agricultural sectors of the economy, as commercial and producing enterprises are not supposed to give credit to each other, with certain limited exceptions. Enterprises and organs have to settle accounts between each other by payments through the Bank, which is thus the hub of the national clearing system. (This may, however, sometimes be circumvented by barter deals.) The Bank is charged with central control of dealings in gold and silver. The People's Bank is also responsible for handling receipts and payments in foreign currency and for effecting international settlements.[3] This it does mainly through its subordinate institution, the Bank of China, although the People's Bank itself has a Foreign Business Bureau.

All these stipulations put the People's Bank in a position where it should, at least in theory, have a full picture of the operations of every enterprise and institution in the country. This information the Bank is expected to use, not only to ensure the success of its own banking operations and the regulation of the currency or to proffer advice to its customers when asked, but also to enable it to act as a universal economic supervisor, to see that all payments between enterprises are made for purposes that accord with the state plan.[4] For example, it is the Bank's duty to ensure that an enterprise does not pay wages in excess of its planned total.[5]

From 1954 until 1965, the Director General of the People's Bank was Ts'ao Chü-ju. In February 1965 Ts'ao was relieved of the post; no announcement as yet (December 1966) has been made of his successor. The Director General is assisted by several deputy directors. Little information about the Bank's internal organization is available for the period after 1952.[6]

The local network of the People's Bank was swiftly established. By the spring of 1950, branches apparently existed in all *hsien* and municipalities.[7]

[1] *New China Monthly (Xinhua Yuebao)*, No. 7, May 1950, p. 128. This regulation may not, of course, always be obeyed.

[2] See pp. 161 and 164 above.

[3] *Economic Research (Jingji Yanjiu)*, No. 10, October 1962, p. 15. Kao Hsiang: loc. cit., and *Handbook on People's China*, Peking, 1957, p. 128.

[4] Hsü Ti-hsin: *An Analysis of China's Economy in the Transitional Period* (in Chinese). Revised edition, Peking, 1959, p. 235.

[5] The Bank 'must plug the wage fund hole and exercise strict supervision over enterprises' implementation of the wage plans approved by the state'. *Economic Research (Jingji Yanjiu)*, No. 1, January 1965, p. 42. Lin Chi-k'en: 'How Should the Regularity of the Circulation of the Currency Be Assessed and Maintained?'

[6] In 1952 the People's Bank had fourteen functional departments and bureaux and five regional offices which, with the Bank's North China Administrative Bureau, corresponded to the six great regions into which the country was then divided. See *People's Handbook (Renmin Shouce) 1952*, pp. 168–9. Around 1953–4, three new functional bureaux were added. Cheng Cho-yuan: *Monetary Affairs of Communist China* (mimeographed). Union Research Institute, Hongkong, 1954, p. 21.

[7] In March 1950 the Ministry of Trade entrusted the People's Bank with the management of commercial funds in every *hsien* and municipality. See *New China Monthly (Xinhua Yuebao)*, No. 6, April 1950. p. 1408.

In May 1951, the Director General of the Bank stated that it had over 2,000 branches with a staff of 160,000.[1] Two years later the employment roll was reported to have swollen to over 300,000;[2] perhaps this number also included personnel of credit co-operatives which, as we shall see, were closely linked with the People's Bank.

The chain of command between the Bank's branches parallels the civil administrative system. Thus, for example, provincial level branches (*fen hang*) of the Bank control the branches (*chih hang*) at *hsien* (and equivalent) level, which in turn have small offices (*yingyeh so*) subordinate to them. The Bank has also its own offices or representatives attached to large factories and mines. In addition, the Bank's savings offices exist in institutions and enterprises of all types; more will be said below about this side of its activities.

Contact between head office and branches is maintained by regular reports, by periodic meetings of the managers of provincial level branches to review current work and by special meetings to discuss particular problems. Apart from such meetings in Peking, 'on the spot conferences' are convened from time to time at other places.

The official status of the Bank of China is that of a joint state-private bank subordinate to the People's Bank and acting as its agent in handling foreign exchange and international settlements.[3] Its nominally separate existence was continued by the Communists, partly to lay claim to investments abroad made in its name in the days of the Nationalist Government, and also for the purpose of retaining commercial goodwill overseas.

The Bank of China is prominent in the business of remittances from Overseas Chinese.[4] Its Hong Kong branch is particularly important in this connection; also in supervising the several smaller banks in Hong Kong that are controlled from the mainland and which engage mainly in remittance business, and in collecting payment for Chinese exports to Hong Kong.

The Bank of China traces its origin to 1904 and was a powerful semi-official bank under the Kuomintang. That part of its capital belonging to 'bureaucratic capitalists' was confiscated by the Communists, while they permitted a few private shareholders, deemed less obnoxious, to retain an interest. For all practical purposes, however, the Bank of China is a state concern, forming virtually a part of the People's Bank. The head office of the Bank of China is in Peking, and it has branches at the chief ports of China and in the main home districts of Overseas Chinese. In addition, there are a number of branches abroad, notably in South East Asia and in Europe. Bank of China branches in countries not recognizing the Peking government, are controlled by the rival Bank of China with its head office in Taiwan. The Chairman of the Board of Directors of the (Mainland) Bank of China ever since 1950 has been Nan Han-ch'en who, until 1954, was also Director General of the People's Bank. In addition Nan is Chairman of the China Council for the Promotion of International Trade.

The Joint State-Private Bank was established as a result of a series of

[1] *New China Monthly* (*Xinhua Yuebao*), No. 21, July 1951, p. 673.
[2] *Chinese Currency* (*Zhongguo Jinrong*), No. 11, June 7, 1954, p. 1. Editorial.
[3] *Handbook on People's China*, pp. 128–9, and Hsü Ti-hsin: op. cit., p. 235.
[4] See Appendix 1 for further information on Overseas Chinese remittances.

mergers between some sixty or more private banks that underwent 'socialist transformation'. It is completely subordinate to the People's Bank of which it handles savings deposits.[1]

Three different agricultural banks, to undertake the provision of rural credit, have existed at various dates since 1949. Their histories suggest that this is the most difficult aspect of banking operations to organize satisfactorily.

In 1951, the Agricultural Co-operation Bank was established to undertake rural banking and to be responsible for state investment in agriculture (both collective and state farms), forestry, water conservancy, and fisheries.[2] Presumably it was abolished before long because in March 1955 another institution, the Agricultural Bank of China, was founded. This, like its predecessor, was to be subordinate to the People's Bank and its functions were to manage funds provided from the budget for investment in agriculture, livestock, fisheries, and water conservancy, and to issue long and short term loans to agricultural producer co-operatives, state farms and individual peasants, to guide and assist rural credit co-operatives and to accept savings deposits in rural areas.[3] Probably this bank was responsible for administering the special fund for making loans to poor peasants entering agricultural producer co-operatives. The original intention was to establish a wide network of branches which were to be guided simultaneously by the Bank's own head office, by the provincial people's councils and Party committees, and by the local branches of the People's Bank. Such a multiplicity of masters may have proved fatal. In any case, it was not feasible to divide the new Bank's credit tasks from those of the People's Bank. Consequently, in March 1957, the Agricultural Bank was abolished.[4] The fact that the movement to form agricultural producer co-operatives had by then been successfully completed, may have had a bearing on the Bank's demise.

From the early 1960s greater priority was given to agriculture and another attempt was made to establish a specialized bank to bring order into the provision of funds for the rural economy. In addition to the People's Bank's involvement with short loans to agriculture, the Ministries of Finance, Agriculture, Forestry and Water Conservancy were concerned with handling budgetary appropriations for their respective interests. At times, organs of several different ministries might be giving out funds to the same commune or production team. Their operations overlapped and sometimes duplicated each other. 'Therefore it is absolutely necessary to set up agricultural banking organs at all levels, and to place all agricultural loans and credit under unified control.'[5]

Consequently in November 1963, once again an Agricultural Bank of China was established. This time it was to be under the direct jurisdiction of the State Council,[6] that is on a level equal to the People's Bank to which the previous agricultural banks had been subordinate.

---

[1] *Handbook on People's China*, p. 129, and Hsü Ti-hsin: op. cit., pp. 235–6.

[2] *New China Monthly (Xinhua Yuebao)*, No. 22, August 1951, p. 875.

[3] *Handbook on People's China*, p. 128, and *New China Monthly (Xinhua Yuebao)*, No. 67, May 1955, p. 176–7, and *People's Handbook (Renmin Shouce) 1956*, p. 540.

[4] *People's Handbook (Renmin Shouce)1956*, p. 540, and Hsü Ti-hsin: op. cit., p. 235, fn.

[5] *Ta Kung Daily (Dagong Bao)*, Peking, November 13, 1963, p. 1. Editorial.

[6] Ibid.

The new Bank was to be staffed by transferring personnel conversant with the relevant operations from both the People's Bank and from the ministries that had been engaged in rural appropriations.[1] In view of the shortage of trained and experienced financial personnel, one of the reasons for the failure of the earlier experiments in agricultural banks may have been the unwillingness of the People's Bank and other organs to release enough staff of the right calibre. Hence the specific instruction to the People's Bank in November 1963 to transfer all the staff of its loan department (presumably only rural loan department staff is meant) together with a number of accountants and senior executives.[2]

By the end of 1963, thirteen provincial branches of the Agricultural Bank had been opened and also a certain number of branches in special districts and *hsien*. Below the *hsien* level, the work of the Agricultural Bank and that of the People's Bank was to be closely co-ordinated.[3]

It was announced that from September 1964 the Agricultural Bank would gradually take over the supervision, previously divided among several ministries, of both investment grants and of loans to state-owned enterprises and institutions in the sphere of agriculture.[4] As yet it is too early to judge whether this time the attempt to launch a specialized agricultural bank has met with success.

One of the objects of the new Agricultural Bank, as of its predecessors, is to guide and help the rural credit co-operatives. Before the Communist era, both traditional and modern types of credit co-operatives existed in the countryside. However, at that time co-operatives were much less important than landlords, other rich farmers, and merchants, as providers of credit for the peasants. When these latter sources of credit largely disappeared after land reform and the socialist transformation of trade, credit co-operatives were rapidly set up to fill the gap.[5] The initiative for this came from above. By February 1955 more than 130,000 credit co-operatives were reported to exist, in addition to credit groups and departments (sometimes forming part of a supply and marketing co-operative) which performed similar functions.[6] They took an important part in assisting the formation of agricultural producers' co-operatives.

On the setting up of the rural communes in 1958, the credit co-operatives were directed to merge into the new unit and become credit departments of

[1] *Ta Kung Daily (Dagong Bao)*, Peking, November 13, 1963, p. 1. Editorial.
[2] Ibid.
[3] Ibid., December 25, 1963, p. 1. *Hsien* branches of the People's Bank were apprehensive lest they be eclipsed by the local branches of the Agricultural Bank. See ibid., May 7, 1964, p. 1.
[4] Ibid., August 27, 1964, p. 1.
[5] John C. H. Wong: *A Study of Communist Land Reform in Post-War China with Special Reference to Policy and Its Implementation* (Unpublished Ph.D. Thesis, London University, 1966). For figures for credit co-operatives before 1949, see *People's Handbook (Renmin Shouce) 1955*, p. 443.
[6] *New China Monthly (Xinhua Yuebao)*, No. 67, May 1955, p. 177. An analysis of credit co-operatives in mid-1953 according to region is given in *People's Handbook (Renmin Shouce) 1955*, p. 443. At that date, the spread over the country was very uneven. Of the 6,864 credit co-operatives in existence, over 40 per cent were found in the two provinces of Shansi and Kiangsi, while Chekiang had only two credit co-operatives. Ibid.

communes. These departments were also to act as local offices of the People's Bank. All the spare cash of every constituent part and enterprise of a commune was to be deposited with the credit department which, in turn, was to deposit its cash balances with the higher offices of the People's Bank.[1] In many cases credit organs were also established in production brigades and teams. As with the supply and marketing co-operatives which, in 1958, were transformed (at least officially) into commune departments, but later regained their old appellation, so with the credit co-operatives. After a time, references to credit departments of communes were replaced by news of credit co-operatives, with the *hsien* appearing to be the significant level for their supervision.[2] It was authoritatively stated that there was no need for uniformity in the organization of credit co-operatives,[3] implying that there was room for wide local variations.

Credit co-operatives draw their funds from bank loans and from rural deposits. According to a *People's Daily* editorial in 1964, in making loans the credit co-operatives should give priority to individual peasants' requirements for both productive purposes and for livelihood needs. Only when these requirements are met should loans be made to production teams.[4] It is not known whether these instructions represented a change in policy or merely reiterated early directives. It is probable that at all times the purposes for which loans might be made have been determined largely at the local (e.g. *hsien*) level.[5]

The credit co-operatives act essentially as rural auxiliaries to the banks, conducting a substantial proportion of the lower level banking functions in the countryside. At the end of 1963, it was stated that about 60 per cent of the banks' credit business with the basic accounting units of communes was transacted through credit co-operatives. In addition, all personal loans to commune members were made through these organs.[6] Credit co-operatives, like banks, have supervisory duties, such as keeping a check on the financial affairs of units of collective agriculture.[7]

Credit co-operatives derive the main portion of their funds from short-

[1] *New China Fortnightly (Xinhua Banyuekan)*, No. 147, January 10, 1959, p. 64.

[2] See e.g. *Ta Kung Daily (Dagong Bao)*, Peking, September 29, 1961, p. 2. 'Fifteen Credit Co-operatives in Wenshui *Hsien* Call A Meeting of Members' Representatives', and ibid., January 31, 1962, p. 2. 'Rural Credit Co-operatives Act as Assistants to State Bank.'

[3] *Red Flag (Hongqi)*, No. 23, December 12, 1963, p. 26. Teng Tzu-hüi: 'The Historic Mission of Credit Co-operatives in Our Country at the Present Stage'.

[4] *People's Daily (Renmin Ribao)*, September 11, 1964, p. 1. Editorial. However, this policy appears not to have stopped some credit co-operatives giving priority to loans for purposes connected with collective agriculture (whether the loans were made to individuals or collective units) over those for production on private plots and in domestic handicrafts, e.g. *Rural Finance (Nongcun Jinrong)*, No. 10, May 21, 1965 (SCMM 490). Kuanti Credit Co-operative, Weinan *hsien*, Shensi: 'The Way to Help Poor and Lower Middle Peasants Overcome Their Production and Livelihood Difficulties.' Here it is reported that 'since (*sc.* in the past two years' work of this co-operative) 80 per cent of the production loans were used to buy farm tools and only 20 per cent for family sideline undertakings, the enthusiasm of commune members for collective production was greatly aroused'.

[5] Chao Shu-li: *Sanliwan Village* (English edition), Peking, 1957, p. 159.

[6] *Red Flag (Hongqi)*, No. 23, December 12, 1963, p. 23. Teng Tzu-hui: loc. cit.

[7] *Rural Finance (Nongcun Jinrong)*, No. 11, June 6, 1965 (SCMM 479). Ch'engchiang *hsien* Branch, Agricultural Bank of China: 'Strengthen Supervision over Financial and Accounting Work, Move Spring Ploughing and Production Forward.'

term deposits drawn from peasants who share both similar seasonal demands for cash and also risks that are likely to be cumulative. This inhibits the co-operatives from making loans for periods longer than a year.[1] Thus there appears to be no source, other than borrowing from private persons, from which individual peasants can get long-term loans. However, their demand for long-term credit for productive purposes (private plots and domestic sideline occupations) is not likely to be great and might in any case be regarded by the Communist authorities with disfavour on political grounds.

The authorities have urged that the leading positions in credit co-operatives should be filled by poor and lower middle peasants and declared that 'landlords, rich peasants, counter-revolutionaries, and bad types who have infiltrated credit co-operatives' should be expelled.[2] Credit workers have frequently been told to make a point of helping poor teams and poor and lower middle peasants. They are instructed not to take ability to repay as the sole criterion for the granting of loans.[3] Apparently the former landlords and rich and upper middle peasants are still the most credit-worthy groups in the rural community.

The People's Construction Bank of China is by far the most important of the two banks which have come under the Ministry of Finance. It was founded in 1954 as a channel for paying out to enterprises and institutions the funds provided by the budget for investment.[4] The Construction Bank was also charged with supervising the use of enterprises' and organs' own 'self-provided' (extra-budgetary) funds ploughed back for capital purposes.[5] Presumably these funds should be paid into an enterprise's account with the People's Bank as soon as they are earned. In 1959 it was laid down that the Construction Bank and the People's Bank should jointly determine the management of investment funds deposited with the People's Bank.[6] From what we know of extra-budgetary funds, the task of supervising their use is likely to be difficult.

In addition to giving out non-repayable investment grants, the Construction Bank issues short-term loans to construction units and enterprises undertaking contracts for capital projects (see pp. 170–1 above), and supervises the use of those funds. From 1964 the Bank began giving loans to finance technical innovations in small- and medium-sized industrial enterprises.[7]

[1] *People's Daily* (*Renmin Ribao*), July 11, 1963, p. 5. Hu Li-chiao: 'Conduct Rural Financial Work Well, Help the Collective Economy Effectively.'

[2] *Red Flag* (*Hongqi*), No. 23, December 12, 1963, p. 25. Teng Tzu-hui: loc. cit.

[3] e.g. *Ta Kung Daily* (*Dagong Bao*), Peking, March 10, 1965, p. 2., and ibid., March 11, 1966, p. 3. Chang Hsiu-min: 'Implement the Class Line While Obtaining Repayment of Loans.'

[4] Two years previously an Investment Bank for Capital Construction had been established under the control of the regional authorities of north-east China (see Cheng Cho-yuan: op. cit., p. 26). It is not known what became of this bank and whether or not it was absorbed into the People's Construction Bank.

[5] *New China Monthly* (*Xinhua Yuebao*), No. 61, November 1954, p. 171. On extra-budgetary funds, see pp. 389–93 above.

[6] *Collected Laws and Regulations of the People's Republic of China* (in Chinese), Vol. 10, p. 272.

[7] *People's Daily* (*Renmin Ribao*), March 19, 1965, p. 2, and *Peking Review*, May 7, 1965, p. 31, and *New China Monthly* (*Xinhua Yuebao*), No. 61, November 1954, p. 171, and Hsü Ti-hsin: op. cit., p. 236.

The Construction Bank has been responsible for investment funds for all sectors of the economy with the sporadic exception of agriculture. In the periods when an Agricultural Bank has been in existence, agricultural investment has naturally come under its control. At times, the People's Bank has been reported as engaging in long- as well as short-term loans to agriculture. However, early in 1963, before the formation of the new Agricultural Bank, the Construction Bank had been directed to establish branches in all *hsien* and municipalities where agricultural investments exceeded ¥500,000.[1]

The Bank of Communications, which before 1958 was subordinate to the Ministry of Finance, in the same manner as was the Construction Bank, resembled the Bank of China in having been founded in the Ch'ing Dynasty, in having been important under the Kuomintang and then having been taken over and transformed by the Communists into a joint state-private concern. Again, as in the case of the Bank of China, Nan Han-ch'en became the first Chairman of the reorganized board.[2]

The Bank of Communications was designated to handle state investment in joint state-private enterprises and to supervise their financial affairs. After the institution of fixed dividends, when the method of management of joint state-private enterprises became almost identical with that of wholly state-owned concerns, the Bank of Communications lost its chief functions.[3]

In 1958 the local branches of this bank were absorbed into the local financial departments, while its head office was put under the People's Bank. Local discretion was allowed as to whether or not Bank of Communications signboards should still be displayed. In these circumstances, it is difficult to determine whether or not the Bank of Communications can still be said to exist.[4]

The main tasks of the Construction Bank and of the Bank of Communications have been to act as organs of the Ministry of Finance for distributing non-repayable budgetary grants for capital investment and to supervise their use: in other words, they are administrative organs of the Ministry of Finance (and were defined as such in 1958) rather than banks in a proper sense of the term. As such they were subject to local control to the same extent as other organs of the Ministry of Finance's 'system'—e.g. the local departments of finance.[5] However, it is convenient to discuss them in this chapter, as some of their functions, notably the financial supervision of enterprises, are common to all Chinese banking institutions.

Apart from specific budgetary allocations for investment purposes laid down in state plans, funds for unplanned investment purposes have derived from increases in the note issue,[6] from retained profits of enterprises and other extra-budgetary funds and from the diversion of working capital to capital investment.

---

[1] *Finance (Caizheng)*, No. 3, February 7, 1963 (SCMM 360). Tseng Chih, Vice Minister of Finance: Speech to Conference of Branch Managers of the Construction Bank.

[2] *Handbook on People's China*, p. 128, and *New China Monthly (Xinhua Yuebao)*, No. 9, July 1950, p. 618. Another point of resemblance between the two banks is that a Bank of Communications exists in Taiwan claiming to be the continuation of the pre-1949 bank.

[3] Hsü Ti-hsin: op. cit., p. 236.

[4] *Collected Financial Laws and Regulations of the Central Government* (in Chinese), 1958, July–December, p. 134.

[5] *Collected Laws and Regulations* ... Vol. 7, pp. 279–80.

[6] Choh-ming Li: *Economic Development in Communist China*, Berkeley, 1959, p. 163.

Two Western banks, the Hong Kong and Shanghai Banking Corporation and the Chartered Bank, both British, still have branches in Shanghai. These branches engage solely in the financing of foreign trade and in foreign exchange transactions, and do not offer either current or savings account facilities nor grant loans. The two banks were each compelled by the Chinese Government to retain a foreign member of staff in Shanghai as a kind of hostage against Chinese-owned US dollar credits held by the banks but frozen as a result of the American embargo. In 1966 foreign members of staff of the British banks were still stationed in Shanghai but by that date, as a result of improved prospects of business, it is unlikely that the banks would have desired to withdraw them if permitted to do so.

Three Overseas Chinese banks, the Overseas Chinese Banking Corporation, the Bank of East Asia and the Chi-Yu Bank, also have branches in Shanghai. They engage in the business of remittances from Overseas Chinese.

Certain points should be noted about the Chinese banking system. First, the People's Bank of China is simultaneously the central bank and the largest bank in direct contact with customers. It is not a bankers' bank and in many ways does not resemble a central bank in the Western sense of the term. The cruder and more direct type of controls operating in China, and the absence of anything like a money market, make irrelevant the arguments for keeping a central bank at one remove from the ultimate customer.

Second, in banking, as in other spheres of the economy, the executive functions of the Communist Party organization at all levels must be borne in mind. Both the banks and the Party are supervisory organs and their duties often overlap. The role of the Party in relation to banks is especially important in rural dealings, in keeping with the notably direct part the Party has played in the administrative control of agriculture. In 1960, for example, new measures of financial control in the rural communes were announced as having been decided by the Central Committee of the Party.[1] The Party's concern with agricultural banking affairs would seem to be especially in evidence at the level of the *hsien*.[2] This is one example of the growing significance of *hsien* Party committees in the early 1960s. The Party organisation is, nevertheless, also active in relation to urban banking. In 1960, to quote an example, the Central Committee's Department of Finance and Trade held a large on-the-spot conference in Shanghai to consider financial and banking work in cities.[3]

Third, the influence of the Soviet banking system on the development of the Chinese Communist banks has been strong. There are obvious parallels between the position and functions of the People's Bank and Gosbank, the Bank of China and Vneshtorgbank, the Construction Bank and Stroibank (but it should be noted that Stroibank was not established until 1959, when it replaced four specialist investment banks—while the Construction Bank dated from 1954). The centralizing of accounts and clearances in the People's Bank and Gosbank is similar, as is the supervisory role of the banks over

---

[1] *Red Flag (Hongqi)*, No. 16, August 16, 1960, p. 20. Huang Ya-kuang, Deputy Director, the People's Bank: 'Non-Cash Settlement of Accounts through the Bank in Our Country'.
[2] *Ta Kung Daily (Dagong Bao)*, Peking, October 17, 1963, p. 1. Editorial, and *Red Flag (Hongqi)*, No. 23, December 12, 1963, p. 28. Teng Tze-hui: loc. cit.
[3] *People's Daily (Renmin Ribao)*, March 29, 1960, p. 1.

enterprises. In the Soviet Union, 'the importance of Gosbank as an organ capable of enforcing centrally determined financial and credit policies' grew after the decentralization measures of 1957.[1] It is probable that in China the significance of the People's Bank also increased after the similar, although not identical, reforms in that country.

Fourth, the banks in China, as in the Soviet Union, perform an all-important role of supervision over the whole economy. This will be further considered when we come to treat of credit policy.

2. CURRENCY

The issue and control of currency is undertaken by the People's Bank. The ban on any other source of currency has been strongly maintained, as when attempts of communes to issue currency were forbidden,[2] with an insistence all the stronger from memories of China's earlier monetary experiences.

For a long period before 1949, China had been split into a number of separate monetary areas, reflecting the political fragmentation of the country under the successive impacts of the Japanese invasion and the civil war.[3] In addition, the circulation inside China of foreign currency (especially Hong Kong dollars) and of gold and silver, had been encouraged by the inflation. One of the great early achievements of the Communist Government after 1949, second only to the political unification of the country, was the monetary unification and the ending of inflation.

The Communist currency unit, the People's Currency (*Jenminpi* or JMP, also known as the *yuan*), was first issued in December 1948, at the same time as the formation of the People's Bank, and some months before the establishment of the People's Republic. It superseded first the various currencies issued in the different areas under Communist control and then, in the wake of further Communist advances, the other currencies circulating in China. The last of the local currencies were withdrawn in 1951, except in Tibet where local notes circulated until 1959. The circulation of gold, silver and foreign currencies had already been prohibited and the JMP became the sole currency in the country.[4]

Measures which the new government took to stabilize the currency (which had already been subject to severe inflation since the first issue of JMP in December 1948) included the decree of April 1950 by which all state undertakings had to deposit their spare cash with the People's Bank and make all important transactions by bank transfer. Subsequently, restrictions on holding cash were extended to individuals and private undertakings. The drives of 1950–2 for subscription to bonds for the Korean war and punitive fines on private enterprises in the course of the 'five-antis' campaign,[5] all had an anti-

---

[1] A. Nove: op. cit., p. 118.
[2] See p. 71 fn. 3 above.
[3] Shun-hsin Chou: op. cit., pp. 1–5, and R. Hsia: *Price Control in Communist China*, New York, 1953, pp. 73–4.
[4] *People's Handbook* (*Renmin Shouce*) *1952*, pp. 276–7, and Cheng Cho-yüan: op. cit., pp. 65–7 and 152, and *Economic Research* (*Jingji Yanjiu*), No. 1, January 1965, p. 32. Yang P'ei-hsin: 'Brief Discussion of the Stability of the *Jenminpi*.'
[5] This campaign was against bribery, tax evasion, fraud, theft of state property and of state economic secrets.

inflationary effect. The fundamental measure which curbed the inflation was, of course, the raising of adequate revenues instead of reliance on deficit financing. The initial inflation of the JMP, however, meant that it circulated in very large denominations. In 1955 this was remedied by a new currency issue, one *yuan* of which was exchanged for ten thousand *yuan* of the old. The new JMP was issued in notes of ten, five, three, two and one *yuan*. Notes and (from 1957) coin were issued also in denominations of less than one *yuan*.[1]

In 1964, the ten, five and three *yuan* notes issued in 1955 (but printed in 1953) were withdrawn from circulation.[2] The five *yuan* notes of 1956 remained in use, but none of any higher denomination. One reason for this measure may have been that the withdrawn notes were printed in the Soviet Union and that it was feared the Russians might infiltrate large quantities of identical notes with the purpose of disrupting China's financial stability. It has been suggested that the withdrawal of many notes of higher denomination, without the promise of anonymity for those exchanging them for new notes that was a feature of the 1955 new issue, may have been directed at 'spontaneous capitalists' and corrupt cadres who would thereby lose their hoarded wealth.[3] Ten *yuan* notes were again issued in 1966.

The backing of the JMP is a subject of considerable ambiguity and debate among Chinese economists. Unlike the rouble, the JMP is not even nominally on a gold standard. Many Chinese economists, however, maintain that a link with gold still exists. Huang Ta, a prominent monetary economist, describes gold as the 'monetary commodity of the socialist economy', the intrinsic value of which is symbolized by the JMP.[4] According to Hsü Ti-hsin, another notable economist, the first guarantee for the currency is commodities in circulation, a second essential being 'an appropriate quantity of precious metals'.[5] The discussion on this topic continues.

Without any legal limitation to the note issue, there is general agreement that 'the circulation of money should be adapted to the circulation of commodities'. Furthermore, it is agreed, only the circulation of consumer goods and services are really relevant, as almost all means of production are paid for through bank transfers and not in cash.[6] In 1959 non-cash transfers accounted for about 85 per cent of the total number of transactions passing through the People's Bank.[7] Cash (meaning here notes and coin) is used by enterprises and

[1] *Collected Laws and Regulations* ... Vol. 1, p. 265, and ibid., Vol. 6, p. 348.

[2] *People's Daily* (*Renmin Ribao*), April 14, 1964, p. 6.

[3] *China Monthly* (*Zuguo*), No. 3, June 1964, pp. 154–5. Tai Ho-cho: 'Communist China's Withdrawal of *Jenminpi*.'

[4] *Economic Research* (*Jingji Yanjiu*), No. 4, August 1957, p. 68. Huang Ta: '*Jenminpi* Is the Symbol of the Intrinsic Value of the Monetary Commodity', and Huang Ta: *Currency and Currency Circulation in China's Socialist Economy* (in Chinese), Peking, 1964, pp. 70–6.

[5] Hsü Ti-hsin: op. cit., p. 193. For further discussion of the subject, see also *Economic Research* (*Jingji Yanjiu*), No. 2, April 1957, pp. 36–50. Shih Wu: 'A Tentative Discussion of *Jenminpi* on the Basis of the Marxist Theory of Currency', and ibid., No. 5, May 1965, pp. 15–19. Yü Lin: 'Price Stability and Our Monetary System', and ibid., No. 2, February 1966, pp. 45–8. Wang K'e-hua and Wang P'ei-chen: 'What *Jenminpi* Really Represents', and *China Weekly* (*Zuguo*), No. 464, December 4, 1961, p. 203. Liu Yung-hua: 'The Chinese Communist Currency System.'

[6] *Economic Research* (*Jingji Yanjiu*), No. 2, February 1963, pp. 27–8. Lin Chi-k'en: 'The Role of the Law of the Circulation of Money in the Socialist System.'

[7] *Red Flag* (*Hongqi*), No. 16, August 16, 1960, p. 17. Huang Ya-kuang: loc. cit.

organs for wage payments (including payments by units of collective agriculture to peasants for wage points earned), for purchasing agricultural produce from individual peasants (as distinct from purchases from agricultural collectives, when payment is for the most part by bank transfer),[1] and for certain miscellaneous expenditures.

The restriction of cash payments to these purposes, among which after-harvest wage payments to peasants and the purchase of agricultural produce ranks high, results in marked seasonal fluctuations in the note issue. The peak period, in December and January, comes after payment has been made for state agricultural purchases and just before the Spring Festival (the old-style New Year—the greatest festival of the year, before which private debts are customarily settled, as well as extra consumer goods purchased). At this period, the note issue runs about 50 per cent above the lowest point which occurs in May and June.[2]

Figures for note issues are not published, but Choh-ming Li, in the *Economic Development of Communist China*, has calculated the average volume of circulation in 1956 as ¥12,770 million, with a velocity of circulation of only three. The slowness of the velocity is accounted for by peasant hoarding which developed markedly from 1956; after collectivization, individual peasant families were not able to hold stocks of grain, cotton and other crops and were thus driven to keep their savings in cash.[3]

Both capital investment and increases in working capital have been financed out of increases in the note issue. An analysis by Choh-ming Li concludes that the chief reason for the rise in the note issue during the First Five Year Plan period was the financing of investment.[4] In 1962 and 1963 references were made to an increase in the note issue as a possible source of loanable funds for working capital.[5] The demand for bank loans for working capital should, in accordance with official regulations, have been limited by the insistence on material backing for these loans. However, during the Great Leap, such precautions were disregarded and in practice there were no limits set to the granting of bank loans for working capital.[6] As we shall see, diversion to investment purposes of loans given for working capital was not an uncommon phenomenon.

While there is no official gold exchange rate for the JMP, the People's Bank pays (or in 1957 paid) ¥95 a *liang* for gold already held by the general public. From October 1957 all newly produced gold was to be bought by the Bank for ¥130 a *liang* of 100 per cent gold content, the previous price having been

---

[1] 'After agricultural producer co-operatives had been formed, non-cash settlement of accounts began to be practised in the countryside. After the establishment of the communes, over 80 per cent of the payments for farm produce went through non-cash settlement.' *Red Flag* (*Hongqi*), No. 16, August 16, 1960, p. 17. Huang Ya-kuang: loc. cit.

[2] Hsü Ti-hsin: op. cit., p. 195.

[3] Choh-ming Li: op. cit., p. 159, and *People's Daily* (*Renmin Ribao*), February 27, 1957, p. 5, and *People's Handbook* (*Renmin Shouce*) *1958*, p. 216.

[4] Choh-ming Li: op. cit., p. 163.

[5] *Economic Research* (*Jingji Yanjiu*), No. 10, October 1962, p. 17. Kao Hsiang: loc. cit., and ibid., No. 10, October 1963, p. 7. Ko Chih-ta: 'The Problem of Comprehensive Equilibrium of Finance, Credit and Raw Materials.'

[6] *Ta Kung Daily* (*Dagong Bao*), Peking, August 17, 1958, p. 4. Ko Chih-ta and Yang Che-hsing: 'Give Correct Consideration to the Question of Equilibrium in the Planning of Finance and Banking.'

¥110·25 for gold mined in north-east China, and ¥95 for that mined in the rest of the country; ¥95 a *liang* had also been paid for gold produced by co-operatives and individual peasants. The 1957 rise in purchasing price was intended to stimulate production which, in 1956, had fallen to half the maximum recorded level. For many mines, costs of production were, before October 1957, above the price obtainable. Peasant production, especially after agricultural co-operativization, had fallen even more severely than the output of mines. In 1957, simultaneously with the rise in price, the 5 per cent tax on peasant gold production was lifted.[1] It should be noted that the post-1957 price of ¥130 a *liang* of 100 per cent gold content was still a little below the world market level.[2]

Private persons are allowed to hold gold and silver although, at least at times, the amount permitted to be held has been stringently restricted,[3] and confiscations have been reported. Apart from jewellery sales, gold and silver (and also foreign exchange) may not be sold except to banks which are also the only licit source of gold for medical, industrial and other uses.[4] It has not, however, been possible entirely to suppress black market transactions in precious metals.

The only exchange rates of the JMP described by the Chinese authorities as official have been the commercial rates with the rouble which, in 1965, stood at ¥2·222 to one new rouble (the equivalent of two old roubles to one *yuan*) and with the Rumanian *lei* which, in the same year, was ¥0·333 to one *lei*. In addition are the non-commercial rates (applying to the expenditure of diplomatic missions, on cultural activities, etc.) fixed in April 1963 between the Chinese *yuan* and the currencies of eleven Communist countries. With the rouble, the non-commercial rate is given as ¥1·29 to one new rouble (as compared with ¥1·66 for this rate before 1963). In 1965 no quotation had been set for the Cuban peso because accounts between China and Cuba were kept and settled in sterling. At this date, foreign exchange quotations were quoted by Chinese banks between the *yuan* and twenty non-communist currencies. The buying and selling rates for sterling were given as ¥6·859 and ¥6·927 respectively; this results in a cross rate between the rouble and sterling at variance with that officially ruling.[5]

Considerable research has been done outside China to elucidate the course of the rouble-*yuan* exchange rates since 1950. One study, to which the reader is referred for a thorough treatment of this involved topic, concludes that the effective rouble-*yuan* rate has greatly overvalued the rouble.[6]

[1] *Collected Laws and Regulations* ... Vol. 6, pp. 403–9.

[2] ¥130 a *liang* is equivalent at the exchange rate against sterling mentioned below to 235s 10d per fine oz. The average price of gold on the London market in October 1957 was 249s 10d a fine oz. The difference of about 6 per cent may not be unreasonable, in view of the costs of purchasing and of transporting the gold from the point of purchase to any centre where the world market price would be obtainable.

[3] Cheng Cho-yuan: op. cit., p. 39.

[4] *Economic Research* (*Jingji Yanjiu*), No. 10, October 1962, p. 21. Kao Hsiang: loc. cit.

[5] *Current Events* (*Shishi Shouce*), No. 3, February 1965, pp. 37–8, and Foreign Business Bureau, Head Office of the People's Bank: *Handbook of the Currencies of All Nations* (in Chinese), Peking, 1963, pp. 13–14.

[6] *China Quarterly*, No. 17, January–March 1964, pp. 192–204. Kang Chao and Ma Feng-hwa: 'A Study of the Rouble-*Yuan* Exchange Rate.' See M. A. Klochko: *Soviet Scientist in China*, London, 1964, p. 62. 'At the official exchange rate, one *yuan* was worth two old

For some years a large part of China's foreign reserves was held in sterling. However, the possibility of sterling devaluation, and also the fear that sterling assets might be frozen if the Vietnam War escalated, led China in 1965 to switch from sterling to gold and other precious metals and to Swiss francs. Experience in the early 1950s when, at the time of the Korean war, the United States froze some of China's foreign holdings, no doubt influenced China's policy. Officially, China refuses to hold American dollars, although some Chinese dollar holdings through nominees are rumoured to exist. The question of foreign currency reserves is, in some respects, even more pressing for China than for other under-developed countries which have access to the facilities of the International Monetary Fund and also have greater possibilities of bilateral assistance from other lands.

3. CREDIT POLICY

The tight control exercised by the People's Bank over business dealings, arising from the obligation of state enterprises, institutions and organs to deposit their cash with the Bank and to conduct all financial transactions with other concerns through the Bank, is reinforced by giving to the Bank a virtual monopoly, shared however with the rural credit co-operatives and now with the Agricultural Bank, of most types of short-term credit. The prohibition of short-term commercial credit between state enterprises, institutions, organs, military units, mass organizations and co-operative concerns in their mutual dealings, was promulgated in the currency control regulations of 1950 with the proviso that this item, like the rest of the regulations, should be introduced gradually and in stages.[1] In 1953, the measures regarding commercial credit were further tightened 'according to Soviet experience and China's actual circumstances'.[2] However, the exceptions allowed or, in any case, practised, were considerable,[3] and in 1955 a further attempt was made to curb their extent.[4] It still remained permissible for advance payments to be made to organs of the Ministry of Foreign Trade for imports, to private enterprises for goods being processed (this was 1955 when many privately owned concerns still existed), and to peasants for purchases of their products.[5] In 1959, the sale on credit of large items of agricultural machinery to communes was regarded as licit.[6]

It has not always proved possible to enforce the ban on commercial credit. Complaints were made about the selling of coal on credit in 1956.[7] In 1959,

---

roubles, but in purchasing power, it was worth more. In reports on the Chinese national economy, Soviet economists placed the purchasing power of one *yuan* at about six old roubles. It was at an unofficial rate of ten roubles to a *yuan* that we bought Chinese money from one another.'

[1] *New China Monthly (Xinhua Yuebao)*, No. 16, February 1951, pp. 841–2.
[2] *Collected Laws and Regulations* . . . Vol. 1, pp. 271–2.
[3] In 1954 a study of five industrial ministries showed that 15·4 per cent of their working capital was currently lent out as commercial credit, and 17·2 per cent of the working capital used by them was borrowed from others. *Collected Laws and Regulations* . . . Vol. 1, p. 270.
[4] *Collected Laws and Regulations* . . . Vol. 1, pp. 269–73 and 278–86.
[5] Ibid., p. 272.
[6] *People's Daily (Renmin Ribao)*, August 16, 1959 (SCMP 2081). Editorial.
[7] *People's Handbook (Renmin Shouce) 1957*, p. 516.

an editorial in the *People's Daily* stated that 'as a rule, credit sales should be stopped in future'.[1] Five years later the 'non-antagonistic' struggle to abolish commercial credit still continued: 'a struggle between the planned nature of socialist credit and the force of traditional custom'. Only those cases of credit extension included in state plans should, it was insisted, be allowed.[2]

There is no formal ban on private money-lending. 'Among the masses it continues of course to be legal for those with money to lend to those without, so long as the rate of interest is not high', wrote Teng Tzu-hui, Director of the Party Central Committee's Rural Work Department in 1963.[3] Nevertheless, the revival of money lending in the countryside has been a source of anxiety to the government, especially from 1963 onwards. Credit co-operatives are prescribed as the remedy. According to a survey made in Fukien province in 1955, after the formation of credit co-operatives the interest charged by private money lenders fell from 10–15 per cent a month to $1 \cdot 4$–2 per cent a month.[4] However, as we are not told the date when credit co-operatives were established in this province, it is not possible to say if part of the reported fall in interest rates was due to currency stabilization rather than to the co-operatives. In 1958, a case is recorded in Honan where grain was lent privately for six months at 50 per cent interest.[5] For urban workers, mutual aid savings associations perform the same type of service, the provision of personal credit, as do credit co-operatives for the peasants. Trade unions are active in organizing these associations.[6] Pawnshops are another source of credit. On occasion, trade warehouses also fulfil this function, although in this case it is uncertain whether loans are made to individual clients or only to clients in their corporate business capacities.[7]

The sources of the loanable funds of the banks are budgetary grants, budgetary surpluses, the bank's own capital (deriving originally from budgetary grants and supplemented by ploughed back profits),[8] deposits of state organs, enterprises and of other bodies held in the bank and deposits belonging to individuals, and lastly, the expansion of the note issue.[9] We shall now briefly review these several sources.

[1] *People's Daily* (*Renmin Ribao*), August 16, 1959 (SCMP 2081). Editorial.

[2] *Red Flag* (*Hongqi*), No. 1, January 4, 1964, p. 24. Tuan Yün: loc. cit.

[3] Ibid., No. 23, December 12, 1963, p. 24. Teng Tzu-hui: loc. cit. However, a reader of the *Daily Worker* was told that money lending between individuals for the purpose of getting interest constituted exploitation. *Daily Worker* (*Gongren Ribao*), August 17, 1963, p. 4.

[4] Hsü Ti-hsin: op. cit., p. 244.

[5] *Honan Daily* (*Honan Ribao*), July 25, 1958 (SCMP 1838).

[6] *Daily Worker* (*Gongren Ribao*), December 9, 1964, p. 2. Trade Union of Poketu Mechanical Section, Tsitsihar Railway Bureau: 'Some Lessons Learned on the Efficient Operation of Mutual Savings Associations.'

[7] *Collected Laws and Regulations* . . . Vol. 6, p. 380. On trade warehouses, see p. 292 and p. 306 above.

[8] The income of the People's Bank is derived mainly from the difference between interest paid on deposits and obtained on loans; also from remittance charges, handling charges and other miscellaneous items. Since 1958 its income has been exempt from industrial and commercial tax. See *People's Taxation* (*Renmin Shuiwu*), September 19, 1958, p. 13.

[9] *Economic Research* (*Jingji Yanjiu*), No. 3, March 1964, pp. 6–7. Li Ch'eng-jui: 'An Exploratory Discussion of the General Equilibrium of the Budget, Credit and Material Supplies.'

Budgetary grants for capital purposes are non-returnable and interest-free. The grants made, for example, by the Construction Bank are of this nature. In the budget, provision is also made for additional working capital: we shall see that the banks have been a major, and at times the main channel, through which budgetary funds for working capital have flowed to enterprises.

In Chapter 14, reference has been made to the use of budget surpluses by the People's Bank as a source for making additional loans for working capital. We have also seen that all types of enterprises and undertakings are compelled to hold their spare cash on deposit at the People's Bank. This provides a considerable fund available for lending.

The urban population is constantly urged, and at times has been subject to strong pressure, to put money on deposit with the People's Bank (either in current deposits or, preferably, in fixed period savings deposits). The People's Bank has opened many special offices to deal with savings and sometimes, too, street associations act as agents of the People's Bank in savings matters. In 1959, over 100,000 establishments were reported to be handling savings deposits;[1] these, no doubt, were in addition to the similar number of rural credit co-operatives which perform the same function of mobilizing small savings in the countryside. It was estimated that at the end of the First Five Year Plan, about 5 per cent of urban wages was currently being deposited in savings accounts;[2] it is not stated if this figure is exclusive of purchases of savings bonds, although that would appear to be the case. Figures published for savings are either percentages or absolute increases on an unknown base[3] or absolute figures for isolated periods.

Official pronouncements have frequently emphasized that savings should be voluntary and withdrawals permitted. Insistent reports, however, tell of savings being deducted compulsorily from wages and of restrictions on withdrawals.

Interest is paid on bank deposits, except on a part of the deposits of departments of finance and of other state organs; it is paid on deposits of state enterprises.[4] Interest rates were lowered abruptly in 1950 from the fantastic levels reached during the inflation.[5] By stages they were lowered still further until, from the beginning of 1959, 0·18 per cent *per mensem* was paid on current accounts, 0·3 per cent *per mensem* on half-year period deposits, and 0·4 per cent *per mensem* on one-year period deposits. Subsequently rates may have been raised, as rates of 0·51 per cent a month on one-year deposits were reported in 1964, falling by 1966, however, to 0·33 per cent. Deposits owned by Overseas Chinese have attracted higher rates of interest.[6] Devices combining

---

[1] *Ta Kung Daily* (*Dagong Bao*), Peking, October 12, 1959, p. 3. Ts'ao Chü-ju: loc. cit.
[2] Ibid., August 17, 1958, p. 4. Ko Chih-ta and Yang Che-hsing: loc. cit.
[3] e.g. *Ten Great Years*, Peking, 1960, p. 219.
[4] *Red Flag* (*Hongqi*), No. 11, June 1, 1959, p. 12. Tuan Yün: 'The Problem of Working Capital, Credit Funds and Their Management', and *Collected Banking Laws and Regulations* (in Chinese), 1957, p. 57.
[5] Until the inflation was brought under control, various forms of 'principal and value preserving deposits' were in operation. Hsin Ying: *The Price Problems of Communist China*, Hong Kong, 1954, pp. 61–6.
[6] *New China Fortnightly* (*Xinhua Banyuekan*), No. 147, January 10, 1959, p. 64, and *Far*

savings deposits with lottery tickets have also been used from time to time.[1]

The great bulk of bank loans are made to enterprises (*ch'iyeh*). Institutions (*shihyeh*), administrative organs and individuals are not eligible for loans from banks.[2]

Apart from the investment grants made by the Construction Bank and the Bank of Communications, funds from banks are in general supposed to be given only for short-term purposes, mainly for working capital. A partial exception is made in the case of agriculture, for which medium-term loans (for up to five years) have been provided by the successive agricultural banks and by the People's Bank.

Control over working capital has caused continuous anxiety. Frequent complaints have been made about the wrongful conversion to investment purposes of funds provided for working capital, leading to shortage of working capital on the one hand and, on the other, to unplanned investment projects straining still further the tight supplies of equipment and raw materials. In an attempt to introduce more stringent controls, changes have been made from time to time in the method of supplying working capital to enterprises. These changes we shall now review.

In the period of rehabilitation before 1953, the People's Bank made loans to central government ministries, not to individual enterprises. This was in line with the centralizing policy of that time, a policy dictated both for political reasons and in order to stem inflation. The ministries were responsible for distributing the loan funds down the various levels of the hierarchy, until eventually they reached the enterprise. This method of credit control by the ministries enabled them to use credit as a weapon to strengthen the position of state enterprises within yet unsocialized branches of industry and to facilitate state control of raw materials. Before long, however, more independence was given to the enterprises themselves to manage their own affairs: this was signalled by the adoption of the economic accounting system. The banks, therefore, began to make loans directly to enterprises.[3]

Total working capital in the economy was increasing very rapidly in the later 1950s with the increase in production. The total sum of enterprises' 'self-owned funds'[4] rose from ¥12,380 million in 1955 to ¥21,430 million in 1959, largely due to the increase in retainable profits accruing to enterprises at the time of the Great Leap.[5]

In 1957, bank credit was reported to account for 54·7 per cent of the

---

Eastern Economic Review, April 7, 1966, p. 5, but see *People's Handbook* (*Renmin Shouce*) *1959*, p. 370, for divergent rates of interest on deposits of various types. It should be noted that at the same time that interest rates were reduced in January 1959, income from interest was exempted from income tax; see p. 380 above. From July 1965 no interest was payable on accounts of foreigners in Peking. On the subject of remittance from Overseas Chinese, see Appendix I below.

[1] Hsin Ying: op. cit., pp. 66–8.
[2] *China Monthly* (*Zuguo*), No. 11, January 1, 1966. Li Ch'a: 'The Chinese Communist Plans for Industrial Finance', p. 6.
[3] Hsü Ti-hsin: op. cit., p. 240.
[4] See p. 26 above.
[5] *Finance* (*Caizheng*), No. 18, September 24, 1959, p. 21, and p. 166 above.

working capital in the whole of the state-owned sector of the economy.[1] In 1958, the budget envisaged an increase in enterprises' working capital totalling ¥2,760 million, of which ¥700 million was allocated from the budget, while the bank credit plan of that year provided for ¥2,060 million in additional loans to enterprises.[2] Thus the 1958 plan envisaged bank loans accounting for some 75 per cent of that part of the rise in enterprises' working capital which derived from sources external to the enterprises themselves.

The banks were able to act more quickly than financial departments. Bank branches were numerous and in closer touch with enterprises; bank representatives, as we have seen, were stationed at large factories and mines. The same circumstances put the banks in a better position to check the widespread abuses of working capital—above all its improper conversion to investment purposes. In addition, the continued centralization of the banking system, in contrast to the financial departments, may have been thought to make the banks the better instruments for enforcing central policy in this respect.

For these reasons, it was decided that from 1958 the banks should supply 70 per cent of the increased needs for working capital for enterprises under local authorities, the remaining 30 per cent to come from the local budgets.[3] One factor which must have limited the importance of this step is that bank credit already accounted for 70 per cent of the working capital of state commerce (or at least had done so in 1955) and commerce, in its turn, accounted for some 85 per cent of the total bank loans outstanding to industry and commerce at the end of September 1957.[4] Another change in 1958 was the announcement that a small part of the fixed quota working capital of central government industrial enterprises would come from bank loans, instead of the whole amount being drawn from budgetary appropriations:[5] here the

---

[1] *Economic Research* (*Jingji Yanjiu*), No. 9, September 1962, p. 5. Huang Ta: 'The Credit Policy of Banks and the Circulation of Currency.' Bank loans outstanding at the end of September 1957 to state industry and commerce and to handicraft co-operatives were as follows:

Bank loans to:	¥ million
Industry under central ministries	1,389
Local Industry	625
Commerce	13,889
Handicraft co-operatives	347
Total	¥16,250

Source: Computed from figures given in *Collected Laws and Regulations* . . . Vol. 6, pp. 345–7. The decentralization measures had not become effective at that date, which explains the relatively small volume of loans to local industry. The overwhelming proportion of bank credit going to commerce is apparent.

[2] *Collected Laws and Regulations* . . . Vol. 7, p. 132.

[3] Ibid., Vol. 6, p. 330. This is consonant with the banks supplying 75 per cent of the increase for all enterprises in 1958, see above.

[4] *New China Monthly* (*Xinhua Yuebao*), No. 69, July 1955, p. 192. Hu Ching-yün, Vice-President of the People's Bank of China: Report at the Second National Conference on the Credit and Loan System of State Commerce, and see fn. 1 above.

[5] *Collected Laws and Regulations* . . . Vol. 7, pp. 132–3.

phrase 'fixed-quota working capital' appears to be used almost interchangeably with 'self-owned working capital' although later, as we shall see, it was given a more specific meaning.

The process was carried still further by the decision that from the beginning of 1959 all working capital of state enterprises, including the former 'self-owned funds', should be in the form of interest-bearing loans from the People's Bank. It was insisted that this did not mean that the financial departments and the economic departments at all levels in charge of enterprises were to be free of responsibility in respect of working capital. They were still supposed to supervise its use and also had to enter into their budget the estimates for increased needs of working capital. However, these sums were all to be channelled to the enterprises through the local branches of the People's Bank.[1] It should be noted that now for the first time, enterprises had to pay interest on the whole of their working capital (apart from any that had come from retained profits); this was meant as an incentive to economize in the amount used. The subject of interest payments will be further treated below.

Exceptions to this general unification under the control of the People's Bank of working capital were made for enterprises under the Military Council and under the Second Ministry of Machine Building, for handicraft cooperatives, factories ancillary to state organs and institutions, for Overseas Chinese investment corporations, for seed funds under the Ministry of Agriculture, and for certain other cases; these were to retain the former system. Nor were funds amassed by enterprises from their retained profits to be transformed into bank loans.[2]

As a result of the change in the method of control of working capital introduced in 1959, by the beginning of 1961 over 95 per cent of the total working capital of industry and commerce was estimated to be in the form of bank credit.[3]

The new system still did not solve the difficulty of controlling the use of working capital. The People's Bank was incapable of giving sufficient supervision on its own, and the acquired expertise of the Ministry of Finance in this field was wasted. From July 1961 a reversion was made in the case of industry and transport to something like the earlier system and in 1962 a similar change was extended also to commerce. The working capital requirements of enterprises were now divided into fixed quota working capital (the minimum permanent requirements) and above-quota working capital (to cover seasonal and other temporary needs). In the case of industry and transport, some 80 per cent of fixed quota working capital was to be channelled from the Ministry of Finance or its local departments to the enterprises through the relevant industrial and other economic ministries and departments and only 20 per cent was to go through the People's Bank. The Bank, however, was to be responsible for supplying all above-quota working capital. Bank loans for this purpose were to carry the same interest charges as before

[1] *Collected Laws and Regulations* . . . Vol. 8, p. 158 and Vol. 9, pp. 121–5.
[2] Ibid., Vol. 9, pp. 125–6.
[3] *Economic Research* (*Jingji Yanjiu*), No. 2, February 1961, p. 7. Chi Ts'ai-ch'eng: 'The Form of Comprehensive Financial Plans and the Inter-Relations between Items in Them.'

(0·6 per cent *per mensem*) but interest on fixed quota working capital from the Bank was reduced to 0·18 per cent *per mensem*.[1]

These choppings and changings in methods of providing working capital spotlight a persistent problem. The misappropriation of these funds by enterprises for capital purposes has gone against all the canons of planning, as well as introducing an inflationary element into the economy by over-expanding investment. However, it must be borne in mind that in China, where the marginal efficiency of capital is very high and the capital invested in a new factory can often be recovered within a year,[2] the distinction between working capital and investment capital loses much of its significance, and the inflationary effect of the diversion of working capital is not likely to be so great. This only holds, of course, if the investment project is wisely chosen; and would not, for example, apply to funds sunk and presumably lost in the backyard steel campaign of 1958.

On loans for working capital, interest is payable in contrast to the interest-free budgetary grants for capital investment. Rates of interest on bank loans in China since 1949 have, in almost all cases, been well above the 2 per cent per annum normally charged to state enterprises in the Soviet Union.[3] However, the Chinese rates are low in relation to the marginal efficiency of capital in China and to the rates that could obtain if there were a free market for credit. This must even have been the case with the discriminatory rates charged to private undertakings before 'socialist transformation'. Here the most important discrimination is likely to have been in the direct rationing of loans to private applicants, rather than in the higher rates charged.[4] In the case of state enterprises, too, the function of the rate of interest has been to encourage economy in the use of loans, not to ration credit, which is done by direct means. The effect of interest payments is, of course, to diminish enterprises' profits. Therefore the extent to which interest rates cause an enterprise to economize on borrowing depends on its eagerness to maximize profits. This, in turn, depends on the importance to it of profits as a success indicator, or the strength of its desire to maximize its retainable share of profits. In any case, interest rates play a minor, not a regulatory, role in the Chinese economy.

From the early 1950s up to 1957, there was a general downward trend of interest rates on bank loans. This was reflected in the lowered rates announced in 1955. These rates, in the case of industrial concerns, were fixed at 0·48 per cent *per mensem* for state enterprises, at 0·69 per cent for joint state-private enterprises, and at 0·99 per cent for private undertakings. Rates to commercial enterprises were somewhat higher, but differing similarly between categories of borrowers. As far as agriculture was concerned, the special funds to help poor peasants on entering co-operatives carried 0·4 per cent *per*

---

[1] *Economic Research (Jingji Yanjiu)*, Vol. 12, pp. 72–4, and *Ta Kung Daily (Dagong Bao)*, Peking, August 3, 1962, p. 1, and Unpublished paper of Ezra Vogel of Harvard University, relating to the financial system in Mainland China.

[2] See p. 371 above.

[3] A. Nove: op. cit., p. 118.

[4] The People's Bank had an important role in assisting 'socialist transformation' by giving loans to help newly established handicraft co-operatives and joint state-private enterprises. *Ta Kung Daily (Dagong Bao)*, Peking, October 12, 1959, p. 3. Ts'ao Chü-ju: loc. cit.

mensem, loans to agricultural producer co-operatives 0·6 per cent, to mutual aid teams, to disaster areas and to individual peasants buying equipment, 0·75 per cent, and to individual peasants for other productive purposes, 0·9 per cent. Interest on overdue loans of all types was surcharged 10 per cent, a penalty which would still leave the interest payable far below the marginal rate of efficiency of capital in China.[1] This factor, as well as the poverty of the borrowers, must contribute to the difficulty often experienced in recovering loans made to agricultural collectives and individual peasants.[2] (Most urban loans, being made to state enterprises, are simpler to recover.) No instances have come to our knowledge of interest rates in China in recent years varying according to the length of time for which the bank loans were originally made.

Two years later, in 1957, difference in rates on loans to state industry and commerce, which had obtained since 1949, was abolished by raising the industrial rate to the level of the commercial at 0·6 per cent *per mensem*. This reversal of the movement towards lower rates was made to encourage economy in the use of working capital. At the same time, the higher rates on loans to joint state-private industrial and commercial concerns were assimilated to that for state enterprises in the case of those joint undertakings which had gone over to the system of fixed dividends. The 0·6 per cent rate was also to apply to handicraft co-operatives. Small pedlars and other independent workers would continue to be charged 0·72 per cent *per mensem*. Bank loans made to credit co-operatives were to bear 0·51 per cent *per mensem* interest, the same rate as was paid on sums deposited in the bank by these co-operatives. In certain places, where much of the credit co-operatives borrowing from their members took the form of fixed term deposits which carried relatively high interest, the co-operatives would make a loss if their own bank deposits earned only 0·51 per cent a month. Such co-operatives might be paid 0·66 per cent *per mensem* on deposits made with the banks for periods of over a year.[3] However, this rate would still be quite inadequate when, as reported in Kirin province in 1955, credit co-operatives were paying 17 per cent per annum on deposits made with them.[4]

On loans to agriculture in 1957, it was announced that the interest rate would remain unchanged at 0·48 per cent a month: apparently, although we have found no such report, the rate had at some time in the period 1955-7 been lowered from 0·6 per cent to 0·48 per cent a month. Rates on loans to individual members of agricultural co-operatives remained unchanged at 0·72 per cent a month and to poor peasants entering co-operatives at 0·4 per cent a month. Now, therefore, interest on loans to state and collective agriculture stood at a lower level than that on loans to other sectors of the economy and at a lower rate than for loans to rural credit co-operatives.[5] This caused

[1] *People's Handbook (Renmin Shouce) 1956*, pp. 536-7.
[2] e.g., see *Collected Laws and Regulations* ... Vol. 4, p. 302, and *Ta Kung Daily (Dagong Bao)*, Peking, April 26, 1966, p. 1.
[3] *Collected Laws and Regulations* ... Vol. 6, pp. 345-7.
[4] Administrative Office of the Central Committee of the CCP (ed.): *The High Tide of Socialism in the Chinese Countryside* (in Chinese), Peking, 1956, Vol. 1, p. 431. I am indebted to Jack Gray of the University of Glasgow for drawing my attention to this reference.
[5] *Collected Laws and Regulations* ... Vol. 6, pp. 345-7.

confusion after the setting up of the communes because these new units combined activities of many types. So it was decided that from January 1959, all loans to the communes, whether for agriculture, industry or commerce with the exceptions to be noted, were to carry interest at 0·6 per cent *per mensem*. This rate thus became common to all bank loans to state and collective undertakings, with the exception of loans to enterprises handed down to communes, and of loans to credit departments of communes, in both of which cases only 0·42 per cent *per mensem* was to be charged.[1] The 0·42 per cent *per mensem* paid by credit departments of communes on bank loans was the same rate as these organs received on their bank deposits.[2]

In 1961 we have seen that different interest rates were fixed for bank loans for fixed-quota and above-quota working capital, the former to carry only 0·18 per cent *per mensem*, but the latter (on which pressure to economize was concentrated), to continue at the general rate of 0·6 per cent.

The rate on loans to agriculture was reduced in 1961 to 0·48 per cent *per mensem*, so that once more it was below the rate for other sectors. This was, of course, in accord with the current policy of giving priority to agriculture. It is significant that the lower rates now applied not only to loans to communes and their constituent units, and to state farms, but even to loans to individual commune members.[3] Many of these loans, especially those to individuals, were probably channelled through credit co-operatives which, as we have seen, undertake much of the basic level rural banking tasks on behalf of the banks.

On a number of occasions, interest-free bank loans are reported to have been given to rural borrowers, notably disaster areas and, in a different category, grain-surplus districts.[4] In addition to these, there have been the non-returnable grants as made, for example, to poor communes in 1959 and 1960.

In theory, the allocation of working capital should be determined by the state on the basis of enterprises' production and other circumstances and should be entered into the budget or economic plan at the beginning of each year.[5] However, it has been found difficult to keep the total of loans down to the figure in the budget. The disparity between budgetary estimates for additional allotment of credit funds to the bank and realized figures illustrates this point. For 1958 and 1959, the last years for which final accounts were published, the figures are as follows:

---

[1] *People's Handbook (Renmin Shouce) 1959*, p. 368, and *Collected Laws and Regulations* ... Vol. 9, p. 127.

[2] *People's Handbook (Renmin Shouce) 1959*, p. 368. These credit departments were supposed to be basic level agencies of the People's Bank and hence their dealings with the higher levels of the Bank were internal to the banking system, and thus in a different category from loans by banks to outside enterprises. Presumably some institutional arrangement prevented communes from doing all their borrowing through the medium of their credit departments and forced them to undertake much of their borrowing through direct bank loans at 0·6 per cent *per mensem*. The special rates on loans in respect of enterprises transferred to communal control is more difficult to understand.

[3] *Ta Kung Daily (Dagong Bao)*, Peking, April 30, 1961, p. 1.

[4] Ibid., October 13, 1962, p. 1.

[5] Ibid., July 6, 1962, p. 3. Ch'en Tsu-wen: 'The Conservation of State Capital', and *Red Flag (Hongqi)*, No. 1, January 4, 1964, p. 31. Tuan Yün: loc. cit.

Additional Allotment of Credit Funds to the
Banks from the Budget

(Million Yuan)	1958	1959
Sums budgeted	800	3,170
Sums actually expended	1,650	4,430

Sources: *People's Handbook* (*Renmin Shouce*) *1959*, p. 229, and ibid., *1960*, p. 182, and *Collected Laws and Regulations* ... Vol. 9, pp. 64 and 71.

Among the chief items of planning stipulated in 1958 for retention in the hands of the central government was the balancing of credit.[1] From the context it appears that not only monetary equilibrium was meant, but also the appropriate inter-provincial allocation of credit.

According to an article in 1962, the target for loans to enterprises directly controlled by the central government was supposed to be decided and handed down by the central ministry concerned to the enterprises, and also decided and handed down by the head office of the People's Bank to the local branch of the Bank. It is not clear how the power of decision was to be divided between the ministries and the Bank. In the case of locally controlled enterprises, the loan target was to be handed down by the head office of the People's Bank to the Bank's branch in the province, city, or autonomous region where the enterprise was situated. This branch of the Bank was then to consult with the relevant departments of the local authority before the loans were finally paid over to the enterprise.[2]

A major gap in our knowledge of the Chinese economy consists in our ignorance of the relations between local branches of the People's Bank and the corresponding local administrations—notably between provincial branches of the Bank and the provincial authorities. Connected with this is, of course, the degree of control exercised over bank branches by the head office in Peking. At the time of the 1957–8 decentralization, the organization of the banks was not, to our knowledge, affected. However, it might be surmised that relations with the provincial authorities became more complex as these authorities acquired more latitude in their own activities. The onus for enforcing the limits laid down by the central government on the total loans and wage payments permitted for any province, must lie with the provincial branch of the People's Bank (also, in its sphere, with the provincial branch of the Agricultural Bank). In relation to the stability of the currency, it is crucial that over-spending the wage fund should be curbed; that this is difficult to prevent is indicated by a number of press references. However, such over-spending has not occurred on a scale to undermine the value of the currency and this suggests that the Bank has, on this vital matter, been able to stand up to pressure from organs of the provincial governments.

In 1965, local autonomy won a victory at the expense of the centralized authority of the banks. It is perhaps significant that this victory was gained over the Agricultural Bank and not over the more powerful People's Bank. Indeed, it may be surmised that the creation of an Agricultural Bank independent of the People's Bank in itself constituted a victory for local forces,

---

[1] *Collected Laws and Regulations* ... Vol. 8, p. 97.
[2] *People's Daily* (*Renmin Ribao*), April 27, 1962, p. 5. Chin Ch'un: 'A Discussion of Banks' Credit Extension.'

in that it was believed that it would be more vulnerable than if it had been a subsidiary of the People's Bank.

The decentralization of some functions of the Agricultural Bank in 1965 followed earlier experimentation in Hunan. It represented a radical change in the system of distributing agricultural loan funds. Previously the funds available had been centralized under the control first of the People's Bank and, from 1963, of the Agricultural Bank. Allotment of the funds between provinces was a matter internal to the Bank (although negotiations on this matter with the provinces and other interested parties may be presumed), the funds still remaining under the Bank's control after the decision had been made. From 1965 this was altered by the introduction of the 'fixed management system'. The total loanable funds were divided out among the provincial level authorities to provide separate revolving funds for rural credit in each province (and possibly within individual lower local administrative units as well). These funds then came under the control of the local departments of finance which were responsible for planning their further distribution. Funds allocated between localities were 'in principle' to remain undisturbed for three years. However, provinces in temporary need of extra funds might arrange loans from the head office of the Agricultural Bank, which also reserved the right to transfer funds from provincial level units when necessary. The Agricultural Bank appears to remain the channel through which the allotment of funds down to the lower levels are made, and it still supervises the use made of funds by borrowers. The choice of who these borrowers should be, would seem now to be out of the Bank's hands.[1]

The advantages envisaged from the new system were that it would give incentive to local authorities to speed up the repayment of loans and to see that these were used to best advantage. At the same time a danger was foreseen that discipline might be relaxed in loan extension work and that planned totals might be exceeded.[2] Information has not yet come through to enable the success or otherwise of the new system to be judged by outsiders.

The loan allocations received by an enterprise should, in theory, be just sufficient to enable it to finance its production plan (or for a commercial concern, its purchasing and sales plan). In other words, the provision of working funds ought to march in step with the provision of the non-capital factors of production (i.e. raw materials and labour), all in accordance with what was laid down in the enterprise's plan. This result is supposed to be secured by the operation of the 'first principle of socialist credit policy'—that bank loans must be backed by material guarantee.[3]

---

[1] *Rural Finance* (*Nongcun Jinrong*), No. 4–5, February 28, 1965 (SCMM 468). The Agricultural Bank of China: 'Review of the Work in 1964 and Arrangements for the Work in 1965', and *Kuang Ming Daily* (*Guangming Ribao*), June 21, 1965, p. 4. Yü Jui-hsiang: 'Many Advantages from Implementing the Fixed Management System for Funds for Agricultural Loans', and *Ta Kung Daily* (*Dagong Bao*), Peking, November 12, 1965, p. 3. Kuo Hung-hsia: 'Financial Departments Should Orientate Themselves More Towards Rural Problems.'

[2] *Kuang Ming Daily* (*Guangming Ribao*), June 21, 1965, p. 4. Yü Jui-hsiang: loc. cit.

[3] *Ta Kung Daily* (*Dagong Bao*), Peking, August 3, 1962, p. 1, and ibid., June 13, 1962, p. 2. Ch'eng Yüan-yeh: 'Emphasize a Broad Outlook and Manage Credit Funds Efficiently', and *Red Flag* (*Hongqi*), No. 11, June 1, 1959, p. 15. Tuan Yün: loc. cit.

This theoretical harmony between material supplies, bank loans, production and plans, was impossible when all the emphasis came to be placed, during the Great Leap of 1958, on surpassing plans. The banks were in fact enjoined to supply as much credit as enterprises themselves considered they needed. The supervisory function of the banks was whittled away and replaced by that of the Party committees. 'If the quality of products of some enterprises is poor, and the type does not accord with market demand . . . or if some kinds of goods are in surplus, we must rely on the Party, the enterprise, and the masses to correct production, or adjust the production plan. We should not rely on credit restriction to solve the problem.'[1] For banks to set rigid targets for loans was condemned as a mechanical approach. Even the ban on bank loans for investment purposes was modified. Loans might be given for quickly maturing medium and small industrial investment projects operated by organs below the *hsien* level.[2] This policy was reversed in 1959 when the order was given to stop all loans for small capital projects,[3] after, it may be surmised, heavy losses, especially in the loans to the tune of ¥2,000 million which the People's Bank had made to finance the iron and steel campaign, 'both native and modern', of 1958.[4]

Enforcement of the ban on using bank loans for capital investment has proved continuously difficult. In 1964, 'contradictions' between the Banks and enterprises included the proclivity of enterprises to use bank loans for capital purposes.[5] On occasion, the use of working capital to acquire fixed assets might be the only way of keeping production going,[6] and in such a case a manager might argue that on balance the benefits accruing to him, his staff and the enterprise (in the form of higher bonuses or of official approval) in maintaining output, outweighed the risk of disapproval for disregarding regulations. Managers were criticized for this attitude and also for applying for loans to solve difficulties arising from their own inefficiency—thinking that in such circumstances they could 'lean against the big mountain', the state.[7]

After the Great Leap, when strenuous efforts were made to restore order into the economy, especial publicity was given to the supervisory role of the banks. Their control of credit and the rule that all payments between enterprises must be made through the banking system, ought to provide banks with knowledge of the operations of all enterprises. They should thus be able to

[1] *Ta Kung Daily* (*Dagong Bao*), Peking, August 17, 1958, p. 4. Ko Chih-ta and Yang Che-hsing: loc. cit.
[2] Ibid.
[3] *Chinese Currency* (*Zhongguo Jinrong*), May 25, 1959 (ECMM 178). Ch'en Hsi-yu, Vice-Director, People's Bank: 'The 1958 Banking Work and the 1959 Tasks'—excerpts of a report to the National Conference of Branch Managers of the People's Bank.
[4] *Ta Kung Daily* (*Dagong Bao*), Peking, October 12, 1959, p. 3. Ts'ao Chü-ju: loc. cit. However, some of the financial loss incurred by the 'backyard' iron and steel campaign of 1958 may have been borne by reductions in profit remittances permitted to enterprises using the high cost material produced by primitive means. *Collected Financial Laws and Regulations* . . . 1958, July–December, p. 147.
[5] *Red Flag* (*Hongqi*), No. 1, January 4, 1964, p. 27. Tuan Yün: loc. cit.
[6] *People's Daily* (*Renmin Ribao*), September 4, 1963, p. 2. 'Protect the Interests of the State, Observe Regulations Firmly.'
[7] *Red Flag* (*Hongqi*), No. 19, October 1, 1961, p. 20. Li Ch'eng-jui and Tso Ch'un-t'ai: 'Some Problems Concerning Economic Accounting in Socialist Enterprises.'

check that plans are being duly fulfilled, and to spot any deviation from plans. Excess stockpiling of raw material, for example, would lead enterprises to ask for more loans. Large enterprises often have bank staff posted to them to exercise oversight on the spot. Banks are reported to search enterprises' warehouses to reveal malpractices such as unauthorized stockpiling. It is also the duty of banks to refuse to release funds from an enterprise's account for purposes contrary to its plan and to refuse it loans in these circumstances. Similarly, banks supervise rural economic activities. For example, bank workers are reported to have visited production teams to discover why a certain supply and marketing co-operative had not fulfilled its purchasing plan.[1] Of course, the ability of the banks to cope effectively with their supervisory duties depends on the competence of their staff, a factor which is likely to result in very uneven degrees of surveillance over the economy.

In the case of agriculture, both short-term credit and long-term investment funds have been channelled through the same institution—the People's Bank or, when such has existed, the Agricultural Bank. In the period 1953 to 1960 inclusive, the state was reported to have made ¥19,000 million available through the banks as loans to agriculture:[2] this was presumably the sum total of loans made from a revolving fund which, at any one time was considerably less.[3] Loans to agriculture have been in addition to the non-repayable grants to agriculture which included ¥2,500 million allocated to rural communes in 1959 and 1960 together.

A large part of the funds for investment in agriculture was expected to come from agriculture itself, more especially for small projects undertaken by units of collective agriculture. Even in the case of tractor stations, a survey of seven showed that 37 per cent of the funds invested from 1958 to 1960 was provided from the local countryside.[4] Collective agriculture raised nearly 80 per cent of the investment required in the extensive power transmission and electric pump system set up in the Pearl River delta in the early 1960s.[5]

In addition to loans made directly to agricultural units, bank credit is extended to state purchasing agencies to enable them to pay in advance for farm output, thus providing working capital for agriculture, particularly in those areas where the marketed proportion of output is high. These advances are given on the signing of contracts to sell and are used by the state as incentives to encourage the cultivation of priority crops. They are interest free.[6]

[1] *Ta Kung Daily (Dagong Bao)*, Peking, August 30, 1965, p. 3.
[2] Ibid., February 23, 1961, p. 3. Ko Chih-ta: 'A Discussion of the Relations Between Agriculture and Finance.'
[3] Figures for agricultural loans given by different sources appear to be mutually inconsistent. Possibly this is due to confusion between additions to the revolving fund and loans made from the revolving fund; some references are ambiguous on which is meant. We cannot here digress on this topic, but refer the curious reader to the following sources: *Collected Laws and Regulations* . . . Vol. 7, p. 137, Li Hsien-nien: Report on Final Accounts for 1957 and Draft Budget for 1958, and *Economic Research (Jingji Yanjiu)*, No. 9, September 1962, p. 5. Huang Ta: loc. cit., and *Peking Review*, April 17, 1964, p. 18. Yang P'ei-hsin: 'Rural Finance.'
[4] *Economic Research (Jingji Yanjiu)*, No. 6, June 1963, p. 11. Yang P'ei-hsin: 'The Problem of Financing the Process of Agricultural Mechanization in Our Country.'
[5] NCNA Canton, January 10, 1966.
[6] *Rural Finance (Nongcun Jinrong)*, No. 4–5, February 28, 1965, loc. cit.

State credit to the agricultural sector is given mainly for productive purposes. Apart from advance payments, two types of production loans are extended, called respectively 'loans for production expenses' (i.e. short term) and 'loans for production equipment' (i.e. longer term).[1] The granting of bank loans to cover living expenses for poor peasants in the pre-harvest season is mentioned in a work published in 1959.[2] By 1961 policy had apparently changed and it was laid down that loans from the state were intended only for production and that seasonal difficulties in consumption must be met by developing subsidiary production such as pigs, poultry, and handicrafts.[3] This contrasts sharply with the position before 1949 when peasants borrowed mainly for consumption, which included expenditure for weddings, funerals, and other occasions as well as for livelihood in the lean months.[4] Nowadays economy in family celebrations is repeatedly enjoined.

Some exceptions are permitted to the general ban on state credit for peasant consumption. Loans are given to disaster areas and also to individuals for medical expenses. This later type of loan, like most credit to individual peasants, would probably be channelled through co-operatives. Credit co-operatives, as we have seen, make loans from their own funds to individuals for purposes of both consumption and production.[5] An acute shortage of credit for consumption purposes is shown to exist by the survival of private lending at high rates of interest. However, this credit shortage is no new phenomenon, but a perpetuation of what has always been the case in the Chinese countryside.

We have seen that credit co-operatives are not supposed to make loans for periods of above one year. Bank loans for agriculture are not often given in the first place for more than three to five years. Five years was the term applied to the special credits to provide poor peasants with share capital on their entry to agricultural producer co-operatives, and three to five years to loans for water conservancy and for the purchase of large agricultural implements, and three years for livestock. In 1955 it was laid down that loans for capital investment to any agricultural co-operative should not exceed its annual accumulation fund.[6] In 1962 we read that loans for small items of investment, such as the purchase of draught cattle, were supposed to be restricted to half the current year's accumulation fund of the production team concerned.[7]

---

[1] *Kuang Ming Daily (Guangming Ribao)*, June 21, 1965, p. 4. Yü Jui-hsiang: loc. cit. In the mid-1960s, loans for draught animals accounted for approximately 60 per cent of the bank loans given every year to production teams for 'production equipment'. *Ta Kung Daily (Dagong Bao)*, Peking, September 25, 1964, p. 3. Chang Shu-jen: 'A Short Cut Solution to the Problem of Funds for Draught Cattle.' Loans given for production expenses are spent on chemical fertilizer (accounting for around 70 per cent of the total of this category of loan in some provinces in the spring of 1964) and on fodder, farm tools, and seed. Ibid., May 8, 1964, p. 1.

[2] Hsü Ti-hsin: op. cit., p. 243.

[3] *Ta Kung Daily (Dagong Bao)*, Peking, May 7, 1961, p. 2.

[4] J. L. Buck: *Land Utilization in China*, Nanking, 1937 (reprinted New York, 1964), p. 461.

[5] *People's Daily (Renmin Ribao)*, September 11, 1964, p. 1. Editorial.

[6] *Collected Laws and Regulations* . . . Vol. 2, pp. 545–6.

[7] *Ta Kung Daily (Dagong Bao)*, Peking, February 22, 1962, p. 1. Editorial.

According to regulations of 1955, loans for 'production expenses' (for the purchase of seed, fertilizers, insecticides, fodder, and similar items) are repayable within one year. The 1955 regulations specified that loans were not in general to exceed 20 per cent of such expenditure for the year in which cooperatives were formed, nor above 10 per cent in succeeding years unless natural disasters occurred.[1] These limitations show the restricted scale of such assistance and the reason for the continual harping on the need for self-reliance by each unit of collective agriculture. However, against this must be set the fact that in 1956 agricultural credit outstanding came to 81 per cent of the sales of agricultural producer goods in that year.[2]

Brief mention must be made of several points bearing on the capacity of Chinese agriculture to absorb capital profitably. At times, especially in the 1950s, the willingness of the peasants to accept equipment and the accompanying loans must have been affected by the unsuitability of some of the goods offered.[3] After the Great Leap, more attention was given to providing appropriate goods. In the words of an article in 1963 'when agricultural loans are issued, attention must be paid to whether there are goods and whether these goods are suitable. The production teams,' it continued, 'must voluntarily choose and buy the producer goods so that selling them unsuitable items is avoided'.[4] This emphasis on greater discrimination in the supply of agricultural producer goods, and on their acceptability to the purchasers, may be expected greatly to increase the effectiveness of investment.

Efficiency in the use of limited funds, in the sense of increasing the return from their investment, also depends on the judicious selection of recipients. This criterion may conflict with social or political objectives, such as concentrating credit on poorer peasants. Poor peasants in any area, or poor communes had, until the 1960s, been priority recipients. From around 1962 a change occurred in this respect in line with the general tendency towards more careful economic calculation. In that year, production teams in major grain producing areas, together with those in areas hit by disasters, received priority for loans.[5] In 1963, priority in credit allocation was given to important grain surplus and industrial crop districts.[6] In 1964 it was explicitly stated that agricultural investment must not be spread widely and indiscriminately, but should be concentrated where it would yield the highest returns, that is to say in the most favourable areas for providing grain surpluses and industrial crops.[7]

From the technical point of view, the capacity of China's agriculture to absorb capital may appear almost unlimited. The shortage of fertilizers compared, for example, with Japan, and the need for improved seed and implements, all indicate vast prospects of profitable returns. The limiting factors to

[1] *Collected Laws and Regulations* . . . Vol. 2, pp. 545–6.
[2] Choh-ming Li: op. cit., p. 132.
[3] *People's Handbook (Renmin Shouce)1957*, p. 170. Liao Lu-yen, Minister of Agriculture: Speech to the Third Session of the First National People's Congress on June 15, 1956.
[4] *People's Daily (Renmin Ribao)*, July 11, 1963, p. 5. Hu Li-chiao: loc. cit.
[5] Ibid., October 22, 1962, p. 1.
[6] *Ta Kung Daily (Dagong Bao)*, Peking, October 31, 1963, p. 1. Editorial.
[7] *People's Daily (Renmin Ribao)*, January 1, 1964, p. 1. Editorial, and ibid., March 11, 1964, p. 1. Editorial.

the speed with which investment funds can be usefully employed are likely to be in the spheres of organization and of education. They include the supply of competent staff to handle rural credit extension, the provision of adequate incentives to encourage peasants to invest, whether in collective agriculture or their private plots, the spread of technical knowledge, and the successful adaptation of equipment, fertilizers, and improved seeds to different localities. Above all, the absorbative capacity for investment of Chinese agriculture must depend on the general level of education among the peasants, so that they can make intelligent use of technical improvements.

Chapter 16

PRICE POLICY

Measures for indirect control of prices through state control of commerce or through monetary and fiscal means have already been mentioned in earlier chapters. We shall now briefly summarize the Chinese Government's anti-inflationary policies and for further treatment refer the reader to studies of the subject by D. H. Perkins.[1]

Throughout the First Five Year Plan period and during the Great Leap, an increasing proportion of resources, including labour, was devoted to the output of producer goods. This sector of the economy generated a large amount of purchasing power through wage payments, but did not immediately increase the quantity of consumer goods to satisfy this purchasing power. The export surplus which China ran from 1956 also aggravated the situation.

The official index of retail prices, however, remained very stable, rising by little more than 8 per cent between 1950 and 1958.[2] This index is thought to have a downward bias, although seldom of more than 3–4 per cent except during the bad years after the Great Leap when, in any case, index figures were not published.[3]

The existence of excess demand was nevertheless seen in the need for rationing, in price increases on the free market (which has existed all along, except in 1955–6 and during the Great Leap in 1958–9) and in the appearance of a black market in the post-Leap crisis. It must be noted that the existence of a free market, mainly in subsidiary farm products, absorbed the purchasing power of urban residents rather than that of the rural population. Although Chinese peasants are by no means altogether self-sufficient for food, so that habitually there has been buying and selling of commodities within the farming community, yet the main outlet for their cash income is the purchase of industrial goods. A considerable proportion of the rural purchasing power was, as Perkins points out, channelled into the buying of agricultural producer goods through government control over the cadres of agricultural co-operatives and communes. Yet there remained a cash income sizeable, in

---

[1] *Journal of Political Economy*, Vol. 72, No. 4, August 1964, pp. 360–75. D. H. Perkins: 'Price Stability and Development in Mainland China (1951–63)', and D. H. Perkins: *Price Formation in Communist China* (unpublished Ph.D Thesis, Harvard University, 1963), and D. H. Perkins: *Market Control and Planning in Communist China*, Cambridge, Mass., 1966.

[2] *Ten Great Years*, Peking, 1960, p. 173. On the price indices, both wholesale and retail, see Choh-ming Li: *Economic Development of Communist China*, Berkeley, 1959, pp. 25–8, and P. Schran: *The Structure of Income in Communist China* (unpublished Ph.D Thesis, University of California, 1961), pp. 14–16.

[3] *Journal of Political Economy*, Vol. 72, No. 4, August 1964, pp. 361–2. D. H. Perkins: loc. cit.

aggregate, in the hands of individual peasants, with evidence of hoarding. This peasant hoarding was said to have become important from the time of the 1956 collectivization drive. Early in 1957 about one-third of the note circulation in rural areas was estimated to be hoarded.[1] This may have been a significant factor in checking the inflationary tendencies of the time. Presumably the hoarding was due to the unavailability of acceptable industrial consumer goods in the countryside and to the lack of non-collective investment openings for the rural population after collectivization.

The basic policy to prevent the emergence of excess demand for consumer goods has been to control the size both of the total wage bill and also of expenditure by state organs and supply and marketing co-operatives on the purchase of agricultural produce. However, this two-pronged policy, while necessary to counter inflation, is liable to have disincentive effects on production, while being also subject to evasion. Measures to control procurement prices of agricultural output as part of an anti-inflationary policy have in addition been restricted by the circumstance that procurement price policy has also other functions to fulfil; changes in relative prices are, for example, a means for the government to influence the supply of particular farm crops. Minor preventatives of inflation have included limits on expenditure on consumer goods by collective units and on state extensions of agricultural credit, and the postponement of advance payments for agricultural output; all these, however, can normally be of only very limited scope. Taxes on consumer goods, notably the industrial and commercial tax, absorb surplus purchasing power as do savings drives, while the running down of stock piles may at times proffer some slight assistance.[2] These measures helped to restrict the size of the inflationary gap but were not able to prevent its existence, as evidenced by the need for rationing. It is noteworthy that the Chinese have relied more than the Soviet Union on non-price measures, such as rationing, to reduce consumption.[3] In the important sphere of housing, prices have played virtually no role in allocation. Rents comprise only around 5 per cent of income for most urban residents and dwellings are allocated mainly according to jobs.

Despite the limitations to which anti-inflationary policies have been subject, the conclusion reached by Perkins is that, except during the Great Leap, the control of suppressed inflationary pressures was 'handled about as well as it was reasonable to expect in the light of the basic goals of the regime'.[4] The relative success of the anti-inflationary policy must have owed a good deal to the high marginal efficiency of capital in China, which meant that total capital could in some industries be recovered within a year of the investment, thus greatly lessening the inflationary effects of at least that part of the investment programme devoted to the expansion of consumer industries.[5]

[1] *People's Daily* (*Renmin Ribao*), February 27, 1957, p. 5.
[2] *Journal of Political Economy*, Vol. 72, No. 4, August 1964, pp. 363 passim. D. H. Perkins: loc. cit.
[3] *Journal of Asian Studies*, Vol. XXV, No. 4, August 1966, p. 656. S. H. Chou: 'Prices in Communist China.'
[4] *Journal of Political Economy*, Vol. 72, No. 4, August 1964, p. 373. D. H. Perkins: loc. cit.
[5] It should be noted that these profits are in addition to the industrial and commercial tax levied on the products of these industries. This increases still further the rate of return to the state on its investment in them.

It is to the credit of the Chinese authorities that they realized the difficulties besetting price determination in a command economy. In 1956 the Minister of Finance, Li Hsien-nien, admitted that 'one of the important reasons why we have failed to . . . make timely readjustments in prices which have always been unreasonable, or have since become unreasonable, is that, generally speaking, there is no price competition in our country, so shortcomings in our price policy are not easily detectable'.[1]

In the rest of this chapter we shall examine the different types of prices that exist, the machinery for determining prices and how far responsibility for such decisions is centralized or dispersed, the extent to which official prices are fixed in theory and in fact, and the criteria used for fixing prices. First, however, we shall consider the influence of the Marxist theory of value on pricing policy.

1. PRICING POLICY AND THE LABOUR THEORY OF VALUE

In all economies, the manner in which prices are determined is apt to diverge rather widely from that described by theoretical writers. When listing the various sorts of prices below, we will mention the elements (average costs, profits, taxes, etc.) of which they are composed and later we shall consider empirical instances of price formation. Now, however, we must glance at the role in price formation ascribed to the Marxist theory of value.

A commodity's value, in Marxist terminology, depends on the quantity of socially necessary labour time devoted to its production; this may differ from costs arising out of the production circumstances of an individual producer. Goods are supposed to be exchanged at parity of value. Among Chinese economists, discussions on prices usually begin with respectful reference to the primacy of the law of value, such as that 'value is the basis of price and price is the monetary form of value'.[2] It is recognized, however, that some divergence between 'values' and prices is unavoidable. Value cannot be precisely calculated, because the amount of labour needed to produce the same kind of product varies between enterprises. In addition, other factors must be taken into account when fixing prices: these include supply and demand, the distribution of the national income, the needs of 'planned and proportional development of the national economy', and of the division of the national income between savings and consumption.[3]

Another question raised when the basis of price formation is debated

[1] *The Eighth National Congress of the Communist Party of China*, Vol. II. Speeches. Peking, 1956, p. 214.

[2] *Red Flag (Hongqi)*, No. 7–8, April 16, 1963, p. 1. Hsüeh Mu-ch'iao: 'The Law of Value and Our Price Policy.' In September 1963 Hsüeh was appointed Chairman of the State Price Commission.

[3] *Economic Research (Jingji Yanjiu)*, No. 4, April 1958, pp. 50–61. Chang Yi-fei: 'The Basis for State Fixing of Market Prices of Commodities', and ibid., No. 3, March 1963, pp. 28–9. Pien Ching-chung: 'The Problem of Price Necessarily Being Based on Social Value', and ibid., No. 2, April 1957, p. 13. Nan Ping and So Chen: 'Some Problems in the Pricing of Producer Goods', and ibid., No. 3, June 1957, pp. 56–7. Fan Jo-yi: 'A Further Discussion of Price Policy for Products of Heavy Industry', and *China Youth Newspaper (Zhongguo Qingnian Bao)*, August 30, 1961 (SCMP 2586). Wang Kuei-ch'en: 'Carrying Out Seriously the Principle Underlying Exchange of Equal Values.'

among Chinese economists is whether prices should reflect imputed capital costs in the industries concerned.[1] This discussion is closely linked with that noted in an earlier chapter on whether profits should be calculated as returns on costs (which, in China, would exclude the fixed capital element, except for depreciation charges) or on capital; it reflects the fact that in China, enterprises receive their original grants for fixed assets free, and do not have to pay interest on them.[2] We must now expand on this topic.

It will be noted that for industrial and mineral products the basic price is the ex-factory (or pithead) price, other prices being derived from this. Ex-factory prices, as we will see, are formed by adding an 'appropriate margin of profit' (plus tax) to the average or 'normal' cost of production in the industry concerned, using 'cost of production' in the Chinese sense just noted. This concept obviously bristles with uncertainty. Apart from this cost-profit rate, two alternative ways have been mooted of reckoning the mark up for profit—the wage-profit rate (profit as a ratio of wages) or the capital-profit rate (profit as a ratio of fixed capital). Prices formed by using the capital-profit rate are known as 'production prices'.[3]

In 1964, a Chinese economist, Yü Lin, described the process of price determination as follows: 'In fixing prices, the first thing to do is to work out, for each type of product separately, the average production costs for the whole industry, i.e. the average expenditure of labour transformed into materials and of wages in each article. The next thing is to calculate separately for each type of product, the amount of profit that should be added. With respect to the size of this profit, should it maintain a fixed ratio to wages, to costs, or to capital?'[4] Yü went on to point out that whichever kind of profit ratio is used will encourage wasteful expenditure on the item (wages, total current costs, or capital) that forms its base. This is because it is in the interest of the individual enterprise and its ministry to maximize the absolute amount of its profit since (apart from awards on above-plan profits) they are entitled to a fixed proportion of total profits for certain specified purposes.[5] This is a difficulty which always arises when administered prices are fixed on a cost plus basis. Yü's conclusions were empirical: 'The economic accounting of a socialist country needs to make use of many indicators and cannot rely on one sole indicator. To use the sole indicator of production price comes to the same thing as using profit as the sole indicator to guide the planned and proportionate development of the national economy; it is a scheme to rely on one sole indicator to regulate complex economic relationships. This manner of thinking is not realistic.'[6] In industries with approximately the same technical level, Yü expresses the opinion that the fixing of prices according to the same wage-profit rate may be appropriate, but not when technical levels diverge

[1] *Economic Research (Jingji Yanjiu)*, No. 5, May 1963, pp. 1–2. Hsüeh Mu-ch'iao: 'Some Problems Awaiting Discussion on Commodity Prices in a Socialist Society.'
[2] See pp. 26 and 162–3 above.
[3] *Economic Research (Jingji Yanjiu)*, No. 12, December 1963, p. 42. Yang Chien-pai: 'The Problem of National Economic Equilibrium and "Production Price".'
[4] *Economic Research (Jingji Yanjiu)*, No. 5, May 1964, p. 4. Yü Lin: 'The Correct Manner of Determining Prices of Different Kinds of Products.'
[5] See p. 166 above.
[6] *Economic Research (Jingji Yanjiu)*, No. 5, May 1964, p. 8. Yü Lin: loc. cit.

widely.[1] The use of the cost-profit rate in setting prices is justified on empirical grounds, 'because in most circumstances, the level of cost-profit frequently falls between those of wage-profit and of capital-profit and approaches the median of these two profit rates. At the present time we often use cost-profit rates to check the price levels of different types of products, this is a comparatively simple method learned from practical experience.'[2]

Yü's final conclusion is that both in capitalist and socialist economies, for different reasons, profit rates in different industries diverge, a conclusion interesting in that it appears to justify a socialist phenomenon by the existence of a similar phenomenon under capitalism. 'In a capitalist society, although there is the objective law of profit equalization, yet, because of subjective conditions, the profit rates in each industry diverge. The tendency towards profit equalization persists together with actual divergence in profit rates. In a socialist society, the state often adjusts prices appropriately where the profit rates in different industries differ too much, in order to make the prices of all types of product approach more nearly to their values. But still, the objective conditions of each industry are not the same and their profit rates generally diverge. The demand for absolute profit equalization does not accord with actual conditions.'[3]

Yü's statements do in fact appear to tally with the methods actually used in price fixing in China in which empiricism bulks large. We have seen that capital costs are considered in the pricing of different forms of transport and we shall have occasion to note that this also occurs in prices of heavy industrial goods. However, while this is an important factor, it is not a paramount consideration in fixing prices, for profits on capital diverge between industries, as Yü states.

The divorce between price formation and the allocation of capital is regarded by Chinese writers as complete. 'The fixing of prices is one matter (this is decided by whether price tallies with value) and the distribution of investment between different departments and industries of the national economy is quite another matter (this is decided by the need to ensure the proportional development of different departments of the national economy).'[4] While occasional daring economists may propound the advantages of allocating capital for investment according to profits on capital,[5] none has, to our knowledge, actually suggested that capital has in fact been so allocated in recent years; yet expected profit on capital is likely to have been significant in determining the distribution of the considerable investment made from extra-budgetary funds.[6]

The root of these questions lies in the tension between the labour theory of value and price as an instrument for the allocation of scarce resources. According to the former concept, goods should exchange at 'parity of values'; according to the latter, their prices should reflect conditions of supply and

[1] *Economic Research (Jingji Yanjiu)*, No. 5, May 1964, p. 2, and p. 10.
[2] Ibid., p. 10.
[3] Ibid., p. 11.
[4] Ibid., p. 8.
[5] Ibid., p. 16. Ho Chien-chang and Chang Ling: 'A Tentative Discussion on "Production Price" in the Socialist Economy.'
[6] See pp. 389–93 above.

demand, so that commodities whose market prices do not cover total costs (including capital charges) would, in the long run, cease to be produced.

Our general conclusion must be that, despite verbal respect paid to the labour theory of value, the economic function of price as the mechanism for the allocation of scarce resources has not been wholly neglected, either in pronouncements on price policy or in practical decisions on pricing. Nor, on the other hand, has it usually been allowed to be dominant. Normally, the price mechanism is permitted freer play in the sphere of consumption decisions than of investment decisions. It is dangerous to generalize about the criteria used for price fixing: each item needs separate study. Later in this chapter we will briefly mention some considerations that have influenced the determination of official prices for certain categories of products. The overall impression is that empiricism and flexibility have had a larger part in Chinese price policy than in that of some other Marxist lands.

2. TYPES OF PRICES

Ex-factory prices (pithead prices in the case of minerals) and *purchasing prices of agricultural produce* (also known as procurement prices) are those received by the producers of industrial and of farm commodities respectively. *Wholesale prices* are those usually charged by commercial ministries[1] to lower commercial organs, notably those engaged in retailing which, in turn, sell to the ultimate customers at *retail prices*. In addition, industrial goods are exchanged between state enterprises (between two producing enterprises, e.g. factories or mines or between a producing enterprise and a commercial enterprise) at *allocation prices*, which are commonly fixed on an annual basis.[2]

Ex-factory prices are supposed to be fixed by 'the state and the controlling (industrial) ministry' on a cost plus basis by adding 'an appropriate margin of profit' to the average or 'normal' cost of production (using 'cost' in the Marxist sense) for the whole industry, with another addition made for industrial and commercial tax. Adjustments to ex-factory prices are also made for 'relevant national policies' and to maintain desired differentials between prices of different goods and qualities: insufficient price differentials for quality have, however, been a frequent complaint.[3]

---

[1] All the ministries which control trade in some type or other of commodities are included in the term. See p. 276 above.

[2] *Financial and Economic Research (Caijing Yanjiu)*, No. 9, December 15, 1958, pp. 19–21. Meng Ch'u-lin: 'Some Remarks on Price Problems Relating to People's Communes', and *Economic Research (Jingji Yanjiu)*, No. 12, December 1959, p. 46. Ch'in Liu-fang: 'A Preliminary Analysis of the Price of Cotton Yarn in Our Country.' The terms translated above as 'allocation price' is sometimes rendered into English as 'transfer price'. This term superseded the earlier term 'industrial wholesale price', see *Economic Research (Jingji Yanjiu)*, No. 3, June 1956, p. 30, fn. Lo Keng-mo: 'Problems of the Turnover Tax on Heavy Industrial Products.'

[3] *Ta Kung Daily (Dagong Bao)*, Peking, July 16, 1962, p. 3. Yang Fang-hsün: 'Determine Price According To Quality—Higher Price for Higher Quality', and *Kuang Ming Daily (Guangming Ribao)*, February 25, 1963, p. 4. Hsiang Ching-ch'üan: 'A Draft Discussion on the Function of Price in Promoting Agricultural and Industrial Production at the Present Time', and *Economic Research (Jingji Yanjiu)*, No. 9, September 1963, p. 2. Tan Ku: 'Some Problems in the Determination of the Prices of Light Industrial Commodities.'

Procurement prices of agricultural produce will be discussed below, where it will be seen that both historic costs and the need for incentives to increase the output of particular crops have influenced pricing decisions. More theoretically, agricultural procurement prices are said to be fixed a little lower than their value (in Marxist terms) the difference being taken by the state as a form of tax.[1]

Wholesale prices are composed of the ex-factory prices together with the expenses and profit of wholesaling (whether done by an organ of the producing ministry or by a commercial organ).[2] The wholesale price may be identical (although this is uncertain) with the so-called 'market price' (also known as the 'commercial price') fixed by the state for sales of producer goods to undertakings not under ownership by the whole people.[3] The state of the market—i.e. the relation between demand and supply of a commodity—is in one account specifically mentioned as a consideration in setting the 'market price'.[4]

The retail price is made up of the wholesale price plus the expenses and profit of the retailing concern, and the 3 per cent industrial and commercial tax on retail sales (reckoned on total retail prices, inclusive of tax).[5] The margin between the wholesale and retail prices was stated, in 1958, to be complex 'and in the case of some products, possibly excessive'.[6] However, retail margins tend to be smaller in low-income countries than in wealthier ones, and in state-run stores in China in 1958 they stood at probably less than 20 per cent.[7] Sometimes two official retail prices have existed for one type of product, one price for on-ration purchases, and another and higher one for off-ration purchases, or the ration may be sold at the official retail price, and above ration purchases at free market prices.[8]

If it is desired to insulate wholesale and retail prices from the effects of changes in prices paid to the producers (ex-factory prices or procurement prices of farm output) this is sometimes done by compensatory changes in the industrial and commercial tax.[9] Alternatively, the same effect may be obtained by squeezing or expanding profits.

Ex-factory prices are taken as the starting point for calculating allocation

---

Special ex-factory prices may be fixed for individual enterprises in a few cases, e.g. for salt wells and mines. Ibid., p. 4, and *Planned Economy* (*Jingji Jihua*), No. 3, March 1957, p. 18. Ts'ui Ch'i: 'Analysis of Accounting in the Plan for Drawing Up Ex-Factory Prices for Producer Goods.'

[1] *Economic Research* (*Jingji Yanjiu*), No. 9, September 1963, p. 2. Tan Ku: loc. cit.

[2] Niu Chung-huang: *Accumulation and Consumption in the National Income of Our Country* (in Chinese), Peking, 1959, p. 89.

[3] *Economic Research* (*Jingji Yanjiu*), No. 2, April 1957, p. 24, fn. Nan Ping and So Chen: loc. cit.

[4] *Ta Kung Daily* (*Dagong Bao*), Peking, July 16, 1962, p. 3. Yang Fang-hsün: loc. cit.

[5] Niu Chung-huang: op. cit., p. 89, and *Collected Laws and Regulations of the People's Republic of China* (in Chinese), Vol. 8, p. 136, and see p. 373 above.

[6] *Financial and Economic Research* (*Caijing Yanjiu*), No. 9, December 15, 1958, p. 20. Meng Ch'u-lin: loc. cit.

[7] See p. 315 above. Some agricultural producer co-operatives had margins of 16·3 per cent which were said to be 'almost as much as that of a state-run store'.

[8] See p. 311 above. Retail prices are frequently lowered by about 5 per cent before national festivals (e.g. May 1st and October 1st) and afterwards raised again.

[9] e.g. *People's Handbook* (*Renmin Shouce*) *1960*, p. 388.

prices of industrial goods; to ex-factory prices (which, it will be remembered, include industrial and commercial tax) are added various expenses of distribution.[1] In the case of some commodities, allocation prices include transport costs in whole or in part.[2]

Certain exceptions have been made to the general rule that allocation prices apply only to goods circulating between state-owned concerns, and that another unvarying price applies to sales to other undertakings. Before 1958, handicraft producer co-operatives in some areas bought supplies from the state at allocation prices.[3] At that period, it appears that producer goods may have on occasion been sold to agricultural producer co-operatives at a price somewhat lower than that normally charged to non-state bodies, although at other times the ordinary wholesale, or even retail prices, ruled in these transactions.[4] When the communes were established, comprising within themselves both the former handicraft co-operatives and the agricultural producer co-operatives, three types of prices—allocation, wholesale and retail—were sometimes being paid by the same commune for state supplies.[5] Although allocation prices are normally below wholesale prices, on occasion they have been higher.[6]

The ministry producing the commodity in question charges the allocation price to the ministry receiving it. However, the price paid by the enterprise that eventually uses the product may be considerably higher owing to commissions taken by the various levels of its own ministry's supply organization.[7]

New industrial products (i.e. those being made for the first time in China) may temporarily be priced below cost. In the initial stages of production, costs may be so high that prices based on costs would inhibit sales. In 1957, an economist advocated that new products should be priced at about the same level as that of the imported goods they were replacing.[8]

Pricing in China's international trade has been treated in Chapter 12, where was noted the divorce between domestic and foreign prices, which stems from the current Chinese concept of foreign trade and the method of its planning.

---

[1] *Planned Economy (Jihua Jingji)*, No. 8, August 1957, p. 23. Liu Jui-hua: 'An Exploratory Discussion of the Problem of Decentralizing Authority for Planning the Market Supplies of Goods Subject to Unified Distribution and to Ministry Control.'

[2] Ibid., No. 10, October 1957, p. 24. Chang Shih: 'A Major Problem in Promoting a Rational System of Coal Transport.'

[3] *Financial and Economic Research (Caijing Yanjiu)*, No. 9, December 15, 1958, p. 19. Meng Ch'u-lin: loc. cit.

[4] *Economic Research (Jingji Yanjiu)*, No. 2, April 1957, p. 24. Nan Ping and So Chen: loc. cit. In February 1958 it was laid down that irrigation machinery should be sold retail to peasants at the ex-factory price plus cost of distribution. *Collected Laws and Regulations . . .* Vol. 7, p. 314.

[5] *Financial and Economic Research (Caijing Yanjiu)*, No. 9, December 15, 1958, p. 19. Meng Ch'u-lin: loc. cit.

[6] *Economic Research (Jingji Yanjiu)*, No. 3, June 1957, p. 65. Fan Jo-yi: loc. cit.

[7] *People's Daily (Renmin Ribao)*, May 17, 1962, p. 2. Wang Hsü: 'Reduce the Number of Middlemen and Lower the Cost of Timber'—A reader's letter. For this reason the price of spare parts to the individual enterprise or bureau under the Ministry of Forestry could come to 30 to 50 per cent above the state allocation price.

[8] *Economic Research (Jingji Yanjiu)*, No. 3, June 1957, p. 66. Fan Jo-yi: loc. cit.

3. THE MACHINERY AND SCOPE OF PRICE FORMATION AND CONTROL

In this section we will discuss the administrative levels and the administrative organs concerned with the formation and control of prices. Logically the two concepts of formation and control might be considered distinct. The diffusion of responsibility for price fixing in China, together with the vagueness of the regulations and, it would seem, an even greater flexibility in practice, means that the two functions cannot always be distinguished.

In 1950, the then Ministry of Trade was required to fix wholesale prices for state trading corporations at the major markets, while regional and provincial departments of trade had to fix prices for the corporations at the smaller centres.[1] During the period of the socialist transformation of private commerce, responsibility for price control in town and country was divided between the Ministry of Commerce and the supply and marketing co-operatives respectively,[2] and apparently no commodities were, explicitly at least, excluded from price control. Probably no more was done than to attempt to fix prices at the centres at which these organizations then operated, without trying to exercise direct control of prices in the smaller places. As the state commercial network spread and began to establish organs at and below the *hsien* level, so the sphere of officially controlled prices also spread—at least in theory. This widening of the attempt at central price control brought difficulties in its train. Great local price variations, inevitable where transport is as primitive as in rural China, made efforts of central authorities to determine appropriate prices for each small area quite impossible. As a result central control looked like collapsing. From the second half of 1956, prices of subsidiary farm produce, handicrafts and industrial goods were in many places reported to have been raised 'spontaneously'.[3]

In price formation, as in other spheres, decentralization was clearly desirable and a series of measures in 1957–8 was designed to bring this to pass, while attempting to strengthen central control over the general lines of policy and over certain all-important prices in particular. This dual aim was reflected in the establishment of the National Price Commission in July 1957 and the directives of the following month that price commissions should be established by local authorities in provinces, in municipalities under provinces, in *hsien* and market towns equivalent to *hsien*. Henceforward, it was also announced, a national price conference would be convened every year.[4] This would provide an opportunity for the central authorities to keep in touch with the provincial commissions. The functions of these conferences were to discuss and determine the general level of prices in accordance with central policy, and to lay

[1] *New China Monthly* (*Xinhua Yuebao*), No. 6, April 1950, p. 1408. For a full treatment of price control in the early years of the regime, see R. Hsia: *Price Control in Communist China*, New York, 1953.

[2] *Collected Laws and Regulations* ... Vol. 6, p. 360.

[3] Ibid., and *Statistical Research* (*Tongji Yanjiu*), No. 4, April 1958, p. 25. Editorial Information Department: 'The Circumstances of the 1957 Price Changes and Their Influence on the Standard of Living.'

[4] *Collected Laws and Regulations* ... Vol. 6, pp. 359–61.

down policy on prices of major commodities, on local price differentials, and on differences between buying and selling prices of agricultural products.[1]

Regulations issued in October 1958 divided the duties of price control between the centre and the local authorities. The appropriate ministries of the central government were to control the procurement prices of the major agricultural products: grain, raw cotton, vegetable oils, jute, ramie, tea, tobacco, timber and live pigs.[2] They were also still to control the selling prices (presumably both wholesale and retail) at important commercial centres, of grain, edible oil, pork, timber, cotton yarn and cloth, woollen cloth, edible salt, sugar, coal, petroleum, chemical fertilizers and wrist watches. The centrally fixed prices of both kinds were to apply to standard types of the goods in question, while prices of other types of these goods (and of standard types at places other than the main commercial centres) were to be determined by the local authorities, with reference to the prices of standard types and at the main centres. The prices of all other goods, both agricultural and manufactured, were also to be under local control. The central government ministries were, however, to continue to be responsible for the overall price equilibrium of all the commodities in their respective spheres. They were ordered to intensify research into price questions although it is more than doubtful if they had the staff for this.[3]

Such was the system of price control decreed in 1957-8. The degree and manner in which it was realized in practice is more difficult to expound. The National Price Commission, the first part of the new system to be established, was before long apparently abolished or allowed to fade away. At any rate, nothing was heard of its operations and then, in 1963, once again the formation was announced of a National Price Commission, without any indication being given that such a body had previously existed.[4] Hsüeh Mu-ch'iao, at one time Director of the State Statistical Bureau, was appointed Chairman of the new Commission. Uncertainty also surrounds the fate of this new State Price Commission—it was not included in a list of State Council commissions published in January 1965[5] and this may signal its abolition.

Nor is it clear how far local price commissions were ever set up as directed in 1958. Committees supervising prices at individual rural markets appear to have been widespread—at least, Press references to them often occur, but little is heard of similar bodies at the various higher levels of local administration.[6]

---

[1] *Collected Laws and Regulations* ... Vol. 8, p. 168.

[2] Ibid. Six months before this directive, another directive had stipulated that the annual price conference was to fix prices of first and second category agricultural produce; third category produce was to remain subject to provincial price control. Ibid., Vol. 7, p. 316.

[3] Ibid., Vol. 8, pp. 168-9. In 1965 an announcement of price reductions for seventy-six kinds of chemical fertilizer, agricultural insecticide and agricultural machinery mentioned that the prices of five of these items were controlled by the central government and of seventy-one by provincial departments. In addition, the prices of some other types of agricultural producer goods were controlled by *hsien* and municipalities. *Southern Daily* (*Nanfang Ribao*), December 10, 1965 (SCMP 3609).

[4] *People's Daily* (*Renmin Ribao*), April 14, 1963, p. 1.

[5] Ibid., January 5, 1965, p. 2.

[6] A *hsien* committee for rural market price stabilization was reported to have been set up in a *hsien* in Hopei. NCNA Tientsin, July 9, 1959.

It may be that although price fixing was undertaken at these levels, the organs for fulfilling this task were seldom as formal as envisaged in 1958. Thus in a south China *hsien*, prices of certain industrial products were in 1960 being fixed by the accounting section of the *hsien* bureau of industry and mining.[1] In 1963, the office of the supply and marketing co-operative of a special district was mentioned as altering the prices of over a hundred agricultural and 'native product' commodities.[2] But whatever the machinery of price fixing employed, the *hsien*, the special district and the province do seem to have exercised authority in this field after 1958.

While it is thus far from clear what happened about national and local price commissions, the annual national price conference, also decreed in 1958, is enveloped in similar mystery. At least five national price conferences were held before the date of this decree,[3] but no reference can be traced to any held after the decree.

At least one instance has come to our knowledge of a province changing the procurement price of grain, the most important commodity of all; a responsibility supposedly reserved to the central government. In 1959 the Kweichow Provincial People's Council was reported to have decided to raise the procurement prices of rice, millet and beans, in order to provide incentive for greater production.[4] No indication was given in the report that this action by a provincial authority was anything out of the ordinary.

Officially it would appear that almost all categories of agricultural, industrial and handicraft products might come under price control by either central or local authorities. However, to this there have been important exceptions, either open or tacit. Third category agricultural products (for the meaning of this term see Chapter 11) seem to have been subject only to fitful and vague forms of price control. In 1956–7, in order to reduce inflationary tendencies, even farm output subject to unified purchase was permitted to be sold at free market prices at rural markets after compulsory sales quotas had been met, a restriction which was not always observed. When these markets were suppressed during the Great Leap, third category commodities were sold by communes to state commercial organs under contract but, according to one account, this system was rendered difficult by unstable prices.[5] Apparently the state's power to control prices of these products was less than might be thought. The Regulations on the Organization of Rural Markets, issued in September 1959 when these markets were being reopened, insisted that first and second category commodities must be sold at state purchasing prices, while those of the third category should be subject to market control committees. For the more important third category products, the state might set

---

[1] *Current Scene*, Vol. 1, No. 28, March 27, 1962, p. 7. Choh-ming Li: 'Statistics and Planning at the *Hsien* Level in Communist China.'

[2] *Ta Kung Daily* (*Dagong Bao*), Peking, June 19, 1963, p. 1.

[3] See a reference to 'the 5th National Price Conference in 1955' in Hsien Yi-yü: 'An Investigation of Local Price Differentials of Industrial Goods in Peking and a Study of Some Problems' in *Selected Essays of Chinese Economists on Problems of Commodities, Value and Price Under the Socialist System* (in Chinese), Vol II, Peking, 1959, pp. 338 and 345.

[4] *Kweichow Daily* (*Guizhou Ribao*), August 30, 1959 (SCMP 2142).

[5] See p. 299 above.

prices, or maximum and minimum prices might be set. In the case of 'odd and petty' products, prices might be settled between buyer and seller 'with the guidance of market control committees'. The need for price stability and for control to prevent prices going 'beyond reasonable limits' was laid down by the regulations of September 1959.[1] We have seen that the reopening of rural markets was reported, from Hopei, to have had a stabilizing effect on prices.[2]

In November 1959, two months after the Regulations on the Organization of Rural Markets had been promulgated, an article in the *People's Daily* said that sales to the state of surplus first and second category commodities, after the compulsory deliveries had been fulfilled, might be made at slightly higher prices than those set for compulsory sales.[3] A year later, a directive of the Kwangtung Provincial People's Council suggested that prices 10–20 per cent above the official state purchasing prices might be given for above-quota sales to the state.[4] In addition, of course, was the produce sold to the state under contracts in which prices were stipulated. In 1961, it became permissible for the prices 'of a minority of ordinary farm products' to be negotiated on purchase by the state at rural markets.[5] Prices in the intermittent and marginal free market for grain have been treated in Chapter 13, although the examples of price flexibility just mentioned for first and second category products probably covered grain as well as other items in these categories.

Effective price control at rural markets proved difficult to maintain. This explains the gradual erosion of the strict principles enunciated at the revival of the rural markets in 1959. By March 1961 the *People's Daily* was stating that sellers might fix the prices of all farm produce offered for sale at these markets, or alternatively that prices might be settled by haggling.[6] It must, however, be mentioned that by 1961 trade in first category commodities at markets was banned; but the ban may not have been consistently enforced, for in the following year a *Ta Kung Daily* editorial referred to the purchase 'at negotiated prices' of certain first and second category commodities.[7] Farm produce brought by individual peasants for sale in cities appears to have been sold at free prices.

An article in the *Ta Kung Daily* in January 1964 suggests that little attempt was made to control prices of third category commodities at rural markets by administrative means, and that the chief method used was through the influence of the purchasing activities of official commercial organs. The prices at which supply and marketing co-operatives buy third category commodities on contract or at markets have, the article stated, an extremely important influence over market prices, but only if they are sufficiently realistic so as not to be out of touch with market prices. 'If these purchasing prices are too much

---

[1] *People's Handbook (Renmin Shouce) 1960*, p. 381.
[2] p. 299 above.
[3] *People's Daily (Renmin Ribao)*, November 21, 1959, p. 7. Kuan Ta-t'ung: 'On Trade at Rural Markets.'
[4] *Southern Daily (Nanfang Ribao)*, December 28, 1960 (SCMP 2421).
[5] *Ta Kung Daily (Dagong Bao)*, Peking, October 19, 1961, p. 1. Editorial.
[6] *People's Daily (Renmin Ribao)*, March 14, 1961, p. 7. Ho Wei and Yang Ch'un-hsü: 'Rural Market Trade'.
[7] *Ta Kung Daily (Dagong Bao)*, Peking, September 22, 1962, p. 1. Editorial.

lower than market prices, it will not be easy to control the sources of goods and so it will not be possible to regulate the relation between supply and demand on the market.' Prices paid by the co-operatives 'are normally the lower limit of market prices', which is reasonable in view of the convenience to the peasants of selling in large quantities.[1] The power of the state to control prices at rural markets would seem, therefore, to be severely limited.

Many industrial products may have been almost as unamenable to price control. More particularly this is likely to be the case with goods made by small establishments, such as handicraft co-operatives. At times the managements of individual factories also appear to have been allowed, or to have assumed, some initiative in price fixing. Probably this happens when they manufacture goods for which there are no fixed prices, in which case it is licit for prices to be settled mutually between seller and buyer, or with reference to prices fixed for similar goods.[2] For new products, or for items such as custom-built machinery, the price suggested by the producing factories is usually accepted, while they have little influence over the price of homogeneous goods already in production.[3] The great number of small industrial concerns in China means that considerable autonomy in price fixing for enterprises does not entail so much danger of monopoly pricing as would be the case in European Communist countries. Also, of course, administrative difficulties prevent rigid price fixing by higher levels for numerous small producers.

Goods in state stores are sold at fixed prices, not subject to haggling. In the case of commodities of any importance, these prices are determined by the appropriate level of government. There is, nevertheless, some room for flexibility and experiment in price-setting, even on occasion by an individual store. In 1957 it was complained that in some cities, purchasing agents from other parts had been buying up scarce goods (including manufactures, industrial raw materials and subsidiary farm products) by offering higher than normal prices.[4] This suggests that, for a wide range of merchandise, price control was not seriously enforced, even in the cities.

Price control is, of course, evaded in the case of that considerable volume of goods, including producer goods, which is the subject of deals, both barter and cash, of varying degrees of illegality. We have referred to these in Chapter 11, and shall have occasion to do so again. It is impossible to estimate, and very difficult to infer, how important such deals are in total, but as they presumably have included the output of the numerous illicit workshops and have been the source of much of the equipment and other producer goods for enterprises' expansion financed by extra-budgetary funds, the total of these uncontrolled transactions must have been very considerable.

[1] *Ta Kung Daily* (*Dagong Bao*), Peking, January 20, 1964, p. 3. Kao Ti-ch'en: 'Emphasize the Supply and Marketing Co-operatives' Role in Guiding Rural Market Trade.'

[2] *China Quarterly*, No. 17, January–March 1964, p. 78. Franz Schurmann: 'China's "New Economic Policy"—Transition or Beginning?', and *Economic Research* (*Jingji Yanjiu*), No. 2, February 1965, p. 37. Sung Chi-shan: 'A Brief Discussion of the Nature and Function of Industrial Contracts in Our Country.'

[3] Information kindly supplied by Barry M. Richman, Chairman, Management and Industrial Relations Divisions, Graduate School of Business Administration, University of California, Los Angeles.

[4] *Collected Laws and Regulations* ... Vol. 6, p. 375.

4. AGRICULTURAL PROCUREMENT PRICES

General considerations governing prices of farm produce have already been discussed in Chapter 13, together with a more detailed study of the procurement prices of grain, and these prices have already been mentioned in the previous section of this present chapter. Here we will review certain other aspects of policy on agricultural procurement prices.

Prices of other agricultural commodities are frequently expressed in terms of grain in discussing price changes in China. The relative procurement prices of different agricultural commodities were stated, in 1958, to be normally based on historic comparative costs. This was explained as being an unfortunate necessity, due to the weakness of production costing in agriculture. As a result, the prices of different products had got out of line as relative costs had changed. The remedy suggested was sampling to discover costs.[1]

Grain prices had originally been fixed on the basis of 1953 prices, before the free market in grain was abolished. For other commodities the same approximate date line was used, which came a couple of years after inflation had been brought under control and after an initial peace-time shake-up in relative prices to make them conform with changed circumstances of supply and demand. In this shake-up, in 1950–1, relative prices of industrial crops (cotton, tobacco and vegetable oils) had risen. In 1950, a government decree fixed the state purchasing prices of raw cotton in terms of grain at about 30 per cent above the pre-war (average for 1931–6) level. The relative price of cotton was lowered a little in succeeding years but in general appears to have remained somewhat above the pre-war level.[2] The high price of cotton relative to grain in 1950 can be explained by its greater relative fall in output compared with the pre-1949 peak figure. With the pre-1949 peak as 100, the outputs of grain crops and of cotton respectively were reported to be 78 and 52 in 1949. However, in the next few years, cotton output rose steeply and from 1952–8 was considerably higher than that of grain crops, compared with the pre-1949 peak outputs of each.[3]

The question of how far agricultural output is influenced by absolute prices, and by the relative procurement prices of different crops, is not susceptible to a clear cut answer. In 1956 the prices of a number of crops were raised but in 1957 the production of each of these crops fell, despite the absence of particularly severe natural disasters. This was because compulsory purchase quotas for other crops, notably cotton and grain, were raised and this had more influence on production decisions than did the price changes.[4] However, prices have not been without their influence. Thus, in 1958, it was feared that a rise in the state price for sugar cane might lead peasants to grow cane instead

---

[1] *Ta Kung Daily* (*Dagong Bao*), Peking, March 23, 1958, p. 4. Chiang Yen-ling: 'On the Purchase Price for Farm Products.'

[2] *Study* (*Xuexi*), No. 7, April 3, 1957, p. 16. Ho Wei: 'Significance and Method of Comparing Present and Pre-War Prices of Agricultural Commodities', and *New China Monthly* (*Xinhua Yuebao*), No. 30, April 1962, p. 161, and ibid., No. 43, May 1953, pp. 180–1, and ibid., No. 54, April 1954, p. 166, and *Collected Laws and Regulations* . . . Vol. 1, p. 232.

[3] *Ten Great Years*, p. 120.

[4] D. H. Perkins: *Market Control and Planning in Communist China*, pp. 68–9 and 71.

of grain, while if the state price for sugar went up without a corresponding rise in the price of cane, peasants might refine the sugar themselves, which would mean a reduction in the raw material for the modern sugar refineries.[1] These examples illustrate the uncertainties that surround government control over the peasants in China. Direct commands to deliver grain or cane to the state are not invariably effective against the pull of higher prices for other products. In any case, of course, even when direct control can be enforced, it is more expensive in men and money than control through the price mechanism.

The prices of many agricultural products were notably affected by changes in policy towards both free markets and peasants' private plots. In the summer of 1956, greater freedom was given to rural markets; while a few months later, policy temporarily became more favourable to peasants' private plots, which could be used, among other purposes, for growing fodder for pigs. As a result, many more pigs were reared in the following year, which led to a drastic fall in price and this, in turn, to a slaughtering of sows[2]—a clear example of a pig cycle set off by exogenous factors.

Chinese publications, when discussing rural welfare, make frequent reference to the 'scissors' relationship, well known to students of the Soviet economy. This is the relationship between the procurement prices of agricultural output paid to the peasants and the prices of industrial goods in rural areas, and is calculated as follows:[3]

$$\frac{\text{Index figure of retail price of industrial goods in rural areas} \times 100}{\text{Index figure of the procurement price of agricultural products}}$$

Thus a figure below 100 indicates that, since the base year, the 'terms of trade' have moved in favour of the peasants, and conversely. During the war the 'scissors' opened against rural interests, and in 1950 was estimated at 131·8 with 1930–6 as base.[4] This figure then fell steadily (except for a slight setback in 1955, due presumably to the ending of price preferences favouring supply and marketing co-operatives), but did not reach 100 until 1958–9, while by 1963 it is reckoned to have been just under 90, and in 1964 stood at 88.[5] The fall in the 1960s must have been greatly influenced by the price reductions

[1] *Ta Kung Daily* (*Dagong Bao*), Peking, March 23, 1958, p. 4. Chiang Yen-ling: loc. cit.
[2] *Collected Laws and Regulations* . . . Vol. 7, pp. 292–3. This interpretation seems more probable than that given by Ta-chung Liu and Kung-chia Yeh: *The Economy of the Chinese Mainland: National Income and Economic Development 1933–59*, Vol. 1, Rand Corporation, Santa Monica, 1963, pp. 77–8, where it is assumed that the rise in pig numbers resulted from a rise in government procurement price which took effect in March 1957. Due to the unlikelihood of a substantial rise in the number of pigs between then and the end of the year, Liu and Yeh question the Chinese figure for pigs in 1957. Also they argue that there was not the fodder available to support this increase. This last factor will have accounted for the fact that the rise reported in *Collected Laws and Regulations* . . . Vol. 7, p. 292, is of piglets brought to market. Shortage of feed may have influenced peasants to sell piglets rather than rear them to maturity. When the price of piglets dropped steeply, sows were slaughtered.
[3] *Statistical Research* (*Tongji Yanjiu*), No. 4, April 23, 1958, p. 25.
[4] *Statistical Bulletin* (*Tongji Gongzuo*), No. 17, September 14, 1957, p. 4.
[5] Ibid., and *Ten Great Years*, p. 173, and *East Wind* (*Dongfeng*), No. 20, October 1959 (ECMM 198). Li Feng and Yü Hang: 'Refute the Idea the General Situation of the Market is Tense', and *Peking Review*, November 20, 1964, p. 7, Yang Po: 'New China's Price

made at that time for agricultural producer goods as well as by higher procurement prices for farm produce.[1]

These figures are not reliable measures of rural welfare because information is seldom given about their method of calculation (e.g. geographical and commodity weighting) and it is not known if this is uniform for each date, nor is it known if allowance is made for changes in quality of agricultural or of industrial goods or for the suitability or even availability of industrial goods in rural areas, nor which price is used when more than one exists for one commodity (for example, compulsory purchase price and free market price) nor if non-monetary inducements to sell are taken into account.[2] While some of these points operate in opposite directions, there is no reason to suppose that they would exactly counterbalance each other. Finally, the scissors index does not allow for the adverse effect on rural welfare of the fact that higher prices do not apparently obtain for compulsory sales in years of poor harvests, when peasants have less to sell and when, on a free market, their produce would fetch higher prices; this must have been especially important in 1959 to 1961. That prices do not fall in years of good harvests is no adequate compensation, as in such periods the marginal utility of money must be deemed to be lower than in times of hardship.

Nevertheless, the general trend towards better rural terms of trade since 1949 may be accepted. It is certainly to be expected during a period when transport improved and law and order was maintained. These facts would, of course, also operate to improve the urban terms of trade by reducing the cost and risk of bringing farm produce to the towns.

5. PRICES OF PRODUCER GOODS

Unlike the Soviet Union, China has not followed a policy of low prices for products of heavy industry. Prices of Soviet producer goods have been fixed by adding 3–5 per cent to average cost. In 1956 a similar pricing system for these items was proposed in China, but was successfully thwarted by the Ministry of Finance on the grounds that even at existing prices, supply could not meet demand. The actual level at which prices of producer goods in China have been fixed, owes much to historical accident—to the prices that happened to exist when stabilization was enforced in 1953 and 1954.[3] One reason suggested for the failure to follow the Soviet example by lowering prices for producer goods, is that the very different relative scarcities of capital and labour in China meant that it was not thought necessary or desirable to encourage capital-intensive production by low pricing of capital goods.[4] Other reasons may be that high prices were considered preferable to giving

---

Policy', and *China Reconstructs*, July 1966, p. 48. Sung Kuang-wei: 'Factors behind Price Stability.' On preferential treatment given until 1955 to supply and marketing co-operatives see p. 279 above, and *New China Monthly (Xinhua Yuebao)*, No. 65, March 1955, p. 148.

[1] See p. 360 above.
[2] Some of these matters are mentioned in Chapter 13 above.
[3] D. H. Perkins: *Market Control and Planning in Communist China*, pp. 110 and 201, and *Economic Research (Jingji Yanjiu)*, No. 3, June 1957, p. 55. Fan Jo-yi: loc. cit.
[4] *Journal of Asian Studies*, Vol. XXV, No. 4, August 1966, p. 656. S. H. Chou: loc. cit.

direct subsidies to the numerous small enterprises that made industrial producer goods; enterprises whose costs were much higher than those of the large modern concerns. Also, high prices for these products fulfilled a distributive function which the planning machinery was inadequate to perform.[1]

In 1957, despite a price reduction in the previous year, the price index of products of heavy industry on a 1936 base (in terms of JMP) stood at around 500, compared with approximately 300 for commodity prices in general and 200 for agricultural produce. Prices of heavy industry products were also reported to be above the international level, presumably at official rates of exchange.[2]

Profits, calculated on costs, have been high in modern plants making producer goods. The Anshan Steel Works, for example, was operating at a 120 per cent profit in 1957, despite a 30 per cent price reduction in the previous year.[3] In smaller, less highly-capitalized concerns, profits on this basis were much lower. (In 1955, the profit on cost in the whole of heavy industry was stated to have been 40 per cent.)[4] However, when reckoned as profit on capital, the discrepancy in profit rates between the two types of enterprises was much less.[5] The making of high (on cost) profits, most of which accrue to the state, may therefore be taken as a way of getting a return from capital which was nominally provided free.

In the case of timber the (on cost) profit rate was even higher than that of heavy industry, being 98 per cent in 1955. This resulted in timber prices being above both international, and earlier Chinese, levels, as well as higher than the prices of timber substitutes.[6] That is to say that timber prices (which, it will be remembered, are subject to central control) have been deliberately set at a level which, at least in some measure, reflects current scarcities.

A controversy was carried on, especially in the greater freedom of 1956–7, between economists who defended and opposed the high price policy for capital goods.[7] An argument in favour of reducing prices was that this would discourage the duplication that occurred when firms made their own equipment in preference to buying it from specialist producers. Also it would prevent the situation which arose in 1954–5 when ministries often ordered imported equipment, or goods from private factories, in preference to supplies from state factories.[8] Those opposing lower prices argued that demand far outran supply for capital equipment and that even the 1956 price reduction had hit hard the smaller and less well-equipped producers.[9]

---

[1] D. H. Perkins: *Market Control and Planning in Communist China*, pp. 112–13.
[2] *Economic Research (Jingji Yanjiu)*, No. 3, June 1957, p. 58. Fan Jo-yi: loc. cit.
[3] Ibid., p. 62.
[4] *Finance (Caizheng)*, No. 2, November 5, 1956, p. 20. Jen Jui-lin: 'A Study of the Present Price of Timber.'
[5] *Economic Research (Jingji Yanjiu)*, No. 3, June 1957, p. 58. Fan Jo-yi: loc. cit.
[6] *Finance (Caizheng)*, No. 2, November 5, 1956, p. 20. Jen Jui-lin: loc. cit.
[7] e.g. *Economic Research (Jingji Yanjiu)*, No. 2, April 1957, pp. 12–24. Nan Ping and So Chen: loc. cit., and ibid., No. 3, June 1957, pp. 54–67. Fan Jo-yi: loc. cit.
[8] Ibid., No. 3, June 1957, p. 61. Fan Jo-yi: loc. cit.
[9] It is interesting to note that in order to help such enterprises in their ensuing difficulties, Shanghai Municipality had not brought in the new lower allocation prices for producer

From 1961 onwards, the prices of capital goods for farm use were repeatedly lowered as part of the programme to aid agricultural development.

One of the producer goods for which prices have not been high is coal. The price of coal in terms of flour or grain was reported to have declined between 1936 and 1956 by 16–49 per cent in the case of three major mines, while in the country as a whole the price ratio between equal weights of steel and coal in 1958 stood at 22:1 compared with 15·51:1 for the United States, 7·98:1 for the Soviet Union, 7·75:1 for France and 3·78:1 for Britain (all figures as given in the Chinese source).[1] One reason for the disparity of the Chinese ratio is the difference in profit levels between the two industries. Profits in the steel industry in China are high, as we have seen, while profits on coal have been low. Usually, it was stated in 1958, profits (on cost) in coalmining, including ancillary processes such as washing, ran at about half the level found in other branches of industry, notably in such major coal consumers as electricity and transport.[2] However, the situation is clouded by the accounting confusion that existed in the coal mining industry, where capital expenditure was often wrongfully included in production costs, thus artificially lowering profit rates reckoned on costs.[3] Once again it must be noted that electricity and modern transport are much more heavily capitalized than coal mining, which in China in 1957 was still largely dependent on manual operations, and here, once more, the same point about concealed return from capital is relevant. Nevertheless, even profits reckoned on capital were said to be much lower in coal mining than in other industries.[4]

Coal subject to central allocation included all the output of the centrally controlled mines and the output of the more accessible local mines.[5] The allocation price for this coal included transport from the pit to the railhead (including loading on rail trucks) but no further. This was held to make the producing interests (the Ministry of Coal and the local mining departments) heedless of the need to bring about local equilibrium between demand and supply by developing production in coal-deficient areas. An allocation price

---

goods, but had fixed temporary prices at a higher level—an indication of the latitude allowed to (or taken by) local authorities in pricing matters even before the 1957–8 decentralization measures. *Economic Research (Jingji Yanjiu)*, No. 2, April 1957, pp. 22–3. Nan Ping and So Chen: loc. cit.

[1] *Finance (Caizheng)*, No. 3, March 1958, p. 14. Chang Meng-tseng: 'Price Problems of the Products of the State Coal Mining Industry.'

[2] Ibid., p. 14. In 1957 the planned rate of profit (on cost) in coal mining was only 2·64 per cent, although achieved profits reached 8·6 per cent (figure probably for first half year) compared with 13 per cent in 1956. Ibid., p. 15 and ibid., No. 7, July 1957, p. 30. Chang Pen-lien: 'Some Questions Influencing the Raising of the Profit Level in the State Coal Mining Industry.' However, another source gives the average profit in coal mining in China in 1956 as 11 per cent of costs: some difference in definition may account for this divergence. *People's Power Industry (Renmin Dianye)*, No. 3, February 5, 1958, p. 21.

[3] *Finance (Caizheng)*, No. 7, July 1957, p. 30. Chang Pen-lien: loc. cit.

[4] Ibid., No. 3, March 1958, p. 15. Chang Meng-tseng: loc. cit.

[5] *Economic Research (Jingji Yanjiu)*, No. 2, February 1959, p. 35. 'A Discussion among Staff of Economic Departments on Problems of Distribution and Pricing of Industrial Commodities.'

which included transport to station of destination would, it was argued in 1957, provide the necessary incentive.¹

In the case of wholesale prices of coal, this system of pricing appears to have been already in operation in 1957. In that year we read of a standard wholesale price for the whole north-east, based on the price in the Shenyang area. This price, probably ¥11·31 a ton (type and quality of coal unspecified), compared with a regional price of ¥13·20 in the coal-deficient north-west, and a national average of ¥12·70.² The vicinity of Shenyang includes Fushun, one of the country's largest coal-mining centres, at which the allocation price in 1957 was probably around ¥9 a ton,³ giving a margin of approximately 25 per cent between allocation price and wholesale price. In some parts of the north-east, notably in the Harbin locality, the standard wholesale price resulted in all the mines working at a loss.⁴ Harbin had a coal surplus, and owing to transport difficulties, there was a tendency for stockpiles to accumulate. If prices were raised to cover the losses, it was feared that even more coal would pile up; so evidently some positive price elasticity of supply or of demand (or both) was assumed.⁵ However, the influence of price was not sufficiently strong to cause output to decline to a point where losses were no longer made. Presumably an output target had been set and the achievement of this ranked as a more important success indicator than the reduction of loss.

In 1957–8, the introduction of an internal accounting price for coal, as used in the Soviet Union, was mooted. By this system, pithead prices would be fixed individually for each mine, based on 'reasonable costs and reasonable profits', and would be divorced from allocation prices. The profits and losses resulting from the difference between the two prices would accrue to the allocating organ. Evidently this proposal was not adopted but was still under discussion in 1963.⁶

In 1958 the pithead prices of coal were raised as had earlier been suggested,

---

¹ *Planned Economy* (*Jihua Jingji*), No. 10, October 1957, pp. 24–5. Chang Shih: loc. cit.

² *Finance* (*Caizheng*), No. 7, July 1957, p. 31. Chang Pen-lien: loc. cit. The figure of ¥11·31 was given as the price in the Harbin area in *Economic Research* (*Jingji Yanjiu*), No. 3, June 1957, p. 65. Fan Jo-yi: loc. cit. Here it is not specifically stated that this is the *wholesale* price, although this would seem to be indicated by the context. Chang Pen-lien: loc. cit., writing at almost the same date, refers to a standard wholesale price of coal for the whole of the north-east, so we have taken ¥11·31 as being this price.

³ The figure of ¥9 a ton as a hypothetical allocation price for Fushun coal (inclusive of transport to railhead only) was given in the course of a numerical example of the effect of charging allocation prices inclusive of different stages of transport. See *Planned Economy* (*Jihua Jingji*), No. 10, October 1957, p. 25. Chang Shih: loc. cit. We have presumed that the hypothetical figure is approximately correct.

⁴ *Economic Research* (*Jingji Yanjiu*), No. 3, June 1957, p. 65. Fan Jo-yi: loc. cit., and *Finance* (*Caizheng*), No. 7, July 1957, p. 31. Chang Pen-lien: loc. cit. Fan says the average loss of all the Harbin coal mines was 14·6 per cent of costs. Chang gives the loss per ton of untreated coal from the mines in the Harbin area as ¥6 to ¥7. It does not seem possible to reconcile these figures with the information on prices given above.

⁵ *Economic Research* (*Jingji Yanjiu*), No. 3, June 1957, p. 65. Fan Jo-yi: loc. cit.

⁶ *Finance* (*Caizheng*), No. 7, July 1957, p. 31. Chang Pen-lien: loc. cit., and ibid., No. 3, March 1958, pp. 14–15, Chang Meng-tseng: loc. cit., and *Economic Research* (*Jingji Yanjiu*), No. 5, May 1963, p. 4. Hsüeh Mu-ch'iao: loc. cit.

but the extent of the rise is not known. 'Market prices' (probably, as we have seen, meaning wholesale prices) remained unchanged. This was achieved by squeezing commercial profits: the result therefore being a transfer of profits from commerce to coal mining.[1]

The pithead prices of coal from local mines were, because of lower costs, below those of the central mines, and still lower were the prices of 'the small native mines' opened in such numbers during the Great Leap and in which quality was also likely to have been lower.[2] In the case of the local and native mines, pithead prices appear to be fixed by the local mining department on an individual basis for each mine. In 1959 the practice was that profits made on all the sales of small mine coal within any given area were divided between the producing and the marketing units 'according to the principle of industrial profit being higher than commercial profit', while losses were absorbed by the commercial department.[3]

The price differentials between coal from central and local mines were compensated, at least in part, by the higher transport costs to outside markets of the coal from the local mines.[4] (The more conveniently transportable coal from local mines was in any case subject to central allocation and hence sold at centrally-fixed prices.)

The price of coal has been treated at length both because of the importance of the commodity and also because it illustrates a number of aspects of price policy. First, despite the command nature of the economy, price plays a definite role in resource allocation and utilization. Before the 1958 price rise of coal, economists were urging a rise on the grounds that this would provide incentive to raise output. Also, it was argued that an all-in allocation price to station of destination, would encourage the expansion of output in coal-deficient areas.

The case of coal demonstrates that for one commodity there can co-exist both a national market to which supplies are centrally allocated at centrally determined prices, and also a series of local markets, served by smaller units of production, for which greater flexibility is allowed. It also shows that even —or perhaps more particularly—in the national market, the existence of central control offers no assurance of rational pricing. We have seen, too, that it is not easy to decide what is the rational price of any one commodity when other prices are irrational.

6. LOCAL PRICE DIFFERENTIALS

In a country of China's size, with poor transport, great variations in prices are liable to be found from one region to another. As in other under-developed lands, these differences may be considerable even within a small area. In China, before 1949, such differences were very marked.

---

[1] *Finance (Caizheng)*, No. 3, March 1958, p. 15. Chang Meng-tseng: loc. cit., and *Economic Research (Jingji Yanjiu)*, No. 3, March 1959, p. 28. Keng Tsun-san: 'Brief Remarks on the Current Price of Coal.'
[2] *Economic Research (Jingji Yanjiu)*, No. 2, February 1959, p. 35., loc. cit.
[3] Ibid., No. 3, March 1959, p. 28. Keng Tsun-san: loc. cit.
[4] Ibid., No. 2, February 1959, p. 35. loc. cit.

In the early years of the Communist regime, local prices of industrial goods had been based on prices at the main centres of production plus handling and transport charges to the place of sale. For cotton cloth, for example, Shanghai prices were taken as the base and the prices in the interior were considerably higher. However, as industry became more widespread, the interior market could be supplied from nearer sources and the disparity with Shanghai prices diminished. Improved transport also worked towards this end.[1] There appears to have been a time lag before these price reductions took effect, during which cotton mills in the interior made higher profits than those on the coast. Such a time lag is likely to occur when price changes are made by administrative order.

The tendency to a narrowing of local price differentials was not unchecked. After the Fifth National Price Conference, held in 1955, to which reference has already been made, a directive was issued that price differentials for industrial goods, between cities in the large and medium range, should be from 3 to 5 per cent in addition to transport expenses. In the case of many goods from other places sold in Peking, this meant a widening of local price differentials. Three years later in 1958, a survey indicated that—at least in Peking—differentials were in fact mainly within or near to the range laid down in 1955. On goods from nearby Tientsin the differential was lower (1–2 per cent) but became progressively higher for goods from the north-east, Shanghai and Canton. On consumer goods, the local price differentials were larger than on producer goods; this too being in accordance with national policy.[2] These differentials, it must be noted, applied to commodities moving from one city to another, not to prices of similar goods made and sold in each city. The prices of these latter must have diverged by much more than the margins permitted for inter-city trade, as can be seen from the divergences in the cost of living between different cities. One study estimates that the cost of living in 1952 to 1955 in the most expensive of the eight chief cities of China (Canton) was some 38 per cent above that of the cheapest (Shenyang).[3]

In 1958, doubts were expressed whether it was still desirable to follow the policy, on price differentials of goods traded between cities, that had been laid down in 1955. A new situation had arisen, especially with the 1957–8 decentralization of pricing decisions.[4] In 1966 a visitor to Shanghai, Peking and Canton noted that price differentials for identical commodities were of the order of 10 per cent between the three cities.[5] This would be inclusive of transport costs.

---

[1] *The Eighth National Congress of the Communist Party of China*, Vol. 2. Speeches, p. 213. Speech by Li Hsien-nien, Minister of Finance, and *Economic Research (Jingji Yanjiu)*, No. 12, December 1959, pp. 46–7. Ch'in Liu-fang: loc. cit.

[2] *Education and Research (Jiaoyu yu Yanjiu)*, October 1958. Hsien Yi-yü: 'A Survey of Local Price Differentials of Industrial Goods in Peking and a Study of Some Problems'— (in *Selected Essays of Chinese Economists* . . . Vol. 2, pp. 338–40).

[3] P. Schran: op. cit., p. 60. For Canton the information is for the average cost of living 1952–4, while for Shenyang it is for May 1955. However, the degree of price stability over these years was sufficient to make this difference of dates relatively unimportant.

[4] *Education and Research (Jiaoyu yu Yanjiu)*, October 1958. Hsien Yi-yü: loc. cit. (in *Selected Essays of Chinese Economists* . . . Vol. 2, p. 340).

[5] Information kindly supplied by Barry M. Richman.

No single policy on local price differentials appears to be applied to those producer goods whose prices are centrally fixed. We have seen that the price of coal (at least the wholesale price) is determined on a regional basis. This also applied (or did, in 1956–7) to electric power and petroleum products.[1] For chemical fertilizers, in contrast, the retail price of any one type was reported in 1959 to be 'basically uniform' throughout the country, irrespective of transport costs.[2]

The allocation of important producer goods is centrally decided and is, therefore, not directly affected by price. For example, by a central government decision, cotton cultivation was given priority for the supply of chemical fertilizers.[3] However, price may affect willingness of the consumer to use the product. Thus the government may have been prompted to bring in a uniform national price for chemical fertilizers, with its element of subsidy for remote areas, by the fact that peasants, especially in the more backward parts of the country, may still need persuasion to use such products. The industrial users of coal and petroleum, on the other hand, would not need convincing of the desirability of these commodities.

In 1966 we read that elimination of unnecessary links in the distributive apparatus had reduced freight costs and prices and that government regulations limited to 3–5 per cent the addition that could be made to prices of producer goods intended for the countryside.[4] The implication appears to be that previously a larger addition had been permitted.

With respect to prices of goods controlled, after 1957–8, at the provincial level, we find an example in 1959 of the central government laying down the general principles while the provinces settled the definite prices, as provided by the decentralization measures. This happened in the case of powered irrigation and drainage machinery and resulted in relatively small local retail price differentials throughout the country as a whole, while uniformity of retail prices within each province was stipulated.[5]

Deliberate government policy, as well as improvements in transport, contributed to reducing local differentials in the procurement prices of agricultural output. In the early days of the regime, 'in some places the purchasing prices of agricultural products were mechanically arrived at by taking the prices at the centres of collection and distribution as the starting point, and then working backwards, deducting transportation charges all along the

[1] *Hydro-Electric Power* (*Shuili Fadian*), No. 4, January 1958, p. 4. (Quoted from Yuan-li Wu: *Economic Development and The Uses of Energy Resources in Communist China*, New York, 1963, p. 258), and *Economic Research* (*Jingji Yanjiu*), No. 3, June 1957, pp. 64–5. Fan Jo-yi: loc. cit.

[2] *Economic Research* (*Jingji Yanjiu*), No. 3, March 1959, p. 31. Chiao Yü-pao: 'The Circumstances Surrounding the Prices of Some Kinds of Important Producer Goods for Agriculture.' In 1962 chemical fertilizers were being sold in Kiangsu 'at the unified price for the whole province fixed by the state. This price has been unchanged for five years'. *Ta Kung Daily* (*Dagong Bao*), July 9, 1962, p. 2. Kuan Sen: 'Give Out Agricultural Loans at the Proper Time and Help Needy Production Teams.' The statement that prices were uniform within one province does not necessarily conflict with their being *basically* uniform throughout the country.

[3] *Economic Research* (*Jingji Yanjiu*), No. 3, March 1959, p. 32. Chiao Yü-pao: loc. cit.

[4] NCNA Peking, February 19, 1966.

[5] *Economic Research* (*Jingji Yanjiu*), No. 3, March 1959, pp. 31–2. Chiao Yü-pao: loc. cit.

route'.[1] As a result, procurement prices were sometimes disproportionately below the local sales prices of grain, which 'violates the principle that the prices of products at places where they are sold should be fixed on the basis of prices at places where they are produced'.[2] Special increases in procurement prices were made in remote, mountainous and backward areas.[3] In 1957, it was stated that the greatest narrowing of the 'scissors' had occurred in the national minority areas, which include the most distant and backward parts of the country.[4] However, in 1957, in the opinion of a prominent economist, procurement prices in such districts were still unduly low.[5]

On the free market, large local price differentials for agricultural commodities have evidently emerged at times. Long distance private trade, which would have had the effect of reducing these differentials, is banned, although enforcement may not have been complete.[6] Pedlars have made their living through the considerable local price differentials which have existed for many products between even nearby places.

Insufficient information is available to decide whether the years since decentralisation of price control have seen a widening of local price differentials in the case of prices newly under local control. This might have been expected to occur if the delegation of authority to the provinces has been effective, which itself is one of the most interesting points in the study of the economics and politics of contemporary China.

[1] *The Eighth National Congress of the Communist Party of China*, Vol. 2. Speeches. p. 213. Speech by Li Hsien-nien, Minister of Finance.
[2] Ibid., pp. 213–14.
[3] Ibid., p. 215, and *People's Handbook* (*Renmin Shouce*) *1956*, p. 524, and p. 359 above.
[4] *Statistical Work* (*Tongji Gongzuo*), No. 17, September 14, 1957, p. 6.
[5] Niu Chung-huang: op. cit., p. 90.
[6] See p. 298 above, and *Red Flag* (*Hongqi*), No. 7–8, April 16, 1963, p. 7. Hsüeh Mu-ch'iao: loc. cit.

Chapter 17

ECONOMIC PLANNING[1]

1. THE DEVELOPMENT OF ECONOMIC PLANNING

China's economic planning has been restricted mainly to the setting of targets, to drawing up lists of resolutions. It does not attempt to effect close integration of different economic sectors, nor is it much concerned with optimum allocation of resources. Throughout, and this can scarcely be stressed too much, economic planning in China is constrained by the deficiencies of the information on which it has to work, as well as by weaknesses in the administrative and supervisory organs charged with implementation of plans and with checking this implementation.

Long-range plans are formulated by the State Planning Commission, while annual and shorter plans come under the State Economic Commission. The State Construction Commission is closely associated with the investment aspects of planning.[2] The Ministry of Finance is naturally concerned with the financial side of planning as is its supervisory body, the State Council Office for Finance and Trade. The Ministry of Allocation of Materials and the State Technological Commission may be presumed to participate prominently in planning in their respective spheres. The economic and other ministries have their own internal planning organs. In the Party organization there is no organ specifically charged with responsibility for economic planning, although the Central Committee's Finance and Trade Work Department is active in this field. However, the state organs connected with planning are headed by members of the Politburo.[3]

A brief account of the history and development of these organs is necessary for an understanding of their present relationships and operations.

Economic planning in China was pioneered in the north-east, the region formerly known as Manchuria, which was economically more advanced than the rest of the country owing to development by the Japanese. This region came under Communist rule relatively early and even in 1949 a rough rehabilitation plan for its industry was formulated. Two years later a regional planning commission was established. The North-East Administrative Area, at the time under the chairmanship of Kao Kang, was—as we have earlier

[1] An early draft of part of this chapter appeared in *China Quarterly*, No. 17, January–March 1964, pp. 111–24, entitled 'China's Economic Planning and Industry.'

[2] State Investment Commission might be a more satisfactory translation of *kuochia chienshe weiyuanhui* (cf. p. 27 above for definition of *chipen chienshe*). However, we shall keep to the usual English translation of the title of this body, which is the one used in official translations issued from Peking.

[3] In this and succeeding paragraphs, I am indebted to an unpublished paper of Ezra Vogel of Harvard University relating to the financial system of Mainland China.

had occasion to notice—a testing ground for practices new to China, especially those deriving from the Soviet Union. After preliminary trials in the north-east, several such practices (e.g. the economic accounting system) were then adopted in the rest of the country. So it was with economic planning.

Preliminary steps in nation-wide planning were taken in 1951, when the Central Financial and Economic Planning Bureau, under the State Council's Financial and Economic Commission, put out control figures for production and capital investment in industry and transport and drew up a plan for state-owned industrial concerns. In November 1952, after it had been announced that the First Five Year Plan was to begin in the following year, a State Planning Commission was set up under Kao Kang. We read that, in 1953, 'a relatively complete set of plans was mapped out and handed down to the lower levels for execution'.[1] However, the First Five Year Plan, as a whole, was not published until 1955, half way through the period (1953–7) which it was supposed to cover.

By the end of 1953, some kind of statistical organs, though usually, no doubt, of a rudimentary type, were in existence in all provinces and autonomous regions except Tibet. On the national level, a State Statistical Bureau had been established in October 1952.

After the adoption of China's new constitution in 1954, the State Planning Commission was one of the bodies directly under the State Council. Meanwhile Kao Kang had been expelled from the Party and had died in mysterious circumstances. His former assistant in the north-east, Li Fu-ch'un, was appointed Chairman of the new State Planning Commission. The general oversight of capital investment under the Plan was entrusted to a new organ, the State Construction Commission, under the chairmanship of Po I-po who, from 1949 to 1953, had been Minister of Finance.

Two years later, in 1956, long-term and short-term planning were separated. The State Planning Commission, which formerly dealt with both long-term and short-term planning, was now to be left free to concentrate on the long-term planning, that is on five year plans and on the longer perspective plans. However, no more than casual references have been made to perspective planning.[2] Short-term planning (the formulation and adjustment of plans of up to one year's duration) was made the responsibility of the newly formed State Economic Commission to which Po I-po was transferred as Chairman and which, like the State Planning Commission and the State Construction Commission, was directly subordinate to the State Council.[3]

[1] *Planning and Statistics* (*Jihua yu Tongji*), No. 13, July 1959 (ECMM 204). Ku Tso-hsin: 'The Development of the Planning of Industrial Construction in the Past Decade.' Many of the first staff of the Communist economic planning organs came from the Kuomintang's National Resources Commission. (Unpublished paper by Ezra Vogel.)

[2] On the difficulties that arose as a result of the State Planning Commission trying to combine both long- and short-term planning, see Li Fu-ch'un's Speech to the Eighth National Congress of the CCP. *The Eighth National Congress of the Communist Party of China*, Vol. II. Speeches. Peking, 1956, pp. 293–4. An Indian Mission which visited the State Planning Commission in 1956 and reported on its organization just before these changes, stated that no special group was working on perspective plans, but that each department concerned itself with them in addition to five year plans—(unpublished mimeographed report).

[3] *Collected Laws and Regulations of the People's Republic of China* (in Chinese), Vol. 3, p. 82.

Another new organ, also established in 1956 directly under the State Council, was the General Bureau for the Supply of Raw Materials, formed for the purpose of controlling raw material supplies and reserves. The State Technological Commission, established at the same time, had among its duties that of formulating five year and perspective plans for technical development.[1] Two reasons may account for the formation of these three new bodies in 1956. First, preparations were under way for the Second Five Year Plan to begin in 1958. Second, 1956 saw the completion of the 'socialist transformation' of all licit private businesses of any size. As a result, many more concerns became subject to direct state planning which thus became more complex but, at the same time, in theory anyhow, more feasible. Direct planning of the activities of the state sector had been in the hands of the State Planning Commission and of its local offices, while indirect planning (for the collective and private sector) was done by the offices of the State Council, the ministries, and local authorities.[2] Hence an increase in the size of the state sector threw an added burden on the State Planning Commission. This led to the need for the new bodies established in 1956.

The State Economic Commission was given the task of effecting balances on the national level between supply and demand of raw materials. Chinese planning is primarily 'planning by material balances', a practice learned from the Soviet Union. At least to begin with, the Soviet methods were roughly followed. According to these, calculations are made of future requirements of raw materials and capital equipment on the basis of technical co-efficients.[3] Then the demand worked out in this fashion is compared with the supply likely to be available in the country as a whole (national balancing) or in the particular area (e.g. province) for which the balancing is being done. In the light of this, decisions are taken for imports or exports nationally or between localities: these latter are called 'balance transfers' (*ch'a e tiaopo*). In the course of the year, quarterly adjustments are made as necessary, particularly in financial and material allocations.[4]

Summing up the achievements in the field of economic planning during the First Five Year Plan period, an article written on the basis of reports made by Soviet experts in Peking claimed that 'a system for the balancing and distribution of products was introduced. The Stock reserve system and the comprehensive financial plan of the state . . . were brought close to perfection'; (the comprehensive financial plan will be discussed more fully below). Other achievements were said to include the inauguration of a

[1] *Collected Laws and Regulations* . . . Vol. 3, p. 82. See also p. 156 above for the other functions of the State Technological Commission.

[2] *The Eighth National Congress of the Communist Party of China*, Vol. II, Speeches, pp. 291–2. Speech by Li Fu-ch'un.

[3] *Planned Economy* (*Jihua Jingji*), No. 1, January 1958, pp. 38–41. Sun Hui-ch'ing: 'Lecture No. 13: Charts of Supply Plans of Raw Materials and Technical Equipment', and *People's Daily* (*Renmin Ribao*), November 12, 1957, p. 7. Hsüeh Mu-ch'iao: 'Our Country's Planning and Statistical Work Must Learn from the Soviet Union.'

[4] *Report of the Indian Delegation to China on Agricultural Planning and Techniques*, Delhi, 1956, pp. 55–6, and *Planned Economy* (*Jihua Jingji*), No. 10, October 1958, pp. 34–5. She Yi-san: 'A Discussion of the Change in the Allocation System for Raw Materials', and *Planning and Statistics* (*Jihua yu Tongji*), No. 13, July 1959 (ECMM 204). Ku Tso-hsin: loc. cit., and unpublished paper of Ezra Vogel.

planning and control system for capital construction, the fixing of targets, arrangements for control at different levels and the laying down of procedure for the approval of reports on tasks planned.[1]

It would be useful if we could assess the validity of these claims to improvement in planning techniques during the First Five Year Plan period by comparing the First and Second Five Year Plans as technical documents. Certainly it is not difficult to demonstrate the weaknesses of the First Plan. This was in the nature of a list of targets, some ill co-ordinated. Thus, as we have seen,[2] during the First Five Year Plan period, plans for electric power generation were not always co-ordinated with the plans for the development of manufacturing industry. The allocation to agriculture, water conservancy and forestry together in the First Five Year Plan of less than 8 per cent of total investment funds,[3] also proved inconsistent with increased demands for food and agricultural raw materials. Unfortunately, the information published about the Second Five Year Plan (for 1958–62) was so scanty that a comparison with its predecessor in regard to technical competence is unfeasible. The annual plans, which were published up to and including 1960, do not appear to demonstrate any great technical advance. However, this may not be the fault of the actual planning staff, for we do not know what truncating or mauling of their plans occurred before publication.

The Second Five Year Plan came into operation almost simultaneously with a radical change of policy which ushered in the Great Leap Forward of 1958 and which caused the plan to be stillborn. Before charting the very chequered story of economic planning in the years of what was to have been the Second Five Year Plan period, we must study the radical change in the circumstances of planning that stemmed from the administrative decentralization movement of 1957–8.

We have already had occasion to comment on the overloading of China's central administration towards the end of the First Five Year Plan period. Ever since the abolition of the six great administrative regions in 1954, the government had attempted to maintain a centralized control over the whole economy. The effort to do so, and the bureaucracy involved in this attempt, were hampering the pace of development. Indeed, it appears that the unworkability of this degree of centralization had caused the system to break down. Some areas were said to 'decide on major items of capital construction without the approval of the state or of higher levels. For these purposes they divert raw materials from key construction projects of the state, and in some cases even detain materials that are in transit.'[4] This led, in places, to investment far exceeding the planned total. Careless plan formulation, followed by repeated revisions, had resulted in priorities being disregarded, in waste of both capital and raw materials and in unbalanced plan fulfilment.[5]

[1] *Planning and Statistics (Jihua yu Tongji)*, No. 13, July 1959 (ECMM 204). Ku Tso-hsin: loc. cit.
[2] See p. 133 above.
[3] *First Five Year Plan for the Development of the National Economy of the People's Republic of China in 1953–7* (in Chinese), Peking, 1956, p. 29.
[4] *Planned Economy (Jihua Jingji)*, No. 11, November 1958, pp. 3–4. Yang Ying-chieh, Vice-Chairman, State Planning Commission: 'On Unified Planning and Decentralized Control.' [5] Ibid.

The local authorities found the demands of higher-level planning authorities for information exceedingly burdensome and were swamped with the paper work entailed in replying to these requests. The situation was aggravated by the existence of three central government planning agencies—the State Planning Commission, the State Economic Commission, and the State Construction Commission. Provinces and lower local authorities, in contrast, at that time had but one planning organ each. Thus 'three large rivers flow into one small stream, so the waters are bound to flood over'. These complaints were voiced loudly in 1957 by even such a relatively advanced province as Kiangsu, where the staff of the local planning commissions must have been considerably more efficient than in most provinces.[1]

The decision to decentralize appears, at least in part, to have been a belated recognition that highly centralized control was impossible and that in fact local authorities had already taken over some of the functions supposedly reserved for the centre. The directive on the reform of the planning system, promulgated jointly by the Central Committee of the Party and the State Council, was dated September 1958, some ten months after the parallel decree on industrial management. Its object was to change the former system of planning, which had been primarily vertical, on a production branch basis, with the central ministries holding the dominant position. Instead, what was called a 'double-track' system (i.e. both vertical and horizontal) was decreed, in which, under central leadership, predominance was to be given to local equilibrium, with central ministries and local authorities co-operating. The territorial principle was, in other words, to have priority over that of the production branch; horizontal links (*k'uai k'uai*) over vertical (*t'iao t'iao*).[2] In this reform of the planning system, as in the other decentralization measures of 1957–8, the Chinese were undoubtedly influenced by the economic decentralization which had been carried out in the Soviet Union shortly before. China, however, retained the central industrial ministries which, in the Soviet Union, were abolished. Nevertheless, the local counterparts of these ministries were under the dual leadership of both ministry and local authority, with the latter paramount. In practice, the degree of influence exercised by a ministry in distant Peking may often have been very slight compared with that of the local authority on the spot. The whole system of planning, as formulated in the decentralization directive, would tend to put the local authority in a dominant position, relative to the industrial ministries, in determining local industrial plans. The fact that in China the industrial ministries were retained should not be taken to indicate that the degree of local control over planning, or industrial management, was less than in the Soviet Union where the ministries were abolished.

The chief items of planning which were to remain under central control,

---

[1] *Planned Economy (Jihua Jingji)*, No. 3, March 1957, p. 16. Mao Chün-i, Kiangsu Provincial Planning Commission: 'Further Discussion on the Method of Reforming Local Planning Organs.' Subsequently, however, provinces are reported as having provincial economic commissions, as well as provincial planning commissions.
[2] *Planned Economy (Jihua Jingji)*, No. 9, September 1958, p. 13. Wang Kuei-wu: 'An Important Change in the Method of Drawing up Annual Plans.'

according to the September 1958 directive on the reform of the planning system, were the following:

(1) The output targets of the most important industrial and agricultural commodities (e.g. steel and grain).[1]

(2) Total national capital investment, major capital projects, and new productive capacity for important commodities.

(3) The balancing and transfers (*sc.* inter-provincial) of important types of raw materials, of equipment and of consumer goods.

(4) Totals for imports and exports and the volume of important import and export commodities.

(5) Receipts and payments of the national budget; the upward remittances payable and subsidies receivable by local authorities (*sc.* provincial level); credit equilibrium and the transfer of funds for capital purposes.

(6) The overall arrangements for the enrolment plan for institutions of higher education and for the plan for sending students abroad.

(7) Total wages, total number of employees, the allocation, at national level, of labour, and especially of scientific and technical manpower.

(8) Volume of railway freight and of freight turnover (the latter possibly including non-railway freight).

(9) The plans, and important items of technical capacity, of the individual enterprises and institutions directly under central ministries.[2]

The directive describes the nine listed items as being the 'chief' or the 'important' items remaining under central control. The phrasing leaves it ambiguous whether any other items of lesser importance also remained similarly controlled.

Other targets which now ceased to be fixed by the central authorities included total value of industrial output, irrigated acreage, arable acreage, total circulation of commodities, total retail sales, turnover of goods, local transport, rate of and total cost reduction, and the volume of building and installation work. These targets were in future to be settled by the local authorities and the ministries between themselves. In order to provide flexibility, even the centrally-controlled targets might be adjusted by local authorities so long as state plans were fulfilled and more especially those plans concerning construction projects, productive capacity, level of production, balance transfers and revenue.[3]

The provincial level authorities had to draw together and co-ordinate the plans of their subordinate *hsien* and of the enterprises and institutions (both those under central and under local control) within their territory. To undertake these tasks, provinces and at least some municipalities under provinces, now had both planning commissions and also economic commissions, corresponding to the State Planning Commission and State Economic Commission on the national level; and also local departments and bureaux for the supply of raw materials corresponding to the central government organ (bureau or

---

[1] In fact central interest in grain was concentrated on inter-provincial transfers. See p. 349 above.

[2] *Collected Laws and Regulations*... Vol 8, pp. 96–7.

[3] *Planned Economy (Jihua Jingji)*, No. 9, September 1958, p. 14. Wang Kuei-wu: loc. cit.

ministry at different dates) existing for that purpose. Subject to the overall fulfilment of state plans, provincial level authorities were to be allowed wide powers of re-arranging and adjusting output targets for both industry and agriculture. Similarly they were empowered to switch around the use of investment funds and make adjustments to the scale of investment and to individual projects, always provided that the main targets for new productive capacity and for especially important projects were achieved. So long as state plans were fulfilled for the main raw materials, types of equipment and consumer goods, the provinces might distribute these as they willed; more particularly was this the case with above-plan output of all commodities, apart from a few unspecified ones reserved for central allocation. In financial matters a similar latitude was allowed to provinces; provided that the payments due to the central government were made, or alternatively, that subsidies receivable did not have to be increased, they had considerable freedom in the arrangement of their expenditure. Parallel provisions were laid down with regard to plans for labour, commerce, local transport, electric power, education, culture and health matters and urban building.[1]

The aim of the post-1958 planning organization, as we have already had occasion to mention, has been to carry out the 'double-track' planning system, in order to effect the 'organic integration of balancing by production branches and local balancing' with the leading role ascribed to the local balancing.[2] This policy has not been conspicuously successful. In August 1962, in the course of an academic discussion on the topic, it was said that local authorities and central government ministries were frequently at odds on planning, and that local planning bodies found it difficult to incorporate the plans of central government enterprises in their areas, into the plans for achieving local balance of commodities. 'The relations of the two sides in planning', it was stated, 'are thus restricted to sending reports backwards and forwards, and the double-track system exists only in form'.[3] However, all agreed that when local balancing was properly organized, the central government enterprises should not be omitted.

The increased authority of provinces in the field of planning must have widened the gap between the types of plans compiled in the more sophisticated provinces and in the more backward ones. In Anhwei, a coastal province not far from Shanghai, the provincial statistical bureau as early as 1956 drew up an equilibrium chart for certain 'social commodities', as well as attempting to work out provincial 'national income' figures. 'The commodities which our province cannot produce, or produces in insufficient quantities, are supplied by the state through balance transfers from outside the province, and surplus commodities are transferred by the state from the province to outside areas.'[4] Despite a reference in this article to the way in which provincial calculations differ from those made on a national basis, it is easy to see how such exercises

[1] *Collected Laws and Regulations* ... Vol. 8, pp. 97–8.
[2] *Ta Kung Daily* (*Dagong Bao*), Peking, August 29, 1962, p. 3, and *Planned Economy* (*Jihua Jingji*), No. 9, September 1958, p. 13. Wang Kuei-wu: loc. cit.
[3] *Ta Kung Daily* (*Dagong Bao*), Peking, August 29, 1962, p. 3, loc. cit.
[4] *Statistical Research* (*Tongji Yanjiu*), No. 1, January 1958, p. 29. Anhwei Provincial Statistical Bureau: 'The Uses and Special Features of Compiling Local Balance Charts.'

furthered the tendencies to provincial self-sufficiency inherent in the whole system. From 1962, as we have seen in Chapter 11, economic disadvantages, and perhaps also political dangers, were seen in this growth of provincial autarky and an attempt was made to set contrary tendencies in motion. However, even in 1964 an article on local equilibrium was urging each province and autonomous region to become as self-sufficient as possible.[1] We shall revert to this theme below.

In 1958, when the Directive on the Reform of the Planning System was promulgated, China was divided—at least in theory—into seven economic co-ordinating regions. One section of the 1958 Directive was, therefore, devoted to the responsibilities of these units for planning. They were to organize, co-ordinate, and adjust the compilation and fulfilment of plans by their subordinate provincial level units and, in the course of the Second Five Year Plan period, to set up a 'relatively complete' industrial system in each of these regions.[2] As the economic co-ordinating regions do not seem ever to have been very substantial entities with administrative organs of their own, and as in any case they were soon heard of no more, these provisions can have had little, if any, practical effect. However, the Party regional bureaux, as existing from 1962, may have fulfilled some of the functions of co-ordinating the plans of groups of provinces, intended in 1958 to be performed by the co-ordinating regions.

The planning duties of central ministries were set down in the 1958 directive as being to effect a rational distribution on a national scale, and on the basis of the plans drawn up by provincial level authorities and by the co-ordinating regions, of the productive capacity of the particular branches of industry under the care of each ministry. The ministries had to compile national plans for production and capital investment from the draft plans produced by both centrally and locally controlled enterprises and institutions in their particular sector of the economy. Each ministry was to arrange 'balance transfers' between provinces of the commodities falling under its aegis, leaving, however, scope for provincial initiative. The central authorities reserved to themselves the right to alter local plans when need arose.[3]

The plan was to be constructed from the bottom up, primarily on the basis of horizontal, territorial balances. The decentralization of planning powers from the central government to the provinces was paralleled by a similar decentralization within provinces to special districts (and municipalities) and below them to *hsien*. It should be noted that the special districts apparently form a distinct planning level, although not a separate budgetary level.[4] At the lowest level, the *hsien* plan was to bring together the planned investment of its component communes, *ch'ü* and *hsiang*. The plans of *hsien* and of special districts were, in turn, to be co-ordinated by their respective provincial level authorities and to be entered into the plans of these. After

[1] *Kuang Ming Daily* (*Guangming Ribao*), November 16, 1964, p. 4. Liu Ch'eng-jui: 'A Tentative Discussion on Comprehensive Local Economic Equilibrium.'

[2] *Collected Laws and Regulations* ... Vol. 8, p. 98.

[3] Ibid., pp. 98–9.

[4] *Planned Economy* (*Jihua Jingji*), No. 7, July 1958, p. 21. Kiangsu Provincial Planning Commission: 'Kiangsu Provincial Planning Commission's Draft Plans for a Leap Forward', and p. 394 above.

provincial plans had been balanced by the economic co-ordinating regions, they were to form part of the unified national plan. These successive horizontal balances (of raw materials, of capital and consumer goods, and of labour, paralleled by financial balancing) were to comprise the primary plans; the vertical, functional plans compiled by the ministries were to take second place. The final national plan would be on the foundation of both these types of plan together. The national plan would restrict itself to balancing certain major items only; the lower administrative levels would successively control balances of less important items. The central ministries were given the task of drawing up lists of industrial commodities to be controlled at each level, together with methods of allocating raw materials and granting approval to investment projects.[1]

On September 24, 1958, the same day as the promulgation of the Directive on the Reform of the Planning System, another decree laid down further provisions on the methods of allocating raw materials and capital equipment. As mentioned in Chapter 6, this directive extended the allocation powers of provincial level authorities to cover even the requirements of central government enterprises within their territories; exception being made for certain raw materials and other items of the highest national priority.[2] Previously, central enterprises had applied for their allocations to central authorities. As a result of the reduced role of the central ministries in the allocation of raw materials, the supply agencies which had previously existed inside the ministries were retrenched or even abolished.[3]

The added responsibilities of provinces for allocation must have necessitated changes in provincial administrative machinery. An article in the State Planning Commission's journal, *Planned Economy*, of October 1958, suggested three possible methods of raw material allocation by provinces and came down in favour of the provincial departments (or bureaux) supplying those enterprises under central or provincial control, while special districts, *hsien* and municipalities allocated supplies to enterprises under lower authorities.[4] A visitor reported that in 1959 provincial departments of industry had their own allocation units; that the central government would reserve a certain amount of a province's production of any given material, the rest being left to be allocated by the provincial authorities.[5] Probably the system actually adopted has differed from province to province and, indeed, also within provinces. Only isolated illustrations come to our knowledge. In Kwangtung in 1960 we hear of timber for an emergency purpose being allocated by the provincial planning commission.[6] In the same province two years later we read of the provincial department of light industry allocating steel pro-

---

[1] *Collected Laws and Regulations* . . . Vol. 8, p. 99. On the making of balances at *hsien* level, see *Planned Economy (Jihua Jingji)*, No. 5, May 1957, pp. 15–17. Liu Feng-lin: 'Some Opinions on Developing *Hsien* (and Municipal) Comprehensive Balances.'

[2] p. 174 above, and *Collected Laws and Regulations* . . . Vol. 8, pp. 100–1. In case of emergency, central ministries were empowered to arrange for national balancing of certain locally controlled materials. Ibid., p. 100.

[3] *Planned Economy (Jihua Jingji)*, No. 10, October 1958, p. 34. She Yi-san: loc. cit.

[4] Ibid., p. 35. She Yi-san: loc. cit.

[5] Private communication to the author.

[6] NCNA, March 15, 1960.

ducts, coal and caustic soda to various large factories under these departments and being commended for giving priority to the production of goods included in the state plan.¹ From this it appears that the highest provincial allocatory organ, presumably still the provincial planning commission, restricted itself to allocating raw materials between production branches, i.e. to the separate provincial economic departments, and that it was left to these departments to make allocations to individual enterprises. In 1959 in Ninghsia, factories that had moved from Shanghai were reported to be receiving raw material allocations from *hsien* and municipalities.²

The Chairman of the State Planning Commission, Li Fu-ch'un, writing in 1960, picked out the distribution for investment purposes of raw materials, equipment and labour, as tasks which were the especial responsibility of provincial level Party committees.³ Organs of provincial level authorities are commended for giving priority for supplies of raw materials to customers outside their province, which suggests that the reverse practice may be frequent.⁴

The enlarged powers of local authorities in compiling labour plans were intended to remedy a difficult situation. In the past, two types of labour plan had existed, the one vertical (by production branch) and the other local, with consequent difficulties in drawing up unified plans for the distribution of labour or for establishing similar wage levels in any one area. As a result, great discrepancies in wages and amenities were apt to exist within a city between factories coming under central ministries and those under the local authority. From 1959 onwards, the labour plans of both categories of enterprises were to be incorporated into the local labour plan.⁵

In future, in accordance with the 1958 changes, the State Economic Commission, at the end of the planning process, was to send down two types of formal plan, the one type local, handed down to the provincial level authorities, and the other type by production branches, handed down to the central ministries.⁶

In order to co-ordinate plans, it was suggested that the local authorities and the ministries might invite each other to planning conferences. The provincial level authorities, after drawing up their draft plans, were to send copies to the central ministries for reference purposes and the ministries were to use these as the basis for their own draft plans. There was also to be a general exchange of copies of plans between the ministries and the local authorities. The Ministries of Labour and of Education were enjoined to maintain close contact with other ministries concerned when formulating their nation-wide plans. In accordance with the principle of 'balance transfer', embodied in the

¹ *Ta Kung Daily (Dagong Bao)*, Peking, February 23, 1962, p. 1.
² Ibid., April 3, 1959, p. 3. Liu Ko-p'ing, Secretary of the Secretariat of the CCP Committee of Ninghsia Hui Autonomous Region and Chairman of the People's Council of Ninghsia Hui Autonomous Region: 'How Ninghsia Develops Light Industry and Commune Industry.'
³ *Red Flag (Hongqi)*, No. 16, August 16, 1960, p. 12. Li Fu-ch'un: 'Raise High the Red Flag of the General Line and Advance Continuously.'
⁴ *People's Daily (Renmin Ribao)*, January 7, 1962, p. 1.
⁵ *Planned Economy (Jihua Jingji)*, No. 9, September 1958, p. 13. Wang Kuei-wu: loc. cit.
⁶ Ibid., pp. 13–14.

new regulations, each local authority had first to make a preliminary balance of industrial and agricultural products within its own area and then forward to the central government its scheme for transfers into and out of its area. On the basis of such local schemes, the central ministries and planning authorities would then effect balances on a national scale; for the chief producer materials, the task of making these balances was transferred from the State Economic Commission to the State Planning Commission. A final, and no doubt welcome, reform embodied in the new regulations was to be a reduction of 70 per cent in the number of forms used in the process of planning.[1]

The 1959 annual plan was the first to be drawn up under this new system. The drafting of this began in the previous June, discussions with the co-ordinating regions took place in July, the central government set a control target in August (the source clearly indicates a single figure—*yiko k'ungchih shutze*—this might have been the combined gross output value of industry and agriculture but this is only speculation).[2] The formal drafting of local plans was carried out from September to November and (in an article appearing in November) it was thought that the final plan would be completed during November and December.[3] Target figures for the four most important items— steel, grain, coal and cotton—were set by the sixth plenary session of the eighth CCP Central Committee which met at Wuchang in November-December 1958.[4] The plan, as a whole, was approved by the State Council on April 16, 1959, and the report on it delivered by Li Fu-ch'un to the NPC five days later. In August of that year the principal targets for the year's plan were readjusted—in plain words were drastically reduced. Originally the targets for 1959 had been calculated on the basis of the supposed output of 1958, the year of the Great Leap. The original 1958 figures were, however, found to be greatly exaggerated, with the result that the 1959 targets based on them were clearly unattainable.

The Second Five Year Plan period witnessed a breakdown of planning, first under the frenzy of the Great Leap of 1958 and then under the weight of crisis in 1959–61. Later, as the economy revived, the machinery of planning was built up once again, presumably to prepare the Third Five Year Plan which, after long postponements, was announced as having begun in January 1966. Information on economic planning since the Great Leap has been scanty, and we can only gather together a few gleanings on the subject. No plans, whether annual or longer term, have been published since 1960.

First, we must note the changes in the organs concerned with planning which have been announced from 1958 onwards. In February 1958 the State Construction Commission was abolished, because it overlapped with the State Planning and State Economic Commissions, and also perhaps because of the

[1] *Planned Economy* (*Jihua Jingji*), No. 9, September 1958, pp. 14–15. Wang Kuei-wu: loc. cit., and ibid., No. 10, October 1958, p. 34. She yi-san: loc. cit.
[2] Ibid., No. 11, November 1958, p. 31. Chao Po: 'Comprehensive Financial Plans.' This speculation is based on the fact that the combined gross output value of industry and agriculture is the first figure given in the Draft National Economic Plan for 1959 and also that it receives pride of place among the economic statistics presented in *Ten Great Years*, Peking, 1960, pp. 15–19.
[3] Ibid., Chao Po: loc. cit.
[4] *People's Daily* (*Renmin Ribao*), February 2, 1959, p. 1. Editorial.

complaints of local authorities at the extra work loaded on to them owing to the existence of three central planning bodies.[1] The work of the State Construction Commission was then divided between the other two commissions and the Ministry of Construction Engineering. Soon, however, there were second thoughts as the great volume of investment undertaken in 1958 had proved more than these other bodies could manage to supervise. Therefore, in November 1958, the establishment of a State Capital Construction Commission was decreed with Ch'en Yün, a former Minister of Commerce, as Chairman. This body was, in turn, abolished in January 1961, at a time when investment was being slashed, and its duties transferred to the State Planning Commission.[2] In 1965, a State Construction Commission was once more revived. By then capital projects had again been put in hand, and investment schemes under the Third Five Year Plan are likely to have occupied the re-established Commission. The Chairman this time was Ku Mu, previously a Vice-Chairman of the State Economic Commission.

In November 1962, the authority of the State Planning Commission was reinforced when it received an accretion of seven notable new vice-chairmen (already it had fifteen), four of the new men being vice-premiers. The new vice-chairmen were: Po I-po, Director of the State Council's Office of Industry and Communications and concurrently Chairman of the State Economic Commission; T'an Chen-lin, Director of the State Council's Office of Agriculture and Forestry; Li Hsien-nien, the Director of the State Council's Office of Finance and Trade and concurrently Minister of Finance; Teng Tze-hui, the Director of the Rural Work Department of the Central Committee of the Party; Ch'en Po-ta, the Editor-in-Chief of the *Red Flag* and Vice Director of the Party Central Committee's Propaganda Department, and two economists, Sung Shao-wen and Yang Ying-chieh.[3] These appointments are thought to have been made in order to strengthen the Commission when it was engaged on drawing up the Third Five Year Plan which, at that time, was scheduled for 1963–7. Three months later, in February 1963, three of the old vice-chairmen were relieved of their posts.

In 1963, the Prime Minister, Chou En-lai, said that the Third Five Year Plan, which had been due to begin that year, was still under preparation and that meanwhile they were operating on the basis of annual plans. In January 1964, Chou was reported to have stated that China was now in the first year of the Third Five Year Plan. Three months earlier, in October 1963, Ch'en Yi, the Foreign Minister, had told Japanese journalists that further readjustment would be needed before another long-term plan could be undertaken. Eventually, in January 1966, the Third Five Year Plan was said to have begun.

In November 1965 a national conference of capital investment had been held in Peking, 'which summed up the experience gained in the past year's

[1] *Planned Economy* (*Jihua Jingji*), No. 3, March 1957, p. 16. Mao Chün-i: loc. cit.

[2] *Collected Laws and Regulations* . . . Vol. 7, p. 61, and ibid., Vol. 8, p. 95. and *People's Daily* (*Renmin Ribao*), January 31, 1961, p. 1 and unpublished paper of Ezra Vogel.

[3] Yang's case is interesting because, in 1959, he had been dismissed from the position to which he was now once again appointed, that of Vice-Chairman of the State Planning Commission, for criticizing the Great Leap Forward. In November 1965, when political tension was again mounting, he was once more dismissed.

work, and made arrangements for 1966 and for the whole period of the Third Five Year Plan'.¹ Of the content of this Plan, little enough is known. Visitors to China have been told that it retains the same order of priority—agriculture first, light industry second, and then heavy industry—which has been proclaimed over the past few years. No target figures have so far (December 1966) been announced (except some, if figures they be called, for the agricultural plan of Liaoning province mentioned below).² References to the Third Five Year Plan in the Chinese press have mostly been in the form of sloganeering.³

The State Planning Commission, the State Economic Commission, and the State Construction Commission, are all co-ordinating bodies which bring together the plans of both the various ministries and of the provinces (the ministries, as well as the provinces, each have their own planning organs). For this purpose, the State Planning and Economic Commissions (and presumably the State Construction Commission as well) have within them bureaux corresponding both to ministries and to provinces.⁴ Conferences are an important instrument in effecting co-ordination. To quote one example at random, early in 1966 the State Economic Commission held a conference with the appropriate ministries to discuss possibilities of popularizing the use of low alloy steel and of producing more of this material.⁵

The three State Commissions involved in economic planning have the reputation of being among the more pragmatic elements in Chinese official life. Thus their influence is apt to be strongest at times of political relaxation, when more moderate policies are in favour, and to diminish when politics are more stridently in command.

Supervising and controlling the execution of plans poses a constant problem which has necessitated various administrative devices. In 1954 a Ministry of Supervision was established, with oversight of supervisory organs within ministries and other state bodies, as well as of those at the levels of provinces, special districts and *hsien*, and also of those in enterprises. The Ministry's duties included the general supervision of activities of all kinds; implicit in this, of course, was the checking on plan fulfilment. The Ministry was abolished in April 1959, and it was said that its duties would thenceforth be performed by other state organs under the guidance of Party committees at various levels.⁶ In the course of the Great Leap, Party organs had come to take a more direct role in administrative and economic life and, as a result, the Ministry of Supervision and its subordinate agencies had lost importance. This was, as Franz Schurmann says, 'part of a general shift, from a system of

¹ NCNA Peking, November 29, 1965.
² See p. 494 below.
³ e.g. 'Demonstrate the Spirit of Taching and Tachai (*sc.* two exemplary economic models) and Manifest the Aggressive Role of Youth in Fulfilling the Third Five-Year Plan.' *China Youth Newspaper* (*Zhongguo Qingnian Bao*), May 4, 1966, p. 1. Communique of the Third Plenary Session of the Ninth Central Committee of the Communist Youth League.
⁴ Unpublished paper of Ezra Vogel.
⁵ NCNA, February 10, 1966.
⁶ *People's Handbook* (*Renmin Shouce*) *1956*, pp. 228–9. Speech of Ch'ien Ying, Minister of Supervision, to the First Session of the First National People's Congress, and ibid., *1957*, pp. 340–1, and ibid., *1958*, p. 360, and *Collected Laws and Regulations* . . . Vol. 9, p. 109.

parallel bureaucracies on the Soviet model towards a system of Party-dominated lateral integration.'[1]

Apart from the Ministry of Supervision, other bodies have been charged with supervising the implementation of plans. In 1958 a number of specialized organs had been newly established in addition to those previously existing, 'to inspect and ensure the carrying out of state plans of all kinds' and to make quarterly checks on the progress of the plans for agricultural and industrial production, transport and capital investment. Before 1958, quarterly plans had been left to ministries and local authorities to draw up on the basis of the state's annual plan. 'According to the practical experience of the last few years', wrote Yang Ying-chieh, 'the arrangements made (for quarterly plans) by the ministries and local authorities alone were insufficient',[2] and hence the establishment of the new organs to carry out this task. 'Punishment according to law,' Yang wrote, 'should be meted out to those who wilfully refuse to fulfil the state plan or intentionally damage it.' 'Repeated propaganda' was to be the first and chief method to ensure plan implementation, 'but when necessary, legal penalties might and should be employed'.[3] There may have been some connection between the setting up of these new control organs in 1958 and the demise of the Ministry of Supervision in 1959.

The abolition of the Ministry of Supervision did not, of course, mean that the supervisory functions of individual economic ministries were also discontinued. These functions included such activities as the dispatch of technical teams to visit factories to check on quality of output.[4] When state supervisory organs of one kind or another discover that substandard goods are being turned out they are empowered to regrade them, to lower their prices, suspend delivery, or even production.[5]

The banks are expected to take a major part in ensuring that production proceeds as planned. They have to see that plans for credit loans to enterprises accord closely with national economic plans. Banks are supposed to prevent the hoarding of raw materials by enterprises (which the banks should spot through the undue running down of the enterprises' bank balances) and they are charged with insisting that the distinction between working capital and long-term investment funds, is maintained. The Construction Bank has responsibility for seeing that grants for investment and the use made of them, both tally with state plans: more will be said of this below.

Organs of the Ministry of Finance, particularly the revenue bureaux at different levels, also have a supervisory role in relation to enterprises. They have to see that tax payments are made regularly and that they are in line with output and sales.[6]

[1] F. Schurmann: *Ideology and Organization in Communist China*, Berkely, 1966, p. 314. For a fuller account of the machinery of supervision and control, see ibid., Chapter 5.
[2] *Planned Economy* (*Jihua Jingji*), No. 11, November 1958, p. 5. Yang Ying-chieh: loc. cit.
[3] Ibid.
[4] *Electric Motor Industry* (*Dianji Gongye*), No. 10, May 25, 1959, p. 1.
[5] *Red Flag* (*Hongqi*), No. 24, December 16, 1961, p. 4. Han Kuang: 'Some Problems in Technical Work in Industry.'
[6] *Finance* (*Caizheng*), No. 11, June 7, 1961, pp. 27–8. Tientsin Municipal Finance Bureau: 'Conscientiously Implement the System of Checking Revenue Collection.'

Other state bodies concerned with supervision in the widest sense include the procuracy (which supervises the execution of the law) and the public security system. Both were copied from the Soviet Union, although the procuracy also had old Chinese roots.[1]

The Party, and its organs at each level of the administration and in every enterprise, might be considered the supreme supervisory body in the economy. However, we must hesitate to accord it this role. From 1958 onwards, the Party has taken such a direct part in administration, both political and economic, that it cannot also operate as an independent supervisor, because it would be in the position of overseeing its own work. It is true that the Party has its own control committee, which absorbed some of the erstwhile executives of the former Ministry of Supervision.[2] When we enquire how far it has the staff or the strength to check on operations of Party organs at lower levels of the economy, we enter the hazy realm of speculation on intra-Party politics.

2. THE COMPREHENSIVE FINANCIAL PLAN

The comprehensive financial plan, mentioned above, is one instrument for checking at least some of the main ratios involved in drawing up economic plans. It is formed from six components: the plans for the national budget, for extra-budgetary receipts and expenditures, for the granting and repayment of bank loans, for cash receipts and payments, for the receipts and payments of ministries in charge of enterprises and for those items concerned with investment and working expenses in the budgets of units of collective agriculture.[3] The comprehensive financial plan is supposed to be not merely the sum total of all these various plans but a 'chain reaction' of them; that is a dynamic and not just a static concept. In drawing up the comprehensive financial plan, we are told that study was to be made of the 'calculating levers' (such as the rate of profit, the rate of reduction of cost, and the economic laws governing the circulation of money), after which the plan should be worked out in accordance with the targets set in the national plan and with the price level. It was not to be an operational plan but was to provide a useful background for other types of planning.[4]

During the First Five Year Plan period, the comprehensive financial plan was compiled by the State Planning Commission at the same time as it drew up the national economic plan. In those years the comprehensive financial plan was in fact far from comprehensive, as in addition to the central planners only a few provincial level units' planning organs interested themselves in it. Extra-budgetary funds were as yet insignificant and the chief task of comprehensive financial planning was to co-ordinate the national budget and

[1] L. T. C. Lee: 'Towards an Understanding of Law in Communist China' in E. F. Szczepanik (ed.) *Symposium on Economic and Social Problems of the Far East*, Hong Kong, 1962, pp. 340–1, and F. Schurmann, op. cit. Chapter V, passim.
[2] F. Schurmann, op. cit., p. 364.
[3] *Economic Research* (*Jingji Yanjiu*), No. 2, February 1960, p. 17. Ko Chih-ta and Ling Han: 'Outline Discussion of Comprehensive Financial Plans.'
[4] *Planned Economy* (*Jingji Jihua*), No. 11, November 1958, pp. 30–1. Chao Po: loc. cit., and *Economic Research* (*Jingji Yanjiu*), No. 2, February 1960, pp. 13 and 20. Ko Chih-ta and Ling Han: loc. cit.

the plans for credit. With the great growth of extra-budgetary funds in 1958 and 1959, more attention was given to comprehensive financial planning and in January 1960 the State Council decreed that the practice should be implemented more vigorously and that even the lower local authorities should gradually take it up.[1]

Soviet experts had advised on the early attempts to compile comprehensive financial plans. By 1958 the Chinese were saying that the methods used had been unsuited to conditions in their country and in this, as in other matters, they determined to strike out on their own.[2]

The financial plans for economic ministries are supposed to be geared to their production plans. However, even in the last years of the First Five Year Plan, when both the budgetary and the planning systems were working relatively smoothly (compared with the years before and after), discrepancies arose. The financial calculations of investment plans were usually 6–10 per cent above those of the corresponding budgetary figures. This resulted from the fact that the investment plans were made some months earlier and did not take into account the expected rate of improvement in productive efficiency and in cost reduction. (Before the budget was ready—i.e. for the first few months of the year—the investment plan figures were used as a basis for the payment of capital grants by the Construction Bank.)[3] In 1958 discrepancies between financial plans and production plans increased enormously. Ministries and enterprises had their targets repeatedly raised without any changes being made in their budgetary appropriations. Therefore they had to finance expansion by improvising a variety of 'self-provided' extra-budgetary sources of revenue.[4]

3. PLANNING AND CONTROL OF INVESTMENT

The State Construction Commission, in the periods when such a body has existed (i.e. September 1954–February 1958; September 1958 to January 1961 and from March 1965 onwards), has had the task of overall control of the investment programme. The range of its responsibilities may be gauged from the scope of an article by its then Chairman, Ch'en Yün, in *Red Flag* of March 1959, in which he discusses at length the location of industry, the determination of the priority of investment projects, co-operation between central organs and local authorities, co-ordination of supplies and materials, and of equipment and labour, the general supervision of technical designing and problems of management.[5] The relationship between the State Construction Commission and the Ministry of Construction Engineering is uncertain; presumably the Commission deals with broad policy, while the Ministry is concerned with more immediate matters.

[1] *Economic Research* (*Jingji Yanjiu*), No. 2, February 1960, pp. 13–14. Ko Chih-ta and Ling Han: loc. cit., and *Collected Laws and Regulations* . . . Vol. 11, pp. 94–6.
[2] *Planned Economy* (*Jihua Jingji*), No. 11, November 1958, p. 31. Chao Po: loc. cit.
[3] Ibid., No. 4, April 1957, p. 29, and unpublished document of Ezra Vogel.
[4] Unpublished paper of Ezra Vogel, and see p. 398 above and p. 476 below.
[5] *Red Flag* (*Hongqi*), No. 5, March 1, 1959, pp. 1–16. Ch'en Yün: 'Some Important Problems in Capital Investment at the Present Time.'

The Construction Bank is the channel through which budgetary grants for investment are paid out. This is no passive role. The Bank's branches must 'resolutely refuse appropriations for all those construction projects not included in the state plan, no matter whether they are newly undertaken, left over from last year, or undertaken by some sections of people on their own and no matter whoever arranges them'. For projects included in the plan, costs must be fixed item by item. 'Should it be discovered that some people exclude the most urgently needed projects from the plan' (i.e. with a view to forcing higher authorities to increase appropriations subsequently), 'the matter should be promptly reported.'[1]

The 1958 Directive on the Reform of the Planning System provided, as we have seen, for the retention by the central government of control over the total national figure for capital investment, over major capital investment projects and over new productive capacity for important products.[2]

All capital projects (new, rebuilt or restored) are classified as either 'above norm' or 'below norm', with different norms laid down for different types of projects.[3] According to regulations in force in 1957, 'above-norm' projects— that is any project of a size equal to or greater than the norm for its particular category—came, even as regards approval of specifications, 'under the unified control of the state', a phrase which usually denotes control either by the State Planning Commission or by the State Economic Commission, or the State Construction Commission: the last, in this case, was presumably the controlling organ. This contrasts with control by a particular ministry; in 1957 permission of the relevant central ministry had still to be obtained for the acquisition of even small fixed assets (anything over ¥200) by enterprises. Before 1957 all new power plants, coal mines, petroleum mines, refineries, railways, highways and ports, and even tractor stations were reckoned as 'above norm' regardless of their cost. This was changed in 1957, with these projects, like others, being divided into above or below norm, according to the sum invested in any project.[4] Apart from this change, the norms for investment projects in different industries around 1956–7 were the same as set down in the First Five Year Plan—that is:[5]

[1] *Finance* (*Caizheng*), No. 3, February 7, 1963 (SCMM 360). Tseng Chih, Vice-Minister of Finance: 'Excercise Strict, Practical and Proper Control over Appropriations for Capital Construction, Increase the Return on Investments.' Excerpts from a Speech to Branch Managers of the Construction Bank.
[2] In 1957, the investment targets reserved for central control comprised—(1) Total figure for investment. (2) Above-norm projects. (3) Utilizable productive capacity and (4) the amount of building and installation to be undertaken. So long as these targets were complied with, provinces were permitted to make adjustments in their investment programmes—*Collected Laws and Regulations* ... Vol. 6, pp. 395–6.
[3] *First Five Year Plan for Development of the National Economy of the People's Republic of China in 1953–7*, p. 21.
[4] *People's Daily* (*Renmin Ribao*), November 18, 1957, p. 1. Editorial, and *Planned Economy* (*Jihua Jingji*), No. 5, May 1957, p. 32. P'eng Jung-ch'üan: 'Tabulation Charts for Plans for Capital Investment.'
[5] *First Five Year Plan for Development of the National Economy of the People's Republic of China in 1953–7*, pp. 21–2 fn., and Ko Chih-ta: *China's Budgets During the Transition Period* (in Chinese), Peking, 1957, p. 106, where, on this topic, the Five Year Plan list is quoted, thereby implying that the same norms were still in force when Ko's book was written as when the plan was published in 1955.

1955–7 Investment Norms ¥ *million*

Iron and steel, motor vehicle, tractor, and rolling stock manufacturing industries, and shipbuilding	10
Non-ferrous metals, chemical and cement industries	6
Electric power plants, transmission lines and substations; coalmines; plants for the extraction and refining of petroleum, most types of machine building, and textile mills	5
Rubber, paper, cigarette and pharmaceutical industries, sugar refineries	4
Ceramics, food processing (apart from sugar) and other light industries	3

In September 1958, a decree divided above-norm projects into those whose specifications must be centrally approved and those for which local approval was sufficient. Appended to this decree was a list of criteria, according to industries, to determine the projects which require central approval for their specifications. It is noteworthy that the phrase 'above norm' is not used for this list, being replaced by the phrase 'important investment items', and that the criteria are couched mostly in physical terms, e.g. by productive capacity to be provided, or by quantity of raw material used a year.[1] As this list of criteria was promulgated on the same day as the Directive on the Reform of the Planning System and was issued as a supplement to it, it might be thought that the types of capital projects listed as needing central approval of specifications, corresponded to the 'major capital projects' mentioned in the Decree as one of the items of planning still to remain under central control.

Despite the evident disuse in September 1958 of the terms 'above and below norm', six months later, in March 1959, the State Planning Commission and the State Construction Commission were mentioned as 'taking a firm grasp of the above-norm projects and demanding monthly reports'.[2] In a note appended to the Minister of Finance's budget speech of March 1960, we are told that 'to define the scope of capital-investment projects of various categories and to facilitate their management at various levels, the state has set an investment norm for every category of capital investment'. The norm figures were given in financial terms and had in some cases been raised from the earlier levels as follows:[3]

1960 Investment Norms ¥ *million*

Integrated iron and steel plants; reservoirs	20
Motor vehicle and tractor industries and coal mining	10
Textiles, paper, salt and sugar industries	5

No post-1960 statement about norms for capital projects has come to our attention. In the next year or two, the central authorities' attempts to control investment were directed first and foremost to implementing the crisis orders, given in 1961, that all capital projects should be stopped forthwith, with few exceptions.[4] When the economy, and with it capital investment, began to pick up again, we hear of the state attempting to control specifications of capital

[1] *Collected Laws and Regulations* ... Vol. 8, pp. 102–5.

[2] *Planning and Statistics (Jihua yu Tongji)*, No. 5, March 8, 1959 (ECMM 173). T'ao Jan, Deputy Director, State Statistical Bureau: 'Arrange Well This Year's Statistical Work in the Field of Capital Construction.'

[3] *Collected Laws and Regulations* ... Vol. 11, p. 35, fn.

[4] *Seventy Important Points of Communist Industrial Policy 1961*. (From Taiwan source), Nos. 3 and 4.

projects, but without mention of the levels of administration—central, provincial and so forth—at which this attempt was being made in relation to projects of different types.[1]

The phrase 'specifications of investment projects', which is used to translate more than one Chinese phrase, is of broader scope than the English implies. The specifications of investment projects, according to an article of 1963, were supposed to include 'the scope of construction, the scheme of products, the methods of production, the conditions of resources, the required amount and sources of raw materials, materials, fuel, power and labour, the required number and source of technical personnel, the conditions for supply of the means of subsistence, the locality of construction, the area of land for construction purpose, the progress of construction, the estimate of investments, the main conditions for co-operation and co-ordination, as well as the economic and technical basis for quantity, speed, quality and economy, and the main technical and economic targets'.[2] Thus the term covers the economic as well as the technical background and plans for the project.

In 1963, it was stipulated that capital items might not be entered in annual plans, nor might work begin, until the specifications of design had been approved. However, delays in preparing the technical documents often led to projects being begun before proper technical designs had been drawn up.[3] This failing is common to many lands at a similar stage of economic development to China . . . 'the weakness in most developing countries', wrote an experienced staff member of the World Bank, 'is not the lack of an elegantly integrated comprehensive plan based on economic potentialities, but the lack of well-planned individual projects that can really be carried out. . . . Unless pre-investment and investment studies of projects for implementing a comprehensive plan are sufficiently advanced, it does little good to prepare such a plan. Yet all too often this is exactly what happens. Few projects are carefully worked out before the work of implementing them begins. As a result, many projects and programmes are not carried out at reasonable cost and in reasonable periods of time.'[4] The thorough preparation of plans for individual projects was one of the chief contributions made by Soviet experts in China in the 1950s and it was perhaps in this sphere that the damage caused by their sudden departure was most serious.

In connection with control over specifications, the influence of financial decentralization on central control of individual investment items must be considered. In 1959, as we have seen, financial relations between the central and provincial level authorities were mainly a matter of negotiations on transfers between the two. It will be recalled that in addition to any block grants as general subsidies to the budgets of certain provincial level units, grants from the central government were to continue to be made for capital

[1] *Building Construction (Jianju)*, No. 5, 1963 (SCMM 367). Yang Pang-chieh: 'Strictly Carry Out the Procedures of Capital Construction Laid Down by the State.'
[2] Ibid. Yang Pang-chieh: loc. cit. We have not been able to consult the original Chinese version of this article and so are unable to say if the phrase used for 'specifications' is exactly the same as in the directive of September 1958 given in *Collected Laws and Regulations* . . . Vol. 8, p. 102. [3] Ibid.
[4] *Finance and Development*, Vol. III, No. 2, June 1966, pp. 89–90. A. Waterston: 'A Hard Look at Development Planning.'

purposes. Direct central control over specifications might be expected in the case of projects for which specific central grants have been made, but would be more difficult to enforce over other items of investment.

Other factors have made difficult the implementation of direct control over investment projects, over the actual direction and size of investment as well as over details. The first is that a considerable volume of investment has been financed out of extra-budgetary funds. Although many attempts (as we have seen in treating of the comprehensive financial plan) have been made to subject the use of these funds to some kind of higher control, this has been hard to enforce. Investment out of extra-budgetary funds, it will be remembered, were reckoned in 1957 to be equivalent to be only 4 per cent of investment from budgetary grants, rising steeply to 23 per cent in 1958 and 19 per cent in 1959. In the early 1960s, the percentage probably fell with the shrinking of the volume of extra-budgetary funds.

In 1958, local authorities were indeed encouraged to use their initiative to provide funds for above-plan investment, for example, by tapping new sources of revenue (i.e. extra-budgetary sources) or by diversion of funds from other uses.[1] The central government gave local authorities something over ¥3,000 million for investment purposes in 1958. But the provincial level authorities so arranged things as to be able to invest more than ¥5,000 million. The context indicates that improvization rather than normal budgetary measures yielded the extra ¥2,000 million.[2]

With the revival of economic prosperity in the mid-1960s, the problem of unplanned investment with extra-budgetary funds once more presented itself.[3]

It is not clear if the figures for investment from extra-budgetary funds include funds ploughed back by great local verticalized concerns, such as the PLA Construction and Production Corps in Sinkiang. This Corps, it will be remembered, through economizing in consumption, accumulated funds from its own resources, 'asking for no state investment nor commandeering not a brick or tile from the masses', with which it built a considerable industrial base in Sinkiang, complete with iron and steel plants, coal mines, electric power stations, cement plants, flour mills and textile mills.[4] If all these investments and corresponding projects undertaken by other similar concerns (e.g. in the major forest areas) are not included in the figures for investment from extra-budgetary funds quoted above, then the total sums invested other than from budgetary grants must be put at still higher figures.

Another type of investment peculiarly intractable to control, has been that financed by the illicit diversion of working capital, a problem which, as we have earlier noted, has chronically proved beyond the authorities' power to stop.

The ability of higher authorities to control the details of investment pro-

---

[1] *Economic Research* (*Jingji Yanjiu*), No. 10, October 1958, p. 47 and No. 11, November 1958, p. 45. Lin Yün: 'The 1958 Reform of Our Country's Financial Management System.' Parts 1 and 2.   [2] Ibid., No. 11, November 1958, p. 45.

[3] *People's Daily* (*Renmin Ribao*), July 5, 1964, p. 5. Teng Chia-jung: 'The Relationship between the Work of Economic Ministries and the Issue of People's Currency.'

[4] *Nationalities Unity* (*Minzu Tuanjie*), No. 12, December 6, 1961. (SCMM 301). Wang Chi-lung, Director of Political Department, Sinkiang Production and Construction Corps: 'Strive to Strengthen Further the Solidarity of All Nationalities in Building a New Sinkiang Together.'

jects has also been curtailed by the exercise of the 'responsibility system for capital investment' under which, as we have seen in Chapter 6, enterprises and ministries have a wide margin of latitude in the manner they expend budgetary grants for capital purposes so long as the project's productive capacity attains at least the minimum productive capacity laid down and the total permitted expenditure is not exceeded. Otherwise, with curbs on diversion to nonproductive uses, the enterprise or ministry is allowed a free hand. This system gives incentive for the efficient use of investment funds and lessens the burden of supervision to be exercised over capital projects. It has been the difficulty of supervision, due to lack of competent personnel and deficiencies in the administrative apparatus, that has prevented the authorities from exercising thorough control over expenditure from extra-budgetary funds and from working capital.

As a result of all these factors, in 1963 and 1964 the authorities still needed to reiterate that no capital investment might be undertaken except as laid down in the state plans.[1] The ability of the central government, indeed of local authorities as well, to exercise direct control of the total and the direction of investment has, therefore, been subject to severe limits. In addition, however, to direct control of investment are the powers of indirect control through allocation of capital goods or of raw materials or of labour, and the use to this end of credit control and of pricing policy both in the case of capital goods and of the products of different types of investment projects. These types of indirect control of investment we shall now review.

Equipment and raw materials produced and used within one province were, by the regulations of 1958, not even nominally under direct central control, except for items of the greatest importance such as steel, and even for these we may suspect that the centre's interest was mainly in the inter-provincial transfers. For other goods, the central authorities' attempts to control distribution were to be limited to these inter-provincial transfers.

The central mechanism for controlling inter-provincial transfers is somewhat obscure. In 1958, as we have seen, the State Planning Commission had been made responsible for effecting a nation-wide balance of raw materials. In the same year, the General Bureau for the Supply of Raw Materials which, it will be remembered, was supposed to co-ordinate the allocation of raw materials, was put under the State Economic Commission. In May 1963, it was announced that a State General Bureau of Raw Materials had been established directly under the State Council. No mention was made of the earlier bureau, although it may be surmised that the new body was its organizational successor and that the change simply meant that the Bureau regained its independence of the State Economic Commission. In 1964, the Bureau was transformed into the Ministry of Allocation of Materials.[2] It is not clear how the division of labour between the various bodies worked out in this sphere. In September 1959, we read of steel for farm tools being allocated by the State Planning Commission.[3] Then six months later, in March

---

[1] *Building Construction (Jianju)*, No. 5, 1963. Yang Pang-chieh: loc. cit., and *People's Daily (Renmin Ribao)*, July 5, 1964, p. 5. Teng Chia-jung: loc. cit.

[2] *Collected Laws and Regulations* . . . Vol. 7, p. 64, and *People's Daily (Renmin Ribao)*, May 26, 1963, p. 1, and ibid., November 1, 1964, p. 1.

[3] NCNA Peking, September 16, 1959.

1960, the 'State Economic Commission and other departments concerned' were allocating rolled steel, tinplate, copper, rubber, quicksilver, and other products to supply urgent needs. In yet another instance, in December 1959, the directive in a shock campaign to collect factory rejects and waste materials was issued jointly by the State Planning Commission, the Ministry of Commerce and the Ministry of Health.[1] We have seen that, within individual provinces, responsibility for allocations was similarly split among several organs.

The apparent confusion in the roles of the different bodies concerned with allocation of raw materials must have been an important contributory factor to the weakness of control which has been evident in this sphere. One example of the centre's inability to maintain a firm grip on the distribution of even the most important raw materials, is seen in the deal reported (by a visiting delegation in 1959) between the municipality of Shanghai and the province of Anhwei, by which steel was bartered for coal; the two parties were said to have been severely reprimanded by the central authorities.[2] Such barter deals probably go on at all levels. Lobbying by provinces for raw material allocations (together with concealment of the size of their own production) is also a likely concomitant of a planning and allocation system which concentrates attention on inter-provincial transfers.

The lack of control over raw material allocations is illustrated by the apparent ease with which raw materials have been acquired for unplanned investments made out of extra-budgetary funds, as well as by the subsequent obtaining of raw materials for the operation of these unplanned factories once they have been completed.[3]

As far as machinery is concerned, national level allocation was in 1958 in the hands of various central ministries, normally the user ministries rather than the ministries producing machinery. Thus, allocation of equipment for metallurgical purposes was by the Ministry of Metallurgy, power equipment by the Ministry of Water Conservancy and Electric Power, chemical fertilizer, cement and coal mining plant by the Ministries of Chemical Industry, Construction Engineering and Coal respectively, equipment for oil extraction and refining by the Ministry of Petroleum, textile machinery by the Ministry of Textiles, tractors and other agricultural machinery by the Ministry of Agriculture (at the time when this Ministry controlled tractor stations), engines, rolling stock and steel rails by the Ministry of Railways, and motor vehicles and ships by the Ministry of Communications. The allocation responsibilities of the First Ministry of Machine Building (which controlled production of most types of machinery for civilian use) were limited to any major items of machinery not specified in this list. The Ministry of Metallurgical Industry was to allocate intermediate iron and steel products.[4] It was to these various allocating ministries that the provincial level authorities were supposed to send requests for machinery, other than could be supplied from factories under their own control. The supply agencies of the

---

[1] NCNA Canton, March 27, 1960, and ibid., Peking, February 23, 1960.
[2] Private communication to the author.
[3] On the allocation of raw materials and other producer goods, see also pp. 173–5 above.
[4] *Collected Laws and Regulations* . . . Vol. 8, pp. 100–1.

central ministries, which had been much reduced or abolished at the time of the decentralization movement of 1957–8, were revived in the 1960s, at least in some ministries.[1]

The dominating position of the main user ministry in the allocation system for machinery of each type, must have encouraged the self-provision of machinery, i.e. verticalization, by enterprises coming under other ministries. For example, a power plant in a complex under the Ministry of Coal or of Metallurgy may have been worse placed to obtain power equipment than was a power plant under the Ministry of Water Conservancy and Electric Power, and therefore will have had greater incentive to develop self-sufficiency in the supply of such equipment. The tendency to verticalization, in turn, made the task of planning, both of investment and of output, much more complicated. Indeed, a large part of these verticalized developments, being internal to a ministry, to a local department or even to an enterprise, may have evaded the planners' control altogether. In 1964 and 1965, a campaign was waged to reverse the trend to verticalized integration in favour of greater specialization. The State Economic Commission, representing the planning interests, may have taken a lead in this campaign.[2]

It may be surmised that changes have occurred in the locus of investment decisions in consequence of changes in the sources from which investment goods are obtained. Thus, when imports accounted for a high proportion of the new capital equipment available, the role of the central government in deciding the types to be imported and their disposition when imported, must have been paramount. Later, when a higher proportion of machinery and other capital goods came to be made in China, much in locally controlled factories, it can be expected that as a result some investment decisions were more widely dispersed. This tendency must have been reinforced by another decentralization measure by which the provinces received a percentage of the foreign currency proceeds of certain exports.

Apart from direct control over investment, a government may attempt to influence the size or direction of investment by indirect means, such as through price policy, including the price of credit (i.e. the rate of interest) and the provision of appropriate economic or other incentives to elicit the desired response from producers and purchasers, actual or potential, of capital goods.

We have seen that for steel and machinery, China has not followed the low price policy of the Soviet Union. This provided another reason for the growth of verticalization in China, because it made it more worthwhile for enterprises and ministries to make their own capital equipment themselves.[3] Also, the relatively high prices of producer goods may have had the effect of switching some production of illegal workshops from consumer to producer goods. However, in both these cases, the shortage of producer goods from official

[1] Local supply and marketing offices of the First Ministry of Light Industry are mentioned in 1966. *Economic Research (Jingji Yanjiu)*, No. 2, February 1966, p. 42. T'ung Wan: 'The Problem of Fixed Point Supply of Third Category Raw Materials for Enterprises of Light Industry.'
[2] pp. 169–70 above.
[3] *Economic Research (Jingji Yanjiu)*, No. 3, June 1957, pp. 54–5. Fan Jo-yi: 'A Further Discussion of Price Policy for Products of Heavy Industry.'

sources is likely to have been more important than the level of official prices for them, as can be seen by the fact that verticalization has also occurred in the Soviet Union. Anyway, the purpose of pricing policy of producer goods has not in general been to influence the level of their output.

The role allotted to prices in the planning process is more modest. 'Important commodities are dependent on planning and lesser commodities on adjustment by demand and supply,' wrote an economist in 1957, 'but both important and lesser commodities are mutually dependent and influence each other.... Plans must be based on equilibrium between output and sales.... Therefore in fixing prices, attention must be paid not only to cost but also to the conditions of supply and demand hidden behind the plans.'[1] The burden of this is that an appropriate pricing system can make planning easier to administer.

Another possible function of prices in a planned economy can be to assist planners in choosing between different priorities, by giving a clear indication of the real costs involved in each choice. This can be done only if prices are rational, that is if they accurately reflect existing scarcities. The most important price in this connection is the price of capital, that is the rate of interest. As the Managing Director of the International Monetary Fund said in 1964: 'Even in cases where the authorities have complete discretionary powers to determine investment priorities, a system of pricing capital at its true scarcity value will enable them to perform this function with much clearer awareness of all the implications of their choices.'[2] In China, budgetary grants for fixed capital carry no interest; bank loans for working capital bear interest, but not at a sufficiently high level to reflect the scarcity of capital in the economy.

So far we have been discussing the use of prices to assist in implementing investment plans which have already been determined by other criteria. In addition, however, the price of capital as fixed by supply and demand (based on the relative profits of different industries or enterprises) may be used as a determinant of the direction of investment. This is what happens in a market economy where different enterprises can compete for capital; as a result capital will flow to those believed to be able to use it most profitably. The allocation of investment on the basis of relative profitability has been suggested by Soviet economists, but it does not form part of the new system adopted in the Soviet Union by which profits become the chief success indicator for enterprises. In China, the profitability criterion as a determinant of investment was cautiously commended in the pages of *Economic Research* by Yang Chien-pai in 1963 and by Ho Chien-chang and Chang Ling in 1964;[3] another notable protagonist of this line of thought was Sun Yeh-fang, director, until his dismissal in 1966, of the Economics Institute of the Chinese

---

[1] *Economic Research* (*Jingji Yanjiu*), No. 3, June 1957, p. 62. Fan Jo-yi: loc. cit.

[2] *International Financial News Service*, Vol. XVI, No. 41, Supplement, October 16, 1964, p. 375. P. P. Schweitzer: 'Some Financial Aspects of Economic Development'—Address before the Indian Institute of Public Administration, New Delhi, October 5, 1964.

[3] *Economic Research* (*Jingji Yanjiu*), No. 12, December 1963, pp. 45, 47 and 50. Yang Chien-pai: 'The Problem of National Economic Equilibrium and "Production Price",' and ibid., No. 5, May 1964, pp. 15 and 17. Ho Chien-chang and Chang Ling: 'A Tentative Discussion on "Production Price" in the Socialist Economy.' See also p. 162 above.

Academy of Sciences.[1] This idea was attacked in a number of articles, with obvious official backing, in the same journal in 1964 and 1965; the attack was renewed in more popular publications and more strident tones in 1966. An opponent of the idea, Ho Kuei-lin, set out the officially approved criteria for investment decisions as follows: (1) the policies decided by the Party and the state according to current political and economic circumstances at home and abroad; (2) the requirements of social needs compared with those of social production, and (3) the requirements of the speedy and proportionate development of the national economy.[2] All these are admirable criteria, it might be conceded (granted the objects of the Party), for national planning, but insufficiently specific to guide a harassed official trying to weigh the relative merits of two projects, both of which appear desirable on these three criteria.

In fact, however, the Chinese are not oblivious of the rate of return on capital. Their accountancy practice, it is true, uses the concept of profit on cost, and thus gives no indication of profitability reckoned on capital. Nevertheless, on many occasions the rate of profit of an industry or enterprise on capital invested in it is stated, which shows that the concept is thought worthy of consideration. Similarly, in assessing the relative importance of an industry to the national economy, and thus indirectly its priority as a recipient of investment, we can infer that its 'accumulation rate' is taken into account and that rate measured on capital as well as on cost. The high rate of profits on cost obtained on modern steel plants in China relative to older ones has been one way of moving towards an equalization of rate of return on capital invested (the difference in profit on capital between the two types of steel plant has been less than in profit on cost). In this case, the higher planned profit margins in modern plants are a way of imposing a charge for capital.

The concept of maximizing return on capital can be said to be at the base of the Great Leap campaign to promote small, quickly maturing, capital-extensive and labour-intensive industrial plants (e.g. the 'backyard' iron and steel furnaces). For other reasons, much of this investment was ill-advised, but the implicit idea was right from the point of view of China's capital shortage. The distribution of investment in the electrical power industry between thermal and hydro-electric plants has depended on some system of weighing the lower capital costs of the former against the lower operating costs of the latter. Thus, as we have seen, when estimates (perhaps mistaken) showed a reduction of the differential between the two for capital costs per unit of output, it was decided to expand the proportion of hydro-electric capacity. Relative capital costs have also been taken into account in decisions on the division of traffic (and consequent division of investment) between rail and river transport. While we know that capital costs are considered when making decisions of this type, we do not know what technique is used to do so, or whether the whole matter is left to the planners' hunch.[3]

[1] *People's Daily* (*Renmin Ribao*), August 12, 1966, p. 5. Tung-fang Wei: 'An Examination of the "Profit in Command" Theory.' As early as 1959 Sun had stressed the importance of return on capital. *Economic Research* (*Jingji Yanjiu*), No. 9, September 1959, p. 64. Sun Yeh-fang: 'A Discussion on Value.'
[2] *Economic Research* (*Jingji Yanjiu*), No. 1, January 1965, p. 22. Ho Kuei-lin: 'The True Quality of the "Theory of Socialist Production Prices".'
[3] We must not exaggerate the importance of scientific calculations in the making of such

Expected return on capital may be presumed to have been a major determinant of the considerable proportion of investment coming from extrabudgetary funds, and also of that which has occurred in the private sector (licit and illicit) as well as of some investment by collective concerns.

The absence of an actual charge on fixed capital (other than amortization) has deprived the Chinese planners of a means of instilling discipline in the use of this scarce resource. For example, extravagance by enterprises in the standard of their buildings has been encouraged by lack of payment for the use of capital. For working capital obtained from bank loans, an interest charge is levied, and at higher rates than have prevailed in the Soviet Union. Yet Chinese rates are still well below the rate of the marginal efficiency of capital in the Chinese economy and thus are insufficient by themselves as a device for rationing funds for working capital, while a strong incentive is provided for diversion of working capital to long-term investment purposes.

A snag arises when prescribing the use of profit in a non-market economy as an indicator of the direction either of investment or of production. The profit indicator can only fulfil its function of indicating the economically most advantageous ways of distributing resources if the other prices on which profit is worked out are themselves formed by the free play of the market and thus accurately reflect relative shortages; while in a command economy, other prices are irrational. Moreover antagonists of the profit on capital indicator have no difficulty in showing that, in the context of the Chinese economy it will not encourage enterprises to economize on capital because demand for capital would be very inelastic.[1] Another difficulty lies in the valuation of capital assets to give the capital sum on which profit on capital should be reckoned. In the USSR, capital assets have been assessed in a series of censuses. We have not heard of a similar census in China.

4. PLANNING OF CURRENT PRODUCTION

We must now turn from the planning of investment to the planning of current production. This, as it affects individual enterprises, has been discussed in Chapter 6. Here we will treat it in a wider setting.

As already mentioned, the directive on planning of September 1958 limited the centre's control of current output targets to the most important commodities, for which, also, the central authorities were to work out the national balances and the inter-provincial transfers.[2] The tendency, as often noted, is to concentrate central control on the inter-provincial transfers. This reflects

---

decisions in the Western world. An engineer once told the author that when the acquisition of new equipment was being considered in his plant, elaborate reckonings were made of its expected profitability. 'These reckonings usually indicate that we ought not to get it, and we usually go ahead and get it.' In other words, there may be a decided bias, especially when technical men have a part in the decision, to give undue weight to the 'technicians' preference' for new equipment for the joy of it.

[1] e.g. *Economic Research (Jingji Yanjiu)*, No. 5, May 1964, p. 8. Yü Lin: 'The Correct Manner of Determining Prices of Different Kinds of Products.'
[2] *Collected Laws and Regulations* . . . Vol 8, p. 96, and *Planned Economy (Jihua Jingji)*, No. 9, September 1958, p. 14. Wang Kuei-wu: loc. cit.

the growth of local self-sufficiency, especially within administrative units. Local self-sufficiency is bound to be far-reaching in any land with poor transport, but in China it has been deliberately fostered from 1954, when a rationalization scheme for transport encouraged the balancing of production and sales within given areas for certain bulky commodities including grain, coal, timber, petroleum, salt, cement, pig iron and building materials of mineral origin.[1] The planning of the greater part of production, therefore, to the extent it is attempted at all, devolves on provincial and lower level authorities.

Material allocation should, in theory, be easier to implement within the smaller economies of individual provinces than on a national scale. The number of producers and consumers of each commodity would be greatly reduced. Even so, however, the problems of control may be beyond the powers of many provincial administrations.

Methods of eliciting enterprises' compliance with production plans include direct allocation to them of important raw materials, scarce skills and working capital for planned production and the supposed non-availability of these factors for production that is unplanned. This has already been discussed when treating of the planning of investment. Economic incentives given for fulfilling or over-fulfilling production plans have been considered in Chapters 6 and 7, when reviewing the types of success indicators and of bonuses (to ministries and enterprises, staff and workers) used at various times. Finally, there are the various forms of political pressure and incentives used to obtain plan fulfilment; these have been mentioned in Chapter 7. We have seen that with regard to success indicators, the current circumstances and atmosphere, both political and economic, have done more to determine the significance of any type than have the formal regulations supposedly in force at any period. The swings in policy, between relying mainly on economic incentives or mainly on political pressure (e.g. through campaigns), have followed the general oscillations in the political temperature of the country. At times such as the Great Leap, or in 1966, politics have been more obviously in command. During the economic crisis in the early 1960s, more reliance had perforce to be given to economic motives and incentives.

During the First Five Year Plan period, the maximization of physical output was the chief material success indicator or target put before an enterprise.[2] In 1958, such quantitative measures were the only economic indicators that mattered and the intense political pressure of that time was directed at obtaining increases of output at all costs.

At the same time, a change was made in the categories into which targets

---

[1] *Economic Research (Jingji Yanjiu)*, No. 7, July 1959, p. 4. Kao Yü-huang. 'The Need for Vigorous Organization of Rational Transport in the Economic Activities of the Nation.'

[2] However, even in the First Five Year Plan period, profit maximization seems to have ranked high as a target, at least in some cases. For example, in an article of 1957 we read that enterprises in the petroleum industry preferred to produce gasoline and kerosene, which carried a higher profit margin, rather than diesel oil, on which the margin was lower. 'The difference in profit margin mentioned above, causes drastic divergence between production and needs. It means that the assortment plan cannot be fulfilled . . . and intensifies the contradiction between the demand and supply of diesel oil.' *Economic Research (Jingji Yanjiu)*, No. 3, June 1957, pp. 65–6. Fan Jo-yi: loc. cit.

were divided. Before 1958, the targets put out in the official documents of the State Planning Commission were of three types: those which had the nature of a command, those which were for reference and those for computational purposes (the last two were sometimes given as those which were adjustable and those for reference). From 1958 onwards, in accordance with the directive on the reform of the industrial management system, there were to be only two categories of planning targets: those of the nature of commands and those not of this nature, i.e. the mandatory and the non-mandatory. Both, it was stressed, formed part of the state plan and should be seriously regarded, but the second, non-mandatory, type might be adjusted by provincial level authorities.[1]

On being sent down to lower levels, the distinction between targets of different types appears, in the course of the Great Leap, to have undergone a process of modification. Instead of targets being categorized as mandatory or non-mandatory according to the nature of their object (e.g. output and transfer of vital commodities being mandatory), as by the directive of 1957, a distinction was made between less or more ambitious targets pertaining to the same object. Targets might, according to an article of January 1959,[2] be divided into 'those hoped for' and 'those which must be realized' or 'those which are guaranteed' and 'those striven after'. Those which were guaranteed and must be realized, were to be decided 'after more accurate computation and made to conform with objective realities as much as possible'; the other sort suffered no such restriction. The situation was formalized by the official use of two sets of targets under the 'system of planning with dual accounts' which was instituted in 1958. By this system, the authorities at each level had two sets of targets, the first being the targets handed down to them by the level above them and the second and larger being the set they in their turn passed down to the level beneath, for which it formed the first set; while a new and yet larger second set would be sent down to the next lower level. The second set formed 'a target for struggle' which, it was held, would give fuller scope to the initiative of the masses which had been restrained by the planners during the First Five Year Plan period. In one province in 1958, the second set of accounts, as far as industry was concerned, exceeded the first set by 33 per cent. At the beginning of 1960, the practice of dual targets was being condemned. However, in 1961 the 'target for guaranteed output' of production brigades was said to be generally around 10 per cent below their 'production target', which suggests that the system had not died out, although it was being used with greater moderation than previously. Five years later, in June 1965, an editorial in the *People's Daily* had to inveigh against the continued use of dual targets.[3]

[1] *Planned Economy (Jihua Jingji)*, No. 1, January 1958, p. 37, and *The Eighth National Congress of the Communist Party of China*, Vol. II. Speeches, p. 301, and *Collected Laws and Regulations* . . . Vol. 6, p. 395.

[2] *The Masses (Qunzhong)*, January 16, 1959 (ECMM 165). Chiang Hsia: 'On High Targets.'

[3] *Planned Economy (Jihua Jingji)*, No. 5, May 1958, pp. 8–10. Liao Chi-li: 'Some Remarks on Dual Accounting', and *Study (Xuexi)*, No. 8, April 18, 1958, p. 10. Wei Yi: 'A Revolution in Methods of Planning', and *Kiangsi Daily (Jiangxi Ribao)*, January 2, 1960 (SCMP 2226). Liu Chün-hsiu: 'Continue to Oppose Rightist Tendencies, Exert

As each level felt it obligatory to report fulfilment or over-fulfilment of the targets handed down to it, the result was the gross inflation of output statistics which occurred in 1958 and which was in part corrected by the revised figure issued in the summer of 1959.

In the years after the Great Leap, as we have seen in Chapter 6, chief emphasis was put on non-quantitative targets, among which profit ranked high. Here again the question of return on capital arises. In 1962, one of the incentive systems in force was to base bonuses to enterprises on the realized rates of profit—including both the rate of profit on costs and on capital.[1] In the course of the 'great socialist cultural revolution' of 1966, profit targets came under attack and their overt significance, at any rate, may be presumed to have been diminished. Indeed, anything in the nature of a material incentive to any desired economic performance, was also opposed. At the time of writing, it is hard to say how far precept and practice have marched in step in this respect.

5. PLANNING OF TRADE

The planning of trade is an essential part of the system of effecting local balances. Those goods which are directly allocated to the users are outside the scope of trade. Others are supposed to be balanced at the national, provincial or lower levels, according to commodity. After the main decisions on local balances are taken, the specific deals are embodied in contracts. Commercial enterprises have profit plans, purchasing plans, and/or sales plans. They are forbidden, except in certain special cases, to achieve plan fulfilment by means of giving advance payments or by making sales on credit.[2]

A planning system based on a series of local balances, leaves trade only a residual place in the economy. This is true for trade between administrative units within a country and even more so for international trade. The 1958 reform of the planning system, as we have seen, listed the total figures for imports and exports, together with the volume of major import and export commodities, as among the targets to be retained under central control. The planning of foreign trade has been treated in Chapter 12. It will be remembered that after decentralization, the provinces received for their own use a percentage of the foreign exchange earned by certain exports. This implies an extension of local control over the import plan.

Touching on the planning of trade is the question of commodity reserves,

---

Efforts and Take a Big Leap Forward in Agricultural Production this Year', and *Kuang Ming Daily* (*Guangming Ribao*), September 18, 1961, p. 4. Yen Yung-ch'ien: 'A Tentative Discussion on Differential Net Land Rent and Its Distribution', and *People's Daily* (*Renmin Ribao*), June 2, 1965, p. 2. Editorial, and Choh-ming Li: *Statistical System of Communist China*, Berkeley, 1962, pp. 71–2.

[1] *Ta Kung Daily* (*Dagong Bao*), Peking, August 22, 1962, p. 3. Ch'en P'ei-yi: 'A Tentative Discussion of Certain Practical Problems in the Bonus System.' See also p. 167 above.

[2] Ibid., June 29, 1965, p. 2. T'u Han-kuo, Finance and Accounting Section, Bureau of Commerce, Huangshih Municipality, Hupeh Province: 'How Should It Be Judged if "Politics Is in Command" of an Enterprise?'

both of raw materials and of finished goods. In 1959, in connection with stockpiling of timber, we hear of a State Bureau of Raw Material Reserves[1] but do not know what, if any, clear division of responsibility existed between this bureau and the commercial ministries. An article in 1965 stressed the role of commerce in providing a reservoir of goods as an insurance against those fluctuations of supply and demand which no planning can even out.[2] Responsibility for stockpiling reserves of export goods to enable sales to be maintained in the face of changes in supply or in foreign demand rests, or at least in 1958 rested, with the organs of foreign trade.[3] The experience of the Great Leap, when reserves were allowed to run down dangerously, must have brought home their importance both to the maintenance of smooth production at home and to the building up of export markets abroad.

Further discussion of topics connected with the planning of trade may be found in Chapter 11 above.

6. PLANNING OF AGRICULTURE

So far we have treated mainly of the planning of industry. Agricultural planning brings its special problems. First, there is the intrinsic instability of farming, dependent on weather. Second, most of China's agriculture, unlike its industry, comes under collective, not state, ownership. Third, the dispersed nature of farming carried on by large numbers of scattered production teams, makes operational planning, or any kind of control, more difficult to implement than in factory industry. The fluctuations in policy on agricultural planning, which we shall now review, have depended mainly on changes in political circumstances. During times of greater political fervour, more thorough planning of agriculture has been propounded, while at times of greater relaxation, policy has favoured limiting planning to figures for off-farm transfers. Behind and beyond these policy shifts, however, have stood the inherent difficulties of plan implementation in agriculture.

The list of centrally controlled targets, as laid down in 1958, included both the output and the 'balance transfer' of major agricultural products. However, in September 1956, a directive of the Central Committee and the State Council had laid down that there should be a gradual transition from central planning of agricultural production to planning only procurement of farm produce (literally the 'purchase and collection plan' also called the 'transfer plan'). It envisaged, nevertheless, that the central authorities would still hand down agricultural output plans to the provinces but that the provinces would be allowed to adjust them.[4] The provinces would in turn hand down production plans to the *hsien* which were to be the basic units of agricultural planning. Because agricultural producer co-operatives were under collective, not state, ownership, production plans issued to them would be for guidance

---

[1] *Collected Laws and Regulations* ... Vol. 9, p. 211.

[2] *Kuang Ming Daily* (*Guangming Ribao*), September 20, 1965, p. 4. Shen Li-jen: 'The "Reservoir" Role of Socialist Commerce.'

[3] *Planned Economy* (*Jihua Jingji*), No. 2, February 1958, p. 28. Li Pai-fang: 'Actively Strengthen the Organization of the Sources of Export Goods.'

[4] *Collected Laws and Regulations* ... Vol. 4, p. 376.

only and would not be in the form of commands as to state enterprises including, of course, state farms.[1]

The agricultural production targets to be passed down by the centre to the provincial level authorities for 1957 included the planted area, production per unit area, and total production of grain (but not specifying types), soya beans, cotton, jute, groundnuts and rapeseed; the number of pigs; and area of newly planted forest land; the total quantity of 'cultivated' fish, and other aquatic products (i.e. excluding catches of 'wild' fish). The provinces were then to send down plans to their *hsien*. For both long-term and annual plans, figures for the total value of national agricultural output were to be worked out by the State Planning Commission and the State Economic Commission. However, these figures were not to be apportioned between, and handed down to, the provincial level authorities.[2]

In pursuance of the intention to change from the planning of agricultural production to procurement planning, in 1957 a plan for this latter was drawn up tentatively, to cover seventeen major items (a longer list than that obtaining for those with production targets fixed by the centre). The intention was that these plans would in time be substituted for production plans, and therefore they were said to correspond with the production plans (despite the longer list of commodities) rather than with the commercial plans for agricultural produce. These commercial plans were based on the previous year's output, not on that planned for the current year.[3]

Articles in *Financial and Economic Research* in January and February 1958 argued the case for the proposed change to procurement planning, but said that in the course of discussions of the topic in the second half of 1956 and the first half of 1957, the general opinion expressed was that conditions were not ripe and that 'for a relatively long period ahead the present system of planning agricultural production could not be changed'. They suggested that the transition should be made piecemeal. 'The characteristics of our country are its vast area and its uneven local development. Actual circumstances differ greatly from place to place. In some areas, natural circumstances are relatively favourable and the foundations of co-operativization and planning have been firmly laid, and there the collection and purchase plan system may be introduced first. In places where less favourable circumstances obtain, the change can be deferred for a bit. The system of agricultural planning need not be changed simultaneously all over the country.'[4]

Later in that year, 1958, political pressure became intense. On the formation during that summer of the people's communes, these units supplanted the *hsien* as the basic units for agricultural planning. This entailed the sending down to the communes of plans for the acreage and output of different crops.

[1] *Collected Laws and Regulations* . . . Vol. 4, p. 376, and *Planned Economy* (*Jihua Jingji*) No. 4, April 1957, p. 30. Liao Hsien-kao: 'Agricultural Production Planning Charts.' On the role of state farms in state planning, see p. 111 above.
[2] *Planned Economy* (*Jihua Jingji*), No. 4, April 1957, pp. 30–2. Liao Hsien-kao: loc. cit.
[3] Ibid., p. 33.
[4] *Financial and Economic Research* (*Caijing Yanjiu*), No. 1, January 1958, p. 54 and No. 2, February 1958, p. 55. Chang K'ai-min and Ch'en Sheng-ya: 'A Discussion of the Transition from a System of Planning Agricultural Production to a System of Planning the Collection and Purchase of Agricultural Output.' Parts I and II.

Officially these plans should have been for guidance only, but during the Great Leap some cadres 'were not clear about the difference between socialist collective ownership and socialist ownership by the whole people', and consequently thought that these plans should take the form of direct orders to the communes. In the politically more relaxed, but economically more critical, years that followed, this attitude was disapproved.[1] By 1961, actual decisions about planning of agricultural production were left to the basic accounting units of collective agriculture. In any case, state plans were usually sent down too late in the year to affect the planting of the first crop. Articles published in 1961 reaffirmed that, at least at the level of communes and below, the state would, in the main, not seek to lay down production plans, but would rest content with plans for procurement.[2]

Four years later, in the more intense political atmosphere of 1965, an article in *Economic Research* contradicted the tenor of former pronouncements on agricultural planning. 'The state,' it ran, 'must control agricultural production plans; that is to say, the collective economy of the people's communes must compile their agriculture production plans under the unified guidance of the state and they may not autonomously arrange their own agricultural production.' The notion that production plans were not applicable to the collective sector was opposed on the grounds that all concerns, both state-owned and collective, should be subordinate to the will of the people as reflected in the state plan. The writers castigated those economists who had favoured procurement planning; no mention was made that procurement planning had ever been proposed in an official directive of the Central Committee and the State Council.[3] The argument put forward was that unless the state controlled the production plan, it would not be able to control the procurement plan. 'If the state does not control agricultural production plans and if the subjective estimates of the planning organs are the basis for action, the upshot would be that the tax and compulsory sales quotas would be exceptionally heavy for some areas and communes and exceptionally light for others. Thus, it can be seen that if the state does not control agricultural production plans, it cannot correctly arrange the plans for tax and compulsory sales. For example, if the quotas for tax and compulsory sales of cotton are fixed, but not the area to be sown to cotton, it often occurs that in places cotton fields are sown to grain, so that cotton quotas cannot be fulfilled, while in other places grain fields are sown to cotton, so that grain quotas cannot be fulfilled.[4] This implies that unless the state directly controls production plans, it has no way of gauging the production potentialities of an area (despite the surveys on which agricultural tax is based); also that for some unexplained and astonishing reason, it is easier for the state to

[1] *Economic Research* (*Jingji Yanjiu*), No. 7, July 1961, p. 19. Liu Jih-hsin: 'Reflections on the Reform of Our Country's Agricultural Planning System.'
[2] Ibid., pp. 20–2, and *Daily Worker* (*Gongren Ribao*), December 12, 1961, p. 3. Yeh Hsi-wen: 'In Organizing Production, Why Should the Various Levels of Rural People's Communes Be Guided by State Plans and Consider Local Conditions?'
[3] *Economic Research* (*Jingji Yanjiu*), No. 3, March 1965, p. 33. Wang Hsiang-ch'un, Chiang Hsing-wei and Ch'en K'un-hsiu: 'Problems of Controlling Plans for Agricultural Production in Our Country.'
[4] Ibid., p. 34.

enforce control of total production than of off-farm transfers. The implausibility of this argument strengthens our contention that swings of policy on agricultural planning arise primarily from changes in the political situation.

In Chapter 16 we have seen that the Chinese authorities are not averse to using relative prices to influence the supply of different crops, although apparently they have not been willing to make sufficient use of price policy to achieve their ends by this means alone. As noted in Chapter 3, the absence of ground rent lessens the likelihood of land being devoted to its economically most advantageous use. Direct state planning of production has been regarded as a supplement to, if not a substitute for, price policy in this respect. This is illustrated in the 1965 article from *Economic Research* quoted above. 'Rational location of agricultural production is of great advantage to the development of our country's agriculture', it stated. 'According to surveys of certain provinces, other conditions being equal, when industrial crops are planted in appropriate soil, output can generally be raised some 20 per cent. . . . In order to improve the rational location of agricultural production everywhere . . . it is necessary to compile agricultural production plans on the basis of complete studies and surveys under the unified guidance of the state. . . . If the state relaxes its hold and does not control agricultural production plans, then arrangements will not be made correctly for planting the different crops in the right proportions, because while every commune and team knows a lot about its own local weather and geographic circumstances, it knows very little about these conditions in other places. Still more serious is the fact that some communes and teams, in arranging production, take a partial view and do not consider wider interests.'[1] Reasons of political control in the countryside were also given as arguments in favour of state planning of production. This, it was hoped, would 'help prevent the peasants' spontaneous tendencies towards capitalism'.[2]

All along remained unstated the grounds for thinking that the required control could be kept, and the required information obtained, when the state increased the scope of its planning to embrace all farm production, although it had apparently been unable to exercise this control, or elicit this information, while confining itself to the easier task of procurement planning. This reveals the basic problem of state control of agriculture—that direct control would require more people than are available with ability and experience in surveying and checking output and accounts and that these people would have to be incorruptible, as well as loyal first and foremost to the aims of the state rather than to those of the peasantry. The crux of the problem lies in the capabilities of rural cadres and the state's control over them.

The article from *Economic Research* 1965 cited above is a straw in the wind, showing the drift of official policy at that time. It must not, however, be taken as indicating what was actually happening either then or later. Something about this may be gleaned from an article in *People's Daily* in 1966, which presumably was published in order to guide the actions of rural cadres. It instanced a *hsien* in Chekiang which previously had taken the initiative in compiling production plans and then had handed them down to communes

---

[1] *Economic Research (Jingji Yanjiu)*, No. 3, March 1965, p. 35. Wang Hsiang-ch'un, Chiang Hsing-wei and Ch'en K'un-hsiu: loc. cit.   [2] Ibid., p. 36.

and thence to brigades and teams. But in 1966 the *hsien*, communes and brigades 'except for controlling figures for sown acreage of some economic crops, according to state plans', did not give targets to the teams. Instead the teams drafted their own cropping plans which were then submitted to the higher levels. This was said to have produced better results in terms of output than the previous method. 'Plan figures, such as for a production team's sown area (except for items which it is essential for the state to control), if handed down from above, can very easily be subjectively one-sided, and although intentions are good, damage may ensue'[1]—an interesting comment on the centralizing views expressed in the *Economic Research* articles of the previous year; strange, too, in view of the political climate of 1966.

In addition to attempts by the state to enforce either direct planning of production or procurement planning, other methods used to influence agricultural output in desired directions have been through price policy, through the provision of credit (by banks, credit co-operatives or advance payment for produce), through the priority provision of fertilizers, machinery and other means of production (and also of incentive consumer goods) and through contracts. Price policy has already been discussed. Credit for agriculture (from bank loans, credit co-operatives and by way of advance payments for produce) was treated in Chapter 15, and priorities for agricultural producer goods have recurrently been mentioned. Contracts embrace a number of different methods of persuasion (or compulsion), as one and the same contract may provide for advance payment, the provision of fertilizers, etc., as well as for the delivery of farm produce to state organs. The use made of contracts has been reviewed in Chapter 11.

A combination of several of the above instruments of control has been employed in the case of the areas of 'high and stable yield'. These represent one of the most striking examples of systematic planning of agriculture in China in recent years. From 1963, much of the state's agricultural investment (especially, it may be surmised, of investment from central government funds) has been concentrated on certain areas which produce large agricultural surpluses, both of industrial crops and of grain. These areas, designated as being of 'high and stable yield' are in any case already favoured by climate, soil and communications. Priority for loans, fertilizers and machinery has been given to those areas which include the Yangtze and Pearl River deltas, the Hangchow-Kashing-Huchow area in Chekiang, the Han River valley in Hupeh, the Chengtu Plain and parts of the north China plains. This widens still further the gap between the relative prosperity of these areas and the conditions in less fortunate parts of China. This policy, then, contrasts sharply with the egalitarianism of 1958-9, when central investment went primarily to the poorer areas.[2] The extent of state investment in these areas makes possible a greater degree of state control of agricultural production there—both of cropping decisions and of procurement—than over the countryside as a whole.

[1] *People's Daily* (*Renmin Ribao*), April 22, 1966, p. 2.
[2] See p. 76 and p. 432 above, and *People's Daily* (*Renmin Ribao*), January 1, 1964, p. 1. Editorial, and ibid., March 11, 1964, p. 1. Editorial, and *Peking Review*, December 11, 1964, p. 27. Hu Chi: 'How Industry Helps Agriculture.'

7. GENERAL REFLECTIONS ON THE OPERATION OF ECONOMIC PLANNING

As well as setting targets for separate sectors of the economy, an economic plan should attemp to co-ordinate the economy by bringing about the necessary proportionate development between the various sectors. The theoretical problems of planned and proportionate development, of balance and imbalance, have generated much discussion in China. Yang Chien-pai, whose name we have mentioned in connection with the controversy over returns on capital, stated in 1959 that it was an 'objective law of socialist construction that the national economy could be developed at the same time both rapidly and in correct proportions'. Nevertheless, 'balance is relative and temporary; imbalance is absolute and regular. Therefore, whatever subjective efforts are made to achieve balance,' he continued, 'imbalance may still result.'[1] In 1961, when the results of disproportionate development of industry and neglect of agriculture had underlined the lesson, Yang Chien-pai was giving more emphasis to the need for balance and proportion.[2] Another economist, writing in 1961, rationalized the series of current economic disasters by putting forward the view that 'the wave-like development of the national economy in the manner of imbalance— balance—imbalance represents the unity of two contradictions, the high-speed development, and the planned, proportionate development, of the national economy'.[3] In fact this 'wave-like development' arose from the fact that much capital investment in industry during the First Five Year Plan period and in the Great Leap, had outrun production of the necessary raw materials. As a result, many factories had to be shut down or run at below capacity, so that the returns on capital invested in them were much below what might otherwise have been expected. In effect, much capital had been wasted.

An article by Yang Ying-chieh in November 1962, in which month he was re-appointed a Vice-Chairman of the State Planning Commission, gave the six ratios to be kept in balance in the national economy as those between agriculture and industry; between the output of means of production and the output of consumption goods; between saving and consumption in the national income; between transport on one hand, and agriculture and industry on the other; between the supply of commodities and total purchasing power; and finally between investment for cultural purposes and economic investment.[4] Three years earlier, the same author writing on the same theme had added that while much could be learned from 'a study of the experience of construction in fraternal countries', nevertheless the ratios used by them were not to be introduced, without modification, into the Chinese plans.[5] In 1962,

[1] *People's Daily* (*Renmin Ribao*), November 18, 1959, p. 7. Yang Chien-pai: 'The Search for Balance in the Midst of High Speed Development.'

[2] Ibid., July 25, 1961, p. 7. Yang Chien-pai: 'An Exploratory Discussion of Some Problems of Comprehensive Equilibrium.'

[3] *Ta Kung Daily* (*Dagong Bao*), Peking, May 17, 1961 (ECMP 13). Ou-yang Ch'eng: 'On the Wave-Like Advance in the Development of the National Economy.'

[4] *Economic Research* (*Jingji Yanjiu*), No. 11, November 1962, pp. 4–8. Yang Ying-chieh: 'Comprehensive Equilibrium'.

[5] Ibid., No. 5, May 1959, p. 13. Yang Ying-chieh: 'Problems of Ratios, Key Points and Speed in the National Economy'.

apparently he no longer felt this warning was necessary. In this connection it is interesting to note that at one time there must have been a considerable number of Soviet experts working in the State Planning Commission. Two volumes of their reports were published in Peking in September 1958 and further volumes were then in preparation.[1]

Many of the mistakes of the past years had been due to a disregard of the type of ratios listed by Yang Ying-chieh, as exemplified by the excessive concentration on industry and neglect of agriculture and of transport, the over-emphasis on producer goods, or, to quote a more specific instance already mentioned, in the lack of co-ordination in plans for electric power and for industry.

When it comes to drawing up material balances, reasonably accurate technical co-efficients are required, relating inputs to outputs. Here the encouragement of small plants and workshops in the Great Leap complicated matters. In the words of Kang Chao, a Chinese economist working in the United States, 'with the technical dualism that rapidly developed in 1958-9, most technical co-efficients or input-output ratios had so greatly diverged between modern and native industries that national averages became less meaningful', and balances between industries more difficult to maintain.[2]

The lack of relevant technical co-efficients is but one example of the inadequacy of numerical information which has frustrated China's planners. The vicissitudes of the State Statistical Bureau and of other organs charged with statistical tasks have been reviewed by Choh-ming Li in his *Statistical System of Communist China*. It will be remembered that the State Statistical Bureau was established in 1952; and by May 1953 it had opened offices in all provincial level units except Tibet, and in provincially controlled municipalities. In 1954, statistical units were set up at the levels of special districts and of *hsien*, while in the next two years an attempt was made to get statistical work going in *hsiang* and *chen* as well. However, below the level of the *hsien*, organization was very patchy. In particular, the collection of agricultural statistics depended on 'a small number of part-time statistical workers'.[3] Indeed, 'agricultural statistical services had failed even to grow roots in the rural areas'.[4]

As well as the local statistical offices established by the State Statistical Bureau, each ministry's 'system' has included statistical units at different levels.[5] The State Statistical Bureau had in 1953 been given authority to supervise and control the work of these units. Throughout the First Five Year Plan period, the Bureau was attempting to assert this authority, especially in such matters as the methods to be used for computing success indicators for enterprises.[6]

The efforts to build up a national statistical network under the professional supervision of the State Statistical Bureau were shattered in 1958 by administrative decentralization, by political pressure leading to false reporting of

---

[1] *Planned Economy (Jihua Jingji)*, No. 9, September 1958, p. 15.
[2] *Asian Survey*, Vol. IV, No. 5, May 1964, p. 853. Kang Chao: 'Economic Aftermath of the Great Leap in Communist China.'
[3] Choh-ming Li: op. cit. pp. 18-19, and 57.
[4] Ibid., p. 33.   [5] Ibid., p. 23.   [6] Ibid., pp. 35-50.

output figures, and by that hostility towards professionalism which characterized the Great Leap. Many statistical units were abolished and their personnel scattered to other tasks.[1] The result can be seen in the statistical fiasco of 1958 and 1959 when wild claims had eventually to be retracted; the task of revising output figures of 1958 was given to the State Statistical Bureau. Almost simultaneously came the dismissal of Hsüeh Mu-ch'iao, Director of the State Statistical Bureau since its inception, who had led the opposition to the dismantling of its network and to direction of statistical work by local Party officials during the Great Leap. His dismissal was probably meant to indicate that renewal of authority for the Bureau was to be conditional on its working in partnership with the Party organization at all levels.[2] In the course of 1959, it was announced that the statistical units in the ministries' systems were to be integrated at all levels with the offices of the State Statistical Bureau's system.[3]

The relative authority over statistical work of the Bureau's local offices and those of local Party organs, has remained ambiguous.[4] In 1962 the position was thus stated in *Red Flag*: 'In respect of statistical work, the state's statistical departments at all levels are subject to vertical leadership by the State Statistical Bureau. In respect of Party administrative work they are subject to leadership by the local Party and government organs.'[5] The year 1962 was one of comparative political relaxation. Therefore, this article went on to stress the need for professional control over the technical side of statistical work. At a period of greater political tension, the emphasis is likely to be otherwise; and statistical (as well as other) errors due to political reasons may be expected to be cumulative as these errors are all liable to work in the same direction at any one time as each cadre is apt to feel obliged to go to more extreme lengths than the last, in order to prove his zeal. It should be noted that from 1960 onwards, few statistics about the Chinese economy have been published.

From 1959, extensive use was made of model surveys in the estimation of agricultural statistics.[6] This is simpler and quicker than the collection of comprehensive figures, but is beset with statistical perils, largely arising from the lack of well-trained statistical workers. The low level of education, above all of numeracy, among the rural population, restricts the possibility of compiling accurate statistics. It is difficult to ensure that output is weighed.[7] Divergencies and ambiguities exist in the system of weights to be employed. Although the metric system has been adopted, the use of older measures still persists.

Lighthearted examples may be quoted to show that the country people are unaccustomed to thinking in terms of accurate statistics. In July 1958, a

[1] Cho-ming Li: op. cit., Chapter 7, passim.
[2] Ibid., Chapter 8, passim and pp. 111–16. From 1954 to 1959 Hsüeh was a Vice-Chairman of the State Planning Commission and was re-appointed as such in December 1960. In 1963 he was made Chairman of the State Price Commission.
[3] Ibid., pp. 116.
[4] Ibid., pp. 119-121.
[5] *Red Flag* (*Hongqi*), No. 18, September 16, 1962, p. 16. Wang Ssu-hua: 'Bring Out to the Fullest Extent the Function of Statistical Work in Socialist Construction.'
[6] Choh-ming Li: op. cit. Chapter 10 and p. 147.
[7] e.g. *People's Daily* (*Renmin Ribao*), November 30, 1960, p. 1.

hsiang in Kwangtung with some 20,000 inhabitants was reported to have drawn up a three year construction plan which called for setting up a farm with 10,000 pigs, another with 10,000 chickens, a third with 10,000 ducks, yet another with 10,000 head of cattle, the opening of 10,000 *mow* of orchards and tea gardens, 10,000 *mow* of fish ponds, a bee farm of 10,000 hives, and new villages for 10,000 people.[1] Similarly, in 1965, a Vice-Governor of Liaoning province (one of the most economically advanced parts of China) said that the province's agricultural development during the Third Five Year Plan period should aim at 'creating five "10 million *mows*".' This meant 'to reclaim 10 million *mow* of swamps, reclaim 10 million *mow* of terraced fields, irrigate 10 million *mow* of land, plant 10 million *mow* of trees, and sow 10 million *mow* of green manure crops'.[2] In colloquial Chinese ten thousand commonly means a 'very great number' (and ten million is expressed in Chinese as 'a thousand ten thousands') so that all these plans amounted to, were expressed intentions of doing a lot in the directions indicated. Given the circumstances of rural life, this was probably the only kind of plan that could be honest, avoiding the veneer of mock accuracy. Nevertheless, this sets severe limits to national agricultural planning. Until reliable agricultural statistics exist, comprehensive planning of the national economy is scarcely possible.

The lack of firm data on which to base plans, has inhibited the use of mathematical techniques in planning. In East Europe and the Soviet Union the use of such techniques has been a way of freeing the work of economists from close supervision by Party men, who are unlikely to understand what is written in mathematical terms. In China, certain articles were published in 1960 and 1961 on 'operations and programming' (*yün ch'ou hsüeh*), a term which covers at least in part the fields of programming (linear and non-linear), the theory of games, and the theory of 'queue-forming'[3]. The province of Shantung was, for some reason, particularly prominent in this field and linear programming was said to have been applied there, especially to transport problems.[4] In 1964, experiments in the use of mathematical techniques (mainly critical path analysis) were initiated in planning technical operations in certain branches of the economy, notably engineering and transport.[5] However, no information has come to our knowledge that econometric or other mathematical approaches to macroscale economic planning are being used in China; nor are such methods likely to be fruitful until better statistical data are available for the economy.

A major criticism that must be levelled at the economic planning system set up in the first decade of Communist rule is that of being over-ambitious for

[1] *Economic Research (Jingji Yanjiu)*, No. 8, August 1958, p. 38. Wang Shao-fei: 'Collectivization as Seen from the Viewpoint of a *Hsiang* Federation of Co-operatives.'

[2] *BBC Summary of World Broadcasts*, Second Series, FE/2039/B/11–12 (Shenyang, December 6, 1965). These figures are the first and, up to the time of writing (October 1966) the only, target figures published for the Third Five Year Plan!

[3] S. Kirby (ed.): *Contemporary China*, Vol. VI, P. Luey: 'The *Yün Ch'ou Hsüeh* Movement.'

[4] *People's Daily (Renmin Ribao)*, July 29, 1960, p. 4, and *Red Flag (Hongqi)*, Nos. 20–1, November 1, 1960, pp. 44–9. Liu Chi-p'ing, Secretary of the Secretariat of the CCP Shantung Provincial Committee: 'Extensive Use of Operations and Programming in the Service of Socialist Construction.' See also the articles translated in CB 649.

[5] *Red Flag (Hongqi)*, No. 11, October 1, 1965, p. 22. Hua Lo-keng: 'Scattered Notes on Experiments in Methods of Overall Planning.'

China's stage of development. We have seen that for agriculture, both statistical weaknesses and vagaries of weather played havoc with attempts to plan. In an economy where farming is so important, lack of meaningful plans, or even of reliable forecasts, for agriculture, together with annual harvest fluctuations, rebound in turn on plans for other sectors. Crop failures diminish the output of light industry, largely dependent on agricultural raw materials; they also reduce supplies of export goods and cut the government's revenues. Thus, plans made for all these activities are in turn thrown into disorder. This is an example of how the need to make short-term adjustments imposes a limitation on long-term planning,[1] a phenomenon which economists in many countries have had occasion to observe without looking to China. Indeed, it is not only in China that, contrary to the intentions of the rulers, improvization has often ousted planning in the conduct of economic policy.

Apart from these difficulties, China's administrative machinery is not capable of enforcing compliance with planning directives, nor of supervising and checking plan fulfilment. Even in such an elementary matter as seeing that bank loans for working capital are not diverted to long-term investment, enforcement is chronically weak—and the banks are one of the most efficient parts of the country's administration. In view of this, any description of China's economic planning must carry a strong warning that the system viewed at close quarters is likely to appear very different from what it is supposed to be in theory. Illustrations of this have been given above. However, a further cautionary note to this end is not out of place. Attention must also be drawn to two especially notable gaps in our knowledge. This first is that of the activities of provincial level units in the field of economic planning; the second concerns the influence of the political factor, of Party organs and of intra-Party feuds, on the efforts of those professionally concerned with matters of economic planning.

The meaning of economic planning in China is far from clear. Often economic planning appears to be a synonym for government control over the economy, commanding obedience from all enterprises, other units and individuals.[2] Although this is assumed to have economic advantages, the deeper reasons for wanting such control are political. Administrative difficulties in China have meant that, in fact, market forces have a larger part in economic life than is apparent from regulations and policy statements. Realization of the difficulties of control, however, increase the authorities' fear of the market, because they are frightened of completely losing control over the economy, and of giving opportunity for the growth of hostile forces. Another factor lessening the strength of market workings is that in a system such as China's, non-economic criteria are even more important than elsewhere in the world in determining economic conduct. The desire to minimize political difficulties, and not to run foul of current political trends, is likely on many occasions to exert more influence than either formal targets or material incentives.

[1] A. Cairncross, Head of the United Kingdom Government Economic Service: *The Short-Term and the Long in Economic Planning*, Lecture to the Economic Development Institute, Washington, DC, 1966, passim.

[2] cf. P. J. D. Wiles: *The Political Economy of Communism*, Oxford, 1962, p. 55. 'Note the emphasis on accounting and control. This is still what Communists really mean by economic planning.'

Chapter 18

CONCLUSIONS[1]

Before drawing together some conclusions from our study, we must first remind ourselves of the limited character of our aims. We have not set out to pass judgment on the degree of success or failure of the economic policy of the Chinese government as a whole, nor to chart quantitatively the course of production and investment. Our primary purpose has been to consider the institutional framework of the Chinese economy, the relationships between its various parts, and their manner of operation, although at times we have given an opinion on the appropriateness of institutional arrangements to their purposes. The limits of our knowledge must equally be stressed and the large margin of uncertainty which, as the reader will by now have seen, surrounds so much of the discussion of the Chinese economy.

How closely can the central government impose its will throughout the country in economic matters? Within what limits is the Chinese economy effectively subject to central direction? These are the questions to which we shall now turn our attention.

We will first review those categories of economic undertakings which, in the course of this study, we have noted as still remaining under the direct management of the central government, as well as those economic targets which the centre apparently still lays down. We will then discuss the extent to which central authorities have been able to maintain the control of the economy, despite administrative decentralization, through the Party organization or other agents, after which we shall consider features of the Chinese scene which render close control difficult by any level of government, central or local.

The decree of November 1957 on the reform of the industrial management system, was implemented faster than originally anticipated and, by the middle of 1958, the central government directly controlled virtually no manufacture of consumer goods. In producer goods industries, most undertakings of importance were, by the terms of the decree, to remain under direct control of the central ministries. The decentralization of heavy industry and of mining apparently covered a wider range than indicated by the original decree. Also, of course, it must be remembered that even enterprises retained under direct control of central ministries, have been subject to 'dual subordination', i.e. to local authorities as well as to the ministries, although for such enterprises, ministry control was to be paramount. As things turned out, local influence

[1] Much of this chapter was incorporated in a paper given to the China Conference in Chicago in February 1966 and later published in the *Bulletin of the Atomic Scientists*, June 1966 and in R. Adams (ed.): *Contemporary China*, New York, 1966.

may often have been stronger than originally intended: this also applies in other economic spheres besides industry.

Important groups of state farms in Sinkiang, Heilungkiang, and Inner Mongolia, have come under the immediate control of the Ministry of State Farms and Land Reclamation. This was intended to give the central government a close hold over certain strategic areas, as well as providing sources of grain supplies under its immediate control.

In transport, the main railway system (other than small local railways and lines built to serve individual coalfields, factories or lumber areas) is under central control, although provincial influence has probably become more far-reaching than envisaged in 1957. Major civil aviation services also come directly under the central government. Road transport is mainly under local control, but the central government has been responsible for building (and presumably maintaining) certain major highways, notably some of strategic importance. The main coastal shipping services are directly under the central government, although there may be some difference in this respect between shipping along the north China and the south China coasts. A central government organ—the Yangtze Navigation Administrative Bureau—exercises general supervision of shipping on the Yangtze; in addition to the Bureau's own vessels, local authorities and joint state-private companies also run ships on the river. Trans-ocean shipping under the Chinese flag, whether Chinese-owned or chartered, may be presumed to come directly under the central government, as also the China Ocean Steamship Agency, which handles the clearing of foreign ships and agency work at all ports at which foreign ships are accustomed to call.

The central government has direct control of the river conservancy commissions, of which the chief are the Yellow River Water Conservancy Commission, the Huai River Water Conservancy Commission and the Yangtze River Planning Office. These commissions span several provinces and are charged with the multi-purpose development of their respective rivers. Similarly, the Grand Canal Commission, established to improve the Grand Canal for purposes of both navigation and water conservancy, was placed under the chairmanship of the Minister of Communications.

The banking system, coming directly under the central government, and especially the ubiquitous People's Bank, is an all-important instrument of supervision and control over the entire economy. The national corporations engaged in foreign and internal trade, also fall under direct central control; although local internal trade corporations probably have considerable independence in their dealings, and even some scope for independence is possessed by local foreign trade corporations.

The chief institutions of higher learning and of scientific research have been maintained as national, rather than provincial, organs, and their subordination to the central government might be expected to have furthered its control over the economy. The main national-level organs of radio, telecommunications and the press are supposed to come directly under the central authorities. However, both the national press and the national universities appear to have fallen under a large measure of local control; at least local Party committees were blamed in 1966 for their alleged failings.

After considering those economic undertakings which remained directly under the central government after the 1957-8 administrative decentralization, our attention must now turn to the economic targets which the centre announced its intention of still controlling.

In the early days of the regime, the emphasis was placed on overall control by the central government of the whole national economy. Gradually this emphasis shifted until it became concentrated on inter-provincial (including provincial-central) transfers of different types. Even where targets under formal central control included total figures (e.g. for production, revenue, etc.), the centre's primary concern appears to have been with the marginal transfers. Thus in financial matters, while the figures for total national revenue and expenditure were stipulated as remaining under central control, the provinces had (or took) such scope for initiative in raising funds (budgetary or extra-budgetary) that central control over national totals cannot have been firm. However, the other financial targets retained under formal central control—transfers of revenue between provinces and the central government, and credit transfers—may be presumed to have been grasped much more firmly by the central authorities. The apparent high degree of centralization of the People's Bank must have enabled credit policy to remain more centralized than most other economic matters; although as we have seen, from 1965, centralized control probably weakened in respect of loans made through the Agricultural Bank.

Overall control of the rate and direction of investment and of major investment projects, is another target officially retained in the hands of the central government, although it is difficult for it to maintain a hold over investment by local authorities, especially from extra-budgetary funds. Central control of overall plans for enrolment in institutions of higher education and for the allocation of graduates can be seen to be a special instance, and a vitally important one, of the control of investment.

Closely connected with central control of investment is another centrally controlled target—that of total wages, which, if inflation is to be avoided, must be kept in step with the supply of consumer goods; here again, the strength of the People's Bank is vitally important in enabling central control to be maintained. Joined with the target for total wages is that of the total number of employees: together they constitute control of wage levels and, given the system of urban residence permits, of immigration into towns. Control over the disposition of the country's foreign exchange reserves strengthens the central government's control over both investment and allocation of certain key commodities, notably (in the past few years) grain and machinery: provincial level authorities, however, control an unspecified amount of the foreign currency proceeds of foreign trade. Central control of the volume of freight carried by railways (and of the major modern transport enterprises) helps to reinforce central controls over other targets.

In respect of material allocation, the central government since 1959 has concentrated on trying to control inter-provincial transfers of certain major commodities, both agricultural and industrial. Here again, it is true that the list of targets included the output as well as the transfer balances of such commodities. However, we have seen that in agriculture from 1956 onwards (except in periods of political pressure) the intention has been to change from unrealistic production planning to procurement planning, at least as far as central government plans are concerned. And in procurement planning, the central authorities are not immediately concerned with what happens within any province so long as that province meets its external obligations, i.e. so long as it delivers its required quota for inter-provincial transfer or for export, or, in the case of a province deficient in any given commodity, so long as it does not demand more than its stipulated inward transfer. While the circumstances of agriculture make production planning particularly hazardous, this is also very difficult with that substantial proportion of China's industrial output which comes from small enterprises.

Lastly, it will be recalled that certain prices have officially remained subject to central control—procurement prices of major agricultural commodities and the sales prices (both wholesale and retail), at the main commercial centres, of the chief foodstuffs and of some major industrial products. The list excludes those industrial goods subject to central allocation, the allocation prices of which would also be centrally fixed.

This account of items under the control of the central government dates largely from the decentralization measures of 1957-8. Since then, the ban on the export (and possibly on the open circulation within China) of journals on economic planning, and the paucity of other sources, makes it difficult to speak with assurance about the regulations in force at later dates. In 1961-2 reports were current of a move back towards greater financial centralization.[1] This, however, as far as can be seen, consisted mainly of improvements in accounting procedures. If this was successful, it would, of course, effect more than any organizational change in actually increasing the financial powers of the centre for, as we have often had occasion to note, the chief limits on central control (or control by lower levels of the government) lie in administrative and accounting weaknesses.

In general, instead of greater centralization, such evidence as we have suggests that in the early 1960s relaxation (whether *de jure* or just *de facto*) of central control occurred in the case of some items, such as procurement prices of grain, which earlier had been reserved to the central authorities. This too, is what might be expected after the decentralization of 1957-8 gave great powers to the provinces, powers which it would be difficult for the centre to confine within the limits it had drawn. The period of political tension that included the 'cultural revolution' might be thought to be leading to changes in the situation. At the time of writing, it is too early to judge the effects of this movement on economic life. The attack on local Party committees which formed a feature of the political campaigns of 1966, appeared to be directed at their hold over political and cultural affairs, and to have had relatively little repercussions on the control by the local Party committees of economic affairs. However, this can be only an interim conclusion relating to a situation still in flux.

Before further discussion of the relative roles in economic life of the central government and the provincial level authorities, we must review the operation of the main centripetal and centrifugal forces, among which

[1] See pp. 398-9 above.

it is impossible to draw a line between the political and the economic.

Apart from the underlying sense of cultural identity and the more recent sentiments of nationalism, the chief forces welding the country together since 1949 have been the Party (although for more recent years this statement, as we shall see, needs serious modification), the Army, modern transport and telecommunications, mass media, national institutions of higher education and of advanced scientific research, the banking system, regional power grids and multi-purpose river valley commissions, national trading corporations for internal and for international trade, the various technical institutes of the central ministries, the frequent national conferences on economic and other matters, the mobility over the country of professional and skilled manpower as well as large-scale migration of the less skilled. These we must now briefly discuss with special reference to their implications for economic control by the central government.

The role of the Communist Party, originally intended as the chief instrument of the centre's control over the economy, demands that its branches should be omnipresent, extending into all units of the economy, and yet that it should maintain its own separate identity; that it should be amenable to central commands and yet be on good terms with the masses. These requirements have often proved incompatible. As we have seen, the scarcity of educated people makes the staffing of two distinct hierarchies in political and economic life difficult and sometimes impossible. As a result of this, and of the Party's ideological suspicions of many of the professional and managerial classes, there has been a constant tendency for the Party to supplant managers and to exert direct authority in economic enterprises, as in political bodies. This desire for immediate Party control was especially strong at the time of the Great Leap when the Party overreached itself by trying to do more than it was administratively capable of doing. The outcome was to hasten the process by which the local Party branches and Party branches in enterprises were, through assimilation to management, being transformed from a revolutionary controlling group into a managerial elite, a club for meritocrats. This transformation has been inevitable, because of the type of person who has in recent years been recruited into the Party from economic and administrative circles, and also because of the nature of the responsibilities of Party branches in local administrations and in enterprises.

The old types of Party member who joined before 1949 are rugged characters, drawn in youth to a revolutionary movement and since then schooled by hard experience, but frequently lacking the education or the qualities to administer the complex undertakings of a modern economy. We have seen that difficulties have often arisen between such persons, when appointed managers of enterprises, and their professional engineering staff. The new generation of Party recruits drawn from administrative organs and economic enterprises, however, is of different calibre. Many are likely to have been attracted into the Party from career motives.[1] A large proportion of new members are already

[1] R. MacFarquhar (ed.): *The Hundred Flowers*, London, 1960, pp. 51, 68, 73–5, 92, 93, 211 and 222, and *Daily Worker* (*Gongren Ribao*), April 28, 1966, p. 4. Wang Hsiang-t'ing, Nanch'ang Diesel Engine Plant: 'The Right Motive for Joining the Party Can only Be the Service of Communism.' Wang writes: 'at that time my motive for wanting to join the

non-Party cadres—such as production team leaders, or those in other positions of leadership[1]—while other recruits are often workers with exceptional achievements in production. Such people are not usually dominated by political motives, but are more likely to regard Party membership as a useful aid to forward their ambitions for their enterprises or for themselves. The tendency for Party cadres to identify with their enterprises is furthered by the fact that, at least at some periods, their bonuses have been calculated within their enterprise and have depended on the enterprise's achievements.

Civilian life, however, has not been the sole—or perhaps even the most important—channel of recruitment into the Chinese Communist Party. The Army also has this role and a high proportion of servicemen are Party members. In many of the developing countries of the world, the Army provides the most significant ladder for social mobility. Even where education is available to the poor, a student from an illiterate home is usually at a serious disadvantage in competition with those from educated families. In the profession of arms, the odds against him are much less.

The Army was the original centralizing force in the country, the instrument by which the country was united under the Communist Party. The military characteristics of the regime must never be overlooked. However, the Army's role as a unifying force in *economic* life is very limited. Ex-servicemen have been given economic appointments, notably in the new political departments, in the hope that they will provide a stiffening element to maintain the Party line in economic spheres. The difficulty has been that such ex-servicemen have seldom sufficient understanding of economic matters to enable them to exert the desired influence.

Another instrument of central influence and control is the public security system, inside the Party yet in some way additional to it. In the public security system, vertical lines of responsibility are thought to be especially strong, at least up to the level of the province. Above this level, less certainty is felt about their strength.[2]

The control of appointments is probably one of the chief means available to the central authorities for controlling affairs within provinces, although it is by no means clear what degree of control over appointments is still exercised by the centre. We have seen that behind the formal state regulations for official appointments, lies the Party *nomenklatura* system, by which Party committees at different levels are responsible for specific appointments in state and other organs. Thus, the degree of central control over appointments must depend on the degree of central control over the Party committees making them, and this depends in part on the degree of central control of central appointees to Party committees once they have been appointed—that is, the extent to which the centre could afford to dismiss them if they championed local interests, or

---

Party was that I was just going to graduate and after graduation, if I was a Party member, I would have better prospects and, when I took a job, my superiors would certainly place more confidence in me'.

[1] J. W. Lewis: *Leadership in Communist China*, Ithaca, New York, 1963, p. 118.
[2] I am indebted to A. Doak Barnett, of Columbia University, for allowing me in this paragraph to draw on the findings of his research.

whether such dismissal would generate ill will between centre and provinces which the centre would be unwilling to risk. We know of cases where the central authorities have dismissed high provincial Party officials, we do not know how often the centre may have wished to order dismissals but refrained because of reasons cited above. In such matters, the currents of intra-Party conflicts must often be all important.

We have already seen how modern developments in transport, tele-communications and mass media have provided the technical basis which has enabled the Communist Government of China to exercise a much greater and more direct control throughout the country than any of its predecessors; and that these developments have all been employed for this purpose, often with considerable skill. The banking system has been an all-important instrument of supervision and control over the entire economy. It falls to the banks, and notably to the People's Bank, to try to force local authorities and enterprises to obey central plans, through refusing payment for expenditure on excess wages, or on production, purchases or investment not in accordance with these plans. River conservancy commissions spanning several provinces are essential if the hydro-electric and irrigation potential of China's great rivers is to be exploited, and such exploitation is required to meet the needs of a growing population. These river conservancy commissions, and also the regional electricity grids, necessitate supra-provincial control to solve disputes between provinces, such as we have seen broke out between the provinces affected by the scheme for controlling the Huai River. This, in effect, has usually meant control by the central government; the various attempts to set up large regional authorities between the provinces and the central government have been short-lived.

These are the centripetal factors operating in China today which make possible a greater degree of unification and of control by the central government than has ever existed before. Relying on these factors and reacting against the fragmentation of China during the previous decades, the Communist government during the First Five Year Plan period attempted a degree of centralization in the hands of the ministries in Peking which could neither be effectively operated nor long maintained. Recognition of this found expression in the decentralization measures of 1957–8. However, this policy of the more realistic administrators, was temporarily blunted by the attempt in 1958 to enforce highly centralized policies through the mechanism, not of the government, but of the Party. It was not until the failure of the Great Leap was apparent, that the 1957–8 decentralization decrees could take full effect. The strains caused by the Great Leap may indeed, over the subsequent few years, actually have hastened the process of decentralization and brought into play the centrifugal forces which we must now discuss.

The policies of the Great Leap led to a breakdown in the allocation system and in transport. Hence it made it more necessary than ever for each administrative unit to reach for the highest possible degree of self-sufficiency. Self-sufficiency, whether industrial (by each industrial ministry), or by enterprises, or by localities, is endemic in the type of economic planning practised by China, when the complexities of allocating raw materials, and the uncertainties involved, encourage individual units to become self-sufficient.

This, as we have seen, was at the root of the trend towards industrial verticalization which we have earlier discussed. Trade between local administrative units, and trade between enterprises, becomes marginal; 'imports' from other units being limited to those items which individual units cannot produce themselves, little regard being had for comparative costs.

Provincial autarky increased during the Leap, to the embarrassment of the central government which, for example, was unable to prevent a decline in inter-provincial grain transfers, despite the good harvest. The growing autonomy of the provinces meant increased authority for the provincial Party secretaries, who were supposed to be agents for maintaining the Party's centralised hold on the provinces. However, once a provincial Party secretary had become *de facto* responsible for the government of a province, he necessarily became identified with the provincial administration, with its particular interests and policies.

The process of the assimilation of the Party with management, which we have mentioned, has applied with particular force to Party committees of provinces and *hsien*, and of other units of local government. These committees have shouldered direct responsibility for a host of practical economic and administrative matters, often of a routine nature. To quote an example at random, the Hupeh Provincial Party Committee 'convened an urgent telephone conference of *hsien* Party committees to analyse the current state of agricultural production and drought-fighting.... If it is desired to make holes in the embankments to get water to the fields, the permission of the Provincial Party Committee must be obtained.'[1] The secretary of a Party committee, with this kind of immediate managerial responsibility for economic matters in a large province must, together with his subordinates, become engrossed with practical work.

Among other results of this situation, the provincial secretaries of the Party have found themselves making their provinces' cases in negotiations with the central government. The vital matters between the provinces and the centre are the net transfer of grain out of or into a province, and similarly with the other key commodities for which the inter-provincial transfer balances are centrally controlled; the net transfer of revenue (including central grants for investment and other purposes) and the allocation between provinces of loanable funds through the banks. The fact that a large part of the central government's revenues is collected by provincial organs and forwarded by the provinces to the central Ministry of Finance, is likely to strengthen the provinces' position in negotiations with the central government, at least in those provinces which have a net outward transfer of revenue. Those authorities, such as Sinkiang, which are subsidized by the central government are likely to be in a weaker position in this respect.

The economic relations between centre and provinces are concerned only with marginal transfers. The great bulk of production, consumption and exchange is intra-provincial, if not intra-*hsien*. What goes on within a province is, as we have seen, of little direct concern to the central government, so long as the province meets its external obligations. The Party, of course, demands

[1] *BBC Summary of World Broadcasts*, Second Series, FE/W379/A/5–6 (Wuhan, August 6, 1966.)

more—it demands from its provincial branches, and thus indirectly from the local administrations they control, obedience to policies, programmes and campaigns. The degree of verbal obedience it receives is overwhelming. A slogan launched one day in the capital will be repeated on the morrow throughout the country. Deeds, however, do not always march with words, we shall return to this theme later.

The overwhelming advantage of the provincial level authorities as against the national government in the task of economic control and development, is that of size. Averaging 20–30 million population each (30–40 million if only the provinces of China proper are taken into account), their administrations are better placed than the ministries at Peking for deciding on the policies and priorities of most types of industrial growth and agricultural improvement. We have seen, for example, how the provinces have become the main unit for policy making and implementation in the field of agricultural mechanization. In addition, the promotion of powered irrigation and electrically motivated processing industries has been based on transmission lines radiating mainly from provincial capitals. These power systems rarely seem to span provincial boundaries, unlike the regional electric grids mentioned earlier. For many agricultural functions the province is, of course, too large a unit: this explains the leadership of the *hsien* in activities such as demonstration farms. For the development of industry, except on the very largest and the very smallest scales, the provincial level is now the most significant; although in some places, municipalities under provinces are important in this respect.

When we consider relations between the province and its subordinate units —(i.e. the special administrative districts, *hsien* and municipalities)—we know even less than when studying central-provincial dealings. The latter are the subject of national directives, many of which are readily accessible in the volumes of *Collected Laws and Regulations*. These directives occasionally have something to say about the provincial level's relations with lower units, as when maximum permitted rates of agricultural tax are specified; but much less is related about such matters. A large degree of latitude is left to the major local authorities in the manner and extent of their control of the affairs of subordinate authorities. This presumably means that, in different provinces and autonomous regions, the amount of power exercised by these subordinate authorities may differ considerably. However, we hazard the opinion that political and economic factors combine to make the province and its equivalents the key units for economic development in China today.

These provincial level authorities vary in resources (even after making allowance for the greater levies made by the centre on the wealthier ones) and in efficiency. The latitude given to the provinces by the decentralization measures (which in practice has been more extensive than on paper), together with the natural differences between the provinces, must have resulted in a growing differentiation of local policies. Differences in policy are manifest in matters such as the inter-provincial variations in size of communes (not always accounted for by differing circumstances); as the formation of communes among the Yi national minority in Yunnan but not among the Yi in neighbouring Szechuan, among whom the unit or organization is reported still to be the agricultural producers' co-operative[1] (whether this difference is merely verbal or more substantial is admittedly uncertain); the development of linear programming, notably in transport, appears to have been especially encouraged in Shantung.

In any large country or organization, centripetal and centrifugal trends are liable to alternate. This is natural and need cause no surprise. However, the 'norm' around which these oscillations take place must vary with the size, nature and traditions of the units in question. All of these factors point to a greater degree of decentralization from the national government to the next lower level in China than in most other countries. Thus, we may judge the degree of centralization attempted in the First Five Year Plan period as abnormal. The corollary is that the decentralization that subsequently occurred in China is even less likely to be reversed than the somewhat earlier movement in the Soviet Union, to which it bore many resemblances, and by which the Chinese decrees were no doubt influenced.

The position of the provinces might be thought threatened by the campaign to restore commerce to its former channels and directions according to economic regions, instead of according to administrative units as had tended to be the case since the growth of local self-sufficiency in 1958. The evident promotion of this policy by the Party regional bureaux is probably due in good measure to a desire to decrease the power and lessen the independence of the provincial party committees and secretaries, especially in economic and financial matters. It was these matters which became the first concern of the new political departments established in 1964 to prevent the assimilation of the old Party committees with the general political and economic administration. We have already raised the question of how far political and economic administrative units can be disjoined without affecting control by the Party of the unit concerned, and have surmised that such a severance would lead to a considerable weakening of control. If this occurred at the provincial level, it may assuage the anxiety of the centre about waxing provincial autonomy, but it would leave in its place the problem which decentralization was designed to solve—the administrative impossibility of far-reaching, direct control throughout the country from Peking.

The future of China, we may conclude, lies in great measure with the provinces. Our present ignorance of what is happening at the provincial level, in both political and economic matters, is profound. Presumably in some provinces, strong administrations are being built up. Negotiations between provinces and the central government are likely to be tough on the matter of transfer balances—the net transfers of revenue, of grain and other major commodities, the allocations between provinces of raw materials, of central budgetary investment and of banks' loanable funds. The permitted total wage payments within a province may also be the subject of hard bargaining and even harder struggle in enforcement. The onus for enforcing it must fall largely on the provincial branches of the People's Bank, for it is their duty to refuse to release cash for unauthorized wage payments. We have seen that overspending the wage fund has been difficult to prevent. However, it has not occurred on a scale to undermine the value of the currency and for this the

[1] NCNA Kunming, July 26, 1965, and NCNA Chengtu, July 19, 1965.

People's Bank must take a good share of the credit. Thus, the provincial branches of the People's Bank must have been kept under firm central control on all vital matters, and be able to stand up to pressure from organs of provincial authorities. Indeed, it may be that the Bank has succeeded in this respect where the Party has failed, in that it has kept its identity as an organ of central control while local Party branches have tended to be assimilated with their corresponding local authorities. In the past, weakness in organizing the large impersonal undertakings of modern economic life had characterized the Chinese scene. Without an opportunity of close study on the spot at the present time, we must speak with caution, but it seems at least probable that the People's Bank has, to a large extent, overcome this weakness.

It may be surmised that a certain amount of friction has been generated at times between the People's Bank and the local Party committees, representing the relatively autonomous local economic and political administrations. During the Great Leap, when the power of the Party committees shot up, the Bank's supervisory role over economic life was whittled away. After the Leap, this function of the Bank was again emphasized, although how far it regained the strength it enjoyed in this respect during the First Five Year Plan period, it is difficult to determine. The establishment of the Agricultural Bank as an entity independent of the People's Bank, may have represented a victory for local interests which became more apparent in 1965, when the Agricultural Bank changed its method of loan management to one which gave greater control to local authorities in decisions over agricultural credit.

The People's Bank presumably is the channel through which the Army is paid. Thus the continued loyalty of dispersed Army units to the central command is bound up with the maintenance of the centralized nature of the People's Bank. It is perhaps no coincidence that during the 'cultural revolution' of 1966 there has not, up to the time of writing, come to our knowledge any instance in which the forces of the cultural revolution (linked closely with the Army) have criticized the People's Bank or its staff, despite the fact that these must include many persons of bourgeois background such as have been targets of attack in other institutions. This suggests that some kind of understanding or even of alliance may exist between Army and Bank, those two great vertical pillars of contemporary Chinese society. Both have found themselves in opposition to the horizontal elements, to localized authority, particularly as represented by provincial level Party committees.

Despite the strength of vertical centralizing forces in political life, as displayed in the 'cultural revolution', and despite the far-reaching power of the People's Bank, there is no sign that the hold of local Party committees over economic enterprises in their areas has been seriously threatened.

China is not a monolithic society or economy, but a cellular one. This is the burden of the evidence. We must indicate certain consequences which flow from this. Any direct revenue or expenditure by the central government (e.g. on the nuclear programme, other military expenditure, foreign aid, etc.) should—to determine its relative internal significance—be calculated as a percentage of total *central government* revenue or expenditure, and not only as a percentage of total budgetary revenue or expenditure; similarly, with the quantities of grain and other commodities at the disposal of the central authorities. The centre can always, of course, call on the major local authorities to increase their contributions of cash or commodities; even when a definite period of years is stipulated before changes can be made in any regulations, there are always loopholes left, and anyway we have, in the course of this study, amassed plenty of examples of the free way in which law is interpreted, or ignored, according to requirements. The real limit on the expansion of central revenues lies in the relations between the centre and the major local authorities. The centre depends on the co-operation of these authorities in many different ways and only in an extreme situation can it afford openly to use crude force—i.e. its control over the armed forces —to secure increased levies of revenue or commodities. The tension between centre and provinces in respect to transfers in cash and kind must be seen in the context of their mutual dependence.

When linked with the question of provincial-central relations, China's imports of grain take on an additional significance. As already pointed out, while 5 to 6 million tons a year (the approximate rate at which these imports were running in the early 1960s) represents only some 3 per cent of China's total grain output, it is the equivalent of around 12 per cent of total grain procurement, and probably a good deal more of total inter-provincial transfers. Hence the imports of grain serve to ease relations between the centre and the provinces, as otherwise Peking would be forced to try to squeeze larger grain transfers out of grain-surplus provinces. Thus, this supply of imported grain, which is under its direct control, strengthens the central government by making it to that extent less dependent on provincial compliance with its levies. Foreign trade in this way fulfils the same role as the 'key economic areas' which in days past gave the imperial government of China much of the grain supplies for its own needs. As well as importing grain, the present government of China is also fostering 'key economic areas', i.e. the areas of 'high and stable yield', for the same purpose. By means of centrally allocated investment in these areas, the government can keep closer control over them and over their surpluses of grain and cotton.

While we stress the cellular nature of the present-day Chinese economy, a word of warning is necessary. As the economy becomes modernized, the tendency will be for its cellular nature to evolve into more complex systems of relationships. Even now the economy is less cellular than in the past, as exemplified in particular by the countrywide operations of the People's Bank, and also by the changes taking place in the more modernized parts of the country.

Another point must be emphasized. Given the size and circumstances of China, the surprising thing is not the amount of provincial autonomy, but the extent of central control; not any fissiparous strains we may have noted, but the sense of underlying and persisting unity which binds this quarter of the human family even in periods of civil strife, and which must claim our tribute of admiration.

Apart from the growth of local autonomy, other factors weaken the control both of the centre and also of local authorities, over the economy. Deficiencies in statistical and accounting work have repeatedly been mentioned in our study. These weaknesses set very severe limits to the possibility of any kind of control. The same result follows from the shortage of competent administrators and managers. In discussing the difference between developed and under-developed economies, too much prominence is usually given to technological matters and not enough to management, and to financial and statistical know-how. Administrative failures may have been one reason for the frequent choppings and changings of policy which have marked the economic scene in Communist China.

The concentration of central control on marginal transfer balances is due very largely to the virtual impossibility, given the deficiencies just mentioned, of trying to ascertain, much less to control, output and revenue totals; transfers are easier to check. Similarly with the importance which devolved on profits as a success indicator for enterprises. Whether a given sum of profits has or has not been remitted to the state by an enterprise, is less liable to uncertainty or abuse (although we have seen that it can be abused) than is the use of output, quality, cost reduction or labour productivity as success indicators. This is apart from the economic superiority of the profit index over the alternatives.

To return to the limitations placed on economic control by administrative and accountancy weaknesses in China, a major example is the inability to prevent the illicit use of extra-budgetary funds. Large sums from these sources have been diverted to unplanned investment, thus making nonsense of state investment plans. Also this unplanned investment often led to the diversion of state-allocated raw materials from their planned uses. Apparently, the People's Bank was not able to prevent all this, possibly because the transactions involved may have been settled in cash, contrary to regulations.

The Chinese have a sophisticated attitude to outward expression of opinion, which renders government control simultaneously easier and more difficult. Words are regarded as symbolic counters, to be moved about the chessboard of life in order to produce the desired effect. This leads to reservations and subtleties of expression and action which need to be interpreted within the framework of the Chinese environment and which a stranger might not understand. There commonly lacks the sense of an obligation for words and beliefs, or words and actions, to correspond. While this phenomenon is certainly present in other cultures, it is not normally so strong as in China. It has the result that outward compliance is easily obtained but that an individual's or a group's 'public face' must not be taken as an indication of their 'private face'. Thus conformity, although easily won, is apt to remain superficial. It is relatively simple in these circumstances for a government to see that stipulated formulae are repeated throughout the country and that demonstrations are held when ordered, but quite another thing for it to secure that its writ should run in enforcing policies against local interests. In such a case, there may be little in the way of outward protest (although occasionally, as in the Hundred Flowers period, submerged feelings may well out), but sabotage need be none the less effective for being done in silence. Indeed, the more contrary to central orders that local cadres may be acting, the more loudly they may give verbal support to those orders.

Connected with this trait is another, the strong tradition in China of not discussing family difficulties and dissensions with outsiders. This is prevalent not only in respect of families but also of larger groups and of the nation itself. Thus the Chinese are apt to present a seemingly monolithic front to foreigners. Added to this, foreigners at present are restricted mainly to contact with those places and sectors of Chinese life which are directly controlled by the central government, the capital and other large cities and their environs, diplomacy and international trade. In consequence, the picture given to the outside world is of a gigantic slab of humanity under tight centralized control, whose actions are based on certain highly simplified slogans. An impression so untrue, so dull, and so terrifying, may be thought to serve the purposes of prestige: certainly it ill serves the cause of international understanding, of world peace, and even of China's national safety.

Certain other features of the Chinese economy deserve to be reviewed in our conclusions. The importance of the private and semi-private sector has frequently been mentioned in our study. A substantial part of the peasant's livelihood is drawn from their private plots and domestic handicrafts; the produce from these, too, forms the mainstay of the rural markets. In 1959, as we have seen, there were estimated to be several million private undertakings in industry and commerce. Most of these would be very small, often one-man, concerns. In addition, many officially recognized handicraft co-operatives may, we have noted, be in essence family workshops. The same probably applies to a proportion of the joint state-private undertakings. When tracing the course of 'socialist transformation' it was remarked that joint state-private enterprises became almost indistinguishable from state-owned ones, and that numerous amalgamations took place between former private undertakings after conversion to the joint state-private status. However, reports indicate that new businesses, especially in such lines as restaurants, have been opened as joint state-private concerns from the beginning; in these, the private element is likely to be more to the fore, with the manager-proprietor being in effect a concessionaire of the state. The administrative machinery for close control of all this private economic activity does not exist. Many of these private businesses are probably subject to less state control than are their counterparts in many Western market economies. This is one illustration of the impossibility of tight universal administrative supervision in a relatively underdeveloped country.

The wholesale borrowing by China from the Soviet Union of forms of organization and of method of operation, as well as of technical matters, will have become evident to the reader. It can be seen in agriculture in the formal organization of agricultural producer co-operatives, of state farms and agricultural machinery stations; in much of the general organization of industry (with the 1957 to 1958 changes, following shortly after similar measures in the Soviet Union), in the economic accounting system, in the definition of costs and profits and in many other economic concepts, including that of the enterprise; in the role of trade unions, in the grading and bonus systems of workers in state enterprises and in some aspects of the allocation system; in the conduct of foreign trade through special corporations; in compulsory sales of grain; in similarity (not, however, complete) between the Chinese industrial and commercial tax and the Soviet turnover tax and in many budgetary forms and practices, in the supervisory role of the banks and above all in the watchdog function in the economy formally assigned to the Communist Party. This borrowing occurred in the early years of the regime during the period of rehabilitation and during the First Five Year Plan period.

The Great Leap of 1958 represented a revulsion against the adoption of foreign ways. This was signalled most clearly by the formation of the people's communes and by the prominence given to development through labour-intensive small-scale industry. The practice of 'sending down' Party and government cadres, staff of enterprises and professional people for spells of manual work, is also a divergence from the Soviet model. Other differences in economic organization from the Soviet Union include agricultural tax in kind, the proportionately greater contribution of profits to the budget, the greater local powers of price-fixing, the relatively higher procurement prices for agricultural produce (at least before the Khruschev reforms), the function of the biennial Canton Export Fair in the country's foreign trade, the existence of joint state-private enterprises, the economic role of the street associations and the short-lived urban communes and, very prominently, the more direct part played by the Party in economic life compared with the Soviet practice.

China derived both advantages and disadvantages in copying the Soviet model. The Soviet economy was much more advanced than the Chinese and, on that account, as well as from differences of national tradition and temperament, not all borrowed methods were suited to the Chinese circumstances. For example, Soviet practices of organization, such as the economic accounting system, are extravagent of educated manpower. However, copying Soviet forms and methods was simpler and quicker than working out new forms and methods all at once. All countries benefit from borrowing from abroad in matters in which they are relatively backward and what is borrowed often needs lengthy adaptation before suiting local conditions. So there was nothing unusual in the fact that China copied a foreign model when re-shaping her economy, although the amount that was borrowed within a few short years was exceptional. Doubt may be felt whether the Soviet model was the most appropriate. Impartial consideration might have preferred Japan's example in many respects. Indeed, much must have been learned and copied from Japanese patterns of economic activity. Manchuria, under Kao Kang in the early days of the Communist regime, is likely to have been the channel for transmitting this experience, as also of Soviet methods, to the rest of China.

The breach with the Soviet Union occasioned a defiant enthusiasm for simple old-style Chinese ways, and for improvization instead of sophisticated professionalism. In the early 1960s, frequent praise was bestowed on 'traditional' methods of production or organization: 'traditional' being contrasted with 'foreign'. The traditions thus lauded were of the humble type, culled from the way of life of peasant and artisan. The attack on more exalted traditions, those of the literati and their culture, was renewed with great vigour in the mid-1960s. The 'cultural revolution' of 1966 extolled the new, but it was a newness contrasted with the professional, 'foreign' standards of doing things, which had often come to be accepted by practical men, such as those in control of local Party committees. Many atavistic elements became apparent in the 'cultural revolution' which was, in fact, directed against the burgeoning meritocracy, or at least against some sections of this new class.

Conclusions

Many examples have been instanced in this study of reversion to old ways after the over-hasty adoption of things foreign. Sometimes, indeed, the student of contemporary China may exaggerate the extent to which the country is relaxing back into 'traditional' methods: the truth probably being that these had never been abandoned as much as official pronouncements gave to believe. Here once again we must repeat a warning that while the width of the gap between regulations that are promulgated and what actually happens, should be apparent to anyone who has read thus far, yet it may be even wider than suspected. Whatever the degree of enforcement, we know enough to realize its patchiness from time to time, place to place, sector to sector, instance to instance. The sprawling, disjointed nature of the Chinese economy must never be forgotten.

However, although modernization may not have gone far in many parts of the economy, we can be sure that movement in this direction will continue, despite nostalgic harking back to primitive simplicity. Two factors make for this. The first is growth of population, which means that the economy must be dynamic in order to remain stable; the second is the spread of modern science and technology, which has gone too far to be checked. These two factors together, will necessarily lead to a transformation of the productive forces of the country. The Communist Government, both in its early days and more especially during the Great Leap, sought to transform the relations of production, the superstructure, before the methods of production had been changed. At great cost some, at least, of China's leaders learned the wisdom not to struggle against well-tried patterns of organization more suited to the existing level of the economy. In future years, the gradual and inevitable process of modernization will render these old patterns obsolete. New patterns will emerge, but in the long run they will be moulded by economic requirements and not primarily by political desire. For the superstructure of even a Marxist state is not above being shaped by the play of productive forces.

Appendix I

REMITTANCES FROM OVERSEAS CHINESE

Remittances from Overseas Chinese have provided a notable contribution to the Chinese balance of payments. These remittances have been estimated at US $150 million a year in prosperous periods before the Second World War, at an annual average of about US $35 million for 1950–60, and at a rate of around US $55 million a year early in 1964.[1] Total remittances have fluctuated with the prosperity of the Overseas Chinese communities, which are predominantly in South East Asia, with the closeness of their ties with their families in China, and with the extent to which the Overseas Chinese think their families will in fact benefit from remittances sent to them. The loosening of ties during the Second World War, when further emigration and home visits were impossible, was a major cause of the lower level of post-war remittances. The fear that under an egalitarian regime in China the recipients would not derive advantages from remittances, a fear that was strengthened on the formation of the communes, also restricted the flow. The greater moderation in China's internal policies in the early 1960s caused remittances to rise again; the political campaigns of 1966 may have caused another fall.

The Chinese government, wanting to encourage this useful source of foreign exchange, and also to make a good impression on Overseas Chinese, took measures to favour recipients of remittances. Extra rations were made available to them, the quantity being proportionate to the size of the remittance. This compensated for the unrealistic exchange rate of the Chinese yuan. Attractive houses and flats in special villages in south-east China were provided for sale to dependants of Overseas Chinese. Special Overseas Chinese investment corporations were formed, offering higher rates of interest on bonds bought by Overseas Chinese than paid on state bonds sold inside China, interest rates on savings deposits held by Overseas Chinese have also been above the level paid on residents' savings deposits. A State Council Order of 1955 enjoined officials to treat dependants of Overseas Chinese with consideration and in no case to force them to enter co-operatives or to put money into savings deposits or bonds against their will or to interfere with their expenditure on weddings, funerals, and other occasions.[2] Throughout, the Chinese authorities have maintained that the remittances are 'the fruit of the labour of Overseas Chinese',[3] a declaration in which nationalist sentiment triumphs over class standpoint in relation to some of the most bourgeois communities in the world.

The Overseas Chinese investment corporations, operating under regulations of 1957, are state concerns in which Overseas Chinese, including Chinese residents of Hong Kong and Macao, are encouraged to invest. Interest of 8 per cent per annum

[1] Soloman Adler: *The Chinese Economy*, London, 1957, p. 228, and E. F. Szczepanik (ed.): *Symposium on Economic and Social Problems of the Far East*, Hong Kong, 1962, p. 117. E. F. Szczepanik: 'Balance of Payments of Mainland China', and *Sunday Times*, April 19, 1964.

[2] *Collected Laws and Regulations of the People's Republic of China* (in Chinese), Vol. 1, p. 532, and *People's Handbook* (*Renmin Shouce*) *1959*, p. 370.

[3] *Ta Kung Daily* (*Dagong Bao*), Peking, October 12, 1959, p. 3. Ts'ao Chü-ju: 'Banking in the Past Ten Years.'

is paid (free of Chinese taxes), half being exchangeable into foreign currency. The capital may be withdrawn in Chinese currency after twelve years, or the investment may be renewed on a choice of terms.[1] By 1963 Overseas Chinese investment corporations had been formed in eleven provinces and municipalities and had been responsible for opening or expanding more than 100 enterprises including sugar refineries, textile and paper mills, plantations, rubber factories, and hydro-electric plants, mainly in areas from which Overseas Chinese originated.[2] This scheme was designed to appeal to the local patriotism of the emigrant communities for their home districts.

At the time of the 'cultural revolution', reports indicated that the privileges given to Overseas Chinese and their dependents in China, might be diminished.

[1] *Collected Laws and Regulations* . . . Vol. 6, p. 570, and *Overseas Chinese Affairs Bulletin* (*Qiaowu Bao*), No. 1, February 1964, p. 31. Ch'ing Hsing: 'Achievements of Thoroughly Implementing Policy on Overseas Chinese Investment and Remittances.' Several such investment corporations were already in existence before 1957. See *People's Handbook* (*Renmin Shouce*) *1955*, p. 442.

[2] *Overseas Chinese Affairs Bulletin* (*Qiaowu Bao*), No. 1, February 1963, p. 32.

Appendix II

INSURANCE

The insurance companies—the People's Insurance Company of China, the Pacific Ocean Insurance Company (also known as the Taiping Insurance Company) and the China Insurance Company—have been classed as part of the Ministry of Finance's 'system' in the same way as have the Construction Bank and (formerly) the Bank of Communications. The Pacific Ocean Insurance Company and the China Insurance Company are joint state-private concerns and appear to be subsidiaries of, or closely associated with, the People's Insurance Company.[1]

The insurance companies, like the Construction Bank and the Bank of Communications, can be considered as administrative rather than as commercial organs. As far as insurance by state and joint state-private enterprises are concerned, the collection of premiums and the payment of claims are matters of governmental accounting rather than commercial transactions. The reasons for charging premiums are likely to be, first, a desire to discover the real costs of enterprises' operations (although this is vitiated by the provision of capital free of charge), and second, the desirability of increasing the proportion of enterprises' revenues which is channelled to the state in the form of taxes and other fixed charges rather than in the form of profits—the arguments for this were given in Chapter 14. In addition, voluntary insurance was offered to individuals and collective bodies to cover fire, livestock and crops, travel and transport risks, and also life insurance.[2]

The Pacific Ocean Insurance Company, a joint state-private concern, was formed by the amalgamation of a number of private insurance companies. It operates under the guidance of the People's Insurance Company, specializing in overseas business.[3] Probably it, like the Bank of China, has been kept in existence to retain the goodwill of its predecessor abroad, especially among Overseas Chinese communities.

Insurance with the People's Insurance Company against certain specified risks was made compulsory in 1951 for all state organs and enterprises and for co-operative organizations at the level of the *hsien* and higher.[4]

In 1958, in line with the other decentralization measures of that time, most forms of insurance were handed over to provincial level authorities to conduct through local companies. Exceptions were insurance connected with foreign trade or placed by overseas insurers, and the compulsory insurance of passengers by rail, air, or ship; these categories of business were, according to the 1958 regulations, still to be a monopoly of the national insurance companies, although reports state that passenger insurance was transferred to the Ministries of Railways and Communications.

[1] Hsü Ti-hsin: *An Analysis of China's Economy in the Transitional Period* (in Chinese). Revised edition, Peking, 1959, pp. 236–7, and China Council for the Promotion of International Trade: *National Organizations of Foreign Trade and Organizations of Other Foreign Business of the People's Republic of China*, Peking, 1964, p. 21, and private communication to the author, to which she is also indebted for other points in this Appendix.

[2] Ko Chih-ta: *China's Budget During the Transition Period* (in Chinese), Peking, 1957, pp. 88–9.

[3] Hsü Ti-hsin: op. cit., pp. 236–7.

[4] *New China Monthly* (*Xinhua Yuebao*), No. 20, June 1951, p. 367.

From 1959 onwards, central government enterprises were no longer to be compelled to insure their property; local enterprises would be governed by local authority directives on this matter. The local authorities were also to decide whether local insurance activities were to be placed under the guidance of the local branch of the People's Bank or of the local department of finance. The local insurance companies under provincial level authorities were ordered to establish funds to meet claims. The nucleus of these local funds would be provided by the division of part of the funds built up by the national insurance companies.[1] This change in the system of insurance went parallel to the change in the system of taxation, by which a high degree of autonomy was given to provinces and equivalent authorities in arranging local revenues and expenditures.

It was rumoured that in or around 1959 the People's Insurance Company had been abolished. In any case, nothing more was heard of it until in October 1964 the resumption of business by its Canton branch was announced.[2] More recently, advertisements have appeared for the People's Insurance Company, and also for the China Insurance Company.

A beginning has been made with agricultural insurance. In 1956 to 1958, and again in 1964, reports came of livestock and crops being insured with the People's Insurance Company, but the references suggested that this was on an experimental scale.[3]

Regulations on voluntary insurance of many types were published in 1957.[4] It should be noted that labour insurance comes under the aegis of trade unions, not of insurance companies.

Chinese insurance companies place reinsurance abroad for the foreign exchange element of the risks they cover, e.g. their foreign business and some marine risks. Reinsurance is placed with foreign companies, usually on a reciprocal basis.

[1] *Collected Laws and Regulations of the People's Republic of China* (in Chinese), Vol. 8, pp. 124–5, and R. Diao: *Communist China's Finance in 1964* (Mimeographed paper published by Union Research Institute, Hong Kong), 1965, p. 21.

[2] R. Diao: op. cit., p. 21.

[3] *People's Handbook (Renmin Shouce) 1957*, p. 538, and NCNA, July 16, 1958, and NCNA Changsha, September 21, 1958, and *Finance (Caizheng)*, No. 10, October 1958, p. 1. Yang Shao-ch'iao: 'Financial Work Must Serve the Party's General Line', and *Ta Kung Daily (Dagong Bao)*, Peking, June 25, 1964, p. 1.

[4] *Collected Laws and Regulations* . . . Vol. 5, pp. 134–40.

Appendix III

(Information available up to October 1966. I am indebted to my colleague Tsu-t'ung Emslie for compiling this chart and to Don Klein of Harvard University for supplying valuable information.)

ab. abolished
amal. amalgamated
est. established
n.c. no change

I. STATE COUNCIL OFFICES

	1954	1955[3]	1956[4]	1957[5]	1958[6]	1959[7]	1960[9]	1961[11]	1962[13]	1963[16]	1964/6[17]
1st General Office (Political & Legal Affairs) Controlled Ministries of Internal Affairs, Public Security, Justice and Supervision.	est. Nov. '54[1] Lo Jui-ch'ing[2]	n.c.	n.c.	n.c.	n.c.	Office of Political and Legal Affairs Hsieh Fu-chih[8] Aug.–Sept. '59	n.c.	n.c.	Office of Internal Affairs[14] Hsieh Fu-chih	n.c.	n.c.
2nd General Office (Culture and Education) Controlled Ministries of Culture, Higher Education, Education, Health, New China News Agency, and Broadcasting Administrative Bureau.	est. Nov. '54[1] Lin Feng[2]	n.c.	n.c	n.c.	n.c.	Office of Culture and Education Chang Chi-ch'un[8] Aug.–Sept. '59	n.c.	n.c.	n.c.	n.c.	n.c.
3rd General Office (Heavy Industry) Controlled Ministries of Heavy Industry, 1st and 2nd Machine Building, Fuel, Geology, and Construction Engineering.	est. Nov. '54[1] Po I-po[2]	n.c.	n.c.	n.c.	n.c.	Office of Industry and Communications Li Fu-ch'un[8] Aug.–Sept. '59 (Former 3rd, 4th and 6th General Offices)		Po I-po[12] April '61	n.c.	n.c.	n.c.
4th General Office (Light Industry) Controlled Ministries of Textiles, Light Industry, Local Industry, Labour, and Central Bureau of Handicraft Industry.	est. Nov. '54[1] Chia T'o-fu[2]	n.c.	n.c.	n.c.	n.c.						
5th General Office (Finance and Trade) Controlled Ministries of Finance, Food, Commerce, Foreign Trade, People's Bank of China, also directs the works of the All-China Supply and Marketing Co-operative.	est. Nov. '54[1] Li Hsien-nien[2]	n.c.	n.c	n.c.	n.c.	Office of Finance and Trade Li Hsien-nien[8] Aug.–Sept. '59	n.c.	n.c.	n.c.	n.c.	n.c.
6th General Office (Communications) Controlled Ministries of Railways, Communications, Post and Telecommunications, and Civil Aviation Administration.	est. Nov. '54[1] Wang Shou-tao[2]	n.c.	n.c.	n.c.	n.c.	(amal. into new Office of Industry and Communications)					
7th General Office (Agriculture and Conservation) Controlled Ministries of Agriculture, Forestry, Water Conservancy, State Farms and Land Reclamation, and Central Bureau of Meteorology.	est. Nov. '54[1] Teng Tzu-hui[2]	n.c.	n.c.	n.c.	n.c.	Office of Agriculture and Forestry Teng Tzu-hui[8] Aug.–Sept. '59	n.c.	n.c.	Tan Chen-lin[15] Oct. '62	n.c.	n.c.
8th General Office (National Capitalism) Controlled socialization work of capitalist industrial and commercial enterprises and Central Bureau of Industry and Commerce.	est. Nov. '54[1] Li Wei-han[2]	n.c.	n.c.	n.c.	n.c.						
General Office of Foreign Affairs.					Ch'en Yi[10] March '58	n.c.	n.c.	n.c.	n.c.	n.c.	n.c.

II. ORGANS UNDER STATE COUNCIL

	1949[18]	1952[19]	1954[20]	1955[8]	1956[4]
State Planning Commission		est. Nov. '52[21] Kao Kang	Li Fu-ch'un Sept. '54	n.c.	n.c.
State Economic Commission					est. May '5 Po I-po[24] May '56
State Construction Commission			est. Sept. '54 Po I-po[22] Sept. '54	n.c.	Wang Ho-s May '56
State Capital Construction Commission					
State Technological Commission					est. May ' Huang Ch May '56
Scientific Planning Commission					est. March Chen Yi
Scientific and Technological Commission					
Foreign Economic Relations Commission					
Ministry of Internal Affairs	Hsieh Chüeh-tsai		n.c.	n.c.	n.c.
Ministry of Foreign Affairs	Chou En-lai		n.c.	n.c.	n.c.
Ministry of National Defence			est. Sept. '54 Peng Te-huai[22] Sept. '54	n.c.	n.c.
Ministry of Public Security	Lo Jui-ch'ing		n.c.	n.c.	n.c.
Ministry of Finance	Po I-po	Teng Hsiao-p'ing[30] Sept. '53	Li Hsien-nien[31] July '54	n.c.	n.c.
Ministry of Food		est. Aug. '52 Chang Nai-ch'i	n.c.	n.c.	n.c.
Ministry of Trade	Yeh Chi-chuang	ab. Aug. '52 Work taken over by two new ministries.	Ministry of Commerce Ministry of Foreign Trade see below		
Ministry of Commerce		est. Aug. '52 Tseng Shan	n.c.	n.c.	Ch'en Yi Nov. '56
Ministry of Urban Services					est. May Yang Yi- Nov. '56
Ministry for the Purchase of Agricultural Produce				est. July '55[35] Yang Yi-ch'en[36] July '55	ab. Nov
Ministry of Foreign Trade		est. Aug. '52 Yeh Chi-chuang	n.c.	n.c.	n.c.
Ministry of Heavy Industry	Ch'en Yün	Wang Ho-shou Aug. '52	n.c.	n.c.	ab. May
Ministry of Metallurgy					est. May Wang H
Ministry of Chemical Industry					est. May P'eng T

APPENDIX III   519

1958[6]	1959[7]	1960[9]	1961[11]	1962[13]	1963[16]	1964–6[17]
n.c.	n.c.	n.c.	n.c.	n.c.	n.c.	n.c.
n.c.	n.c.	n.c.	n.c.	n.c.	n.c.	n.c.
ab. Feb. '58[88] work taken over by	⎫ State Planning Commission ⎬ State Economic Commission ⎭ Ministry of Construction Engineering					
est. Nov. '58[26] Ch'en Yün	n.c.		ab. Jan. '61[48]			Re-est. March '65[88] Ku Mu[89] March '65
⎫ amal. to form ⎪ Scientific and ⎬ Technological ⎪ Commission ⎭ Nov. '58[26]						
est. Nov. '58[26] Nieh Jung-chen	n.c.	n.c.	n.c.	n.c.	n.c.	n.c.
						est. June '64[27] Fang Yi[16]
	Ch'ien Ying[28] April '59	Tseng Shan	n.c.	n.c.	n.c.	n.c.
Chen Yi[29] Feb. '58	n.c.	n.c.	n.c.	n.c.	n.c.	n.c.
n.c.	Lin Piao[8] Sept. '59	n.c.	n.c.	n.c.	n.c.	n.c.
n.c.	Hsieh Fu-chih[8] Sept. '59	n.c.	n.c.	n.c.	n.c.	n.c.
n.c.	n.c.	n.c.	n.c.	n.c.	n.c.	n.c.
Sha Ch'ien-li[29] Feb. '58	n.c.	n.c.	n.c.	n.c.	n.c.	n.c.
Changed to 1st Ministry of Commerce Feb. '58[88] Ch'en Yün Changed to 2nd Ministry of Commerce Feb. '58[88] Yang Yi-ch'en[29] Feb. '58	Sept. '58[66] Amal. to form Ministry of Commerce Ch'eng Tzu-hua[66] Sept. '58	Yao Yi-lin[34] Feb. '60	n.c.	n.c.	n.c.	n.c.
n.c.	n.c.	n.c.	n.c.	n.c.	n.c.	n.c.
n.c.	n.c.	n.c.	n.c.	n.c.	n.c.	Lü Tung[42] July '64
n.c.	n.c.	n.c.	Died in office[40] Nov. '61	Kao Yang[41] July '62	n.c.	n.c.

520 CHINA'S ECONOMIC SYSTEM

	1949[18]	1952[19]	1954[20]	1955[3]	1956[4]
Ministry of Building Materials					est. May '56 Lai Chi-fa[24]
Ministry of Construction Engineering		est. Aug. '52 Ch'en Cheng-jen[21] Nov. '52	Liu Hsiu-feng[22] Sept. '54	n.c.	n.c.
Ministry of Urban Construction					est. May '5 Wan Li[24]
1st Ministry of Machine Building		est. Aug. '52 Huang Ching	n.c.	n.c.	n.c.
2nd Ministry of Machine Building		est. Aug. '52 Chao Erh-lu	n.c.	n.c.	n.c.
3rd Ministry of Machine Building				est. April '55[44] Chang Lin-chih[48] April '55	ab. May ' re-est. No Sung Jen- Nov. '56
New 3rd Ministry of Machine Building					
4th Ministry of Machine Building					
5th Ministry of Machine Building					
6th Ministry of Machine Building					
7th Ministry of Machine Building					
8th Ministry of Machine Building					
Ministry of Electrical Equipment					est. May Chang L
Ministry of Agricultural Machinery					
Ministry of Textiles		Tseng Shan	Chiang Kuang-nai n.c.	n.c.	n.c.
Ministry of Light Industry		Huang Yen-pei	Chia T'o-fu[22] Sept. '54	n.c.	Sha Ch' May '56
2nd Ministry of Light Industry					
Ministry of Food Industry		Yang Li-san ab. Dec. '50[31]			re-est. M Li Chu-d
Ministry of Local Industry			est. Sept. '54 Sha Ch'ien-li[22] Sept. '54	n.c.	ab. May
Ministry of Fuel Industries		Ch'en Yü	n.c.	ab. July '55[35]	
Ministry of Coal				est. July '55[35] Chen Yü[36] July '55	n.c.
Ministry of Petroleum				est. July '55[35] Li Chü-k'uei[36]	n.c.

Appendix III

	1958[6]	1959[7]	1960[9]	1961[11]	1962[13]	1963[16]	1964–6[17]
'58[33] amalgamated to Ministry of Construction Engineering. *Tsiu-feng*		n.c.	n.c.	n.c.	n.c.	*Li Jen-tsün*[43] Nov. '64.	Divided to form two new ministries March '65.[38] Ministry of Construction Engineering *Liu Yu-min*[39] March '65. Ministry of Building Materials *Lai Chi-fa*[39] March '65
58[33] amal. with ry of Electrical ment to form new 1st ry of Machine Building *Erh-lu*[29]		n.c.	*Tuan Chün-yi*	n.c.	n.c.	n.c.	n.c.
	Feb. '58[33] became new 2nd Ministry of Machinery *Sung Jen-ch'iung*	n.c.	*Liu Chieh*	n.c.	n.c.	n.c.	n.c.
			est. Sept '60[45] *Sun Chih-yüan*	n.c.	n.c.	n.c.	n.c.
						est. May '63[46] *Wang Cheng*	n.c.
						est. Sept. '63[47] *Ch'iu Ch'uang-ch'eng*	n.c.
						est. Sept. '63[47] *Fang Ch'iang*	n.c.
							est. date not known[49] *Wang Ping-chang* Jan. '65.
							est. date not known[49] *Ch'en Cheng-jen* Jan. '65
	Feb. '58[33] amalgamated with 1st Ministry of Machinery						
		est. Aug. '59[50] *Ch'en Cheng-jen*	n.c.	n.c.	n.c.	n.c.	
	n.c.	n.c.	n.c.	n.c.	n.c.	n.c.	n.c.
	Li Chu-ch'en[29] Feb. '58	n.c.	n.c.	n.c.	n.c.	n.c.	Became 1st[52] Ministry of Light Industry Feb. '65
							est. Feb. '65[52] *Hsü Yün-pei*
	Amalgamated with Ministry of Light Industry[38] Feb. '58						
chih[52]	n.c.	n.c.	n.c.	n.c.	n.c.	n.c.	n.c.
	Yü Ch'iu-li[29] Feb. '58	n.c.	n.c.	n.c.	n.c.	n.c.	n.c.

	1949[18]	1952[19]	1954[20]	1955[3]	1956[4]
Ministry of Electric Power				est. July '55[J8] Liu Lan-po[36]	n.c.
Ministry of Water Conservancy	Fu Tso-yi		n.c.	n.c.	n.c.
Ministry of Aquatic Products					est. May ' Hsü Te-he
Ministry of Geology		est. Aug. '52 Li Szu-kuang	n.c.	n.c.	n.c.
Ministry of Forestry and Land Reclamation	Liang Hs	Nov. '51 Renamed Ministry of Forestry[54]			
Ministry of Forestry			Liang Hsi	n.c.	n.c.
Ministry of Forestry Industry					est. May ' Lo Lung-,
Ministry of Agriculture	Li Shu-ch'eng		Liao Lu-yen[22] Sept. '54	n.c.	n.c.
Ministry of State Farms and Land Reclamation					est. May Wang Ch
Ministry of Railways	T'eng Tai-yuan		n.c.	n.c.	n.c.
Ministry of Communications	Chang Po-chün		n.c.	n.c.	n.c.
Ministry of Post and Telecommunications	Chu Hsüeh-fan		n.c.	n.c.	n.c.
Ministry of Labour	Li Li-san		Ma Wen-jui[22] Sept. '54	n.c.	n.c.
Ministry of Culture	Shen Yen-ping		n.c.	n.c.	n.c.
Ministry of Education	Ma Hsü-lun	Chang Hsi-jo[21] Nov. '52	n.c.	n.c.	n.c.
Ministry of Higher Education		est. Nov. '52[21] Ma Hsü-lun	Yang Hsiu-feng[22] Sept. '54	n.c.	n.c.
Ministry of Health	Li Te-chüan		n.c.	n.c.	n.c.
Ministry of Justice	Shih Liang		n.c.	n.c.	n.c.
Ministry of Supervision			Chi'en Ying[22] Sept. '54	n.c.	n.c.
Ministry of Allocation of Materials					
State Statistical Bureau			est. Nov. '54[1] Hsüeh Mu-ch'iao[2] Nov. '54	n.c.	n.c.
State General Bureau of Survey and Cartography					est. 'Jan. Ch'en W July '56
State Bureau of Weights and Measures			est. Nov. '54[1]	Li Ch'eng-kan[4] April '55	n.c.
People's Bank of China	Nan Han-ch'en		Ts'ao Chü-ju[2] Nov. '54	n.c.	n.c.
Agricultural Bank of China					
Central Bureau of Meteorology			est. Nov. '54[1] T'u Ch'ang-Wang[2] Nov. '54	n.c.	n.c.

APPENDIX III

1958[6]	1959[7]	1960[9]	1961[11]	1962[13]	1963[16]	1964–5[17]
Feb. '58[33] amal. to form Ministry of Water Conservancy and Electric Power Fu Tso-yi[29]	n.c.	n.c.	n.c.	n.c.	n.c.	n.c.
n.c.	n.c.	n.c.	n.c.	n.c	n.c.	n.c.
n.c.	n.c.	n.c.	n.c.	n.c.	n.c.	n.c.
Feb. '58[33] amalgamated with Ministry of Forestry	Liu Wen hui[28] April '59	n.c.	n.c.	n.c.	n.c.	n.c.
n.c.	n.c.	n.c.	n.c.	n.c.	n.c.	n.c.
n.c.	n.c.	n.c.	n.c.	n.c.	n.c.	n.c.
n.c.	n.c.	n.c.	n.c.	n.c.	n.c.	Lü Cheng ts'ao[49] Jan. '65
Wang Shou-tao[29] Feb. '58	n.c.	n.c.	n.c.	n.c.	n.c.	Sun Ta-kuang[42] July '64
n.c.	n.c.	n.c.	n.c.	n.c.	n.c.	n.c.
n.c.	n.c.	n.c.	n.c.	n.c.	n.c.	n.c.
n.c.	n.c.	n.c.	n.c.	n.c.	n.c.	Lu Ting-yi[79] Jan. '65
Feb. '58[33] amalgamated to form Ministry of Education Yang Hsiu-feng[23]	n.c.	n.c.	n.c.	n.c.	Divided to form two new ministries[27]	Ministry of Education Ho Wei July '64[42] Ministry of Higher Education Yang Hsiu-feng July '64[42] Later Chiang Nan-hsiang Jan. '65[49]
n.c.	n.c.	n.c.	n.c.	n.c.	n.c.	Ch'ien Hsin-chung[49] Jan. '65
n.c.	ab. April '59[55]					
n.c.	ab. April '59[55]					
						est. Oct. '64[43] Yuan Pao-hua[43] Nov. '64
n.c.	Chia Ch'i-yün[8] Aug–Sept. '59		Wang Szu-hua[56] July '61	n.c.	n.c.	n.c.
n.c.	Li T'ing-tsan	n.c.	n.c.	Ch'en Wai-ou[15] Oct. '62	n.c.	n.c.
Put under State Technological Commission March 1958[33]						
n.c.	n.c.	n.c.	n.c.	n.c.	n.c.	Relieved from post Feb. '65[78]
				est. Oct. '63[60] Hu Ching-yün[61] Nov. '63	n.c.	n.c.
n.c	n.c.	n.c.		Jao Hsing (Deputy)	n.c.	Jao Hsing[6] Oct. '64

	1949[18]	1952[19]	1954[20]	1955[3]	1956[4]
Central Administration of Industry and Commerce			est. Nov. '54[1] *Hsü Ti-hsin*[2] Nov. '54	n.c.	n.c.
Central Handicrafts Administrative Bureau			est. Nov. '54[1] *Pai Ju-ping*[2] Nov. '54	n.c.	n.c.
Central General Bureau of Handicraft Industry					
Civil Aviation Administration of China			est. Nov. '54[1]		*K'uang Jen* June '56
Civil Aviation General Administration of China					
State Housing Administrative Bureau					
New China News Agency			est. Nov. '54[1] *Wu Leng-hsi*[2] Nov. '54	n.c.	n.c.
Broadcasting Administrative Bureau			est. Nov. '54[1] *Mei Yi*[2] Nov. '54	n.c.	n.c.
State Council Bureau of Religious Affairs			est. Nov. '54[1] *Ho Ch'eng-hsiang*[2] Nov. '54	n.c.	n.c.
State Archives Bureau			est. Nov. '54[1] *Tseng San*[2] Nov. '54	n.c.	n.c.
State Council Councillor's Office			est. Nov. '54[1] *T'ao Hsi-chin*[2] Nov. '54	n.c.	n.c.
State Council Administrative Bureau of Government Offices			est. Nov. '54[1] *Liu Yung-ju*[2] Nov. '54	n.c.	*Kao Teng* March '5
State Council Bureau for the Affairs of Experts			est. Nov. '54[1] *Yang Fang-chih*[2] Nov. '54	n.c.	Changed Council of Forei Experts,
State Council Bureau of Foreign Experts					See abov
State Council Bureau of Experts					est. May *Ch'i Yen* c. July '
Premier's Secretariat			est. Nov. '54[1] *Ch'i Yen-ming* Nov. '54	n.c.	n.c.
Secretariat of the State Council			est. Sept. '54[2] *Ch'ang Li-fu* Nov. '54	n.c.	n.c.
Bureau for Cultural Relations with Foreign Countries			est. Nov. '54[1] *Hung Shen*[2] Nov. '54		
Commission for Cultural Relations with Foreign Countries					
General Bureau of Foreign Economic Relations					
Bureau of Legal Codification (former Commission of Legal Codification)			est. Nov. '54[1] *T'ao Hsi-chin*[2] Nov. '54	n.c.	n.c.

APPENDIX III

	1958[6]	1959[7]	1960[9]	1961[11]	1962[13]	1963[16]	1964–5[17]
[5]	n.c.	n.c.	n.c.	n.c.	n.c.	n.c.	n.c.
	Put under Ministry of Light Industry, March '58[33]						
				est. Oct. '61[45]	Teng Chieh[15] Oct. '62		ab. Feb. '65[52]
	Put under Ministry of Communications, March '58[33]						
					est. April '62[64] K'uang Jen-Nung	n.c.	n.c.
					est. June '62[64] Chao P'eng-fei[63] Dec. '62	n.c.	n.c.
	n.c.	n.c.	n.c.	n.c.	n.c.	n.c.	n.c.
	n.c.	n.c.	n.c.	n.c.	n.c.	n.c.	n.c.
	n.c.	n.c.		Hsiao Hsien-fa[56] July '61			
	n.c.	n.c.	n.c.	n.c.	n.c.	n.c.	n.c.
	n.c.	Tseng Yi-fan[8] c. Aug. '59	n.c.	n.c.	n.c.	n.c.	n.c.
	n.c.	n.c.	n.c.	n.c.	n.c.	n.c.	n.c.
ang-chih	n.c.	n.c.	n.c.	n.c.	n.c.	n.c.	Mi Yung[62] Oct. '64
	Chao Shou-kung[66] c. Aug. '58	ab. June '59. Work taken over by Scientific and Technological Commission					
	T'ung Hsiao-peng[10] April '58	n.c.	n.c.	n.c.	n.c.	n.c.	n.c.
		Yang Fang-chih[8] Aug.–Sept. '59	n.c.	n.c.	n.c.	n.c.	n.c.
	Changed to Commission for Cultural Relations with Foreign Countries, Feb. '58[33]						
	est. Feb. '58[33] Chang Hsi-jo[29] Feb. '58	n.c.	n.c.	n.c.	n.c.	n.c.	n.c.
			est. Jan. '60[68]	Fang Yi[12] April '61	n.c.		Changed to Foreign Economic Relations Commission June '64
	n.c.	ab. June '59. Work taken over by Secretariat of State Council[55]					

526 China's Economic System

	1949[18]	1952[19]	1954[20]	1955[3]	1956[4]
Personnel Bureau		(former Ministry of Personnel)	est. Nov. '54[1] Chang Yi-pai[2] Nov. '54	n.c.	n.c.
Central Bureau of Confidential Communication			est. Nov. '54[1] Wang K'ai[2] Nov. '54	n.c.	n.c.
General Bureau for the Supply of Raw Materials					est. May '5... Han Che-y... Nov. '56
State General Bureau of Raw Materials					
General Bureau of Urban Construction				est. April '55[1] Wan Li[48]	ab. May '... form Min... Urban Construct...
Physical Culture and Sports Commission		est. Nov. '52[21] Ho Lung	n.c.	n.c.	n.c.
Nationalities Affairs Commission	Li Wei-han	n.c.	Ulanfu Sept. '54	n.c.	n.c.
Overseas Chinese Affairs Commission	Ho Hsiang-ning	n.c.	n.c.	n.c.	n.c.
Commission for Reform of the Written Language			est. Nov. '54[1] Wu Yü-chang[2] Nov. '54	n.c.	n.c.
Anti-Illiteracy Commission		est. Nov. '52[21] Ch'u T'u nan	ab. Nov. '54. Work taken over by Ministry of Education[1]		Re-est. M... Ch'en Y...
Central Commission for Phoneticization of Standard Spoken Chinese					est. Feb. Ch'en Y...
Commission for Phoneticization of the Chinese Language					est. Oct... Kuo Mo...
Commission of Legal Codification		Ch'en Shao-yü	n.c.	ab. Nov. '54 to form Bureau of Legal Codification[1]	
People's Supervisory Commission		T'an P'ing-shan	n.c.	ab. Nov. '54 to form Ministry of Supervision[1]	
Commission of Culture and Education		Kuo Mo-jo	n.c.	ab. Nov. '54[1]	
Commission of Finance and Economics		Ch'en Yün	n.c.	ab. Nov. '54[1]	
Commission for Political and Legal Affairs		Tung Pi-wu	n.c.	ab. Nov. '54[1]	
Academy of Sciences		Kuo Mo-jo	n.c.	Became independen... of State Council, but still under its supervision. Nov. '54[1]	
Intelligence General Office		Tsou Ta-p'eng	ab. Aug. '52		
Maritime Customs General Office		K'ung Yüan		Put under Ministry of Foreign Trade. Jan. '53[74]	
Information General Office		Hu Ch'iao-mu	ab. Aug. '52		
Publications General Office		Hu Yü-chih		ab. Nov. '54. Work taken over by Ministry of Culture[1]	

Appendix III   527

	1958[6]	1959[7]	1960[9]	1961[11]	1962[13]	1963[16]	1964–6[17]
	n.c.	ab. June '59. Work taken over by Ministry of Internal Affairs[55]					
	n.c.	ab. June '59[58]					
	Put under State Economic Commission, March '58[33], [59]						
						est. May '63[46] Yuan Pao-hua[70] Sept. '63	ab. Oct. '64[48] to become Ministry of Allocation of Materials
	n.c.	n.c.	n.c.	n.c.	n.c.	n.c.	n.c.
	n.c.	n.c.	n.c.	n.c.	n.c.	n.c.	n.c.
	Liao Ch'eng-chih	n.c.	n.c.	n.c.	n.c.	n.c.	n.c.
	n.c.	n.c.	n.c.	n.c.	n.c.	n.c.	n.c.

} date of abolition not known

	1957	1963	1964–6[17]
anguage Publication and Distribution trative Bureau		est. May '63[46] Lo Tsün[70] Sept. '63	n.c.
rice Commission	est. July '57[76] date of ab. not known	Re-est. May '63[46] Hsüeh Mu-ch'iao[70] Sept. '63	n.c.
nnel Organization Commission[75]		est. May '63[46] Chou Jung-hsin[61] Sept. '63	n.c.
time Bureau			est. June '64[27] Ch'i Ying[68] Oct. '64
el and Tourism Administrative Bureau			est. June '64[27]
nd Technological Personnel Administrative			est. June '64[27] Yüeh Chih-chien[62] Oct. '64
n for Reception and Settlement of Overseas Chinese			est. Sept. '66[77]

Sources—Unless other source noted, all changes are taken from the source given at top of column.

1. *Collected Laws and Regulations of the People's Republic of China* (in Chinese), Vol. 1, pp. 151–3.
2. *New China Monthly (Xinhua Yuebao)*, No. 62, December 1954, pp. 4–5.
3. *People's Handbook (Renmin Shouce) 1956*, pp. 250–1.
4. Ibid., *1957*, pp. 310–13.
5. Ibid., *1958*, pp. 327–8.
6. Ibid., *1959*, pp. 259–60.
7. Ibid., *1960*, pp. 279–80.
8. *New China Fortnightly (Xinhua Banyuekan)*, No. 165, October 12, 1959, pp. 116–18.
9. *People's Handbook (Renmin Shouce) 1961*, pp. 59–61.
10. *New China Fortnightly (Xinhua Banyuekan)*, No. 132, May 25, 1958, pp. 48–9. We can find no notification of the establishment of the State Council Office of Foreign Affairs, but only of the appointment of Chen Yi as its director.
11. *People's Handbook (Renmin Shouce) 1962*, pp. 49–51.
12. *People's Daily (Renmin Ribao)*, May 6, 1961, p. 4.
13. *People's Handbook (Renmin Shouce) 1963*, pp. 133–5.
14. It is not known when this office was established. Hsieh Fu-chih was appointed director in 1963. *China Monthly (Zuguo)*, No. 2, May 1964, p. 2.
15. *People's Daily (Renmin Ribao)*, November 9, 1962, pp. 1–2.
16. *People's Handbook (Renmin Shouce) 1964*, pp. 273–5.
17. Ibid., *1965*, pp. 125–7.
18. *New China Monthly (Xinhua Yuebao)*, No. 2, December 1949, pp. 329–35.
19. Ibid., No. 35, September 1952, pp. 14–15.
20. *Collected Laws and Regulations . . .* Vol. 1, pp. 119–21.
21. *New China Monthly (Xinhua Yuebao)*, No. 38, December 1952, pp. 4–5.
22. Ibid., No. 60, October 1954, p. 150.
23. *Collected Laws and Regulations . . .* Vol. 3, p. 79.
24. *New China Fortnightly (Xinhua Banyuekan)*, No. 85, June 6, 1956, pp. 8–9.
25. *People's Daily (Renmin Ribao)*, March 10, 1956, p. 1.
26. *Collected Laws and Regulations . . .* Vol. 8, pp. 94–5.
27. *People's Daily (Renmin Ribao)*, June 6, 1964, p. 1 and June 10, 1964, p. 2.
28. *New China Fortnightly (Xinhua Banyuekan)*, No. 155, May 10, 1959, p. 26.
29. Ibid., No. 127, March 10, 1958, p. 106.
30. *New China Monthly (Xinhua Yuebao)*, No. 48, October 1953, p.12.
31. Ibid., No. 57, July 1954, pp. 19–21.
32. *New China Fortnightly (Xinhua Banyuekan)*, No. 98, December 21, 1956, p. 3.
33. *Collected Laws and Regulations . . .* Vol. 7, pp. 61–4.
34. *People's Daily (Renmin Ribao)*, February 18, 1960, p. 4.
35. *Collected Laws and Regulations . . .* Vol. 2, p. 62.
36. *New China Monthly (Xinhua Yuebao)*, No. 70, August 1955, pp. 251–2.
37. *Current Background*, No. 461, June 29, 1957. Cover page.
38. *People's Daily (Renmin Ribao)*, March 28, 1965, p. 2.
39. Ibid., April 1, 1965, p. 1.
40. Ibid., November 15, 1961, p. 1.
41. Ibid., July 7, 1962, p. 1.
42. *Daily Worker (Gongren Ribao)*, July 23, 1964, p. 1.
43. *Kuang Ming Daily (Guangming Ribao)*, November 6, 1964, p. 1.
44. *People's Daily (Renmin Ribao)*, April 10, 1955, p. 1.
45. *Collected Laws and Regulations . . .* Vol. 12, pp. 24–5.
46. *People's Daily (Renmin Ribao)*, May 26, 1963, p. 1.
47. *Ta Kung Daily (Dagong Bao)*, Peking, September 29, 1963, p. 1.

48. *New China Monthly* (*Xinhua Yuebao*), No. 68, June 1955, pp. 13–14.
49. Date of establishment of Seventh and Eighth Ministries of Machine Building not known, first mention appeared in *People's Daily* (*Renmin Ribao*), January 5, 1965, p. 2.
50. *Collected Laws and Regulations* . . . Vol. 10, p. 63. Presumably this Ministry later became the Eighth Ministry of Machinery Building which was listed with Ch'en Cheng-jen as minister in *People's Daily* (*Renmin Ribao*), January 5, 1965, p. 2.
51. *People's Handbook* (*Renmin Shouce*) *1951*, p. 'hai' 33.
52. *Ta Kung Daily* (*Dagong Bao*), Peking, February 21, 1965, p. 1.
53. *New China Fortnightly* (*Xinhua Banyuekan*), No. 118, October 25, 1957, p. 122.
54. *People's Daily* (*Renmin Ribao*), November 6, 1951, p. 1.
55. *Collected Laws and Regulations* . . . Vol. 9, pp. 108–9.
56. *People's Daily* (*Renmin Ribao*) July 24, 1961, p. 2.
57. *Collected Laws and Regulations* . . . Vol. 3, p. 53.
58. *New China Fortnightly* (*Xinhua Banyuekan*), No. 91, September 6, 1956, p. 2.
59. Presumably this became the State Bureau of Raw Material Reserves under the State Economic Commission as in *Collected Laws and Regulations* . . . Vol. 9, p. 211.
60. *Ta Kung Daily* (*Dagong Bao*), Peking, October 24, 1963, p. 1.
61. *People's Daily* (*Renmin Ribao*), November 28, 1963, p. 2.
62. Ibid., November 18, 1964, p. 2.
63. Ibid., December 23, 1962, p. 2.
64. *Collected Laws and Regulations* . . . Vol. 13, p. 37.
65. *New China Fortnightly* (*Xinhua Banyuekan*), No. 82, April 21, 1956, p. 2.
66. Ibid., No. 141, October 10, 1958, pp. 38–9.
67. Ibid., No. 97, December 6, 1956, p. 36.
68. *Collected Laws and Regulations* . . . Vol. 11, p. 92.
69. *New China Fortnightly* (*Xinhua Banyuekan*), No. 106, April 25, 1957, p. 24.
70. *People's Daily* (*Renmin Ribao*), October 8, 1963, p. 2.
71. *People's Handbook* (*Renmin Shouce*) 1957, pp. 313 and 579.
72. *People's Daily* (*Renmin Ribao*), February 12, 1956, p. 3.
73. Ibid., October 11, 1956, p. 1.
74. *New China Monthly* (*Xinhua Yuebao*), No. 40, February 1953, p. 8.
75. See F. Schurmann: *Ideology and Organization in Communist China*, Berkeley, 1966, pp. 184 and 186.
76. *Collected Laws and Regulations* . . . Vol. 6, p. 359 footnote. It is not known when this was abolished, presumably this occurred not long after its establishment, because it is not in any *People's Handbook* (*Renmin Shouce*) List of State Council organs.
77. *Ta Kung Daily* (*Dagong Bao*), Hong Kong, September 14, 1966. (Quoted in *China News Summary* No. 138, Hong Kong.)
78. *People's Daily* (*Renmin Ribao*), February 25, 1965, p. 2.
79. *People's Daily* (*Renmin Ribao*), January 5, 1965, p. 2. In July 1966, Lu was dismissed from his concurrent post of Director of the CCP Central Committee Propaganda Department and was subject to violent criticism but his dismissal as Minister of Culture was not announced.

BIBLIOGRAPHY

I. BOOKS—CHINESE

Central College for Political and Law Cadres, Education Research Dept. (ed.): *Basic Questions in the Civil Law of People's Republic of China*, Peking, 1958.

Chang Chien: *The Question of Cadres in the Socialist Construction of Our Country*, Peking, 1956.

Chi Yu: *New China's Railway Construction*, Peking, 1953.

China Council for the Promotion of International Trade (ed.): *New China's Economic Achievements 1949-52*, Peking, 1953. Po I-po: 'On the Question of Tax Re-adjustment.'

China, People's Republic of: *The Agrarian Reform Law of the People's Republic of China*, Peking, 1950.

China, People's Republic of, *Collected Laws and Regulations of the People's Republic of China*, Vol. 1, September 1954–June 1955; Vol. 2, July–December 1955; Vol. 3, January–June 1956; Vol. 4, July–December 1956; Vol. 5, January–June 1957; Vol. 6, July–December 1957; Vol. 7, January–June 1958; Vol. 8, July–December 1958; Vol. 9, January–June 1959; Vol. 10, July–December 1959; Vol. 11, January–June 1960; Vol. 12, July 1960–December 1961; Vol. 13, January 1962–December 1963.

China, People's Republic of: *Collected Papers of The Third Session of the First National People's Congress*, Peking, 1956.

China, People's Republic of: *Proceedings of the Fourth Session of the First National People's Congress*.

China, People's Republic of, Finance and Economic Commission: *Collected Laws and Regulations on Financial and Economic Policies of the Central Government*, Vol. 1, 1950; Vol. 2, 1951; Vol. 3, 1952.

China, People's Republic of, Ministry of Finance: *Collected Financial Laws and Regulations of the Central Government*, 1955; 1956; July–December 1958.

China, People's Republic of, Ministry of Foreign Affairs: *Collected Treaties of the People's Republic of China*, Vols. 1-7.

China, People's Republic of, State Planning Commission: *Simple Explanation of Terms Used in the First Five Year Plan for the Development of the National Economy of the People's Republic of China*, Peking, 1955.

China, Republic of (Nationalist), Ministry of Defence Intelligence Bureau (ed.): *The Collected Documents Obtained by the Anti-Communist Guerrillas in the Raid on Lienchiang, Fukien*, Taipei, 1964.

Chinese Academy of Sciences, Institute of Economics, Department of Political Economy: *Selected Essays of Chinese Economists on Problems of Commodities, Value and Price Under the Socialist System*, Vols. I and II, Peking, 1959.

Chinese Communist Party Central Committee: *Documents of the Eighth National Congress of the Communist Party of China*, Peking, 1956.

Chinese Communist Party Central Committee: *Draft Articles on Rural Communes*, 1961 (Taiwan edition, and Union Research Institute, Hong Kong edition).

Chinese Communist Party Central Committee: *Seventy Important Points of Communist Industrial Policy*, 1961. (From Taiwan source.)

Chinese Communist Party Central Committee: *Policy Directive on the Socialist Education Campaign in Rural Communes* (Draft) 1963. Published by National Security Bureau, Taipei, Taiwan.

Chinese Communist Party Central Committee Administrative Office (ed.): *The High Tide of Socialism in the Chinese Countryside*, Peking, 1956. Vol. 1.

Chinese Maritime Customs: *Tariff of Import Duties of the Chinese People's Republic*, Peking, 1951.

Chinese Trade Unions, Eighth National Congress: *Constitution of Chinese Trade Unions*, Peking, 1957.

Chou Fang: *Our Country's State Organs*, Peking, 1957.

Hsü Ti-hsin: *An Analysis of China's Economy in the Transitional Period*, Revised edition, Peking, 1959.

Hua Shang Daily, Hong Kong: *1949 Handbook* (1949 *Shouce*), Hong Kong.

Huang Ta: *Currency and Currency Circulation in China's Socialist Economy*, Peking, 1964.

Kao Kang: *Stand in the Forefront of the North East's Economic Construction*. Report to the CCP North East Region's First Congress. Canton, 1950.

Ko Chih-ta: *China's Budget during the Transition Period*, Peking, 1957.

Kozpov, G. A. and S. P. Pervashin: *Simple Economic Dictionary*. Translated by Ho Ching into Chinese. Peking, 1958.

Ma Yin-ch'u: *My Economic Theory, Philosophical Ideas and Political Standpoint*, Peking, 1958.

Mao Tse-tung: *Mao Tse-tung Nineteen Poems*, Peking, 1958.

Niu Chung-huang: *Accumulation and Consumption in the National Income of Our Country*, Peking, 1959.

Pan Hsü-lun and Yu Wen-ch'ing: *Principles of Accounting for State Enterprises*, Shanghai, 1952.

People's Bank of China: *Collected Banking Laws and Regulations*, 1957.

People's Bank of China, Foreign Business Bureau of the Head Office: *Handbook of the Currencies of All Nations*, Peking, 1963.

Shishi Shouce Editorial Department: *Explanation of Certain Terms Used in the First Five Year Plan*, Peking, 1955.

Sun Ping-yen: *The Communist System of Grain Control*, Taipei, 1958.

Ta Kung Daily Publications: *People's Handbook* (*Renmin Shouce*), *1951, 1952* published in Shanghai; *1953, 1955, 1956* published in Tientsin; *1957–65* published in Peking.

Tso Ch'un-t'ai and Li Hai: *The Problem of Accumulating Funds for Our Country's Socialist Industrialization*, Peking, 1957.

Wen Chün-t'ien: *The Chinese Pao-Chia System*, Fourth edition, Changsha, 1939.

Wu Tan-ko: *Labour and Wages under the Socialist System*, Shanghai, 1956.

Yen Chung-ping and others (ed.): *Selected Statistical Material on the Modern Economic History of China*, Peking, 1955.

II. BOOKS—OTHER LANGUAGES

Adams, R. (ed.): *Contemporary China*, New York, 1966.

Adler, Solomon: *The Chinese Economy*, London, 1957.

Allen, G. C.: *Japan's Economic Recovery*, London, 1958.

Allen, G. C. and A. G. Donnithorne: *Western Enterprise in Far Eastern Economic Development: China and Japan*, London, 1954.

Berezina, Julia: *Power Resources of the Chinese Peoples' Republic* (in Russian), Moscow, 1959.

Boorman H. L., A. Eckstein, P. E. Mosley and B. Schwartz: *Moscow-Peking Axis*, New York, 1957.

Buck, J. L.: *China's Farm Economy*, Nanking, 1930.

Buck, J. L.: *Land Utilization in China*, Nanking, 1937. (Reprinted New York, 1964.)

Buck, J. L., O. L. Dawson and Y. L. Wu: *Food and Agriculture in Communist China*, New York, 1966.

Cairncross A., Head of the United Kingdom Government Economic Service: *The Short Term and the Long in Economic Planning*. Lecture to the Economic Development Institute, Washington, D.C., 1966.

Carin, R.: *River Control in Communist China*, Hong Kong, 1962.

Carin, R.: *State Farms in Communist China*, Hong Kong, 1962.

Chang Kia-ngau: *The Inflationary Spiral*, London, 1958.

Chao Kuo-chun: *Agrarian Policies of Mainland China: A Documentary Study (1949–56)*, Cambridge, Mass., 1957.

Chao Shu-li: *Sanliwan Village* (English edition), Peking, 1957.

Cheng Cho-yuan: *Monetary Affairs of Communist China* (Mimeographed), Union Research Institute, Hong Kong, 1954.

Cheng, Cho-yuan: *Scientific and Engineering Manpower in Communist China, 1949–63*, Washington, D.C., 1965.

Chi Ch'ao-ting: *Key Economic Areas in Chinese History*, 2nd ed., New York, 1963.

China Association, London: *China Association Annual Report, 1963–4, 1964–5, 1965–6*. London.

China Committee for the Promotion of International Trade: *New China's Economic Achievements 1949–52*, Peking, 1952.

China Council for the Promotion of International Trade: *National Organizations of Foreign Trade and Organizations of Other Foreign Business of the People's Republic of China*, Peking, 1964.

China, People's Republic of: *First Five Year Plan for Development of the National Economy of the People's Republic of China in 1953–7*, Peking, 1956.

China, People's Republic of: *Handbook on People's China*, Peking, 1957.

China, People's Republic of: *Labour Laws and Regulations of the People's Republic of China*, Peking, 1956.

China, People's Republic of: *Important Labour Laws and Regulations of the People's Republic of China*, Peking, 1961.

China, People's Republic of, National People's Congress: *Constitution of the People's Republic of China*, Peking, 1954.

China, People's Republic of, State Statistical Bureau: *Ten Great Years*, Peking, 1960.

Chinese Communist Party: *The Constitution of the Communist Party of China*, Peking, 1965.

Chinese Communist Party Central Committee: *The Eighth National Congress of the Communist Party of China*, Vol. 1, Documents, Peking, 1956.

Chou Shun-hsin: *The Chinese Inflation 1937–49*, New York, 1963.

Crook, I. and D.: *The First Years of Yangyi Commune*, London, 1966.

Crosfield & Son, Ltd.: *The Chinese Coal Industry*, Warrington, 1961.

Diao, Richard: *Communist China's Finance in 1964* (mimeographed paper published by Union Research Institute, Hong Kong, 1965).

Durand, F. J.: *Le Financement du Budget en Chine Populaire*, Hong Kong, 1965.

Eckstein, A.: *Communist China's Economic Growth and Foreign Trade*, New York, 1966.

Emerson, J. P.; *Non-Agricultural Employment in Mainland China 1949–58*, US Bureau of Census, Washington, D.C., 1965.

Feurwerker, A.: *China's Early Industrialization*, Cambridge, Mass., 1958.
Foreign Language Press (ed.): *People's Communes in China*, Peking, 1958.
Foreign Language Press (ed.): *Ten Glorious Years*, Peking, 1960.
Gamble, S. D.: *North China Villages*, Berkeley and Los Angeles, 1963.
Geddes, W. R.: *Peasant Life in Communist China* (Monograph). Published by Society for Applied Anthropology, Ithaca, 1963.
Gould, S. H. (ed.): *Sciences in Communist China*, Washington, D.C., 1961.
Gray, J. (ed.): *China's Search for a Political Form*. To be published by Oxford University Press.
Halperin, Morton, H.: *China and the Bomb*, London, 1965.
Ho Ping-ti: *Studies on the Population of China, 1368–1953*, Cambridge, Mass., 1959.
Hollister, W. W.: *China's Gross National Product and Social Accounts 1950–7*, Glencoe, Ill., 1958.
Hsia, R.: *Government Acquisition of Agricultural Output in Mainland China 1953–6* (Rand Research Memorandum, R.M. 2207), Santa Monica, 1958.
Hsia, R.: *Price Control in Communist China*, New York, 1953.
Hsia, R.: *The Role of Labour Intensive Investment Projects in China's Capital Formation*, Cambridge, Mass., 1954.
Hsia, T. A.: *The Commune in Retreat as Evidenced in Terminology and Semantics*, Berkeley, 1964.
Hsin Ying: *The Price Problems of Communist China*, Hong Kong, 1954.
Hsüeh Mu-ch'iao, Su Hsing and Lin Tse-li: *The Socialist Transformation of the National Economy in China*, Peking, 1960.
Huang Han-liang: *The Land Tax in China*, Columbia University Studies—History, Economics and Public Law, Vol. 80, No. 3, New York, 1918.
Hughes, T. J. and D. E. T. Luard: *The Economic Development of Communist China 1949–60*. Second edition, London, 1961.
Il'yin, A. I. and M. P. Voronichev: *Railroad Transport of the Chinese People's Republic*, Moscow, 1959. (Translated from the Russian in JPRS 3484.)
Indian Delegation to China: *Report on Agricultural Planning and Techniques*, Delhi, 1956.
International Tin Council: *Statistical Bulletin*, London, December 1963.
Jamieson, G.: *Chinese Family and Commercial Law*, Shanghai, 1921.
Kaser, M.: *Comecon*, London, 1965.
Kirby, E. S. (ed.): *Contemporary China*, Hong Kong. Vol. 1, 1955 (pub. 1956); Vol. 2, 1956–7 (pub. 1958); Vol. 3, 1958–9 (pub. 1960); Vol. 4, 1959–60 (pub. 1961); Vol. 5, 1961–2 (pub. 1963); Vol. 6 (to be published).
Klochko, M. A.: *Soviet Scientist in China*, London, 1964.
Kornai, J.: *Overcentralization in Economic Administration*, London, 1959.
Kuan Ta-tung: *The Socialist Transformation of Capitalist Industry and Commerce in China*, Peking, 1960.
Lang Fang-chung: *The Single-Whip Method of Taxation in China*. Translated from Chinese by Wang Yü-ch'uan. Cambridge, Mass. 1956.
Lewin, P.: *The Foreign Trade of Communist China*, New York, 1964.
Lewis, J. W., *Leadership in Communist China*, Ithaca, N.Y., 1963.
Li, Choh-ming: *Economic Development of Communist China*, Berkeley, 1959.
Li, Choh-ming: *The Statistical System of Communist China*, Berkeley, 1962.
Li, Chuan-shih: *Central and Local Finance in China*, New York, 1922.
Lindqvist, S.: *China in Crisis*, London, 1965.
Liu, Ta-chung and Kung-chia Yeh: *The Economy of the Chinese Mainland: National Income and Economic Development 1933–59*. Vols. 1 and 2, Rand Corp., Santa Monica, 1963.

Lu, C. T. *An Interim Understanding of the Concept of Handicraft as the Term is Used in Communist China*. (Mimeographed paper prepared for the First Research Conference of the Social Science Research Council Committee on the Economy of China. Berkeley, January–February 1963.)

Lysenko, I. A.: *Economic Co-operation Between China and the Countries of the Socialist Camp* (in Russian), Moscow, 1960.

MacFarquhar, R. (ed.): *The Hundred Flowers*, London, 1960.

Mao Tse-tung: *Nineteen Poems* (English edition), Peking, 1958.

Mao Tse-tung: *On the Question of Agricultural Co-operation*. English edition, Peking, 1962.

Mao-Tse-tung: *Selected Works of Mao Tse-tung*. Vols. 1–4 (English ed.), Peking.

Mehnert, Klaus: *Peking and Moscow*. Translated by Vennewitz, Leila, London, 1963.

Mu Fu-sheng: *The Wilting of the Hundred Flowers—Free Thought in China Today*, London, 1962.

Myrdal, J., *Report from a Chinese Village*, London, 1965.

Nove, A., *The Soviet Economy* (revised ed.), London, 1965.

Nove, A. and D. Donnelly: *Trade with Communist Countries*, London, 1960.

Oksenberg, Michel: *Local Government and Politics in China 1955–8*. Unpublished paper presented to Columbia University Faculty Seminar on Modern East Asia: China, May 4, 1966.

Oksenberg, Michel: Unpublished papers of Michel Oksenberg, Stanford University, relating to the financial system in Mainland China.

Orleans, L. A.: *Professional Manpower and Education in Communist China*, Washington, D.C., 1961,

Perkins, D. H.: *Market Control and Planning in Communist China*, Cambridge, Mass., 1966.

Perkins, D. H.: *Price Formation in Communist China* (unpublished Ph.D. Thesis, Harvard University, 1963).

Pryor, F. L.: *The Communist Foreign Trade System*, London, 1963.

Remer, C. F. (ed.): *Three Essays on the International Economics of Communist China*, Ann Arbor, 1959.

Remer, C. F.: *The Trade Agreements of Communist China*, Rand Corp., Santa Monica, 1961.

Richardson, H. L.: *The Use of Fertilizers in the Far East*. Paper read before the Fertilizer Society in London, 1956.

Schanz, J. J.: *The United States and a Postwar Tin Control Agreement*. (Unpublished Ph.D. Thesis, Pennsylvania State University, 1954).

Schran, P.: *The Structure of Income in Communist China*. (Unpublished Ph.D. Thesis, University of California, 1961.)

Schultz, T.: *Transforming Traditional Agriculture*, New Haven, 1964.

Schumpeter, E. B. (ed).: *The Industrialization of Japan and Manchukuo 1930–40*, New York, 1940.

Schurmann, F.: *Ideology and Organization in Communist China*, Berkeley, 1966.

Shabad, T.: *China's Changing Map*, London, 1956.

Shen, T. H.: *Agricultural Resources of China*, Ithaca, N.Y., 1951.

Shih, Kuo-heng: *China Enters the Machine Age*, Cambridge, Mass., 1944.

Smith, A.: *The Wealth of Nations* (ed. E. Cannan, 6th Edition, London, 1950).

Snow, E.: *The Other Side of the River: Red China Today*, London, 1963.

Strong, A. L.: *Letters from China*, Peking, 1963 and 1964.

Strong, A. L.: *The Rise of the Chinese People's Communes—and Six Years After*, Peking, 1964.

Szczepanik, E. F. (ed.): *Symposium on Economic and Social Problems of the Far East*, Hong Kong, 1962.

Ta Kung Daily, Hong Kong. *Trade with China: A Practical Guide*, Hong Kong, 1957.

Teng Tze-hui: *Report on the Multiple Purpose Plan for Permanently Controlling the Yellow River and Exploiting Its Water Resources*, Peking, 1955.

Tung Ta-lin: *Agricultural Co-operation in China*, Peking, 1959.

Ullman, M. B.: *Cities of Mainland China 1953 and 1958*, US Department of Commerce, Washington, D.C., 1961.

Union Research Institute, Hong Kong: *Who's Who in Communist China*, Hong Kong, 1966.

United Nations: *Economic Survey of Asia and the Far East* (Annual), Bangkok.

US Bureau of Mines: *Mineral Trade Notes Special Supplement*, No. 59, March 1960.

US Central Intelligence Agency: *Taxation in Communist China 1950–9*, Washington, D.C., 1961.

US Consulate General, Hong Kong: *Biographic information—Directory of Chinese Communist Leadership*, Reports No. 1 and No. 2, Hong Kong, 1959 and 1962.

US Dept. of Agriculture: *Trends and Developments in Communist China's World Trade in Farm Products 1955–60*, Washington, D.C., 1962.

USSR: *External Trade of the USSR* (Annual) (in Russian), Moscow.

USSR: *1965 Yearbook of the Great Soviet Encyclopaedia* (in Russian), Moscow.

Vogel, Ezra: Unpublished paper of Ezra Vogel of Harvard University, relating to the Financial System in Mainland China.

Walker, K. R.: *Planning in Chinese Agriculture: Socialization and the Private Sector*, London, 1965.

Wiles, P. J. D.: *Communist International Economics*, New York, 1967.

Wiles, P. J. D.: *The Political Economy of Communism*, Oxford, 1962.

Wong, John, C. H.: *A Study of Communist Land Reform in Post-War China with Special Reference to Policy and Its Implementation* (unpublished Ph.D. Thesis, London University, 1966).

Wu, Yuan-li: *An Economic Survey of Communist China*, New York, 1956.

Wu, Yuan-li: *Economic Development and the Use of Energy Resources in Communist China*, New York, 1963.

Wu, Yuan-li, F. P. Hoeber and M. M. Rockwell: *The Economic Potentials of Communist China*, Vols. 1–3, Menlo Park, California, 1963.

Yin, H. and Yi-chang Yin: *Economic Statistics of Mainland China*, Cambridge, Mass., 1960.

Zagoria, D. Z., *The Sino-Soviet Conflict 1956–61*. Princeton, 1962.

III. ARTICLES—CHINESE

Agricultural Bank of China: 'Review of the Work in 1964 and Arrangements for the Work in 1965.' *Rural Finance* (*Nongcun Jinrong*), No. 4–5, February 28, 1965. (SCMM 468.)

Agricultural Bank of China, Ch'engchiang *hsien* Branch: 'Strengthen Supervision over Financial and Accounting Work. Move Spring Ploughing and Production Forward.' *Rural Finance* (*Nongcun Jinrong*), No. 11, June 6, 1965. (SCMM 479.)

Agricultural Bank of China, Huailai Branch, Correspondence Team: 'Help Poor and Lower Middle Peasants Obtain All the Small Tools They Need.' *Rural Finance* (*Nongcun Jingrong*), No. 10, May 21, 1965. (SCMM 477.)

Ai T'o-ya: 'The Communist Organs of Foreign Trade.' *Mainland Today (Jinri Dalu)*, No. 153, February 1, 1962.

An Hsing-ts'un: 'Make Full Use of Old Craftsmen in Arts and Crafts.' *People's Daily (Renmin Ribao)*, March 21, 1962. p. 2.

An Tze-wen: 'Further Strengthen the Rôle of the Party Organization in the People's Communes.' *Red Flag (Hongqi)*, No. 24, December 16, 1959.

Anhwei Department of Water Conservancy: 'The Circumstances of Controlling the Huai River in Anhwei in the Past Seven Years and Some Views on this Work from 1958 to 1962.' *Chinese Water Conservancy (Zhongguo Shuili)*, No. 3, March 14, 1958. (SCMM 130.)

Anhwei Provincial Statistical Bureau: 'The Uses and Special Features of Compiling Local Balance Charts.' *Statistical Research (Tongji Yanjiu)*, No. 1, January 1958.

Chai Mao: 'The Superiority of the People's Communes from the Viewpoint of Finance and Trade.' *Economic Research (Jingji Yanjiu)*, No. 11, November 1959.

Ch'ai Yen-hsieh: 'Some Problems in Correctly Regulating the Financial Relations between the State and State Enterprises.' *Economic Research (Jingji Yanjiu)*, No. 10, October 1965.

Chan Han-ying: 'Agricultural Water Conservation and Fields of High and Stable Yields.' *New Construction (Xin Jianshe)*, No. 10–11, October–November 1964.

Chang Chien-ming: 'Some Problems in Organizing and Developing Rural Handicraft Production.' *Ta Kung Daily (Dagong Bao)*, Peking, May 29, 1961. p. 3.

Chang Ch'in-jen: 'The Creative Conditions for a Great Development of Local Coal Mining.' *Coal Industry (Meitan Gongye)*, No. 7, April 4, 1958.

Chang Ch'ing-t'ai: 'The Problems of Consolidating the Operational Management of Tractor Stations.' *Chinese Agricultural Journal (Zhongguo Nongbao)*, No. 11, November 1963.

Chang Ch'iu: 'Ten Years of Hard Work and Happiness.' *Southern Daily (Nanfang Ribao)*, November 13, 1962. (SCMP 2877.)

Chang Chung-han, Deputy Commission of the Sinkiang Production and Construction Army Corps and Vice Minister of State Farms and Land Reclamation: 'The Production and Construction Corps in Sinkiang.' *People's Daily (Renmin Ribao)*, July 31, 1960. p. 7.

Chang Chung-liang, First Secretary of the Kansu Provincial CCP Committee: Report at Second Session of CCP Kansu Second Provincial Congress. *Kansu Daily (Gansu Ribao)*, August 16, 1958. (CB 528.)

Chang Chung-lien: 'A Consideration of Basic Level Accounting in the Coal Industry.' *Coal Industry (Meitan Gongye)*, No. 22, November 19, 1957.

Chang Feng-lin: 'Distribute Enterprises' Bonus Funds Reasonably.' *Labour (Laodong)*, No. 8, August 1964.

Chang Feng-shih, Vice-Minister of Agricultural Machinery: 'Produce Suitable Agricultural Machinery to Support Agriculture.' *Daily Worker (Gongren Ribao)*, January 18, 1962. p. 1.

Chang Feng-shih, Vice-Minister of Agricultural Machinery: 'The Technical Transformation of Agriculture Must Be Better Served by the Agricultural Machinery Industry.' *Daily Worker (Gongren Ribao)*, January 5, 1963. p. 1.

Chang Han-ch'ing: 'Huahsien Has Truly Changed into a Flowery *Hsien*.' *Red Flag (Hongqi)*, No. 4, February 26, 1964.

Chang Ho-wei: 'An Outline Discussion of the Worker-Peasant System in Finance and Trade.' *New Construction (Xin Jianshe)*, No. 1–2, February 1966.

Chang Hou-hsing: 'Some Remarks on Problems in the Cattle Market.' *Chinese Agricultural Journal (Zhongguo Nongbao)*, No. 8, August 1963.

Chang Hua, Yang Kun-ch'uan and Li Kuang: 'An Introduction to the Leadership Methods of Three Production Teams.' *People's Daily (Renmin Ribao)*, July 22, 1960. p. 2.

Chang Hsiu-min: 'Implement the Class Line While Obtaining Repayment of Loans.' *Ta Kung Daily (Dagong Bao)*, Peking, March 11, 1966, p. 3.

Chang Hung-hsing: 'We Must Humbly Listen to the Opinions of Technologists.' *Daily Worker (Gongren Ribao)*, June 26, 1962. p. 2.

Chang K'ai-min and Ch'en Sheng-ya: 'A Discussion of the Transition from a System of Planning Agricultural Production to a System of Planning the Collection and Purchase of Agricultural Output.' Parts 1 and 2. *Financial and Economic Research (Caijing Yanjiu)*, No. 1, January 1958 and No. 2, February 1958.

Chang Ken-sheng: A Report Delivered at the Conference of Directors of Rural Work Departments of the District and *Hsien* CCP Committees in Kwangtung Province. *Southern Daily (Nanfang Ribao)*, October 28, 1960. (SCMP 2401.)

Chang K'uang-yu and T'an P'ei-ch'uan: 'A Revolutionary Agricultural Machinery Station.' *People's Daily (Renmin Ribao)*, July 28, 1965. p. 2.

Chang Kuei-ying: 'Why I Agreed to the Children's Father Selling Castor Beans to the State.' *Ta Kung Daily (Dagong Bao)*, Peking, February 11, 1962, p. 2.

Chang Lin-chih, Minister of Coal: 'Struggle for the Swift Development of The Coal Industry.' *People's Daily (Renmin Ribao)*, October 7, 1959, p. 7.

Chang Lin-chih, Vice-Minister of State Farms and Land Reclamation and First Secretary of the Hokiang District CCP Committee, Heilungkiang, and Wang Cheng-lin, Director of Yu-yi State Farm: 'The Yu-yi State Farm—A Model and a Training Centre for Mechanized Farms.' *People's Daily (Renmin Ribao)*, November 12, 1959, p. 4.

Chang Meng-tseng: 'Price Problems of the Products of the State Coal Mining Industry.' *Finance (Caizheng)*, No. 3, March 1958.

Chang Nai-ch'i, Minister of Food: 'Grain Work in the Past Year.' *People's Handbook (Renmin Shouce) 1957*.

Chang Pang-ying: 'Transport Undertaken by People's Communes.' *Red Flag (Hongqi)*, No. 17, September 1, 1959.

Chang Pen-lien: 'Some Questions Influencing the Raising of the Profit Level in the State Coal Mining Industry.' *Finance (Caizheng)*, No. 7, July 1957.

Chang Shih: 'A Major Problem in Promoting a Rational System of Coal Transport.' *Planned Economy (Jihua Jingji)*, No. 10, October 1957.

Chang Shu-jen: 'A Short Cut Solution to the Problem of Funds for Draught Cattle.' *Ta Kung Daily (Dagong Bao)*, Peking, September 25, 1964, p. 3.

Chang T'ing-tung: 'Fixed Norm Management in Industrial Production.' *Kuang Ming Daily (Guangming Ribao)*, March 4, 1963, p. 4.

Chang Wu-tung and Yang Kuan-hsiung: 'Function of Transport in the Development of Agricultural Production.' *People's Daily (Renmin Ribao)*, June 6, 1964, p. 5.

Chang Yi-fei: 'The Basis for State Fixing of Market Prices of Commodities.' *Economic Research (Jingji Yanjiu)*, No. 4, April 1958.

Chang Ying: 'A Discussion of Some Problems in Rearing Pigs.' *Ta Kung Daily (Dagong Bao)*, Peking, July 17, 1964, p. 3.

Chang Yü-ching: 'The Great Victory of the Half-Work (Farming) and the Half-Study Educational System—Introducing Kiangsi Communist Labour University.' *China's Agriculture and Land Reclamation (Zhongguo Nongken)*, No. 1, January 5, 1965. (SCMM 466.)

Chang Yuan-kuang: 'New China's Sea Transport.' *Geographical Knowledge (Dili Zhishi)*, No. 3, March 1958.

Changchun First Automobile Plant, CCP Committee: 'Promote Multiple Utilization of Factors of Production and Develop Many Kinds of Operation.' *Red Flag (Hongqi)*, No. 19, October 1, 1960.

Chao Ch'uang-shih, Secretary of the League Branch of Miaoti Production Brigade, Ch'engkuan Commune, Juich'eng *hsien*, Shansi: 'Our Young People Here Are Very Lively.' *China Youth (Zhongguo Qingnian)*. No. 13, July 1, 1965.

Chao Fu-chi: 'The One *Hsien* One Commune System as Demonstrated by Chaoyuan *Hsien* Commune.' *Financial and Economic Research (Caijing Yanjiu)*, No. 9, December 1958.

Chao Han: 'Government and Commune May Be One, but Party and Commune May Not Be One.' *People's Daily (Renmin Ribao)*, December 24, 1958, p. 7.

Chao Hsiang and Ai Ting: 'Technical Innovations Introduced by Workers in the Greater Hsingan Forestry Area.' *People's Daily (Renmin Ribao)*, December 4, 1960, p. 7.

Chao Jung-an and Wang Chao-lin: 'A Labour System Mutually Beneficial to Industry and Agriculture.' *People's Daily (Renmin Ribao)*, August 28, 1964, p. 5.

Chao Lü-k'uan and Hsiang Ching-ch'uan: 'On the Objective Foundation of Commodity Price Differentials under Socialism and the Basis for Determining these Differentials.' *Economic Research (Jingji Yanjiu)*, No. 2, February 1964.

Chao Ming-fu, Vice-Chairman, Yellow River Conservancy Commission: 'Water and Soil Conservation in Regions along the Middle Reaches of the Yellow River.' *Water Conservancy and Electric Power (Shuili yu Dianli)*, No. 13, July 5, 1963. (SCMM 380.)

Chao Po: 'Comprehensive Financial Plans.' *Planned Economy (Jihua Jingji)*, No. 11, November 1958.

Chao Te-huan, Jen Chung-te and Ma Yu-t'ien: 'How Do We Rouse the Masses to Cancel the Piece Wage System?' *Daily Worker (Gongren Ribao)* August 29, 1958. (SCMP 1862.)

Chao Tzu-yang: 'We Must Surely Make a Success of the Mess Halls.' *Southern Daily (Nanfang Ribao)*, April 3, 1960. (SCMP 2262.)

Ch'en Cheng-jen, Minister of Agricultural Machinery: 'Speed Up the Technical Transformation of Agriculture.' *Red Flag (Hongqi)*, No. 4, February 16, 1960.

Ch'en Cheng-jen: 'Start Up a Large Scale Mass Campaign to Get the People's Communes in Order.' *Red Flag (Hongqi)*, No. 2, January 16, 1959.

Chen Chi, An Pai-k'ang and Liu Hsing-san: 'A Review of Honan's Finance in the Past Ten Years.' *Finance (Caizheng)*, No. 19, October 9, 1959.

Chen Chih: 'How to Strengthen and Perfect the Responsibility System in Production Teams.' *Current Events (Shishi Shouce)*, No. 18, September 21. 1961.

Ch'en Ching-fang: 'Step up Work of Tax Collection in Connection with Trade in Rural Fairs.' *Ta Kung Daily (Dagong Bao)*, Peking, July 26, 1961, p. 3.

Ch'en Han-ch'üan: 'How Yüant'an Commune Controls Rural Market Trade.' *Ta Kung Daily (Dagong Bao)*, Peking, January 15, 1962, p. 2.

Ch'en Hsi-yu, Vice-Director, People's Bank: 'The 1958 Banking Work and the 1959 Tasks.' *Chinese Currency (Zhongguo Jinrong)*, May 25, 1959. (ECMM 178.)

Ch'en Hsing: 'Strengthen the Economic Work of State Commerce in Trade at Rural Fairs.' *Ta Kung Daily (Dagong Bao)*, Peking, March 6, 1961. (SCMP 2504.)

Ch'en Hsüeh: 'Further Strengthen Local Responsibility for Financial Management.' *Finance (Caizheng)*, No. 1, October 5, 1956.

Ch'en Hung-yung: 'Handicraft Production: at the Same Time Both Planned and Adaptable.' *Ta Kung Daily (Dagong Bao)*, Peking, March 23, 1962, p. 3.

Ch'en Mao-li, Engineer and Deputy Manager, Steel Refinery, Wuhan Iron and Steel Works: 'Competent, Responsible and with Authority.' *Daily Worker (Gongren Ribao)*, July 19, 1962, p. 2.

Ch'en Pao-sen: 'A Preliminary Discussion of the Renewal and Technical Transformation of the Equipment of Industrial Enterprises.' *People's Daily* (*Renmin Ribao*), July 20, 1964, p. 5.

Ch'en P'ei-yi: 'A Tentative Discussion of Certain Practical Problems in the Bonus System.' *Ta Kung Daily* (*Dagong Bao*), Peking, August 22, 1962, p. 3.

Ch'en Shih-ho, Technical Department, Shanghai Municipal Industrial Production Commission: 'Raise Quality by Interviewing Consumers.' *People's Daily* (*Renmin Ribao*), June 29, 1961, p. 3.

Ch'en Ta-lun: 'The Change in Our Country's Industrial Administrative System.' *Economic Research* (*Jingji Yanjiu*), No. 3, March 1958.

Ch'en Tsu-wen: 'The Conservation of State Capital.' *Ta Kung Daily* (*Dagong Bao*), Peking, July 6, 1962, p. 3.

Ch'en Yang-p'ing and Liao Yen-chih: 'On What Principles Should Office Blocks Be Built?' *People's Daily* (*Remnin Ribao*), December 9, 1964, p. 2.

Ch'en Yi-fan, Chairman, All-China Federation of Handicraft Co-operatives Council: Report to the Second General Meeting of the All-China Federation of Handicraft Co-operatives. *People's Daily* (*Renmin Ribao*), October 27, 1963, p. 2.

Ch'en Yi-yen: 'On the So-Called Four Magic Wands and the Like.' *Southern Daily* (*Nanfang Ribao*), November 10, 1962. (SCMP 2881.)

Ch'en Yi-yen: 'Small Freedoms and Spontaneous Influences.' *Southern Daily* (*Nanfang Ribao*). December 28, 1960. (SCMP 2429.)

Ch'en Yi-yen: 'Whose Words are Final?' *Southern Daily* (*Nanfang Ribao*), March 21, 1962. (SCMP 2722.)

Ch'en Yün: 'Some Important Problems in Capital Investment at the Present Time.' *Red Flag* (*Hongqi*), No. 5, March 1, 1959.

Cheng Ch'i-chang: 'Regular Attendance Bonuses Are Very Harmful and Have Few Advantages.' *Labour* (*Laodong*), No. 8, August 1964.

Ch'eng Chih-ting and Hsü Yin-t'ung (ed.): 'The Views of Kiangsu Province on the Project for Controlling the Huai River.' *Chinese Water Conservancy* (*Zhongguo Shuili*), No. 3, March 14, 1958. (SCMM 130.)

Ch'eng Fang: 'Balance in the Financial and Economic System and Planning.' *New Construction* (*Xin Jianshe*), No. 8, August 1958.

Ch'eng Hsi-hai, Secretary, CCP Huainan Municipal Committee: 'How Was Labour Organization Overhauled in Huainan Municipality?' *Anhwei Daily* (*Anhui Ribao*), March 15, 1959. (SCMP 1993.)

Ch'eng Tze-hua, Chairman, All-China Federation of Supply and Marketing Co-operatives: 'The Development of Supply and Marketing Co-operatives in the Past Five Years.' *People's Handbook* (*Renmin Shouce*) *1955*.

Ch'eng Tze-hua: 'Struggle to Fulfil the Task Assigned to Supply and Marketing Co-operatives by the National First Five Year Plan.' *People's Handbook* (*Renmin Shouce*) *1956*.

Ch'eng Yüan-yeh: 'Emphasize a Broad Outlook and Manage Credit Funds Efficiently.' *Ta Kung Daily* (*Dagong Bao*), Peking, June 13, 1962, p. 2.

Ch'engchiang *hsien* Work Team, Rural Work Dept., Yunnan Provincial CCP Committee: 'Ch'engchiang *hsien*'s Preliminary Experience of Improvement of Labour Organization.' *Yunnan Daily* (*Yunnan Ribao*), July 30, 1959. (SCMP 2091.)

Chengtu Measuring Instruments and Cutting Tools Factory, CCP Committee: 'A New Example of the Socialist Enterprise Management System.' *People's Daily* (*Renmin Ribao*), June 24, 1960, p. 1.

Chi Ch'eng: 'Understand the Role of State Taxation Correctly.' *Ta Kung Daily* (*Dagong Bao*), Peking, August 11, 1961, p. 3.

Chi Ch'ung-wei, Li lan-ch'ing and Lo Ching-fen: 'Specialization and Co-operation Are an Important Short Cut to Greater, Faster, Better, and More Economical Development of Industrial Productive Capacity.' *People's Daily (Renmin Ribao)*, February 20, 1965, p. 5.

Chi Hsi-ch'en and Li Chi-ch'eng: 'Innovations in Forestry.' *People's Daily (Renmin Ribao)*, December 18, 1964, p. 2.

Chi Kuang: 'Problems of Distributing Productive Materials.' *Economic Research (Jingji Yanjiu)*, No. 3, March 1960.

Chi Ts'ai-ch'eng: 'The Form of Comprehensive Financial Plans and the Inter-Relations between Items in Them.' *Economic Research (Jingji Yanjiu)*, No. 2, February 1961.

Ch'i Yen-yung: 'What is the Rational Disposition of Grade 2 Wholesale Depots?' *Ta Kung Daily (Dagong Bao)*, Peking, October 27, 1964, p. 2.

Chia T'o-fu, Director of the Fourth Office of the State Council: 'Our Task after Co-operativization of the Handicrafts Industry.' Report on handicrafts co-operatives. *People's Handbook (Renmin Shouce) 1958*.

Chiang Hsia: 'On High Targets.' *The Masses (Qunzhong)*, January 16, 1959. (ECMM 165.)

Chiang Hsüeh-mo: 'A Discussion on the Use of the Law of Value in the Economy of the Rural People's Commune.' *Ta Kung Daily (Dagong Bao)*, Peking, June 15, 1962, p. 3.

Chiang Huai: 'A Discussion of the Socialist Channels of Commodity Flow.' *Economic Research (Jingji Yanjiu)*, No. 5, May 1963.

Chiang Kuang-nai, Minister of Textiles: 'Only Socialism Can Save China.' *Chinese Textiles (Zhongguo Fangzhi)*, No. 14, July 30, 1957.

Chiang Kuang-nai: 'Ten Glorious Years of the Textile Industry.' *People's Daily (Renmin Ribao)*, September 18, 1959, p. 9.

Chiang Wei-ch'ing: 'Develop Widely the Mass Movement to Aid Agriculture.' *Red Flag (Hongqi)*, No. 14, July 16, 1960.

Chiang Yen-ling: 'On the Purchase Price for Farm Products.' *Ta Kung Daily (Dagong Bao)*, Peking, March 23, 1958, p. 4.

Chiao Yü-pao: 'The Circumstances Surrounding the Prices of Some Kinds of Important Producer Goods for Agriculture.' *Economic Research (Jingji Yanjiu)*, No. 3, March 1959.

Chieh Yuan: 'Practical and Theoretical Economists in Peking Discuss How to Conduct Further Study on the Question of Developing Agricultural Production through Implementing the Principle of Taking Agriculture as the Foundation.' *Economic Research (Jingji Yanjiu)*, No. 12, December 1962.

Ch'ien Ying, Minister of Supervision: Speech to the First Session of the National People's Congress. *People's Handbook (Renmin Shouce) 1956*.

Chih Chung: 'The Conditions for "Ownership by the Whole People" in People's Communes.' *Financial and Economic Research (Caijing Yanjiu)*, No. 1, January 15, 1959.

Chin Chang-chün, Tientsin Fourth Metal Wire Factory: 'Numerous Conferences Are Bad for Production.' *People's Daily (Renmin Ribao)*, June 21, 1964, p. 6.

Chin Chao, Sung Kuai-chih and Hao Hsien-pin: 'Growing Up Steeled in Struggle.' *People's Daily (Renmin Ribao)*, November 27, 1963, p. 5.

Chin Chüeh: 'The Question of Raw Material Bases for Light Industry.' *Ta Kung Daily (Dagong Bao)*, Peking, December 6, 1961, p. 3.

Chin Ch'un: 'A Discussion of Banks' Credit Extension.' *People's Daily (Renmin Ribao)*, April 27, 1962, p. 5.

Chin Chün, Shantung Provincial Finance Department: 'Use Extra-Budgetary Funds Advantageously for Developing Production.' *Finance (Caizheng)*, No. 5, May 5, 1958.

Chin Li: 'A Discussion in Recent Years of Our Country's Economists on the Question of Socialist Economic Results.' *Economic Research (Jingji Yanjiu)*, No. 1, January 1963.

Chin Li: 'A Recent Discussion among Economists on Problems of Socialist Economic Accounting.' *Economic Research (Jingji Yanjiu)*, No. 11, November 1962.

Ch'in Liu-fang: 'A Preliminary Analysis of the Price of Cotton Yarn in Our Country.' *Economic Research (Jingji Yanjiu)*, No. 12, December 1959.

Chin Ming: 'The Way in Which the Financial Work in People's Communes Serves Distribution.' *Red Flag (Hongqi)*, No. 22, November 16, 1960.

Chinese Communist Party: 'Resolution of the Eighth Plenary Session on Developing the Movement for Economy, August 16, 1959.' *New China Fortnightly (Xinhua Banyuekan)*, No. 163, September 12, 1959.

Chinese Communist Party Central Committee Directive, September 14, 1957. *New China Fortnightly (Xinhua Banyuekan)*, No. 117, October 10, 1957.

Chinese Communist Party Central Committee: 'Resolution on the Establishment of the People's Communes in Rural Areas, passed by the enlarged conference of the Political Bureau at Peitaiho, Hopei, on August 29, 1958.' *People's Handbook (Renmin Shouce) 1959*.

Chinese Communist Party Central Committee: 'Resolution on Certain Problems of the People's Communes, December 10, 1958.' *People's Handbook (Renmin Shouce) 1959*.

Chinese Communist Party Central Committee and State Council: 'Decree on the Reform of the Administration of Finance and Trade in Rural Areas to Fit the Situation Arising from the Establishment of People's Communes.' *New China Fortnightly (Xinhua Banyuekan)*, No. 147, January 10, 1959.

CCP Central Committee, Central-South Bureau, Agricultural Committee Work Team, and a Kwangtung Provincial CCP Committee Work Team: 'The Pearl River State Farm—a Red Flag.' *Southern Daily (Nangfang Ribao)*, September 2, 1964. (SCMP 3312.)

Chinchow Railway Administrative Bureau, CCP Committee: 'Continuously Raise the Quality of Equipment: Realize the Potential of Rail Transport.' *Red Flag (Hongqi)*, No. 22, November 16, 1960.

Ching Tung: 'Why Should Private Ownership Still Predominate in Pig Rearing?' *Ta Kung Daily (Dagong Bao)*, Peking, August 14, 1964, p. 3.

Ching Tung: 'Some Problems in Developing Collective Pig Rearing.' *Ta Kung Daily (Dagong Bao)*, Peking, August 21, 1964, p. 3.

Ch'iu Fang-chen: 'A Report on Conditions in Red Star People's Commune, Kwangtze *hsien*, Fukien.' *Mainland Today (Jinri Dalu)*, No. 176, January 25, 1963.

Ch'iu Hsien-chung, Deputy Director, Communications Department, Szechuan Province: 'Improve Field Transport and Save Labour.' *People's Daily (Renmin Ribao)*, December 8, 1960, p. 4.

Chou En-lai; Premier: Report to the 1957 Session of the National People's Congress on the Work of the Government. *People's Handbook (Renmin Shouce) 1958*.

Chou K'e-yung, Deputy Commissioner, Department of Public Security, Kiangsi: 'The Great Achievement Made in the Work of Reforming Criminals through Labour.' *Kiangsi Daily (Jiangxi Ribao)*, December 17, 1959. (SCMP 2230.)

Chou Li-po: 'On a Sunday.' *Red Flag (Hongqi)*, No. 24, December 16, 1961.

Chou Lin: 'The Struggle between the Two Forces of Old and New in the Great Leap Forward.' *People's Daily (Renmin Ribao)*, December 31, 1959, p. 7.

Chou Yen-pin: 'The Conditions for Implementing the Piece Wage System.' *Ta Kung Daily (Dagong Bao)*, Peking, November 2, 1962, p. 3.

Chou Yung-liang, Assistant Secretary, CCP Committee, Min-Sheng Pharmaceutical Manufacturing Factory, Hangchow: 'They Are Working Class Intellectuals.' *Daily Worker* (*Gongren Ribao*), June 21, 1962, p. 2.

Chu Fu-lin, P'an Tsu-yi and Liu Wen-pin: 'Correctly Implement Tax Policy, Continuously Reform Methods of Working.' *Ta Kung Daily* (*Dagong Bao*), Peking, September 2, 1962, p. 2.

Chu Hang: 'Suggested Solution of the Problem of the Procurement of Sweet Potatoes.' *Ta Kung Daily* (*Dagong Bao*), Peking, April 27, 1958, p. 2.

Chu Huai-chen: 'Some Problems on Rural Electrification: Views for Deliberation.' *Water Conservancy and Electric Power* (*Shuili yu Dianli*), No. 7, April 5, 1963. (SCMM 372.)

Chu Nai-k'ang: 'Strengthen Financial Work in Production Teams of State Farms.' *Ta Kung Daily* (*Dagong Bao*), Peking, November 4, 1962, p. 2.

Chu Yen: 'A Preliminary Consideration of Certain Problems in Planning Transport Rates.' *Planned Economy* (*Jihua Jingji*), No. 12, December 1956.

Chung Chieh: 'A Discussion of the Modernization of Agriculture in Our Country.' *Economic Research* (*Jingji Yanjiu*), No. 12, December 1963.

Chung Fu: 'A Discussion of Some Commercial Problems in People's Communes.' *Ta Kung Daily* (*Dagong Bao*), Peking, September 28, 1958, p. 3.

Chung Tze-yün, Vice Minister of Coal: 'Current Problems of Capital Construction in Coal Mining.' *Coal Industry* (*Meitan Gongye*), No. 22, October 13, 1959.

Chungking Municipal CCP Committee, Finance and Trade Department, Survey Team: 'Everyone Attends to Everyone's Business, the Masses Control the Life of the Masses.' *People's Daily* (*Renmin Ribao*), March 11, 1960, p. 7.

Coal, Ministry of: 'Decree Concerning the Regulations for Reforming the Administrative System of the Enterprises and Units of the Ministry.' *Coal Industry* (*Meitan Gongye*), No. 2, January 19, 1958.

Coal, Ministry of, Local Industry Bureau: 'Energetically Develop the Local Coal Industry.' *Coal Industry* (*Meitan Gongye*), No. 7, April 4, 1958.

Commerce, Ministry of, Planning Bureau, Long Term Planning Dept.: 'Production and Consumption of Sugar.' *Central Co-operation Bulletin* (*Zhongyang Hozuo Tongxun*), No. 59, June 11, 1959. (ECMM 194.)

Commerce, Ministry of, Wages Office of Technical Organization Bureau: 'Certain Problems in Improving the Comprehensive Bonus System in State Commerce.' *Labour* (*Laodong*), No. 4, February 18, 1962.

Communist Youth League, Third Plenary Session of the Ninth Central Committee Communique. *China Youth Newspaper* (*Zhongguo Quignian Bao*), May 4, 1966, p. 1.

Fan Jo-yi: 'A Further Discussion of Price Policy for Products of Heavy Industry.' *Economic Research* (*Jingji Yanjiu*), No. 3, June 1957.

Fan Jung-k'ang and Ch'en Ch'ih: 'Bring About Co-operation between Large, Medium and Small Concerns, Take the Road of Specialized Production and Coordination.' *People's Daily* (*Renmin Ribao*), June 10, 1965, p. 5.

Fan Yeh-chün, Li Te-sheng and Chang Chih-tao: 'The Centralization and Unification of Financial Work.' *Ta Kung Daily* (*Dagong Bao*), Peking, June 25, 1962, p. 3.

Fang Ch'eng-p'ing: 'The Fundamental Reform of the Industrial and Financial System.' *Financial and Economic Research* (*Caijing Yanjiu*), No. 7, October 15, 1958.

Fang Ch'i-meng: 'A Necessary Understanding of the Comprehensive Guarantee System of State Grain Purchase and Supply.' *Theoretical Study* (*Lilun Xuexi*), No. 11, June 1, 1958. (ECMM 147.)

Fang Ch'ün: 'Be a Zealous Upholder of all Sprouts of Communism.' *China Youth* (*Zhongguo Qingnian*), No. 22, November 16, 1958.

Fang Nan: 'Common Prosperity and Individual Riches.' *Southern Daily* (*Nanfang Ribao*), February 20, 1963. (SCMP 2945.)

Fang Nan: 'For Those Who Are Drifting with the Main Current: On Cadres Participation in Collective Labour.' *Southern Daily* (*Nanfang Ribao*), July 13, 1963. (SCMP 3039.)

Feng Ch'un-lin: 'Return Enough Funds for Expenses of Agricultural Production.' *Ta Kung Daily* (*Dagong Bao*), Peking, November 25, 1962, p. 2.

Feng P'ing-fei: 'Handicraft Industry Is an Important Component of the National Economy.' *Ta Kung Daily* (*Dagong Bao*), Peking, August 28, 1961. p. 3.

Feng Ta-chih: 'The Need to Make a Good Job of a Four-Sided Relationship.' *Daily Worker* (*Gongren Ribao*), August 14, 1962, p. 2.

The Fifth Oil Factory: 'A Summary of the Progress in Basic Construction in the Fifth Oil Factory in 1958.' *Oil Refining* (*Shiyou Lianzhi*), No. 10, October 9, 1958.

Finance, Ministry of, and Second Ministry of Commerce: Joint Notice to the Supply and Marketing Co-operatives. *People's Taxation* (*Renmin Shuiwu*), No. 11, June 4, 1958.

Finance, Ministry of, General Tax Bureau, Agricultural Tax Office: 'The Progress of the Collection of Agricultural Tax on the Summer Crop.' *People's Taxation* (*Renmin Shuiwu*), No. 18, September 19, 1958.

Finance, Ministry of, Investment Finance Office: 'Actively Organize the Supply of Capital: Sustain Investment with All One's Strength.' *Finance* (*Caizheng*), No. 12, December 1958.

First Ministry of Machine Building, Eighth Bureau: Directive on the Swift Adoption of Measures to Maintain the Quality of Electrical Goods. *Electric Motor Industry* (*Dianji Gongye*), No. 10, May 25, 1959.

Forestry Capital Construction Conference: 'Exploit the Victories and Advance, Strive for Greater Victories in Capital Construction.' *China's Forestry* (*Zhongguo Linye*), No. 3, March 1964. (SCMM 414.)

Forestry, Ministry of: 'Summing Up Forestation Work in the Past Thirteen Years.' *China's Forestry* (*Zhongguo Linye*), No. 5, May 1963. (SCMM 367.)

Forestry, Ministry of, Hunting Control Office: 'A Discussion on the Development of Hunting in National Minority Areas.' *Nationalities Unity* (*Minzu Tuanjie*), No. 2–3, February–March 1964.

Han Kuang: 'Some Problems in Technical Work in Industry.' *Red Flag* (*Hongqi*), No. 24, December 16, 1961.

Heilungkiang Provincial CCP Committee, Work Team of Agricultural Work Dept.: 'A Survey of the Method of Setting Aside Reserve Funds in Communes.' *People's Commune Construction* (*Renmin Gongshe Jianshe*) No. 21, November 5, 1964. (SCMM 452.)

Ho Ch'ang-kung, Vice Minister of Geology: 'The Glorious Road of Our National Geological Work.' *People's Daily* (*Renmin Ribao*), October 11, 1959, p. 6.

Ho Ch'ang-kung: 'Survey Underground Water Resources and Help Agricultural Production.' *Red Flag* (*Hongqi*), No. 9–10, May 5, 1961.

Ho Ch'eng: 'Carry Out Well the "Three Co-ordinations" in Tax Inspection.' *Finance* (*Caizheng*), No. 11, June 9, 1959.

Ho Chen-lu and Li Hui-chao: 'The Origin of The Evaluation of a Work-Day at ¥2.' *Southern Daily* (*Nanfang Ribao*), December 21, 1962. (SCMP 2899.)

Ho Ch'eng: 'Energetically Develop the Production of Tussah Silk.' *Ta Kung Daily* (*Dagong Bao*), Peking, December 17, 1963, p. 2.

Ho Cheng and Wei Wan: 'A Discussion of Rural Market Trade.' *Economic Research* (*Jingji Yanjiu*), No. 4, April 1962.

Ho Chi: 'The Superiority of the People's Communes as Seen from Kohsiang Commune.' *Economic Research* (*Jingji Yanjiu*), No. 1, January 1960.

Ho Chi-feng, Vice-Minister of Agriculture: 'Energetically Continue to Build Water Conservancy Projects.' *Chinese Agricultural Journal (Zhongguo Nongbao)*, No. 17, September 8, 1959.

Ho Chien-chang and Chang Ling: 'A Tentative Discussion on "Production Price" in the Socialist Economy.' *Economic Research (Jingji Yanjiu)*, No. 5, May 1964.

Ho Chien-chang, Kuei Shih-yung and Chao Hsiao-min: 'The Content of Economic Accounting of Socialist Enterprises.' *Economic Research (Jingji Yanjiu)*, No. 4, April 1962.

Ho Hui: 'Rely on the Masses, Emphasize Self-Dependence and Small Scale Production.' *Ta Kung Daily (Dagong Bao)*, Peking, October 23, 1964, p. 3.

Ho Ju: 'The Positive Role of Handicrafts in Our National Economy.' *People's Daily (Renmin Ribao)*, June 30, 1964, p. 5.

Ho Kuei-lin: 'The True Quality of the "Theory of Socialist Production Price".' *Economic Research (Jingji Yanjiu)*, No. 1, January 1965.

Ho Kuei-lin, Hsüeh Chung-chang and P'eng Chen-yüan: ' "Production Price" Cannot Form the Basis of Socialist Price Formation.' *Economic Research (Jingji Yanjiu)*, No. 4, April 1964.

Ho Pai-sha, Director of Coal Industry Planning Bureau, State Economic Commission: 'Increase Local Initiative, Energetically Develop Coal Mines.' *Planned Economy (Jihua Jingji)*, No. 2, February 1958.

Ho Po: 'A Tentative Discussion of the System of Determining the Wages of the Senior Administrators, Engineers, and Staff of Industrial Enterprises according to Positions Held.' *Chinese Industry (Zhongguo Gongye)*, No. 2, 1956.

Ho T'ing-shih: 'How to Compile a Survey Study of Residents' Needs of Commodities.' *Planned Economy (Jihua Jingji)*, No. 4, April 1957.

Ho Wei: 'Significance and Method of Comparing Present and Pre-War Prices of Agricultural Commodities.' *Study (Xuexi)*, No. 7, April 3, 1957.

Ho Wei and Yang Ch'un-hsü: 'Rural Market Trade.' *People's Daily (Renmin Ribao)*, March 14, 1961, p. 7.

Ho Yi-fu: 'Encourage Traditional Business Methods.' *Daily Worker (Gongren Ribao)*, November 21, 1961, p. 2.

Honan Provincial CCP Committee: 'Plan on Overhaul Consolidation and Elevation of People's Commune This Winter and Next Spring.' *Honan Daily (Honan Ribao)*, January 14, 1959. (SCMP 1965.)

Hopei Ch'engte Special District Office and Forestry Bureau of Hopei Province, Joint Survey Team: 'A Survey Report on the "Afforestation as Well as Agriculture" Contract Labour System Used by the Huangtuliang State Forest Farm.' *People's Daily (Renmin Ribao)*, January 23, 1965, p. 5.

Hou Chih-yüan: 'The Reason for Differential Rent in Rural People's Communes at the Present Stage.' *Kuang Ming Daily (Guangming Ribao)*, August 6, 1962, p. 4.

Hsiang Ching-ch'üan: 'A Draft Discussion on the Function of Price in Promoting Agricultural and Industrial Production at the Present Time.' *Kuang Ming Daily (Guangming Ribao)*, February 25, 1963, p. 4.

Hsiang Kan-ch'eng: 'Control the Wage Fund Severely and Use It Rationally.' *Labour (Laodong)*, No. 14, August 18, 1962.

Hsiang Kan-ch'eng, Deputy Director, Kirin Provincial Department of Labour: 'The Great Superiority of Comprehensive Bonuses.' *Labour (Laodong)*, No. 9, May 3, 1959.

Hsiang Nan: 'Certain Problems in the Mechanization of Agriculture.' *People's Daily (Renmin Ribao)*, December 22, 1962, p. 5.

Hsiao Ch'uan: 'We Should Pay Close Attention to the Development of Light Industry.' *People's Daily (Renmin Ribao)*, August 8, 1959, p. 7.

Hsiao Lin: 'Commercial Work in the Great Leap Forward.' *Financial and Economic Research (Caijing Yanjiu)*, No. 3, June 1958.

Hsiao Liu: 'The Problem of Building Industrial Bases and the Balanced Development of Local Economies.' *Planned Economy (Jihua Jingji)*, No. 7, July 1958.

Hsiao Mei and Yü Ch'ing: 'Economic Aid to Production Teams Must Fit the Actual Circumstances.' *People's Daily (Renmin Ribao)*, February 21, 1963, p. 2.

Hsieh Chia-jung: 'Close Co-ordination of Geological Work with State Demand.' *People's Daily (Renmin Ribao)*, March 12, 1957, (CB 443.)

Hsieh Ho-ch'ou, Vice Chairman, Nationalities' Affairs Commission: 'Further Strengthen Commercial Work Among Minority Nationalities.' *Nationalities Unity (Minzu Tuanjie)*, No. 2–3, February–March 1963.

Hsieh Kuang-ch'eng: 'After Implementing the System of Production Bonuses for Senior Personnel.' *Labour (Laodong)*, No. 11, June 3, 1957.

Hsieh Li: 'A Preliminary Discussion of the Financial Problem of the People's Communes.' *Economic Research (Jingji Yanjiu)*, No. 10, October 1958.

Hsieh Ming: 'On Contract System.' *Political and Legal Research (Zhengfa Yanjiu)*, No. 2, April 1959.

Hsieh Yin-chi: 'Ways to Increase Productivity in Agriculture in Our Country.' *People's Daily (Renmin Ribao)*, March 12, 1959, p. 7.

Hsien Li: 'A Preliminary Discussion on the Financial Problems of People's Communes.' *Economic Research (Jingji Yanjiu)*, No. 10, October 1958.

Hsien Yi-yü: 'A Survey of Local Price Differentials of Industrial Goods in Peking and a Study of Some Problems.' *Education and Research (Jiaoyu yu Yanjiu)*, October 1958 (in *Selected Essays of Chinese Economists* . . . Vol. II).

Hsing Huan and P'ei Ch'uan: 'When the Root Is Firm, the Branches Will Flourish.' *People's Daily (Renmin Ribao)*, February 5, 1963, p. 2.

Hsinhsiang CCP Committee, Political Department for Finance and Trade: 'Report on the Rural Market.' *People's Daily (Renmin Ribao)*, June 4, 1965, p. 2.

Hsinyang Special District, Honan Province, Commercial Bureau General Office Study Team: 'Use the Thought of Mao Tse-tung to Resolve Contradictions in Sending Industrial Goods to the Countryside.' *Ta Kung Daily (Dagong Bao)*, Peking, December 28, 1964, p. 2.

Hsü An-ch'eng, Assistant Manager, Seamless Steel Tube Plant, Anshan Iron and Steel Works: 'When Our Consumers Are Satisfied, We Shall be Satisfied.' *People's Daily (Renmin Ribao)*, December 8, 1965, p. 2.

Hsü Fei-ch'ing: 'Centralized Leadership and Decentralized Administration Is the Correct Policy for the National Budgetary Management.' *Finance (Caizheng)*, No. 19, October 9, 1959.

Hsü Fen and Li Yuan: 'Why Is the Cost of Yangtze River Transport Higher than that of Railway Transport?' *Planned Economy (Jihua Jingji)*, No. 3, March 1958.

Hsü Kang: 'Some Views on How to Compare Standards of Living of Workers and Peasants.' *Statistical Work (Tongji Gongzuo)*, No. 16, August 29, 1957.

Hsü Li-chih, Deputy Director, Resettlement Bureau, Ministry of State Farms and Land Reclamation: 'Reply to Young Friends Clamouring to Go to the Frontiers.' *China Youth (Zhongguo Qingnian)*, No. 1, January 1, 1959.

Hsü Shou-po: 'Rural Electrification.' *Popular Science (Kexue Dazhong)*, No. 5, May 1963.

Hsü Ti-hsin: 'Advance the Transformation of Capitalist Industry and Commerce to a New Stage.' *Study (Xuexi)*, No. 1, January 1956.

Hsüeh An-fu: 'Wholeheartedly for the Thirteen Households of Poor Peasants.' *China Youth (Zhongguo Qingnian)*, No. 1, January 1, 1965.

Hsüeh Cheng-hsiu: 'Tentative Discussion of the Relationship between the Increase in Population in Socialist Cities and the Development of Industrial and

s

Agricultural Production.' *Kuang Ming Daily* (*Guangming Ribao*), October 7, 1963, p. 4.

Hsüeh Ch'iu-lun: 'Reply to a Question Whether the *Hsiang* Organization Remains Necessary Where Co-operatives Have Been Formed.' *Study* (*Xuexi*), No. 8, August 1956.

Hsüeh Mu-ch'iao: 'The Law of Value and Our Price Policy.' *Red Flag* (*Hongqi*), No. 7–8, April 16, 1963.

Hsüeh Mu-ch'iao: 'National Construction and the General Arrangement of the People's Livelihood.' *Study* (*Xuexi*), No. 3, February 3, 1958.

Hsüeh Mu-ch'iao: 'Our Country's Planning and Statistical Work Must Learn from the Soviet Union.' *People's Daily* (*Renmin Ribao*), November 12, 1957, p. 7.

Hsüeh Mu-ch'iao: 'Some Problems Awaiting Discussion on Commodity Prices in a Socialist Society.' *Economic Research* (*Jingji Yanjiu*), No. 5, May 1963.

Hsüeh Nung: 'The Objective Necessity of Rural People's Communes.' *Daily Worker* (*Gongren Ribao*), November 7, 1961, p. 4.

Hu Ching-yün, Vice-President of the People's Bank: Report at the Second National Conference on the Credit and Loan System of State Commerce. *New China Monthly* (*Xinhua Yuebao*), No. 69, July 1955.

Hu Feng-chi: 'Why Should the Development of Basic Industries Be Further Speeded Up?' *Kuang Ming Daily* (*Guangming Ribao*), February 22, 1965, p. 4.

Hu Jui-liang and Yuan Tai-hsu: 'A Discussion of Handicraft Industry and Its Economic Forms.' *Economic Research* (*Jingji Yanjiu*), No. 7, July 1962.

Hu Li-chiao: 'Conduct Rural Financial Work Well, Help the Collective Economy Effectively.' *People's Daily* (*Renmin Ribao*), July 11, 1963, p. 5.

Hu Sheng: 'Commodity Production in Our Country at the Present Time.' *Red Flag* (*Hongqi*), No. 14, December 16, 1958.

Hu Tze-ming: 'A Consideration of Certain Problems in Local Budgets.' *Finance* (*Caizheng*), No. 8, August 1957.

Hu Yü-yuan: 'On the Formation of Seasonal Price Differentials of Agricultural Commodities under the Socialist System.' *Economic Research* (*Jingji Yanjiu*), No. 6, June 1965.

Hua Lo-keng: 'Scattered Notes on Experiments in Methods of Overall Planning.' *Red Flag* (*Hongqi*), No. 11, October 1, 1965.

Huan Wen: 'Some Problems in Local Budgetary Management after the Implementation of the New Financial System.' *Finance* (*Caizheng*), No. 1, January 1958.

Huang Chih-kang: 'Strengthen Guidance of Study by Basic Level Rural Cadres.' *Red Flag* (*Hongqi*), No. 19, October 1, 1961.

Huang Ching, Chairman of the State Technological Commission: 'Problems of Agricultural Mechanization in Our Country.' *People's Daily* (*Renmin Ribao*), October 25, 1957. p. 4.

Huang Ching-ya: 'Certain Problems in the Development of Agricultural Electrification.' *People's Daily* (*Renmin Ribao*), September 12, 1963, p. 5.

Huang Chung-hsiang: 'Persistently Hold Examination and Rating, Firmly Carry Out the Party's Policy.' *Southern Daily* (*Nanfang Ribao*), August 5, 1962. (SCMP 2806.)

Huang Hua-ch'ing, First Secretary, Liaoning Provincial CCP Committee: 'Promote the Spirit of Communist Co-operation.' *People's Daily* (*Renmin Ribao*), January 23, 1960. (SCMP 2201.)

Huang Ta: 'The Credit Policy of Banks and the Circulation of Currency.' *Economic Research* (*Jingji Yanjiu*), No. 9, September 1962.

Huang Ta, Vice-Governor of Liaoning Province: 'Even Industrial Centres Can Become Self-Sufficient in Vegetables.' *Red Flag* (*Hongqi*), No. 14, July 16, 1960.

Huang Ta: '*Jenminpi* Is the Symbol of the Intrinsic Value of the Monetary Commodity.' *Economic Research* (*Jingji Yanjiu*), No. 4, August 1954.

Huang T'ien-hsiang: 'Energetically Develop Spare Time Education for Rural Young People.' *China Youth (Zhongguo Qingnian)*, No. 4, February 16, 1964.

Huang Tsu-yu: 'The Problem of the Training and Distribution of Middle-Ranking Specialist Cadres.' *Planned Economy (Jihua Jingji)*, No. 4, April 1957.

Huang Ya-kuang, Deputy Director of People's Bank: 'Non-Cash Settlement of Accounts Through the Bank in Our Country.' *Red Flag (Hongqi)*, No. 16, August 16, 1960.

Huang Ying-sung, Financial Office, Lunghsi Special District, Fukien: 'Some Points on Efficiency in *Hsiang (Chen)* Financial Work.' *Finance (Caizheng)*, No. 11, November 1957.

Huimin North Canal United Water Conservancy Administrative Committee: 'When the Masses Manage an Irrigation District Themselves, the Development of Production Is on a Firm Basis.' *People's Daily (Renmin Ribao)*, December 13, 1963, p. 2.

Hunan Provincial Federation of Handicraft Co-operatives, Accounting Department: 'In What Ways Should a Handicraft Co-operative Publish Its Accounts?' *Ta Kung Daily (Dagong Bao)*, Peking, January 20, 1964, p. 2.

Huo Chi-ch'ao, Finance and Fund Office, Shensi Provincial Planning Committee: 'Some of the Points We Learn in Comprehensive Fiscal Planning Work.' *Planning and Statistics (Jihua yu Tongji)*, No. 2, January 23, 1959. (ECMM 176.)

Hupeh Provincial CCP Committee, Rural Work Department: 'Report of a Survey on the Relation between Accumulation and Expenditure in Agricultural Co-operatives.' *New China Fortnightly (Xinhua Banyuekan)*, No. 144, November 25, 1958.

Jen Jui-lin: 'A Study of the Present Price of Timber.' *Finance (Caizheng)*, No. 2, November 1956.

Jen Po-ke: 'Organizing Urban Residents' Economic Life Is an Important Aspect of Building New Socialist Cities.' *Red Flag (Hongqi)*, No. 5, March 1, 1960.

Jen Yuan-shou: 'Arouse the Masses, Plant Trees and Create Forests.' *Economic Research (Jingji Yanjiu)*, No. 4, April 1965.

Jung Tze-ho, Vice Minister of Finance: 'China's Finance in the Past Ten Years.' *Finance (Caizheng)*, No. 18, September 24, 1959.

Jung Tze-ho, Vice-Minister of Finance: Speech at the National Conference for the Exchange of Experience on Budgetary Work. *Finance (Caizheng)*, No. 10, October 1960.

Jung Wen-tsuo: 'Develop Light Industry Production Based on Industrial Raw Materials.' *Ta Kung Daily (Dagong Bao)*, Peking, February 22, 1963, p. 3.

K'ang Li-jen: 'Some Problems in the Present Collection of Agricultural Tax in Kind.' *Ta Kung Daily (Dagong Bao)*, Peking, November 17, 1962, p. 2.

Kao Feng, First Secretary, Tsinghai Provincial CCP Committee: 'Energetically Open Waste Land, Quickly Develop Agriculture and Ensure the Continuous Leap Forward of the National Economy.' *People's Daily (Renmin Ribao)*, July 11, 1960, p. 7.

Kao Hsiang: 'The Functions of the State Bank in Socialist Construction.' *Economic Research (Jingji Yanjiu)*, No. 10, October 1962.

Kao Jun-chih, Deputy Chief Engineer, Shihchingshan Iron and Steel Corporation, Peking, and Deputy Manager, Steel Refinery: 'How to Train and Employ Technical Personnel.' *Daily Worker (Gongren Ribao)*, July 3, 1962, p. 2.

Kao Ti-ch'en: 'Emphasize the Supply and Marketing Co-operatives' Role in Guiding Rural Market Trade.' *Ta Kung Daily (Dagong Bao)*, Peking, January 20, 1964, p. 3.

Kao-wan-pao-cha-pu, First Secretary, CCP Committee for Silongol League: 'A Great Victory Achieved for Agriculture on the Grasslands.' *People's Daily (Renmin Ribao)*, September 26, 1960, p. 7.

Kao Yang-wen: 'Put Mining in the Forefront of the Metallurgical Industry.' *Red Flag (Hongqi)*, Nos. 15–16, August 10, 1961

Kao Yü-huang: 'The Need for Vigorous Organization of Rational Transport in the Economic Activities of the Nation.' *Economic Research (Jingji Yanjiu)*, No. 7, July 1959.

Keng Tsün-san: 'Brief Remarks on the Current Price of Coal.' *Economic Research (Jingji Yanjiu)*, No. 3, March 1959.

Kiangsu Provincial Planning Commission: 'Kiangsu Provincial Planning Commission's Draft Plans for a Leap Forward.' *Planned Economy (Jihua Jingji)*, No. 7, July 1958.

Kirin Provincial Labour Dept. Working Group and Kirin Municipal Federation of Trade Unions and Bureau of Labour: 'After Kirin Municipal Wooden Implement Factory Had Experimented with Comprehensive Bonuses.' *Labour (Laodong)*, No. 13, July 3, 1959.

Ko Chih-ta: 'A Discussion of the Relations Between Agriculture and Finance.' *Ta Kung Daily (Dagong Bao)*, Peking, February 23, 1961, p. 3.

Ko Chih-ta: 'The Problem of Comprehensive Equilibrium of Finance, Credit and Raw Materials.' *Economic Research (Jingji Yanjiu)*, No. 10, October 1963.

Ko Chih-ta and Ling Han: 'Outline Discussion of Comprehensive Financial Plans.' *Economic Research (Jingji Yanjiu)*, No. 2, February 1960.

Ko Chih-ta and Wang Cho: 'Some Inter-Relationships between Finance and Currency Work.' *Ta Kung Daily (Dagong Bao)*, Peking, November 17, 1961.

Ko Chih-ta and Yang Che-hsing: 'Give Correct Consideration to the Question of Equilibrium in the Planning of Finance and Banking.' *Ta Kung Daily (Dagong Bao)*, August 17, 1958, p. 4.

Ko Fu-chih: 'Actively Implement the Expenditure Budget Responsibility System.' *Finance (Caizheng)*, No. 12, December 1960.

Korniev: 'Some Problems in the Further Development of Water Conservancy in China.' *Water Conservancy and Electric Power (Shuili yü Dianli)*, No. 4, February 20, 1959.

Ku Lien-ch'i and Chu Tso-ch'un: 'Why Must Industrial Production Take the Road of Specialization and Co-ordination?' *Ta Kung Daily (Dagong Bao)*, Peking, March 5, 1965, p. 3.

Ku Ming (ed.): 'A Discussion of the Question of Differential Rent in Rural People's Communes.' *Red Flag (Hongqi)*, No. 23, December 1, 1961.

Ku Ta-ch'un: 'Trade Unions Must Energetically Take the Initiative to Be Good Assistants of the Party.' *Chinese Workers* (Zhongguo Gongren), No. 19, October 12, 1959.

Ku To-ching: ' "Responsibility for Investment" Is a Very Important System for Regulating Production Relationships and for Developing Productive Capacity in Capital Construction.' *Economic Research (Jingji Yanjiu)*, No. 3, March 1960.

Ku Tso-hsin: 'The Development of the Planning of Industrial Construction in the Past Decade.' *Planning and Statistics (Jihua yu Tongji)*, No. 13, July 1959. (ECMM 204.)

Kuan Sen: 'Give Out Agricultural Loans at the Proper Time and Help Needy Production Teams.' *Ta Kung Daily (Dagong Bao)*, Peking, July 9, 1962, p. 2.

Kuan Ta-t'ung: 'Commerce Should Improve Its Service to Production and Consumption.' *People's Daily (Renmin Ribao)*, October 23, 1962, p. 5.

Kuan Ta-t'ung: 'On Trade at Rural Markets.' *People's Daily (Renmin Ribao)*, November 21, 1959, p. 7.

Kuan Ta-t'ung: 'Our Country's Unified, Socialist Internal Market.' *Red Flag (Hongqi)*, No. 6, April 1963.

Kuan Ta-t'ung: 'Rural Market Trade.' *Red Flag (Hongqi)*, No. 18, September 16, 1961.

Kuan Ta-t'ung: 'Strengthen Links between Town and Country, Promote the Flow of Commodities.' *People's Daily (Renmin Ribao)*, July 15, 1961, p. 7.

K'uang Ch'ang-ch'eng, First Secretary, Toushan Commune CCP Committee, Toishan *hsien*, Kwangtung: 'Production Teams that Have Increased Output Should Not Distribute and Consume All Their Output.' *Southern Daily (Nanfang Ribao)*, August 21, 1962. (SCMP 2814.)

Kuanti Credit Co-operative, Weinan *hsien*, Shensi: 'The Way to Help Poor and Lower Middle Peasants Overcome Their Production and Livelihood Difficulties.' *Rural Finance (Nongcun Jinrong)*, No. 10, May 21, 1965. (SCMM 490.)

K'ung Fan-chi: 'Rates of Work Attendance and Manure Delivery Must Be Fixed Seriously to Improve the Relationship between Public and Private Interests.' *Southern Daily (Nanfang Ribao)*, July 20, 1962. (SCMP 2804.)

K'ung Hsiang-chen: 'Organize a High Tide in Production and Construction in Light Industry in Harmony with the General Line.' *Ta Kung Daily (Dagong Bao)*, Peking, April 18, 1965, p. 2.

'K'ung Hsiang-chen, Vice Minister of Light Industry: 'A Short Cut Solution of the Raw Material Supply Problem of Light Industry.' *Red Flag (Hongqi)*, No. 6, March 16, 1961.

Kung Wen: 'Sideline Occupations of Rural Households: Parts 1 and 2,' *Daily Worker (Gongren Ribao)*, August 2 and 3, 1961, p. 3.

Kuo Hung-hsia: 'Financial Departments Should Orientate Themselves More Towards Rural Problems.' *Ta Kung Daily (Dagong Bao)*, Peking, November 12, 1965, p. 3.

Kuo Hung-te and Wang Ch'eng-yao: 'The Accumulation of State Enterprises Must Be Remitted in the Two Forms of Tax and Profit.' *Ta Kung Daily (Dagong Bao)*, Peking, August 5, 1962, p. 3.

Kuo Kuo-sheng: 'Development of Tractor Ploughing Potential from the Viewpoint of Two Tractor Stations.' *Daily Worker (Gongren Ribao)*, May 17, 1962, p. 1.

Kwangtung Provincial Department of Finance: 'Promote the Development of Undertakings through Budgetary Responsibility and Financial Decentralization.' *Finance (Caizheng)*, No. 13, November 24, 1958.

Kweichow Provincial Finance Department, Budget Office: 'Some Problems that Must Be Solved in the Management of Extra-Budgetary Funds.' *Finance (Caizheng)*, No. 20, October 24, 1959.

Lei Chih-p'ing: 'Technical and Administrative Staff and Political and Mass Organization Cadres Ought to Get Bonuses.' *Labour (Laodong)*, No. 11, June 3, 1957.

Li Ch'a: 'Chinese Communist Plans for Industrial Finance.' *China Monthly (Zuguo)*, No. 1, January 1966.

Li Ch'ao-jui: 'Fully Develop the Use of Tractors for Ploughing.' *People's Daily (Renmin Ribao)*, December 16, 1963, p. 2.

Li Ch'eng-jui: 'An Exploratory Discussion of the General Equilibrium of the Budget, Credit and Material Supplies.' *Economic Research (Jingji Yanjiu)*, No. 3, March 1964.

Li Ch'eng-jui: 'Socialist Economic Accounting.' *Ta Kung Daily (Dagong Bao)*, Peking, December 10, 1962, p. 3.

Li Ch'eng-jui and Tso Ch'un-t'ai: 'Some Problems Concerning Economic Accounting in Socialist Enterprises.' *Red Flag (Hongqi)*, No. 19, October 1, 1961.

Li Ch'eng-jui and Yang Ch'un-hsü: 'Apply the Contract System Extensively.' *Ta Kung Daily (Dagong Bao)*, Peking, February 20, 1959. (SCMP 1980.)

Li Chien-pai, First Secretary, CCP Heilungkiang Provincial Committee: 'Some Problems of Agricultural Mechanization.' *Study* (Xuexi), Nos. 10–11, May 31, 1958.

Li Chih-sheng: 'Co-ordinate Revolutionary Responsibility and the Responsibility System.' *Red Flag (Hongqi)*, No. 20, October 28, 1964.

Li Fu-ch'un: 'Raise High the Red Flag of the General Line and Advance Continuously.' *Red Flag (Hongqi)*, No. 16, August 16, 1960.

Li Fu-ch'un: 'Report on Achievements of Our First Five Year Plan and Future Tasks and Aims of Socialist Construction.' *People's Handbook (Remain Shouce) 1958*.

Li Feng and Yü Hang: 'Refute the Idea the General Situation of the Market Is Tense.' *East Wind (Dongfeng)*, No. 20, October 1959. (ECMM 198.)

Li Fu-hsiang: 'Take the Mass Line and Manage Rural Supply and Marketing Co-operatives Efficiently.' *Ta Kung Daily (Dagong Bao)*, Peking, November 10, 1961, p. 3.

Li Fu-tu, Vice-Chairman of the Yellow River Water Conservancy Commission: 'Soil and Conservation Work in the Middle Reaches of the Yellow River Must Be Carried Out Firmly.' *People's Daily (Renmin Ribao)*, July 8, 1957, p. 6.

Li Hai: 'The Organization of Rural Handicrafts.' *Ta Kung Daily (Dagong Bao)*, Peking, December 18, 1961, p. 3.

Li Ho-ting, Yin Chün-k'ai, Hsieh Hung-te, Tseng Li-t'ing and Mao Shih-sheng: 'A Report of a Survey of Flexibility in Planting Crops in Aikuo Commune.' *People's Daily (Renmin Ribao)*, October 25, 1961, p. 2.

Li Hsi-mu: 'Many-Sided Operation Is the Road to the Development of Greater, Quicker, Better and More Economical Production by Industrial Enterprises.' *People's Daily (Renmin Ribao)*, October 8, 1960, p. 7.

Li Hsien-nien, Minister of Finance: Report on Final Accounts for 1956 and Draft Budget for 1957. *People's Handbook (Renmin Shouce) 1958*.

Li Hsien-nien, Minister of Finance: Report on Final Accounts for 1957 and Draft Budget for 1958, *Collected Laws and Regulations . . .* Vol. 7.

Li Hsien-nien, Minister of Finance: Report on Final Accounts for 1959 and Draft Budget for 1960. *People's Handbook (Renmin Shouce) 1960*.

Li Hsien-nien, Minister of Finance: 'A Look at the People's Communes.' *Red Flag (Hongqi)*, No 10, October 16, 1958.

Li Hsien-nien, Minister of Finance: 'How to Recognize Improvements in the Management of Rural Finance and Trade.' *Red Flag (Hongqi)*, No. 2, January 16, 1959.

Li Hsien-nien, Minister of Finance: 'Some Problems in Finance and Currency Work.' *Red Flag (Hongqi)*, No. 1, January 1, 1960.

Li Hsien-nien, Minister of Finance: Speech to the All-China Cultural and Educational Advanced Workers' Conference. *People's Daily (Renmin Ribao)*, June 5, 1960, p. 2.

Li Hui-hung, Sung Chi-jen and Wang Hua-hsin: 'Some Opinions on the Division Between Light and Heavy Industry.' *Statistical Work (Tongji Gongzuo)*, No. 18, September 14, 1957.

Li Jen, Kan Fu and Tsung Shun: 'Several Views on the Problem of Establishing a Supply and Marketing Department for the Agricultural Producers' Co-operative.' *Ta Kung Daily (Dagong Bao)*, Peking, May 26, 1958. (SCMP 1797.)

Li Ju-mei, Member of the Secretariat of the Hochien *Hsien* CCP Committee: 'Functions of Commune Trade Markets.' *Hopei Daily (Hobei Ribao)*, August 3, 1959. (SCMP 2134.)

Li Ming-hsin, Chairman of the Changchiak'ou Municipal Federation of Trade Unions: 'Pay Attention to all Aspects of the Training of New Workers.' *Daily Worker (Gongren Ribao)*, August 9, 1959. (SCMP 2097.)

Li Pai-fang: 'Actively Strengthen the Organization of the Sources of Export Goods.' *Planned Economy (Jihua Jingji)*, No. 2, February 1958.

Li Po-fang: 'Energetically Organize the Supply of Exports.' *Planned Economy (Jihua Jingji)*, No. 2, February 1958.

Li She-nan: 'Some Problems in the Economic Accounting of Agricultural Machinery Stations.' *Economic Research (Jingji Yanjiu)*, No. 7, July 1965.

Li She-nan: 'Some Problems in Lowering Operational Costs of Agricultural Mechanization.' *People's Daily (Renmin Ribao)*, June 30, 1964, p. 5.

Li Shu-te: 'Agricultural Taxation in the Past Ten Years.' *Finance (Caizheng)*, No. 19, October 9, 1959.

Li Szu-kuang, Minister of Geology: 'Current Geological Work in China.' NCNA Peking, April 28, 1959.

Li T'i: 'Shihotzu: A New City to the North of the Tienshan.' China News Service, Peking, April 7, 1959. (SCMP 2018.)

Li Tse-wen, Szechuan Provincial Department of Industry: 'Certain Measures Taken by Szechuan Province to Develop the Local Coal Industry.' *Coal Industry (Meitan Gongye)*, No. 7, April 4, 1958.

Li Wei-fu, Deputy Secretary of CCP Committee of Changshih Commune, Shaokuan, Kwangtung: 'Agriculture Needs More Educated Young People.' *China Youth (Zhongguo Qingnian)*, No. 15, August 1, 1960.

Li Yin: 'Chinglienko Tea-House in Shanghai Enters a New Era.' *Liberation Daily (Jiefang Ribao)*, May 7, 1958. (SCMP 1794.)

Liang Chen-hai and Ts'en Hung-lin: 'Dividend Distribution Must Not Be Overlooked in Supply and Marketing Co-operatives.' *Southern Daily (Nanfang Ribao)*, March 6, 1963. (SCMP 2948.)

Liang Chih and Kan T'ieh-ya: 'A Study in the Development of Comprehensive Financial Planning at *Hsien* Level.' *Economic Research (Jingji Yanjiu)*, No. 1, January 1961.

Liang Hsi, Minister of Forestry: 'The Forestry Situation in China.' Reports to Third Session of First National People's Congress. NCNA Peking, June 19, 1956.

Liang Hung-mou and Lung Cheng-yuan: 'The Completion of Tax Collection Tasks in Successive Years by Muko Tax Office.' *Ta Kung Daily (Dagong Bao)*, Peking, July 16, 1962, p. 2.

Liang Yao: 'The Current Task of Supply and Marketing Co-operatives.' *New Industry and Commerce (Xin Gongshang)*, No. 2, February 18, 1964. (SCMM 421.)

Liang Yao, Vice-Chairman, All-China Federation of Supply and Marketing Co-operatives: 'Improve the Supply of Means of Production for Agriculture, Help Agricultural Production and Strengthen the Collective Economy of the People's Communes.' *Daily Worker (Gongren Ribao)*, February 12, 1963, p. 1.

Liao Chi-li: 'Some Remarks on Dual Accounting.' *Planned Economy (Jihua Jingji)*, No. 5, May 1958.

Liao Hsien-kao: 'Agricultural Production Planning Charts.' *Planned Economy (Jihua Jingji)*, No. 4, April 1957.

Liao Lu-yen, Minister of Agriculture: 'The 1959 Task on the Agricultural Front.' *Red Flag (Hongqi)*, No. 1, January 1, 1959.

Liao Lu-yen, Minister of Agriculture: Speech to the Third Session of the First National People's Congress on June 15, 1956. *People's Handbook (Renmin Shouce) 1957.*

Liao Lu-yen, Minister of Agriculture: 'Summon Up Vigour, Energetically Win a Bountiful Harvest.' *Red Flag (Hongqi)*, No. 3–4, February 1, 1961.

Liaoning CCP Provincial Committee, Rural Work Department: 'The System and Organization of the Communes.' *People's Daily (Renmin Ribao)*, December 2, 1958, p. 3.

Liaoning Provincial CCP Committee Work Groups: Report on Conditions in Rural Community Mess Halls. (Excerpts) *Liaoning Daily (Liaoning Ribao)*, May 24, 1960. (SCMP 2289.)

Lien Lan: 'Inside the "Labour Education" Camps of Canton Municipality.' *China Weekly* (*Zuguo*), No. 505, September 17, 1962.

Lien Po-sheng: 'The Past Ten Years' Achievements in Building Highways.' *Geographical Knowledge* (*Dili Zhishi*), No. 9, September 1959.

Lin Ch'eng-ts'ai: 'Strengthen Guidance over Financial Work in Production Teams.' *Southern Daily* (*Nanfang Ribao*), June 22, 1963. (SCMP 3022.)

Lin Chai-mu and Wu Shu-ch'ing: 'Do Not Let the Equalizing of Profit and "Production Price" Choke Up the Socialist Economy.' *Kuang Ming Daily* (*Guangmin Ribao*), October 12, 1964, p. 4.

Lin Chi-k'en: 'How Should the Regularity of the Circulation of the Currency Be Assessed and Maintained?' *Economic Research* (*Jingji Yanjiu*), No. 1, January 1965.

Lin Chi-k'en: 'The Role of the Law of the Circulation of Money in the Socialist System.' *Economic Research* (*Jingji Yanjiu*), No. 2, February 1963.

Lin Chiang, Member of the Technical Staff of the Red Flag Chemical Fertilizer Factory, Yangchow: 'Technologists and "Conservatives".' *Daily Worker* (*Gongren Ribao*), August 5, 1962, p. 2.

Lin Fang: 'A Tentative Dissertation on Forms of Wages.' *People's Daily* (*Renmin Ribao*), October 28, 1961, p. 7.

Lin Hsi: 'What I Have Seen, Heard and Thought about in Places Where I Once Worked.' *People's Daily* (*Renmin Ribao*), June 16, 1962, p. 2.

Lin Yao: 'Rely on the Masses, Uphold Policy, Activate Rural Market Trade.' *People's Daily* (*Renmin Ribao*), March 14, 1961, p. 7.

Lin Yün: 'The 1958 Reform of Our Country's Financial Management System.' Parts 1 and 2. *Economic Research* (*Jingji Yanjiu*), No. 10, October 1958 and No. 11 November 1958.

Ling Han: 'The Interests of the State, of the Collective, and of the Individual, Must All Be Considered When Dividing the Income of Rural People's Communes.' *Ta Kung Daily* (*Dagong Bao*), Peking, May 31, 1961, p. 3.

Liu Chang-liang, First Secretary of Yümen Municipal CCP Committee, Secretary of CCP Committee of Yümen Petroleum Administrative Bureau: 'Extend the Functions of the Petroleum Base.' *People's Daily* (*Renmin Ribao*), November 6, 1960, p. 7.

Liu Ch'eng-jui: 'A Tentative Discussion on Comprehensive Local Economic Equilibrium.' *Kuang Ming Daily* (*Guangming Ribao*), November 16, 1964, p. 4.

Liu Chi-p'ing, Secretary of the Secretariat of the Shangtung Provincial CCP Committee: 'Extensive Use of Operations and Programming in the Service of Socialist Construction.' *Red Flag* (*Hongqi*), No. 20–21, November 1, 1960.

Liu Ch'ing: 'Always Remember to Rely Upon the Masses.' *Overseas Chinese Affairs Journal* (*Qiaowu Bao*), No. 2, April 1962.

Liu Ch'ing: 'Train Accountants and Take Inventories of Warehouses.' *Overseas Chinese Affairs Journal* (*Qiaowu Bao*), No. 3, June 1962.

Liu Chün-hsiu: 'Continue to Oppose Rightist Tendencies, Exert Efforts and Take a Big Leap Forward in Agricultural Production this Year.' *Kiangsi Daily* (*Jiangxi Ribao*), January 2, 1960. (SCMP 2226.)

Liu Chün-hsiu, Secretary, Kiangsi Provincial CCP Committee and Principal of The Communist Labour University: 'How We Founded the Communist Labour University.' *People's Daily* (*Renmin Ribao*), April 17, 1965, p. 6.

Liu Chün-hsiu, Secretary, Kiangsi Provincial CCP Committee: Report delivered to the Kiangsi Provincial Representatives' Conference of State Owned Comprehensive Reclamation Farms and the Communist Labour University on February 13, 1959. *Kiangsi Daily* (*Jiangxi Ribao*), February 28, 1959. (SCMP 2027.)

Liu Feng-lin: 'Some Opinions on Developing *Hsien* (and Municipality) Comprehensive Balances.' *Planned Economy* (*Jihua Jingji*), No. 5, May 1957.

Liu Hung-ju and Tai Ch'ien-ting: 'The Stability of the *Jenminpi* Demonstrates the Incomparable Superiority of New China's Socialist System.' *Kuang Ming Daily (Guangming Ribao)*, February 8, 1965, p. 4.

Liu Jih-hsin: 'Reflections on the Reform of Our Country's Agricultural Planning System.' *Economic Research (Jingji Yanjiu)*, No. 7, July 1961.

Liu Jui-hua: 'An Exploratory Discussion of the Problem of Decentralizing Authority for Planning the Market Supplies of Goods Subject to Unified Distribution and to Ministry Control.' *Planned Economy (Jihua Jingji)*, No. 8, August 1957.

Liu Ko-p'ing, Secretary of the Secretariat of the CCP Committee of Ninghsia Hui Autonomous Region and Chairman of the People's Council of Ninghsia Hui Autonomous Region: 'How Ninghsia Develops Light Industry and Commune Industry.' *Ta Kung Daily (Dagong Bao)*, Peking, April 3, 1959, p. 3.

Liu Shih-pai: 'A Tentative Discussion on Remnants of Private Ownership under the Socialist System.' *New Construction (Xin Jianshe)*, No. 1, January 1964.

Liu Yung-hua: 'The Chinese Communist Currency System.' *China Weekly (Zuguo)*, No. 464, December 4, 1961.

Lo Ching-fen: 'Actively Develop Specialized Production in the Machine Building Industry.' *Ta Kung Daily (Dagong Bao)*, Peking, July 10, 1964, p. 3.

Lo Keng-mo: 'The Nature of Rural People's Communes at the Present Stage.' *Daily Worker (Gongren Ribao)*, July 19, 1961, p. 3.

Lo Keng-mo: 'The Problem of the Transition from Socialism to Communism.' *New Construction (Xin Jianshe)*, No. 8, August 1959.

Lo Keng-mo: 'Problems of the Turnover Tax on Heavy Industrial Products.' *Economic Research (Jingji Yanjiu)*, No. 3, June 1956.

Lü Cheng-ts'ao, Vice Minister of Railways: Speech to First Session of the Second National People's Congress. NCNA Peking, April 25, 1959.

Lü Cheng-ts'ao, Vice-Minister of Railways: Speech to the Second Session of the Second National People's Congress. *People's Daily (Renmin Ribao)*, April 9, 1960, p. 10.

Lu Ch'i-mo and Li Ch'ung-ch'ing: 'Why the Delay in Sending Industrial Products to Rural Areas?' *Southern Daily (Nanfang Ribao)*, September 29, 1962. (SCMP 2864.)

Lü Liang-p'ing: 'With Revolutionary Energy Organize Specialization and Co-operation in Processing Industries.' *People's Daily (Renmin Ribao)*, April 12, 1965, p. 5.

Lu Mu-lan: 'An Unexpected Meeting with Premier Chou.' *China Youth (Zhongguo Qingnian)*, No. 19, October 1, 1958.

Ma Ch'ang-tsung: 'Communist China's Agricultural Machinery Stations.' *China Weekly (Zuguo)*, No. 583, March 9, 1964, p. 7.

Ma I-hang, Vice-Chairman of Shanghai Economic Planning Committee and Director of the Shanghai Bureau of Finance: Report on 1958 Final Accounts and 1959 Draft Budget of Shanghai Municipality. *Wen wui Pao (Wenhui Bao)*, June 14, 1959. (SCMP 2061.)

Ma Ming-fang, Minister of Commerce: Speech in *People's Daily (Renmin Ribao)*, June 23, 1958, quoted in *People's Handbook (Renmin Shouce) 1959*.

Ma Shang-wu, Councillor, Tsinghai Provincial People's Council: 'Views on Resettlement and State-Operated Farms in Tsinghai.' *Tsinghai Daily (Qinghai Ribao)*, September 12, 1956. (SCMP 1433.)

Ma T'ien-shui, Secretary of the Secretariat, Shanghai Municipal CCP Committee: 'Strengthen Mass Work and Fundamental Work: Promote Technical Innovation and Technical Revolution.' *Daily Worker (Gongren Ribao)*, July 14, 1965, p. 1.

Ma Wen-kuei: 'The Characteristics, Responsibilities and Methods of Planning for Socialist Industrial Enterprises.' *Economic Research (Jingji Yanjiu)*, No. 7, July 1964.

Ma Wen-kuei: 'The Nature and Tasks of State Industrial Enterprises in Our Country.' *People's Daily (Renmin Ribao)*, March 3, 1964, p. 5.

Ma Yi-hsing: Report on Shanghai's Final Accounts of 1959 and Draft Budget for 1960. *Liberation Daily (Jiefang Ribao)*, May 18, 1960. (SCMP 2291.)

Mach'eng *Hsien*, Paikao Commune Party Committee: 'The Circumstances in Which the "Two Decentralizations, Three Unifications and One Guarantee" Are Being Implemented in Paikao Commune. Mach'eng *hsien*.' *Finance (Caizheng)*, No 15, December 24, 1958.

Mao Ch'i-hua, Vice-Minister of Labour: 'The Way to Treat the Problem of Adjusting Organization of Labour.' *Chinese Worker (Zhongguo Gongren)*, No. 13, July 12, 1959.

Mao Chün-i, Kiangsu Provincial Planning Commission: 'Further Discussion on the Method of Reforming Local Planning Organs.' *Planned Economy (Jihua Jingji)*, No. 3, March 1957.

Mei Chi-lun: 'Some Questions on the Work of Credit Departments.' *Ta Kung Daily (Dagong Bao)*, Peking, August 8, 1958, p. 2.

Men Tso-min: 'Learn from the Experience of Supplying Raw Materials in 1956.' *Planned Economy (Jihua Jingji)*, No. 2, February 1957.

Meng Chao-liang: 'Basic Conditions of Labour Reform Work in the Last Nine Years.' *Political and Legal Research (Zhengfa Yanjiu)*, No. 5, October 1958.

Meng Chao-liang: 'Preliminary Achievements of Labour Education.' *Political and Legal Research (Zhengfa Yanjiu)*, No. 3, June 1959.

Meng Ch'ing-p'eng: 'Some Problems of Agricultural Mechanization.' *Economic Research (Jingji Yanjiu)*, No. 2, February 1964.

Meng Ch'u-lin: 'Some Remarks on Price Problems Relating to People's Communes.' *Financial and Economic Research (Caijing Yanjiu)*, No. 9, December 15, 1958.

Meng Shao-wen: 'Do Not Forget Party Work.' *People's Daily (Renmin Ribao)*, April 6, 1966, p. 5.

Nan Ping and So Chen: 'Some Problems in the Pricing of Producer Goods.' *Economic Research (Jingji Yanjiu)*, No. 2, April 1957.

Nankai University, Economic Research Institute, Criticises the 'Theory of Production Price'. *Economic Research (Jingji Yanjiu)*, No. 2, February 1965.

Niu Chung-huang: 'The Composite Economic Management of Large-Scale Factories and Mines.' *Red Flag (Hongqi)*, No. 9, May 1, 1959.

Niu Chung-huang: 'The Technical Transformation of the Agriculture of Our Country.' *People's Daily (Renmin Ribao)*, August 26, 1960, p. 7.

Ou-yang Ch'eng: 'On the Wave-Like Advance in the Development of the National Economy.' *Ta Kung Daily (Dagong Bao)*, Peking, May 17, 1961. (ECMP 13.)

Overseas Chinese Affairs Journal, Editorial Department: 'Replies to Questions about Overseas Chinese Farms.' *Overseas Chinese Affairs Journal (Qiaowu Bao)*, No. 9, September 1959.

Pai Hung: 'Further Comments on the Basis of Price Formation under the Socialist System.' *Economic Research (Jingji Yanjiu)*, No. 6, June 1964.

Paikao Commune CCP Committee, Mach'eng *hsien*, Hupeh: 'The Circumstances in Which Paikao Commune Implemented the "Two Transfers, Three Unifications and One Guarantee".' *Finance (Caizheng)*, No. 15, December 24, 1958.

P'an Ching-yüan: 'The Struggle between the "Two Roads" on the Free Market.' *New Construction (Xin Jianshe)*, No. 3, March 1958.

Pathan Sugerpaev: 'To Build Socialism Well in Sinkiang, We Must Depend on Support from the State and from the Han Nationality.' Speech to Fifth Session of the First National People's Congress. *People's Daily (Renmin Ribao)*, February 14, 1958, p. 10.

Peking Municipal Agricultural Mechanization Research Institute, Investigation Group: 'Some Problems of Raising the Utilization Rate of Tractors.' *Chinese Agricultural Journal (Zhongguo Nongbao)*, No. 8, August 1964.

P'eng Jung-ch'üan: 'Tabulation Charts for Plans for Capital Investment.' *Planned Economy (Jihua Jingji)*, No. 5, May 1957.

P'eng Men-yü, Vice Governor of Kiangsi Province: 'Struggle to Consolidate and Improve State Farms.' *Chinese Agricultural Journal (Zhongguo Nongbao)*, No. 1, January 1962.

Pi Ming: 'The Work of Tax Collection Must Serve to Aid Agriculture and to Consolidate the Collective Economy of the People's Communes.' *Ta Kung Daily (Dagong Bao)*, Peking, November 27, 1962, p. 2.

Pieh-szu-to-fu-szu-chi (name transliterated), Chief of the Team of Soviet Electric Power Experts: 'Some Important Problems in Development and Investment in China's Power Industry at the Present Time.' *Water Conservancy and Electric Power (Shuili yu Dianli)*, No. 4, February 20, 1959.

Pien Ching-chung: 'The Problem of Price Necessarily Being Based on Social Value.' *Economic Research (Jingji Yanjiu)*, No. 3, March 1963.

Pilman, A. M.: 'The Role of Finance in Enforcing Economy.' *Economic Research (Jingji Yanjiu)*, No. 4, October 1955.

Po I-po, Director of State Council Office of Industry and Communications: Speech to National Radio Conference on the Emulation Drive among Railway Workers. NCNA Peking, March 31, 1959.

Sha Ch'ien-li, Minister of Food: 'Brilliant Achievements on the Food Grain Front.' *People's Daily (Renmin Ribao)*, October 25, 1959, p. 6.

Sha Yao-chien: 'The Problem of Tractors in the Paddy Fields of Our Country.' *People's Daily (Renmin Ribao)*, November 4, 1964, p. 5.

Shang Chien-ming: 'Some Problems in Organizing and Developing Rural Handicraft Production.' *Ta Kung Daily (Dagong Bao)*, Peking. May 29, 1961, p. 3.

Shang Chih-lung and Ma Ching-p'o: 'Fifteen Years of Agricultural Mechanization on State Farms.' *Technology of Agricultural Machinery (Nongye Jixie Jishu)*, No. 11, November 13, 1964. (SCMM 451.)

Shang Hsiu-lien: 'Farmers with Culture Needed for Agricultural Work.' *China Youth Newspaper (Zhongguo Qingnian Bao)*, May 15, 1962. (SCMP 2753.)

Shanghai Municipal Department of Finance: 'Strengthen Inspection, Prevent Evasion.' *Finance (Caizheng)*, No. 11, June 9, 1959.

Shansi Provincial Finance Department, Investigation Group: 'Some Opinions on Strengthening the Control of Extra-Budgetary Funds.' *Finance (Caizheng)*, No. 22, November 24, 1959.

Shantung Provincial Economic Research Institute, *Agricultural Economics Unit*: 'Rely on Accumulation by Labour for Agricultural Irrigation and Other Forms of Capital Investment.' *Economic Research (Jingji Yanjiu)*, No. 9, September 1965.

Shantung Provincial Institute of Economic Research, Agricultural Economics Group and the Politics and Economics Teaching Research Office of Shantung University: 'A Survey of the Formation of a New Socialist Country by the Tungkuo Production Brigade.' *Economic Research (Jingji Yanjiu)*, No. 2, February 1966.

Shao Ch'ang, 'The Masses are Sages.' *People's Daily (Renmin Ribao)*, September 19, 1961, p. 2.

Shao Shih-ping, Secretary, Kiangsi Provincial CCP Committee: 'Push on the Construction of Great Undertakings in Mountainous Districts.' *People's Daily (Renmin Ribao)*, December 25, 1960, p. 7.

Shao Yen: 'A Preliminary Discussion of Some Problems Concerning Handicraft Co-operatives.' *Ta Kung Daily (Dagong Bao)*, Peking, September 17, 1963, p. 3.

Shao Yen: 'Wholeheartedly Encourage the Role of Handicraft Industry in Aiding Agriculture.' *People's Daily (Renmin Ribao)*, April 19, 1963, p. 5.

She Yi-san: 'A Discussion of the Change in the Allocation System for Raw Materials.' *Planned Economy (Jihua Jingji)*, No. 10, October 1958.

Shen Chen-hsin: 'Improve the Bonus System for Administrative Personnel According to the Special Features of the Job.' *Labour (Laodong)*, No. 17, November 18, 1962.

Shen Li-jen: 'The "Reservoir" Role of Socialist Commerce.' *Kuang Ming Daily (Guangming Ribao)*, September 20, 1965, p. 4.

Shen P'ing: 'Our Country's Industrial and Commercial Tax in the Past Ten Years.' *Finance (Caizheng)*, No. 18, September 24, 1959.

Shen Yün: 'A Discussion on the Nature, Special Characteristics and System of Socialist National Finance.' *Economic Research (Jingji Yanjiu)*, No. 6, June 1965.

Shih Che: 'Preliminary Examination of Certain Questions Concerning Accumulation and Expenditure in Rural People's Communes.' *Economic Research (Jingji Yanjiu)*, No. 3, March 1965.

Shih Hsiang-sheng, Secretary of the Secretariat, Honan Provincial CCP Committee: 'Some Problems Concerning the Consolidation and Development of People's Communes.' *People's Daily (Renmin Ribao)*, March 14, 1960, p. 7.

Shih Hsiu-lin: 'A Tentative Dissertation of Industrial Enterprises' Bonus System.' *People's Daily (Renmin Ribao)*, March 6, 1962, p. 5.

Shih Hsiu-lin: 'Some Problems of Enterprises' Bonus Systems.' *Ta Kung Daily (Dagong Bao)*, Peking, May 14, 1962, p. 3.

Shih K'e-chien: 'Fully Tap the Strength of Technical Staff.' *Red Flag (Hongqi)*, No. 8–9, April 25, 1962.

Shih Man: 'The Bright Youthfulness of an Ancient City—Urumchi.' *Daily Worker (Gongren Ribao)*, April 13, 1961, p. 2.

Shih P'ing: 'Some Suggestions Concerning the Use and Study of Electrical Appliances for Farming Purposes.' *Machine Building Industry (Jixie Gongye)*, No. 3, February 1963. (SCMM 362.)

Shih Wu: 'A Tentative Discussion of *Jenminpi* on the Basis of the Marxist Theory of Currency.' *Economic Research (Jingji Yanjiu)*, No. 2, April 1957.

Shih Yen-nung: 'Some Problems in Raising the Utilization Rate of Tractors.' *Ta Kung Daily (Dagong Bao)*, Peking, June 9, 1963, p. 3.

The Sixth Oil Factory: 'An Introduction to Experience in Decentralizing and Enforcing the Responsibility System from Level to Level.' *Oil Refining (Shiyou Lianzhi)*, No. 10, October 9, 1958.

State Farms and Land Reclamation, Ministry of, Bureau of People's Communes. 'The Policy of Self-Reliance and Running Enterprises with Frugality and Industry Works Well on the Nantakang Farm.' *Chinese Agriculture and Land Reclamation (Zhongguo Nongken)*, No. 2, February 1965. (SCMM 478.)

Statistical Research, Editorial Information Dept.: 'The Circumstances of the 1957 Price Changes and Their Influence on the Standard of Living.' *Statistical Research (Tongji Yanjiu)*, No. 4, April 1958.

Statistical Research, Editorial Information Dept.: 'The Basic Circumstances of Our Country's Coal Industry.' *Statistical Research (Tongji Yanjiu)*, No. 4, April 1958.

Statistical Research, Editorial Information Dept.: 'The Great Leap Forward in Basic Construction.' *Statistical Research (Tongji Yanjiu)*, No. 9, September 1958.

Statistical Research Information Department: 'Changes in the "Price Scissors" Between Industrial and Agricultural Commodities Over All the Country Since Liberation.' *Statistical Work (Tongji Gongzuo)*, No. 17, September 14, 1957.

Statistical Work Bulletin Information Room: 'The National Figures, Composition and Distribution of the Employed Labour Force in 1955.' *New China Fortnightly (Xinhua Banyuekan)*, No. 100, January 25, 1957.

Su Tsung-sung, Irrigation Research Institute of the Chinese Academy of Agricultural Science: 'Adapt to Local Conditions the Measures to Curb Salinization and Alkalization in Irrigated Areas.' *People's Daily (Renmin Ribao)*, May 25, 1962, p. 2.

Suihsi *Hsien* CCP Committee, Correspondence Section: 'Poor and Lower Middle Peasants Must Be the Masters of the House.' *Southern Daily (Nanfang Ribao)*, January 25, 1963. (SCMP 2959.)

Sun Chih-yuan, Vice-Chairman, National Economic Commission: 'The Great Historical Significance of Industry of the People's Communes.' *People's Daily (Renmin Ribao)*, October 26, 1959, p. 7.

Sun Hui-ch'ing: 'Lecture No. 13: Charts of Supply Plans of Raw Materials and Technical Equipment.' *Planned Economy (Jihua Jingji)*, No. 1, January 1958.

Sun Shang-ch'ing: 'Current Problems Concerning the Nature and Destiny of Piece-Work Wages in Our Country.' *Economic Research (Jingji Yanjiu)*, No. 4, April 1959.

Sun Ting: 'The Need to Strengthen and Promote Economic Accounting by Teams.' *Coal Industry (Meitan Gongye)*, No. 22, November 19, 1957.

Sun Wei-tsu: 'The Principles for Compiling Grain Circulation Plans.' *Planned Economy (Jihua Jingji)*, No. 2, February 1958.

Sun Yeh-fang: 'A Discussion on Value'. *Economic Research (Jingji Yanjiu)*, No. 9, September 1959.

Sun Yeh-fang: 'A Talk on Gross Value of Output.' *Statistical Work (Tongji Gongzuo)*, No. 13, July 14, 1957.

Sung Chi-shan: 'A Brief Discussion of the Nature and Function of Industrial Contracts in Our Country.' *Economic Research (Jingji Yanjiu)*, No. 2, February 1965.

Sung Chih-ho: 'On Development of a Many-Sided Economy.' *Ta Kung Daily (Dagong Bao)*, Peking, July 18, 1959, p. 1.

Sung Chun, Deputy Director, United Front Work Dept., CCP Committee of Sinkiang Uighur Autonomous Region: 'Resolutely Change Our Political Stand and Take the Road of Socialism under Party Leadership.' *Sinkiang Daily (Xinjiang Ribao)*, March 11, 1959. (SCMP 1998.)

Sung Hsien-min, Deputy Director, Honan Department of Water Conservancy: 'Some Views on Controlling the Upper Reaches of the Huai River.' *Chinese Water Conservancy (Zhongguo Shuili)*, No. 3, March 14, 1958. (SCMM 129.)

Sung Hsin-chung: 'The System of Enterprises' Retainable Percentage of Profits.' *Ta Kung Daily (Dagong Bao)*, Peking, May 12, 1961. p. 3.

Sung P'ing: 'The Problems of Employment.' *Labour (Laodong)*, No. 21, October 4, 1957.

Sung T'ao: 'The Problem of Accumulation and Investment by Production Teams.' *New Construction (Xin Jianshe)*, No. 11–12, December 1965.

Sung Yi-min: 'Strengthen Leadership Over the Free Market.' *Planned Economy (Jihua Jingji)*, No. 12, December 1956.

Sung Yi-p'ing: 'Street Industry—A New Force Not to Be Neglected.' *People's Daily (Renmin Ribao)*, April 26, 1959, p. 9.

Szechuan Finance and Economics Institute, Industrial Economics Department, Class 56, Production Study Group at the Chengtu Measuring Instruments and Cutting Tools Factory: 'Small Group Administration in Industrial Enterprises Is a Necessary Product of the Political and Economic Development of Our Country'. *Economic Research (Jingji Yanjiu)*, No. 6, June 1960.

Tai Ho-cho: 'Communist China's Withdrawal of *Jenminpi*.' *China Monthly (Zuguo)*, No. 3, June 1964.

Tai Yüan-ch'en: 'A Criticism of "Production Price" and the Theory of Equalizing Profit on Capital.' *Economic Research (Jingji Yanjiu)*, No. 9, September 1964.

T'an Chen-lin: 'A Preliminary Study of the Income and Standard of Living of the Peasants of Our Country.' *People's Daily (Renmin Ribao)*, May 5, 1957, p. 3.

Tan Ku: 'Some Problems in the Determination of the Prices of Light Industrial Commodities.' *Economic Research (Jingji Yanjiu)*, No. 9, September 1963.

T'ao Chu, First Secretary of Kwangtung Provincial CCP Committee: 'The People's Communes are Progressing.' *Red Flag (Hongqi)*, No. 4, February 26, 1964.

T'ao Chu, First Secretary of Kwangtung Provincial CCP Committee: 'Report on a Survey of Humen Commune', *People's Daily (Renmin Ribao)*, February 25, 1959, p. 7.

T'ao Chu, First Secretary of Kwangtung Provincial CCP Committee: 'Some Problems of Leadership Over Factory and Mining Enterprises.' *Red Flag (Hongqi)*, No. 12, June 16, 1960.

T'ao Jan, Deputy Director, State Statistical Bureau: 'Arrange Well This Year's Statistical Work in the Field of Capital Construction.' *Planning and Statistics (Jihua yu Tongji)*, No. 5, March 8, 1959. (ECMM 173.)

T'ao Lu-chia: 'Let the Tachai Spirit Blossom and Bear Fruit Everywhere.' *Red Flag (Hongqi)*, No. 11, October 1, 1965.

Ta'o Sheng-yü: 'A Study of Enterprise Bonus Funds for State Enterprises.' *Finance (Caizheng)*, No. 3, December 5, 1956.

T'ao Ting-lai: 'The Direction and Order of Our Country's Agricultural Mechanization Development.' *Red Flag (Hongqi)*, No. 7–8, April 20, 1964.

T'ao Yu-liang: 'A Good Way for Departments of Building Construction to Help Agricultural Production.' *Economic Research (Jingji Yanjiu)*, No. 8, August 1965.

Te San: 'On Afforestation in Our Country.' *Ta Kung Daily (Dagong Bao)*, Peking, January 27, 1964, p. 3.

Teng Chia-jung: 'The Relationship Between the Work of Economic Ministries and the Issue of People's Currency.' *People's Daily (Renmin Ribao)*, July 5, 1964, p. 5.

Teng Chieh, Chairman of All-China Federation of Handicraft Co-operatives: 'Be Content and Skilful in the Production of Small Things.' *Daily Worker (Gongren Ribao)*, September 20, 1961, p. 1.

Teng Chieh: 'The Great Victory of the Socialist Transformation of China's Handicraft Industry.' *People's Daily (Renmin Ribao)*, September 17, 1959, p. 4.

Teng Cho-jung and Feng Wu-ch'u: 'Investigation on Tractors for Wet Rice Areas in Our Country.' *People's Daily (Renmin Ribao)*, November 4, 1964, p. 5.

Teng Tzu-hui: 'The Historical Mission of Credit Co-operatives in Our Country at the Present Stage.' *Red Flag (Hongqi)*, No. 23, December 12, 1963.

Teng Tzu-hui, Director of the Rural Work Department of the CCP Central Committee: Speech at Third Plenum of CCP Central Committee. *People's Daily (Renmin Ribao)*, November 14, 1957, p. 3.

Teng Ying-ch'ao: 'Greetings to University Students Who Are to Graduate This Year.' *China Youth Newspaper (Zhongguo Qingnian Bao)*, May 30, 1963. (SCMP 3000.)

Tientsin Municipal Finance Bureau: 'Conscientiously Implement the System of Checking Revenue Collection.' *Finance (Caizheng)*, No. 11, June 7, 1961.

Ting Lü-ch'u: 'An Exploratory Discussion of the Rational Management of State Farms.' *Economic Research (Jingji Yanjiu)*, No. 12, December 1963.

Ting Yüeh: 'The Disintegration of Commune Cadres under Restrictions.' *Mainland Today (Jinri Dalu)*, No. 180, March 25, 1963.

Ts'ai Chien-hua: 'Controverting the "Production Price" Theory of Comrade Yang Chien-pai and Others.' *Economic Research (Jingji Yanjiu)*, No. 1, January 1965.

Ts'ai Shih, 'The Benefits to Be Gained by Production Teams from Contracting Work for a Short Period, a Season or a Whole Year.' *Daily Worker (Gongren Ribao)*, December 15, 1961, p. 3.

Ts'ai Yüan-yüan and Teng Tse-hui: 'An Exploratory Discussion on Methods of Calculating Labour Remuneration in People's Communes—The System of Recording Work by Piece-Rate.' *Kuang Ming Daily (Guangming Ribao)*, May 20, 1963, p. 4.

Ts'ao Chü-ju, Director General of the People's Bank: 'Banking in the Past Ten Years.' *Ta Kung Daily (Dagong Bao)*, Peking, October 12, 1959, p. 3.

Tsao Hai-chung: 'Bonuses to Technical Administrative Staff for Fulfilling Tasks Should Be Abolished.' *Labour (Laodong)*, No. 11, June 3, 1957.

Ts'ao Shao-ch'iung: 'Deliveries of Farm Produce—Our Glorious Duty as Commune Members.' *People's Daily (Renmin Ribao)*, January 5, 1962, p. 1.

Tseng Chih: 'The Correct Disposition of Certain Relationships in Financial Work.' *Finance (Caizheng)*, No. 10, May 24, 1959.

Tseng Chih, Vice Minister of Finance: 'Exercise Strict, Practical and Proper Control over Appropriations for Capital Construction, Increase the Return on Investments.' Speech to Branch Managers of the Construction Bank. *Finance (Caizheng)*, No. 3, February 7, 1963. (SCMM 360.)

Tseng Ch'uan-liu, Vice Minister of Commerce: 'Supply the Countryside Efficiently.' *New China Fortnightly (Xinhua Banyuekan)*, No. 83, May 6, 1956.

Tseng Hsi-sheng: 'The Two Roads in Water Control Problems.' *Red Flag (Hongqi)*, No. 2, June 16, 1958.

Tsitsihar Railway Bureau, Poketu Mechanical Section Trade Union: 'Some Lessons Learned on the Efficient Operation of Mutual Savings Association.' *Daily Worker (Gongren Ribao)*, December 9, 1964, p. 2.

Tso Chi: 'How Should the Problem of Raw Materials be Solved?' *Daily Worker (Gongren Ribao)*, September 8, 1961, p. 3.

Tso Chi: 'Production of Small Commodities Should Be the Main Task of Urban Commune Industry.' *Daily Worker (Gongren Ribao)*, September 5, 1961, p. 3.

Tso Chi: 'Strengthen Planning, Promote Initiative.' *Daily Worker (Gongren Ribao)*, September 6, 1961, p. 3.

Tso Ch'un-t'ai: 'The Institution and Development of the Economic Accounting System in Our Country.' Parts 1 and 2. *Ta Kung Daily (Dagong Bao)*, Peking, June 1 and 4, 1962, p. 3.

Tso Hu: 'Several Problems of Agricultural Electrification.' *Economic Research (Jingji Yanjiu)*, No. 3, March 1963.

Tsou Ming, Deputy Director, General Revenue Bureau, Ministry of Finance: 'Energetically Organize Financial Revenues, Improve Accumulation of Funds for the State.' *Ta Kung Daily (Dagong Bao)*, Peking, August 8, 1963, p. 2.

Tsu Chih-ch'u: 'Base the Lowest Level Supply and Marketing Co-operatives on Market Towns.' *Ta Kung Daily (Dagong Bao)*, Peking, October 25, 1963, p. 3.

Ts'ui Chi: 'Analysis of Accounting in the Plan for Drawing Up Ex-Factory Prices for Producer Goods.' *Planned Economy (Jingji Yanjiu)*, No. 3, March 1957.

T'u Han-kuo, Finance and Accounting Section, Bureau of Commerce, Huangshih Municipality, Hupeh Province: 'How Should It Be Judged if "Politics Is In Command" of an Enterprise?' *Ta Kung Daily (Dagong Bao)*, Peking, June 29, 1965, p. 2.

Tu Hung: 'Energetically Restore Traditional Channels of Commodity Circulation.' *Ta Kung Daily (Dagong Bao)*, Peking, July 3, 1962, p. 2.

Tu Yen-ch'ing, Chairman of the National Committee of the China Light Industry Trade Union: 'Struggle to Produce More and Better Light Industry Products.' *Daily Worker (Gongren Ribao)*, September 13, 1959. (CB 601.)

Tuan Li-chün: 'Waste Land and Pasture is Transformed into Riches, Ponds and Rivers are the Source of Funds.' *Finance (Caizheng)*, No. 9, September 1958.

Tuan Yün: 'The Problem of Working Capital Credit Funds and Their Management.' *Red Flag (Hongqi)*, No. 11, June 1, 1959.

Tuan Yün: 'Several Problems in Our Country's Socialist Banking.' *Red Flag (Hongqi)*, No. 1, January 4, 1964.

T'ung Wan: 'The Problem of Fixed Point Supply of Third Category Raw Materials for Enterprises of Light Industry.' *Economic Research (Jingji Yanjiu)*, No. 2, February 1966.

Tung Yang: 'Establish a Job Responsibility System and Strengthen the Management of Industrial Enterprises.' *Economic Research (Jingji Yanjiu)*, No. 4, April 1965.

Wan Hsing: 'The Problem of Wages on Overseas Chinese State Farms.' *Overseas Chinese Affairs Journal (Qiaowu Bao)*, No. 3, June 1962.

Wang Chen, Minister of State Farms and Land Reclamation: 'Exert Revolutionary Zeal, Make State Farms Take a Great Leap Forward.' *Daily Worker (Gongren Ribao)*, February 1, 1958. Quoted from *New China Fortnightly (Xinhua Banyuekan)*, No. 127, March 10, 1958.

Wang Chen, Minister of State Farms and Land Reclamation: 'Strengthen the Building Up of State Farms.' *Red Flag (Hongqi)*, No. 7, April 1, 1961.

Wang Chi-lung, Director of Political Department, Sinkiang Production and Construction Army Corps: 'Strive to Strengthen Further the Solidarity of All Nationalities in Building a New Sinkiang Together.' *Nationalities Unity (Minzu Tuanjie)*, No. 12, December 6, 1961. (SCMM 301.)

Wang Chi-yi: 'Given Overall Consideration When Planning Dockyards.' *People's Daily (Renmin Ribao)*, March 24, 1957, p. 11.

Wang Chieh: 'Views on Differential Ground Rent.' *Kuang Ming Daily (Guangming Ribao)*, September 18, 1961, p. 4.

Wang Ch'ing and Kung Ch'eng-hua: 'Economic Rationality Is the Best Policy.' *People's Daily (Renmin Ribao)*, March 10, 1963, p. 2.

Wang Cho: 'A Discussion of Some Problems of Financial Management.' *Ta Kung Daily (Dagong Bao)*, Peking, April 26, 1961, p. 3.

Wang Cho: 'Financial and Currency Work in Relation to the Policy of Taking Agriculture as the Foundation.' *People's Daily (Renmin Ribao)*, April 6, 1962, p. 5.

Wang Cho: 'My Views on the Planned and Proportionate Development of the National Economy.' *Economic Research (Jingji Yanjiu)*, No. 6, June 1959.

Wang Ch'ung-lun, Deputy Chief and Engineer, Tool Shop, North Machine Repair Plant, Anshan Iron and Steel Corporation: 'Be Friendly Towards Engineers and Technologists.' *Daily Worker (Gongren Ribao)*, June 19, 1962, p. 2.

Wang Hai-p'o: 'Questions Concerning the Establishment of People's Communes in Urban Streets.' *Teaching and Research (Jiaoxue yu Yanjiu)*, No. 11, November 1958. (ECMM 163).

Wang Ho-feng, Secretary, Heilungkiang Provincial CCP Committee: 'Strengthen and Develop the Two Participations, One Reform and Three Co-ordinations. Improve All Aspects of Enterprise Management.' *Red Flag (Hongqi)*, No. 15, August 1, 1960.

Wang Hsiang-ch'un, Chiang Hsing-wei and Ch'en K'un-hsiu: 'Problems of Controlling Plans for Agricultural Production in Our Country.' *Economic Research (Jingji Yanjiu)*, No. 3, March 1965.

Wang Hsiang-t'ing, Nanch'ang Diesel Engine Plant: 'The Right Motive for Joining the Party Can only Be the Service of Communism.' *Daily Worker (Gongren Ribao)*, April 28, 1966, p. 4.

Wang Hsing-k'ung: 'Communist China's State Farms.' *Mainland Today (Jinri Dalu)*, July 25, 1963.

Wang Hsü: 'Reduce the Number of Middlemen and Lower the Cost of Timber'—a reader's letter. *People's Daily (Renmin Ribao)*, May 17, 1962, p. 2.

Wang Hu-sheng: 'Problems in the Classification of Heavy and Light Industry.' *Economic Research (Jingji Yanjiu)*, No. 4, April 1963.

Wang Hua-yün: 'The Glorious Ideal of Diverting Southern Waters Northwards.' *Red Flag (Hongqi)*, No. 17, September 1, 1959.

Wang Hung-ting: 'The Nature and Functions of Specialized Industrial Companies.' *New Construction (Xin Jianshe)*, No. 2, February 1957.

Wang Ju-ming, Deputy Director of Kwangtung Provincial Dept. of Finance: 'Financial Departments Must Provide Energetic Aid to Agriculture.' *Southern Daily (Nanfang Ribao)*, November 13, 1962. (SCMP 2878.)

Wang K'ai, Chief Engineer, Kuanghua Timber Plant: 'Some Preliminary Considerations.' *Daily Worker (Gongren Ribao)*, June 19, 1962, p. 2.

Wang K'e: 'A Tentative Discussion of Supply and Marketing Departments of Agricultural Producer Co-operatives.' *Ta Kung Daily (Dagong Bao)*, Peking, April 28, 1958, p. 2.

Wang K'e-hua and Wang P'ei-chen: 'What *Jenminpi* Really Represents.' *Economic Research (Jingji Yanjiu)*, No. 2, February 1966.

Wang Kuang-wei: 'Opinions on the Arrangement of Agricultural Labour.' *Planned Economy (Jihua Jingji)*, No. 8, August 1957.

Wang Kuei-ch'en: 'Carrying Out Seriously the Principle Underlying Exchange of Equal Values.' *China Youth Newspaper (Zhongguo Qingnian Bao)*, August 30, 1961. (SCMP 2586.)

Wang Kuei-wu: 'An Important Change in the Method of Drawing Up Annual Plans.' *Planned Economy (Jihua Jingji)*, No. 9, September 1958.

Wang Lien, Secretary of Party Branch of Tungshihtzukou Brigade, Shihtzukou Commune, Chungli *hsien*, Hopei: 'A Party Branch Must Conscientiously Control and Educate Party Members.' *People's Daily (Renmin Ribao)*, April 14, 1966, p. 6.

Wang Luan-sheng, Tu Chia-hsing and Hsiang Shao-t'ang: 'Give a Lead to Production by Participation.' *Red Flag (Hongqi)*, No. 13–14. July 10, 1963.

Wang Shao-fei: 'Collectivization as Seen from the Viewpoint of a *Hsiang* Federation of Co-operatives.' *Economic Research (Jingji Yanjiu)*, No. 8, August 1958.

Wang Shao-min: 'Strengthen the Control of Tax Collection at Rural Markets.' *Ta Kung Daily (Dagong Bao)*, Peking, May 15, 1962, p. 2.

Wang Shih-hsin: 'Open the Source and Economize the Flow: Pay Wages Monthly in Advance.' *People's Daily (Renmin Ribao)*, August 8, 1960, p. 3.

Wang Shou-li: 'Certain Problems in Demarcating Economic Regions within Provinces.' *Economic Research (Jingji Yanjiu)*, No. 3, March 1960.

Wang Shou-tao, Director of the Sixth Office of State Council: 'Develop Transport, Postal and Telecommunication Undertaking.' Speech to Third Session of First NPC. *New China Fortnightly (Xinhua Banyuekan)*, No. 88, July 21, 1956.

Wang Shou-tao, Minister of Communications: 'Continuously Develop Communitions and Transport Undertakings: Improve Service to Production and Livelihood.' *People's Daily (Renmin Ribao)*, May 26, 1961, p. 7.

Wang Shou-tao, Minister of Communications: 'Raise High the Banner of the General Line: Speed Up the Development of Transport Undertakings.' *People's Daily (Renmin Ribao)*, September 23, 1959, p. 9.

Wang Ssu-hua: 'Bring Out to the Fullest Extent the Function of Statistical Work in Socialist Construction.' *Red Flag (Hongqi)*, No. 18, September 16, 1962.

Wang Te-ho: 'Experience Gained by Being Secretary of a Party Branch.' *People's Daily (Renmin Ribao)*, July 1, 1960, p. 4.

Wang Ti: 'Stop Up Holes through Which Foreign Exchange Is Leaking Out to Waste.' *Planned Economy (Jihua Jingji)*, No. 3, March 1958.

Wang To, Secretary of CCP Committee of Inner Mongolia: 'Deepen the Socialist Education Movement Centred on Waging a Struggle between Two Roads and on the Implementation of the General Line.' *Inner Mongolia Daily (Neimenggu Ribao)*, November 15, 1959. (SCMP 2159.)

Wang Tsai-t'ien, Vice-Chairman, Inner Mongolia Autonomous Region: 'Inner Mongolia Makes Rapid Advance in Agriculture and Animal Husbandry over the Past Ten Years.' *Chinese Agricultural Journal (Zhongguo Nongbao)*, No. 20, October 23, 1959. (SCMM 192.)

Wang Tsu-k'ang: 'Certain Problems of Fixed Norm Management in Industrial Enterprises.' *Ta Kung Daily (Dagong Bao)*, Peking, October 4, 1963, p. 3.

Wang Tung-hsing: 'The Struggle for the Construction of Strong and Modernized Socialist State-Owned Bases for the Production of Commodities.' *Kiangsi Daily (Jiangxi Ribao)*, December 15, 1959. (SCMP 2217.)

Wang Wen: 'A Continuous Supply of Electricity for the Villages.' *Daily Worker (Gongren Ribao)*, September 24, 1963, p. 2.

Wang Wen-ting and P'eng Wei-ts'ai: 'Reform of the Tax System Must Be Done in Two Steps.' *Ta Kung Daily (Dagong Bao)*, Peking. August 11, 1957, p. 3.

Wang Yi-ming and Liu Hua-chen: 'The Nature and Tasks of Our Country's State Agricultural Machinery Stations.' *Kuang Ming Daily (Guangming Ribao)*, November 30, 1964, p. 6.

Wang Yu-chang, T'ieh Yün, Hsieh Feng, Lo Hsuan and Yeh Chieh-yün: 'Make Careful Arrangements for the Livelihood of Employees.' *People's Daily (Renmin Ribao)*, May 19, 1961, p. 2.

Wang Yuan-hsing and Yu Yang-tsu: 'Overseas Chinese Farms in the Great Leap Forward'—a joint statement at the National People's Congress, *People's Daily (Renmin Ribao)*, May 3, 1959, p. 11.

Wang Yung-hsing, Secretary to the General Party Branch, Hsiatingchia Production Brigade, Talüchia Commune, Huanghsien, Shantung. 'We Cannot Sit and Wait for Socialist Undertakings to Develop.' *Red Flag (Hongqi)*, No. 1, January 1, 1966.

Weifang Diesel Engine Factory: 'The Circumstances and Problems of Instituting a Staff Bonus System in Our Factory.' *Labour (Laodong)*, No. 5, March 3, 1957.

Wei Li: 'The Supplementary Wage System Must Be Radically Reformed.' *Planned Economy (Jihua Jingji)*, No. 5, May 1958.

Wei Yi: 'A Revolution in Methods of Planning.' *Study (Xuexi)*, No. 8, April 18, 1958.

Wen Li: 'The Superiority of Large-Sized Urban People's Communes.' *Yangtze Daily (Changjian Ribao)*, May 6, 1960. (SCMP 2276.)

Wen Ping-yuan: 'A Discussion on the Trial Reform of the Industrial and Commercial Tax System.' *Finance (Caizheng)*, No. 5, May 1958.

Weng Chan: 'The Problem of Developing Fixed Co-operation and Fixed Point Supply in Local Industry.' *Economic Research (Jingji Yanjiu)*, No. 4, April 1965.

Wu Chih-pu: 'The Strengthening and Development of the People's Communes.' *Red Flag (Hongqi)*, No. 1, January 1, 1960.

Wu Ch'ing-yu: 'Is the Socialist State Bank an Organ or an Enterprise?' *Study (Xuexi)*, No. 2, January 18, 1957.

Wu Hsing-feng, Director, Political Dept., Ministry of Petroleum: 'Deal Satisfactorily with the Problem of the Orientation of Socialist Enterprises.' *People's Daily (Renmin Ribao)*, May 12, 1964, p. 5.

Wu Jen-k'uei, Director, Kiangsi Provincial Dept. of Commerce: 'Carry Out Policy, Strengthen Leadership and Enliven Trade at Rural Markets.' *Ta Kung Daily (Dagong Bao)*, Peking, February 20, 1961. (SCMP 2460.)

Wu Po, Vice Minister of Finance: 'An Explanation of the Draft Regulations of the People's Republic of China on the Consolidated Industrial and Commercial Tax.' *People's Taxation (Renmin Shuiwu)*, No. 18, September 19, 1958.

Wu Wen-pin: 'Irrational Regulations and System Must Be Reformed.' *Philosophical Research (Zhexue Yanjiu)*, No. 4, August 1958.

Wu Ying-t'ang: 'The Production and Construction Corps of the PLA in Sinkiang.' NCNA Urumchi, September 10, 1959.

Wuan *hsien* Tractor Station, Hopei: 'The Experience of the Wuan Tractor Station in Practising Cost Accounting at Three Levels.' *Chinese Agricultural Journal (Zhongguo Nongbao)*, No. 2, February 1964.

Wuhsiang *Hsien* CCP Committee, the Central Correspondence Unit, the Work Unit of the Department of Commerce of Shansi Province and the Correspondence Unit of the Bureau of Commerce of Wuhsiang *Hsien*: 'Implement the Policies, Strengthen the Leadership, Make Trade through Rural Markets Brisk Without Becoming Chaotic.' *Ta Kung Daily (Dagong Bao)*, Peking, April 17, 1961. (SCMP 2499.)

Yang Ch'eng-min, Vice-Mayor of Tientsin: 'Organize the Machine-Building Industry on the Basis of "Small but Specialized" and "Medium-sized but Specialized" Units.' *People's Daily (Renmin Ribao)*, March 13, 1965, p. 5.

Yang Chien-pai: 'An Exploratory Discussion of Some Problems of Comprehensive Equilibrium.' *People's Daily (Renmin Ribao)*, July 25, 1961, p. 7.

Yang Chien-pai: 'The Problem of National Economic Equilibrium and "Production Price".' *Economic Research (Jingji Yanjiu)*, No. 12, December 1963.

Yang Chien-pai: 'The Search for Balance in the Midst of High Speed Development.' *People's Daily (Renmin Ribao)*, November 18, 1959, p. 7.

Yang Ch'ing: 'The New Circumstances and Duties of Financial Work after the Formation of the People's Communes.' *Finance (Caizheng)*, No. 10, October 1958.

Yang Ch'ing-wen: 'Two Problems of Industrial Location.' *Planned Economy (Jihua Jingji)* No. 8, August 1957.

Yang Chün-sheng and Sa Pen-hsin: 'New Achievements of China's Shipbuilding Industry.' Speech to 1st Session of 2nd National People's Congress. *People's Daily (Renmin Ribao)*, May 5, 1959, p. 9.

Yang Fang-hsün: 'Determine Price According to Quality—Higher Price for Higher Quality.' *Ta Kung Daily (Dagong Bao)*, Peking, July 16, 1962, p. 3.

Yang Hu-ch'en, Director, Resettlement Bureau, Ministry of State Farms and Land Reclamation: 'The Great Victory in Mobilizing Youth to Participate in Borderland Nationalities Areas.' *Nationalities Unity (Minzu Tuanjie)*, No. 1 January 6, 1960. (ECMM 201.)

Yang Jun-jui and Li Hsün: 'A Tentative Discussion of Economic Accounting in Industrial Enterprises.' *People's Daily (Renmin Ribao)*, July 19, 1962, p. 5.

Yang Pang-chieh: 'Strictly Carry Out the Procedures of Capital Construction Laid Down by the State.' *Building Construction (Jianju)*, No. 5, 1963. (SCMM 367.)

Yang Pang-ch'un: 'Enterprises' Bonus Fund Should Be Based on the Numbers of Productive Workers.' *Finance (Caizheng)*, No. 1, June 1957.

Yang P'ei-hsin: 'Brief Discussion of the Stability of the *Jenminpi*.' *Economic Research (Jingji Yanjiu)*, No. 1, January 1965.

Yang P'ei-hsin: 'The Problem of Financing the Process of Agricultural Mechanization in Our Country.' *Economic Research (Jingi Yanjiu)*, No. 6, June 1963.

Yang Shang-k'uei, First Secretary, Kiangsi Provincial CCP Committee: 'Care for and Educate New Workers, Strengthen and Raise the Ranks of Workers.' *Daily Worker (Gongren Ribao)*, July 14, 1959. (SCMP 2069.)

Yang Shao-ch'iao: 'Financial Work Must Serve the Party's General Line.' *Finance (Caizheng)*, No. 10, October 1958.

Yang Yi-ch'en, Secretary, Heilungkiang Provincial CCP Committee: 'On Establishing a Network of Commodity Production Bases.' *People's Daily (Renmin Ribao)*, February 12, 1960, p. 7.

Yang Ying-chieh: 'Comprehensive Equilibrium.' *Economic Research (Jingji Yanjiu)*, No. 11, November 1962.

Yang Ying-chieh, Vice-Chairman, State Planning Commission: 'On Unified Planning and Decentralized Control.' *Planned Economy (Jihua Jingji)*, No. 11, November 1958.

Yang Ying-chieh: 'Problems of Ratios, Key Points and Speed in the National Economy.' *Economic Research (Jingji Yanjiu)*, No. 5, May 1962.

Yao Fang-yu: 'My Views on the Nature of Private Plots.' *Ta Kung Daily (Dagong Bao)*, Peking, June 12, 1961, p. 3.

Yao Yi-lin, Minister of Commerce: 'Some Hopes for Commercial Work in 1964.' *People's Handbook (Renmin Shouce) 1964*.

Yeh Chi-chuang, Minister of Foreign Trade: 'A Talk on Foreign Trade.' *People's Handbook (Renmin Shouce) 1958*.

Yeh Chi-chuang, Minister of Foreign Trade: 'China's Foreign Trade during the Past Decade.' China News Service, Canton, September 2, 1959.

Yeh Chin-t'ang: 'Concentrate Financial Authority and Strengthen Control.' *Ta Kung Daily (Dagong Bao)*, Peking, December 1, 1961, p. 3.

Yeh Fang-t'ien: 'On Developing the Role of Industrial Crops Production.' *Ta Kung Daily (Dagong Bao)*, Peking, June 23, 1961, p. 3.

Yeh Hsi-wen: 'In Organizing Production, Why Should the Various Levels of Rural People's Communes Be Guided by State Plans and Consider Local Conditions?' *Daily Worker (Gongren Ribao)*, December 12, 1961, p. 3.

Yeh Ta-hsin and Liu Ch'ao-yeh: 'Do Not Believe Too Much in Figures of Goods in Stock.' *Southern Daily (Nanfang Ribao)*, March 2, 1963. (SCMP 2946).

Yen Yung-ch'ien: 'A Tentative Discussion on Differential Net Land Rent and Its Distribution.' *Kuang Ming Daily (Guangming Ribao)*, September 18, 1961, p. 4.

Yi Hsin: 'Give Serious Consideration to the Management of Water Conservancy Work.' *Ta Kung Daily (Dagong Bao)*, Peking, January 8, 1965, p. 3.

Yi T'ung: 'Warehouse Trade.' *Ta Kung Daily (Dagong Bao)*, Peking, January 24, 1962, p. 3.

Yin Ch'eng-chang: 'Be Efficient in Budgetary Administration and Go All Out to Fulfil the National Budget for 1959.' *Finance (Caizheng)*, No. 9, May 9, 1959.

Yü Chieh, Vice Minister of Commerce: 'Raise the Efficiency of Commercial Work among Minority Nationalities.' *Nationalities Unity (Minzu Tuanjie)*, No. 2–3, February–March, 1963.

Yü Jui-hsiang: 'Many Advantages from Implementing the Fixed Management System for Funds for Agricultural Loans.' *Kuang Ming Daily (Guangming Ribao)*, June 21, 1965, p. 4.

Yü Lin: 'Price Stability and Our Monetary System.' *Economic Research (Jingji Yanjiu)*, No. 5, May 1965.

Yü Lin: 'The Correct Manner of Determining Prices of Different Kinds of Products.' *Economic Research (Jingji Yanjiu)*, No. 5, May 1964.

Yü Shu-fang: 'Enterprises' Political and Mass Organization Cadres Who Are Not Engaged in Production Should Not Receive Bonuses.' *Labour (Laodong)*, No. 11, June 3, 1957.

Yü T'ung-li: 'A Short Cut to the Reduction of the Operating Costs of Tractor Stations.' *Ta Kung Daily (Dagong Bao)*, Peking, November 6, 1964, p. 3.

Yuan Fang: 'The Relationship between Increase in Labour Productivity and in Wages in Our Country.' *New Construction (Xin Jianshe)*, No. 12, December 1956.

Yueh Wei: 'A Discussion of Socio-Economic Research Surveys.' *Economic Research (Jingji Yanjiu)*, No. 6, June 1965.

Yunghsiu *Hsien* CCP Committee, Rural Work Dept.: 'Spread the Work of Distribution of Income Over the Whole Year.' *Agricultural and Forestry Work Bulletin (Nonglin Gongzuo Tongxun)*, No. 6, June 1964. (SCMM 430.)

IV. ARTICLES—ENGLISH

Alexandrov, Eugene A.: 'Red China Steps Up Its Geological Service.' *Mining Engineering*, March 1960.

Ashdown, J.: 'China's Proletarian Problems.' *Far Eastern Economic Review*, March 12, 1965.

Baker, J. E.: 'Transportation in China.' *Annals of the American Academy of Political and Social Science*, Vol. 152, November 1930.

Chang Chi, Vice-Chairman of Hupeh Provincial Economic Commission: 'Hupeh Begins to Mechanize Its Farming.' *China Reconstructs*, December 1964.

Chang Chuan-wen: 'How Higher Production Targets Are Fulfilled.' *China Reconstructs*, August 1965.

Chang Yen: 'The Commune Gave Us Wings: Report from Huatung Commune.' —Parts 1 and 2. *China Reconstructs*, June and July 1964.

Chen Hsüeh-nung: 'Full Market Counters in Peking.' *Peking Review*, January 15, 1965.

Chen Ti-pao: 'Supervision and Control of Imports and Exports by the Chinese Customs Administration.' *Foreign Trade of the People's Republic of China*, No. 2, June 1963.

Chi, Wen-shun: 'Water Conservancy in Communist China.' *China Quarterly*, No. 23, July–September 1965.

Chi Yu-ching: 'Rebuilding the Grand Canal.' *China Reconstructs*, July 1963.

Chinese Communist Party Central Committee: 'Letter of February 29, 1964, to the Central Committee of the CPSU.' *Peking Review*, May 8, 1964.

Chou En-lai: Report on the Work of the Government at the First Session of the Third National People's Congress. *Peking Review*, January 1, 1965.

Chou, S. H.: 'Prices in Communist China" *Journal of Asian Studies*, Vol. XXV, No. 4, August 1966.

Chu Chi-lin: 'The Great Victory in Steel.' *Peking Review*, March 24, 1961.

Close, A.: 'Bombs or Trousers?' *Far Eastern Economic Review*, October 29, 1964.

Close, A.: 'Correcting the Cadres.' *Far Eastern Economic Review*, February 18, 1965.

Cohen, J. A.: 'The Criminal Process in the People's Republic of China: An Introduction.' *Harvard Law Review*, Vol. 79, No. 3, January 1966.

Crossman, R. H. S.: 'Chinese Notebook.' *Encounter*, March 1959.

Chung Huang: 'Basing Industry on Agriculture.' *Peking Review*, May 10, 1963.

Davies, D.: 'A Kwangtung Commune.' *Far Eastern Economic Review*, December 17, 1964.

Donnithorne, A.: 'Background to the People's Communes: Changes in China's Economic Organization in 1958.' *Pacific Affairs*, Vol. XXXII, No. 4, December 1959.

Donnithorne, A.: 'China's Economic Planning and Industry.' *China Quarterly*, No. 17, January–March, 1964.

Donnithorne, A.: 'The Council for Mutual Economic Aid.' *The Banker's Magazine*, April 1959.

Donnithorne, A.: 'Extra-Budgetary Funds in the Chinese Fiscal System.' *The China Mainland Review*, Vol. I, No. 4, March 1966.

Donnithorne, A.: 'The Organization of Rural Trade in China since 1958.' *China Quarterly*, No. 8, October–December 1961.

Emerson, J. P.: 'Chinese Communist Party Views on Labour Utilization Before and After 1958.' *Current Scene*, Vol. I, No. 3, April 20, 1962.

Emerson, J. P.: 'Manpower Absorption in the Non-Agricultural Branches of the Economy of Communist China, 1953–8.' *China Quarterly*, No. 7, July–September 1961.

Galenson, W. and Eriksson, J. R.: 'Industrial Labour Productivity in Non-Western Countries since 1945.' (Paper presented to the International Economic Association's International Congress on Economic Development, Vienna, 1962.)

Gillan, D. G.: 'China's First Five Year Plan: Industrialization under the Warlords as Reflected in the Policies of Yen Hsi-shan in Shansi Province, 1930–7.' *Journal of Asian Studies*, Vol. XXIV, No. 2, February 1965.

Garratt, C.: 'China as a Foreign Aid Donor.' *Far Eastern Economic Review*, January 19, 1961.

Gray, J.: 'Collectivization in China: The Experimental Year, 1952.' (Unpublished paper given to a working group at the Royal Institute of International Affairs.)

Gray, J.: 'The Communist Party and the System of Government.' *The Political Quarterly*, Vol. 35, No. 3, July–September 1964.

Gray, J.: 'Political Aspects of the Land Reform Campaign in China, 1947–52.' *Soviet Studies*, Vol. XIV, No. 2, October 1964.

Harper, P.: 'Closing the Education Gap.' *Current Scene*, Vol. III, No. 15, March 15, 1965.

Hoffman, C.: 'Work Incentives in Communist China.' *Industrial Relations*, Vol. 3, No. 2, February 1964.

Hofheinz, R.: 'Rural Administration in Communist China.' *China Quarterly*, No. 11, July–September 1962.

Hollister, W. W.: 'Capital Formation in Communist China.' *China Quarterly*, No. 17, January–March, 1964.

Hough, J. F.: 'Technical Elite versus the Party—A First-hand Report.' *Problems of Communism*, Vol. 8, No. 5, September–October 1959.

Hu, Ch'ang-tu: 'The Yellow River Administration in the Ch'ing Dynasty.' *Far Eastern Quarterly*, Vol. XIV, No. 4, August 1955.

Hu Chi: 'How Industry Helps Agriculture.' *Peking Review*, December 11, 1964.

Huang Han-liang: 'The Land Tax in China.' *Columbia University Studies in History, Economics and Public Law*, Vol. LXXX, No. 3, 1918.

Inner Mongolian Autonomous Region: Report on 1957 Final Budget and 1958 Draft Budget. (Translated in JPRS 482-D.)

Jones, P. H. M.: 'Creeping Modernization.' *Far Eastern Economic Review*, October 28, 1964.

Kang Chao: 'Economic Aftermath of the Great Leap in Communist China.' *Asian Survey*, Vol. IV, No. 5, May 1964.

Kang Chao: 'Pitfalls in the Use of China's Foreign Trade Statistics.' *China Quarterly*, No. 19, July–September 1964.

Kang Chao and Ma Feng-hwa: 'A Study of the Rouble-Yuan Exchange Rate.' *China Quarterly*, No. 17, January–March 1964.

Karol, K. S.: 'Maoism: China's Secular Religion. A Twentieth-Century Experiment in Puritan Ethics.' *New Statesman*, September 3, 1965.

Kuo, T. C.: 'Agricultural Mechanization in Communist China.' *China Quarterly*, No. 17, January–March 1964.

Lee, T. C.: 'China's Food, Population, Agricultural Exports—Parts 1 and 2.' *Far Eastern Economic Review*, December 10 and 17, 1959.

Leng, C. S.: 'The Lawyer in Communist China.' *Journal of the International Commission of Jurists*, Vol. 4, No. 1, Summer 1962.

Li, Choh-ming: 'Statistics and Planning at *Hsien* Level in Communist China.' *Current Scene*, Vol. I, No. 28, March 27, 1962.

Li Fu-ch'un, Chairman of the State Planning Commission: Report on the Draft 1960 National Economic Plan. *Peking Review*, April 5, 1960.

Li Hsien-nien, Minister of Finance: 'China's Great Financial Achievements during the Past Ten Years.' *Peking Review*, November 24, 1959.

Li Hsien-nien, Minister of Finance: Report on the Final State Accounts for 1959 and the Draft State Budget for 1960. *Peking Review*, April 5, 1960.

Liao Lu-Yen, Minister of Agriculture: 'Collectivization of Agriculture in China.' *Peking Review*, November 1, 1963.

Lim, E. R.: 'The Role of Profit in China's Industrial Planning.' *The China Mainland Review*, Vol. I, No. 4, March 1966.

Lindqvist, S.: 'Inside China—Parts 1 and 2.' *Guardian*, January 23 and 24, 1963.

Liu, Jung-chao: 'Fertilizer Application in Communist China.' *China Quarterly*, No. 24, October–December 1965.

Liu Tzu-mo: Sinkiang 1957 and 1958 Final Budgets and 1959 Draft Budget. *Sinkiang Daily* (*Sinjiang Ribao*) February 1, 1959. (JPRS 1070–D).

Lung Yeh: 'Vegetables in Abundance for Peking.' *China Reconstructs*, August 1963.

Ma Wen-kuei: 'Industrial Management in China.' *Peking Review*, February 26, 1965.

MacDougall, Colina: 'The Reds and the Experts.' *Far Eastern Economic Review*, February 6, 1964.

Mah, Feng-hwa: 'The Terms of Sino-Soviet Trade.' *China Quarterly*, No. 17, January–March 1964.

Mendershausen, H.: 'The Terms of Soviet-Satellite Trade: A Broadened Analysis.' *The Review of Economics and Statistics*, Vol. XLII, No. 2, May 1960.

Meng Kuei and Hsiao Lin: 'On Sun Yeh-fang's Reactionary Political Stand and Economic Programme.' *Peking Review*, October 21, 1966.

Mikesell, R. F. and Wells, D. A.: 'State Trading in the Sino-Soviet Bloc.' *Law and Contemporary Problems*, Vol. 24, No. 3, Summer 1959.

Munthe-Kaas, H.: 'Easy Atoms.' *Far Eastern Economic Review*, December 9, 1965.

Munthe-Kaas, H.: 'Roads and Rails in China.' *Far Eastern Economic Review*, February 17, 1966.

Munthe-Kaas, H.: 'Chinese Afloat.' *Far Eastern Economic Review*, March 3, 1966.

Munthe-Kaas, H.: 'China's Steel.' *Far Eastern Economic Review*, March 31, 1966.

Munthe-Kaas, H.: 'China's "Four Clean-Ups".' *Far Eastern Economic Review*, June 9, 1966.

Perkins, D. H.: 'Price Stability and Development in Mainland China (1951–63).' *Journal of Political Economy*, Vol. 72, No. 4, August 1964.

Pfeffer, R. M.: 'The Institution of Contracts in the Chinese People's Republic.' Parts 1 and 2, *China Quarterly*, No. 14, April–June 1963; No. 15, July–September 1963.

Schurmann, F.: 'China's "New Economic Policy"—Transition or Beginning?' *China Quarterly*, No. 17, January–March 1964.

Schurmann, F.: 'Economic Policy and Political Power in Communist China.' *Annals of the American Academy of Political and Social Science*, Vol. 349, September 1963.

Schweitzer, P. P.: 'Some Financial Aspects of Economic Development.' *International Financial News Service*, Vol. XVI, No. 41. Supplement, October 16, 1964.

Sieh, M.: 'Medicine in China: Wealth for the State.' Part II, *Current Scene*, Vol. III, No. 6, November 1, 1964.

Skinner, G. W.: 'Marketing and Social Structure in Rural China.' Parts 1, 2 and 3. *Journal of Asian Studies*, Vol. XXIV, No. 1, November 1964; No. 2, February 1965 and No. 3, May 1965.

Skinner, G. W.: Communications in reply to note by A. Donnithorne. *Journal of Asian Studies*, Vol. XXIV, No. 2, February 1966.

Strong, A. L.: 'Some Comments on the Chinese People's Communes.' *Peking Review*, June 12, 1964.

Su Tsung-sung: 'Irrigation Renews the Land.' *China Reconstructs*, November 1964.

Sung, Kayser: 'Shipping—Charter, Purchase, Construction, Salvage.' *Far Eastern Economic Review*, October 1, 1959.

Sung Kuang-wei: 'Factors behind Price Stability.' *China Reconstructs*, July 1966.

T'ao Chu, First Secretary of the Kwangtung Provincial Party Committee: 'The People's Communes Forge Ahead.' Parts 1 and 2. *Peking Review*, March 27 and April 10, 1964.

Ts'ao Ti-ch'iu: 'Shanghai—Growth of a Socialist Industrial Centre.' *Peking Review*, October 9, 1964.

Tung Shao-sheng, Vice Director of the Yangtze Navigation Administration Bureau: 'The Yangtze Belongs to the People.' *China Reconstructs*, March 1960.

Wang, K. P.: 'The Mineral Industry of Mainland China.' US Bureau of Mines: *1964 Year Book* pre-print.

Waterson, A.: 'A Hard Look at Development Planning.' *Finance and Development*. Vol. III, No. 2, June 1966.

Wen Yu: 'The New Generation of Skilled Workers.' *China Reconstructs*, August 1960.

Wolfstone, Daniel: 'Economics of the Split.' *Far Eastern Economic Review*, May 28, 1964.

Wu, Y. L.: 'Expansion of the Chinese Research and Development Industry.' *The China Mainland Review*, Vol. I, No. 2, September 1965.

Yang Po: 'New China's Price Policy.' *Peking Review*, November 20, 1964.

V. LIST OF PERIODICALS AND NEWSPAPERS:

PERIODICALS—Chinese

Agricultural and Forestry Work Bulletin (Nonglin Gongzuo Tongxun), Peking.
Agricultural Mechanization (Nongye Jixie), Peking.
Agricultural Work Bulletin (Nongcun Gongzuo Tongxun), Peking.
Building Construction (Jianzhu), Peking.
Central Co-operation Bulletin (Zhongyang Hozuo Tongxun), Peking.
Chemical Industry (Huaxue Gongye), Peking.
China Monthly (Zuguo),[1] Hong Kong.
China Weekly (Zuguo),[1] Hong Kong.
China Youth (Zhongguo Qingnian), Peking.
China's Foreign Trade (Duiwai Maoyi), Peking.
China's Forestry (Zhongguo Linye), Peking.
Chinese Agricultural Journal (Zhongguo Nongbao), Peking.
Chinese Agricultural Machinery (Zhongguo Nongye Jixie), Peking.
Chinese Agriculture and Land Reclamation (Zhongguo Nongken), Peking.
Chinese Currency (Zhongguo Jinrong), Peking.
Chinese Industry (Zhongguo Gongye), Peking.
Chinese Textiles (Zhongguo Fangzhi), Peking.
Chinese Water Conservancy (Zhongguo Shuili), Peking.
Chinese Worker (Zhongguo Gongren), Peking.

[1] *China Monthly* is the successor of *China Weekly*. The English and the Chinese names of this journal given here are those carried by the journal. In this case the English title is not a translation of the Chinese ('Zuguo' means 'fatherland').

BIBLIOGRAPHY

Coal Industry (Meitan Gongye), Peking.
Commercial Work (Shangye Gongzuo), Peking.
Communist Affairs Research (Feiqing Yanjiu), Taipei.
Current Events (Shishi Shouce), Peking.
East Wind (Dongfeng), Peking.
Economic Research (Jingji Yanjiu), Peking.
Education and Research (Jiaoyu yu Yangjiu), Peking.
Electric Motor Industry (Dianji Gongye), Peking.
Finance (Caizheng), Peking.
Financial and Economic Research (Caijing Yanjiu), Peking.
Geographical Knowledge (Dili Zhishi), Peking.
Highway (Gonglu), Peking.
Journal of Railway Commerce (Tielu Shangwu Zhuankan), Peking.
Labour (Laodong), Peking.
Liberation (Jiefang), Peking.
Literary Gazette (Wenyi Bao), Peking.
Machine Building Industry (Jixie Gongye), Peking.
Mainland Today (Jinri Dalu), Taipei.
The Masses (Qunzhong), Peking.
Nationalities Unity (Minzu Tuanjie), Peking.
New China Fortnightly (Xinhua Banyuekan), Peking.
New China Monthly (Xinhua Yuebao), Peking.
New Construction (Xin Jianshe), Peking.
New Industry and Commerce (Xin Gongshang), Peking.
Oil Prospecting (Shiyou Kantan), Peking.
Oil Refining (Shiyou Lianzhi), Peking.
Overseas Chinese Affairs Journal (Qiaowu Bao), Peking.
Pao An Bulletin (Baoan Tongxun), Pao An, Kwangtung.
People's Communes Construction (Renmin Gongshe Jianshe), Peking.
People's Power Industry (Renmin Dianye), Peking.
People's Railways (Renmin Tiedao), Peking.
People's Taxation (Renmin Shuiwu), Peking.
People's Water Transport Paper (Renmin Hangyun Bao), Peking.
Philosophical Research (Zhexue Yanjiu), Peking.
Planned Economy (Jihua Jingji), Peking.
Planning and Statistics (Jihua yu Tongji), Peking.
Political and Legal Research (Zhengfa Yanjiu), Peking.
Popular Science (Kexue Dazhong), Peking.
Railway Weekly (Tiedao Zhoukan), Peking.
Red Flag (Hongqi), Peking.
Rural Finance (Nongcun Jinrong), Peking.
Science News (Kexue Tongbao), Peking.
State Council Bulletin (Guowuyuan Gongbao), Peking.
Statistical Research (Tongji Yangjiu), Peking.
Statistical Work (Tongji Gongzuo), Peking.
Statistical Work Bulletin (Tongji Gongzuo Tongxun), Peking.
Study (Xuexi), Peking.
Teaching and Research (Jiaoxue yu Yanjiu), Peking.
Technology of Agricultural Machinery (Nongye Jixie Jishu), Peking.
Theoretical Study (Lilun Xuexi), Peking.
Water Conservancy and Electric Power (Shuili yu Dianli), Peking.
Water Transport (Shuiyun), Peking.
Work Bulletin (Gongzuo Tongxun), Peking.

PERIODICALS—English

Annals of the American Academy of Political and Social Science, Philadelphia.
Asian Survey, University of California, Berkeley.
The Bankers' Magazine, London.
BBC Summary of World Broadcasts, London.
The China Mainland Review, University of Hong Kong, Hong Kong.
China News Analysis, Hong Kong.
China News Summary, Hong Kong.
China Quarterly, London.
China Reconstructs, Peking.
Current Background, US Consulate General, Hong Kong.
Current Scene, US Consulate General, Hong Kong.
Economist, London.
Encounter, London.
Extracts from China Mainland Magazines, US Consulate General, Hong Kong.
Extracts from China Mainland Publications, US Consulate General, Hong Kong.
Far Eastern Economic Review, Hong Kong.
Far Eastern Quarterly, Menasha, Wisconsin.
Finance and Development, International Monetary Fund, Washington, D.C.
Foreign Trade of the People's Republic of China, Peking.
Harvard Law Review, Harvard University, Cambridge, Mass.
Industrial Relations, University of California, Berkeley.
International Financial News Service, International Monetary Fund, Washington, D.C.
Journal of Asian Studies, Ann Arbor, Michigan.
Journal of the International Commission of Jurists, The Hague.
Journal of Political Economy, University of Chicago, Chicago.
Law and Contemporary Problems, Duke University, Durham, N.C.
Mining Engineering, American Institute of Mining Engineers.
News from Chinese Regional Radio Stations, Hong Kong.
New Statesman, London.
Pacific Affairs, Institute of Pacific Relations, Honolulu.
Peking Review, Peking.
Political Quarterly, London.
Problems of Communism, US Information Agency, Washington, D.C.
Review of Economics and Statistics, Cambridge, Mass.
Selections from China Mainland Magazines, US Consulate General, Hong Kong.
Soviet News, Soviet Embassy, London.
Soviet Studies, University of Glasgow.
Statistical Bulletin, International Tin Council, London.
Survey of China Mainland Press, US Consulate General, Hong Kong.

NEWSPAPERS—Chinese

Anhwei Daily (Anhui Ribao), Hofei.
Chekiang Daily (Zhejiang Ribao), Hangchow.
China Youth Newspaper (Zhongguo Qingnian Bao), Peking.
Daily Worker (Gongren Ribao), Peking.
Honan Daily (Honan Ribao), Chengchow.
Hopei Daily (Hobei Ribao), Tientsin.
Hupeh Daily (Hubei Ribao), Wuhan.
Inner Mongolia Daily (Neimenggu Ribao), Huhehot.

Kansu Daily (*Gansu Ribao*), Lanchow.
Kiangsi Daily (*Jiangxi Ribao*), Nanchang.
Kuang Ming Daily (*Guangming Ribao*), Peking.
Kweichow Daily (*Guizhou Ribao*), Kweiyang.
Liaoning Daily (*Liaoning Ribao*), Shenyang.
Liberation Daily (*Jiefang Ribao*), Shanghai.
New Hunan Daily (*Xin Hunan Bao*), Changsha.
People's Daily (*Renmin Ribao*), Peking.
Shensi Daily (*Shanxi Ribao*), Sian.
Shenyang Daily (*Shenyang Ribao*), Shenyang.
Sinkiang Daily (*Xinjiang Ribao*), Urumchi.
Southern Daily, (*Nanfang Ribao*), Canton.
Ta Kung Daily (*Dagong Bao*), Hong Kong, 1948–
Ta Kung Daily (*Dagong Bao*), Shanghai, 1946–53; Tientsin, 1953–55; Peking, 1955–66.
Tsinghai Daily (*Qinghai Ribao*), Sining.
Tsitsihar Daily (*Qiqihaer Ribao*), Tsitsihar.
Wen Hui Pao (*Wenhui Bao*), Shanghai.
Yangch'eng Evening Paper (*Yangcheng Wanbao*), Canton.
Yangtze Daily (*Changjiang Ribao*), Wuhan.
Yunnan Daily (*Yunnan Ribao*), Kunming.

NEWSPAPERS—Other Languages

Guardian, London.
New York Times, New York.
Pravda, Moscow.
Sunday Times, London.
The Times, London.

INDEX

Academy of Agricultural Sciences, 42, 127
Academy of Sciences, 127, 155, 237, 238, 526–7
  Economic Institute, 480–1
  Geological Institute, 237
Accountancy and accountants, 43–4, 71, 178, 195, 202, 399, 507
Accounting
  Provisional Regulation Governing the Authority of Accounting Personnel, 202
Administration, expenditure on, 384
Administrative decentralization movement, *see* Decentralization, administrative
Administrative staff, shortage of, 507–8
Administrative units, 20–3, 64, 277, 303, 307–9, 385, 505
  See also under Provinces; *Hsien*, etc.
Advance payments, 418, 430, 435, 480
Advertising, 314, 325, 326
Agents, purchasing, 175, 290–1, 307, 446
Agrarian Reform Law, 36
Agricultural Bank of China, *see under* Banks
Agricultural Co-operation Bank, *see under* Banks
Agricultural Land Water Conservancy Bureau, 126
Agricultural loans, *see* Bank loans, agricultural; Credit co-operatives
Agricultural machinery and mechanization, 60, 92n, 93, 96, 104, 112–20, 142, 418, 443n, 474, 478, 490, 504
  See also Pumps, mechanized; Tractors
Agricultural Machinery, Ministry of, 112, 261n, 520–1
Agricultural machinery stations, 60, 112–20, 372, 430, 473, 509
Agricultural planning, 56, 486–90, 499
Agricultural producer co-operatives, 17, 26, 338, 343, 346, 347, 349, 408, 409, 416n, 425, 440n, 486, 509, 513
  'Higher', 38–9, 43–4, 48, 49n
  'Lower', 26n, 38–9
  Numbers of, 43, 46, 48
  Size of, 43
Agricultural production
  National survey of, 345
  'Normal yield', 338, 339, 341, 346
  Official estimates, 341, 351
  Targets, 462, 463, 486–8
  Subsidiary, 42, 82–8 *passim*, 351–3
    See also Commodities, third category

Agricultural products
  Categories of, *see* Commodities
  Compulsory sale, Ch. 13; 40, 57, 273, 292, 294, 295, 297, 304, 488, 509
  Foreign trade in, 319, 329
  Prices, 273, 344, 347, 358–63, 383, 435, 439, 442, 447–9, 455, 456, 499
  Processing of, 135, 149, 279, 283–7, 328, 361, 474
  Subsidiary, 35, 284, 299, 304, 337, 349, 352, 353, 434
  See also Pigs; Poultry; Vegetables, etc.
Agricultural Tax, Ch. 13; 57, 72, 89, 109, 273, 367n, 372, 377–8, 382, 394, 396, 488, 510
  Local supplementary, 338, 339, 342, 363, 389, 393
Agricultural Tax Bureau, 345, 366
Agriculture, Chs. 2, 3 and 4; 15–19, 21n, 33, 142, 310, 338, 339, 343, 408, 426, 462, 469, 486–90, 495
  See also Communes, rural people's; Agricultural producer co-operatives; Water conservancy, etc.
Agriculture, Ministry of, 41, 42, 93, 94, 103, 112, 127, 129, 408, 413, 423, 486–90, 522–3
Agriculture and Forestry, State Council Office of, 20, 41, 42, 156, 468, 517
Aid to foreign countries, *see* Foreign aid given by China
Albania, 264, 320n
Algeria, 320n
Alkalization of soil, 130
All-China Federation of Handicraft Co-operatives, 222–3, 296n
All-China Federation of Industry and Commerce, 147
All-China Federation of Supply and Marketing Co-operatives, 274, 279, 296n, 303–5, 315, 330
All-China Federation of Trade Unions, 29, 189, 191–2, 314
Allocation of Materials, Ministry of, 275, 457, 477, 522–3, 527
Allocation price, *see* Price, allocation
Allocation of raw materials and producer goods, 168, 173–5, 273, 282, 285, 453, 455, 459, 478, 483, 498–9, 502, 509
Alum, 239
Aluminium, 150, 238–9, 283n, 284
Amoy, 257

INDEX 573

Amur River, 127, 240
Anhwei, 78, 97, 99, 117n, 129, 133, 182, 478
Anshan Iron and Steel Works, 153n, 174, 188, 210, 241, 247, 450
Anti-Illiteracy Commission, 526-7
Antimony, 238-9
Antropov (Soviet Minister of Geology), 239
Apprenticeship system, 188, 224-5
Aquatic products, 284
  See also Fish and fisheries
Aquatic Products, Ministry of, 41, 61n, 151, 277n, 286, 287n, 369, 522-3
Argentine, grain imports from, 320
Armed Forces, 174
  See also People's Liberation Army; Military Council; Military equipment; Military expenditure; Nuclear weapons programme
Asbestos, 239
Assets, 25-6
Assets, absence of charge on, 26, 370, 437, 482
Assets, fixed, 25-6, 157, 161, 370, 385, 395, 399, 473, 482
Assets, income arising from changes in price of, 163, 369
Australia, grain imports from, 320
Autonomous *chou*, 21, 22
Autonomous *hsien*, 21, 22
Autonomous regions, 19-22, 396
Aviation, civil, *see* Civil aviation

Balances, year end, 171-2, 386, 388n-9n, 395
Balancing of commodities
  Local, 459, 463-5, 485
  National, 366, 459, 462, 464-5, 482, 505
  Vertical, 463
  See also Transfers
Bamboo, 15, 120, 284
Bank accounts and deposits, 365, 382, 405, 406, 412, 418, 420, 421
Bank agents at factories, etc., 422
Bank capital, 419
Bank loans, 75n, 157, 385, 388, 397, 405, 406, 408, 410-12, 416, 418-33 *passim*, 425, 429, 471, 482, 495, 503
  See also Capital, working
Bank loans, agricultural, 75, 76, 109-10, 405, 408, 409, 411, 412, 421, 424-33, 490, 505
  See also Credit Co-operatives
Banks and banking, Ch. 15; 23, 26, 368, 372, 385
  Foreign, 402, 412-13
  Joint State-Private, 402, 407
  'Native', 402
  Overseas Chinese, 403, 413
  Private, 402
  'Shansi', 402

Banks and banking (*cont.*)
  Supervisory role of banks, 316, 406, 413, 414, 422, 429-30, 470, 497, 506, 508
Banks (named)
  Agricultural Bank of China (1955), 75, 408, 412, 430
  Agricultural Bank of China (1963), 75, 275, 366, 404, 405, 408-9, 412, 418, 427-8, 430, 498, 522-3
  Agricultural Co-operation Bank, 408
  Central Bank, 403
  Chartered Bank, 412
  Chi-Yu Bank, 413
  China, Bank of, 248, 330, 332, 333, 403, 404, 406, 407, 413
  Communications, Bank of, 366, 403, 404, 405, 412, 421, 515
  Construction Bank of China, 171, 172, 366, 404, 405, 411, 412, 413, 420, 421, 470, 472, 473, 515
  East Asia, Bank of, 413
  Farmers' Bank of China, 403
  Gosbank, 403, 413
  Hong Kong and Shanghai Banking Corporation, 412
  International Bank for Reconstruction and Development, 475
  Investment Bank for Capital Construction, 411n
  Joint State-Private Bank, 402, 403-4, 407-8
  Overseas Chinese Banking Corporation, 413
  People's Bank of China, Ch. 15 *passim*; 20, 26, 71, 75, 240, 248, 275, 276, 365, 366, 497-8, 500, 502, 506-7, 522-3
    Director-General of, 365, 406, 407
    Foreign Business Bureau, 406
    Gold and silver, dealings in, 406
    Gold, involvement in production of, 240, 248
    Income of, 419n
    Loan department, 409
    Local branches, 44, 405, 407, 422, 423, 427, 505-6
    Note issue, 402, 405, 412, 414, 416, 419
    Staff and employees, 403, 407, 409
  People's Construction Bank of China, *see* Construction Bank
Barnett, A. D., 501n
Barter trade, 175, 321, 324, 334-5, 406, 446, 478
Basic construction, *see* 'Capital construction'
Bicycles, 149, 285, 312
Bismuth, 239
Black market, 311, 434
  In gold and silver, 417

574 CHINA'S ECONOMIC SYSTEM

Blacksmiths, 225
Bonds, 381, 382, 385, 391, 396, 405, 414, 420, 513
Bonuses, 164–7, 205–12, 216, 483
Borax, 239
British economic activities, 145
Broadcasting Administrative Bureau, 524
Brokers, independent, 291
Buck, J. L., 31–5 *passim*, 77n, 125, 359n
Budget Bureau, 366
Budgets and budgeting, Ch. 14; 109–10, 157, 171, 316, 340, 405, 412, 419, 420, 462, 471, 472, 498
  See also Taxation; Expenditure, budgetary; Revenue, budgetary
Budgets, conferences on, 387–8, 503
Budgets, local, 365, 369, 393–400, 422
Building co-operatives, 170n
Building materials, 141, 275, 462, 463, 483
  See also Cement; Timber, etc.
Building Materials, Ministry of, 149, 150, 153n, 240, 520–1
Burma, 266, 320n
Bus services, 261

Cadres, Ch. 7; 415
  Definition of, 29
  Financial, 375, 377, 400, 401, 409
  Industrial, Ch. 7 *passim*
  Participation in labour, 62, 69, 510
  Party, 18, 55–6, 194–6, 198, 200, 210–11, 501
  Remuneration of, 66–7, 206–11
  Rural, 43, 65–71, 75, 206, 489
Cambodia, 266, 320n
Canada, grain imports from, 320
Canton, 134, 254, 256, 258, 263, 265, 326, 454
Canton Export Fairs, 333, 510
Canton Sea Transport Administrative Bureau, 263
Capital
  Allocation of, 438
  Commercial, 275, 276, 314–17, 422
  Marginal efficiency of, 375, 393, 424, 425, 435, 482
  Working, 25–6, 109–10, 155, 157, 163, 167, 316, 369, 385, 388, 399, 412, 416, 420–3, 426, 470, 476, 477, 482, 483, 495
  See also Assets, fixed; Investment
'Capital Construction', 27
  See also Investment
Capital goods, 140, 421, 450, 459
  Agricultural, 293
    See also Agricultural machinery, etc.
  Allocation of, 465, 477
  Balancing and transfer of, 462

Capital goods (*cont.*)
  Import of, 479
  Planning of, 463, 472–82 *passim*
  Prices of, Ch. 16 *passim*
  Provincial distribution of, 463, 477
Capitalism, 'spontaneous', 235, 280, 290, 415
Carpenters, 225
Cattle, *see* Draught animals
Cement, 140, 143, 145, 151, 173n, 474, 476, 478, 483
Boats, 265
Central Administration of Industry and Commerce, 25, 147, 275, 302, 524–5
Central African Republic, 320n
Central Bank, *see under* Banks
Central Bureau of Meteorology, 41, 42, 522–3
Central Finance Cadres School, 366, 387
Central Financial and Economic Planning Bureau, 458
Central Flood Prevention Headquarters, 127
Central General Bureau of Handicraft Industry, 149, 222, 524–5
Central Government control, Ch. 18 *passim*; 17, 23, 460–1
  Of agricultural production, 93, 111, 486, 488, 489
  Of appointments, 176–9, 501
  Of banking, 23, 405, 421, 422, 427, 497, 498, 500, 506
  Of commerce, 287–8, 324–5, 479, 485
  Of fiscal system, 294, 393–401, 499
  Of inter-provincial transfers, 285, 324, 349, 397–8, 459, 462–7, 477, 498–9, 503
  Of investment, 473–9
  Of planning, Ch. 17 *passim*; 294
  Of prices, Ch. 16 *passim*; 499
Central Handicrafts Administrative Bureau, 222, 524–5
Ceramics, 474
Ceylon, 320n, 334
Chang Chung-han, 99
Chang Ling, 480
Chang Po-chun, 252
Changchun, 227
Changchun Motor Works, 153n, 188, 196
Changchun Railway, 26, 251, 254, 257, 265, 271, 272
Charcoal, 15, 59
Chartered Bank, *see under* Banks
Chekiang, 97, 133, 135n, 264, 340, 409n, 489–90
Chemical industry, 140, 141, 150, 152, 153, 172, 248, 401, 474
Chemical Industry, Ministry of, 149, 150, 153n, 240, 478, 518–19

INDEX 575

Chemicals
  Agricultural, 285
  Industrial, 150, 290
  See also Fertilizers, chemical; Insecticides
Chen, see Market town
Ch'en Yi, 468
Ch'en Po-ta, 468
Ch'en Yün, 145, 158, 159, 224, 275, 281–3, 468, 472
Ch'eng Tzu-hua, 275
Chengchow, 227, 228
Chengtu, 168, 256–7, 267, 292n
Chengtu Plain, 114, 125, 490
Chi-Yu Bank, *see under* Banks
China, Bank of, *see under* Banks
China Council for the Promotion of International Trade, 264, 323, 329–30, 358n, 407
China General Goods Company, 276
China Industrial Co-operatives, 221
China Insurance Company, 515–16
China National Animal By-Products Import and Export Corporation, 325
China National Arts and Crafts Import and Export Corporation, 325
China National Aviation Corporation, 266
China National Cereals, Oils and Foodstuffs Import and Export Corporation, 325
China National Chartering and Shipbroking Corporation, 264
China National Chemicals Import and Export Corporation, 325
China National Complete Plant Export Corporation, 325
China National Foreign Trade Transportation Corporation, 264, 326
China National Garments Import and Export Corporation, 325
China National Instruments Import and Export Corporation, 325
China National Light Industrial Products Import and Export Corporation, 325
China National Machinery Import and Export Corporation, 325
China National Metals and Minerals Import and Export Corporation, 325, 326
China National Tea and Native Produce Import and Export Corporation, 325
China National Technical Import Corporation, 325
China National Textiles Import and Export Corporation, 325
China Ocean Shipping Co, 264
China Ocean Steamship Agency, 265, 497
China, People's Republic of, 17
  Chairman of, 20, 176, 210n
  Constitution of, 20, 22, 25, 176, 366, 458

China Publications Centre, 325
China Resources Co, 326, 332
China Silk Corporation, 321
China Travel and Tourism Administrative Bureau, 527
China Vegetable Oil Corporation, 321
China's Foreign Trade, 325
Chinese Academy of Sciences, *see* Academy of Sciences
Chinese Communist Party, 17–19, 21n, 23
  Assimilation with administration and management, 19, 55–6, 65, 196–9, 503
  Branch committees, 19, 29n, 55, 195, 242, 298n, 304, 385n, 500
  Branch committees, secretaries of, 18, 55–6, 65–71 *passim*, 195, 198, 200
    See also Provincial committees and secretaries
  Cadres, 194, 196, 210–11, 501
  Central Committee, 19, 20, 44n, 331, 413, 460
    Plenary sessions of, 19, 467
    Publications of, 29, 167, 314
  Communications Work Department, 19, 148, 252
  Constitution of, 19, 195, 210
  Finance and Trade Work Department, 19, 275, 365, 413, 457
    Director of, 365
  Government subsidies to, 384, 385n
  Industrial Work Department, 19, 148, 196
    Director of, 148, 196
    Members, 19, 196, 385, 500
  National Party Congress, 19
    Eighth, 158, 192, 224, 281
  North China Bureau, 148
    First Secretary of, 148
  Organization Work Department, 19
  Peking Municipal Committee, 148, 290
  Politburo, 19, 457
  Political Departments, 19, 505
    Agriculture and Forestry, 19, 41
    Finance and Trade, 19, 275, 365
    Industry and Communications, 19, 148, 252
  Propaganda Work Department, 19
    Director of, 468
  Provincial committees, 19, 111, 184, 503, 505
  Provincial secretaries, 40, 93, 184, 352, 502, 503, 505
  Regional bureaux, 19, 56, 387, 464, 500–1, 505
  Rural Work Department, 19, 41, 42
    Director of, 42, 419, 468
  Secretaries, *see under* Chinese Communist Party—Branch committees, secretaries of

Chinese Communist Party (*cont.*)
  Supervisory role of, 56, 199–200, 413
  United Front Work Department, 19
Chingwangtao, 265
Chou En-lai, 20, 24n, 468
Ch'ü (districts), 22, 23, 48, 55n, 62, 303, 394
Chuan ch'ü (special districts), 22, 42, 394, 464
Chungking, 144, 227, 228, 254, 256–7, 262, 263, 267, 272, 280, 289
Cigarettes, 273, 274, 281, 312, 474
Cinemas, 386
Civil aviation, 174, 252, 253, 265–6, 270, 497, 524–5
Civil Aviation General Administration of China, 253, 266, 524–5
Clocks, 149
Clothing industry, 233, 293, 325
Coal and coal mining, Ch. 9 *passim*; 63, 145, 154, 172, 281, 285, 286, 316, 451, 455, 466, 467, 473, 474, 478
  Distribution, 245, 259, 275, 418, 451, 483
  Transport of, 247, 259, 264
  Prices, 242, 269, 443, 451–3, 455
Coal Construction Company, 245
Coal Industry, 244
Coal, Minister of, 244
Coal, Ministry of, 126, 150, 153n, 154n, 189, 237, 240, 241, 243, 244, 245, 248, 451, 478, 479, 520–1
  Provincial bureaux, 243
Coal Planning Bureau, 245
Coke, 59, 239, 243, 245
Collective ownership, *see* Ownership, collective
Collectivization and 'Socialist Transformation', 374, 459, 509
  Of Agriculture, 17, 38–43, 218, 224, 279, 338, 408, 409, 425, 435
Collectivization of banking, 402–3
Collectivization of commerce, 146, 277–81, 301, 321, 409, 442, 459
Collectivization of handicrafts, 193, 220–4, 235, 424n
Collectivization of industry, 146–7, 193, 194, 281, 459
Collectivization of mining, 241
Collectivization of social life, 45, 62–4, 77, 90–1, 241, 293
Collectivization of transport, 146, 252
Comecon, *see* Council for Mutual Economic Assistance
Commerce, Chs. 11, 12 and 13
  See also Exports; Foreign trade; Imports; Warehouses, trade; Corporations, foreign trade; Corporations, internal trade, etc.
  Alignment with administrative units or with economic regions, 308–9, 505

Commerce (*cont.*)
  Co-operative, 274–5, 277–80, 301, 309, 310
  See also Supply and marketing co-operatives
  Finance of, 275, 287, 314–16, 418, 422n
  See also Capital, working; Tax, commercial; Tax, industrial and commercial
  Foreign merchants, 273–4, 320, 321, 329
  Joint state-private, 275, 277–8, 292, 309, 310
  Labour force, 181, 280, 287
  Planning of, 275, 287, 295, 304, 323, 324, 462, 485–6
  Political departments of, 19, 275, 316
  Private, 220, 233, 235, 273–80, 283, 290–1, 297–8, 300–1, 310, 316, 321, 362–3, 374, 377, 409, 456, 509
  See also Markets, rural; Pedlars
  Retail, 220, 233, 276, 277–81, 289, 293, 294, 302, 304, 309–10, 315, 327n, 372, 439–40, 446, 462
  See also Markets, rural; Pedlars
  Rural, 220, 275, 276, 280, 291–307, 376–7
  See also Markets, rural; Marketing systems; Pedlars; Co-operatives, supply and marketing
  State, Chs. 11, 12 and 13 *passim*; 442, 497
  Urban, 228, 275, 288–91, 306
  Wholesale, 175n, 276–8, 281–2, 287, 291, 306, 309, 315
Commerce, Minister of, 158, 275, 281, 365, 468
Commerce, Ministry of, 21, 151, 153n, 173, 232n, 274, 275, 276n, 284, 286, 287n, 288, 289, 296, 297, 310, 316, 345, 369, 404, 442, 478, 518–19
  See also Trade, Ministry of
  Local departments and bureaux, 234, 276, 282, 287, 288, 289, 294, 295, 297, 309, 315, 328, 442
Commerce, First Ministry of, 274, 275, 519
Commerce, Second Ministry of, 274, 378n, 519
Commercial Management System, Decree on the Reform of, 287
Commissions, commercial, 281, 289, 291, 310, 315
Commodities, division into categories, 284, 285
  First category commodities, 285, 291, 293, 297, 306n, 443n, 444, 445
  Second category commodities, 284, 285, 291, 292, 298, 299n, 305, 306, 351, 352n, 443n, 444, 445
  Third category commodities, 284, 285, 295, 296, 297, 300, 305, 306, 443n, 444, 445

Commodity exchange meetings, 291, 296, 297
Communes, Rural People's, Chs. 2 and 3; 17, 22, 110–11, 224, 304, 307, 376, 426
 Commercial departments, 72, 293–7
 Credit departments, 71–2, 409–10, 426
 Draft Articles on Rural Communes, 48, 55, 67, 69, 85, 341, 352
 Federations of, 48
 Finances of, 71–82, 383, 393, 416n, 426
 Industrial departments, 294
 Number of, 46, 49–50
 Policy Directive on the Socialist Education Campaign in Rural Communes, 68
 Resolution on the Establishment of the People's Communes in Rural Areas, 44n, 46, 48, 51, 84, 226
 Size of, 46–9, 52, 305, 504
 Suburban, 88
 Tax payments by, 72, 89, 340–1, 376
Communes, urban, 226–31, 307, 510
 Number of, 228
 Size of, 228
 Types, 228
Communications, Bank of, *see under* Banks
Communications, Minister of, 264, 497
Communications, Ministry of, 127, 150, 252, 259–63, 266, 270n, 272, 478, 515, 522–3, 525
Communist Labour University, 101n
Communist Party, *see* Chinese Communist Party
Communist Youth League, 56, 65, 186, 191, 196, 211n, 384, 385n
Confidential Communications, Central Bureau of, 253, 526–7
Construction, Bank of, *see under* Banks
Construction Engineering, Ministry of, 149, 150, 170, 468, 472, 478, 519, 520–1
Construction Units, 170–1
Consumer research, 313–14
Contracts, commercial, 28–9, 80, 117, 123, 171, 174, 291, 294–6, 299, 303, 350, 351, 430, 490
Contracts, foreign trade, 329, 331, 333
Contracts, labour, 186–7, 209
Cooking in households, 91, 242
Cooking at mess halls, 62–3, 241
Cooking utensils, 149, 293, 312
Co-operative ownership, *see* Ownership, collective
Co-operatives, *see* Agricultural producer co-operatives; Building co-operatives; Handicraft co-operatives; Salt co-operatives; Supply and marketing co-operatives
Coopers, 225
Copper, 238–9, 241, 284, 478
T

Corporations, advertising, 314
Corporations, foreign trade, 321–3 *passim*, 336, 497, 509
 See also under individual (named) corporations
Corporations, industrial, 25, 157
Corporations, internal trade, 274–7, 282, 284, 288, 291, 316, 442, 497
Cost of living, 208, 454
Cost of living allowances, 205, 208, 210
Costs, definition of, 161
Costs, reduction of, 158, 159, 161, 400, 462, 471
Cotton, 15, 34, 287, 363
 See also Textiles and textile industry
 Cloth, 281, 284, 286, 310–11, 363, 373
 Growing, 34, 90, 99, 111, 114, 323, 337, 338, 347, 371, 447, 455, 467, 487
 Industry, 149, 371, 454
 Prices, 298n, 359, 443, 447, 454
 Procurement, sale and transport, 259, 275, 295, 298n, 338, 344, 347, 356
 Raw, 284, 286, 323, 349, 443, 446
 Yarn, 281, 283–6, 373
Council for Mutual Economic Assistance (Comecon), 331–2
Counties, *see Hsien*
Credit, 32, 37, 329, 402, 418–33, 462, 477, 480, 485, 490, 498
 See also Agricultural loans; Bank loans; Loans from private sources; Advance payments
Credit co-operatives, 27, 37, 43, 44, 62, 75, 87, 365, 382, 401, 407, 409–11, 418, 419, 420, 426, 431
Crockery and porcelain, 149
Cropping, multiple, 31, 33, 347
Crystal mines, 240
Cuba, 320n
Cultural Relations with Foreign Countries, Commission for, 524–5
'Cultural Revolution', 18, 163, 167, 199, 300, 401, 485, 499, 506, 510, 513, 514
Culture and Education, Commission of, 526–7
Culture and Education, State Council Office of, 20
Culture, Ministry of, 286, 522–3
Currency (*jenminpi* or *yuan*), 71n, 414–18, 419, 427, 435, 471, 506
 Foreign currency, 331, 414, 435
 Foreign exchange rates, 319–20, 322, 328, 333–5, 406, 407, 412, 417–18, 479, 485, 498, 513
Czechoslovakia, 92n

Daily Worker, 29, 191, 314
Dairen, 265, 326

Decentralization, Ch. 18 *passim*; 17, 19, 45, 283, 293, 315, 349, 377, 382, 403, 405, 413, 460, 479, 485, 492
  See also Central Government control
  Of banking, 427–8
  Of commerce, 287–8, 324–5, 327, 328
  Of finance, 394–401, 475–6
  Of forestry, 121
  Of industry, 133n, 151–4, 156, 157, 172, 328
  Of mining, 241–6
  Of planning, 323, 460–7, 473, 477, 482, 485–8
  Of price control, 288, 442, 454–6
  Provincial, 464
  Of railways, 254–7
  Of road transport, 259
  Of state farms, 98, 106–7
Defence, *see* Military equipment; Nuclear weapons programme; People's Liberation Army
'Democratic Parties', 19, 384
'Departmentalism', 290
Depreciation, 161, 163–4, 371, 75n, 109, 119, 153, 268n, 369, 370
Design, engineering, 155, 171, 475
Diamonds, 239, 240n
Diseases, crop, 384
Diseases, malnutrition and deficiency, 312
Districts (*ch'ü*), 22, 23, 48, 62, 228, 303, 394
Districts, rural (*hsiang*), 22, 23, 37, 43–8, 64, 183, 393, 400
Districts, special or administrative (*chuan ch'ü*), 22, 42, 57, 130–1, 394, 464
Dividends, fixed, 412, 425
Dockyards, 265, 272
Downer, G., 321n
Draught animals, 34, 41, 58–9, 75n, 76, 301–2, 431
'Dual subordination', 244, 248, 255, 496
Dyers and dyestuffs, 225, 274
Dzungaria, 98n

East Asia, Bank of, *see under* Banks
East China Oil Administrative Bureau, 249
Economic accounting system, 26, 257, 271, 276, 385–7, 421, 458, 509
Economic accounting units, 26, 51, 57, 64, 107, 132, 157, 159, 232, 246–7, 376, 410, 488
Economic commissions, local, 462
Economic co-ordinating regions, 20, 399n, 464, 465
Economic planning, Ch. 17; 15, 25–6, 158, 160, 234, 289, 290, 367, 384, 387, 428–9
  Annual, 158, 457, 467, 487
  Conferences, 466, 469

Economic planning (*cont.*)
  Decentralization, 323, 460–7, 473, 477, 482, 485–8
  Local, 457, 461–3, 465–6
  Meaning of, 457, 495
  Five-Year Plan, First, 17, 41, 73, 124, 134, 136, 137, 142, 144, 145, 155, 165, 168, 173, 182, 184, 200, 203, 213, 215, 216, 226, 231, 242, 271, 272, 283, 306, 338, 354, 356, 363, 370, 371, 377, 383, 394, 401, 416, 420, 434, 458–60, 471–4, 483–4, 491–2, 502, 505, 510
  Five-Year Plan, Second, 18, 126, 133, 136, 137, 338, 363, 377, 395, 459–60, 464, 467
  Five-Year Plan, Third, 18, 467–9, 494
  Perspective plans, 458, 459
  Planning System, Directive on Reform of, 397, 464–5, 473, 474, 482, 485
  Quarterly, 158, 457, 459, 470
  Supervision of, 457, 469–71, 490
  See also Agricultural planning; Commercial planning; Industry, planning of; Investment, planning of; Labour, planning of; State Planning Commission; State Economic Commission
Economic Research, 107, 282, 480, 488–90
Education, 63, 64, 82n, 178, 187, 206, 363, 384, 385, 389, 393, 493
Education, higher, 178, 194, 255, 384, 462, 497, 498, 500
  Graduates of, 117, 193–4, 498
  Students sent abroad, 178, 194, 462
Education, Ministry of, 466, 522–3, 526
Education, Ministry of Higher, 178, 552–3
Education, spare-time, 63, 187
Eggs, 285, 286, 307, 313n, 351, 352
Electric power, Ch. 5; 140, 145, 152, 463, 473–6
  Capacity and output, 126, 132, 245n
  Consumption by sectors, 135–6
  Costs and pricing, 137–8, 455
  Grids, 132–5, 138, 152, 153, 500, 502, 504
  Hydro-electric, 124, 127, 128, 132, 133, 136–8, 172, 245n, 481, 514
  Thermal, 136–7, 481
Electric Power, Ministry of, 126, 149n, 153n, 522–3
  See also Water Conservancy and Electric Power, Ministry of
Electrical equipment, 136, 152, 153, 314n, 478
Electrical Equipment, Ministry of, 149n, 153n, 520–1
Electricity Administration, North-East, 132
Electrification, rural, 124, 125, 133–6, 138, 430
Embargo, strategic, 334, 336, 413

Emerson, J. P., 180–1, 280
Employees, *see* Labour
Engineering, 152n, 156, 171, 475
Engineers, 188–9, 193–4, 202, 482n
Enterprises, Chs. 6 and 7 *passim*; 372, 375, 385, 400, 409, 418, 420, 421, 427–8, 446, 470
   See also Ownership, joint state-private, private, and state
   Allocation to, 173–5
   Definition of, 25–6
   Operations and plans, 157–68, 428, 462, 482–5
   Party organization in, 195–201, 210, 500–1
   Profits of, 25, 153–4, 158–68, 315, 368–71, 375–6, 378, 389–93, 395–8, 400–1, 412, 423
   See also Profits
   Staff of, 192–204, 210–12, 500–1
Etienne, Gilbert, 342
Exhibitions
   Abroad, 330
   Foreign, in China, 330, 333
Expenditure, budgetary, 366–78, 383–9, 394–8, 462, 498
Experts, foreign, 177
Experts, State Council Bureau of, 177
Experts, State Council Bureau for the Affairs of, 524–5
Experts, State Council Bureau of Foreign, 177, 524–5
Exports, Ch. 12; 174, 274, 286, 313n, 319, 354, 355n, 459, 462, 485, 486, 499
   See also Foreign trade; Corporations, foreign trade
Export duties, 381
Ex-servicemen, 68, 82, 100, 111, 177, 179, 200, 317, 501
Extra-budgetary funds, 211, 260, 365, 369, 389–93, 398, 399, 400, 401, 412, 471, 472, 476–8, 482, 508

Factories, *see* Industry; Street factories
Fairs, *see* Markets, rural, occasional
Fairs, abroad, 330
Fairs, Canton Export, 333, 510
Fairs, Chinese Export Garments Trade, 333
Farm tools, 34, 75n, 80n, 220, 224, 225, 233, 269, 294, 310n, 410n, 431n
Farms, demonstration and experimental, 61, 504
   See also Agriculture; State farms
Farmers, Bank of, *see under* Banks
Fertilizers
   Animal manure, 34, 41, 58, 82, 91
   Chemical, 34, 61, 76, 93, 104, 109, 138, 142–4, 149, 150, 267, 269, 283, 285, 319, 373, 431n, 432, 443, 455, 478, 490

Fertilizers (*cont.*)
   Green manure, 34, 58
   Mud, 34, 58
   Nightsoil, 34, 35, 58, 82, 91, 389
   Soya bean cake, 34
Fibres, 285, 286, 338, 343, 443
   See also Cotton; Hemp; Jute; Kenafe; Ramie; Silk
Film studios, 386
Finance, 30
Finance, *see* Budgets and budgeting; Taxation; Expenditure, budgetary; Revenue, budgetary
Finance and Economics, Commission of, 526–7
Finance, Minister of, 71n, 166, 275, 294, 359, 365, 366, 436, 458, 474
Finance, Ministry of, 30, 155, 260, 275, 340, 345, 365–6, 378n, 385n, 387, 390, 392, 394, 403, 408, 412, 423, 449, 457, 470, 503, 515, 518–19
   Local bureaux and departments, 294, 365–6, 387, 390, 423, 470
Finance Research Institute, 366
Finance and Trade, State Council Office of, 20, 156, 275, 322, 365, 457, 468, 517
Finland, trade with, 331
Fish and fisheries, 61, 286, 313n, 351, 487
   See also Aquatic products
'Five-antis' Campaign, 146, 414
Flood control, 125, 127, 138
Flour mills, 476
Fluorite, 239
Food Industry, Ministry of, 149, 153n, 248, 286, 520–1
Food, Minister of, 358, 359
Food, Ministry of, 151, 153n, 154n, 274, 275, 276n, 286, 287n, 310, 345, 518–19
   Local departments, 350
Food processing, *see* Agricultural products, processing of
Foreign Affairs, Ministry of, 468, 518–19
Foreign Affairs, State Council Office of, 20, 517, 528
Foreign aid given by China, 174, 320, 330, 334, 385, 506
Foreign currency, *see under* Currency
Foreign exchange rates, *see under* Currency
Foreign Economic Relations Commission, 518–19
Foreign Economic Relations, General Bureau of, 330, 524–5
Foreign Language Institute, 177
Foreign Language Press, 177
Foreign Language Publication and Distribution Administrative Bureau, 526–7

Foreign trade, Ch. 12; 485-6
  Agreements, 324, 330-4
  Corporations, 274, 321, 322, 324-9, 332-6, 509
    See also under the individual (named) corporations
  Financing of, 329, 331, 333-4, 407, 412, 418
  Plans, 322-4, 485
  Prices, 334-6
  Profits, 288
    See also Corporations, foreign trade; and under separate foreign countries
Foreign Trade Arbitration Commission, 330
Foreign Trade, Minister of, 335
Foreign Trade, Ministry of, 151, 153, 154n, 156, 274, 275, 276n, 286, 287n, 321-4, 327-9, 380-1, 418, 518-19
  Local bureaux, 322, 326
Forestry, Ministry of, 94, 121, 149n, 151, 277n, 286, 408, 522-3
  Local bureaux and departments, 121-2
Forestry Industry, Ministry of, 121, 149n, 153n, 522-3
Forestry and Land Reclamation, Ministry of, 522-3
Forests and forestry, 94, 120-3, 259, 266, 441n, 476, 487
'Four Cleansings' Campaign, 70
'Four Fixed' factors of production, 53, 57-8
France, grain imports from, 330
Free market, *see under* Prices
Fruit and fruit trees, 84, 91, 284, 296, 351
Fu Tso-yi, 126
Fuel, *see* Coal; Petroleum; Electric power, etc.
Fuel Industries, Ministry of, 126, 151n, 520-1
Fukien, 48, 54, 78, 97, 98, 103-4, 243-4, 257, 400n, 419
Funnell, Victor, 78n, 199n
Fushun, 249, 452n

Gas, 140, 248, 249
Geological surveying, 237-40
Geology, Ministry of, 127, 153n, 237, 239, 522-3
Germany, East, 327
Germany (pre-war), trade with, 321
Glass industry, 140
Gold
  Circulation and holdings, 414, 417
  Price paid for, 416-7
  Production and mineral reserves, 239, 240, 248
Gosbank, *see under* Banks
Government Administrative Council, 275, 322, 346

Graduates of higher educational institutions, 117, 193-4, 498, 501n
Grain, Ch. 8 *passim*; 33, 95-7, 99, 109, 259, 276, 288, 323, 507
  Compulsory sales, 284, 346-64
  Corporations for grain trade, 375-6
  Definition of, 96n, 346, 357n
  Exports, 319, 354
  Free market sales, 292n, 298, 362-3
  Imports, 264, 312, 319, 332, 356, 507
  Output, 41, 90, 94-6, 99n, 138, 338, 343, 346, 347, 350, 354, 356, 357, 364, 447, 467, 487, 507
  Prices, 76n, 90, 298, 358-64, 443, 444, 447-9, 499
  Processing, 135, 361
  Rationing, 76-7, 284, 310-11, 363, 346-8
  Reserves, 57, 90, 335, 345n, 348, 354, 397
  Storage, 57, 89-90, 287, 359
    See also Agricultural Tax
Granaries, *see* Grain storage
Grand Canal, 263-4, 497
Graphite, 239
Gray, J., 425n
'Great Administrative Regions', 20-1, 276, 394, 399, 406n, 460
Great Hsingan Mountains, 121
Great Leap Forward, 17-18, 45-6, 59, 70, 74, 124, 129, 130, 133, 134, 138, 158, 166, 168, 169, 187, 193, 200, 203, 207, 215, 216, 217, 224, 226, 229, 246, 248, 253, 271, 282, 283, 290, 306, 349, 351, 363, 375n, 391, 399, 400, 401, 416, 429, 434, 460, 467, 468n, 469, 481, 483, 488, 491, 500, 502, 506, 510, 511
Groundnuts, *see* Peanuts
Guilds, 188n
Guinea, 320n
Gypsum, 239

Hainan Island, 92n, 98, 100, 102
Hami, 314n
'Han' Chinese, 21n, 93, 100
Han River Valley, 490
Handicraft co-operatives, 27, 44, 140, 219-26, 232-6, 291, 378-9, 423, 441, 509
  See also All-China Federation of Handicraft Co-operatives
Handicrafts and handicraftsmen, Ch. 8; 27, 42, 81-2, 91, 140-2, 149, 184, 193, 245, 295-6, 325, 329, 379, 410n, 422n, 442, 509
  See also Street industry
Hangchow, 490
Harbin, 189, 228, 254
Harvests, *see* Agricultural production
Hats, 151n, 233
Hawkers, *see* Pedlars

Health, institutions and services, 15, 64, 182, 191–2, 209n, 212, 213, 226, 372, 384, 463
Health, Ministry of, 153n, 277n, 286, 287n, 478, 522–3
Heavy Industry, Ministry of, 150, 518–19
Heilungkiang, 40n, 74, 77, 92, 97, 98–100, 106–7, 109, 114–16, 120, 172, 179, 200, 228, 240, 243–4, 248, 254, 256, 263, 313n
Hemp, 284
Hides and skins, 284
'High and stable yield' areas, 18, 76, 79, 103, 114, 125, 490, 507
Highways, see Roads
Hire purchase, 312
Ho Ch'ang-kung, 239
Ho Chien-chang, 480
Ho Kuei-lin, 481
Hofheinz, R., 22
Hogs, see Pigs
Hokiang reclamation area, 98, 106
Honan, 48, 58, 62, 77, 97, 98, 99, 129, 131, 133, 144, 182, 227, 228, 263, 298n, 350, 351, 400, 419
Hong Kong, 193, 263, 326, 329, 332–3, 351, 407, 414, 513
Hong Kong and Shanghai Banking Corporation, see under Banks
Hopei, 97, 115, 117n, 133, 172, 182, 228, 242, 264, 265, 280, 299
Horses, 301–2
Hospitals, 385
Hot'ung, see Contract
Hours of work, 214
Housing, 435, 513
  State Housing Administrative Bureau, 524–5
Hsiang (rural district), 22, 23, 37, 43–8, 50, 55, 64, 71, 122n, 183, 393, 400
Hsien (county), 18, 22, 23n, 25, 35, 37, 42, 48, 52, 57, 60–4 *passim*, 66n, 68, 98, 115–18, 122n, 125, 130–3, 138, 199, 222, 253, 259, 260, 263, 279, 302, 303, 306, 308, 309, 339, 340, 350, 366, 383–91, 393, 399–400, 406–7, 409, 410, 413, 429, 442, 444, 464, 469, 486–7, 489–90, 503–4
Hsin Hua Book Store, 286
Hsinkang, 265
Hsit'ung, see System
Hsü Ti-hsin, 25, 207, 340, 415
Hsüeh Mu-ch'iao, 361–2, 443, 493
Huai River, 129, 502
Huai River Water Conservancy Commission, 127, 129, 497
Huang Ta, 415
Huchow, 490
Hulunbuir reclamation area, 98

Hunan, 19, 47, 97, 99, 125, 225, 240
'Hundred Flower' period, 29, 192, 252, 265, 272, 508
Hungary, 320n
Hunting Control Bureau, 121
Hupeh, 74, 97, 99, 114, 131, 257, 299, 326, 341, 353, 503
Hydro-electricity, see Electric power

Ichang, 262, 267
Ili, 98n
Imports, Ch. 12; 274, 372, 388n, 418, 458, 462, 485
  See also Foreign trade; Corporations, foreign trade; Grain imports
Import duties, 322–3, 380–1, 383, 394, 397, 398
Incentives
  Material, see Wages; Bonuses
  Non-material, 207, 212
Income, national, see National income
Income tax, 315, 373n, 378–80, 396, 421n
India, 103, 321
Indonesia, 103, 264, 320n
Industrial and commercial tax, 72, 137n, 164, 169, 300–1, 316, 360, 372–7, 394, 396, 419n, 422n, 435, 439–41, 509
  Local supplement to, 373n, 389, 393, 394n
Industry, Chs. 6, 7, 8; 16, 17, 18, 19, 99, 245, 280–3, 372, 411, 514
  Control of, see Central Government control; Decentralization; Ownership
  Definitions, 140–1, 219–20
  Industrial Management System, Decree on the Reform of, 151–4, 165, 177, 197, 209, 484, 496
  Industrial Policy, Seventy Points on, 190, 282, 308
  Local bureaux and departments, 156–7, 328, 465
  Location, 133, 144–5, 472
  Managers, 147, 165, 177–8, 192–204, 208, 210–12, 500–1, 507–8
  Operation of, 157–68
  Output, 141–4, 151, 153, 169, 391–2, 462–3
  Party organization in, 195–201, 210, 500–1
  Planning, Ch. 17 *passim*; 133, 141, 158–67, 229, 428–9
  Rural, 44, 45, 59, 61–2, 64, 88–9, 135, 142, 183, 224, 293, 295–6, 376–7
    See also Handicrafts
  Small-scale, Ch. 8 *passim*; 17, 61, 141, 411, 510
  Street, see Street industry
  Verticalization, 99–100, 121, 151, 168–70, 175n, 229, 479, 503

Industry, Verticalization (*cont.*)
  See also Enterprises; Ownership; Government control; Decentralization; Industrial and commercial tax; Labour; Wages; Prices; Handicrafts; Success indicators; Allocation of raw materials; Profits; Training; Trade Unions, etc.
Industry and Communications, State Council Office of, 20, 148, 176, 252, 468, 517
  Director of, 148, 252, 468
Information General Office, 526, 527
Inner Mongolia, 21, 22, 96, 97, 98, 100, 120, 122, 134, 144, 258, 497
Innovations, technical, 212, 262, 411
Insecticides, 149, 373, 443n
'Institutions' (*shihyeh*), 25n, 368–70, 385–7, 389, 397, 404, 409, 418, 421, 462
Insurance, 267, 366, 372, 404–5, 515–16
  Labour, 182, 192, 212–13
Intelligence and General Office, 526–7
Interest, 36, 479, 480
  On bank deposits, 378, 380, 419n, 420, 421n
  On bank loans, 419n, 423–6
  On bonds, 380, 381–2, 513–14
  On private lending, 32, 36, 419, 431
  To ex-capitalists, 146–7
Interest-free loans, 426, 430
Internal Affairs, Minister of, 252
Internal Affairs, Ministry of, 94, 105, 177, 518–19, 527
Internal Affairs, State Council Office of, 20, 517, 520, 528
International Economic Conference, Moscow (1952), 329
Inventions, 212
Investment, 17, 18, 170n, 416, 421, 468–9, 477
  Budgetary grants for, 93, 270–2, 315, 365–71, 383–5, 397, 408, 409, 411–12, 505
  From extra-budgetary funds, 167, 390–3, 412, 498
  Planning and control of, 167, 365, 458, 462, 470, 472–82, 498
  Projects, 170–2, 473–6, 498
    Above norm, 145, 473–4
    Below norm, 473–4
  See also State Construction Commission; Construction Bank; and under separate sectors of economy
Investment Bank for Capital Construction, *see under* Banks
Iron mining and ore, 238–9, 241, 243
Iron, pig, 232, 259, 483

Iron and steel industry and products, 75n, 143, 145, 150–2, 243, 284, 429, 467, 474, 476
  Allocation and transport of products, 173n, 259, 286, 477–8
  Imports, 324
  Prices and profits, 450–1, 481
  Small-scale, 18, 59, 142, 224, 225, 232, 429
  See also under individual iron and steel works; Metallurgy, Ministry of
Irrigation, *see* Water conservancy
Irrigation Control Board, 126
Irrigation districts, 60, 129–30, 132

Japan and Japanese economic activities, 16, 92, 145, 187, 193, 264, 274, 321, 330, 510
Jenminpi (JMP), *see* Currency
'Job Groups', 52–3
Joint State-Private Bank, *see under* Banks
Joint state-private ownership, *see* Ownership, joint state-private
Justice, Ministry of, 522–3
Jute, 487

Kaifeng, 228
Kailan mines, 242, 244n
Kang Chao, 492
Kansu, 97, 98, 128, 133, 144, 172, 182, 248, 258
Kao Kang, 457, 458, 510
Kaoliang, 33
Karamai Oilfield, 248, 249
Kashing, 490
Kenafe, 284
Kenya, 320n
Kerosene, 273
Khruschev, 510
Kiangsi, 63n, 97, 98, 101, 106, 108, 110, 340, 361, 409n
Kiangsu, 97, 99, 102, 114, 129, 133, 135n, 182, 264, 361n, 461
Kirin, 97, 115, 120, 172, 227, 253, 425
Kirin Chemical Corporation, 188
Kochiu Tin Mines, 248
Korea, North, 266, 318, 320, 322
Korean War, 17, 319, 334, 382, 414, 418
Ku Mu, 148, 252, 468
Kuan Ta-t'ung, 302, 308
Kuang Ming Daily, 29
Kunming, 78, 134, 201, 254, 257
Kuomintang Government, 16, 145, 188n, 193, 221, 248, 251, 266, 321, 343, 346, 394, 458n
Kuusinen, 192
Kwangsi, 21, 46, 51, 97, 103, 144, 145, 257

INDEX 583

Kwangtung, 247n, 252, 265, 312
  Agriculture, 31, 47, 53, 54, 58, 59, 63, 65, 66, 69, 76, 77, 87, 97, 100, 102, 103-4, 109, 111, 114, 131, 342, 494
  Allocation of raw materials, 465-6
  Commerce, 282, 315
  Industry and handicrafts, 160, 172, 223
  Mining, 247, 249
  Provincial organs, 111, 445, 465
Kweichow, 197, 257, 391, 444
  Agriculture, 47, 97, 103
  Mining, 154, 241, 249

Labour, 27, 475
  Building, 170n
  Commercial, 181, 280, 287
  Industrial, Ch. 7
  Insurance, 182, 192, 209n, 212-13, 516
  Mining, 181, 189, 191, 246
  Plans, 462-6, 498
  Private hiring of, 27, 87, 236
  Productivity, 159, 161, 165n, 207, 208, 215-16
  Rural, 32, 33, 58, 62, 63, 91, 107
  See also Bonuses; Hours of work; Migration; Trade unions; Training; Wages, etc.
Labour, Minister of, 182
Labour, Ministry of, 176, 466, 522-3
'Labour Reform', 105, 257, 391-2
Labour theory of value, 436-9
Ladakh, 260
Lai Jo-yu, 192
Lanchow, 128, 133, 144, 248n, 258
Land reform, 17, 36-8, 40, 338, 409
Landless labourers, 36, 37
Landlords, 35, 37, 409
Laos, 320n, 321
Law, 23-4
Lead, 238-9, 284
Leather industry, 149
Legal Codification, Bureau of, 524-6
Legal Codification, Commission of, 526-7
Lewis, John W., 309n
Lhasa, 258
Li, Choh-ming, 30, 416, 492
Li Fu-ch'un, 227, 453, 466, 467
Li Hsien-nien, 166, 275, 294, 365, 366, 436, 468
Li Hsueh-feng, 148, 196, 197
Liao Lu-yen, 42
Liao-Takasaki Agreement, 330
Liaoning, 228, 315, 326, 454
  Agriculture, 97, 115, 116, 118, 131, 315, 469, 494
  Industry and transport, 169-70, 172, 253, 256, 265
  Mining, 249

Liaoning (*cont.*)
  Revenue, 154, 396
  Supplies for, 307, 312-13
'Liberated areas', 36, 38, 337
Liberman, 158, 162
Licences for vehicles and boats, 381, 396
Light Industry, Ministry of, 102, 148-50, 152, 153n, 154, 222, 240, 248, 276n-277n, 286, 287n, 296, 380, 520-1, 525
  First Ministry of, 149, 150, 154, 479n, 521
  Second Ministry of, 149, 223, 520-1
Liho Dam, 133
Limestone, 239
Lineages, 31, 36, 53, 66
Linear programming, 258, 494, 505
Liu P'ei-chih, 109
Liu Shao-ch'i, 20
Liuchia Dam, 133, 136
Livestock, 33-4, 42, 58, 85, 97, 99, 100
  See also Draught animals; Pigs; Poultry
Loans, *see* Bank loans; Communes, credit departments; Credit; Credit co-operatives; Interest
Loans, from private sources, 32, 37, 87, 419, 431
Local authorities, *see* Administrative units; and under each level of local authority
Local Industry, Ministry of, 148, 149, 520-1
Locomotives, 255, 258, 272
Lorries, 14, 143, 261
Losses of enterprises, 26, 109n, 154n, 159, 242, 268, 316, 327, 359, 361, 376, 429, 441, 452, 453
Lotteries, 382n, 421
Loyang, 144
Luhsien, 268
Lunghai Railway, 258, 267-8

Ma Ming-fang, 275, 365
Ma Wen-jui, 176
Ma Yin-ch'u, 130
Macao, 513
Machine Building, Ministries of, 149-51, 520-1
Machine Building, First Ministry of, 127, 149n, 150, 151n, 153n, 240, 255, 261, 265, 478, 520-1
Machine Building, Second Ministry of, 128, 137, 149n, 150, 153, 165n, 240, 423, 520-1
Machine Building, Third Ministry of, 148, 150, 520-1
Machine Building, Fourth Ministry of, 150, 520-1
Machine Building, Fifth Ministry of, 150, 520-1

Machine Building, Sixth Ministry of, 150, 520–1
Machine Building, Seventh Ministry of, 150, 520–1, 529
Machine Building, Eighth Ministry of, 112, 127, 150, 261, 520–1, 529
Machine tools, 150, 173n
Machinery, 141, 151n, 152, 173, 175n, 269, 285, 319, 325, 474
 Allocation of, 478–9, 498
 Prices of, 397, 455
 Textile, 149, 478
 See also Agricultural machinery
Magnesite, 239
Magnesium, 239
Maize, 15, 33
Mali, 320n
Managers, *see* Industry, managers
Manchouli, 254
Manchuria, *see* 'North-East'
Manganese, 238–9
Mannass River Basin, 98n
Manure, *see* Fertilizers
Mao Tse-tung, 15, 19, 38, 41, 169, 270, 385
Maritime Arbitration Commission, 264
Maritime Customs, 322
 See also Import duties
Maritime Customs General Office, 526–7
Market, free, *see under* Prices
Market research, 282, 313–14, 322
Market towns (*chen*), 18, 22, 23, 35, 44, 45n, 89, 232, 303, 304, 310, 400
Markets, cattle, 301–2
Markets, rural, 87, 90, 111n, 232, 280, 288, 291–309, 329, 377, 445, 448, 509
 Rural marketing systems, 35, 47, 49, 50, 277, 300, 308
 Higher level, 296, 298
 Occasional (fairs), 298, 301–2
 Prices at, 443–6
 Taxation of, 306, 377
Mass campaigns, 23, 130
Mass organizations, 211n, 384
Matches, 149, 281
Meat, 285–6, 307, 313n, 319
Medical services, *see* Health
Medicinal materials, 284, 292n, 325n
Medicinal Materials Corporation, 153n
Merchants, *see* Commerce
Mercury, 239
Mess halls, industrial, 191, 196
 Rural, 57, 62–3, 80, 85, 91, 229, 230, 241, 289, 293, 353, 372
Metallurgical industry, *see* Iron and steel
Metallurgy, Ministry of, 141, 149, 150, 152, 153, 172, 237, 240, 241, 247, 248, 324, 478, 479, 518–19
Meteorological services, 41–2, 384, 522–3
Mexico, grain imports from, 320
Mica, 239
Migration, 98, 99, 111, 180, 182–4, 217–18, 311, 498
Military Council, 423
Military equipment, 142, 152, 174
Military expenditure, 368, 384, 506
Millet, 15, 33
Mines and mining, Ch. 9; 140–2, 152–3, 259, 451, 496
 See also under Coal; Petroleum, etc.
Ministries of central government
 Appointment of ministers, 176
 Duties, 154–5, 398, 464–5, 470
Minority nationalities, *see* Nationalities, minority
Molybdenum, 239
Mongolia, People's Republic of, 257, 266, 318, 320, 322, 332
Motor vehicles, 188, 196, 261, 381, 396, 474, 478
Moutankiang reclamation area, 98, 106
Mow, standard, 116n, 118n
Mud, *see under* Fertilizers
Municipalities, centrally controlled, 19–22 *passim*
Mutual Aid Savings Association, 419
Mutual aid teams, 17, 37–40 *passim*, 346

Nan Han-ch'en, 330, 412
Nanch'ung Oilfield, 248–50
Nankai University, 151n
Nanking, 133, 243, 249, 257, 267
National defence, *see* Military equipment; Military expenditure; Nuclear weapons programme; People's Liberation Army
National Defence, Ministry of, 518–19
National income, 367, 436, 463
National People's Congress, 20, 24, 176, 227, 366
 Standing Committee of, 20, 176
National Price Commission, 361, 442–4, 527–9
National Resources Commission, 248, 458n
National Water and Soil Conservation Commission, 127
Nationalist Government, *see* Kuomintang Government
Nationalities Affairs Commission, 526–7
Nationalities, minority, 21, 50, 301–2, 313, 504
'Native products', 275, 325
Navigation, local bureaux of, 263
Nepal, 320
New China News Agency, 524–5
Newspapers and journals, 29–30, 499
Nightsoil, *see under* Fertilizers
Ninghsia, 21, 46, 98, 115, 144, 154, 172, 241, 256n, 466

Niu Chung-huang, 355
Nomenklatura system, 179, 501
Norms
  Above-norm projects, 145, 473–4
  Below-norm projects, 473–4
'North-East' (formerly Manchuria), 16, 26, 34, 92, 98, 106, 132, 133, 144, 145, 154, 193, 228, 381n, 411n, 457, 510
North-east administrative area, 457
North-East Electricity Administration, 132
North-East General Bureau of Land Reclamation, 98, 106, 107n
Note issue, 402, 405, 412, 414, 416, 419
Nuclear weapons programme, 126n, 128, 137, 138, 194, 240, 384, 506
Nuts, 284
  See also Peanuts

Oil, *see* Petroleum; Vegetable oil
Oil-bearing crops, *see* Vegetable oil
Oksenberg, M., 386n, 390n
Organization for European Economic Co-operation, 332
Overseas Chinese, 264, 313, 387, 420
  Commission for Reception and Settlement of Returned Overseas Chinese, 527
  Investment corporations, 103n, 151, 423, 513–14
  Remittances, 312n, 313, 407, 413, 420, 513–14
  State farms, 100, 103, 105, 108, 110, 111, 514
Overseas Chinese Affairs Commission, 94, 103, 526–7
Overseas Chinese Banking Corporation, *see under* Banks
Ownership, 25–7
  Collective, 25–7, 31, 103n, 509
    See also Agricultural Producer Co-operatives; Collectivization; Commerce, co-operative; Communes, rural peoples; Credit co-operatives; Handicraft co-operatives; Supply and marketing co-operatives
  Co-operative, *see* Collective
  Joint state-private, 27, 103n, 145–8, 165, 193, 194, 205, 235, 252, 275, 291, 316n, 321, 367, 369, 372, 378, 412, 424n, 509, 510
    See also Commerce, joint state-private
  Private, 25, 27, 31, 145–6, 148, 234, 235, 241n, 277, 279, 280, 321, 372, 374, 378, 379, 418, 482, 509
    See also Commerce, private
  State, 25–6, 92, 112, 369n, 372
    See also Commerce, state; State farms; Collectivization; and Ch. 6 *passim*

Pacific Ocean Insurance Co, 515
Pai national minority, 301–2
Pakistan, 320n, 334
Pan-American Airways, 266
Pan Fu-sheng, 40, 352
Paoan, 54, 351
Paoki, 258, 267
Paotow, 134, 144, 258
Paper and paper industry, 120n, 149, 152n, 281, 284, 285, 474, 514
Patent rights, absence of, 212
Pawnshops, 419
Payments, advance, *see* Advance payments
Peanuts, 343, 359, 487
Pearl River
  Basin, 33, 111n
  Delta, 102, 114, 125, 134, 430, 490
Pearl River Navigation Administrative Bureau, 263
Peasants, Chs. 2 and 3 *passim*
  Middle, 35–7, 80n, 411
  Poor, 35–7, 80n, 408, 411
  Rich, 35–7, 347, 409
    See also Agricultural producer co-operatives; Communes, rural people's; Private plots, etc.
Pedlars, 298, 301, 304, 307, 374, 456
  Licensed, 280, 297, 310
  Tax on, 377, 379
  Unlicensed, 279, 280, 310
Peking, 21, 47, 55n, 68, 78, 97, 102, 115, 133, 154, 169, 170, 231, 258, 266, 281, 290, 307, 313, 396, 421n, 454
Peking Agricultural University, 68
Peking Correspondence College, 68
Penhsi Iron and Steel Works, 153n, 241
Pensions, 204, 214, 384
People's Bank of China, *see under* Banks
People's Construction Bank of China, *see under* Banks
People's Daily, 29, 155, 159, 171, 201, 227, 233, 308, 314, 350, 353, 410, 419, 445, 484, 489
People's Insurance Co, 404, 515–16
People's Liberation Army, 23, 98, 106, 151, 248, 313n, 378n, 387, 501
  See also Ex-servicemen; Military Council; Military equipment; Military expenditure
People's Liberation Army Production and Construction Corps, Sinkiang, 97–100, 106, 151, 240, 257, 260, 476
People's Liberation Army Railway Engineering Corps, 99, 257, 259, 260, 354
People's Supervisory Commission, 526–7
People's University, 387
Pepper growing, 104n
Perkins, D. H., 434, 435

Personnel appointments and assignments, 176–80
Personnel Bureau, 23n, 526–7
Petroleum, 145, 172, 237–41, 248–50, 265–6, 455
  Distribution, 274, 285–6, 478, 483
  Equipment, 478
  Local bureaux, 249
  Mining, 153, 240, 241, 248–50, 473, 474
  Oilfields, 242, 248–50
  Pricing, 261, 443, 455
  Prospecting, 237, 239–40, 249
  Refining, 152, 153, 241, 248–9, 474, 478, 483
  Reserves, 239, 240n
  Shale, 248, 249
Petroleum, Ministry of, 126, 150, 153n, 237, 240, 241, 248, 520–1
Pharmaceuticals, 150, 474
Phoneticization of the Chinese Language, Commission for, 526–7
Phosphates, 34, 239
Physical Culture and Sports Commission, 526–7
Pig cycle, 448
Pigs and pork, 15, 34, 313n, 487
  Manure, *see under* Fertilizers
  Prices, 359, 443, 448
  Rearing, 58–9, 86, 91, 296, 299, 311, 352, 353
  Sale, 101, 284–5, 297, 319, 351, 353
  See also Commodities, third category
'Planned purchase and planned supply', 284, 291, 310, 345, 346
Planning, *see* Economic planning
Plastics, 18, 150
Plots, private, *see* Private plots
Plough, double-wheeled and double-share, 313n
Po I-po, 148, 252, 458, 468
Police, expenditure on, 384
Polish economic activities, 265
Political and Legal Affairs, Commission for, 526–7
Popularization of Standard Spoken Chinese, Central Commission for, 526–7
Population, 15, 31, 32, 43, 98, 138, 183, 185, 502, 504, 511
Pork, *see* Pigs
Ports, 264–5, 326, 473
  Bureaux, 264–5, 322
  Treaty, 273–4
Post Office and posts, 270, 405
Posts and Telecommunications, Ministry of, 153, 253, 522–3
Potassium ore, 239
Potatoes, 15, 33, 90, 96n, 242, 307, 310n, 313n, 338, 346, 347, 357n
Poultry, 34, 91, 101, 285, 299, 307, 313n, 319, 351, 352
Poyang Lake, 101
Prices, Ch. 16; 166, 170, 327, 479–82
  See also under Grain
  Agricultural, 109, 184, 273, 291–307 *passim*, 358–64, 383, 439–40, 442–6, 447–9, 450, 455–6, 489–90, 510
  See also 'Scissors' index
  Decentralization of price control, 288, 442, 446, 450n–451n, 453, 454–6, 510
  Foreign trade, prices in, 323, 327, 334–6, 441
  Free market, 160, 162, 173, 184, 235–6, 273, 275, 281, 292, 298, 300, 359, 362–3, 434, 440, 442, 445–9, 480, 482
  Local differentials, 208, 280, 442–3, 453–6
  Machinery and scope of price policy, 276, 290, 297, 434–6, 442–7, 454–6
  National Price Conferences, 442–4, 454
  Objectives of price policy, 358, 434–6, 453, 477, 479
  Producer goods, 168, 438, 449–53, 479–82
  'Production price', 162n–163n, 437
  Retail, 279, 315, 434, 439–41, 446
  'Scissors' index, 78n, 448–9, 456
  Seasonal price differentials, 359
  Types of, 437, 439–41
  Wholesale, 275, 279, 315, 439, 440–2, 452
Printing industry, 140, 388
Private money lending, *see* Loans from private sources
Private plots, 27n, 42–3, 45, 53, 58, 82–8, 89–91 *passim*, 111n, 299, 319, 338, 410n, 448, 509
  Exemption from tax and compulsory sales, 341, 352
  On state farms, 110–11
Procuracy, 471
Producer goods, *see* Allocation of raw materials and producer goods; Prices, producer goods
Production brigades, 26, 42, 43, 51, 53n, 296, 297, 298n, 329, 350, 351, 410, 484
  As basic units of economic accounting, 51, 57, 341
  Tax payments by, 341, 376
  Total number of, 52
Production teams, 26, 42, 51–3, 56–7, 73, 294, 295, 410, 490
  As basic units of economic accounting, 51, 57, 73, 341
  In forestry, 123
  In state farms, 106, 107, 110
  Tax payments by, 341, 376
  Total number of, 52
Profits, 25, 146, 242, 369–71, 375–6, 378–9, 391–2, 429n, 436–41, 450–3, 471, 482n
  Above-plan, 164–5, 166, 375, 437

INDEX 587

Profits (*cont.*)
  As source of budgetary revenue, 164, 270–1, 358–64, 368–71, 376, 400, 401, 510
  As source of extra-budgetary revenue, 389–92, 412
  As success indicator, 26, 158–67, 287–8, 315, 369, 471, 480–2, 483n, 485, 508
  Commercial, 287–8, 298, 315–16, 327, 358–64, 369–71, 453
  Division of profits with local authorities, 153–4, 166, 241, 288, 316, 327, 345n, 395–6
  Industrial, 157–68 *passim*, 370–1, 401, 438, 450–4, 480–2
  Method of remittance, 375ns
  Ploughing back of, 164, 168, 230, 365, 405, 411, 419, 476
  Reckoned on capital, 137, 162–3, 167, 268, 370–1, 393, 437–8, 450–1, 480–2, 485
  Reckoned on cost, 137, 161–2, 167, 268, 370–1, 437–9, 450–1, 481, 485
  Reckoned on wages, 437–8
  Retained by enterprises and ministries, 155, 164–8, 209, 214, 216, 315, 369, 375, 389, 391, 412, 437
Provincial level authorities, 17, 19–22, 42, 135, 151–7, 174, 175, 256, 387, 388, 393–400 *passim*, 428, 442–4, 455–6, 460–6, 475–6, 492; Ch. 18 *passim*
  See also Central Government control; Decentralization; Budgets, local; Industry, local bureaux; Chinese Communist Party provincial committees; Chinese Communist Party provincial secretaries
Public Security, Ministry of, 23, 94, 105, 183, 384, 471, 501, 518–19
Public utilities, 140–2, 389, 393
  See also under separate utilities
Publications General Office, 526–7
Publishing, 325, 386
Pumps, mechanized, 125, 134, 136, 138, 430, 504
  See also Electrification, rural; Water conservancy
Purchase of Agricultural Products, Ministry of, 274, 518–19
Purchasing agents, 175, 290–1, 307

Quartz, 239

Radio, central control of, 497
Radios, 312
Rails, 255, 258, 478
Railways, Ch. 10 *passim*; 26, 92, 172, 174, 247n, 497

Railways (*cont.*)
  Freight and freight rates, 252, 259, 267, 268, 451, 462, 498
  Local bureaux, 254–6
  Local railways, 258, 259, 497
  Investment in railways, 172, 270–1, 473
  Rolling stock, 255, 474, 478
Railways, Ministry of, 150, 151n, 153, 253–5 *passim*, 258, 259, 266, 478, 515, 522–3
Ramie, 284, 443
Rapeseed, 487
Rations and rationing, 309–13, 180, 183, 229, 289, 348, 434, 435, 440, 513
Raw Materials Reserves, State Bureau of, 486, 529
Raw materials, *see* Agricultural products; Allocation of raw materials and producer goods
Reclamation of waste land, 109, 339, 397
  See also State farms
Red Flag, 29, 85, 145, 167, 308, 468, 472, 493
Red Guards, 27
Reform of the Written Language, Commission for, 526–7
Refrigerating plants, 287
Regions, *see* Autonomous regions; Economic co-ordinating regions; Great administrative regions
Rehabilitation period (1949–52), 17, 196, 382, 421
Relief, expenditure on, 384
Religious Affairs, State Council Bureau of, 524–5
Remittances from overseas Chinese, *see under* Overseas Chinese
Rent of agricultural land, 32, 36, 78–9, 339, 489
Rent of housing, 208, 389
Repairs, major repair fund, 371, 389, 406
Reserves, commodity (general), 174, 275, 435, 459, 485–6
  Financial, 394, 397
  Grain, 57, 90, 335, 345n, 348, 354, 397
Residence permits, 180, 311, 498
'Responsibility System' (*paokan chihtu*), 27–8, 53–4, 107, 118, 171, 195, 198, 249, 306, 349, 353, 386, 401, 477
Restaurants, 147, 311, 312, 509
Retailing, *see* Commerce, retailing
Revenue, budgetary, 166, 300, 361, 365–83, 385, 393–401, 498, 507
  See also Budgets and budgeting; Taxation
Revolving Fund for Agricultural Loans, 428, 430
Revolving Fund for Local Authorities, 385
Rice, *see* Grain

Richman, Barry, 157n, 163n, 167n, 208n, 211n, 446n, 454n
River Conservancy Commissions, 127–33 *passim*, 138, 498, 500, 502
Roads, 64, 252–3, 259–62, 266, 270, 272, 381, 384, 473, 497
Rolling stock, *see under* Railway
Royalties, Chairman Mao's, 385
Rubber
  Allocation, 478
  Growing, 100
  Manufacture, 150, 474, 514
  Synthetic, 150

Salinization of soil, 130
Salt, 239, 263n, 443
  Production, 149, 240, 248, 380, 474, 483
  Distribution, 248, 275, 285, 380, 483
  Tax, 380, 383, 394
Salt co-operatives, 248
Sanmen Gorge Dam, 128, 133
Sarawak, 104n
Savings, 73–4, 208, 382, 420, 435, 513
  See also Bank accounts and deposits; Bonds
Schools, *see* Education
Schran, P., 78
Schurmann, F., 469
Science and scientists, 155–6, 177, 178, 372, 384, 462, 497, 500, 511
  See also Technical manpower
Scientific Planning Commission, 156, 518–19
Scientific and Technological Commission, 156, 177, 518–19
Scientific and Technological Personnel Administrative Bureau, 177, 526–7
'Scissors' index, *see under* Prices
Seamen, foreign, 327n
Secret societies, 36
Seed, 42, 102, 111, 423, 431n
Self sufficiency
  Local, 21, 89, 101–2, 104, 111, 135, 137, 139, 229, 243, 245, 247, 258, 269, 273, 290, 293, 303, 307–9, 323, 356, 464, 483, 485, 502–3, 505
  Industrial, 102, 168–70, 479, 502–3
    See also Verticalization
  National, 323–4, 331, 485
'Sending down' (*hsiafang*) movement, 56, 106, 130, 183, 185–6, 203, 510
Servicemen, *see* People's Liberation Army; Ex-servicemen
Sewing machines, 149, 312
Sha Ch'ien-li, 358–9
Shanghai, 21, 133, 135n, 228
  Agriculture, 21, 47, 97, 134
  Banking, 412–13

Shanghai (*cont.*)
  Commerce, 175, 290, 300n, 307, 313, 314, 326, 327n, 478
  Finance, 154, 378, 382n, 396
  Industry, 16, 133–4, 144–5, 148, 168–70, 174, 197, 201, 212, 215, 230, 249, 314, 450n–451n, 466
  Prices, 450n–451n, 454
  Transport, 256, 258, 263, 265
Shanghai Sea Transport Administrative Bureau, 263
Shansi, 97, 133–4, 135n, 144, 198, 225, 258, 391n, 409n
Shantung, 97, 98, 114–15, 131, 172, 182, 264, 494, 505
Shensi, 97, 133, 172, 182, 253, 258
Shenyang, 169, 170, 201, 228, 454
Shih, *see* Municipality
Shihchingshan Iron and Steel Works, 153n, 171, 172, 241
Shihhotzu, 99
Shihyeh, *see* Institutions
Shipbuilding, 265, 272, 274
Shipping co-operatives, 263, 266
Ships and shipping, Ch. 10 *passim*; 145, 247n, 478
  Coastal, 153, 262–7, 270, 497
  Chartered, 264, 497
  Foreign, 251, 263–5, 497
  Freight and freight rates, 252, 253, 262, 264, 266–8
  Ocean, 262, 264, 265, 270, 272, 497
  River, 153, 251, 252, 262–8, 270, 272, 497
Shoes, 149, 225, 233, 285, 293, 312, 313n
Shops, *see* Commerce, retailing
Silica, 239
Silk, 103, 284, 321, 328
Silver, 239, 248, 414, 417
Sinankiang Dam, 133, 135n
Sining, 258
Sinkiang, 21, 46, 93, 98–100, 145n, 179, 208
  Agriculture, 46, 92n, 93, 97–100, 114, 116, 497
  Commerce, 314n
  Finance, 396, 503
  Industry, 99, 133, 145n, 172, 182
  Mining, 99, 240, 248–9, 478
  Transport, 257, 258, 260, 266
Sinofracht Chartering and Shipbroking Corporation, 264, 326
Skinner, G. W., 35, 47, 49, 50, 277, 300, 308
Skins, *see* Hides and skins
Slaughter tax, 381, 396
Snow, E., 342, 354–5
Soap, 149
'Socialist Transformation', *see* Collectivization and 'Socialist Transformation'
Somalia, 320n

South Manchurian Railway, 92
Soviet Union, *see* Union of Soviet Socialist Republics
Soya beans, 34, 92n, 99, 346, 347, 357n, 358n, 487
Spirits, tax on, 376
Stamp Duty, 374, 381, 396
State Archives Bureau, 524–5
State Capital Construction Commission, 468, 518–19
State Construction Commission, 145, 156, 457–69 *passim*, 472, 473, 474, 518–19,
  Chairman of, 275, 458, 472
State Council, 20, 24, 176, 177, 183, 264, 266, 284, 285, 287, 291, 292, 461, 472, 524–5
State Council Offices, 20, 387, 517
  For post-1959 offices, see under name of each office. Pre-1959 offices as follows:
  First, 517
  Second, 517
  Third, 148, 517
  Fourth, 148, 517
  Fifth, 275, 365, 517
  Sixth, 148, 252, 266, 517
  Seventh, 517
  Eighth, 517
State Economic Commission, 20, 156, 170, 173, 270, 284, 296n, 387, 457–69 *passim*, 473, 477, 478, 479, 487, 518–19, 527, 529
  Chairman of, 458, 468
State farms, 42, 92–111, 112, 114, 259, 338, 347, 408, 509
  Army farms, 106
    See also PLA Production and Construction Corps, Sinkiang
  Demonstration and experimental, 102, 111, 114
  Ex-servicemen's farms, 98–100
    See also PLA Production and Construction Corps, Sinkiang
  Fish farms, 101n
  Forestry farms, *see* Forests and forestry
  Game farms and reserves, 94
  Labour reform farms, 105
  Mulberry plantations, 103
  Overseas Chinese state farms, *see under* Overseas Chinese
  PLA Production and Construction Corps farms, *see under* that heading
  Seed farms, 102, 111
  Silk farms, 103
  Suburban farms, 102, 111
  Tea plantations, 103
State Farms and Land Reclamation, Minister of, 93

State Farms and Land Reclamation, Ministry of, 41, 93, 94, 96, 97, 99, 102, 107, 151, 153n, 497, 522–3
State Housing Administrative Bureau, 524–5
State Maritime Bureau, 253, 527
State Personnel Organization Commission, 526–7
State Planning Commission, 20, 30, 156, 173, 182, 227, 284, 387, 457–69 *passim*, 471, 473, 474, 477, 478, 484, 487, 491, 492, 493n, 518–19,
  Chairman of, 227, 458, 466
State Price Commission, 442–3, 527
  Chairman of, 361, 443, 493n
State Statistical Bureau, 345, 354, 458, 492, 522–3
  Director of, 183, 361, 443, 493
State Technological Commission, 156, 457, 459, 518–19, 523
Statistical work, 314, 343, 458, 463, 485, 492–4, 507
  See also State Statistical Bureau
Stocks and stockpiling, *see under* Reserves
Storage of grain, *see under* Grain
Stores, *see under* Commerce
Street associations, 224, 226–8, 231, 289, 420, 510
Street industry, 169, 182, 231, 379
Students, *see* Education, higher
Success indicators, 26, 158–68 *passim*, 199, 209–11, 287–8, 304, 315, 480–5, 495, 508
Sugar, 149, 281, 284–6, 338, 371, 448, 474, 514
Sulphur, 239
Sun Yat-sen, 36
Sun Yeh-fang, 162, 480
Sung Shao-wen, 468
Sungari River, 262
Supervision, Ministry of, 469, 470, 522–3, 526
Supply and Marketing Co-operatives, 27, 37, 44, 62, 72, 205, 206, 219, 276, 277–9, 284, 288, 291–307 *passim*, 315, 328, 345, 369n, 378, 379, 410, 435, 442, 444
  See also All-China Federation of Supply and Marketing Co-operatives
Supply of Raw Materials, General Bureau for, 477, 526–7
'Supply system', 27n, 210, 229
Survey and Cartography, State General Bureau of, 522–3
Swatow, 168
Syria, 320n
'Systems' (ministerial, etc.), 21
Szechuan, 47, 50, 228, 289, 504–5
  Agriculture, 47, 50, 97, 102, 114, 120, 125, 490, 504–5

Szechuan (cont.)
  Commerce, 247, 280, 289, 292n
  Industry, 144, 168, 227
  Mining, 247–50
  Transport, 247, 252, 254, 256–8, 260, 262, 263, 267, 272

Ta Kung Daily, 29, 308, 314, 343, 353, 355, 399, 445
Tach'ing Oilfield, 248–50
Taihu Lake, 102
Taiping Insurance Co, 515
Taiwan, 8, 21, 50, 193, 251, 257, 318, 403, 407, 412n
Taiwan Straits, 263
Taiyuan, 134, 144, 153n, 241
Taklamakan Desert, 98n
Talc, 239
T'an Chen-lin, 42, 468
Tangku New Harbour, 252
Tangshan, 133, 309
Tanzania, 264, 320n
Tarim Basin, 98n
Tat'ung, 45
Taxation, 36, 45, 166, 337–46, 365–83, 389–98, 401
  Agricultural, see Agricultural tax
  Business tax, 373n, 374
  Cattle transactions tax, 381, 396
  Commodity circulation tax, 373n, 374, 396
  Entertainment tax, 381, 396
  Extra-budgetary taxes, see Extra-budgetary funds
  Goods tax, 373n, 374
  Incidence of taxes, 383
  Income tax, see under Income tax
  Industrial and commercial tax, see under Industrial and commercial tax
  Land tax, 32, 394
  Licences from vehicles and boats, 381, 396
  Pastoral tax, 342, 396
  Road tax, 260, 381
  Slaughter tax, 381, 396
  Urban real estate tax, 381, 396
  See also Budgets and budgeting; Revenue, budgeting
Tea, 103, 284, 285, 325, 443
Technical innovations, see Innovations, technical
Technical manpower, 155–6, 177, 178, 192–204 passim, 208, 210–11, 333, 462, 475
  See also Science and scientists
'Technical Organization Measures', 165
Telecommunications, 23, 88n, 270, 497, 500, 502, 503
Teng Chieh, 223
Teng Tsu-hui, 42, 419, 468

Textiles, Ministry of, 148, 149, 150, 153n, 154, 478, 520–1
Textiles and textile industry, 145, 149, 152, 273, 319, 325, 370, 371n, 376, 474, 476, 514
  Machinery for, see Machinery, textiles
  Synthetic textiles, 149
  See also Cotton; Silk
Thailand, 321
Theatres, 386
Tibet, 21n, 46, 50, 97, 98, 208, 252, 260, 414, 458
T'ien P'ing, 223
Tienshan Mountains, 120
Tientsin, 21, 97, 154, 231, 396
  Commerce, 290, 313, 454
  Industry, 16, 133, 144, 151n, 169, 170
  Transport, 258, 265, 326
Timber, 120–3 passim, 141, 486
  Distribution, 173n, 232, 284, 286, 291n, 483
  Prices, 443, 450
  See also Forests and forestry
Tin, 150, 238–9, 240n, 247–8, 283n, 286
Tinplate, 478
Tobacco, 284, 285, 286, 338, 343, 376, 443, 447
Tourism, 327n, 526–7
Tractors, see Agricultural machinery
Tractor stations, see Agricultural machinery stations
Trade, see Commerce
Trade, Ministry of, 274–6, 321, 406n, 442, 518–19
Trade unions, 21n, 29, 189–92, 203, 209n, 211n, 213, 314, 419n, 509
  See also All-China Federation of Trade Unions
Trade warehouses, see Warehouses, trade
Training, industrial, 187–9
  See also Education
Transfers, extra-provincial, 459, 498, 508
  Commodities (general), 285, 324, 459, 463, 464, 466, 477–8, 482, 486, 498, 499, 503
  Financial, 393, 397–8, 498, 503
  Grain, 349, 364, 503, 505, 507
Transport, Ch. 10; 34, 53n, 64, 148, 290, 293, 308, 462, 463, 483, 494, 500, 502, 505
  Finances of, 266–71, 272, 379, 438, 441, 451–3, 481
  See also Civil aviation; Railways; Roads; Shipping
Trucks, see Lorries
Tsaidam Basin, 208, 248, 249, 258
Tsamkong, 252, 265
Ts'ao Chü-ju, 365, 406
Tseng Shan, 252, 281–2

Tsinghai, 22, 98, 133, 208, 313n
  Agriculture, 97, 100
  Mining, 243–4, 248–9, 258
  Transport, 258, 260
Tung oil, 120, 284
Tungsten, 238–9, 283n
Tungting Lake, 125
Turfan Basin, 249n

Unemployment
  Rural, 185
  Urban, 184–5, 387
Union of Soviet Socialist Republics, 27,83n, 111, 145, 257, 320, 333, 403, 479
  Aid to China, 17, 142, 155, 194, 240, 249, 331, 382, 385
  Exchange rate (rouble-yuan), 319–20, 417–18
  Experts, 126n, 128, 194, 201, 240, 272, 459, 472, 475, 492
  Influence of Soviet model on China, 19, 25, 26, 505, 509
    On agriculture, 92, 106, 313n
    On commerce, 321, 330
    On economic planning, 458, 459, 461, 470, 471
    On finance and banking, 367, 369, 372, 403, 413, 418
    On industry and mining, 148–9, 162, 195, 204
    On transport, 268, 271, 272
    On water conservancy, 124, 128, 130, 132, 133
  Joint Sino-Soviet undertakings, 127, 240, 257, 265, 266, 271
United Arab Republic, 320n
United States of America, 128, 266, 412–13, 418
Uranium, 126n, 239, 240
Urban communes, *see* Communes, urban
Urban Construction, General Bureau of, 526–7
Urban Construction, Ministry of, 149n, 150, 520–1, 526
Urban Services, Ministry of, 153n, 274, 287n, 315, 369, 518–19
Urumchi, 99, 133, 257
Urumchi River Administrative Bureau, 130

Vegetable oil, 149, 284, 286, 287, 310–11, 321, 338, 347, 352n, 353, 356, 363, 443, 447
  See also Peanuts; Soya beans; Rapeseed
Vegetables, 15, 35, 58, 285, 299, 311, 329, 338, 351, 352
  See also Agricultural production, subsidiary; Commodities, third category
Verticalization, industrial, *see* Industry, verticalization

Vietnam, North, 83n, 257, 263, 266, 318, 320, 322

Wages, 66n, 107, 167, 176, 184, 185, 191, 204–18, 406, 415, 435, 462, 466, 498, 502, 505
  Grade scales, 205, 206, 210n
  Local differentials, 204, 208
  Piece rates, 38, 80, 205, 207–8, 217
  'Supply system', 27n, 210, 229
  See also Bonuses; Labour
Walker, K. R., 83
Wang Chen, 93
Wang Shou-tao, 252, 266
Warehouses, trade, 292, 296, 301, 306–7, 309, 377, 419
Watches, wrist, 149, 312, 443
Water conservancy, Ch. 5; 36, 46, 59–60, 266, 293, 339, 462, 474
  Finances of, 131–2, 389, 441n, 474
  Powered irrigation, 131, 135, 138, 504
  See also Irrigation districts
Water Conservancy, Ministry of, 126, 127, 149n, 522–3
Water Conservancy and Electric Power, Ministry of, 126, 127, 129, 132, 133, 137, 149n, 264, 408, 478, 479, 523
  Local departments, 127, 129
Water supply (piped), 140, 373
Weights, 13, 156, 493
Weights and Measures, State Bureau of, 156, 522–3
Weihsing Commune, 54, 67, 84
Wheat, *see* Grain
Wholesaling, *see* Commerce, wholesaling
Wiles, P. J. D., 160, 269, 320n
Wolfram, *see* Tungsten
Wong, John Chiu-hon, 22n
Wool and woollen goods, 145, 149, 284, 312, 443
Work days, 66, 76, 77, 77n, 82, 215
Work points, 58n, 66, 76, 79, 80, 108
Workers, *see* Labour; Wages, etc.
Workers' conferences, 200, 203
Working capital, *see* Capital, working
Workshops, *see* Industry, small-scale; Handicrafts; Communes, urban; Street industry
World Bank, *see under* Banks, International Bank for Reconstruction and Development
Wu Po, 365
Wu Yuan-li, 125, 136
Wuhan, 47, 290, 467
  Industry, 109, 134, 144, 198, 227, 235
  Transport, 257, 263, 272
Wusu, 99

Yang Chien-pai, 162, 480, 490
Yang Ying-chieh, 468, 470, 492
Yangtze River, 17, 33, 128, 133, 263
  Bridges, 271, 272
  Delta, 114, 125, 134, 135n, 490
  Plan, 127, 128, 130, 497
  Shipping, 153, 262–4, 266–8, 497
Yangtze River Navigation Administrative Bureau, 263, 497
Yao Yi-lin, 275, 289, 365
Yeh Chi-chuang, 321–2
Yellow River, 120
  Plan, 127–8
  Shipping, 252, 262
Yellow River Water Conservancy Commission, 127, 128, 497
Yemen, 320n
Yenchang Oilfield, 242

Yi national minority, 50, 504–5
Yingtang, 257
Young Communist League, *see* Communist Youth League
Yü Lin, 437–8
Yuan, see Currency
Yümen, 248, 249
Yung Lung-kwei, 358n
Yunnan, 98, 504
  Agriculture, 46, 50, 78, 97, 100, 103, 120, 504
  Commerce, 301–2, 321
  Industry, 133, 134, 201
  Mining, 154, 241, 248
  Transport, 254, 257

Zinc, 238–9

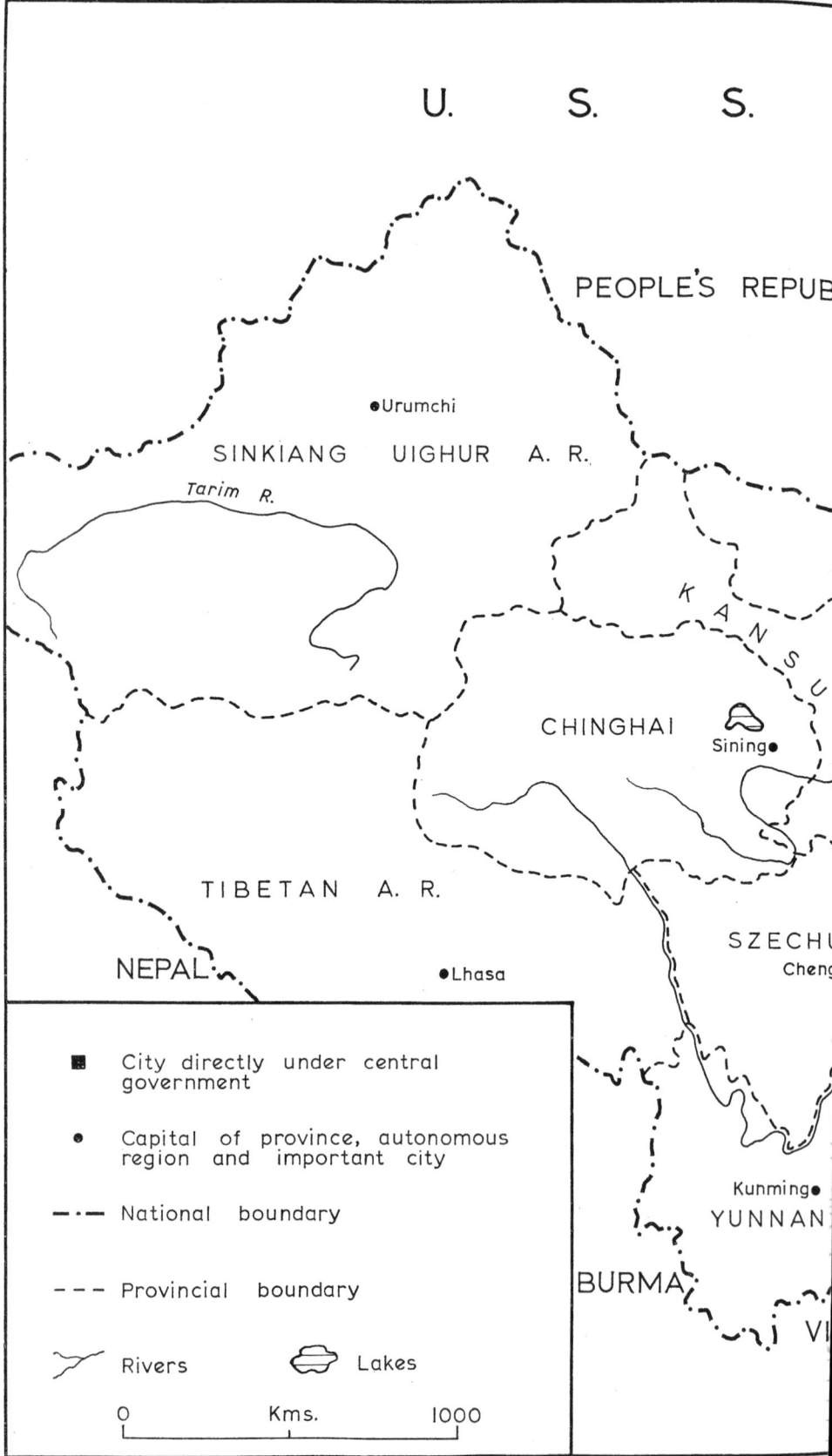